DAVID PLATT

THE
RADICAL
QUESTION

A
RADICAL
IDEA

MULTNOMAH
BOOKS

THE RADICAL QUESTION AND A RADICAL IDEA
PUBLISHED BY MULTNOMAH BOOKS
12265 Oracle Boulevard, Suite 200
Colorado Springs, Colorado 80921

Details in some anecdotes and stories have been changed to protect the identities of the persons involved.

ISBN 978-1-60142-489-1
ISBN 978-1-60142-490-7 (electronic)

Published in association with Yates & Yates, LLP, Attorneys and Counselors, Orange, California.

Published in the United States by WaterBrook Multnomah, an imprint of the Crown Publishing Group, a division of Random House Inc., New York.

MULTNOMAH and its mountain colophon are registered trademarks of Random House Inc.

Printed in the United States of America
2012

10 9 8 7 6 5 4 3 2 1

SPECIAL SALES
Most WaterBrook Multnomah books are available at special quantity discounts when purchased in bulk by corporations, organizations, and special-interest groups. Custom imprinting or excerpting can also be done to fit special needs. For information, please e-mail Special Markets @WaterBrookMultnomah.com or call 1-800-603-7051.

THE
RADICAL
QUESTION

Imagine a scene that took place in Asia not long ago:

A room in an ordinary house, dimly lit, all the blinds on the windows closed. Twenty leaders from churches in the region sit quietly in a circle on the floor, their Bibles open. They speak in hushed tones or not at all. Some still glisten with sweat; others' clothes and shoes are noticeably dusty. They have been walking or riding bicycles since early morning when they left distant villages to get here.

Whenever a knock is heard or a suspicious sound drifts in, everyone freezes while a burly, tough-looking man gets up to check things out.

These men and women have gathered in secret, arriving intentionally at different times throughout the day so as not to draw attention. In this country it is illegal for Christians to come together like this. If caught, the people here could lose their land, their jobs, their families, even their lives…

■ ■ ■

I was in that dimly lit room that day, a visitor from America. I huddled next to an interpreter, who helped me understand their stories as they began to share.

The tough-looking man—our "head of security"—was the first to speak up. But as he spoke, his intimidating appearance quickly gave way to reveal a tender heart.

"Some of the people in my church have been pulled away by a cult," he said. Tears welled up in his eyes. "We are hurting. I need

God's grace to lead my church through these attacks."

The cult that had been preying on his church is known for kidnapping Christians, taking them to isolated locations, and torturing them, my interpreter explained. Many brothers and sisters in the area would never tell the good news again. At least not with words. Their tongues had been cut out.

■ *The tough-looking man*
■ *was the first to speak up.*

A woman on the other side of the room spoke next. "Some of the members in my church were recently confronted by government officials," she said. "They threatened their families, saying that if they did not stop gathering to study the Bible, they were going to lose everything they had." She asked for

prayer, then said, "I need to know how to lead my church to follow Christ even when it costs them everything."

I looked around the room. Now everyone was in tears. They looked at one another, then several said at once, "We need to pray."

Immediately they went to their knees, and with their faces on the floor, they began to cry out with muted intensity to God. Their praying was not marked by lofty language but by heartfelt praise and pleading.

"O God, thank you for loving us!"

"O God, we need you!"

"Jesus, we trust in you!"

"Jesus, you are worthy!"

One after another they prayed while others wept.

After about an hour the room grew silent, and the men and women rose from the floor.

All around the room, on the floor where each had prayed, I saw puddles of tears.

■ ■ ■

The brothers and sisters in that Asian country have shown by their sacrifices just how much Jesus is worth to them. He is worth *everything* to them.

And they are not alone.

They are joined by brothers and sisters in Sudan who believe Jesus is worthy of their trust, even amid pain and persecution of genocidal proportions.

They are joined by brothers and sisters in India who believe Jesus is worthy of their devotion, even when they face threats from Muslim extremists in the north and Hindu extremists in the south.

They are joined by brothers and sisters all

over the Middle East who believe Jesus is worthy of their love, even when their family members threaten to kill them for professing belief in him.

They are joined by brothers and sisters around the world who believe Jesus is worthy of all their hopes, all their dreams, all their desires, all their possessions, all their plans, and all their lives.

But are they joined by you and me?

A DIFFERENT SCENE

Three weeks after traveling to underground house churches in Asia, I began my first Sunday as the pastor of a church in America. The scene was much different. No dimly lit rooms here; we were occupying an auditorium with theater-style lighting. Instead of traveling for miles by foot or bicycle to gather for worship, we had all arrived in millions of dollars' worth

of vehicles. Dressed in our fine clothes, we sat in cushioned chairs.

To be honest, there was not much at stake. Many had come because this was their normal routine. Some had come simply to check out the new pastor. I don't think any had come at the risk of their lives.

> *In America, the scene was much different. We had all arrived in millions of dollars' worth of vehicles.*

That afternoon crowds filled the parking lot of our sprawling multimillion-dollar church campus for a celebration. Moms, dads, and their kids jumped around together on inflatable games brought in for the occasion. Church members discussed a plan for using the adjacent open land to build state-of-the-art

recreation fields and facilities to support more events like this. Everyone, it seemed, looked forward to a successful future.

Please don't misunderstand this scene I'm describing. It was filled with wonderful, Bible-believing Christians who genuinely wanted to welcome me and enjoy one another. People like you and me—people who desire community, who want to be involved in church, and who believe God is important in their lives. But as a new pastor comparing the images around me that day with the pictures, still fresh in my mind, of brothers and sisters on the other side of the world, I could not help but think that somewhere along the way we in America have lost touch with what is essential, radical—even dangerous— about our faith and replaced it with what is comfortable.

In the days that followed, I began look-

ing further at my own life, at the church God has entrusted to me to pastor, and at the church culture around me. As I did, I was overwhelmed by the differences between our version of Christianity and the version of Christianity that prevails among our brothers and sisters around the world.

Instead of weeping together on our faces before God, we calmly sit on plush chairs in beautiful buildings.

Instead of going against the grain in our culture, we settle into our culture with lifestyles that are virtually indistinguishable from the world around us.

Instead of a simple, costly, humble, authentic, passionate, risky pursuit of Christ, we prioritize clean, elaborate, entertaining, slick, innovative church programs and performances that cater to our personal tastes.

And in light of these differences, I am

convinced we need to answer a fundamentally important question. What is Jesus worth to us?

REDEFINING JESUS

Do we believe that Jesus is worthy of sacrifice in our lives? Our immediate thought would probably be, *Yes. Sure. Of course.*

But listen to how we describe what it means to follow him.

Ask Jesus to come into your heart.

Invite Jesus to come into your life.

Pray this prayer, sign this card, or walk down this aisle, and accept Jesus as your personal Savior.

You will not find one of these casual, contemporary catch phrases in Scripture. Instead, in Jesus' mouth you will find words that are foreign to us today. You will find phrases that

show us he is worthy of far more than a polite invitation. He is worthy of supreme devotion. Let me give you a few examples.

At the end of Luke 9, we find the stories of three men who approach Jesus, eager to follow him. Surprisingly, in each case Jesus seems to try to talk them *out* of doing so!

The first guy says, "I will follow you wherever you go."

Jesus responds, "Foxes have holes and birds of the air have nests, but the Son of Man has no place to lay his head."[1] In other words, Jesus tells this man that he can expect homelessness on the journey ahead. Even when the basic need of shelter is not guaranteed, Jesus is worthy of all our trust.

The second man tells Jesus that his father has just died. The man wants to go back, bury his father, and then follow Jesus.

Jesus replies, "Let the dead bury their own dead, but you go and proclaim the kingdom of God."[2]

What could he mean by that?

> *I remember the moment I learned that my own dad had died of a heart attack.*

I remember distinctly the moment I learned that my own dad had died of a heart attack. In the days that followed, my heart was filled with an immense heaviness and a deep desire to honor my dad at his funeral. I cannot imagine hearing at that point these words from Jesus: "Don't even go to your dad's funeral. There are more important things to do." Yet that's the essence of what Jesus tells the second man who comes up to him. Jesus is worthy of total allegiance and immediate obedience.

A third man approaches Jesus and tells him that he wants to follow him, but before he does, he needs to say good-bye to his family.

Makes sense. But Jesus tells the man, "No one who puts his hand to the plow and looks back is fit for service in the kingdom of God."3 Plainly put, a relationship with Jesus requires absolute, undivided, exclusive affection.

Trust me, even if it means becoming homeless.

Follow me, even if it means letting someone else bury your dad.

Love me, even if it means not saying good-bye to your family.

Jesus is worthy of radical devotion.

The first time I heard this text from Luke 9 preached, it was from the lips of Dr. Jim Shaddix. He was my preaching professor, and I had moved to New Orleans specifically to study under him. Soon after I got there, Dr. Shaddix invited me to travel with him to an

event where he was speaking. I sat in the front row in a crowd of hundreds of people, and I listened as he began to speak.

"Tonight my goal is to talk you out of following Jesus."

My eyebrows shot up in amazement and confusion. What was he thinking? What was *I* thinking? My wife and I had moved to New Orleans to study under a guy who persuades people *not* to follow Jesus?

Dr. Shaddix preached the sermon exactly as Luke 9 describes, warning potential disciples about what is involved in following Jesus. At the end he invited people who wanted to follow Christ to come down to the front. To my surprise, many in the crowd got up from their seats and came down.

I sat there dumbfounded. Then insight struck. *So this is just a preaching tactic, kind of a sanctified reverse psychology. And it works. Tell*

them you're going to talk them out of following Jesus, and they will respond in droves.

I decided I was going to try it.

- *My eyebrows shot up in*
- *amazement and confusion.*
- *What was he thinking?*
- *What was I thinking?*

The next week I was preaching at a youth event. Taking my cue from Dr. Shaddix, I proudly stood before the students assembled that night and announced, "My goal tonight is to talk you out of following Jesus." I could see the leaders of the event raise their eyebrows in concern, but I knew what I was doing. After all, I'd been in seminary for a few weeks, and I'd seen this done before. So I preached the message and then invited students who wanted to follow Christ to come forward.

Apparently I was more successful than Dr. Shaddix in preaching that message. Let's just say that I stood alone at the front until the event organizer finally decided it was time for me to call it a night. For some reason I was never invited back.

Unlike what I thought about Dr. Shaddix, Jesus was not pulling a gimmick in order to get more followers. On the contrary, Jesus often seemed totally unwilling to cater to the crowds. He is so unlike us. We will do whatever it takes to draw the masses, but Jesus was constantly turning them away. Whenever the crowd would get big, he'd say something like, "Unless you eat the flesh of the Son of Man and drink his blood, you have no life in you."[4] Not exactly the sharpest church-growth tactic. I can picture the look on the disciples' faces. I can imagine their minds racing. *No, not the drink-my-blood speech! We'll never make*

the list of fastest-growing movements if you keep asking them to eat you!

> ***Can you imagine your church deciding to stream those words across its home page for every new visitor to see? Jesus just lost most of us at hello.***

On another occasion when Jesus was surrounded by a throng of eager followers, he turned to them and remarked, "If anyone comes to me and does not hate his father and mother, his wife and children, his brothers and sisters—yes, even his own life—he cannot be my disciple."[5] Can you imagine your church deciding to stream those words across its home page for every new visitor to see? Jesus just lost most of us at hello.

But Jesus had more to say: "Anyone who

does not carry his cross and follow me cannot be my disciple."[6]

Now this is taking it to another level. *Pick up an instrument of torture and follow me.* This is getting weird…and kind of creepy. Imagine a leader coming on the scene today and inviting all who would come after him to pick up an electric chair and become his disciples. Any takers?

As if this were not enough, Jesus rounded out his seeker-sensitive plea with a pull-at-your-heartstrings conclusion. "Any of you who does not give up everything he has cannot be my disciple."[7] Give up everything you have, carry a cross, and hate your family. You have to agree, this sounds a lot different than "Admit, believe, confess, and pray a prayer after me."

Yet one more potential disciple approached Jesus and asked what he needed to

do in order to be a part of Christ's kingdom. This eager seeker was young, rich, intelligent, and influential—a prime prospect for any growing movement.

But what was Jesus' reply? "Sell everything you have and give to the poor.... Then come, follow me."[8]

The man turned away, persuaded that the cost was too high.

Let's put ourselves in the shoes of these followers of Jesus in the first century. What if you were the man Jesus told not to even say good-bye to his family? What if we were told to hate our families and give up everything we had in order to follow Jesus? What if we were told to sell all our possessions in order to give to the poor?

This is where we come face to face with a dangerous reality. We *do* have to give up everything we have to follow Jesus. We *do*

have to love him in a way that makes our closest relationships in this world look like hate. And it is entirely possible that he *will* tell any one of us to sell everything we have and give it to the poor.

But we don't want to believe it.

> *We take the Jesus of the Bible and begin twisting him into a version of Jesus that we are more comfortable with.*

We are afraid of what this might mean for our lives. So we rationalize these passages away. "Jesus wouldn't really tell us not to bury our father or not to say good-bye to our family. Jesus didn't literally mean to sell all we have and give it to the poor. What Jesus really meant was…"

And this is where we need to pause. We

need to pause because we are redefining Christianity according to our preferences. We are giving in to the dangerous temptation to take the Jesus of the Bible and begin twisting him into a version of Jesus that we are more comfortable with.

A nice, middle-class, American Jesus.

A Jesus who doesn't mind material security and would never call us to give away everything we have.

A Jesus who would not expect us to forsake our closest relationships so that he receives all our affection.

A Jesus who wants us to be balanced, who wants us to avoid dangerous extremes, who for that matter wants us to avoid danger altogether.

A Jesus who is fine with a devotion from us that does not infringe on our comforts, because after all he loves us just the way we are.

But do you and I realize what we are doing at this point? We are molding Jesus into our image and making him look like us. And the danger now is that when we gather to sing and lift our hands in worship, we are not actually worshiping the Jesus of the Bible. Instead, we are worshiping ourselves.

Meanwhile, the Jesus of the Bible is supremely worthy of sacrificial devotion. His portrait in Scripture evokes immediate and total submission. He is the Alpha and Omega, the Beginning and the End, the First and the Last, the Final Amen. He is the Bread of Life, Christ our Creator, our Deliverer, our Everlasting Father—he is God. He is the Good Shepherd, the Great High Priest, the Holy One, the image of the invisible God. He is King of kings and Lord of lords, majestic and mighty, and no one compares to him, the only begotten Son of the Father, full of grace

and truth. He is the power of God, the Resurrection and the Life, the Supreme Sacrifice, the Way, the Truth, and the Life, the very Word of God made flesh.

When we see a biblical picture of Jesus, we realize that the greatness of who he is demands the surrender of all we are and have.

A NEW AMERICAN DREAM

Yet we are tempted to give him less than he deserves. Instead of radical devotion to Christ, we so easily settle for nominal devotion to him while we indulge ourselves in other pursuits. We are captivated by an American dream. Told at every turn to believe in ourselves, trust in ourselves, and promote ourselves, we work to gain it all: a comfortable life, a good career, a decent family, and an easy retirement. Sure, we tack church attendance onto the end of everything, but at the core our

lives are consumed with a dream of success, security, safety, and satisfaction in all this world has to offer.

> *What if Jesus is worthy*
> *of more in our lives than*
> *a Christian spin on the*
> *American dream?*

But what if there is another way? What if we were created for a much greater purpose? What if we were created, not to advance ourselves, but to deny ourselves? What if Jesus is worthy of more in our lives than a Christian spin on the American dream? And what if there is greater, more lasting success, security, safety, and satisfaction that can be found only in radical devotion to him?

Imagine the American dream in action.

Imagine a university student preparing for

his profession. All his life he has been told to work hard at school so he can go to college, get a degree, and build a career. With the right amount of motivation, dedication, and intuition, he can make something of himself one day. So he presses on toward that goal.

Or imagine a gifted businessman who has reached his aspirations. He started with humble roots and faced daunting challenges, but he persevered through long days at the office and short nights at home to get to the top. He arrived there faster than he expected, and though it was not always easy, in the end he believes it was worth it. He now lives in an expansive suburban home with his wife and children, a self-made man with all he needs.

And then there is the married couple beginning retirement. Finally the wait is over, and the options abound. Settle into a quiet, secluded home, or travel across the country?

Renovate the house, or take out a second mortgage on one in the mountains? Buy a fishing boat, or take up golf lessons? The pleasures they now enjoy are a monument to the years of labor that have made it all possible.

> *Imagine these common scenarios, and then ask the question, "What if we were created for something much greater than this?"*

Imagine these common scenarios, and then ask the question, "What if we were created for something much greater than this?"

Let me introduce you to Daniel, a college student like the one I mentioned earlier. He is a member of our faith family and recently graduated with honors from a nearby university with a degree in mechanical engineering.

Coming out of school, he was given two attractive offers: take an extremely high-paying job at a nuclear power plant, or have all his expenses paid to complete master's and doctorate degrees in engineering.

Taking either one of these offers would certainly not have been bad, but two years ago Daniel came to faith in Christ. The focus of his entire life shifted to using the grace of God in his life to make much of the glory of God in the world. Consequently, he turned down both options before him and instead went to work with an engineering program designed to help impoverished communities in third-world countries.

His dad e-mailed me soon after Daniel made this decision. "Daniel has made a very radical departure from my long-held and traditional value system," he wrote. "I have raised my children with solid Christian values

and naturally have expected them to grab the brass ring of opportunity and settle into a productive family life." In the rest of the e-mail, though, his dad described how proud he was that his son had let go of the pursuits of this world in order to "take the gospel to places and peoples unknown to him."

> *Jeff climbed the ladder of success only to realize that success in the kingdom of God involves moving down, not up.*

And God has been faithful to Daniel. I met with him in my office a few weeks ago, and he told me about unprecedented opportunities that God is now giving him from America to Africa to Asia as he pursues a much greater dream than he ever had before.

Or let me introduce you to Jeff, a businessman like the one I mentioned earlier, who climbed the ladder of success only to realize that success in the kingdom of God involves moving down, not up. As a young professional, he scaled the heights of success in our culture in almost every conceivable way. I'll let him tell his story in excerpts from a speech he gave to other executives in his company:

> My career has been a complete whirlwind in ways more successful than I ever anticipated it could be. I am paying more in taxes than I ever expected to make in a full year! I have been incredibly blessed. I was able to bring my wife home from work. Then we purchased our dream home in the exact neighborhood where we always wanted to live. I purchased the BMW; I bought

the big beach house; and we went on great vacations. On top of all this, I was growing a business that I truly loved in an industry that I am passionate about. But somehow something was missing from my life, and I couldn't figure out what it was. I have been a Christian since I was seven years old, but through my pursuit of business and success, I somehow had replaced seeking the Lord with pursuing stuff and success.

Then something happened last year that changed my life. I stood in a city dump in Tegucigalpa, Honduras. I saw men, women, and children who were living in a dump where they scoured for food and shelter. Humbled by the reality of parents raising their kids in a dump, I reached my breaking point when I saw a woman eight

months pregnant walk by me, looking for food. I couldn't decide which was worse—the fact that the baby was conceived in a dump or that it was going to be born there. In the middle of this scene, God asked me, "What are you going to do with what I have given you? How are you going to use your influence, your leadership, and your resources in the world around you?"

For the first time, Jeff realized that God had a purpose for his life that was greater than the pursuit of the next and bigger thing. So Jeff decided to walk away from the American dream. He still runs his business and makes a lot of money but not to make much of himself. He and a couple of other guys in our faith family have begun a ministry that works with local churches around the world to provide

clean water in communities where thousands are dying every day of preventable waterborne diseases.

Finally, let me introduce you to Ed and Patty. A few years ago when they got to retirement, they had plenty of options for what to do together. But they chose an uncommon path. This year, between July and October, Ed and Patty were home a total of eleven days. Why? Not because they were vacationing, but because they were doing disaster relief in cities and towns that had experienced flooding in the United States. Then they both went to Nigeria. Then Ed went to Sri Lanka, where he cooked meals for the hungry in the middle of rebel fighting. Patty usually travels with him, but Ed told me she doesn't like sleeping under trucks in the middle of rebel fighting, so she passed on the Sri Lanka trip. Ed told me once, "What else am I going to do with

my retirement? I just want to tell as many people about the gospel as I can."

> ■ *They have been conquered*
> ■ *by a superior ambition...*
> ■ *and they are not alone.*

If you were to meet Daniel, Jeff, Ed, or Patty, you wouldn't notice anything extraordinary about them. They are ordinary people who have achieved varying levels of success in this world. But all of them have this in common: They believe that they were created for more than a Christian spin on the American dream. They believe the purpose of their lives is deeper than having a nice job, raising a decent family, living a comfortable life, and tacking church attendance onto the end of it. They believe Jesus has called them to a much higher plane and given them a much greater

dream. They are Christians who have been conquered by a superior ambition, and they are surrendering every facet of their lives to knowing Jesus and making his worth known in all the world.

■ *Will you join the*
■ *movement?*

And they are not alone. They are joined by wealthy doctors who are selling their homes and giving to the poor or moving overseas, business leaders who are mobilizing their companies to help the hurting, young couples who are moving into the inner city to live out the gospel, and senior adults, stay-at-home moms, college students, and teenagers who are reorienting their lives around radical devotion to Jesus.

They are part of a movement of Chris-

tians in American churches today who are re-discovering what it means to follow Jesus for who he is, not for who we have created him to be. A movement of Christians who have decided they do not have time to play games with their lives and in church while billions around the globe suffer and die without Christ. A movement of Christians who are forsaking the priorities and pursuits of this world so that their lives might count in this world for the spread of the gospel and the glory of Christ. A movement of Christians who have decided that settling for casual, comfortable, complacent, business-as-usual Christianity is no longer an option. A movement of Christians who are taking Jesus at his word and sacrificing everything to declare Jesus to the world, no matter what it costs them, because they believe he is worth it.

Will you join the movement?

THE WORLD AS IT IS

Look at the world.

See a world where, over the last few years, more than half a million people have died instantly—in tsunamis in southeast Asia, cyclones in Myanmar, earthquakes in China and Pakistan, or floods in Nepal and Bangladesh—and where most of those half-million people had never once heard the gospel. They are joined today by a billion others who at this moment still have not heard that Christ came to save them from their sins.

See a world where half the population is living on less than two dollars a day while you and I, by contrast, are extremely rich.

See the nation of India, where there are more people living below the poverty line than there are total people in the United States.

See a world where today alone twenty-six

thousand children will die either of starvation or a preventable disease.

See our dogs and cats eating better than our brothers and sisters in central Africa.

See a world where last fall, in one week alone, fifty thousand people died of AIDS, more than a hundred thousand children died of hunger-related diseases, thousands of other children were trafficked around the world for sexual exploitation, and hundreds were killed in an earthquake in Pakistan. All in one week. And yet, during that same week, the greatest concerns for many of us were how our football teams played and how our 401(k) accounts fared.

In addition to all this, see thousands upon thousands of our brothers and sisters in China and North Korea and Laos and Saudi Arabia imprisoned and killed because of their faith in Christ.

See all these things, and realize that the purpose of our lives is not just to have a comfortable life, a good career, a decent family, and an easy retirement in this world. We were created for so much more than this. Jesus is worthy of so much more than this.

We have a choice. We can settle for casual devotion to Jesus, sitting comfortably in our nice church buildings, where we are insulated and isolated from the inner city and the spiritual lostness of the world. We can give a tip of our hats to the purpose of Christ in the world while we go on designing endless activities that revolve around us. We can retreat into our nice, cozy communities where we can live nice, decent lives while we pretend the starving millions do not exist. We can hide behind our catchy phrases and our easy prayers that dilute the awesome reality of who

Jesus is and what it means to follow him. We can spend our Christian lives sitting comfortably in the nurseries of our churches while drinking spiritual milk.

> *We can hide behind our catchy phrases and our easy prayers. Or we can decide that Jesus is worth more.*

Or we can decide that Jesus is worth more than this.

We can decide that he has created us for a much greater purpose. We can decide to die to ourselves and our dreams and our plans, and we can decide to let our hearts be conquered by a superior ambition. Ultimately, we can decide to sacrifice our lives, our gifts, our skills, our time, our families, and our resources

to make the great worth of Christ known amid urgent spiritual and physical needs in all the world.

Here's what I want to say to my brothers and sisters in America: let's sacrifice it all!

For the glory of Christ among a billion people who have not even heard the gospel…

For the sake of men, women, and children who are starving, suffering, and dying every single day…

For the millions in your city and my city who do not know Christ and are headed for a Christless eternity…

For ourselves, for our churches, for our families, for our children who will come behind us…

For all of this and more, let's sacrifice it all!

And when we do, we will discover that Jesus is, indeed, absolutely worthy of all our plans and all our dreams and all our ambitions.

THE COST OF
NONDISCIPLESHIP

We realize, of course, that following Christ for who he is will be costly. To sacrifice everything in radical devotion to Jesus means to surrender our lives, our rights, our ambitions, our plans, our dreams, our families, our relationships, our possessions, our safety, our security, our past, our present, and our future to the absolute lordship of Jesus. It is to relinquish to him our control of the way we think, the way we feel, the way we act, the way we relate, and the way we live. As Dietrich Bonhoeffer wrote in his classic book entitled *The Cost of Discipleship,* "When Christ calls a man, he bids him come and die."

Based on what we have heard from Jesus in the Gospels, we would have to agree that the cost of discipleship is great. But before we let this reality dissuade us from following

Christ wholeheartedly, I want to propose that the cost of nondiscipleship is far greater.

> *The cost of discipleship is great. But I want to propose that the cost of nondiscipleship is far greater.*

When Christians shrink back from self-denying faith and settle into self-indulging faith, the price is high. The cost of nondiscipleship is extremely high for people around the world who don't know Christ. Even the most liberal estimates put the number of Christians at one-third of the world's population. This means that at least 4.5 billion people today are without Christ and are destined for an eternal hell. As long as Christians choose to play games in their churches while they spend their

lives fulfilling an American dream, billions in need of the gospel will remain hopelessly in the dark. The cost will be high for the lost if we do not follow Christ radically.

The cost of nondiscipleship is also high for the poor in the world. Consider the price when Christians ignore Jesus' commands to give away their possessions for the sake of the poor and instead choose to spend their resources on larger homes, nicer cars, and more stuff. Consider the cost when these Christians gather in churches and choose to spend millions of dollars on nice buildings to drive up to, cushioned chairs to sit in, and endless programs to enjoy for themselves. Consider the cost for the starving multitudes who sit outside the gate of contemporary Christian affluence.

I remember preparing to take my first trip

to Sudan in 2004. The country was still at war, and the Darfur region in western Sudan had just begun to make headlines. A couple of months before we left, I received a Christian news publication in the mail. The front cover had two headlines side by side. I'm not sure if the editor planned for these particular headlines to be next to each other or if he just missed it in a really big way.

On the left the headline read, "First Baptist Church Celebrates New $23 Million Building." A lengthy article followed, celebrating the church's expensive new sanctuary. It described in detail the building's exquisite marble, intricate design, and beautiful stained glass.

On the right was a much smaller article. The headline for it read, "Baptist Relief Helps Sudanese Refugees." Knowing I was about to go to Sudan, my attention was drawn. As I

read the article, it described how 350,000 refugees in western Sudan were dying of malnutrition and might not live to the end of the year. It briefly explained their plight and sufferings. When I got to the end of the article, the last sentence said that Baptists had sent money to help relieve the suffering of the Sudanese. I was excited until I got to the amount.

Now, remember what was on the left: "First Baptist Church Celebrates New $23 Million Building." On the right, the article said, "Baptists have raised $5,000 to send to refugees in western Sudan."

Five thousand dollars.

That is not enough to get a plane into Sudan, much less one drop of water to people who need it.

Twenty-three million dollars for an elaborate sanctuary and five thousand dollars for

hundreds of thousands of starving men, women, and children, most of whom were dying apart from faith in Christ.

> *Where have we gone wrong? How did we get to the place where this is tolerable?*

Where have we gone wrong?

How did we get to the place where this is tolerable?

Yes, the cost of nondiscipleship is great. The cost of believers not taking Jesus' worth seriously is vast for those who don't know Christ and devastating for those who are starving and suffering around the world.

But they are not the only ones who pay the cost of nondiscipleship. We pay it as well.

IS HE WORTH IT?

Look at what Jesus says when he tells the rich man to abandon his possessions and give to the poor: "Go, sell everything you have and give to the poor, *and you will have treasure in heaven.*"[9]

If we are not careful, we can misconstrue the radical statements from Jesus in the Gospels and begin to think that he does not want the best for us. But he does. Jesus was not trying to strip this rich man of all his pleasure. Instead he was offering him the satisfaction of eternal treasure. Jesus was saying, "It will be better, not just for the poor, but for you too, when you abandon the stuff you are holding on to."

We see the same thing in Matthew 13. There Jesus tells his disciples, "The kingdom of heaven is like treasure hidden in a field.

When a man found it, he hid it again, and then in his joy went and sold all he had and bought that field."[10]

I love this picture. Imagine walking in a field and stumbling upon a treasure that is more valuable than anything else you could ever work for or find in this life. It is more valuable than all you have now or will ever have in the future.

> *In an instant a plan drops fully formed into your imagination.*

You look around and notice that no one else realizes the treasure is there. In an instant a plan drops fully formed into your imagination. You cover up the treasure quickly and walk away, pretending you haven't seen anything. You go into town and begin to sell all

your possessions to have enough to buy that field. People think you're crazy. "What are you doing? What are you thinking?" worried friends and family ask.

"See that field over there?" you tell them. "I'm buying it."

They look at you in disbelief. "That's a ridiculous investment," they say. "Why are you trading away everything you have just for that?"

You respond, "I've got a hunch." And you smile to yourself as you walk away.

You smile because you know. You know that in the end you are not really giving away anything at all. Instead you are gaining. Yes, you are abandoning everything you have, but you are also gaining more than you could ever have in any other way. So with joy—with joy!—you sell your possessions. You sacrifice it all.

Why? Because you have found something worth losing everything for.

This is the picture of Jesus in the Gospels. He is something—someone—worth losing everything for. And if we walk away from the Jesus of the Gospels, then we walk away from eternal riches. The cost of nondiscipleship is profoundly greater for us than the cost of discipleship. For if we cling to the trinkets of this world and reject the radical invitation of Jesus, we will miss out on the infinite treasure of knowing and experiencing him.

This brings us to the crucial question for every professing or potential follower of Jesus. What is Jesus worth to you?

Do you believe he is worth abandoning everything for? Do you really believe Jesus is so good, so satisfying, and so rewarding that you will leave all you own and all you are to find your fullness in him? Do you believe him

enough to obey him and to follow him however and wherever he leads, even when the crowds in our culture—and maybe in our churches—turn the other way?

> *Let's stop living as though we need more possessions, greater positions, or greater pleasures in this world.*

Let's trust that Jesus is worthy of radical devotion. Let's take him at his word when he says that he is a treasure worth giving everything in this world for. Let's stop living as though we need more possessions, greater positions, more plaudits, or greater pleasures in this world. For that matter, let's stop living as if this world is even our home. And let's start living as if we were created for another world, where a Savior waits for all who have forsaken

this world because they believe in his great worth. Let's start living as though this world has nothing for us because Christ is truly everything to us.

Let's join our brothers and sisters around the world who have joyfully sacrificed the comforts, safety, security, pleasures, and priorities of this world in order to follow Christ. Let's join our brothers and sisters who have decided to spend their lives for his glory in the world. Let's join them in trusting that Jesus is, indeed, someone worth losing everything for.

Let's believe that Jesus is worthy of all our trust—even though we may not always be safe in this world, we will always be secure in his hands.

Let's believe that Jesus is worthy of all our plans—he alone knows what is best for our

lives, and we will follow him wherever, however, and whenever he leads.

Let's believe that Jesus is worthy of all our obedience—his word demands total allegiance, so when he speaks, we will respond without question or hesitation.

Let's believe that Jesus is worthy of all our dreams—he has created us for so much more than acclaim in this world, and we will settle for nothing less than his fame in all the world.

> ### *Is Jesus worth this to you?*

Let's believe that Jesus is worthy of all our possessions—he has given them to us, not so we will indulge ourselves with more stuff, but so we will spend ourselves on behalf of those in spiritual and physical need.

Let's believe that Jesus is worthy of all our desire—he is utterly satisfying, and we have no need to seek the pleasures of this world, because we have found ultimate delight in him.

Let's believe that Jesus is worthy of all our affections—he has loved us completely, so we will adore him supremely.

Let's believe that Jesus is worthy of all our lives—we will gladly lose them in this world because our eyes are fixed on the world to come.

O Christian, is Jesus worth this to you?

NOTES

1. Luke 9:57–58
2. Luke 9:60
3. Luke 9:62
4. John 6:53
5. Luke 14:26
6. Luke 14:27
7. Luke 14:33
8. Luke 18:22
9. Mark 10:21, emphasis added
10. Matthew 13:44

A
RADICAL
IDEA

High atop the Andes Mountains, the rays of the sun strike ice, and a single drop of water forms. It begins to trace a hesitant course downward, gradually joining with other drops of water to become a steady stream. The stream gains speed and strength. Thousands of feet below and hundreds of miles later, what were once single drops have converged to become the mightiest river on earth: the Amazon. Flowing into the Atlantic Ocean at a rate of more than seven million cubic feet per second, the Amazon is more powerful than the next ten largest rivers in the world combined.

In my book *Radical*, I explored how the biblical gospel affects individual Christian lives. Simply put, in a world of urgent spiritual and physical need, gospel-believing, God-exalting men and women do not have time to waste their lives pursuing a Christian spin on the American dream. Using the imagery above, I tried to picture what happens when the truth of Christ penetrates our hearts, melts our assumptions, and propels us on a journey of abandonment to God.

 You and I are not intended to plunge down the mountain of radical obedience alone.

But you and I are not intended to plunge down the mountain of radical obedience alone. That's one of the reasons I love this

imagery of the Amazon. The force of a single drop of water descending the Andes is minuscule. Similarly, as long as individual Christians journey alone—no matter how "radical" they are—their effect will be minimal. But as men and women who are surrendered to the person of Christ join together in churches that are committed to the purpose of Christ, then nothing can stop the spread of the gospel to the ends of the earth.

In *A Radical Idea,* I want to consider what happens—or can happen—when we apply the revolutionary claims and commands of Christ to our communities of faith. I want to contemplate the force of a people who come together to enjoy God's grace in the church while they extend God's glory in the world. And I want to propose that a movement of such people in such churches

has the potential to permeate nations with the praise of God.

I am speaking to believers who are ready to lead, influence, or simply be a part of such a movement in their local church. You may be a follower of Christ who desires to live out a more biblical gospel, and you want to see your church do the same. You may be a pastor, staff person, or leader of some other description in the church, and you want your local fellowship to count for the spread of God's glory in the world. You may even be a Christian who is tempted to throw in the towel and say, "My church will never be radical."

Whatever your circumstance, I invite you to engage God's Word and God's world with a fresh, honest, and open perspective so that together we might answer one question:

How can we in the church
best unleash the people of God
in the Spirit of God with the Word of God
for the glory of God in the world?

As I pose this question, I do not claim to be an expert on how to answer it. I am merely one pastor in one church, and I have so much to learn. Yet I know that, as leaders and members of churches, we are called to spur one another toward Christ and his agenda in the world.

Throughout the history of humankind, God has chosen to call out not just individuals but a people for himself. He told the Israelites, "I will walk among you and be your God, and you will be my people." Through Christ, God brought Jews and Gentiles together as "one body" in which "each member

belongs to all the others." Peter told the church, "You are a chosen people,…a people belonging to God, that you may declare the praises of him who called you out of darkness into his wonderful light." Indeed, God's intention is that "through the church, the manifold wisdom of God should be made known to the rulers and authorities in the heavenly realms."[1]

If you and I want our lives to count for God's purpose in the world, we need to begin with a commitment to God's people in the church. God has called us to lock arms with one another in single-minded, death-defying obedience to one objective: the declaration of his gospel for the demonstration of his glory to all nations. This is God's design for his people, and it is worth giving our lives to see it accomplished. It is worth it for billions of

people who do not yet know that Jesus is the grave-conquering, life-giving, all-satisfying King. And it is worth it for you and me, because we were made to enjoy the great pleasures of God in the context of total abandonment to his global purpose.

 God has called us to lock arms with one another in single-minded, death-defying obedience to one objective: the declaration of his gospel for the demonstration of his glory to all nations.

THE GENIUS OF WRONG

I was sitting at a table with an old friend who leads a large and thriving church. "We try to make everything easy for the members of our

church," he said to me. "We encourage them to get to know people in our community, whether in their neighborhood or office or anywhere else. Then all they have to do is invite those people to church. At church, those people will hear relevant, gifted communicators in a warm, attractive, and appealing environment where their children can be a part of top-of-the-line programs."

He concluded, "If our members will just invite their friends to the environment we create, then we can take care of the rest."

Then he asked me what we do at Brook Hills.

Hesitantly I said, "We actually do the exact opposite."

"Oh really," he said. "What do you mean?"

"Well, when we gather as the church, our

main focus is on the church. In other words, we organize our worship environment around believers, not unbelievers."

He looked confused. "Why would you do that?" he asked. "If your worship environment on Sunday is not appealing to non-Christians, then how is your church going to intentionally lead unbelievers in Birmingham to Christ?"

"We're going to equip our people every Sunday to lead unbelievers in Birmingham to Christ all week long," I said.

"Your members are going to lead them to Christ?"

"That's our plan."

"Well," he said, "once those unbelievers become believers, how are they going to grow in Christ?"

"Our people are going to be equipped to

show new believers how to live as followers of Christ," I said. "I want people in the church to be able to fulfill the purpose for which they were created without being dependent on gifted preachers, nice buildings, and great programs to do it for them."

Looking puzzled, he said, "Well, that's a new approach."

Now, I am a young pastor, and I have a lot to learn, particularly from pastors like this one, whom I respect greatly. But I don't think I'm coming up with something new here.

I believe in the people of God. Or more specifically, I believe in the work of God's Spirit through God's Word in God's people. The last thing I want to do is rob Christians of the joy of making disciples by telling them that I or anyone or anything else can take care of that for them.

Someone might ask, "But if a church has a gifted communicator or a gifted leader, wouldn't we want as many people as possible to hear that person?"

 The last thing I want to do is rob Christians of the joy of making disciples by telling them that I or anyone or anything else can take care of that for them.

The answer is "not necessarily." The goal of the church is never for one person to be equipped and empowered to lead as many people as possible to Christ. The goal is always for all of God's people to be equipped and empowered to lead as many people as possible to Christ.

I also believe in the plan of God. In Jesus' simple command to "make disciples," he has invited every one of his followers to share the life of Christ with others in a sacrificial, intentional, global effort to multiply the gospel of Christ through others. He never intended to limit this invitation to the most effective communicators, the most brilliant organizers, or the most talented leaders and artists—all the allegedly right people that you and I are prone to exalt in the church. Instead, the Spirit of God has empowered every follower of Christ to accomplish the purpose of God for the glory of God in the world. This includes the so-called wrong people: those who are the least effective, least brilliant, or least talented in the church.

Building the right church, then, is dependent on using all the wrong people.

MANUFACTURED ELEMENTS

At one point in *Radical,* I described the various elements that we in America have manufactured for growing a church.[2] I want to revisit the discussion I began there and take it further so we can better explore what a church might look like if it properly valued the wrong people.

It's commonly assumed that if you and I want to be a part of a growing church today, we need a few simple elements.

First, we need a good performance. In an entertainment-driven culture, we need someone who can captivate the crowds. If we don't have a charismatic communicator, we're sunk from the start. Even if we have to show him on video, we get a good speaker. And for a bonus, we surround the speaker with quality music and arts.

Next, we need a place to hold the crowds who will come. This usually means investing hundreds of thousands, if not millions, of dollars in a facility to house the performance. The more attractive the environment, the better.

 There it is: a performance at a place filled with programs run by professionals. The problem is the one p we have left out of the equation: the people of God.

Then once the crowds get there, we need something to keep them coming back. So we start programs—first-class, top-of-the-line programs—for kids, youth, and families, for every age and stage. And in order to have those programs, we need professionals to run

them. That way parents can drop their kids off at the door, and the professionals can handle ministry for them. We don't want people trying this at home.

There it is: a performance at a place filled with programs run by professionals. The problem, though, is the one *p* we have left out of the equation: the people of God.

PEOPLE, NOT PERFORMANCES

What if growing the church was never intended to depend on creating a good performance with all the right people on the stage?

Where did we get the idea that this was necessary? Certainly Scripture instructs us to gather for worship.[3] This is nonnegotiable but not necessarily in the way we usually think about it.

Imagine being in a church on the other

side of the world where it is illegal for the church even to exist. You wait until midnight, when everyone else in the village is asleep, to quietly leave your house. Under the cover of darkness, you sneak down winding roads and past silent houses, looking around every corner to make sure no one is following you. You know that if you or anyone else from your church is caught, you may never see your home again. For that matter, you may never see the light of day again.

Yet you continue on until you round a bend, and there you see a small house with a faint light emanating from it. Checking one last time to make sure you have not been tailed, you slip inside. There you are greeted by a small band of brothers and sisters who have made the same long trek. As you look at their weary but expectant faces, you realize something: Not one of them has come

because a great communicator has been scheduled to speak. Not one is present because a cool band is scheduled to play. No, all are there simply because they desire to gather with the people of God, and they are willing to risk their lives to be together.

Performance has nothing to do with it. People have everything to do with it.

 What if the church itself is intended to be the attraction, regardless of who is teaching or singing that day?

Whenever I am in churches overseas like the one just depicted, I am reminded of how much we have filled our contemporary worship environments with performance elements such as elaborate stage sets, state-of-the-art sound systems, and high-definition

video screens. I am also struck by our reliance upon having just the right speaker and just the right musician who can attract the most people to a worship service. But what if the church itself—the people of God gathered in one place—is intended to be the attraction, regardless of who is teaching or singing that day? This is enough for our brothers and sisters around the world.

But is it enough for us?

I am haunted by this question on Sundays as I stand in a nice auditorium with a quality sound system and large video screens on the wall, all designed to spotlight select people on stage. It's not that everything in this scene is necessarily wrong, but I do wonder what in this scene is biblically best and practically healthy for the people of God. I have more questions than I have answers on this issue, and I am grateful for leaders in our

worship ministry who are willing to ask the questions with me.

We recently cut 83 percent of our worship budget. We did this not only to free up resources for urgent needs around the world but also to scale back our emphasis on nonessential elements of corporate worship. We want to focus on ways we can cultivate the best people: a people who love to pray together, fast together, confess sin together, sing together, and study together; a people who depend more on the Word that is spoken than on the one who speaks it; a people who are gripped in music more by the content of the song than by the appeal of the singer; and a people who define worship less by the quality of a slick performance and more by the commitment of a humble people who gather week after week simply to behold the glory of God as they surrender their lives to him.

PEOPLE, NOT PLACES

When the church is fundamentally a gathering of committed people, the place where the church gathers hardly matters.

Over the last few years, I have had many conversations, both inside and outside Brook Hills, about church buildings. Admittedly, I pastor a church that gathers in and enjoys the luxuries of one of these multimillion-dollar edifices. Because we have this building, I want us to steward it well, whether that means maximizing it for ministry or selling it and spending our resources differently. Everything is on the table, and the Lord will lead us in what is best. I realize that a lot of people in our church have sacrificed greatly to make our facility a reality, and I am deeply grateful for God's grace in them. At the same time, I am not convinced that large

buildings are the best or only way to use God's resources.

You may ask (as members of our church and leaders of other churches have asked me in countless conversations), "What's wrong with constructing church buildings? Nowhere does the New Testament say we shouldn't construct church buildings."

 Why would we spend an inordinate amount of our resources on something that is never prescribed or even encouraged in the New Testament?

But that's just it. There's also nothing in the New Testament that says we *should* construct church buildings. So whenever we

plant a church or whenever a church starts to grow, why is the first thing we think, *We need to spend masses of our resources on a building*? Why would we spend an inordinate amount of our resources on something that is never prescribed or even encouraged in the New Testament? Why would we not instead use those resources on that which is explicitly promoted in the New Testament, such as sharing the gospel with the lost or helping the poor in the church?[4] As I write this, more than seven hundred million people around the world live in slums. Many of them are our brothers and sisters in Christ. Should we really be prioritizing bigger buildings for ourselves?

I spoke recently with the pastor of an inner-city church plant in the southern United States. His congregation numbers around one hundred people, and recently

twenty of them went on a short-term mission trip to a third-world country. As they traveled, they read and discussed *Radical* and the truths from God's Word that the book presents. By the time the team came back, God had transformed their hearts and minds in surprising ways.

They began reevaluating how they had been spending their lives and resources, both personally and corporately. When they looked at the church budget, they realized that their little church was spending five thousand dollars a month to lease building space downtown. So some of the members asked the pastor, "Why don't we take this sixty thousand dollars a year and use it for something more eternally valuable?"

"Then where are we going to meet as a church?" he asked.

They pointed to the parking deck next

to the space they were leasing. "We can meet over there," they said.

"Outside?" he asked.

"It's covered, it's empty on Sundays, and we already know that it's available for our use."

The pastor gave it some thought and then said, "Let's do it." The church is now meeting outside every Sunday on a parking deck.

This is the beauty of New Testament Christianity, and I wonder if too many of us are missing it. We definitely do not have to construct buildings as houses of worship. In the words of Stephen before he was martyred by the Sanhedrin, "The Most High does not live in houses made by men."[5]

Stephen was speaking to resistant people who were undergoing a major shift in the redemptive plan of God. They were used to

seeing the presence of God symbolized in the temple, a monumental edifice. But with Jesus' death on the cross, the way had been opened for people to dwell in the presence of God in any place.[6] No central building was necessary. And as a result, they no longer needed to focus on a building as a house of worship.

Well, what would the house of worship be, then?

You guessed it: people.

Paul says to the church at Corinth, "Don't you know that you yourselves are God's temple and that God's Spirit lives in you?" He later tells them that their bodies are the temple of God.[7] This is the astounding reality of New Testament religion: we as Christians are the house of worship.

So let's gather wherever we can—in homes, in offices, in workspaces, in parks, in any facilities we can find. Let's remember

that many of our brothers and sisters around the world simply meet outside. And let's at least consider not spending such a large portion of our resources on building places when the priority of the New Testament is decidedly on building people.

PEOPLE, NOT PROGRAMS

The challenge, though, is that we need our places to sustain our programs. How will we have thriving children and adult programs if we don't have a place to host them? This is when we begin to realize that redefining place in ministry leads to rethinking the importance of programs in ministry.

Imagine that your church had no building or facilities whatsoever. Could you still make disciples? Certainly the answer is yes. Churches all around the world make do. So

how would your church make disciples completely separate from a church building? This is the question we started asking at Brook Hills, and it has led us to some significant changes. I'll share just one.

 Imagine that your church had no building or facilities whatsoever. Could you still make disciples?

For years we had hosted a Vacation Bible School for one week every summer in our building. Members of the church would spend hours decorating rooms and preparing facilities for the time when kids in our community would come to our building for ministry. But then our children's ministry leaders asked, "If we didn't have a build-

ing, how could we teach the gospel to kids throughout our community?"

That's when they began equipping parents, children's ministry leaders, and small-group leaders in our faith family to host Bible clubs for kids in their homes. We already had homes spread all around our immediate community. Why not make our homes the place of ministry instead of the church building? Why not invite people from our neighborhoods, not to go to a church building with us, but to come across the street and into our homes with us? Home is where we could show the gospel to their children while we also shared life with them.

So during the summer, members of our church started hosting neighbors in their homes for Bible clubs. Crowds of kids came—far more than we could ever have

hosted in our church building at one time. And all of it took place in diverse neighborhoods far away from our building.

The outcome? Scores of non-Christian neighbors are hearing a gospel-centered witness and seeing a gospel-centered family right next door, and the gospel is multiplying throughout our community.

One day I visited a home during a Bible club event. As kids played in the yard and parents visited, the host mom and dad hit me with a proposal. "We were thinking that we could invite these kids and their families to our home throughout the year. We'd be doing ministry here instead of trying to do it all at the church building on a Wednesday night. Would that be okay with you?"

Yes! That would be okay with me! I am okay when people discover that God has built

into our everyday lives opportunities and platforms to spread the gospel. I am okay when people realize that we are not dependent on well-crafted programs at designated places to accomplish the mission God has created us for as his people.

This is just one small illustration in the area of children's ministry. But imagine what could happen if this picture were multiplied across the church: men and women seeing that the most effective avenues for ministry are found not in programs created for them but amid the people who surround them where they live. God has given every follower of Christ natural avenues to spread the gospel and declare his glory. Which means that the last thing leaders should do is pull people away from those avenues in order to participate in our activities.

At one point at Brook Hills, we were trying to organize and centralize all the types of ministry in which people were involved. For example, we created community ministry programs so people could participate in outreach efforts in our city. We encouraged every small group to get involved in one of the programs we had organized. The only problem was that the more Christ compelled the members of our faith family to see the opportunities he had built into their lives for the spread of the gospel, the less time they had to participate in our programs. I have to admit: when people started giving themselves to ministries we had not organized, we didn't know what to do about it.

That's when we woke up and said to ourselves, "Why are we trying to organize how and where and when our people minister?

God has already given them opportunities for ministry where they live and work and play." So we decided to stop planning, creating, and managing outreach programs and to start unleashing people to maximize the ministry opportunities God had already planned and created for them.

 We woke up and said to ourselves, "Why are we trying to organize how and where and when our people minister?"

From that point the impact of our church in the community changed radically. Now our people are busy leading Bible studies in their workplaces and neighborhoods, helping addicts in rehabilitation centers, supplying food in homeless shelters, loving orphans in

learning centers, caring for widows in retirement homes, providing hospice care for the elderly, training men and women in job skills, tutoring men and women in reading, helping patients in AIDS clinics, teaching English to internationals, and serving in a variety of other ways. And now our leadership team understands that it's good when people are so involved in ministry where they live that they don't have time to participate in the programs we create.

If you are a leader in the church, think about the individuals in your care. See their faces, hear their names, and picture their lives. Consider how God has written a different story in each of their lives, filled with varied circumstances and challenges, trials and temptations, experiences and encounters. He has sovereignly led them to the life

stage and situation where they now find themselves, surrounded by people you will never meet and opportunities you will never have. And you have been called by God to serve them in the accomplishment of God's purpose for their lives. If you're like me, the last thing you want to do is sideline them to sit during a performance while you do the work or to participate in a program you have created. Instead, you want to equip them, train them, support them, and set them free to use everything God has given them to make his glory known in ways you could never design or imagine.

And if you are a member of the church, start dreaming and strategizing. Consider where God has placed you, whom God has put around you, and how God desires to use you for his glory where you live and work. If

you are single, how can you make the most of your singleness for ministry?[8] If you are married, how can you serve together with your spouse in your community? If you have kids, how can you make your home a ministry to children in your neighborhood? If you work outside the home, how can you share Christ in your workplace? Be careful not to let programs in the church keep you from engaging people in the world with the gospel. Make the most of the opportunities for ministry that God has built into your life.

I think of Darren and Julia, a married couple in our church. Darren works in automobile service, and he intentionally uses his work as an avenue for sharing the gospel. He often tells me stories about guys he works with who have come to Christ and whom he is now personally teaching to follow Christ.

Meanwhile, he and Julia serve together in a residential facility that provides shelter and rehabilitation for women. Christ is transforming numerous people's lives in our city through this one couple.

Imagine the spread of the gospel for the glory of God if every follower of Christ were involved in ministry like this. Who can fathom the potential of the church when we stop programming ministry for people and start propelling people into ministry?

PEOPLE, NOT PROFESSIONALS

That question leads to a right understanding of leaders in the church.

Unfortunately, we have a tendency to overlook God's plan for people when we organize churches around professionals. We single out people who seem especially gifted,

and we craft the community of faith around them. Everything we do is dependent on their speaking ability, organizational aptitude, and creative skill. But the ministry of making disciples was not intended for professionals alone; it was intended for the whole people of God.

All men and women who have placed their faith in Christ have the Spirit in them so they might be witnesses for Christ to the ends of the earth. When you read Acts 2, you realize that the giving of the Spirit was never to be a special anointing on a select few. This is about a supernatural anointing on every single one of God's people.[9]

Think about the time Jesus was talking with his disciples about the coming of the Holy Spirit. "I tell you the truth," he said, "anyone who has faith in me will do what I

have been doing. He will do even greater things than these, because I am going to the Father."[10]

What did Jesus mean? Was he saying that the anointing of the Holy Spirit on us would be stronger than it was on him? Yes. But the key is *why* it would be stronger.

The Spirit's anointing on us is not stronger in quality than it was on Jesus. After all, he was sinless. And as a result, his relationship with the Spirit of God was totally unhindered. So how will the Spirit's anointing on our lives enable us to do greater things than Jesus could do?

We will do greater things, not because of the quality of the Spirit in select ones among us, but because of the quantity of the Spirit spread throughout all of us. The Spirit of God does not rest on just one individual, as we

observe in Jesus. No, the Spirit of God rests on every disciple of Jesus, and because of the filling of the Spirit all across the community of faith, we can see greater things than anyone ever saw in the ministry of Jesus.

 Because of the filling of the Spirit all across the community of faith, we can see greater things than anyone ever saw in the ministry of Jesus.

At this moment, while you read this sentence, men and women around the world are being saved from their sins through the proclamation of the gospel. At this moment, people are being delivered from addictions and healed of diseases. At this moment,

brothers and sisters are advancing the gospel in power amid unreached people groups. All of this is happening right now because the Spirit of God has been poured out on all his people all over the world.

Let us not, then, be so foolish as to confine the work of the Spirit to one professional, speaking in one place, at one time of the week. Let us not be so unwise as to bank the spread of the gospel on a certain person at a certain place when all week long the Spirit of God is living in every single man and woman of God, empowering each of us to advance the kingdom of God for his glory.

I was having a conversation the other day with a seminary buddy who jokingly accused me of campaigning to end paid leadership in the church, his salary (and mine) included. You might be wondering the same thing. Is

there a place for paid leaders—that is, professionals—in the church?

Absolutely. And I don't think I'm saying this out of self-interest. When we look in the New Testament, we clearly see a warrant, even a command, to provide financially for certain teachers and leaders in the church. Paul says it is good for leaders who sow spiritual blessings among God's people to reap material blessings from God's people. Of course, leaders in the church must be careful to honor God by their use of money.[11]

What, then, is the responsibility of such leaders in the church? Paul answers this question in Ephesians 4. God has given leaders to the church to equip God's people for ministry and "prepare God's people for works of service."[12] The church has been entrusted by God with stewards of God's Word to equip

God's people to be servants with God's Word. This goes to the essence of being radical together, and it changes everything about how we view leaders in the church.

There is clearly no way that I as a pastor can minister to all the needs in our church, much less in our city. Realizing this, some people might say, "Well, that's what the rest of the church staff is for." But that can't be true either. We will never have enough staff members to meet all the needs in our church or our city. If we want to multiply the gospel from our faith family to all the families of the earth, it will require not just a pastor or church staff but the entire body of Christ built up in love "as each part does its work."[13]

What this means, then, is that church leaders are intended by God not to plan events but to equip people. Leaders do not

exist to provide services; they exist to serve people. Realizing this, we who are leaders in our faith family have made a concentrated effort to take resources (most notably our time) away from organizing ministry for people and to invest them more in mobilizing people for ministry.

 Church leaders are intended by God not to plan events but to equip people.

As I write this, an overseas church leader I'll call Dominic comes to mind. I met him once while visiting a communist nation.

Dominic is now in his sixties, and he has been the pastor of a relatively small house church for most of his life. Dominic's passion is telling people about Christ. He was

once brought before the communist council in his community to be questioned about his evangelistic work. He walked into the interrogation room with a large rock in his hands and set it down on the table in front of the men who were about to question him.

Surprised, one of the men asked Dominic, "Why did you bring this rock with you?"

Dominic replied, "Before we begin my questioning today, I want you to know something. If you try to stop me from telling people about the greatness of Jesus Christ, then this rock is going to start speaking for me." Dominic was alluding to Luke 19:40, where Jesus says that if the disciples didn't proclaim his glory, the stones would cry out instead. The communist leaders, of course, had no idea what Dominic was talking about.

They conferred and decided he was out of his mind, so they released him without further questioning!

Dominic's passion to tell people about Christ translates into a commitment to train people in the church. When he leads someone to Christ, Dominic takes personal responsibility for helping that person grow in Christ. His goal is for that person to become a leader in the church and then eventually to leave and plant another church somewhere else. (Almost all church planters in that part of the world are bivocational.) Dominic's church has now planted more than sixty other churches in his country, with nearly every one of the pastors trained by Dominic. His life and leadership are a picture of what it means, not to organize ministry for people, but to mobilize people for ministry.

WHERE WILL OUR LIVES COUNT?

Isn't this the model of Jesus? During his ministry on earth, he spent more time with twelve men than with everyone else put together. In John 17, where he recounts his ministry before going to the cross, he doesn't mention the multitudes he preached to or the miracles he performed. As spectacular as those events were, they were not his primary focus. Instead, forty times Jesus speaks to and about the men in whom he had invested his life. They were his focus. When he came to his ascension, Jesus had no buildings or programs to point to and no crowds to boast of. Indeed, most of the crowds had walked away. Just 120 unschooled, ordinary people were gathered—a small group with a small band of leaders.

And he had given them one command

as their commission: make disciples. Do with others what I have done with you, Jesus had said. Don't sit in a classroom; share your lives. Don't build extravagant places; build extraordinary people. Make disciples who will make disciples who will make disciples, and together multiply this gospel to all peoples. This is the simple command that was to drive the church. And this is the simple command that is to drive each of our lives.

I don't want this command to be treated as optional in my life or in anyone else's life in the church I pastor. Personally, I have an intentional disciple-making plan that involves sharing life with and multiplying the gospel through my family, a small group of men within our church, and church planters we are sending out from our church. I don't want to imply that this plan is always smooth

in practice or easy to implement. Like you, I am constantly beset by the busyness of life and the responsibilities of leadership, and if I am not careful, disciple making fades into the background. As a result, I want to act intentionally, for if I forsake the priority of people, then I will miss the purpose of God.

 You may at times feel like the wrong person, thinking you are not gifted enough, smart enough, talented enough, or qualified enough to engage in effective ministry. This is simply not true.

Every one of our pastors and church staff has designed similar disciple-making plans. In addition, we help all new members

in our church to outline their plans for how they will be involved in making disciples of all nations. The key for all of us is an intense desire and intentional effort to make every one of our lives count for the multiplication of the gospel in the world.

Regardless of your place in the church, remember that you are not intended to be sidelined in the kingdom of God. You may at times feel like the wrong person, thinking you are not gifted enough, smart enough, talented enough, or qualified enough to engage in effective ministry. This is simply not true. You have the Word of God before you, the Spirit of God in you, and the command of God to you: make disciples of all nations. So whether you are a businessman or a businesswoman, a lawyer or a doctor, a consultant or a construction worker, a teacher or

a student, an on-the-go professional or an on-the-go stay-at-home mom, I implore you to ask God to make your life count where you live for the spread of the gospel and the declaration of his glory to the ends of the earth.

A BETTER WAY

We will never have enough resources, staff, buildings, events, or activities to reach all the people in our community, much less all the peoples in the world. But we will always have enough people. Even if they seem like the wrong people.

If eleven disciples on a mountain in Galilee were enough to launch the gospel to the ends of the earth, then a church with a handful of members can spread the gospel in and beyond a community, regardless of the amount of material resources it has. The plan

of God is certainly not confined to large churches or gifted leaders. The plan of God is for every person among the people of God to count for the advancement of the kingdom of God.

 If eleven disciples on a mountain in Galilee were enough to launch the gospel to the ends of the earth, then a church with a handful of members can spread the gospel in and beyond a community.

What if each of us were actually making disciples who were making disciples who were making disciples? Is it too idealistic to dream that the church of God, unleashed for the purpose of God, might actually reach the

ends of the earth with the gospel? Is that re-
alistic? You bet it is. In fact, it's guaranteed.
Jesus has promised that every nation, tribe,
tongue, and people are going to hear the
gospel, and it is going to happen through all
of us.[14]

Notes

1. Leviticus 26:12; Romans 12:5;
 1 Peter 2:9; Ephesians 3:10.
2. David Platt, *Radical: Taking Back
 Your Faith from the American Dream*
 (Colorado Springs, CO: Multnomah,
 2010), 48–50.
3. Hebrews 10:24–25.
4. Acts 4:32–35; 2 Corinthians 8–9.
5. Acts 7:48.
6. Matthew 27:51.
7. 1 Corinthians 3:16; 6:18–20.
8. 1 Corinthians 7:32–34.
9. Acts 1:8; 2:17–18; Joel 2:28–29.
10. John 14:12.
11. 1 Timothy 5:17–18; 1 Corinthians
 9:8–18; 1 Timothy 3:2–3, 8.

12. Ephesians 4:12.
13. Ephesians 4:16.
14. Matthew 24:14; Revelation 7:9–10; Romans 10:13–15.

About the Author

Dr. David Platt is the senior pastor of the Church at Brook Hills, Birmingham, Alabama. He and his wife, Heather, have two sons. David is the author of *Radical* and *Radical Together*, both *New York Times* bestsellers. For more information, see radical thebook.com and radicaltogether.com.

What is Jesus worth to you?

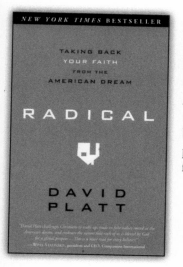

Take the next step of radical discipleship...together.

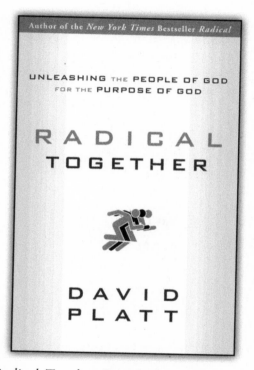

In *Radical Together,* David Platt follows up his revolutionary call to authentic discipleship with the next big step: showing how it can work in your church.

SHARE THE MESSAGE

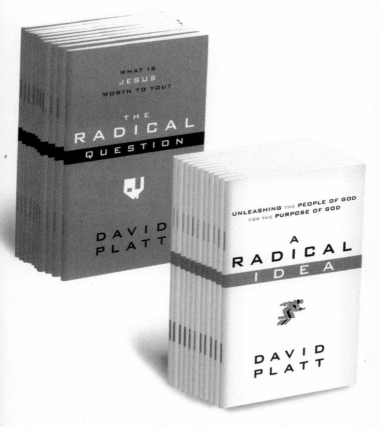

Available as 10-packs

DEEPEN YOUR UNDERSTANDING

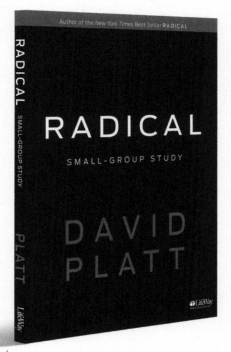

This resource will help you discover what could happen if the message of *Radical* and *Radical Together* were lived out by every member of your church.

30. $\displaystyle\int \cos au \cos bu \, du = \frac{\sin(a-b)u}{2(a-b)} + \frac{\sin(a+b)u}{2(a+b)} + C \quad \text{if } a^2 \neq b^2$

31. $\displaystyle\int \sin au \cos bu \, du = -\frac{\cos(a-b)u}{2(a-b)} - \frac{\cos(a+b)u}{2(a+b)} + C \quad \text{if } a^2 \neq b^2$

32. $\displaystyle\int \sin^n u \, du = -\frac{1}{n} \sin^{n-1} u \cos u + \frac{n-1}{n} \int \sin^{n-2} u \, du$

33. $\displaystyle\int \cos^n u \, du = \frac{1}{n} \cos^{n-1} u \sin u + \frac{n-1}{n} \int \cos^{n-2} u \, du$

34. $\displaystyle\int \tan^n u \, du = \frac{1}{n-1} \tan^{n-1} u - \int \tan^{n-2} u \, du \quad \text{if } n \neq 1$

35. $\displaystyle\int \cot^n u \, du = -\frac{1}{n-1} \cot^{n-1} u - \int \cot^{n-2} u \, du \quad \text{if } n \neq 1$

36. $\displaystyle\int \sec^n u \, du = \frac{1}{n-1} \sec^{n-2} u \tan u + \frac{n-2}{n-1} \int \sec^{n-2} u \, du \quad \text{if } n \neq 1$

37. $\displaystyle\int \csc^n u \, du = -\frac{1}{n-1} \csc^{n-2} u \cot u + \frac{n-2}{n-1} \int \csc^{n-2} u \, du \quad \text{if } n \neq 1$

38. $\displaystyle\int u \sin u \, du = \sin u - u \cos u + C$

39. $\displaystyle\int u \cos u \, du = \cos u + u \sin u + C$

40. $\displaystyle\int u^n \sin u \, du = -u^n \cos u + n \int u^{n-1} \cos u \, du$

41. $\displaystyle\int u^n \cos u \, du = u^n \sin u - n \int u^{n-1} \sin u \, du$

FORMS INVOLVING $\sqrt{u^2 \pm a^2}$

42. $\displaystyle\int \sqrt{u^2 \pm a^2} \, du = \frac{u}{2} \sqrt{u^2 \pm a^2} \pm \frac{a^2}{2} \ln\left|u + \sqrt{u^2 \pm a^2}\right| + C$

43. $\displaystyle\int \frac{du}{\sqrt{u^2 \pm a^2}} = \ln\left|u + \sqrt{u^2 \pm a^2}\right| + C$

FORMS INVOLVING $\sqrt{a^2 - u^2}$

44. $\displaystyle\int \sqrt{a^2 - u^2} \, du = \frac{u}{2} \sqrt{a^2 - u^2} + \frac{a^2}{2} \sin^{-1}\frac{u}{a} + C$

45. $\displaystyle\int \frac{\sqrt{a^2 - u^2}}{u} \, du = \sqrt{a^2 - u^2} - a \ln\left|\frac{a + \sqrt{a^2 - u^2}}{u}\right| + C$

(Continued on Rear Endpaper)

DIFFERENTIAL EQUATIONS
AND BOUNDARY VALUE PROBLEMS

Computing and Modeling

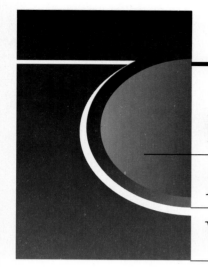

DIFFERENTIAL EQUATIONS AND BOUNDARY VALUE PROBLEMS

Computing and Modeling

C. H. Edwards, Jr.
David E. Penney

The University of Georgia

PRENTICE HALL, Englewood Cliffs, New Jersey 07632

Library of Congress Cataloging-in-Publication Data

Edwards, C. H. (Charles Henry)
 Differential equations and boundary value problems : computing and
modeling / C.H. Edwards, Jr., David E. Penney.
 p. cm.
 Includes bibliographical references (p. -) and index.
 ISBN 0-13-382094-7
 1. Differential equations. 2. Boundary value problems.
I. Penney, David E. II. Title.
QA371.E28 1996
515'.35--dc20 95-33185
 CIP

EDITOR-IN-CHIEF, Tim Bozik

ACQUISITION EDITOR, George Lobell

MANAGING EDITOR, Jeanne Hoeting

DIRECTOR OF DESIGN, Amy Rosen

INTERIOR DESIGN, Lee Goldstein

COVER DESIGN, Mary De Franco

PRODUCTION EDITOR, Nicholas Romanelli

MANUFACTURING BUYER, Alan Fischer

EDITORIAL ASSISTANTS, Nancy Bauer, Mary De Luca, Gale A. Epps

 ©1996 by Prentice-Hall, Inc.
Simon & Schuster / A Viacom Company
Englewood Cliffs, NJ 07632

Printed in the United States of America
10 9 8 7 6 5 4 3 2 1

ISBN 0-13-382094-7

Prentice-Hall International (UK) Limited, London
Prentice-Hall of Australia Pty. Limited, Sydney
Prentice-Hall Canada, Inc., Toronto
Prentice-Hall Hispanoamericana, S.A., Mexico
Prentice-Hall of India Private Limited, New Delhi
Prentice-Hall of Japan, Inc., Tokyo
Simon & Schuster Asia Pte. Ltd., Singapore
Editoria Prentice-Hall do Brasil, Ltda., Rio de Janeiro

Contents

8 Power Series Methods 457

9 Fourier Series Methods 529

10 Eigenvalues and Boundary Value Problems 599

Preface

For the past half century many (if not most) introductory differential equations courses for science and engineering students have emphasized the formal solution of standard types of differential equations using a (seeming) grab-bag of systematic solution techniques. Students in such courses frequently have seen the subject as largely a game of matching memorized methods with memorized equations. The evolution of the present text from our earlier elementary differential equations book is based on experience teaching a new course (assisted by a National Science Foundation grant) with a greater emphasis on conceptual ideas and the use of computer lab projects to involve students in more intense and sustained problem-solving experiences.

The availability of technical computing environments like *Maple, Mathematica,* and MATLAB is now reshaping the role and applications of differential equations in science and engineering, and has shaped our approach in this text. New technology motivates a shift in emphasis from traditional manual methods to both qualitative and computer-based methods that

- render accessible a wider range of more realistic applications;
- permit the use of both numerical computation and graphical visualization to develop greater conceptual understanding; and
- encourage empirical investigations that involve deeper thought and analysis than standard textbook problems.

Major Features

The following features of this text are intended to support a contemporary differential equations course that augments traditional core skills with conceptual perspectives that students will need for the effective use of differential equations in their subsequent work and study:

- We have trimmed the coverage of seldom-used topics and added new topics in order to place throughout a greater emphasis on core techniques as well as qualitative aspects of the subject associated with slope fields, solution curves, phase portraits, and dynamical systems. To this end we combine symbolic, graphic, and numeric solution methods wherever it seems advantageous. A fresh new computational flavor should be evident in figures, examples, problems, and projects throughout the text.

- The organization of the book places an increased emphasis on linear systems of differential equations, which are covered in Chapters 4 and 5 (together with the necessary linear algebra), followed by a substantial treatment in Chapter 6 of nonlinear systems and phenomena (including chaos in dynamical systems).

- This book begins and ends with discussions and examples of the mathematical modeling of real-world phenomena. The fact that differential equations have diverse and important applications is obvious enough—whole areas of the subject exist mainly because of their applications. Students learn through mathematical modeling and empirical investigation to balance the questions of what equation to formulate, how to solve it, and whether a solution will yield useful information.

- While according real-world applications their due, we also think the first course in differential equations should be a window on the world of mathematics. While it is neither feasible nor desirable to include proofs of the fundamental existence and uniqueness theorems along the way in an elementary course, students need to see precise and clear-cut statements of these theorems, and to understand their role in the subject. We include appropriate existence and uniqueness proofs in the Appendix, and occasionally refer to them in the main body of the text.

- While our approach reflects the widespread use of new computer methods for the solution of differential equations, we continue to believe that certain elementary analytical methods of solution (as in Chapters 1 and 3) are important for students to learn. One reason is that effective and reliable use of numerical methods often requires preliminary analysis using standard elementary techniques; the construction of a realistic numerical model often is based on the study of a simpler analytical model. We therefore continue to stress the mastery of traditional solution techniques (especially through the inclusion of extensive problem sets).

Computing Features

The following features highlight the flavor of computing technology that distinguishes much of our exposition.

- About 180 new *computer-generated graphics* throughout the text show students vivid pictures of slope fields, solution curves, and phase plane portraits that bring symbolic solutions of differential equations to life.

- About 40 new *computing projects,* which follow key sections throughout the text, illustrate the use of computer algebra systems like *Maple, Mathematica,*

and MATLAB—and actively engage students in the application of new technology. The companion Computing Projects Manual provides separate and detailed instruction on *Maple, Mathematica,* and MATLAB syntax and techniques. It also supplements the text projects with additional and sometimes more challenging investigations.

- A fresh *numerical emphasis* that is afforded by the early introduction of numerical solution techniques in Chapter 2 (on mathematical models and numerical methods). Here and in Chapter 4, where numerical techniques for systems are treated, a concrete and tangible flavor is achieved by the inclusion of numerical algorithms presented in parallel fashion for systems ranging from the TI-85 graphics calculator to MATLAB.

- A *conceptual perspective* shaped by the availability of computational aids, which permits a leaner and more streamlined coverage of certain traditional manual topics (like exact equations and variation of parameters) in Chapters 1, 3, and 5.

Modeling Features

We take mathematical modeling as a goal and constant motivation for the study of differential equations. To sample the range of applications in this text, take a look at the following questions:

- What makes the difference between doomsday and extinction in alligator populations? (Section 2.1)

- How do a unicycle and a two-axle car react differently to road bumps? (Sections 3.7 and 5.3)

- What shape for a rocket nose-cone minimizes its air resistance? (Section 4.3)

- Why might an earthquake demolish one building and leave standing the one next door? (Section 5.3)

- What determines whether two species will live harmoniously together, or whether competition will result in the extinction of one of them and the survival of the other? (Section 6.3)

- Why and when does non-linearity lead to chaos in biological and mechanical systems? (Section 6.5)

- Why are flagpoles hollow instead of solid? (Section 8.6)

- What explains the difference in the sounds of a guitar, a xylophone, and a drum? (Sections 9.6, 10.2, and 10.4)

Organization and Content

We have reshaped the usual approach and sequence of topics to accommodate new technology and new perspectives. For instance:

- After a precis of first-order equations in Chapter 1 (though with the coverage of certain traditional symbolic methods somewhat streamlined), Chapter 2 offers

an unusually early introduction to mathematical modeling, stability and qualitative properties of differential equations, and numerical methods—a combination of topics that usually are dispersed later in an introductory course.

- Chapters 4 and 5 provide a flexible treatment of linear systems. Motivated by current trends in science and engineering education and practice, Chapter 4 offers an early, intuitive introduction to first-order systems, models, and numerical approximation techniques. Chapter 5 begins with a self-contained treatment of the linear algebra that is needed both for conceptual understanding and for numerical solution, and then presents the eigenvalue approach to linear systems. It includes an unusual number of applications (ranging from railway cars to earthquakes) of all the various cases of the eigenvalue method.

- Chapter 6 on nonlinear systems and phenomena ranges from phase plane analysis to ecological and mechanical systems to a concluding section on chaos and bifurcation in dynamical systems—Section 6.5 presents an elementary introduction to such contemporary topics as period-doubling in biological and mechanical systems, the pitchfork diagram, and the Lorenz strange attractor (all illustrated with vivid computer graphics).

- Laplace transform methods (Chapter 7) and power series methods (Chapter 8) follow the material on linear and nonlinear systems, but can be covered at any earlier point (after Chapter 3) the instructor desires.

- Chapters 9 and 10 treat the applications of Fourier series, separation of variables, and Sturm-Liouville theory to partial differential equations and boundary value problems. After the introduction of Fourier series, the three classical equations—the wave and heat equations and Laplace's equation—are discussed in the last three sections of Chapter 9. The Sturm-Liouville methods of Chapter 10 are developed sufficiently to include some rather significant and realistic applications.

This book includes enough material appropriately arranged for different courses varying in length from one quarter to two semesters. The briefer version, **Differential Equations: Computing and Modeling,** ends with Chapter 7 on Laplace transform methods (and thus omits the material on power series methods, Fourier series, separation of variables, and partial differential equations).

Problems and Projects

Probably no other mathematics course beyond calculus relies so much on the exercises and problem sets to promote adequate student learning. We therefore devoted great effort to the development and selection of the approximately 1800 problems in this book. Each section contains more computational problems ("solve the following equations," and so on) than any class will ordinarily use, plus an ample number of applied problems.

The answer section includes the answers to most odd-numbered problems and to some of the even-numbered ones. The 385-page **Student Solutions Manual** accompanying this book provides worked-out solutions for slightly over a quarter of the problems in the book—a majority of these solutions are for even-numbered problems, a

brief hint or suggestion for another quarter, and an answer alone for most of the remaining problems in the text that do not include answers in their statements.

The approximately 40 project sections in the text contain much additional and extended problem material designed to engage students in the exploration and application of computational technology. These project sections are "technology neutral" in character, with illustrative references to *Maple, Mathematica,* and MATLAB commands as well as occasional comments on the use of graphics calculators or other systems. These projects are expanded considerably in the **Computing Projects Manual** that accompanies the text and includes additional projects not contained in the text. Each project in this manual has parallel **Using *Maple*, Using *Mathematica*,** and **Using MATLAB** sections that detail the applicable methods and techniques of each system, and will afford student users an opportunity to compare the merits and styles of different computational systems.

Acknowledgments

In preparing this revision we profited greatly from the advice and assistance of the following very able reviewers:

Len Bruening, Cleveland State University; Patricia Clark, Rochester Institute of Technology; Philip Crooke, Vanderbilt University; George Giordano, Ryerson Polytechnic University; Rebecca E. Hill, Rochester Institute of Technology; Dar-Veig Ho, Georgia Institute of Technology; Joe A. Marlin, North Carolina State University, and Michael Stecher, Texas A&M University.

We thank also our editor, George Lobell, for his enthusiastic encouragement and advice, and Nick Romanelli for his efficient coordination of the process of book production. Once again, we are unable to express adequately our debts to Alice F. Edwards and Carol W. Penney for their continued assistance, encouragement, support, and patience.

C. H. E., Jr.
D. E. P.

1 First-Order Differential Equations

1.1 Differential Equations and Mathematical Models

The laws of the universe are written in the language of mathematics. Algebra is sufficient to solve many static problems, but the most interesting natural phenomena involve change and are described only by equations that relate changing quantities.

Because the derivative $dx/dt = f'(t)$ of the function f is the rate at which the quantity $x = f(t)$ is changing with respect to the independent variable t, it is natural that equations involving derivatives are frequently used to describe the changing universe. An equation relating an unknown function and one or more of its derivatives is called a **differential equation.**

EXAMPLE 1 The differential equation

$$\frac{dx}{dt} = x^2 + t^2$$

involves both the unknown function $x(t)$ and its first derivative. The differential equation

$$\frac{d^2y}{dx^2} + 3\frac{dy}{dx} + 7y = 0$$

1

involves the unknown function y of the independent variable x and the first two derivatives y' and y'' of y. ■

The study of differential equations has three principal goals:

1. To discover the differential equation that describes a specified physical situation.
2. To find—either exactly or approximately—the appropriate solution of that equation;
3. To interpret the solution that is found.

In algebra, we typically seek the unknown *numbers* that satisfy an equation such as $x^3 + 7x^2 - 11x + 41 = 0$. By contrast, in solving a differential equation, we are challenged to find the unknown *functions* $y = y(x)$ for which an identity such as $y'(x) = 2xy(x)$—that is, the differential equation

$$\frac{dy}{dx} = 2xy$$

—holds on some interval of real numbers. Ordinarily, we will want to find *all* solutions of the differential equation if possible.

EXAMPLE 2 If C is a constant and

$$y(x) = Ce^{x^2}, \tag{1}$$

then

$$\frac{dy}{dx} = C(2xe^{x^2}) = (2x)(Ce^{x^2}) = 2xy.$$

Thus every function $y(x)$ of the form in (1) is a solution of the differential equation

$$\frac{dy}{dx} = 2xy \tag{2}$$

for all x. In particular, Eq. (1) defines an *infinite* family of different solutions of this differential equation, one for each choice of the "arbitrary constant" C. By the method of separation of variables (Section 1.4) it can be shown that every solution of the differential equation in (2) is of the form in Eq. (1). ■

Differential Equations and Mathematical Models

The following three examples illustrate the process of translating scientific laws and principles into differential equations. In each of these examples the independent variable is time t, but we will see numerous examples in which some quantity other than time is the independent variable.

EXAMPLE 3 Newton's law of cooling may be stated in this way: The *time rate of change* (the rate of change with respect to time t) of the temperature $T(t)$ of a body is proportional to the difference between T and the temperature A of the surrounding medium (Fig.

1.1.1). That is,

$$\frac{dT}{dt} = -k(T - A), \tag{3}$$

where k is a positive constant. Observe that if $T > A$, then $dT/dt < 0$, so the temperature $T(t)$ is a decreasing function of t and the body is cooling. On the other hand, if $T < A$, then $dT/dt > 0$, so that T is increasing.

Thus the physical law is translated into a differential equation. If we are given the values of k and A, we should be able to find an explicit formula for $T(t)$, and then—with the aid of this formula—we can predict the future temperature of the body.

Temperature A

Temperature T

FIGURE 1.1.1. Newton's law of cooling, Eq. (3), describes the cooling of a hot rock in cold water.

EXAMPLE 4 Torricelli's law implies that the *time rate of change* of the volume V of water in a draining tank (Fig. 1.1.2) is proportional to the square root of the depth y of water in the tank:

$$\frac{dV}{dt} = -k\sqrt{y}, \tag{4}$$

where k is a constant. If the tank is a cylinder with vertical axis and cross-sectional area A, then $V = Ay$, so $dV/dt = A \cdot (dy/dt)$. In this case Eq. (4) takes the form

$$\frac{dy}{dt} = -h\sqrt{y}, \tag{5}$$

where $h = k/A$ is a constant.

Volume V

FIGURE 1.1.2. Torricelli's law of draining, Eq. (4), describes the draining of a water tank.

EXAMPLE 5 The *time rate of change* of a population $P(t)$ with constant birth and death rates is, in many simple cases, proportional to the size of the population. That is,

$$\frac{dP}{dt} = kP, \tag{6}$$

where k is the constant of proportionality. ∎

Discussion: Let us discuss Example 5 further. Note first that each function of the form

$$P(t) = Ce^{kt} \tag{7}$$

is a solution of the differential equation

$$\frac{dP}{dt} = kP$$

in (6). We verify this assertion as follows:

$$P'(t) = Cke^{kt} = k(Ce^{kt}) = kP(t)$$

for all real numbers t. Because substitution of each function of the form given in (7) into Eq. (6) produces an identity, all these functions are solutions of Eq. (6).

Thus, even if the value of the constant k is known, the differential equation dP/dt has *infinitely many* different solutions of the form $P(t) = Ce^{kt}$, one for each choice of the "arbitrary" constant C. This is typical of differential equations. It is also fortunate, because it may allow us to use additional information to select from all the solutions a particular one that fits the situation under study.

EXAMPLE 6 Suppose that $P(t) = Ce^{kt}$ is the population of a colony of bacteria at time t, that the population at time $t = 0$ (hours, h) was 1000, and that the population doubled after 1 h. This additional information about the function $P(t)$ yields the following equations:

$$1000 = P(0) = Ce^0 = C,$$

$$2000 = P(1) = Ce^k.$$

It follows that $C = 1000$ and that $e^k = 2$, so $k = \ln 2 \approx 0.693147$. With this value of k the differential equation in (6) is

$$\frac{dP}{dt} = (\ln 2)P \approx (0.693147)P,$$

and the value $C = 1000$ yields the particular solution

$$P(t) = 1000e^{t\ln 2} \approx 1000e^{(0.693147)t}$$

that satisfies the given conditions. Therefore, we can predict the population at any future time. For instance, the number of bacteria in the population after one and a half hours (when $t = 1.5$ h) will be

$$P(1.5) = 1000e^{(1.5)\ln 2} \approx 2828. \qquad \blacksquare$$

The condition $P(0) = 1000$ in Example 6 is called an **initial condition** because we frequently write differential equations for which $t = 0$ is the "starting time." Figure 1.1.3 shows a number of different graphs of the form $P(t) = Ce^{kt}$ with $k = \ln 2$. The graphs of all the infinitely many solutions of $dP/dt = kP$ in fact fill the entire two-dimensional plane, and no two intersect. Moreover, the selection of any point on the P-axis amounts to a determination of the value $P(0)$. Because exactly one solution passes through each such point, we see in this case that an initial condition $P(0) = P_0$ determines a unique solution agreeing with the given data.

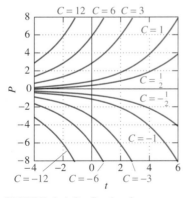

FIGURE 1.1.3. Graphs of $P(t) = Ce^{kt}$ with $k = \ln 2$

Mathematical Models

Our brief discussion of population growth in Examples 5 and 6 illustrates the crucial process of *mathematical modeling* (Fig. 1.1.4), which involves:

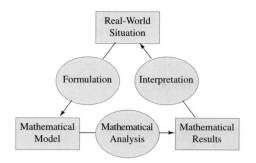

FIGURE 1.1.4. The process
of mathematical modeling

1. The formulation of a real-world problem in mathematical terms—that is, the construction of a mathematical model;

2. The analysis or solution of the resulting mathematical problem;

3. The interpretation of the mathematical results in the context of the original real-world situation—for example, answering the question originally posed.

In the population example, the real-world problem is that of determining the population at some future time. A **mathematical model** consists of a list of variables (P and t) that describe the given situation, together with one or more equations relating these variables ($dP/dt = kP$, $P(0) = P_0$) that are known or are assumed to hold. The mathematical analysis consists of solving these equations (here, for P as a function of t). Finally, we apply these mathematical results to attempt to answer the original real-world question.

Nevertheless, it is quite possible that no one solution of the differential equation fits *all* the known information. In such a case we must suspect that the differential equation may not adequately describe the real world. For instance, the solutions of Eq. (6) are of the form $P(t) = Ce^{kt}$, where C is a positive constant, but for *no* choice of the constants k and C does $P(t)$ accurately describe the actual growth of the human population of the world over the past hundred years. We must therefore write a perhaps more complicated differential equation, one that takes into account the effects of population pressure on the birth rate, the declining food supply, and other factors. This should not be regarded as a failure of the model in Example 5, but as an insight into what additional factors must be considered in studying the growth of populations. Indeed, Eq. (6) is quite accurate under certain circumstances—for example, the growth of a bacterial population under conditions of unlimited food and space.

But in our population example we ignored the effects of such factors as varying birth and death rates. This made the mathematical analysis quite simple, perhaps unrealistically so. A satisfactory mathematical model is subject to two contradictory requirements: It must be sufficiently detailed to represent the real-world situation with relative accuracy, yet it must be sufficiently simple to make the mathematical analysis practical. If the model is so detailed that it fully represents the physical situation, then the mathematical analysis may be too difficult to carry out. If the model is too simple, the results may be so inaccurate as to be useless. Thus there is an inevitable tradeoff between what is physically realistic and what is mathematically possible. The construction of a model that adequately bridges this gap between realism and feasibility is

therefore the most crucial and delicate step in the process. Ways must be found to simplify the model mathematically without sacrificing essential features of the real-world situation.

Mathematical models are discussed throughout this book. The remainder of this introductory section is devoted to simple examples and to standard terminology used in discussing differential equations and their solutions.

Examples and Terminology

EXAMPLE 7 If C is a constant and $y(x) = 1/(C - x)$, then

$$\frac{dy}{dx} = \frac{1}{(C - x)^2} = y^2$$

if $x \neq C$. Thus,

$$y(x) = \frac{1}{C - x} \tag{8}$$

defines a solution of the differential equation

$$\frac{dy}{dx} = y^2 \tag{9}$$

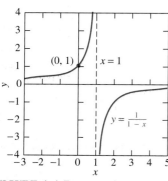

FIGURE 1.1.5. The solution of $y' = y^2$ defined by $y(x) = 1/(1 - x)$

on any interval of real numbers not containing the point $x = C$. Actually, Eq. (8) defines a *one-parameter family* of solutions of $dy/dx = y^2$, one for each value of the arbitrary constant or "parameter" C. With $C = 1$ we get the particular solution $y(t) = 1/(1 - x)$ that satisfies the initial condition $y(0) = 1$. As indicated in Fig. 1.1.5, this solution is continuous on the interval $(-\infty, 1)$ but has a vertical asymptote at $x = 1$.

EXAMPLE 8 Verify that the function $y(x) = 2x^{1/2} - x^{1/2} \ln x$ satisfies the differential equation

$$4x^2 y'' + y = 0 \tag{10}$$

for all $x > 0$.

Solution First we compute the derivatives

$$y'(x) = -\frac{1}{2} x^{-1/2} \ln x \quad \text{and} \quad y''(x) = \frac{1}{4} x^{-3/2} \ln x - \frac{1}{2} x^{-3/2}.$$

Then substitution into Eq. (10) yields

$$4x^2 y'' + y = 4x^2 \left(\frac{1}{4} x^{-3/2} \ln x - \frac{1}{2} x^{-3/2} \right) + 2x^{1/2} - x^{1/2} \ln x = 0$$

if x is positive, so the differential equation is satisfied for all $x > 0$. ∎

The fact that we can write a differential equation is not enough to guarantee that it has a solution. For example, it is clear that the differential equation

$$(y')^2 + y^2 = -1 \tag{11}$$

has *no* (real-valued) solution because the sum of nonnegative numbers cannot be negative. For another variation on this theme, note that the equation

$$(y')^2 + y^2 = 0 \tag{12}$$

obviously has only the (real-valued) solution $y(x) \equiv 0$. In our previous examples any differential equation having at least one solution indeed had infinitely many.

The **order** of a differential equation is the order of the highest derivative that appears in it. The differential equation of Example 8 is of second order, those in Examples 2 through 7 are first-order equations, and

$$y^{(4)} + x^2 y^{(3)} + x^5 y = \sin x$$

is a fourth-order equation. The most general form of an ***n*th-order** differential equation with independent variable x and unknown function or dependent variable $y = y(x)$ is

$$F(x, y, y', y'', \ldots, y^{(n)}) = 0, \tag{13}$$

where F is a specific real-valued function of $n + 2$ variables.

Our use of the word *solution* has been until now somewhat informal. To be precise, we say that the function $u = u(x)$ is a **solution** of the differential equation in (13) **on the interval** I provided that the derivatives $u', u'', \ldots, u^{(n)}$ exist on I and

$$F(x, u, u', u'', \ldots, u^{(n)}) = 0$$

for all x in I. When brevity is important, we say that $u = u(x)$ **satisfies** the differential equation in (13) on I.

EXAMPLE 9 If A and B are constants and

$$y(x) = A \cos 3x + B \sin 3x, \tag{14}$$

then two successive differentiations yield

$$y'(x) = -3A \sin 3x + 3B \cos 3x,$$

$$y''(x) = -9A \cos 3x - 9B \sin 3x = -9y(x)$$

for all x. Consequently, Eq. (14) defines what it is natural to call a *two-parameter family* of solutions of the second-order differential equation

$$y'' + 9y = 0 \tag{15}$$

on the whole real number line. ∎

Although the differential equations in (11) and (12) are exceptions to the general rule, we will see that an *n*th-order equation ordinarily has an n-parameter family of solutions—one involving n different arbitrary constants or parameters.

In both Eqs. (11) and (12), the appearance of y' as an implicitly defined function causes complications. For this reason, we will ordinarily assume that any differential equation under study can be solved explicitly for the highest derivative that appears; that is, that the equation may be written in the form

$$y^{(n)} = G(x, y, y', y'', \ldots, y^{(n-1)}), \tag{16}$$

where G is a real-valued function of $n + 1$ variables. In addition, we will always seek only real-valued solutions unless we warn the reader otherwise.

All the differential equations we have mentioned so far are **ordinary** differential equations, meaning that the unknown function (dependent variable) depends on only a *single* independent variable. For this reason only ordinary derivatives appear in the equation. If the dependent variable is a function of two or more independent variables, partial derivatives are likely to be involved; if so, the equation is called a **partial** differential equation. For example, the temperature $u = u(x, t)$ of a long thin rod at the point x at time t satisfies (under appropriate simple conditions) the partial differential equation

$$\frac{\partial u}{\partial t} = k \frac{\partial^2 u}{\partial x^2},$$

where k is a constant (called the *thermal diffusivity* of the rod). In Chapters 1 through 8 we will be concerned only with *ordinary* differential equations, and will refer to them simply as differential equations.

In this chapter we concentrate our attention on first-order differential equations of the general form

$$\frac{dy}{dx} = f(x, y). \tag{17}$$

We also will sample the wide range of applications of such equations. A typical mathematical model of an applied situation will be an **initial value problem,** consisting of a differential equation of the form in (17) together with an **initial condition** $y(x_0) = y_0$. Note that we call $y(x_0) = y_0$ an initial condition whether or not $x_0 = 0$. To solve the initial value problem

$$\blacktriangleright \qquad \frac{dy}{dx} = f(x, y), \qquad y(x_0) = y_0 \tag{18}$$

means to find a differentiable function $y(x)$ that satisfies both conditions in Eq. (18) on some interval containing x_0.

EXAMPLE 10 Given the solution $y(x) = 1/(C - x)$ of the differential equation $dy/dx = y^2$ discussed in Example 7, solve the initial value problem

$$\frac{dy}{dx} = y^2, \qquad y(1) = 2.$$

Solution We need only find a value of C so that the solution $y(x) = 1/(C - x)$ satisfies the initial condition $y(1) = 2$. Substitution of the values $x = 1$ and $y = 2$ in the solution yields

$$2 = y(1) = \frac{1}{C - 1},$$

so $2C - 2 = 1$, and hence $C = \frac{3}{2}$. With this value of C we obtain the desired solution

$$y(x) = \frac{1}{\frac{3}{2} - x} = \frac{2}{3 - 2x}. \qquad \blacksquare$$

The central question of greatest immediate interest to us is this: If we are given a differential equation known to have a solution satisfying a given initial condition, how do we actually *find* or *compute* that solution? And, once found, what can we do with it? We will see that a relatively few simple techniques—separation of variables (Section 1.4), solution of linear equations (Section 1.5), elementary substitution methods (Section 1.6)—are enough to enable us to solve a diversity of first-order equations having impressive applications.

1.1 Problems

In Problems 1 through 12, verify by substitution that each given function is a solution of the given differential equation.

1. $y' = 3x^2$; $y = x^3 + 7$

2. $y' + 2y = 0$; $y = 3e^{-2x}$

3. $y'' + 4y = 0$; $y_1 = \cos 2x$, $y_2 = \sin 2x$

4. $y'' = 9y$; $y_1 = e^{3x}$, $y_2 = e^{-3x}$

5. $y' = y + 2e^{-x}$; $y = e^x - e^{-x}$

6. $y'' + 4y' + 4y = 0$; $y_1 = e^{-2x}$, $y_2 = xe^{-2x}$

7. $y'' - 2y' + 2y = 0$; $y_1 = e^x \cos x$, $y_2 = e^x \sin x$

8. $y'' + y = 3 \cos 2x$; $y_1 = \cos x - \cos 2x$,
$y_2 = \sin x - \cos 2x$

9. $y' + 2xy^2 = 0$; $y = \dfrac{1}{1 + x^2}$

10. $x^2y'' + xy' - y = \ln x$; $y_1 = x - \ln x$, $y_2 = \dfrac{1}{x} - \ln x$

11. $x^2y'' + 5xy' + 4y = 0$; $y_1 = \dfrac{1}{x^2}$, $y_2 = \dfrac{\ln x}{x^2}$

12. $x^2y'' - xy' + 2y = 0$; $y_1 = x \cos(\ln x)$, $y_2 = x \sin(\ln x)$

In Problems 13 through 16, substitute $y = e^{rx}$ into the given differential equation to determine all values of r for which $y = e^{rx}$ is a solution of the equation.

13. $3y' = 2y$

14. $4y'' = y$

15. $y'' + y' - 2y = 0$

16. $3y'' + 3y' - 4y = 0$

In Problems 17 through 26, first verify that $y(x)$ satisfies the given differential equation. Then determine a value of the constant C so that $y(x)$ satisfies the given initial condition.

17. $y' + y = 0$; $y(x) = Ce^{-x}$, $y(0) = 2$

18. $y' = 2y$; $y(x) = Ce^{2x}$, $y(0) = 3$

19. $y' = y + 1$; $y(x) = Ce^x - 1$, $y(0) = 5$

20. $y' = x - y$; $y(x) = Ce^{-x} + x - 1$, $y(0) = 10$

21. $y' + 3x^2y; = 0$; $y(x) = Ce^{-x^3}$, $y(0) = 7$

22. $e^y y' = 1$; $y = \ln(x + C)$, $y(0) = 0$

23. $x\dfrac{dy}{dx} + 3y = 2x^5$; $y(x) = \dfrac{1}{4}x^5 + Cx^{-3}$, $y(2) = 1$

24. $xy' - 3y = x^3$; $y(x) = x^3(C + \ln x)$, $y(1) = 17$

25. $y' = 3x^2(y^2 + 1)$; $y(x) = \tan(x^3 + C)$, $y(0) = 1$

26. $y' + y \tan x = \cos x$; $y(x) = (x + C)\cos x$, $y(\pi) = 0$

In Problems 27 through 31, a function $y = g(x)$ is described by some geometric property of its graph. Write a differential equation of the form $dy/dx = f(x, y)$ having the function g as its solution (or as one of its solutions).

27. The slope of the graph of g at the point (x, y) is the sum of x and y.

28. The tangent line to the graph of g at the point (x, y) intersects the x-axis at the point $(x/2, 0)$.

29. Every straight line normal to the graph of g passes through the point $(0, 1)$.

30. The graph of g is normal to every curve of the form $y = k + x^2$ (k is a constant) where they meet.

31. The line tangent to the graph of g at (x, y) passes through the point $(-y, x)$.

In Problems 32 through 36, write—in the manner of Eqs. (3) through (6) of this section—a differential equation that is a mathematical model of the situation described.

32. The time rate of change of a population P is proportional to the square root of P.

33. The time rate of change of the velocity v of a coasting motorboat is proportional to the square of v.

34. The acceleration dv/dt of a Lamborghini is proportional to the difference between 250 km/h and the velocity of the car.

35. In a city having a fixed population of P persons, the time rate of change of the number N of those persons who have heard a certain rumor is proportional to the number of those who have not yet heard the rumor.

36. In a city with a fixed population of P persons, the time rate of change of the number N of persons infected with a certain contagious disease is proportional to the product of the number who have the disease and the number who do not.

In Problems 37 through 42, determine by inspection at least one solution of the given differential equation. That is, use your knowledge of derivatives to make an intelligent guess. Then test your hypothesis.

37. $y'' = 0$ **38.** $y' = y$

39. $xy' + y = 3x^2$ **40.** $(y')^2 + y^2 = 1$

41. $y' + y = e^x$ **42.** $y'' + y = 0$

43. In Example 7 we saw that $y(x) = 1/(C - x)$ defines a one-parameter family of solutions of the differential equation $dy/dx = y^2$. (a) Determine a value of C so that $y(10) = 10$. (b) Is there a value of C such that $y(0) = 0$? Can you nevertheless find by inspection a solution of $dy/dx = y^2$ such that $y(0) = 0$? (c) Figure 1.1.6 shows typical graphs of solutions of the form $1/(C - x)$. Does it appear that these solution graphs fill the xy-plane? Can you conclude that, given any point (a, b) in the plane, the differential equation $dy/dx = y^2$ has exactly one solution $y(x)$ satisfying the condition $y(a) = b$?

44. (a) Show that $y(x) = Cx^4$ defines a one-parameter family of

solutions of the differential equation $xy' = 4y$. **(b) Show that**

$$y(x) = \begin{cases} -x^4 & \text{if } x \le 0, \\ +x^4 & \text{if } x \ge 0 \end{cases}$$

defines a solution of $xy' = 4y$ for all x but is not of the form $y = Cx^4$.

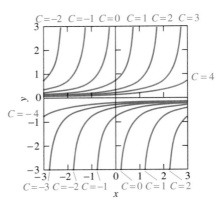

FIGURE 1.1.6. Graphs of solutions of the equation $dy/dx = y^2$

1.2 Integrals as General and Particular Solutions

The first-order differential equation $dy/dx = f(x, y)$ takes an especially simple form if the function f is independent of the dependent variable y:

$$\frac{dy}{dx} = f(x). \tag{1}$$

In this special case we need only integrate both sides of Eq. (1) to obtain

$$y = \int f(x)\, dx + C. \tag{2}$$

This is a **general solution** of Eq. (1), meaning that it involves an arbitrary constant C, and for every choice of C it is a solution of the differential equation. If $G(x)$ is a particular antiderivative of f—that is, if $G'(x) \equiv f(x)$—then

$$y(x) = G(x) + C. \tag{3}$$

The graphs of any two such solutions $y_1(x) = G(x) + C_1$ and $y_2(x) = G(x) + C_2$ on the same interval I are "parallel" in the sense illustrated by Figs. 1.2.1 and 1.2.2. There we see that the constant C is geometrically the vertical distance between the curves $y(x) = G(x)$ and $y(x) = G(x) + C$.

To satisfy an initial condition $y(x_0) = y_0$, we need only substitute $x = x_0$ and $y = y_0$ into Eq. (3) to obtain $y_0 = G(x_0) + C$, so that $C = y_0 - G(x_0)$. With this choice

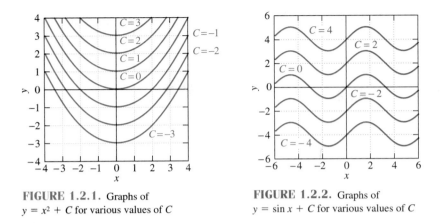

FIGURE 1.2.1. Graphs of
$y = x^2 + C$ for various values of C

FIGURE 1.2.2. Graphs of
$y = \sin x + C$ for various values of C

of C, we obtain the **particular solution** of (1) satisfying the initial value problem

$$\frac{dy}{dx} = f(x), \qquad y(x_0) = y_0.$$

We will see that this is the typical pattern for solutions of first-order differential equations. Ordinarily, we will first find a *general solution* involving an arbitrary constant C. We can then attempt to obtain, by appropriate choice of C, a *particular solution* satisfying a given initial condition $y(x_0) = y_0$.

Remark: As the term is used above, a *general solution* of a first-order differential equation is simply a one-parameter family of solutions. A natural question is whether a given general solution contains *every* particular solution of the differential equation. When this is known to be true, we call it **the** general solution of the differential equation. For example, because any two antiderivatives of the same function $f(x)$ can differ only by a constant, it follows that every solution of Eq. (1) is of the form in (2). Thus Eq. (2) serves to define **the** general solution of (1).

EXAMPLE 1 Solve the initial value problem

$$\frac{dy}{dx} = 2x + 3, \qquad y(1) = 2.$$

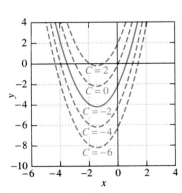

FIGURE 1.2.3. Solution curves for the differential equation in Example 1

Solution Integration of both sides of the differential equation as in Eq. (2) immediately yields the general solution

$$y = \int (2x + 3)\, dx = x^2 + 3x + C.$$

Figure 1.2.3 shows the graph $y = x^2 + 3x + C$ for various values of C. The particular solution we seek corresponds to the curve that passes through the point $(1, 2)$, thereby satisfying the initial condition

$$y(1) = (1)^2 + 3 \cdot (1) + C = 2.$$

It follows that $C = -2$, so the desired particular solution is

$$y(x) = x^2 + 3x - 2. \qquad \blacksquare$$

The observation that the special first-order equation $dy/dx = f(x)$ is readily solvable (provided that the function f can be integrated) extends to second-order differential equations of the special form

$$\frac{d^2y}{dx^2} = g(x), \tag{4}$$

in which the function g on the right-hand side involves neither the independent variable y nor its derivative dy/dx. We simple integrate once to obtain

$$\frac{dy}{dx} = \int y''(x)\,dx = \int g(x)\,dx = G(x) + C_1,$$

where G is an antiderivative of g and C_1 is an arbitrary constant. Then another integration yields

$$y(x) = \int y'(x)\,dx = \int [G(x) + C_1]\,dx = \int G(x)\,dx + C_1 x + C_2,$$

where C_2 is a second arbitrary constant. In effect, the second-order differential equation in (4) is one that can be solved by solving successively the *first-order* differential equations

$$\frac{dv}{dx} = g(x) \qquad \text{and} \qquad \frac{dy}{dx} = v(x).$$

Velocity and Acceleration

Direct integration is sufficient to allow us to solve a number of important problems concerning the motion of a particle (or *mass point*) in terms of the forces acting on it. The motion of a particle along a straight line (the x-axis) is described by its **position function**

$$x = f(t) \tag{5}$$

giving its x-coordinate at time t. The **velocity** of the particle is defined to be

$$\blacktriangleright \qquad v(t) = f'(t); \qquad \text{that is,} \quad v = \frac{dx}{dt}. \tag{6}$$

Its **acceleration** $a(t)$ is $a(t) = v'(t) = x''(t)$; in Leibniz notation,

$$\blacktriangleright \qquad a = \frac{dv}{dt} = \frac{d^2x}{dt^2}. \tag{7}$$

Newton's *second law of motion* implies that if a force $F(t)$ acts on the particle and is directed along its line of motion, then

$$ma(t) = F(t); \qquad \text{that is,} \quad F = ma, \tag{8}$$

where m is the mass of the particle. If the force F is known, then the equation $x''(t) = F(t)/m$ can be integrated twice to obtain the position function $x(t)$ in terms of two constants of integration. These two arbitrary constants are frequently determined by the **initial position** $x_0 = x(0)$ and the **initial velocity** $v_0 = v(0)$ of the particle.

For instance, suppose that the force F, and therefore the acceleration $a = F/m$, are

constant. Then we begin with the equation

$$\frac{dv}{dt} = a \qquad (a \text{ is a constant}) \tag{9}$$

and integrate both sides to obtain

$$v = \int a \, dt = at + C_1.$$

We know that $v = v_0$ when $t = 0$, and substitution of this information into the preceding equation yields the fact that $C_1 = v_0$. So

$$v = \frac{dx}{dt} = at + v_0. \tag{10}$$

A second integration gives

$$x(t) = \int v \, dt = \int (at + v_0) \, dt = \frac{1}{2} at^2 + v_0 t + C_2,$$

and the substitution $t = 0$, $x = x_0$ gives $C_2 = x_0$. Therefore

$$x(t) = \frac{1}{2} at^2 + v_0 t + x_0. \tag{11}$$

Thus, with Eq. (10) we can find the velocity, and with (11) the position, of the particle at any time t in terms of its *constant* acceleration a, its initial velocity v_0, and its initial position x_0.

EXAMPLE 2 A lunar lander is falling freely toward the surface of the moon at a speed of 1000 miles per hour (mi/h). Its retrorockets, when fired, provide a constant deceleration of 20,000 miles per hour per hour (mi/h²) (the gravitational acceleration produced by the moon is assumed to be included in the given deceleration). At what height above the lunar surface should the retrorockets be activated to ensure a "soft touchdown" ($v = 0$ at impact)?

Solution We denote by $x(t)$ the height of the lunar lander above the surface, as indicated in Fig. 1.2.4. Then $v_0 = -1000$ (mi/h, negative because the height $x(t)$ is decreasing), and $a = +20,000$ because an upward thrust increases the velocity v (although it decreases the *speed* $|v|$). Then Eqs. (10) and (11) become

$$v(t) = 20,000t - 1000 \tag{12}$$

and

$$x(t) = 10,000t^2 - 1000t + x_0, \tag{13}$$

where x_0 is the height of the lander above the lunar surface at the time $t = 0$ at which the retrorockets should be activated.

From Eq. (12) we see that $v = 0$ (soft touchdown) occurs when $t = \frac{1}{20}$ (h; thus 3 min); then substitution of $t = \frac{1}{20}$, $x = 0$ into (13) yields

$$x_0 = -10,000 \left(\frac{1}{20}\right)^2 + 1000 \left(\frac{1}{20}\right) = 25$$

Lunar surface

FIGURE 1.2.4. The lunar lander of Example 2

(mi). Thus the retrorockets should be activated when the lunar lander is 25 mi above the surface, and it will reach the surface 3 min later.

Gravitational Attraction and Physical Units

A common application of Eqs. (10) and (11) involves vertical motion near the surface of the earth. Recall that the **weight** W of a body is the force exerted by gravity upon the body at the surface of the earth. Hence Newton's second law implies that

$$W = mg, \tag{8'}$$

where m is the mass of the body and g is the gravitational acceleration at the surface of the earth. (The value of g depends on the precise location of its measurement, but it is nearly constant; we assume it constant in the remainder of this section.) Although it was convenient to use units of miles and hours in Example 2, we will ordinarily employ one of the three systems of units summarized in the following table.

	fps system	cgs system	mks system
Force	pound (lb)	dyne (dyn)	newton (N)
Mass	slug	gram (g)	kilogram (kg)
Distance	foot (ft)	centimeter (cm)	meter (m)
Time	second (s)	second (s)	second (s)
g	32 ft/s²	980 cm/s²	9.8 m/s²

The values listed for g are approximations; more accurate values are 980.665 m/s² and 32.1740 ft/s². All three unit systems are compatible with Newton's law in (8'). For example, the weight of a mass of 1 slug is

$$W = (1 \text{ slug})(32 \text{ ft/s}^2) = 32 \text{ lb.}$$

Similarly, a mass of 1 g has a weight of 980 dyn, whereas a mass of 1 kg has a weight of 9.8 N. It follows that 9.8 N $= 1000 \times 980$ dyn, so 1 N $= 10^5$ dyn. For conversions between fps and metric units it helps to remember that

$$1 \text{ ft} = 12 \text{ in.} \times 2.54 \frac{\text{cm}}{\text{in.}} = 30.48 \text{ cm} \quad \text{(exactly)}$$

and that

$$1 \text{ lb} = 453.59 \text{ g} \quad \text{(approximately),}$$

meaning that a *mass* of about 454 g has a *weight* of about 1 lb (and hence a mass of about 1/32 slug). Consequently,

$$1 \text{ lb} \approx 453.59 \text{ g} \times 980 \frac{\text{dyn}}{\text{g}}$$

$$\approx 4.4452 \times 10^5 \text{ dyn} = 4.4452 \text{ N.}$$

Because we intend to deal here with vertical motion, it is natural to choose the y-axis as the coordinate system for position. If we choose the upward direction as the

positive direction, the effect of gravity on the moving body is to *decrease* its height y and also to *decrease* its velocity $v = dy/dt$, so we see that if air resistance is ignored, then the acceleration of the body is

$$a = \frac{dv}{dt} = -g = -32 \; (\text{ft/s}^2).$$

Equations (10) and (11) then take the forms

$$v = -32t + v_0 \qquad\qquad (10')$$

and

$$y = -16t^2 + v_0 t + y_0. \qquad\qquad (11')$$

Here y_0 is the initial height of the body in feet and v_0 its initial velocity in feet per second. If the initial ($t = 0$) values v_0 and y_0 are given, the subsequent velocity and height of the body are given by Eqs. (10') and (11').

EXAMPLE 3 Suppose that a ball is thrown straight upward from the ground ($y_0 = 0$) with initial velocity $v_0 = 96$ ft/s. Then it reaches its maximum height when its velocity is zero,

$$v = -32t + 96 = 0,$$

and thus when $t = 3$ s. Hence the maximum height the ball attains is

$$y(3) = -16 \cdot 3^2 + 96 \cdot 3 = 144 \quad (\text{ft}). \qquad\qquad \blacksquare$$

A Swimmer's Problem

FIGURE 1.2.5. A swimmer's problem (Example 4)

Figure 1.2.5 shows a northward-flowing river of width $w = 2a$. The lines $x = \pm a$ represent the banks of the river and the y-axis its center. Suppose that the velocity v_R with which the water flows increases as one approaches the center of the river, and indeed is given in terms of distance x from the center by

$$v_R = v_0 \left(1 - \frac{x^2}{a^2} \right). \qquad\qquad (14)$$

You can verify that the water does flow the fastest at the center, where $v_R = v_0$, whereas $v_R = 0$ at each riverbank.

Suppose that a swimmer starts at the point $(-a, 0)$ on the west bank and swims due east (relative to the water) with constant speed v_S. As indicated in Fig. 1.2.5, his velocity vector (relative to the ground) has horizontal component v_S and vertical component v_R. Hence the swimmer's direction angle α is given by

$$\tan \alpha = \frac{v_R}{v_S}.$$

Because $\tan \alpha = dy/dx$, substitution of (14) gives the differential equation

$$\frac{dy}{dx} = \frac{v_0}{v_S} \left(1 - \frac{x^2}{a^2} \right) \qquad\qquad (15)$$

for the swimmer's trajectory $y = y(x)$ as he crosses the river.

EXAMPLE 4 Suppose that the river is 1 mile wide and that its midstream velocity is $v_0 = 9$ mi/h. If the swimmer's velocity is $v_S = 3$ mi/h, Eq. (15) takes the form

$$\frac{dy}{dx} = 3(1 - 4x^2).$$

Integration yields

$$y = \int (3 - 12x^2)\,dx = 3x - 4x^3 + C$$

for the swimmer's trajectory. The initial condition $y(-\frac{1}{2}) = 0$ yields $C = 1$, so

$$y(x) = 3x - 4x^3 + 1.$$

Then

$$y\left(\frac{1}{2}\right) = 3\left(\frac{1}{2}\right) - 4\left(\frac{1}{2}\right)^3 + 1 = 2,$$

so the swimmer drifts two miles downstream while he swims 1 mile across the river. ■

1.2 Problems

In Problems 1 through 10, find a function $y = f(x)$ satisfying the given differential equation and the prescribed initial condition.

1. $\dfrac{dy}{dx} = 2x + 1;\quad y(0) = 3$

2. $\dfrac{dy}{dx} = (x - 2)^2;\quad y(2) = 1$

3. $\dfrac{dy}{dx} = \sqrt{x};\quad y(4) = 0$

4. $\dfrac{dy}{dx} = \dfrac{1}{x^2};\quad y(1) = 5$

5. $\dfrac{dy}{dx} = \dfrac{1}{\sqrt{x + 2}};\quad y(2) = -1$

6. $\dfrac{dy}{dx} = x\sqrt{x^2 + 9};\quad y(-4) = 0$

7. $\dfrac{dy}{dx} = \dfrac{10}{x^2 + 1};\quad y(0) = 0$

8. $\dfrac{dy}{dx} = \cos 2x;\quad y(0) = 1$

9. $\dfrac{dy}{dx} = \dfrac{1}{\sqrt{1 - x^2}};\quad y(0) = 0$

10. $\dfrac{dy}{dx} = xe^{-x};\quad y(0) = 1$

In Problems 11 through 17, find the position function $x(t)$ of a moving particle with the given acceleration $a(t)$, initial position $x_0 = x(0)$, and initial velocity $v_0 = v(0)$.

11. $a(t) = 50,\quad v_0 = 10,\quad x_0 = 20$

12. $a(t) = -20,\quad v_0 = -15,\quad x_0 = 5$

13. $a(t) = 3t,\quad v_0 = 5,\quad x_0 = 0$

14. $a(t) = 2t + 1,\quad v_0 = -7,\quad x_0 = 4$

15. $a(t) = 4(t + 3)^2,\quad v_0 = -1,\quad x_0 = 1$

16. $a(t) = \dfrac{1}{\sqrt{t + 4}},\quad v_0 = -1,\quad x_0 = 1$

17. $a(t) = \dfrac{1}{(t + 1)^3}.\quad v_0 = 0,\quad x_0 = 0$

18. A ball is dropped from the top of a building that is 400 ft high. How long does it take to reach the ground? With what speed does the ball strike the ground?

19. The brakes of a car are applied when it is moving at 100 km/h and provide a constant deceleration of 10 meters per second per second (m/s²). How far does the car travel before coming to a stop?

20. A ball is thrown straight upward from ground level with an initial speed of 160 ft/s. What is the maximum height that the ball attains? How long does it remain aloft?

21. A ball is thrown straight downward from the top of a tall building. The initial speed of the ball is 10 m/s. It strikes the ground with a speed of 60 m/s. How tall is the building?

22. A baseball is thrown straight downward with an initial speed of 40 ft/s from the top of the Washington Monument (555 ft high). How long does it take to reach the ground, and with what speed does the baseball strike the ground?

23. A bomb is dropped from a balloon hovering at an altitude of 800 ft. A gun emplacement is located on the ground directly below the balloon. The gun fires a projectile straight upward toward the bomb exactly 2 s after the bomb is released. With what initial speed should the projectile be fired in order to intercept the bomb at an altitude of exactly 400 ft?

24. A car traveling at 60 mi/h (88 ft/s) skids 176 ft after its brakes are suddenly applied. Under the assumption that the braking system provides constant deceleration, what is that deceleration? For how long does the skid continue?

25. The skid marks made by an automobile indicate that its brakes were fully applied for a distance of 225 ft before it came to a stop. The car in question is known to have a constant deceleration of 50 feet per second per second (ft/s²) under these conditions. How fast was the car traveling when the brakes were first applied?

26. Suppose that a car skids 15 m if it is moving at 50 km/h when the brakes are applied. Assuming that the car has the same constant deceleration, how far will it skid if it is moving at 100 km/h when the brakes are applied?

27. On the planet Gzyx, a ball dropped from a height of 20 ft hits the ground in 2 s. If a ball is dropped from the top of a 200-ft-tall building on Gzyx, how long will it take to hit the ground? With what speed will it hit?

28. A person can throw a ball straight upward from the surface of the earth to a maximum height of 144 ft. How high could this person throw the ball on the planet Gzyx of Problem 27?

29. A stone is dropped from rest at initial height h above the surface of the earth. Show that the speed at which it strikes the ground is $v = \sqrt{2gh}$.

30. If a woman has enough "spring" in her legs to jump vertically to a height of 2.25 ft on the earth, how high could she jump on the moon, where the surface gravitational acceleration is (approximately) 5.3 ft/s²?

31. At noon a car starts from rest at point A and proceeds with constant acceleration along a straight road toward point B. If the car reaches B at 12:50 P.M. with a velocity of 60 mi/h, what is the distance from A to B?

32. At noon a car starts from rest at point A and proceeds with constant acceleration along a straight road toward point C, 35 miles away. If the constantly accelerated car arrives at C with a velocity of 60 mi/h, at what time does it arrive there?

33. If $a = 0.5$ mi and $v_0 = 9$ mi/h as in Example 4, what must the swimmer's speed v_S be in order that he drift only 1 mile downstream as he crosses the river?

34. Suppose that $a = 0.5$ mi, $v_0 = 9$ mi/h, and $v_S = 3$ mi/h as in Example 4, but the velocity of the river is given by the fourth degree function

$$v_R = v_0\left(1 - \frac{x^4}{a^4}\right)$$

rather than the quadratic function in (14). Now find how far downstream the swimmer drifts as he crosses the river.

1.3 Slope Fields and Solution Curves

In the case of a general first-order differential equation of the form

$$\frac{dy}{dx} = f(x, y), \tag{1}$$

we cannot simply integrate each side as in Section 1.2, because now the right-hand side involves the unknown function $y(x)$. Before one spends much time trying to solve a differential equation, it is wise to know that solutions actually *exist*. We may also want to know whether there is only one solution of the equation satisfying a given initial condition — that is, whether solutions are *unique*. For instance, such a simple-looking initial value problem as

$$\frac{dy}{dx} = 2\sqrt{y}, \qquad y(0) = 0 \tag{2}$$

has the two different solutions $y_1(x) = x^2$ and $y_2(x) \equiv 0$.

The questions of existence and uniqueness also bear on the process of mathematical modeling. Suppose that we are studying a physical system whose behavior is determined completely by certain initial conditions, but that our proposed mathematical model involves a differential equation *not* having a unique solution. This raises an immediate question as to whether the mathematical model adequately represents the physical system.

Slope Fields

In order to investigate the possible behavior of solutions of a differential equation of the form $dy/dx = f(x, y)$, we may think of it in a very geometric way: At various points (x, y) of the two-dimensional coordinate plane, the value of $f(x, y)$ determines a slope y'. A *solution* of this differential equation is a differentiable function with graph having slope y' at each point (x, y) through which the graph passes. The graph of a solution of a differential equation is sometimes called a **solution curve** of the equation. From this geometric viewpoint, a solution curve of a differential equation is then a curve in the plane whose tangent at each point (x, y) has slope $m = f(x, y)$.

This idea of a solution curve suggests the following *graphical method* for constructing approximate solutions of the differential equation $dy/dx = f(x, y)$. Through each of a representative collection of points (x, y) we draw a short line segment having slope $m = f(x, y)$. The set of all these line segments is called a **slope field** (or *direction field*) for the equation $dy/dx = f(x, y)$. We can attempt to sketch a solution curve that threads its way through the slope field in such a way that it is tangent to each of the short line segments that it intersects.

EXAMPLE 1 Figures 1.3.1 (a)–(d) show slope fields and solution curves for the differential equation

$$\frac{dy}{dx} = ky \tag{3}$$

with the values $k = 2, 0.5, -1$, and -3 of the parameter k in Eq. (3). Note that each slope field yields important qualitative information about the set of all solutions of the differential equation. For instance, Figs. 1.3.1 (a)–(b) suggest that each solution $y(x)$ approaches $\pm\infty$ as $x \to +\infty$ if $k > 0$, whereas Figs. 1.3.1 (c)–(d) suggest that $y(x) \to 0$ as $x \to +\infty$ if $k < 0$. Moreover, although the sign of k determines the *direction* of increase or decrease of $y(x)$, its absolute value $|k|$ appears to determine the rate of change of $y(x)$. All this is apparent from slope fields like those in Fig. 1.3.1 even without knowing that the general solution of Eq. (3) is given explicitly by $y(x) = Ce^{kx}$. ∎

Isoclines

It is easy to instruct a computer to draw a slope field for a given differential equation $dy/dx = f(x, y)$, and programs for doing this are readily available. There is also an older manual method still useful on occasion: An **isocline** of the differential equation $dy/dx = f(x, y)$ is a curve of the form

$$f(x, y) = c \qquad (c \text{ is a constant}) \tag{4}$$

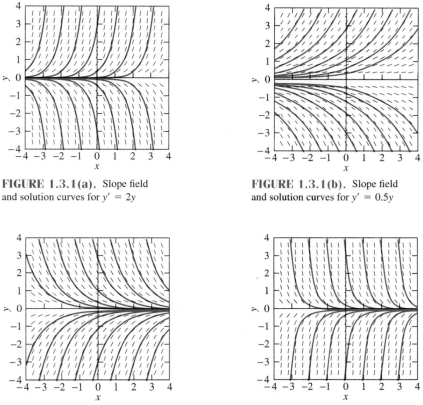

FIGURE 1.3.1(a). Slope field and solution curves for $y' = 2y$

FIGURE 1.3.1(b). Slope field and solution curves for $y' = 0.5y$

FIGURE 1.3.1(c). Slope field and solution curves for $y' = -y$

FIGURE 1.3.1(d). Slope field and solution curves for $y' = -3y$

FIGURE 1.3.2. Isoclines and slope field for $y' = -y$

on which the slope $y'(x)$ is *constant*. If these isoclines are simple and familiar curves, we first sketch several of them, then draw short line segments with the same slope c at representative points of each isocline $f(x, y) = c$.

For example, $f(x, y) = -y$ for the equation $dy/dx = -y$ of Fig. 1.3.1(c), so the isoclines are horizontal straight lines of the form $y = -c$. Several of these isoclines, each embellished with short line segments of slope $m = c$, are shown in Fig. 1.3.2. Observe that the resulting slope field is consistent with the more detailed one shown in Fig. 1.3.1(c).

EXAMPLE 2 The typical isocline of the differential equation

$$\frac{dy}{dx} = x^2 + y^2 \tag{5}$$

has the equation $x^2 + y^2 = c > 0$, and thus is a circle centered at the origin and having radius $r = \sqrt{c}$. Several of these circles are shown in Fig. 1.3.3, each marked with its direction lines of slope $m = r^2$, together with some typical solution curves of the differential equation in (5). It happens that the equation $dy/dx = x^2 + y^2$ is quite difficult to solve explicitly; its general solution involves the Bessel functions of Section

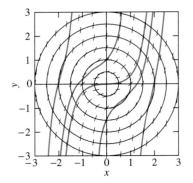

FIGURE 1.3.3. Isoclines, slope field, and solution curves for $y' = x^2 + y^2$.

8.5. But even without an explicit knowledge of the solutions, it seems apparent from Fig. 1.3.3 that on each solution curve, $y(x) \to +\infty$ as x increases. This observation is correct and illustrates the qualitative information about solutions of a differential equation that frequently is revealed by an easily constructed slope field.

EXAMPLE 3 The isoclines of the differential equation

$$\frac{dy}{dx} = \sin(x - y) \tag{6}$$

are of the form

$$\sin(x - y) = c;$$

that is, $x - y = \sin^{-1} c$, and thus of the form

$$y = x - \sin^{-1} c.$$

Therefore, the isoclines of Eq. (6) are all straight lines of slope 1 in the xy-plane. The slope field and some typical solution curves are shown in Fig. 1.3.4. Most of the solution curves one sees in this figure appear to exhibit the oscillatory behavior suggested by the presence of the sine function in Eq. (6). Yet there is one solution curve that appears to be a straight line! This observation prompts us to inspect Eq. (6) more closely. When we do, we spot the particular solution

$$y = x - \frac{\pi}{2}$$

for which $y'(x) \equiv 1$ and $x - y = \pi/2$, so that $\sin(x - y) \equiv 1$ as well. Do you see in Fig. 1.3.4 any indication of *another* straight line solution curve for Eq. (6)?

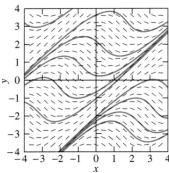

FIGURE 1.3.4. Slope field and solution curves for $y' = \sin(x - y)$.

EXAMPLE 4 Consider the differential equation

$$y^2 + x^2 y' = 0. \tag{7}$$

If we write this equation in the form

$$\frac{dy}{dx} = -\frac{y^2}{x^2}, \tag{8}$$

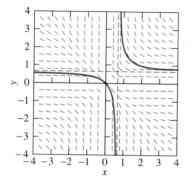

FIGURE 1.3.5. Slope field for $y^2 + x^2y' = 0$ and the graph of one solution of the equation

we see that the isoclines are of the form $-y^2/x^2 = C$—that is, $y = kx$—and thus are straight lines through the origin. We show a slope field and a typical solution curve for this equation in Fig. 1.3.5. Indeed, because $dy/dx = -(y/x)^2$, we see that each differentiable solution must be decreasing except on the coordinate axes (where x or y is zero). Much additional qualitative information can be read from the slope field of Eq. (7).

In Section 1.4 we will solve equations like this one—known as **separable** differential equations—by separating the variables. Here's how: First we rewrite Eq. (8) in the "separated form"

$$-\frac{dy}{y^2} = \frac{dx}{x^2}.$$

Next we integrate each side,

$$-\int \frac{dy}{y^2} = \int \frac{dx}{x^2} + C,$$

to obtain

$$\frac{1}{y} = -\frac{1}{x} + C.$$

Finally, we solve for y to obtain

$$y = y(x) = \frac{x}{Cx - 1}. \tag{9}$$

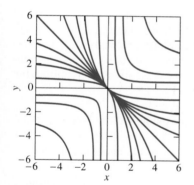

FIGURE 1.3.6. Solution curves for $y^2 + x^2y' = 0$

Figure 1.3.6 shows a number of solution curves calculated with different values of C. Each solution curve of the form in Eq. (9) with $C \neq 0$ has a pair of vertical and horizontal asymptotes $x = 1/C$ and $y = 1/C$ (like the ones shown in Fig. 1.3.5). In fact, each of these solution curves consists of the two branches of a rectangular hyperbola, one branch of which passes through the origin. When $C = 0$ we obtain the "different" solution $y = -x$. Moreover, the solution process displayed here excludes the function $y(x) \equiv 0$, which (by substitution in Eq. (7)) is yet another solution. ∎

The remarkable feature of the differential equation in (7) and its solutions is this: First, there are *infinitely many* different solutions satisfying the initial condition $y(0) = 0$. But it follows from Eq. (7) that $y(0) = 0$, so if $b \neq 0$, there is *no* solution satisfying the initial condition $y(0) = b$. Finally, if $a \neq 0$ and b is arbitrary, there is exactly one solution with $y(a) = b$. All these observations are evident from inspection of Fig. 1.3.6.

Existence and Uniqueness of Solutions

Example 4 shows that an initial value problem may have either no solution, a unique (that is, one and only one) solution, or many—even infinitely many—solutions. The following theorem provides sufficient conditions to ensure existence and uniqueness of solutions, so that neither extreme case (no solution or nonunique solutions) can occur. Methods of proving existence and uniqueness theorems are discussed in the Appendix.

THEOREM 1: Existence and Uniqueness of Solutions

Suppose that the real-valued function $f(x, y)$ is continuous on some rectangle in the plane containing the point (a, b) in its interior. Then the initial value problem

$$\frac{dy}{dx} = f(x, y), \qquad y(a) = b \tag{10}$$

has at least one solution defined on some open interval J containing the point $x = a$. If, in addition, the partial derivative $\partial f/\partial y$ is continuous on that rectangle, then the solution is unique on some (perhaps smaller) open interval J_0 containing the point $x = a$. ∎

Remark 1: In the case of the differential equation $dy/dx = -y$ of Example 1, both the function $f(x, y) = -y$ and the partial derivative $\partial f/\partial y = -1$ are continuous everywhere, so the theorem implies the existence of a unique solution for any initial data (a, b). Although the theorem ensures existence only on some open interval about $x = a$, each solution $y(x) = Ce^{-x}$ actually is defined for all x.

Remark 2: In the case of the differential equation $dy/dx = 2\sqrt{y}$ in Eq. (2), the function $f(x, y) = 2\sqrt{y}$ is continuous wherever $y > 0$, but the partial derivative $\partial f/\partial y = 1/\sqrt{y}$ is discontinuous when $y = 0$, and hence at the point $(0, 0)$. This is why it is possible for there to exist two different solutions $y_1(x) = x^2$ and $y_2(x) \equiv 0$, each of which satisfies the initial condition $y(0) = 0$.

Remark 3: In Example 4 we analyzed the differential equation $y^2 + x^2 y' = 0$ and found that there was no solution passing through $(0, 1)$. If we take $f(x, y) = -(y/x)^2$, we see that Theorem 1 cannot guarantee existence of a solution through $(0, 1)$ because f is not continuous there. (Note that f is also not continuous at $(0, 0)$, but some solutions *do* pass through this point. Thus, the continuity of f is a sufficient condition, but not a necessary condition, for the existence of solutions.)

Remark 4: Finally, in Example 7 of Section 1.1 we examined the especially simple differential equation $dy/dx = y^2$. Here we have $f(x, y) = y^2$ and $\partial f/\partial y = 2y$. Both of these functions are continuous everywhere in the plane, and in particular on the rectangle $-2 < x < 2, 0 < y < 2$. Because the point $(0, 1)$ lies in the interior of this rectangle, Theorem 1 guarantees a unique solution—necessarily a continuous function—of the initial value problem

$$\frac{dy}{dx} = y^2, \qquad y(0) = 1$$

on some open interval containing $x_0 = 0$. This is the solution

$$y(x) = \frac{1}{1 - x}$$

that we discussed in Example 7. But $1/(1 - x)$ is discontinuous at $x = 1$, so we do *not* have *existence* of a solution on the entire interval $-2 < x < 2$. This means that the interval J of the theorem may not be as wide as the rectangle; even though the hypothe-

ses of the theorem are satisfied for all x in an interval I (and all y in an appropriate interval), the solution may, as in Example 7, exist only on a smaller interval J. Similarly, the interval J_0 of uniqueness may be even smaller than J.

EXAMPLE 5 Consider the first-order differential equation

$$xy' = 2y. \tag{11}$$

Applying Theorem 1 with $f(x, y) = 2y/x$, we see that Eq. (11) has a unique solution near any point where $x \neq 0$. Indeed, we see readily that

$$y(x) = Cx^2 \tag{12}$$

satisfies Eq. (11) for any value of the constant C and for all values of x.

With these preliminary observations in mind, let us consider the initial value problem

$$xy' = 2y, \qquad y(-1) = 1. \tag{13}$$

The initial condition $y(-1) = 1$ implies that $C = 1$ in Eq. (12), so on some open interval about $x = -1$ we have the unique solution $y(x) = x^2$ which passes through the origin $(0, 0)$. But to the right of the origin we may choose any value we please for C in Eq. (12). That is, for any fixed C, a solution of the initial value problem in (13) is given by

$$y(x) = \begin{cases} x^2 & \text{if } x \leq 0, \\ Cx^2 & \text{if } x > 0. \end{cases}$$

Thus, this initial value problem has infinitely many different solutions, despite the fact that (in accord with Theorem 1) there is a unique solution in *some* open interval about the point $x = -1$. Figure 1.3.7 shows three of these different solutions of (13). ■

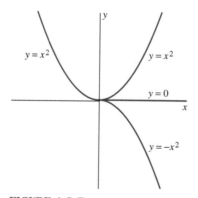

FIGURE 1.3.7. Three solutions of the initial value problem in (13)

The point is that Theorem 1 guarantees uniqueness *near* the point (a, b), but the solution curve may branch elsewhere and uniqueness will be lost. Similarly, Theorem 1 can guarantee existence of a solution *near* the point (a, b), but the differential equation may have no solution for some other values of x.

1.3 Problems

In Problems 1 through 10, we have provided the slope field of the indicated differential equation, together with one or more solution curves. Sketch likely solution curves through the additional points marked in each slope field. (One method: Photocopy the slope field and draw your solution curve in a second color. Another method: Use tracing paper.)

1. $\dfrac{dy}{dx} = -y - \sin x$

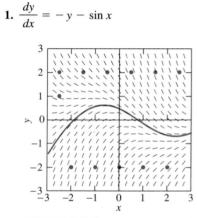

FIGURE 1.3.8.

2. $\dfrac{dy}{dx} = x + y$

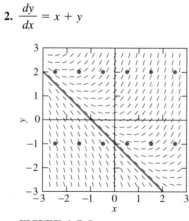

FIGURE 1.3.9.

3. $\dfrac{dy}{dx} = y - \sin x$

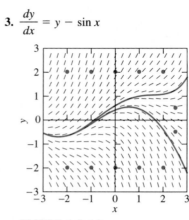

FIGURE 1.3.10.

4. $\dfrac{dy}{dx} = x - y$

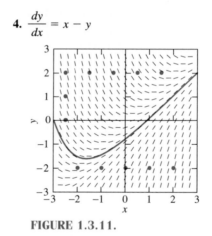

FIGURE 1.3.11.

5. $\dfrac{dy}{dx} = y - x + 1$

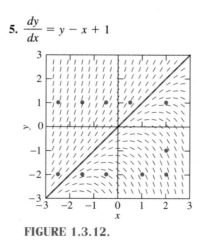

FIGURE 1.3.12.

6. $\dfrac{dy}{dx} = x - y + 1$

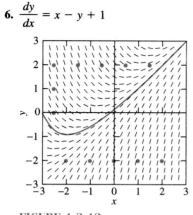

FIGURE 1.3.13.

7. $\dfrac{dy}{dx} = \sin x + \sin y$

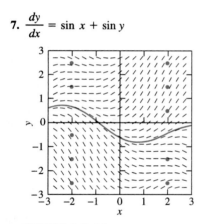

FIGURE 1.3.14.

8. $\dfrac{dy}{dx} = x^2 - y$

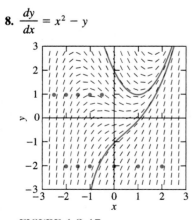

FIGURE 1.3.15.

9. $\dfrac{dy}{dx} = x^2 - y - 2$

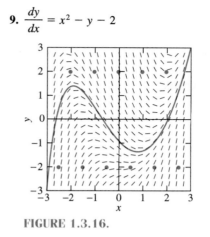

FIGURE 1.3.16.

10. $\dfrac{dy}{dx} = -x^2 + \sin y$

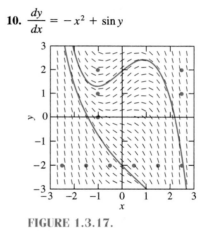

FIGURE 1.3.17.

In Problems 11 through 20, identify the isoclines of the given differential equation. Draw a sketch showing several of these isoclines, each marked with short line segments having the appropriate slope.

11. $\dfrac{dy}{dx} = x - 1$ **12.** $\dfrac{dy}{dx} = x + y$

13. $\dfrac{dy}{dx} = y^2$ **14.** $\dfrac{dy}{dx} = y^{1/3}$

15. $\dfrac{dy}{dx} = \dfrac{y}{x}$ **16.** $\dfrac{dy}{dx} = x^2 - y^2$

17. $\dfrac{dy}{dx} = xy$ **18.** $\dfrac{dy}{dx} = x - y^2$

19. $\dfrac{dy}{dx} = y - x^2$ **20.** $\dfrac{dy}{dx} = ye^{-x}$

In Problems 21 through 30, determine whether Theorem 1 does or does not guarantee existence of a solution of the given initial value problem. If existence is guaranteed, determine whether Theorem 1 does or does not guarantee uniqueness of that solution.

21. $\dfrac{dy}{dx} = 2x^2y^2$; $\quad y(1) = -1$

22. $\dfrac{dy}{dx} = x \ln y$; $\quad y(1) = 1$

23. $\dfrac{dy}{dx} = y^{1/3}$; $\quad y(0) = 1$

24. $\dfrac{dy}{dx} = y^{1/3}$; $\quad y(0) = 0$

25. $\dfrac{dy}{dx} = \sqrt{x - y}$; $\quad y(2) = 2$

26. $\dfrac{dy}{dx} = \sqrt{x - y}$; $\quad y(2) = 1$

27. $y\dfrac{dy}{dx} = x - 1$; $\quad y(0) = 1$

28. $y\dfrac{dy}{dx} = x - 1$; $\quad y(1) = 0$

29. $\dfrac{dy}{dx} = \ln(1 + y^2)$; $\quad y(0) = 0$

30. $\dfrac{dy}{dx} = x^2 - y^2$; $\quad y(0) = 1$

The next six problems illustrate that if the hypotheses of Theorem 1 fail at a point (a, b), then there may be no solutions, finitely many solutions, or infinitely many solutions passing through (a, b).

31. Show that on the interval $[0, \pi]$, the functions $y_1(x) \equiv 1$ and $y_2(x) = \cos x$ both satisfy the initial value problem

$$\frac{dy}{dx} + \sqrt{1 - y^2} = 0, \qquad y(0) = 1.$$

Why does this fact not contradict Theorem 1? Explain your answer carefully.

32. Find by inspection two different solutions of the initial value problem

$$\frac{dy}{dx} = 3y^{2/3}, \qquad y(0) = 0.$$

Why does the existence of different solutions not contradict Theorem 1?

33. Use Fig. 1.3.18 as a suggestion for showing that the initial value problem

$$\frac{dy}{dx} = 3y^{2/3}, \qquad y(-1) = -1$$

has infinitely many solutions. Why does this not contradict Theorem 1?

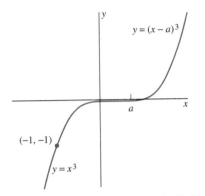

FIGURE 1.3.18. A suggestion for Problem 33

34. Verify that if k is a constant, then $y = kx$ satisfies the differential equation $xy' = y$. Hence conclude that the initial value problem

$$xy' = y, \qquad y(0) = 0$$

has infinitely many solutions on any open interval containing $x = 0$.

35. Use isoclines to construct a slope field for the differential equation $xy' = y$. Explain why this slope field suggests that the initial value problem

$$xy' = y, \qquad y(a) = b$$

has (a) a unique solution if $a \neq 0$, (b) no solution if $a = 0$ and $b \neq 0$, (c) infinitely many solutions if $a = b = 0$. Are these results consistent with Theorem 1?

36. Consider the differential equation $dy/dx = 4x\sqrt{y}$ for $y \geq 0$. Apply Theorem 1 to find those points (a, b) such that a solution of the differential equation *must* exist on an open interval J containing a. Find those points (a, b) such that a unique solution exists on an open interval J_0 containing a. Then find how many solutions pass through $(0, 0)$. (*Suggestion:* Note that $y_1(x) \equiv 0$ is a solution, as is $y_2(x) = (x^2 + C)^2$ if $x^2 + C \geq 0$.)

1.3 Computing Project

If appropriate computer software is available, it will be instructive for you to generate for yourself the slope fields of Problems 1 through 10. Generate additional slope fields for differential equations $dy/dx = f(x, y)$ of your own choice, and manually sketch some typical solution curves. Assemble a portfolio containing your most interesting and visually attractive results.

A number of specialized differential equations software packages are available, and typically include a facility for the ready construction of slope fields. Systems such as *MacMath* (Macintosh) and *Phaser* (DOS)—as well as the **dfield** function in John Polking's *MATLAB Manual for ODE* (Englewood Cliffs, N.J.: Prentice Hall, 1995)—plot both a slope field and, at the click of a mouse button, the solution curve through a desired point. The *Maple* command

dfieldplot(diff(y(x),x) = f(x,y), [x,y], a..b, y = c..d)

(using the **DEtools** package) and the *Mathematica* command

PlotVectorField[{1,f[x,y]}, {x,a,b}, {y,c,d}]

(using the **PlotField.m** package) generate a slope field for the equation $dy/dx = f(x, y)$ in the rectangle $a \leqq x \leqq b, c \leqq y \leqq d$.

For a project involving computer-generated solution curves, plot a slope field and typical solution curves for the differential equation $dy/dx = \sin(x - y)$ of Example 3, but with a larger "window" than that of Fig. 1.3.4. With $-8 \leqq x \leqq 8$, $-8 \leqq y \leqq 8$, for instance, a number of apparent straight line solution curves should be visible. Substitute $y = ax + b$ in the differential equation to determine what the coefficients a and b must be for a straight line solution curve. Having done this, can you now infer from your figure how $y(x)$ behaves as $x \to \infty$ (perhaps in terms of the initial value $y(0) = y_0$)?

For a personalized project, carry out a similar analysis for the differential equation

$$\frac{dy}{dx} = \frac{1}{n} \cos(x - ny)$$

where n is the smallest integer in your student ID number other than 0 or 1.

1.4 Separable Equations and Applications

The first-order differential equation

$$\frac{dy}{dx} = H(x, y) \tag{1}$$

is called **separable** provided that $H(x, y)$ can be written as the product of a function of x and a function of y:

$$\frac{dy}{dx} = g(x)\phi(y) = \frac{g(x)}{f(y)},$$

where $\phi(y) = 1/f(y)$. In this case the variables x and y can be *separated*—isolated on opposite sides of an equation—by writing informally the equation

$$f(y)\,dy = g(x)\,dx,$$

which we understand to be concise notation for the differential equation

$$f(y)\frac{dy}{dx} = g(x). \tag{2}$$

It is easy to solve this special type of differential equation simply by integrating both sides with respect to x:

$$\int f(y(x))\frac{dy}{dx}\,dx = \int g(x)\,dx + C;$$

equivalently,

$$\int f(y)\,dy = \int g(x)\,dx + C. \tag{3}$$

All that is required is that the antiderivatives $F(y) = \int f(y)\,dy$ and $G(x) = \int g(x)\,dx$ can be found. To see that Eqs. (2) and (3) are equivalent, note the following consequence of the chain rule:

$$D_x F(y(x)) = F'(y(x))\,y'(x) = f(y)\frac{dy}{dx} = g(x) = D_x G(x),$$

which in turn is equivalent to

$$F(y(x)) = G(x) + C, \tag{4}$$

because two functions have the same derivative on an interval if and only if they differ by a constant on that interval.

EXAMPLE 1 Solve the initial value problem

$$\frac{dy}{dx} = -6xy; \qquad y(0) = 7.$$

Solution Informally, we divide each side of the differential equation by y and multiply each side by dx to get

$$\frac{dy}{y} = -6x\,dx.$$

Hence

$$\int \frac{dy}{y} = \int (-6x)\,dx;$$

$$\ln|y| = -3x^2 + C.$$

We see from the initial condition $y(0) = 7$ that $y(x)$ is positive near $x = 0$, so we may delete the absolute value symbols:

$$\ln y = -3x^2 + C,$$

and hence

$$y(x) = e^{-3x^2 + C} = e^{-3x^2}e^C = Ae^{-3x^2},$$

where $A = e^C$. The condition $y(0) = 7$ yields $A = 7$, so the desired solution is

$$y(x) = 7e^{-3x^2}.$$

EXAMPLE 2 Solve the differential equation

$$\frac{dy}{dx} = \frac{10 - 2x}{y^3 - y - 6}. \tag{5}$$

Solution When we separate the variables and integrate both sides, we get

$$\int (y^3 - y - 6)\,dy = \int (10 - 2x)\,dx;$$

$$\frac{1}{4}y^4 - \frac{1}{2}y^2 - 6y = 10x - x^2 + C. \tag{6}$$

∎

As Example 2 illustrates, it may not be possible or practical to solve Eq. (4) explicitly for y as a function of x. If not, we call (4) an *implicit solution* of the differential equation in (2). Thus, Eq. (6) gives an implicit solution of the differential equation in (5). Although it is not convenient to solve Eq. (6) explicitly for y in terms of x, we see that each solution curve $y = y(x)$ lies on a contour (or level) curve where the function

$$H(x, y) = \frac{1}{4}y^4 - \frac{1}{2}y^2 - 6y + x^2 - 10x$$

is constant. Figure 1.4.1 shows several of these contour curves; each is an oval enclosing the point $(5, 2)$.

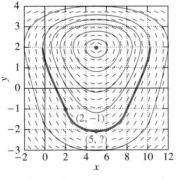

FIGURE 1.4.1. Contour curves of
$H(x, y) = \frac{1}{4}y^4 - \frac{1}{2}y^2 - 6y + x^2 - 10x$

EXAMPLE 3 To solve the initial value problem

$$\frac{dy}{dx} = \frac{10 - 2x}{y^3 - y - 6}, \qquad y(2) = -1,$$

we substitute $x = 2$ and $y = -1$ in Eq. (6) and find that $C = -\frac{41}{4}$. Thus, the desired particular solution $y = y(x)$ is defined implicitly by the equation

$$\frac{1}{4} y^4 - \frac{1}{2} y^2 - 6y = 10x - x^2 - \frac{41}{4}. \tag{7}$$

In Fig. 1.4.1 it is evident that $y = y(x)$ lies on the lower part of the contour curve through the point $(2, -1)$. When a specific value of x is substituted in Eq. (7) we can attempt to solve for y numerically. For instance, $x = 5$ yields the equation

$$f(y) = \frac{1}{4} y^4 - \frac{1}{2} y^2 - 6y - \frac{59}{4} = 0. \tag{8}$$

Figure 1.4.2 shows the graph of f. Clearly the *negative* solution near -2 is the value of $y(5)$. With a graphics calculator we can readily solve Eq. (8) for $y(5) \approx 2.0608$. ∎

In general, the equation $K(x, y) = 0$ is called an **implicit solution** of a differential equation if it is satisfied (on some interval) by some solution $y = y(x)$ of the differential equation. But note that a particular solution $y = y(x)$ of $K(x, y) = 0$ may or may not satisfy a given initial condition. For example, differentiation of $x^2 + y^2 = 4$ yields

$$x + y \frac{dy}{dx} = 0,$$

so $x^2 + y^2 = 4$ is an implicit solution of the differential equation $x + yy' = 0$. But only the first of the two explicit solutions

$$y(x) = +\sqrt{4 - x^2} \quad \text{and} \quad y(x) = -\sqrt{4 - x^2}$$

satisfies the initial condition $y(0) = 2$.

The argument preceding Example 1 shows that every particular solution of (2) satisfies (4) for some choice of C; *this* is why it is appropriate to call (4) a **general solution** of (2).

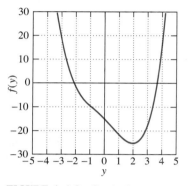

FIGURE 1.4.2. Graph of $f(y) = \frac{1}{4} y^4 - \frac{1}{2} y^2 - 6y - \frac{59}{4}$

Warning: Suppose, however, that we begin with the differential equation

$$\frac{dy}{dx} = g(x) h(y) \tag{9}$$

and divide by $h(y)$ to obtain the separated equation

$$\frac{1}{h(y)} \frac{dy}{dx} = g(x) \tag{10}$$

If y_0 is a root of the equation $h(y) = 0$—that is, if $h(y_0) = 0$—then the constant function $y(x) \equiv y_0$ is clearly a solution of (9), but may *not* be contained in the general solution of Eq. (10). Thus, solutions of a differential equation may be lost upon division by a vanishing factor. (Indeed, false solutions may be gained upon multiplication by a vanishing factor. This phenomenon is similar to the introduction of extraneous roots in solving algebraic equations.)

In Section 1.5 we shall see that every particular solution of a *linear* first-order differential equation is contained in its general solution. By contrast, it is common for a nonlinear first-order differential equation to have both a general solution involving an

arbitrary constant C and one or several particular solutions that cannot be obtained by selecting a value for C. These exceptional solutions are frequently called **singular solutions.** In Example 4 of Section 1.3 we found that the solution $y(x) \equiv 0$ was a singular solution of the equation $y^2 + x^2 y' = 0$; this solution cannot be obtained from the general solution $y(x) = x/(Cx - 1)$ by any choice of the constant C.

EXAMPLE 4 Find all solutions of the differential equation

$$\frac{dy}{dx} = 2x\sqrt{y - 1}.$$

Solution We note first the constant solution $y(x) \equiv 1$. If $y \neq 1$, we can divide both sides by $\sqrt{y - 1}$ to obtain

$$(y - 1)^{-1/2}\frac{dy}{dx} = 2x.$$

Integration gives $2\sqrt{y - 1} = x^2 + C$; upon solving for y we get the general solution

$$y(x) = 1 + \frac{1}{4}(x^2 + C)^2.$$

Note that no value of C gives the particular solution $y(x) \equiv 1$. It was lost when we divided by $\sqrt{y - 1}$. ∎

Natural Growth and Decay

The differential equation

▶ $$\frac{dy}{dx} = ky \quad (k \text{ a constant}) \tag{11}$$

serves as a mathematical model for a remarkably wide range of natural phenomena— any involving a quantity whose time rate of change is proportional to its current value. Here are some examples.

Population Growth. Suppose that $P(t)$ is the number of individuals in a population (of humans, or insects, or bacteria) having *constant* birth and death rates β and δ (in births or deaths per individual per unit of time). Then, during a short time interval Δt, approximately $\beta P(t) \, \Delta t$ births and $\delta P(t) \, \Delta t$ deaths occur, so the change in $P(t)$ is given approximately by

$$\Delta P = (\beta - \delta) \, P(t) \, \Delta t,$$

and therefore

$$\frac{dP}{dt} = \lim_{\Delta t \to 0} \frac{\Delta P}{\Delta t} = kP, \tag{12}$$

where $k = \beta - \delta$.

Compound Interest. Let $A(t)$ be the number of dollars in a savings account at time t (in years), and suppose that the interest is *compounded continuously* at an annual interest rate r. (Note that 10% annual interest means that $r = 0.10$.) Continuous

compounding means that during a short time interval Δt, the amount of interest added to the account is approximately $\Delta A = rA(t) \, \Delta t$, so that

$$\frac{dA}{dt} = \lim_{\Delta t \to 0} \frac{\Delta A}{\Delta t} = rA \, . \tag{13}$$

Radioactive Decay. Consider a sample of material that contains $N(t)$ atoms of a certain radioactive isotope at time t. It has been observed that a constant fraction of these radioactive atoms will spontaneously decay (into atoms of another element or into another isotope of the same element) during each unit of time. Consequently, the sample behaves exactly like a population with a constant death rate but with no births occurring. To write a model for $N(t)$, we use Eq. (12) with N in place of P, with $k > 0$ in place of δ, and with $\beta = 0$. We thus get the differential equation

$$\frac{dN}{dt} = -kN. \tag{14}$$

The value of k depends upon the particular radioactive isotope.

The key to the method of *radiocarbon dating* is that a constant proportion of the carbon atoms in any living creature is made up of the radioactive isotope ^{14}C of carbon. This proportion remains constant because the fraction of ^{14}C in the atmosphere remains almost constant, and living matter is continuously taking up carbon from the air or is consuming other living matter containing the same constant ratio of ^{14}C atoms to ordinary ^{12}C atoms. The same ratio permeates all life, because organic processes seem to make no distinction between the two isotopes.

The ratio of ^{14}C to normal carbon remains constant in the atmosphere because, although ^{14}C is ratioactive and slowly decays, the amount is continuously replenished through the conversion of nitrogen to ^{14}C by cosmic rays in the upper atmosphere. Over the long history of the planet, this decay and replenishment process has come into nearly steady state.

Of course, when a living organism dies, it ceases its metabolism of carbon and the process of radioactive decay begins to deplete its ^{14}C content. There is no replenishment of this ^{14}C, and consequently the ratio of ^{14}C to normal carbon begins to drop. By measuring this ratio, the amount of time elapsed since the death of the organism can be estimated. For such purposes it is necessary to measure the decay constant k; for ^{14}C, it is known that $k \approx 0.0001216$ if t is measured in years.

(Matters are not as simple as we have made them appear. In applying the technique of radiocarbon dating, extreme care must be taken to avoid contaminating the sample with organic matter or even with ordinary fresh air. In addition, the cosmic ray levels apparently have not been constant, so the ratio of radioactive carbon in the atmosphere has varied over the past centuries. By using independent methods of dating samples, researchers in this area have compiled tables of correction factors to enhance the accuracy of the process.)

Drug Elimination. In many cases the amount $A(t)$ of a certain drug in the bloodstream, measured by the excess over the natural level of the drug, will decline at a rate

proportional to the current excess amount. That is,

$$\frac{dA}{dt} = -\lambda A, \tag{15}$$

where $\lambda > 0$. The parameter λ is called the **elimination constant** of the drug.

The Natural Growth Equation

The prototype differential equation $dx/dt = kx$ with $x(t) > 0$ and k a constant (either negative or positive) is readily solved by separating the variables and integrating:

$$\int \frac{1}{x} \, dx = \int k \, dt;$$

$$\ln x = kt + C.$$

Then we solve for x:

$$e^{\ln x} = e^{kt + C}; \qquad x = e^{C} e^{kt} = A e^{kt}.$$

Because C is a constant, so is $A = e^{C}$. It is also clear that $A = x(0) = x_0$, so the particular solution of Eq. (11) with the initial condition $x(0) = x_0$ is simply

$$x(t) = x_0 e^{kt}. \tag{16}$$

Because of the presence of the natural exponential function in its solution, the differential equation

$$\frac{dx}{dt} = kx \tag{17}$$

is often called the **exponential** or **natural growth equation.** Figure 1.4.3 shows a typical graph of $x(t)$ in the case $k > 0$; the case $k < 0$ is illustrated in Fig. 1.4.4.

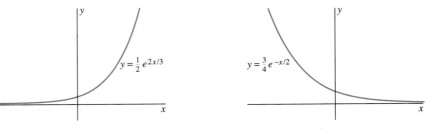

FIGURE 1.4.3. Natural growth **FIGURE 1.4.4.** Natural decay

EXAMPLE 5 In March 1987 the world population had reached 5 billion and was increasing then at the rate of 380 thousand persons each day. Assuming constant birth and death rates, when should a world population of 10 billion be expected?

Solution From Eq. (16) with P in place of x, we know that $P(t) = P_0 e^{kt}$. We measure the world population $P(t)$ in billions and measure time t in years. We shall take $t = 0$ to correspond to 1987, so that $P_0 = 5$. The fact that P was increasing by 380 thousand, or 0.00038 billion, persons per day at time $t = 0$ means that

$$P'(0) = (0.00038)(365.25) \approx 0.1388$$

billion per year. From Eq. (12) we now obtain

$$k = \left[\frac{1}{P} \cdot \frac{dP}{dt} \right]_{t=0} = \frac{P'(0)}{P(0)} \approx \frac{0.1388}{5} \approx 0.0278.$$

Thus the population was growing at the rate of about 2.78% in 1987.

To find when the population will be 10 billion, we need only solve the equation

$$10 = P(T) = 5e^{(0.0278)T}$$

for

$$T = \frac{\ln(10/5)}{0.0278} \approx 25 \quad \text{(years)},$$

which corresponds to the year 2012. Assuming that birth and death rates held constant, the world population thereafter would continue to double every quarter century. ∎

The decay constant of a radioactive isotope is often specified in terms of another empirical constant, the *half-life* of the isotope, because this parameter is more convenient. The **half-life** τ of a radioactive isotope is the time required for *half* of it to decay. To find the relationship between k and τ, we set $t = \tau$ and $N = \frac{1}{2}N_0$ in the equation $N(t) = N_0 e^{-kt}$, so that $\frac{1}{2}N_0 = N_0 e^{-k\tau}$. When we solve for τ, we find that

$$\tau = \frac{\ln 2}{k}. \tag{18}$$

For example, the half life of ^{14}C is $\tau \approx (\ln 2)/(0.00001216)$, approximately 5700 years.

EXAMPLE 6 A specimen of charcoal found at Stonehenge turns out to contain 63% as much ^{14}C as a sample of present-day charcoal of equal mass. What is the age of the sample?

Solution We take $t = 0$ as the time of the death of the tree from which the Stonehenge charcoal was made and N_0 as the number of ^{14}C atoms it contained then. We are given that $N = (0.63)N_0$ now, so we solve the equation $(0.63)N_0 = N_0 e^{-kt}$ with the value $k = 0.0001216$. Thus we find that

$$t = -\frac{\ln(0.63)}{0.0001216} \approx 3800 \quad \text{(years)}.$$

The sample is about 3800 years old, and if it has any connection with the builders of Stonehenge, our computations suggest that this observatory, monument, or temple—whichever it may be—dates from 1800 B.C. or earlier. ∎

Cooling and Heating

According to Newton's law of cooling (Eq. (3) of Section 1.1), the time rate of change of the temperature $T(t)$ of a body immersed in a medium of constant temperature A is proportional to the difference $A - T$. That is,

$$\frac{dT}{dt} = k(A - T), \tag{19}$$

where k is a positive constant. This is an instance of the linear first-order differential equation with constant coefficients:

$$\frac{dx}{dt} = ax + b. \tag{20}$$

It includes the exponential equation as a special case ($b = 0$) and is also easy to solve by separation of variables.

EXAMPLE 7 A 5-lb roast, initially at 50°F, is placed in a 375°F oven at 5:00 P.M. After 75 min it is found that the temperature $T(t)$ of the roast is 125°F. When will the roast be 150°F (medium rare)?

Solution We take time t in minutes, with $t = 0$ corresponding to 5:00 P.M. We also assume (somewhat unrealistically) that at any instant the temperature $T(t)$ of the roast is uniform throughout. We have $T(t) < A = 375$, $T(0) = 50$, and $T(75) = 125$. Hence

$$\frac{dT}{dt} = k(375 - T);$$

$$\int \frac{1}{375 - T} \, dT = \int k \, dt;$$

$$-\ln(375 - T) = kt + C;$$

$$375 - T = Be^{-kt}.$$

Now $T(0) = 50$ implies that $B = 325$, so $T(t) = 375 - 325e^{-kt}$. We also know that $T = 125$ when $T = 75$. Substitution of these values in the preceding equation yields

$$k = -\frac{1}{75} \ln\left(\frac{250}{325}\right) \approx 0.0035.$$

Hence we finally solve the equation

$$150 = 375 - 325e^{(-0.0035)t}$$

for $t = -[\ln(225/325)]/(0.0035) \approx 105$ min, the total cooking time required. Because the roast was placed in the oven at 5:00 P.M., it should be removed at about 6:45 P.M.

Torricelli's Law

Suppose that a water tank has a hole with area a at its bottom, from which water is leaking. Denote by $y(t)$ the depth of water in the tank at time t, and by $V(t)$ the volume of water in the tank then. It is plausible—and true, under ideal conditions—that the velocity of water exiting through the hole is

$$v = \sqrt{2gy}, \tag{21}$$

which is the velocity a drop of water would acquire in falling freely from the surface of the water to the hole (see Problem 29 of Section 1.2). Under real conditions, taking into account the constriction of a water jet from an orifice, $v = c\sqrt{2gy}$, where c is an empirical constant between 0 and 1 (usually about 0.6 for a small continuous stream of water). For simplicity we take $c = 1$ in the following discussion.

As a consequence of Eq. (21), we have

$$\frac{dV}{dt} = -av = -a\sqrt{2gy}; \tag{22a}$$

equivalently,

$$\frac{dV}{dt} = -k\sqrt{y} \quad \text{with} \quad k = a\sqrt{2g}. \tag{22b}$$

This is a statement of Torricelli's law for a draining tank. If $A(y)$ denotes the horizontal cross-sectional area of the tank at height y above the hole, the method of volume by cross sections gives

$$V = \int_0^y A(y)\,dy,$$

so the fundamental theorem of calculus implies that $dV/dy = A(y)$ and therefore that

$$\frac{dV}{dt} = \frac{dV}{dy}\frac{dy}{dt} = A(y)\frac{dy}{dt}. \tag{23}$$

From Eqs. (22) and (23) we finally obtain

$$A(y)\frac{dy}{dt} = -a\sqrt{2gy} = -k\sqrt{y}, \tag{24}$$

an alternative form of Torricelli's law.

EXAMPLE 8 A hemispherical tank has top radius 4 ft and at time $t = 0$ is full of water. At that moment a circular hole with diameter 1 in. is opened in the bottom of the tank. How long will it take for all the water to drain from the tank?

FIGURE 1.4.5. Draining a hemispherical tank

Solution From the right triangle in Fig. 1.4.5, we see that

$$A(y) = \pi r^2 = \pi[16 - (4 - y)^2] = \pi(8y - y^2).$$

With $g = 32$ ft/s^2, Eq. (24) becomes

$$\pi(8y - y^2)\frac{dy}{dt} = -\pi\left(\frac{1}{24}\right)^2\sqrt{64y};$$

$$\int (8y^{1/2} - y^{3/2})\,dy = -\int \frac{1}{72}\,dt;$$

$$\frac{16}{3}y^{3/2} - \frac{2}{5}y^{5/2} = -\frac{1}{72}t + C.$$

Now $y(0) = 4$, so

$$C = \frac{16}{3}\cdot 4^{3/2} - \frac{2}{5}\cdot 4^{5/2} = \frac{448}{15}.$$

The tank is empty when $y = 0$, thus when

$$t = 72 \cdot \frac{448}{15} \approx 2150 \quad \text{(s)};$$

that is, about 35 min 50 s. So it takes slightly less than 36 min for the tank to drain. ∎

1.4 Problems

Find general solutions (implicit if necessary, explicit if convenient) of the differential equations in Problems 1 through 18. Primes denote derivatives with respect to x.

1. $\dfrac{dy}{dx} + 2xy = 0$

2. $\dfrac{dy}{dx} + 2xy^2 = 0$

3. $\dfrac{dy}{dx} = y \sin x$

4. $(1 + x)\dfrac{dy}{dx} = 4y$

5. $2\sqrt{x}\,\dfrac{dy}{dx} = \sqrt{1 - y^2}$

6. $\dfrac{dy}{dx} = 3\sqrt{xy}$

7. $\dfrac{dy}{dx} = (64xy)^{1/3}$

8. $\dfrac{dy}{dx} = 2x \sec y$

9. $(1 - x^2)\dfrac{dy}{dx} = 2y$

10. $(1 + x^2)\dfrac{dy}{dx} = (1 + y)^2$

11. $y' = xy^3$

12. $yy' = x(y^2 + 1)$

13. $y^3 \dfrac{dy}{dx} = (y^4 + 1) \cos x$

14. $\dfrac{dy}{dx} = \dfrac{1 + \sqrt{x}}{1 + \sqrt{y}}$

15. $\dfrac{dy}{dx} = \dfrac{(x - 1)\,y^5}{x^2(2y^3 - y)}$

16. $(x^2 + 1)y' \tan y = x$

17. $y' = 1 + x + y + xy$ (*Suggestion:* Factor the right-hand side.)

18. $x^2 y' = 1 - x^2 + y^2 - x^2 y^2$

Find explicit particular solutions of the initial value problems in Problems 19 through 26.

19. $\dfrac{dy}{dx} = ye^x, \quad y(0) = 2e$

20. $\dfrac{dy}{dx} = 3x^2 (y^2 + 1), \quad y(0) = 1$

21. $2y\dfrac{dy}{dx} = \dfrac{x}{\sqrt{x^2 - 16}}, \quad y(5) = 2$

22. $\dfrac{dy}{dx} = 4x^3 y - y, \quad y(1) = -3$

23. $\dfrac{dy}{dx} + 1 = 2y, \quad y(1) = 1$

24. $(\tan x)\dfrac{dy}{dx} = y, \quad y\left(\dfrac{\pi}{2}\right) = \dfrac{\pi}{2}$

25. $x\dfrac{dy}{dx} - y = 2x^2 y, \quad y(1) = 1$

26. $\dfrac{dy}{dx} = 2xy^2 + 3x^2 y^2, \quad y(1) = -1$

27. (Population growth) A certain city had a population of 25,000 in 1960 and a population of 30,000 in 1970. Assume that its population will continue to grow exponentially at a constant rate. What population can its city planners expect in the year 2000?

28. (Population growth) In a certain culture of bacteria, the number of bacteria increased sixfold in 10 h. How long did it take for the population to double?

29. (Radiocarbon dating) Carbon extracted from an ancient skull contained only one-sixth as much radioactive ^{14}C as carbon extracted from present-day bone. How old is the skull?

30. (Radiocarbon dating) Carbon taken from a purported relic of the time of Christ contained 4.6×10^{10} atoms of ^{14}C per gram. Carbon extracted from a present-day specimen of the same substance contained 5.0×10^{10} atoms of ^{14}C per gram. Compute the approximate age of the relic. What is your opinion as to its authenticity?

31. (Continuously compounded interest) Upon the birth of their first child, a couple deposited $5000 in an account that pays 8% interest compounded continuously. The interest payments are allowed to accumulate. How much will the account contain on the child's eighteenth birthday?

32. (Continuously compounded interest) Suppose that you dis-

cover in your attic an overdue library book on which your great-great-grandfather owed a fine of 30 cents 100 years ago. If an overdue fine grows exponentially at a 5% annual rate compounded continuously, how much would you have to pay if you returned the book today?

33. (Drug elimination) Suppose that sodium pentobarbital is used to anesthetize a dog. The dog is anesthetized when its bloodstream concentration contains at least 45 milligrams (mg) of sodium pentobarbitol per kilogram of the dog's body weight. Suppose also that sodium pentobarbitol is eliminated exponentially from the dog's bloodstream, with a half-life of 5 h. What single dose should be administered in order to anesthetize a 50-kg dog for 1 h?

34. The half-life of radioactive cobalt is 5.27 years. Suppose that a nuclear accident has left the level of cobalt radiation in a certain region at 100 times the level acceptable for human habitation. How long will it be before the region is again habitable? (Ignore the probable presence of other radioactive isotopes.)

35. Suppose that a mineral body formed in an ancient cataclysm—perhaps the formation of the earth itself—originally contained the uranium isotope ^{238}U (which has a half-life of 4.51×10^9 years) but no lead, the end product of the radioactive decay of ^{238}U. If today the ratio of ^{238}U atoms to lead atoms in the mineral body is 0.9, when did the cataclysm occur?

36. A certain moon rock was found to contain equal numbers of potassium and argon atoms. Assume that all the argon is the result of radioactive decay of potassium (its half-life is about 1.28×10^9 years) and that one of every nine potassium atom disintegrations yields an argon atom. What is the age of the rock, measured from the time it contained only potassium?

37. A pitcher of buttermilk initially at 25°C is to be cooled by setting it on the front porch, where the temperature is 0°C. Suppose that the temperature of the buttermilk has dropped to 15°C after 20 min. When will it be at 5°C?

38. When sugar is dissolved in water, the amount A that remains undissolved after t minutes satisfies the differential equation $dA/dt = -kA$ ($k > 0$). If 25% of the sugar dissolves after 1 min, how long does it take for half of the sugar to dissolve?

39. The intensity I of light at a depth of x meters below the surface of a lake satisfies the differential equation $dI/dt = (-1.4) I$. (a) At what depth is the intensity half the intensity I_0 at the surface (where $x = 0$)? (b) What is the intensity at a depth of 10 m (as a fraction of I_0)? (c) At what depth will the intensity be $\frac{1}{100}$ of that at the surface?

40. The barometric pressure p (in inches of mercury) at an altitude x miles above sea level satisfies the initial value problem $dp/dx = (-0.2) p$, $p(0) = 29.92$. (a) Calculate the barometric pressure at 10,000 ft and again at 30,000 ft. (b) Without prior conditioning, few people can survive when the pressure drops to less than 15 in. of mercury. How high is that?

41. Consider a savings account that contains A_0 dollars initially and earns interest at the annual rate r compounded continuously. Suppose that deposits are added to this account at the rate of Q dollars per year. To simplify the mathematical model, assume that these deposits are made continuously rather than (for instance) monthly. (a) Derive the differential equation for the amount $A(t)$ in the account at time t years. (b) Suppose that you wish to arrange, at the time of her birth, for your daughter to have $40,000 available for college expenses at her eighteenth birthday. You plan to do so by making small—essentially continuous—deposits in a savings account, at the rate of Q thousand dollars per year. This account accumulates interest at an annual rate of 11%, compounded continuously. What should Q be so that you may achieve your goal?

42. According to one cosmological theory, there were equal amounts of the two uranium isotopes ^{235}U and ^{238}U at the creation of the universe in the "big bang." At present there are 137.7 atoms of ^{238}U for each atom of ^{235}U. Using the half-lives 4.51×10^9 years for ^{238}U and 7.1×10^8 years for ^{235}U, calculate the age of the universe.

43. A cake is removed from an oven at 210°F and left to cool at room temperature, which is 70°F. After 30 min the temperature of the cake is 140°F. When will it be 100°F?

44. (a) Payments are made continuously on a mortgage of P_0 dollars at the constant rate of c dollars per month. Let $P(t)$ denote the principal (amount still owed to the lender) after t months, and let r denote the monthly interest rate paid by the borrower (for instance, $r = (0.12)/12 = 0.01$ if the annual interest rate is 12%). Derive the differential equation

$$\frac{dP}{dt} = rP - c, \qquad P(0) = P_0.$$

(b) An automobile loan of $10,800 is to be paid off continuously over a period of 60 months. Determine the monthly payment required if the annual interest rate is (i) 12%; (ii) 18%.

45. A certain piece of dubious information about phenylethylamine in the drinking water began to spread one day in a city with a population of 100,000. Within a week, 10,000 people had heard this rumor. Assume that the rate of increase of the number who have heard the rumor is proportional to the number who have not yet heard it. How long will it be until half the population of the city has heard the rumor?

46. A tank is shaped like a vertical cylinder; it initially contains water to a depth of 9 ft, and a bottom plug is removed at time $t = 0$ (hours). After 1 h the depth has dropped to 4 ft. How long does it take for all the water to drain from the tank?

47. Suppose that the tank of Problem 46 has a radius of 3 ft and that its bottom hole is circular with radius 1 in. How long will it take the water (initially 9 ft deep) to drain completely?

48. At time $t = 0$ the bottom plug (at the vertex) of a full conical water tank 16 ft high is removed. After 1 h the water in the tank is 9 ft deep. When will the tank be empty?

49. Suppose that a cylindrical tank initially containing V_0 gallons of water drains (through a bottom hole) in T minutes. Use Torricelli's law to show that the volume of water in the tank after $t \leq T$ minutes is $V = V_0 [1 - (t/T)]^2$.

50. A water tank has the shape obtained by revolving the curve $y = x^{4/3}$ around the y-axis. A plug at the bottom is removed at 12 noon, when the depth of water in the tank is 12 ft. At 1 P.M. the depth of the water is 6 ft. When will the tank be empty?

51. A water tank has the shape obtained by revolving the parabola $x^2 = by$ around the y-axis. The water depth is 4 ft at 12 noon, when a circular plug in the bottom is removed. At 1 P.M. the depth of the water is 1 ft. (a) Find the depth $y(t)$ of water remaining after t hours. (b) When will the tank be empty? (c) If the initial radius of the top surface of the water is 2 ft, what is the radius of the circular hole in the bottom?

52. A cylindrical tank with length 5 ft and radius 3 ft is situated with its axis horizontal. If a circular bottom hole with a radius of 1 in. is opened and the tank is initially half full of xylene, how long will it take for the liquid to drain completely?

53. A spherical tank with radius 4 ft is full of gasoline when a circular bottom hole with radius 1 in. is opened. How long will be required for all the gasoline to drain from the tank?

54. (The clepsydra, or water clock) A 12-h water clock is to be designed with the dimensions shown in Fig. 1.4.6, shaped like the surface obtained by revolving the curve $y = f(x)$ around the y-axis. What should be this curve, and what should be the radius of the circular bottom hole, in order that the water level will fall at the *constant* rate of 4 inches per hour (in./h)?

55. Just before midday the body of an apparent homicide victim is found in a room that is kept at a constant temperature of 70°F. At 12 noon the temperature of the body is 80°F and at 1 P.M. it is 75°F. Assume that the temperature of the body at the time of death was 98.6°F and that it has cooled in accord with Newton's law. What was the time of death?

56. Early one morning it began to snow at a constant rate. At 7:00 A.M. a snowplow set off to clear a road. By 8:00 A.M. it had traveled 2 miles, but it took two more hours (until 10:00 A.M.) for the snowplow to go an additional 2 miles. (a) Let $t = 0$ when it began to snow and let x denote the distance traveled by the snowplow at time t. Assuming that the snowplow clears snow from the road at a constant rate (in cubic feet per hour, say), show that

$$k\frac{dx}{dt} = \frac{1}{t},$$

where k is a constant. (b) What time did it start snowing? (*Answer:* 6:00 A.M.)

57. A snowplow sets off at 7:00 A.M. as in Problem 56. Suppose now that by 8:00 A.M. it had traveled 4 miles and that by 9 A.M. it had moved an additional 3 miles. What time did it start snowing? This is a more difficult snowplow problem because now a transcendental equation must be solved numerically to find the value of k. (*Answer:* 4:27 A.M.)

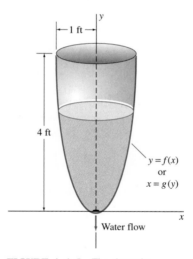

FIGURE 1.4.6. The clepsydra

1.4 Computing Project

As in Eq. (3), the solution of a separable differential equation reduces to the evaluation of two indefinite integrals. Thus it is tempting to use a symbolic algebra system such as *Maple* or *Mathematica* that can compute such integrals. Using *Mathematica* we would write Eq. (3) in the form

```
genSolution := Integrate[ f[y],y ] == Integrate[ g[x],x ] + C
```

For an example of the symbolic algebra solution of a differential equation, consider the logistic equation

$$\frac{dy}{dt} = ky(M - y)$$

which (as we'll see in Section 2.1) models the growth of certain human and animal populations. Using *Maple* we would separate the variables and write

```
> genSolution := int(1/(y*(M-y)),y) = int(k,t) + C;
```

$$genSolution := \frac{\ln(y)}{M} - \frac{\ln(M - y)}{M} = kt + C$$

The following sequence of successive simplifications is then fairly self-explanatory.

```
> genSolution := simplify(M*lhs(") = M*rhs("));
```

$$genSolution := \ln(y) - \ln(M - y) = M(kt + C)$$

```
> genSolution := exp(lhs(")) = exp(rhs("));
```

$$genSolution := e^{\ln(y) - \ln(M - y)} = e^{M(kt + C)}$$

```
> genSolution := simplify(lhs(")) = simplify(rhs("));
```

$$genSolution := -\frac{y}{-M + y} = e^{M(kt + C)}$$

```
> explicitSolution := y = solve(genSolution, y);
```

$$explicitSolution := y = \frac{e^{(M(kt + C))}M}{1 + e^{(M(kt + C))}}$$

From the first line of *Maple* output above we see that

```
> C := (ln(y0) - ln(M - y0))/M:
```

With this value of the arbitrary constant C we get

```
> partSolution := simplify(explicitSolution);
```

$$partSolution := y = \frac{e^{(ktM)}y0\,M}{M - y0 + e^{(ktM)}y0}$$

Thus the particular solution of the logistic equation satisfying the initial condition $y(0) = y_0$ is given by

$$y(t) = \frac{My_0 e^{ktM}}{M + y_0(e^{ktM} - 1)}.$$

If a symbolic algebra system is available, you should use it to carry out this or a similar solution of the logistic equation. Then attempt to solve similarly some separable differential equations such as those in Problems 1 through 26 of this section.

1.5 Linear First-Order Equations

In Section 1.4 we saw how to solve a separable differential equation by integrating *after* multiplying both sides by an appropriate factor. For instance, to solve the equation

$$\frac{dy}{dx} = 2xy \qquad (y > 0),$$
(1)

we multiply both sides by the factor $1/y$ to get

$$\frac{1}{y}\frac{dy}{dx} = 2x; \qquad \text{that is,} \quad D_x(\ln y) = D_x(x^2).$$
(2)

Because each side of the equation in (2) is recognizable as a *derivative* (with respect to the independent variable x), all that remains are two simple integrations, which yield $\ln y = x^2 + C$. For this reason, the function $\rho(y) = 1/y$ is called an *integrating factor* for the original equation in (1). An **integrating factor** for a differential equation is a function $\rho(x, y)$ such that multiplication of each side of the differential equation by $\rho(x, y)$ yields an equation in which each side is recognizable as a derivative.

With the aid of the appropriate integrating factor, there is a standard technique for solving the *linear* **first-order equation**

▶
$$\frac{dy}{dx} + P(x)y = Q(x)$$
(3)

on an interval on which the coefficient functions $P(x)$ and $Q(x)$ are continuous. We multiply each side in Eq. (3) by the integrating factor

▶
$$\rho = \rho(x) = e^{\int P(x)\,dx}.$$
(4)

The result is

$$e^{\int P(x)\,dx}\frac{dy}{dx} + P(x)e^{\int P(x)\,dx}y = Q(x)e^{\int P(x)\,dx}.$$
(5)

Because $D_x\left[\int P(x)\,dx\right] = P(x)$, the left-hand side is the derivative of the *product* $y(x) \cdot e^{\int P(x)\,dx}$, so (5) is equivalent to

$$D_x\left[y(x)e^{\int P(x)\,dx}\right] = Q(x)e^{\int P(x)\,dx}.$$

Integration of both sides of this equation gives

$$y(x)e^{\int P(x)\,dx} = \int \left(Q(x)e^{\int P(x)\,dx}\right) dx + C.$$

Finally solving for y, we obtain the general solution of the linear first-order equation in (3):

$$y(x) = e^{-\int P(x)\,dx}\left[\int \left(Q(x)e^{\int P(x)\,dx}\right) dx + C\right].$$
(6)

The formula in (6) should **not** be memorized. In a specific problem it is generally simpler to use the *method* by which we developed this formula. That is, in order to solve Eq. (3), carry out the following steps:

1. Begin by calculating the integrating factor $\rho(x) = e^{\int P(x)\,dx}$.
2. Then multiply both sides of the differential equation by $\rho(x)$.
3. Next, recognize the left-hand side of the resulting equation as the derivative of a product:

$$D_x[\rho(x)y(x)] = \rho(x)Q(x).$$

4. Finally, integrate this equation,

$$\rho(x)\,y(x) = \int \rho(x)Q(x)\,dx + C,$$

then solve for y to obtain the general solution of the original differential equation.

Moreover, given an initial condition $y(x_0) = y_0$, we can substitute $x = x_0$ and $y = y_0$ in (6) to solve for the value of C yielding the particular solution of Eq. (3) that satisfies this initial condition.

The integrating factor $\rho(x)$ is determined only to within a multiplicative constant. If we replace $\int P(x)\,dx$ by $\int P(x)\,dx + c$ in (4), the result is

$$\rho(x) = e^{c + \int P(x)\,dx} = e^c e^{\int P(x)\,dx}.$$

But the constant factor e^c does not affect the result of multiplying both sides of the differential equation in (3) by $\rho(x)$. Hence we may choose for $\int P(x)\,dx$ any convenient antiderivative of $P(x)$.

EXAMPLE 1 Solve the initial value problem

$$\frac{dy}{dx} - 3y = e^{2x}, \qquad y(0) = 3.$$

Solution Here we have $P(x) = -3$ and $Q(x) = e^{2x}$, so the integrating factor is

$$\rho(x) = e^{\int (-3)\,dx} = e^{-3x}.$$

Multiplication of both sides of the given equation by e^{-3x} yields

$$e^{-3x}\frac{dy}{dx} - 3e^{-3x}y = e^{-x},$$

which we recognize as

$$\frac{d}{dx}(e^{-3x}y) = e^{-x}.$$

Hence integration with respect to x gives

$$e^{-3x}y = \int e^{-x}\,dx = -e^{-x} + C,$$

so multiplication by e^{3x} yields the general solution

$$y(x) = Ce^{3x} - e^{2x}.$$

Substitution of $x = 0$ and $y = 3$ now gives $C = 4$. Thus the desired particular solution is

$$y(x) = 4e^{3x} - e^{2x}.$$

EXAMPLE 2 Find a general solution of

$$(x^2 + 1)\frac{dy}{dx} + 3xy = 6x.$$

Solution After division of both sides of the equation by $x^2 + 1$, we recognize the result

$$\frac{dy}{dx} + \frac{3x}{x^2 + 1}y = \frac{6x}{x^2 + 1}$$

as a first-order linear equation with $P(x) = 3x/(x^2 + 1)$ and $Q(x) = 6x/(x^2 + 1)$. Multiplication by

$$\rho(x) = \exp\left(\int \frac{3x}{x^2 + 1}\,dx\right) = \exp\left(\frac{3}{2}\ln(x^2 + 1)\right) = (x^2 + 1)^{3/2}$$

yields

$$(x^2 + 1)^{3/2}\frac{dy}{dx} + 3x\,(x^2 + 1)^{1/2}y = 6x(x^2 + 1)^{1/2},$$

and thus

$$D_x\,[(x^2 + 1)^{3/2}y] = 6x(x^2 + 1)^{1/2}.$$

Integration then yields

$$(x^2 + 1)^{1/2}y = \int 6x(x^2 + 1)^{1/2}\,dx = 2(x^2 + 1)^{3/2} + C.$$

Multiplication of both sides by $(x^2 + 1)^{-3/2}$ gives the general solution

$$y(x) = 2 + C(x^2 + 1)^{-3/2}. \qquad \blacksquare$$

Frequently the integrations are not so simple as those in Examples 1 and 2. We may apply the fundamental theorem of calculus, however, to write an antiderivative of an arbitrary continuous function f in the form

$$F(x) = \int_a^t f(t)\,dt.$$

EXAMPLE 3 Solve the initial value problem

$$x^2\frac{dy}{dx} + xy = \sin x, \qquad y(1) = y_1. \tag{7}$$

Solution Division by x^2 gives

$$\frac{dy}{dx} + \frac{1}{x}y = \frac{\sin x}{x^2},$$

so an integrating factor is $\rho(x) = e^{\int (1/x)\,dx} = e^{\ln x} = x$. Hence

$$x\frac{dy}{dx} + y = \frac{\sin x}{x}; \qquad D_x(xy) = \frac{\sin x}{x}; \qquad xy = \int_0^x \frac{\sin t}{t}\,dt + C. \qquad (8)$$

The lower limit of integration $a = 0$ is permissible because $(\sin t)/t \to 1$ as $t \to 0$. Consequently, we can define the integrand in (8) to have the value 1 when $t = 0$. Then the integral is not improper. Substitution of the initial conditions $x = 1$, $y = y_1$ in (8) yields

$$C = y_1 - \int_0^1 \frac{\sin t}{t}\,dt,$$

so

$$y(x) = \frac{1}{x}\int_0^x \frac{\sin t}{t}\,dt + \frac{C}{x} = \frac{1}{x}\int_0^x \frac{\sin t}{t}\,dt + \frac{y_1}{x} - \frac{1}{x}\int_0^1 \frac{\sin t}{t}\,dt$$

$$= \frac{y_1}{x} + \frac{1}{x}\int_1^x \frac{\sin t}{t}\,dt. \qquad (9)$$

Comment: In general, an integral such as the one in Eq. (9) would (for a given x) have to be approximated numerically—using Simpson's rule, for instance—to find the value $y(x)$ of the solution at x. In this case, however, we have the sine integral function

$$\text{Si}(x) = \int_0^x \frac{\sin t}{t}\,dt,$$

which appears with sufficient frequency in applications that its values have been tabulated. A good set of tables of special functions is Abramowitz and Stegun, *Handbook of Mathematical Functions* (New York: Dover, 1965). Then the particular solution in (9) reduces to

$$y(x) = \frac{1}{x}\,[y_1 + \text{Si}(x) - \text{Si}(1)]. \qquad (10)$$

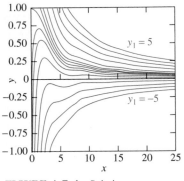

FIGURE 1.5.1. Solution curves defined by Eq. (10) with $y_1 = -5, -4, \ldots, 4, 5$

The *Mathematica* function `SinIntegral[x]` can be used to plot typical solution curves. Figure 1.5.1 shows a selection of solution curves with initial values $y(1) = y_1$ ranging from $y_1 = 5$ to $y_1 = -5$. It appears that on each solution curve, $y(x) \to 0$ as $x \to +\infty$, and this is in fact true because the sine integral function is bounded.

In the sequel we will see that it is an exception—rather than the rule—when a solution to a differential equation can be expressed in terms of elementary functions. We will study various devices for obtaining good approximations to the values of the nonelementary functions we encounter; in Chapter 2 we will discuss numerical integration of differential equations in some detail.

A Closer Look at the Method

The preceding derivation of the solution in (6) of the linear first-order equation in (3) bears a closer examination. Suppose that the functions $P(x)$ and $Q(x)$ are continuous on the (possibly unbounded) open interval I. Then the antiderivatives

$$\int P(x)\,dx \quad \text{and} \quad \int \left(Q(x)e^{\int P(x)\,dx}\right) dx$$

exist on I. Our derivation of Eq. (6) shows that *if* $y = y(x)$ is a solution of Eq. (3) on I, *then* $y(x)$ is given by the formula in (6) for some choice of the constant C. Conversely, you may verify by direct substitution (Problem 31) that the function $y(x)$ given in Eq. (6) satisfies Eq. (3). Finally, given a point x_0 of I and any number y_0, there is—as previously noted—a unique value of C such that $y(x_0) = y_0$. Consequently, we have proved the following existence-uniqueness theorem.

THEOREM 1: The Linear First-Order Equation

If the functions $P(x)$ and $Q(x)$ are continuous on the open interval I containing the point x_0, then the initial value problem

$$\frac{dy}{dx} + P(x)y = Q(x), \qquad y(x_0) = y_0$$

has a unique solution $y(x)$ on I, given by the formula in Eq. (6) with an appropriate value of C. ∎

Remark 1: Theorem 1 gives a solution on the *entire* interval I for a *linear* differential equation, in contrast with Theorem 1 of Section 1.3, which guarantees only a solution on a possibly smaller interval J.

Remark 2: Theorem 1 tells us that every solution of Eq. (3) is included in the general solution given in (6). Thus a *linear* first-order differential equation has *no* singular solutions.

EXAMPLE 4 If we write the equation

$$x\frac{dy}{dx} + y = 1$$

in the standard form shown in (3), we see that it has coefficient functions $P(x) = Q(x) = 1/x$ that are continuous on the intervals $x < 0$ and $x > 0$, but discontinuous at $x = 0$. Because the equation as written is equivalent to $D_x(xy) = 1$, integration gives $xy = x + C$; thus

$$y(x) = 1 + \frac{C}{x}.$$

Some typical solution curves are shown in Fig. 1.5.2. The solution with $y(1) = 2$ is $y = 1 + (1/x)$ for $x > 0$, whereas the solution with $y(-1) = 2$ is $y = 1 - (1/x)$ for $x < 0$. The only solution that is continuous on the whole real line is the constant solution $y(x) \equiv 1$. We see also that if $y_0 \neq 1$, then there is *no* solution with $y(0) = y_0$. Note that in accord with Theorem 1, all solutions are continuous expect possibly at the discontinuity $x = 0$ of $P(x)$ and $Q(x)$, and that most solutions are singular at the singularity $x = 0$ of the differential equation. ∎

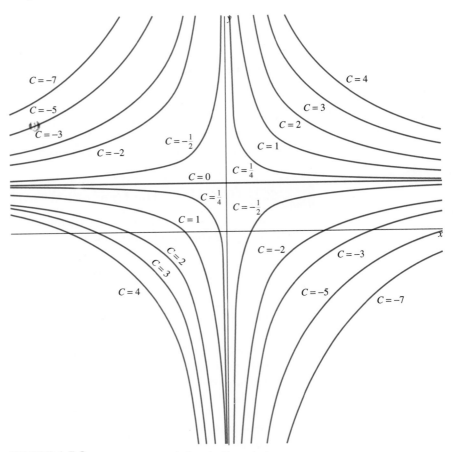

FIGURE 1.5.2. Graphs of some solutions for Example 4

Mixture Problems

As a first application of linear first-order equations, we consider a tank containing a solution—a mixture of solute and solvent—such as salt dissolved in water. There is both inflow and outflow, and we want to compute the *amount* $x(t)$ of solute in the tank at time t, given the amount $x(0) = x_0$ at time $t = 0$. Suppose that solution with a concentration of c_i grams of solute per liter of solution flows into the tank at the constant rate of r_i liters per second, and that the solution in the tank—kept thoroughly mixed by stirring—flows out at the constant rate of r_o liters per second.

To set up a differential equation for $x(t)$, we estimate the change Δx in x during the brief time interval $[t, t + \Delta t]$. The amount of solute that flows into the tank during Δt seconds is $r_i c_i \, \Delta t$ grams. To check this, note how the cancellation of dimensions checks our computations:

$$\left(r_i \frac{\text{liters}}{\text{second}}\right)\left(c_i \frac{\text{grams}}{\text{liter}}\right)(\Delta t \text{ seconds})$$

yields a quantity measured in grams.

Input: r_i L/s, c_i gm/L

Amount $x(t)$
Volume $V(t)$
Concentration $c_o(t) = \frac{x}{V}$

Output:
r_o L/s,
c_o gm/L

FIGURE 1.5.3. The single-tank mixture problem

The amount of solute that flows out of the tank during the same time interval depends on the concentration $c_o(t)$ in the tank at time t. But as noted in Fig. 1.5.3, $c_o(t) = x(t)/V(t)$, where $V(t)$ denotes the volume (not constant unless $r_i = r_o$) of solution in the tank at time t. Then

$$\Delta x = \{\text{grams input}\} - \{\text{grams output}\} \approx r_i c_i \Delta t - r_o c_o \Delta t.$$

We now divide by Δt:

$$\frac{\Delta x}{\Delta t} \approx r_i c_i - r_o c_o.$$

Finally, we take the limit as $\Delta t \to 0$; if all the functions involved are continuous and $x(t)$ is differentiable, then the error in this approximation also approaches zero, and we obtain the differential equation

$$\frac{dx}{dt} = r_i c_i - r_o c_o, \tag{11}$$

in which r_i, c_i, and r_o are constants, but c_o denotes the variable concentration

$$c_o(t) = \frac{x(t)}{V(t)} \tag{12}$$

of solute in the tank at time t. Thus the *amount* $x(t)$ of solute in the tank satisfies the differential equation

$$\frac{dx}{dt} = r_i c_i - \frac{r_o}{V} x. \tag{13}$$

If $V_0 = V(0)$, then $V(t) = V_0 + (r_i - r_o)t$, so Eq. (13) is a linear first-order differential equation for the amount $x(t)$ of solute in the tank.

Important. Equation (13) is *not* one you should commit to memory. It is the process we used to obtain that equation—examination of the behavior of the system over a short time interval $[t, t + \Delta t]$—that you should strive to understand, because it is a very useful tool for obtaining all sorts of differential equations.

EXAMPLE 5 Lake Erie has a volume of 458 km³, and its rate of inflow and outflow are both 175 km³/year. Suppose that at the time $t = 0$ (years), its pollutant concentration is 0.05%, and that thereafter the concentration of pollutants in the inflowing water is 0.01%. Assuming that the outflow is perfectly mixed lake water, how long will it take to reduce the pollution concentration in the lake to 0.02%?

Solution Here we have $V = 458$ (km³) and $r_i = r_o = 175$ (km³/year). Let $x(t)$ denote the volume of pollutants in the lake at time t. We are given

$$x(0) = (0.0005)(458) = 0.2290 \text{ (km}^3),$$

and we want to find when

$$x(t) = (0.0002)(458) = 0.0916 \text{ (km}^3).$$

The change Δx in Δt years is

$$\Delta x \approx (0.0001)\,(175)\,\Delta t - \left(\frac{x}{458}\right)(175)\,\Delta t$$

$$= (0.0175 - 0.3821x)\,\Delta t,$$

so our differential equation is

$$\frac{dx}{dt} + (0.3821)x = 0.0175.$$

An integrating factor is $\rho = e^{(0.3821)t}$; it yields

$$D_t[e^{(0.3821)t}x] = (0.0175)e^{(0.3821)t};$$

$$[e^{(0.3821)t}]x = (0.0458)e^{(0.3821)t} + C.$$

Substitution of $x(0) = 0.2290$ into the preceding equation gives

$$C = 0.2290 - 0.0458 = 0.1832,$$

so the solution is

$$x(t) = 0.0458 + (0.1832)e^{-(0.3821)t}.$$

Finally, we solve the equation

$$0.0916 = 0.0458 + (0.1832)e^{-(0.3821)t}$$

for

$$t = -\frac{1}{0.3821}\ln\frac{0.0916 - 0.0458}{0.1832} \approx 3.63.$$

Thus the answer to the problem is: After about 3.63 years.

EXAMPLE 6 A 120-gallon (gal) tank initially contains 90 lb of salt dissolved in 90 gal of water. Brine containing 2 lb/gal of salt flows into the tank at the rate of 4 gal/min, and the mixture flows out of the tank at the rate of 3 gal/min. How much salt does the tank contain when it is full?

Solution The interesting feature of this example is that, due to the differing rates of inflow and outflow, the volume of brine in the tank increases steadily with $V(t) = 90 + t$ gallons. The change Δx in the amount x of salt in the tank from time t to time $t + \Delta t$ (minutes) is given by

$$\Delta x \approx (4)\,(2)\,\Delta t - 3\left(\frac{x}{90 + t}\right)\Delta t,$$

so our differential equation is

$$\frac{dx}{dt} + \frac{3}{90 + t}x = 8.$$

An integrating factor is

$$\rho(x) = \exp\left(\int \frac{3}{90 + t}\,dt\right) = e^{3\ln(90 + t)} = (90 + t)^3,$$

which gives

$$D_t[(90 + t)^3 x] = 8(90 + t)^3;$$

$$(90 + t)^3 x = 2(90 + t)^4 + C.$$

Substitution of $x(0) = 90$ gives $C = -(90)^4$, so the amount of salt in the tank at time t is

$$x(t) = 2(90 + t) - \frac{90^4}{(90 + t)^3}.$$

The tank is full after 30 min, and when $t = 30$, we have

$$x(30) = 2(90 + 30) - \frac{90^4}{120^3} \approx 202 \text{ (lb)}$$

of salt. ∎

1.5 Problems

Find general solutions of the differential equations in Problems 1 through 25. If an initial condition is given, find the corresponding particular solution. Throughout, primes denote derivatives with respect to x.

1. $y' + y = 2, \quad y(0) = 0$

2. $y' - 2y = 3e^{2x}, \quad y(0) = 0$

3. $y' + 3y = 2xe^{-3x}$

4. $y' - 2xy = e^{x^2}$

5. $xy' + 2y = 3x, \quad y(1) = 5$

6. $xy' + 5y = 7x^2, \quad y(2) = 5$

7. $2xy' + y = 10\sqrt{x}$

8. $3xy' + y = 12x$

9. $xy' - y = x; \quad y(1) = 7$

10. $2xy' - 3y = 9x^3$

11. $xy' + y = 3xy; \quad y(1) = 0$

12. $xy' + 3y = 2x^5, \quad y(2) = 1$

13. $y' + y = e^x, \quad y(0) = 1$

14. $xy' - 3y = x^3, \quad y(1) = 10$

15. $y' + 2xy = x, \quad y(0) = -2$

16. $y' = (1 - y) \cos x, \quad y(\pi) = 2$

17. $(1 + x) y' + y = \cos x, \quad y(0) = 1$

18. $xy' = 2y + x^3 \cos x$

19. $y' + y \cot x = \cos x$

20. $y' = 1 + x + y + xy, \quad y(0) = 0$

21. $xy' = 3y + x^4 \cos x, \quad y(2\pi) = 0$

22. $y' = 2xy + 3x^2 \exp(x^2), \quad y(0) = 5$

23. $xy' + (2x - 3)y = 4x^4$

24. $(x^2 + 4)y' + 3xy = x, \quad y(0) = 1$

25. $(x^2 + 1) \dfrac{dy}{dx} + 3x^3 y = 6x \exp\left(-\dfrac{3}{2}x^2\right), \quad y(0) = 1$

Solve the differential equations in Problems 26 through 28 by regarding y as the independent variable rather than x.

26. $(1 - 4xy^2) \dfrac{dy}{dx} = y^3$

27. $(x + ye^y) \dfrac{dy}{dx} = 1$

28. $(1 + 2xy) \dfrac{dy}{dx} = 1 + y^2$

29. Express the general solution of $dy/dx = 1 + 2xy$ in terms of the **error function**

$$\text{erf}(x) = \frac{2}{\sqrt{\pi}} \int_0^x e^{-t^2} dt.$$

30. Express the solution of the initial value problem

$$2x \frac{dy}{dx} = y + 2x \cos x, \qquad y(1) = 0$$

as an integral as in Example 3.

31. (a) Show that $y_c(x) = Ce^{-\int P(x)\,dx}$ is a general solution of $dy/dx + P(x)y = 0$. (b) Show that

$$y_p(x) = e^{-\int P(x)\,dx}\left[\int \left(Q(x)e^{\int P(x)\,dx}\right)dx\right]$$

is a particular solution of $dy/dx + P(x)y = Q(x)$. (c) Suppose that $y_c(x)$ is any general solution of $dy/dx + P(x)y = 0$ and $y_p(x)$ is any particular solution of $dy/dx + P(x)y = Q(x)$. Show that $y(x) = y_c(x) + y_p(x)$ is a general solution of $dy/dx + P(x)y = Q(x)$.

32. (a) Find constants A and B such that $y_p(x) = A\sin x + B\cos x$ is a solution of $dy/dx + y = 2\sin x$. (b) Use the result of part (a) and the method of Problem 31 to find the general solution of $dy/dx + y = 2\sin x$. (c) Solve the initial value problem $dy/dx + y = 2\sin x,\; y(0) = 1$.

33. A tank contains 1000 liters (L) of a solution consisting of 100 kg of salt dissolved in water. Pure water is pumped into the tank at the rate of 5 L/s, and the mixture—kept uniform by stirring—is pumped out at the same rate. How long will it be until only 10 kg of salt remain in the tank?

34. Consider a reservoir with a volume of 8 billion cubic feet (ft^3) and an initial pollutant concentration of 0.25%. There is a daily inflow of 500 million ft^3 of water with a pollutant concentration of 0.05% and an equal daily outflow of the well-mixed water in the reservoir. How long will it take to reduce the pollutant concentration in the reservoir to 0.10%?

35. Rework Example 5 for the case of Lake Ontario. The only differences are that this lake has a volume of 1636 km^3 and an inflow-outflow rate of 209 km^3/year.

36. A tank initially contains 60 gal of pure water. Brine containing 1 lb of salt per gallon enters the tank at 2 gal/min, and the (perfectly mixed) solution leaves the tank at 3 gal/min; thus the tank is empty after exactly 1 h. (a) Find the amount of water in the tank after t minutes. (b) What is the maximum amount of salt ever in the tank?

37. A 400-gal tank initially contains 100 gal of brine containing 50 lb of salt. Brine containing 1 lb of salt per gallon enters the tank at the rate of 5 gal/s, and the well-mixed brine in the tank flows out at the rate of 3 gal/s. How much salt will the tank contain when it is full of brine?

38. Consider the *cascade* of two tanks shown in Fig. 1.5.4, with $V_1 = 100$ (gal) and $V_2 = 200$ (gal) the volumes of brine in the two tanks. Each tank initially contains 50 lb of salt. The three flow rates are each 5 gal/s, with pure water flowing into tank 1. (a) Find the amount $x(t)$ of salt in tank 1 at time t. (b) Suppose that $y(t)$ is the amount of salt in tank 2 at time t. Show first that

$$\frac{dy}{dt} = \frac{5x}{100} - \frac{5y}{200},$$

Tank 1
Volume V_1
Amount x

Tank 2
Volume V_2
Amount y

FIGURE 1.5.4. A cascade of two tanks

and then solve for $y(t)$, using the function $x(t)$ found in part (a). (c) Finally, find the maximum amount of salt ever in tank 2.

39. Suppose that in the cascade shown in Fig. 1.5.4, tank 1 initially contains 100 gal of pure ethyl alcohol and tank 2 initially contains 100 gal of pure water. Pure water flows into tank 1 at 10 gal/min, and the other two flow rates are also 10 gal/min. (a) Find the amounts $x(t)$ and $y(t)$ of alcohol in the two tanks at time $t \geq 0$. (b) Find the maximum amount of alcohol ever in tank 2.

40. A multiple cascade is shown in Fig. 1.5.5. At time $t = 0$, tank 0 contains 1 gal of alcohol and 1 gal of water, whereas each

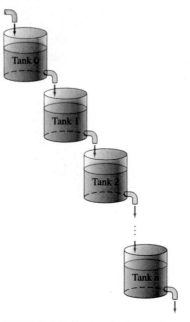

Tank 0

Tank 1

Tank 2

Tank n

FIGURE 1.5.5. A multiple cascade

of the other tanks contains 2 gal of pure water. Pure water is pumped into tank 0 at 1 gal/min, and the varying mixture in each tank is pumped into the one to its right at the same rate. Assume, as usual, that the mixtures are kept perfectly uniform by stirring. Let $x_n(t)$ denote the amount of alcohol in tank n at time t. (a) Show that $x_0(t) = e^{-t/2}$. (b) Show by induction on n that

$$x_n(t) = \frac{t^n e^{-t/2}}{n! \, 2^n} \qquad \text{for } n > 0.$$

(c) Show that the maximum value of $x_n(t)$ for $n > 0$ is $M_n = n^n e^{-n}/n!$. (d) Conclude from **Stirling's approximation** $n! \approx n^n e^{-n}\sqrt{2\pi n}$ that $M_n \approx (2\pi n)^{-1/2}$.

41. A 30-year-old woman accepts an engineering position with a starting salary of \$30,000 per year. Her salary $S(t)$ increases exponentially, with $S(t) = 30e^{t/20}$ thousand dollars after t years. Meanwhile, 12% of her salary is deposited continuously in a re-

tirement account, which accumulates interest at a continuous annual rate of 6%. (a) Estimate ΔA in terms of Δt to derive the differential equation satisfied by the amount $A(t)$ in her retirement account after t years. (b) Compute $A(40)$, the amount available for her retirement at age 70.

42. Suppose that a falling hailstone with density $\delta = 1$ starts from rest with negligible radius $r = 0$. Thereafter its radius is $r = kt$ (k is a constant) as it grows by accretion during its fall. Set up and solve the initial value problem

$$\frac{d}{dt}(mv) = mg, \qquad v(0) = 0,$$

where m is the variable mass of the hailstone, $v = dy/dt$ is its velocity, and the positive y-axis points downward. Then show that $dv/dt = g/4$. Thus the hailstone falls as though it were under *one-fourth* the influence of gravity.

1.5 Computing Project

The algorithm described by Steps 1 through 4 on page 42 for solving the linear differential equation

$$\frac{dy}{dx} + p(x)\, y = q(x)$$

is well-adapted to automatic symbolic computation. To solve the initial value problem

$$\frac{dy}{dx} - 3y = e^{2x}, \qquad y(0) = 3,$$

of Example 1 using *Mathematica* (for instance), we first define the coefficient functions

```
p[x_] := -3
q[x_] := Exp[2*x]
```

Then we calculate the integrating factor

```
r[x_] := Exp[ Integrate[p[x], x] ]
```

Then Eq. (6) in this section gives

```
genSolution = y == (1/r[x])*(c + Integrate[q[x]*r[x], x])
```

$$y == E^3 \; x \; (c - E^{-x})$$

If we want a particular solution, we apply the initial condition $x \rightarrow x0$, $y \rightarrow y0$ and solve for the constant **c**.

```
Solve[ genSolution, c ] /. {x -> 0, y -> 3}
{{c -> 4}}
```

Thus the desired particular solution is given by

partSolution = genSolution /. c -> 4

$y == E^{3\ x}\ (4 - E^{-x})$

The commands shown here constitute a "template" that you can apply to any given linear first-order differential equation. First redefine the coefficient functions $p(x)$ and $q(x)$ as specified by your linear equation, then work through the subsequent steps.

You should apply whatever computer algebra system is available to carry out the solution process shown here for the initial value problem in Example 1, then apply it to a selection of other examples and problems in this section.

1.6 Substitution Methods and Exact Equations

The first-order differential equations we have solved in the previous sections have all been either separable or linear. But many applications involve differential equations that are neither separable nor linear. In this section we illustrate (mainly with examples) substitution methods that sometimes can be used to transform a given differential equation into one that we already know how to solve.

For instance, the differential equation

$$\frac{dy}{dx} = f(x, y), \tag{1}$$

with dependent variable y and independent variable x, may contain a conspicuous combination

$$v = \alpha(x, y) \tag{2}$$

of x and y that suggests itself as a new dependent variable v. Thus the differential equation

$$\frac{dy}{dx} = (x + y + 3)^2$$

practically demands the substitution $v = x + y + 3$ of the form in (2).

If the substitution relation in (2) can be solved for

$$y = \beta(x, v), \tag{3}$$

then application of the chain rule—regarding v as an (unknown) function of x—yields

$$\frac{dy}{dx} = \frac{\partial \beta}{\partial x} \frac{dx}{dx} + \frac{\partial \beta}{\partial v} \frac{dv}{dx} = \frac{\partial \beta}{\partial x} + \frac{\partial \beta}{\partial v} \frac{dv}{dx}, \tag{4}$$

where the partial derivatives $\partial\beta/\partial x = \beta_x(x, v)$ and $\partial\beta/\partial v = \beta_v(x, v)$ are *known* functions of x and v. If we substitute the right-hand side in (4) for dy/dx in Eq. (1) and then solve for dv/dx, the result is a *new* differential equation of the form

$$\frac{dv}{dx} = g(x, v) \tag{5}$$

with *new* dependent variable v. If this new equation is either separable or linear, then we can apply the methods of preceding sections to solve it.

If $v = v(x)$ is a solution of Eq. (5), then $y = \beta(x, v(x))$ is a solution of the original Eq. (1). The trick is to select a substitution such that the transformed Eq. (5) is one we can solve. Even when possible, this is not always easy; it may require a fair amount of ingenuity or trial and error.

EXAMPLE 1 Solve the differential equation

$$\frac{dy}{dx} = (x + y + 3)^2.$$

Solution As indicated earlier, let's try the substitution

$$v = x + y + 3; \qquad \text{that is,} \quad y = v - x - 3.$$

Then

$$\frac{dy}{dx} = \frac{dv}{dx} - 1,$$

so the transformed equation is

$$\frac{dv}{dx} = 1 + v^2.$$

This is a separable equation, and we have no difficulty in obtaining its solution

$$x = \int \frac{dv}{1 + v^2} = \tan^{-1} v + c.$$

So $v = \tan(x - C)$. Because $v = x + y + 3$, the general solution of the original equation $dy/dx = (x + y + 3)^2$ is $x + y + 3 = \tan(x - C)$; that is,

$$y(x) = \tan(x - C) - x - 3. \qquad ■$$

Example 1 illustrates the fact that any differential equation of the form

$$\frac{dy}{dx} = F(ax + by + c) \tag{6}$$

can be transformed into a separable equation by use of the substitution $v = ax + by + c$ (see Problem 31). The paragraphs that follow deal with other classes of first-order equations for which there are standard substitutions that are known to succeed.

Homogeneous Equations

A **homogeneous** first-order differential equation is one that can be written in the form

▶
$$\frac{dy}{dx} = F\left(\frac{y}{x}\right). \tag{7}$$

If we make the substitutions

$$v = \frac{y}{x}, \qquad y = vx, \qquad \frac{dy}{dx} = v + x\frac{dv}{dx}, \tag{8}$$

then Eq. (7) is transformed into the *separable* equation

$$x\frac{dv}{dx} = F(v) - v.$$

Thus every homogeneous first-order differential equation can be reduced to an integration problem by means of the substitutions in (8).

EXAMPLE 2 Solve the differential equation

$$2xy\frac{dy}{dx} = 4x^2 + 3y^2.$$

Solution This equation is neither separable nor linear, but we recognize it as a homogeneous equation by writing it in the form

$$\frac{dy}{dx} = \frac{4x^2 + 3y^2}{2xy} = 2\left(\frac{x}{y}\right) + \frac{3}{2}\left(\frac{y}{x}\right).$$

The substitutions in (8) then take the form

$$y = vx, \qquad \frac{dy}{dx} = v + x\frac{dv}{dx}, \qquad v = \frac{y}{x}, \qquad \text{and} \qquad \frac{1}{v} = \frac{x}{y}.$$

These yield

$$v + x\frac{dv}{dx} = \frac{2}{v} + \frac{3}{2}v,$$

and hence

$$x\frac{dv}{dx} = \frac{2}{v} + \frac{v}{2} = \frac{v^2 + 4}{2v};$$

$$\int \frac{2v}{v^2 + 4}\,dv = \int \frac{1}{x}\,dx;$$

$$\ln(v^2 + 4) = \ln|x| + \ln C.$$

We apply the exponential function to both sides of the last equation to obtain

$$v^2 + 4 = C|x|;$$

$$\frac{y^2}{x^2} + 4 = C|x|;$$

$$y^2 + 4x^2 = Cx^3,$$

because the sign of x can be absorbed by the arbitrary constant C.

EXAMPLE 3 Solve the initial value problem

$$x\frac{dy}{dx} = y + (x^2 - y^2)^{1/2}, \qquad y(1) = 0.$$

Solution We divide both sides by x and find that

$$\frac{dy}{dx} = \frac{y}{x} + \left[1 - \left(\frac{y}{x}\right)\right]^{1/2},$$

so we make the substitutions in (8); we get

$$v + x\frac{dv}{dx} = v + (1 - v^2)^{1/2};$$

$$\int \frac{1}{(1 - v^2)^{1/2}} \, dv = \int \frac{1}{x} \, dx;$$

$$\sin^{-1} v = \ln x + C.$$

There is no need to use $\ln|x|$ because $x > 0$ near $x = 1$ (part of the given initial condition). Next we note that $v(1) = y(1)/1 = 0$, so

$$C = \sin^{-1} 0 - \ln 1 = 0.$$

Hence

$$v = \frac{y}{x} = \sin(\ln x),$$

and therefore $y(x) = x \sin(\ln x)$ is the desired solution. ■

Bernoulli Equations

A first-order differential equation of the form

▶
$$\frac{dy}{dx} + P(x)y = Q(x)y^n \tag{9}$$

is called a **Bernoulli equation.** If either $n = 0$ or $n = 1$, then Eq. (9) is linear. Otherwise, as we ask you to show in Problem 32, the substitution

$$v = y^{1-n} \tag{10}$$

transforms Eq. (9) into the linear equation

$$\frac{dv}{dx} + (1 - n) P(x)v = (1 - n)Q(x).$$

Rather than memorizing the form of this transformed equation, it is more efficient to make the substitution in (10) explicitly, as in the following examples.

EXAMPLE 4 If we rewrite the homogeneous equation $2xyy' = 4x^2 + 3y^2$ of Example 2 in the form

$$\frac{dy}{dx} - \frac{3}{2x}y = \frac{2x}{y},$$

we see that it is also a Bernoulli equation with $P(x) = -3/(2x)$, $Q(x) = 2x$, $n = -1$, and $1 - n = 2$. Hence we substitute

$$v = y^2, \quad y = v^{1/2}, \quad \text{and} \quad \frac{dy}{dx} = \frac{dy}{dv}\frac{dv}{dx} = \frac{1}{2}v^{-1/2}\frac{dv}{dx}.$$

This gives

$$\frac{1}{2} v^{-1/2} \frac{dv}{dx} - \frac{3}{2x} v^{1/2} = 2xv^{-1/2}.$$

Then multiplication by $2v^{1/2}$ produces the linear equation

$$\frac{dv}{dx} - \frac{3}{x} v = 4x$$

with integrating factor $\rho = e^{\int (-3/x)\, dx} = x^{-3}$. So we obtain

$$D_x(x^{-3}v) = \frac{4}{x^2};$$

$$x^{-3}v = -\frac{4}{x} + C;$$

$$x^{-3}y^2 = -\frac{4}{x} + C;$$

$$y^2 = -4x^2 + Cx^3.$$

EXAMPLE 5 The equation

$$x\frac{dy}{dx} + 6y = 3xy^{4/3}$$

is neither separable nor linear nor homogeneous, but it is a Bernoulli equation with $n = \frac{4}{3}$, $1 - n = -\frac{1}{3}$. The substitutions

$$v = y^{-1/3}, \qquad y = v^{-3}, \qquad \text{and} \qquad \frac{dy}{dx} = \frac{dy}{dv}\frac{dv}{dx} = -3v^{-4}\frac{dv}{dx}$$

transform it into

$$-3xv^{-4}\frac{dv}{dx} + 6v^{-3} = 3xv^{-4}.$$

Division by $-3xv^{-4}$ yields the linear equation

$$\frac{dv}{dx} - \frac{2}{x} v = -1$$

with integrating factor $\rho = e^{\int (-2/x)\, dx} = x^{-2}$. This gives

$$D_x(x^{-2}v) = -\frac{1}{x^2}; \qquad x^{-2}v = \frac{1}{x} + C; \qquad v = x + Cx^2;$$

and finally,

$$y(x) = \frac{1}{(x + Cx^2)^3}.$$

EXAMPLE 6 The equation

$$2xe^{2y}\frac{dy}{dx} = 3x^4 + e^{2y} \tag{11}$$

is neither separable, nor linear, nor homogeneous, nor is it a Bernoulli equation. But we observe that y appears only in the combinations e^{2y} and $(e^{2y})' = 2e^{2y}y'$. This prompts the substitution

$$v = e^{2y}, \qquad \frac{dv}{dx} = 2e^{2y}\frac{dy}{dx}$$

that transforms Eq. (11) into the linear equation $xv' = 3x^4 + v$; that is,

$$\frac{dv}{dx} - \frac{1}{x}v = 3x^3.$$

After multiplying by the integrating factor $\rho = 1/x$, we find that

$$\frac{1}{x}v = \int 3x^2\,dx = x^3 + C, \qquad \text{so} \quad e^{2y} = v = x^4 + Cx,$$

and hence

$$y(x) = \frac{1}{2}\ln|x^4 + Cx|.$$

Flight Trajectories

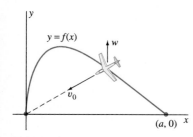

Suppose that an airplane starts at the point $(a, 0)$ located due east of its intended destination—an airport located at the origin $(0, 0)$. The plane travels with constant speed v_0 relative to the wind, which is blowing due north with constant speed w. As indicated in Fig. 1.6.1, we assume that the plane's pilot maintains its heading directly toward the origin.

Figure 1.6.2 helps us derive the plane's velocity components relative to the ground. They are

$$\frac{dx}{dt} = -v_0\cos\theta = -\frac{v_0 x}{\sqrt{x^2 + y^2}},$$

$$\frac{dy}{dt} = -v_0\sin\theta + w = -\frac{v_0 y}{\sqrt{x^2 + y^2}} + w.$$

FIGURE 1.6.1. The airplane headed for the origin

Hence the trajectory $y = f(x)$ of the plane satisfies the differential equation

$$\frac{dy}{dx} = \frac{dy/dt}{dx/dt} = \frac{1}{v_0 x}\left(v_0 y - w\sqrt{x^2 + y^2}\right). \tag{12}$$

If we set

$$k = \frac{w}{v_0}, \tag{13}$$

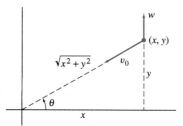

FIGURE 1.6.2. The components of the velocity vector of the airplane

the ratio of the windspeed to the plane's airspeed, then Eq. (12) takes the homogeneous form

$$\frac{dy}{dx} = \frac{y}{x} - k\left[1 + \left(\frac{y}{x}\right)^2\right]^{1/2}. \tag{14}$$

The substitution $y = vx$, $y' = v + xv'$ then leads routinely to

$$\int \frac{dv}{\sqrt{1 + v^2}} = -\int \frac{k}{x}\,dx. \tag{15}$$

By trigonometric substitution, or by consulting a table for the integral on the left, we find that

$$\ln\left(v + \sqrt{1 + v^2}\right) = -k \ln x + C, \tag{16}$$

and the initial condition $v(a) = y(a)/a = 0$ yields

$$C = k \ln a. \tag{17}$$

According to Problem 56, the result of substituting (17) in (16) and then solving for v is

$$v = \frac{1}{2}\left[\left(\frac{x}{a}\right)^{-k} - \left(\frac{x}{a}\right)^{k}\right]. \tag{18}$$

Because $y = vx$, we finally obtain

$$y = \frac{a}{2}\left[\left(\frac{x}{a}\right)^{1-k} - \left(\frac{x}{a}\right)^{1+k}\right] \tag{19}$$

for the equation of the plane's trajectory.

Note that only in the case $k < 1$ (that is, $w < v_0$) does the curve in (19) pass through the origin, so that the plane reaches its destination. If $w = v_0$ (so that $k = 1$), then Eq. (19) takes the form $y = \frac{1}{2}a(1 - x^2/a^2)$, so the plane's trajectory approaches the point $(0, a/2)$ rather than $(0, 0)$. The situation is even worse if $w > v_0$ (so $k > 1$)— in this case it follows from Eq. (19) that $y \to +\infty$ as $x \to 0$.

EXAMPLE 7 If $a = 200$ mi, $v_0 = 500$ mi/h, and $w = 100$ mi/h, then $k = w/v_0 = \frac{1}{5}$, so the plane will succeed in reaching the airport at $(0, 0)$. With these values, Eq. (19) yields

$$y(x) = 100\left[\left(\frac{x}{200}\right)^{4/5} - \left(\frac{x}{200}\right)^{6/5}\right]. \tag{20}$$

Now suppose that we want to find the maximum amount by which the plane is blown off course during its trip. That is, what is the maximum value of $y(x)$ for $0 \leq x \leq 200$?

Solution Differentiation of (20) yields

$$\frac{dy}{dx} = \frac{1}{2}\left[\frac{4}{5}\left(\frac{x}{200}\right)^{-1/5} - \frac{6}{5}\left(\frac{x}{200}\right)^{1/5}\right],$$

and we readily solve the equation $y'(x) = 0$ for $(x/200)^{2/5} = \frac{2}{3}$. Hence

$$y_{max} = 100\left[\left(\frac{2}{3}\right)^2 - \left(\frac{2}{3}\right)^3\right] = \frac{400}{27} \approx 14.81.$$

Thus the plane is blown almost 15 mi north at one point during its westward journey. (The graph of the function in Eq. (20) is the one used to construct Fig. 1.6.1. The vertical scale there is exaggerated by a factor of 4.) ∎

Exact Differential Equations

We have seen that a general solution $y(x)$ of a first-order differential equation is often defined implicitly by an equation of the form

$$F(x, y(x)) = C, \tag{21}$$

where C is a constant. On the other hand, given the identity in (21), we can recover the original differential equation by differentiating each side with respect to x. Provided that Eq. (21) implicitly defines y as a differentiable function of x, this gives the original differential equation in the form

$$\frac{\partial F}{\partial x} + \frac{\partial F}{\partial y} \frac{dy}{dx} = 0;$$

that is,

$$M(x, y) + N(x, y)\frac{dy}{dx} = 0, \tag{22}$$

where $M(x, y) = F_x(x, y)$ and $N(x, y) = F_y(x, y)$.

It is sometimes convenient to rewrite Eq. (22) in the form

▶ $$M(x, y)\,dx + N(x, y)\,dy = 0, \tag{23}$$

called its **differential** form. The general first-order differential equation $y' = f(x, y)$ can be written in this form with $M = f(x, y)$ and $N = -1$. The discussion above shows that, *if* there exists a function $F(x, y)$ such that

$$\frac{\partial F}{\partial x} = M \quad \text{and} \quad \frac{\partial F}{\partial y} = N,$$

then the equation

▶ $$F(x, y) = C$$

implicitly defines a general solution of Eq. (23). In this case, Eq. (23) is called an **exact** differential equation — the differential

$$dF = F_x\,dx + F_y\,dy$$

of $F(x, y)$ is exactly $M\,dx + N\,dy$.

A natural question is this: How can we determine whether the differential equation in (23) is exact? And if it is exact, how can we find the function F such that $F_x = M$ and $F_y = N$? To answer the first question, let us recall that if the mixed second-order partial derivatives F_{xy} and F_{yx} are continuous on an open set in the xy-plane, then they are equal: $F_{xy} = F_{yx}$. If Eq. (23) is exact and M and N have continuous partial derivatives, it then follows that

$$\frac{\partial M}{\partial y} = F_{xy} = F_{yx} = \frac{\partial N}{\partial x}.$$

Thus the equation

▶ $$\frac{\partial M}{\partial y} = \frac{\partial N}{\partial x} \tag{24}$$

is a *necessary condition* that the differential equation $M\,dx + N\,dy = 0$ be exact. That is, if $M_y \neq N_x$, then the differential equation in question is not exact, so we need not attempt to find a function $F(x, y)$ such that $F_x = M$ and $F_y = N$—there is no such function.

EXAMPLE 8 The differential equation

$$y^3\,dx + 3xy^2\,dy = 0 \tag{25}$$

is exact because we can immediately see that the function $F(x, y) = xy^3$ has the property that $F_x = y^3$ and $F_y = 3xy^2$. Thus a general solution of Eq. (25) is

$$xy^3 = C;$$

if you prefer, $y(x) = kx^{-1/3}$. ∎

But suppose that we divide each term of the differential equation in Example 1 by y^2 to obtain

$$y\,dx + 3x\,dy = 0. \tag{26}$$

This equation is not exact because, with $M = y$ and $N = 3x$, we have

$$\frac{\partial M}{\partial y} = 1 \neq 3 = \frac{\partial N}{\partial x}.$$

Hence the necessary condition in (24) is not satisfied.

We are confronted with a curious situation here: The differential equations in (25) and (26) are essentially equivalent, and they have exactly the same solutions, yet one is exact and the other is not. In brief, whether a given differential equation is exact or not is related to the precise form $M\,dx + N\,dy = 0$ in which it is written. Theorem 1 tells us that (subject to differentiability conditions usually satisfied in practice) the necessary condition in (24) is also a *sufficient* condition for exactness. That is, if $M_y = N_x$, then the differential equation $M\,dx + N\,dy = 0$ is exact.

THEOREM 1: Criterion for Exactness

Suppose that the functions $M(x, y)$ and $N(x, y)$ are continuous and have continuous first-order partial derivatives in the open rectangle R: $a < x < b$, $c < y < d$. Then the differential equation

$$M(x, y)\,dx + N(x, y)\,dy = 0 \tag{23}$$

is exact in R if and only if

$$\frac{\partial M}{\partial y} = \frac{\partial N}{\partial x} \tag{24}$$

at each point of R. That is, there exists a function $F(x, y)$ defined on R with $\partial F/\partial x = M$ and $\partial F/\partial y = N$ if and only if Eq. (24) holds on R.

Proof: We have seen already that it is necessary for Eq. (24) to hold if Eq. (23) is to be exact. To prove the converse, we must show that if Eq. (24) holds, then we can

construct a function $F(x, y)$ such that $\partial F/\partial x = M$ and $\partial F/\partial y = N$. Note first that, for *any* function $g(y)$, the function

$$F(x, y) = \int M(x, y)\,dx + g(y) \tag{27}$$

satisfies the condition $\partial F/\partial x = M$. (In Eq. (27), the notation $\int M(x, y)\,dx$ denotes an antiderivative of $M(x, y)$ with respect to x.) We plan to choose $g(y)$ so that

$$N = \frac{\partial F}{\partial y} = \left(\frac{\partial}{\partial y} \int M(x, y)\,dx \right) + g'(y)$$

as well; that is, so that

$$g'(y) = N - \frac{\partial}{\partial y} \int M(x, y)\,dx. \tag{28}$$

To see that there *is* such a function of y, it suffices to show that the right-hand side in (28) is a function of y alone. We can then find $g(y)$ by integrating with respect to y. Because the right-hand side in (28) is defined on a rectangle, and hence on an interval as a function of x, it suffices to show that its derivative with respect to x is identically zero. But

$$\frac{\partial}{\partial x}\left(N - \frac{\partial}{\partial y} \int M(x, y)\,dx \right) = \frac{\partial N}{\partial x} - \frac{\partial}{\partial x}\frac{\partial}{\partial y} \int M(x, y)\,dx$$

$$= \frac{\partial N}{\partial x} - \frac{\partial}{\partial y}\frac{\partial}{\partial x} \int M(x, y)\,dx$$

$$= \frac{\partial N}{\partial x} - \frac{\partial M}{\partial y} = 0$$

by hypothesis. So we can, indeed, find the desired function $g(y)$ by integrating Eq. (28). We substitute this result in Eq. (27) to obtain

$$F(x, y) = \int M(x, y)\,dx + \int \left[N(x, y) - \frac{\partial}{\partial y} \int M(x, y)\,dx \right] dy \tag{29}$$

as the desired function with $F_x = M$ and $F_y = N$. ∎

Instead of memorizing Eq. (29), it is usually better to solve an exact equation $M\,dx + N\,dy = 0$ by carrying out the process indicated by Eqs. (27) and (28). First we integrate $M(x, y)$ with respect to x and write

$$F(x, y) = \int M(x, y)\,dx + g(y),$$

thinking of the function $g(y)$ as an "arbitrary constant of integration" as far as the variable x is concerned. Then we determine $g(y)$ by imposing the condition that $\partial F/\partial y = N(x, y)$. This yields a general solution in the implicit form $F(x, y) = C$.

EXAMPLE 9 Solve the differential equation

$$(6xy - y^3)\,dx + (4y + 3x^2 - 3xy^2)\,dy = 0.$$

Solution This equation is exact because

$$\frac{\partial M}{\partial y} = 6x - 3y^2 = \frac{\partial N}{\partial x}.$$

Integrating $\partial F/\partial x = M$ with respect to x, we get

$$F(x, y) = \int (6xy - y^3)\, dx = 3x^2 y - xy^3 + g(y).$$

Then we differentiate with respect to y and set $\partial F/\partial y$ equal to N. This yields

$$\frac{\partial F}{\partial y} = 3x^2 - 3xy^2 + g'(y) = 4y + 3x^2 - 3xy^2,$$

and it follows that $g'(y) = 4y$. Hence $g(y) = 2y^2 + C_1$, and thus

$$F(x, y) = 3x^2 y - xy^3 + 2y^2 + C_1.$$

Therefore, a general solution of the given differential equation is defined implicitly by the equation

$$3x^2 y - xy^3 + 2y^2 = C$$

(we have absorbed the constant C_1 into the constant C). ■

1.6 Problems

Find general solutions of the differential equations in Problems 1 through 30. Primes denote derivatives with respect to x throughout.

1. $(x + y)y' = x - y$

2. $2xyy' + y^3 = e^{-x}$

3. $xy' = y + 2\sqrt{xy}$

4. $(x - y)y' = x + y$

5. $x(x + y)y' = y(x - y)$

6. $(x + 2y)y' = y$

7. $xy^2 y' = x^3 + y^3$

8. $x^2 y' = xy + x^2 e^{y/x}$

9. $x^2 y' = xy + y^2$

10. $xyy' = x^2 + 3y^2$

11. $(x^2 - y^2)y' = 2xy$

12. $xyy' = y^2 + x\sqrt{4x^2 + y^2}$

13. $xy' = y + \sqrt{x^2 + y^2}$

14. $yy' + x = \sqrt{x^2 + y^2}$

15. $x(x + y)y' + y(3x + y) = 0$

16. $y' = \sqrt{x + y + 1}$

17. $y' = (4x + y)^2$

18. $(x + y)y' = 1$

19. $x^2 y' + 2xy = 5y^3$

20. $y^2 y' + 2xy^3 = 6x$

21. $y' = y + y^3$

22. $x^2 y' + 2xy = 5y^4$

23. $xy' + 6y = 3xy^{4/3}$

24. $2xy' + y^3 e^{-2x} = 2xy$

25. $y^2(xy' + y)(1 + x^4)^{1/2} = x$

26. $3y^2 y' + y^3 = e^{-x}$

27. $3xy^2 y' = 3x^4 + y^3$

28. $xe^y y' = 2(e^y + x^3 e^{2x})$

29. $(2x \sin y \cos y)y' = 4x^2 + \sin^2 y$

30. $(x + e^y)y' = xe^{-y} - 1$

In Problems 31 through 42, verify that the given differential equation is exact; then solve it.

31. $(2x + 3y)\, dx + (3x + 2y)\, dy = 0$

32. $(4x - y)\, dx + (6y - x)\, dy = 0$

33. $(3x^2 + 2y^2)\, dx + (4xy + 6y^2)\, dy = 0$

34. $(2xy^2 + 3x^2)\, dx + (2x^2 y + 4y^3)\, dy = 0$

35. $\left(x^3 + \dfrac{y}{x}\right)dx + (y^2 + \ln x)\, dy = 0$

36. $(1 + ye^{xy})\, dx + (2y + xe^{xy})\, dy = 0$

37. $(\cos x + \ln y)\, dx + \left(\dfrac{x}{y} + e^y\right)dy = 0$

38. $(x + \tan^{-1} y)\, dx + \dfrac{x + y}{1 + y^2}\, dy = 0$

39. $(3x^2 y^3 + y^4)\, dx + (3x^3 y^2 + y^4 + 4xy^3)\, dy = 0$

40. $(e^x \sin y + \tan y)\, dx + (e^x \cos y + x \sec^2 y)\, dy = 0$

41. $\left(\dfrac{2x}{y} - \dfrac{3y^2}{x^4}\right)dx + \left(\dfrac{2y}{x^3} - \dfrac{x^2}{y^2} + \dfrac{1}{\sqrt{y}}\right)dy = 0$

42. $\dfrac{2x^{5/2} - 3y^{5/3}}{2x^{5/2}y^{2/3}}\,dx + \dfrac{3y^{5/3} - 2x^{5/2}}{3x^{3/2}y^{5/3}}\,dy = 0$

43. Show that the substitution $v = ax + by + c$ transforms the differential equation $y' = F(ax + by + c)$ into a separable equation.

44. Suppose that $n \neq 0$ and $n \neq 1$. Show that the substitution $v = y^{1-n}$ transforms the Bernoulli equation $y' + P(x)y = Q(x)y^{n}$ into the linear equation

$$\frac{dv}{dx} + (1 - n)P(x)v(x) = (1 - n)Q(x).$$

45. Show that the substitution $v = \ln y$ transforms the differential equation $y' + P(x)y = Q(x)y \ln y$ into the linear equation $v' + P = Qv$.

46. Use the method of Problem 45 to solve the equation $xy' - 4x^{2}y + 2y \ln y = 0$.

47. Solve the equation

$$\frac{dy}{dx} = \frac{x - y - 1}{x + y + 3}$$

by finding h and k so that the substitutions $x = u + h$, $y = v + k$ transform it into the homogeneous equation

$$\frac{dv}{du} = \frac{u - v}{u + v}.$$

48. Use the method of Problem 47 to solve the equation

$$\frac{dy}{dx} = \frac{2y - x + 7}{4x - 3y - 18}.$$

49. Make an appropriate substitution to find a solution of the equation $dy/dx = \sin(x - y)$. Does this general solution contain the solution $y \equiv x - \pi/2$ that we noted in Example 3 of Section 1.3?

50. Show that the solution curves of the differential equation

$$\frac{dy}{dx} = -\frac{y(2x^{3} - y^{3})}{x(2y^{3} - x^{3})}$$

are of the form $x^{3} + y^{3} = 3Cxy$.

51. The equation $dy/dx = A(x)y^{2} + B(x)y + C(x)$ is called a **Riccati equation.** Suppose that one particular solution $y_{1}(x)$ of this equation is known. Show that the substitution

$$y = y_{1} + \frac{1}{v}$$

transforms the Riccati equation into the *linear* equation

$$\frac{dv}{dx} + (B + 2Ay_{1})v = -A.$$

Use the method of Problem 51 to solve the equations in Problems 52 and 53, give that $y_{1}(x) = x$ is a solution of each.

52. $y' + y^{2} = 1 + x^{2}$

53. $y' + 2xy = 1 + x^{2} + y^{2}$

54. An equation of the form

$$y = xy' + g(y') \tag{30}$$

is called a **Clairaut equation.** Show that the one-parameter family of straight lines described by

$$y = Cx + g(C) \tag{31}$$

is a general solution of Eq. (30).

55. Consider the Clairaut equation

$$y = xy' - \frac{1}{4}(y')^{2}$$

with $g(y') = -\frac{1}{4}(y')^{2}$ in Eq. (30). Show that the line

$$y = Cx - \frac{1}{4}C^{2}$$

is tangent to the parabola $y = x^{2}$ at the point $(C/2,\, C^{2}/4)$. Explain why this implies that $y = x^{2}$ is a singular solution of the given Clairaut equation. This singular solution and the one-parameter family of straight line solutions are illustrated in Fig. 1.6.3.

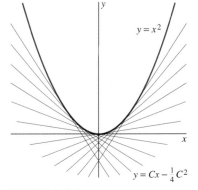

FIGURE 1.6.3. Solutions of the Clairaut equation of Problem 43. The "typical" straight line with equation $y = Cx - \dfrac{1}{4}C^{2}$ is tangent to the parabola at the point $\left(\dfrac{1}{2}C,\, \dfrac{1}{4}C^{2}\right)$.

56. Derive Eq. (18) in the text from Eqs. (16) and (17).

57. In the situation of Example 7, suppose that $a = 100$ mi, $v_{0} = 400$ mi/h, and $w = 40$ mi/h. Now how far northward does the wind blow the airplane?

58. As in the text discussion, suppose that an airplane maintains a heading toward an airport at the origin. If $v_0 = 500$ mi/h and $w = 50$ mi/h (with the wind blowing due north), and the plane begins at the point (200, 150), show that its trajectory is defined by

$$y + \sqrt{x^2 + y^2} = 2(200x^9)^{1/10}.$$

59. A river 100 ft wide is flowing north at w feet per second. A dog starts at (100, 0) and swims at $v_0 = 4$ ft/s, always heading toward a tree at (0, 0) on the west bank directly across from the dog's starting point. (a) If $w = 2$ ft/s, show that the dog reaches the tree. (b) If $w = 4$ ft/s, show that the dog reaches instead the point on the west bank 50 ft north of the tree. (c) If $w = 6$ ft/s, show that the dog never reaches the west bank.

1.6 Computing Project

The substitutions of this section are readily carried out using a computer algebra system such as *Mathematica* or *Maple*. To solve the differential equation

```
diffEq1 := y'[x] == (x + y[x] + 3)^2
```

of Example 1 using *Mathematica,* for instance, we first define the substitution

```
v[x_] := x + y[x] + 3
```

then calculate the derivative *dv/dx*

```
v'[x]
1 + y'[x]
```

and finally solve for *dy/dx* in terms of *dv/dx*.

```
Clear[v]
Solve[ v'[x] == 1 + y'[x], y'[x] ]
{{y'[x] -> -1 + v'[x]}}
```

We can now substitute to get the transformed equation.

```
diffEq2 = diffEq1 /. {x + y[x] + 3 -> v[x],
                      y'[x] -> -1 + v'[x] }

-1 + v'[x] == v[x]²
```

Having gotten this far, we might as well ask *Mathematica* to solve the new differential equation.

```
DSolve[ diffEq2, v[x], x ]

{{v[x] -> Tan[x + C[1]]}}

genSolution = v[x] == Tan[x + c1] /.
                      v[x] -> x + y[x] + 3

3 + x + y[x] == Tan[c1 + x]

Solve[ genSolution, y[x] ]

{{y[x] -> -3 - x + Tan[c1 + x]}}
```

The differential equation **diffEq1** is quite simple, but the commands shown here provide a "template" that can be used with more complicated equations.

In slightly abbreviated form, the corresponding template of *Maple* commands is

```
> diffeq1 := diff(y(x),x) = (x + y(x) + 3)^2;
> diffeq2 := subs(diff(y(x),x) = -1 + diff(v(x),x),
                   x + y(x) + 3 = v(x), diffeq1 );
> genSolution := dsolve( diffeq2, v(x) );
> genSolution := subs(v(x) = x + y(x) + 3, genSolution );
> y(x) = solve( genSolution, y(x) );
```

$$y(x) = \tan(x - _C1) - x - 3$$

If an appropriate computer algebra system is available, try your hand at the computer solution of some of Problems 1 through 30 in this section.

Chapter *1* Summary

In this chapter we have discussed applications of and solution methods for several important types of first-order differential equations, including those that are separable (Section 1.4), linear (Section 1.5), or exact (Section 1.6). In Section 1.6 we also discussed substitution techniques that can sometimes be used to transform a given first-order differential equation into one that is either separable, linear, or exact.

Lest it appear that these methods constitute a "grab bag" of special and unrelated techniques, it is important to note that they are all versions of a single idea. Given a differential equation

$$f(x, y, y') = 0, \tag{1}$$

we attempt to write it in the form

$$\frac{d}{dx}[G(x, y)] = 0. \tag{2}$$

It is precisely to attain the form in (2) that we multiply the terms in Eq. (1) by an appropriate integrating factor (even if all we are doing is separating the variables). But once we have found a function $G(x, y)$ such that (1) and (2) are equivalent, a general solution is defined implicitly by means of the equation

$$G(x, y) = C \tag{3}$$

that one obtains by integrating (2).

Given a specific first-order differential equation to be solved, we can attack it by means of the following steps:

- Is it *separable?* If so, separate the variables and integrate (Section 1.4).
- Is it *linear?* That is, can it be written in the form

$$\frac{dy}{dx} + P(x)y = Q(x)?$$

If so, multiply by the integrating factor $\rho = \exp\left(\int P\,dx\right)$ of Section 1.5.

- Is it *exact?* That is, when the equation is written in the form $M\,dx + N\,dy = 0$, is $\partial M/\partial y = \partial N/\partial x$ (Section 1.6)?

- If the equation as it stands is not separable, linear, or exact, is there a plausible substitution that will make it so? For instance, is it homogeneous (Section 1.6)?

Many first-order differential equations succumb to the line of attack outlined above. Nevertheless, many more do not. Because of the wide availability of computers, numerical techniques are commonly used to *approximate* the solutions of differential equations that cannot be solved readily or explicitly by the methods of this chapter. Indeed, most of the solution curves shown in figures in this chapter were plotted using numerical approximations rather than exact solutions. Several numerical methods for the approximate solution of differential equations will be discussed in Chapter 2.

Chapter *1* Review Problems

Find general solutions of the differential equations in Problems 1 through 30. Primes denote derivatives with respect to x.

1. $x^3 + 3y - xy' = 0$

2. $xy^2 + 3y^2 - x^2y' = 0$

3. $xy + y^2 - x^2y' = 0$

4. $2xy^3 + e^x + (3x^2y^2 + \sin y)y' = 0$

5. $3y + x^4y' = 2xy$ **6.** $2xy^2 + x^2y' = y^2$

7. $2x^2y + x^3y' = 1$ **8.** $2xy + x^2y' = y^2$

9. $xy' + 2y = 6x^2\sqrt{y}$

10. $y' = 1 + x^2 + y^2 + x^2y^2$

11. $x^2y' = xy + 3y^2$

12. $6xy^3 + 2y^4 + (9x^2y^2 + 8xy^3)y' = 0$

13. $4xy^2 + y' = 5x^4y^2$ **14.** $x^3y' = x^2y - y^3$

15. $y' + 3y = 3x^2e^{-3x}$ **16.** $y' = x^2 - 2xy + y^2$

17. $e^x + ye^{xy} + (e^y + xe^{xy})y' = 0$

18. $2x^2y - x^3y' = y^3$

19. $3x^5y^2 + x^3y' = 2y^2$

20. $xy' + 3y = 3x^{-3/2}$

21. $(x^2 - 1)y' + (x - 1)y = 1$

22. $xy' = 6y + 12x^4y^{2/3}$

23. $e^y + y\cos x + (xe^y + \sin x)y' = 0$

24. $9x^2y^2 + x^{3/2}y' = y^2$

25. $2y + (x + 1)y' = 3x + 3$

26. $9x^{1/2}y^{4/3} - 12x^{1/5}y^{3/2} + (8x^{3/2}y^{1/3} - 15x^{6/5}y^{1/2})y' = 0$

27. $3y + x^3y^4 + 3xy' = 0$

28. $y + xy' = 2e^{2x}$

29. $(2x + 1)y' + y = (2x + 1)^{3/2}$

30. $y' = \sqrt{x + y}$

Chapter *1* Computing Review Project

In the Section 1.6 project we mentioned the *Maple* and *Mathematica* commands for the symbolic solution of first-order differential equations. The computer algebra system *Derive* has some features that are especially useful for review purposes. The *Derive* utility file ODE1.MTH contains separate commands for the solution of separable, linear, exact, homogeneous, and Bernoulli equations (among others). Thus the user must first classify the particular differential equation at hand, then apply the ap-

propriate *Derive* command. The pertinent commands are shown in the following table, together with the form and type of equation to which each applies

Form of Equation	Type	*Derive* Command
$\dfrac{dy}{dx} = p(x)q(y)$	Separable	`SEPARABLE_GEN(p(x),q(y),x,y)`
$\dfrac{dy}{dx} + p(x)y = q(x)$	Linear	`LINEAR_GEN(p(x),q(x),x,y)`
$\dfrac{dy}{dx} + p(x)y = q(x)y^k$	Bernoulli	`BERNOULLI_GEN(p(x),q(x),k,x,y)`
$\dfrac{dy}{dx} = r(x, y) = F\left(\dfrac{y}{x}\right)$	Homogeneous	`HOMOGENEOUS_GEN(r(x,y),x,y)`
$p(x, y)\,dx + q(x, y)\,dy = 0$	Exact	`EXACT_GEN(p(x,y),q(x,y),x,y)`

The suffix GEN in each case indicates that a general solution (perhaps implicit) containing an arbitrary constant c is produced. If this suffix is omitted and initial values are inserted then a particular solution results. For instance, the command

> `SEPARABLE(p(x),q(y),x,y,x0,y0)`

generates the particular solution satisfying the initial condition $y(x_0) = y_0$.

EXAMPLE The differential equation $(y^2 + 1)\,dx + 2xy\,dy = 0$ is simultaneously exact, separable, and a Bernoulli equation. The *Derive* command

> `EXACT_GEN(y^2 + 1, 2 x y, x, y)`

yields after simplification the solution $x(y^2 + 1) = c$, which results also (in equivalent forms) from the commands

> `SEPARABLE_GEN(-1/(2x), (y^2 + 1)/y, x, y)`

and

> `BERNOULLI_GEN(1/(2x), -1/(2x), -1, x, y)`

Do you see where the entries in these last two commands came from? ∎

If *Derive* is available, solve each of the following differential equations in both of the indicated ways. Even if *Derive* software is not available, you can still analyze the equations and write the two pertinent *Derive* commands.

1. $\dfrac{dy}{dx} = 3(y + 7)x^2$ (separable and linear)

2. $\dfrac{dy}{dx} + xy = xy^3$ (separable and Bernoulli)

3. $(2y^2 + 3x^2)\,dx + 4xy\,dy = 0$ (exact and homogeneous)

4. $(x + 3y)\,dx + (3x - y)\,dy = 0$ (exact and homogeneous)

5. $\dfrac{dy}{dx} = \dfrac{2x(y+1)}{x^2+1}$ (separable and linear)

6. $(\tan x)\dfrac{dy}{dx} = \sqrt{y} - y$ (separable and Bernoulli)

It may be even more instructive for you to produce your own examples of such differential equations — ones that are simultaneously separable and linear, exact and Bernoulli, etc. See how many such combinations you can achieve.

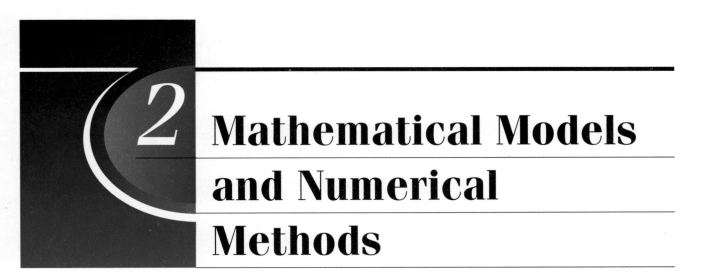

2 Mathematical Models and Numerical Methods

2.1 Population Models

In Section 1.4 we introduced the exponential differential equation $dP/dt = kP$, with solution $P(t) = P_0 e^{kt}$, as a mathematical model for natural population growth that occurs as a result of constant birth and death rates. Here we present a more general population model that accommodates birth and death rates that are not necessarily constant. As before, however, our population function $P(t)$ will be a *continuous* approximation to the actual population, which of course grows by integral increments.

Suppose that the population changes only by the occurrence of births and deaths—there is no immigration or emigration. Let $B(t)$ and $D(t)$ denote, respectively, the numbers of births and deaths that have occurred (since $t = 0$) by time t. Then the *birth rate* $\beta(t)$ and *death rate* $\delta(t)$, in births or deaths per individual per unit of time, are defined as follows:

$$\beta(t) = \lim_{h \to 0} \frac{B(t + h) - B(t)}{hP(t)} = \frac{1}{P}\frac{dB}{dt},$$

$$\delta(t) = \lim_{h \to 0} \frac{D(t + h) - D(t)}{hP(t)} = \frac{1}{P}\frac{dD}{dt}.$$

(1)

Thus the birth rate $\beta(t)$ is the number of births per unit time per unit of population, whereas the death rate $\delta(t)$ is the number of deaths per unit time per unit of population. Then

$$P'(t) = \lim_{h \to 0} \frac{P(t + h) - P(t)}{h}$$

$$= \lim_{h \to 0} \frac{[B(t + h) - B(t)] - [D(t + h) - D(t)]}{h} = B'(t) - D'(t).$$

Therefore

$$P'(t) = [\beta(t) - \delta(t)]P(t). \tag{2}$$

We will also use the briefer notation

▶
$$\frac{dP}{dt} = (\beta - \delta)P.$$

Equation (2) is the **general population equation.** If β and δ are constant, it reduces to the natural growth equation with $k = \beta - \delta$. But it also includes the possibility that β and δ are variable functions of t. The birth and death rates need not be known in advance; they may well depend upon the unknown function $P(t)$.

Limited Populations and the Logistic Equation

In situations as diverse as the human population of a nation and a fruit fly population in a closed container, it is often observed that the birth rate decreases as the population itself increases. The reasons may range from increased scientific or cultural sophistication to a limited food supply. Suppose, for example, that the birth rate β is a *linear* decreasing function of the population size P, so that $\beta = \beta_0 - \beta_1 P$, where β_0 and β_1 are positive constants. If the death rate $\delta = \delta_0$ remains constant, then Eq. (2) takes the form

$$\frac{dP}{dt} = (\beta_0 - \beta_1 P - \delta_0)P;$$

that is,

▶
$$\frac{dP}{dt} = kP(M - P) \tag{3}$$

where $k = \beta_1$ and $M = (\beta_0 - \delta_0)/\beta_1$. We assume that $\beta_0 > \delta_0$ so that $M > 0$.

Equation (3) is called the **logistic equation.** If we assume that $0 < P < M$, then it may be solved by separation of variables as follows.

$$\int \frac{dP}{P(M - P)} = \int k\,dt;$$

$$\frac{1}{M} \int \left(\frac{1}{P} + \frac{1}{M - P} \right) dP = \int k\,dt;$$

$$\ln \left(\frac{P}{M - P} \right) = kMt + C.$$

Exponentiation gives

$$\frac{P}{M - P} = Ae^{kMt},$$

where $A = e^C$. We substitute $t = 0$ into each side of this equation to find that $A = P_0/(M - P_0)$. So

$$\frac{P}{M - P} = \frac{P_0 e^{kMt}}{M - P_0}.$$

This equation is easy to solve for

▶ $$P(t) = \frac{MP_0}{P_0 + (M - P_0)e^{-kMt}}. \qquad (4)$$

While we made the assumption that $0 < P < M$ in order to derive Eq. (4), this restriction is unnecessary, because we can verify by direct substitution into Eq. (3) that $P(t)$ as given in (4) satisfies the logistic equation whether $0 < P < M$ or $P \geqq M$.

Limiting Populations

If the initial population satisfies $0 < P_0 < M$, then Eq. (4) shows that $P(t) < M$ for all $t \geqq 0$, and also that

$$\lim_{t \to \infty} P(t) = M. \qquad (5)$$

Thus a population that satisfies the logistic equation is *not* like a naturally growing population; it does not grow without bound, but instead approaches the finite **limiting population** M as $t \to +\infty$. Figure 2.1.1 (in which $M = k = 1$) shows typical solution curves corresponding to different initial populations, and illustrates the fact that, whatever the (positive) initial population P_0 may be, $P(t) \to M$ as $t \to +\infty$. Because

$$P'(t) = kP(M - P) > 0$$

if $0 < P < M$, we see in this case that the population is steadily increasing toward the limiting population M.

Moreover, differentiation of $P'(t) = kP(M - P)$ with respect to t gives

$$\frac{d^2 P}{dt^2} = \left[\frac{d}{dP}\left(\frac{dP}{dt}\right)\right]\left(\frac{dP}{dt}\right) = (kM - 2kP)[kP(M - P)]$$

$$= 2k^2 P\left(P - \frac{M}{2}\right)(P - M).$$

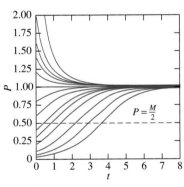

FIGURE 2.1.1. Typical solution curves of the logistic equation (with $M = k = 1$)

Thus

- $P'' > 0$ if $0 < P < \dfrac{M}{2}$;

- $P'' = 0$ if $P = \dfrac{M}{2}$;

- $P'' < 0$ if $\dfrac{M}{2} < P < M$.

Hence any solution curve that crosses the line $P = M/2$ has an inflection point where it crosses that line, and therefore looks like one of the lower S-shaped curves in Fig. 2.1.1. In this case the population increases at an increasing rate until $P = M/2$ and thereafter increases at a decreasing rate.

If $P_0 > M$, so that the initial population exceeds the limiting population, then a similar analysis (Problem 8) shows that $P(t)$ is a steadily decreasing function with a graph resembling one of the upper curves in Fig. 2.1.1.

Can you see—both from Eq. (3) and in Fig. 2.1.1—that if $P_0 = M$, then $P(t) = M$ for all $t \geq 0$? In this case the population remains constant.

Historical Note

In 1845 the Belgian demographer Verhulst used the 1790–1840 U.S. population data to predict the U.S. population through the year 1930, under his assumption that it would continue to satisfy the logistic equation. With $P_0 = 3.9$ and $M = 197.5$ (in millions) and $k = 0.000159$, Eq. (4) is

$$\frac{dP}{dt} = (0.0314)P - (0.000159)P^2,$$

and its solution

$$P(t) = \frac{770.25}{3.9 + (193.6)e^{(-0.0314)t}}$$

[from Eq. (4)] gives the remarkable results shown in the table in Fig. 2.1.2. Of course, the assumed limiting population of $M = 197.5$ millions has now been exceeded, so the population of the United States has not continued to satisfy the same logistic equation in the decades following 1930.

Year	Actual U.S. Population (millions)	Logistic Predicted Population	Percent Error
1790	3.9	3.9	0.0
1800	5.3	5.3	0.0
1810	7.2	7.2	0.0
1820	9.6	9.7	−1.0
1830	12.9	13.0	−0.8
1840	17.1	17.4	−1.8
1850	23.2	23.1	0.4
1860	31.4	30.3	3.5
1870	38.6	39.3	−1.8
1880	50.2	50.1	0.2
1890	63.0	62.7	0.5
1900	76.2	76.9	−0.9
1910	92.2	92.0	0.2
1920	106.0	107.5	−1.4
1930	123.2	122.5	0.6

FIGURE 2.1.2. Actual and predicted U.S. population data

EXAMPLE 1 Suppose that in 1885 the population of a certain country was 50 million and was growing at the rate of 750,000 people per year at that time. Suppose also that in 1940 its population was 100 million and was then growing at the rate of 1 million per year. Assume that this population satisfies the logistic equation. Determine both the limiting population M and the predicted population for the year 2000.

> **Solution** We substitute the two given pairs of data in Eq. (3) and find that
>
> $$0.75 = 50k(M - 50), \qquad 1.00 = 100k(M - 100).$$
>
> We solve simultaneously for $M = 200$ and $k = 0.0001$. Thus the limiting population of the country in question is 200 million. With these values of M and k and with $t = 0$ corresponding to the year 1940 (in which $P_0 = 100$), we find that, as a consequence of Eq. (4), the population in the year 2000 will be
>
> $$P(60) = \frac{100 \cdot 200}{100 + (200 - 100)e^{-(0.0001)(200)(60)}},$$

about 153.7 million people. ∎

More Applications of the Logistic Equation

We next describe some situations that illustrate the varied circumstances in which the logistic equation is a satisfactory mathematical model.

1. *Limited environment situation.* A certain environment can support a population of at most M individuals. It's then reasonable to expect the growth rate $\beta - \delta$ (the combined birth and death rates) to be proportional to $M - P$, because we may think of $M - P$ as the potential for further expansion. Then $\beta - \delta = k(M - P)$, so that

$$\frac{dP}{dt} = (\beta - \delta)P = kP(M - P).$$

 The classic example of a limited environment situation is a fruit fly population in a closed container.

2. *Competition situation.* If the birth rate β is constant but the death rate δ is proportional to P, so that $\delta = \alpha P$, then

$$\frac{dP}{dt} = (\beta - \alpha P)P = kP(M - P).$$

 This might be a reasonable working hypothesis in a study of a cannibalistic population, in which all deaths result from chance encounters between individuals. Of course, competition between individuals is not usually so deadly, nor its effects so immediate and decisive.

3. *Joint proportion situation.* Let $P(t)$ denote the number of individuals in a constant-size susceptible population M who are infected with a certain contagious and incurable disease. The disease is spread by chance encounters. Then $P'(t)$ should be proportional to the product P of the number of individuals having the disease and the number $M - P$ of those not having it, and therefore $dP/dt = kP(M - P)$. Again we discover that the mathematical model is the logistic

equation. The mathematical description of the spread of a rumor in a population of M individuals is identical.

EXAMPLE 2 Suppose that at time $t = 0$, 10 thousand people in a city with population $M = 100$ thousand people have heard a certain rumor. After 1 week the number $P(t)$ of those who have heard it has increased to $P(1) = 20$ thousand. Assuming that $P(t)$ satisfies a logistic equation, when will 80% of the city's population have heard the rumor?

Solution Substituting $P_0 = 10$ and $M = 100$ (thousand) in Eq. (4), we get

$$P(t) = \frac{1000}{10 + 90e^{-100kt}}. \tag{6}$$

Then substitution of $t = 1, P = 20$ gives the equation

$$20 = \frac{1000}{10 + 90e^{-100k}}$$

that is readily solved for

$$e^{-100k} = \frac{4}{9}, \quad \text{so} \quad k = \frac{1}{100} \ln \frac{9}{4} \approx 0.008109.$$

With $P(t) = 80$, Eq. (6) takes the form

$$80 = \frac{1000}{10 + 90e^{-100kt}},$$

which we solve for $e^{-100kt} = \frac{1}{36}$. It follows that 80% of the population has heard the rumor when

$$t = \frac{\ln 36}{100k} = \frac{\ln 36}{\ln \frac{9}{4}} \approx 4.42,$$

thus after about 4 weeks and 3 days. ∎

Doomsday Versus Extinction

Consider a population $P(t)$ of unsophisticated animals that rely solely on chance encounters to meet mates for reproductive purposes. It is reasonable to expect such encounters to occur at a rate that is proportional to the product of the number $P/2$ of males and the number $P/2$ of females, hence at a rate proportional to P^2. Hence we assume that births occur at the rate $dB/dt = kP^2$ (k is a constant), so that $\beta = kP$ by Eq. (1). If the death rate δ is constant, then the general population equation in (2) yields the differential equation

$$\frac{dP}{dt} = kP^2 - \delta P = kP(P - a), \tag{7}$$

where $a = \delta/k > 0$, as a mathematical model of the population. The solution of Eq. (7) depends upon whether the initial population $P_0 = P(0)$ is greater than or less than a.

Case 1. $P_0 > a$. From Eq. (7) we see that $P'(0) = kP_0(P_0 - a) > 0$, so $P(t)$ starts out increasing. Hence $P'(t)$ remains positive, so $P(t)$ continues to increase, and therefore $P(t) > a$ for all $t \geq 0$. We note that

$$\frac{1}{P(P - a)} = -\frac{1}{a}\left(\frac{1}{P} - \frac{1}{P - a}\right).$$

We separate variables in Eq. (7) and integrate as follows:

$$\int \frac{dP}{P(P - a)} = \int k\, dt;$$

$$\int \left(\frac{1}{P} - \frac{1}{P - a}\right) dP = -\int ka\, dt;$$

$$\ln \frac{P}{P - a} = -kat + C_1.$$

Substitution of P_0 for P and 0 for t then gives

$$C_1 = \ln \frac{P_0}{P_0 - a} = \ln C$$

where $C = P_0/(P_0 - a) > 1$. Exponentiation then yields $P/(P - a) = Ce^{-kat}$, which we solve for

$$P(t) = \frac{Cae^{-kat}}{Ce^{-kat} - 1}. \tag{8}$$

Note that the denominator in (8) approaches zero as

$$t \rightarrow T = \frac{\ln C}{ka} = \frac{1}{ka}\ln\frac{P_0}{P_0 - a} > 0.$$

Thus $\lim_{t \to T} P(t) = +\infty$. This is a *doomsday* situation.

Case 2. $0 < P_0 < a$. In this case $P'(0) < 0$, and it follows that $P(t) < a$ for all $t \geq 0$. A similar separation of variables (Problem 14) now leads to

$$P(t) = \frac{Cae^{-kat}}{Ce^{-kat} + 1}, \tag{9}$$

where $C = P_0/(a - P_0) > 0$. The difference between this case and the doomsday situation of Case 1 is that the denominator in Eq. (9) remains greater than 1. It follows that $\lim_{t \to \infty} P(t) = 0$. This is an *extinction* situation.

Thus the population either explodes or is an endangered species threatened with extinction, depending on its initial size. An approximation to this phenomenon is sometimes observed with certain animal populations, such as the alligator population in certain areas of the southern United States.

The slope field and solution curves for Eq. (7) with $a = k = 1$ shown in Fig. 2.1.3 summarize cases 1 and 2 for such a population. If $P_0 = a$, then the population remains

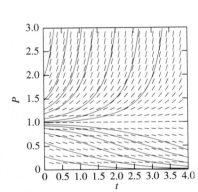

FIGURE 2.1.3. Slope field and solution curves for Equation (7) (with $a = k = 1$)

constant. But if P_0 exceeds a even slightly, then $P(t)$ rapidly increases without bound, whereas if the initial (positive) population is less than a then it decreases (more gradually) toward zero.

2.1 Problems

1. Suppose that the fish population $P(t)$ in a lake is attacked by a disease at time $t = 0$, with the result that the fish cease to reproduce (so that the birth rate is $\beta = 0$) and the death rate δ (deaths per week per fish) is thereafter proportional to $\sqrt{1/P}$. If there were initially 900 fish in the lake and 441 were left after 6 weeks, how long did it take all the fish in the lake to die?

2. Suppose that when a certain lake is stocked with fish, the birth and death rates β and δ are both inversely proportional to \sqrt{P}. (a) Show that $P(t) = \left(\frac{1}{2} kt + \sqrt{P_0}\right)^2$, where k is a constant. (b) If $P_0 = 100$ and after 6 months there are 169 fish in the lake, how many will there be after 1 year?

3. Consider a prolific breed of rabbits whose birth and death rates, β and δ, are each proportional to the rabbit population $P = P(t)$, with $\beta > \delta$. (a) Show that

$$P(t) = \frac{P_0}{1 - kP_0 t}, \qquad k \text{ constant.}$$

Note that $P(t) \to +\infty$ as $t \to 1/(kP_0)$. This is doomsday. (b) Suppose that $P_0 = 2$ and that there are four rabbits after 3 months. When does doomsday occur?

4. Repeat part (a) of Problem 3 in the case $\beta < \delta$. What now happens to the rabbit population in the long run?

5. Consider a human population $P(t)$ with constant birth and death rates β and δ, but also with I persons per year entering the country through immigration. Estimate the change ΔP during the short time interval Δt to derive the differential equation

$$\frac{dP}{dt} = kP + I \qquad (k = \beta - \delta).$$

Use the result of Problem 5 in Problems 6 and 7.

6. A certain city had a population of 1.5 million in 1980. Assume that it grows continuously at a 4% annual rate (this implies that $\beta - \delta = 0.04$) and also absorbs 50,000 newcomers per year. What will be its population in the year 2000?

7. Consider the U.S. population with $P_0 = 222$ million in 1980. (a) Compute the population in the year 2000, assuming a natural growth rate of 1% annually. (b) Rework part (a) with the additional assumption that immigration will remain at a constant 500,000 people per year.

8. Derive the solution in Eq. (4) of the logistic equation in (3) under the assumption that $P > M$, and show in this case that the graph of $P(t)$ resembles the upper curves in Fig. 2.1.1.

9. Figure 2.1.4 shows a slope field for the logistic equation

$$\frac{dP}{dt} = P - P^2$$

for which $k = M = 1$. Sketch some solution curves for negative as well as positive initial values. Although an actual population function $P(t)$ would be positive-valued, one nevertheless can discuss solutions of $dP/dt = P - P^2$ in the case $P'(0) = P_0 < 0$. Does Fig. 2.1.4 indicate that such a solution is negative-valued for all $t > 0$? Describe the behavior of $P(t)$ as t increases. Verify your answer by deriving and analyzing the solution

$$P(t) = \frac{P_0 e^t}{1 - P_0(1 - e^t)}$$

in the case $P_0 < 0$.

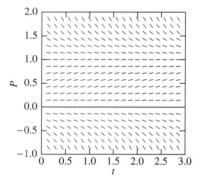

FIGURE 2.1.4. Slope field for $P' = P - P^2$

10. Suppose that at time $t = 0$, half of a "logistic" population of 100,000 persons have heard a certain rumor, and that the number of those who have heard it is then increasing at the rate of 1000 persons per day. How long will it take for this rumor to spread to 80% of the population? *Suggestion:* Find the value of k by substituting $P(0)$ and $P'(0)$ in the logistic equation, Eq. (3).

11. Suppose that as a certain salt dissolves in a solvent, the number $x(t)$ of grams of the salt in solution after t seconds satisfies the logistic equation $dx/dt = (0.8)x - (0.004)x^2$. (a) What is the maximum amount of the salt that will dissolve in this solvent? (b) If $x = 50$ when $t = 0$, how long will it take for an additional 50 g of the salt to dissolve?

12. Suppose that a community contains 15,000 people who are susceptible to a spreading contagious disease. At time $t = 0$ the number $N(t)$ of people who have the disease is 5000 and is increasing by 500 per day. How long will it take for another 5000 people to contract the disease? Assume that $N'(t)$ is proportional to the product of the numbers of those who have the disease and those who do not.

13. The data in the table in Fig. 2.1.5 are given for a certain population $P(t)$ that satisfies the logistic equation in (3). (a) What is the limiting population M? (*Suggestion:* Use the approximation

$$P'(t) \approx \frac{P(t + h) - P(t - h)}{2h}$$

with $h = 1$ to estimate the values of $P'(t)$ when $P = 25.00$ and when $P = 47.54$. Then substitute these values in the logistic equation and solve for k and M.) (b) Use the values of k and M found in part (a) to determine when $P = 75$. (*Suggestion:* Take $t = 0$ to correspond to the year 1925.)

Year	P (millions)
1924	24.63
1925	25.00
1926	25.38
⋮	⋮
1974	47.04
1975	47.54
1976	48.04

FIGURE 2.1.5. Population data for Problem 13

14. A population $P(t)$ of small rodents has birth rate $\beta = (0.001)P$ (births per month per rodent) and *constant* death rate δ.

If $P(0) = 100$ and $P'(0) = 8$, how long (in months) will it take this population to double to 200 rodents? (*Suggestion:* First find the value of δ.)

15. Consider an animal population $P(t)$ with constant death rate $\delta = 0.01$ and with birth rate β proportional to P. Suppose that $P(0) = 200$ and $P'(0) = 2$. (a) When is $P = 1000$? (b) When does doomsday occur?

16. Derive the solution in Eq. (9) of Eq. (7) in the case $0 < P(0) < a$.

17. A tumor may be regarded as a population of multiplying cells. It is found empirically that the "birth rate" of the cells in a tumor decreases exponentially with time, so that $\beta(t) = \beta_0 e^{-\alpha t}$ (where α and β_0 are positive constants), and hence

$$\frac{dP}{dt} = \beta_0 e^{-\alpha t} P, \qquad P(0) = P_0.$$

Solve this initial value problem for

$$P(t) = P_0 \exp\left(\frac{\beta_0}{\alpha}\left(1 - e^{-\alpha t}\right)\right).$$

Observe that $P(t)$ approaches the finite limiting population $P_0 \exp(\beta_0/\alpha)$ as $t \to +\infty$.

18. For the tumor of Problem 17, suppose that at time $t = 0$ there are $P_0 = 10^6$ cells and that $P(t)$ is then increasing at the rate of 3×10^5 cells per month. After 6 months the tumor has doubled (in size and in number of cells). Solve numerically for α, and then find the limiting population of the tumor.

19. Consider two population functions $P_1(t)$ and $P_2(t)$, both of which satisfy the logistic equation with the same limiting population M, but with different values k_1 and k_2 of the constant k in Eq. (3). Assume that $k_1 < k_2$. Which population approaches M the most rapidly? You can reason *geometrically* by examining slope fields (especially if appropriate software is available), *symbolically* by analyzing the solution given in Eq. (4), or *numerically* by substituting successive values of t.

2.1 Computing Project

This project deals with the problem of fitting a logistic model to given population data. Thus we want to determine the numerical constants a and b so that the solution $P(t)$ of the initial value problem

$$\frac{dP}{dt} = aP + bP^2, \qquad P(0) = P_0 \tag{1}$$

approximates the given values P_0, P_1, \ldots, P_n of the population at the times $t_0 = 0, t_1, \ldots, t_n$. If we rewrite Eq. (1) (the logistic equation with $kM = a$ and $k = -b$) in the form

$$\frac{1}{P}\frac{dP}{dt} = a + bP, \tag{2}$$

then we see that the points

$$\left(P(t_i), \frac{P'(t_i)}{P(t_i)}\right), \qquad i = 0, 1, 2, \ldots , n,$$

should all lie on the straight line with y-intercept a and slope b (as defined by the function of P on the right-hand side in Eq. (2)).

This observation provides a way to find a and b. If we can determine the approximate values of the derivatives P'_1, P'_2, . . . corresponding to the given population data, then we can proceed with the following agenda.

- First plot the points $(P_1, P'_1/P_1)$, $(P_2, P'_2/P_2)$, . . . on a sheet of graph paper with horizontal P-axis.

- Then use a ruler to draw a straight line that appears to approximate these points well.

- Finally measure this straight line's y-intercept a and slope b.

But where are we to find the needed values of the derivative $P'(t)$ of the (as yet) unknown function P? It is easiest to use the approximation

$$P'_i = \frac{P_{i+1} - P_{i-1}}{t_{i+1} - t_{i-1}} \tag{3}$$

suggested by Fig. 2.1.6. For instance, using the U.S. population data given in Fig. 2.1.2, we obtain these results:

$$\text{For 1800:} \quad P'_1 = \frac{7.2 - 3.9}{20} = 0.165$$

$$\text{For 1810:} \quad P'_2 = \frac{9.6 - 5.3}{20} = 0.215$$

$$\vdots$$

$$\text{For 1920:} \quad P'_{13} = \frac{123.2 - 92.2}{20} = 1.550$$

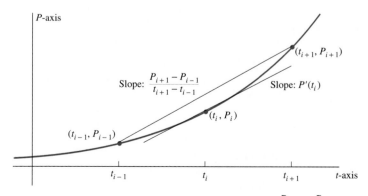

FIGURE 2.1.6. The symmetric difference approximation $\dfrac{P_{i+1} - P_{i-1}}{t_{i+1} - t_{i-1}}$ to the derivative $P'(t_i)$

FIGURE 2.1.7.

Year	Actual U.S. Population (millions)
1900	76.2
1910	92.2
1920	106.0
1930	123.2
1940	132.2
1950	151.3
1960	179.3
1970	203.3
1980	225.6
1990	248.7

FIGURE 2.1.8. Twentieth-century U.S. population data

Investigation 1

Finish the computation indicated above, then plot the points

$$(P_1, P_1'/P_1), \quad (P_2, P_2'/P_2), \quad \ldots, \quad (P_{13}, P_{13}'/P_{13})$$

as indicated by the small dots in Fig. 2.1.7. Draw your own straight line approximating these points, then measure its y-intercept and slope as accurately as you can. Solve Eq. (1) with the resulting numerical parameters a and b. How do your predicted populations for the years 1800 through 2000 compare with the population data given in Figs. 2.1.2 and 2.1.8?

Investigation 2

Repeat Investigation 1, but take $t = 0$ in 1900 and use only 20th century population data. Do you get a better approximation for the U.S. population during the final decades of the 20th century?

Year	World Population (billions)
1960	3.049
1965	3.358
1970	3.721
1975	4.103
1980	4.473
1985	4.882
1990	5.249
1995	5.679
2000	6.127

FIGURE 2.1.9. World population data

Investigation 3

Model similarly the world population data shown in Fig. 2.1.9. The Population Division of the United Nations predicts a world population of 8.177 billion in the year 2025. What do you predict?

2.2 Equilibrium Solutions and Stability

In previous sections we have often used explicit solutions of differential equations to answer specific numerical questions. But even when a given differential equation is difficult or impossible to solve explicitly, it still may be possible to extract *qualitative* information about general properties of its solutions. For example, we may be able to establish that every solution $x(t)$ grows without bound as $t \to +\infty$, or approaches a finite limit, or is a periodic function of t. In this section we introduce—mainly by consideration of simple differential equations that *can* be solved explicitly—some of the more important qualitative questions that can sometimes be answered for less tractable equations.

EXAMPLE 1 Let $x(t)$ denote the temperature of a body with initial temperature $x(0) = x_0$. At time $t = 0$ this body is immersed in a medium with constant temperature A. Assuming Newton's law of cooling,

$$\frac{dx}{dt} = -k(x - A) \qquad (k > 0 \quad \text{constant}), \tag{1}$$

we readily solve (by separation of variables) for the explicit solution

$$x(t) = A + (x_0 - A)e^{-kt}.$$

It follows immediately that

$$\lim_{t \to \infty} x(t) = A, \tag{2}$$

so the temperature of the body approaches that of the surrounding medium (as is evident to one's intuition). Note that the constant function $x(t) \equiv A$ is a solution of Eq. (1); it corresponds to the temperature of the body when it is in thermal equilibrium with the surrounding medium. In Fig. 2.2.1 (in which $A = 100$ and $k = 1$) the limit in (2) means that every other solution curve approaches the equilibrium solution curve $x = A$ asymptotically as $t \to +\infty$. ∎

In Section 2.1 we introduced the general population equation

$$\frac{dx}{dt} = (\beta - \delta)x, \tag{3}$$

FIGURE 2.2.1. Slope field and solution curves for $x' = -(x - 100)$

where β and δ are the birth and death rates, respectively, in births or deaths per individual per unit of time. The question of whether a population $x(t)$ is bounded or unbounded as $t \to +\infty$ is of evident interest.

If β and δ are constants, we have the case of natural population growth, and the solution of Eq. (3) is

$$x(t) = x_0 e^{kt},$$

where $k = \beta - \delta$ and $x_0 = x(0)$. If $k > 0$, it is clear that $x(t) \to +\infty$ as $t \to +\infty$ if $x_0 > 0$, whereas $x(t) \to -\infty$ if $x_0 < 0$. (Although an actual population would not be negative, we can discuss the initial value problem $x' = kx$, $x(0) = x_0 < 0$.) On the other hand, if $k < 0$, then $x(t) \to 0$ as $t \to +\infty$ for every value of x_0. In either case we see that given k, the qualitative behavior as $t \to +\infty$ of a solution $x(t)$ of $x' = kx$ is determined by the initial condition $x(0) = x_0$.

In more interesting situations β and δ are (known) functions of x. Then Eq. (3) takes the form

$$\frac{dx}{dt} = f(x). \tag{4}$$

This is an **autonomous** first-order differential equation—one in which the independent variable t does not appear explicitly. As in Example 1, the solutions of the equation $f(x) = 0$ play an important role, and are called **critical points** of the autonomous differential equation $dx/dt = f(x)$.

If $x = c$ is a critical point of Eq. (4), then the differential equation has the constant solution $x(t) \equiv c$. A constant solution of a differential equation is sometimes called an **equilibrium solution** (one may think of a population that remains constant because it is in "equilibrium" with its environment). Thus the critical point $x = c$, a number, corresponds to the equilibrium solution $x(t) \equiv c$, a constant-valued function.

Example 2 illustrates the fact that the qualitative behavior (as t increases) of the solutions of an autonomous first-order equation can be described in terms of its critical points.

EXAMPLE 2 Consider the differential equation

$$\frac{dx}{dt} = 4x - x^2, \tag{5}$$

a logistic equation (as in Section 2.1) with $k = 1$ and $M = 4$. It has two critical points—the roots $x = 0$ and $x = 4$ of the equation

$$f(x) = 4x - x^2 = x(4 - x) = 0.$$

By separating the variables in Eq. (5) we readily find the solution

$$x(t) = \frac{4x_0}{x_0 + (4 - x_0)e^{-4t}} \tag{6}$$

that satisfies the initial condition $x(0) = x_0$. Note that Eq. (6) includes the equilibrium solutions $x(t) \equiv 0$ (if $x_0 = 0$) and $x(t) \equiv 4$ (if $x_0 = 4$).

If $x_0 > 0$, then the denominator on the right-hand side in Eq. (6) is positive for all $t > 0$ and approaches x_0 as $t \to +\infty$, so

$$\lim_{t \to \times} x(t) = 4 \qquad \text{if } x_0 > 0. \tag{7a}$$

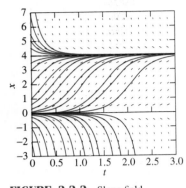

FIGURE 2.2.2. Slope field and solution curves for $x' = 4x - x^2$

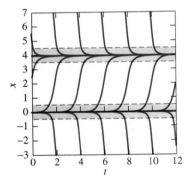

FIGURE 2.2.3. Solution curves, funnel and spout for $x' = 4x - x^2$

FIGURE 2.2.4. The phase portrait shows a stable critical point and an unstable critical point.

That is, if $x_0 > 0$, then $x(t)$ approaches the critical point $x = 4$ as $t \to +\infty$. On the other hand, if $x_0 < 0$, then the denominator in Eq. (6) is initially positive but approaches zero as

$$t \to t_0 = \frac{1}{4} \ln \frac{x_0 - 4}{x_0} > 0,$$

so

$$\lim_{t \to t_0^-} x(t) = -\times \qquad \text{if } x_0 < 0. \tag{7b}$$

From Eqs. (7a) and (7b) we see that solution curves of Eq. (5) with different initial values appear as shown in Fig. 2.2.2. ∎

This figure illustrates the concept of stability. A critical point $x = c$ of an autonomous first-order equation is called *stable* provided that if the initial value x_0 is sufficiently close to c, then $x(t)$ remains close to c for all $t > 0$. More precisely, the critical point c is **stable** if, for each $\varepsilon > 0$, there exists $\delta > 0$ such that

$$|x_0 - c| < \delta \qquad \text{implies that} \qquad |x(t) - c| < \varepsilon \tag{8}$$

for all $t > 0$. The critical point $x = c$ is **unstable** if it is not stable.

Figure 2.2.3 shows a "wider view" of the solution curves of $dx/dt = 4x - x^2$. Note that the strip $3.5 < x < 4.5$ enclosing the stable equilibrium curve $x = 4$ acts like a *funnel*—solution curves (moving from left to right) enter this strip and thereafter remain within it. By contrast the strip $-0.5 < x < 0.5$ enclosing the unstable solution curve $x = 0$ acts like a *spout*—solution curves leave this strip and thereafter remain outside it.

In Problem 14 we ask you to carry out the analysis of Example 2 for the original logistic population equation

$$\frac{dx}{dt} = ax - bx^2 = kx(M - x) \tag{9}$$

with $a, b > 0$. The critical point $x = M = a/b$ is stable (M is the *limiting population*), whereas the critical point $x = 0$ is unstable. The solution curves of Eq. (9) look just like those shown in Fig. 2.2.2 (with the equilibrium solution $x(t) \equiv 4$ replaced with $x(t) = M = a/b$). We can summarize the behavior of solutions of Eq. (9)—in terms of their initial values—by means of the *phase portrait* shown in Fig. 2.2.4. It indicates that $x(t) \to M$ as $t \to +\infty$ if either $x_0 > M$ or $0 < x_0 < M$, whereas $x(t) \to -\infty$ as t increases if $x_0 < 0$. The fact that M is a stable critical point would be important, for instance, if we wished to conduct an experiment with a population of M bacteria. It is impossible to count precisely M bacteria for M large, but any initially positive population will approach M as t increases.

Here is another aspect of stability. The coefficients a and b in Eq. (9) are unlikely to be known precisely for an actual population. But if they are replaced with close approximations a^* and b^*, then the approximate limiting population $M^* = a^*/b^*$ will be close to the actual limiting population $M = a/b$. Thus the limiting population that Eq. (9) predicts is stable with respect to small perturbations of its constant coefficients.

Harvesting a Logistic Population

The autonomous differential equation

$$\frac{dx}{dt} = ax - bx^2 - k \tag{10}$$

(with a, b, and k all positive) may be considered to describe a logistic population *with harvesting*. For instance, we might think of the population of fish in a lake from which k fish per year are removed by fishing.

EXAMPLE 3 If $a = 4$ and $b = 1$, as in Example 2, and $k = 3$, then Eq. (10) is

$$\frac{dx}{dt} = 4x - x^2 - 3 \tag{11}$$

with

$$f(x) = 4x - x^2 - 3 = -(x - 1)(x - 3),$$

so it has the two critical points $x = 1$ and $x = 3$.

Separation of variables in (11) yields the solution

$$x(t) = \frac{3(x_0 - 1) - (x_0 - 3)e^{-2t}}{(x_0 - 1) - (x_0 - 3)e^{-2t}} \tag{12}$$

in terms of the initial value $x(0) = x_0$. In order to analyze the stability of the two critical points $x = 1$ and $x = 3$, we analyze the behavior of $x(t)$ for different initial values—in the open intervals $x_0 > 3$, $1 < x_0 < 3$, and $x_0 < 1$ into which the critical points separate the x-axis.

If $x_0 > 3$, then each of the quantities within parentheses in Eq. (12) is positive. Hence it follows (because of the negative exponents) that

$$\lim_{t \to \times} x(t) = 3 \qquad \text{if } x_0 > 3. \tag{13}$$

If $1 < x_0 < 3$, then we write Eq. (12) in the form

$$x(t) = \frac{(3x_0 - 3) + (3 - x_0)e^{-2t}}{(x_0 - 1) + (3 - x_0)e^{-2t}} \tag{14}$$

with each of the quantities within parentheses positive. Now it also follows that

$$\lim_{t \to \times} x(t) = 3 \qquad \text{if } 1 < x_0 < 3. \tag{15}$$

If $x_0 < 1$, then we write Eq. (12) in the form

$$x(t) = \frac{(3 - x_0)e^{-2t} - (3 - 3x_0)}{(3 - x_0)e^{-2t} - (1 - x_0)} \tag{16}$$

with each quantity within parentheses again positive. The numerator and denominator in Eq. (16) both are positive initially, but the denominator approaches zero as

$$t \to t_0 = \frac{1}{2} \ln \frac{3 - x_0}{1 - x_0},$$

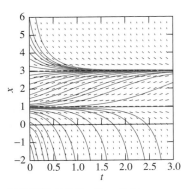

FIGURE 2.2.5. Slope field and solution curves for $x' = 4x - x^2 - 3$.

and the numerator approaches zero as

$$t \to t_1 = \frac{1}{2} \ln \frac{3 - x_0}{3(1 - x_0)} < t_0.$$

Hence it follows that

$$\lim_{t \to t_0^-} x(t) = -\times \quad \text{if} \quad x_0 < 1. \tag{17}$$

From Eqs. (13), (15), and (17) we see that the solution curves of Eq. (11) appear as shown in Fig. 2.2.5. Hence we conclude that the critical point $x = 3$ is stable, whereas the critical point $x = 1$ is unstable. Do you see in Fig. 2.2.5 a funnel along the line $x = 3$ and a spout along the line $x = 1$? ∎

For a concrete application of our stability conclusions in Example 3, suppose that $x(t)$ in Eq. (11) denotes the fish population in hundreds after t years (so 300 fish per year are removed by fishing). If the lake is stocked initially with more than 100 fish, then as t increases the fish will approach a stable population of 300 fish. But if the lake is stocked initially with fewer than 100 fish, the lake will be "fished out" and the fish will disappear in a finite period of time.

2.2 Problems

In Problems 1 through 12, first solve explicitly for $x(t)$ in terms of t and the initial value $x_0 = x(0)$. Then construct a sketch like the ones in Figs. 2.2.3 and 2.2.5, showing the nature of the trajectories for a wide variety of possible values of x_0. Finally, determine the stability or instability of each critical point.

1. $\dfrac{dx}{dt} = -x$

2. $\dfrac{dx}{dt} = x - 2$

3. $\dfrac{dx}{dt} = x - x^2$

4. $\dfrac{dx}{dt} = x^2 - 2x$

5. $\dfrac{dx}{dt} = x + x^2$

6. $\dfrac{dx}{dt} = (x - 1)^2$

7. $\dfrac{dx}{dt} = 1 - x^2$

8. $\dfrac{dx}{dt} = x^2 - 4$

9. $\dfrac{dx}{dt} = 2 - x - x^2$

10. $\dfrac{dx}{dt} = x - x^3$

11. $\dfrac{dx}{dt} = x^2 - 5x + 6$

12. $\dfrac{dx}{dt} = (2 - x)^3$

13. Consider the equation

$$\frac{dx}{dt} = kx - x^3.$$

(a) Show that the critical point $x = 0$ is stable if $k \leqq 0$.

(b) Suppose that $k > 0$. Show that the critical point $x = 0$ is now unstable, but that the critical points $x = \pm\sqrt{k}$ are stable. The value $k = 0$ of the parameter, for which the qualitative nature of the solutions of $x' = kx - x^3$ changes as k increases, is called a **bifurcation point** for the differential equation.

14. Solve the logistic equation

$$\frac{dx}{dt} = ax - bx^2, \qquad x(0) = x_0$$

explicitly (with $a, b > 0$) to show that the critical point $x = 0$ is unstable whereas the critical point $x = a/b$ is stable.

15. Consider the initial value problem

$$\frac{dx}{dt} = bx^2 - ax, \qquad x(0) = x_0$$

(with $a, b > 0$) for a population of unsophisticated animals in which deaths occur at a natural linear rate, but births occur as a result of chance encounters (as in the "doomsday versus extinction" example of Section 2.1). Show that the critical point $x = 0$ is stable but that the critical point $x = a/b$ is unstable (the reverse of the situation for the logistic equation of Problem 14).

16. Suppose that the equation $x' = ax - bx^2$ of Example 2 describes the fish population $x(t)$ in a lake after t months in which no fishing occurs. Now suppose that, because of fishing, fish are removed from the lake at the rate of kx fish per month.

(a) What is the new limiting population in the case $0 < k < a$?

(b) Show that if $k \geq a$, then $x(t) \to 0$ as $t \to +\infty$.

Problems 17 through 19 deal with the phenomenon of harvesting a logistic population (as illustrated in Example 3 of this section). If k is the [constant] rate at which individuals are removed from the population by harvesting, then the differential equation is

$$\frac{dx}{dt} = ax - bx^2 - k. \tag{18}$$

The long-range situation depends upon the values of the positive parameters a, b, and k in Eq. (18).

17. Suppose that $4bk = a^2$. Show that $x(t) \to a/(2b)$ (*half the limiting population in the logistic case $k = 0$*) as $t \to +\infty$.

18. Suppose that $4bk > a^2$. Show that $x(t) = 0$ after a finite period of time. In this case the harvesting rate k is too large, and extinction of the population results.

19. Suppose that $4bk < a^2$. Show that $x(t)$ approaches the limiting population

$$M_k = \frac{a + \sqrt{a^2 - 4bk}}{2b}$$

as $t \to +\infty$. Note that $M_k \to M = a/b$ as $k \to 0$. (*Suggestion:* Complete the square on the right-hand side in Eq. (18). The re-

sults of this and the previous two problems show that when the harvesting rate k is gradually increased, the limiting population M_k gradually decreases to half its original ($k = 0$) value $M = a/b$, until k reaches the critical value $k = a^2/(4b)$, above which extinction of the population occurs.)

20. This problem deals with the initial value problem

$$\frac{dx}{dt} = bx^2 - ax - k, \qquad x(0) = x_0 \tag{19}$$

(with a, b, $k > 0$) that describes the harvesting of an unsophisticated population (such as alligators) of the type mentioned in Problem 15. The two critical points of the equation in Eq. (19) are

$$\alpha = \frac{a + \sqrt{a^2 + 4bk}}{2b} > 0$$

and

$$\beta = \frac{a - \sqrt{a^2 + 4bk}}{2b} < 0.$$

Show that the critical point $x = \alpha$ is unstable, whereas $x = \beta$ is stable. In particular, show that if $x_0 > \alpha$, then $x(t) \to +\infty$ in a finite period of time, but that if $x_0 < \alpha$, then $x(t) \to 0$ in a finite period of time. Thus $x_0 = \alpha$ is a threshold value that increases when the harvesting rate k is increased—naturally enough, for the more alligators are killed annually, the greater must be their initial number to prevent extinction from resulting.

2.2 Computing Project

Every autonomous first-order differential equation

$$\frac{dx}{dt} = f(x) \tag{1}$$

is immediately separable, so its solution reduces to an integration:

$$t = \int \frac{dx}{f(x)}. \tag{2}$$

For instance, consider the case

$$\frac{dx}{dt} = (x - a)(x - b)(x - c) \tag{3}$$

in which $f(x)$ is a cubic polynomial with distinct real zeros a, b, and c. Then the integral

$$t = G(x) = \int \frac{dx}{(x - a)(x - b)(x - c)} \tag{4}$$

can be evaluated explicitly using a computer algebra system such as *Derive*, *Maple*, or

Mathematica, or even manually using a partial fractions decomposition of the form

$$\frac{1}{(x-a)(x-b)(x-c)} = \frac{A}{x-a} + \frac{B}{x-b} + \frac{C}{x-c}. \tag{5}$$

Thus the resulting antiderivative will have the form

$$G(x) = A \ln|x-a| + B \ln|x-b| + C \ln|x-c|. \tag{6}$$

The corresponding formal solution of Eq. (3) is given by

$$G(x) = t + K, \tag{7}$$

where K is a constant of integration. Hence the particular solution $x = x(t)$ satisfying the initial condition $x(t_0) = x_0$ is defined implicitly by the equation

$$G(x) = t + G(x_0) - t_0. \tag{8}$$

But instead of attempting to solve for x as a function, why not take the easy way out and solve for t as a function of x:

$$t = t_0 + G(x) - G(x_0). \tag{9}$$

If a computer graphing utility is available, then "solution curves" of Eq. (3) are readily plotted in the xt-plane with horizontal x-axis and vertical t-axis. Assuming that this has been done, is it clear how to convert the resulting figure into a picture showing "ordinary" solution curves in the tx-plane with horizontal t-axis and vertical x-axis?

For your own individual project, carry out the program described above with $|a|$, $|b|$, and $|c|$ being the three smallest distinct nonzero digits in your student I.D. number; choose signs for a, b, and c however you wish. If you're more ambitious numerically, you can solve in this manner the differential equation

$$\frac{dx}{dt} = x^3 - 3x^2 + 1. \tag{10}$$

In this case you'll have to begin by solving numerically for the three distinct real solutions a, b, and c of the equation

$$f(x) = x^3 - 3x^2 + 1 = 0. \tag{11}$$

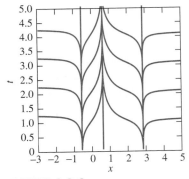

FIGURE 2.2.6. $t(x)$-curves
for $x' = x^3 - 3x^2 + 1$

Figure 2.2.6 shows four curves of the form $t = t(x)$ plotted on each of the intervals $(-3, a)$, (a, b), (b, c), and $(c, 5)$ with $a < b < c$, together with the vertical asymptotes $x = a$, $x = b$, and $x = c$. When you convert this xt-figure into a tx-figure, do you see two spouts and a funnel?

2.3 Acceleration-Velocity Models

In Section 1.2 we discussed vertical motion near the surface of the earth under the influence of constant gravitational acceleration, $g \approx 32$ ft/s$^2 \approx 9.8$ m/s^2. Beginning with the acceleration $dv/dt = -g$, we integrated twice to obtain the equations

$$\frac{dy}{dt} = v = -gt + v_0 \quad \text{and} \quad y = -\frac{1}{2}gt^2 + v_0 t + y_0$$

for the velocity v and height y at time t. We saw that these equations can be used to answer specific questions.

EXAMPLE 1 Suppose that we want to predict the maximum height that will be attained by a bolt shot from a crossbow aimed directly upward from ground level ($y_0 = 0$). A modern crossbow can impart an initial velocity of 288 ft/s to a lightweight bolt, so let us take $v_0 = 288$. We take $g = 32$ (exactly) for simplicity, and the equations of motion of the bolt take the form

$$v = -32t + 288, \qquad y = -16t^2 + 288t.$$

Of course, here we assume that the crossbow is fired at time $t = 0$. Then $v = 0$ when $t = 9$, so the maximum height attained by the bolt will be

$$y_{max} = y(9) = -(16)(9^2) + (288)(9) = 1296 \quad \text{(ft)}.$$ ∎

In the computations of Example 1 we have, however, ignored the effects of air resistance. This makes the mathematical analysis quite simple, but perhaps unrealistic. We now construct a more complete mathematical model, one that takes air resistance into account.

Empirical studies indicate that the force F_R of air resistance on a moving body with velocity v is approximately of the form

$$F_R = kv^p,$$

where $1 \leqq p \leqq 2$ and the value of k depends upon the size and shape of the body, as well as the density and viscosity of the air. Generally speaking, $p = 1$ for relatively low speeds and $p = 2$ for high speeds, whereas $1 < p < 2$ for intermediate speeds. But how slow "low speed" and how fast "high speed" are depends upon the same factors that determine the value of the coefficient k.

Thus air resistance is a complicated physical phenomenon. But the simplifying assumption that F_R is exactly of the form given here, with either $p = 1$ or $p = 2$, yields a tractable mathematical model that exhibits the most important qualitative features of motion with resistance.

Resistance Proportional to Velocity

Let us first consider the vertical motion of a body with mass m near the surface of the earth, subject to two forces: a downward gravitational force F_G and a force F_R of air resistance that is proportional to velocity (so that $p = 1$) and of course directed opposite the direction of motion of the body. If we set up a coordinate system with the positive y-direction upward and $y = 0$ at ground level, then $F_G = -mg$ and

$$F_R = -kv, \tag{1}$$

where k is a positive constant and $v = dy/dt$ is the velocity of the body. Note that the minus sign in Eq. (1) makes F_R positive (an upward force) if the body is falling (v is negative), whereas it makes F_R negative (a downward force) if the body is rising (v is positive). As indicated in Fig. 2.3.1, the net force acting on the body is then

$$F = F_R + F_G = -kv - mg,$$

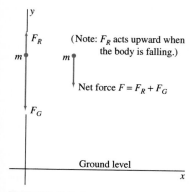

FIGURE 2.3.1. Vertical motion with air resistance

and Newton's law of motion $F = m(dv/dt)$ yields the equation

$$m\frac{dv}{dt} = -kv - mg.$$

Thus

$$\frac{dv}{dt} = -\rho v - g \tag{2}$$

where $\rho = k/m > 0$. The reader should verify that, if the positive y-axis were directed downward, then Eq. (2) would take the form $dv/dt = -\rho v + g$.

Equation (2) is a separable first-order differential equation, and its solution is

$$v(t) = \left(v_0 + \frac{g}{\rho}\right)e^{-\rho t} - \frac{g}{\rho}. \tag{3}$$

Here, $v_0 = v(0)$ is the initial velocity of the body. Note that

$$\lim_{t \to \times} v(t) = -\frac{g}{\rho}. \tag{4}$$

Thus the speed of a body falling with air resistance does *not* increase indefinitely; instead, it approaches a *finite* limiting speed, or **terminal speed,**

$$v_\tau = \frac{g}{\rho} = \frac{mg}{k}. \tag{5}$$

This fact is what makes the parachute a practical invention; it even helps explain the occasional survival of people who fall without parachutes from high-flying airplanes.

We now rewrite Eq. (3) in the form

$$\frac{dy}{dt} = (v_0 + v_\tau)e^{-\rho t} - v_\tau. \tag{6}$$

Integration gives

$$y(t) = -\frac{1}{\rho}(v_0 + v_\tau)e^{-\rho t} - v_\tau t + C.$$

We substitute 0 for t and let $y_0 = y(0)$ denote the initial height of the body. Thus we find that $C = y_0 + (v_0 + v_\tau)/\rho$, and so

$$y(t) = y_0 - v_\tau t + \frac{1}{\rho}(v_0 + v_\tau)(1 - e^{-\rho t}). \tag{7}$$

Equations (6) and (7) give the velocity v and height y of a body moving vertically under the influence of gravity and air resistance. The formulas depend upon the initial height y_0 of the body, its initial velocity v_0, and the *drag coefficient* ρ, the constant such that the acceleration due to air resistance is $a_R = -\rho v$. The two equations also involve the terminal speed v_τ.

EXAMPLE 2 We consider again a bolt shot straight upward with initial velocity $v_0 = 288$ ft/s from a crossbow at ground level. But now let us also take into account air resistance, with $\rho = 0.04$. What will be the maximum height reached by the bolt, and when will that maximum be attained? When and with what speed will the bolt strike the ground?

Solution We substitute $y_0 = 0$, $v_0 = 288$, and $v_\tau = g/\rho = 800$ into Eqs. (3) and (7). We obtain

$$v(t) = 1088e^{-t/25} - 800 \quad \text{and} \quad y(t) = 27{,}200\,(1 - e^{-t/25}) - 800t.$$

To find the time required for the bolt to reach its maximum height (when $v = 0$), we solve the equation

$$1088e^{-t/25} - 800 = 0$$

for $t = 25\ln(34/25) \approx 7.687$ s. Its maximum height is then

$$y_{\max} \approx 27{,}200(1 - e^{-0.3075}) - (800)(7.687) \approx 1050 \quad \text{(ft)}.$$

To find when the bolt strikes the ground ($y = 0$), we must solve the equation $27{,}200(1 - e^{-t/25}) - 800t = 0$, which can be written in the simpler form

$$34(1 - e^{-t/25}) - t = 0.$$

To solve the latter equation, we use the iterative formula of Newton's method:

$$t_{n+1} = t_n - \frac{f(t_n)}{f'(t_n)}. \tag{8}$$

Recall that this iteration successively improves an initial estimate t_0 of a solution of the equation $f(t) = 0$. (See, for example, Section 3.9 of Edwards and Penney, *Calculus with Analytic Geometry,* 4th ed. (Englewood Cliffs, N.J.: Prentice Hall, 1994).) With

$$f(t) = 34(1 - e^{-t/25}) - t,$$

Eq. (8) takes the form

$$t_{n+1} = t_n - \frac{34[1 - \exp(-t_n/25)] - t_n}{(34/25)\exp(-t_n/25) - 1}. \tag{9}$$

If we begin with $t_0 = 18$ s (the total time aloft in the case of no air resistance), the iteration in (9) yields $t_1 = 16.374$ s and $t_2 = t_3 = 16.252$ s. Thus the bolt is in the air for about 16.25 s and hits the ground with velocity

$$v_{\text{imp}} = 1088e^{-0.65} - 800 \approx -232 \text{ (ft/s)}.$$

The effect of air resistance is to decrease the maximum height, the total time spent aloft, and the final impact speed. Note also that when the effect of air resistance is included, the bolt spends more time in descent (about 8.565 s) than in ascent (about 7.687 s). ∎

For a person descending with the aid of a parachute, a typical value of ρ is 1.5, which corresponds to a terminal speed of $v_\tau \approx 21.3$ ft/s, or about 14.5 mi/h. With an unbuttoned overcoat flapping in the wind in place of a parachute, an unlucky skydiver might increase ρ to perhaps as much as 0.5, which gives a terminal speed of $v_\tau \approx 65$ ft/s, about 44 mi/h. See Problems 10 and 11 for some parachute-jump computations.

Resistance Proportional to Square of Velocity

Now let us assume that the force of air resistance is proportional to the *square* of the velocity:

$$F_R = \pm kv^2, \tag{10}$$

where k is a positive constant. Then Newton's second law gives

$$m\frac{dv}{dt} = F_G + F_R = \pm mg \pm kv^2;$$

that is,

$$\frac{dv}{dt} = \pm g \pm \rho v^2, \tag{11}$$

where $\rho = k/m > 0$. The choice of signs in Eq. (11) depends upon the direction of motion, as well as the choice of the direction of the positive y-axis. Consequently, we must discuss the two cases—upward and downward motion—separately.

Downward Motion. Suppose that the body is dropped from a given height with initial velocity $v(0) = 0$. In this case it is more convenient to choose the y-axis with the positive numbers *downward*, with $y_0 = y(0) = 0$, so $y(t)$ denotes the distance the body has fallen at time t. Then F_G is a downward force, thus positive, whereas F_R is an upward (negative) force. So we choose the signs in Eq. (11) to obtain

$$\frac{dv}{dt} = +g - \rho v^2 = g\left(1 - \frac{\rho}{g}v^2\right). \tag{12}$$

Recall that the hyperbolic tangent function may be defined as

$$\tanh u = \frac{\sinh u}{\cosh u} = \frac{e^u - e^{-u}}{e^u + e^{-u}}.$$

In Problem 13 we ask you to apply the integral

$$\int \frac{du}{1 - u^2} = \tanh^{-1} u + C$$

to solve Eq. (12) with $v(0) = 0$ for

$$v(t) = \sqrt{\frac{g}{\rho}}\,\tanh\left(t\sqrt{\rho g}\right). \tag{13}$$

Because $v = dy/dt$, another integration (see Problem 14) yields

$$y(t) = \frac{1}{\rho}\ln\cosh\left(t\sqrt{\rho g}\right) \tag{14}$$

for the distance the body has fallen at time t.

In the case of downward motion with resistance proportional to the velocity, $F_R = -kv$, we saw earlier that a body acquires a terminal speed $v_\tau = g/\rho$ (where $\rho = k/m$). Because

$$\lim_{t\to\times}\tanh at = \lim_{t\to\times}\frac{e^{at} - e^{-at}}{e^{at} + e^{-at}} = 1$$

if $a > 0$, it follows from Eq. (13) that, in the present case of downward motion with resistance $F_R = kv^2$, the body approaches the terminal speed

$$v_\tau = \sqrt{\frac{g}{\rho}} = \sqrt{\frac{mg}{k}}. \tag{15}$$

Upward Motion. Now let us consider a body that is projected straight upward from ground level $y_0 = 0$ with initial velocity $v(0) = v_0$ and with the positive y-axis now directed upward. Our differential equation now takes the form

$$\frac{dv}{dt} = -g - \rho v^2 \tag{16}$$

because F_G and F_R are each directed downward.

In Problem 16 we ask you to deduce that the velocity and height of the body at time t are given by

$$v = \sqrt{\frac{g}{\rho}} \tan\left(C - t\sqrt{\rho g}\right) \tag{17}$$

and

$$y = \frac{1}{\rho} \ln \left| \frac{\cos\left(C - t\sqrt{\rho g}\right)}{\cos C} \right|, \tag{18}$$

where

$$C = \tan^{-1}\left(v_0 \sqrt{\frac{\rho}{g}}\right). \tag{19}$$

The motion of the body continues to be described by Eqs. (17) and (18) as long as the velocity given in (17) is still positive; that is, as long as the body is still moving upward. It reaches its maximum height when $t\sqrt{\rho g} = C$ (so that $v = 0$); hence Eq. (18) gives

$$y_{\max} = -\frac{1}{\rho} \ln \cos C. \tag{20}$$

Thereafter the body falls back toward the ground, with its (downward) velocity and distance fallen (t seconds after beginning to fall) given by Eqs. (13) and (14).

Let us now reconsider the crossbow bolt of Example 2, which we assume shot straight upward from the ground with initial velocity $v_0 = 288$ ft/s. Instead of air resistance proportional to velocity v, we assume air resistance proportional to v^2, with $\rho = 0.0002$ in Eqs. (12) and (16). In Problems 18 and 19 we ask you to verify the entries in the last line of the following table.

Air Resistance	Maximum Height (ft)	Ascent Time (s)	Descent Time (s)	Impact Speed (ft/s)
0.0	1296	9.000	9.000	288
$0.04v$	1050	7.687	8.565	232
$0.0002v^2$	1044	7.800	8.362	234

Comparison of the last two lines of data here suggests a qualitative similarity between the cases $F_R = kv$ and $F_R = kv^2$.

Variable Gravitational Acceleration

Unless a projectile in vertical motion remains in the immediate vicinity of the earth's surface, the gravitational acceleration acting upon it is not constant. According to

Newton's law of gravitation, the gravitational force of attraction between two point masses M and m located at distance r apart is given by

$$F = \frac{GMm}{r^2}, \tag{21}$$

where G is a certain empirical constant ($G \approx 6.67260 \times 10^{-11}$ N·(m/kg)2 in mks units). The formula is also valid if either or both of the two masses are homogeneous spheres; in this case, the distance r is measured between the centers of the spheres.

Let M denote the mass of the earth and R its radius. We obtain the gravitational acceleration $a = g$ of a particle of mass m at the earth's surface by combining Eq. (21) with the equation $F = ma$:

$$ma = mg = \frac{GMm}{r^2} = \frac{GMm}{R^2},$$

so that

$$g = \frac{GM}{R^2} \quad \text{(about 32 ft/s}^2\text{).} \tag{22}$$

We will use Eq. (22) from time to time in our computations to remove the necessity for the actual determination of G in our examples and problems. For instance, the mass M_1 of the moon is approximately $(0.0123)M$ and its radius R_1 is approximately $(0.2725)R$, so we can use Eq. (22) to compute the lunar gravitational acceleration g_1 at the surface of the moon:

$$g_1 = \frac{GM_1}{(R_1)^2} = G\frac{(0.0123)M}{(0.2725R)^2} \approx (0.1656)\frac{GM}{R^2}$$

$$= (0.1656)g \approx (0.1656)(32) \approx 5.3 \quad \text{(ft/s}^2\text{).}$$

We now calculate the *escape velocity* from the earth—the minimal initial velocity with which an object must be launched straight upward from the earth's surface so that it will continue forever to move away from the earth. The condition that the upward motion will continue forever becomes the relation $v = dy/dt > 0$ for all $t \geqq 0$. We will use $y = y(t)$ to denote the distance from the object to the earth's *center* (because of the way in which Newton's law of gravitation is phrased). Our launch site, though, will be on the earth's *surface*, where we take $y_0 = y(0) = 6370$ km; that is, 6,370,000 m. The solution to the escape velocity problem will be the initial velocity $v_0 = v(0)$ that is just sufficient to insure that $v(t)$ is never zero or negative.

Now imagine the launched object as it is shown in Fig. 2.3.2,. with mass m, at distance $y = y(t)$ from the center of the earth at time $t \geqq 0$, and with velocity $v = v(t)$ then. The only force acting on the mass m as it ascends is the pull of gravity of the earth, given by Eq. (21), Newton'a law of gravitation, as $F = -GMm/y^2$. The resulting acceleration of m is then given, with the *same* values of F and m, by Newton's second law of motion, $F = ma$. We eliminate F by equating the other sides of each equation:

$$ma = m\frac{dv}{dt} = -\frac{GMm}{y^2},$$

which we simplify to

$$\frac{dv}{dt} = -\frac{GM}{y^2}.$$

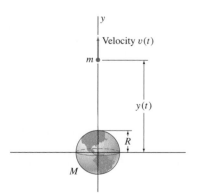

FIGURE 2.3.2. A mass m at a great distance from the earth

To solve this differential equation, we use the chain rule:

$$\frac{dv}{dt} = \frac{dv}{dy}\frac{dy}{dt} = v\frac{dv}{dy}.$$

Thus

$$v\frac{dv}{dy} = -\frac{GM}{y^2}; \qquad \text{that is,} \quad D_y\left(\frac{1}{2}v^2\right) = D_y\left(\frac{GM}{y}\right).$$

Note that we think of y as the independent variable, rather than the more natural t. It follows immediately that

$$\frac{1}{2}v^2 = \frac{GM}{y} + C. \tag{23}$$

To evaluate the constant C, we use the fact that when $t = 0$, we have $v = v_0$ and $y = R$. Thus

$$\frac{1}{2}v_0^2 = \frac{GM}{R} + C;$$

we substitute the resulting value of C in Eq. (23) to obtain

$$v^2 = v_0^2 + 2GM\left(\frac{1}{y} - \frac{1}{R}\right).$$

In particular,

$$v^2 > v_0^2 - \frac{2GM}{R}.$$

Therefore, v will remain positive provided that $v_0^2 \geqq 2GM/R$. With the aid of Eq. (22), we can now write a formula for the escape velocity for the earth:

$$v_0 = \sqrt{\frac{2GM}{R}} = \sqrt{2Rg}. \tag{24}$$

With $g = 9.8$ m/s^2 and $R = 6.37 \times 10^6$ m, this gives $v_0 \approx 11{,}174$ m/s, about 36,000 ft/s, about 24,995 mi/h, about 6.94 mi/s.

The following example is a refinement of Example 2 of Section 1.2; we now take lunar gravity into account.

EXAMPLE 3 A lunar lander is free-falling toward the moon's surface at a speed of 1000 mi/h. Its retrorockets, when fired in free space, provide a deceleration of 33,000 mi/h^2. At what height above the lunar surface should the retrorockets be activated to insure a "soft" touchdown ($v = 0$ at impact)?

Solution We use units of kilomiles and hours, and denote by $y(t)$ the lunar lander's distance from the center of the moon at time t. The moon's radius is about 1.08 kilomiles, so we want $v = 0$ when $y = 1.08$. The moon's *surface* gravitational acceleration is, as computed earlier, 5.3 ft/s^2; this is approximately 13 kilomiles/h^2. Because gravitational acceleration is inversely proportional to the square of the distance, the lunar gravitational acceleration at distance y (from its center) is approximately

$$\left(\frac{1.08}{y}\right)^2 (13) \approx \frac{15.16}{y^2}$$

kilomiles/h². We subtract this from the retrorocket acceleration of 33 kilomiles/h² to obtain

$$\frac{dv}{dt} = 33 - \frac{15.16}{y^2},$$

where $v = dy/dt$. We change the independent variable to y by using the chain rule (as before) to write

$$\frac{dv}{dt} = \frac{dv}{dy}\frac{dy}{dt} = v\frac{dv}{dy} = 33 - \frac{15.16}{y^2}.$$

Integration with respect to y gives

$$\frac{1}{2}v^2 = 33y + \frac{15.16}{y} + C.$$

The desired condition $v = 0$ when $y = 1.08$ implies that $C = -49.68$, so

$$\frac{1}{2}v^2 = 33y + \frac{15.16}{y} - 49.68.$$

Finally, we want to know the value of $y = y_0$ when $v_0 = -1$ (the initial velocity of the rocket, in kilomiles/h). We substitute $v = -1$ into the last equation and simplify; the result is the quadratic equation

$$33y^2 - (50.18)y + 15.16 = 0.$$

The only roots of this equation are $y = 1.105$ and $y = 0.416$ (approximately). The second corresponds to a height *below* the lunar surface, so the first of the two is the solution we seek. And $1.105 - 1.080 = 0.025$ kilomiles, so the retrorockets should be activated at a distance of 25 miles above the lunar surface. ∎

2.3 Problems

1. The acceleration of a Maserati is proportional to the difference between 250 km/h and the velocity of the sports car. If this machine can accelerate from rest to 100 km/h in 10 s, how long will it take for the car to accelerate from rest to 200 km/h?

2. Suppose that a body moves through a resisting medium with resistance proportional to its velocity v, so that $dv/dt = -kv$.
(a) Show that its velocity and position at time t are given by

$$v(t) = v_0 e^{-kt}$$

and

$$x(t) = x_0 + \left(\frac{v_0}{k}\right)(1 - e^{-kt}).$$

(b) Conclude that the body travels only a finite distance, and find that distance.

3. Suppose that a motorboat is moving at 40 ft/s when its mo-

tor suddenly quits, and that 10 s later the boat has slowed to 20 ft/s. Assume, as in Problem 2, that the resistance it encounters while coasting is proportional to its velocity. How far will the boat coast in all?

4. Consider a body that moves horizontally through a medium whose resistance is proportional to the *square* of the velocity, so that $dv/dt = -kv^2$. Show that

$$v(t) = \frac{v_0}{1 + v_0 kt}$$

and that

$$x(t) = x_0 + \frac{1}{k}\ln(1 + v_0 kt).$$

Note that, in contrast with the result of Problem 2, $x(t) \to +\infty$ as $t \to +\infty$.

5. Assuming resistance proportional to the square of the velocity as in Problem 4, how far does the motorboat of Problem 3 coast in the first minute after its motor quits?

6. Assume that a body moving with velocity v encounters resistance of the form $dv/dt = -kv^{3/2}$. Show that

$$v(t) = \frac{4v_0}{(kt\sqrt{v_0} + 2)^2}$$

and

$$x(t) = x_0 + \frac{2}{k}\sqrt{v_0}\left(1 - \frac{2}{kt\sqrt{v_0} + 2}\right).$$

Conclude that under a (3/2)-power resistance a body travels only a finite distance before coasting to a stop.

7. Calculate $v(t)$ and $x(t)$ under the assumption that

$$\frac{dv}{dt} = -kv^{1+r}, \quad \text{where} \quad 0 < r < 1.$$

Also compute the coasting distance.

8. A car starts from rest $(x_0 = v_0 = 0)$ and travels along a straight road. Its engine provides a constant acceleration of 18 ft/s². The combination of air and road resistance provides a deceleration of 0.12 ft/s² for every foot per second of the car's velocity v. (a) Set up and solve a first-order differential equation for v. (b) Find v when $t = 10$ s and also the limiting velocity as $t \to +\infty$, both in miles per hour.

9. A motorboat weighs 32,000 lb and its motor provides a thrust of 5000 lb. Assume that the water resistance is 100 pounds for each foot per second of the speed v of the boat. Then

$$1000\frac{dv}{dt} = 5000 - 100v.$$

If the boat starts from rest, what is the maximum velocity that it can attain?

10. A woman bails out of an airplane at an altitude of 10,000 ft, falls freely for 20 s, then opens her parachute? How long will it take her to reach the ground? Assume that $\rho = 0.15$ without the parachute and that $\rho = 1.5$ with the parachute. (*Suggestion:* First determine her height and velocity when the parachute opens.)

11. According to a newspaper account, a paratrooper survived a training jump from 1200 ft when his parachute failed to open but provided some resistance by flapping unopened in the wind. Allegedly he hit the ground at 100 mi/h after falling for 8 s. Test the accuracy of this account. (*Suggestion:* Find ρ (in Eq. (2)) by assuming a terminal velocity of 100 mi/h. Then calculate the time required to fall 1200 ft.)

12. It is proposed to dispose of nuclear wastes—in drums with weight $W = 640$ lb and volume 8 ft³—by dropping them into the ocean $(v_0 = 0)$. The force equation for a drum falling

through water is

$$m\frac{dv}{dt} = -W + B + F_R,$$

where the buoyant force B is equal to the weight of the volume of water displaced by the drum (Archimedes' principle) and F_R is the force of water resistance, found empirically to be 1 lb per foot per second of the velocity of a drum. If the drums are likely to burst upon an impact of more than 75 ft/s, what is the maximum depth to which they can be dropped in the ocean without likelihood of bursting?

13. Derive Eq. (13).

14. Derive Eq. (14); note that

$$\int \tanh u\, du = \int \frac{\sinh u}{\cosh u}\, du = \ln \cosh u + C.$$

15. A motorboat starts from rest (initial velocity $v(0) = v_0 = 0$). Its motor provides a constant acceleration of 4 ft/s², but water resistance causes a deceleration of $v^2/400$ ft/s². Find v when $t = 10$ s, and also find the *limiting velocity* as $t \to +\infty$ (that is, the maximum possible speed of the boat).

16. Derive Eqs. (17) through (19) of the text.

17. If a ball is projected upward from the ground with initial velocity v_0, deduce from Eq. (20) that the maximum height it attains is

$$y_{\max} = \frac{1}{2\rho}\ln\left(1 + \frac{\rho v_0^2}{g}\right).$$

18. Suppose that a crossbow bolt is shot straight upward with initial velocity 288 ft/s. Assume that air resistance is proportional to v^2, the square of the velocity, with $\rho = 0.0002$ in Eqs. (12) and (16). Find the maximum height that the bolt attains and its time of ascent.

19. In a continuation of Problem 18, find the descent time of the bolt and the speed with which it strikes the ground.

20. Suppose that $\rho = 0.075$ in Eq. (12) for a paratrooper falling with parachute open. If he jumps from an altitude of 10,000 ft and opens his parachute immediately, what will be his terminal speed? How long will it take him to reach the ground?

21. Suppose that the paratrooper of Problem 20 freefalls for 30 s with $\rho = 0.00075$ before opening his parachute. How long will it now take him to reach the ground?

22. The mass of the sun is 329,320 times that of the earth, and its radius is 109 times the radius of the earth. (a) To what radius (in meters) would the earth have to be compressed in order for it to become a *black hole*—the escape velocity from its surface equal to the velocity $c = 3 \times 10^8$ m/s of light? (b) Repeat part (a) with the sun in place of the earth.

23. (a) Show that if a projectile is launched upward from the

surface of the earth with initial velocity v_0 less than escape velocity, then the maximum distance from the center of the earth that the projectile will attain is

$$y_{max} = \frac{2gR^2}{2gR - v_0^2},$$

where g and R are the surface gravity and radius of the earth, respectively. (b) With what initial velocity v_0 (in miles per hour) must such a projectile be launched to yield a maximum height of 100 mi above the surface of the earth? (Take the radius of the earth to be 3960 mi.) (c) Find the maximum distance from the center of the earth, expressed in terms of earth radii, attained by a projectile launched from the surface of the earth with 90% of escape velocity.

24. (a) Suppose that a body is dropped ($v_0 = 0$) from a distance y_0 from the earth's center, so that its gravitational acceleration is $dv/dt = -ky^2$ with $k = GM = R^2g$. Ignore air resistance and show that it reaches the height y at time

$$t = \sqrt{\frac{y_0}{2R^2g}}\left(\sqrt{yy_0 - y^2} + y_0 \cos^{-1}\sqrt{\frac{y}{y_0}}\right).$$

(*Suggestion:* Substitute $y = y_0 \cos^2 \theta$ to evaluate the antiderivative of $\sqrt{y/(y_0 - y)}$.) (b) If a body is dropped from a height of 1000 mi above the earth's surface and air resistance is neglected, how long does it fall and with what speed will it strike the earth's surface?

25. Suppose that a projectile is fired straight upward from the surface of the earth with initial velocity v_0. Then its height $x(t)$ at time t satisfies the initial value problem

$$\frac{d^2x}{dt^2} = -\frac{gR^2}{(x+R)^2}; \qquad x(0) = 0, \quad x'(0) = v_0.$$

Let us use the values $g = 32.15$ (ft/s^2) or 0.006089 (mi/s^2) for the gravitational acceleration of the earth at its surface and $R = 3960$ (mi) as the radius of the earth. (a) Substitute $dv/dt = v(dv/dx)$ and then integrate to obtain

$$v^2 = \frac{v_0^2 R - (2gR - v_0^2)x}{R + x}$$

for the velocity of the projectile at altitude x. If $v_0 = 1$ (mi/s), what is the maximum height x_{max} attained by the projectile? (*Answer:* About 84 mi.) (b) Assume that $v_0^2 < 2gR$. Conclude from part (a) that the time required for the projectile to ascend to its maximum height x_{max} is

$$t_{max} = \int_0^{x_{max}} \sqrt{\frac{R+x}{\alpha^2 - \beta^2 x}}\, dx$$

where $\alpha^2 = v_0^2 R$ and $\beta^2 = 2gR - v_0^2$. Make the rationalizing substitution $u^2 = (R + x)/(\alpha^2 - \beta^2 x)$, and then integrate to obtain

$$t_{max} = \frac{2gR^2}{\beta^3}\left[\frac{\pi}{2} - \tan^{-1}\left(\frac{\beta}{v_0}\right) + \frac{\beta v_0}{2gR}\right].$$

In the case $v_0 = 1$ (mi/s), conclude that $t_{max} \approx 169$ (s).

2.4 Numerical Approximation: Euler's Method

It is the exception rather than the rule when a differential equation of the general form

$$\blacktriangleright \qquad \frac{dy}{dx} = f(x, y)$$

can be solved exactly and explicitly by elementary methods like those discussed in Chapter 1. For example, consider the simple equation

$$\frac{dy}{dx} = e^{-x^2}. \tag{1}$$

A solution of Eq. (1) is simply an antiderivative of e^{-x^2}. But it is known that every antiderivative of $f(x) = e^{-x^2}$ is a **nonelementary** function—one that cannot be expressed as a finite combination of the familiar functions of elementary calculus. Hence no particular solution of Eq. (1) is finitely expressible in terms of elementary functions.

Finding a particular solution of a differential equation is, in most applications, merely a means to an end. The goal is to be able to predict—with a reasonable degree of accuracy—the shape of a column, the trajectory of a particle, or the modes of vibration of a mechanical system. Suppose that the system under investigation is modeled by the initial value problem

$$\frac{dy}{dx} = f(x, y), \qquad y(a) = y_0 . \qquad (2)$$

For purposes such as those mentioned above, it might be quite adequate to have a table of values of the unknown solution $y(x)$ at selected points of some interval $[a, b]$. In this section we discuss **Euler's method** for computing a table of numerical approximations to the solution of the initial value problem in (2).

To describe Euler's method, we first choose a fixed **step size** $h > 0$ and consider the points

$$x_0 = a, \quad x_1, \quad x_2, \quad \ldots , \quad x_n, \quad \ldots ,$$

where $x_n = a + nh$, so that

$$x_{n+1} = x_n + h$$

for $n = 0, 1, 2, \ldots$. Our goal is to find suitable *approximations*

$$y_1, \quad y_2, \quad y_3, \quad \ldots , \quad y_n, \quad \ldots$$

to the true values

$$y(x_1), \quad y(x_2), \quad y(x_3), \quad \ldots , \quad y(x_n), \quad \ldots$$

of the solution $y(x)$ of Eq. (2) at the points x_1, x_2, x_3, \ldots . Thus we seek reasonably accurate approximations

$$y_n \approx y(x_n) \qquad (3)$$

for $n = 1, 2, 3, \ldots$. The question is this: How do we "step" from the approximate value y_n at x_n to the approximate value y_{n+1} at x_{n+1}?

When $x = x_0$, the rate of change of y with respect to x is $y' = f(x_0, y_0)$. If y continued to change at this same rate from $x = x_0$ to $x = x_1 = x_0 + h$, the change in y would be exactly $h \cdot f(x_0, y_0)$. We therefore take

$$y_1 = y_0 + h \cdot f(x_0, y_0) \qquad (4)$$

as our approximation to the true value $y(x_1)$ of the solution at $x = x_1$. Similarly, we take

$$y_2 = y_1 + h \cdot f(x_1, y_1) \qquad (5)$$

as our approximation to $y(x_2)$. In general, having reached the nth approximate value $y_n \approx y(x_n)$, we take

$$y_{n+1} = y_n + h \cdot f(x_n, y_n) \qquad (6)$$

as our approximation to the true value $y(x_{n+1})$.

Equation (6) tells us how to make the typical step from y_n to y_{n+1}, and is the heart of Euler's method. Note that the formulas in Eqs. (4) and (5) are the first two cases, $n = 0$ and $n = 1$, of the general iterative formula in Eq. (6).

ALGORITHM: The Euler Method

Given the initial value problem

▶
$$\frac{dy}{dx} = f(x, y), \qquad y(a) = y_0, \tag{2}$$

Euler's method with step size h consists in applying the iterative formula

▶
$$y_{n+1} = y_n + h \cdot f(x_n, y_n) \qquad (n \geq 0) \tag{6}$$

to compute successive approximations y_1, y_2, y_3, . . . to the [true] values $y(x_1)$, $y(x_2)$, $y(x_3)$, . . . of the [exact] solution $y = y(x)$ at the points x_1, x_2, x_3, . . . , respectively. ■

Although the most important practical applications of Euler's method are to nonlinear differential equations, we will first illustrate the method with the linear initial value problem

$$\frac{dy}{dx} = x + y, \qquad y(0) = 1, \tag{7}$$

in order that we may compare our approximate solution with the exact solution

$$y(x) = 2e^x - x - 1. \tag{8}$$

(This solution is readily found using the methods of Section 1.5.)

EXAMPLE 1 Apply Euler's method with step size $h = 0.1$ to approximate the solution of the initial value problem in (7) on the interval $0 \leq x \leq 1$.

Solution Here $f(x, y) = x + y$, so the iterative formula in (6) takes the form

$$y_{n+1} = y_n + h \cdot (x_n + y_n). \tag{9}$$

Beginning with $x_0 = 0$, $y_0 = 1$, and rounding values to four decimal places, the first three approximate values given by (9) are

$$y_1 = 1.0000 + (0.1) \cdot (0.0 + 1.0000) = 1.1000,$$

$$y_2 = 1.1000 + (0.1) \cdot (0.1 + 1.1000) = 1.2200,$$

$$y_3 = 1.2200 + (0.1) \cdot (0.2 + 1.2200) = 1.3620.$$

The table in Fig. 2.4.1 shows the approximate values obtained in all ten steps, together with the actual value $y(x_n)$ given by (8) and the error

$$y_{\text{actual}} - y_{\text{approx}} = y(x_n) - y_n$$

at each step. Observe that the error in y_n increases as n increases—that is, as x_n gets further and further from the starting point x_0. The final column of the table shows the percentage error $100 \cdot (y_{\text{actual}} - y_{\text{approx}})/y_{\text{actual}}$ in each approximate value; these percentage errors increase from 0.93% at $x_1 = 0.1$ to 7.25% at $x_{10} = 1.0$. ■

Local and Cumulative Errors

There are several sources of error in Euler's method that may make the approximation y_n to $y(x_n)$ unreliable for large values of n, those for which x_n is not sufficiently close

n	x_n	Approximate y_n	Actual $y(x_n)$	Error $y(x_n) - y_n$	Percent Error
0	0.0	1.0000	1.0000	0.0000	0.00%
1	0.1	1.1000	1.1103	0.0103	0.93%
2	0.2	1.2200	1.2428	0.0228	1.84%
3	0.3	1.3620	1.3997	0.0377	2.69%
4	0.4	1.5282	1.5836	0.0554	3.50%
5	0.5	1.7210	1.7974	0.0764	4.25%
6	0.6	1.9431	2.0442	0.1011	4.95%
7	0.7	2.1974	2.3275	0.1301	5.59%
8	0.8	2.4872	2.6511	0.1639	6.18%
9	0.9	2.8159	3.0192	0.2033	6.73%
10	1.0	3.1875	3.4366	0.2491	7.25%

FIGURE 2.4.1. Using Euler's method to approximate the solution of Eq. (7)

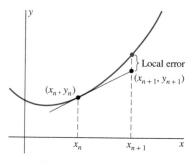

FIGURE 2.4.2. The local error in Euler's method

to x_0. The error in the linear approximation formula

$$y(x_{n+1}) \approx y_n + h \cdot f(x_n, y_n) = y_{n+1} \tag{10}$$

is the amount by which the tangent line at (x_n, y_n) departs from the solution curve through (x_n, y_n), as illustrated in Fig. 2.4.2. This error, introduced at each step in the process, is called the **local error** in Euler's method.

The local error indicated in Fig. 2.4.2 *would be* the total error in y_{n+1} *if* the starting point y_n in (10) were an exact value, rather than merely an approximation to the actual value $y(x_n)$. But y_n itself suffers from the accumulated effects of all the local errors introduced at the previous steps. Thus the tangent line in Fig. 2.4.2 is tangent to the "wrong" solution curve—the one through (x_n, y_n) rather than the actual solution curve through the initial point (x_0, y_0). Figure 2.4.3 illustrates the **cumulative error** in Euler's method; it is the amount by which the polygonal stepwise path from (x_0, y_0) departs from the actual solution curve through (x_0, y_0).

The usual way of attempting to reduce the cumulative error in Euler's method is to decrease the step size h. The table in Fig. 2.4.4 shows the results obtained in approximating the solution of the initial value problem

$$\frac{dy}{dx} = x + y, \qquad y(0) = 1,$$

of Example 1, using the successively smaller step sizes $h = 0.1$, $h = 0.02$, $h = 0.005$, and $h = 0.001$. We show computed values only at intervals of $\Delta x = 0.1$. For instance, with $h = 0.001$, the computation required 1000 Euler steps, but the value y_n is shown only when n is a multiple of 100, so that x_n is an integral multiple of 0.1.

By scanning the columns in Fig. 2.4.4 we observe that, for each fixed step size h, the error $y_{\text{actual}} - y_{\text{approx}}$ increases as x gets further from the starting point $x_0 = 0$. But by scanning the rows of the table we see that for each fixed x, the error decreases as the step size h is reduced. The percentage errors at the final point $x = 1$ range from 7.25% with $h = 0.1$ down to only 0.08% with $h = 0.001$. Thus the smaller is the step size h, the more slowly does the error grow with increasing distance from the starting point.

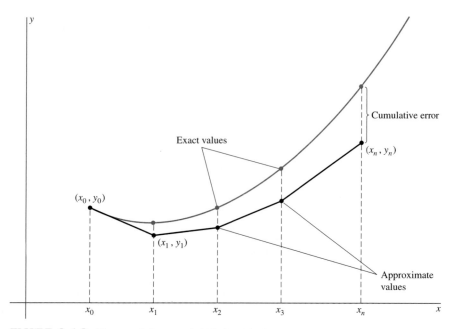

FIGURE 2.4.3. The cumulative error in Euler's method

The column of data for $h = 0.1$ in Fig. 2.4.4 requires only 10 steps, so Euler's method can be carried out (as in Example 1) with a hand-held calculator. But 50 steps are required to reach $x = 1$ with $h = 0.02$, 200 steps with $h = 0.005$, and 1000 steps with $h = 0.001$. A computer is almost always used to implement Euler's method when more than 10 or 20 steps are required. Once an appropriate computer program has been written, one step size is—in principle—just as convenient as another; after all, the computer hardly cares how many steps it is asked to carry out.

Why, then, do we not simply choose an exceedingly small step size (such as

x	y with $h = 0.1$	y with $h = 0.02$	y with $h = 0.005$	y with $h = 0.001$	Actual y
0.1	1.1000	1.1082	1.1098	1.1102	1.1103
0.2	1.2200	1.2380	1.2416	1.2426	1.2428
0.3	1.3620	1.3917	1.3977	1.3993	1.3997
0.4	1.5282	1.5719	1.5807	1.5831	1.5836
0.5	1.7210	1.7812	1.7933	1.7966	1.7974
0.6	1.9461	2.0227	2.0388	2.0431	2.0442
0.7	2.1974	2.2998	2.3205	2.3261	2.3275
0.8	2.4872	2.6161	2.6422	2.6493	2.6511
0.9	2.8159	2.9757	3.0082	3.0170	3.0192
1.0	3.1875	3.3832	3.4230	3.4338	3.4266

FIGURE 2.4.4. Approximating the solution of $dy/dx = x + y$, $y(0) = 1$ with successively smaller step sizes

$h = 10^{-9}$), with the expectation that very great accuracy will result? There are two reasons for not doing so. The first is obvious: the time required for the computation. For example, the data in Fig. 2.4.4 were obtained using a pocket computer that carried out nine Euler steps per second. Thus it required slightly over one second to approximate $y(1)$ with $h = 0.1$ and about 1 min 50 s with $h = 0.001$. But with $h = 10^{-9}$ it would require over three years!

The second reason is more subtle. In addition to the local and cumulative errors discussed previously, the computer itself will contribute **roundoff error** at each stage because only finitely many significant digits can be used in each calculation. An Euler's method computation with $h = 0.0001$ will introduce roundoff errors 1000 times as often as one with $h = 0.1$. Hence with certain differential equations, $h = 0.1$ could actually produce more accurate results than those obtained with $h = 0.0001$, because the cumulative effect of roundoff error in the latter case might exceed combined cumulative and roundoff error in the case $h = 0.1$.

The "best" choice of h is difficult to determine in practice as well as in theory. It depends on the nature of the function $f(x, y)$ in the initial value problem in (2), on the exact code in which the program is written, and on the specific computer used. With a step size that is too large, the approximations inherent in Euler's method may not be sufficiently accurate, while if h is too small, then roundoff errors may accumulate to an unacceptable degree or the program may require too much time to be practical. The subject of *error propagation* in numerical algorithms is treated in numerical analysis courses and textbooks.

A Word of Caution

The data shown in Fig. 2.4.4 indicate that Euler's method works well in approximating the solution of $dy/dx = x + y$, $y(0) = 1$ on the interval $[0, 1]$. That is, for each fixed x it appears that the approximate values approach the actual value of $y(x)$ as the step size h is decreased. For instance, the approximate values in the rows corresponding to $x = 0.3$ and $x = 0.5$ suggest that $y(0.3) \approx 1.40$ and $y(0.5) \approx 1.80$, in agreement with the actual values shown in the final column of the table.

Example 2, in contrast, shows that some initial value problems are not so well-behaved.

EXAMPLE 2 Use Euler's method to approximate the solution of the initial value problem

$$\frac{dy}{dx} = x^2 + y^2, \qquad y(0) = 1 \tag{11}$$

Solution Here $f(x, y) = x^2 + y^2$, so the iterative formula of Euler's method is

$$y_{n+1} = y_n + h \cdot (x_n^2 + y_n^2). \tag{12}$$

With step size $h = 0.1$ we obtain

$$y_1 = 1 + (0.1) \cdot [(0)^2 + (1)^2] = 1.1,$$
$$y_2 = 1.1 + (0.1) \cdot [(0.1)^2 + (1.1)^2] = 1.222,$$
$$y_3 = 1.222 + (0.1) \cdot [(0.2)^2 + (1.222)^2] \approx 1.3753,$$

and so forth. Rounded to four decimal places, the first ten values obtained in this manner are

$$y_1 = 1.1000 \qquad y_6 = 2.1995$$

$$y_2 = 1.2220 \qquad y_7 = 2.7193$$

$$y_3 = 1.3753 \qquad y_8 = 3.5078$$

$$y_4 = 1.5735 \qquad y_9 = 4.8023$$

$$y_5 = 1.8371 \qquad y_{10} = 7.1895$$

But instead of naively accepting these results as accurate approximations, we decided to use a computer to repeat the computations with smaller values of h. The table in Fig. 2.4.5 shows the results obtained with step sizes $h = 0.1$, $h = 0.02$, and $h = 0.005$. Observe that now the "stability" of our earlier table is missing. Indeed, it seems obvious that something is going wrong near $x = 1$.

x	y with $h = 0.1$	y with $h = 0.02$	y with $h = 0.005$
0.1	1.1000	1.1088	1.1108
0.2	1.2220	1.2458	1.2512
0.3	1.3753	1.4243	1.4357
0.4	1.5735	1.6658	1.6882
0.5	1.8371	2.0074	2.0512
0.6	2.1995	2.5201	2.6104
0.7	2.7193	3.3612	3.5706
0.8	3.5078	4.9601	5.5763
0.9	4.8023	9.0000	12.2061
1.0	7.1895	30.9167	1502.2090

FIGURE 2.4.5. Attempting to approximate the solution of $dy/dx = x^2 + y^2$, $y(0) = 1$

Figure 2.4.6 provides a graphical clue to the difficulty. It shows a slope field for $dy/dx = x^2 + y^2$, together with a solution curve through $(0, 1)$ plotted using one of the more accurate approximation methods of the following two sections. It appears that this solution curve may have a vertical asymptote near $x = 0.97$. Indeed, an exact solution using Bessel functions (see Problem 16 in Section 8.6) can be used to show that $y(x) \to +\infty$ as $x \to 0.969811$ (approximately). Although Euler's method gives values (albeit spurious ones) at $x = 1$, the actual solution does not exist on the entire interval $[0, 1]$. Moreover, Euler's method is unable to "keep up" with the rapid changes in $y(x)$ that occur as x approaches the infinite discontinuity near 0.969811. ∎

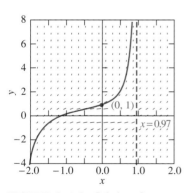

FIGURE 2.4.6. Solution of $y' = x^2 + y^2$, $y(0) = 1$

The moral of Example 2 is that there are pitfalls in the numerical solution of certain types of initial value problems. Certainly it's pointless to attempt to approximate a solution on an interval where it doesn't even exist (or where it is not unique, in which case there's no generally applicable way to predict which way the numerical approximations will branch at a point of nonuniqueness). One should never accept as accurate the results of applying Euler's method with a single fixed step size h. A second "run" with smaller step size ($h/2$, say, or $h/5$, or $h/10$) may give seemingly consistent re-

sults, thereby suggesting their accuracy, or it may—as in Example 2— reveal the presence of some hidden difficulty in the problem. Many problems simply require the more accurate and powerful methods that are discussed in subsequent sections of this chapter.

2.4 Problems

A hand-held calculator will suffice for Problems 1 through 10. In each problem, find the exact solution of the given initial value problem. Then apply Euler's method twice to approximate (to four decimal places) this solution on the interval $[0, 0.5]$, first with step size $h = 0.1$, then with $h = 0.05$. Make a table showing the approximate values with $h = 0.1$, the approximate values with $h = 0.05$, and the actual values of the solution at the points $x = 0.1, 0.2, 0.3, 0.4$, and 0.5.

1. $\dfrac{dy}{dx} = -y \quad y(0) = 2$

2. $\dfrac{dy}{dx} = 2y, \quad y(0) = \frac{1}{2}$

3. $\dfrac{dy}{dx} = y + 1, \quad y(0) = 1$

4. $\dfrac{dy}{dx} = x - y, \quad y(0) = 1$

5. $\dfrac{dy}{dx} = y - x - 1, \quad y(0) = 1$

6. $\dfrac{dy}{dx} = -2xy, \quad y(0) = 2$

7. $\dfrac{dy}{dx} = -3x^2y, \quad y(0) = 3$

8. $\dfrac{dy}{dx} = e^{-y}, \quad y(0) = 0$

9. $\dfrac{dy}{dx} = \frac{1}{4}(1 + y^2), \quad y(0) = 1$

10. $\dfrac{dy}{dx} = 2xy^2, \quad y(0) = 1$

Note: The project following this problem set lists illustrative calculator/computer programs that can be used in the remaining problems.

A programmable calculator or a computer will be useful for Problems 11 through 16. In each problem find the exact solution of the given initial value problem. Then apply Euler's method twice to approximate (to four decimal places) this solution on the given interval, first with step size $h = 0.01$, then with step size $h = 0.005$. Make a table showing the approximate values and the actual value, together with the percentage error in the

more accurate approximation, for x an integral multiple of 0.2. Throughout, y' is an abbreviation for dy/dx.

11. $\dfrac{dy}{dx} = y - 2, \quad y(0) = 1; \quad 0 \leq x \leq 1$

12. $\dfrac{dy}{dx} = \frac{1}{2}(y - 1)^2, \quad y(0) = 2; \quad 0 \leq x \leq 1$

13. $yy' = 2x^3, \quad y(1) = 3; \quad 1 \leq x \leq 2$

14. $xy' = y^2, \quad y(1) = 1; \quad 1 \leq x \leq 2$

15. $xy' = 3x - 2y, \quad y(2) = 3; \quad 2 \leq x \leq 3$

16. $y^2y' = 2x^5, \quad y(2) = 3; \quad 2 \leq x \leq 3$

A computer with a printer is required for Problems 17 through 24. In these initial value problems, use Euler's method with step sizes $h = 0.1, 0.02, 0.004$, and 0.0008 to approximate to four decimal places the values of the solution at ten equally spaced points of the given interval. Print the results in tabular form with appropriate headings to make it easy to gauge the effect of varying the step size h.

17. $y' = x^2 + y^2, \quad y(0) = 0; \quad 0 \leq x \leq 1$

18. $y' = x^2 - y^2, \quad y(0) = 1; \quad 0 \leq x \leq 2$

19. $y' = x + \sqrt{y}, \quad y(0) = 1; \quad 0 \leq x \leq 2$

20. $\dfrac{dy}{dx} = x + \sqrt[3]{y}, \quad y(0) = -1; \quad 0 \leq x \leq 2$

21. $y' = \ln y, \quad y(1) = 2; \quad 1 \leq x \leq 2$

22. $y' = x^{2/3} + y^{2/3}, \quad y(0) = 1; \quad 0 \leq x \leq 2$

23. $y' = \sin x + \cos y, \quad y(0) = 0; \quad 0 \leq x \leq 1$

24. $\dfrac{dy}{dx} = \dfrac{x}{1 + y^2}, \quad y(-1) = 1; \quad -1 \leq x \leq 1$

25. Consider the initial value problem

$$7x\frac{dy}{dx} + y = 0, \qquad y(-1) = 1.$$

(a) Solve this problem for the exact solution

$$y(x) = -\frac{1}{x^{1/7}},$$

which has an infinite discontinuity at $x = 0$. (b) Apply Euler's method with step size $h = 0.15$ to approximate this solution on

the interval $-1 \leq x \leq 0.5$. Note that, from these data alone, you might not suspect any difficulty near $x = 0$. The reason is that the numerical approximation "jumps across the discontinuity" to another solution of $7xy' + y = 0$ for $x > 0$. (c) Finally, apply Euler's method again with step sizes $h = 0.03$ and $h = 0.006$, but still printing results only at the original points $x = -1.00$, $-0.85, -0.70, \ldots, 1.20, 1.35, 1.50$. Would you now suspect a discontinuity in the exact solution?

26. Apply Euler's method with successively smaller step sizes on the interval $[0, 2]$ to verify empirically that the solution of the initial value problem

$$\frac{dy}{dx} = x^2 + y^2, \qquad y(0) = 0$$

has a vertical asymptote near $x = 2.003147$. (Contrast this with Example 2, in which $y(0) = 1$.)

27. The general solution of the equation

$$\frac{dy}{dx} = (1 + y^2)\cos x$$

is $y(x) = \tan(C + \sin x)$. With the initial condition $y(0) = 0$ the solution $y(x) = \tan(\sin x)$ is well-behaved. But with $y(0) = 1$ the solution $y(x) = \tan(\frac{1}{4}\pi + \sin x)$ has a vertical asymptote at $x = \sin^{-1}(\pi/4) \approx 0.90334$. Use Euler's method to verify this fact empirically.

2.4 Computing Project

One's understanding of a numerical algorithm is sharpened by considering its implementation in the form of a calculator or computer program. Figure 2.4.7 lists TI-85 and BASIC programs implementing Euler's method to approximate the solution of the initial value problem

$$\frac{dy}{dx} = x + y, \qquad y(0) = 1$$

considered in Example 1 of this section. The comments provided in the final column should make these programs intelligible even if you have little familiarity with the BASIC and Texas Instruments programming languages.

To increase the number of steps (and thereby decrease the step size) you need only change the value of **N** specified in the first line of the program. To apply Euler's method to a different equation $dy/dx = f(x, y)$, you need only change the single line that calculates the function value **F**.

Any other procedural programming language (such as FORTRAN or Pascal) would follow the pattern illustrated by the parallel lines of TI-85 and BASIC code in

TI-85	BASIC	Comment
PROGRAM:EULER	Program EULER	Program title
:10→N	N = 10	Number of steps
:0→X	X = 0	Initial x
:1→Y	Y = 1	Initial y
:1→X1	X1 = 1	Final x
:(X1-X)/N→H	H = (X1-X)/N	Step size
:For(I,1,N)	FOR I=1 TO N	Begin loop
:X+Y→F	F = X + Y	Function value
:Y+H*F→Y	Y = Y + H*F	Euler iteration
:X+H→X	X = X + H	New x
:Disp X,Y	PRINT X,Y	Display results
:End	NEXT I	End loop

FIGURE 2.4.7. TI-85 and BASIC Euler's method programs

```
function yp = f(x,y)
yp = x + y;                          % yp = y'

function  [X,Y] = euler(x,y,x1,n)
h = (x1 - x)/n;                      % step size
X = x;                               % initial x
Y = y;                               % initial y
for i = 1:n                          % begin loop
    y = y + h*f(x,y);                % Euler iteration
    x = x + h;                       % new x
    X = [X;x];                       % update x-column
    Y = [Y;y];                       % update y-column
end                                  % end loop
```

FIGURE 2.4.8. MATLAB implementation of Euler's method

Fig. 2.4.7. Some of the modern functional programming languages mirror standard mathematical notation even more closely. Figure 2.4.8 exhibits a MATLAB implementation of Euler's method. The **euler** function takes as input the initial value **x**, the initial value **y**, the final value **x1** of x, and the desired number **n** of subintervals. As output it produces the resulting column vectors **X** and **Y** of x- and y-values. For instance, the MATLAB command

 [X, Y] = euler(0, 1, 1, 10)

then generates the x_n- and y_n-columns of data shown in the table of Fig. 2.4.1.

For this project, you should implement Euler's method on your calculator or in a programming language of your choice. Test your program by application first to the initial value problem of Example 1, and then to some of the problems for this section.

2.5 A Closer Look at the Euler Method

The Euler method as presented in Section 2.4 is not often used in practice, mainly because more accurate methods are available. But Euler's method has the advantage of simplicity, and a careful study of this method yields insights into the workings of the more accurate methods, because many of the latter are extensions or refinements of the Euler method. In order to compare two different methods of numerical approximation, we need some way to measure the accuracy of each. Theorem 1 tells what degree of accuracy we can expect when we use Euler's method.

THEOREM 1: The Error in the Euler Method

Suppose that the initial value problem

$$\frac{dy}{dx} = f(x, y), \qquad y(a) = y_0 \tag{1}$$

has a unique solution $y(x)$ on the closed interval $[a, b]$, and assume that $y(x)$ has a continuous second derivative on $[a, b]$. (This would follow from the assumption that $f, f_x,$

and f_y are all continuous for $a \leqq x \leqq b$ and $c \leqq y \leqq d$, where $c \leqq y(x) \leqq d$ for all x in $[a, b]$.) Then there exists a constant C such that the following is true: If the approximations $y_1, y_2, y_3, \ldots, y_k$ to the actual values $y(x_1), y(x_2), y(x_3), \ldots, y(x_k)$ at points of $[a, b]$ are computed using Euler's method with step size $h > 0$, then

$$|y_n - y(x_n)| \leqq Ch \tag{2}$$

for each $n = 1, 2, 3, \ldots, k$. ■

> *Remark:* The **error**
>
> $$y_{\text{actual}} - y_{\text{approx}} = y(x_n) - y_n$$
>
> in (2) denotes the [cumulative] error in Euler's method after n steps in the approximation, *exclusive* of roundoff error (as though we were using a perfect machine that made no roundoff errors). The theorem can be summarized by saying that *the error in Euler's method is of order h*; that is, the error is bounded by a [predetermined] constant C multiplied by the step size h. It follows, for instance, that (on a given closed interval) halving the step size cuts the maximum error in half; similarly, with step size $h/10$ we get 10 times the accuracy (that is, $1/10$ the maximum error) as with step size h. Consequently, we can—in principle—get any degree of accuracy we want by choosing h sufficiently small.

We will omit the proof of this theorem, but one can be found in Chapter 7 of G. Birkhoff and G.-C. Rota, *Ordinary Differential Equations,* 4th ed. (New York: John Wiley, 1989). The constant C deserves some comment. Because C tends to increase as the maximum value of $|y''(x)|$ on $[a, b]$ increases, it follows that C must depend in a fairly complicated way upon y, and actual computation of a value of C such that (2) holds is usually impractical. In practice, the following type of procedure is commonly employed.

1. Apply Euler's method to the initial value problem in (1) with a reasonable value of h.

2. Repeat with $h/2$, $h/4$, and so forth, at each stage halving the step size for the next application of Euler's method.

3. Continue until the results obtained at one stage agree—to an appropriate number of significant digits—with those obtained at the previous stage. Then the approximate values obtained at this stage are considered likely to be accurate to the indicated number of significant digits.

EXAMPLE 1 Carry out this procedure with the initial value problem

$$\frac{dy}{dx} = -\frac{2xy}{1 + x^2}, \qquad y(0) = 1 \tag{3}$$

to approximate accurately the value $y(1)$ of the solution at $x = 1$.

Solution Using an Euler method program, perhaps one of those listed in Figs. 2.4.7 and 2.4.8, we begin with a step size $h = 0.04$ requiring $n = 25$ steps to reach $x = 1$. The table in Fig. 2.5.1 shows the approximate values of $y(1)$ obtained with suc-

h	Approximate $y(1)$	Actual $y(1)$	$\lvert\text{Error}\rvert/h$
0.04	0.50451	0.50000	0.11
0.02	0.50220	0.50000	0.11
0.01	0.50109	0.50000	0.11
0.005	0.50054	0.50000	0.11
0.0025	0.50027	0.50000	0.11
0.00125	0.50013	0.50000	0.10
0.000625	0.50007	0.50000	0.11
0.0003125	0.50003	0.50000	0.10

FIGURE 2.5.1. Table of values in Example 1

cessively smaller values of h. The data suggest that the true value of $y(1)$ is exactly 0.5. Indeed, the exact solution of the initial value problem in (3) is $y(1) = 1/(1 + x^2)$, so the true value of $y(1)$ is exactly $\frac{1}{2}$. ∎

The final column of the table in Fig. 2.5.1 displays the ratio of the magnitude of the error to h; that is, $\lvert y_{\text{actual}} - y_{\text{approx}}\rvert/h$. Observe how the data in this column substantiate the theorem above—in this computation, the error bound in (2) appears to hold with a value of C perhaps slightly larger than $1/10$.

An Improvement in Euler's Method

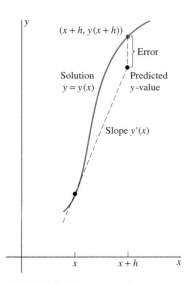

As Fig. 2.5.2 shows, Euler's method is rather unsymmetrical. It uses the predicted slope $k = f(x_n, y_n)$ of the graph of the solution at the left-hand endpoint of the interval $[x_n, x_n + h]$ as if it were the actual slope of the solution over that entire interval. We now turn our attention to a way in which increased accuracy can easily be obtained; it is known as the *improved Euler method*.

Given the initial value problem

$$\frac{dy}{dx} = f(x, y), \qquad y(x_0) = y_0, \tag{4}$$

suppose that after carrying out n steps with step size h we have computed the approximation y_n to the actual value $y(x_n)$ of the solution at $x_n = x_0 + nh$. We can use the Euler method to obtain a first estimate—which we now call u_{n+1} rather than y_{n+1}—of the value of the solution at $x_{n+1} = x_n + h$. Thus

▶ $$u_{n+1} = y_n + h \cdot f(x_n, y_n) = y_n + h \cdot k_1.$$

Now that $u_{n+1} \approx y(x_{n+1})$ has been computed, we can take

▶ $$k_2 = f(x_{n+1}, u_{n+1})$$

as a prediction of the slope of the solution curve $y = y(x)$ at $x = x_{n+1}$.

Of course, the approximate slope $k_1 = f(x_n, y_n)$ at $x = x_n$ has already been calculated. Why not *average* these two slopes to obtain a more accurate estimate of the average slope of the solution curve over the entire subinterval $[x_n, x_{n+1}]$? This idea is the essence of the *improved* Euler method. Figure 2.5.3 shows the geometry behind this method.

FIGURE 2.5.2. True and predicted values in Euler's method

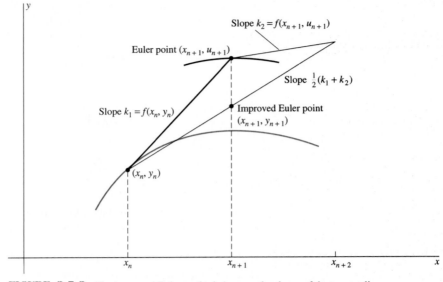

FIGURE 2.5.3. The improved Euler method: Average the slopes of the tangent lines at (x_n, y_n) and (x_{n+1}, u_{n+1}).

ALGORITHM: The Improved Euler Method

Given the initial value problem

$$\frac{dy}{dx} = f(x, y), \qquad y(x_0) = y_0,$$

the **improved Euler method with step size** h consists in applying the iterative formulas

$$k_1 = f(x_n, y_n),$$
$$u_{n+1} = y_n + h \cdot k_1,$$
$$k_2 = f(x_{n+1}, u_{n+1}),$$
$$y_{n+1} = y_n + h \cdot \frac{1}{2}(k_1 + k_2) \tag{5}$$

to compute successive approximations y_1, y_2, y_3, \ldots to the [true] values $y(x_1)$, $y(x_2), y(x_3), \ldots$ of the [exact] solution $y = y(x)$ at the points x_1, x_2, x_3, \ldots, respectively. ∎

Remark: Note that the final formula in (5) takes the "Euler form"

$$y_{n+1} = y_n + h \cdot k$$

if we write

$$k = \frac{k_1 + k_2}{2}$$

for the approximate *average slope* on the interval $[x_n, x_{n+1}]$.

The improved Euler method is one of a class of numerical techniques known as **predictor–corrector** methods. First a predictor u_{n+1} of the next y-value is computed; then it is used to correct itself. Thus the **improved Euler method** with step size h consists in using the **predictor**

▶
$$u_{n+1} = y_n + h \cdot f(x_n, y_n) \tag{6}$$

and the **corrector**

▶
$$y_{n+1} = y_n + h \cdot \frac{1}{2}[f(x_n, y_n) + f(x_{n+1}, u_{n+1})] \tag{7}$$

iteratively to compute successive approximations y_1, y_2, y_3, \ldots to the values $y(x_1)$, $y(x_2)$, $y(x_3)$, . . . of the actual solution of the initial value problem in (4).

Remark: Note that each improved Euler step requires two evaluations of the function $f(x, y)$, as compared with the single function evaluation required for an ordinary Euler step. We naturally wonder whether this doubled computational labor is worth the trouble.

Answer: Under the assumption that the exact solution $y = y(x)$ of the initial value problem in (4) has a continuous third derivative, it can be proved—see Chapter 7 of Birkhoff and Rota—that the error in the improved Euler method is of order h^2. This means that on a given bounded interval $[a, b]$, each approximate value y_n satisfies the inequality

▶
$$|y(x_n) - y_n| \le Ch^2 \tag{8}$$

where the constant C does not depend upon h. Because h^2 is much smaller than h if h itself is small, this means that the improved Euler method is more accurate than Euler's method itself. This advantage is offset by the fact that about twice as many computations are required. But the factor h^2 in (8) means that halving the step size results in $1/4$ the maximum error, while with step size $h/10$ we get 100 times the accuracy (that is, $1/100$ the maximum error) as with step size h.

EXAMPLE 2 In Example 1 of Section 2.4 we applied Euler's method to the initial value problem

$$\frac{dy}{dx} = x + y, \qquad y(0) = 1 \tag{9}$$

with exact solution $y(x) = 2e^x - x - 1$. With $f(x, y) = x + y$ in (6) and (7), the predictor–corrector formulas for the improved Euler method are

$$u_{n+1} = y_n + h \cdot (x_n + y_n),$$

$$y_{n+1} = y_n + h \cdot \frac{1}{2}[(x_n + y_n) + (x_{n+1} + u_{n+1})].$$

With step size $h = 0.1$ we calculate

$$u_1 = 1 + (0.1) \cdot (0 + 1) = 1.1,$$

$$y_1 = 1 + (0.05) \cdot [(0 + 1) + (0.1 + 1.1)] = 1.11,$$

$$u_2 = 1.11 + (0.1) \cdot (0.1 + 1.11) = 1.231,$$

$$y_2 = 1.11 + (0.05) \cdot [(0.1 + 1.11) + (0.2 + 1.231)] = 1.24205,$$

x	Euler method, $h = 0.1$, Values of y	Euler method, $h = 0.005$, Values of y	Improved Euler, $h = 0.1$, Values of y	Actual y
0.1	1.1000	1.1098	1.1100	1.1103
0.2	1.2200	1.2416	1.2421	1.2428
0.3	1.3620	1.3977	1.3985	1.3997
0.4	1.5282	1.5807	1.5818	1.5836
0.5	1.7210	1.7933	1.7949	1.7974
0.6	1.9431	2.0388	2.0409	2.0442
0.7	2.1974	2.3205	2.3231	2.3275
0.8	2.4872	2.6422	2.6456	2.6511
0.9	2.8159	3.0082	3.0124	3.0192
1.0	3.1875	3.4230	3.4282	3.4366

FIGURE 2.5.4. Euler and improved Euler approximations to the solution of $dy/dx = x + y$, $y(0) = 1$

and so forth. The table in Fig. 2.5.4 compares the results obtained using the improved Euler method with those obtained previously using the "unimproved" Euler method. When the same step size $h = 0.1$ is used, the error in the Euler approximation to $y(1)$ is 7.25%, whereas the error in the improved Euler approximation is only 0.24%.

Indeed, the improved Euler method with $h = 0.1$ is more accurate (in this example) than the original Euler method with $h = 0.005$. The latter requires 200 evaluations of the function $f(x, y)$, while the former requires only 20 such evaluations, so in this case the improved Euler method yields greater accuracy with only about one-tenth the work!

Figure 2.5.5 shows the results obtained when the improved Euler method is applied to the initial value problem in (9) using step size $h = 0.005$. Accuracy of five significant figures is apparent in the table. This suggests that, in contrast with the original Euler method, the improved Euler method is sufficiently accurate for certain types of practical applications—such as plotting solution curves. ■

An improved Euler program (similar to the ones listed in the project material for this section) was used to compute approximations to the exact value $y(1) = 0.5$ of the solution $y(x) = 1/(1 + x^2)$ of the initial value problem

$$\frac{dy}{dx} = -\frac{2xy}{1 + x^2}, \qquad y(0) = 1 \tag{3}$$

of Example 1. The results obtained by successively halving the step size appear in the table in Fig. 2.5.6. Note that the final column of this table impressively corroborates the form of the error bound in (8), and that each halving of the step size reduces the error by a factor of almost exactly 4, as should happen if the error is proportional to h^2.

Taylor Series Methods

Another way to improve Euler's method of approximating the solution of $dy/dx = f(x, y)$, $y(x_0) = y_0$ is to use the Taylor series

x	Improved Euler, Approximate y	Actual y
0.0	1.00000	1.00000
0.1	1.11034	1.11034
0.2	1.24280	1.24281
0.3	1.39971	1.39972
0.4	1.58364	1.58365
0.5	1.79744	1.79744
0.6	2.04423	2.04424
0.7	2.32749	2.32751
0.8	2.65107	2.65108
0.9	3.01919	3.01921
1.0	3.43654	3.43656

FIGURE 2.5.5. Improved Euler approximations to the solution of Eq. (9) with step size $h = 0.005$

h	Improved Euler Approximation to y(1)	Error	\|Error\|/h^2
0.04	0.500195903	-0.000195903	0.12
0.02	0.500049494	-0.000049494	0.12
0.01	0.500012437	-0.000012437	0.12
0.005	0.500003117	-0.000003117	0.12
0.0025	0.500000780	-0.000000780	0.12
0.00125	0.500000195	-0.000000195	0.12
0.000625	0.500000049	-0.000000049	0.12
0.0003125	0.500000012	-0.000000012	0.12

FIGURE 2.5.6. Improved Euler approximation to $y(1)$ for $dy/dx = -2xy/(1 + x^2)$, $y(0) = 1$

$$y(a + h) = y(a) + hy'(a) + \frac{h^2}{2!} y''(a) + \frac{h^3}{3!} y'''(a) + \cdots \tag{10}$$

at each step. If we substitute $a = x_n$, $a + h = x_{n+1}$ and retain only the first two terms on the right-hand side, then (10) yields the linear approximation

$$y(x_{n+1}) \approx y(x_n) + h \cdot y'(x_n).$$

With $y(x_n) \approx y_n$ and $y'(x_n) \approx f(x_n, y_n)$ this is simply the iterative formula

$$y_{n+1} = y_n + h \cdot f(x_n, y_n)$$

of the original Euler method.

The idea now is to improve the accuracy at each step by retaining more terms of the Taylor series in (10). Retention of *three* terms gives

$$y(x_{n+1}) \approx y(x_n) + h \cdot y'(x_n) + \frac{1}{2} h^2 \cdot y''(x_n). \tag{11}$$

Because $y'(x) = f(x, y)$ is our differential equation, the second derivative on the right in (11) is given by the chain rule:

$$y''(x) = \frac{d}{dx} [f(x, y)] = f_x(x, y) + f_y(x, y)f(x, y). \tag{12}$$

When the indicated derivatives are evaluated at the point (x_n, y_n), Eq. (11) therefore yields the approximation

$$y_{n+1} = y_n + h \cdot f(x_n, y_n) + \frac{1}{2} h^2 \cdot [f_x(x_n, y_n) + f_y(x_n, y_n)f(x_n, y_n)] \tag{13}$$

to the actual value $y(x_{n+1})$ of the solution.

The use of the iterative formula in (13), to compute successive approximations y_1, y_2, y_3, . . . to the actual values $y(x_1)$, $y(x_2)$, $y(x_3)$, . . . of the solution of the initial value problem in (4), constitutes the **three-term Taylor series method** with step size h. Like the improved Euler method on a given bounded interval $[a, b]$, this method has a [cumulative] error of order h^2. For this reason, and also because it results from re-

taining terms through h^2 in the Taylor series, it is sometimes called the **Taylor series method of order 2.** The Taylor series method of order 1 is simply Euler's method.

EXAMPLE 3 Compare the improved Euler method with the three-term Taylor series method when each is applied to the initial value problem

$$\frac{dy}{dx} = 2xy, \qquad y(0) = 1 \tag{14}$$

on the interval [0, 1].

Solution Figure 2.5.7 lists a simple TI-85 program that implements the three-term Taylor series method. The first three lines define the function $f(x, y)$ and its partial derivatives $\partial f/\partial z$ and $\partial f/\partial y$; the remaining lines are explained by the comments.

TI-85	Comment
PROGRAM:TAYLOR3	Program title
:F=2*X*Y	Function f(x,y)
:FX=2*Y	Derivative wrt x
:FY=2*X	Derivative wrt y
:100→N	No. of steps
:0→X	Initial x
:1→Y	Initial y
:1→X1	Final x
:(X1–X)/N→H	Step size
:For(I,1,N)	Begin loop
:Y+H*F+(H*H/2)*(FX+F*FY)→Y	Taylor formula
:X+H→X	New x
:Disp X,Y	Display results
:End	End loop

FIGURE 2.5.7. TI-85 program implementing the three-term Taylor series method

The table in Fig. 2.5.8 shows the results obtained using the improved Euler method and the three-term Taylor series method, each with step size $h = 0.01$. The final column shows values of the exact solution $y(x) = e^{x^2}$. In this particular problem

x	Improved Euler y	Three-term Taylor y	Actual y
0.1	1.01005	1.01005	1.01005
0.2	1.04081	1.04081	1.04081
0.3	1.09417	1.09416	1.09417
0.4	1.17351	1.17349	1.17351
0.5	1.28402	1.28399	1.28403
0.6	1.43332	1.43327	1.43333
0.7	1.63230	1.63222	1.63232
0.8	1.89645	1.89634	1.89648
0.9	2.24786	2.24768	2.24791
1.0	2.71819	2.71793	2.71828

FIGURE 2.5.8. Approximating the solution in Example 3 with $h = 0.01$

the improved Euler method is slightly more accurate than the three-term Taylor series method, though in another problem the reverse might be true. ∎

If the function $f(x, y)$ is sufficiently simple that the calculation of higher order partial derivatives is feasible, then more than three terms of the Taylor series

$$y(x_{n+1}) = y(x_n) + h \cdot y'(x_n) + \frac{h^2}{2!} \cdot y''(x_n) + \frac{h^3}{3!} \cdot y'''(x_n) + \cdots \tag{15}$$

can be retained at each step. The **Taylor series method of order** k consists of using at each step all terms in (15) through the one involving h^k, and it is known that (on a fixed bounded interval) the [cumulative] error in the Taylor series method of order k is of order h^k; that is, $|y(x_n) - y_n| \leq C|h|^k$ for some constant C. The disadvantage of these methods is that the higher order derivatives in (15) may be very tedious to compute analytically. Example 4 illustrates the great accuracy that higher order Taylor series offer when they are practical. It also demonstrates the use of a *negative* step size to step backward rather than forward.

EXAMPLE 4 Consider the initial value problem

$$\frac{dy}{dx} = y^2, \qquad y(1) = 1, \tag{16}$$

whose exact solution for $x < 2$ is $y(x) = 1/(2 - x)$. To obtain the Taylor polynomial of degree 4, for instance, we begin with the differential equation in (16) and compute the following derivatives:

$$\begin{aligned} y' &= y^2, \\ y'' &= 2yy' = 2y^3, \\ y^{(3)} &= 6y^2y' = 6y^4, \\ y^{(4)} &= 24y^3y' = 24y^5. \end{aligned} \tag{17}$$

Thus

$$y(x + h) \approx y + hy^2 + h^2y^3 + h^3y^4 + h^4y^5,$$

with y in place of $y(x)$ on the right-hand side. Hence the iterative formula for the Taylor series method of order 4 is

$$y_{n+1} = y_n + hy_n^2 + h^2y_n^3 + h^3y_n^4 + h^4y_n^5;$$

that is,

$$y_{n+1} = y_n(1 + hy_n\{1 + hy_n[1 + hy_n(1 + hy_n)]\}) \tag{18}$$

in the "stacked" form that is more convenient for automated computation.

It is clear from the pattern in (17) that $y^{(p)} = p!y^{p+1}$ for all $p > 0$. It follows that the iterative formula for the Taylor series of order p for the problem in (16) is the pth degree analogue of the 4th degree (in h) stacked polynomial in (18). Figure 2.5.9 shows an *ad hoc* program written to carry out Taylor series approximations to the solution of (16) when the desired order p is entered. Figure 2.5.10 shows the results of applying the Taylor series method with orders $p = 4$, $p = 6$, $p = 8$, and step size $h = -0.05$, so that only 20 steps are required to reach $x = 0$, where $y(0) = \frac{1}{2}$. With $p = 8$ the results are correct to 10 decimal places on the entire interval.

BASIC	Comment
Program EX4	Program title
P = 4	Order of method
X = 1	Initial x-value
Y = 1	Initial y-value
N = 20	Number of steps
H = -0.05	Step size
For I = 1 to N	Begin I-loop
V = 0	Initialize poly
For J = 1 to P	Calculating the stacked
V = H*Y*(1 + V)	poly in Eq. (18)
NEXT J	End J-loop
Y = Y*(1+V)	Update y
X = X + H	Update x
NEXT I	End I-loop

FIGURE 2.5.9. BASIC program for Example 4

x	Order $m = 4$ Approximate y	Order $m = 6$ Approximate y	Order $m = 8$ Approximate y	Actual y
1.0	1.0000000000	1.0000000000	1.0000000000	1.0000000000
0.8	0.8333340327	0.8333333349	0.8333333333	0.8333333333
0.6	0.7142864839	0.7142857158	0.7142857143	0.7142857143
0.4	0.6250006974	0.6250000013	0.6250000000	0.6250000000
0.2	0.5555561577	0.5555555566	0.5555555556	0.5555555556
0.0	0.5000005139	0.5000000009	0.5000000000	0.5000000000

FIGURE 2.5.10. Using the Taylor series method with step size $h = -0.05$ to approximate the solution of the initial value problem in Eq. (16)

2.5 Problems

A hand-held calculator will suffice for Problems 1 through 10. In each problem, find the exact solution of the given initial value problem. Then apply both (a) the improved Euler method, and (b) the three-term Taylor series method to approximate to four decimal places this solution on the interval [0, 0.05] with step size $h = 0.1$. Make a table showing the approximate values and the actual values of the solution at the points $x = 0.1, 0.2, 0.3, 0.4,$ and 0.5.

1. $\dfrac{dy}{dx} = -y, \quad y(0) = 2$

2. $\dfrac{dy}{dx} = 2y, \quad y(0) = \frac{1}{2}$

3. $\dfrac{dy}{dx} = y + 1, \quad y(0) = 1$

4. $\dfrac{dy}{dx} = x - y, \quad y(0) = 1$

5. $\dfrac{dy}{dx} = y - x - 1, \quad y(0) = 1$

6. $\dfrac{dy}{dx} = -2xy, \quad y(0) = 2$

7. $\dfrac{dy}{dx} = -3x^2 y, \quad y(0) = 3$

8. $\dfrac{dy}{dx} = e^{-y}, \quad y(0) = 0$

9. $\dfrac{dy}{dx} = \dfrac{1}{4}(1 + y^2), \quad y(0) = 1$

10. $\dfrac{dy}{dx} = 2xy^2, \quad y(0) = 1$

Note: The project following this problem set lists illustrative calculator/computer programs that can be used in Problems 11 through 24.

A programmable calculator or a computer will be useful for Problems 11 through 16. In each problem, find the exact solution of the given initial value problem. Then apply the improved Euler method twice to approximate (to five decimal places) this solution on the given interval, first with step size $h = 0.01$, then with step size $h = 0.005$. Make a table showing the approximate values and the actual values, together with the percentage errors in the more accurate approximations, when x is an integral multiple of 0.2. Throughout, y' is an abbreviation for dy/dx.

11. $\dfrac{dy}{dx} = y - 2, \quad y(0) = 1; \quad 0 \le x \le 1$

12. $\dfrac{dy}{dx} = \frac{1}{2}(y - 1)^2, \quad y(0) = 2; \quad 0 \le x \le 1$

13. $yy' = 2x^3, \quad y(1) = 3; \quad 1 \le x \le 2$

14. $xy' = y^2, \quad y(1) = 1; \quad 1 \le x \le 2$

15. $xy' = 3x - 2y, \quad y(2) = 3; \quad 2 \le x \le 3$

16. $y^2y' = 2x^5, \quad y(2) = 3; \quad 2 \le x \le 3$

A computer with a printer is required for Problems 17 through 24. In each of these initial value problems, use the improved Euler method with step sizes $h = 0.1, 0.02, 0.004$, and 0.0008 to approximate to five decimal places the values of the solution at ten equally spaced points of the given interval. Print the results in tabular form to make it easy to gauge the effect of varying the step size.

17. $y' = x^2 + y^2, \quad y(0) = 0; \quad 0 \le x \le 1$

18. $y' = x^2 - y^2, \quad y(0) = 1; \quad 0 \le x \le 2$

19. $y' = x + \sqrt{y}, \quad y(0) = 1; \quad 0 \le x \le 2$

20. $\dfrac{dy}{dx} = x + \sqrt[3]{y}, \quad y(0) = -1; \quad 0 \le x \le 2$

21. $y' = \ln y, \quad y(1) = 2; \quad 1 \le x \le 2$

22. $y' = x^{2/3} + y^{2/3}, \quad y(0) = 1; \quad 0 \le x \le 2$

23. $y' = \sin x + \cos y, \quad y(0) = 0; \quad 0 \le x \le 1$

24. $\dfrac{dy}{dx} = \dfrac{x}{1 + y^2}, \quad y(-1) = 1; \quad -1 \le x \le 1$

For each of the differential equations in Problems 25 through 27, write the iterative formula (for y_{n+1} in terms of y_n) for the Taylor series method of order 3.

25. $y' = 1 + y^2$

26. $y' = y + y^2$

27. $y' = (x + y)^2$

28. Show that for the initial value problem

$$\frac{dy}{dx} = y, \qquad y(0) = 1,$$

the iterative formula for the Taylor series method of order p is

$$y_{n+1} = \left(1 + h + \frac{h^2}{2!} + \cdots + \frac{h^p}{p!}\right) y_n.$$

Use this formula with various combinations of $h = 0.1, 0.2$, and $p = 4, 6, 8$ to approximate to nine decimal places the number $y(1) = e \approx 2.718281828$.

29. For the initial value problem

$$\frac{dy}{dx} = xy, \qquad y(0) = 1,$$

show that the successive derivatives of the solution are given by

$$y^{(k+1)} = xy^{(k)} + ky^{(k-1)}.$$

Then write a program to apply the Taylor series method of order p (with the value of p to be entered when the program is executed) to approximate the actual solution $y(x) = e^{x^2/2}$, $0 \le x \le 1$.

30. For the initial value problem

$$\frac{dy}{dx} = e^{-y}, \qquad y(0) = 0,$$

with exact solution $y(x) = \ln(1 + x)$ for $x > -1$, show that successive derivatives are given by

$$y^{(k)} = (-1)^{k+1}(k - 1)! \, e^{-ky}.$$

Hence conclude that the iterative formula for the Taylor series method of order p is

$$y_{n+1} = y_n + he^{-y_n} - \frac{1}{2}h^2e^{-2y_n} + \cdots + (-1)^{p+1}\frac{h^p}{p}e^{-py_n}.$$

31. Here is one idea that might yield an improvement in both the improved Euler method and the Taylor series method, and it depends upon combining the two. Suppose that x_n and y_n have both been computed for some value of n (and, of course, all previous values) in the initial value problem

$$\frac{dy}{dx} = f(x, y), \qquad y(a) = y_0. \tag{19}$$

Use the differential equation in (19) to compute estimates of $y'(x_n)$ and $y''(x_n)$, then use the Taylor series method to obtain a first estimate u_{n+1} of the solution at x_{n+1}. Next use the differential equation in (19) to compute estimates of $y'(x_{n+1})$ and $y''(x_{n+1})$. Then average the approximate first derivatives at the points x_n and x_{n+1}, and also average the approximate second derivatives there, to obtain [possibly better] estimates of y' and y'' over the interval $[x_n, x_{n+1}]$. Write a flowchart for this new algo-

rithm, write a program to implement it, and apply it to the initial value problem

$$\frac{dy}{dx} = 2xy, \qquad y(0) = 1$$

on [0, 1] discussed in Example 3 of this section. Comment on the results. (*Note:* Data for the improved Euler method and the three-term Taylor series method are shown in Fig. 2.5.8.)

2.5 Computing Project

Figure 2.5.11 lists TI-85 and BASIC programs implementing the improved Euler method to approximate the solution of the initial value problem

$$\frac{dy}{dx} = x + y, \qquad y(0) = 1$$

considered in Example 2 of this section. The comments provided in the final column should make these programs intelligible even if you have little familiarity with the BASIC and TI programming languages.

To apply the improved Euler method to a differential equation $dy/dx = f(x, y)$, one need only change the initial line of the program, in which the function f is defined. To increase the number of steps (and thereby decrease the step size) one need only change the value of **N** specified in the second line of the program.

Figure 2.5.12 exhibits one MATLAB implementation of the improved Euler method. The **impeuler** function takes as input the initial value **x**, the initial value **y**, the final value **x1** of x, and the desired number **n** of subintervals. As output it produces

TI-85	BASIC	Comment
`PROGRAM:IMPEULER`	`Program IMPEULER`	Program title
`:F=X+Y`	`DEF FN F(X,Y) = X+Y`	Define function f
`:10→N`	`N = 10`	No. of steps
`:0→X`	`X = 0`	Initial x
`:1→Y`	`Y = 1`	Initial y
`:1→X1`	`X1= 1`	Final x
`:(X1-X)/N→H`	`H = (X1-X)/N`	Step size
`:For(I,1,N)`	`FOR I=1 TO N`	Begin loop
`:Y→Y0`	`Y0 = Y`	Save previous y
`:F→K1`	`K1 = FNF(X,Y)`	First slope
`:Y0+H*K1→Y`	`Y = Y0 + H*K1`	Predictor
`:X+H→X`	`X = X + H`	New x
`:F→K2`	`K2 = FNF(X,Y)`	Second slope
`:(K1+K2)/2→K`	`K = (K1 + K2)/2`	Average slope
`:Y0+H*K→Y`	`Y = Y0 + H*K`	Corrector
`:Disp X,Y`	`PRINT X,Y`	Display results
`:End`	`NEXT I`	End loop

FIGURE 2.5.11. TI-85 and BASIC improved Euler programs

```
function yp = f(x,y)
yp = x + y;                          % yp = y'

function  [X,Y] = impeuler(x,y,x1,n)
h = (x1 - x)/n;                      % step size
X = x;                               % initial x
Y = y;                               % initial y
for i = 1 : n                        % begin loop
    k1 = f(x,y);                     % first slope
    k2 = f(x+h,y+h*k1);              % second slope
    k = (k1 + k2)/2;                 % average slope
    x = x + h;                       % new x
    y = y + h*k;                     % new y
    X = [X;x];                       % update x-column
    Y = [Y;y];                       % update y-column
    end                              % end loop
```

FIGURE 2.5.12. MATLAB implementation of the improved Euler method

the resulting column vectors **X** and **Y** of *x*- and *y*-values. For instance, the MATLAB command

```
[X, Y] = impeuler(0, 1, 1, 10)
```

then generates the first and fourth columns of data shown in the table of Fig. 2.5.4.

For this project, you should implement the improved Euler method in your calculator or programming language of choice. Test your program by application first to the initial value problem of Example 2, and then to some of the problems for this section.

2.6 The Runge–Kutta Method

We now discuss a method for approximating the solution $y = y(x)$ of the initial value problem

$$\frac{dy}{dx} = f(x, y), \qquad y(x_0) = y_0 \tag{1}$$

that is considerably more accurate than the improved Euler method, and is more widely used in practice than any of the numerical methods discussed in Sections 2.4 and 2.5. It is called the *Runge–Kutta method* and is named for the German mathematicians Carl Runge (1856–1927) and Wilhelm Kutta (1867–1944).

With the usual notation, suppose that we have computed the approximations y_1, y_2, y_3, . . . , y_n to the actual values $y(x_1)$, $y(x_2)$, $y(x_3)$, . . . , $y(x_n)$ and now want to compute $y_{n+1} \approx y(x_{n+1})$. Then

$$y(x_{n+1}) - y(x_n) = \int_{x_n}^{x_{n+1}} y'(x)\,dx = \int_{x_n}^{x_n+h} y'(x)\,dx \tag{2}$$

by the fundamental theorem of calculus. Next, Simpson's rule for numerical integra-

tion yields

$$y(x_{n+1}) - y(x_n) = \frac{h}{6}\left[y'(x_n) + 4y'\left(x_n + \frac{h}{2}\right) + y'(x_{n+1}) \right]. \tag{3}$$

Hence we want to define y_{n+1} so that

$$y_{n+1} \approx y_n + \frac{h}{6}\left[y'(x_n) + 2y'\left(x_n + \frac{h}{2}\right) + 2y'\left(x_n + \frac{h}{2}\right) + y'(x_{n+1}) \right]; \tag{4}$$

we have split $4y'(x_n + \frac{1}{2}h)$ into a sum of two terms because we intend to approximate the slope $y'(x + \frac{1}{2}h)$ at the midpoint $x_n + \frac{1}{2}h$ of the interval $[x_n, x_{n+1}]$ in two different ways.

On the right-hand side in (4), we replace the [true] slopes $y'(x_n)$, $y'(x_n + \frac{1}{2}h)$, $y'(x_n + \frac{1}{2}h)$, and $y'(x_{n+1})$, respectively, by the following estimates.

▶
$$k_1 = f(x_n, y_n). \tag{5a}$$

- This is the Euler method slope at x_n.

▶
$$k_2 = f\left(x_n + \frac{1}{2}h, y_n + \frac{1}{2}hk_1\right). \tag{5b}$$

- This is an estimate of the slope at the midpoint of the interval $[x_n, x_{n+1}]$ using the Euler method to predict the ordinate there.

▶
$$k_3 = f\left(x_n + \frac{1}{2}h, y_n + \frac{1}{2}hk_2\right). \tag{5c}$$

- This is an improved Euler value for the slope at the midpoint.

▶
$$k_4 = f(x_{n+1}, y_n + hk_3). \tag{5d}$$

- This is the Euler method slope at x_{n+1}, using the improved slope k_3 at the midpoint to step to x_{n+1}.

When these substitutions are made in (4), the result is the iterative formula

▶
$$y_{n+1} = y_n + \frac{h}{6}(k_1 + 2k_2 + 2k_3 + k_4). \tag{6}$$

The use of this formula to compute the approximations y_1, y_2, y_3, . . . successively constitutes the **Runge–Kutta method.** Note that Eq. (6) takes the "Euler form"

$$y_{n+1} = y_n + h \cdot k$$

if we write

$$k = \frac{1}{6}(k_1 + 2k_2 + 2k_3 + k_4)$$

for the approximate *average slope* on the interval $[x_n, x_{n+1}]$.

It happens that this method is equivalent in accuracy to the five-term (fourth degree) Taylor formula that uses in place of (6) the iterative formula

$$y_{n+1} = y_n + y'_n h + \frac{y''_n}{2!}h^2 + \frac{y^{(3)}_n}{3!}h^3 + \frac{y^{(4)}_n}{4!}h^4. \tag{7}$$

The Runge–Kutta method is, however, simpler to apply in practice because the computation of the numbers k_1, k_2, k_3, and k_4 in (5a) through (5d) involves only evaluation of the original function $f(x, y)$ in (1), whereas use of the Taylor formula in (7) requires high-order partial derivatives of f.

The Runge-Kutta method is a *fourth-order* method—it can be proved that the cumulative error on a bounded interval $[a, b]$ with $a = x_0$ is of order h^4. (Thus the iteration in (6) is sometimes called the *fourth-order* Runge–Kutta method because it is possible to develop Runge–Kutta methods of other orders.) That is,

▶
$$|y(x_n) - y_n| \leq Ch^4, \tag{8}$$

where the constant C depends on the function $f(x, y)$ and the interval $[a, b]$, but does not depend on the step size h. The following example illustrates this high accuracy in comparison with the lower-order accuracy of our previous numerical methods.

EXAMPLE 1 We first apply the Runge–Kutta method to the illustrative initial value problem

$$\frac{dy}{dx} = x + y, \qquad y(0) = 1 \tag{9}$$

that we considered in Example 1 of Section 2.4 and again in Example 2 of Section 2.5. The exact solution of this problem is $y(x) = 2e^x - x - 1$. To make a point we use $h = 0.5$, a larger step size than in any previous example, so only two steps are required to go from $x = 0$ to $x = 1$.

In the first step we use the formulas in (5) and (6) to calculate

$$k_1 = 0 + 1 = 1,$$

$$k_2 = (0 + 0.25) + (1 + (0.25) \cdot (1)) = 1.5,$$

$$k_3 = (0 + 0.25) + (1 + (0.25) \cdot (1.5)) = 1.625,$$

$$k_4 = (0.5) + (1 + (0.5) \cdot (1.625)) = 2.3125,$$

and thence

$$y_1 = 1 + \frac{0.5}{6} [1 + 2 \cdot (1.5) + 2 \cdot (1.625) + 2.3125] \approx 1.7969.$$

Similarly, the second step yields $y_2 \approx 3.4347$.

Figure 2.6.1 presents these results together with the results (from Fig. 2.5.4) of applying the improved Euler method with step size $h = 0.1$. We see that even with the larger step size, the Runge–Kutta method gives (for this problem) four to five times the accuracy (in terms of relative percentage errors) of the improved Euler method. ■

	Improved Euler		Runge–Kutta		
x	y with $h = 0.1$	Percent Error	y with $h = 0.5$	Percent Error	Actual y
0.0	1.0000	0.00%	1.0000	0.00%	1.0000
0.5	1.7949	0.14%	1.7969	0.03%	1.7974
1.0	3.4282	0.24%	3.4347	0.05%	3.4366

FIGURE 2.6.1. Runge–Kutta and improved Euler results for the initial value problem $dy/dx = x + y, y(0) = 1$

It is customary to measure the computational labor involved in solving $dy/dx = f(x, y)$ numerically by counting the number of evaluations of the function $f(x, y)$ that are required. In Example 1, the Runge–Kutta method required eight evaluations of $f(x, y) = x + y$ (four at each step), while the improved Euler method required 20 such evaluations (two for each of 10 steps). Thus the Runge–Kutta method gave over four times the accuracy with only 40% of the labor.

Computer programs implementing the Runge–Kutta method are listed in the project material for this section. Figure 2.6.2 shows the results obtained by applying the improved Euler and Runge–Kutta methods to the problem $dy/dx = x + y$, $y(0) = 1$ with the same step size $h = 0.1$. The relative error in the improved Euler value at $x = 1$ is about 0.24%, whereas for the Runge–Kutta value it is 0.00012%. In this comparison the Runge–Kutta method is about 2000 times as accurate, but requires only twice as many function evaluations, as the improved Euler method.

x	**Improved Euler y**	**Runge–Kutta y**	**Actual y**
0.1	1.1100	1.110342	1.110342
0.2	1.2421	1.242805	1.242806
0.3	1.3985	1.399717	1.399718
0.4	1.5818	1.583648	1.583649
0.5	1.7949	1.797441	1.797443
0.6	2.0409	2.044236	2.044238
0.7	2.3231	2.327503	2.327505
0.8	2.6456	2.651079	2.651082
0.9	3.0124	3.019203	3.019206
1.0	3.4282	3.436559	3.436564

FIGURE 2.6.2. Runge–Kutta and improved Euler results for the initial value problem $dy/dx = x + y$, $y(0) = 1$, with the same step size $h = 0.1$

The error bound

$$|y(x_n) - y_n| \leqq Ch^4 \tag{8}$$

for the Runge–Kutta method results in a rapid decrease in errors when the step size h is reduced (except for the possibility that very small step sizes may result in unacceptable roundoff errors). It follows from Eq. (8) that (on a fixed bounded interval) halving the step size decreases the absolute error by a factor of $(\frac{1}{2})^4 = \frac{1}{16}$. Consequently, the common practice of successively halving the step size until the computed results "stabilize" is particularly effective with the Runge–Kutta method.

EXAMPLE 2 In Example 2 of Section 2.4 we saw that Euler's method is not adequate to approximate the solution $y(x)$ of the initial value problem

$$\frac{dy}{dx} = x^2 + y^2, \qquad y(0) = 1 \tag{10}$$

as it approaches the infinite discontinuity near $x = 0.969811$ (see Fig. 2.6.3). Now we apply the Runge–Kutta method to this initial value problem.

Figure 2.6.4 shows Runge–Kutta results on the interval [0, 0.9], computed with

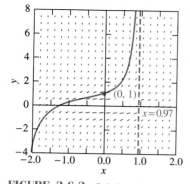

FIGURE 2.6.3. Solution of $y' = x^2 + y^2$, $y(0) = 1$

x	y with $h = 0.1$	y with $h = 0.05$	y with $h = 0.025$
0.1	1.1115	1.1115	1.1115
0.3	1.4397	1.4397	1.4397
0.5	2.0670	2.0670	2.0670
0.7	3.6522	3.6529	3.6529
0.9	14.0218	14.2712	14.3021

FIGURE 2.6.4. Approximating the solution of the initial value problem in (10)

step sizes $h = 0.1$, $h = 0.05$, and $h = 0.025$. There is still some difficulty near $x = 0.9$, but it seems safe to conclude from these data that $y(0.5) \approx 2.0670$.

We therefore start afresh and apply the Runge–Kutta method to the initial value problem.

$$\frac{dy}{dx} = x^2 + y^2, \qquad y(0.5) = 2.0670. \tag{11}$$

Figure 2.6.5 shows results on the interval [0.5, 0.9], obtained with step sizes $h = 0.01$, $h = 0.005$, and $h = 0.0025$. We now conclude that $y(0.9) \approx 14.3049$.

Finally, Fig. 2.6.6 shows results on the interval [0.90, 0.95] for the initial value problem

$$\frac{dy}{dx} = x^2 + y^2, \qquad y(0.9) = 14.3049, \tag{12}$$

x	y with $h = 0.01$	y with $h = 0.005$	y with $h = 0.0025$
0.5	2.0670	2.0670	2.0670
0.6	2.6440	2.6440	2.6440
0.7	3.6529	3.6529	3.6529
0.8	5.8486	5.8486	5.8486
0.9	14.3048	14.3049	14.3049

FIGURE 2.6.5. Approximating the solution of the initial value problem in (11)

x	y with $h = 0.002$	y with $h = 0.001$	y with $h = 0.0005$
0.90	14.3049	14.3049	14.3049
0.91	16.7024	16.7024	16.7024
0.92	20.0617	20.0617	20.0617
0.93	25.1073	25.1073	25.1073
0.94	33.5363	33.5363	33.5363
0.95	50.4722	50.4723	50.4723

FIGURE 2.6.6. Approximating the solution of the initial value problem in (12)

obtained using step sizes $h = 0.002$, $h = 0.001$, and $h = 0.0005$. Our final approximate result is $y(0.95) \approx 50.4723$. The actual value of the solution at $x = 0.95$ is $y(0.95) \approx 50.471867$. Our slight overestimate results mainly from the fact that the four-place initial value in (12) is (in effect) the result of rounding *up* the actual value $y(0.9) \approx 14.304864$; such errors are magnified considerably as we approach the vertical asymptote.

EXAMPLE 3 A skydiver jumps from an aircraft at an initial altitude of 10,000 ft. Assume that she falls vertically with initial velocity zero, weighs 128 lb, and experiences an upward force F_R of air resistance given in terms of her velocity v (in feet per second) by

$$F_R = (0.01)v + (0.001)v^2 + (0.0001)v^3$$

(in pounds, and with the coordinate axis directed downward so that $v > 0$). If she does not open her parachute, what will be her terminal velocity? How fast will she be falling after 5 s have elapsed? After 10 s? After 20 s?

> **Solution** With $g = 32$ ft/s^2, the skydiver's mass is $m = 4$ slugs, so Newton's law $F = ma$ yields

$$m \frac{dv}{dt} = mg - F_R;$$

that is,

$$4 \frac{dv}{dt} = 128 - (0.01)v - (0.001)v^2 - (0.0001)v^3. \tag{13}$$

Thus the velocity $v(t)$ satisfies the initial value problem

$$\frac{dv}{dt} = f(v), \qquad v(0) = 0, \tag{14}$$

where

$$f(v) = 32 - (0.000025) \cdot (100v + 10v^2 + v^3). \tag{15}$$

The skydiver reaches her terminal velocity when the forces of gravity and air resistance balance, so $f(v) = 0$. We therefore can calculate her terminal velocity immediately by the simple expedient of solving the equation

$$32 - (0.000025) \cdot (100v + 10v^2 + v^3) = 0. \tag{16}$$

Using Newton's method we find that her terminal velocity is approximately 105.046 ft/s, approximately 71.6 mi/h.

Figure 2.6.7 shows the results of Runge–Kutta approximations to the solution of the initial value problem in (14); the step sizes $h = 0.2$ and $h = 0.1$ yield the same results (to three decimal places). Observe that the terminal velocity is effectively attained in only 16 s. But the skydiver's velocity is 95.35% of her terminal velocity after only 5 s, and 99.94% after 10 s. ∎

t (s)	v (ft/s)
1	31.675
2	60.264
3	81.423
4	93.933
5	100.163
6	102.972
7	104.178
8	104.685
9	104.897
10	104.984
11	105.020
12	105.035
13	105.042
14	105.044
15	105.045
16	105.046
17	105.046
18	105.046
19	105.046
20	105.046

FIGURE 2.6.7. Data in Example 3

The final example of this section contains a *warning:* For certain types of initial value problems, the numerical methods we have discussed are not nearly so successful as in the previous examples.

x	Runge–Kutta y with $h = 0.2$	Runge–Kutta y with $h = 0.1$	Runge–Kutta y with $h = 0.05$	Actual y
0.4	0.66880	0.67020	0.67031	0.67032
0.8	0.43713	0.44833	0.44926	0.44933
1.2	0.21099	0.29376	0.30067	0.30199
1.6	− 0.46019	0.14697	0.19802	0.20190
2.0	− 4.72142	− 0.27026	0.10668	0.13534
2.4	− 35.53415	− 2.90419	− 0.12102	0.09072
2.8	− 261.25023	− 22.05352	− 1.50367	0.06081
3.2	− 1,916.69395	− 163.25077	− 11.51868	0.04076
3.6	− 14,059.35494	− 1205.71249	− 85.38156	0.02732
4.0	− 103,126.5270	− 8903.12866	− 631.03934	0.01832

FIGURE 2.6.8. Runge–Kutta attempts to solve numerically the initial value problem in (17)

EXAMPLE 4 Consider the seemingly innocuous initial value problem

$$\frac{dy}{dx} = 5y - 6e^{-x}, \qquad y(0) = 1 \tag{17}$$

whose exact solution is $y(x) = e^{-x}$. The table in Fig. 2.6.8 shows the results obtained by applying the Runge–Kutta method on the interval [0, 4] with step sizes $h = 0.2$, $h = 0.1$, and $h = 0.05$. Obviously, these attempts are spectacularly unsuccessful. Although $y(x) = e^{-x} \to 0$ as $x \to +\infty$, it appears that our numerical approximations are headed toward $-\infty$ rather than zero.

The explanation lies in the fact that the general solution of the equation $dy/dx = 5y - 6e^{-x}$ is

$$y(x) = e^{-x} + Ce^{5x}. \tag{18}$$

The particular solution of (17) satisfying the initial condition $y(0) = 1$ is obtained with $C = 0$. But any departure, however small, from the exact solution $y(x) = e^{-x}$—even if due only to roundoff error—introduces [in effect] a nonzero value of C in (18). And as indicated in Fig. 2.6.9, all solution curves of the form in (18) with $C \neq 0$ diverge strongly away from the one with $C = 0$, even if their initial values are close to 1. ■

Difficulties of the sort illustrated by Example 4 sometimes are unavoidable, but one can at least hope to recognize such a problem when it appears. Approximate values whose order of magnitude varies with changing step size are a common indicator of such instability. These difficulties are discussed in numerical analysis textbooks and are the subject of current research in the field.

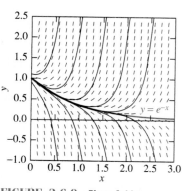

FIGURE 2.6.9. Slope field and solution curves for $y' = 5y - 6e^{-x}$

2.6 Problems

A hand-held calculator will suffice for Problems 1 through 10. In each problem, find the exact solution of the given initial value problem. Then apply the Runge–Kutta method with step size $h = 0.25$ to approximate to five decimal places this solution on the interval [0, 0.5]. Make a table showing the approximate values and the actual values of the solution at the points $x = 0.25$ and $x = 0.50$.

1. $\dfrac{dy}{dx} = -y, \quad y(0) = 2$

2. $\dfrac{dy}{dx} = 2y, \quad y(0) = \dfrac{1}{2}$

3. $\dfrac{dy}{dx} = y + 1, \quad y(0) = 1$

4. $\dfrac{dy}{dx} = x - y, \quad y(0) = 1$

5. $\dfrac{dy}{dx} = y - x - 1, \quad y(0) = 1$

6. $\dfrac{dy}{dx} = -2xy, \quad y(0) = 2$

7. $\dfrac{dy}{dx} = -3x^2y, \quad y(0) = 3$

8. $\dfrac{dy}{dx} = e^{-y}, \quad y(0) = 0$

9. $\dfrac{dy}{dx} = \dfrac{1}{4}(1 + y^2), \quad y(0) = 1$

10. $\dfrac{dy}{dx} = 2xy^2, \quad y(0) = 1$

Note: The project following this problem set lists illustrative calculator/computer programs that can be used in the remaining problems.

A programmable calculator or a computer will be useful for Problems 11 through 16. In each problem, find the exact solution of the given initial value problem. Then apply the Runge–Kutta method twice to approximate (to five decimal places) this solution on the given interval, first with step size $h = 0.2$, then with step size $h = 0.1$. Make a table showing the approximate values and the actual values, together with the percentage errors in the more accurate approximations, when x is an integral multiple of 0.2. Throughout, y' is an abbreviation for dy/dx.

11. $\dfrac{dy}{dx} = y - 2, \quad y(0) = 1; \quad 0 \leq x \leq 1$

12. $\dfrac{dy}{dx} = \dfrac{1}{2}(y - 1)^2, \quad y(0) = 2; \quad 0 \leq x \leq 1$

13. $yy' = 2x^3, \quad y(1) = 3; \quad 1 \leq x \leq 2$

14. $xy' = y^2, \quad y(1) = 1; \quad 1 \leq x \leq 2$

15. $xy' = 3x - 2y, \quad y(2) = 3; \quad 2 \leq x \leq 3$

16. $y^2y' = 2x^5, \quad y(2) = 3; \quad 2 \leq x \leq 3$

A computer with a printer is required for Problems 17 through 24. In each of these initial value problems, use the Runge–Kutta method with step sizes $h = 0.2, 0.1, 0.05$, and 0.025 to approximate to six decimal places the values of the solution at five equally spaced points of the given interval. Print the results in tabular form to make it easy to gauge the effect of varying the step size h.

17. $y' = x^2 + y^2, \quad y(0) = 0; \quad 0 \leq x \leq 1$

18. $y' = x^2 - y^2, \quad y(0) = 1; \quad 0 \leq x \leq 2$

19. $y' = x + \sqrt{y}, \quad y(0) = 1; \quad 0 \leq x \leq 2$

20. $\dfrac{dy}{dx} = x + \sqrt[3]{y}, \quad y(0) = -1; \quad 0 \leq x \leq 2$

21. $y' = \ln y, \quad y(1) = 2; \quad 1 \leq x \leq 2$

22. $y' = x^{2/3} + y^{2/3}, \quad y(0) = 1; \quad 0 \leq x \leq 2$

23. $y' = \sin x + \cos y, \quad y(0) = 0; \quad 0 \leq x \leq 1$

24. $\dfrac{dy}{dx} = \dfrac{x}{1 + y^2}, \quad y(-1) = 1; \quad -1 \leq x \leq 1$

Velocity–Acceleration Problems

In each of Problems 25 through 30, the linear acceleration $a = dv/dt$ of a moving particle is given by a formula

$$\frac{dv}{dt} = f(t, v), \tag{19}$$

where the velocity $v = ds/dt$ is the time derivative of the distance function $s = s(t)$. The velocity $v(t)$ is approximated by using the Runge–Kutta method to solve numerically the initial value problem

$$\frac{dv}{dt} = f(t, v), \qquad v(0) = v_0. \tag{20}$$

Suppose that we also want to compute the distance $s(t)$ traveled by the particle, beginning with $s(0) = s_0$. We can do this by calculating

$$s_{n+1} = s_n + v_n h + \frac{1}{2}a_n h^2 \tag{21}$$

at each step, where $a_n = f(t_n, v_n)$. (The formula in (21) would give the correct increment in the distance s if the acceleration a_n remained *constant* during the time interval $[t_n, t_{n+1}]$.) Thus at each step we compute

$$a_n = f(t_n, v_n),$$

$$s_{n+1} = s_n + v_n h + \frac{1}{2}a_n h^2,$$

$$v_{n+1} = v_n + \frac{h}{6}(k_1 + 2k_2 + 2k_3 + k_4), \tag{22}$$

$$t_{n+1} = t_n + h.$$

Here, k_1, k_2, k_3, and k_4 are given by Eqs. (5a) through (5d) with t in place of x and v in place of y.

25. If the skydiver of Example 3 jumped from an altitude of 10,000 ft and there were *no* air resistance, then (by the formula

$s = \frac{1}{2}gt^2$) she would fall 1600 ft in the first 10 s, 6400 ft in the first 20 s, and (if the parachute remained unopened) would hit the ground in a total of 25 s. Use the equations in (22) with $h = 0.2$ to find the distance fallen after 10 and 20 s and the time elapsed at impact with the ground, under the assumption that her acceleration due to gravity *and* air resistance is that given in Eq. (15).

26. Suppose that a skydiver steps out of an airplane at an altitude of 10,000 ft and that his downward acceleration is given by

$$\frac{dv}{dt} = 32 - (0.005)v^2.$$

(a) Show that his velocity and distance fallen are given [exactly] by

$$v(t) = 80 \tanh(0.4t), \qquad s(t) = 200 \ln(\cosh(0.4t)).$$

(b) Use the method outlined in (22) to approximate (with $h = 0.1$) the distance fallen after 5, 10, and 15 s. Compare with the actual values. (c) What terminal velocity will the skydiver attain and when will he hit the ground (with no parachute)?

27. Suppose that a car starts from rest and its engine provides an acceleration of 10 ft/s². Assume also that it experiences a deceleration of $(0.1)v$ ft/s² ($v = v(t)$ denotes its velocity at time t seconds) due to friction and air resistance, so that its net acceleration is given by

$$\frac{dv}{dt} = 10 - (0.1)v.$$

Find Runge–Kutta approximations (with $h = 0.2$) to $v(t)$ and $s(t)$ in order to answer the following questions. (a) What is the limiting velocity of the car? (b) How far will it travel in the first 10 s, and what will its velocity be then? (c) How long will it take to reach a velocity of 60 mi/h (88 ft/s) and how far will it travel during that time?

28. Repeat Problem 27, but use acceleration

$$\frac{dv}{dt} = 10 - (0.001)v^2.$$

29. Suppose that a ball is thrown straight upward from the ground with initial velocity $v_0 = 160$ ft/s. If there were no resistance, it would reach a maximum height of 400 ft in 5 s, then fall back to the ground in another 5 s. But assume, more realistically, that the effect of air resistance is to give the ball acceleration

$$\frac{dv}{dt} = -32 - (0.1)v.$$

Find Runge–Kutta approximations (with $h = 0.1$) to the velocity $v(t)$ and height $s(t)$ of the ball in order to answer the following questions. (a) What is the maximum height that the ball reaches, and at what time t is that height attained? (b) How long will it take the ball to fall from its maximum height back to the ground, and with what velocity will it strike the ground?

30. Repeat Problem 29, but take

$$\frac{dv}{dt} = -32 - (0.001)\, v\,|v|$$

as the acceleration of the ball. Note that $dv/dt = -32 - (0.001)v^2$ during the ascent of the ball, whereas $dv/dt = -32 + (0.001)v^2$ during its descent. The answers should be comparable to those found in Problem 29.

2.6 Computing Project

Figure 2.6.10 lists TI-85 and BASIC programs implementing the Runge–Kutta method to approximate the solution of the initial value problem

$$\frac{dy}{dx} = x + y, \qquad y(0) = 1$$

considered in Example 1 of this section. The comments provided in the final column should make these programs intelligible even if you have little familiarity with the BASIC and TI programming languages.

To apply the Runge–Kutta method to a different equation $dy/dx = f(x, y)$, one need only change the initial line of the program, in which the function f is defined. To increase the number of steps (and thereby decrease the step size) one need only change the value of **N** specified in the second line of the program.

Figure 2.6.11 exhibits a MATLAB implementation of the Runge–Kutta method. Suppose that the function f describing the differential equation $x' = f(t, x)$ has been

TI-85	BASIC	Comment
PROGRAM:RK	Program RK	Program title
:F=X+Y	DEF FN F(X,Y) = X+Y	Define function f
:10→N	N = 10	No. of steps
:0→X	X = 0	Initial x
:1→Y	Y = 1	Initial y
:1→X1	X1= 1	Final x
:(X1-X)/N→H	H = (X1-X)/N	Step size
:For(I,1,N)	FOR I=1 TO N	Begin loop
:X→X0	X0 = X	Save previous x
:Y→Y0	Y0 = Y	Save previous y
:F→K1	K1 = FNF(X,Y)	First slope
:X0+H/2→X	X = X0 + H/2	Midpoint
:Y0+H*K1/2→Y	Y = Y0 + H*K1/2	Midpt predictor
:F→K2	K2 = FNF(X,Y)	Second slope
:Y0+H*K2/2→Y	Y = Y0 + H*K2/2	Midpt predictor
:F→K3	K3 = FNF(X,Y)	Third slope
:X0+H→X	X = X0 + H	New x
:Y0+H*K3→Y	Y = Y0 + H*K3	Endpt predictor
:F→K4	K4 = FNF(X,Y)	Fourth slope
:(K1+2*K2+2*K3 +K4)/6→K	K = (K1+2*K2+2*K3 +K4)/6	Average slope
:Y0+H*K→Y	Y = Y0 + H*K	Corrector
:Disp X,Y	PRINT X,Y	Display results
:End	NEXT I	End loop

FIGURE 2.6.10. TI-85 and BASIC Runge–Kutta programs

```
function yp = f(x,y)
yp = x + y;                          % yp = y'

function [X,Y] = rk(x,y,x1,n)
h = (x1 - x)/n;                      % step size
X = x;                               % initial x
Y = y;                               % initial y
for i = 1 : n                        % begin loop
    k1 = f(x, y);                    % first slope
    k2 = f(x+h/2,y+h*k1/2);          % second slope
    k3 = f(x+h/2,y+h*k2/2);          % third slope
    k4 = f(x+h  ,y+h*k3  );          % fourth slope
    k  = (k1+2*k2+2*k3+k4)/6;        % average slope
    x  = x + h;                      % new x
    y  = y + h*k;                    % new y
    X = [X;x];                       % update x-column
    Y = [Y;y];                       % update y-column
    end                              % end loop
```

FIGURE 2.6.11. MATLAB implementation of the Runge–Kutta method

defined. Then the **rk** function takes as input the initial value **x**, the initial value **y**, the final value **x1** of *x*, and the desired number **n** of subintervals. As output it produces the resulting column vectors **X** and **Y** of *x*- and *y*-values. For instance, the MATLAB command

```
[X, Y] = rk(0, 1, 1, 10)
```

then generates the first and third columns of data shown in the table of Fig. 2.6.2.

For this project, you should implement the Runge–Kutta method in your calculator or programming language of choice. Test your program by application first to the initial value problem of Example 1, and then to some of the problems for this section.

3 Linear Equations of Higher Order

3.1 Introduction: Second-Order Linear Equations

In Chapters 1 and 2 we confined our attention to first-order differential equations. We now turn to equations of higher order $n \geqq 2$, beginning in this chapter with equations that are linear. The general theory of linear differential equations parallels the case of second-order linear equations (the case $n = 2$), which we outline in this initial section.

Recall that a second-order differential equation in the (unknown) function $y(x)$ is one of the form

$$G(x, y, y', y'') = 0. \tag{1}$$

This differential equation is said to be **linear** provided that G is linear in the dependent variable y and its derivatives y' and y''. Thus a linear second-order equation takes the form

▶ $$A(x)y'' + B(x)y' + C(x)y = F(x). \tag{2}$$

Unless otherwise noted, we will always assume that the (known) coefficient functions $A(x)$, $B(x)$, $C(x)$, and $F(x)$ are continuous on some open interval I (perhaps unbounded) on which we wish to solve this differential equation, but they need not be

linear functions. Thus the differential equation

$$e^x y'' + (\cos x) y' + (1 + \sqrt{x}) y = \tan^{-1} x$$

is linear because the dependent variable and its derivatives appear linearly, whereas the equations

$$y'' = yy' \qquad \text{and} \qquad y'' + 3(y')^2 + 4y^3 = 0$$

and not linear because products and powers of y or its derivatives appear.

If the function $F(x)$ on the right-hand side of Eq. (2) vanishes identically on I, then we call Eq. (2) a **homogeneous** linear equation; otherwise, it is **nonhomogeneous.** For example, the second-order equation

$$x^2 y'' + 2xy' + 3y = \cos x$$

is nonhomogeneous; its *associated* homogeneous equation is

$$x^2 y'' + 2xy' + 3y = 0.$$

The homogeneous linear equation **associated** with Eq. (2) is

$$A(x) y'' + B(c) y' + C(x) y = 0. \tag{3}$$

In case the differential equation in (2) models a physical system, the nonhomogeneous term $F(x)$ frequently corresponds to some *external* influence on the system.

A Typical Application

Spring Mass Dashpot

$x(t)$

$x = 0 \qquad x > 0$
Equilibrium
position

FIGURE 3.1.1. A mass-spring-dashpot system

Linear differential equations frequently appear as mathematical models of mechanical systems and electrical circuits. For example, suppose that a mass m is attached both to a spring that exerts on it a force F_S and to a dashpot (shock absorber) that exerts a force F_R on the mass (Fig. 3.1.1). Assume that the restoring force F_S of the spring is proportional to the displacement x (positive to the right, negative to the left) of the mass from equilibrium, and that the dashpot force F_R is proportional to the velocity $v = dx/dt$ of the mass. With the aid of Fig. 3.1.2 we also get the appropriate directions of action of these two forces:

$$F_S = -kx \qquad \text{and} \qquad F_R = -cv \qquad (k, c > 0).$$

m

$F_S \longleftarrow \qquad \longleftarrow F_R$

$x, v > 0$

FIGURE 3.1.2. Directions of the forces acting on m

The minus signs are correct—F_S is negative when x is positive, F_R is negative when v is positive. Newton's law $F = ma$ now gives

$$mx'' = F_S + F_R; \tag{4}$$

that is,

$$m\frac{d^2x}{dt^2} + c\frac{dx}{dt} + kx = 0. \tag{5}$$

Thus we have a differential equation in the position function $x(t)$ of the mass m. This homogeneous second-order linear equation governs the *free vibrations* of the mass; we will return to this problem in detail in Section 3.4.

If, in addition to F_S and F_R, the mass m is acted on by an external force $F(t)$—which must then be added to the right-hand side in Eq. (4)—the resulting equation is

$$m\frac{d^2x}{dt^2} + c\frac{dx}{dt} + kx = F(t). \tag{6}$$

This nonhomogeneous linear differential equation governs the *forced vibrations* of the mass under the influence of the external force $F(t)$.

Homogeneous Second-Order Linear Equations

Consider the general second-order linear equation

$$A(x)\, y'' + B(x)\, y' + C(x)\, y = F(x), \tag{7}$$

where the coefficient functions A, B, C, and F are continuous on the open interval I. Here we will assume in addition that $A(x) \neq 0$ at each point of I, so we can divide each term in Eq. (7) by $A(x)$ and write it in the form

▶
$$y'' + p(x)\, y' + q(x)\, y = f(x). \tag{8}$$

We will discuss first the associated homogeneous equation

▶
$$y'' + p(x)\, y' + q(x)\, y = 0. \tag{9}$$

A particularly useful property of this *homogeneous* linear equation is the fact that the sum of any two solutions of (9) is again a solution, as is any constant multiple of a solution. This is the central idea of the following theorem.

THEOREM 1: Principle of Superposition

Let y_1 and y_2 be two solutions of the homogeneous linear Eq. (9) on the interval I. If c_1 and c_2 are constants, then the linear combination

$$y = c_1 y_1 + c_2 y_2 \tag{10}$$

is also a solution of (9) on I.

Proof: The conclusion follows almost immediately from the *linearity* of the operation of differentiation, which gives

$$y' = c_1 y_1' + c_2 y_2' \qquad \text{and} \qquad y'' = c_1 y_1'' + c_2 y_2'' \,.$$

Then

$$
\begin{aligned}
y'' + py' + qy &= (c_1 y_1 + c_2 y_2)'' + p(c_1 y_1 + c_2 y_2)' + q(c_1 y_1 + c_2 y_2) \\
&= (c_1 y_1'' + c_2 y_2'') + p(c_1 y_1' + c_2 y_2') + q(c_1 y_1 + c_2 y_2) \\
&= c_1 (y_1'' + py_1' + qy_1) + c_2 (y_2'' + py_2' + qy_2) \\
&= c_1 \cdot 0 + c_2 \cdot 0 = 0
\end{aligned}
$$

because y_1 and y_2 are solutions. Thus $y = c_1 y_1 + c_2 y_2$ is also a solution. ■

EXAMPLE 1 We can see by inspection that

$$y_1(x) = \cos x \qquad \text{and} \qquad y_2(x) = \sin x$$

are two solutions of the equation

$$y'' + y = 0.$$

Theorem 1 tells us that any linear combination of these solutions, such as

$$y(x) = 3y_1(x) - 2y_2(x) = 3 \cos x - 2 \sin x$$

is also a solution. We will see later that, conversely, *every* solution of $y'' + y = 0$ is a linear combination of these two particular solutions y_1 and y_2. Thus a general solution of $y'' + y = 0$ is

$$y(x) = c_1 \cos x + c_2 \sin x. \qquad\blacksquare$$

Earlier in this section we gave the linear equation $mx'' + cx' + kx = F(t)$ as a mathematical model of the motion of the mass shown in Fig. 3.1.1. Physical considerations suggest that the motion of the mass should be determined by its initial position and initial velocity. Hence, given any preassigned values of $x(0)$ and $x'(0)$, Eq. (6) ought to have a *unique* solution satisfying these initial conditions. More generally, in order to be a "good" mathematical model of a deterministic physical situation, a differential equation must have unique solutions satisfying any appropriate initial conditions. The following existence and uniqueness theorem (proved in the Appendix) gives us this assurance for the general second-order linear equation.

THEOREM 2: Existence and Uniqueness

Suppose that the functions p, q, and f are continuous on the open interval I containing the point a. Then, given any two numbers b_0 and b_1, the equation

$$y'' + p(x)y' + q(x)y = f(x) \qquad (8)$$

has a unique (that is, one and only one) solution on the entire interval I that satisfies the initial conditions

$$y(a) = b_0, \qquad y'(a) = b_1. \qquad (11)$$

\blacksquare

Remark 1: Equation (8) and the conditions in (11) constitute a second-order linear **initial value problem.** Theorem 2 tells us that any such initial value problem has a unique solution on the *whole* interval I where the coefficient functions in (8) are continuous. Recall from Section 1.3 that a *nonlinear* differential equation generally has a unique solution on only a smaller interval.

Remark 2: Whereas a *first-order* differential equation $dy/dx = F(x, y)$ generally admits only a single solution curve $y = y(x)$ passing through a given initial point (a, b), Theorem 2 implies that the *second-order* equation in (8) has infinitely many solution curves passing through the point (a, b_0)—namely, one for each (real number) value of the initial slope $y'(a) = b_1$. That is, instead of there being only one line through (a, b_0) tangent to a solution curve, *every* nonvertical straight line through (a, b_0) is tangent to a solution curve of Eq. (8). Figure 3.1.3 shows a variety of solution curves of the equation

$$y'' + 3y' + 2y = 0,$$

all passing through the point $(0, 1)$. The project material for this section suggests how to construct such a family of solution curves for a given homogeneous second-order linear differential equation.

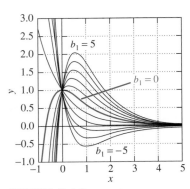

FIGURE 3.1.3. Solution curves of $y'' + 3y' + 2y = 0$ passing through the point $(0, 1)$

EXAMPLE 1
Continued
We saw in the first part of Example 1 that $y(x) = 3 \cos x - 2 \sin x$ is a solution (on the entire real line) of $y'' + y = 0$. It has the initial values $y(0) = 3$, $y'(0) = -2$. Theorem 2 tells us that this is the *only* solution with these initial values. More generally, the solution

$$y(x) = b_0 \cos x + b_1 \sin x$$

satisfies the *arbitrary* initial conditions $y(0) = b_0, y'(0) = b_1$; this illustrates the *existence* of such a solution, also as guaranteed by Theorem 2. ∎

Example 1 suggests how, given a *homogeneous* second-order linear equation, we might actually find the solution whose existence is assured by Theorem 2. First, we find two "essentially different" solutions y_1 and y_2; second, we attempt to impose on the general solution

$$y = c_1 y_1 + c_2 y_2 \tag{12}$$

the initial conditions $y(a) = b_0, y'(a) = b_1$. That is, we attempt to solve the simultaneous equations

$$c_1 y_1(a) + c_2 y_2(a) = b_0, \qquad c_1 y_1'(a) + c_2 y_2'(a) = b_1 \tag{13}$$

for the coefficients c_1 and c_2.

EXAMPLE 2
Verify that the functions

$$y_1(x) = e^x \qquad \text{and} \qquad y_2(x) = xe^x$$

are solutions of the differential equation

$$y'' - 2y' + y = 0,$$

and then find a solution satisfying the initial conditions $y(0) = 3, y'(0) = 1$.

Solution: The verification is routine; we omit it. We impose the given initial conditions on the general solution

$$y(x) = c_1 e^x + c_2 xe^x,$$

for which

$$y'(x) = (c_1 + c_2)e^x + c_2 xe^x,$$

to obtain the simultaneous equations

$$y(0) = c_1 \qquad = 3,$$
$$y'(0) = c_1 + c_2 = 1.$$

The resulting solution is $c_1 = 3, c_2 = -2$. Hence the solution of the original initial value problem is

$$y(x) = 3e^x - 2xe^x. \qquad \blacksquare$$

In order for the procedure of Example 2 to succeed, the two solutions y_1 and y_2 must have the elusive property that the equations in (13) can always be solved for c_1

and c_2, no matter what the initial conditions b_0 and b_1 might be. The following definition tells precisely how different the two functions y_1 and y_2 must be.

> ### DEFINITION: Linear Independence of Two Functions
>
> Two functions defined on an open interval are said to be **linearly independent** provided that neither is a constant multiple of the other. ∎

Two functions are said to be **linearly dependent** on an open interval provided that they are not linearly independent; that is, one of them is a constant multiple of the other. We can always determine whether two given functions f and g are linearly dependent on an interval I by noting at a glance whether either of the two quotients f/g or g/f is a constant on I.

EXAMPLE 3 Thus it is clear that the following pairs of functions are linearly independent on the entire real line:

$$\sin x \quad \text{and} \quad \cos x;$$
$$e^x \quad \text{and} \quad e^{-2x};$$
$$e^x \quad \text{and} \quad xe^x;$$
$$x + 1 \quad \text{and} \quad x^2;$$
$$x \quad \text{and} \quad |x|.$$

But the identically zero function and any other function g are linearly dependent on every interval because $0 = 0 \cdot g(x)$. Also, the functions

$$f(x) = \sin 2x \quad \text{and} \quad g(x) = \sin x \cos x$$

are linearly dependent on any interval because $f(x) = 2g(x)$ for all x (a familiar trigonometric identity). ∎

General Solutions

But does the homogeneous equation $y'' + py' + qy = 0$ always have two linearly independent solutions? Theorem 2 says yes! We need only choose y_1 and y_2 so that

$$y_1(a) = 1, \quad y_1'(a) = 0 \quad \text{and} \quad y_2(a) = 0, \quad y_2'(a) = 1.$$

It is then impossible that either $y_1 = ky_2$ or $y_2 = ky_1$ because $k \cdot 0 \neq 1$ for any constant k. Theorem 2 tells us that two such linearly independent solutions *exist;* actually finding them is a crucial matter that we will discuss briefly at the end of this section, and in greater detail beginning in Section 3.3.

We want to show, finally, that given *any* two linearly independent solutions y_1 and y_2 of the homogeneous equation

$$y''(x) + p(x)y'(x) + q(x)y(x) = 0, \tag{9}$$

every solution y of Eq. (9) can be expressed as a linear combination

$$y = c_1 y_1 + c_2 y_2 \tag{12}$$

of y_1 and y_2. This means that the function in (12) is the *general solution* of Eq. (9).

As suggested by the equations in (13), the determination of the constants c_1 and c_2 in (12) depends upon a certain 2×2 determinant of values of y_1, y_2, and their derivatives. Given two functions f and g, the **Wronskian** of f and g is the determinant

▶
$$W = \begin{vmatrix} f & g \\ f' & g' \end{vmatrix} = fg' - f'g.$$

We write either $W(f, g)$ or $W(x)$, depending upon whether we wish to emphasize the two functions or the point x at which their Wronskian is to be evaluated. For example,

$$W(\cos x, \sin x) = \begin{vmatrix} \cos x & \sin x \\ -\sin x & \cos x \end{vmatrix} = \cos^2 x + \sin^2 x = 1$$

and

$$W(e^x, xe^x) = \begin{vmatrix} e^x & xe^x \\ e^x & e^x + xe^x \end{vmatrix} = e^{2x}.$$

These are examples of linearly *independent* pairs of solutions of differential equations (see Examples 1 and 2). Note that in both cases the Wronskian is everywhere *nonzero*.

On the other hand, if the functions f and g are linearly dependent, with $f = kg$ (for example), then

$$W(f, g) = \begin{vmatrix} kg & g \\ kg' & g' \end{vmatrix} = kgg' - kg'g \equiv 0.$$

Thus the Wronskian of two linearly *dependent* functions is identically zero. In Section 3.2 we will prove that, if the two functions y_1 and y_2 are solutions of a homogeneous second-order linear equation, then the strong converse stated in part (b) of Theorem 3 holds.

THEOREM 3: Wronskians of Solutions

Suppose that y_1 and y_2 are two solutions of the homogeneous second-order linear equation (Eq. (9))

$$y'' + p(x)y' + q(x)y = 0$$

on an open interval I on which p and q are continuous.

(a) If y_1 and y_2 are linearly dependent, then $W(y_1, y_2) \equiv 0$ on I;
(b) If y_1 and y_2 are linearly independent, then $W(y_1, y_2) \neq 0$ at each point of I.

■

Thus, given two solutions of Eq. (9), there are just two possibilities: The Wronskian W is identically zero if the solutions are linearly dependent; the Wronskian is never zero if the solutions are linearly independent. The latter fact is what we need to show that $y = c_1 y_1 + c_2 y_2$ is the general solution of Eq. (9) if y_1 and y_2 are solutions.

THEOREM 4: General Solutions

Let y_1 and y_2 be two linearly independent solutions of the homogeneous equation (Eq. (9))

$$y'' + p(x)y' + q(x)y = 0$$

with p and q continuous on the open interval I. If Y is any solution whatsoever of Eq. (9), then there exist numbers c_1 and c_2 such that

$$Y(x) = c_1 y_1(x) + c_2 y_2(x)$$

for all x in I.

∎

In essence, Theorem 4 tells us that when we have found *two* linearly independent solutions of the homogeneous equation in (9), then we have found *all* of its solutions.

Proof of Theorem 4: Choose a point a of I, and consider the simultaneous equations

$$c_1 y_1(a) + c_2 y_2(a) = Y(a),$$
$$c_1 y_1'(a) + c_2 y_2'(a) = Y'(a). \tag{14}$$

The determinant of the coefficients in this system of linear equations in the unknowns c_1 and c_2 is simply the Wronskian $W(y_1, y_2)$ evaluated at $x = a$. By Theorem 3, this determinant is nonzero, so by elementary algebra it follows that the equations in (14) can be solved for c_1 and c_2. With these values of c_1 and c_2, we define the solution

$$G(x) = c_1 y_1(x) + c_2 y_2(x)$$

of Eq. (9); then

$$G(a) = c_1 y_1(a) + c_2 y_2(a) = Y(a)$$

and

$$G'(a) = c_1 y_1'(a) + c_2 y_2'(a) = Y'(a).$$

Thus the two solutions Y and G have the same initial values at a, as do Y' and G'. By the uniqueness of a solution determined by such initial values (Theorem 2), it follows that Y and G agree on I. Thus we see that

$$Y(x) \equiv G(x) = c_1 y_1(x) + c_2 y_2(x),$$

as desired. ∎

EXAMPLE 4 It is evident that

$$y_1(x) = e^{2x} \quad \text{and} \quad y_2(x) = e^{-2x}$$

are linearly independent solutions of

$$y'' - 4y = 0. \tag{15}$$

But $y_3(x) = \cosh 2x$ and $y_4(x) = \sinh 2x$ are also solutions of (15) because

$$\frac{d^2}{dx^2}(\cosh 2x) = \frac{d}{dx}(2 \sinh 2x) = 4 \cosh 2x$$

and, similarly, $(\sinh 2x)'' = 4 \sinh 2x$. It therefore follows from Theorem 4 that the functions $\cosh 2x$ and $\sinh 2x$ can be expressed as linear combinations of $y_1(x) = e^{2x}$ and $y_2(x) = e^{-2x}$. Of course, this is no surprise, because

$$\cosh 2x = \frac{1}{2} e^{2x} + \frac{1}{2} e^{-2x} \qquad \text{and} \qquad \sinh 2x = \frac{1}{2} e^{2x} - \frac{1}{2} e^{-2x}$$

by the definitions of the hyperbolic cosine and sine. ∎

Linear Second-Order Equations with Constant Coefficients

As an illustration of the general theory introduced in this section, we discuss the homogeneous second-order linear differential equation

$$ay'' + by' + cy = 0 \tag{16}$$

with constant coefficients a, b, and c. We first look for a *single* solution of Eq. (16) and begin with the observation that

$$(e^{rx})' = re^{rx} \qquad \text{and} \qquad (e^{rx})'' = r^2 e^{rx}, \tag{17}$$

so any derivative of e^{rx} is a constant multiple of e^{rx}. Hence, if we substituted $y = e^{rx}$ in Eq. (16), each term would be a constant multiple of e^{rx}, with the constant coefficients dependent upon r and the coefficients a, b, and c. This suggests that we try to find a value of r so that these multiples of e^{rx} will have sum zero. If we succeed, then $y = e^{rx}$ will be a solution of Eq. (16).

For example, if we substitute $y = e^{rx}$ in the equation

$$y'' - 5y' + 6y = 0,$$

we obtain

$$r^2 e^{rx} - 5re^{rx} + 6e^{rx} = 0.$$

Thus

$$(r^2 - 5r + 6)e^{rx} = 0; \qquad (r - 2)(r - 3)e^{rx} = 0.$$

Hence $y = e^{rx}$ will be a solution if either $r = 2$ or $r = 3$. So, in searching for a single solution, we actually have found two solutions: $y_1(x) = e^{2x}$ and $y_2(x) = e^{3x}$.

To carry out this procedure in the general case, we substitute $y = e^{rx}$ in Eq. (16). With the aid of Eq. (17), we find the result to be

$$ar^2 e^{rx} + bre^{rx} + ce^{rx} = 0.$$

Because e^{rx} is never zero, we conclude that $y(x) = e^{rx}$ will satisfy the differential equation in (16) precisely when r is a root of the *algebraic* equation

▶
$$ar^2 + br + c = 0. \tag{18}$$

This quadratic equation is called the **characteristic equation** of the homogeneous linear differential equation

$$ay'' + by' + cy = 0. \tag{16}$$

If Eq. (18) has two *distinct* (unequal) roots, r_1 and r_2, then the corresponding solutions

$y_1(x) = e^{r_1 x}$ and $y_2(x) = e^{r_2 x}$ of (16) are linearly independent. (Why?) This gives the following result.

THEOREM 5: Distinct Real Roots

If the two roots r_1 and r_2 of the characteristic equation in (18) are real and distinct, then

$$y(x) = c_1 e^{r_1 x} + c_2 e^{r_2 x} \tag{19}$$

is the general solution of Eq. (16). ∎

EXAMPLE 5 Find the general solution of

$$2y'' - 7y' + 3y = 0.$$

Solution: We can solve the characteristic equation

$$2r^2 - 7r + 3 = 0$$

by factoring:

$$(2r - 1)(r - 3) = 0.$$

The roots $r_1 = \frac{1}{2}$ and $r_2 = 3$ are real and distinct, so Theorem 5 yields the general solution

$$y(x) = c_1 e^{x/2} + c_2 e^{3x}.$$

EXAMPLE 6 The differential equation $y'' + 2y' = 0$ has characteristic equation

$$r^2 + 2r = r(r + 2) = 0$$

with distinct real roots $r_1 = 0$ and $r_2 = -2$. Because $e^{0 \cdot x} \equiv 1$, we get the general solution

$$y(x) = c_1 + c_2 e^{-2x}.$$ ∎

Remark: Note that Theorem 5 changes a problem involving a differential equation into a problem involving only the solution of an *algebraic* equation.

If the characteristic equation in (18) has equal roots $r_1 = r_2$, we get (at first) only the single solution $y_1(x) = e^{r_1 x}$ of Eq. (16). The problem in this case is to produce the "missing" second solution of the differential equation.

A double root $r = r_1$ will occur precisely when the characteristic equation is a constant multiple of the equation

$$(r - r_1)^2 = r^2 - 2r_1 r + r_1^2 = 0.$$

Any differential equation with this characteristic equation is equivalent to

$$y'' - 2r_1 y' + r_1^2 y = 0. \tag{20}$$

But it is easy to verify by direct substitution that $y = x e^{r_1 x}$ is a second solution of Eq. (20). It is clear (but you should verify) that

$$y_1(x) = e^{r_1 x} \qquad \text{and} \qquad y_2(x) = x e^{r_1 x}$$

are linearly independent functions, so the general solution of the differential equation in (20) is

$$y(x) = c_1 e^{r_1 x} + c_2 x e^{r_1 x}.$$

 THEOREM 6: Repeated Roots

If the characteristic equation in (18) has equal (necessarily real) roots $r_1 = r_2$, then

$$y(x) = (c_1 + c_2 x)\, e^{r_1 x} \qquad (21)$$

is the general solution of Eq. (16). ∎

EXAMPLE 7 To solve the initial value problem

$$y'' + 2y' + y = 0;$$

$$y(0) = 5, \quad y'(0) = -3,$$

we note first that the characteristic equation

$$r^2 + 2r + 1 = (r + 1)^2 = 0$$

has equal roots $r_1 = r_2 = -1$. Hence the general solution provided by Theorem 6 is

$$y(x) = c_1 e^{-x} + c_2 x e^{-x}.$$

Differentiation yields

$$y'(x) = -c_1 e^{-x} + c_2 e^{-x} - c_2 x e^{-x},$$

so the initial conditions yield the equations

$$y(0) = \quad c_1 \qquad = 5,$$

$$y'(0) = -c_1 + c_2 = -3,$$

which imply that $c_1 = 5$ and $c_2 = 2$. Thus the desired particular solution of the initial value problem is

$$y(x) = 5e^{-x} + 2x e^{-x}.$$ ∎

The characteristic equation in (18) may have either real or complex roots. The case of complex roots will be discussed in Section 3.3.

3.1 Problems

In Problems 1 through 16, a homogeneous second-order linear differential equation, two functions y_1 and y_2, and a pair of initial conditions are given. First verify that y_1 and y_2 are solutions of the differential equation. Then find a particular solution of the form $y = c_1 y_1 + c_2 y_2$ that satisfies the given initial conditions.

1. $y'' - y = 0$; $\quad y_1 = e^x, \quad y_2 = e^{-x}$; $\quad y(0) = 0$,
$\quad y'(0) = 5$

2. $y'' - 9y = 0$; $\quad y_1 = e^{3x}, \quad y_2 = e^{-3x}$; $\quad y(0) = -1$,
$\quad y'(0) = 15$

3. $y'' + 4y = 0$; $\quad y_1 = \cos 2x, \quad y_2 = \sin 2x$; $\quad y(0) = 3$,
$\quad y'(0) = 8$

4. $y'' + 25y = 0$; $\quad y_1 = \cos 5x, \quad y_2 = \sin 5x$;
$\quad y(0) = 10, \quad y'(0) = -10$

5. $y'' - 3y' + 2y = 0$; $\quad y_1 = e^x, \quad y_2 = e^{2x}$; $\quad y(0) = 1$,
$\quad y'(0) = 0$

6. $y'' + y' - 6y = 0$; $y_1 = e^{2x}$, $y_2 = e^{-3x}$; $y(0) = 7$,
$y'(0) = -1$

7. $y'' + y' = 0$; $y_1 = 1$, $y_2 = e^{-x}$; $y(0) = -2$,
$y'(0) = 8$

8. $y'' - 3y' = 0$; $y_1 = 1$, $y_2 = e^{3x}$; $y(0) = 4$,
$y'(0) = -2$

9. $y'' + 2y' + y = 0$; $y_1 = e^{-x}$, $y_2 = xe^{-x}$; $y(0) = 2$,
$y'(0) = -1$

10. $y'' - 10y' + 25y = 0$; $y_1 = e^{5x}$, $y_2 = xe^{5x}$; $y(0) = 3$,
$y'(0) = 13$

11. $y'' - 2y' + 2y = 0$; $y_1 = e^x \cos x$, $y_2 = e^x \sin x$;
$y(0) = 0$, $y'(0) = 5$

12. $y'' + 6y' + 13y = 0$; $y_1 = e^{-3x} \cos 2x$,
$y_2 = e^{-3x} \sin 2x$; $y(0) = 2$, $y'(0) = 0$

13. $x^2 y'' - 2xy' + 2y = 0$; $y_1 = x$, $y_2 = x^2$;
$y(1) = 3$, $y'(1) = 1$

14. $x^2 y'' + 2xy' - 6y = 0$; $y_1 = x^2$, $y_2 = x^{-3}$;
$y(2) = 10$, $y'(2) = 15$

15. $x^2 y'' - xy' + y = 0$; $y_1 = x$, $y_2 = x \ln x$; $y(1) = 7$,
$y'(1) = 2$

16. $x^2 y'' + xy' + y = 0$; $y_1 = \cos(\ln x)$, $y_2 = \sin(\ln x)$;
$y(1) = 2$, $y'(1) = 3$

The following three problems illustrate the fact that the superposition principle does not generally hold for nonlinear equations.

17. Show that $y = 1/x$ is a solution of $y' + y^2 = 0$, but that if $c \neq 0$ and $c \neq 1$, then $y = c/x$ is not a solution.

18. Show that $y = x^3$ is a solution of $yy'' = 6x^4$, but that if $c^2 \neq 1$, then $y = cx^3$ is not a solution.

19. Show that $y_1 = 1$ and $y_2 = x^{1/2}$ are solutions of $yy'' + (y')^2 = 0$, but that their sum $y = y_1 + y_2$ is not a solution.

Determine whether the pairs of functions in Problems 20 through 26 are linearly independent or linearly dependent on the real line.

20. $f(x) = \pi$, $g(x) = \cos^2 x + \sin^2 x$

21. $f(x) = x^3$, $g(x) = x^2 |x|$

22. $f(x) = 1 + x$, $g(x) = 1 + |x|$

23. $f(x) = xe^x$, $g(x) = |x| e^x$

24. $f(x) = \sin^2 x$, $g(x) = 1 - \cos 2x$

25. $f(x) = e^x \sin x$, $g(x) = e^x \cos x$

26. $f(x) = 2 \cos x + 3 \sin x$, $g(x) = 3 \cos x - 2 \sin x$

27. Let y_p be a particular solution of the nonhomogeneous equation $y'' + py' + qy = f(x)$ and let y_c be a solution of its associated homogeneous equation. Show that $y = y_c + y_p$ is a solution of the given nonhomogeneous equation.

28. With $y_p = 1$ and $y_c = c_1 \cos x + c_2 \sin x$ in the notation of Problem 27, find a solution of $y'' + y = 1$ satisfying the initial conditions $y(0) = -1 = y'(0)$.

29. Show that $y_1 = x^2$ and $y_2 = x^3$ are two different solutions of $x^2 y'' - 4xy' + 6y = 0$, both satisfying the initial conditions $y(0) = 0 = y'(0)$. Explain why these facts do not contradict Theorem 2 (with respect to the guaranteed uniqueness).

30. (a) Show that $y_1 = x^3$ and $y_2 = |x^3|$ are linearly independent solutions on the real line of the equation $x^2 y'' - 3xy' + 3y = 0$. (b) Verify that $W(y_1, y_2)$ is identically zero. Why do these facts not contradict Theorem 3?

31. Show that $y_1 = \sin x^2$ and $y_2 = \cos x^2$ are linearly independent functions, but that their Wronskian vanishes at $x = 0$. Why does this imply that there is *no* differential equation of the form $y'' + p(x)y' + q(x)y = 0$, with both p and q continuous everywhere, having both y_1 and y_2 as solutions?

32. Let y_1 and y_2 be two solutions of $A(x)y'' + B(x)y' + C(x)y = 0$ on an open interval I where A, B, and C are continuous and $A(x)$ is never zero. (a) Let $W = W(y_1, y_2)$. Show that

$$A(x) \frac{dW}{dx} = y_1 (Ay_2'') - y_2 (Ay_1'').$$

Then substitute for Ay_2'' and Ay_1'' from the original differential equation to show that

$$A(x) \frac{dW}{dx} = -B(x)W(x).$$

(b) Solve this first-order equation to deduce **Abel's formula**

$$W(x) = K \exp\left(-\int \frac{B(x)}{A(x)} dx \right),$$

where K is a constant. (c) Why does Abel's formula imply that the Wronskian $W(y_1, y_2)$ is either zero everywhere or nonzero everywhere (as stated in Theorem 3)?

Apply Theorems 5 and 6 to find general solutions of the differential equations given in Problems 33 through 42.

33. $y'' - 3y' + 2y = 0$ **34.** $y'' + 2y' - 15y = 0$

35. $y'' + 5y' = 0$ **36.** $2y'' + 3y' = 0$

37. $2y'' - y' - y = 0$ **38.** $4y'' + 8y' + 3y = 0$

39. $4y'' + 4y' + y = 0$ **40.** $9y'' - 12y' + 4y = 0$

41. $6y'' - 7y' - 20y = 0$ **42.** $35y'' - y' - 12y = 0$

3.1 Computing Project

If a graphics calculator or a computer graphing program is available, you can construct for yourself a picture like Fig. 3.1.3, illustrating a family of solution curves of the differential equation

$$y'' + 3y' + 2y = 0 \tag{1}$$

passing through the (same) point $(0, 1)$. Proceed as follows:

- First show that the general solution of Eq. (1) is

$$y(x) = c_1 e^{-x} + c_2 e^{-2x}. \tag{2}$$

- Then show that the general solution of Eq. (1) satisfying the initial conditions $y(0) = 1$, $y'(0) = b$ is

$$y(x) = (2 + b)e^{-x} - (1 + b)e^{-2x}. \tag{3}$$

The MATLAB loop

```
x = -1 : 0.025 : 5,
for b = -5 : 1 : 5
    y = (2 + b)*exp(-x) - (1 + b)*exp(-2*x);
    plot(x,y)
end
```

was used to generate Fig. 3.1.3.

After reproducing Fig. 3.1.3 in such a way, construct for each of the following second-order differential equations a variety of typical solution curves passing through the point $(0, 1)$.

1. $y'' - y = 0$
2. $y'' - 3y' + 2y = 0$
3. $2y'' + 3y' + y = 0$
4. $y'' + y = 0$ (see Example 1)
5. $y'' + 2y' + 2y = 0$, which has general solution
 $y(x) = e^{-x}(c_1 \cos x + c_2 \sin x)$.

3.2 General Solutions of Linear Equations

Only in very special cases can an nth-order differential equation of the general form $G(x, y, y', y'', \ldots y^{(n)}) = 0$ be solved exactly and explicitly. But we now show that our discussion in Section 3.1 of second-order linear equations generalizes in a very natural way to the general **nth-order linear** differential equation of the form

$$P_0(x)y^{(n)} + P_1(x)y^{(n-1)} + \cdots + P_{n-1}(x)y' + P_n(x)y = F(x). \tag{1}$$

Unless otherwise noted, we will always assume that the coefficient functions $P_i(x)$ and $F(x)$ are continuous on some open interval I (perhaps unbounded) where we wish to solve the equation. Under the additional assumption that $P_0(x) \neq 0$ at each point of I, we can divide each term in Eq. (1) by $P_0(x)$ to obtain an equation with leading coefficient 1, of the form

▶
$$y^{(n)} + p_1(x)y^{(n-1)} + \cdots + p_{n-1}(x)y' + p_n(x)y = f(x). \tag{2}$$

The **homogeneous** linear equation **associated** with Eq. (2) is

▶
$$y^{(n)} + p_1(x)y^{(n-1)} + \cdots + p_{n-1}(x)y' + p_n(x)y = 0. \tag{3}$$

Just as in the second-order case, a *homogeneous* nth-order linear differential equation has the valuable property that any superposition, or *linear combination,* of solutions of the equation is again a solution. The proof of the following theorem is essentially the same—a routine verification—as that of Theorem 1 of Section 3.1.

THEOREM 1: Principle of Superposition

Let y_1, y_2, \ldots, y_n be n solutions of the homogeneous linear equation in (3) on the interval I. If c_1, c_2, \ldots, c_n are constants, then the linear combination

$$y = c_1 y_1 + c_2 y_2 + \cdots + c_n y_n \tag{4}$$

is also a solution of Eq. (3) on I. ■

EXAMPLE 1 It is easy to verify that the three functions

$$y_1(x) = e^{3x}, \quad y_2(x) = \cos 2x, \quad \text{and} \quad y_3(x) = \sin 2x$$

are all solutions of the homogeneous third-order equation

$$y^{(3)} - 3y'' + 4y' - 12y = 0$$

on the entire real line. Theorem 1 tells us that any linear combination of these solutions, such as

$$y(x) = 7y_1(x) + 3y_2(x) - 2y_3(x) = 7e^{3x} + 3\cos 2x - 2\sin 2x,$$

is also a solution on the entire real line. We will see that, conversely, every solution of the differential equation of this example is a linear combination of the three particular solutions y_1, y_2, and y_3. Thus its general solution has the form

$$y(x) = c_1 e^{3x} + c_2 \cos 2x + c_3 \sin 2x.$$ ■

Existence and Uniqueness of Solutions

We saw in Section 3.1 that a particular solution of a *second-order* linear differential equation is determined by *two* initial conditions. Similarly, a particular solution of an nth-order linear differential equation is determined by n initial conditions. The following theorem, proved in the Appendix, is the natural generalization of Theorem 2 of Section 3.1.

THEOREM 2: Existence and Uniqueness

Suppose that the functions p_1, p_2, \ldots, p_n, and f are continuous on the open interval I containing the point a. Then, given n numbers $b_0, b_1, b_2, \ldots b_{n-1}$, the nth-order linear equation (Eq. (2))

$$y^{(n)} + p_1(x)y^{(n-1)} + \cdots + p_{n-1}(x)y' + p_n(x)y = f(x)$$

has a unique (that is, one and only one) solution on the entire interval I that satisfies the n initial conditions

$$y(a) = b_0, \qquad y'(a) = b_1, \qquad \ldots, \qquad y^{(n-1)}(a) = b_{n-1}. \qquad (5)$$

∎

Equation (2) and the conditions in (5) constitute an nth-order **initial value problem.** Theorem 2 tells us that any such initial value problem has a unique solution on the *whole* interval I where the coefficient functions in (2) are continuous. It tells us nothing, however, about how to find this solution. In Section 3.3 we will see how to construct explicit solutions of initial value problems in the *constant* coefficient case that occurs often in applications.

EXAMPLE 1
Continued

We saw earlier that

$$y(x) = 7e^{3x} + 3 \cos 2x - 2 \sin 2x$$

is a solution of

$$y^{(3)} - 3y'' + 4y' - 12y = 0$$

on the real line. The solution has the initial values $y(0) = 10$, $y'(0) = 17$, and $y''(0) = 51$. Theorem 2 assures us that this is the *only* solution with these initial values. ∎

Note that Theorem 2 implies that the *trivial* solution $y(x) \equiv 0$ is the only solution of the *homogeneous* equation

$$y^{(n)} + p_1(x)y^{(n-1)} + \cdots + p_{n-1}(x)y' + p_n(x)y = 0 \qquad (3)$$

that satisfies the *trivial* initial conditions

$$y(a) = y'(a) = \cdots = y^{(n-1)}(a) = 0.$$

EXAMPLE 2 It is easy to verify that

$$y_1(x) = x^2 \qquad \text{and} \qquad y_2(x) = x^3$$

are two different solutions of

$$x^2 y'' - 4xy' + 6y = 0,$$

and that both satisfy the initial conditions $y(0) = y'(0) = 0$. Why does this not contradict the uniqueness part of Theorem 2? It is because the leading coefficient in this differential equation vanishes at $x = 0$, so this equation cannot be written in the form of Eq. (3) with coefficient functions *continuous* on an open interval containing the point $x = 0$. ∎

Linearly Independent Solutions

On the basis of our knowledge of general solutions of second-order linear equations, we anticipate that a general solution of the *homogeneous n*th-order linear equation

$$y^{(n)} + p_1(x)y^{(n-1)} + \cdots + p_{n-1}(x)y' + p_n(x)y = 0 \qquad (3)$$

will be a linear combination

$$y = c_1 y_1 + c_2 y_2 + \cdots + c_n y_n, \qquad (4)$$

where y_1, y_2, \ldots, y_n are particular solutions of Eq. (3). But these n particular solutions must be "sufficiently independent" that we can always choose the coefficients c_1, c_2, \ldots, c_n in (4) to satisfy arbitrary initial conditions of the form in (5). The question is this: What should be meant by *independence* of three or more functions?

Recall that *two* functions f_1 and f_2 are linearly *dependent* if one is a constant multiple of the other; that is, if either $f_1 = kf_2$ or $f_2 = kf_1$ for some constant k. If we write these equations as

$$(1)f_1 + (-k)f_2 = 0 \qquad \text{or} \qquad (k)f_1 + (-1)f_2 = 0,$$

we see that the linear dependence of f_1 and f_2 implies that these exist two constants c_1 and c_2 *not both zero* such that

$$c_1 f_1 + c_2 f_2 = 0. \qquad (6)$$

Conversely, if c_1 and c_2 are not both zero, then Eq. (6) certainly implies that f_1 and f_2 are linearly dependent.

By analogy with Eq. (6), we say that n functions f_1, f_2, \ldots, f_n are *linearly dependent* provided that some *nontrivial* linear combination

$$c_1 f_1 + c_2 f_2 + \cdots + c_n f_n$$

of them vanishes identically; "nontrivial" means that *not all* of the coefficients c_1, c_2, \ldots, c_n are zero (although some of them may be zero).

DEFINITION: Linear Dependence of Functions

The n functions f_1, f_2, \ldots, f_n are said to be **linearly dependent** on the interval I provided that there exist constants c_1, c_2, \ldots, c_n not all zero such that

$$c_1 f_1 + c_2 f_2 + \cdots + c_n f_n = 0 \qquad (7)$$

on I; that is,

$$c_1 f_1(x) + c_2 f_2(x) + \cdots + c_n f_n(x) = 0$$

for all x in I. ■

If not all the coefficients in (7) are zero, then clearly we can solve for at least one of the functions as a linear combination of the others, and conversely. Thus the functions f_1, f_2, \ldots, f_n are linearly dependent if and only if at least one of them is a linear combination of the others.

EXAMPLE 3 The functions

$$f_1(x) = \sin 2x, \quad f_2(x) = \sin x \cos x, \quad \text{and} \quad f_3(x) = e^x$$

are linearly dependent on the real line because

$$(1)f_1 + (-2)f_2 + (0)f_3 = 0$$

(by the familiar trigonometric identity $\sin 2x = 2 \sin x \cos x$). ∎

The n functions f_1, f_2, \ldots, f_n are called **linearly independent** on the interval I provided that they are not linearly dependent there. Equivalently, they are linearly independent on I provided that the identity

$$c_1 f_1 + c_2 f_2 + \cdots + c_n f_n = 0 \tag{7}$$

holds on I only in the trivial case

$$c_1 = c_2 = \cdots = c_n = 0;$$

that is, *no* nontrivial linear combination of these functions vanishes on I. Put yet another way, the functions f_1, f_2, \ldots, f_n are linearly independent if no one of them is a linear combination of the others. (Why?)

Sometimes one can show that n given functions are linearly dependent by finding, as in Example 3, nontrivial values of the coefficients so that Eq. (7) holds. But in order to show that n given functions are linearly independent, we must prove that nontrivial values of the coefficients *cannot* be found, and this is seldom easy to do in any direct or obvious manner.

Fortunately, in the case of n solutions of a homogeneous nth-order linear equation, there is a tool that makes the determination of their linear dependence or independence a routine matter. This tool is the Wronskian determinant, which we introduced (for the case $n = 2$) in Section 3.1. Suppose that the n functions f_1, f_2, \ldots, f_n are each $n - 1$ times differentiable. Then their Wronskian is the $n \times n$ determinant

$$W = \begin{vmatrix} f_1 & f_2 & \cdots & f_n \\ f_1' & f_2' & \cdots & f_n' \\ \vdots & \vdots & & \vdots \\ f_1^{(n-1)} & f_2^{(n-1)} & \cdots & f_n^{(n-1)} \end{vmatrix}. \tag{8}$$

We write $W(f_1, f_2, \ldots, f_n)$ or $W(x)$, depending upon whether we wish to emphasize the functions or the point x at which their Wronskian is to be evaluated. The Wronskian is named after the Polish mathematician J. M. H. Wronski (1778–1853).

We saw in Section 3.1 that the Wronskian of two linearly dependent functions vanishes identically. More generally, *the Wronskian of n linearly dependent functions f_1, f_2, \ldots, f_n is identically zero.* To prove this, assume that Eq. (7) holds on the interval I for some choice of the constants c_1, c_2, \ldots, c_n not all zero. We then differentiate this equation $n - 1$ times in succession, obtaining the n equations

$$\begin{aligned} c_1 f_1(x) + c_2 f_2(x) &+ \cdots + c_n f_n(x) = 0, \\ c_1 f_1'(x) + c_2 f_2'(x) &+ \cdots + c_n f_n'(x) = 0, \\ &\vdots \\ c_1 f_1^{(n-1)}(x) + c_2 f_2^{(n-1)}(x) &+ \cdots + c_n f_n^{(n-1)}(x) = 0, \end{aligned} \tag{9}$$

which hold for all x in I. We recall from linear algebra that a system of n linear *homogeneous* equations in n unknowns has a nontrivial solution if and only if the determinant of coefficients vanishes. In Eq. (9) the unknowns are the constants c_1, c_2, \ldots, c_n and the determinant of coefficients is simply the Wronskian $W(f_1, f_2, \ldots, f_n)$ evaluated at the typical point x of I. Because we know that the c_i are not all zero, it follows that $W(x) \equiv 0$, as we wanted to prove.

Therefore, to show that the functions f_1, f_2, \ldots, f_n are *linearly independent* on the interval I, it suffices to show that their Wronskian is nonzero at just one point of I.

EXAMPLE 4 Show that the functions $y_1(x) = e^{3x}$, $y_2(x) = \cos 2x$, and $y_3(x) = \sin 2x$ (of Example 1) are linearly independent.

Solution: Their Wronskian is

$$W = \begin{vmatrix} e^{3x} & \cos 2x & \sin 2x \\ 3e^{3x} & -2\sin 2x & 2\cos 2x \\ 9e^{3x} & -4\cos 2x & -4\sin 2x \end{vmatrix}$$

$$= e^{3x}\begin{vmatrix} -2\sin 2x & 2\cos 2x \\ -4\cos 2x & -4\sin 2x \end{vmatrix} - 3e^{3x}\begin{vmatrix} \cos 2x & \sin 2x \\ -4\cos 2x & -4\sin 2x \end{vmatrix}$$

$$+ 9e^{3x}\begin{vmatrix} \cos 2x & \sin 2x \\ -\sin 2x & 2\cos 2x \end{vmatrix} = 26e^{3x} \neq 0.$$

Because $W \neq 0$ everywhere, it follows that y_1, y_2, and y_3 are linearly independent on any open interval (including the whole real line).

EXAMPLE 5 Show first that the three solutions

$$y_1(x) = x, \quad y_2(x) = x\ln x, \quad \text{and} \quad y_3(x) = x^2$$

of the third-order equation

$$x^3 y^{(3)} - x^2 y'' + 2xy' - 2y = 0 \tag{10}$$

are linearly independent on the open interval $x > 0$. Then find a particular solution of Eq. (10) that satisfies the initial conditions

$$y(1) = 3, \quad y'(1) = 2, \quad y''(1) = 1. \tag{11}$$

Solution: Note that for $x > 0$, we could divide each term in (10) by x^3 to obtain a homogeneous linear equation of the standard form in (3). When we compute the Wronskian of the three given solutions, we find that

$$W = \begin{vmatrix} x & x\ln x & x^2 \\ 1 & 1+\ln x & 2x \\ 0 & \dfrac{1}{x} & 2 \end{vmatrix} = x.$$

Thus $W \neq 0$ for $x > 0$, so y_1, y_2, and y_3 are linearly independent on the interval $x > 0$. To find the desired particular solution, we impose the initial conditions in (11) on

$$y(x) = c_1 x + c_2 x \ln x \quad + c_3 x^2,$$
$$y'(x) = c_1 \quad + c_2(1 + \ln x) + 2c_3 x,$$
$$y''(x) = 0 \quad + \frac{c_2}{x} \quad + 2c_3.$$

This yields the simultaneous equations

$$y(1) = c_1 \quad + c_3 = 3,$$
$$y'(1) = c_1 + c_2 + 2c_3 = 2,$$
$$y''(1) = \quad c_2 + 2c_3 = 1;$$

we solve to find $c_1 = 1$, $c_2 = -3$, and $c_3 = 2$. Thus the particular solution in question is

$$y(x) = x - 3x \ln x + 2x^2. \qquad \blacksquare$$

Provided that $W(y_1, y_2, \ldots, y_n) \neq 0$, it turns out (Theorem 4) that we can always find values of the coefficients in the linear combination

$$y = c_1 y_1 + c_2 y_2 + \cdots + c_n y_n$$

in order to satisfy any given initial conditions of the form in (5). Theorem 3 provides the necessary nonvanishing of W in the case of linearly independent solutions.

THEOREM 3: Wronskians of Solutions

Suppose that y_1, y_2, \ldots, y_n are n solutions of the homogeneous nth-order linear equation

$$y^{(n)} + p_1(x)y^{(n-1)} + \cdots + p_{n-1}(x)y' + p_n(x)y = 0 \qquad (3)$$

on an open interval I where each p_i is continuous. Let

$$W = W(y_1, y_2, \ldots, y_n).$$

(a) If y_1, y_2, \ldots, y_n are linearly dependent, then $W \equiv 0$ on I.
(b) If y_1, y_2, \ldots, y_n are linearly independent, then $W \neq 0$ at each point of I.

Thus there are just two possibilities: Either $W = 0$ everywhere on I, or $W \neq 0$ everywhere on I.

Proof: We have already proven part (a). To prove part (b), it is sufficient to assume that $W(a) = 0$ at some point of I, and show that this implies the solutions y_1, y_2, \ldots, y_n are linearly dependent. But $W(a)$ is simply the determinant of coefficients of the system of n homogeneous linear equations

$$c_1 y_1(a) + c_2 y_2(a) \quad + \cdots + \quad c_n y_n(a) = 0,$$
$$c_1 y_1'(a) + c_2 y_2'(a) \quad + \cdots + \quad c_n y_n'(a) = 0,$$
$$\vdots \qquad (12)$$
$$c_1 y_1^{(n-1)}(a) + c_2 y_2^{(n-1)}(a) + \cdots + c_n y_n^{(n-1)}(a) = 0$$

in the n unknowns c_1, c_2, \ldots, c_n. Because $W(a) = 0$, the basic fact from linear algebra quoted just after (9) implies that the equations in (12) have a nontrivial solution. That is, the numbers c_1, c_2, \ldots, c_n are not all zero.

We now use these values to define the particular solution

$$Y(x) = c_1 y_1(x) + c_2 y_2(x) + \cdots + c_n y_n(x) \tag{13}$$

of Eq. (3). The equations in (12) then imply that Y satisfies the trivial initial conditions

$$Y(a) = Y'(a) = \cdots = Y^{(n-1)}(a) = 0.$$

Theorem 2 (uniqueness) therefore implies that $Y(x) \equiv 0$ on I. In view of (13) and the fact that c_1, c_2, \ldots, c_n are not all zero, this is the desired conclusion that the solutions y_1, y_2, \ldots, y_n are linearly dependent. This completes the proof of Theorem 3. ∎

General Solutions

We can now show that every solution of a *homogeneous* nth-order solution is a linear combination of n given linearly independent solutions. Using the fact from Theorem 3 that the Wronskian of n linearly independent solutions is nonzero, the proof of the following theorem is essentially the same as the proof of Theorem 4 of Section 3.1 (the case $n = 2$).

THEOREM 4: General Solutions of Homogeneous Equations

Let y_1, y_2, \ldots, y_n be n linearly independent solutions of the homogeneous equation

$$y^{(n)} + p_1(x)y^{(n-1)} + \cdots + p_{n-1}(x)y' + p_n(x)y = 0 \tag{3}$$

on an open interval I where the p_i are continuous. If Y is any solution whatsoever of Eq. (3), then there exist numbers c_1, c_2, \ldots, c_n such that

$$Y(x) = c_1 y_1(x) + c_2 y_2(x) + \cdots + c_n y_n(x)$$

for all x in I. ∎

Thus *every* solution of a homogeneous nth-order linear differential equation is a linear combination

$$y = c_1 y_1 + c_2 y_2 + \cdots + c_n y_n$$

of any n given linearly independent solutions. On this basis we call such a linear combination the **general solution** of the differential equation.

Nonhomogeneous Equations

We now consider the *nonhomogeneous* nth-order linear differential equation

$$Ly = y^{(n)} + p_1(x)y^{(n-1)} + \cdots + p_{n-1}(x)y' + p_n(x)y = f(x) \tag{2}$$

with associated homogeneous equation

$$Ly = y^{(n)} + p_1(x)y^{(n-1)} + \cdots + p_{n-1}(x)y' + p_n(x)y = 0. \tag{3}$$

FIGURE 3.2.1. The idea of L "operating" on the function y

Here we introduce the symbol L to represent an **operator;** given an n times differentiable function y, L *operates* on y (as suggested in Fig. 3.2.1) to produce the linear combination

$$Ly = y^{(n)} + p_1 y^{(n-1)} + \cdots + p_{n-1} y' + p_n y \tag{14}$$

of y and its first n derivatives. The principle of superposition (Theorem 1) means simply that the operator L is *linear;* that is,

$$L(c_1 y_1 + c_2 y_2) = c_1 L y_1 + c_2 L y_2 \tag{15}$$

if c_1 and c_2 are constants.

Suppose that a single particular solution y_p of the nonhomogeneous equation in (2) is known and that Y is any other solution of Eq. (2). Then Eq. (15) implies that

$$L(Y - y_p) = LY - Ly_p = f - f = 0.$$

Thus $y_c = Y - y_p$ is a solution of the associated homogeneous equation in (3). Then

$$Y = y_c + y_p, \tag{16}$$

and it follows from Theorem 4 that

$$y_c = c_1 y_1 + c_2 y_2 + \cdots + c_n y_n, \tag{17}$$

where y_1, y_2, \ldots, y_n are linearly independent solutions of the associated *homogeneous* equation. We call y_c a **complementary function** of the nonhomogeneous equation and have thus proved that a *general solution* of the nonhomogeneous equation in (2) is the sum of its complementary function y_c and a single particular solution y_p of Eq. (2).

THEOREM 5: Solutions of Nonhomogeneous Equations

Let y_p be a particular solution of the nonhomogeneous equation in (2) on an open interval I where the functions p_i and f are continuous. Let y_1, y_2, \ldots, y_n be linearly independent solutions of the associated homogeneous equation in (3). If Y is any solution whatsoever of Eq. (2) on I, then there exist numbers c_1, c_2, \ldots, c_n such that

$$Y(x) = c_1 y_1(x) + c_2 y_2(x) + \cdots + c_n y_n(x) + y_p(x) \tag{18}$$

for all x in I. ∎

EXAMPLE 6 It is evident that $y_p(x) = 3x$ is a particular solution of the equation

$$y'' + 4y = 12x, \tag{19}$$

and that $y_c(x) = c_1 \cos 2x + c_2 \sin 2x$ is its complementary solution. Find a solution of Eq. (19) that satisfies the initial conditions $y(0) = 5$, $y'(0) = 7$.

Solution: The general solution of Eq. (19) is

$$y(x) = c_1 \cos 2x + c_2 \sin 2x + 3x.$$

Now

$$y'(x) = -2c_1 \sin 2x + 2c_2 \cos 2x + 3.$$

Hence the initial conditions give

$$y(0) = c_1 = 5,$$
$$y'(0) = 2c_2 + 3 = 7.$$

We find that $c_1 = 5$ and $c_2 = 2$. Thus the desired solution is

$$y(x) = 5\cos 2x + 2\sin 2x + 3x.$$

3.2 Problems

In Problems 1 through 6, show directly that the given functions are linearly dependent on the real line. That is, find a nontrivial linear combination of the given functions that vanishes identically.

1. $f(x) = 2x$, $g(x) = 3x^2$, $h(x) = 5x - 8x^2$

2. $f(x) = 5$, $g(x) = 2 - 3x^2$, $h(x) = 10 + 15x^2$

3. $f(x) = 0$, $g(x) = \sin x$, $h(x) = e^x$

4. $f(x) = 17$, $g(x) = 2\sin^2 x$, $h(x) = 3\cos^2 x$

5. $f(x) = 17$, $g(x) = \cos^2 x$, $h(x) = \cos 2x$

6. $f(x) = e^x$, $g(x) = \cosh x$, $h(x) = \sinh x$

In Problems 7 through 12, use the Wronskian to prove that the given functions are linearly independent on the indicated interval.

7. $f(x) = 1$, $g(x) = x$, $h(x) = x^2$; the real line

8. $f(x) = e^x$, $g(x) = e^{2x}$, $h(x) = e^{3x}$; the real line

9. $f(x) = e^x$, $g(x) = \cos x$, $h(x) = \sin x$; the real line

10. $f(x) = e^x$, $g(x) = x^{-2}$, $h(x) = x^{-2}\ln x$; $x > 0$

11. $f(x) = x$, $g(x) = xe^x$, $h(x) = x^2 e^x$; the real line

12. $f(x) = x$, $g(x) = \cos(\ln x)$, $h(x) = \sin(\ln x)$; $x > 0$

In Problems 13 through 20, a third-order homogeneous linear equation and three linearly independent solutions are given. Find a particular solution satisfying the given initial conditions.

13. $y^{(3)} + 2y'' - y' - 2y = 0$; $y(0) = 1$, $y'(0) = 2$, $y''(0) = 0$; $y_1 = e^x$, $y_2 = e^{-x}$, $y_3 = e^{-2x}$

14. $y^{(3)} - 6y'' + 11y' - 6y = 0$; $y(0) = 0$, $y'(0) = 0$, $y''(0) = 3$; $y_1 = e^x$, $y_2 = e^{2x}$, $y_3 = e^{3x}$

15. $y^{(3)} - 3y'' + 3y' - y = 0$; $y(0) = 2$, $y'(0) = 0$, $y''(0) = 0$; $y_1 = e^x$, $y_2 = xe^x$, $y_3 = x^2 e^x$

16. $y^{(3)} - 5y'' + 8y' - 4y = 0$; $y(0) = 1$, $y'(0) = 4$, $y''(0) = 0$; $y_1 = e^x$, $y_2 = e^{2x}$, $y_3 = xe^{2x}$

17. $y^{(3)} + 9y'' = 0$; $y(0) = 3$, $y'(0) = -1$, $y''(0) = 2$; $y_1 = 1$, $y_2 = \cos 3x$, $y_3 = \sin 3x$

18. $y^{(3)} - 3y'' + 4y' - 2y = 0$; $y(0) = 1$, $y'(0) = 0$, $y''(0) = 0$; $y_1 = e^x$, $y_2 = e^x\cos x$, $y_3 = e^x\sin x$

19. $x^3 y^{(3)} - 3x^2 y'' + 6xy' - 6y = 0$; $y(1) = 6$, $y'(1) = 14$, $y''(1) = 22$; $y_1 = x$, $y_2 = x^2$, $y_3 = x^3$

20. $x^3 y^{(3)} + 6x^2 y'' + 4xy' - 4y = 0$; $y(1) = 1$, $y'(1) = 5$, $y''(1) = -11$; $y_1 = x$, $y_2 = x^{-2}$, $y_3 = x^{-2}\ln x$

In Problems 21 through 24, a nonhomogeneous differential equation, a complementary solution y_c, and a particular solution y_p are given. Find a solution satisfying the given initial conditions.

21. $y'' + y = 3x$; $y(0) = 2$, $y'(0) = -2$; $y_c = c_1\cos x + c_2\sin x$; $y_p = 3x$

22. $y'' - 4y = 12$; $y(0) = 0$, $y'(0) = 10$; $y_c = c_1 e^{2x} + c_2 e^{-2x}$; $y_p = -3$

23. $y'' - 2y' - 3y = 6$; $y(0) = 3$, $y'(0) = 11$; $y_c = c_1 e^{-x} + c_2 e^{3x}$; $y_p = -2$

24. $y'' - 2y' + 2y = 2x$; $y(0) = 4$, $y'(0) = 8$; $y_c = c_1 e^x\cos x + c_2 e^x\sin x$; $y_p = x + 1$

25. Let $Ly = y'' + py' + qy$. Suppose that y_1 and y_2 are two functions such that

$$Ly_1 = f(x) \qquad \text{and} \qquad Ly_2 = g(x).$$

Show that their sum $y = y_1 + y_2$ satisfies the nonhomogeneous equation $Ly = f(x) + g(x)$.

26. (a) Find by inspection particular solutions of the two nonhomogeneous equations

$$y'' + 2y = 4 \qquad \text{and} \qquad y'' + 2y = 6x.$$

(b) Use the method of Problem 25 to find a particular solution of the differential equation $y'' + 2y = 6x + 4$.

ily real. Finding the exact values of these zeros may be difficult or even impossible; the quadratic formula is sufficient for second-degree equations, but for equations of high degree we may need to spot a fortuitous factorization, or restore to numerical techniques (such as Newton's method or Müller's method—see any numerical analysis text).

Distinct Real Roots

Whatever the method we use, let us suppose that we have solved the characteristic equation. Then we can always write a general solution of the differential equation. The situation is slightly more complicated in the case of repeated roots or complex roots of Eq. (3), so let us first examine the simplest case—in which the characteristic equation has n distinct (no two equal) *real* roots r_1, r_2, \ldots, r_n. Then the functions

$$e^{r_1 x}, \quad e^{r_2 x}, \quad \ldots, \quad e^{r_n x}$$

are all solutions of Eq. (1), and (by Problem 34 of Section 3.2) these n solutions are linearly independent on the entire real line. In summary, we have proved Theorem 1.

THEOREM 1: Distinct Real Roots

If the roots r_1, r_2, \ldots, r_n of the characteristic equation in (3) are real and distinct, then

$$y(x) = c_1 e^{r_1 x} + c_2 e^{r_2 x} + \cdots + c_n e^{r_n x} \tag{4}$$

is the general solution of Eq. (1). ■

EXAMPLE 1 Solve the initial value problem

$$y'' + 2y' - 8y = 0; \quad y(0) = 5, \quad y'(0) = -2.$$

Solution: According to Theorem 1 we need only solve the characteristic equation

$$r^2 + 2r - 8 = (r - 2)(r + 4) = 0$$

for $r = 2, -4$. Hence the general solution is

$$y(x) = c_1 e^{2x} + c_2 e^{-4x}.$$

Then

$$y'(x) = 2c_1 e^{2x} - 4c_2 e^{-4x},$$

so the given initial conditions yield the equations

$$y(0) = \quad c_1 + \quad c_2 = 5,$$
$$y'(0) = 2c_1 - 4c_2 = -2$$

that we readily solve for $c_1 = 3$, $c_2 = 2$. Thus the desired particular solution is

$$y(x) = 3e^{2x} + 2e^{-4x}.$$

EXAMPLE 2 Find a general solution of

$$y^{(3)} - y'' - 6y' = 0.$$

Solution: The characteristic equation of this differential equation is

$$r^3 - r^2 - 6r = 0,$$

which we solve by factoring:

$$r(r^2 - r - 6) = r(r - 3)(r + 2) = 0,$$

so the three roots are $r = 0$, $r = 3$, and $r = -2$. They are real and distinct, and there-fore—because $e^0 = 1$—a general solution of the given differential equation is

$$y(x) = c_1 + c_2 e^{3x} + c_3 e^{-2x}.$$ ■

Polynomial Operators

If the roots of the characteristic equation in (3) are *not* distinct—there are repeated roots—then we cannot produce n linearly independent solutions of Eq. (1) by the method of Theorem 1. For example, if the roots are 1, 2, 2, and 2, we obtain only the *two* functions e^x and e^{2x}. The problem, then, is to produce the missing linearly inde-pendent solutions. For this purpose it is convenient to adopt the operator notation in-troduced near the conclusion of Section 3.2. Equation (1) corresponds to the operator equation $Ly = 0$ where L is the operator

$$L = a_n \frac{d^n}{dx^n} + a_{n-1} \frac{d^{n-1}}{dx^{n-1}} + \cdots + a_2 \frac{d^2}{dx^2} + a_1 \frac{d}{dx} + a_0. \tag{5}$$

We also denote by $D = d/dx$ the operation of differentiation with respect to x, so that

$$Dy = y', \qquad D^2 y = y'', \qquad D^3 y = y^{(3)},$$

and so on. In terms of D, the operator L in (5) may be written

$$L = a_n D^n + a_{n-1} D^{n-1} + \cdots + a_2 D^2 + a_1 D + a_0, \tag{6}$$

and we will find it useful to think of the right-hand side in (6) as a (formal) nth-degree polynomial in the "variable" D; it is a **polynomial operator.**

A first-degree polynomial operator has the form $D - a$ where a is a real number. It operates on the function $y = y(x)$ to produce

$$(D - a)y = Dy - ay = y' - ay.$$

The important fact about such operators is that any two of them *commute:*

$$(D - a)(D - b)y = (D - b)(D - a)y \tag{7}$$

for any twice differentiable function $y = y(x)$. The proof of the formula in (7) is the following computation:

$$
\begin{aligned}
(D - a)(D - b)y &= (D - a)(y' - by) \\
&= D(y' - by) - a(y' - by) \\
&= y'' - (b + a)y' + aby = y'' - (a + b)y' + bay \\
&= D(y' - ay) - b(y' - ay) \\
&= (D - b)(y' - ay) = (D - b)(D - a)y.
\end{aligned}
$$

Repeated Roots

Let us now consider the possibility that the characteristic equation

$$a_n r^n + a_{n-1} r^{n-1} + \cdots + a_2 r^2 + a_1 r + a_0 = 0 \qquad (3)$$

has *repeated* roots. For example, suppose that Eq. (3) has only two distinct roots, r_0 of multiplicity 1 and r_1 of multiplicity $k > 0$. Then Eq. (3) can be rewritten in the form

$$(r - r_1)^k (r - r_0) = (r - r_0)(r - r_1)^k = 0. \qquad (8)$$

Similarly, the operator L in (6) can be written as

$$L = (D - r_1)^k (D - r_0) = (D - r_0)(D - r_1)^k, \qquad (9)$$

the order of the factors making no difference because of the formula in (7).

Two solutions of the differential equation $Ly = 0$ are certainly $y_0 = e^{r_0 x}$ and $y_1 = e^{r_1 x}$. This is, however, not sufficient; we need $k + 1$ linearly independent solutions in order to construct a general solution, because the equation is of order $k + 1$. To find the missing $k - 1$ solutions, we note that

$$Ly = (D - r_0)[(D - r_1)^k y] = 0.$$

Consequently, *every* solution of the kth-order equation

$$(D - r_1)^k y = 0 \qquad (10)$$

will also be a solution of the original equation $Ly = 0$. Hence our problem is reduced to that of finding the general solution of the differential equation in (10).

The fact that $e^{r_1 x}$ is one solution of (10) suggests that we try the substitution

$$y(x) = u(x) e^{r_1 x}, \qquad (11)$$

where $u(x)$ is a function yet to be determined. Observe that

$$(D - r_1)[ue^{r_1 x}] = (Du)e^{r_1 x} + r_1 u e^{r_1 x} - r_1 u e^{r_1 x},$$

so

$$(D - r_1)[ue^{r_1 x}] = (Du)e^{r_1 x}. \qquad (12)$$

It therefore follows by induction on k that

$$(D - r_1)^k [ue^{r_1 x}] = (D^k u) e^{r_1 x} \qquad (13)$$

for any function $u(x)$. Hence $y = ue^{r_1 x}$ will be a solution of (10) if and only if $D^k u = u^{(k)} = 0$. But this is so if and only if

$$u(x) = c_1 + c_2 x + c_3 x^2 + \cdots + c_k x^{k-1},$$

a polynomial of degree at most $k - 1$. Hence our desired solution of (10) is

$$y(x) = ue^{r_1 x} = (c_1 + c_2 x + \cdots + c_k x^{k-1})e^{r_1 x}.$$

In particular, we see here the additional solutions $xe^{r_1 x}, x^2 e^{r_1 x}, \ldots, x^{k-1} e^{r_1 x}$ of the original differential equation $Ly = 0$.

The preceding analysis can be carried out with the operator $D - r_0$ replaced with an arbitrary polynomial operator. When this is done, the result is a proof of the following theorem.

THEOREM 2: Repeated Roots

If the characteristic equation in (3) has a repeated root r of multiplicity k, then the part of the general solution of the differential equation in (1) corresponding to r is of the form

▶
$$(c_1 + c_2 x + c_3 x^2 + \cdots + c_k x^{k-1})e^{rx}. \qquad (14)$$
■

We may observe that according to Problem 29 of Section 3.2, the k functions e^{rx}, xe^{rx}, $x^2 e^{rx}$, . . . , and $x^{k-1}e^{rx}$ involved in (14) are linearly independent on the real line. Thus a root of multiplicity k corresponds to k linearly independent solutions of the differential equation.

EXAMPLE 3 The differential equation

$$y'' + 4y' + 4y = 0$$

has the characteristic equation

$$r^2 + 4r + 4 = (r + 2)^2 = 0$$

with double root $r = -2, -2$. Hence with $k = 2$ Theorem 2 yields the general solution

$$y(x) = (c_1 + c_2 x)e^{-2x}.$$

EXAMPLE 4 Find a general solution of

$$y^{(4)} + 3y^{(3)} + 3y'' + y' = 0.$$

Solution: The characteristic equation of this differential equation is

$$r^4 + 3r^3 + 3r^2 + r = r(r + 1)^3 = 0.$$

It has the simple root $r_1 = 0$, which contributes $y_1 \equiv c_1$ to the general solution. It has also the triple ($k = 3$) root $r_2 = -1$, which contributes $y_2 = (c_2 + c_3 x + c_4 x^2)e^{-x}$ to the solution. Hence the general solution of the differential equation is

$$y(x) = c_1 + (c_2 + c_3 x + c_4 x^2)e^{-x}.$$
■

Complex-Valued Functions and Euler's Formula

Because we have assumed that the coefficients of the differential equation and its characteristic equation are real, any complex (nonreal) roots will occur in complex conjugate pairs $a \pm bi$ where a and b are real and $i = \sqrt{-1}$. This raises the question as to what might be meant by an exponential such as $\exp([a + bi]x)$.

To answer this question, we recall from elementary calculus the Taylor series for the exponential function:

$$e^t = \sum_{n=0}^{\infty} \frac{t^n}{n!} = 1 + t + \frac{t^2}{2!} + \frac{t^3}{3!} + \frac{t^4}{4!} + \cdots.$$

If we substitute $t = ix$ in this series, we get

$$e^{ix} = \sum_{n=0}^{\infty} \frac{(ix)^n}{n!}$$

$$= 1 + ix - \frac{x^2}{2!} - \frac{ix^3}{3!} + \frac{x^4}{4!} + \frac{ix^5}{5!} - \cdots$$

$$= \left(1 - \frac{x^2}{2!} + \frac{x^4}{4!} - \cdots\right) + i\left(x - \frac{x^3}{3!} + \frac{x^5}{5!} - \cdots\right).$$

Because the two real series in the last line are the Taylor series for $\cos x$ and $\sin x$, respectively, this implies that

$$e^{ix} = \cos x + i \sin x. \tag{15}$$

This result is known as **Euler's formula.** Because of it we *define* the exponential function e^z, for $z = x + iy$ an arbitrary complex number, to be

$$e^z = e^{x+iy} = e^x e^{iy} = e^x(\cos y + i \sin y). \tag{16}$$

Thus it appears that complex roots of the characteristic equation will lead to complex-valued solutions of the differential equations. A **complex-valued function** F of the real variable x associates with each real number x (in its domain of definition) the complex number

$$z = F(x) = f(x) + ig(x). \tag{17}$$

The real-valued functions f and g are called the **real** and **imaginary** parts, respectively, of F. If they are differentiable, we define the **derivative** F' of F to be

$$F'(x) = f'(x) + ig'(x). \tag{18}$$

Thus we simply differentiate the real and imaginary parts of F separately. Similarly, we say that the complex-valued function $y = F(x)$ **satisfies** the differential equation in (1) provided that its real and imaginary parts separately satisfy that differential equation.

The particular complex-valued functions of interest here are of the form $F(x) = e^{rx}$ where $r = a \pm bi$. We note from Euler's formula that

$$e^{(a+bi)x} = e^{ax}(\cos bx + i \sin bx). \tag{19a}$$

and

$$e^{(a-bi)x} = e^{ax}(\cos bx - i \sin bx). \tag{19b}$$

The most important property of e^{rx} is

$$D_x(e^{rx}) = re^{rx} \tag{20}$$

even if r should be a complex number. The proof of this assertion is a straightforward computation based on the definitions and formulas given earlier:

$$D_x(e^{rx}) = D_x(e^{ax}\cos bx) + iD_x(e^{ax}\sin bx)$$

$$= [ae^{ax}\cos bx - be^{ax}\sin bx] + i[ae^{ax}\sin bx + be^{ax}\cos bx]$$

$$= (a+bi)(e^{ax}\cos bx + ie^{ax}\sin bx) = re^{rx}.$$

Complex Roots

It follows from Eq. (20) that when r is complex (just as when r is real), e^{rx} will be a solution of the differential equation in (1) if and only if r is a root of its characteristic equation. If the complex conjugate pairs of roots $r_1 = a + bi$ and $r_2 = a - bi$ are simple (nonrepeated), then the corresponding part of a general solution of (1) is

$$C_1 e^{(a + bi)x} + C_2 e^{(a - bi)x} = C_1 e^{ax}(\cos bx + i \sin bx) + C_2 e^{ax}(\cos bx - i \sin bx)$$
$$= e^{ax}(c_1 \cos bx + c_2 \sin bx),$$

where $c_1 = C_1 + C_2$ and $c_2 = (C_1 - C_2)i$. Thus the conjugate pair of roots $a \pm bi$ leads to the linearly independent *real-valued* solutions $e^{ax} \cos bx$ and $e^{ax} \sin bx$. This yields the following result.

THEOREM 3: Complex Roots

If the characteristic equation in (3) has an unrepeated pair of complex conjugate roots $a \pm bi$ (with $b \neq 0$), then the corresponding part of a general solution of (1) is of the form

$$e^{ax}(c_1 \cos bx + c_2 \sin bx). \qquad \blacksquare \quad (21)$$

EXAMPLE 5 The characteristic equation of

$$y'' + b^2 y = 0 \qquad (b > 0)$$

is $r^2 + b^2 = 0$, with roots $r = \pm bi$. So Theorem 3 (with $a = 0$) gives the general solution

$$y(x) = c_1 \cos bx + c_2 \sin bx.$$

EXAMPLE 6 Find the particular solution of

$$y'' - 4y' + 5y = 0$$

for which $y(0) = 1$ and $y'(0) = 5$.

Solution: The characteristic equation is

$$r^2 - 4r + 5 = (r - 2)^2 + 1 = 0,$$

with roots $2 + i$ and $2 - i$. Hence a general solution is

$$y(x) = e^{2x}(c_1 \cos x + c_2 \sin x).$$

Then

$$y'(x) = 2e^{2x}(c_1 \cos x + c_2 \sin x) + e^{2x}(-c_1 \sin x + c_2 \cos x),$$

so the initial conditions give

$$y(0) = c_1 = 1 \qquad \text{and} \qquad y'(0) = 2c_1 + c_2 = 5.$$

It follows that $c_2 = 3$, and so the desired particular solution is

$$y(x) = e^{2x}(\cos x + 3 \sin x).$$

EXAMPLE 7 Find a general solution of $y^{(4)} + 4y = 0$.

Solution: The characteristic equation is

$$r^4 + 4 = (r^2 + 2i)(r^2 - 2i) = 0,$$

and its four roots are $\pm\sqrt{\pm 2i}$. Now $i = e^{i\pi/2}$ and $-i = e^{3i\pi/2}$, so

$$\sqrt{i} = (e^{i\pi/2})^{1/2} = e^{i\pi/4} = \frac{1 + i}{\sqrt{2}}$$

and

$$\sqrt{-i} = (e^{3i\pi/2})^{1/2} = e^{3i\pi/4} = \frac{-1 + i}{\sqrt{2}}.$$

Thus the four (distinct) roots of the characteristic equation are $r = \pm(1 \pm i)$. These two pairs of complex conjugate roots, $1 \pm i$ and $-1 \pm i$, give a general solution

$$y(x) = e^x(c_1 \cos x + c_2 \sin x) + e^{-x}(c_3 \cos x + c_4 \sin x)$$

of the differential equation $y^{(4)} + 4y = 0$. ∎

In Example 7 we employed the polar form

$$x + iy = re^{i\theta} \tag{22}$$

of a complex number. The relation between the real and imaginary parts x, y and the **modulus** r and **argument** θ is indicated in Fig. 3.3.1. One consequence of (22) is that the nonzero complex number $x + iy$ has the two square roots

$$\pm(x + iy)^{1/2} = \pm(re^{i\theta})^{1/2} = \pm r^{1/2}e^{i\theta/2}. \tag{23}$$

FIGURE 3.3.1. Modulus and argument of the complex number $x + iy$

Repeated Complex Roots

Theorem 2 holds for repeated complex roots. If the conjugate pair $a \pm bi$ has multiplicity k, then the corresponding part of the general solution has the form

$$(A_1 + A_2 x + \cdots + A_k x^{k-1})e^{(a + bi)x} + (B_1 + B_2 x + \cdots + B_k x^{k-1})e^{(a - bi)x}$$

$$= \sum_{p=0}^{k-1} x^p e^{ax}(c_i \cos bx + d_i \sin bx). \tag{24}$$

It can be shown that the $2k$ functions

$$x^p e^{ax} \cos bx, \qquad x^p e^{ax} \sin bx, \qquad 0 \le p \le k - 1$$

that appear in (24) are linearly independent.

EXAMPLE 8 Find a general solution of $(D^2 + 6D + 13)^2 y = 0$.

Solution By completing the square, we see that the characteristic equation

$$(r^2 + 6r + 13)^2 = [(r + 3)^2 + 4]^2 = 0$$

has as its roots the conjugate pair $-3 \pm 2i$ of multiplicity 2. Hence Eq. (24) gives the general solution

$$y(x) = e^{-3x}(c_1 \cos 2x + d_1 \sin 2x) + xe^{-3x}(c_2 \cos 2x + d_2 \sin 2x). \qquad ∎$$

In applications we are seldom presented in advance with a factorization as convenient as the one in Example 8. Often the most difficult part of solving a homogeneous linear equation is finding the roots of its characteristic equation. Example 9 illustrates an approach that may succeed when a root of the characteristic equation can be found by inspection. The project material for this section illustrates other possibilities.

EXAMPLE 9 The characteristic equation of the differential equation

$$y^{(3)} + y' - 10y = 0$$

is the cubic equation

$$r^3 + r - 10 = 0.$$

By a standard theorem of elementary algebra, the only possible rational roots are the factors ± 1, ± 2, ± 5, and ± 10 of the constant term 10. By trial-and-error (if not by immediate inspection) we discover the root $r = 2$. The factor theorem of elementary algebra implies that $r - 2$ is a factor of $r^3 + r - 10$, and division of the former into the latter produces as quotient the quadratic polynomial

$$r^2 + 2r + 5 = (r + 1)^2 + 4.$$

The roots of this quotient are the complex conjugates $-1 \pm 2i$. The three roots we have found now yield the general solution

$$y(x) = c_1 e^{2x} + e^{-x}(c_2 \cos 2x + c_3 \sin 2x).$$

EXAMPLE 10 The roots of the characteristic equation of a certain differential equation are 3, -5, 0, 0, 0, 0, -5, $2 \pm 3i$, and $2 \pm 3i$. Write the general solution of this homogeneous differential equation.

Solution The solution can be read directly from the list of roots. It is

$$y(x) = c_1 + c_2 x + c_3 x^2 + c_4 x^3 + c_5 e^{3x} + c_6 e^{-5x} + c_7 x e^{-5x}$$
$$+ e^{2x}(c_8 \cos 3x + c_9 \sin 3x) + xe^{2x}(c_{10} \cos 3x + c_{11} \sin 3x).$$

3.3 Problems

Find the general solutions of the differential equations in Problems 1 through 20.

1. $y'' - 4y = 0$

2. $2y'' - 3y' = 0$

3. $y'' + 3y' - 10y = 0$

4. $2y'' - 7y' + 3y = 0$

5. $y'' + 6y' + 9y = 0$

6. $y'' + 5y' + 5y = 0$

7. $4y'' - 12y' + 9y = 0$

8. $y'' - 6y' + 13y = 0$

9. $y'' + 8y' + 25y = 0$

10. $5y^{(4)} + 3y^{(3)} = 0$

11. $y^{(4)} - 8y^{(3)} + 16y'' = 0$

12. $y^{(4)} - 3y^{(3)} + 3y'' - y' = 0$

13. $9y^{(3)} + 12y'' + 4y' = 0$

14. $y^{(4)} + 3y'' - 4y = 0$

15. $y^{(4)} - 8y'' + 16y = 0$

16. $y^{(4)} + 18y'' + 81y = 0$

17. $6y^{(4)} + 11y'' + 4y = 0$

18. $y^{(4)} = 16y$

19. $y^{(3)} + y'' - y' - y = 0$

20. $y^{(4)} + 2y^{(3)} + 3y'' + 2y' + y = 0$ (*Suggestion:* Compute $(r^2 + r + 1)^2$.)

Solve the initial value problems given in Problems 21 through 26.

21. $y'' - 4y' + 3y = 0$; $y(0) = 7$, $y'(0) = 11$

22. $9y'' + 6y' + 4y = 0$; $y(0) = 3$, $y'(0) = 4$

23. $y'' - 6y' + 25y = 0$; $y(0) = 3$, $y'(0) = 1$

24. $2y^{(3)} - 3y'' - 2y' = 0$; $y(0) = 1$, $y'(0) = 1$, $y''(0) = 3$

25. $3y^{(3)} + 2y'' = 0$; $y(0) = -1$, $y'(0) = 0$,
$y''(0) = 1$

26. $y^{(3)} + 10y'' + 25y' = 0$; $y(0) = 3$, $y'(0) = 4$,
$y''(0) = 5$

Find the general solutions of the equations in Problems 27 through 32. First find a small integral root of the characteristic equation by inspection; then factor by division.

27. $y^{(3)} + 3y'' - 4y = 0$

28. $2y^{(3)} - y'' - 5y' - 2y = 0$

29. $y^{(3)} + 27y = 0$

30. $y^{(4)} - y^{(3)} + y'' - 3y' - 6y = 0$

31. $y^{(3)} + 3y'' + 4y' - 8y = 0$

32. $y^{(4)} + y^{(3)} - 3y'' - 5y' - 2y = 0$

In Problems 33 through 36, one solution of the differential equation is given. Find the general solution.

33. $y^{(3)} + 3y'' - 54y = 0$; $y = e^{3x}$

34. $3y^{(3)} - 2y'' + 12y' - 8y = 0$; $y = e^{2x/3}$

35. $6y^{(4)} + 5y^{(3)} + 25y'' + 20y' + 4y = 0$; $y = \cos 2x$

36. $9y^{(3)} + 11y'' + 4y' - 14y = 0$; $y = e^{-x}\sin x$

Problems 37 through 41 pertain to the solution of differential equations with complex coefficients.

37. (a) Use Euler's formula to show that every complex number can be written in the form $re^{i\theta}$, where $r \geq 0$ and $-\pi < \theta \leq \pi$. **(b)** Express the numbers 4, -2, $3i$, $1 + i$, and $-1 + i\sqrt{3}$ in the form $re^{i\theta}$. **(c)** The two square roots of $re^{i\theta}$ are $\pm e^{i\theta/2}\sqrt{r}$. Find the square roots of the numbers $2 - 2i\sqrt{3}$ and $-2 + 2i\sqrt{3}$.

38. Use the quadratic formula to solve the following equations. Note in each case that the roots are not complex conjugates. **(a)** $x^2 + ix + 2 = 0$. **(b)** $x^2 - 2ix + 3 = 0$.

39. Find a general solution of $y'' - 2iy' + 3y = 0$.

40. Find a general solution of $y'' - iy' + 6y = 0$.

41. Find a general solution of $y'' = (-2 + 2i\sqrt{3})y$.

42. Solve the initial value problem

$$y^{(3)} = y; \qquad y(0) = 1, \qquad y'(0) = y''(0) = 0.$$

(*Suggestion:* Impose the given initial conditions on the general solution

$$y(x) = Ae^x + Be^{\alpha x} + Ce^{\beta x},$$

where α and β are the complex conjugate roots of $r^3 - 1 = 0$, to discover that

$$y(x) = \frac{1}{3}\left(e^x + 2e^{-x/2}\cos\frac{x\sqrt{3}}{2}\right)$$

is a solution.)

43. Solve the initial value problem

$$y^{(4)} = y^{(3)} + y'' + y' + 2y;$$

$$y(0) = y'(0) = y''(0) = 0, \qquad y^{(3)}(0) = 30.$$

44. The differential equation

$$y'' + (\operatorname{sgn} x)y = 0 \qquad\qquad (25)$$

has the discontinuous coefficient function

$$\operatorname{sgn} x = \begin{cases} +1 & \text{if } x > 0, \\ -1 & \text{if } x < 0. \end{cases}$$

Show that Eq. (25) nevertheless has two linearly independent solutions $y_1(x)$ and $y_2(x)$ defined for all x such that:

- Each satisfies Eq. (25) at each point $x \neq 0$.
- Each has a continuous derivative at $x = 0$.
- $y_1(0) = y_2'(0) = 1$ and $y_2(0) = y_1'(0) = 0$.

(*Suggestion:* Each $y_i(x)$ will be defined by one formula for $x \leq 0$ and by another for $x \geq 0$.)

3.3 Computing Project

To meet the needs of applications such as those of this section, polynomial-solving utilities are now a common feature of calculator and computer systems, and can be used to solve a characteristic equation numerically even when no simple factorization is evident or even possible. For instance, suppose that we want to solve the homogeneous linear differential equation

$$y^{(3)} - 3y'' + y = 0 \qquad\qquad (1)$$

with characteristic polynomial

$$r^3 - 3r^2 + 1 = 0. \tag{2}$$

With a calculator (like the TI-85) having a built-in polynomial solver, we can simply enter the coefficients $1, -3, 0, 1$ of this cubic polynomial and get the three (approximate) roots $r = -0.5321, 0.6527, 2.8794$ at the press of a key.

With a system like *Maple* or *Mathematica* we can enter a one-line command like

```
NSolve[ r^3 - 3 r^2 + 1 == 0, r ]
```

to solve Eq. (2) numerically for the approximate roots of the characteristic equation. However we find them, it follows that a general solution of the differential equation in (1) is given (approximately) by

$$y(x) = c_1 e^{-0.5321x} + c_2 e^{0.6527x} + c_3 e^{2.8794x}. \tag{3}$$

Systems like *Maple* and *Mathematica* also offer simple commands for the direct solution of differential equations. Using *Maple,* for instance, we can first define the differential equation in (1) by entering the command

```
> diffeq := diff(y(x),x$3) - 3*diff(y(x),x$2) + y(x) = 0;
```

$$diffeq := \left(\frac{\partial^3}{\partial x^3} y(x)\right) - 3\left(\frac{\partial^2}{\partial x^2} y(x)\right) + y(x) = 0$$

and then ask for the solution by means of the command

```
> dsolve( diffeq, y(x) );
```

$$y(x) = _C1 \ e^{(2\cos(1/9 \ \pi) + 1)x}$$

$$+ _C2 \ e^{-(\cos(1/9 \ \pi) - 1 + \sqrt{3} \sin(1/9 \ \pi))x}$$

$$+ _C3 \ e^{-x(\cos(1/9 \ \pi) - 1 - \sqrt{3} \sin(1/9 \ \pi))}$$

Evidently *Maple* has solved the cubic characteristic equation exactly in terms of trigonometric functions! To compare this result with the solution given in (3), we can apply the function **evalf** to convert exact expressions to floating point approximations:

```
> evalf(");
```

$$y(x) = _C1 \ e^{2.8794x} + _C2 \ e^{-.53209x} + _C3 \ e^{.65271x}$$

Use calculator or computer methods like those indicated above to find general solutions (in approximate numerical form) of the following differential equations.

1. $y^{(3)} - 3y' + y = 0$
2. $y^{(3)} + 3y'' - 3y = 0$
3. $y^{(3)} + y' + y = 0$
4. $y^{(3)} + 3y' + 5y = 0$
5. $y^{(4)} + 2y^{(3)} - 3y = 0$
6. $y^{(4)} + 3y' - 4y = 0$

3.4 Mechanical Vibrations

The motion of a mass attached to a spring serves as a relatively simple example of the vibrations that occur in more complex mechanical systems. For many such systems, the analysis of these vibrations is a problem in the solution of linear differential equations with constant coefficients.

We consider a body of mass m attached to one end of an ordinary spring that resists compression as well as stretching; the other end of the spring is attached to a fixed wall, as shown in Fig. 3.4.1. Assume that the body rests on a frictionless horizontal plane, so that it can move only back and forth as the spring stretches and compresses. Denote by x the distance of the body from its **equilibrium position**—its position when the spring is unstretched. We take $x > 0$ when the spring is stretched, and thus $x < 0$ when it is compressed.

Equilibrium
position

FIGURE 3.4.1. A mass-spring-dashpot system

According to Hooke's law, the restorative force F_S that the spring exerts on the mass is proportional to the distance x that the spring has been stretched or compressed. Because this is the same as the displacement x of the mass m from its equilibrium position, it follows that

$$F_S = -kx. \tag{1}$$

The positive constant of proportionality k is called the **spring constant.** Note that F_S and x have opposite signs: $F_S < 0$ when $x > 0$, $F_S > 0$ when $x < 0$.

Figure 3.4.1 shows the mass attached to a dashpot—a device, like a shock absorber, that provides a force directed opposite to the instantaneous direction of motion of the mass m. We assume the dashpot is so designed that this force F_R is proportional to the velocity $v = dx/dt$ of the mass; that is,

$$F_R = -cv = -c\frac{dx}{dt}. \tag{2}$$

The positive constant c is the **damping constant** of the dashpot. More generally, we may regard (2) as specifying frictional forces in our system (including air resistance to the motion of m).

If, in addition to the forces F_S and F_R, the mass is subjected to a given **external force** $F_E = F(t)$, then the total force acting on the mass is $F = F_S + F_R + F_E$. Using Newton's law

$$F = ma = m\frac{d^2x}{dt^2} = mx'',$$

we obtain the second-order linear differential equation

$$\blacktriangleright \qquad mx'' + cx' + kx = F(t) \tag{3}$$

that governs the motion of the mass.

If there is no dashpot (and we ignore all frictional forces), then we set $c = 0$ in (3) and call the motion **undamped;** it is **damped** motion if $c > 0$. If there is no external force we replace $F(t)$ by 0 in (3). We refer to the motion as **free** in this case and **forced** in the case $F(t) \neq 0$. Thus the homogeneous equation

$$\blacktriangleright \qquad mx'' + cx' + kx = 0 \tag{4}$$

FIGURE 3.4.2. A mass suspended vertically from a spring

describes free motion of a mass on a spring with dashpot but with no external forces applied. We will defer discussion of forced motion until Section 3.6.

For an alternative example, we might attach the mass to the lower end of a spring that is suspended vertically from a fixed support, as in Fig. 3.4.2. In this case the weight $W = mg$ of the mass would stretch the spring a distance s_0 determined by Eq. (1) with $F_S = -W$ and $x = s_0$. That is, $mg = ks_0$, so that $s_0 = mg/k$. This gives the **static** equilibrium position of the mass. If y denotes the displacement of the mass in motion, measured downward from its static equilibrium position, then we ask you to show in Problem 9 that y satisfies Eq. (3); specifically, that

$$my'' + cy' + ky = F(t) \tag{5}$$

if we include damping and external forces.

The Simple Pendulum

The importance of the differential equation that appears in Eqs. (3) and (5) stems from the fact that it describes the motion of many other simple mechanical systems. For example, a **simple pendulum** consists of a mass m swinging back and forth on the end of a string (or better, a *massless rod*) of length L, as shown in Fig. 3.4.3. We may specify the position of the mass at time t by giving the counterclockwise angle $\theta = \theta(t)$ that the string or rod makes with the vertical at time t. To analyze the motion of the mass m, we will apply the law of the conservation of mechanical energy, according to which the sum of the kinetic energy and the potential energy of m remains constant.

The distance along the circular arc from 0 to m is $s = L\theta$, so the velocity of the mass is $v = ds/dt = L(d\theta/dt)$, and therefore its kinetic energy is

$$T = \frac{1}{2} mv^2 = \frac{1}{2} m \left(\frac{ds}{dt} \right)^2 = \frac{1}{2} mL^2 \left(\frac{d\theta}{dt} \right)^2.$$

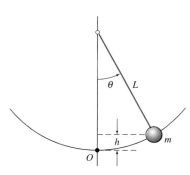

FIGURE 3.4.3. The simple pendulum

We next choose as reference point the lowest point O reached by the mass (see Fig. 3.4.3). Then its potential energy V is the product of its weight mg and its vertical height $h = L(1 - \cos \theta)$ above O, so

$$V = mgL(1 - \cos \theta).$$

The fact that the sum of T and V is a constant C therefore gives

$$\frac{1}{2} mL^2 \left(\frac{d\theta}{dt} \right)^2 + mgL(1 - \cos \theta) = C.$$

We differentiate both sides of this identity with respect to t to obtain

$$mL^2 \left(\frac{d\theta}{dt} \right) \left(\frac{d^2\theta}{dt^2} \right) + mgL (\sin \theta) \frac{d\theta}{dt} = 0,$$

so

$$\frac{d^2\theta}{dt^2} + \frac{g}{L} \sin \theta = 0 \tag{6}$$

after removal of the common factor $mL^2(d\theta/dt)$.

Now recall that $\sin \theta \approx \theta$ when θ is small; in fact, $\sin \theta$ and θ agree to two decimal places when $|\theta|$ is at most $\pi/12$ ($15°$). In a typical pendulum clock, for example, θ would never exceed $15°$. It therefore seems reasonable to simplify our mathematical

model of the simple pendulum by replacing $\sin \theta$ with θ in Eq. (6). If we also insert a term $c\theta'$ to account for the frictional resistance of the surrounding medium, the result is an equation of the form of Eq. (4):

$$\theta'' + c\theta' + k\theta = 0, \tag{7}$$

where $k = g/L$. Note that this equation is independent of the mass m on the end of the rod. We might, however, expect for the effects of the discrepancy between θ and $\sin \theta$ to accumulate over a period of time, so that Eq. (7) will probably not describe accurately the actual motion of the pendulum over a long period of time.

In the remainder of this section, we first analyze free undamped motion and then free damped motion.

Free Undamped Motion

If we have only a mass on a spring, with neither damping nor external force, then Eq. (3) takes the simpler form

$$mx'' + kx = 0. \tag{8}$$

It is convenient to define

$$\omega_0 = \sqrt{\frac{k}{m}}, \tag{9}$$

and rewrite Eq.(8) as

$$x'' + \omega_0^2 x = 0. \tag{8'}$$

The general solution of Eq. (8′) is

$$x(t) = A \cos \omega_0 t + B \sin \omega_0 t. \tag{10}$$

To analyze the motion described by this solution, we choose constants C and α so that

$$C = \sqrt{A^2 + B^2}, \qquad \cos \alpha = \frac{A}{C}, \qquad \text{and} \qquad \sin \alpha = \frac{B}{C}, \tag{11}$$

as indicated in Fig. 3.4.4. Note that, though $\tan \alpha = B/A$, the angle α is *not* given by the principal branch of the inverse tangent function (which gives values only in the interval $(-\pi/2, \pi/2)$). Instead, α is the angle between 0 and 2π whose cosine and sine have the signs given in (11), where either A or B or both may be negative.

In any event, from (10) and (11) we get

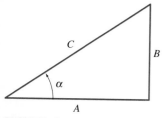

FIGURE 3.4.4. The angle α

$$x(t) = C\left(\frac{A}{C} \cos \omega_0 t + \frac{B}{C} \sin \omega_0 t\right) = C(\cos \alpha \cos \omega_0 t + \sin \alpha \sin \omega_0 t).$$

With the aid of the cosine addition formula, we find that

$$x(t) = C\cos(\omega_0 t - \alpha). \tag{12}$$

Thus the mass oscillates to-and-fro about its equilibrium position with

Amplitude $\qquad C$,

Circular frequency $\qquad \omega_0,$ and

Phase angle $\qquad \alpha$.

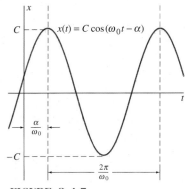

FIGURE 3.4.5. Simple harmonic motion

Such motion is called **simple harmonic motion.** A typical graph of $x(t)$ is shown in Fig. 3.4.5. If time t is measured in seconds, the circular frequency ω_0 has dimensions of radians per second (rad/s). The **period** of the motion is the time required for the system to complete one full oscillation, so is given by

$$T = \frac{2\pi}{\omega_0} \tag{13}$$

seconds; its **frequency** is

$$\frac{1}{T} = \frac{\omega_0}{2\pi} \tag{14}$$

in hertz (Hz), which measures the number of complete cycles per second. Note that frequency is measured in cycles per second, whereas circular frequency has the dimensions of radians per second.

If the initial position $x(0) = x_0$ and initial velocity $x'(0) = v_0$ of the mass are given, we first determine the values of the coefficients A and B in (10), and then find the amplitude C and phase angle α by carrying out the transformation of $x(t)$ to the form in (12), as indicated above.

EXAMPLE 1 A body with mass $m = \frac{1}{2}$ kilogram (kg) is attached to the end of a spring that is stretched 2 meters (m) by a force of 100 Newtons (N). It is set in motion with initial position $x_0 = 0.5$ (m) and initial velocity $v_0 = -10$ (m/s). (Note that these data indicate that the body is displaced to the right and moving to the left at time $t = 0$.) Find the position function of the body as well as the amplitude, frequency, period of oscillation, and phase angle of its motion.

Solution The spring constant is $k = (100 \text{ N})/(2 \text{ m}) = 50$ (N/m), so Eq. (8) yields $\frac{1}{2}x'' + 50x = 0$; that is,

$$x'' + 100x = 0.$$

Consequently, the circular frequency will be $\omega_0 = 10$ (rad/s). So the body will oscillate with

$$\text{frequency:} \quad \frac{10}{2\pi} \approx 1.59 \text{ Hz}$$

and

$$\text{period:} \quad \frac{2\pi}{10} \approx 0.63 \text{ s}.$$

We now impose the initial conditions $x(0) = 0.5$ and $x'(0) = 10$ on the general solution $x(t) = A \cos 10t + B \sin 10t$, and it follows that $A = 0.5$ and $B = -1$. So the position function of the body is

$$x(t) = \frac{1}{2} \cos 10t - \sin 10t.$$

Hence its amplitude of motion is

$$C = \sqrt{\left(\frac{1}{2}\right)^2 + 1^2} = \frac{1}{2}\sqrt{5} \approx 1.12 \quad \text{(m)}.$$

To find the phase angle, we write

$$x(t) = \frac{\sqrt{5}}{2}\left(\frac{1}{\sqrt{5}}\cos 10t - \frac{2}{\sqrt{5}}\sin 10t\right) = \frac{\sqrt{5}}{2}\cos(10t - \alpha).$$

Thus we require $\cos\alpha = 1/\sqrt{5} > 0$ and $\sin\alpha = -2/\sqrt{5} < 0$. Hence α is the fourth-quadrant angle

$$\alpha = 2\pi - \tan^{-1}\left(\frac{2/\sqrt{5}}{1/\sqrt{5}}\right) \approx 5.1760 \quad (\text{rad}).$$

In the form in which the amplitude and phase angle are made explicit, the position function is

$$x(t) \approx \frac{\sqrt{5}}{2}\cos(10t - 5.1760).$$

Free Damped Motion

With damping but no external force, the differential equation we have been studying takes the form $mx'' + cx' + kx = 0$; alternatively,

$$x'' + 2px' + \omega_0^2 x = 0, \tag{15}$$

where $\omega_0 = \sqrt{k/m}$ is the corresponding *undamped* circular frequency and

$$p = \frac{c}{2m} > 0. \tag{16}$$

The characteristic equation $r^2 + 2pr + \omega_0^2 = 0$ of (15) has roots

$$r_1, r_2 = -p \pm (p^2 - \omega_0^2)^{1/2} \tag{17}$$

that depend upon the sign of

$$p^2 - \omega_0^2 = \frac{c^2}{4m^2} - \frac{k}{m} = \frac{c^2 - 4km}{4m^2}.$$

The **critical damping** c_{CR} is given by $c_{CR} = \sqrt{4km}$, and we distinguish three cases, according as $c > c_{CR}$, $c = c_{CR}$, or $c < c_{CR}$.

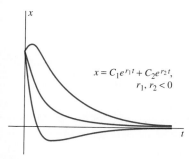

$x = C_1 e^{r_1 t} + C_2 e^{r_2 t},$
$r_1, r_2 < 0$

FIGURE 3.4.6. Overdamped motion

Overdamped Case: $c > c_{CR}$ ($c^2 > 4km$). Because c is relatively large in this case, we are dealing with a strong resistance in comparison with a relatively weak spring or small mass. Then (17) gives distinct real roots r_1 and r_2, both of which are negative. The position function has the form

$$x(t) = c_1 e^{r_1 t} + c_2 e^{r_2 t}. \tag{18}$$

It is easy to see that $x(t) \to 0$ as $t \to +\infty$ and that the body settles to its equilibrium position without any oscillations (Problem 27). Fig. 3.4.6 shows some typical graphs of the position function for the overdamped case; we chose x_0 a fixed positive number and illustrated the effects of changing the initial velocity v_0. In every case the would-be oscillations are damped out.

Critically Damped Case: $c = c_{CR}$ *($c^2 = 4km$).* In this case (17) gives equal roots $r_1 = r_2 = -p$ of the characteristic equation, so the general solution is

$$x(t) = e^{-pt}(c_1 + c_2 t). \tag{19}$$

Because $e^{-pt} > 0$ and $c_1 + c_2 t$ has at most one positive zero, the body passes through its equilibrium position at most once, and it is clear that $x(t) \to 0$ as $t \to +\infty$. Some graphs of the motion in the critically damped case appear in Fig. 3.4.7, and they resemble those of the overdamped case (Fig. 3.4.6). In the critically damped case, the resistance of the dashpot is just large enough to damp out any oscillations, but even a slight decrease in resistance will bring us to the remaining case, the one that shows the most dramatic behavior.

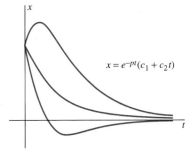

FIGURE 3.4.7. Critically damped motion

Underdamped Case: $c < c_{CR}$ *($c^2 < 4km$).* The characteristic equation now has the two complex conjugate roots $-p \pm i\sqrt{\omega_0^2 - p^2}$, and the general solution is

$$x(t) = e^{-pt}(c_1 \cos \omega_1 t + c_2 \sin \omega_1 t), \tag{20}$$

where

$$\omega_1 = \sqrt{\omega_0^2 - p^2} = \frac{\sqrt{4km - c^2}}{2m}. \tag{21}$$

Using the cosine addition formula as in the derivation of Eq. (12), we may rewrite (20) as

$$x(t) = Ce^{-pt} \cos(\omega_1 t - \alpha), \tag{22}$$

where $C = \sqrt{c_1^2 + c_2^2}$ and $\tan \alpha = c_2 / c_1$.

The solution in (22) represents exponentially damped oscillations of the body about its equilibrium position. The graph of $x(t)$ lies between the curves $x = Ce^{-pt}$ and $x = Ce^{-pt}$ and touches them when $\omega_1 t - \alpha$ is an integral multiple of π. The motion is not actually periodic, but it nevertheless is useful to call ω_1 its **circular frequency**, $T_1 = 2\pi/\omega_1$ its **pseudoperiod** of oscillation, and Ce^{-pt} its **time-varying amplitude.** Most of these quantities are shown in the typical graph of underdamped motion shown in Fig. 3.4.8. Note from Eq. (21) that in this case ω_1 is less than the undamped circular frequency ω_0, so T_1 is larger than the period T of oscillation of the same mass without damping on the same spring. Thus the action of the dashpot has at least three effects:

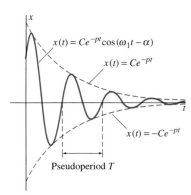

FIGURE 3.4.8. Underdamped oscillations

1. It exponentially damps the oscillations, in accord with the time-varying amplitude.

2. It slows the motion; that is, the dashpot decreases the frequency of the motion.

3. It delays the motion—this is the effect of the phase angle in Eq. (22).

EXAMPLE 2 The mass and spring of Example 1 are now attached also to a dashpot that provides 6 N of resistance for each meter per second of velocity. The mass is set in motion with the same initial position $x(0) = 0.5$ (m) and the same initial velocity $x'(0) = -10$ (m/s). Find the position function of the mass, its new frequency and pseudoperiod, its phase angle, and the amplitudes of its first four (local) maxima and minima.

Solution Rather than memorizing the various formulas given in the preceding discussion, it is better practice in a particular case to set up the differential equation and then solve it directly. Recall that $m = \frac{1}{2}$ and $k = 50$; we are now given $c = 6$ in mks units. Hence Eq. (3) is $\frac{1}{2} x'' + 6x' + 50x = 0$; that is,

$$x'' + 12x' + 100x = 0.$$

The roots of the characteristic equation $r^2 + 12r + 100 = 0$ are

$$\frac{-12 \pm \sqrt{144 - 400}}{2} = -6 \pm 8i,$$

so the general solution is

$$x(t) = e^{-6t}(A \cos 8t + B \sin 8t). \tag{23}$$

The new circular frequency is $\omega_1 = 8$ (rad/s) and the pseudoperiod and new frequency are

$$T_1 = \frac{2\pi}{8} \approx 0.79 \quad (s)$$

and

$$\frac{1}{T_1} = \frac{8}{2\pi} \approx 1.27 \quad (Hz)$$

(in contrast with 0.63 s and 1.59 Hz, respectively, in the undamped case).

From (23) we compute

$$x'(t) = e^{-6t}(-8A \sin 8t + 8B \cos 8t) - 6e^{-6t}(A \cos 8t + B \sin 8t).$$

The initial conditions therefore produce the equations

$$x(0) = A = \frac{1}{2} \quad \text{and} \quad x'(0) = -6A + 8B = -10,$$

so $A = \frac{1}{2}$ and $B = -\frac{7}{8}$. Thus

$$x(t) = e^{-6t}\left(\frac{1}{2}\cos 8t - \frac{7}{8}\sin 8t\right),$$

and so with

$$C = \sqrt{\left(\frac{1}{2}\right)^2 + \left(\frac{7}{8}\right)^2} = \frac{1}{8}\sqrt{65}$$

we have

$$x(t) = \frac{\sqrt{65}}{8} e^{-6t}\left(\frac{4}{\sqrt{65}}\cos 8t - \frac{7}{\sqrt{65}}\sin 8t\right).$$

We require $\cos \alpha = 4/\sqrt{65} > 0$ and $\sin \alpha = -7/\sqrt{65} < 0$, so α is the fourth-quadrant angle

$$\alpha = 2\pi - \tan^{-1}\left(\frac{7}{4}\right) \approx 5.2315 \quad (rad).$$

Finally,

$$x(t) \approx \frac{\sqrt{65}}{8} e^{-6t} \cos(8t - 5.2315). \tag{24}$$

The local maxima and minima of $x(t)$ occur when

$$0 = x'(t)$$

$$\approx \frac{\sqrt{65}}{8} [-6e^{-6t} \cos(8t - 5.2315) - 8e^{-6t} \sin(8t - 5.2315)],$$

and thus when

$$\tan(8t - 5.2315) \approx -0.75.$$

Because $\tan^{-1}(-0.75) \approx -0.6435$, we want to find the first four positive values of t such that $8t - 5.2315$ is the sum of -0.6435 and an integral multiple of π. These values of t and the corresponding values of x computed with the aid of (24) are as follows:

t (s)	0.1808	0.5735	0.9662	1.3589
x (m)	-0.2725	0.0258	-0.0024	0.0002

We see that the oscillations are damped out very rapidly, with their amplitude decreasing by a factor of about 10 every half-cycle. See Problems 30 and 31 for a more general discussion of this phenomenon. ∎

3.4 Problems

1. Determine the period and frequency of the simple harmonic motion of a 4-kg mass on the end of a spring with spring constant 16 N/m.

2. Determine the period and frequency of the simple harmonic motion of a body of mass 0.75 kg on the end of a spring with spring constant 48 N/m.

3. A mass of 3 kg is attached to the end of a spring that is stretched 20 cm by a force of 15 N. It is set in motion with initial position $x_0 = 0$ and initial velocity $v_0 = -10$ m/s. Find the amplitude, period, and frequency of the resulting motion.

4. A body with mass 250 g is attached to the end of a spring that is stretched 25 cm by a force of 9 N. At time $t = 0$ the body is pulled 1 m to the right, stretching the spring, and set in motion with an initial velocity of 5 m/s to the left. (a) Find $x(t)$ in the form $C \cos(\omega_0 t + \alpha)$. (b) Find the amplitude and period of the motion of the body.

In Problems 5 through 8, assume that the differential equation of a simple pendulum of length L is $L\theta'' + g\theta = 0$, where $g = GM/R^2$ is the gravitational acceleration at the location of

the pendulum (at distance R from the center of the earth; M denotes the mass of the earth).

5. Two pendulums are of lengths L_1 and L_2, and—when located at the respective distances R_1 and R_2 from the center of the earth—have periods p_1 and p_2. Show that

$$\frac{p_1}{p_2} = \frac{R_1 \sqrt{L_1}}{r_2 \sqrt{L_2}}.$$

6. A certain pendulum clock keeps perfect time in Paris, where the radius of the earth is $R = 3956$ (mi). But this clock loses 2 min 40 s per day at a location on the equator. Use the result of Problem 5 to find the amount of the equatorial bulge of the earth.

7. A pendulum of length 100.10 in., located at a point at sea level where the radius of the earth is $R = 3960$ (mi), has the same period as does a pendulum of length 100.00 in. atop a nearby mountain. Use the result of Problem 5 to find the height of the mountain.

8. Most grandfather clocks have pendulums with adjustable

lengths. One such clock loses 10 min per day when the length of its pendulum is 30 in. With what length pendulum will this clock keep perfect time?

9. Derive Eq. (5) describing the motion of a mass attached to the bottom of a vertically suspended spring. (*Suggestion:* First denote by $x(t)$ the displacement of the mass below the un-stretched position of the spring; set up the differential equation for x. Then substitute $y = x - x_0$ in this differential equation.)

10. Consider a floating cylindrical buoy with radius r, height h, and density $\rho \leqq 0.5$ (recall that the density of water is 1 g/cm³). The buoy is initially suspended at rest with its bottom at the top surface of the water and is released at time $t = 0$. Thereafter it is acted on by two forces: a downward gravitational force equal to its weight $mg = \rho\pi r^2 hg$ and an upward force of buoyancy equal to the weight $\pi r^2 xg$ of water displaced, where $x = x(t)$ is the depth of the bottom of the buoy beneath the surface at time t (Fig. 3.4.9). Conclude that the buoy undergoes simple harmonic motion about the equilibrium position $x_e = \rho h$ with period $p = 2\pi\sqrt{\rho h/g}$. Compute p and the amplitude of the motion if $\rho = 0.5$ g/cm³, $h = 200$ cm, and $g = 980$ cm/s².

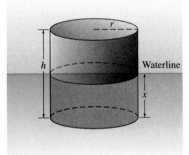

FIGURE 3.4.9. The buoy of Problem 10

11. A cylindrical buoy weighing 100 lb (thus of mass $m = 3.125$ slugs in ft-lb-s (fps) units) floats in water with its axis vertical (as in Problem 10). When depressed slightly and released, it oscillates up and down four times every 10 s. Assume that friction is negligible. Find the radius of the buoy.

12. Assume that the earth is a solid sphere of uniform density, with mass M and radius $R = 3960$ (mi). For a particle of mass m *within* the earth at distance r from the center of the earth, the gravitational force attracting m toward the center is $F_r = -GM_r m/r^2$, where M_r is the mass of the part of the earth within a sphere of radius r. (a) Show that $F_r = -GMmr/R^3$. (b) Now suppose that a hole is drilled straight through the center of the earth, thus connecting two antipodal points on its surface. Let a particle of mass m be dropped at time $t = 0$ into this hole with initial speed zero, and let $r(t)$ be its distance from the center of the earth at time t (Fig. 3.4.10). Conclude from Newton's second law and part (a) that $r''(t) = -k^2 r(t)$, where

FIGURE 3.4.10. A mass m falling down a hole through the center of the earth (Problem 12)

$k^2 = GM/R^3 = g/R$. (c) Take $g = 32.2$ ft/s², and conclude from part (b) that the particle undergoes simple harmonic motion back and forth between the ends of the hole, with a period of about 84 min. (d) Look up (or derive) the period of a satellite that just skims the surface of the earth; compare with the results in part (c). How do you explain the coincidence? Or *is* it a coincidence? (e) With what speed (in miles per hour) does the particle pass through the center of the earth? (f) Look up or derive the orbital velocity of a satellite that just skims the surface of the earth; compare the value with the result in part (e). How do you explain the coincidence? Or *is* it a coincidence?

The remaining problems in this section deal with free damped motion. In Problems 13 through 19, a mass m is attached to both a spring (with given spring constant k) and a dashpot (with given damping constant c). The mass is set in motion with initial position x_0 and initial velocity v_0. Find the position function $x(t)$ and determine whether the motion is over-damped, critically, damped, or underdamped. If it is under-damped, write $x(t)$ in the form $Ce^{-pt}\cos(\omega_1 t - \alpha)$.

13. $m = \frac{1}{2}$, $c = 3$, $k = 4$; $x_0 = 2$, $v_0 = 0$

14. $m = 3$, $c = 30$, $k = 63$; $x_0 = 2$, $v_0 = 2$

15. $m = 1$, $c = 8$, $k = 16$; $x_0 = 5$, $v_0 = -10$

16. $m = 2$, $c = 12$, $k = 50$; $x_0 = 0$, $v_0 = -8$

17. $m = 4$, $c = 20$, $k = 169$; $x_0 = 4$, $v_0 = 16$

18. $m = 2$, $c = 16$, $k = 40$; $x_0 = 5$, $v_0 = 4$

19. $m = 1$, $c = 10$, $k = 125$; $x_0 = 6$, $v_0 = 50$

20. A 12-lb weight (mass $m = 0.375$ slugs in fps units) is attached both to a vertically suspended spring that it stretches 6 in. and to a dashpot that provides 3 lb of resistance for every foot per second of velocity. (a) If the weight is pulled down 1 ft below its static equilibrium position and then released from rest at time $t = 0$, find its position function $x(t)$. (b) Find

the frequency, time-varying amplitude, and phase angle of the motion.

21. This problem deals with a highly simplified model of a car of weight 3200 lb (mass $m = 100$ slugs in fps units). Assume that the suspension system of the car acts like a single spring and its shock absorbers like a single dashpot, so that its vertical vibrations satisfy Eq. (4) with appropriate values of the coefficients. (a) Find the stiffness coefficient k of the spring if the car undergoes free vibrations at 80 cycles per minute (cycles/min) when its shock absorbers are disconnected. (b) With the shock absorbers connected the car is set into vibration by driving it over a bump, and the resulting damped vibrations have a frequency of 78 cycles/min. After how long will the time-varying amplitude be 1% of its initial value?

Problems 22 through 32 deal with a mass-spring-dashpot system having position function $x(t)$ satisfying Eq. (4). We write $x_0 = x(0)$ and $v_0 = x'(0)$ and recall that $p = c/(2m)$, $\omega_0^2 = k/m$, and $\omega_1^2 = \omega_0^2 - p^2$. The system is critically damped, overdamped, or underdamped, as specified in each problem.

22. (Critically damped) Show in this case that

$$x(t) = (x_0 + v_0 t + p x_0 t) e^{-pt}.$$

23. (Critically damped) Deduce from Problem 22 that the mass passes through $x = 0$ at some instant $t > 0$ if and only if x_0 and $v_0 + p x_0$ have opposite signs.

24. (Critically damped) Deduce from Problem 22 that $x(t)$ has a local maximum or minimum at some instant $t > 0$ if and only if v_0 and $v_0 + p x_0$ have the same sign.

25. (Overdamped) Show in this case that

$$x(t) = \frac{1}{2\gamma} [(v_0 - r_2 x_0) e^{r_1 t} - (v_0 - r_1 x_0) e^{r_2 t}],$$

where $r_1, r_2 = -p \pm \sqrt{p^2 - \omega_0^2}$ and $\gamma = (r_1 - r_2)/2 > 0$.

26. (Overdamped) If $x_0 = 0$, deduce from Problem 25 that

$$x(t) = \frac{v_0}{\gamma} e^{-pt} \sinh \gamma t.$$

27. (Overdamped) Prove that in this case the mass can pass through its equilibrium position $x = 0$ at most once.

28. (Underdamped) Show that in this case

$$x(t) = e^{-pt} \left(x_0 \cos \omega_1 t + \frac{v_0 + p x_0}{\omega_1} \sin \omega_1 t \right).$$

29. (Underdamped) If the damping constant c is small in comparison with $\sqrt{8mk}$, apply the binomial series to show that

$$\omega_1 \approx \omega_0 \left(1 - \frac{c^2}{8mk} \right).$$

30. (Underdamped) Show that the local maxima and minima of $x(t) = Ce^{-pt} \cos(\omega_1 t - \alpha)$ occur where

$$\tan(\omega_1 t - \alpha) = -\frac{p}{\omega_1}.$$

Conclude that $t_2 - t_1 = 2\pi/\omega_1$ if two consecutive maxima occur at times t_1 and t_2.

31. (Underdamped) Let x_1 and x_2 be two consecutive local maximum values of $x(t)$. Deduce from the result of Problem 30 that

$$\ln \frac{x_1}{x_2} = \frac{2\pi p}{\omega_1}.$$

The constant $\Delta = 2\pi p/\omega_1$ is called the **logarithmic decrement** of the oscillation. Note also that $c = m\omega_1 \Delta/\pi$ because $p = c/(2m)$.

Note: The result of Problem 31 provides an accurate method for measuring the *viscosity* of a fluid, which is an important parameter in fluid dynamics, but which is not easy to measure directly. According to Stokes' drag law, a spherical body of radius a moving at a (relatively slow) speed v through a fluid of viscosity m experiences a resistive force $F_R = 6\pi\mu av$. Thus if a spherical mass on a spring is immersed in the fluid and set in motion, this drag resistance damps its oscillations with damping constant $c = 6\pi a\mu$. The frequency ω_1 and logarithmic decrement Δ of the oscillations can be measured by direct observation. The final formula in Problem 31 then gives c and hence viscosity of the fluid.

32. (Underdamped) A body weighing 100 lb (mass $m = 3.125$ slugs in fps units) is oscillating attached to a spring and a dashpot. Its first two maximum displacements of 6.73 in. and 1.46 in. are observed to occur at times 0.34 s and 1.17 s, respectively. Compute the damping constant (in pound-seconds per foot) and spring constant (in pounds per foot).

Differential Equations and Determinism

Given a mass m, a dashpot constant c, and a spring constant k, Theorem 2 of Section 3.1 implies that the equation

$$mx'' + cx' + kx = 0 \tag{25}$$

has a *unique* solution for $t \geq 0$ satisfying given initial conditions $x(0) = x_0$, $x'(0) = v_0$. Thus the future motion of an ideal mass-spring-dashpot system is completely determined by the differential equation and the initial conditions. Of course in a real physical system it is impossible to measure the parameters m, c, and k *precisely*. Problems 33 through 36 explore the resulting uncertainty in predicting the future behavior of a physical system.

33. Suppose that $m = 1$, $c = 2$, and $k = 1$ in Eq. (25). Show that the solution with $x(0) = 0$ and $x'(0) = 1$ is

$$x_1(t) = te^{-t}.$$

34. Suppose that $m = 1$ and $c = 2$ but $k = 1 - 10^{-2n}$. Show that the solution of Eq. (25) with $x(0) = 0$ and $x'(0) = 1$ is

$$x_2(t) = 10^n e^{-t} \sinh 10^{-n} t.$$

35. Suppose that $m = 1$ and $c = 2$ but $k = 1 + 10^{-2n}$. Show that the solution of Eq. (25) with $x(0) = 0$ and $x'(0) = 1$ is

$$x_3(t) = 10^n e^{-t} \sin 10^{-n} t.$$

36. Whereas the graphs of $x_1(t)$ and $x_2(t)$ resemble those shown in Figs. 3.4.6 and 3.4.7, the graph of $x_3(t)$ exhibits damped oscillations like those illustrated in Fig. 3.4.8, but with a very long pseudoperiod. Nevertheless, show that for each fixed $t > 0$ it is true that

$$\lim_{n \to \infty} x_2(t) = \lim_{n \to \infty} x_3(t) = x_1(t).$$

Conclude that *on a given finite time interval* the three solutions are in "practical" agreement if n is sufficiently large.

3.5 Nonhomogeneous Equations and the Method of Undetermined Coefficients

We learned in Section 3.3 how to solve homogeneous linear equations wth constant coefficients, but we saw in Section 3.4 that an external force in a simple mechanical system contributes a nonhomogeneous term to its differential equation. The general nonhomogeneous nth-order linear equation with constant coefficients has the form

$$a_n y^{(n)} + a_{n-1} y^{(n-1)} + \cdots + a_1 y' + a_0 y = f(x). \tag{1}$$

By Theorem 5 of Section 3.2, a general solution of (1) has the form

$$\blacktriangleright \qquad y = y_c + y_{p'} \tag{2}$$

where the complementary function $y_c(x)$ is a general solution of the associated homogeneous equation

$$a_n y^{(n)} + a_{n-1} y^{(n-1)} + \cdots + a_1 y' + a_0 y = 0, \tag{3}$$

and $y_p(x)$ is a particular solution of (1). Thus our remaining task is to find y_p.

The **method of undetermined coefficients** is a straightforward way of doing this when the given function $f(x)$ in (1) is sufficiently simple that we can make an intelligent guess as to the general form of y_p. For example, suppose that $f(x)$ is a polynomial of degree m. Then, because the derivatives of a polynomial are themselves polynomials of lower degree, it is reasonable to suspect a particular solution

$$y_p(x) = A_m x^m + A_{m-1} x^{m-1} + \cdots + A_1 x + A_0$$

that is also a polynomial of degree m, but with as yet undetermined coefficients. We may, therefore, substitute this expression for y_p into (1), and then—by equating coefficients of like powers of x on the two sides of the resulting equation—attempt to determine the coefficients A_0, A_1, \ldots, A_m so that y_p will, indeed, be a particular solution of Eq. (1).

Similarly, suppose that

$$f(x) = a \cos kx + b \sin kx.$$

Then it is reasonable to expect a particular solution of the same form:

$$y_p(x) = A \cos kx + B \sin kx,$$

a linear combination with undetermined coefficients A and B. The reason is that any derivative of such a linear combination of $\cos kx$ and $\sin kx$ has the same form. We

may therefore substitute this form of y_p in (1), and then—by equating coefficients of $\cos kx$ and of $\sin kx$ on both sides of the resulting equation—attempt to determine the coefficients A and B so that y_p will, indeed, be a particular solution.

It turns out that this approach does succeed whenever all the derivatives of $f(x)$ have the same form as $f(x)$ itself. Before describing the method in full generality, we illustrate it with several preliminary examples.

EXAMPLE 1 Find a particular solution of $y'' + 3y' + 4y = 3x + 2$.

Solution Here $f(x) = 3x + 2$ is a polynomial of degree 1, so our guess is that

$$y_p(x) = Ax + B.$$

Then $y_p' = A$ and $y_p'' = 0$, so y_p will satisfy the differential equation provided that

$$(0) + 3(A) + 4(Ax + B) = 3x + 2.$$

This is so if and only if $4A = 3$ and $3A + 4B = 2$. These two equations yield $A = \frac{3}{4}$ and $B = -\frac{1}{16}$, so we have found the particular solution

$$y_p(x) = \frac{3}{4}x - \frac{1}{16}.$$

EXAMPLE 2 Find a particular solution of $y'' - 4y = 2e^{3x}$.

Solution Any derivative of e^{3x} is a constant multiple of e^{3x}, so it is reasonable to try

$$y_p(x) = Ae^{3x}.$$

Then $y_p'' = 9Ae^{3x}$, so the given differential equation will be satisfied provided that

$$9Ae^{3x} - 4(Ae^{3x}) = 2e^{3x};$$

that is, $5A = 2$, so that $A = \frac{2}{5}$. Thus our particular solution is $y_p(x) = \frac{2}{5}e^{3x}$.

EXAMPLE 3 Find a particular solution of $3y'' + y' - 2y = 2\cos x$.

Solution A first guess might be $y_p(x) = A\cos x$, but the presence of y' on the left-hand side signals that we probably need a term involving $\sin x$ as well. So we try

$$y_p(x) = A\cos x \quad + B\sin x;$$
$$y_p'(x) = -A\sin x + B\cos x,$$
$$y_p''(x) = -A\cos x - B\sin x.$$

Then substitution of y_p and its derivatives into the given differential equation yields

$$3(-A\cos x - B\sin x) + (-A\sin x + B\cos x) - 2(A\cos x + B\sin x) = 2\cos x.$$

We equate the coefficient of $\cos x$ on the left-hand side with that of $\cos x$ on the right and do the same with $\sin x$ to get the equations

$$-5A + B = 2,$$
$$-A - 5B = 0,$$

with solution $A = -\frac{5}{13}$, $B = \frac{1}{13}$. Hence a particular solution is

$$y_p(x) = -\frac{5}{13}\cos x + \frac{1}{13}\sin x.$$ ∎

The following example, which superficially resembles Example 2, indicates that the method of undetermined coefficients is not always quite so simple as we have made it appear.

EXAMPLE 4 Find a particular solution of $y'' - 4y = 2e^{2x}$.

Solution If we try $y_p(x) = Ae^{2x}$, we find that

$$y_p'' - 4y_p = 4Ae^{2x} - 4Ae^{2x} = 0 \neq 2e^{2x};$$

so, no matter what A is, Ae^{2x} cannot satisfy the given nonhomogeneous equation. In fact, the above computation shows that Ae^{2x} satisfies instead the associated *homogeneous* equation. Therefore, we should begin with a trial function $y_p(x)$ whose derivative involves both e^{2x} *and something else* that can cancel upon substitution into the differential equation to leave the e^{2x} term that we need. A reasonable guess is

$$y_p(x) = Axe^{2x},$$

with

$$y_p'(x) = Ae^{2x} + 2Axe^{2x} \quad \text{and} \quad y_p''(x) = 4Ae^{2x} + 4Axe^{2x}.$$

Substitution into the original differential equation yields

$$(4Ae^{2x} + 4Axe^{2x}) - 4(Axe^{2x}) = 2e^{2x}.$$

The terms involving xe^{2x} obligingly cancel, leaving only $4Ae^{2x} = 2e^{2x}$, so that $A = \frac{1}{2}$. Thus a particular solution is

$$y_p(x) = \frac{1}{2}xe^{2x}.$$ ∎

The General Approach

Our initial difficulty in Example 4 resulted from the fact that $f(x) = 2e^{2x}$ satisfied the associated homogeneous equation. Rule 1, given shortly, tells what to do when we do not have this difficulty, and Rule 2 tells what to do when we do have it.

The method of undetermined coefficients applies whenever the function $f(x)$ in Eq. (1) is a linear combination of (finite) products of functions of the following three types:

1. A polynomial in x;
2. An exponential function e^{rx}; (4)
3. $\cos kx$ or $\sin kx$.

Any such function, for example

$$f(x) = (3 - 4x^2)e^{5x} - 4x^3\cos 10x,$$

has the crucial property that only *finitely* many linearly independent functions appear as terms (summands) in $f(x)$ and its derivatives of all orders. In Rules 1 and 2 below we assume that $Ly = f(x)$ is a nonhomogeneous linear equation with constant coefficients and that $f(x)$ is a function of this kind.

RULE 1: Method of Undetermined Coefficients

Suppose that no term appearing either in $f(x)$ or in any of its derivatives satisfies the associated homogeneous equation $Ly = 0$. Then take as a trial solution for y_p a linear combination of all linearly independent such terms and their derivatives. Determine the coefficients by substitution of this trial solution into the nonhomogeneous equation $Ly = f(x)$. ∎

Note that this rule is not a theorem requiring proof; it is merely a procedure to be following in searching for a particular solution y_p. If we succeed in finding y_p, then nothing more need be said. It can be proved, however, that this procedure will always succeed under the conditions specified here.

In practice we check the supposition made in Rule 1 by first using the characteristic equation to find the complementary function y_c, and then write a list of all the terms appearing in $f(x)$ and its successive derivatives. If none of the terms in this list duplicates a term in y_c, then we're in business!

EXAMPLE 5 Find a particular solution of

$$y'' + 4y = 3x^3. \tag{5}$$

Solution The (familiar) complementary function of this equation is

$$y_c(x) = c_1 \cos 2x + c_2 \sin 2x.$$

The function $f(x) = 3x^3$ and its derivatives are constant multiples of the linearly independent functions x^3, x^2, x, and 1. Because none of these appears in y_c, we try

$$y_p = Ax^3 + Bx^2 + Cx + D,$$
$$y_p' = 3Ax^2 + 2Bx + C,$$
$$y_p'' = 6Ax + 2B.$$

Substitution in Eq. (5) gives

$$y_p'' + 4y_p = (6Ax + 2B) + 4(Ax^3 + Bx^2 + Cx + D)$$
$$= 4Ax^3 + 4Bx^2 + (6A + 4C)x + (2B + D)$$
$$= 3x^3.$$

We equate coefficients of like powers of x to get the equations

$$4A = 3, \qquad\qquad 4B = 0,$$
$$6A + 4C = 0, \qquad 2B + D = 0$$

with solution $A = \frac{3}{4}$, $B = 0$, $C = -\frac{9}{8}$, and $D = 0$. Hence a particular solution of Eq.

(5) is

$$y_p(x) = \frac{3}{4}x^3 - \frac{9}{8}x.$$

EXAMPLE 6 Solve the initial value problem

$$y'' - 3y' + 2y = 3e^{-x} - 10\cos 3x;$$
$$y(0) = 1, \qquad y'(0) = 2.$$

(6)

Solution The characteristic equation $r^2 - 3r + 2 = 0$ has roots $r = 1$ and $r = 2$, so the complementary function is

$$y_c(x) = c_1 e^x + c_2 e^{2x}.$$

The terms involved in $f(x) = 3e^{-x} - 10\cos 3x$ and its derivatives are e^{-x}, $\cos 3x$, and $\sin 3x$. Because none of these appears in y_c, we try

$$y_p = Ae^{-x} \quad + B\cos 3x \ + C\sin 3x,$$
$$y_p' = -Ae^{-x} - 3B\sin 3x + 3C\cos 3x,$$
$$y_p'' = Ae^{-x} \quad - 9B\cos 3x - 9C\sin 3x.$$

After we substitute these expressions into the differential equation in (6) and collect coefficients, we get

$$y_p'' - 3y_p' + 2y_p = 6Ae^{-x} + (-7B - 9C)\cos 3x + (9B - 7C)\sin 3x$$
$$= 3e^{-x} - 10\cos 3x.$$

We equate the coefficients of the terms involving e^{-x}, those involving $\cos 3x$, and those involving $\sin 3x$. The result is the system

$$6A = 3,$$
$$-7B - 9C = -10,$$
$$9B - 7C = 0$$

with solution $A = \frac{1}{2}$, $B = \frac{7}{13}$, and $C = \frac{9}{13}$. This gives the particular solution

$$y_p(x) = \frac{1}{2}e^{-x} + \frac{7}{13}\cos 3x + \frac{9}{13}\sin 3x$$

which, however, does not have the required initial values in (6).

To satisfy those initial conditions, we begin with the *general* solution

$$y(x) = y_c(x) + y_p(x)$$
$$= c_1 e^x + c_2 e^{2x} + \frac{1}{2}e^{-x} + \frac{7}{13}\cos 3x + \frac{9}{13}\sin 3x,$$

with derivative

$$y'(x) = c_1 e^x + 2c_2 e^{2x} - \frac{1}{2}e^{-x} - \frac{21}{13}\sin 3x + \frac{27}{13}\cos 3x.$$

The initial conditions in (6) lead to the equations

$$y(0) = c_1 + c_2 + \frac{1}{2} + \frac{7}{13} = 1,$$

$$y'(0) = c_1 + 2c_2 - \frac{1}{2} + \frac{27}{13} = 2$$

with solution $c_1 = -\frac{1}{2}$, $c_2 = \frac{6}{13}$. The desired particular solution is therefore

$$y(x) = -\frac{1}{2}e^x + \frac{6}{13}e^{2x} + \frac{1}{2}e^{-x} + \frac{7}{13}\cos 3x + \frac{9}{13}\sin 3x.$$

EXAMPLE 7 Find the general form of a particular solution of

$$y^{(3)} + 9y' = x \sin x + x^2 e^{2x}. \tag{7}$$

Solution The characteristic equation $r^3 + 9r = 0$ has roots $r = 0$, $r = -3i$, and $r = 3i$. So the complementary function is

$$y_c(x) = c_1 + c_2 \cos 3x + c_3 \sin 3x.$$

The derivatives of the right-hand side in Eq. (7) involve the terms

$$\cos x, \quad \sin x, \quad x \cos x, \quad x \sin x,$$

$$e^{2x}, \quad xe^{2x}, \quad \text{and} \quad x^2 e^{2x}.$$

Because there is no duplication with the terms of the complementary function, the trial function takes the form

$$y_p(x) = A \cos x + B \sin x + Cx \cos x + Dx \sin x + Ee^{2x} + Fxe^{2x} + Gx^2 e^{2x}.$$

Upon substituting y_p in (7) and equating coefficients of like terms, we get seven equations determining the seven coefficients A, B, C, D, E, F, and G. ∎

The Case of Duplication

Now we turn our attention to the situation in which Rule 1 does not apply: Some of the terms involved in $f(x)$ and its derivatives satisfy the associated homogeneous equation. For instance, suppose that we want to find a particular solution of the differential equation

$$(D - r)^3 y = (2x - 3)e^{rx}. \tag{8}$$

Proceeding as in Rule 1, our first guess would be

$$y_p(x) = Ae^{rx} + Bxe^{rx}. \tag{9}$$

This form of $y_p(x)$ will not be adequate because the complementary function of (8) is

$$y_c(x) = c_1 e^{rx} + c_2 xe^{rx} + c_3 x^2 e^{rx}, \tag{10}$$

so substitution of (9) in the left-hand side of (8) would yield zero rather than $(2x - 3)e^{rx}$.

To see how to amend our first guess, we observe that

$$(D - r)^2[(2x - 3)e^{rx}] = [D^2(2x - 3)]e^{rx} = 0$$

by Eq. (13) of Section 3.3. If $y(x)$ is *any* solution of Eq. (8) and we apply the operator $(D - r)^2$ to both sides, we therefore see that $y(x)$ is also a solution of the equation $(D - r)^5 y = 0$. The general solution of this *homogeneous* equation can be written as

$$y(x) = \underbrace{c_1 e^{rx} + c_2 x e^{rx} + c_3 x^2 e^{rx}}_{y_c} + \underbrace{Ax^3 e^{rx} + Bx^4 e^{rx}}_{y_p}.$$

Thus *every* solution of our original equation in (8) is the sum of a complementary function and a *particular solution* of the form

$$y_p(x) = Ax^3 e^{rx} + Bx^4 e^{rx}. \tag{11}$$

Note that (11) may be obtained by multiplying each term of our first guess in (9) by the least power of x (in this case, x^3) that suffices to eliminate duplication between the terms of the resulting trial solution $y_p(x)$ and the complementary function $y_c(x)$ given in (10). This procedure succeeds in the general case.

To simplify the general statement of Rule 2, we observe that in order to find a particular solution of the nonhomogeneous linear differential equation

$$Ly = f_1(x) + f_2(x), \tag{12}$$

it suffices to find *separately* particular solutions Y_1 and Y_2 of the two equations

$$Ly = f_1(x) \quad \text{and} \quad Ly = f_2(x), \tag{13}$$

respectively. For linearity then gives

$$L[Y_1 + Y_2] = LY_1 + LY_2 = f_1(x) + f_2(x),$$

and therefore $y_p = Y_1 + Y_2$ is a particular solution of (12). This is the **principle of superposition** for nonhomogeneous linear equations.

Now our problem is to find a particular solution of the equation $Ly = f(x)$, where $f(x)$ is a linear combination of products of the elementary functions listed in (4). Thus $f(x)$ can be written as a sum of terms each of the form

$$P_m(x)e^{rx} \cos kx \quad \text{or} \quad P_m(x)e^{rx} \sin kx, \tag{14}$$

where $P_m(x)$ is a polynomial in x of degree m. Note that any derivative of such a term is of the same form but with *both* sines and cosines appearing. The procedure by which we arrived earlier at the particular solution in (11) of Eq. (8) can be generalized to show that the following procedure is always successful.

RULE 2: Method of Undetermined Cofficients

If the function $f(x)$ is of either form in (14), take as the trial solution

$$y_p(x) = x^s[(A_0 + A_1 x + \cdots + A_m x^m)e^{rx} \cos kx$$
$$+ (B_0 + B_1 x + \cdots + B_m x^m)e^{rx} \sin kx], \tag{15}$$

where s is the smallest nonnegative integer such that no term in y_p duplicates a term in the complementary function y_c. Then determine the coefficients in (15) by substituting y_p into the nonhomogeneous equation. ∎

$f(x)$	y_p
$P_m(x) = b_0 + b_1x + b_2x^2 + \cdots + b_mx^m$	$x^s(A_0 + A_1x + A_2x^2 + \cdots + A_mx^m)$
$a \cos kx + b \sin kx$	$x^s(A \cos kx + B \sin kx)$
$e^{rx}(a \cos kx + b \sin kx)$	$x^se^{rx}(A \cos kx + B \sin kx)$
$P_m(x)e^{rx}$	$x^s(A_0 + A_1x + A_2x^2 + \cdots + A_mx^m)e^{rx}$
$P_m(x)\,(a \cos kx + b \sin kx)$	$x^s[(A_0 + A_1x + \cdots + A_mx^m) \cos kx$
	$\qquad + (B_0 + B_1x + \cdots + B_mx^m) \sin kx]$

FIGURE 3.5.1. Substitutions in the method of undetermined coefficients

In practice we seldom need to deal with a function $f(x)$ exhibiting the full generality in (14). The table in Fig. 3.5.1 lists the form of y_p in various common cases, corresponding to the possibilities $m = 0$, $r = 0$, and $k = 0$.

On the other hand, it is not uncommon to have

$$f(x) = f_1(x) + f_2(x),$$

where $f_1(x)$ and $f_2(x)$ are different functions of the sort listed in the table of Fig. 3.5.1. In this event we take as y_p the sum of the indicated particular functions, choosing s *separately* for each part to eliminate duplication with the complementary function. This procedure is illustrated in Examples 8 through 10.

EXAMPLE 8 Find a particular solution of

$$y^{(3)} + y'' = 3e^x + 4x^2. \tag{16}$$

Solution The characteristic equation $r^3 + r^2 = 0$ has roots $r_1 = r_2 = 0$ and $r_3 = -1$, so the complementary function is

$$y_c(x) = c_1 + c_2x + c_3e^{-x}.$$

As a first step toward our particular solution, we form the sum

$$(Ae^x) + (B + Cx + Dx^2).$$

The part Ae^x corresponding to $3e^x$ does not duplicate any part of the complementary function, but the part $B + Cx + Dx^2$ must be multiplied by x^2 to eliminate duplication. Hence we take

$$y_p = Ae^x + Bx^2 + Cx^3 + Dx^4,$$
$$y_p' = Ae^x + 2Bx + 3Cx^2 + 4Dx^3,$$
$$y_p'' = Ae^x + 2B + 6Cx + 12Dx^2, \quad \text{and}$$
$$y_p^{(3)} = Ae^x + 6C + 24Dx,$$

Substitution of these derivatives in (16) yields

$$2Ae^x + (2B + 6C) + (6C + 24D)x + 12Dx^2 = 3e^x + 4x^2.$$

The system of equations

$$2A = 3, \qquad 2B + 6C = 0,$$
$$6C + 24D = 0, \qquad 12D = 4$$

has the solution $A = \frac{3}{2}$, $B = 4$, $C = -\frac{4}{3}$, and $D = \frac{1}{3}$. Hence the desired particular solution is

$$y_p(x) = \frac{3}{2} e^x + 4x^2 - \frac{4}{3} x^3 + \frac{1}{3} x^4.$$

EXAMPLE 9 Determine the appropriate form for a particular solution of

$$y'' + 6y' + 13y = e^{-3x} \cos 2x.$$

Solution The characteristic equation $r^2 + 6r + 13 = 0$ has roots $-3 \pm 2i$, so the complementary function is

$$y_c(x) = e^{-3x}(c_1 \cos 2x + c_2 \sin 2x).$$

This is the same form as a first attempt $e^{-3x}(A \cos 2x + B \sin 2x)$ at a particular solution, so we must multiply by x to eliminate duplication. Hence we would take

$$y_p(x) = e^{-3x}(Ax \cos 2x + Bx \sin 2x).$$

EXAMPLE 10 Determine the appropriate form for a particular solution of the fifth-order equation

$$(D - 2)^3(D^2 + 9)y = x^2 e^{2x} + x \sin 3x.$$

Solution The characteristic equation $(r - 2)^3(r^2 + 9) = 0$ has roots $r = 2, 2, 2, 3i$, and $-3i$, so the complementary function is

$$y_c(x) = c_1 e^{2x} + c_2 x e^{2x} + c_3 x^2 e^{2x} + c_4 \cos 3x + c_5 \sin 3x.$$

As a first step toward the form of a particular solution, we examine the sum

$$[(A + Bx + Cx^2)e^{2x}] + [(D + Ex)\cos 3x + (F + Gx)\sin 3x].$$

To eliminate duplication with terms of $y_c(x)$, the first part—corresponding to $x^2 e^{2x}$—must be multiplied by x^3, and the second part—corresponding to $x \sin 3x$—must be multiplied by x. Hence we would take

$$y_p(x) = (Ax^3 + Bx^4 + Cx^5)e^{2x} + (Dx + Ex^2)\cos 3x + (Fx + Gx^2)\sin 3x. \quad \blacksquare$$

Variation of Parameters

Finally, let us point out the kind of situation in which the method of undetermined coefficients cannot be used. Consider, for instance, the equation

$$y'' + y = \tan x, \tag{17}$$

which at first glance may appear similar to those considered in the preceding examples. Not so; the function $f(x) = \tan x$ has *infinitely many* linearly independent derivatives

$$\sec^2 x, \quad 2 \sec^2 x \tan x, \quad 4 \sec^2 x \tan^2 x + 2 \sec^4 x, \quad \ldots.$$

Therefore we do not have available a *finite* linear combination to use as a trial solution.

We discuss here the method of **variation of parameters** which—in principle (that is, if the integrals that appear can be evaluated)—can always be used to find a

particular solution of the nonhomogeneous linear differential equation

$$y^{(n)} + p_{n-1}(x)y^{(n-1)} + \cdots + p_1(x)y' + p_0(x)y = f(x), \tag{18}$$

provided that we already know the general solution

$$y_c = c_1 y_1 + c_2 y_2 + \cdots + c_n y_n \tag{19}$$

of the associated homogeneous equation

$$y^{(n)} + p_{n-1}(x)y^{(n-1)} + \cdots + p_1(x)y' + p_0(x)y = 0. \tag{20}$$

Here, in brief, is the basic idea of the method of variation of parameters. Suppose that we replace the constants, or *parameters,* c_1, c_2, \ldots, c_n in the complementary function in (19) by variables: functions u_1, u_2, \ldots, u_n of x. We ask whether it is possible to choose these functions in such a way that the combination

$$y_p(x) = u_1(x)y_1(x) + u_2(x)y_2(x) + \cdots + u_n(x)y_n(x) \tag{21}$$

is a particular solution of the nonhomogeneous Eq. (18). It turns out that this *is* always possible.

The method is essentially the same for all orders $n \geqq 2$, but we will describe it in detail only for the case $n = 2$. So we begin with the second-order nonhomogeneous equation

$$\blacktriangleright \qquad L[y] = y'' + P(x)y' + Q(x)y = f(x) \tag{22}$$

with complementary function

$$y_c = c_1 y_1 + c_2 y_2 \tag{23}$$

on some open interval I where the functions P and Q are continuous. We want to find functions u_1 and u_2 such that

$$\blacktriangleright \qquad y_p = u_1 y_1 + u_2 y_2 \tag{24}$$

is a particular solution of Eq. (22).

One condition on the two functions u_1 and u_2 is that $L[y_p] = f(x)$. Because two conditions are required to determine two functions, we are free to impose an additional condition of our choice. We will do this in a way that simplifies the computations as much as possible. But first, to impose the condition $L[y_p] = f(x)$, we must compute the derivatives y'_p and y''_p. The product rule gives

$$y'_p = (u_1 y'_1 + u_2 y'_2) + (u'_1 y_1 + u'_2 y_2).$$

To avoid the appearance of the second derivatives u''_1 and u''_2, our additional condition will be that the second sum here must vanish:

$$u'_1 y_1 + u'_2 y_2 = 0. \tag{25}$$

Then

$$y'_p = u_1 y'_1 + u_2 y'_2, \tag{26}$$

and the product rule gives

$$y''_p = (u_1 y''_1 + u_2 y''_2) + (u'_1 y'_1 + u'_2 y'_2). \tag{27}$$

But both y_1 and y_2 satisfy the homogeneous equation

$$y'' + Py' + Qy = 0$$

associated with the nonhomogeneous equation in (22), so

$$y_i'' = -Py_i' - Qy_i \qquad (28)$$

for $i = 1, 2$. It therefore follows from Eq. (27) that

$$y_p'' = (u_1'y_1' + u_2'y_2') - P \cdot (u_1y_1' + u_2y_2') - Q \cdot (u_1y_1 + u_2y_2).$$

In view of Eqs. (24) and (26), this means that

$$y_p'' = (u_1'y_1' + u_2'y_2') - Py_p' - Qy_p;$$

that is, that

$$L[y_p] = u_1'y_1' + u_2'y_2'. \qquad (29)$$

The requirement that y_p satisfy the nonhomogeneous equation in (22)—that is, that $L[y_p] = f(x)$—therefore implies that

$$u_1'y_1' + u_2'y_2' = f(x). \qquad (30)$$

Finally, Eqs. (25) and (30) determine the functions u_1 and u_2 that we need. Collecting these equations, we obtain a system

$$\blacktriangleright \qquad \begin{aligned} u_1'y_1 + u_2'y_2 &= 0, \\ u_1'y_1' + u_2'y_2' &= f(x) \end{aligned} \qquad (31)$$

of two linear equations in the two *derivatives* u_1' and u_2'. Note that the determinant of coefficients in (31) is simply the Wronskian $W(y_1, y_2)$. Once we have solved the equations in (31) for the derivatives u_1' and u_2', we integrate each to obtain the functions u_1 and u_2 such that

$$\blacktriangleright \qquad y_p = u_1y_1 + u_2y_2$$

is the desired particular solution of Eq. (22).

EXAMPLE 11 Find a particular solution of $y'' + y = \tan x$.

Solution The complementary function is $y_c(x) = c_1 \cos x + c_2 \sin x$, so

$$y_1 = \cos x, \qquad y_2 = \sin x,$$
$$y_1' = -\sin x, \qquad y_2' = \cos x.$$

Hence the equations in (31) are

$$u_1'(\cos x) + u_2'(\sin x) = 0,$$
$$u_1'(-\sin x) + u_2'(\cos x) = \tan x.$$

We easily solve these equations for

$$u_1' = -\sin x \tan x = -\frac{\sin^2 x}{\cos x} = \cos x - \sec x,$$

$$u_2' = \cos x \tan x = \sin x.$$

Hence we take

$$u_1 = \int (\cos x - \sec x)\, dx = \sin x - \ln|\sec x + \tan x|$$

and

$$u_2 = \int \sin x \, dx = -\cos x.$$

Thus our particular solution is

$$y_p(x) = u_1(x)y_1(x) + u_2(x)y_2(x)$$
$$= (\sin x - \ln|\sec x + \tan x|)\cos x + (-\cos x)\sin x;$$

that is,

$$y_p(x) = -(\cos x)\ln|\sec x + \tan x|.$$

3.5 Problems

In Problems 1 through 20, find a particular solution y_p of the given equation.

1. $y'' + 16y = e^{3x}$

2. $y'' - y' - 2y = 3x + 4$

3. $y'' - y' - 6y = 2\sin 3x$

4. $4y'' + 4y' + y = 3xe^x$

5. $y'' + y' + y = \sin^2 x$

6. $2y'' + 4y' + 7y = x^2$

7. $y'' - 4y = \sinh x$

8. $y'' - 4y = \cosh 2x$

9. $y'' + 2y' - 3y = 1 + xe^x$

10. $y'' + 9y = 2\cos 3x + 3\sin 3x$

11. $y^{(3)} + 4y' = 3x - 1$

12. $y^{(3)} + y' = 2 - \sin x$

13. $y'' + 2y' + 5y = e^x \sin x$

14. $y^{(4)} - 2y'' + y = xe^x$

15. $y^{(5)} + 5y^{(4)} - y = 17$

16. $y'' + 9y = 2x^2 e^{3x} + 5$

17. $y'' + y = \sin x + x\cos x$

18. $y^{(4)} - 5y'' + 4y = e^x - xe^{2x}$

19. $y^{(5)} + 2y^{(3)} + 2y'' = 3x^2 - 1$

20. $y^{(3)} - y = e^x + 7$

In Problems 21 through 30, set up the appropriate form of a particular solution y_p, but do not determine the values of the coefficients.

21. $y'' - 2y' + 2y = e^x \sin x$

22. $y^{(5)} - y^{(3)} = e^x + 2x^2 - 5$

23. $y'' + 4y = 3x\cos 2x$

24. $y^{(3)} - y'' - 12y' = x - 2xe^{-3x}$

25. $y'' + 3y' + 2y = x(e^{-x} - e^{-2x})$

26. $y'' - 6y' + 13y = xe^{3x}\sin 2x$

27. $y^{(4)} + 5y'' + 4y = \sin x + \cos 2x$

28. $y^{(4)} + 9y'' = (x^2 + 1)\sin 3x$

29. $(D - 1)^3(D^2 - 4)y = xe^x + e^{2x} + e^{-2x}$

30. $y^{(4)} - 2y'' + y = x^2 \cos x$

Solve the initial value problems in Problems 31 through 40.

31. $y'' + 4y = 2x$; $y(0) = 1$, $y'(0) = 2$

32. $y'' + 3y' + 2y = e^x$; $y(0) = 0$, $y'(0) = 3$

33. $y'' + 9y = \sin 2x$; $y(0) = 1$, $y'(0) = 0$

34. $y'' + y = \cos x$; $y(0) = 1$, $y'(0) = -1$

35. $y'' - 2y' + 2y = x + 1$; $y(0) = 3$, $y'(0) = 0$

36. $y^{(4)} - 4y'' = x^2$; $y(0) = y'(0) = 1$,
$y''(0) = y^{(3)}(0) = -1$

37. $y^{(3)} - 2y'' + y' = 1 + xe^x$; $y(0) = y'(0) = 0$,
$y''(0) = 1$

38. $y'' + 2y' + 2y = \sin 3x$; $y(0) = 2$, $y'(0) = 0$

39. $y^{(3)} + y'' = x + e^{-x}$; $y(0) = 1$, $y'(0) = 0$,
$y''(0) = 1$

40. $y^{(4)} - y = 5$; $y(0) = y'(0) = y''(0) = y^{(3)}(0) = 0$

41. Find a particular solution of the equation

$$y^{(4)} - y^{(3)} - y'' - y' - 2y = 8x^5.$$

42. Find the solution of the initial value problem consisting of the differential equation of Problem 41 and the initial conditions

$$y(0) = y'(0) = y''(0) = y^{(3)}(0) = 0.$$

43. (a) Write

$$\cos 3x + i\sin 3x = e^{3ix} = (\cos x + i\sin x)^3$$

by Euler's formula, expand, and equate real and imaginary parts to derive the identities

$$\cos^3 x = \frac{3}{4}\cos x + \frac{1}{4}\cos 3x,$$

$$\sin^3 x = \frac{3}{4}\sin x - \frac{1}{4}\sin 3x.$$

(b) Use the result of part (a) to find a general solution of

$$y'' + 4y = \cos^3 x.$$

Use trigonometric identities to find general solutions of the equations in Problems 44 through 46.

44. $y'' + y' + y = \sin x \sin 3x$

45. $y'' + 9y = \sin^4 x$

46. $y'' + y = x\cos^3 x$

In Problems 47 through 56, use the method of variation of parameters to find a particular solution of the given differential equation.

47. $y'' + 3y' + 2y = 4e^x$

48. $y'' - 2y' - 8y = 3e^{-2x}$

49. $y'' - 4y' + 4y = 2e^{2x}$

50. $y'' - 4y = \sinh 2x$

51. $y'' + 4y = \cos 3x$

52. $y'' + 9y = \sin 3x$

53. $y'' + 9y = 2\sec 3x$

54. $y'' + y = \csc^2 x$

55. $y'' + 4y = \sin^2 x$

56. $y'' - 4y = xe^x$

57. You can verify by substitution that $y_c = c_1 x + c_2 x^{-1}$ is a complementary function for the nonhomogeneous second-order equation $x^2 y'' + xy' - y = 72x^5$. But before applying the method of variation of parameters, you first must divide this equation by the leading coefficient x^2 to rewrite it in the standard form

$$y'' + \frac{1}{x}y' - \frac{1}{x^2}y = 72x^3.$$

Thus $f(x) = 72x^3$ in Eq. (22). Now proceed to solve the equations in (31) and thence derive the particular solution $y_p = 3x^5$.

In Problems 58 through 63 a nonhomogeneous second-order linear equation and a complementary function y_c are given. Apply the method of Problem 57 to find a particular solution of the equation.

58. $x^2 y'' - 4xy' + 6y = x^3$; $y_c = c_1 x^2 + c_2 x^3$

59. $x^2 y'' - 3xy' + 4y = x^4$; $y_c = x^2(c_1 + c_2\ln x)$

60. $4x^2 y'' - 4xy' + 3y = 8x^{4/3}$; $y_c = c_1 x + c_2 x^{3/4}$

61. $x^2 y'' + xy' + y = \ln x$; $y_c = c_1\cos(\ln x) + c_2\sin(\ln x)$

62. $(x^2 - 1)y'' - 2xy' + 2y = x^2 - 1$; $y_c = c_1 x + c_2(1 + x^2)$

3.5 Computing Projects

The use of a computer algebra system can lighten the burden of algebraic computation associated with the method of undetermined coefficients. For example, consider the differential equation

$$L[y] = y^{(5)} + 2y^{(4)} + 2y^{(3)} - 300x^2 - 30e^x = 0 \tag{1}$$

with complementary function

$$y_c(x) = A + Bx + Cx^2 + e^{-x}(D\cos x + E\sin x).$$

Using *Mathematica,* for instance, we first specify the form

 y = a x^3 + b x^4 + c x^5 + d E^x;

of the desired particular solution. We then calculate the result of substituting **y** in the left-hand side of Eq. (1) with the command

 Ly = D[y,{x,5}] + 2 D[y,{x,4}] +
 2 D[y,{x,3}] - 300 x^2 - 30 E^x
 120 c - 30 E^x + d E^x - 300 x^2 + 2 (24 b + d E^x + 120 c x) +
 2 (6 a + d E^x + 24 b x + 60 c x^2)

where **D[y, {x,n}]** yields the *n*th derivative of the expression **y** with respect to the variable **x**. Upon collecting coefficients of the types of terms that appear,

> **Collect[Ly, {1, x, x^2, E^x}]**
>
> 12 a + 48 b + 120 c + (−30 + 5 d) EX + (48 b + 240 c) x +
>
> (−300 + 120 c) x^2

we can readily read off the four linear equations to be solved for the four coefficients a, b, c, d.

> **Solve [{ 12 a + 48 b + 120 c == 0,**
>
> **−30 + 5 d == 0,**
>
> **(48 b + 240 c) == 0,**
>
> **−300 + 120 c == 0}, {a, b, c, d}]**
>
> {{a -> 25, d -> 6, b -> − ($\frac{25}{2}$), c -> $\frac{5}{2}$ }}

Thus the desired particular solution of Eq. (1) is

$$y_p(x) = \frac{1}{2}(50x^3 - 25x^4 + 5x^5) + 6e^x.$$

If a computer algebra system is available, use it to find particular solutions of the differential equations given in Problems 21 through 30 of this section.

The method of variation of parameters also is readily automated using a computer algebra system. To solve Example 11 using *Maple,* for instance, we first enter the given homogeneous solutions y_1 and y_2 and the nonhomogeneous term $f(x)$ in the equation $y'' + y = \tan x$.

> **>y1 := cos(x):**
>
> **y2 := sin(x):**
>
> **f := tan(x):**

We next set up and solve the equations in (31).

> **>y1p := diff(y1, x):**
>
> **y2p := diff(y2, x): # Derivatives of y1 and y2**
>
> **eqs := { u1p*y1 + u2p*y2 = 0,**
>
> **u1p*y1p + u2p*y2p = f }:**
>
> **soln := solve(eqs, {u1p, u2p});**
>
> soln:=$\left\{u2p = \dfrac{\cos(x)\,\tan(x)}{\sin(x)^2 + \cos(x)^2}\, ,\ u1p = -\dfrac{\tan(x)\,\sin(x)}{\sin(x)^2 + \cos(x)^2}\right\}$
>
> **>u1p := rhs(soln[2]): # Select the derivatives**
>
> **u2p := rhs(soln[1]): # of u1 and u2**

Finally we integrate **u1p** $= u'_1$ and **u2p** $= u'_2$ and assemble the desired particular solution $y_p = u_1 y_1 + u_2 y_2$.

```
>u1 := int(u1p, x):

 u2 := int(u2p, x);

 y := simplify( u1*y1 + u2*y2);

 y := ln(1 - cos(x) - sin(x)) cos(x)
         - ln(1 - cos(x) + sin(x)) cos(x) - sin(x)
```

By combining the two logarithms on the right and then converting sines and cosines into secants and tangents, you should be able to verify that this solution is equivalent to the one we found manually in the text.

To solve a different second-order variation of parameters problem (as in Problems 47 through 62 in this section), one need only substitute the appropriate functions y_1, y_2, and $f(x)$ in the initial lines above, then re-execute the remaining lines.

3.6 Forced Oscillations and Resonance

In Section 3.4 we derived the differential equation

$$mx'' + cx' + kx = F(t) \tag{1}$$

that governs the one-dimensional motion of a mass m that is attached to a spring (with constant k) and a dashpot (with constant c) and is also acted on by an external force $F(t)$. Machines with rotating components commonly involve mass-spring systems (or their equivalents) in which the external force is simple harmonic:

$$F(t) = F_0 \cos \omega t \quad \text{or} \quad F(t) = F_0 \sin \omega t, \tag{2}$$

where the constant F_0 is the amplitude of the periodic force and ω is its circular frequency.

For an example of how a rotating machine component can provide a simple harmonic force, consider the cart with a rotating vertical flywheel shown in Fig. 3.6.1. The cart has mass $m - m_0$, not including the flywheel of mass m_0. The centroid of the flywheel is off-center at distance a from its center, and its angular speed is ω radians per second. The cart is attached to a spring (with constant k) as shown. Assume that the centroid of the cart itself is directly beneath the center of the flywheel, and denote by $x(t)$ its displacement from its equilibrium position (where the spring is unstretched). Figure 3.6.1 helps us to see that the displacement \bar{x} of the centroid of the combined cart plus flywheel is given by

FIGURE 3.6.1. The cart-with-flywheel system

$$\bar{x} = \frac{(m - m_0) x + m_0 (x + a \cos \omega t)}{m} = x + \frac{m_0 a}{m} \cos \omega t.$$

Let us ignore friction and apply apply Newton's second law $m\bar{x}'' = -kx$, because the force exerted by the spring is $-kx$. We substitute for \bar{x} in the last equation to obtain

$$mx'' - m_0 a\omega^2 \cos \omega t = -kx;$$

that is,

$$mx'' + kx = m_0 a \omega^2 \cos \omega t. \tag{3}$$

Thus the cart with its rotating flywheel acts like a mass on a spring under the influence of a simple harmonic external force with amplitude $F_0 = m_0 a \omega^2$. Such a system is a reasonable model of a front-loading washing machine with the clothes being washed loaded off-center. This illustrates the practical importance of analyzing solutions of Eq. (1) with external forces as in (2).

Undamped Forced Oscillations

To study undamped oscillations under the influence of the external force $F(t) = F_0 \cos \omega t$, we set $c = 0$ in Eq. (1), and thereby begin with the equation

▶
$$mx'' + kx = F_0 \cos \omega t \tag{4}$$

whose complementary function is $x_c = c_1 \cos \omega_0 t + c_2 \sin \omega_0 t$. Here,

$$\omega_0 = \sqrt{\frac{k}{m}}$$

is the (circular) **natural frequency** of the mass-spring system. Let us assume initially that the external and natural frequencies are *unequal:* $\omega \neq \omega_0$. We substitute $x_p = A \cos \omega t$ in (4) to find a particular solution. (No sine term is needed in x_p because there is no term involving x' on the left-hand side in Eq. (4).) This gives

$$-m\omega^2 A \cos \omega t + kA \cos \omega t = F_0 \cos \omega t,$$

so

$$A = \frac{F_0}{k - m\omega^2} = \frac{F_0/m}{\omega_0^2 - \omega^2}, \tag{5}$$

and thus

$$x_p(t) = \frac{F_0/m}{\omega_0^2 - \omega^2} \cos \omega t. \tag{6}$$

Therefore the general solution $x = x_c + x_p$ is given by

$$x(t) = c_1 \cos \omega_0 t + c_2 \sin \omega_0 t + \frac{F_0/m}{\omega_0^2 - \omega^2} \cos \omega t, \tag{7}$$

where the constants c_1 and c_2 are determined by the initial values $x(0)$ and $x'(0)$. Equivalently, as in Eq. (12) of Section 3.4, we can rewrite Eq. (7) as

$$x(t) = C \cos(\omega_0 t - \alpha) + \frac{F_0/m}{\omega_0^2 - \omega^2} \cos \omega t, \tag{8}$$

so we see that the resulting motion is a superposition of two oscillations, one with natural circular frequency ω_0, the other with the frequency ω of the external force.

EXAMPLE 1 Suppose that $m = 1$, $k = 9$, $F_0 = 80$, and $\omega = 5$, so the differential equation in (4) is

$$x'' + 9x = 80 \cos 5t.$$

Find $x(t)$ if $x(0) = x'(0) = 0$.

Solution Here the natural frequency $\omega_0 = 3$ and the frequency $\omega = 5$ of the external force are unequal, as in the preceding discussion. First we substitute $x_p = A \cos 5t$ in the differential equation and find that $-25A + 9A = 80$, so that $A = -5$. Thus a particular solution is

$$x_p(t) = -5 \cos 5t.$$

The complementary function is $x_c = c_1 \cos 3t + c_2 \sin 3t$, so the general solution of the given nonhomogeneous equation is

$$x(t) = c_1 \cos 3t + c_2 \sin 3t - 5 \cos 5t,$$

with derivative

$$x'(t) = -3c_1 \sin 3t + 3c_2 \cos 3t + 25 \sin 5t.$$

The initial conditions $x(0) = 0$ and $x'(0) = 0$ now yield $c_1 = 5$ and $c_2 = 0$, so the desired particular solution is

$$x(t) = 5 \cos 3t - 5 \cos 5t. \qquad \blacksquare$$

Beats

If we impose the initial conditions $x(0) = x'(0) = 0$ on the solution in (7), we find that

$$c_1 = -\frac{F_0}{m(\omega_0^2 - \omega^2)} \qquad \text{and} \qquad c_2 = 0,$$

so the particular solution is

$$x(t) = \frac{F_0}{m(\omega_0^2 - \omega^2)} (\cos \omega t - \cos \omega_0 t). \tag{9}$$

The trigonometric identity $2 \sin A \sin B = \cos(A - B) - \cos(A + B)$, applied with $A = \frac{1}{2}(\omega_0 + \omega)t$ and $B = \frac{1}{2}(\omega_0 - \omega)t$, enables us to rewrite Eq. (9) in the form

$$x(t) = \frac{2F_0}{m(\omega_0^2 - \omega^2)} \sin \frac{1}{2}(\omega_0 - \omega)t \sin \frac{1}{2}(\omega_0 + \omega)t. \tag{10}$$

Suppose now that $\omega \approx \omega_0$, so that $\omega_0 + \omega$ is very large in comparison with $|\omega_0 - \omega|$. Then $\sin \frac{1}{2}(\omega_0 + \omega)t$ is a *rapidly* varying function, whereas $\sin \frac{1}{2}(\omega_0 - \omega)t$ is a *slowly* varying function. We may therefore interpret (10) as a rapid oscillation with circular frequency $\frac{1}{2}(\omega_0 + \omega)$,

$$x(t) = A(t) \sin \frac{1}{2}(\omega_0 + \omega)t,$$

but with a slowly varying amplitude

$$A(t) = \frac{2F_0}{m(\omega_0^2 - \omega^2)} \sin \frac{1}{2}(\omega_0 - \omega)t.$$

EXAMPLE 2 With $m = 0.1$, $F_0 = 50$, $\omega_0 = 55$, and $\omega = 45$, Eq. (10) gives

$$x(t) = \sin 5t \sin 50t.$$

Figure 3.6.2 shows the corresponding oscillation of frequency $\frac{1}{2}(\omega_0 + \omega) = 50$ that is "modulated" by the amplitude function $A(t) = \sin 5t$ of frequency $\frac{1}{2}(\omega_0 - \omega) = 5$. ∎

A rapid oscillation with a (comparatively) slowly varying periodic amplitude exhibits the phenomenon of *beats*. For example, if two horns not exactly attuned to one another simultaneously play their middle C, one at $\omega_0/(2\pi) = 258$ Hz and the other at $\omega/(2\pi) = 254$ Hz, then one hears a beat—an audible variation in the *amplitude* of the combined sound—with a frequency of

Resonance
$$\frac{(\omega_0 - \omega)/2}{2\pi} = \frac{1}{2}(258 - 254) = 2 \text{ Hz}.$$

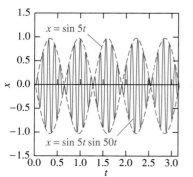

FIGURE 3.6.2. The phenomenon of beats

Looking at Eq. (6), we see that the amplitude A of x_p is large when the natural and external frequencies ω_0 and ω are approximately equal. It is sometimes useful to rewrite (5) in the form

$$A = \frac{F_0}{k - m\omega^2} = \frac{F_0/k}{1 - (\omega/\omega_0)^2} = \pm\frac{\rho F_0}{k}, \tag{11}$$

where F_0/k is the **static displacement** of a spring with constant k due to a *constant* force F_0, and the **amplification factor** ρ is defined to be

$$\rho = \frac{1}{|1 - (\omega/\omega_0)^2|}. \tag{12}$$

It is clear that $\rho \rightarrow +\infty$ as $\omega \rightarrow \omega_0$. This is the phenomenon of **resonance**—the increase without bound (as $\omega \rightarrow \omega_0$) in the amplitude of the oscillations of an undamped system with natural frequency ω_0 in response to an external force with frequency $\omega \approx \omega_0$.

We have been assuming that $\omega \neq \omega_0$. What sort of catastrophe should one expect if ω and ω_0 are precisely equal? Then Eq. (4), upon division of each term by m, becomes

$$x'' + \omega_0^2 x = \frac{F_0}{m} \cos \omega_0 t. \tag{13}$$

Because $\cos \omega_0 t$ is a term of the complementary function, the method of **undetermined coefficients** calls for us to try

$$x_p = t(A \cos \omega_0 t + B \sin \omega_0 t).$$

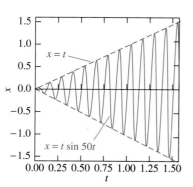

FIGURE 3.6.3. The phenomenon of resonance

We substitute this in (13), and thereby find that $A = 0$ and $B = F_0/(2m\omega_0)$. Hence the particular solution is

$$x_p(t) = \frac{F_0}{2m\omega_0} t \sin \omega_0 t. \tag{14}$$

The graph of $x_p(t)$ in Fig. 3.6.3 (in which $m = 1$, $F_0 = 100$, and $\omega_0 = 50$) shows vividly how the amplitude of the oscillation theoretically would increase without bound in this case of *pure resonance, $\omega = \omega_0$*. We may interpret the phenomenon as reinforcement of the natural vibrations of the system by externally impressed vibrations at the same frequency.

EXAMPLE 3 Suppose that $m = 5$ kg and that $k = 500$ N/m in the cart with the flywheel of Fig. 3.6.1. Then the natural frequency is $\omega_0 = \sqrt{k/m} = 10$ rad/s; that is, $10/(2\pi) \approx 1.59$ Hz. We would therefore expect oscillations of very large amplitude to occur if the flywheel revolves at about $(1.59)(60) \approx 95$ revolutions per minute (rpm). ∎

In practice, a mechanical system with very little damping can be destroyed by resonance vibrations. A spectacular example can occur when a column of soldiers marches in step over a bridge. Any complicated structure such as a bridge has many natural frequencies of vibration. If the frequency of the soldiers' cadence is approximately equal to one of the natural frequencies of the structure, then—just as in our simple example of a mass on a spring—resonance will occur. Indeed, the resulting resonance vibrations can be of such large amplitude that the bridge will collapse. This has actually happened—for example, the collapse of Broughton Bridge near Manchester, England, in 1831—and it is the reason for the now-standard practice of breaking cadence when crossing a bridge. Resonance may have been involved in the 1981 Kansas City disaster in which a hotel balcony (called a *skywalk*) collapsed with dancers on it. The collapse of a building in an earthquake is sometimes due to resonance vibrations caused by the ground oscillating at one of the natural frequencies of the structure; this happened to many buildings in the Mexico City earthquake of September 19, 1985. On occasion an airplane has crashed because of resonant wing oscillations caused by vibrations of the engines. It is reported that for some of the first commercial jet aircraft, the natural frequency of the vertical vibrations of the airplane during turbulence was almost exactly that of the mass-spring system consisting of the pilot's head (mass) and spine (spring). Resonance occurred, causing pilots to have difficulty in reading the instruments. Large modern commercial jets have different natural frequencies, so that this resonance problem no longer occurs.

Modeling Mechanical Systems

The avoidance of destructive resonance vibrations is a constant factor in the design of mechanical structures and systems of all types. Often the most important step in determining the natural frequency of vibration of a system is the formulation of its differential equation. In addition to Newton's law $F = ma$, the principle of conservation of energy is sometimes useful for this purpose (as in the derivation of the pendulum equation in Section 3.4). The following kinetic and potential energy formulas are often useful.

1. *Kinetic energy:* $T = \frac{1}{2}mv^2$ for translation of a mass with velocity v;

2. *Kinetic energy:* $T = \frac{1}{2}I\omega^2$ for rotation of a body of moment of inertia I with angular velocity ω;

3. *Potential energy:* $V = \frac{1}{2}kx^2$ for a spring with constant k stretched or compressed a distance x;

4. *Potential energy:* $V = mgh$ for the gravitational potential energy of a mass m at height h above the reference level (the level at which $V = 0$), provided that g may be regarded as essentially constant.

EXAMPLE 4 Find the natural frequency of a mass m on a spring (with constant k) if, instead of sliding without friction, it is a uniform disk of radius a that rolls without slipping, as shown in Fig. 3.6.4.

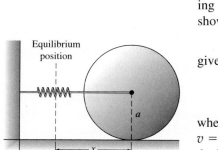

FIGURE 3.6.4. The rolling disk

Solution With the preceding notation, the principle of conservation of energy gives

$$\frac{1}{2} mv^2 + \frac{1}{2} I\omega^2 + \frac{1}{2} kx^2 = E$$

where E is a constant (the total mechanical energy of the system). We note that $v = a\omega$, and recall that $I = ma^2/2$ for a uniform circular disk. Thus we may simplify the last equation to

$$\frac{3}{4} mv^2 + \frac{1}{2} kx^2 = E.$$

Differentiation ($v = x'$, $v' = x''$) now gives

$$\frac{3}{2} mx'x'' + kxx' = 0.$$

We divide each term by $\frac{3}{2} mx'$ to obtain

$$x'' + \frac{2k}{3m} x = 0.$$

Thus the natural circular frequency is $\omega_0 = \sqrt{2k/3m}$, which is $\sqrt{2/3} \approx 0.8165$ times the frequency in the previous situation of sliding without friction.

EXAMPLE 5 Suppose that a car oscillates vertically as if it were a mass $m = 800$ kg on a single spring (with constant $k = 7 \times 10^4$ N/m), attached to a single dashpot (with constant $c = 2000$ N-s/m). Suppose that this car with the dashpot *disconnected* is driven along a washboard road surface with an amplitude of 5 cm and a wavelength of $L = 10$ m (Fig. 3.6.5). At what car speed will resonance vibrations occur?

FIGURE 3.6.5. The washboard road surface of Example 5

Solution We think of the car as a unicycle, as pictured in Fig. 3.6.6. Let $x(t)$ denote the upward displacement of the mass m from its equilibrium position; we ignore the force of gravity, because it merely displaces the equilibrium position as in Problem 9 of Section 3.4. We write the equation of the road surface as

$$y = a \cos \frac{2\pi s}{L} \qquad (a = 0.05 \text{ m}, L = 10 \text{ m}). \tag{15}$$

When the car is in motion, the spring is stretched by the amount $x - y$, so Newton's second law, $F = ma$, gives

$$mx'' = -k(x - y);$$

that is,

$$mx'' + kx = ky \tag{16}$$

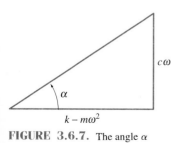

FIGURE 3.6.6. The "unicycle model" of a car

If the velocity of the car is v, then $s = vt$ in (15), so Eq. (16) takes the form

$$mx'' + kx = ka \cos \frac{2\pi v t}{L}. \tag{16'}$$

This is the differential equation that governs the vertical oscillations of the car. In comparing it with Eq. (4), we see that we have forced oscillations with circular frequency $\omega = 2\pi v/L$. Resonance will occur when $\omega = \omega_0 = \sqrt{k/m}$. We use our numerical data to find the speed of the car at resonance:

$$v = \frac{L}{2\pi}\sqrt{\frac{k}{m}} = \frac{10}{2\pi}\sqrt{\frac{7 \times 10^4}{800}} \approx 14.89 \quad \text{(m/s)};$$

that is, about 33.3 mi/h (using the conversion factor of 2.237 mi/h per m/s). ∎

Damped Forced Oscillations

In real physical systems there is always some damping, from frictional effects if nothing else. The complementary function x_c of the equation

▶
$$mx'' + cx' + kx = F_0 \cos \omega t \tag{17}$$

is given by Eq. (18), (19), or (20) of Section 3.4, depending upon whether $c > c_{CR}$, $c = c_{CR}$, or $c < c_{CR}$. The specific form is not important here. What is important is that, in any case, these formulas show that $x_c(t) \to 0$ as $t \to +\infty$. Thus x_c is a **transient solution** of (17)—one that dies out with the passage of time, leaving only the particular solution x_p.

The method of undetermined coefficients indicates that we should substitute

$$x_p = A \cos \omega t + B \sin \omega t$$

in (17). When we do so, collect terms, and equate coefficients of $\cos \omega t$ and $\sin \omega t$, we obtain the two equations

$$(k - m\omega^2)A + c\omega B = F_0, \qquad -c\omega A + (k - m\omega^2)B = 0 \tag{18}$$

that we solve without difficulty for

$$A = \frac{(k - m\omega^2)F_0}{(k - m\omega^2)^2 + (c\omega)^2}, \qquad B = \frac{(c\omega)F_0}{(k - m\omega^2)^2 + (c\omega)^2}.$$

To simplify the notation, it is convenient to introduce the quantity

$$\rho = \frac{k}{\sqrt{(k - m\omega^2)^2 + (c\omega)^2}} \tag{19}$$

and the angle α of Fig. 3.6.7. Then we find that

$$A = \rho\frac{F_0}{k}\cos\alpha, \qquad B = \rho\frac{F_0}{k}\sin\alpha.$$

Hence our particular solution is

$$x_p = A \cos \omega t + B \sin \omega t = \rho\frac{F_0}{k}(\cos \omega t \cos \alpha + \sin \omega t \sin \alpha);$$

FIGURE 3.6.7. The angle α

more concisely,

$$x_p(t) = \rho \frac{F_0}{k} \cos(\omega t - \alpha). \tag{20}$$

Thus we get a **steady periodic solution** that remains after the transient solution has died away. This steady-state solution has amplitude $\rho F_0 / k$, circular frequency ω, and phase angle α given by

$$\alpha = \tan^{-1} \frac{c\omega}{k - m\omega^2}, \qquad 0 \leq \alpha \leq \pi. \tag{21}$$

Note that α lies in the first or second quadrant, so the formula in (21) does not simply involve the principal value of the inverse tangent function. If a calculator gives a negative value for α, simply add π to obtain the correct value of α.

The **amplification factor** ρ, defined in (19), is the amount by which the static displacement F_0 / k must be multiplied to get the amplitude of the steady periodic oscillation. Note that when $c > 0$, the amplitude always remains finite (unlike the undamped case). The amplitude may reach a maximum for some value of ω; this is *practical resonance*. To see when it occurs for various values of the constants m, c, and k, it is useful to express ρ in terms of the dimensionless ratios

$$\tilde{\omega} = \frac{\omega}{\omega_0} = \frac{\omega}{\sqrt{k/m}} \qquad \text{and} \qquad \tilde{c} = \frac{c}{c_{CR}} = \frac{c}{\sqrt{4km}}.$$

Then (19) is equivalent to

$$\rho = \frac{1}{\sqrt{(1 - \tilde{\omega}^2)^2 + 4\tilde{c}^2\tilde{\omega}^2}}. \tag{19'}$$

Figure 3.6.8 shows the graph of ρ versus $\tilde{\omega}$ for various values of \tilde{c}. It can be shown that if $c \geqq c_{CR}/\sqrt{2}$, then ρ steadily decreases as ω increases, but if $c < c_{CR}/\sqrt{2}$, then ρ reaches a maximum value—practical resonance—at some value of ω less than ω_0, and then approaches zero as $\omega \to +\infty$. It follows that an underdamped system typically will undergo forced oscillations whose amplitude is:

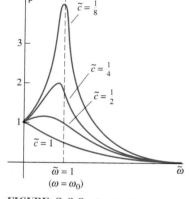

FIGURE 3.6.8. Practical resonance

1. Large if ω is close to the critical resonance frequency;
2. Close to F_0 / k is ω is very small;
3. Very small if ω is very large.

EXAMPLE 6 Find the transient and steady periodic solutions of

$$x'' + 2x' + 2x = 20 \cos 2t, \qquad x(0) = x'(0) = 0.$$

Solution Instead of applying the general formulas derived above, it is better in a concrete problem to work the problem directly. The roots of the characteristic equation $r^2 + 2r + 2 = 0$ are $-1 \pm i$, so the complementary function is

$$x_c(t) = e^{-t}(c_1 \cos t + c_2 \sin t).$$

When we substitute

$$x_p(t) = A \cos 2t + B \sin 2t$$

in the given equation, collect coefficients, and equate coefficients of cos $2t$ and sin $2t$, we obtain the equations

$$-2A + 4B = 20,$$

$$-4A - 2B = 0,$$

with solution $A = -2, B = 4$. Hence the general solution is

$$x(t) = e^{-t}(c_1 \cos t + c_2 \sin t) - 2 \cos 2t + 4 \sin 2t.$$

At this point we impose the initial conditions $x(0) = x'(0) = 0$, and find easily that $c_1 = 2$ and $c_2 = -6$. Therefore, the transient solution x_{tr} and the steady periodic solution x_{sp} are given by

$$x_{tr}(t) = e^{-t}(2 \cos t - 6 \sin t)$$

and

$$x_{sp}(t) = -2 \cos 2t + 4 \sin 2t = 2\sqrt{5}\left(-\frac{1}{\sqrt{5}} \cos 2t + \frac{2}{\sqrt{5}} \sin 2t\right).$$

The latter can also be written in the form

$$x_{sp}(t) = 2\sqrt{5} \cos(2t - \alpha),$$

where $\alpha = \pi - \tan^{-1}(2) \approx 2.0344$. ∎

Figure 3.6.9 shows graphs of the solution

$$x(t) = x_{sp}(t) + x_{tr}(t)$$

of the initial value problem

$$x'' + 2x' + 2x = 20 \cos t, \tag{22}$$

$$x(0) = x_0, \qquad x'(0) = 0$$

for the different values $x_0 = -10, -8, -6, \ldots, 8$, and 10 of the initial position. Here we see clearly what it means for the transient solution $x_{tr}(t)$ to "die out with the passage of time," leaving only the steady periodic solution $x_{sp}(t)$. Indeed, because $x_{tr}(t) \to 0$ exponentially, within a few cycles the full solution $x(t)$ and the steady periodic solution $x_{sp}(t)$ are visually indistinguishable.

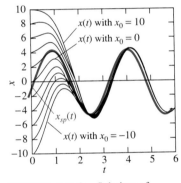

FIGURE 3.6.9. Solutions of the initial value problem (22) for $x_0 = -10, -8, -6, \ldots, 8, 10$

3.6 Problems

In Problems 1 through 6, express the solution of the given initial value problem as a sum of two oscillations (as in Eq. (8)).

1. $x'' + 9x = 10 \cos 2t$; $x(0) = x'(0) = 0$

2. $x'' + 4x = 5 \sin 3t$; $x(0) = x'(0) = 0$

3. $x'' + 100x = 15 \cos 5t + 20 \sin 5t$; $x(0) = 25$, $x'(0) = 0$

4. $x'' + 25x = 10 \cos 4t$; $x(0) = 0$, $x'(0) = 10$

5. $mx'' + kx = F_0 \cos \omega t$ with $\omega \neq \omega_0$; $x(0) = x_0$, $x'(0) = 0$

6. $mx'' + kx = F_0 \cos \omega t$ with $\omega = \omega_0$; $x(0) = 0$, $x'(0) = v_0$

In Problems 7 through 14, find the steady periodic solution in the form $x_{sp}(t) = C \cos(\omega t - \alpha)$ with $C > 0$. If initial conditions are given, also find the transient solution.

7. $x'' + 4x' + 4x = 10 \cos 3t$

8. $x'' + 3x' + 5x = -4 \cos 5t$

9. $2x'' + 2x' + x = 3 \sin 10t$

10. $x'' + 3x' + 3x = 8 \cos 10t + 6 \sin 10t$

11. $x'' + 4x' + 5x = 10 \cos 3t; \quad x(0) = x'(0) = 0$

12. $x'' + 6x' + 13x = 10 \sin 5t; \quad x(0) = x'(0) = 0$

13. $x'' + 2x' + 6x = 3 \cos 10t; \quad x(0) = 10,$
$x'(0) = 0$

14. $x'' + 8x' + 25x = 5 \cos t + 13 \sin t; \quad x(0) = 5,$
$x'(0) = 0$

15. A mass weighing 100 lb (mass $m = 3.125$ slugs in fps units) is attached to the end of a spring that is stretched 1 in. by a force of 100 lb. A force $F_0 \cos \omega t$ acts on the mass. At what frequency (in hertz) will resonance oscilllations occur? Neglect damping.

16. A front-loading washing machine is mounted on a thick rubber pad that acts like a spring; the weight $W = mg$ (with $g = 9.8$ m/s^2) of the machine depresses the pad exactly $\frac{1}{2}$ cm. When its rotor spins at ω radians per second, the rotor exerts a vertical force $F_0 \cos \omega t$ pounds on the machine. At what speed (in revolutions per minute) will resonance vibrations occur? Neglect damping.

17. See Fig. 3.6.10, which shows a mass m on the end of a pendulum (of length L) also attached to a horizontal spring (with constant k). Assume small oscillations of m so that the spring remains essentially horizontal, and neglect damping. Find the natural circular frequency ω_0 of motion of the mass in terms of L, k, m, and the gravitational constant g.

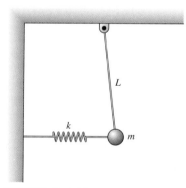

FIGURE 3.6.10. The pendulum-and-spring system of Problem 17

18. A mass m hangs on the end of a cord around a pulley of radius a and moment of inertia I, as shown in Fig. 3.6.11. The rim of the pulley is attached to a spring (with constant k). Assume small oscillations so that the spring remains essentially horizontal, and neglect friction. Find the natural circular frequency of the system in terms of m, a, k, I, and g.

19. A building consists of two floors. The first floor is attached rigidly to the ground, and the second floor is of mass $m = 1000$

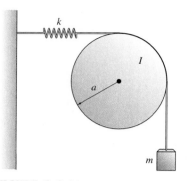

FIGURE 3.6.11. The mass-spring-pulley system of Problem 18

slugs (fps units) and weighs 16 tons (32,000 lb). The elastic frame of the building behaves as a spring that resists horizontal displacements of the second floor; it requires a horizontal force of 5 tons to displace the second floor a distance of 1 ft. Assume that in an earthquake the ground oscillates horizontally with amplitude A_0 and circular frequency ω, resulting in an external horizontal force $F(t) = mA_0\omega^2 \sin \omega t$ on the second floor. (a) What is the natural frequency (in hertz) of oscillations of the second floor? (b) If the ground undergoes one oscillation every 2.25 s with an amplitude of 3 in., what is the amplitude of the resulting forced oscillations of the second floor?

20. A mass on a spring without damping is acted on by the external force $F(t) = F_0 \cos^3 \omega t$. Show that there are *two* values of ω for which resonance occurs, and find both.

21. Derive the steady periodic solution of

$$mx'' + cx' + kx = F_0 \sin \omega t.$$

In particular, show that it is what one would expect—the same as the formula in (20) with the same values of ρ and ω, except with $\sin(\omega t - \alpha)$ in place of $\cos(\omega t - \alpha)$.

22. Given the differential equation

$$mx'' + cx' + kx = E_0 \cos \omega t + F_0 \sin \omega t$$

—with both cosine and sine forcing terms—derive the steady periodic solution

$$x_{sp}(t) = \frac{\sqrt{E_0^2 + F_0^2}}{\sqrt{(k - m\omega^2)^2 + (c\omega)^2}} \cos(\omega t - \alpha - \beta),$$

where α is defined in Eq. (21) and $\beta = \tan^{-1}(F_0/E_0)$. *Suggestion:* Add the steady periodic solutions separately corresponding to $E_0 \cos \omega t$ and $F_0 \sin \omega t$ (see Problem 21).

23. Recall that the amplification factor ρ is given in terms of the impressed frequency ω by

$$\rho = \frac{k}{\sqrt{(k - m\omega^2)^2 + (c\omega)^2}}.$$

(a) If $c \geq c_{CR}/\sqrt{2}$, where $c_{CR} = \sqrt{4km}$, show that ρ steadily decreases as ω increases. (b) If $c < c_{CR}/\sqrt{2}$, show that ρ attains a maximum value (practical resonance) when

$$\omega = \omega_m = \sqrt{\frac{k}{m} - \frac{c^2}{2m^2}} < \omega_0 = \sqrt{\frac{k}{m}}.$$

24. As indicated by the cart-with-flywheel example discussed in this section, an unbalanced rotating machine part typically results in a force having amplitude proportional to the *square* of the frequency ω. (a) Show that the amplitude of the steady periodic solution of the differential equation

$$mx'' + cx' + kx = mA\omega^2 \cos \omega t$$

(with a forcing term similar to that in Eq. (17)) is $\rho(mA/k)$, where the amplification factor is

$$\rho = \frac{k\omega^2}{\sqrt{(k - m\omega^2)^2 + (c\omega)^2}}.$$

(b) Suppose that $c^2 < 2mk$. Show that the maximum amplitude occurs at the frequency ω_m given by

$$\omega_m = \sqrt{\frac{k}{m}\left(\frac{2mk}{2mk - c^2}\right)}.$$

Thus the resonance frequency in this case is *larger* (in contrast to the result of Problem 23) than the natural frequency $\omega_0 = \sqrt{k/m}$. (*Suggestion:* Maximize the *square* of ρ.)

3.6 Computing Projects

Steady Periodic and Transient Solutions

For your personal project let $p = 2a$ and $q = a^2 + b^2$ where a and b are the two smallest nonzero digits of your student I.D. number (with $a < b$), and let r be the largest such digit. Then solve the initial value problem

$$x'' + px' + qx = r \cos t,$$

$$x(0) = x_0, \qquad x'(0) = v_0$$

in terms of x_0 and v_0. If a computer algebra system is available, you can use the *Mathematica* command

```
DSolve[ {x"[t] + p x'[t] + q x[t] == r Cos[t],
           x[0] == x0, x'[0] == v0}, x[t], t ]
```

the very similar *Maple* **dsolve** command, or the *Derive* command

```
DSOLVE_IV(p, q, r cos(t), t, 0, x0, v0)
```

(in the ODE2.MTH utility file). Then generate a figure like Fig. 3.6.9, except showing solution curves with $x_0 = 0$ and various different values of v_0.

Automobile Vibrations

The upward displacement function $x(t)$ of the car of Example 5 satisfies the equation

$$mx'' + cx' + kx = cy' + ky \tag{1}$$

when the car's shock absorber is connected (so $c > 0$). With $y = a \sin \omega t$ for the road surface, this equation becomes

$$mx'' + cx' + kx = E_0 \cos \omega t + F_0 \sin \omega t, \tag{2}$$

where $E_0 = c\omega a$ and $F_0 = ka$. Apply the result of Problem 22 in this section to show

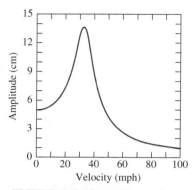

FIGURE 3.6.12. Amplitude of vibrations of the car on a washboard surface

that the amplitude C of the resulting steady periodic oscillation for the car is given by

$$C = \frac{a\sqrt{k^2 + (c\omega)^2}}{\sqrt{(k - m\omega^2)^2 + (c\omega)^2}}. \tag{3}$$

Because $\omega = 2\pi v/L$ when the car is moving with velocity v, this gives C as a function of v.

Using the numerical data given in Example 5 (including $c = 3000$ N-s/m), see whether you can use Eq. (3) to reproduce the plot in Fig. 3.6.12 showing the amplitude of the car's vibrations as a function of its velocity over the washboard surface. The graph indicates that, as the car accelerates gradually from rest, it initially oscillates with amplitude slightly over 5 cm. Maximum resonance oscillations with amplitude about 14 cm occur around 32 mi/h, but then subside to more tolerable levels at high speeds.

Can you verify the maximum point on the graph by maximizing C as a function of ω in Eq. (3)?

*3.7 Electrical Circuits

FIGURE 3.7.1. The series RLC circuit

Here we examine the RLC circuit that is a basic building block in more complicated electrical circuits and networks. As shown in Fig. 3.7.1, it consists of

A **resistor** with a resistance of R *ohms,*

An **inductor** with an inductance of L *henries,* and

A **capacitor** with a capacitance of C *farads*

in series with a source of electromotive force (such as a battery or generator) that supplies a voltage of $E(t)$ *volts* at time t. If the switch shown in the circuit of Fig. 3.7.1 is closed, this results in a current of $I(t)$ *amperes* in the circuit and a charge of $Q(t)$ *coulombs* on the capacitor at time t. The relation between the functions Q and I is

$$\frac{dQ}{dt} = I(t). \tag{1}$$

We will always use mks electric units, in which time is measured in seconds.

According to elementary principles of electricity, the **voltage drops** across the three circuit elements are those shown in the table in Fig. 3.7.2. We can analyze the behavior of the series circuit of Fig. 3.7.1 with the aid of this table and one of Kirchhoff's laws:

> The (algebraic) sum of the voltage drops across the elements in a simple loop of an electrical circuit is equal to the applied voltage.

Circuit Element	Voltage Drop
Inductor	$L\dfrac{dI}{dt}$
Resistor	RI
Capacitor	$\dfrac{1}{C}Q$

FIGURE 3.7.2. Table of voltage drops

As a consequence, the current and charge in the simple RLC circuit of Fig. 3.7.1 satisfy the basic circuit equation

$$L\frac{dI}{dt} + RI + \frac{1}{C}Q = E(t). \tag{2}$$

If we substitute (1) in (2), we get the second-order linear differential equation

$$LQ'' + RQ' + \frac{1}{C}Q = E(t) \tag{3}$$

for the charge $Q(t)$, under the assumption that the voltage $E(t)$ is known.

In most practical problems it is the current I rather than the charge Q that is of primary interest, so we differentiate both sides of Eq. (3) and substitute I for Q' to obtain

▶
$$LI'' + RI' + \frac{1}{C}I = E'(t). \tag{4}$$

We do *not* assume here a prior familiarity with electrical circuits. It suffices to regard the resistor, inductor, and capacitor in an electrical circuit as "black boxes" that are calibrated by the constants R, C, and L. A battery or generator is described by the voltage $E(t)$ that it supplies. When the switch is open, no current flows in the circuit; when the switch is closed, there is a current $I(t)$ in the circuit and a charge $Q(t)$ on the capacitor. All we need to know about these constants and functions is that they satisfy Eqs. (1) through (4), our mathematical model for the RLC circuit. We can then learn a good deal about electricity by studying this mathematical model.

The Mechanical–Electrical Analogy

It is striking that Eqs. (3) and (4) have precisely the same form as the equation

▶
$$mx'' + cx' + kx = F(t) \tag{5}$$

of a mass-spring-dashpot system with external force $F(t)$. The table in Fig. 3.7.3 details this important **mechanical–electrical analogy.** As a consequence, most of the results derived in Section 3.6 for mechanical systems can be applied at once to electrical circuits. The fact that the same differential equation serves as a mathematical model for such different physical systems is a powerful illustration of the unifying role of mathematics in the investigation of natural phenomena. More concretely, the correspondences in Fig. 3.7.3 can be used to construct an electrical model of a given mechanical system, using inexpensive and readily available circuit elements. The performance of the mechanical system can then be predicted by means of accurate and simple measurements in the electrical model. This is especially useful when the actual mechanical system would be expensive to construct and when measurements of displacements and velocities would be inconvenient, inaccurate, or even dangerous. This idea is the basis of *analog computers*—electrical models of mechanical systems.

Mechanical System	Electrical System
Mass m	Inductance L
Damping constant c	Resistance R
Spring constant k	Reciprocal capacitance $1/C$
Position x	Charge Q (using (3) (or current I using (4))
Force F	Electromotive force E (or its derivative E')

FIGURE 3.7.3. Mechanical–electrical analogies

In the typical case of an alternating current voltage $E(t) = E_0 \sin \omega t$, Eq. (4) takes the form

$$LI'' + RI' + \frac{1}{C} I = \omega E_0 \cos \omega t. \tag{6}$$

As in a mass-spring-dashpot system with a simple harmonic external force, the solution of Eq. (6) is the sum of a **transient current** I_{tr} that approaches zero as $t \to +\infty$ (under the assumption that the coefficients in (6) are all positive, so the roots of the characteristic equation have negative real parts), and a **steady periodic current** I_{sp}; thus

$$I = I_{tr} + I_{sp}. \tag{7}$$

Recall from Section 3.6 (Eqs. (19) through (21) there) that the steady periodic solution of Eq. (5) with $F(t) = F_0 \cos \omega t$ is

$$x_{sp}(t) = \frac{F_0 \cos(\omega t - \alpha)}{\sqrt{(k - m\omega^2)^2 + (c\omega)^2}},$$

where

$$\alpha = \tan^{-1} \frac{c\omega}{k - m\omega^2}, \qquad 0 \le \alpha \le \pi.$$

If we make the substitutions L for m, R for c, $1/C$ for k, and ωE_0 for F_0, we get the steady periodic current

$$I_{sp}(t) = \frac{E_0 \cos(\omega t - \alpha)}{\sqrt{R^2 + \left(\omega L - \dfrac{1}{\omega C}\right)^2}} \tag{8}$$

with the phase angle

$$\alpha = \tan^{-1} \frac{\omega RC}{1 - LC\omega^2}, \qquad 0 \le \alpha \le \pi. \tag{9}$$

*Reactance and Impedance

The quantity

$$Z = \sqrt{R^2 + \left(\omega L - \frac{1}{\omega C}\right)^2} \quad \text{(ohms)} \tag{10}$$

is called the **impedance** of the circuit. Then the steady periodic current

$$I_{sp}(t) = \frac{E_0}{Z} \cos(\omega t - \alpha) \tag{11}$$

has amplitude

$$I_0 = \frac{E_0}{Z}, \tag{12}$$

reminiscent of Ohm's law $I = E/R$.

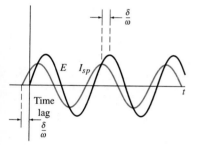

$$\delta = \alpha - \tfrac{\pi}{2}$$

FIGURE 3.7.4. Reactance and delay angle

FIGURE 3.7.5. Time lag of current behind imposed voltage

Equation (11) gives the steady periodic current as a cosine function, whereas the input voltage $E(t) = E_0 \sin \omega t$ was a sine function. To convert I_{sp} to a sine function, we first introduce the **reactance**

$$S = \omega L - \frac{1}{\omega C}. \tag{13}$$

Then $Z = \sqrt{R^2 + S^2}$, and we see from Eq. (9) that α is as in Fig. 3.7.4, with delay angle $\delta = \alpha - \pi/2$. Equation (11) now yields

$$I_{sp}(t) = \frac{E_0}{Z}(\cos \alpha \cos \omega t + \sin \alpha \sin \omega t)$$

$$= \frac{E_0}{Z}\left(-\frac{S}{Z}\cos \omega t + \frac{R}{Z}\sin \omega t\right)$$

$$= \frac{E_0}{Z}(\cos \delta \sin \omega t - \sin \delta \cos \omega t).$$

Therefore

$$I_{sp}(t) = \frac{E_0}{Z}\sin(\omega t - \delta), \tag{14}$$

where

$$\delta = \tan^{-1}\frac{S}{R} = \tan^{-1}\frac{LC\omega^2 - 1}{\omega RC}. \tag{15}$$

This finally gives the **time lag** δ/ω (in seconds) of the steady periodic current I_{sp} behind the input voltage (Fig. 3.7.5).

Initial Value Problems

When we want to find the transient current, we are usually given the initial values $I(0)$ and $Q(0)$. So we first must find $I'(0)$. To do so, we substitute $t = 0$ in Eq. (2) to obtain the equation

$$LI'(0) + RI(0) + \frac{1}{C}Q(0) = E(0) \tag{16}$$

to determine $I'(0)$ in terms of the initial values of current, charge, and voltage.

EXAMPLE 1 Consider an RLC circuit with $R = 50$ ohms, $L = 0.1$ henry (H), and $C = 5 \times 10^{-4}$ farad (F). At time $t = 0$, when both $I(0)$ and $Q(0)$ are zero, the circuit is connected to a 110-V, 60-Hz alternating current generator. Find the current in the circuit and the time lag of the steady periodic current behind the voltage.

Solution A frequency of 60 Hz means that $\omega = (2\pi)(60)$ rad/s, approximately 377 rad/s. So we take $E(t) = 110 \sin 377t$ and use equality in place of the symbol for approximate equality in this discussion. The differential equation in (6) takes the form

$$(0.1)I'' + 50I' + 2000I = (377)(110)\cos 377t.$$

We substitute the given values of R, L, C, and $\omega = 377$ in (10) to find that the imped-

ance is $Z = 59.58$ ohms, so the steady periodic amplitude is

$$I_0 = \frac{110 \text{ (volts)}}{59.58 \text{ (ohms)}} = 1.846 \text{ amperes (A)}.$$

With the same data, Eq. (15) gives the sine phase angle:

$$\delta = \tan^{-1}(0.648) = 0.575.$$

Thus the time lag of current behind voltage is

$$\frac{\delta}{\omega} = \frac{0.575}{377} = 0.0015 \text{ s},$$

and the steady periodic current is

$$I_{sp} = (1.846) \sin(377t - 0.575).$$

The characteristic equation $(0.1)r^2 + 50r + 2000 = 0$ has roots $r_1 \approx -44$ and $r_2 \approx -456$. With these approximations, the general solution is

$$I(t) = c_1 e^{-44t}c + {}_2 e^{-456t} + (1.846) \sin(377t - 0.575),$$

with derivative

$$I'(t) = -44c_1 e^{-44t} - 456c_2 e^{-456t} + 696 \cos(377t - 0.575).$$

Because $I(0) = Q(0) = 0$, Eq. (16) gives $I'(0) = 0$ as well. With these initial values substituted, we obtain the equations

$$I(0) = c_1 + c_2 - 1.004 = 0,$$

$$I'(0) = -44c_1 - 456c_2 + 584 = 0;$$

the solution is $c_1 = -0.307$, $c_2 = 1.311$. Thus the transient solution is

$$I_{tr}(t) = (-0.307)e^{-44t} + (1.311)e^{-456t},$$

and it dies out very rapidly, indeed.

EXAMPLE 2 Suppose that the RLC circuit of Example 1, still with $I(0) = Q(0) = 0$, is connected at time $t = 0$ to a battery supplying a constant 110 V. Now find the current in the circuit.

Solution We now have $E(t) \equiv 110$, so Eq. (16) gives

$$I'(0) = \frac{E(0)}{L} = \frac{110}{0.1} = 1100 \text{ A/s},$$

and the differential equation is

$$(0.1)I'' + 50I' + 2000I = E'(t) = 0.$$

Its general solution is the complementary function we found in Example 1: $I(t) = c_1 e^{-44t} + c_2 e^{-456t}$. We solve the equations

$$I(0) = c_1 + c_2 = 0,$$

$$I'(0) = -44c_1 - 456c_2 = 1100$$

for $c_1 = -c_2 = 2.670$. Therefore

$$I(t) = (2.670)(e^{-44t} - e^{-456t}).$$

Note that $I \to 0$ as $t \to +\infty$, even though the voltage is constant. ∎

Electrical Resonance

Consider again the current differential equation in (6) corresponding to a sinusoidal input voltage $E(t) = E_0 \sin \omega t$. We have seen that the amplitude of its steady periodic current is

$$I_0 = \frac{E_0}{Z} = \frac{E_0}{\sqrt{R^2 + \left(\omega L - \dfrac{1}{\omega C}\right)^2}}. \tag{17}$$

FIGURE 3.7.6. Effect of frequency of I_0

For typical values of the constants R, L, C, and E_0, the graph of I_0 as a function of ω resembles the one shown in Fig. 3.7.6. It reaches a maximum value at $\omega_m = 1/\sqrt{LC}$ and then approaches zero as $\omega \to +\infty$; the critical frequency ω_m is the **resonance frequency** of the circuit.

In Section 3.6 we emphasized the importance of avoiding resonance in most mechanical systems (the violin is an example of a mechanical system in which resonance is *sought*). By contrast, many common electrical devices could not function properly without taking advantage of the phenomenon of resonance. The radio is a familiar example. A highly simplified model of its tuning circuit is the RLC circuit we have discussed. Its inductance L and resistance R are constant, but its capacitance C is varied as one operates the tuning dial.

Suppose that we wanted to pick up a particular radio station that is broadcasting at frequency ω, and thereby (in effect) provides an input voltage $E(t) = E_0 \sin \omega t$ to the tuning circuit of the radio. The resulting steady periodic current I_{sp} in the tuning circuit drives its amplifier, and in turn its loudspeaker, with the volume of sound we hear roughly proportional to the amplitude I_0 of I_{sp}. In order to hear our preferred station (of frequency ω) the loudest (and simultaneously tune out stations broadcasting at other frequencies), we therefore want to choose C to maximize I_0. But examine Eq. (17), thinking of ω as a constant with C the only variable. We see at a glance—no calculus required—that I_0 is maximal when

$$\omega L - \frac{1}{\omega C} = 0;$$

that is, when

$$C = \frac{1}{L\omega^2}. \tag{18}$$

So we merely turn the dial to set the capacitance to this value.

This is the way that old crystal radios worked, but modern AM radios have a more sophisticated design. A *pair* of variable capacitors are used: The first controls the frequency selected as described earlier; the second controls the frequency of a signal that the radio itself generates, kept close to 455 kilohertz (kHz) above the desired frequency. The resulting *beat* frequency of 455 kHz, known as the *intermediate frequency*, is then amplified in several stages. This technique has the advantage that the several RLC circuits used in the amplification stages easily can be designed to resonate at 455 kHz and reject other frequencies, resulting in more selectivity of the receiver as well as better amplification of the desired signal.

3.7 Problems

Problems 1 through 6 deal with the LR circuit of Fig. 3.7.7, a series circuit containing an inductor with an inductance of L henries, a resistor with a resistance of R ohms (Ω), and a source of electromotive force (emf), but no capacitor. In this case Eq. (2) reduces to the linear first-order equation

$$LI' + RI = E(t).$$

FIGURE 3.7.7. The circuit for Problems 1 through 6

1. In the circuit of Fig. 3.7.7, suppose that $L = 5$ H, $R = 25$ Ω, and that the source E of emf is a battery supplying 100 V to the circuit. Suppose also that the switch has been in position 1 for a long time, so that a steady current of 4 A is flowing in the circuit. At time $t = 0$, the switch is thrown to position 2, so that $I(0) = 4$ and $E = 0$ for $t \geq 0$. Find $I(t)$.

2. Given the same circuit as in Problem 1, suppose that the switch is initially in position 2, but is thrown to position 1 at time $t = 0$, so that $I(0) = 0$ and $E = 100$ for $t \geq 0$. Find $I(t)$ and show that $I(t) \to 4$ as $t \to +\infty$.

3. Suppose that the battery in Problem 2 is replaced with an alternating current generator that supplies a voltage of $E(t) = 100 \cos 60t$ volts. With everything else the same, now find $I(t)$.

4. In the circuit of Fig. 3.7.7, with the switch in position 1, suppose that $L = 2$, $R = 40$, $E(t) = 100e^{-10t}$, and $I(0) = 0$. Find the maximum current in the circuit for $t \geq 0$.

5. In the circuit of Fig. 3.7.7, with the switch in position 1, suppose that $E(t) = 100e^{-10t} \cos 60t$, $R = 20$, $L = 2$, and $I(0) = 0$. Find $I(t)$.

6. In the circuit of Fig. 3.7.7, with the switch in position 1, take $L = 1$, $R = 10$, and $E(t) = 30 \cos 60t + 40 \sin 60t$. (a) Substitute $I_{sp} = A \cos 60t + B \sin 60t$ and then determine A and B to find the steady-state current I_{sp} in the circuit. (b) Write the solution in the form $I_{sp} = C \cos(\omega t - \alpha)$.

Problems 7 through 10 deal with the RC circuit shown in Fig. 3.7.8, containing a resistor (R ohms), a capacitor (C farads), a switch, a source of emf, but no inductor. Substitution of $L = 0$

in Eq. (3) gives the linear first-order differential equation

$$R\frac{dQ}{dt} + \frac{1}{C}Q = E(t)$$

for the charge $Q = Q(t)$ on the capacitor at time t. Note that $I(t) = Q'(t)$.

FIGURE 3.7.8. The circuit for Problems 7 through 10

7. (a) Find the charge $Q(t)$ and current $I(t)$ in the RC circuit if $E(t) \equiv E_0$ (a constant voltage supplied by a battery) and the switch is closed at time $t = 0$, so that $Q(0) = 0$. (b) Show that

$$\lim_{t \to +\infty} Q(t) = E_0 C \quad \text{and that} \quad \lim_{t \to +\infty} I(t) = 0.$$

8. Suppose that in the circuit of Fig. 3.7.8, we have $R = 10$, $C = 0.02$, $Q(0) = 0$, and $E(t) = 100e^{-5t}$ (volts). (a) Find $Q(t)$ and $I(t)$. (b) What is the maximum charge on the capacitor for $t \geq 0$ and when does it occur?

9. Suppose that in the circuit of Fig. 3.7.8, $R = 200$, $C = 2.5 \times 10^{-4}$, $Q(0) = 0$, and $E(t) = 100 \cos 120t$. (a) Find $Q(t)$ and $I(t)$. (b) What is the amplitude of the steady-state current?

10. An emf of voltage $E(t) = E_0 \cos \omega t$ is applied to the RC circuit of Fig. 3.7.8 at time $t = 0$, and $Q(0) = 0$. Substitute $Q_{sp} = A \cos \omega t + B \sin \omega t$ in the differential equation to show that the steady periodic charge on the capacitor is

$$Q_{sp} = \frac{E_0 C}{\sqrt{1 + \omega^2 R^2 C^2}} \cos(\omega t - \beta)$$

where $\beta = \tan^{-1}(\omega RC)$.

In Problems 11 through 16, the parameters of an RLC circuit with input voltage $E(t)$ are given. Substitute

$$I_{sp} = A \cos \omega t + B \sin \omega t$$

in Eq. (4), using the appropriate value of ω, to find the steady periodic current in the form $I_{sp} = I_0 \sin(\omega t - \delta)$.

11. $R = 30\ \Omega,\ \ L = 10\ \text{H},\ \ C = 0.02\ \text{F};$
$E(t) = 50 \sin 2t$ volts

12. $R = 200\ \Omega,\ \ L = 5\ \text{H},\ \ C = 0.001\ \text{F};$
$E(t) = 100 \sin 10t$ volts

13. $R = 20\ \Omega,\ \ L = 10\ \text{H},\ \ C = 0.01\ \text{F};$
$E(t) = 200 \cos 5t$ volts

14. $R = 50\ \Omega,\ \ L = 5\ \text{H},\ \ C = 0.005\ \text{F};$
$E(t) = 300 \cos 100t + 400 \sin 100t$ volts

15. $R = 100\ \Omega,\ \ L = 2\ \text{H},\ \ C = 5 \times 10^{-6}\ \text{F};$
$E(t) = 110 \sin 60\pi t$ volts

16. $R = 25\ \Omega,\ \ L = 0.2\ \text{H},\ \ C = 5 \times 10^{-4}\ \text{F};$
$E(t) = 120 \cos 377t$ volts

In Problems 17 through 22, an RLC circuit with input voltage $E(t)$ is described. Find the current $I(t)$ given the initial current (in amperes) and charge on the capacitor (in coulombs).

17. $R = 16\ \Omega,\ \ L = 2\ \text{H},\ \ C = 0.02\ \text{F};\ \ E(t) = 100\ \text{V};$
$I(0) = 0,\ \ Q(0) = 5$

18. $R = 60\ \Omega,\ \ L = 2\ \text{H},\ \ C = 0.0025\ \text{F};\ \ E(t) = 100e^{-t}\ \text{V};$
$I(0) = 0,\ \ Q(0) = 0$

19. $R = 60\ \Omega,\ \ L = 2\ \text{H},\ \ C = 0.0025\ \text{F};\ \ E(t) = 100e^{-10t}\ \text{V};$
$I(0) = 0,\ \ Q(0) = 1$

20. The circuit and input voltage of Problem 11 with $I(0) = 0$ and $Q(0) = 0$

21. The circuit and input voltage of Problem 13 with $I(0) = 0$ and $Q(0) = 3$

22. The circuit and input voltage of Problem 15 with $I(0) = 0$ and $Q(0) = 0$

23. Consider an LC circuit—that is, an RLC circuit with $R = 0$—with input voltage $E(t) = E_0 \sin \omega t$. Show that unbounded oscillations of current occur for a certain resonance frequency; express this frequency in terms of L and C.

24. It was stated in the text that, if R, L, and C are positive, then any solution of $LI'' + RI' + I/C = 0$ is a transient solution—it approaches zero as $t \to +\infty$. Prove this.

25. Prove that the amplitude I_0 of the steady periodic solution of Eq. (6) is maximal at frequency $\omega = 1/\sqrt{LC}$.

*3.8 Endpoint Problems and Eigenvalues

You are now familiar with the fact that a solution of a second-order linear differential equation is uniquely determined by two initial conditions. In particular, the only solution of the initial value problem

$$y'' + p(x)y' + q(x)y = 0; \qquad y(a) = 0; \qquad y'(a) = 0 \qquad (1)$$

is the trivial solution $y(x) \equiv 0$. Most of Chapter 3 has been based, directly or indirectly, on the uniqueness of solutions of linear initial value problems (as guaranteed by Theorem 2 of Section 3.2).

In this section we will see that the situation is radically different for a problem such as

$$y'' + p(x)y' + q(x)y = 0; \qquad y(a) = 0, \qquad y(b) = 0. \qquad (2)$$

The difference between the problems in Eqs. (1) and (2) is that in (2) the two conditions are imposed at two *different* points a and b with (say) $a < b$. In (2) we are to find a solution of the differential equation on the interval (a, b) that satisfies the conditions $y(a) = 0$ and $y(b) = 0$ at the endpoints of the interval. Such a problem is called an **endpoint** or **boundary value problem**. The following two examples illustrate the sorts of complications that can arise in endpoint problems.

EXAMPLE 1 Consider the endpoint problem

$$y'' + 3y = 0; \qquad y(0) = 0, \qquad y(\pi) = 0. \qquad (3)$$

The general solution of the differential equation is

$$y(x) = A \cos x\sqrt{3} + B \sin x\sqrt{3}.$$

The endpoint conditions give

$$y(0) = A = 0 \quad \text{and} \quad y(\pi) = B \sin \pi\sqrt{3} \approx (-0.7458)B = 0,$$

so $B = 0$ as well. Thus the only solution of the endpoint problem in (3) is the trivial solution $y(x) \equiv 0$; there is no surprise here.

EXAMPLE 2 Consider the endpoint problem

$$y'' + 4y = 0; \quad y(0) = 0, \quad y(\pi) = 0. \tag{4}$$

The general solution of the differential equation is

$$y(x) = A \cos 2x + B \sin 2x.$$

The endpoint conditions yield $y(0) = A = 0$ and

$$y(\pi) = A \cos 2\pi + B \sin 2\pi = B \cdot 0 = 0.$$

No matter what the value of B, the condition $y(\pi) = 0$ is automatically satisfied because $\sin 2\pi = 0$. Thus the function

$$y(x) = B \sin 2x$$

satisfies the endpoint problem in (4) for *every* value of B. This is an example of an endpoint problem having infinitely many nontrivial solutions.

Eigenvalue Problems

Rather than being the exceptional cases, these two examples illustrate the typical situation for an endpoint problem as in (2): It may have no nontrivial solutions, or it may have infinitely many nontrivial solutions. Note that the problems in (3) and (4) both can be written in the form

▶ $$y'' + p(x)y' + \lambda q(x)y = 0; \quad y(a) = 0, \quad y(b) = 0, \tag{5}$$

with $p(x) \equiv 0$, $q(x) \equiv 1$, $a = 0$ and $b = \pi$. The number λ is a parameter in the problem (nothing to do with the parameters that were varied in Section 3.5). If we take $\lambda = 3$, we get the equations in (3); with $\lambda = 4$, we obtain the equations in (4). Examples 1 and 2 show that the situation in an endpoint problem containing a parameter can (and generally will) depend strongly on the specific numerical value of the parameter.

An endpoint problem containing a parameter λ, such as the endpoint problem in (5), is called an **eigenvalue problem.** The question we ask in an eigenvalue problem is this: For what (real) values of the parameter λ does there exist a *nontrivial* solution of the endpoint problem? Such a value of λ is called an **eigenvalue** or **characteristic value** of the problem. Thus we saw in Example 2 that $\lambda = 4$ is an eigenvalue of the eigenvalue problem

$$y'' + \lambda y = 0; \quad y(0) = 0, \quad y(\pi) = 0. \tag{6}$$

In Example 1 we saw that $\lambda = 3$ is not an eigenvalue of this problem.

Suppose that λ_* is an eigenvalue of the problem in (5) and that y_* is a nontrivial solution of the problem with this value of λ inserted; that is, that

$$y_*'' + p(x)y_*' + \lambda_* q(x)y_* = 0 \quad \text{and} \quad y_*(a) = 0, \quad y_*(b) = 0.$$

Then we call y_* an **eigenfunction** associated with the eigenvalue λ_*. Thus we saw in Example 2 that $y_*(x) = \sin 2x$ is an eigenfunction associated with the eigenvalue $\lambda_* = 4$, as is any constant multiple of $\sin 2x$.

More generally, note that the problem in (5) is *homogeneous* in the sense that any constant multiple of an eigenfunction is again an eigenfunction; indeed, one associated with the same eigenvalue. That is, if $y = y_*(x)$ satisfies the problem in (5) with $\lambda = \lambda_*$, then so does any constant multiple $cy_*(x)$. It can be proved under mild restrictions on the coefficient functions p and q that any two eigenfunctions associated with the same eigenvalue must be linearly dependent.

EXAMPLE 3 Determine the eigenvalues and associated eigenfunctions of the problem

$$y'' + \lambda y = 0; \qquad y(0) = 0, \qquad y(L) = 0 \qquad (L > 0). \tag{7}$$

Solution We must consider all possible (real) values of λ—positive, zero, and negative.

If $\lambda = 0$, then the equation is simply $y'' = 0$ and its general solution is

$$y(x) = Ax + B.$$

Then the endpoint conditions $y(0) = 0 = y(L)$ immediately imply that $A = B = 0$, so the only solution in this case is the trivial function $y(x) \equiv 0$. Therefore $\lambda = 0$ is *not* an eigenvalue of the problem in (7).

If $\lambda < 0$, let us then write $\lambda = -\alpha^2$ (with $\alpha > 0$) to be specific. Then the differential equation takes the form

$$y'' - \alpha^2 y = 0,$$

and its general solution is

$$y(x) = c_1 e^{\alpha x} + c_2 e^{-\alpha x} = A \cosh \alpha x + B \sinh \alpha x,$$

where $A = c_1 + c_2$ and $B = c_1 - c_2$. (Recall that $\cosh \alpha x = (e^{\alpha x} + e^{-\alpha x})/2$ and that $\sinh \alpha x = (e^{\alpha x} - e^{-\alpha x})/2$.) The condition $y(0) = 0$ then gives

$$y(0) = A \cosh 0 + B \sinh 0 = A = 0,$$

so that $y = B \sinh \alpha x$. But now the second endpoint condition, $y(L) = 0$, gives $y(L) = B \sinh \alpha L = 0$. This implies that $B = 0$, because $\alpha \neq 0$, and $\sinh x = 0$ only for $x = 0$ (examine the graphs of $\sinh x$ and $\cosh x$ in Fig. 3.8.1). Thus the only solution of the problem in (7) in the case $\lambda < 0$ is the trivial solution $y \equiv 0$, and we may therefore conclude that the problem has *no* negative eigenvalues.

The only remaining possibility is that $\lambda = \alpha^2 > 0$ with $\alpha > 0$. In this case the differential equation is

$$y'' + \alpha^2 y = 0,$$

with general solution

$$y(x) = A \cos \alpha x + B \sin \alpha x.$$

The condition $y(0) = 0$ implies that $A = 0$, so $y(x) = B \sin \alpha x$. The condition $y(L) = 0$ then gives

$$y(L) = B \sin \alpha L = 0.$$

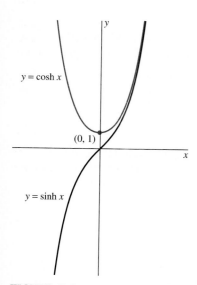

$y = \cosh x$

$(0, 1)$

$y = \sinh x$

FIGURE 3.8.1. The hyperbolic sine and cosine graphs

Can this occur if $B \neq 0$? Yes, but only provided that αL is a (positive) integral multiple of π:

$$\alpha L = \pi, \quad 2\pi, \quad 3\pi, \quad \ldots, \quad n\pi, \quad \ldots ;$$

that is, if

$$\lambda = \alpha^2 = \frac{\pi^2}{L^2}, \quad \frac{4\pi^2}{L^2}, \quad \frac{9\pi^2}{L^2}, \quad \ldots, \quad \frac{n^2\pi^2}{L^2}, \quad \ldots .$$

Thus we have discovered that the problem in (7) has an *infinite sequence* of positive eigenvalues,

$$\lambda_n = \frac{n^2\pi^2}{L^2}, \qquad n = 1, 2, 3, \ldots . \tag{8}$$

With $B = 1$, the eigenfunction associated with the eigenvalue λ_n is

$$y_n(x) = \sin \frac{n\pi x}{L}, \qquad n = 1, 2, 3, \ldots . \tag{9}$$

∎

Example 3 illustrates the general situation. According to a theorem whose precise statement we will defer until Section 10.1, under the assumption that $q(x) > 0$ on the interval $[a, b]$, any eigenvalue problem of the form in (5) has a divergent increasing sequence

$$\lambda_1 < \lambda_2 < \lambda_3 < \cdots < \lambda_n < \cdots \rightarrow +\infty$$

of eigenvalues, each with an associated eigenfunction. This is also true of the following slightly more general type of eigenvalue problem, in which the endpoint conditions involve values of the derivative y' as well as values of y:

$$y'' + p(x)y' + \lambda q(x)y = 0;$$
$$a_1 y(a) + a_2 y'(a) = 0, \qquad b_1 y(b) + b_2 y'(b) = 0, \tag{10}$$

where a_1, a_2, b_1, and b_2 are given constants. With $a_1 = 1 = b_2$ and $a_2 = 0 = b_1$, we get the problem of Example 4 (in which $p(x) \equiv 0$ and $q(x) \equiv 1$, as in the previous examples).

EXAMPLE 4 Determine the eigenvalues and eigenfunctions of the problem

$$y'' + \lambda y = 0; \qquad y(0) = 0, \qquad y'(L) = 0. \tag{11}$$

Solution Virtually the same argument as that used in Example 3 shows that the only possible eigenvalues are positive, so we take $\lambda = \alpha^2 > 0$ ($\alpha > 0$) to be specific. Then the differential equation is

$$y'' + \alpha^2 y = 0,$$

with general solution

$$y(x) = A \cos \alpha x + B \sin \alpha x.$$

The condition $y(0) = 0$ immediately gives $A = 0$, so

$$y(x) = B \sin \alpha x \qquad \text{and} \qquad y'(x) = B\alpha \cos \alpha x.$$

The second endpoint condition $y'(L) = 0$ now gives

$$y'(L) = B\alpha \cos \alpha L = 0.$$

This will hold with $B \neq 0$ provided that αL is an odd positive multiple of $\pi/2$:

$$\alpha L = \frac{\pi}{2}, \quad \frac{3\pi}{2}, \quad \ldots, \quad \frac{(2n-1)\pi}{2}, \quad \ldots \, ;$$

that is, if

$$\lambda = \frac{\pi^2}{4L^2}, \quad \frac{9\pi^2}{4L^2}, \quad \ldots, \quad \frac{(2n-1)^2\pi^2}{4L^2}, \quad \ldots$$

Thus the nth eigenvalue λ_n and associated eigenfunction of the problem in (11) are given by

$$\lambda_n = \frac{(2n-1)^2\pi^2}{4L^2} \quad \text{and} \quad y_n(x) = \sin\frac{(2n-1)\pi x}{2L} \quad \text{for } n = 1, 2, 3, \ldots . \quad (12)$$

∎

A general procedure for determining the eigenvalues of the problem in (10) can be outlined as follows. We first write the general solution of the differential equation in the form

$$y = Ay_1(x, \lambda) + By_2(x, \lambda).$$

We write $y_i(x, \lambda)$ because y_1 and y_2 will depend on λ, as in Examples 3 and 4, in which

$$y_1(x) = \cos \alpha x = \cos x\sqrt{\lambda} \quad \text{and} \quad y_2(x) = \sin \alpha x = \sin x\sqrt{\lambda}.$$

Then we impose the two endpoint conditions, noting that each is linear in y and y', and hence also linear in A and B. When we collect coefficients of A and B in the resulting pair of equations, we therefore get a system of the form

$$\alpha_1(\lambda)A + \beta_1(\lambda)B = 0,$$
$$\alpha_2(\lambda)A + \beta_2(\lambda)B = 0. \quad (13)$$

Now λ is an eigenvalue if and only if (13) has a nontrivial solution (one with A and B not both zero). But such a homogeneous system of linear equations has a nontrivial solution if and only if the determinant of its coefficients vanishes. We therefore conclude that the eigenvalues of the problem in (10) are the (real) solutions of the equation

$$D(\lambda) = a_1(\lambda)\beta_2(\lambda) - a_2(\lambda)\beta_1(\lambda) = 0. \quad (14)$$

This can be a formidable equation to solve and may require a numerical approximation technique such as Newton's method.

Most of the interest in eigenvalue problems is due to their very diverse physical applications. The remainder of this section is devoted to three such applications. Numerous additional applications are included in Chapters 9 and 10 (on partial differential equations and boundary value problems).

The Whirling String

Who of us has not wondered about the shape of a quickly spinning jump rope? Let us consider the shape assumed by a tightly stretched flexible string of length L and con-

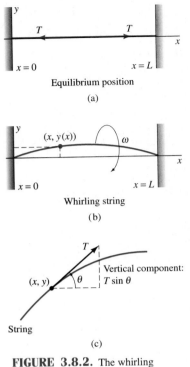

FIGURE 3.8.2. The whirling string

FIGURE 3.8.3. Forces on a short segment of the whirling string

stant linear density ρ (mass per unit length) if it is rotated or whirled (like a jump rope) with constant angular speed ω (in radians per second) about its equilibrium position along the x-axis. We assume that the portion of the string to one side of any point exerts a constant tension force T on the portion of the string to the other side of the point, with the direction of T tangential to the string at that point. We further assume that, as the string whirls around the x-axis, each point moves in a circle centered at that point's equilibrium position on the x-axis. Thus the string is elastic, so that as it whirls it also stretches to assume a curved shape. Denote by $y(x)$ the displacement of the string from the axis of rotation. Finally, we assume that the deflection of the string is so slight that $\sin\theta \approx \tan\theta \approx y'(x)$ in Fig. 3.8.2(c).

We plan to derive a differential equation for $y(x)$ by application of Newton's law $F = ma$ to the piece of string of mass $\rho\,\Delta x$ corresponding to the interval $[x, x + \Delta x]$. The only forces acting on this piece are the tension forces at its two ends. From Fig. 3.8.3 we see that the net vertical force in the positive y-direction is

$$F = T\sin(\theta + \Delta\theta) - T\sin\theta \approx T\tan(\theta + \Delta\theta) - T\tan\theta,$$

so that

$$F \approx Ty'(x + \Delta x) - Ty'(x). \tag{15}$$

Next we recall from elementary calculus or physics the formula $a = r\omega^2$ for the (inward) centripetal acceleration of a body in uniform circular motion (r is the radius of the circle and ω is the angular velocity of the body). Here we have $r = y$, so the vertical acceleration of our piece of string is $a = -\omega^2 y$, the minus sign because the inward direction is the negative y-direction. Because $m = \rho\,\Delta x$, substitution of this and (15) in $F = ma$ yields

$$Ty'(x + \Delta x) - Ty'(x) \approx -\rho\omega^2 y\,\Delta x,$$

so that

$$T \cdot \frac{y'(x + \Delta x) - y'(x)}{\Delta x} \approx -\rho\omega^2 y.$$

We now take the limit as $\Delta x \to 0$ to get the differential equation of motion of the string:

$$Ty'' + \rho\omega^2 y = 0. \tag{16}$$

If we write

$$\lambda = \frac{\rho\omega^2}{T} \tag{17}$$

and impose the condition that the ends of the string are fixed, we get finally the eigenvalue problem

$$y'' + \lambda y = 0; \qquad y(0) = 0, \qquad y(L) = 0 \tag{7}$$

that we considered in Example 3. We found there that the eigenvalues of the problem in (7) are

$$\lambda_n = \frac{n^2\pi^2}{L^2}, \qquad n = 1, 2, 3, \ldots, \tag{8}$$

with the eigenfunction $y_n(x) = \sin(n\pi x/L)$ associated with λ_n.

But what does all this mean in terms of the whirling string? It means that unless λ

in (17) is one of the eigenvalues in (8), then the only solution of the problem in (7) is the trivial solution $y(x) \equiv 0$. In this case the string remains in its equilibrium position with zero deflection. But if we equate (17) and (8) and solve for the value ω_n corresponding to λ_n,

$$\omega_n = \sqrt{\frac{\lambda_n T}{\rho}} = \frac{n\pi}{L}\sqrt{\frac{T}{\rho}} \qquad (18)$$

for $n = 1, 2, 3, \ldots$, we get a sequence of **critical speeds** of angular rotation. Only at these critical angular speeds can the string whirl up out of its equilibrium position. At angular speed ω_n it assumes a shape of the form $y_n = c_n \sin(n\pi x/L)$; our mathematical model is not sufficiently complete to determine the coefficient c_n.

Suppose that we start the string rotating at speed

$$\omega < \omega_1 = \frac{\pi}{L}\sqrt{\frac{T}{\rho}},$$

but gradually increase its speed of rotation. So long as $\omega < \omega_1$, the string remains in its undeflected position $y \equiv 0$. But when $\omega = \omega_1$, the string pops into a whirling position $y = c_1 \sin(\pi x/L)$. And when ω is increased further, the string (theoretically) pops back into its undeflected position along the axis of rotation!

The Deflection of a Uniform Beam

We include now an example of the use of a relatively simple endpoint value problem to explain a complicated physical phenomenon—the shape of a horizontal beam upon which a vertical force is acting.

Consider the horizontal beam shown in Fig. 3.8.4, uniform both in cross section and in material. If it is supported only at its ends, the force of its own weight distorts its longitudinal axis of symmetry into the curve shown as a dashed line in the figure. We want to investigate the shape $y = y(x)$ of this curve, the **deflection curve** of the beam. We will use the coordinate system indicated in Fig. 3.8.5, with the positive y-axis directed downward.

A consequence of the theory of elasticity is that for relatively small deflections of such a beam (so small that $[y'(x)]^2$ is negligible in comparison with unity), an adequate mathematical model of the deflection curve is the fourth-order differential equation

$$EIy^{(4)} = F(x), \qquad (19)$$

where

FIGURE 3.8.4. Distortion of a horizontal beam

Positive
y-values

FIGURE 3.8.5. The deflection curve

E denotes the Young's modulus of the material of the beam,

I denotes the moment of inertia of the cross section of the beam around a horizontal line through the centroid of the cross section, and

$F(x)$ denotes the density of *downward* force acting vertically on the beam at the point x.

Density of force? Yes; this means that the force acting downward on a very short segment $[x, x + \Delta x]$ of the beam is approximately $F(x) \Delta x$. The units of $F(x)$ are those of force per unit length, such as pounds per foot. We will consider here the case in

which the only force distributed along the beam is its own weight, w pounds per foot, so that $F(x) \equiv w$. Then Eq. (19) takes the form

$$EIy^{(4)} = w \tag{20}$$

where E, I, and w are all constant.

Note: We assume no previous familiarity with the theory of elasticity or with Eqs. (19) and (20) here. It is important to be able to begin with a differential equation that arises in a specific applied discipline and the analyze its implications; thus we develop an understanding of the equation by examining its solutions. Observe that, in essence, Eq. (20) implies that the fourth derivative $y^{(4)}$ is proportional to the weight density w. This proportionality involves, however, *two* constants: E, which depends only upon the material in the beam, and I, which depends only upon the shape of the cross section of the beam. Values of the Young's modulus E of various material can be found in handbooks of physical constants; $I = \frac{1}{4}\pi a^4$ for a circular cross section of radius a.

Although (20) is a fourth-order differential equation, its solution involves only the solution of simple first-order equations by successive simple integrations. One integration of Eq. (20) yields

$$EIy^{(3)} = wx + C_1;$$

a second yields

$$EIy'' = \frac{1}{2}wx^2 + C_1 x + C_2;$$

another yields

$$EIy' = \frac{1}{6}wx^3 + \frac{1}{2}C_1 x^2 + C_2 x + C_3;$$

a final integration gives

$$EIy = \frac{1}{24}wx^4 + \frac{1}{6}C_1 x^3 + \frac{1}{2}C_2 x^2 + C_3 x + C_4,$$

where C_1, C_2, C_3, and C_4 are arbitrary constants. Thus we obtain a solution of Eq. (20) of the form

$$y(x) = \frac{w}{24EI}x^4 + Ax^3 + Bx^2 + Cx + D, \tag{21}$$

where A, B, C, and D are constants resulting from the four integrations.

These last four constants are determined by the way in which the beam is supported at its ends, where $x = 0$ and $x = L$. Figure 3.8.6 shows two common types of support. A beam might also be supported one way at one end but another way at the other end. For instance, Fig. 3.8.7 shows a **cantilever**—a beam firmly fastened at $x = 0$ but *free* (no support whatsoever) at $x = L$. The following table shows the **boundary** or **endpoint conditions** corresponding to the three most common cases. We will see that these conditions are applied readily in beam problems, although a discussion here of their origin would take us too far afield.

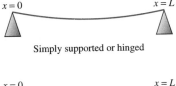

$x = 0$ $x = L$

Simply supported or hinged

$x = 0$ $x = L$

Built -In

FIGURE 3.8.6. Two ways of supporting a beam

Cantilever

FIGURE 3.8.7. The cantilever

Support	Endpoint Condition
Simply supported	$y = y'' = 0$
Build-in or fixed end	$y = y' = 0$
Free end	$y'' = y^{(3)} = 0$

For example, the deflection curve of the cantilever in Fig. 3.8.7 would be given by Eq. (21), with the coefficients A, B, C, and D determined by the conditions

$$y(0) = y'(0) = 0 \quad \text{and} \quad y''(L) = y^{(3)}(L) = 0, \tag{22}$$

corresponding to the fixed end at $x = 0$ and the free end at $x = L$. The conditions in (22) together with the differential equation in (21) constitute an **endpoint value problem.**

EXAMPLE 5 Determine the shape of the deflection curve of a uniform horizontal beam of length L and weight w per unit length and simply supported at each end.

Solution We have the endpoint conditions

$$y(0) = y''(0) = 0 = y(L) = y''(L).$$

Rather than imposing them directly on Eq. (21), let us begin with the differential equation $EIy^{(4)} = w$ and determine the constants as we proceed with the four successive integrations. The first two integrations yield

$$EIy^{(3)} = wx + A; \qquad EIy'' = \frac{1}{2} wx^2 + Ax + B.$$

Hence $y''(0) = 0$ implies that $B = 0$, and then $y''(L) = 0$ gives

$$0 = \frac{1}{2} wL^2 + AL.$$

It follows that $A = -wL/2$ and thus that

$$EIy'' = \frac{1}{2} wx^2 - \frac{1}{2} wLx.$$

Then two more integrations give

$$EIy' = \frac{1}{6} wx^3 - \frac{1}{4} wLx^2 + C,$$

and finally,

$$EIy(x) = \frac{1}{24} wx^4 - \frac{1}{12} wLx^3 + Cx + D. \tag{23}$$

Now $y(0) = 0$ implies that $D = 0$; then, because $y(L) = 0$,

$$0 = \frac{1}{24} wL^4 - \frac{1}{12} wL^4 + CL.$$

It follows that $C = wL^3/24$. Hence from Eq. (23) we obtain

$$y(x) = \frac{w}{24EI}(x^4 - 2Lx^3 + L^3x) \tag{24}$$

as the shape of the supported beam. It is apparent from symmetry (see also Problem 17) that the *maximum deflection* y_{max} of the beam occurs at its midpoint $x = L/2$, and thus has the value

$$y_{max} = y\left(\frac{L}{2}\right) = \frac{w}{24EI}\left(\frac{1}{16}L^4 - \frac{2}{8}L^4 + \frac{1}{2}L^4\right);$$

that is,

$$y_{max} = \frac{5wL^4}{384EI}. \tag{25}$$

∎

For instance, suppose that we want to calculate the maximum deflection of a simply supported steel rod 20 ft long with a circular cross section 1 in. in diameter. From a handbook we find that typical steel has density $\delta = 7.75$ g/cm², and that its Young's modulus is $E = 2 \times 10^{12}$ g/cm · s², so it will be more convenient to work in cgs units. Thus our rod has

$$\text{Length:}\quad L = (20\text{ ft})\left(30.48\,\frac{\text{cm}}{\text{ft}}\right) = 609.60\text{ cm}$$

$$\text{and}\quad \text{Radius:}\quad a = \left(\frac{1}{2}\text{ in.}\right)\left(2.54\,\frac{\text{cm}}{\text{in.}}\right) = 1.27\text{ cm.}$$

Its *linear* mass density (that is, its mass per unit length) is

$$\rho = \pi a^2 \delta = \pi(1.27)^2(7.75) \approx 39.27\,\frac{\text{g}}{\text{cm}},$$

so

$$w = \rho g = \left(39.27\,\frac{\text{g}}{\text{cm}}\right)\left(980\,\frac{\text{cm}}{\text{s}^2}\right) \approx 38484.6\,\frac{\text{dyn}}{\text{cm}}.$$

The area moment of inertia of a circular disk of radius a about a diameter is $I = \frac{1}{4}\pi a^4$, so

$$I = \frac{1}{4}\pi(1.27)^4 \approx 2.04\text{ cm}^4.$$

Therefore Eq. (25) yields

$$y_{max} \approx \frac{(5)(38484.6)(609.60)^4}{(384)(2 \times 10^{12})(2.04)} \approx 16.96\quad(\text{cm}),$$

about 6.68 in., as the maximum deflection of the rod at its midpoint. It is interesting to note that y_{max} is proportional to L^4, so if the rod were only 10 ft long, its maximum de-

flection would be only one-sixteenth as much—only about 0.42 in. Because $I = \frac{1}{4}\pi a^4$, we see from Eq. (25) that the same reduction in maximum deflection could be achieved by doubling the radius a of the rod.

The Buckled Rod

FIGURE 3.8.8. The buckled rod

Figure 3.8.8 shows a uniform rod of length L, hinged at each end, that has been "buckled" by an axial force of compression P applied at each end. We assume this buckling to be so slight that the deflection curve $y = y(x)$ of the rod may be regarded as defined on the interval $0 \leq x \leq L$.

In the theory of elasticity the linear endpoint boundary value problem

$$EIy'' + Py = 0, \qquad y(0) = y(L) = 0 \tag{26}$$

is used to model the actual (nonlinear) behavior of the rod. As in our discussion of the deflection of a uniform beam, E denotes the Young's modulus of the beam material and I denotes the moment of inertia of each cross section of the beam about a horizontal line through its centroid.

If we write

$$\lambda = \frac{P}{EI}, \tag{27}$$

then the problem in (26) becomes the eigenvalue problem

$$y'' + \lambda y = 0; \qquad y(0) = y(L) = 0 \tag{7}$$

that we considered in Example 3. We found that its eigenvalues $\{\lambda_n\}$ are given by

$$\lambda_n = \frac{n^2 \pi^2}{L^2}, \qquad n = 1, 2, 3, \ldots . \tag{8}$$

with the eigenfunction $y_n(x) = \sin(n\pi x/L)$ associated with λ_n. (Thus whirling strings and buckled rods lead to the same eigenvalues and eigenfunctions.)

To interpret this result in terms of the buckled rod, recall from (27) that $P = \lambda EI$. The forces

$$P_n = \lambda_n EI = \frac{n^2 \pi^2 EI}{L^2}, \qquad n = 1, 2, 3, \ldots \tag{28}$$

are the *critical buckling forces* of the rod. Only when the compressive force P is one of these critical forces should the rod "buckle" out of its straight (undeflected) shape. The smallest compressive force for which this occurs is

$$P_1 = \frac{\pi^2 EI}{L^2}. \tag{29}$$

This smallest critical force P_1 is called the *Euler buckling force* for the rod; it is the upper bound for those compressive forces to which the rod can safely be subjected without buckling. (In actual practice a rod may fail at a significantly smaller force due to a contribution of factors not taken into account by the mathematical model discussed here.)

For instance, suppose that we want to compute the Euler buckling force for a steel

rod 10 ft long having a circular cross section 1 in. in diameter. In cgs units we have

$$E = 2 \times 10^{12} \text{ g/cm} \cdot \text{s}^2,$$

$$L = (10 \text{ ft}) \left(30.48 \, \frac{\text{cm}}{\text{ft}} \right) = 304.8 \text{ cm}, \quad \text{and}$$

$$I = \frac{\pi}{4} \left[(0.5 \text{ in.}) \left(2.54 \, \frac{\text{cm}}{\text{in.}} \right) \right]^4 \approx 2.04 \text{ cm}^4.$$

Upon substituting these values in (29) we find that the critical force for this rod is

$$P_1 \approx 4.34 \times 10^8 \text{ dyn} \approx 976 \text{ lb},$$

using the conversion factor 4.448×10^5 dyn/lb.

3.8 Problems

The eigenvalues in Problems 1 through 5 are all nonnegative. First determine whether $\lambda = 0$ is an eigenvalue; then find the positive eigenvalues and associated eigenfunctions.

1. $y'' + \lambda y = 0;$ $y'(0) = 0,$ $y(1) = 0$
2. $y'' + \lambda y = 0;$ $y'(0) = 0,$ $y'(\pi) = 0$
3. $y'' + \lambda y = 0;$ $y(-\pi) = 0,$ $y(\pi) = 0$
4. $y'' + \lambda y = 0;$ $y'(-\pi) = 0,$ $y'(\pi) = 0$
5. $y'' + \lambda y = 0;$ $y(-2) = 0,$ $y'(2) = 0$

6. Consider the eigenvalue problem

$$y'' + \lambda y = 0; \quad y'(0) = 0, \quad y(1) + y'(1) = 0.$$

All the eigenvalues are nonnegative, so write $\lambda = \alpha^2$ with $\alpha \geq 0$. (a) Show that $\lambda = 0$ is not an eigenvalue. (b) Show that $y = A \cos \alpha x + B \sin \alpha x$ satisfies the endpoint conditions if and only if $B = 0$ and α is a positive root of the equation

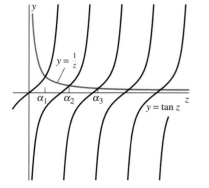

FIGURE 3.8.9. The eigenvalues are determined by the intersection of the graphs of $y = \tan z$ and $y = 1/z$.

$\tan z = 1/z$. These roots $\{\alpha_n\}_1^\infty$ are the abscissas of the points of intersection of the curves $y = \tan z$ and $y = 1/z$, as indicated in Fig. 3.8.9. Thus the eigenvalues and eigenfunctions of this problem are the numbers $\{\alpha_n^2\}_1^\infty$ and the functions $\{\cos \alpha_n x\}_1^\infty$, respectively.

7. Consider the eigenvalue problem

$$y'' + \lambda y = 0; \quad y(0) = 0, \quad y(1) + y'(1) = 0;$$

all its eigenvalues are nonnegative. (a) Show that $\lambda = 0$ is not an eigenvalue. (b) Show that the eigenfunctions are the functions $\{\sin \alpha_n x\}_1^\infty$, where α_n is the nth positive root of the equation $\tan z = -z$. (c) Draw a sketch indicating the roots $\{\alpha_n\}_1^\infty$ as the points of intersection of the curves $y = z$ and $y = -\tan z$.

8. Consider the eigenvalue problem

$$y'' + \lambda y = 0; \quad y(0) = 0, \quad y(1) = y'(1);$$

all its eigenvalues are nonnegative. (a) Show that $\lambda = 0$ is an eigenvalue with associated eigenfunction $y_0(x) = x$. (b) Show that the remaining eigenfunctions are given by $y_n(x) = \sin a_n x$, where α_n is the nth positive root of the equation $\tan z = z$. Draw a sketch showing these roots.

9. Prove that the eigenvalue problem of Example 4 has no negative eigenvalues.

10. Prove that the eigenvalue problem

$$y'' + \lambda y = 0; \quad y(0) = 0, \quad y(1) + y'(1) = 0$$

has no negative eigenvalues. (*Suggestion:* Show graphically that the only root of the equation $\tanh z = -z$ is $z = 0$.)

11. Use a method similar to that suggested in Problem 10 to show that the eigenvalue problem in Problem 6 has no negative eigenvalues.

12. Consider the eigenvalue problem

$$y'' + \lambda y = 0; \qquad y(-\pi) = y(\pi), \qquad y'(-\pi) = y'(\pi),$$

which is not of the type in (10) because the two endpoints conditions are not "separated" between the two endpoints. (a) Show that $\lambda_0 = 0$ is an eigenvalue with associated eigenfunction $y_0(x) \equiv 1$. (b) Show that there are no negative eigenvalues. (c) Show that the nth positive eigenvalue is n^2, and that it has two linearly independent associated eigenfunctions, $\cos nx$ and $\sin nx$.

13. Consider the eigenvalue problem

$$y'' + 2y' + \lambda y = 0; \qquad y(0) = y(1) = 0.$$

(a) Show that $\lambda = 1$ is not an eigenvalue. (b) Show that there is no eigenvalue λ such that $\lambda < 1$. (c) Show that the nth positive eigenvalue is $\lambda_n = n^2\pi^2 + 1$, with associated eigenfunction $y_n(x) = e^{-x}\sin(n\pi x)$.

14. Consider the eigenvalue problem

$$y'' + 2y' + \lambda y = 0; \qquad y(0) = 0, \qquad y'(1) = 0.$$

Show that the eigenvalues are all positive, and that the nth positive eigenvalue is $\lambda_n = \alpha_n^2 + 1$ with associated eigenfunction $y_n(x) = e^{-x}\sin \alpha_n x$, where α_n is the nth positive root of $\tan z = z$.

15. (a) A cantilever beam is fixed at $x = 0$ and free at $x = L$ (its other end). Show that its shape is given by

$$y(x) = \frac{w}{24EI}(x^4 - 4Lx^3 + 6L^2x^2).$$

(b) Show that $y'(x) = 0$ only at $x = 0$, and thus that it follows (why?) that the maximum deflection of the cantilever is $y_{\max} = y(L) = wL^4/(8EI)$.

16. (a) Suppose that a beam is fixed at its ends $x = 0$ and $x = L$. Show that its shape is given by

$$y(x) = \frac{w}{24EI}(x^4 - 2Lx^3 + L^2x^2).$$

(b) Show that the roots of $y'(x) = 0$ are $x = 0$, $x = L$, and $x = L/2$, so it follows (why?) that the maximum deflection of the beam is

$$y_{\max} = y\left(\frac{L}{2}\right) = \frac{wL^4}{384EI},$$

one-fifth that of a beam with simply supported ends.

17. For the simply supported beam whose deflection curve is given by Eq. (24), show that the only root of $y'(x) = 0$ in $[0, L]$ is $x = L/2$, so it follows (why?) that the maximum deflection is indeed that given in Eq. (25).

18. (a) A beam is fixed at its left end $x = 0$ but is simply supported at the other end $x = L$. Show that its deflection curve is

$$y(x) = \frac{w}{48EI}(2x^4 - 5Lx^3 + 3L^2x^2).$$

(b) Show that its maximum deflection occurs where $x = (15 - \sqrt{33})L/16$, and is about 41.6% of the maximum deflection that would occur if it were simply supported at each end.

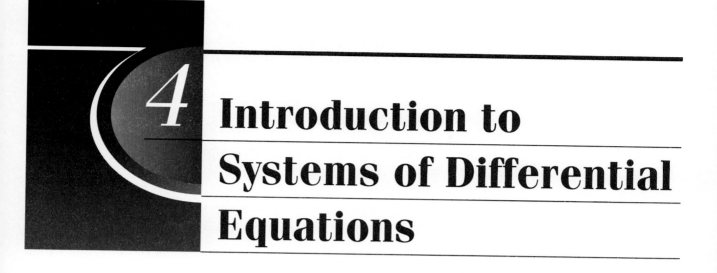

4 Introduction to Systems of Differential Equations

4.1 First-Order Systems and Applications

In the preceding chapters we have discussed methods for solving an ordinary differential equation that involves only one dependent variable. Many applications, however, require the use of two or more dependent variables, each a function of a single independent variable (typically time). Such a problem leads naturally to a *system* of simultaneous ordinary differential equations. We will usually denote the independent variable by t and the dependent variables (the unknown functions of t) by x_1, x_2, x_3, . . . , or by x, y, z, Primes will denote differentiation with respect to t.

We will restrict our attention to systems in which the number of equations is the same as the number of dependent variables (unknown functions). For instance, a system of two first-order equations in the dependent variables x and y has the general form

$$f(t, x, y, x', y') = 0,$$
$$g(t, x, y, x', y') = 0, \tag{1}$$

where the functions f and g are given. A **solution** of this system is a pair $x(t)$, $y(t)$ of functions of t that satisfy both equations identically over some interval of values of t.

For an example of a second-order system, consider a particle of mass m that moves in space under the influence of a force field \mathbf{F} that depends upon time t, the position $(x(t),\, y(t),\, z(t))$ of the particle, and its velocity $(x'(t),\, y'(t),\, z'(t))$. Applying Newton's law $m\mathbf{a} = \mathbf{F}$ componentwise, we get the system

$$
\begin{aligned}
mx'' &= F_1(t,\, x,\, y,\, z,\, x',\, y',\, z'), \\
my'' &= F_2(t,\, x,\, y,\, z,\, x',\, y',\, z'), \\
mz'' &= F_3(t,\, x,\, y,\, z,\, x',\, y',\, z'),
\end{aligned}
\tag{2}
$$

where F_1, F_2, and F_3, are the three components of the vector function \mathbf{F}.

Initial Applications

Examples 1 through 3 illustrate further how systems of differential equations arise naturally in scientific problems.

EXAMPLE 1 Consider the system of two masses and two springs shown in Fig. 4.1.1, with a given external force $f(t)$ acting on the right-hand mass m_2. We denote by $x(t)$ the displacement (to the right) of the mass m_1 from its static equilibrium position (when the system is motionless and in equilibrium and $f(t) = 0$), and by $y(t)$ the displacement of the mass m_2 from its static position. Thus the two springs are neither stretched nor compressed when x and y are zero.

In the configuration in Fig. 4.1.1, the first spring is stretched x units and the second by $y - x$ units. We apply Newton's law of motion to the two "free body dia-

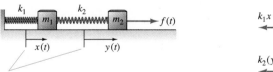

Equilibrium positions

FIGURE 4.1.1. The mass-and-spring system of Example 1

FIGURE 4.1.2. The "free body diagrams" for the system of Example 1

grams" shown in Fig. 4.1.2; we thereby obtain the system

$$
\begin{aligned}
m_1 x'' &= -k_1 x + k_2(y - x) \\
m_2 y'' &= -k_2(y - x) + f(t)
\end{aligned}
\tag{3}
$$

of differential equations that the position functions $x(t)$ and $y(t)$ must satisfy. For instance, if $m_1 = 2$, $m_2 = 1$, $k_1 = 4$, $k_2 = 2$, and $f(t) = 40 \sin 3t$ in appropriate physical units, then the system in (3) reduces to

$$
\begin{aligned}
2x'' &= -6x + 2y \\
y'' &= 2x - 2y + 40 \sin 3t.
\end{aligned}
\tag{4}
$$

EXAMPLE 2 Consider two brine tanks connected as shown in Fig. 4.1.3. Tank 1 contains $x(t)$ pounds of salt in 100 gal of brine and tank 2 contains $y(t)$ pounds of salt in 200 gal of brine. The brine in each tank is kept uniform by stirring, and brine is pumped from

20 gal/min
Fresh water

10 gal/min

$x(t)$ lb
100 gal

$y(t)$ lb
200 gal

30 gal/min

Tank 1

Tank 2

20 gal/min

FIGURE 4.1.3. The two brine tanks of Example 2

each tank to the other at the rates indicated in Fig. 4.1.3. In addition, fresh water flows into tank 1 at 20 gal/min, and the brine in tank 2 flows out at 20 gal/min (so the total volume of brine in the two tanks remains constant). The salt concentrations in the two tanks are $x/100$ pounds per gallon and $y/200$ pounds per gallon, respectively. When we compute the rates of change of the amounts of salt in the two tanks, we therefore get the system of differential equations that $x(t)$ and $y(t)$ must satisfy:

$$x' = -30 \cdot \frac{x}{100} + 10 \cdot \frac{y}{200} = -\frac{3}{10}x + \frac{1}{20}y$$

$$y' = 30 \cdot \frac{x}{100} - 10 \cdot \frac{y}{200} - 20 \cdot \frac{y}{200} = \frac{3}{10}x - \frac{3}{20}y;$$

that is,

$$20x' = -6x + y$$
$$20y' = 6x - 3y. \tag{5}$$

EXAMPLE 3 Consider the electrical network shown in Fig. 4.1.4, where $I_1(t)$ denotes the current in the indicated direction through the inductor L and $I_2(t)$ denotes the current through the resistor R_2. The current through the resistor R_1 is $I = I_1 - I_2$ in the direction indicated.

L: 2 henries C: 0.008 farads

E_0:
100 volts

I_1 R_1:
50 ohms

I_2 R_2:
25 ohms

I

FIGURE 4.1.4. The electrical network of Example 3

We recall Kirchhoff's voltage law to the effect that the (algebraic) sum of the voltage drops around any closed loop of such a network is zero. As in Section 3.7, the voltage drops across the three types of circuit elements are those shown in Fig. 4.1.5. We apply Kirchhoff's law to the left-hand loop of the network to obtain

$$2\frac{dI_1}{dt} + 50(I_1 - I_2) - 100 = 0, \tag{6}$$

because the voltage drop from the negative to the positive pole of the battery is -100. The right-hand loop yields the equation

$$125Q_2 + 25I_2 + 50(I_2 - I_1) = 0 \tag{7}$$

where $Q_2(t)$ is the charge on the capacitor. Because $dQ_2/dt = I_2$, differentiation of each side of Eq. (7) yields

$$-50\frac{dI_1}{dt} + 75\frac{dI_2}{dt} + 125I_2 = 0. \tag{8}$$

Circuit Element	Voltage Drop
Inductor	$L\dfrac{dI}{dt}$
Resistor	RI
Capacitor	$\dfrac{1}{C}Q$

FIGURE 4.1.5. Voltage drops across common circuit elements

Dividing Eqs. (6) and (8) by the factors 2 and -25, respectively, we get the system

$$\frac{dI_1}{dt} + 25I_1 - 25I_2 = 50$$

$$2\frac{dI_1}{dt} - 3\frac{dI_2}{dt} - 5I_2 = 0$$

(9)

of differential equations that the currents $I_1(t)$ and $I_2(t)$ must satisfy. ■

First-Order Systems

Consider a system of differential equations that can be solved for the highest-order derivatives of the dependent variables that appear, as explicit functions of t and of lower-order derivatives of the dependent variables. For instance, in the case of a system of two second-order equations, our assumption is that it can be written in the form

$$x_1'' = f_1(t, x_1, x_2, x_1', x_2')$$
$$x_2'' = f_2(t, x_1, x_2, x_1', x_2').$$

(10)

It is of both practical and theoretical importance that any such higher-order system can be transformed into an equivalent system of *first-order* equations.

To describe how such a transformation is accomplished, we consider first the "system" consisting of the single nth-order equation

▶ $$x^{(n)} = f(t, x\, x', \ldots, x^{(n-1)}).$$ (11)

We introduce the dependent variables x_1, x_2, \ldots, x_n defined as follows:

$$x_1 = x, \quad x_2 = x', \quad x_3 = x'', \quad \ldots, \quad x_n = x^{(n-1)}.$$ (12)

Note that $x_1' = x' = x_2$, $x_2' = x'' = x_3$, and so on. Hence the substitutions of (12) in Eq. (11) yield the system

$$x_1' = x_2$$
$$x_2' = x_3$$
$$\vdots$$

▶ (13)

$$x_{n-1}' = x_n$$
$$x_n' = f(t, x_1, x_2, \ldots, x_n)$$

of n *first-order* equations. Evidently, this system is equivalent to the original nth-order equation in (11), in the sense that $x(t)$ is a solution of Eq. (11) if and only if the functions $x_1(t), x_2(t), \ldots, x_n(t)$ defined in (12) satisfy the system of equations in (13).

EXAMPLE 4 The third-order equation

$$x''' + 3x'' + 2x' - 5x = \sin 2t$$

is of the form in (11) with

$$f(t, x, x', x'') = 5x - 2x' - 3x'' + \sin 2t.$$

Hence the substitutions

$$x_1 = x, \qquad x_2 = x' = x'_1, \qquad x_3 = x'' = x'_2$$

yield the system

$$x'_1 = x_2$$
$$x'_2 = x_3$$
$$x'_3 = 5x_1 - 2x_2 - 3x_3 + \sin 2t$$

of three first-order equations. ∎

It may appear that the first-order system obtained in Example 4 offers little advantage because we could use the methods of Chapter 3 to solve the original (linear) third-order equation. But suppose that we were confronted with the nonlinear equation

$$x'' = x^3 + (x')^3,$$

to which none of our earlier methods can be applied. The corresponding first-order system is

$$x'_1 = x_2$$
$$x'_2 = (x_1)^3 + (x_2)^3, \tag{14}$$

and we will see in Section 4.3 that there exist effective numerical techniques for approximating the solution of essentially any first-order system. So in this case the transformation to a first-order system *is* advantageous. From a practical viewpoint, large systems of higher-order differential equations typically are solved numerically with the aid of a computer, and the first step is to transform such a system into a first-order system for which a standard computer program is available.

EXAMPLE 5 The system

$$2x'' = -6x + 2y$$
$$y'' = 2x - 2y + 40 \sin 3t \tag{4}$$

of second-order equations was derived in Example 1. Transform this system into an equivalent first-order system.

Solution Motivated by the equations in (12), we define

$$x_1 = x, \qquad x_2 = x' = x'_1, \qquad y_1 = y, \qquad y_2 = y' = y'_1.$$

Then the system in (4) yields the system

$$x'_1 = x_2$$
$$2x'_2 = -6x_1 + 2y_1$$
$$y'_1 = y_2$$
$$y'_2 = 2x_1 - 2y_1 + 40 \sin 3t \tag{15}$$

of four first-order equations in the dependent variables $x_1, x_2, y_1,$ and y_2. ∎

Simple Two-Dimensional Systems

The linear second-order differential equation

$$x'' + px' + qx = 0 \tag{16}$$

(with constant coefficients and independent variable t) transforms via the substitutions $x' = y$, $x'' = y'$ into the two-dimensional linear system

$$x' = y$$
$$y' = -qx - py. \tag{17}$$

Conversely, we can solve this system in (17) by solving the familiar single equation in (16).

EXAMPLE 6 To solve the two-dimensional system

$$x' = -2y$$
$$y' = \frac{1}{2}x, \tag{18}$$

we begin with the observation that

$$x'' = -2y' = -2\left(\frac{1}{2}x\right) = -x.$$

This gives the single second-order equation $x'' + x = 0$ with general solution

$$x(t) = A \cos t + B \sin t = C \cos(t - \alpha)$$

where $A = C \cos \alpha$, $B = C \sin \alpha$. Then

$$y(t) = -\frac{1}{2}x'(t) = -\frac{1}{2}(-A \sin t + B \cos t)$$

$$= \frac{1}{2}C \sin(t - \alpha).$$

The identity $\cos^2 \theta + \sin^2 \theta = 1$ therefore implies that, for each value of t, the point $(x(t), y(t))$ lies on the ellipse

$$\frac{x^2}{C^2} + \frac{y^2}{(C/2)^2} = 1$$

with semiaxes C and $C/2$. Figure 4.1.6 shows several such ellipses in the xy-plane. ∎

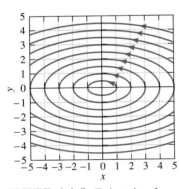

FIGURE 4.1.6. Trajectories of the system $x' = -2y$, $y' = x/2$

A solution $(x(t), y(t))$ of a two-dimensional system

$$x' = f(t, x, y)$$
$$y' = g(t, x, y)$$

may be regarded as a parametrization of a **solution curve** or **trajectory** of the system in the xy-plane. Thus the trajectories of the system in (18) are the ellipses of Fig. 4.1.6. The choice of an initial point $(x(0), y(0))$ determines which one of these trajectories a particular solution parametrizes.

Unfortunately, the picture showing a system's trajectories in the xy-plane—its so-called *phase plane portrait*—fails to reveal precisely how the point $(x(t), y(t))$ moves along its trajectory. This missing information can be shown in the separate graphs of $x(t)$ and $y(t)$ as functions of t.

EXAMPLE 6
Continued

With initial values $x(0) = 2$, $y(0) = 0$, the general solution in Example 6 yields

$$x(0) = A = 2, \qquad y(0) = -\frac{1}{2}B = 0.$$

The resulting particular solution is given by

$$x(t) = 2\cos t, \qquad y(t) = \sin t.$$

The graphs of the two functions are shown in Fig. 4.1.7. We see that $x(t)$ initially decreases while $y(t)$ increases. It follows that, as t increases, the solution point $(x(t), y(t))$ traverses the trajectory $\frac{1}{4}x^2 + y^2 = 1$ in the counterclockwise direction, as indicated by the arrows labeling the elliptical trajectories in Fig. 4.1.6.

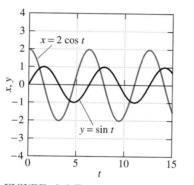

FIGURE 4.1.7. x- and y-solution curves for the initial value problem $x' = -2y$, $y' = x/2$, $x(0) = 2$, $y(0) = 0$

EXAMPLE 7

To find a general solution of the system

$$\begin{aligned} x' &= y \\ y' &= 2x + y, \end{aligned} \tag{19}$$

we begin with the observation that

$$x'' = y' = 2x + y = x' + 2x.$$

This gives the single linear second-order equation

$$x'' - x' - 2x = 0$$

with characteristic equation

$$r^2 - r - 2 = (r + 1)(r - 2) = 0$$

and general solution

$$x(t) = Ae^{-t} + Be^{2t}. \tag{20}$$

Then

$$y(t) = x'(t) = -Ae^{-t} + 2Be^{2t}. \tag{21}$$

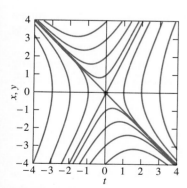

FIGURE 4.1.8. Trajectories of the system $x' = y$, $y' = 2x + y$ of Example 7

Typical phase plane trajectories of the system in (19) parametrized by Eqs. (20) and (21) are shown in Fig. 4.1.8. See Problem 23 for further discussion of these trajectories.

EXAMPLE 8 To solve the initial value problem

$$x' = -y$$
$$y' = (1.01)x - (0.2)y, \tag{22}$$
$$x(0) = 0, \qquad y(0) = -1,$$

we begin with the observation that

$$x'' = -y' = -[(1.01)x - (0.2)y] = (-1.01)x - (0.2)x'.$$

This gives the single linear second-order equation

$$x'' + (0.2)x' + (1.01)x = 0$$

with characteristic equation

$$r^2 + (0.2)r + 1.01 = (r + 0.1)^2 + 1 = 0,$$

characteristic roots $-0.1 \pm i$, and general solution

$$x(t) = e^{-t/10}(A \cos t + B \sin t).$$

Then $x(0) = A = 0$, so

$$x(t) = Be^{-t/10} \sin t,$$
$$y(t) = -x'(t) = \frac{1}{10}Be^{-t/10}\sin t - Be^{-t/10}\cos t.$$

Finally, $y(0) = -B = -1$, so the desired solution of the system in (22) is

$$x(t) = e^{-t/10}\sin t,$$
$$y(t) = \frac{1}{10}e^{-t/10}(-10\cos t + \sin t). \tag{23}$$

These equations parametrize the spiral trajectory in Fig. 4.1.9; the trajectory approaches the origin as $t \to +\infty$. Figure 4.1.10 shows the x- and y-solution curves given in (23). ∎

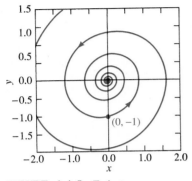

FIGURE 4.1.9. Trajectory parametrized by the equations in Eq. (23)

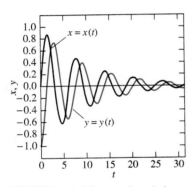

FIGURE 4.1.10. *x*- and *y*-solution curves for the initial value problem of Example 8

When we study linear systems in Chapter 5, we will learn why the superficially similar systems in Examples 6 through 8 have the markedly different trajectories shown in Figs. 4.1.6, 4.1.8, and 4.1.9.

Linear Systems

In addition to practical advantages for numerical computation, the general theory of systems and systematic solution techniques are more easily and more concisely described for first-order systems than for higher-order systems. For instance, consider a *linear* first-order system of the form

$$x_1' = p_{11}(t)x_1 + p_{12}(t)x_2 + \cdots + p_{1n}(t)x_n + f_1(t)$$
$$x_2' = p_{21}(t)x_1 + p_{22}(t)x_2 + \cdots + p_{2n}(t)x_n + f_2(t)$$
$$\vdots \qquad\qquad\qquad\qquad\qquad\qquad\qquad (24)$$
$$x_n' = p_{n1}(t)x_1 + p_{n2}(t)x_2 + \cdots + p_{nn}(t)x_n + f_n(t)$$

We say that this system is **homogeneous** if the functions f_1, f_2, \ldots, f_n are all identically zero; otherwise, it is **nonhomogeneous.** Thus the linear system in (5) is homogeneous, whereas the linear system in (15) is nonhomogeneous. The system in (14) is nonlinear because the right-hand side of the second equation is not a linear function of the dependent variables x_1 and x_2.

A **solution** of the system in (24) is an n-tuple of functions $x_1(t), x_2(t), \ldots, x_n(t)$ that (on some interval) identically satisfy each of the equations in (24). We will see that the general theory of a system of n linear first-order equations shares many similarities with the general theory of a single nth-order linear differential equation. Theorem 1 (proved in the Appendix) is analogous to Theorem 2 of Section 3.2. It tells us that if the coefficient functions p_{ij} and f_j in (24) are continuous, then the system has a unique solution satisfying given initial conditions.

THEOREM 1: Existence and Uniqueness for Linear Systems

Suppose that the functions $p_{11}, p_{12}, \ldots, p_{nn}$ and the functions f_1, f_2, \ldots, f_n are continuous on the open interval I containing the point a. Then, given n numbers b_1, b_2, \ldots, b_n, the system in (24) has a unique solution on the entire interval I that satisfies the n initial conditions

$$x_1(a) = b_1, \qquad x_2(a) = b_2, \qquad \ldots, \qquad x_n(a) = b_n. \qquad (25)$$

∎

Thus n initial conditions are needed to determine a solution of a system of n linear first-order equations, and we therefore expect a general solution of such a system to involve n arbitrary constants. For instance, we saw in Example 5 that the second-order system

$$2x'' = -6x + 2y$$
$$y'' = 2x - 2y + 40 \sin 3t,$$

which describes the position functions $x(t)$ and $y(t)$ of Example 1, is equivalent to the system of *four* first-order linear equations in (15). Hence four initial conditions would be needed to determine the subsequent motions of the two masses in Example 1; typical initial values would be the initial positions $x(0)$ and $y(0)$ and the initial velocities $x'(0)$ and $y'(0)$. On the other hand, we found that the amounts $x(t)$ and $y(t)$ of salt in the two tanks of Example 2 are described by the system

$$20x' = -6x + y$$
$$20y' = 6x + 3y$$

of *two* first-order linear equations. Hence the two initial values $x(0)$ and $y(0)$ should suffice to determine the solution. Given a higher-order system, we often must trans-

form it into an equivalent first-order system to discover how many initial conditions are needed to determine a unique solution. Theorem 1 tells us that the number of such conditions is precisely the same as the number of equations in the equivalent first-order system.

4.1 Problems

In Problems 1 through 10, transform the given differential equation or system into an equivalent system of first-order differential equations.

1. $x'' + 3x' + 7x = t^2$

2. $x^{(4)} + 6x'' - 3x' + x = \cos 3t$

3. $t^2 x'' + tx' + (t^2 - 1)x = 0$

4. $t^3 x''' - 2t^2 x'' + 3tx' + 5x = \ln t$

5. $x''' = (x')^2 + \cos x$

6. $x'' - 5x + 4y = 0, \quad y'' + 4x - 5y = 0$

7. $x'' = -\dfrac{kx}{(x^2 + y^2)^{3/2}}, \quad y'' = -\dfrac{ky}{(x^2 + y^2)^{3/2}}$

8. $x'' + 3x' + 4x - 2y = 0, \quad y'' + 2y' - 3x + y = \cos t$

9. $x'' = 3x - y + 2z, \quad y'' = x + y - 4z, \quad z'' = 5x - y - z$

10. $x'' = (1 - y)x, \quad y'' = (1 - x)y$

Use the method of Examples 6, 7, and 8 to find general solutions of the systems in Problems 11 through 20. If initial conditions are given, find the corresponding particular solutions.

11. $x' = y$
$y' = -x$

12. $x' = y$
$y' = x$

13. $x' = -2y$
$y' = 2x,$
$x(0) = 1, \quad y(0) = 0$

14. $x' = 10y$
$y' = -10x,$
$x(0) = 3, \quad y(0) = 4$

15. $x' = \frac{1}{2}y$
$y' = -8x$

16. $x' = 8y$
$y' = -2x$

17. $x' = y$
$y' = 6x - y,$
$x(0) = 1, \quad y(0) = 2$

18. $x' = -y$
$y' = 10x - 7y,$
$x(0) = 2, \quad y(0) = -7$

19. $x' = -y$
$y' = 13x + 4y,$
$x(0) = 0, \quad y(0) = 3$

20. $x' = y$
$y' = -9x + 6y$

21. (a) Calculate $[x(t)]^2 + [y(t)]^2$ to show that the trajectories of the system $x' = y, y' = -x$ of Problem 11 are circles. (b) Calculate $[x(t)]^2 - [y(t)]^2$ to show that the trajectories of the system $x' = y, y' = x$ of Problem 12 are hyperbolas.

22. (a) Beginning with the general solution of the system $x' = -2y, y' = 2x$ of Problem 13, calculate $x^2 + y^2$ to show that the trajectories are circles. (b) Show similarly that the tra-

jectories of the system $x' = \frac{1}{2}y, y' = -8x$ of Problem 15 are ellipses with equations of the form $16x^2 + y^2 = C^2$.

23. First solve Eqs. (20) and (21) for e^{-t} and e^{2t} in terms of $x(t)$, $y(t)$, and the constants A and B. Then substitute the results in $(e^{2t})(e^{-t})^2 = 1$ to show that the trajectories of the system $x' = y$, $y' = 2x + y$ in Example 7 satisfy an equation of the form

$$4x^3 - 3xy^2 + y^3 = C \quad \text{(constant)}.$$

Then show that $C = 0$ yields the straight lines $y = -x$ and $y = 2x$ that are visible in Fig. 4.1.8.

24. Derive the equations

$$m_1 x_1'' = -(k_1 + k_2)x_1 + k_2 x_2$$
$$m_2 x_2'' = k_2 x_1 - (k_2 + k_3)x_2$$

for the displacements (from equilibrium) of the two masses shown in Fig. 4.1.11.

x_1 x_2

FIGURE 4.1.11. The system of Problem 24

25. Two particles each of mass m are attached to a string under (constant) tension T, as indicated in Fig. 4.1.12. Assume that the particles oscillate vertically (that is, parallel to the y-axis) with amplitudes so small that the sines of the angles shown are accurately approximated by their tangents. Show that the displacements y_1 and y_2 of the two masses satisfy the equations

$$ky_1'' = -2y_1 + y_2, \qquad ky_2'' = y_1 - 2y_2$$

where $k = mL/T$.

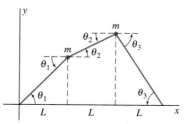

FIGURE 4.1.12. The mechanical system of Problem 25

26. Three 100-gal fermentation vats are connected as indicated in Fig. 4.1.13, and the mixtures in each tank are kept uniform by

FIGURE 4.1.13. The fermentation tanks of Problem 26

stirring. Denote by $x_i(t)$ the amount (in pounds) of alcohol in tank T_i at time t ($i = 1, 2, 3$). Suppose that the mixture circulates between the tanks at the rate of 10 gal/min. Derive the equations

$$10x_1' = -x_1 \qquad + x_3$$
$$10x_2' = \quad x_1 - x_2$$
$$10x_3' = \qquad\quad x_2 - x_3.$$

27. Set up a system of first-order differential equations for the currents in the electrical circuit shown in Fig. 4.1.14.

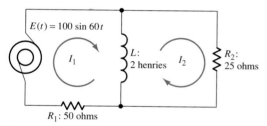

$E(t) = 100 \sin 60t$

I_1

L: 2 henries

I_2

R_2: 25 ohms

R_1: 50 ohms

FIGURE 4.1.14. The electrical circuit of Problem 27

28. Repeat Problem 27, except with the generator replaced with a battery supplying an emf of 100 V and with the inductor replaced by a 1-millifarad (mF) capacitor.

29. A particle of mass m moves in the plane with coordinates $(x(t), y(t))$ under the influence of a force that is directed toward the origin and has magnitude $k/(x^2 + y^2)$—an inverse-square central force field. Show that

$$mx'' = -\frac{kx}{r^3} \qquad \text{and} \qquad my'' = -\frac{ky}{r^3},$$

where $r = \sqrt{x^2 + y^2}$.

30. Suppose that a projectile of mass m moves in a vertical plane in the atmosphere near the surface of the earth under the influence of two forces: a downward gravitational force of magnitude mg, and a resistive force \mathbf{F}_R that is directed opposite to the velocity vector \mathbf{v} and has magnitude kv^2 (where $v = |\mathbf{v}|$ is the speed of the projectile; see Fig. 4.1.15). Show that the equations of motion of the projectile are

$$mx'' = -kvx', \qquad my'' = -kvy' - mg,$$

where $v = \sqrt{(x')^2 + (y')^2}$.

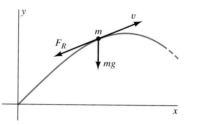

FIGURE 4.1.15. The trajectory of the projectile of Problem 30

31. Suppose that a particle with mass m and electrical charge q moves in the xy-plane under the influence of the magnetic field $\mathbf{B} = B\mathbf{k}$ (thus a uniform field parallel to the z-axis), so the force on the particle is $\mathbf{F} = q\mathbf{v} \times \mathbf{B}$ if its velocity is \mathbf{v}. Show that the equations of motion of the particle are

$$mx'' = +qBy', \qquad my'' = -qBx'.$$

4.2 The Method of Elimination

The most elementary approach to linear systems of differential equations involves the elimination of dependent variables by appropriately combining pairs of equations. The object of this procedure is to eliminate dependent variables in succession until there remains only a single equation containing only one dependent variable. This remaining equation will usually be a linear equation of high order and can frequently be solved by the methods of Chapter 3. After its solution has been found, the other dependent variables can be found in turn, using either the original differential equations or those that have appeared in the elimination process.

This *method of elimination* for linear differential systems is quite similar to the solution of linear algebraic equations by elimination of the variables until only one re-

mains. It is most convenient in the case of manageably small systems: those containing no more than two or three equations. For such systems the method of elimination provides a simple and concrete approach that requires little preliminary theory or formal machinery. But for larger systems of differential equations, as well as for theoretical discussion, the matrix methods of Chapter 5 are preferable.

EXAMPLE 1 Find the particular solution of the system

$$x' = 4x - 3y, \qquad y' = 6x - 7y \tag{1}$$

that satisfies the initial conditions $x(0) = 2$, $y(0) = -1$.

 Solution If we solve the second equation in (1) for x, we get

$$x = \frac{1}{6} y' + \frac{7}{6} y, \tag{2}$$

so that

$$x' = \frac{1}{6} y'' + \frac{7}{6} y'. \tag{3}$$

We then substitute these expressions for x and x' in the first equation of the system in (1); this yields

$$\frac{1}{6} y'' + \frac{7}{6} y' = 4 \left(\frac{1}{6} y' + \frac{7}{6} y \right) - 3y,$$

which can be simplified to

$$y'' + 3y' - 10y = 0.$$

This second-order equation has characteristic equation

$$r^2 + 3r - 10 = (r - 2)(r + 5) = 0,$$

so its general solution is

$$y(t) = c_1 e^{2t} + c_2 e^{-5t}. \tag{4}$$

 Next, substitution of (4) in (2) gives

$$x(t) = \frac{1}{6} (2c_1 e^{2t} - 5c_2 e^{-5t}) + \frac{7}{6} (c_1 e^{2t} + c_2 e^{-5t});$$

that is,

$$x(t) = \frac{3}{2} c_1 e^{2t} + \frac{1}{3} c_2 e^{-5t}. \tag{5}$$

Thus Eqs.(4) and (5) describe the general solution of the system in (1).
 The given initial conditions imply that

$$x(0) = \frac{3}{2} c_1 + \frac{1}{3} c_2 = 2$$

and that

$$y(0) = c_1 + c_2 = -1;$$

these equations are readily solved for $c_1 = 2$ and $c_2 = -3$. Hence the desired solution is

$$x(t) = 3e^{2t} - e^{-5t}, \qquad y(t) = 2e^{2t} - 3e^{-5t}. \qquad \blacksquare$$

Remark: The general solution defined by Eqs. (4) and (5) may be regarded as the pair or vector $(x(t), y(t))$. Recalling the componentwise addition of vectors (and multiplication of vectors by scalars), we can write the general solution in (4) and (5) in the form

$$(x(t), y(t)) = \left(\frac{3}{2} c_1 e^{2t} + \frac{1}{3} c_2 e^{-5t}, c_1 e^{2t} + c_2 e^{-5t} \right)$$

$$= c_1 \left(\frac{3}{2} e^{2t}, e^{2t} \right) + c_2 \left(\frac{1}{3} e^{-5t}, e^{-5t} \right).$$

This expression presents the general solution of the system in (1) as a linear combination of the two particular solutions

$$(x_1, y_1) = \left(\frac{3}{2} e^{2t}, e^{2t} \right) \qquad \text{and} \qquad (x_2, y_2) = \left(\frac{1}{3} e^{-5t}, e^{-5t} \right).$$

Linear Operators

In Example 1 we used an *ad hoc* procedure to eliminate one of the independent variables by expressing it in terms of the other. We now describe a systematic elimination procedure. Operator notation is most convenient for these purposes. A **linear differential operator** of order n with *constant* coefficients is one of the form

$$L = a_n D^n + a_{n-1} D^{n-1} + \cdots + a_1 D + a_0, \tag{6}$$

where D denotes differentiation with respect to the independent variable t. If L_1 and L_2 are two such operators, then their product $L_1 L_2$ is defined in this way:

$$\blacktriangleright \qquad L_1 L_2[x] = L_1[L_2 x]. \tag{7}$$

For instance, if $L_1 = D + a$ and $L_2 = D + b$, then

$$L_1 L_2[x] = (D + a)[(D + b)x] = D(Dx + bx) + a(Dx + bx)$$

$$= [D^2 + (a + b)D + ab]x.$$

This illustrates the fact that two linear operators L_1 and L_2 with constant coefficients can be multiplied as if they were ordinary polynomials in the "variable" D. Because the multiplication of such polynomials is commutative, it follows that

$$L_1 L_2 x = L_2 L_1 x \tag{8}$$

if the necessary derivatives of $x(t)$ exist. By contrast, this property of commutativity generally fails for linear operators with variable coefficients—see Problems 21 and 22.

Any system of two linear differential equations with constant coefficients can be written in the form

$$L_1 x + L_2 y = f_1(t)$$

$$L_3 x + L_4 y = f_2(t), \tag{9}$$

where L_1, L_2, L_3, and L_4, are linear differential operators (perhaps of different orders) as in Eq. (6), and $f_1(t)$ and $f_2(t)$ are given functions. For instance, the system in (1) (Example 1) can be written in the form

$$
\begin{aligned}
(D - 4)x \qquad + 3y &= 0 \\
-6x + (D + 7)y &= 0,
\end{aligned}
$$
(10)

with $L_1 = D - 4$, $L_2 = 3$, $L_3 = -6$, and $L_4 = D + 7$.

To eliminate the dependent variable x from the system in (9), we operate with L_3 on the first equation and with L_1 on the second. Thus we obtain the system

$$
\begin{aligned}
L_3 L_1 x + L_3 L_2 y &= L_3 f_1(t) \\
L_1 L_3 x + L_1 L_4 y &= L_1 f_2(t).
\end{aligned}
$$
(11)

Subtraction of the first from the second of these equations yields the single equation

$$
(L_1 L_4 - L_2 L_3)y = L_1 f_2(t) - L_3 f_1(t)
$$
(12)

in the single dependent variable y. After solving for $y = y(t)$ we can substitute the result into either of the original equations in (9) and then solve for $x = x(t)$.

Alternatively, we could eliminate in like manner the dependent variable y from the original system in (9). If so, we would get the equation

$$
(L_1 L_4 - L_2 L_3)x = L_4 f_1(t) - L_2 f_2(t),
$$
(13)

which can now be solved for $x = x(t)$.

Note that the same operator $L_1 L_4 - L_2 L_3$ appears on the left-hand side in both Eq. (12) and Eq. (13). This is the **operational determinant**

$$
\begin{vmatrix} L_1 & L_2 \\ L_3 & L_4 \end{vmatrix} = L_1 L_4 - L_2 L_3
$$
(14)

of the system in (9). In determinant notation Eqs. (12) and (13) can be rewritten as

$$
\begin{vmatrix} L_1 & L_2 \\ L_3 & L_4 \end{vmatrix} x = \begin{vmatrix} f_1(t) & L_2 \\ f_2(t) & L_4 \end{vmatrix},
$$

$$
\begin{vmatrix} L_1 & L_2 \\ L_3 & L_4 \end{vmatrix} y = \begin{vmatrix} L_1 & f_1(t) \\ L_3 & f_2(t) \end{vmatrix}.
$$
(15)

It is important to note that the determinants on the right-hand side in (15) are evaluated by means of the operators operating on the functions. The equations in (15) are strongly reminiscent of Cramer's rule for the solution of two linear equations in two (algebraic) variables and are thereby easy to remember. Indeed, you can solve a system of two linear differential equations either by carrying out the systematic elimination procedure described above or by directly employing the determinant notation in (15). Either process is especially simple if the system is homogeneous ($f_1(t) \equiv 0$ and $f_2(t) \equiv 0$), because in this case the right-hand sides of the equations in (12), (13), and (15) are zero.

EXAMPLE 2 Find the general solution of the system

$$(D - 4)x \quad\quad + 3y = 0$$

$$-6x + (D + 7)y = 0. \tag{10}$$

Solution The operational determinant of this system is

$$(D - 4)(D + 7) - 3 \cdot (-6) = D^2 + 3D - 10. \tag{16}$$

Hence Eqs. (13) and (12) are

$$x'' + 3x' - 10x = 0,$$

$$y'' + 3y' - 10y = 0.$$

The characteristic equation of each is

$$r^2 + 3r - 10 = (r - 2)(r + 5) = 0,$$

so their (separate) general solutions are

$$x(t) = a_1 e^{2t} + a_2 e^{-5t},$$

$$y(t) = b_1 e^{2t} + b_2 e^{-5t}. \tag{17}$$

At this point we appear to have *four* arbitrary constants a_1, a_2, b_1, and b_2. But it follows from Theorem 1 in Section 4.1 that the general solution of a system of two first-order equations involves only two arbitrary constants. This apparent difficulty demands a resolution.

The explanation is simple: There must be some relations among our four constants. We can discover them by substituting the solutions in (17) into either of the original equations in (10). On substitution in the first equation, we get

$$0 = x' - 4x + 3y$$

$$= (2a_1 e^{2t} - 5a_2 e^{-5t}) - 4(a_1 e^{2t} + a_2 e^{-5t}) + 3(b_1 e^{2t} + b_2 e^{-5t});$$

that is,

$$0 = (-2a_1 + 3b_1) e^{2t} + (-9a_2 + 3b_2)e^{-5t}.$$

But e^{2t} and e^{-5t} are linearly independent functions, and so it follows that $a_1 = \frac{3}{2} b_1$ and $a_2 = \frac{1}{3} b_2$. Therefore the desired general solution is given by

$$x(t) = \frac{3}{2} b_1 e^{2t} + \frac{1}{3} b_2 e^{-5t}, \quad\quad y(t) = b_1 e^{2t} + b_2 e^{-5t}.$$

Note that this result is in accord with the general solution (described by Eqs. (4) and (5)) that we obtained by a different method in Example 1. ∎

As illustrated by Example 2, the elimination procedure ordinarily will introduce a number of interdependent—thus unnecessary and undesirable—arbitrary constants. These must be eliminated by substitution of the proposed general solution into one or more of the original differential equations. If the operational determinant defined in (15) is *not identically zero,* then the number of independent arbitrary constants in a general solution of the system in (9) is equal to the order of the operational

determinant—that is, its degree as a polynomial in D. (For a proof of this fact, see pages 144–150 of E. L. Ince's *Ordinary Differential Equations* (New York: Dover, 1956).) Thus the general solution of the system in (10) of Example 2 involves two arbitrary constants because its operational determinant $D^2 + 3D - 10$ is of order 2.

If the operational determinant is identically zero, then the system is said to be **degenerate.** A degenerate system may have either no solution or infinitely many independent solutions. For instance, the equations

$$Dx - \quad Dy = 0$$

$$2Dx - 2Dy = 1$$

with operational determinant zero are obviously inconsistent and thus have no solutions. On the other hand, the equations

$$Dx + \quad Dy = t$$

$$2Dx + 2Dy = 2t$$

with operational determinant zero are obviously redundant; we can substitute *any* (continuously differentiable) function for $x(t)$ and then integrate to obtain $y(t)$. Roughly speaking, every degenerate system is equivalent to either an inconsistent system or a redundant system.

Although the procedures and results above are described for the case of a system of two equations, they can be generalized readily to systems of three or more equations. For the system

$$L_{11}x + L_{12}y + L_{13}z = f_1(t)$$

$$L_{21}x + L_{22}y + L_{23}z = f_2(t) \tag{18}$$

$$L_{31}x + L_{32}y + L_{33}z = f_3(t)$$

of three linear equations, the dependent variable $x(t)$ satisfies the single linear equation

$$\begin{vmatrix} L_{11} & L_{12} & L_{13} \\ L_{21} & L_{22} & L_{23} \\ L_{31} & L_{32} & L_{33} \end{vmatrix} x = \begin{vmatrix} f_1(t) & L_{12} & L_{13} \\ f_2(t) & L_{22} & L_{23} \\ f_3(t) & L_{32} & L_{33} \end{vmatrix}, \tag{19}$$

with analogous equations for $y = y(t)$ and $z = z(t)$. For most systems of more than three equations, however, the method of operational determinants is too tedious for the method to be practical.

Mechanical Vibrations

A mechanical system typically vibrates or oscillates periodically in one or more specific ways. The methods of this section often can be applied to analyze these "natural modes of oscillation" of a given system. Example 3 illustrates this approach.

EXAMPLE 3 In Example 1 of Section 4.1, we derived the equations

$$(D^2 + 3)x - \qquad y = 0$$

$$-2x + (D^2 + 2)y = 0 \tag{20}$$

Equilibrium positions

FIGURE 4.2.1. The mass-and-spring system of Example 3

for the displacements of the two masses in Fig. 4.2.1. Here $f(t) \equiv 0$ because we assume that there is no external force. Find the general solution of the system in (20).

Solution The operational determinant of the system in (20) is

$$(D^2 + 3)(D^2 + 2) - (-1)(-2) = D^4 + 5D^2 + 4 = (D^2 + 1)(D^2 + 4).$$

Hence the equations for $x(t)$ and $y(t)$ are

$$(D^2 + 1)(D^2 + 4)\, x = 0$$
$$(D^2 + 1)(D^2 + 4)\, y = 0. \tag{21}$$

The characteristic equation $(r^2 + 1)(r^2 + 4) = 0$ has roots i, $-i$, $2i$, and $-2i$. So the general solutions of the equations in (21) are

$$x(t) = a_1 \cos t + a_2 \sin t + b_1 \cos 2t + b_2 \sin 2t,$$
$$y(t) = c_1 \cos t + c_2 \sin t + d_1 \cos 2t + d_2 \sin 2t. \tag{22}$$

Because the operational determinant is of order 4, the general solution should involve four (rather than eight) arbitrary constants. When we substitute $x(t)$ and $y(t)$ from (22) in the first equation in (20), we get

$$0 = x'' + 3x - y$$
$$= (-a_1 \cos t - a_2 \sin t - 4b_1 \cos 2t - 4b_2 \sin 2t)$$
$$+ 3(a_1 \cos t + a_2 \sin t + b_1 \cos 2t + b_2 \sin 2t)$$
$$- (c_1 \cos t + c_2 \sin t + d_1 \cos 2t + d_2 \sin 2t);$$

thus

$$0 = (2a_1 - c_1) \cos t + (2a_2 - c_2) \sin t$$
$$+ (-b_1 - d_1) \cos 2t + (-b_2 - d_2) \sin 2t.$$

Because $\cos t$, $\cos 2t$, $\sin t$, and $\sin 2t$ are linearly independent, it follows that their coefficients in the last equation are zero:

$$c_1 = 2a_1, \qquad c_2 = 2a_2, \qquad d_1 = -b_1, \qquad \text{and} \qquad d_2 = -b_2.$$

Hence the desired general solution $(x(t), y(t))$ is described by

$$x(t) = a_1 \cos t + a_2 \sin t + b_1 \cos 2t + b_2 \sin 2t,$$
$$y(t) = 2a_1 \cos t + 2a_2 \sin t - b_1 \cos 2t - b_2 \sin 2t. \tag{23}$$

∎

The equations in (23) describe **free oscillations** of the mass-and-spring system of Fig. 4.2.1—motion subject to *no* external forces. Four initial conditions (typically, initial displacements and velocities) would be needed to determine the values of a_1, a_2, b_1, and b_2. The expression

$$(x(t), y(t)) = a_1(\cos t, 2 \cos t) + a_2(\sin t, 2 \sin t)$$
$$+ b_1(\cos 2t, -\cos 2t) + b_2(\sin 2t, -\sin 2t) \tag{24}$$

then presents the general solution of the system in (20) as a linear combination of four particular solutions. Moreover, the first two of these particular solutions represent physically similar oscillations of the masses, as do the latter two.

Indeed, we can (by the usual trigonometric machinations) write

$$a_1 \cos t + \; a_2 \sin t = \; A \cos(t - \alpha),$$

$$2a_1 \cos t + 2a_2 \sin t = 2A \cos(t - \alpha)$$

and

$$b_1 \cos 2t + b_2 \sin t = \; B \cos(2t - \beta),$$

$$- b_1 \cos 2t - b_2 \sin t = - B \cos(2t - \beta)$$

with $A = \sqrt{a_1^2 + a_2^2}$, $\tan \alpha = a_2/a_1$, $B = \sqrt{b_1^2 + b_2^2}$, and $\tan \beta = b_2/b_1$. Then Eq. (24) takes the form

$$(x, y) = A(x_1, y_1) + B(x_2, y_2), \tag{25}$$

where the particular solutions

$$(x_1(t), y_1(t)) = (\cos(t - \alpha), 2\cos(t - \alpha)) \tag{26}$$

and

$$(x_2(t), y_2(t)) = (\cos(2t - \beta), - \cos(2t - \beta)) \tag{27}$$

describe the two **natural modes of oscillation** of the mass-and-spring system. Moreover, they exhibit its two (circular) **natural frequencies** $\omega_1 = 1$ and $\omega_2 = 2$.

The linear combination in Eq. (25) represents an arbitrary free oscillation of the mass-and-spring system as a superposition of its two natural modes of oscillation, with the constants A, α, B, and β determined by the initial conditions. Figure 4.2.2 (where $\alpha = 0$) illustrates the natural mode (x_1, y_1) of Eq. (26), in which the two masses move in synchrony in the same direction with the same frequency of oscillation $\omega_1 = 1$, but with the amplitude of oscillation of m_2 twice that of m_1 (because $y_1 = 2x_1$). Figure 4.2.3 (where $\beta = 0$) illustrates the natural mode (x_2, y_2) of Eq. (27), in which they move in synchrony in opposite directions, with the same frequency $\omega_2 = 2$ and with equal amplitudes of oscillation (because $y_2 = - x_2$).

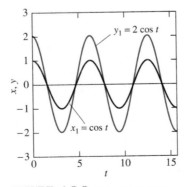

FIGURE 4.2.2. The two masses move in the same direction each with frequency $\omega_1 = 1$

FIGURE 4.2.3. The two masses move in opposite directions with frequency $\omega_2 = 2$

4.2 Problems

Find general solutions of the linear systems in Problems 1 through 20. If initial conditions are given, find the particular solution that satisfies them.

1. $x' = -x + 3y, \quad y' = 2y$

2. $x' = x - 2y, \quad y' = 2x - 3y$

3. $x' = -3x + 2y, \quad y' = -3x + 4y; \quad x(0) = 0, \quad y(0) = 2$

4. $x' = 3x - y, \quad y' = 5x - 3y; \quad x(0) = 1, \quad y(0) = -1$

5. $x' = -3x - 4y, \quad y' = 2x + y$

6. $x' = x + 9y, \quad y' = -2x - 5y; \quad x(0) = 3, \quad y(0) = 2$

7. $x' = 4x + y + 2t, \quad y' = -2x + y$

8. $x' = 2x + y, \quad y' = x + 2y - e^{2t}$

9. $x' = 2x - 3y + 2\sin 2t, \quad y' = x - 2y - \cos 2t$

10. $x' + 2y' = 4x + 5y, \quad 2x' - y' = 3x; \quad x(0) = 1, \quad y(0) = -1$

11. $2y' - x' = x + 3y + e^t, \quad 3x' - 4y' = x - 15y + e^{-t}$

12. $x'' = 6x + 2y, \quad y'' = 3x + 7y$

13. $x'' = -5x + 2y, \quad y'' = 2x - 8y$

14. $x'' = -4x + \sin t, \quad y'' = 4x - 8y$

15. $x'' - 3y' - 2x = 0, \quad y'' + 3x' - 2y = 0$

16. $x'' + 13y' - 4x = 6\sin t, \quad y'' - 2x' - 9y = 0$

17. $x'' + y'' - 3x' - y' - 2x + 2y = 0, \quad 2x'' + 3y'' - 9x' - 2y' - 4x + 6y = 0$

18. $x' = x + 2y + z, \quad y' = 6x - y, \quad z' = -x - 2y - z$

19. $x' = 4x - 2y, \quad y' = -4x + 4y - 2z, \quad z' = -4y + 4z$

20. $x' = y + z + e^{-t}, \quad y' = x + z, \quad z' = x + y$
(*Suggestion:* Solve the characteristic equation by inspection.)

21. Suppose that $L_1 = a_1 D^2 + b_1 D + c_1$ and $L_2 = a_2 D^2 + b_2 D + c_2$, where the coefficients are all constants, and that $x(t)$ is a twice differentiable function. Verify that $L_1 L_2 x = L_2 L_1 x$.

22. Suppose that $L_1 x = tDx + x$ and that $L_2 x = Dx + tx$. Show that $L_1 L_2 \neq L_2 L_1$. Thus linear operators with *variable* coefficients generally do not commute.

Show that the systems in Problems 23 through 25 are degenerate. In each problem determine—by attempting to solve the system—whether it has infinitely many solutions or no solutions.

23. $(D + 2)x + (D + 2)y = e^{-3t}$
$(D + 3)x + (D + 3)y = e^{-2t}$

24. $(D + 2)x + (D + 2)y = t$
$(D + 3)x + (D + 3)y = t^2$

25. $(D^2 + 5D + 6)x + D(D + 2)y = 0$
$(D + 3)x + \qquad Dy = 0$

In Problems 26 through 29, first calculate the operational determinant, then attempt to solve the given system in order to determine the number of arbitrary constants that appear in its general solution.

26. $(D^2 + 1)x + D^2 y = 2e^{-t}$
$(D^2 - 1)x + D^2 y = 0$

27. $(D^2 + 1)x + (D^2 + 2)y = 2e^{-t}$
$(D^2 - 1)x + \qquad D^2 y = 0$

28. $(D^2 + D)x + \qquad D^2 y = 2e^{-t}$
$(D^2 - 1)x + (D^2 - D)y = 0$

29. $(D^2 + 1)x - D^2 y = 2e^{-t}$
$(D^2 - 1)x + D^2 y = 0$

30. Suppose that the salt concentration in each of the two brine tanks of Example 2 of Section 4.1 initially ($t = 0$) is 0.5 lb/gal. Then solve the system in (5) there to find the amounts $x(t)$ and $y(t)$ of salt in the two tanks at time t.

31. Suppose that the electrical network of Example 3 of Section 4.1 is initially open—no currents are flowing. Assume that it is closed at time $t = 0$; solve the system in (9) there to find $I_1(t)$ and $I_2(t)$.

32. Repeat Problem 31, except use the electrical network of Problem 27 of Section 4.1.

33. Repeat Problem 32, except use the electrical network of Problem 28 of Section 4.1. Assume that $I_1(0) = 2$ and that $Q(0) = 0$, so that at time $t = 0$ there is no charge on the capacitor.

34. Three 100-gal brine tanks are connected as indicated in Fig. 4.1.13 of Section 4.1. Assume that the first tank initially contains 100 lb of salt, whereas the other two are filled with fresh water. Find the amounts of salt in each of the three tanks at time t. *Suggestion:* Examine the equations to be derived in Problem 26 of Section 4.1.)

35. From Problem 31 of Section 4.1, recall the equations of motion

$$mx'' = qBy', \qquad my'' = -qBx'$$

for a particle of mass m and electrical charge q under the influence of the uniform magnetic field $\mathbf{B} = B\mathbf{k}$. Suppose that the initial conditions are $x(0) = r_0$, $y(0) = 0$, $x'(0) = 0$, and $y'(0) = -\omega r_0$ where $\omega = qB/m$. Show that the trajectory of the particle is a circle of radius r_0.

36. If, in addition to the magnetic field $\mathbf{B} = B\mathbf{k}$, the charged particle of Problem 35 moves with velocity \mathbf{v} under the influence

of a uniform electric field $\mathbf{E} = E\mathbf{i}$, then the force acting on it is $\mathbf{F} = q(\mathbf{E} + \mathbf{v} \times \mathbf{B})$. Assume that the particle starts from rest at the origin. Show that its trajectory is the cycloid

$$x = a(1 - \cos \omega t), \qquad y = -a(\omega t - \sin \omega t)$$

where $a = E/(\omega B)$ and $\omega = qB/m$. The graph of such a cycloid is shown in Fig. 4.2.4.

FIGURE 4.2.4. The cycloidal path of the particle of Problem 36

37. In the mass-and-spring system of Example 3, suppose instead that $m_1 = 2$, $m_2 = 0.5$, $k_1 = 75$, and $k_2 = 25$. (a) Find the general solution of the equations of motion of the system. In particular, show that its natural frequencies are $\omega_1 = 5$ and $\omega_2 = 5\sqrt{3}$. (b) Describe the natural modes of oscillation of the system.

38. Consider the system of two masses and three springs shown in Fig. 4.2.5. Derive the equations of motion

$$m_1 x'' = -(k_1 + k_2)x + k_2 y$$
$$m_2 y'' = k_2 x - (k_2 + k_3)y.$$

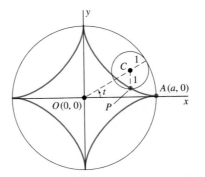

Equilibrium positions

FIGURE 4.2.5. The mechanical system of Problem 38

In Problems 39 through 43, find the general solution of the system in Problem 38 with the given masses and spring constants. Find the natural frequencies of the mass-and-spring systems, and describe their natural modes of oscillation.

39. $m_1 = 1$, $m_2 = 1$, $k_1 = 1$, $k_2 = 4$, $k_3 = 1$

40. $m_1 = 1$, $m_2 = 2$, $k_1 = 1$, $k_2 = 2$, $k_3 = 2$

41. $m_1 = 1$, $m_2 = 1$, $k_1 = 1$, $k_2 = 2$, $k_3 = 1$

42. $m_1 = 1$, $m_2 = 1$, $k_1 = 2$, $k_2 = 1$, $k_3 = 2$

43. $m_1 = 1$, $m_2 = 2$, $k_1 = 2$, $k_2 = 4$, $k_3 = 4$

44. (a) For the system shown in Fig. 4.2.6, derive the equations of motion

$$mx'' = -2kx + ky$$
$$my'' = kx - 2ky + kz$$
$$mz'' = ky - 2kz.$$

(b) Assume that $m = k = 1$. Show that the natural frequencies of oscillation of the system are

$$\omega_1 = \sqrt{2}, \quad \omega_2 = \sqrt{2 - \sqrt{2}}, \quad \text{and} \quad \omega_3 = \sqrt{2 + \sqrt{2}}.$$

FIGURE 4.2.6. The mechanical system of Problem 44

45. Suppose that the trajectory $(x(t), y(t))$ of a particle moving in the plane satisfies the initial value problem

$$x'' - 2y' + 3x = 0,$$
$$y'' + 2x' + 3y = 0;$$
$$x(0) = 4, \quad y(0) = x'(0) = y'(0) = 0.$$

Solve this problem. You should obtain

$$x(t) = 3 \cos t + \cos 3t,$$
$$y(t) = 3 \sin t - \sin 3t.$$

FIGURE 4.2.7. The hypocycloid of Problem 45

Verify that these equations describe the *hypocycloid* traced by a point $P(x, y)$ fixed on the circumference of a circle of radius $b = 1$ that rolls around inside a circle of radius $a = 4$. If P begins at $A(a, 0)$ when $t = 0$, then the parameter t represents the angle AOC shown in Fig. 4.2.7.

4.2 Computing Project

Computer algebra systems can be used to solve systems as well as single differential equations. For instance, using *Maple* let us define the system

```
> deq1 := diff(x(t),t) = 4*x(t) - 3*y(t):
  deq2 := diff(y(t),t) = 6*x(t) - 7*y(t):
```

of Example 1 in this section. Then the command

```
> dsolve( {deq1,deq2}, {x(t),y(t)} );
```

$$\left\{ x(t) = \frac{3}{2}_C1 e^{(2t)} + _C2 e^{(-5t)}, \quad y(t) = _C1 e^{(2t)} + 3_C2 e^{(-5t)} \right\}$$

yields the same general solution we found using the method of elimination (though with the second arbitrary constant multiplied by 3), and the command

```
> dsolve( {deq1,deq2, x(0) = 2, y(0) = -1}, {x(t),y(t)} );
```

$$\{ y(t) = 2 \ e^{(2t)} - 3 \ e^{(-5t)}, \quad x(t) = 3 \ e^{(2t)} - e^{(-5t)} \}$$

solves our initial value problem. For the second-order system of Example 3 we would use the *Maple* commands

```
> deq3 := diff(x(t),t,t) + 3*x(t) -   y(t) = 0;
  deq4 := diff(y(t),t,t) - 2*x(t) + 2*y(t) = 0:
> dsolve( {deq3,deq4}, {x(t),y(t)} );
```

$$\{ y(t) = 2 _C1 \sin(t) + 2 _C2 \cos(t) - _C3 \sin(2\ t)$$
$$- _C4 \cos(2\ t), \quad x(t) = _C1 \sin(t) + _C2 \cos(t)$$
$$+ _C3 \sin(2\ t) + _C4 \cos(2\ t) \}$$

The *Mathematica* syntax for the solution of differential systems is virtually identical. Thus, for the initial value problem above we use the commands

```
deq1 = x'[t] == 4 x[t] - 3 y[t];
deq2 = y'[t] == 6 x[t] - 7 y[t];
DSolve[{deq1,deq2, x[0] == 2, y[0] == -1,
        {x[t],y[t]}, t ]
```

and a bit of simplification gives the same results.

If a computer algebra system is available, use it to solve some of the systems in Problems 1 through 20 of this section. In each case, you should verify that the solution obtained is equivalent to the one obtained manually. For instance, *Mathematica* gives

```
DSolve[ {deq1,deq2}, {x[t],y[t]}, t ]
```

$$\left\{ \left\{ x[t] \rightarrow \left(\frac{-2}{7\ E^{5\ t}} + \frac{9\ E^{2\ t}}{7} \right) C[1] + \left(\frac{3}{7\ E^{5\ t}} - \frac{3\ E^{2\ t}}{7} \right) C[2], \right. \right.$$

$$\left. \left. y[t] \rightarrow \left(\frac{-6}{7\ E^{5\ t}} + \frac{6\ E^{2\ t}}{7} \right) C[1] + \left(\frac{9}{7\ E^{5\ t}} - \frac{2\ E^{2\ t}}{7} \right) C[2] \right\} \right\}$$

for the general solution of Example 1. Is it clear that this solution is equivalent to the one obtained in the text? What is the relation between *Mathematica's* constants C[1] and C[2] and our constants c_1 and c_2?

4.3 Numerical Methods for Systems

We now discuss the numerical approximation of solutions of systems of differential equations. Our goal is to apply the methods of Sections 2.4 through 2.6 to the initial value problem

$$\blacktriangleright \qquad \mathbf{x}' = \mathbf{f}(t, \mathbf{x}), \qquad \mathbf{x}(t_0) = \mathbf{x}_0 \qquad (1)$$

for a system of m first-order differential equations. In (1) the independent variable is the scalar t, whereas

$$\mathbf{x} = (x_1, x_2, \ldots, x_m) \qquad \text{and} \qquad \mathbf{f} = (f_1, f_2, \ldots, f_m)$$

are vector-valued functions. If the component functions of \mathbf{f} and their first-order partial derivatives are all continuous in a neighborhood of the point (t_0, \mathbf{x}_0), then Theorems 3 and 4 of the Appendix guarantee the existence and uniqueness of a solution $\mathbf{x} = \mathbf{x}(t)$ of (1) on some subinterval [of the t-axis] containing t_0. With this assurance we can proceed to discuss the numerical approximation of this solution.

Beginning with step size h, we want to approximate the values of $\mathbf{x}(t)$ at the points t_1, t_2, t_3, \ldots, where $t_{n+1} = t_n + h$ for $n \geq 0$. Suppose that we have already computed the *approximations*

$$\mathbf{x}_1, \quad \mathbf{x}_2, \quad \mathbf{x}_3, \quad \ldots, \quad \mathbf{x}_n$$

to the *actual values*

$$\mathbf{x}(t_1), \quad \mathbf{x}(t_2), \quad \mathbf{x}(t_3), \quad \ldots, \quad \mathbf{x}(t_n)$$

of the exact solution of the system in (1). We can then make the step from \mathbf{x}_n to the next approximation $\mathbf{x}_{n+1} \approx \mathbf{x}(t_{n+1})$ by any one of the methods of Sections 2.4 through 2.6. Essentially all that is required is to write the iterative formula of the selected method in the vector notation of the present discussion.

Euler Methods for Systems

For example, the iterative formula of Euler's method for systems is

$$\blacktriangleright \qquad \mathbf{x}_{n+1} = \mathbf{x}_n + h\mathbf{f}(t, \mathbf{x}_n). \qquad (2)$$

To examine the case $m = 2$ of a pair of first-order differential equations, let us write

$$\mathbf{x} = \begin{bmatrix} x \\ y \end{bmatrix} \qquad \text{and} \qquad \mathbf{f} = \begin{bmatrix} f \\ g \end{bmatrix}.$$

Then the initial value problem in (1) is

$$\begin{aligned} x' &= f(t, x, y), & x(t_0) &= x_0, \\ y' &= g(t, x, y), & y(t_0) &= y_0 \end{aligned} \qquad (3)$$

and the scalar components of the vector formula in (2) are

$$x_{n+1} = x_n + hf(t_n, x_n, y_n),$$
$$y_{n+1} = y_n + hg(t_n, x_n, y_n). \tag{4}$$

Note that each iterative formula in (4) has the form of a single Euler iteration, but with y_n inserted like a parameter in the first formula (for x_{n+1}) and with x_n inserted like a parameter in the second formula (for y_{n+1}). The generalization to the system in (3) of each of the other methods in Section 2.4 through 2.6 follows a similar pattern.

The improved Euler method for systems consists at each step of calculating first the predictor

▶ $$\mathbf{u}_{n+1} = \mathbf{x}_n + h\mathbf{f}(t_n, \mathbf{x}_n) \tag{5}$$

and then the corrector

▶ $$\mathbf{x}_{n+1} = \mathbf{x}_n + \frac{h}{2} [\mathbf{f}(t_n, \mathbf{x}_n) + \mathbf{f}(t_{n+1}, \mathbf{u}_{n+1})]. \tag{6}$$

For the case of the two-dimensional initial value problem in (3), the scalar components of the formulas in (5) and (6) are

$$u_{n+1} = x_n + hf(t_n, x_n, y_n),$$
$$v_{n+1} = y_n + hg(t_n, x_n, y_n) \tag{7}$$

and

$$x_{n+1} = x_n + \frac{h}{2} [f(t_n, x_n, y_n) + f(t_{n+1}, u_{n+1}, v_{n+1})],$$

$$y_{n+1} = y_n + \frac{h}{2} [g(t_n, x_n, y_n) + g(t_{n+1}, u_{n+1}, v_{n+1})]. \tag{8}$$

EXAMPLE 1 Consider the initial value problem

$$x' = 3x - 2y, \qquad x(0) = 3;$$
$$y' = 5x - 4y, \qquad y(0) = 6. \tag{9}$$

The exact solution of the system in (9) is

$$x(t) = 2e^{-2t} + e^t, \qquad y(t) = 5e^{-2t} + e^t. \tag{10}$$

Here we have $f(x, y) = 3x - 2y$ and $g(x, y) = 5x - 4y$ in (3), so the Euler iterative formulas in (4) are

$$x_{n+1} = x_n + h(3x_n - 2y_n), \qquad y_{n+1} = y_n + h(5x_n - 4y_n).$$

With step size $h = 0.1$ we calculate

$$x_1 = 3 + (0.1) \cdot [3 \cdot 3 - 2 \cdot 6] = 2.7,$$
$$y_1 = 6 + (0.1) \cdot [5 \cdot 3 - 4 \cdot 6] = 5.1$$

and

$$x_2 = 2.7 + (0.1) \cdot [3 \cdot (2.7) - 2 \cdot (5.1)] = 2.49,$$
$$y_2 = 5.1 + (0.1) \cdot [5 \cdot (2.7) - 4 \cdot (5.1)] = 4.41.$$

The actual values at $t_2 = 0.2$ given by (10) are $x(0.2) \approx 2.562$ and $y(0.2) \approx 4.573$.

To compute the improved Euler approximations to $x(0.2)$ and $y(0.2)$ with a single step of size $h = 0.2$, we first calculate the predictors

$$u_1 = 3 + (0.2)\cdot[3\cdot3 - 2\cdot6] = 2.4,$$

$$v_1 = 6 + (0.2)\cdot[5\cdot3 - 4\cdot6] = 4.2.$$

Then the corrector formulas in (8) yield

$$x_1 = 3 + (0.1)\cdot\{[3\cdot3 - 2\cdot6] + [3\cdot(2.4) - 2\cdot(4.2)]\} = 2.58,$$

$$y_1 = 6 + (0.1)\cdot\{[5\cdot3 - 4\cdot6] + [5\cdot(2.4) - 4\cdot(4.2)]\} = 4.62.$$

As we would expect, a single improved Euler step gives better accuracy than two ordinary Euler steps. ∎

The Runge–Kutta Method and Second-Order Equations

The vector version of the iterative formula for the Runge-Kutta method is

▶
$$\mathbf{x}_{n+1} = \mathbf{x}_n + \frac{h}{6}(\mathbf{k}_1 + 2\mathbf{k}_2 + 2\mathbf{k}_3 + \mathbf{k}_4) \tag{11}$$

where the vectors $\mathbf{k}_1, \mathbf{k}_2, \mathbf{k}_3, \mathbf{k}_4$ are defined (in analogy with Eqs. (5a)–(5d) of Section 2.6) as follows:

$$\mathbf{k}_1 = f(t_n, \mathbf{x}_n),$$

▶
$$\mathbf{k}_2 = \mathbf{f}\left(t_n + \frac{1}{2}h, \mathbf{x}_n + \frac{1}{2}h\mathbf{k}_1\right),$$

$$\mathbf{k}_3 = \mathbf{f}\left(t_n + \frac{1}{2}h, \mathbf{x}_n + \frac{1}{2}h\mathbf{k}_2\right), \tag{12}$$

$$\mathbf{k}_4 = \mathbf{f}(t_n + h, \mathbf{x}_n + h\mathbf{k}_3).$$

To describe in scalar notation the Runge–Kutta method for the two-dimensional initial value problem

$$x' = f(t, x, y), \qquad x(t_0) = x_0,$$
$$y' = g(t, x, y), \qquad y(t_0) = y_0, \tag{3}$$

let us write

$$\mathbf{x} = \begin{bmatrix} x \\ y \end{bmatrix}, \qquad \mathbf{f} = \begin{bmatrix} f \\ g \end{bmatrix}, \qquad \text{and} \qquad \mathbf{k}_i = \begin{bmatrix} F_i \\ G_i \end{bmatrix}.$$

Then the Runge–Kutta iterative formulas for the step from (x_n, y_n) to the next approximation $(x_{n+1}, y_{n+1}) \approx (x(t_{n+1}), y(t_{n+1}))$ are

$$x_{n+1} = x_n + \frac{h}{6}(F_1 + 2F_2 + 2F_3 + F_4),$$

$$y_{n+1} = y_n + \frac{h}{6}(G_1 + 2G_2 + 2G_3 + G_4), \tag{13}$$

where the values F_1, F_2, F_3, F_4 of the function f are

$$F_1 = f(t_n, x_n, y_n),$$

$$F_2 = f\left(t_n + \frac{1}{2}h, x_n + \frac{1}{2}hF_1, y_n + \frac{1}{2}hG_1\right),$$

$$F_3 = f\left(t_n + \frac{1}{2}h, x_n + \frac{1}{2}hF_2, y_n + \frac{1}{2}hG_2\right),$$

$$F_4 = f(t_n + h, x_n + hF_3, y_n + hG_3);$$

(14)

G_1, G_2, G_3, and G_4 are the similarly defined values of the function g.

Perhaps the most common application of the two-dimensional Runge–Kutta method is to the numerical solution of second-order initial value problems of the form

▶
$$x'' = g(t, x, x'),$$
$$x(t_0) = x_0, \qquad x'(t_0) = y_0.$$
(15)

If we introduce the auxiliary variable $y = x'$, then the problem in (15) translates into the two-dimensional first-order problem

$$x' = y, \qquad\qquad x(t_0) = x_0,$$
$$y' = g(t, x, y), \qquad y(t_0) = y_0.$$
(16)

This is a problem of the form in (3) with $f(t, x, y) = y$.

If the functions f and g are not too complicated, then it is feasible to carry out manually a reasonable number of steps of the two-dimensional Runge–Kutta method described above. But the first operating electronic computers were constructed (during World War II) specifically to implement methods similar to the Runge–Kutta method for the numerical computation of trajectories of artillary projectiles. The project material for this section lists TI-85 and BASIC versions of Program RK2DIM that can be used with two-dimensional systems.

EXAMPLE 2 The exact solution of the initial value problem

$$x'' = -x; \qquad x(0) = 0, \qquad x'(0) = 1$$
(17)

t	$x = \sin t$	$y = \cos t$
0.5	+0.47943	+0.87758
1.0	+0.84147	+0.54030
1.5	+0.99749	+0.07074
2.0	+0.90930	−0.41615
2.5	+0.59847	−0.80114
3.0	+0.14112	−0.98999
3.5	−0.35078	−0.93646
4.0	−0.75680	−0.65364
4.5	−0.97753	−0.21080
5.0	−0.95892	+0.28366

FIGURE 4.3.1. Runge–Kutta values (with $h = 0.05$) for the problem in Eq. (18)

is $x(t) = \sin t$. The substitution $x' = y$ translates (17) into the two-dimensional problem

$$x' = y, \qquad x(0) = 0;$$
$$y' = -x, \qquad y(0) = 1, \tag{18}$$

which has the form in (3) with $f(t, x, y) = y$ and $g(t, x, y) = -x$. The table in Fig. 4.3.1 shows the results produced for $0 \leq t \leq 5$ (radians) using Program RK2DIM with step size $h = 0.05$. The values shown for $x = \sin t$ and $y = \cos t$ are all accurate to five decimal places.

EXAMPLE 3 In Example 3 of Section 2.3 we considered a lunar lander that initially is falling freely toward the surface of the moon at a speed of 1000 mi/h. Its retrorockets, when fired in free space, provide a deceleration of 33,000 mi/h^2. In addition, the lander is subject to the gravitational attraction of the moon. We found that a soft touchdown ($v = 0$ at impact) is achieved by firing the rockets beginning at time $t = 0$ at a height of approximately 25 miles above the lunar surface.

Here we want to compute the *descent time* of the lunar lander. Let the distance $x(t)$ of the lander from the center of the moon be measured in kilomiles and measure time t in hours. According to the analysis in Section 2.3, $x(t)$ satisfies the initial value problem

$$\frac{d^2x}{dt^2} = 33 - \frac{15.1632}{x^2};$$
$$x(0) = 1.10464, \qquad x'(0) = -1. \tag{19}$$

(Actually, in Section 2.3 we used y where here we use x; we also use more precise values of the constants to take advantage of the accuracy of the Runge–Kutta method.) We seek the value of t when $x = 1.080$ (the radius of the moon is 1080 mi).

t	x	v
0.004	+1.10080	−0.91788
0.008	+1.09730	−0.83610
0.012	+1.09412	−0.75462
0.016	+1.09126	−0.67342
0.020	+1.08873	−0.59248
0.024	+1.08652	−0.51175
0.028	+1.08463	−0.43122
0.032	+1.08307	−0.35086
0.036	+1.08183	−0.27062
0.040	+1.08090	−0.19049
0.044	+1.08030	−0.11044
0.048	+1.08002	−0.03043
0.052	+1.08006	+0.04958

FIGURE 4.3.2. The lander's descent to the lunar surface

t	x	v
0.0482	+1.08001	−0.02643
0.0484	+1.08001	−0.02243
0.0486	+1.08001	−0.01843
0.0488	+1.08000	−0.01443
0.0490	+1.08000	−0.01043
0.0492	+1.08000	−0.00643
0.0494	+1.08000	−0.00243
0.0496	+1.08000	+0.00157
0.0498	+1.08000	+0.00557
0.0500	+1.08000	+0.00957

FIGURE 4.3.3. Focusing on the lunar lander's soft touchdown

The problem in (19) is equivalent to the first-order system

$$\frac{dx}{dt} = y, \qquad x(0) = 1.10464;$$

$$\frac{dy}{dt} = 33 - \frac{15.1632}{x^2}, \qquad y(0) = -1. \tag{20}$$

The table in Fig. 4.3.2 shows the result of a run of Program RK2DIM with step size $h = 0.002$. Evidently, touchdown ($x = 1.080$) occurs at some time between $t = 0.048$ and $t = 0.052$. The table in Fig. 4.3.3 shows the result of a second run with $t_0 = 0.048$, $x_0 = 1.08002$, $y_0 = v_0 = -0.03043$, and $h = 0.0002$. Now it is apparent that the lander's time of descent to the lunar surface is about $t = 0.0495$ h—approximately 2 min 58 s. ∎

Higher-Order Systems

As we saw in Section 4.1, any system of higher-order differential equations can be replaced with an equivalent system of first-order differential equations. For example, consider the system

$$x'' = F(t, x, y, x', y'),$$
$$y'' = G(t, x, y, x', y') \tag{21}$$

of second-order equations. If we substitute

$$x = x_1, \quad y = x_2, \quad x' = x_3 = x_1', \quad y' = x_4 = x_2',$$

then we get the equivalent system

$$x_1' = x_3$$
$$x_2' = x_4$$
$$x_3' = F(t, x_1, x_2, x_3, x_4) \tag{22}$$
$$x_4' = G(t, x_1, x_2, x_3, x_4)$$

of four first-order equations in the unknown functions $x_1(t) = x(t)$, $x_2(t) = y(t)$, $x_3(t)$, and $x_4(t)$. It would be a routine (if slightly tedious) matter to write a four-dimensional version of program RK2DIM for the purpose of solving such a system. But, in a programming language that accommodates vectors, an n-dimensional Runge–Kutta program is scarcely more complicated than a one-dimensional program. For instance, the project material for this section lists the n-dimensional MATLAB program **rkn** that closely resembles the one-dimensional program **rk** of Fig. 2.6.11.

EXAMPLE 4 Suppose that a batted ball starts at $x_0 = 0$, $y_0 = 0$ with initial velocity $v_0 = 160$ ft/s and with initial angle of inclination $\theta = 30°$. If air resistance is ignored, we find by the elementary methods of Section 1.2 that the baseball travels a [horizontal] distance of $400\sqrt{3}$ ft (approximately 693 ft) in 5 s before striking the ground. Now suppose that in addition to a downward gravitational acceleration ($g = 32$ ft/s^2), the baseball experiences an acceleration due to air resistance of $(0.0025)v^2$ feet per second per second, directed opposite to its instantaneous direction of motion. Determine how far the baseball will travel horizontally under these conditions.

Solution According to Problem 30 of Section 4.1, the equations of motion of the baseball are

$$\frac{d^2x}{dt^2} = -cv\,\frac{dx}{dt}, \qquad \frac{d^2y}{dt^2} = -cv\,\frac{dy}{dt} - g \tag{23}$$

where $v = \sqrt{(x')^2 + (y')^2}$ is the speed of the ball, and where $c = 0.0025$ and $g = 32$ in fps units. We convert to a first-order system as in (22) and thereby obtain the system

$$
\begin{aligned}
x'_1 &= x_3 \\
x'_2 &= x_4 \\
x'_3 &= -cx_3\sqrt{x_3^2 + x_4^2} \\
x'_4 &= -cx_4\sqrt{x_3^2 + x_4^2} - g
\end{aligned}
\tag{24}
$$

of four first-order differential equations with

$$
\begin{aligned}
x_1(0) &= x_2(0) = 0, \\
x_3(0) &= 80\sqrt{3}, \qquad x_4(0) = 80.
\end{aligned}
\tag{25}
$$

Note that $x_3(t)$ and $x_4(t)$ are simply the x- and y-components of the baseball's velocity vector, so $v = \sqrt{x_3^2 + x_4^2}$.

Without Air Resistance: Figure 4.3.4 shows the numerical results obtained when a Runge–Kutta program such as **rkn** is applied with step size $k = 0.1$ and with $c = 0$ (no air resistance). For convenience in interpreting the results, the printed output at each selected step consists of the horizontal and vertical coordinates x and y of the baseball, its velocity v, and the angle of inclination α of its velocity vector (in degrees measured from the horizontal). These results agree with the exact solution when $c = 0$. The ball travels a horizontal distance of $400\sqrt{3} \approx 692.82$ ft in exactly 5 s, having reached a maximum height of 100 ft after 2.5 s. Note also that it strikes the ground at the same angle and with the same speed as its initial angle and speed.

With Air Resistance: Figure 4.3.5 shows the results obtained with the fairly realistic value of $c = 0.0025$ for the air resistance for a batted baseball. To within a hundredth of a foot in either direction, the same results are obtained with step sizes $h = 0.05$ and $h = 0.025$. We now see that with air resistance the ball travels a distance well under 400 ft in just over 4 s. The more refined data in Fig. 4.3.6 show that the ball now travels horizontally only about 340 ft and that its maximum height is only about 66 ft. As illustrated in Fig. 4.3.7, air resistance has converted a massive home run into a routine fly ball (if hit straightaway to center field). Note also that when the ball strikes the ground, it has slightly under *half* its initial speed (only about 79 ft/s) and is falling at a steeper angle (about 46°). Every baseball fan has observed empirically these aspects of the trajectory of a fly ball.

t	x	y	v	α
0.0	0.00	0.00	160.00	$+30$
0.5	69.28	36.00	152.63	$+25$
1.0	138.56	64.00	146.64	$+19$
1.5	207.85	84.00	142.21	$+13$
2.0	277.13	96.00	139.48	$+7$
2.5	346.41	100.00	138.56	$+0$
3.0	415.69	96.00	139.48	-7
3.5	484.97	84.00	142.21	-13
4.0	554.26	64.00	146.64	-19
4.5	623.54	36.00	152.63	-25
5.0	692.82	0.00	160.00	-30

FIGURE 4.3.4. The batted baseball with no air resistance ($c = 0$)

Variable Step Size Methods

The Runge–Kutta method for a large system requires an appreciable amount of computational labor, even when a computer is employed. Therefore, just as the step size h

t	x	y	v	α
0.0	0.00	0.00	160.00	+30
0.5	63.25	32.74	127.18	+24
1.0	117.11	53.20	104.86	+17
1.5	164.32	63.60	89.72	+8
2.0	206.48	65.30	80.17	−3
2.5	244.61	59.22	75.22	−15
3.0	279.29	46.05	73.99	−27
3.5	310.91	26.41	75.47	−37
4.0	339.67	0.91	78.66	−46

FIGURE 4.3.5. The batted baseball with air resistance ($c = 0.0025$)

t	x	y	v	α
1.5	164.32	63.60	89.72	+8
1.6	173.11	64.60	87.40	+5
1.7	181.72	65.26	85.29	+3
1.8	190.15	65.60	83.39	+1
1.9	198.40	65.61	81.68	−1 ← Apex
2.0	206.48	65.30	80.17	−3
.
.
.
3.8	328.50	11.77	77.24	−42
3.9	334.14	6.45	77.93	−44
4.0	339.67	0.91	78.66	−46
4.1	345.10	−4.84	79.43	−47 ← Impact
4.2	350.41	−10.79	80.22	−49

FIGURE 4.3.6. The batted ball's apex and its impact with the ground

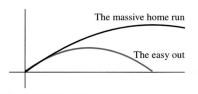

The massive home run

The easy out

FIGURE 4.3.7. An "easy out" or a home run?

should not be so large that the resulting error in the solution is unacceptable, h also ought not to be so small that too many steps are needed, hence requiring an unacceptable amount of computation. Thus the practical numerical solution of differential equations involves a trade-off between accuracy and efficiency.

To facilitate this trade-off, modern *variable step size methods* vary the step size h as the solution process proceeds. Large steps are taken in regions where the dependent variables are changing slowly; smaller steps are taken when these variables are changing rapidly, in order to prevent large errors.

An *adaptable* or *variable step size* Runge–Kutta method employs both a preassigned minimum error tolerance *MinTol* and a maximum error tolerance *MaxTol* to attempt to ensure that the error made in the typical step from \mathbf{x}_n to \mathbf{x}_{n+1} is neither too large (and hence inaccurate) nor too small (and hence inefficient). A fairly simple scheme for doing this may be outlined as follows:

- Having reached \mathbf{x}_n with a Runge–Kutta step of length $t_n - t_{n-1} = h$, let $\mathbf{x}^{(1)}$ denote the result of a further Runge–Kutta step of length h and let $\mathbf{x}^{(2)}$ denote the result of *two* successive Runge–Kutta steps each of length $h/2$.

- On the grounds that $\mathbf{x}^{(2)}$ should be a more accurate approximation to $\mathbf{x}(t_n + h)$ than is $\mathbf{x}^{(1)}$, take

$$Err = \left| \mathbf{x}^{(1)} - \mathbf{x}^{(2)} \right|$$

 as an estimate of the error in $\mathbf{x}^{(1)}$.

- If *Mintol* $\leq Err \leq$ *MaxTol*, then let $\mathbf{x}_{n+1} = \mathbf{x}^{(1)}$, $t_{n+1} = t_n + h$ and proceed to the next step.

- If *Err* < *MinTol*, then the error is too small! Hence let $\mathbf{x}_{n+1} = \mathbf{x}^{(1)}$, $t_{n+1} = t_n + h$ but *double* the step size to $2h$ before making the next step.

- If *Err* > *MaxTol* then the error is too large. Hence reject $\mathbf{x}^{(1)}$, and start afresh at \mathbf{x}_n with the *halved* step size $h/2$.

The detailed implementation of such a scheme can be complicated. For a much more complete but readable discussion of adaptive Runge–Kutta methods, see Section 15.2 of William H. Press et al.: *Numerical Recipes: The Art of Scientific Computing* (Cambridge University Press, 1986).

Several widely available scientific computing packages (such as *Maple*, *Mathematica,* and MATLAB) include sophisticated variable step size programs that will accommodate an essentially arbitrary number of simultaneous differential equations. Such a general-purpose program might be used, for example, to model numerically the major components of the solar system: the sun and the nine (known) major planets. If m_i denotes the mass and $\mathbf{r}_i = (x_i, y_i, z_i)$ denotes the position vector of the *i*th one of these 10 bodies, then—by Newton's laws—the equation of motion of m_i is

$$m_i \mathbf{r}_i'' = \sum_{j \neq i} \frac{Gm_i m_j}{(r_{ij})^3} (\mathbf{r}_j - \mathbf{r}_i), \tag{26}$$

where $r_{ij} = |\mathbf{r}_j - \mathbf{r}_i|$ denotes the distance between m_i and m_j. For each $i = 1,$ 2, . . . , 10, the summation in Eq. (26) is over all values of $j \neq i$ from 1 to 10. The 10 vector equations in (26) constitute a system of 30 second-order scalar equations, and the equivalent first-order system consists of 60 differential equations in the coordinates and velocity components of the 10 major bodies in the solar system. Mathematical models that involve this many (or more) differential equations—and that require sophisticated software and hardware for their numerical analysis—are quite common in science, engineering, and applied technology.

Earth–Moon Satellite Orbits

For an example of a problem whose efficient solution requires adaptive step size methods, we consider an Apollo satellite in orbit about the Earth *E* and Moon *M*. Figure 4.3.8 shows an $x_1 x_2$-coordinate system whose origin lies at the center of mass of the Earth and the Moon, and which rotates at the rate of one revolution per "moon month" of approximately $\tau = 27.32$ days, so the Earth and Moon remain fixed in their positions on the x_1-axis. If we take as unit distance the distance (about 239,000 miles, assumed constant) between the Earth and Moon centers, then their coordinates are $E(-\mu, 0)$ and $M(1 - \mu, 0)$, where $\mu = m_M/(m_E + m_M)$ in terms of the Earth mass m_E and Moon mass m_M. If we take the total mass $m_E + m_M$ as the unit of mass and $\tau/2\pi \approx 4.35$ days as the unit of time, then the gravitational constant is $G = 1$ in Eq. (26), and the equations of motion of the satellite position $S(x_1, x_2)$ are

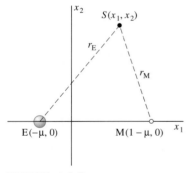

FIGURE 4.3.8. The earth-moon center-of-mass coordinate system

$$x_1'' = x_1 + 2x_2' - \frac{(1 - \mu)(x_1 + \mu)}{(r_E)^3} - \frac{\mu(x_1 - 1 + \mu)}{(r_M)^3},$$

$$x_2'' = x_2 - 2x_1' - \frac{(1 - \mu)x_2}{(r_E)^3} - \frac{\mu x_2}{(r_M)^3}, \tag{27}$$

where r_E and r_M denote the satellite's distances to the Earth and Moon (indicated in Fig. 4.3.8). The initial two terms on the right-hand side of each equation result from the rotation of the coordinate system. In the system of units described here, the lunar mass is approximately $m_M = 0.012277471$. The second-order system in (27) can be converted to an equivalent first-order system (of four differential equations) by substituting

$$x_1' = x_3, \quad x_2' = x_4, \quad \text{so that} \quad x_1'' = x_3', \quad x_2'' = x_4'.$$

Suppose that the satellite initially is in a clockwise circular orbit of radius about 1500 miles about the Moon. At its farthest point from the Earth ($x_1 = 0.994$) it is "launched" into Earth-Moon orbit with initial velocity v_0. The corresponding initial conditions are

$$x_1(0) = 0.994, \qquad x_2(0) = 0, \qquad x_3(0) = 0, \qquad x_4(0) = -v_0.$$

An adaptive step size method **(ode45)** in the MATLAB software system was used to solve numerically the system in (27). The orbits in Figs. 4.3.9 and 4.3.10 were

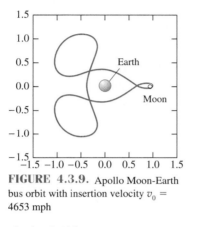

FIGURE 4.3.9. Apollo Moon-Earth bus orbit with insertion velocity $v_0 = 4653$ mph

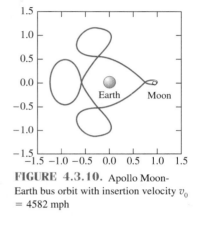

FIGURE 4.3.10. Apollo Moon-Earth bus orbit with insertion velocity $v_0 = 4582$ mph

obtained with

$$v_0 = 2.031732629557 \quad \text{and} \quad v_0 = 2.001585106379,$$

respectively.* [In the system of units used here, the unit of velocity is approximately 2290 mi/h.] In each case a closed but multi-looped periodic trajectory about the Earth and the Moon—a so-called "bus orbit"—is obtained, but a relatively small change in the initial velocity changes the number of loops!

* See NASA Contractor Report CR-61139, "Study of the Methods for the Numerical Solution of Ordinary Differential Equations," prepared by O. B. Francis, Jr. et al. for the NASA–George C. Marshall Space Flight Center, June 7, 1966.

4.3 Problems

A hand-held calculator will suffice for Problems 1 through 8. In each problem an initial value problem and its exact solution are given. Approximate the values of $x(0.2)$ and $y(0.2)$ in three ways: (a) by the Euler method with two steps of size $h = 0.1$; (b) by the improved Euler method with a single step of size $h = 0.2$, and (c) by the Runge–Kutta method with a single step of size $h = 0.2$. Compare the approximate values with the actual values $x(0.2)$ and $y(0.2)$.

1. $x' = x + 2y, \quad x(0) = 0,$
$y' = 2x + y, \quad y(0) = 2;$
$x(t) = e^{3t} - e^{-t}, \quad y(t) = e^{3t} + e^{-t}$

2. $x' = 2x + 3y, \quad x(0) = 1,$
$y' = 2x + y, \quad y(0) = -1;$
$x(t) = e^{-t}, \quad y(t) = -e^{-t}$

3. $x' = 3x + 4y, \quad x(0) = 1,$
$y' = 3x + 2y, \quad y(0) = 1;$
$x(t) = \frac{1}{7}(8e^{6t} - e^{-t}), \quad y(t) = \frac{1}{7}(6e^{6t} + e^{-t})$

4. $x' = 9x + 5y, \quad x(0) = 1,$
$y' = -6x - 2y, \quad y(0) = 0;$
$x(t) = -5e^{3t} + 6e^{4t}, \quad y(t) = 6e^{3t} - 6e^{4t}$

5. $x' = 2x - 5y, \quad x(0) = 2,$
$y' = 4x - 2y, \quad y(0) = 3;$
$x(t) = 2 \cos 4t - \frac{11}{4} \sin 4t, \quad y(t) = 3 \cos 4t + \frac{1}{2} \sin 4t$

6. $x' = x - 2y$, $x(0) = 0$,
$\quad y' = 2x + y$, $y(0) = 4$;
$\quad x(t) = -4e^t \sin 2t$, $y(t) = 4e^t \cos 2t$

7. $x' = 3x - y$, $x(0) = 2$,
$\quad y' = x + y$, $y(0) = 1$;
$\quad x(t) = (t + 2)e^{2t}$, $y(t) = (t + 1)e^{2t}$

8. $x' = 5x - 9y$, $x(0) = 0$,
$\quad y' = 2x - y$, $y(0) = -1$;
$\quad x(t) = 3e^{2t} \sin 3t$, $y(t) = e^{2t}(\sin 3t - \cos 3t)$

A computer will be required for the remaining problems in this section. In Problems 9 through 12, an initial value problem and its exact solution are given. In each of these four problems, use the Runge–Kutta method with step sizes $h = 0.1$ and $h = 0.05$ to approximate to five decimal places the values $x(1)$ and $y(1)$. Compare the approximate values with the actual values.

9. $x' = 2x - y$, $x(0) = 1$,
$\quad y' = x + 2y$, $y(0) = 0$;
$\quad x(t) = e^{2t} \cos t$, $y(t) = e^{2t} \sin t$

10. $x' = x + 2y$, $x(0) = 0$,
$\quad y' = x + e^{-t}$, $y(0) = 0$;
$\quad x(t) = \frac{1}{9}(2e^{2t} - 2e^{-t} - 6te^{-t})$,
$\quad y(t) = \frac{1}{9}(e^{2t} - e^{-t} + 6te^{-t})$

11. $x' = -x + y - (1 + t^3)e^{-t}$, $x(0) = 0$,
$\quad y' = -x - y - (t - 3t^2)e^{-t}$, $y(0) = 1$;
$\quad x(t) = e^{-t}(\sin t - t)$, $y(t) = e^{-t}(\cos t + t^3)$

12. $x'' + x = \sin t$, $x(0) = x'(0) = 0$;
$\quad x(t) = \frac{1}{2}(\sin t - t \cos t)$

13. Suppose that a crossbow bolt is shot straight upward with initial velocity 288 ft/s. If its deceleration due to air resistance is $(0.04)v$, then its height $x(t)$ satisfies the initial value problem

$$x'' = -32 - (0.04)x'; \qquad x(0) = 0, \qquad x'(0) = 288.$$

Find the maximum height that the bolt attains and the time required for it to reach this height.

14. Repeat Problem 13, but assume instead that the deceleration of the bolt due to air resistance is $(0.0002)v^2$.

15. Suppose that a projectile is fired straight upward with initial velocity v_0 from the surface of the earth. If air resistance is not

a factor, then its height $x(t)$ at time t satisfies the initial value problem

$$\frac{d^2 x}{dt^2} = -\frac{gR^2}{(x + R)^2}; \qquad x(0) = 0, \qquad x'(0) = v_0.$$

Use the values $g = 32.15$ ft/s$^2 \approx 0.006089$ mi/s^2 for the gravitational acceleration of the earth at its surface and $R = 3960$ mi as the radius of the earth. If $v_0 = 1$ mi/s, find the maximum height attained by the projectile and its time of ascent to this height.

Problems 16 through 18 deal with the batted baseball of Example 4, having initial velocity 160 ft/s and air resistance coefficient $c = 0.0025$.

16. Find the *range* — the horizontal distance the ball travels before it hits the ground — and its total time of flight with initial inclination angles 40°, 45°, and 50°.

17. Find (to the nearest degree) the initial inclination that maximizes the range. If there were no air resistance it would be exactly 45°, but your answer should be less than 45°.

18. Find (to the nearest half degree) the initial inclination angle greater than 45° for which the range is 300 ft.

19. Find the initial velocity of a baseball hit by Babe Ruth (with $c = 0.0025$ and initial inclination 40°) if it hit the bleachers at a point 50 ft high and 500 horizontal feet from home plate.

20. Consider the crossbow bolt of Problem 14, fired with the same initial velocity of 288 ft/s and with the air resistance deceleration $(0.0002)v^2$ directed opposite its direction of motion. Suppose that this bolt is fired from ground level at an initial angle of 45°. Find how high vertically and how far horizontally it goes, and how long it remains in the air.

21. Suppose that an artillery projectile is fired from ground level with initial velocity 3000 ft/s and initial inclination angle 40°. Assume that its air resistance deceleration is $(0.0001)v^2$. (a) What is the range of the projectile and what is its total time of flight? What is its speed at impact with the ground? (b) What is the maximum altitude of the projectile, and when is that altitude attained? (c) You will find that the projectile is still losing speed at the apex of its trajectory. What is the *minimum* speed that it attains during its descent?

4.3 Computing Projects

Figure 4.3.11 lists TI-85 and BASIC versions of the two-dimensional Runge–Kutta program RK2DIM. You should note that it closely parallels the one-dimensional Runge–Kutta program listed in Fig. 2.6.11, with a single line there replaced (where appropriate) with two lines here to calculate a *pair* of x- and y-values or slopes. Note

TI-85	BASIC	Comment
PROGRAM:RK2DIM	Program RK2DIM	Program title
:F=Y	DEF FN F(T,X,Y) = Y	Define function f
:G=-X	DEF FN G(T,X,Y) = -X	Define function g
:50→N	N = 50	No. of steps
:0→T	T = 0	Initial t
:0→X	X = 0	Initial x
:1→Y	Y = 1	Initial y
:5→T1	T1= 5	Final t
:(T1-T)/N→H	H = (T1-T)/N	Step size
:For(I,1,N)	FOR I=1 TO N	Begin loop
:T→T0	T0 = T	Save previous t
:X→X0	X0 = X	Save previous x
:Y→Y0	Y0 = Y	Save previous y
:F→F1	F1 = FNF(T,X,Y)	First f-slope
:G→G1	G1 = FNG(T,X,Y)	First g-slope
:T0+H/2→T	T = T0 + H/2	Midpoint t
:X0+H*F1/2→X	X = X0 + H*F1/2	Midpt x-predictor
:Y0+H*G1/2→Y	Y = Y0 + H*G1/2	Midpt y-predictor
:F→F2	F2 = FNF(T,X,Y)	Second f-slope
:G→G2	G2 = FNG(T,X,Y)	Second g-slope
:X0+H*F2/2→X	X = X0 + H*F2/2	Midpt x-predictor
:Y0+H*G2/2→Y	Y = Y0 + H*G2/2	Midpt y-predictor
:F→F3	F3 = FNF(T,X,Y)	Third f-slope
:G→G3	G3 = FNG(T,X,Y)	Third g-slope
:T0+H→T	T = T0 + H	New t
:X0+H*F3→X	X = X0 + H*F3	Endpt x-predictor
:Y0+H*G3→Y	Y = Y0 + H*G3	Endpt y-predictor
:F→F4	F4 = FNF(T,X,Y)	Fourth f-slope
:G→G4	G4 = FNG(T,X,Y)	Fourth g-slope
:(F1+2*F2+2*F3 +F4)/6→FA	FA = (F1+2*F2+2*F3 +F4)/6	Average f-slope
:(G1+2*G2+2*G3 +G4)/6→GA	GA = (G1+2*G2+2*G3 +G4)/6	Average g-slope
:X0+H*FA→X	X = X0 + H*FA	x-corrector
:Y0+H*GA→Y	Y = Y0 + H*GA	y-corrector
:Disp T,X,Y	PRINT T,X,Y	Display results
:End	NEXT I	End loop

FIGURE 4.3.11. TI-85 and BASIC two-dimensional Runge–Kutta programs

also that the notation used is essentially that of Eqs. (13) and (14) in this section. The first several lines define the functions and initial data needed for Example 1.

Figure 4.3.12 exhibits an *n*-dimensional MATLAB implementation of the Runge–Kutta method. The MATLAB function **f** defines the vector of right-hand sides of the differential equations in the system $\mathbf{x}' = \mathbf{f}(t, \mathbf{x})$ to be solved. The **rkn** function then takes as input the initial *t*-value **t**, the column vector **x** of initial *x*-values, the final *t*-value **t1**, and the desired number **n** of subintervals. As output it produces the resulting column vector **T** of *t*-values and the matrix **X** whose rows give the corresponding

```
function xp = f(t,x)
xp = x;
xp(1) = x(2);
xp(2) = -x(1);

function  [T,X] = rkn(t,x,t1,n)
h = (t1 - t)/n;                    % step size
T = t;                             % initial t
X = x´;                            % initial x-vector
for i = 1 : n                      % begin loop
    k1 = f(t, x);                  % first k-vector
    k2 = f(t+h/2,x+h*k1/2);        % second k-vector
    k3 = f(t+h/2,x+h*k2/2);        % third k-vector
    k4 = f(t+h  ,x+h*k3  );        % fourth k-vector
    k  = (k1+2*k2+2*k3+k4)/6;      % average k-vector
    t  = t + h;                    % new t
    x  = x + h*k;                  % new x
    T = [T;t];                     % update t-column
    X = [X;x´]                     % update x-matrix
    end                            % end loop
```

FIGURE 4.3.12. MATLAB implementation of the Runge–Kutta method

x-values. For instance, with **f** as indicated in the figure, the MATLAB command

```
[T,X] = rkn(0, [0;1], 5, 50)
```

then generates the data shown in the table of Fig. 4.3.1 (which lists only every fifth values of each variable).

For this project you should implement the Runge–Kutta method in your calculator or programming language of choice. Test your program by application first to the initial value problems of Examples 1 through 3 in this section. Then investigate Kepler's laws as outlined below. The computer lab manual accompanying this text describes additional numerical ODE projects ranging from batted baseballs to the Apollo orbits shown in Figs. 4.3.9 and 4.3.10.

Kepler's Laws of Planetary (or Satellite) Motion

Consider a satellite in elliptical orbit around a planet of mass M, and suppose that physical units are so chosen that $GM = 1$ (where G is the gravitational constant). If the planet is located at the origin in the xy-plane, then the equations of motion of the satellite are

$$\frac{d^2x}{dt^2} = -\frac{x}{(x^2 + y^2)^{3/2}}, \qquad \frac{d^2y}{dt^2} = -\frac{y}{(x^2 + y^2)^{3/2}}. \tag{1}$$

Let T denote the period of revolution of the satellite. Kepler's third law says that the *square* of T is proportional to the *cube* of the major semiaxis a of its elliptical orbit. In particular, if $GM = 1$, then

$$T^2 = 4\pi^2 a^3. \tag{2}$$

(For details, see Section 12.5 of Edwards and Penney, *Calculus with Analytic Geometry*, 4th ed. (Englewood Cliffs, N.J.: Prentice-Hall, 1994).) (a) If the satellite's *x*- and *y*-components of velocity, $x_3 = x' = x_1'$ and $x_4 = y' = x_2'$, are introduced, then the system in (1) translates into a system of four first-order differential equations having the form of those in Eq. (22) of this section.

(a) Solve this 4×4 system numerically with the initial conditions

$$x(0) = 1, \qquad y(0) = 0, \qquad x'(0) = 0, \qquad y'(0) = 1$$

that correspond theoretically to a circular orbit of radius $a = 1$, so Eq. (2) gives $T = 2\pi$. Is this what you get?

(b) Now solve the system numerically with the initial conditions

$$x(0) = 1, \qquad y(0) = 0, \qquad x'(0) = 0, \qquad y'(0) = \frac{1}{2}\sqrt{6}$$

that correspond theoretically to an elliptical orbit with major semiaxis $a = 2$, so Eq. (2) gives $T = 4\pi\sqrt{2}$. Is this what you get?

(c) Investigate what happens when both the *x*-component and the *y*-component of the initial velocity are nonzero.

Newton's Nose Cone

In his great *Principia Mathematica* of 1687, Isaac Newton not only showed in Book I that Kepler's laws imply the inverse-square law of gravitation, but proceeded in Book II to investigate a variety of "practical" problems, including the motion of projectiles subject to air resistance. Figure 4.3.13 illustrates a projectile shaped roughly like a bullet with a "nose cone" having radius *r* and height *h*. This nose cone is a surface of revolution determined by the curve $y = y(x)$. Newton showed that, on the basis of plausible assumptions about the nature of air resistance, the force *F* of air resistance to the projectile moving at velocity *v* is given by

$$F = 2k\rho A v^2, \tag{3}$$

where ρ denotes the density of the air, $A = \pi r^2$ the cross-sectional area of the cylindrical body of the projectile, and the crucial constant *k* is given by

$$k = \int_0^r \frac{2\pi x \, dx}{1 + [y'(x)]^2}. \tag{4}$$

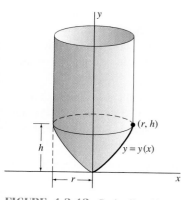

FIGURE 4.3.13. Projectile with nose cone of radius *r* and height *h*

The table in Fig. 4.3.14 lists numerical values of *k* for various shapes of nose cones with $r = h$ that Newton investigated. It may seem surprising that a "rounded" hemisphere and a "pointed" cone provide the same value $k = \frac{1}{2}$; the appropriate parabola — for which $y(r) = h$ — yields the smaller value $k = \frac{1}{4} \ln 5 \approx 0.4024$. But even more surprising is the fact that the optimally angled "flat-tipped" conical frustum (Fig. 4.3.15) yields the still smaller value $k \approx 0.3820$. Newton proceeded to study the much more difficult question of the optimally curved nose-cone-with-flat-tip (Fig. 4.3.16). He found that the minimum possible air resistance coefficient $k \approx 0.3748$ is obtained when the shape function $y(x)$ satisfies the endpoint value problem

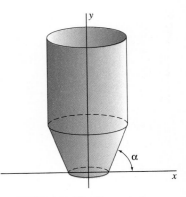

Shape	Value of k
Hemisphere	0.5000
Cone	0.5000
Paraboloid	0.4024
Optimal conical frustum	0.3820
Newton's optimal nose cone	0.3748

FIGURE 4.3.14. Values of k in Eq. (1) for various nose cone shapes

FIGURE 4.3.15. The conical frustum with $r = h$ offers least air resistance when $\tan 2\alpha = 2$.

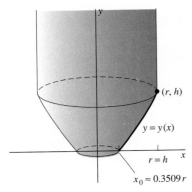

FIGURE 4.3.16. Newton's optimal nose cone has flat tip and gently curved "side surface."

$$xy''[3(y')^2 - 1] = y'[1 + (y')^2];$$

$$y(x_0) = 0, \quad y'(x_0) = 1, \quad y(r) = h. \tag{5}$$

Part of the problem is to determine x_0 so that a solution $y(x)$ exists; this part is discussed in the lab manual. Taking as given the numerical results listed in Fig. 4.3.14, here are *your* problems:

1. Suppose that a projectile with hemispherical nose (so $k = 0.5$) is fired at an initial inclination angle of 45° with initial velocity 300 ft/s, and travels 2000 ft before striking the ground. What is the value of c in Eq. (23) for this projectile? (Take $g = 32$ ft/s².) Answer this question by the "shooting" or "mortar fire" method—solve the appropriate initial value problem numerically with different values of c until you close in on a satisfactory value giving the desired range of 2000 ft.

2. Now the same projectile is fitted with an optimal conical frustum nose cone, so $k = 0.3820$ and therefore c is (0.3820)/(0.5) times the value found in Problem 1 (why?). Try to guess in advance the order of magnitude (10 ft or 100 ft?) of the increase in range due to flattening the tip of the projectile.

3. Repeat Problem 2, but now use Newton's optimal nose cone with $k \approx 0.3748$.

5 Linear Systems of Differential Equations

Although the simple elimination techniques of Section 4.2 suffice for the solution of small linear systems containing only two or three equations with constant coefficients, the general properties of linear systems—as well as solution methods suitable for larger systems—are most easily and concisely described using the language and notation of vectors and matrices. For ready reference and review, this section begins with a complete and self-contained account of the matrix notation and terminology that is needed. Special techniques of linear algebra—specifically, those associated with eigenvalues and eigenvectors—are introduced as needed in subsequent sections of this chapter.

Review of Matrix Notation and Terminology

An $m \times n$ **matrix A** is a rectangular array of mn numbers (or **elements**) arranged in m (horizontal) **rows** and n (vertical) **columns**:

$$A = \begin{bmatrix} a_{11} & a_{12} & a_{13} & \cdots & a_{1j} & \cdots & a_{1n} \\ a_{21} & a_{22} & a_{23} & \cdots & a_{2j} & \cdots & a_{2n} \\ a_{31} & a_{32} & a_{33} & \cdots & a_{3j} & \cdots & a_{3n} \\ \vdots & \vdots & \vdots & & \vdots & & \vdots \\ a_{i1} & a_{i2} & a_{i3} & \cdots & a_{ij} & \cdots & a_{in} \\ \vdots & \vdots & \vdots & & \vdots & & \vdots \\ a_{m1} & a_{m2} & a_{m3} & \cdots & a_{mj} & \cdots & a_{mn} \end{bmatrix} \tag{1}$$

We will ordinarily denote matrices by **boldface** capital letters. Sometimes we use the abbreviation $A = [a_{ij}]$ for the matrix with the element a_{ij} in the ith row and jth column, as in Eq. (1). We denote the **zero matrix,** each entry of which is zero, by

$$0 = \begin{bmatrix} 0 & 0 & \cdots & 0 \\ 0 & 0 & \cdots & 0 \\ \vdots & \vdots & & \vdots \\ 0 & 0 & \cdots & 0 \end{bmatrix}. \tag{2}$$

Actually for each pair of positive integers m and n, there is an $m \times n$ zero matrix, but the single symbol 0 will suffice for all these zero matrices.

Two $m \times n$ matrices $A = [a_{ij}]$ and $B = [b_{ij}]$ are said to be **equal** if corresponding elements are equal; that is, if $a_{ij} = b_{ij}$ for $1 \leqq i \leqq m$ and $1 \leqq j \leqq n$. We **add** A and B by adding corresponding entries:

$$A + B = [a_{ij}] + [b_{ij}] = [a_{ij} + b_{ij}]. \tag{3}$$

Thus the element in row i and column j of $C = A + B$ is $c_{ij} = a_{ij} + b_{ij}$. To multiply the matrix $A = [a_{ij}]$ by the number c, we simply multiply each of its elements by c:

$$cA = Ac = [ca_{ij}]. \tag{4}$$

EXAMPLE 1 If

$$A = \begin{bmatrix} 2 & -3 \\ 4 & 7 \end{bmatrix}, \qquad B = \begin{bmatrix} -13 & 10 \\ 7 & -5 \end{bmatrix}, \quad \text{and} \quad C = \begin{bmatrix} 3 & 0 \\ 5 & -7 \end{bmatrix},$$

then

$$A + B = \begin{bmatrix} 2 & -3 \\ 4 & 7 \end{bmatrix} + \begin{bmatrix} -13 & 10 \\ 7 & -5 \end{bmatrix} = \begin{bmatrix} -11 & 7 \\ 11 & 2 \end{bmatrix}$$

and

$$6C = 6 \cdot \begin{bmatrix} 3 & 0 \\ 5 & -7 \end{bmatrix} = \begin{bmatrix} 18 & 0 \\ 30 & -42 \end{bmatrix}. \qquad \blacksquare$$

We denote $(-1)A$ by $-A$ and define **subtraction** of matrices as follows:

$$A - B = A + (-B). \tag{5}$$

The matrix operations just defined have the following properties, each of which is analogous to a familiar algebraic property of the real number system:

$$\mathbf{A} + \mathbf{0} = \mathbf{0} + \mathbf{A} = \mathbf{A}, \qquad \mathbf{A} - \mathbf{A} = \mathbf{0}; \tag{6}$$

$$\mathbf{A} + \mathbf{B} = \mathbf{B} + \mathbf{A} \qquad \text{(commutativity)}; \tag{7}$$

$$\mathbf{A} + (\mathbf{B} + \mathbf{C}) = (\mathbf{A} + \mathbf{B}) + \mathbf{C} \qquad \text{(associativity)}; \tag{8}$$

$$c(\mathbf{A} + \mathbf{B}) = c\mathbf{A} + c\mathbf{B},$$
$$\qquad\qquad\qquad\qquad \text{(distributivity)} \tag{9}$$
$$(c + d)\mathbf{A} = c\mathbf{A} + d\mathbf{A}.$$

Each of these properties is readily verified by elementwise application of a corresponding property of the real numbers. For example, $a_{ij} + b_{ij} = b_{ij} + a_{ij}$ for all i and j because addition of real numbers is commutative. Consequently,

$$\mathbf{A} + \mathbf{B} = [a_{ij} + b_{ij}] + [b_{ij} + a_{ij}] = \mathbf{B} + \mathbf{A}$$

The **transpose** \mathbf{A}^T of the $m \times n$ matrix $\mathbf{A} = [a_{ij}]$ is the $n \times m$ (note!) matrix whose jth column is the jth row of \mathbf{A} (and consequently, whose ith row is the ith column of \mathbf{A}). Thus $\mathbf{A}^T = [a_{ji}]$, although this is not notationally perfect; you must remember that \mathbf{A}^T will not have the same shape as \mathbf{A} unless \mathbf{A} is a **square** matrix—that is, unless $m = n$.

An $m \times 1$ matrix—one having only a single column—is called a **column vector,** or simply a **vector.** We often denote column vectors by **boldface** lowercase letters, as in

$$\mathbf{b} = \begin{bmatrix} 3 \\ -7 \\ 0 \end{bmatrix} \quad \text{or} \quad \mathbf{x} = \begin{bmatrix} x_1 \\ x_2 \\ \vdots \\ x_m \end{bmatrix}.$$

Similarly, a **row vector** is a $1 \times n$ matrix—one having only a single row, such as $\mathbf{c} = [5 \ 17 \ 0 \ -3]$. For aesthetic and typographical reasons, we will frequently write a column vector as the transpose of a row vector; for example, the two column vectors above may be written in the forms

$$\mathbf{b} = [3 \quad -7 \quad 0]^T \qquad \text{and} \qquad \mathbf{x} = [x_1 \quad x_2 \quad \cdots \quad x_m]^T.$$

Sometimes it is convenient to describe an $m \times n$ matrix in terms of either its m row vectors or its n column vectors. Thus if we write

$$\mathbf{A} = \begin{bmatrix} \mathbf{a}_1 \\ \mathbf{a}_2 \\ \vdots \\ \mathbf{a}_m \end{bmatrix} \qquad \text{and} \qquad \mathbf{B} = [\mathbf{b}_1 \quad \mathbf{b}_2 \quad \cdots \quad \mathbf{b}_n],$$

it is understood that \mathbf{a}_1, \mathbf{a}_2, . . . , \mathbf{a}_m are the *row* vectors of the matrix \mathbf{A} and \mathbf{b}_1, \mathbf{b}_2, . . . , \mathbf{b}_n are the *column* vectors of the matrix \mathbf{B}.

Matrix Multiplication

The properties listed in Eqs. (6) through (9) are quite natural and expected. The first surprises in the realm of matrix arithmetic come with multiplication. We define first the **scalar product a · b** of a row vector **a** and a column vector **b**, each having the same number p of elements. If

$$\mathbf{a} = [a_1 \quad a_2 \quad \cdots \quad a_p] \quad \text{and} \quad \mathbf{b} = [b_1 \quad b_2 \quad \cdots \quad b_p]^T,$$

then **a · b** is defined as follows:

$$\mathbf{a} \cdot \mathbf{b} = \sum_{k=1}^{p} a_k b_k = a_1 b_1 + a_2 b_2 + \cdots + a_p b_p, \tag{10}$$

exactly as in the scalar or *dot* product of two vectors—a familiar topic from elementary calculus.

The product **AB** of two matrices is defined only if the number of columns of **A** is equal to the number of rows of **B**. If **A** is an $m \times p$ matrix and **B** is a $p \times n$ matrix, then their product **AB** is the $m \times n$ matrix $\mathbf{C} = [c_{ij}]$, where c_{ij} is the scalar product of the ith row vector \mathbf{a}_i of **A** and the jth column vector \mathbf{b}_j of **B**. Thus

$$\mathbf{AB} = [\mathbf{a}_i \cdot \mathbf{b}_j]. \tag{11}$$

In terms of the individual entries of $\mathbf{A} = [a_{ij}]$ and $\mathbf{B} = [b_{ij}]$, Eq. (11) can be recast in the form

$$c_{ij} = \sum_{k=1}^{p} a_{ik} b_{kj}. \tag{12}$$

For purposes of hand computation, the definition in (11) and (12) is easy to remember by visualizing the picture

$$\mathbf{a}_i \longrightarrow \begin{bmatrix} a_{11} & a_{12} & \cdots & a_{1p} \\ a_{21} & a_{22} & \cdots & a_{2p} \\ \vdots & \vdots & & \vdots \\ a_{i1} & a_{i2} & \cdots & a_{ip} \\ \vdots & \vdots & & \vdots \\ a_{m1} & a_{m2} & \cdots & a_{mp} \end{bmatrix} \begin{bmatrix} b_{11} & b_{12} & \cdots & b_{1j} & \cdots & b_{1n} \\ b_{21} & b_{22} & \cdots & b_{2j} & \cdots & b_{2n} \\ \vdots & \vdots & & \vdots & & \vdots \\ b_{p1} & b_{p2} & \cdots & b_{pj} & \cdots & b_{pn} \end{bmatrix},$$
$$\underset{\mathbf{b}_j}{\uparrow}$$

in which the row vector \mathbf{a}_i and the column vector \mathbf{b}_j are spotlighted; c_{ij} is simply their scalar product. It may help to think of "pouring the rows of **A** down the columns of **B**." This also reminds us that the number of columns of **A** must be equal to the number of rows of **B**.

EXAMPLE 2 Check your understanding of the definition of matrix multiplication by verifying that if

$$\mathbf{A} = \begin{bmatrix} 2 & -3 \\ -1 & 5 \end{bmatrix} \quad \text{and} \quad \mathbf{B} = \begin{bmatrix} 13 & 9 \\ 4 & 0 \end{bmatrix},$$

then

$$\mathbf{AB} = \begin{bmatrix} 2 & -3 \\ -1 & 5 \end{bmatrix} \begin{bmatrix} 13 & 9 \\ 4 & 0 \end{bmatrix} = \begin{bmatrix} 14 & 18 \\ 7 & -9 \end{bmatrix}.$$

Similarly, verify that

$$\begin{bmatrix} 2 & -3 & 1 \\ 4 & 5 & -2 \\ 6 & -7 & 0 \end{bmatrix} \begin{bmatrix} x \\ y \\ z \end{bmatrix} = \begin{bmatrix} 2x - 3y + z \\ 4x + 5y - 2z \\ 6x - 7y \end{bmatrix}$$

and that

$$\begin{bmatrix} 1 & 2 \\ 3 & 4 \\ 5 & 6 \\ 7 & 8 \end{bmatrix} \begin{bmatrix} 2 & 1 & 3 \\ -1 & 3 & -2 \end{bmatrix} = \begin{bmatrix} 0 & 7 & -1 \\ 2 & 15 & 1 \\ 4 & 23 & 3 \\ 6 & 31 & 5 \end{bmatrix}. \qquad \blacksquare$$

It can be shown by direct (though lengthy) computation based on its definition that matrix multiplication is associative and is also distributive with respect to matrix addition; that is,

$$\mathbf{A(BC)} = \mathbf{(AB)C} \tag{13}$$

and

$$\mathbf{A(B + C)} = \mathbf{AB} + \mathbf{AC}, \tag{14}$$

provided that the matrices are of such sizes that the indicated multiplications and additions are possible.

But matrix multiplication is not commutative. That is, if \mathbf{A} and \mathbf{B} are both $n \times n$ matrices (so that both the products \mathbf{AB} and \mathbf{BA} are defined and have the same dimensions—$n \times n$), then, in general,

$$\mathbf{AB} \neq \mathbf{BA}. \tag{15}$$

Moreover, it can happen that

$$\mathbf{AB} = \mathbf{0} \qquad \text{even though} \qquad \mathbf{A} \neq \mathbf{0} \qquad \text{and} \qquad \mathbf{B} \neq \mathbf{0}. \tag{16}$$

Examples illustrating the phenomena in (15) and (16) may be found in the problems, although you can easily construct your own examples using 2×2 matrices with small integral elements.

Inverse Matrices

A square $n \times n$ matrix is said to have **order** n. The **identity** matrix of order n is the square matrix

$$\mathbf{I} = \begin{bmatrix} 1 & 0 & 0 & 0 & \cdots & 0 \\ 0 & 1 & 0 & 0 & \cdots & 0 \\ 0 & 0 & 1 & 0 & \cdots & 0 \\ 0 & 0 & 0 & 1 & \cdots & 0 \\ \cdot & \cdot & \cdot & \cdot & & \cdot \\ \cdot & \cdot & \cdot & \cdot & & \cdot \\ \cdot & \cdot & \cdot & \cdot & & \cdot \\ 0 & 0 & 0 & 0 & \cdots & 1 \end{bmatrix} \tag{17}$$

for which each entry on the **principal diagonal** is 1 and all off-diagonal entries are zero. It is quite easy to verify that

$$\mathbf{AI} = \mathbf{A} = \mathbf{IA} \tag{18}$$

for every square matrix \mathbf{A} of the same order as \mathbf{I}.

If \mathbf{A} is a square matrix, then an **inverse** of \mathbf{A} is a square matrix \mathbf{B} of the same order as \mathbf{A} such that *both*

$$\mathbf{AB} = \mathbf{I} \quad \text{and} \quad \mathbf{BA} = \mathbf{I}.$$

It is not difficult to show that if the matrix \mathbf{A} has an inverse, then this inverse is unique. Consequently, we may speak of *the* inverse of \mathbf{A}, and we will denote it by \mathbf{A}^{-1}. Thus

$$\mathbf{AA}^{-1} = \mathbf{I} = \mathbf{A}^{-1}\mathbf{A}, \tag{19}$$

given the existence of \mathbf{A}^{-1}. It is clear that some square matrices do not have inverses—consider any square zero matrix. It is also easy to show that if \mathbf{A}^{-1} exists, then $(\mathbf{A}^{-1})^{-1}$ exists and $(\mathbf{A}^{-1})^{-1} = \mathbf{A}$.

In linear algebra it is proved that \mathbf{A}^{-1} exists if and only if the determinant $\det(\mathbf{A})$ of the square matrix \mathbf{A} is nonzero. If so, the matrix \mathbf{A} is said to be **nonsingular;** if $\det(\mathbf{A}) = 0$, then \mathbf{A} is called a **singular** matrix.

Determinants

We assume that the student has computed 2×2 and 3×3 determinants in earlier courses. If $\mathbf{A} = [a_{ij}]$ is a 2×2 matrix, then its **determinant** $\det(\mathbf{A}) = |\mathbf{A}|$ is defined as

$$|\mathbf{A}| = \begin{vmatrix} a_{11} & a_{12} \\ a_{21} & a_{22} \end{vmatrix} = a_{11}a_{22} - a_{12}a_{21}.$$

Determinants of higher order may be defined by induction, as follows. If $\mathbf{A} = [a_{ij}]$ is an $n \times n$ matrix, let \mathbf{A}_{ij} denote the $(n - 1) \times (n - 1)$ matrix obtained from \mathbf{A} by deleting its ith row and its jth column. The *expansion* of the determinant $|\mathbf{A}|$ along its ith row is given by

$$|\mathbf{A}| = \sum_{j=1}^{n} (-1)^{i+j} a_{ij} |\mathbf{A}_{ij}| \qquad (i \text{ fixed}), \tag{20a}$$

and its expansion along its jth column is given by

$$|\mathbf{A}| = \sum_{i=1}^{n} (-1)^{i+j} a_{ij} |\mathbf{A}_{ij}| \qquad (j \text{ fixed}). \tag{20b}$$

It is shown in linear algebra that whichever row we use in Eq. (20a) and whichever column we use in Eq. (20b), the results are the same in all $2n$ cases. Hence $|\mathbf{A}|$ is well-defined by these formulas.

EXAMPLE 3 If

$$\mathbf{A} = \begin{bmatrix} 3 & 1 & -2 \\ 4 & 2 & 1 \\ -2 & 3 & 5 \end{bmatrix},$$

then the expansion of **A** along its second row is

$$|\mathbf{A}| = -4 \cdot \begin{vmatrix} 1 & -2 \\ 3 & 5 \end{vmatrix} + 2 \cdot \begin{vmatrix} 3 & -2 \\ -2 & 5 \end{vmatrix} - 1 \cdot \begin{vmatrix} 3 & 1 \\ -2 & 3 \end{vmatrix}$$

$$= -4 \cdot 11 + 2 \cdot 11 - 1 \cdot 11 = -33.$$

And the expansion of $|\mathbf{A}|$ along its third column is

$$|\mathbf{A}| = -2 \cdot \begin{vmatrix} 4 & 2 \\ -2 & 3 \end{vmatrix} - 1 \cdot \begin{vmatrix} 3 & 1 \\ -2 & 3 \end{vmatrix} + 5 \cdot \begin{vmatrix} 3 & 1 \\ 4 & 2 \end{vmatrix}$$

$$= -2 \cdot 16 - 1 \cdot 11 + 5 \cdot 2 = -33. \qquad \blacksquare$$

Calculators and computers are convenient for the calculation of higher-dimensional determinants and inverse matrices, but determinants and inverses of 2×2 matrices are easy to compute by hand. For instance, if the 2×2 matrix

$$\mathbf{A} = \begin{bmatrix} a & b \\ c & d \end{bmatrix}$$

has nonzero determinant $|\mathbf{A}| = ad - bc \neq 0$, then its inverse matrix is

$$\mathbf{A}^{-1} = \frac{1}{|\mathbf{A}|} \begin{bmatrix} d & -b \\ -c & a \end{bmatrix}. \tag{21}$$

Note that the matrix on the right-hand side of Eq. (21) is obtained from **A** by interchanging the diagonal elements and changing the signs of the off-diagonal elements.

EXAMPLE 4 If

$$A = \begin{bmatrix} 6 & 8 \\ 5 & 7 \end{bmatrix},$$

then $|\mathbf{A}| = 6 \cdot 7 - 5 \cdot 8 = 2$. Hence Eq. (21) gives

$$\mathbf{A}^{-1} = \frac{1}{2} \begin{bmatrix} 7 & -8 \\ -5 & 6 \end{bmatrix} = \begin{bmatrix} \frac{7}{2} & -4 \\ -\frac{5}{2} & 3 \end{bmatrix}.$$

You should pause to verify that

$$\mathbf{A}^{-1}\mathbf{A} = \begin{bmatrix} \frac{7}{2} & -4 \\ -\frac{5}{2} & 3 \end{bmatrix} \begin{bmatrix} 6 & 8 \\ 5 & 7 \end{bmatrix} = \begin{bmatrix} 1 & 0 \\ 0 & 1 \end{bmatrix}.$$

Matrix-Valued Functions

A **matrix-valued function,** or simply **matrix function,** is a matrix such as

$$\mathbf{x}(t) = \begin{bmatrix} x_1(t) \\ x_2(t) \\ \cdot \\ \cdot \\ \cdot \\ x_n(t) \end{bmatrix} \tag{22a}$$

or

$$\mathbf{A}(t) = \begin{bmatrix} a_{11}(t) & a_{12}(t) & \cdots & a_{1n}(t) \\ a_{21}(t) & a_{22}(t) & \cdots & a_{2n}(t) \\ \cdot & \cdot & & \cdot \\ \cdot & \cdot & & \cdot \\ \cdot & \cdot & & \cdot \\ a_{m1}(t) & a_{m2}(t) & \cdots & a_{mn}(t) \end{bmatrix}, \tag{22b}$$

in which each entry is a function of t. We say that the matrix function $\mathbf{A}(t)$ is **continuous** (or **differentiable**) at a point (or on an interval) if each of its elements has the same property. The **derivative** of a differentiable matrix function is defined by elementwise differentiation; that is,

$$\mathbf{A}'(t) = \frac{d\mathbf{A}}{dt} = \left[\frac{da_{ij}}{dt} \right]. \tag{23}$$

EXAMPLE 5 If

$$x(t) = \begin{bmatrix} t \\ t^2 \\ e^{-t} \end{bmatrix} \qquad \text{and} \qquad \mathbf{A}(t) = \begin{bmatrix} \sin t & 1 \\ t & \cos t \end{bmatrix},$$

then

$$\frac{d\mathbf{x}}{dt} = \begin{bmatrix} 1 \\ 2t \\ -e^{-t} \end{bmatrix} \qquad \text{and} \qquad \mathbf{A}'(t) = \begin{bmatrix} \cos t & 0 \\ 1 & -\sin t \end{bmatrix}. \qquad \blacksquare$$

The differentiation rules

$$\frac{d}{dt}(\mathbf{A} + \mathbf{B}) = \frac{d\mathbf{A}}{dt} + \frac{d\mathbf{B}}{dt} \tag{24}$$

and

$$\frac{d}{dt}(\mathbf{AB}) = \mathbf{A}\frac{d\mathbf{B}}{dt} + \frac{d\mathbf{A}}{dt}\mathbf{B} \tag{25}$$

follow readily by elementwise application of the analogous differentiation rules of elementary calculus for real-valued functions. If c is a (constant) real number and \mathbf{C} is a constant matrix, then

$$\frac{d}{dt}(c\mathbf{A}) = c\frac{d\mathbf{A}}{dt}, \qquad \frac{d}{dt}(\mathbf{CA}) = \mathbf{C}\frac{d\mathbf{A}}{dt}, \quad \text{and} \quad \frac{d}{dt}(\mathbf{AC}) = \frac{d\mathbf{A}}{dt}\mathbf{C}. \tag{26}$$

Because of the noncommutativity of matrix multiplication, it is important not to reverse the order of the factors in (25) and (26).

First-Order Linear Systems

The notation and terminology of matrices and vectors may seem rather elaborate when first encountered, but it is readily assimilated with practice. Our main use for matrix

notation will be the simplification of computations with systems of differential equations, especially those computations that would be burdensome in scalar notation.

We discuss here the general system of n first-order linear equations

$$x_1' = p_{11}(t)x_1 + p_{12}(t)x_2 + \cdots + p_{1n}(t)x_n + f_1(t)$$
$$x_2' = p_{21}(t)x_1 + p_{22}(t)x_2 + \cdots + p_{2n}(t)x_n + f_2(t)$$
▶ $$x_3' = p_{31}(t)x_1 + p_{32}(t)x_2 + \cdots + p_{3n}(t)x_n + f_3(t) \qquad (27)$$
$$\vdots$$
$$x_n' = p_{n1}(t)x_1 + p_{n2}(t)x_2 + \cdots + p_{nn}(t)x_n + f_n(t).$$

If we introduce the *coefficient matrix*

$$\mathbf{P}(t) = [p_{ij}(t)]$$

and the column vectors

$$\mathbf{x} = [x_i] \qquad \text{and} \qquad \mathbf{f}(t) = [f_i(t)],$$

then the system in (27) takes the form of a single matrix equation

▶ $$\frac{d\mathbf{x}}{dt} = \mathbf{P}(t)\mathbf{x} + \mathbf{f}(t). \qquad (28)$$

We will see that the general theory of the linear system in (27) closely parallels that of a single nth-order equation. The matrix notation used in Eq. (28) not only emphasizes this analogy, but also saves a great deal of space.

A **solution** of Eq. (28) on the open interval I is a column vector function $\mathbf{x}(t) = [x_i(t)]$ such that the component functions of \mathbf{x} satisfy the system in (27) identically on I. If the functions $p_{ij}(t)$ and $f_i(t)$ are all continuous on I, then Theorem 1 of Section 4.1 guarantees the existence on I of a unique solution $\mathbf{x}(t)$ satisfying preassigned initial conditions $\mathbf{x}(a) = \mathbf{b}$.

EXAMPLE 6 The first-order system

$$x_1' = 4x_1 - 3x_2$$
$$x_2' = 6x_1 - 7x_2$$

can be written as the single matrix equation

$$\frac{d\mathbf{x}}{dt} = \begin{bmatrix} 4 & -3 \\ 6 & -7 \end{bmatrix} \mathbf{x} = \mathbf{Px}.$$

To verify that the vector functions

$$\mathbf{x}_1(t) = \begin{bmatrix} 3e^{2t} \\ 2e^{2t} \end{bmatrix} \qquad \text{and} \qquad \mathbf{x}_2(t) = \begin{bmatrix} e^{-5t} \\ 3e^{-5t} \end{bmatrix}$$

are both solutions of the matrix differential equation with coefficient matrix \mathbf{P}, we need only calculate

$$\mathbf{Px}_1 = \begin{bmatrix} 4 & -3 \\ 6 & -7 \end{bmatrix} \begin{bmatrix} 3e^{2t} \\ 2e^{2t} \end{bmatrix} = \begin{bmatrix} 6e^{2t} \\ 4e^{2t} \end{bmatrix} = \mathbf{x}_1'.$$

and

$$\mathbf{Px}_2 = \begin{bmatrix} 4 & -3 \\ 6 & -7 \end{bmatrix} \begin{bmatrix} e^{-5t} \\ 3e^{-5t} \end{bmatrix} = \begin{bmatrix} -5e^{-5t} \\ -15e^{-5t} \end{bmatrix} = \mathbf{x}_2'. \qquad \blacksquare$$

To investigate the general nature of the solutions of Eq. (28), we consider first the **associated homogeneous equation**

$$\frac{d\mathbf{x}}{dt} = \mathbf{P}(t)\mathbf{x}, \tag{29}$$

which has the form shown in Eq. (28), but with $\mathbf{f}(t) \equiv \mathbf{0}$. We expect it to have n solutions $\mathbf{x}_1, \mathbf{x}_2, \ldots, \mathbf{x}_n$ that are independent in some appropriate sense, and such that every solution of Eq. (29) is a linear combination of these n particular solutions. Given n solutions $\mathbf{x}_1, \mathbf{x}_2, \ldots, \mathbf{x}_n$ of Eq. (29), let us write

$$\mathbf{x}_j(t) = \begin{bmatrix} x_{1j}(t) \\ \cdot \\ \cdot \\ \cdot \\ x_{ij}(t) \\ \cdot \\ \cdot \\ \cdot \\ x_{nj}(t) \end{bmatrix}. \tag{30}$$

Thus $x_{ij}(t)$ denotes the ith component of the vector $\mathbf{x}_j(t)$, so the second subscript refers to the vector function $\mathbf{x}_j(t)$, whereas the first subscript refers to a component of this function. Theorem 1 is analogous to Theorem 1 of Section 3.2.

THEOREM 1: Principle of Superposition

Let $\mathbf{x}_1, \mathbf{x}_2, \ldots, \mathbf{x}_n$ be n solutions of the homogeneous linear equation in (29) on the open interval I. If c_1, c_2, \ldots, c_n are constants, then the linear combination

$$\mathbf{x}(t) = c_1\mathbf{x}_1(t) + c_2\mathbf{x}_2(t) + \cdots + c_n\mathbf{x}_n(t) \tag{31}$$

is also a solution of Eq. (29) on I.

Proof: We know that $\mathbf{x}_i' = \mathbf{P}(t)\mathbf{x}_i$ for each i ($1 \leqq i \leqq n$), so it follows immediately that

$$\begin{aligned} \mathbf{x}' &= c_1\mathbf{x}_1' + c_2\mathbf{x}_2' + \cdots + c_n\mathbf{x}_n' \\ &= c_1\mathbf{P}(t)\mathbf{x}_1 + c_2\mathbf{P}(t)\mathbf{x}_2 + \cdots + c_n\mathbf{P}(t)\mathbf{x}_n \\ &= \mathbf{P}(t)(c_1\mathbf{x}_1 + c_2\mathbf{x}_2 + \cdots + c_n\mathbf{x}_n). \end{aligned}$$

That is, $\mathbf{x}' = \mathbf{P}(t)\mathbf{x}$, as desired. The remarkable simplicity of this proof demonstrates clearly one advantage of matrix notation. ∎

EXAMPLE 6
Continued

If \mathbf{x}_1 and \mathbf{x}_2 are the two solutions of

$$\frac{d\mathbf{x}}{dt} = \begin{bmatrix} 4 & -3 \\ 6 & -7 \end{bmatrix} \mathbf{x}$$

discussed in Example 6, then the linear combination

$$\mathbf{x}(t) = c_1\mathbf{x}_1(t) + c_2\mathbf{x}_2(t) = c_1 \begin{bmatrix} 3e^{2t} \\ 2e^{2t} \end{bmatrix} + c_2 \begin{bmatrix} e^{-5t} \\ 3e^{-5t} \end{bmatrix}$$

is also a solution. In scalar form with $\mathbf{x} = [x_1, \quad x_2]^T$, this gives the solution

$$x_1(t) = 3c_1e^{2t} + c_2e^{-5t}$$

$$x_2(t) = 2c_1e^{2t} + 3c_2e^{-5t},$$

which is equivalent to the general solution we found by the method of elimination in Example 2 of Section 4.2. ∎

Independence and General Solutions

Linear independence is defined in the same way for vector-valued functions as for real-valued functions (Section 3.2). The vector-valued functions $\mathbf{x}_1, \mathbf{x}_2, \ldots, \mathbf{x}_n$ are **linearly dependent** on the interval I provided that there exist constants c_1, c_2, \ldots, c_n *not all zero* such that

$$c_1\mathbf{x}_1(t) + c_2\mathbf{x}_2(t) + \cdots + c_n\mathbf{x}_n(t) = \mathbf{0} \tag{32}$$

for all t in I. Otherwise, they are **linearly independent.** Equivalently, they are linearly independent provided that no one of them is a linear combination of the others. For instance, the two solutions \mathbf{x}_1 and \mathbf{x}_2 of Example 6 are linearly independent because neither is a scalar multiple of the other—this is clear.

Just as in the case of a single nth-order equation, there is a Wronskian determinant that tells us whether or not n given solutions of the homogeneous equation in (29) are linearly dependent. If $\mathbf{x}_1, \mathbf{x}_2, \ldots, \mathbf{x}_n$ are such solutions, then their **Wronskian** is the $n \times n$ determinant

$$W = \begin{vmatrix} x_{11}(t) & x_{12}(t) & \cdots & x_{1n}(t) \\ x_{21}(t) & x_{22}(t) & \cdots & x_{2n}(t) \\ \cdot & \cdot & & \cdot \\ \cdot & \cdot & & \cdot \\ x_{n1}(t) & x_{n2}(t) & \cdots & x_{nn}(t) \end{vmatrix}, \tag{33}$$

using the notation in (30) for the components of the solutions. We may write either $W(t)$ or $W(\mathbf{x}_1, \mathbf{x}_2, \ldots, \mathbf{x}_n)$. Note that W is the determinant of the matrix that has as its *column* vectors the solutions $\mathbf{x}_1, \mathbf{x}_2, \ldots, \mathbf{x}_n$. Theorem 2 is analogous to Theorem 3 of Section 3.2. Moreover, its proof is essentially the same, with the definition of $W(\mathbf{x}_1, \mathbf{x}_2, \ldots, \mathbf{x}_n)$ in Eq. (33) substituted for the definition of the Wronskian of n solutions of a single nth-order equation (see Problems 42 through 44).

THEOREM 2: Wronskians of Solutions

Suppose that \mathbf{x}_1, \mathbf{x}_2, . . . , \mathbf{x}_n are n solutions of the homogeneous linear equation $\mathbf{x}' = \mathbf{P}(t)\mathbf{x}$ on an open interval I. Suppose also that $\mathbf{P}(t)$ is continuous on I. Let

$$W = W(\mathbf{x}_1, \mathbf{x}_2, \ldots, \mathbf{x}_n).$$

Then:

- If \mathbf{x}_1, \mathbf{x}_2, . . . , \mathbf{x}_n are linearly dependent on I, then $W \equiv 0$ on I.
- If \mathbf{x}_1, \mathbf{x}_2, . . . , \mathbf{x}_n are linearly independent on I, then $W \neq 0$ at each point of I.

Thus there are only two possibilities for solutions of homogeneous systems: Either $W \equiv 0$ on I, or $W = 0$ for *no* point of I. ∎

EXAMPLE 7 It is readily verified directly (as in Example 6) that

$$\mathbf{x}_1(t) = \begin{bmatrix} 2e^t \\ 2e^t \\ e^t \end{bmatrix}, \qquad \mathbf{x}_2(t) = \begin{bmatrix} 2e^{3t} \\ 0 \\ -e^{3t} \end{bmatrix}, \qquad \text{and} \qquad \mathbf{x}_3(t) = \begin{bmatrix} 2e^{5t} \\ -2e^{5t} \\ e^{5t} \end{bmatrix}$$

are solutions of the equation

$$\frac{d\mathbf{x}}{dt} = \begin{bmatrix} 3 & -2 & 0 \\ -1 & 3 & -2 \\ 0 & -1 & 3 \end{bmatrix} \mathbf{x}. \tag{34}$$

The Wronskian of these solutions is

$$W = \begin{vmatrix} 2e^t & 2e^{3t} & 2e^{5t} \\ 2e^t & 0 & -2e^{5t} \\ e^t & -e^{3t} & e^{5t} \end{vmatrix} = e^{9t} \begin{vmatrix} 2 & 2 & 2 \\ 2 & 0 & -2 \\ 1 & -1 & 1 \end{vmatrix} = -16e^{9t},$$

which is never zero. Hence Theorem 2 implies that the solutions \mathbf{x}_1, \mathbf{x}_2, and \mathbf{x}_3 are linearly independent (on any open interval). ∎

Theorem 3 is analogous to Theorem 4 of Section 3.2. It says that **the general solution** of the *homogeneous* $n \times n$ system $\mathbf{x}' = \mathbf{P}(t)\mathbf{x}$ is a linear combination

$$\mathbf{x} = c_1\mathbf{x}_1 + c_2\mathbf{x}_2 + \cdots + c_n\mathbf{x}_n \tag{35}$$

of any n given linearly independent solutions \mathbf{x}_1, \mathbf{x}_2, . . . , \mathbf{x}_n.

THEOREM 3: General Solutions of Homogeneous Systems

Let \mathbf{x}_1, \mathbf{x}_2, . . . , \mathbf{x}_n be n linearly independent solutions of the homogeneous linear equation $\mathbf{x}' = \mathbf{P}(t)\mathbf{x}$ on an open interval I where $\mathbf{P}(t)$ is continuous. If $\mathbf{x}(t)$ is any solution whatsoever of the equation $\mathbf{x}' = \mathbf{P}(t)\mathbf{x}$ on I, then there exist numbers c_1,

c_2, \ldots, c_n such that

$$\mathbf{x}(t) = c_1\mathbf{x}_1(t) + c_2\mathbf{x}_2(t) + \cdots + c_n\mathbf{x}_n(t) \tag{35}$$

for all t in I.

Proof: Let a be a fixed point of I. We show first that there exist numbers c_1, c_2, \ldots, c_n such that the solution

$$\mathbf{y}(t) = c_1\mathbf{x}_1(t) + c_2\mathbf{x}_1(t) + \cdots + c_n\mathbf{x}_n(t) \tag{36}$$

has the same initial values at $t = a$ as does the given solution $\mathbf{x}(t)$; that is, such that

$$c_1\mathbf{x}_1(a) + c_2\mathbf{x}_2(a) + \cdots + c_n\mathbf{x}_n(a) = \mathbf{x}(a). \tag{37}$$

Let $\mathbf{X}(t)$ be the $n \times n$ matrix with column vectors $\mathbf{x}_1(t), \mathbf{x}_2(t), \ldots, \mathbf{x}_n(t)$, and let \mathbf{c} be the column vector with components c_1, c_2, \ldots, c_n. Then Eq.(37) may be written in the form

$$\mathbf{X}(a)\mathbf{c} = \mathbf{x}(a). \tag{38}$$

The Wronskian determinant $W(a) = |\mathbf{X}(a)|$ is nonzero because the solutions \mathbf{x}_1, $\mathbf{x}_2, \ldots, \mathbf{x}_n$ are linearly independent. Hence the matrix $\mathbf{X}(a)$ has an inverse matrix $\mathbf{X}(a)^{-1}$. Therefore the vector $\mathbf{c} = \mathbf{X}(a)^{-1}\mathbf{x}(a)$ satisfies Eq. (38), as desired.

Finally, note that the given solution $\mathbf{x}(t)$ and the solution $\mathbf{y}(t)$ of Eq. (36)—with the values of c_i determined by the equation $\mathbf{c} = \mathbf{X}(a)^{-1}\mathbf{x}(a)$—have the same initial values (at $t = a$). It follows from the existence-uniqueness theorem of Section 4.1 that $\mathbf{x}(t) = \mathbf{y}(t)$ for all t in I. This establishes Eq. (35). ∎

Remark: Every $n \times n$ system $\mathbf{x}' = \mathbf{P}(t)\mathbf{x}$ with continuous coefficient matrix does have a set of n linearly independent solutions $\mathbf{x}_1, \mathbf{x}_2, \ldots, \mathbf{x}_n$ as in the hypotheses of Theorem 3. It suffices to choose for $\mathbf{x}_j(t)$ the unique solution such that

$$\mathbf{x}_j(a) = \begin{bmatrix} 0 \\ 0 \\ 0 \\ \cdot \\ \cdot \\ \cdot \\ 0 \\ 1 \\ 0 \\ \cdot \\ \cdot \\ \cdot \\ 0 \end{bmatrix} \longleftarrow \text{position } j$$

—that is, the column vector with all elements zero except for a 1 in row j. (In other words, $\mathbf{x}_j(a)$ is merely the jth column of the identity matrix.) Then

$$W(\mathbf{x}_1, \mathbf{x}_2, \ldots, \mathbf{x}_n)\big|_{t=a} = |\mathbf{I}| = 1 \neq 0,$$

so the solutions $\mathbf{x}_1, \mathbf{x}_2, \ldots, \mathbf{x}_n$ are linearly independent by Theorem 2. How actually to find these solutions explicitly is another matter—one that we address in Section 5.2 (for the case of constant coefficient matrices).

Initial Value Problems and Elementary Row Operations

The general solution in Eq. (35) of the homogeneous linear system $\mathbf{x}' = \mathbf{P}(t)\mathbf{x}$ can be written in the form

$$\mathbf{x}(t) = \mathbf{X}(t)\mathbf{c}, \tag{39}$$

where

$$\mathbf{X}(t) = [\mathbf{x}_1(t) \quad \mathbf{x}_2(t) \quad \cdots \quad \mathbf{x}_n(t)] \tag{40}$$

is the $n \times n$ matrix whose *column vectors* are the linearly independent solutions \mathbf{x}_1, $\mathbf{x}_2, \ldots, \mathbf{x}_n$, and $\mathbf{c} = [c_1 \ c_2 \ \cdots \ c_n]^T$ is the vector of coefficients in the linear combination

$$\mathbf{x}(t) = c_1\mathbf{x}_1(t) + c_2\mathbf{x}_2(t) + \cdots + c_n\mathbf{x}_n(t). \tag{35}$$

Suppose now that we wish to solve the *initial value problem*

$$\blacktriangleright \qquad \frac{d\mathbf{x}}{dt} = \mathbf{P}\mathbf{x}, \qquad \mathbf{x}(a) = \mathbf{b}, \tag{41}$$

where the initial vector $\mathbf{b} = [b_1 \ b_2 \ \cdots \ b_n]^T$ is given. Then, according to Eq. (39), it suffices to solve the system

$$\mathbf{X}(a)\mathbf{c} = \mathbf{b} \tag{42}$$

to find the coefficients c_1, c_2, \ldots, c_n in (35).

We therefore review briefly the elementary technique of *row reduction* to solve an $n \times n$ *algebraic* linear system

$$\begin{aligned}
a_{11}x_1 + a_{12}x_2 + \cdots + a_{1n}x_n &= b_1 \\
a_{21}x_1 + a_{22}x_2 + \cdots + a_{2n}x_n &= b_2 \\
&\vdots \\
a_{n1}x_1 + a_{n2}x_2 + \cdots + a_{nn}x_n &= b_n
\end{aligned} \tag{43}$$

with nonsingular coefficient matrix $\mathbf{A} = [a_{ij}]$, constant vector $\mathbf{b} = [b_i]$, and unknowns x_1, x_2, \ldots, x_n. The basic idea is to transform the system in (43) into the simpler *upper triangular form*

$$\begin{aligned}
\overline{a}_{11}x_1 + \overline{a}_{12}x_2 + \cdots + \overline{a}_{1n}x_n &= \overline{b}_1 \\
\overline{a}_{22}x_2 + \cdots + \overline{a}_{2n}x_n &= \overline{b}_2 \\
&\vdots \\
\overline{a}_{nn}x_n &= \overline{b}_n
\end{aligned} \tag{44}$$

in which only the unknowns $x_j, x_{j+1}, \ldots, x_n$ appear explicitly in the jth equation ($j = 1, 2, \ldots, n$). The transformed system is then easily solved by the process of *back substitution*. First the last equation in (44) is solved for x_n, then the next-to-last is solved for x_{n-1}, and so forth, until the first equation is finally solved for x_1.

The transformation of (43) into upper triangular form is most easily described in

terms of elementary row operations on the *augmented coefficient matrix*

$$[\mathbf{A} \mathbin{\vdots} \mathbf{b}] = \begin{bmatrix} a_{11} & a_{12} & \cdots & a_{1n} & \vdots & b_1 \\ a_{21} & a_{22} & \cdots & a_{2n} & \vdots & b_2 \\ \cdot & \cdot & & \cdot & \vdots & \cdot \\ \cdot & \cdot & & \cdot & \vdots & \cdot \\ \cdot & \cdot & & \cdot & \vdots & \cdot \\ a_{n1} & a_{n2} & \cdots & a_{nn} & \vdots & b_n \end{bmatrix} \tag{45}$$

that is obtained by adjoining the vector \mathbf{b} to the matrix \mathbf{A} as an additional column. The admissible **elementary row operations** are of the following three types:

1. Multiply any (single) row of the matrix by a nonzero constant.

2. Interchange any two rows of the matrix.

3. Subtract a constant multiple of one row from any other row.

The goal is to use a sequence of such operations (one by one, in turn) to transform $[\mathbf{A} \mathbin{\vdots} \mathbf{b}]$ into an upper triangular matrix, one that has only zeros beneath its principal diagonal. This upper triangular augmented coefficient matrix then corresponds to an upper triangular system as in (44). The process of transforming $[\mathbf{A} \mathbin{\vdots} \mathbf{b}]$ is carried out one column at a time, from left to right, as in the next example.

EXAMPLE 8 Use the solution vectors given in Example 7 to solve the initial value problem

$$\frac{d\mathbf{x}}{dt} = \begin{bmatrix} 3 & -2 & 0 \\ -1 & 3 & -2 \\ 0 & -1 & 3 \end{bmatrix} \mathbf{x}, \qquad \mathbf{x}(0) = \begin{bmatrix} 0 \\ 2 \\ 6 \end{bmatrix}. \tag{46}$$

Solution: It follows from Theorem 3 that the linear combination

$$\mathbf{x}(t) = c_1 \mathbf{x}_1(t) + c_2 \mathbf{x}_2(t) + c_3 \mathbf{x}_3(t)$$

$$= c_1 \begin{bmatrix} 2e^t \\ 2e^t \\ e^t \end{bmatrix} + c_2 \begin{bmatrix} 2e^{3t} \\ 0 \\ -e^{3t} \end{bmatrix} + c_3 \begin{bmatrix} 2e^{5t} \\ -2e^{5t} \\ e^{5t} \end{bmatrix}$$

is a general solution of the 3×3 linear system in (46). In scalar form, this gives the general solution

$$x_1(t) = 2c_1 e^t + 2c_2 e^{3t} + 2c_3 e^{5t}$$
$$x_2(t) = 2c_1 e^t \qquad\qquad - 2c_3 e^{5t}$$
$$x_3(t) = c_1 e^t - c_2 e^{3t} + c_3 e^{5t}.$$

We seek the particular solution satisfying the initial conditions

$$x_1(0) = 0, \qquad x_2(0) = 2, \qquad x_3(0) = 6.$$

When we substitute these values in the three scalar equations above, we get the algebraic linear system

$$2c_1 + 2c_2 + 2c_3 = 0$$
$$2c_2 \qquad - 2c_3 = 2$$
$$c_1 - c_2 + c_3 = 6$$

with augmented coefficient matrix

$$\left[\begin{array}{ccc|c} 2 & 2 & 2 & 0 \\ 2 & 0 & -2 & 2 \\ 1 & -1 & 1 & 6 \end{array}\right].$$

Multiplication of each of the first two rows by $\frac{1}{2}$ gives

$$\left[\begin{array}{ccc|c} 1 & 1 & 1 & 0 \\ 1 & 0 & -1 & 1 \\ 1 & -1 & 1 & 6 \end{array}\right],$$

then subtraction of the first row both from the second row and from the third row gives the matrix

$$\left[\begin{array}{ccc|c} 1 & 1 & 1 & 0 \\ 0 & -1 & -2 & 1 \\ 0 & -2 & 0 & 6 \end{array}\right].$$

The first column of this matrix now has the desired form.

Now we multiply the second row by -1, then add twice the result to the third row. Thereby we get the upper triangular augmented coefficient matrix

$$\left[\begin{array}{ccc|c} 1 & 1 & 1 & 0 \\ 0 & 1 & 2 & -1 \\ 0 & 0 & 4 & 4 \end{array}\right]$$

that corresponds to the transformed system

$$
\begin{aligned}
c_1 + c_2 + c_3 &= 0 \\
c_2 + 2c_3 &= -1 \\
4c_3 &= 4.
\end{aligned}
$$

We finally solve in turn for $c_3 = 1$, $c_2 = -3$, and $c_1 = 2$. Thus the desired particular solution is given by

$$\mathbf{x}(t) = 2\mathbf{x}_1(t) - 3\mathbf{x}_2(t) + \mathbf{x}_3(t) = \begin{array}{l} 4e^t - 6e^{3t} + 2e^{5t} \\ 4e^t \qquad\quad - 2e^{5t} \\ 2e^t + 3e^{3t} + e^{5t} \end{array}.$$

Nonhomogeneous Solutions

We finally turn our attention to a *nonhomogeneous* linear system of the form

$$\blacktriangleright \qquad \frac{d\mathbf{x}}{dt} = \mathbf{P}(t)\mathbf{x} + \mathbf{f}(t). \tag{47}$$

The following theorem is analogous to Theorem 5 of Section 3.2 and is proved in precisely the same way, substituting the preceding theorems in this section for the analo-

gous theorems of Section 3.2. In brief, Theorem 4 means that the general solution of Eq. (47) has the form

$$\blacktriangleright \qquad \mathbf{x}(t) = \mathbf{x}_c(t) + \mathbf{x}_p(t), \qquad (48)$$

where $\mathbf{x}_p(t)$ is a single particular solution of Eq. (47) and the **complementary function** $\mathbf{x}_c(t)$ is a general solution of the associated homogeneous equation $\mathbf{x}' = \mathbf{P}(t)\mathbf{x}$.

THEOREM 4: Solutions of Nonhomogeneous Systems

Let \mathbf{x}_p be a particular solution of the nonhomogeneous linear equation in (47) on an open interval I on which the functions $\mathbf{P}(t)$ and $\mathbf{f}(t)$ are continuous. Let \mathbf{x}_1, \mathbf{x}_2, . . . , \mathbf{x}_n be linearly independent solutions of the associated homogeneous equation on I. If $\mathbf{x}(t)$ is any solution whatsoever of Eq. (47) on I, then there exist numbers c_1, c_2, . . . , c_n such that

$$\blacktriangleright \qquad \mathbf{x}(t) = c_1\mathbf{x}_1(t) + c_2\mathbf{x}_2(t) + \cdots + c_n\mathbf{x}_n(t) + \mathbf{x}_p(t) \qquad (49)$$

for all t in I. ∎

Thus finding a general solution of a nonhomogeneous linear system involves two separate steps:

1. Finding the general solution $\mathbf{x}_c(t)$ of the associated homogeneous system;
2. Finding a single particular solution $\mathbf{x}_p(t)$ of the nonhomogeneous system.

The sum $\mathbf{x}(t) = \mathbf{x}_c(t) + \mathbf{x}_p(t)$ will then be a general solution of the nonhomogeneous system.

EXAMPLE 9 The nonhomogeneous linear system

$$
\begin{aligned}
x_1' &= 3x_1 - 2x_2 - 9t + 13 \\
x_2' &= -x_1 + 3x_2 - 2x_3 + 7t - 15 \\
x_3' &= - x_2 + 3x_3 - 6t + 7
\end{aligned}
$$

is of the form in (47) with

$$
\mathbf{P}(t) = \begin{bmatrix} 3 & -2 & 0 \\ -1 & 3 & -2 \\ 0 & -1 & 3 \end{bmatrix}, \qquad \mathbf{f}(t) = \begin{bmatrix} -9t + 13 \\ 7t - 15 \\ -6t + 7 \end{bmatrix}.
$$

In Example 7 we saw that a general solution of the associated homogeneous linear system

$$
\frac{d\mathbf{x}}{dt} = \begin{bmatrix} 3 & -2 & 0 \\ -1 & 3 & -2 \\ 0 & -1 & 3 \end{bmatrix} \mathbf{x}
$$

is given by

$$\mathbf{x}_c(t) = \begin{bmatrix} 2c_1e^t + 2c_2e^{3t} + 2c_3e^{5t} \\ 2c_1e^t \qquad - 2c_3e^{5t} \\ c_1e^t - c_2e^{3t} + c_3e^{5t} \end{bmatrix},$$

and we can verify by substitution that the function

$$\mathbf{x}_p(t) = \begin{bmatrix} 3t \\ 5 \\ 2t \end{bmatrix}$$

(found using a computer algebra system) is a particular solution of the original nonhomogeneous system. Consequently, Theorem 4 implies that a general solution of the nonhomogeneous system is given by

$$\mathbf{x}(t) = \mathbf{x}_c(t) + \mathbf{x}_p(t);$$

that is, by

$$x_1(t) = 2c_1e^t + 2c_2e^{3t} + 2c_3e^{5t} + 3t$$
$$x_2(t) = 2c_1e^t \qquad - 2c_3e^{5t} + 5$$
$$x_3(t) = c_1e^t - c_2e^{3t} + c_3e^{5t} + 2t.$$

5.1 Problems

1. Let

$$\mathbf{A} = \begin{bmatrix} 2 & -3 \\ 4 & 7 \end{bmatrix} \quad \text{and} \quad \mathbf{B} = \begin{bmatrix} 3 & -4 \\ 5 & 1 \end{bmatrix}.$$

Find (a) $2\mathbf{A} + 3\mathbf{B}$; (b) $3\mathbf{A} - 2\mathbf{B}$; (c) \mathbf{AB}; (d) \mathbf{BA}.

2. Verify that (a) $\mathbf{A(BC)} = \mathbf{(AB)C}$ and that (b) $\mathbf{A(B + C)} = \mathbf{AB} + \mathbf{AC}$, where \mathbf{A} and \mathbf{B} are the matrices given in Problem 1 and

$$\mathbf{C} = \begin{bmatrix} 0 & 2 \\ 3 & -1 \end{bmatrix}.$$

3. Find \mathbf{AB} and \mathbf{BA} given

$$\mathbf{A} = \begin{bmatrix} 2 & 0 & -1 \\ 3 & -4 & 5 \end{bmatrix} \quad \text{and} \quad \mathbf{B} = \begin{bmatrix} 1 & 3 \\ -7 & 0 \\ 3 & -2 \end{bmatrix}.$$

4. Let \mathbf{A} and \mathbf{B} be the matrices given in Problem 3 and let

$$\mathbf{x} = \begin{bmatrix} 2t \\ e^{-t} \end{bmatrix} \quad \text{and} \quad \mathbf{y} = \begin{bmatrix} t^2 \\ \sin t \\ \cos t \end{bmatrix}.$$

Find \mathbf{Ay} and \mathbf{Bx}. Are the products \mathbf{Ax} and \mathbf{By} defined? Explain your answer.

5. Let

$$\mathbf{A} = \begin{bmatrix} 3 & 2 & -1 \\ 0 & 4 & 3 \\ -5 & 2 & 7 \end{bmatrix} \quad \text{and} \quad \mathbf{B} = \begin{bmatrix} 0 & -3 & 2 \\ 1 & 4 & -3 \\ 2 & 5 & -1 \end{bmatrix}.$$

Find (a) $7\mathbf{A} + 4\mathbf{B}$; (b) $3\mathbf{A} - 5\mathbf{B}$; (c) \mathbf{AB}; (d) \mathbf{BA}; (e) $\mathbf{A} - t\mathbf{I}$.

6. Let

$$\mathbf{A}_1 = \begin{bmatrix} 2 & 1 \\ -3 & 2 \end{bmatrix}, \quad \mathbf{A}_2 = \begin{bmatrix} 1 & 3 \\ -1 & -2 \end{bmatrix}, \quad \mathbf{B} = \begin{bmatrix} 2 & 4 \\ 1 & 2 \end{bmatrix}.$$

(a) Show that $A_1B = A_2B$ and note that $A_1 \neq A_2$. Thus the cancellation law does not hold for matrices; that is, if $A_1B = A_2B$ and $B \neq 0$, it does not follow that $A_1 = A_2$. (b) Let $A = A_1 - A_2$ and show that $AB = 0$. Thus the product of two nonzero matrices may be the zero matrix.

7. Compute the determinants of the matrices A and B in Problem 6. Are your results consistent with the theorem to the effect that

$$\det(AB) = [\det(A)] \cdot [\det(B)]$$

for any two square matrices A and B of the same order?

8. Suppose that A and B are the matrices of Problem 5. Verify that $\det(AB) = \det(BA)$.

In Problems 9 and 10, verify the product law for differentiation, $(AB)' = A'B + AB'$.

9. $A(t) = \begin{bmatrix} t & 2t-1 \\ t^3 & \dfrac{1}{t} \end{bmatrix}$ and $B(t) = \begin{bmatrix} 1-t & 1+t \\ 3t^2 & 4t^3 \end{bmatrix}$

10. $A(t) = \begin{bmatrix} e^t & t & t^2 \\ -t & 0 & 2 \\ 8t & -1 & t^3 \end{bmatrix}$ and $B(t) = \begin{bmatrix} 3 \\ 2e^{-t} \\ 3t \end{bmatrix}$

In Problems 11 through 20, write the given system in the form $x' = P(t)x + f(t)$.

11. $x' = -3y$
$y' = 3x$

12. $x' = 3x - 2y$
$y' = 2x + y$

13. $x' = 2x + 4y + 3e^t$
$y' = 5x - y - t^2$

14. $x' = tx - e^ty + \cos t$
$y' = e^{-t}x + t^2y - \sin t$

15. $x' = y + z$
$y' = z + x$
$z' = x + y$

16. $x' = 2x - 3y$
$y' = x + y + 2z$
$z' = 5y - 7z$

17. $x' = 3x - 4y + z + t$
$y' = x - 3z + t^2$
$z' = 6y - 7z + t^3$

18. $x' = tx - y + e^tz$
$y' = 2x + t^2y - z$
$z' = e^{-t}x + 3ty + t^3z$

19. $x'_1 = x_2$
$x'_2 = 2x_3$
$x'_3 = 3x_4$
$x'_4 = 4x_1$

20. $x'_1 = x_2 + x_3 + 1$
$x'_2 = x_3 + x_4 + t$
$x'_3 = x_1 + x_4 + t^2$
$x'_4 = x_1 + x_2 + t^3$

In Problems 21 through 30, first verify that the given vectors are solutions of the given system. Then use the Wronskian to show that they are linearly independent. Finally, write the general solution of the system.

21. $x' = \begin{bmatrix} 4 & 2 \\ -3 & -1 \end{bmatrix} x; \quad x_1 = \begin{bmatrix} 2e^t \\ -3e^t \end{bmatrix}, \quad x_2 = \begin{bmatrix} e^{2t} \\ -e^{2t} \end{bmatrix}$

22. $x' = \begin{bmatrix} -3 & 2 \\ -3 & 4 \end{bmatrix} x; \quad x_1 = \begin{bmatrix} e^{3t} \\ 3e^{3t} \end{bmatrix}, \quad x_2 = \begin{bmatrix} 2e^{-2t} \\ e^{-2t} \end{bmatrix}$

23. $x' = \begin{bmatrix} 3 & -1 \\ 5 & -3 \end{bmatrix} x; \quad x_1 = e^{2t}\begin{bmatrix} 1 \\ 1 \end{bmatrix}, \quad x_2 = e^{-2t}\begin{bmatrix} 1 \\ 5 \end{bmatrix}$

24. $x' = \begin{bmatrix} 4 & 1 \\ -2 & 1 \end{bmatrix} x; \quad x_1 = e^{3t}\begin{bmatrix} 1 \\ -1 \end{bmatrix}, \quad x_2 = e^{2t}\begin{bmatrix} 2 \\ -1 \end{bmatrix}$

25. $x' = \begin{bmatrix} 4 & -3 \\ 6 & -7 \end{bmatrix} x; \quad x_1 = \begin{bmatrix} 3e^{2t} \\ 2e^{2t} \end{bmatrix}, \quad x_2 = \begin{bmatrix} e^{-5t} \\ 3e^{-5t} \end{bmatrix}$

26. $x' = \begin{bmatrix} 3 & -2 & 0 \\ -1 & 3 & -2 \\ 0 & -1 & 3 \end{bmatrix} x; \quad x_1 = e^t\begin{bmatrix} 2 \\ 2 \\ 1 \end{bmatrix},$

$x_2 = e^{3t}\begin{bmatrix} -2 \\ 0 \\ 1 \end{bmatrix}, \quad x_3 = e^{5t}\begin{bmatrix} 2 \\ -2 \\ 1 \end{bmatrix}$

27. $x' = \begin{bmatrix} 0 & 1 & 1 \\ 1 & 0 & 1 \\ 1 & 1 & 0 \end{bmatrix} x; \quad x_1 = e^{2t}\begin{bmatrix} 1 \\ 1 \\ 1 \end{bmatrix},$

$x_2 = e^{-t}\begin{bmatrix} 1 \\ 0 \\ -1 \end{bmatrix}, \quad x_3 = e^{-t}\begin{bmatrix} 0 \\ 1 \\ -1 \end{bmatrix}$

28. $x' = \begin{bmatrix} 1 & 2 & 1 \\ 6 & -1 & 0 \\ -1 & -2 & -1 \end{bmatrix} x; \quad x_1 = \begin{bmatrix} 1 \\ 6 \\ -13 \end{bmatrix},$

$x_2 = e^{3t}\begin{bmatrix} 2 \\ 3 \\ -2 \end{bmatrix}, \quad x_3 = e^{-4t}\begin{bmatrix} -1 \\ 2 \\ 1 \end{bmatrix}$

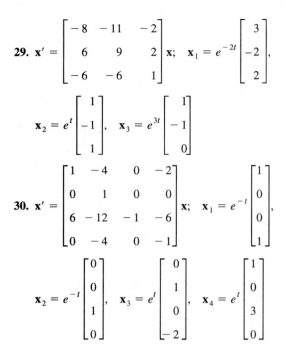

29. $\mathbf{x}' = \begin{bmatrix} -8 & -11 & -2 \\ 6 & 9 & 2 \\ -6 & -6 & 1 \end{bmatrix} \mathbf{x}; \quad \mathbf{x}_1 = e^{-2t} \begin{bmatrix} 3 \\ -2 \\ 2 \end{bmatrix},$

$\mathbf{x}_2 = e^{t} \begin{bmatrix} 1 \\ -1 \\ 1 \end{bmatrix}, \quad \mathbf{x}_3 = e^{3t} \begin{bmatrix} 1 \\ -1 \\ 0 \end{bmatrix}$

30. $\mathbf{x}' = \begin{bmatrix} 1 & -4 & 0 & -2 \\ 0 & 1 & 0 & 0 \\ 6 & -12 & -1 & -6 \\ 0 & -4 & 0 & -1 \end{bmatrix} \mathbf{x}; \quad \mathbf{x}_1 = e^{-t} \begin{bmatrix} 1 \\ 0 \\ 0 \\ 1 \end{bmatrix},$

$\mathbf{x}_2 = e^{-t} \begin{bmatrix} 0 \\ 0 \\ 1 \\ 0 \end{bmatrix}, \quad \mathbf{x}_3 = e^{t} \begin{bmatrix} 0 \\ 1 \\ 0 \\ -2 \end{bmatrix}, \quad \mathbf{x}_4 = e^{t} \begin{bmatrix} 1 \\ 0 \\ 3 \\ 0 \end{bmatrix}$

In Problems 31 through 40, find a particular solution of the indicated linear system that satisfies the given initial conditions.

31. The system of Problem 22: $x_1(0) = 0, \quad x_2(0) = 5$

32. The system of Problem 23: $x_1(0) = 5, \quad x_2(0) = -3$

33. The system of Problem 24: $x_1(0) = 11, \quad x_2(0) = -7$

34. The system of Problem 25: $x_1(0) = 8, \quad x_2(0) = 0$

35. The system of Problem 26: $x_1(0) = 0, \quad x_2(0) = 0,$
$x_3(0) = 4$

36. The system of Problem 27: $x_1(0) = 10, \quad x_2(0) = 12,$
$x_3(0) = -1$

37. The system of Problem 29: $x_1(0) = 1, \quad x_2(0) = 2,$
$x_3(0) = 3$

38. The system of Problem 29: $x_1(0) = 5, \quad x_2(0) = -7,$
$x_3(0) = 11$

39. The system of Problem 30:
$x_1(0) = x_2(0) = x_3(0) = x_4(0) = 1$

40. The system of Problem 30: $x_1(0) = 1, \quad x_2(0) = 3,$
$x_3(0) = 5, \quad x_4(0) = 7$

41. (a) Show that the vector functions

$$\mathbf{x}_1(t) = \begin{bmatrix} t \\ t^2 \end{bmatrix} \quad \text{and} \quad \mathbf{x}_2 = \begin{bmatrix} t^2 \\ t^3 \end{bmatrix}$$

are linearly independent on the real line. (b) Why does it follow from Theorem 2 that there is *no* continuous matrix $\mathbf{P}(t)$ such that \mathbf{x}_1 and \mathbf{x}_2 are both solutions of $\mathbf{x}' = \mathbf{P}(t)\mathbf{x}$?

42. Suppose that one of the vector functions

$$\mathbf{x}_1(t) = \begin{bmatrix} x_{11}(t) \\ x_{21}(t) \end{bmatrix} \quad \text{and} \quad \mathbf{x}_2(t) = \begin{bmatrix} x_{12}(t) \\ x_{22}(t) \end{bmatrix}$$

is a constant multiple of the other on the open interval I. Show that their Wronskian $W(t) = |[x_{ij}(t)]|$ must vanish identically on I. This proves part (a) of Theorem 2 in the case $n = 2$.

43. Suppose that the vectors $\mathbf{x}_1(t)$ and $\mathbf{x}_2(t)$ of Problem 42 are solutions of the equation $\mathbf{x}' = \mathbf{P}(t)\mathbf{x}$, where the 2×2 matrix $\mathbf{P}(t)$ is continuous on the open interval I. Show that if there exists a point a of I at which their Wronskian $W(a)$ is zero, then there exist numbers c_1 and c_2 not both zero such that $c_1\mathbf{x}_1(a) + c_2\mathbf{x}_2(a) = \mathbf{0}$. Then conclude from the uniqueness of solutions of the equation $\mathbf{x}' = \mathbf{P}(t)\mathbf{x}$ that

$$c_1\mathbf{x}_1(t) + c_2\mathbf{x}_2(t) = \mathbf{0}$$

for all t in I; that is, that \mathbf{x}_1 and \mathbf{x}_2 are linearly dependent. This proves part (b) of Theorem 2 in the case $n = 2$.

44. Generalize Problems 42 and 43 to prove Theorem 2 for n an arbitrary positive integer.

45. Let $\mathbf{x}_1(t), \mathbf{x}_2(t), \ldots, \mathbf{x}_n(t)$ be vector functions whose ith components (for some fixed i) $x_{i1}(t), x_{i2}(t), \ldots, x_{in}(t)$ are linearly independent real-valued functions. Conclude that the vector functions are themselves linearly independent.

5.1 Computing Projects

Calculations with numerical matrices of order greater than 3 are most frequently done with the aid of calculators or computers. For instance, recall that in Example 8 we needed to solve the linear system

$$2c_1 + 2c_2 + 2c_3 = 0$$
$$2c_1 \quad\quad\; - 2c_3 = 2$$
$$c_1 - c_2 + c_3 = 6.$$

Writing this system in matrix notation $\mathbf{Ac} = \mathbf{b}$ and working with a TI-85 calculator, for instance, we would store the 3×3 coefficient matrix \mathbf{A} and the column vector \mathbf{b} with the commands

```
[[2,2,2] [2,0,-2] [1,-1,1]] → A
[[0] [2] [6]] → b
```

in which each matrix and each of its successive rows in enclosed within square brackets. Then we calculate and store the solution $\mathbf{c} = \mathbf{A}^{-1}\mathbf{b}$ with the command

```
A⁻¹*b → c
```

which yields the result

```
[[2 ]
[-3]
[1 ]]
```

Thus $c_1 = 2$, $c_2 = -3$, and $c_3 = 1$, as we found using elementary row operations in Example 8.

Matrix notation in a computational system such as *Maple, Mathematica,* or MATLAB is similar. To carry out the same computation using *Mathematica,* for instance, we would enter the commands

```
A = { {2, 2, 2}, {2, 0, -2}, {1, -1, 1} };
b = { {0}, {2}, {6} };
c = Inverse[A] . b
{{2},{-3},{1}}
```

Project A

To practice simple matrix algebra with whatever calculator or computer system is available, you might begin by defining a square matrix \mathbf{A}. Then calculate its inverse matrix \mathbf{B} and check that the matrix product \mathbf{AB} is the identity matrix. Do this with several square matrices of different dimensions. Most calculators and computer algebra systems will produce an error message if you request the inverse of a singular matrix. In this case *Mathematica* reports

```
LinearSolve::nosol: Linear equation encountered
which has no solution.
```

And the TI-85 reports

```
ERROR 03 SINGULAR MAT
```

Project B

Use matrix algebra as indicated above (for the computations of Example 8) to solve Problems 31 through 40 of this section.

5.2 The Eigenvalue Method for Homogeneous Systems

We now introduce a powerful alternative to the method of elimination for constructing the general solution of a *homogeneous* first-order linear system with *constant* coefficients,

$$
\begin{aligned}
x'_1 &= a_{11}x_1 + a_{12}x_2 + \cdots + a_{1n}x_n \\
x'_2 &= a_{21}x_1 + a_{22}x_2 + \cdots + a_{2n}x_n \\
&\;\;\vdots \\
x'_n &= a_{n1}x_1 + a_{n2}x_2 + \cdots + a_{nn}x_n.
\end{aligned}
\tag{1}
$$

By Theorem 3 of Section 5.1, we know that it suffices to find n linearly independent solution vectors $\mathbf{x}_1, \mathbf{x}_2, \ldots, \mathbf{x}_n$; the linear combination

$$
\blacktriangleright \qquad \mathbf{x}(t) = c_1\mathbf{x}_1(t) + c_2\mathbf{x}_2(t) + \cdots + c_n\mathbf{x}_n(t)
\tag{2}
$$

with arbitrary coefficients will then be a general solution of the system in (1).

To search for the n needed linearly independent solution vectors, we proceed by analogy with the characteristic root method for solving a single homogeneous linear equation with constant coefficients (Section 3.3). It is reasonable to anticipate solution vectors of the form

$$
\mathbf{x}(t) =
\begin{bmatrix} x_1 \\ x_2 \\ x_3 \\ \vdots \\ x_n \end{bmatrix}
=
\begin{bmatrix} v_1 e^{\lambda t} \\ v_2 e^{\lambda t} \\ v_3 e^{\lambda t} \\ \vdots \\ v_n e^{\lambda t} \end{bmatrix}
=
\begin{bmatrix} v_1 \\ v_2 \\ v_3 \\ \vdots \\ v_n \end{bmatrix} e^{\lambda t} = \mathbf{v}e^{\lambda t}
\tag{3}
$$

where $\lambda, v_1, v_2, \ldots, v_n$ are appropriate scalar constants. For if we substitute

$$
x_i = v_i e^{\lambda t}, \qquad x'_i = \lambda v_i e^{\lambda t}
$$

$(i = 1, 2, \ldots, n)$ in (1), then the factor $e^{\lambda t}$ will cancel throughout. This will leave us with n linear equations which—for appropriate values of λ—we can hope to solve for values of the coefficients v_1, v_2, \ldots, v_n in (3) so that $\mathbf{x}(t) = \mathbf{v}e^{\lambda t}$ is, indeed, a solution of the system in (1).

To investigate this possibility, it is more efficient to write the system in (1) in the matrix form

$$
\blacktriangleright \qquad\qquad\qquad \mathbf{x}' = \mathbf{A}\mathbf{x}
\tag{4}
$$

where $\mathbf{A} = [a_{ij}]$. When we substitute the trial solution $\mathbf{x} = \mathbf{v}e^{\lambda t}$ with derivative $\mathbf{x}' = \lambda\mathbf{v}e^{\lambda t}$ in Eq. (4), the result is

$$
\lambda\mathbf{v}e^{\lambda t} = \mathbf{A}\mathbf{v}e^{\lambda t}.
$$

We cancel the nonzero scalar factor $e^{\lambda t}$ to get

$$
\blacktriangleright \qquad\qquad\qquad \mathbf{A}\mathbf{v} = \lambda\mathbf{v}.
\tag{5}
$$

This means that $\mathbf{x} = \mathbf{v}e^{\lambda t}$ will be a nontrivial solution of Eq. (4) provided that \mathbf{v} is

a *nonzero* vector and λ is a constant such that Eq. (5) holds; that is, the *matrix product* **Av** *is a scalar multiple of the vector* **v**. The question now is this: How do we find **v** and λ?

To answer this question, we rewrite Eq. (5) in the form

▶ $$(\mathbf{A} - \lambda\mathbf{I})\mathbf{v} = \mathbf{0}. \tag{6}$$

Given λ, this is a system of n nonhomogeneous linear equations in the unknowns v_1, v_2, \ldots, v_n. By a standard theorem of linear algebra, it has a nontrivial solution if and only if the determinant of its coefficient matrix vanishes; that is, if and only if

$$|\mathbf{A} - \lambda\mathbf{I}| = \det(\mathbf{A} - \lambda\mathbf{I}) = 0. \tag{7}$$

In its simplest formulation, the **eigenvalue method** for solving the system $\mathbf{x}' = \mathbf{A}\mathbf{x}$ consists of finding λ so that Eq. (7) holds and next solving Eq. (6) with this value of λ to obtain v_1, v_2, \ldots, v_n. Then $\mathbf{x} = \mathbf{v}e^{\lambda t}$ will be a solution vector. The name of the method comes from the following definition.

DEFINITION: Eigenvalues and Eigenvectors

The number λ (either zero or nonzero) is called an **eigenvalue** of the $n \times n$ matrix **A** provided that

$$|\mathbf{A} - \lambda\mathbf{I}| = 0. \tag{7}$$

An **eigenvector** associated with the eigenvalue λ is a *nonzero* vector **v** such that $\mathbf{A}\mathbf{v} = \lambda\mathbf{v}$, so that

$$(\mathbf{A} - \lambda\mathbf{I})\mathbf{v} = \mathbf{0}. \tag{6} \blacksquare$$

Note that if **v** is an eigenvector associated with the eigenvalue λ, then so is any nonzero constant scalar multiple of $c\mathbf{v}$ of **v**—this follows upon multiplication of each side in Eq. (6) by $c \neq 0$.

The prefix *eigen* is a German word with the approximate translation *characteristic* in this context; the terms *characteristic value* and *characteristic vector* are in common use. For this reason, the equation

$$|\mathbf{A} - \lambda\mathbf{I}| = \begin{vmatrix} a_{11} - \lambda & a_{12} & \cdots & a_{1n} \\ a_{21} & a_{22} - \lambda & \cdots & a_{2n} \\ \vdots & \vdots & & \vdots \\ a_{n1} & a_{n2} & \cdots & a_{nn} - \lambda \end{vmatrix} = 0 \tag{8}$$

is called the **characteristic equation** of the matrix **A**; its roots are the eigenvalues of **A**. Upon expanding the determinant in (8), we evidently get an nth-degree polynomial of the form

$$(-1)^n\lambda^n + b_{n-1}\lambda^{n-1} + \cdots + b_1\lambda + b_0 = 0. \tag{9}$$

By the fundamental theorem of algebra, this equation has n roots—possibly some are complex, possibly some are repeated—and thus an $n \times n$ matrix has n eigenvalues (counting repetitions, if any). Although we assume that the elements of **A** are real

numbers, we allow the possibility of complex eigenvalues and complex-valued eigenvectors.

Our discussion of Eqs. (4) through (7) provides a proof of the following theorem, which is the basis for the eigenvalue method of solving a first-order linear system with constant coefficients.

THEOREM: Eigenvalue Solutions of x′ = Ax

Let λ be an eigenvalue of the [constant] coefficient matrix **A** of the first-order linear system

$$\frac{d\mathbf{x}}{dt} = \mathbf{Ax}.$$

If **v** is an eigenvector associated with λ, then

$$\mathbf{x}(t) = \mathbf{v}e^{\lambda t}$$

is a nontrivial solution of the system. ∎

In outline, the eigenvalue method for solving the $n \times n$ system $\mathbf{x}' = \mathbf{Ax}$ proceeds as follows.

1. We first solve the characteristic equation in (8) for the eigenvalues λ_1, λ_2, . . . , λ_n of the matrix **A**.
2. Next we attempt to find *n linearly independent* eigenvectors \mathbf{v}_1, \mathbf{v}_2, . . . , \mathbf{v}_n associated with these eigenvalues.
3. Step 2 is not always possible, but when it is, we get *n* linearly independent solutions

 $$\mathbf{x}_1(t) = \mathbf{v}_1 e^{\lambda_1 t}, \qquad \mathbf{x}_2(t) = \mathbf{v}_2 e^{\lambda_2 t}, \quad . . . , \quad \mathbf{x}_n(t) = \mathbf{v}_n e^{\lambda_n t}. \qquad (10)$$

 In this case the general solution of $\mathbf{x}' = \mathbf{Ax}$ is a linear combination

 $$\mathbf{x}(t) = c_1 \mathbf{x}_1(t) + c_2 \mathbf{x}_2(t) + \cdots + c_n \mathbf{x}_n(t)$$

 of these *n* solutions.

We will discuss separately the various cases that can occur, depending upon whether the eigenvalues are distinct or repeated, real or complex. The case of repeated eigenvalues—multiple roots of the characteristic equation—will be deferred to Section 5.4.

Distinct Real Eigenvalues

If the eigenvalues λ_1, λ_2, . . . , λ_n are real and distinct, then we substitute each of them in turn in Eq. (6) and solve for the associated eigenvectors \mathbf{v}_1, \mathbf{v}_2, . . . , \mathbf{v}_n. In this case it can be proved that the particular solution vectors given in (10) are always linearly independent. (For instance, see Section 6.2 of Edwards and Penney, *Elementary Linear Algebra* (Englewood Cliffs, N.J.: Prentice Hall, 1988).) In any particular example such linear independence can always be verified by using the Wronskian determinant of Section 5.1. The following example illustrates the procedure.

EXAMPLE 1 Find a general solution of the system

$$x'_1 = 4x_1 + 2x_2$$
$$x'_2 = 3x_1 - x_2. \tag{11}$$

Solution: The matrix form of the system in (11) is

$$\mathbf{x}' = \begin{bmatrix} 4 & 2 \\ 3 & -1 \end{bmatrix} \mathbf{x}. \tag{12}$$

The characteristic equation of the coefficient matrix is

$$\begin{vmatrix} 4 - \lambda & 2 \\ 3 & -1 - \lambda \end{vmatrix} = (4 - \lambda)(-1 - \lambda) - 6$$

$$= \lambda^2 - 3\lambda - 10 = (\lambda + 2)(\lambda - 5) = 0,$$

so we have the distinct real eigenvalues $\lambda_1 = -2$ and $\lambda_2 = 5$.

For the coefficient matrix \mathbf{A} in (12) the eigenvector equation $(\mathbf{A} - \lambda\mathbf{I})\mathbf{v} = \mathbf{0}$ takes the form

$$\begin{bmatrix} 4 - \lambda & 2 \\ 3 & -1 - \lambda \end{bmatrix} \begin{bmatrix} a \\ b \end{bmatrix} = \begin{bmatrix} 0 \\ 0 \end{bmatrix} \tag{13}$$

for the associated eigenvector $\mathbf{v} = [a\ b]^T$.

With $\lambda_1 = -2$:

Substitution of the first eigenvalue $\lambda_1 = -2$ in Eq. (13) yields the system

$$\begin{bmatrix} 6 & 2 \\ 3 & 1 \end{bmatrix} \begin{bmatrix} a \\ b \end{bmatrix} = \begin{bmatrix} 0 \\ 0 \end{bmatrix};$$

that is, the two scalar equations

$$6a + 2b = 0$$
$$3a + b = 0. \tag{14}$$

In contrast with the nonsingular (algebraic) linear systems whose solutions we discussed in Section 5.1, the homogeneous linear system in (14) is *singular*—the two scalar equations obviously are equivalent (each being a multiple of the other). Therefore Eq. (14) has infinitely many nonzero solutions—we can choose a arbitrary (but nonzero) and then solve for b.

Substitution of an eigenvalue λ in the eigenvector equation $(\mathbf{A} - \lambda\mathbf{I})\mathbf{v} = \mathbf{0}$ always yields a singular homogeneous linear system, and among its infinity of solutions we generally seek a "simple" solution with small integer values (if possible). Looking at the second equation in (14), the choice $a = 1$ yields $b = -3$, and thus

$$\mathbf{v}_1 = \begin{bmatrix} 1 \\ -3 \end{bmatrix}$$

is an eigenvector associated with $\lambda_1 = -2$ (as is any nonzero constant multiple of \mathbf{v}_1).

Remark: If instead of the "simplest" choice $a = 1, b = -3$, we had made another choice, $a = c, b = -3c$, we would have obtained the eigenvector

$$\mathbf{v}_1 = \begin{bmatrix} c \\ -3c \end{bmatrix} = c \begin{bmatrix} 1 \\ -3 \end{bmatrix}.$$

Because this is a constant multiple of our previous result, any choice we make leads to [a constant multiple of] the same solution

$$\mathbf{x}_1(t) = \begin{bmatrix} 1 \\ -3 \end{bmatrix} e^{-2t}.$$

With $\lambda_2 = 5$;

Substitution of the second eigenvalue $\lambda = 5$ in (13) yields the pair

$$\begin{aligned} -a + 2b &= 0 \\ 3a - 6b &= 0 \end{aligned} \tag{15}$$

of equivalent scalar equations. With $b = 1$ in the first equation we get $a = 2$, so

$$\mathbf{v}_2 = \begin{bmatrix} 2 \\ 1 \end{bmatrix}$$

is an eigenvector associated with $\lambda_2 = 5$. A different choice $a = 2c, b = c$ would merely give a [constant] multiple of \mathbf{v}_2.

These two eigenvalues and associated eigenvectors yield the two solutions

$$\mathbf{x}_1(t) = \begin{bmatrix} 1 \\ -3 \end{bmatrix} e^{-2t} \quad \text{and} \quad \mathbf{x}_2(t) = \begin{bmatrix} 2 \\ 1 \end{bmatrix} e^{5t}.$$

They are linearly independent because their Wronskian

$$\begin{vmatrix} e^{-2t} & 2e^{5t} \\ -3e^{-2t} & e^{5t} \end{vmatrix} = 7e^{3t}$$

is nonzero. Hence a general solution of the system in (11) is

$$\mathbf{x}(t) = c_1 \mathbf{x}_1(t) + c_2 \mathbf{x}_2(t) = c_1 \begin{bmatrix} 1 \\ -3 \end{bmatrix} e^{-2t} + c_2 \begin{bmatrix} 2 \\ 1 \end{bmatrix} e^{5t};$$

in scalar form,

$$\begin{aligned} x_1(t) &= c_1 e^{-2t} + 2c_2 e^{5t} \\ x_2(t) &= -3c_1 e^{-2t} + c_2 e^{5t}. \end{aligned}$$ ∎

Remark: As in Example 1, it is convenient when discussing a linear system $\mathbf{x}' = \mathbf{A}\mathbf{x}$ to use vectors $\mathbf{x}_1, \mathbf{x}_2, \ldots, \mathbf{x}_n$ to denote different vector-valued solutions of the system, whereas the *scalars* x_1, x_2, \ldots, x_n denote the components of a single vector-valued solution \mathbf{x}.

Compartmental Analysis

Frequently a complex process or system can be broken down into simpler subsystems of "compartments" that can be analyzed separately. The whole system can then be modeled by describing the interactions between the various compartments. Thus a chemical plant may consist of a succession of separate stages (or even physical compartments) in which various reactants and products combine or are mixed. It may happen that a single differential equation describes each compartment of the system, and then the whole physical system is modeled by a system of differential equations.

As a simple example of a three-stage system, Fig. 5.2.1 shows three brine tanks containing V_1, V_2, and V_3 gallons of brine, respectively. Fresh water flows into tank 1, while mixed brine flows from tank 1 into tank 2, from tank 2 into tank 3, and out of tank 3. Let $x_i(t)$ denote the amount (in pounds) of salt in tank i at time t ($i = 1, 2, 3$). If each flow rate is r gallons per minute, then a simple accounting of salt concentrations, as in Example 2 of Section 4.1, yields the first-order system

$$
\begin{aligned}
x_1' &= -k_1 x_1 \\
x_2' &= \quad k_1 x_1 - k_2 x_2 \\
x_3' &= \qquad\qquad k_2 x_2 - k_3 x_3
\end{aligned}
\tag{16}
$$

where

$$
k_i = \frac{r}{V_i}, \qquad i = 1, 2, 3.
\tag{17}
$$

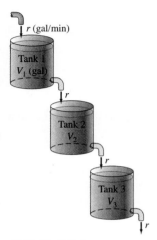

r (gal/min)

Tank 1
V_1 (gal)

r

Tank 2
V_2

r

Tank 3
V_3

r

FIGURE 5.2.1. The three brine tanks of Example 2

EXAMPLE 2 If $V_1 = 20$, $V_2 = 40$, $V_3 = 50$, $r = 10$ (gal/min), and the initial amounts of salt in the three brine tanks, in pounds, are

$$
x_1(0) = 15, \qquad x_2(0) = x_3(0) = 0,
$$

find the amount of salt in each tank at time $t \geqq 0$.

Solution Substituting the given numerical values in (16) and (17), we get the initial value problem

$$
\mathbf{x}'(t) = \begin{bmatrix} -0.5 & 0 & 0 \\ 0.5 & -0.25 & 0 \\ 0 & 0.25 & -0.2 \end{bmatrix} \mathbf{x}, \qquad \mathbf{x}(0) = \begin{bmatrix} 15 \\ 0 \\ 0 \end{bmatrix}
\tag{18}
$$

for the vector $\mathbf{x}(t) = [x_1(t)\ x_2(t)\ x_3(t)]^T$. The simple form of the matrix

$$
\mathbf{A} - \lambda\mathbf{I} = \begin{bmatrix} -0.5 - \lambda & 0 & 0 \\ 0.5 & -0.25 - \lambda & 0 \\ 0 & 0.25 & -0.2 - \lambda \end{bmatrix}
\tag{19}
$$

leads readily to the characteristic equation

$$
|\mathbf{A} - \lambda\mathbf{I}| = (-0.5 - \lambda)(-0.25 - \lambda)(-0.2 - \lambda) = 0.
$$

Thus the coefficient matrix \mathbf{A} in (18) has the distinct eigenvalues $\lambda_1 = -0.5$, $\lambda_2 = -0.25$, and $\lambda_3 = -0.2$.

With $\lambda_1 = -0.5$:

Substituting $\lambda = -0.5$ in (19), we get the equation

$$[A + (0.5) \cdot I]v = \begin{bmatrix} 0 & 0 & 0 \\ 0.5 & 0.25 & 0 \\ 0 & 0.25 & 0.3 \end{bmatrix} \begin{bmatrix} a \\ b \\ c \end{bmatrix} = \begin{bmatrix} 0 \\ 0 \\ 0 \end{bmatrix}$$

for the associated eigenvector $v = [a \; b \; c]^T$. The last two rows, upon division by 0.25 and 0.05, respectively, yield the scalar equations

$$2a + b \qquad = 0$$
$$5b + 6c = 0.$$

The second equation is satisfied by $b = -6$ and $c = 5$, and then the first equation gives $a = 3$. Thus the eigenvector

$$v_1 = [3 \quad -6 \quad 5]^T$$

is associated with the eigenvalue $\lambda_1 = -0.5$.

With $\lambda_2 = -0.25$:

Substituting $\lambda = -0.25$ in (19), we get the equation

$$[A + (0.25) \cdot I]v = \begin{bmatrix} -0.25 & 0 & 0 \\ 0.50 & 0 & 0 \\ 0 & 0.25 & 0.05 \end{bmatrix} \begin{bmatrix} a \\ b \\ c \end{bmatrix} = \begin{bmatrix} 0 \\ 0 \\ 0 \end{bmatrix}$$

for the associated eigenvector $v = [a \; b \; c]^T$. Each of the first two rows implies that $a = 0$, and division of the third row by 0.05 gives the equation

$$5b + c = 0,$$

which is satisfied by $b = 1$, $c = -5$. Thus the eigenvector

$$v_2 = [0 \quad 1 \quad -5]^T$$

is associated with the eigenvalue $\lambda_2 = -0.25$.

With $\lambda_3 = -0.2$:

Substituting $\lambda = -0.2$ in (19), we get the equation

$$[A + (0.2) \cdot I]v = \begin{bmatrix} -0.3 & 0 & 0 \\ 0.5 & -0.05 & 0 \\ 0 & 0.25 & 0 \end{bmatrix} \begin{bmatrix} a \\ b \\ c \end{bmatrix} = \begin{bmatrix} 0 \\ 0 \\ 0 \end{bmatrix}$$

for the eigenvector v. The first and third rows imply that $a = 0$ and $b = 0$, respectively, but the all-zero third column leaves c arbitrary (but nonzero). Thus

$$v_3 = [0 \; 0 \; 1]^T$$

is an eigenvector associated with $\lambda_3 = -0.2$.

The general solution

$$\mathbf{x}(t) = c_1\mathbf{v}_1 e^{\lambda_1 t} + c_2\mathbf{v}_2 e^{\lambda_2 t} + c_3\mathbf{v}_3 e^{\lambda_3 t}$$

therefore takes the form

$$\mathbf{x}(t) = c_1\begin{bmatrix} 3 \\ -6 \\ 5 \end{bmatrix} e^{(-0.5)t} + c_2\begin{bmatrix} 0 \\ 1 \\ -5 \end{bmatrix} e^{(-0.25)t} + c_3\begin{bmatrix} 0 \\ 0 \\ 1 \end{bmatrix} e^{(-0.2)t}.$$

The resulting scalar equations are

$$x_1(t) = 3c_1 e^{(-0.5)t}$$
$$x_2(t) = -6c_1 e^{(-0.5)t} + c_2 e^{(-0.25)t}$$
$$x_3(t) = 5c_1 e^{(-0.5)t} - 5c_2 e^{(-0.25)t} + c_3 e^{(-0.2)t}.$$

When we impose the initial conditions $x_1(0) = 15$, $x_2(0) = x_3(0) = 0$, we get the equations

$$3c_1 = 15$$
$$-6c_1 + c_2 = 0$$
$$5c_1 - 5c_2 + c_3 = 0$$

that are readily solved (in turn) for $c_1 = 5$, $c_2 = 30$, and $c_3 = 125$. Thus, finally, the amounts of salt at time t in the three brine tanks are given by

$$x_1(t) = 15e^{(-0.5)t}$$
$$x_2(t) = -30e^{(-0.5)t} + 30e^{(-0.25)t}$$
$$x_3(t) = 25e^{(-0.5)t} - 150e^{(-0.25)t} + 125e^{(-0.2)t}.$$

Figure 5.2.2 shows the graphs of $x_1(t)$, $x_2(t)$, and $x_3(t)$. As one would expect, tank 1 is rapidly "flushed" by the incoming fresh water, and $x_1(t) \to 0$ as $t \to +\infty$. The amounts $x_2(t)$ and $x_3(t)$ of salt in tanks 2 and 3 peak in turn and then approach zero as the whole three-tank system is purged of salt as $t \to +\infty$. ∎

FIGURE 5.2.2. The salt content functions of Example 2

Complex Eigenvalues

Even if some of the eigenvalues are complex, so long as they are distinct the method described above still yields n linearly independent solutions. The only complication is that the eigenvectors associated with complex eigenvalues are ordinarily complex-valued, so we will have complex-valued solutions.

To obtain real-valued solutions, we note that—because we are assuming that the matrix **A** has **only** real entries—the coefficients in the characteristic equation in (8) will all be real. Consequently any complex eigenvalues must appear in complex conjugate pairs. Suppose then that $\lambda = p + qi$ and $\overline{\lambda} = p - qi$ are such a pair of eigenvalues. If **v** is an eigenvector associated with λ, so that

$$(\mathbf{A} - \lambda\mathbf{I})\mathbf{v} = \mathbf{0},$$

then taking complex conjugates in this equation yields

$$(\mathbf{A} - \overline{\lambda}\mathbf{I})\overline{\mathbf{v}} = \mathbf{0}.$$

Thus the conjugate $\overline{\mathbf{v}}$ of \mathbf{v} is an eigenvector associated with $\overline{\lambda}$. Of course the conjugate of a vector is defined componentwise; if

$$\mathbf{v} = \begin{bmatrix} a_1 + b_1 i \\ a_2 + b_2 i \\ \vdots \\ a_n + b_n i \end{bmatrix} = \begin{bmatrix} a_1 \\ a_2 \\ \vdots \\ a_n \end{bmatrix} + \begin{bmatrix} b_1 \\ b_2 \\ \vdots \\ b_n \end{bmatrix} i = \mathbf{a} + \mathbf{b}i, \tag{20}$$

then $\overline{\mathbf{v}} = \mathbf{a} - \mathbf{b}i$. The complex-valued solution associated with λ and \mathbf{v} is then

$$\mathbf{x}(t) = \mathbf{v}e^{\lambda t} = \mathbf{v}e^{(p + qi)t}$$

$$= (\mathbf{a} + \mathbf{b}i)e^{pt}(\cos qt + i \sin qt);$$

that is,

$$\mathbf{x}(t) = e^{pt}(\mathbf{a} \cos qt - \mathbf{b} \sin qt)$$

$$+ ie^{pt}(\mathbf{b} \cos qt + \mathbf{a} \sin qt). \tag{21}$$

Because the real and imaginary parts of a complex-valued solution are also solutions, we thus get the two *real-valued* solutions

$$\mathbf{x}_1(t) = \mathrm{Re}(\mathbf{x}(t)) = e^{pt}(\mathbf{a} \cos qt - \mathbf{b} \sin qt),$$
$$\mathbf{x}_2(t) = \mathrm{Im}(\mathbf{x}(t)) = e^{pt}(\mathbf{b} \cos qt + \mathbf{a} \sin qt) \tag{22}$$

associated with the complex conjugate eigenvalues $p \pm qi$. It is easy to check that the same two real-valued solutions result from taking real and imaginary parts of $\overline{\mathbf{v}}e^{\overline{\lambda}t}$. Rather than memorizing the formulas in (22), it is preferable in a specific example to:

- First find explicitly a single complex-valued solution $\mathbf{x}(t)$ associated with the complex eigenvalue l;
- Then find the real and imaginary parts $\mathbf{x}_1(t)$ and $\mathbf{x}_2(t)$ of $\mathbf{x}(t)$ to get two independent real-valued solutions corresponding to the two complex conjugate eigenvalues λ and $\overline{\lambda}$.

EXAMPLE 3 Find a general solution of the system

$$\frac{dx_1}{dt} = 4x_1 - 3x_2$$

$$\frac{dx_2}{dt} = 3x_1 + 4x_2. \tag{23}$$

Solution The coefficient matrix

$$\mathbf{A} = \begin{bmatrix} 4 & -3 \\ 3 & 4 \end{bmatrix}$$

has characteristic equation

$$|\mathbf{A} - \lambda\mathbf{I}| = \begin{vmatrix} 4 - \lambda & -3 \\ 3 & 4 - \lambda \end{vmatrix} = (4 - \lambda)^2 + 9 = 0,$$

and hence has the complex conjugate eigenvalues $\lambda = 4 - 3i$ and $\overline{\lambda} = 4 + 3i$. Substituting $\lambda = 4 - 3i$ in the eigenvector equation $(\mathbf{A} - \lambda\mathbf{I})\mathbf{v} = \mathbf{0}$, we get the equation

$$[\mathbf{A} - (4 - 3i) \cdot \mathbf{I}]\mathbf{v} = \begin{bmatrix} 3i & -3 \\ 3 & 3i \end{bmatrix} \begin{bmatrix} a \\ b \end{bmatrix} = \begin{bmatrix} 0 \\ 0 \end{bmatrix}$$

for an associated eigenvalue $\mathbf{v} = [a\ b]^T$. Division of each row by 3 yields the two scalar equations

$$ia - b = 0$$
$$a + ib = 0,$$

each of which is satisfied by $a = 1$ and $b = i$. Thus $\mathbf{v} = [1\ i]^T$ is a complex eigenvector associated with the complex eigenvalue $\lambda = 4 - 3i$.

The corresponding complex-valued solution $\mathbf{x}(t) = \mathbf{v}e^{\lambda t}$ of $\mathbf{x}' = \mathbf{Ax}$ is then

$$\mathbf{x}(t) = \begin{bmatrix} 1 \\ i \end{bmatrix} e^{(4 - 3i)t} = \begin{bmatrix} 1 \\ i \end{bmatrix} e^{4t}(\cos 3t - i \sin 3t) = e^{4t} \begin{bmatrix} \cos 3t - i \sin 3t \\ i \cos 3t + \sin 3t \end{bmatrix}.$$

The real and imaginary parts of $\mathbf{x}(t)$ are the real-valued solutions

$$\mathbf{x}_1(t) = e^{4t} \begin{bmatrix} \cos 3t \\ \sin 3t \end{bmatrix} \quad \text{and} \quad \mathbf{x}_2(t) = e^{4t} \begin{bmatrix} -\sin 3t \\ \cos 3t \end{bmatrix}.$$

A real-valued general solution of $\mathbf{x}' = \mathbf{Ax}$ is then given by

$$\mathbf{x}(t) = c_1\mathbf{x}_1(t) + c_2\mathbf{x}_2(t) = e^{4t} \begin{bmatrix} c_1 \cos 3t - c_2 \sin 3t \\ c_1 \sin 3t + c_2 \cos 3t \end{bmatrix}.$$

Finally, a general solution of (23) in scalar form is

$$x_1(t) = e^{4t}(c_1 \cos 3t - c_2 \sin 3t)$$
$$x_2(t) = e^{4t}(c_1 \sin 3t + c_2 \cos 3t). \qquad \blacksquare$$

Flow rate: r

T_1 T_2 T_3

r r

FIGURE 5.2.3. The three brine tanks of Example 4

Figure 5.2.3 shows a "closed" system of three brine tanks with volumes V_1, V_2, and V_3. The difference between this system and the "open" system of Fig. 5.2.1 is that now the inflow to tank 1 is the outflow from tank 3. With the same notation as in Example 2, the appropriate modification of Eq. (16) is

$$\frac{dx_1}{dt} = -k_1 x_1 + k_3 x_3$$

$$\frac{dx_2}{dt} = k_1 x_1 - k_2 x_2 \qquad (24)$$

$$\frac{dx_3}{dt} = k_2 x_2 - k_3 x_3,$$

where $k_i = r/V_i$ as in (17).

EXAMPLE 4 Find the amounts $x_1(t)$, $x_2(t)$, and $x_3(t)$ of salt in the three brine tanks at time t if $V_1 = 50$ gal, $V_2 = 25$ gal, $V_3 = 50$ gal, and $r = 10$ gal/min.

Solution With the given numerical values, (24) takes the form

$$\frac{d\mathbf{x}}{dt} = \begin{bmatrix} -0.2 & 0 & 0.2 \\ 0.2 & -0.4 & 0 \\ 0 & 0.4 & -0.2 \end{bmatrix} \mathbf{x} \tag{25}$$

with $\mathbf{x} = [x_1 \ x_2 \ x_3]^T$ as usual. When we expand the determinant of the matrix

$$\mathbf{A} - \lambda\mathbf{I} = \begin{bmatrix} -0.2 - \lambda & 0 & 0.2 \\ 0.2 & -0.4 - \lambda & 0 \\ 0 & 0.4 & -0.2 - \lambda \end{bmatrix} \tag{26}$$

along its first row, we find that the characteristic equation of \mathbf{A} is

$(-0.2 - \lambda)(-0.4 - \lambda)(-0.2 - \lambda) + (0.2)(0.2)(0.4)$

$$= -\lambda^3 - (0.8) \cdot \lambda^2 - (0.2) \cdot \lambda$$

$$= -\lambda[(\lambda + 0.4)^2 + (0.2)^2] = 0.$$

Thus \mathbf{A} has the zero eigenvalue $\lambda_0 = 0$ and the complex conjugate eigenvalues $\lambda, \overline{\lambda} = -0.4 \pm (0.2)i$.

With $\lambda_0 = 0$:
 Substitution of $\lambda = 0$ in Eq. (26) gives the eigenvector equation

$$(\mathbf{A} - 0 \cdot \mathbf{I})\mathbf{v} = \begin{bmatrix} -0.2 & 0 & 0.2 \\ 0.2 & -0.4 & 0 \\ 0 & 0.4 & -0.2 \end{bmatrix} \begin{bmatrix} a \\ b \\ c \end{bmatrix} = \begin{bmatrix} 0 \\ 0 \\ 0 \end{bmatrix} \tag{26}$$

for $\mathbf{v} = [a \ b \ c]^T$. The first row gives $a = c$ and the second row gives $a = 2b$, so $\mathbf{v}_0 = [2 \ 1 \ 2]^T$ is an eigenvector associated with the eigenvalue $\lambda_0 = 0$. The corresponding solution $\mathbf{x}_0(t) = \mathbf{v}_0 e^{\lambda_0 t}$ of Eq. (25) is the constant solution

$$\mathbf{x}_0(t) = \begin{bmatrix} 2 \\ 1 \\ 2 \end{bmatrix}. \tag{27}$$

With $\lambda = -0.4 - 0.2i$:
 Substitution of $\lambda = -0.4 - 0.2i$ in (26) gives the eigenvector equation

$$[\mathbf{A} - (-0.4 - 0.2i)\mathbf{I}]\mathbf{v} = \begin{bmatrix} 0.2 + 0.2i & 0 & 0.2 \\ 0.2 & 0.2i & 0 \\ 0 & 0.4 & 0.2 + 0.2i \end{bmatrix} \begin{bmatrix} a \\ b \\ c \end{bmatrix} = \begin{bmatrix} 0 \\ 0 \\ 0 \end{bmatrix}.$$

The second equation $(0.2)a + (0.2)ib = 0$ is satisfied by $a = 1$ and $b = i$. Then the first equation

$$(0.2 + 0.2i)a + (0.2)c = 0$$

gives $c = -1 - i$. Thus $\mathbf{v} = [1 \quad i \quad (-1 - i)]^T$ is a complex eigenvector associated with the complex eigenvalue $\lambda = -0.4 - 0.2i$.

The corresponding complex-valued solution $\mathbf{x}(t) = \mathbf{v}e^{\lambda t}$ of (25) is

$$\mathbf{x}(t) = \begin{bmatrix} 1 \\ i \\ -1 - i \end{bmatrix} e^{(-0.4 - 0.2i)t}$$

$$= \begin{bmatrix} 1 \\ i \\ -1 - i \end{bmatrix} e^{(-0.4)t}(\cos 0.2t - i \sin 0.2t)$$

$$= e^{(-0.4)t} \begin{bmatrix} \cos 0.2t - i \sin 0.2t \\ \sin 0.2t + i \cos 0.2t \\ -\cos 0.2t - \sin 0.2t - i \cos 0.2t + i \sin 0.2t \end{bmatrix}.$$

The real and imaginary parts of $\mathbf{x}(t)$ are the real-valued solutions

$$\mathbf{x}_1(t) = e^{(-0.4)t} \begin{bmatrix} \cos 0.2t \\ \sin 0.2t \\ -\cos 0.2t - \sin 0.2t \end{bmatrix},$$

$$\mathbf{x}_2(t) = e^{(-0.4)t} \begin{bmatrix} -\sin 0.2t \\ \cos 0.2t \\ -\cos 0.2t + \sin 0.2t \end{bmatrix}. \tag{28}$$

The general solution

$$\mathbf{x}(t) = c_0\mathbf{x}_0(t) + c_1\mathbf{x}_1(t) + c_2\mathbf{x}_2(t)$$

has scalar components

$$x_1(t) = 2c_0 + e^{(-0.4)t}(c_1 \cos 0.2t - c_2 \sin 0.2t)$$
$$x_2(t) = c_0 + e^{(-0.4)t}(c_1 \sin 0.2t + c_2 \cos 0.2t) \tag{29}$$
$$x_3(t) = 2c_0 + e^{(-0.4)t}[(-c_1 - c_2)\cos 0.2t + (-c_1 + c_2)\sin 0.2t]$$

giving the amounts of salt in the three tanks at time t.

Observe that

$$x_1(t) + x_2(t) + x_3(t) \equiv 5c_0. \tag{30}$$

Of course the total amount of salt in the closed system is constant; the constant c_0 in

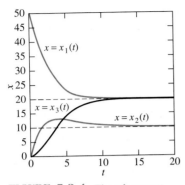

FIGURE 5.2.4. The salt content functions of Example 4

(29) is one-fifth of the total initial amount of salt. Because of the factors of $e^{(-0.4)t}$ in (29), we see that

$$\lim_{t \to \infty} x_1(t) = 2c_0, \qquad \lim_{x \to \infty} x_2(t) = c_0, \qquad \text{and} \qquad \lim_{t \to \infty} x_3(t) = 2c_0.$$

Thus as $t \to +\infty$ the salt in the system approaches a *steady-state* distribution with 40% of the salt in each of the two 50-gallon tanks and 20% in the 25-gallon tank. So, whatever the initial distribution of salt among the three tanks, the limiting distribution is one of uniform concentration throughout the system. Figure 5.2.4 shows the graphs of the three solution functions with $c_0 = 10$, $c_1 = 30$, and $c_2 = -10$, so

$$x_1(0) = 50 \quad \text{and} \quad x_2(0) = x_3(0) = 0.$$

5.2 Problems

In Problems 1 through 16, apply the eigenvalue method of this section to find a general solution of the given system. If initial values are given, find also the corresponding particular solution.

1. $x_1' = x_1 + 2x_2$
$x_2' = 2x_1 + x_2$

2. $x_1' = 2x_1 + 3x_2$
$x_2' = 2x_1 + x_2$

3. $x_1' = 3x_1 + 4x_2$
$x_2' = 3x_1 + 2x_2$
$x_1(0) = x_2(0) = 1$

4. $x_1' = 4x_1 + x_2$
$x_2' = 6x_1 - x_2$

5. $x_1' = 6x_1 - 7x_2$
$x_2' = x_1 - 2x_2$

6. $x_1' = 9x_1 + 5x_2$
$x_2' = -6x_1 - 2x_2$
$x_1(0) = 1, \quad x_2(0) = 0$

7. $x_1' = -3x_1 + 4x_2$
$x_2' = 6x_1 - 5x_2$

8. $x_1' = x_1 - 5x_2$
$x_2' = x_1 - x_2$

9. $x_1' = 2x_1 - 5x_2$
$x_2' = 4x_1 - 2x_2$
$x_1(0) = 2, \quad x_2(0) = 3$

10. $x_1' = -3x_1 - 2x_2$
$x_2' = 9x_1 + 3x_2$

11. $x_1' = x_1 - 2x_2$
$x_2' = 2x_1 + x_2$
$x_1(0) = 0, \quad x_2(0) = 4$

12. $x_1' = x_1 - 5x_2$
$x_2' = x_1 + 3x_2$

13. $x_1' = 5x_1 - 9x_2$
$x_2' = 2x_1 - x_2$

14. $x_1' = 3x_1 - 4x_2$
$x_2' = 4x_1 + 3x_2$

15. $x_1' = 7x_1 - 5x_2$
$x_2' = 4x_1 + 3x_2$

16. $x_1' = -50x_1 + 20x_2$
$x_2' = 100x_1 - 60x_2$

In Problems 17 through 25, the eigenvalues of the coefficient matrix can be found by inspection and factoring. Apply the eigenvalue method to find a general solution of each system.

17. $x_1' = 4x_1 + x_2 + 4x_3$
$x_2' = x_1 + 7x_2 + x_3$
$x_3' = 4x_1 + x_2 + 4x_3$

18. $x_1' = x_1 + 2x_2 + 2x_3$
$x_2' = 2x_1 + 7x_2 + x_3$
$x_3' = 2x_1 + x_2 + 7x_3$

19. $x_1' = 4x_1 + x_2 + x_3$
$x_2' = x_1 + 4x_2 + x_3$
$x_3' = x_1 + x_2 + 4x_3$

20. $x_1' = 5x_1 + x_2 + 3x_3$
$x_2' = x_1 + 7x_2 + x_3$
$x_3' = 3x_1 + x_2 + 5x_3$

21. $x_1' = 5x_1 \qquad - 6x_3$
$x_2' = 2x_1 - x_2 - 2x_3$
$x_3' = 4x_1 - 2x_2 - 4x_3$

22. $x_1' = 3x_1 + 2x_2 + 2x_3$
$x_2' = -5x_1 - 4x_2 - 2x_3$
$x_3' = 5x_1 + 5x_2 + 3x_3$

23. $x_1' = 3x_1 + x_2 + x_3$
$x_2' = -5x_1 - 3x_2 - x_3$
$x_3' = 5x_1 + 5x_2 + 3x_3$

24. $x_1' = 2x_1 + x_2 - x_3$
$x_2' = -4x_1 - 3x_2 - x_3$
$x_3' = 4x_1 + 4x_2 + 2x_3$

25. $x_1' = 5x_1 + 5x_2 + 2x_3$
$x_2' = -6x_1 - 6x_2 - 5x_3$
$x_3' = 6x_1 + 6x_2 + 5x_3$

26. Find the particular solution of the system

$$\frac{dx_1}{dt} = 3x_1 \qquad + x_3$$

$$\frac{dx_2}{dt} = 9x_1 - x_2 + 2x_3$$

$$\frac{dx_3}{dt} = -9x_1 + 4x_2 - x_3$$

that satisfies the initial conditions $x_1(0) = 0$, $x_2(0) = 0$, $x_3(0) = 17$.

The amounts $x_1(t)$ and $x_2(t)$ of salt in the two brine tanks of Fig. 5.2.5 satisfy the differential equations

$$\frac{dx_1}{dt} = -k_1 x_1, \qquad \frac{dx_2}{dt} = k_1 x_1 - k_2 x_2,$$

where $k_i = r/V_i$ for $i = 1, 2$. In Problems 27 and 28 the volumes V_1 and V_2 are given. First solve for $x_1(t)$ and $x_2(t)$, assuming that

$r = 10$ (gal/min), $x_1(0) = 15$ (gal), and $x_2(0) = 0$. Then find the maximum amount of salt ever in tank 2.

Fresh water
Flow rate r

Tank 1
Volume V_1
Salt $x_1(t)$

r

Tank 2
Volume V_2
Salt $x_2(t)$

r

FIGURE 5.2.5. The two brine tanks of Problems 27 and 28

27. $V_1 = 50$ (gal), $V_2 = 25$ (gal)
28. $V_1 = 25$ (gal), $V_2 = 40$ (gal)

The amounts $x_1(t)$ and $x_2(t)$ of salt in the two brine tanks of Fig. 5.2.6 satisfy the differential equations

$$\frac{dx_1}{dt} = -k_1 x_1 + k_2 x_2, \qquad \frac{dx_2}{dt} = k_1 x_1 - k_2 x_2,$$

where $k_i = r/V_i$ as usual. In Problems 29 and 30, solve for $x_1(t)$ and $x_2(t)$, assuming that $r = 10$ (gal/min), $x_1(0) = 15$ (gal), and $x_2(0) = 0$.

r

Tank 1 Tank 2

r

FIGURE 5.2.6. The two brine tanks of Problems 29 and 30

29. $V_1 = 50$ (gal), $V_2 = 25$ (gal)
30. $V_1 = 25$ (gal), $V_2 = 40$ (gal)

Problems 31 and 32 deal with the open three-tank system of Fig. 5.2.1. Find the general solution of the system in (16) with $r = 10$ (gal/min) and the given volumes.

31. $V_1 = 20$ (gal), $V_2 = 50$ (gal), $V_3 = 40$ (gal)
32. $V_1 = 50$ (gal), $V_2 = 25$ (gal), $V_3 = 20$ (gal)

33. Find the general solution of the system in (24) describing the closed three-tank system of Fig. 5.2.3, given that $r = 10$ (gal/min), $V_1 = 20$ (gal), $V_2 = 50$ (gal), and $V_3 = 20$ (gal).

For each matrix **A** given in Problems 34 through 36, the zeros in the matrix make its characteristic polynomial easy to calculate. Find the general solution of $\mathbf{x}' = \mathbf{Ax}$.

34. $\mathbf{A} = \begin{bmatrix} 1 & 0 & 0 & 0 \\ 2 & 2 & 0 & 0 \\ 0 & 3 & 3 & 0 \\ 0 & 0 & 4 & 4 \end{bmatrix}$ **35.** $\mathbf{A} = \begin{bmatrix} -2 & 0 & 0 & 9 \\ 4 & 2 & 0 & -10 \\ 0 & 0 & -1 & 8 \\ 0 & 0 & 0 & 1 \end{bmatrix}$

36. $\mathbf{A} = \begin{bmatrix} 2 & 0 & 0 & 0 \\ -21 & -5 & -27 & -9 \\ 0 & 0 & 5 & 0 \\ 0 & 0 & -21 & -2 \end{bmatrix}$

37. The coefficient matrix **A** of the 4×4 system

$$\begin{aligned} x_1' &= 4x_1 + x_2 + x_3 + 7x_4 \\ x_2' &= x_1 + 4x_2 + 10x_3 + x_4 \\ x_3' &= x_1 + 10x_2 + 4x_3 + x_4 \\ x_4' &= 7x_1 + x_2 + x_3 + 4x_4 \end{aligned}$$

has eigenvalues $\lambda_1 = -3$, $\lambda_2 = -6$, $\lambda_3 = 10$, and $\lambda_4 = 15$. Find the particular solution of this system that satisfies the initial conditions

$$x_1(0) = 3, \quad x_2(0) = x_3(0) = 1, \quad x_4(0) = 3.$$

5.2 Computing Project

Most computational systems offer the capability to find eigenvalues and eigenvectors readily. For instance, for the matrix

$$\mathbf{A} = \begin{bmatrix} -0.5 & 0 & 0 \\ 0.5 & -0.25 & 0 \\ 0 & 0.25 & -0.2 \end{bmatrix}$$

of Example 2, the TI-85 commands

```
[[-0.5,0,0][0.5,-0.25,0][0,0.25,-0.2]] → A
eigVl A
    {-.2, -.25, -.5}
eigVc A
[[0.00    0.00    1.00]
 [0.00    1.00   -2.00]
 [1.00   -5.00    1.67]]
```

produce the three eigenvalues of **A** and display beneath each its (column) eigenvector. Note that with results presented in decimal form, it is up to us to guess (and verify by matrix multiplication) that the exact eigenvector associated with the eigenvalue $\lambda = -\frac{1}{2}$ is $\mathbf{v} = [1 \ -2 \ \frac{5}{3}]^T$. The *Maple* commands

```
with(linalg):
A := matrix(3,3,[-0.5,0,0,0.5,-0.25,0,0,0.25,-0.2]);
eigenvects(A);
```

the *Mathematica* commands

```
A = {{-0.5,0,0}, {0.5,-0.25,0}, {0,0.25,-0.2}}
Eigensystem[A]
```

and the MATLAB commands

```
A = [-0.5,0,0; 0.5,-0.25,0; 0,0.25,-0.2]
[V,D] = eig(A)
```

(where **D** will be a diagonal matrix displaying the eigenvalues of **A** and the column vectors of **V** are the corresponding eigenvectors) produce similar results. You can use these commands to find the eigenvalues and eigenvectors needed for any of the problems in this section.

For a more substantial project, choose a positive integer $n < 10$ ($n = 5$, for example) and let V_1, V_2, \ldots, V_n denote the first n nonzero digits of your student ID number. Now consider an open system of brine tanks as in Fig. 5.2.1, except with n (rather than three) successive tanks having volumes V_1, V_2, \ldots, V_n (in gallons). If each flow rate is r gal/min, then the salt amounts $x_1(t), x_2(t), \ldots, x_n(t)$ satisfy the linear system

$$x_1' = -k_1 x_1$$

$$x_i' = k_{i-1} x_{i-1} - k_i x_i \qquad (i = 2, 3, \ldots, n)$$

where $k_i = r/V_i$. If $r = 1$ gal/min, apply the eigenvalue method to solve this system with initial conditions

$$x_1(0) = 10, \quad x_2(0) = \quad \cdots \quad = x_n(0) = 0.$$

Graph the solution functions, and estimate graphically the maximum amount of salt that each tank ever contains.

*5.3 Second-Order Systems and Mechanical Applications

In this section we apply the matrix methods of Sections 5.1 and 5.2 to investigate the oscillations of typical mass-and-spring systems having two or more degrees of freedom. Our examples are chosen to illustrate phenomena that are generally characteristic of complex mechanical systems.

FIGURE 5.3.1. Three spring-coupled masses

Figure 5.3.1 shows three masses connected to each other and to two walls by the four indicated springs. We assume that the masses slide without friction and that each spring obeys Hooke's law—its extension or compression x and force F of reaction are related by the formula $F = kx$. If the rightward displacements x_1, x_2, and x_3 of the three masses (from the equilibrium positions) are all positive, then:

- The first spring is stretched the distance x_1;
- The second spring is stretched the distance $x_2 - x_1$;
- The third spring is stretched the distance $x_3 - x_2$;
- The fourth spring is compressed the distance x_3.

Therefore application of Newton's law $ma = F$ to the three masses (as in Example 1 of Section 4.1) yields their equations of motion:

$$\begin{aligned} m_1 x_1'' &= -k_1 x_1 && + k_2(x_2 - x_1) \\ m_2 x_2'' &= -k_2(x_2 - x_1) + k_3(x_3 - x_2) \\ m_3 x_3'' &= -k_3(x_3 - x_2) - k_4 x_3. \end{aligned} \qquad (1)$$

In terms of the **displacement vector** $\mathbf{x} = [x_1 \ \ x_2 \ \ x_3]^T$, the **mass matrix**

$$\mathbf{M} = \begin{bmatrix} m_1 & 0 & 0 \\ 0 & m_2 & 0 \\ 0 & 0 & m_3 \end{bmatrix} \qquad (2)$$

and the **stiffness matrix**

$$\mathbf{K} = \begin{bmatrix} -(k_1 + k_2) & k_2 & 0 \\ k_2 & -(k_2 + k_3) & k_3 \\ 0 & k_3 & -(k_3 + k_4) \end{bmatrix}, \qquad (3)$$

FIGURE 5.3.2. A system of n spring-coupled masses

the system in (1) takes the matrix form

$$\blacktriangleright \qquad \mathbf{M}\mathbf{x}'' = \mathbf{K}\mathbf{x}. \qquad (4)$$

The notation in Eqs. (1) through (4) generalizes in a natural way to the system of n spring-coupled masses shown in Fig. 5.3.2. We need only write

* This optional section may be omitted without loss of continuity. It provides a sample of the more technical applications of eigenvalues to physics and engineering problems.

$$\mathbf{M} = \begin{bmatrix} m_1 & 0 & \cdots & 0 \\ 0 & m_2 & \cdots & 0 \\ . & . & & . \\ . & . & & . \\ . & . & & . \\ 0 & 0 & \cdots & m_n \end{bmatrix} \tag{5}$$

and

$$\mathbf{K} = \begin{bmatrix} -(k_1 + k_2) & k_2 & 0 & \cdots & 0 \\ k_2 & -(k_2 + k_3) & k_3 & \cdots & 0 \\ 0 & k_3 & -(k_3 + k_4) & \cdots & 0 \\ 0 & 0 & k_4 & \cdots & 0 \\ . & . & & & . \\ . & . & & & . \\ 0 & 0 & \cdots & -(k_{n-1} + k_n) & k_n \\ 0 & 0 & \cdots & k_n & -(k_n + k_{n+1}) \end{bmatrix} \tag{6}$$

for the mass and stiffness matrices in (4).

The diagonal matrix \mathbf{M} is obviously nonsingular; to get its inverse \mathbf{M}^{-1} we need only replace each diagonal element by its reciprocal. Hence multiplication of each side in (4) by \mathbf{M}^{-1} yields the homogeneous **second-order system**

▶
$$\mathbf{x}'' = \mathbf{A}\mathbf{x}, \tag{7}$$

where $\mathbf{A} = \mathbf{M}^{-1}\mathbf{K}$. There is a wide variety of *frictionless* mechanical systems for which a displacement or position vector \mathbf{x}, a nonsingular mass matrix \mathbf{M}, and a stiffness matrix \mathbf{K} satisfying (4) can be defined.

To seek a solution of Eq. (7), we substitute (as in Section 5.2 for a first-order system) a trial solution of the form

$$\mathbf{x}(t) = \mathbf{v}e^{\alpha t}, \tag{8}$$

where \mathbf{v} is a constant vector. Then $\mathbf{x}'' = \alpha^2 \mathbf{v}e^{\alpha t}$, so substitution of (8) in (7) gives

$$\alpha^2 \mathbf{v}e^{\alpha t} = \mathbf{A}\mathbf{v}e^{\alpha t},$$

which implies that

$$\mathbf{A}\mathbf{v} = \alpha^2 \mathbf{v}. \tag{9}$$

Therefore $\mathbf{x}(t) = \mathbf{v}e^{\alpha t}$ is a solution of $\mathbf{x}'' = \mathbf{A}\mathbf{x}$ if and only if $\alpha^2 = \lambda$, an eigenvalue of the matrix \mathbf{A}, and \mathbf{v} is an associated eigenvector.

If $\mathbf{x}'' = \mathbf{A}\mathbf{x}$ models a mechanical system, then it is typical that the eigenvalues of \mathbf{A} are *negative* real numbers. If

$$\alpha^2 = \lambda = -\omega^2 < 0,$$

then $\alpha = \pm \omega i$. In this case the solution given by (8) is

$$\mathbf{x}(t) = \mathbf{v}e^{i\omega t} = \mathbf{v}(\cos \omega t + i \sin \omega t).$$

The real and imaginary parts

$$\mathbf{x}_1(t) = \mathbf{v} \cos \omega t \qquad \text{and} \qquad \mathbf{x}_2(t) = \mathbf{v} \sin \omega t \qquad (10)$$

of $\mathbf{x}(t)$ are then independent *real-valued* solutions of the system. This analysis leads to the following theorem.

THEOREM 1: Second-Order Homogeneous Linear Systems

If the $n \times n$ matrix \mathbf{A} has distinct negative eigenvalues $-\omega_1^2, -\omega_2^2, \ldots, -\omega_n^2$ with associated [real] eigenvectors $\mathbf{v}_1, \mathbf{v}_2, \ldots, \mathbf{v}_n$, then a general solution of

▶
$$\mathbf{x}'' = \mathbf{A}\mathbf{x}$$

is given by

▶
$$\mathbf{x}(t) = \sum_{i=1}^{n} (a_i \cos \omega_i t + b_i \sin \omega_i t)\mathbf{v}_i \qquad (11)$$

with a_i and b_i arbitrary constants. In the special case of a nonrepeated zero eigenvalue $\lambda_0 = 0$ with associated eigenvector \mathbf{v}_0, the corresponding part of the general solution is

$$\mathbf{x}_0(t) = (a_0 + b_0 t)\mathbf{v}_0. \qquad (12)$$
■

Remark: The nonzero vector \mathbf{v}_0 is an eigenvector corresponding to $\lambda_0 = 0$ provided that $\mathbf{A}\mathbf{v}_0 = \mathbf{0}$. If $\mathbf{x}(t) = (a_0 + b_0 t)\mathbf{v}_0$, then

$$\mathbf{x}'' = 0 \cdot \mathbf{v}_0 = (a_0 + b_0 t) \cdot \mathbf{0} = (a_0 + b_0 t) \cdot (\mathbf{A}\mathbf{v}_0) = \mathbf{A}\mathbf{x},$$

thus verifying the form in Eq. (12).

EXAMPLE 1

Equilibrium positions

FIGURE 5.3.3. The mass-and-spring system of Example 1

Consider the mass-and-spring system with $n = 2$ shown in Fig. 5.3.3. Because there is *no* third spring connected to a right-hand wall, we set $k_3 = 0$. If $m_1 = 2$, $m_2 = 1$ and $k_1 = 100$, $k_2 = 50$, then the equation $\mathbf{M}\mathbf{x}'' = \mathbf{K}\mathbf{x}$ is

$$\begin{bmatrix} 2 & 0 \\ 0 & 1 \end{bmatrix} \mathbf{x}'' = \begin{bmatrix} -150 & 50 \\ 50 & -50 \end{bmatrix} \mathbf{x}, \qquad (13)$$

which reduces to $\mathbf{x}'' = \mathbf{A}\mathbf{x}$ with

$$\mathbf{A} = \begin{bmatrix} -75 & 25 \\ 50 & -50 \end{bmatrix}.$$

The characteristic equation of \mathbf{A} is

$$(-75 - \lambda)(-50 - \lambda) - 50 \cdot 25 = \lambda^2 + 125\lambda + 2500$$

$$= (\lambda + 25)(\lambda + 100) = 0,$$

so \mathbf{A} has the negative eigenvalues $\lambda_1 = -25$ and $\lambda_2 = -100$. By Theorem 1, the system in (13) therefore has solutions with [circular] frequencies $\omega_1 = 5$ and $\omega_2 = 10$.

With $\lambda_1 = -25$:
 The eigenvector equation $(\mathbf{A} - \lambda\mathbf{I})\mathbf{v} = \mathbf{0}$ is

$$\begin{bmatrix} -50 & 25 \\ 50 & -25 \end{bmatrix} \begin{bmatrix} a \\ b \end{bmatrix} = \begin{bmatrix} 0 \\ 0 \end{bmatrix},$$

so an eigenvector associated with $\lambda_1 = -25$ is $\mathbf{v}_1 = [1 \ 2]^T$.

With $\lambda_2 = -100$;
 The eigenvector equation $(\mathbf{A} - \lambda\mathbf{I})\mathbf{v} = \mathbf{0}$ is

$$\begin{bmatrix} 25 & 25 \\ 50 & 50 \end{bmatrix} \begin{bmatrix} a \\ b \end{bmatrix} = \begin{bmatrix} 0 \\ 0 \end{bmatrix},$$

so an eigenvector associated with $\lambda_2 = -100$ is $\mathbf{v}_2 = [1 \ -1]^T$.

By Eq. (11) it follows that a general solution of the system in (13) is given by

$$\mathbf{x}(t) = (a_1 \cos 5t + b_1 \sin 5t)\mathbf{v}_1 + (a_2 \cos 10t + b_2 \sin 10t)\mathbf{v}_2. \tag{14}$$

As in the discussion of Example 3 at the end of Section 4.2, the two terms on the right in (14) represent **free oscillations** of the mass-and-spring system. They describe the physical system's two **natural modes of oscillation** at its two [circular] **natural frequencies** $\omega_1 = 5$ and $\omega_2 = 10$. The natural mode

$$\mathbf{x}_1(t) = (a_1 \cos 5t + b_1 \sin 5t)\mathbf{v}_1 = c_1 \cos(5t - \alpha_1) \begin{bmatrix} 1 \\ 2 \end{bmatrix}$$

(with $c_1 = \sqrt{a_1^2 + b_1^2}$, $\cos \alpha_1 = a_1/c_1$, $\sin \alpha_1 = b_1/c_1$) has the scalar component equations

$$\begin{aligned} x_1(t) &= c_1 \cos(5t - \alpha_1) \\ x_2(t) &= 2c_1 \cos(5t - \alpha_1), \end{aligned} \tag{15}$$

and therefore describes a free oscillation in which the two masses move in synchrony in the same direction and with the same frequency $\omega_1 = 5$, but with the amplitude of motion of m_2 twice that of m_1. The natural mode

$$\mathbf{x}_2(t) = (a_2 \cos 10t + b_2 \sin 10t)\mathbf{v}_2 = c_2 \cos(10t - \alpha_2) \begin{bmatrix} 1 \\ -1 \end{bmatrix}$$

has the scalar component equations

$$\begin{aligned} x_1(t) &= c_2 \cos(10t - \alpha_2) \\ x_2(t) &= -c_2 \cos(10t - \alpha_2), \end{aligned} \tag{16}$$

and therefore describes a free oscillation in which the two masses move in synchrony in opposite directions with the same frequency $\omega_2 = 10$ and with equal amplitudes of oscillation.

EXAMPLE 2 Figure 5.3.4 shows three railway cars connected by buffer springs that react when compressed, but disengage instead of stretching. With $n = 3$, $k_1 = k_3 = k$, and $k_2 = k_4 = 0$ in Eqs. (2) through (4), we get the system

FIGURE 5.3.4. The three railway cars of Example 2

$$\begin{bmatrix} m_1 & 0 & 0 \\ 0 & m_2 & 0 \\ 0 & 0 & m_3 \end{bmatrix} \mathbf{x}'' = \begin{bmatrix} -k & k & 0 \\ k & -2k & k \\ 0 & k & -k \end{bmatrix} \mathbf{x}, \tag{17}$$

which is equivalent to

$$\mathbf{x}'' = \begin{bmatrix} -c_1 & c_1 & 0 \\ c_2 & -2c_2 & c_2 \\ 0 & c_3 & -c_3 \end{bmatrix} \mathbf{x} \tag{18}$$

with

$$c_i = \frac{k}{m_i} \qquad (i = 1, 2, 3). \tag{19}$$

If we assume further that

$$m_1 = m_3, \qquad \text{so that} \quad c_1 = c_3,$$

then a brief computation gives

$$-\lambda(\lambda + c_1)(\lambda + c_1 + 2c_2) = 0 \tag{20}$$

for the characteristic equation of the coefficient matrix \mathbf{A} in Eq. (18). Hence the matrix \mathbf{A} has eigenvalues

$$\lambda_1 = 0, \qquad \lambda_2 = -c_1, \qquad \lambda_3 = -c_1 - 2c_2 \tag{21a}$$

corresponding to the natural frequencies

$$\omega_1 = 0, \qquad \omega_2 = \sqrt{c_1}, \qquad \omega_3 = \sqrt{c_1 + 2c_2} \tag{21b}$$

of the physical system.

For a numerical example, suppose that the first and third railway cars weigh 12 tons each, whereas the middle car weighs 8 tons, and that the spring constant is $k = 1.5$ tons/ft; i.e., $k = 3000$ lb/ft. Then, using fps units with mass measured in slugs (a weight of 32 pounds having a mass of 1 slug), we have

$$m_1 = m_3 = 750, \qquad m_2 = 500,$$

and

$$c_1 = \frac{3000}{750} = 4, \qquad c_2 = \frac{3000}{500} = 6.$$

Hence the coefficient matrix \mathbf{A} is

$$\mathbf{A} = \begin{bmatrix} -4 & 4 & 0 \\ 6 & -12 & 6 \\ 0 & 4 & -4 \end{bmatrix}, \tag{22}$$

and the eigenvalue-frequency pairs given by (21a) and (21b) are $\lambda_1 = 0$, $\omega_1 = 0$; $\lambda_2 = -4$, $\omega_2 = 2$; and $\lambda_3 = -16$, $\omega_3 = 4$.

With $\lambda_1 = 0$, $\omega_1 = 0$:

The eigenvector equation $(\mathbf{A} - \lambda\mathbf{I})\mathbf{v} = \mathbf{0}$ is

$$\mathbf{Av} = \begin{bmatrix} -4 & 4 & 0 \\ 6 & -12 & 6 \\ 0 & 4 & -4 \end{bmatrix}\begin{bmatrix} a \\ b \\ c \end{bmatrix} = \begin{bmatrix} 0 \\ 0 \\ 0 \end{bmatrix},$$

so it is clear that $\mathbf{v}_1 = [1 \ 1 \ 1]^T$ is an eigenvector associated with $\lambda_1 = 0$. According to Theorem 1, the corresponding part of a general solution of $\mathbf{x}'' = \mathbf{Ax}$ is

$$\mathbf{x}_1(t) = (a_1 + b_1 t)\mathbf{v}_1.$$

With $\lambda_2 = -4$, $\omega_2 = 2$:

The eigenvector equation $(\mathbf{A} - \lambda\mathbf{I})\mathbf{v} = \mathbf{0}$ is

$$(\mathbf{A} + 4\mathbf{I})\mathbf{v} = \begin{bmatrix} 0 & 4 & 0 \\ 6 & -8 & 6 \\ 0 & 4 & 0 \end{bmatrix}\begin{bmatrix} a \\ b \\ c \end{bmatrix} = \begin{bmatrix} 0 \\ 0 \\ 0 \end{bmatrix}$$

so it is clear that $\mathbf{v}_2 = [1 \ 0 \ -1]^T$ is an eigenvector associated with $\lambda_2 = -4$. According to Theorem 1, the corresponding part of a general solution of $\mathbf{x}'' = \mathbf{Ax}$ is

$$\mathbf{x}_2(t) = (a_2 \cos 2t + b_2 \sin 2t)\mathbf{v}_2.$$

With $\lambda_3 = -16$, $\omega_3 = 4$:

The eigenvector equation $(\mathbf{A} - \lambda\mathbf{I})\mathbf{v} = \mathbf{0}$ is

$$(\mathbf{A} + 16\mathbf{I})\mathbf{v} = \begin{bmatrix} 12 & 4 & 0 \\ 6 & 4 & 6 \\ 0 & 4 & 12 \end{bmatrix}\begin{bmatrix} a \\ b \\ c \end{bmatrix} = \begin{bmatrix} 0 \\ 0 \\ 0 \end{bmatrix},$$

so it is clear that $\mathbf{v}_3 = [1 \ -3 \ 1]^T$ is an eigenvector associated with $\lambda_2 = -16$. The corresponding part of a general solution is

$$\mathbf{x}_3(t) = (a_3 \cos 4t + b_3 \sin 4t)\mathbf{v}_3.$$

The general solution $\mathbf{x} = \mathbf{x}_1 + \mathbf{x}_2 + \mathbf{x}_3$ of $\mathbf{x}'' = \mathbf{Ax}$ is therefore given by

$$\mathbf{x}(t) = a_1\begin{bmatrix} 1 \\ 1 \\ 1 \end{bmatrix} + b_1 t\begin{bmatrix} 1 \\ 1 \\ 1 \end{bmatrix} + a_2\begin{bmatrix} 1 \\ 0 \\ -1 \end{bmatrix}\cos 2t$$

$$+ b_2\begin{bmatrix} 1 \\ 0 \\ -1 \end{bmatrix}\sin 2t + a_3\begin{bmatrix} 1 \\ -3 \\ 1 \end{bmatrix}\cos 4t + b_3\begin{bmatrix} 1 \\ -3 \\ 1 \end{bmatrix}\sin 4t. \quad (23)$$

To determine a particular solution, let us suppose that the leftmost car is moving to the right with velocity v_0 and at time $t = 0$ strikes the other two cars, which are at rest. The corresponding initial conditions are

$$x_1(0) = x_2(0) = x_3(0) = 0, \tag{24a}$$

$$x_1'(0) = v_0, \qquad x_2'(0) = x_3'(0) = 0. \tag{24b}$$

Then substitution of (24a) in (23) gives the scalar equations

$$a_1 + a_2 + a_3 = 0$$

$$a_1 \qquad - 3a_3 = 0$$

$$a_1 - a_2 + a_3 = 0,$$

which readily yield $a_1 = a_2 = a_3 = 0$. Hence the position functions of the three cars are

$$x_1(t) = b_1 t + b_2 \sin 2t + \ b_3 \sin 4t$$

$$x_2(t) = b_1 t \qquad\qquad - 3b_3 \sin 4t \tag{25}$$

$$x_3(t) = b_1 t - b_2 \sin 2t + \ b_3 \sin 4t$$

and their velocity functions are

$$x_1'(t) = b_1 + 2b_2 \cos 2t + \ 4b_3 \cos 4t$$

$$x_2'(t) = b_1 \qquad\qquad - 12b_3 \cos 4t \tag{26}$$

$$x_3'(t) = b_1 - 2b_2 \cos 2t + \ 4b_3 \cos 4t.$$

Substitution of (24b) in (26) gives the equations

$$b_1 + 2b_2 + \ 4b_3 = v_0$$

$$b_1 \qquad\qquad - 12b_3 = 0$$

$$b_1 - 2b_2 + \ 4b_3 = 0$$

that readily yield $b_1 = \frac{3}{8}v_0$, $b_2 = \frac{1}{4}v_0$, and $b_3 = \frac{1}{32}v_0$. Finally, the position functions in (25) are

$$x_1(t) = \frac{1}{32} v_0(12t + 8 \sin 2t + \ \sin 4t)$$

$$x_2(t) = \frac{1}{32} v_0(12t \qquad\qquad - 3 \sin 4t) \tag{27}$$

$$x_3(t) = \frac{1}{32} v_0(12t - 8 \sin 2t + \ \sin 4t).$$

But these equations hold *only* so long as the two buffer springs remain *compressed;* that is, while both

$$x_2 - x_1 < 0 \qquad \text{and} \qquad x_3 - x_2 < 0.$$

To find what this implies about t, we compute:

$$x_2(t) - x_1(t) = \frac{1}{32} v_0(-8 \sin 2t - 4 \sin 4t)$$

$$= -\frac{1}{32} v_0(8 \sin 2t + 8 \sin 2t \cos 2t)$$

$$= -\frac{1}{4} v_0(\sin 2t)(1 + \cos 2t)$$

and, similarly,

$$x_3(t) - x_2(t) = -\frac{1}{4} v_0(\sin 2t)(1 - \cos 2t).$$

It follows that $x_2 - x_1 < 0$ and $x_3 - x_2 < 0$ until $t = \pi/2 \approx 1.57$ (seconds), at which time the equations in (26) and (27) give the values

$$x_1\left(\frac{\pi}{2}\right) = x_2\left(\frac{\pi}{2}\right) = x_3\left(\frac{\pi}{2}\right) = \frac{3\pi v_0}{16},$$

$$x_1'\left(\frac{\pi}{2}\right) = x_2'\left(\frac{\pi}{2}\right) = 0, \qquad x_3'\left(\frac{\pi}{2}\right) = v_0.$$

We conclude that the three railway cars remain engaged and moving to the right until disengagement occurs at time $t = \pi/2$ (!). Thereafter, cars 1 and 2 remain at rest (!), while car 3 continues to the right with speed v_0. If, for instance, $v_0 = 48$ feet per second (about 33 miles per hour), then the three cars travel a distance of $9\pi \approx 28.27$ (ft) during their 1.57 seconds of engagement, and

$$x_1(t) = x_2(t) = 9\pi, \qquad x_3(t) = 48t - 15\pi \tag{27'}$$

for $t > \pi/2$. Figure 5.3.5 illustrates the "before" and "after" situations, and Fig. 5.3.6 shows the graphs of the functions $x_1(t)$, $x_2(t)$, and $x_3(t)$ in Eqs. (27) and (27').

FIGURE 5.3.5. (a) Before; (b) after

FIGURE 5.3.6. Position functions of the three railway cars of Example 2

Forced Oscillations and Resonance

Suppose now that the ith mass of the mass-and-spring system in Fig. 5.3.2 is subject to an external force F_i ($i = 1, 2, \ldots, n$) in addition to the forces exerted by the springs

attached to it. Then the homogeneous equation $\mathbf{M}\mathbf{x}'' = \mathbf{K}\mathbf{x}$ is replaced by the nonhomogeneous equation

$$\mathbf{M}\mathbf{x}'' = \mathbf{K}\mathbf{x} + \mathbf{F} \tag{28}$$

where $\mathbf{F} = [F_1\ F_2\ \cdots\ F_n]^T$ is the **external force vector** for the system. Multiplication by \mathbf{M}^{-1} yields

$$\mathbf{x}'' = \mathbf{A}\mathbf{x} + \mathbf{f} \tag{29}$$

where \mathbf{f} is the external force vector *per unit mass*. We are especially interested in the case of a *periodic external force*

$$\mathbf{f} = \mathbf{F}_0 \cos \omega t \tag{30}$$

(where \mathbf{F}_0 is a constant vector). We then anticipate a periodic particular solution

$$\mathbf{x}_p(t) = \mathbf{c} \cos \omega t \tag{31}$$

with the known external frequency ω and with a coefficient vector \mathbf{c} yet to be determined. Because $\mathbf{x}_p'' = -\omega^2 \mathbf{c} \cos \omega t$, substitution of (30) and (31) in (29), followed by cancellation of the common factor $\cos \omega t$, gives the linear system

$$(\mathbf{A} + \omega^2 \mathbf{I})\mathbf{c} = -\mathbf{F}_0 \tag{32}$$

to be solved for \mathbf{c}.

Observe that the matrix $\mathbf{A} + \omega^2 \mathbf{I}$ is nonsingular—in which case Eq. (32) can be solved for \mathbf{c}—unless $-\omega^2 = \lambda$, an eigenvalue of \mathbf{A}. Thus a periodic particular solution of the form in Eq. (31) exists provided that the external forcing frequency does **not** equal one of the natural frequencies ω_1, ω_2, . . . , ω_n of the system. The case in which ω **is** a natural frequency corresponds to the phenomenon of **resonance** discussed in Section 3.6.

EXAMPLE 3 Suppose that the second mass in Example 1 is subjected to the external periodic force $50 \cos \omega t$. Then with $m_1 = 2$, $m_2 = 1$, $k_1 = 100$, $k_2 = 50$, and $F_0 = 50$ in Fig. 5.3.7, Eq. (29) takes the form

FIGURE 5.3.7. The forced mass-and-spring system of Example 3

$$\mathbf{x}'' = \begin{bmatrix} -75 & 25 \\ 50 & -50 \end{bmatrix} \mathbf{x} + \begin{bmatrix} 0 \\ 50 \end{bmatrix} \cos \omega t, \tag{33}$$

and the substitution $\mathbf{x} = \mathbf{c} \cos \omega t$ leads to the equation

$$\begin{bmatrix} \omega^2 - 75 & 25 \\ 50 & \omega^2 - 50 \end{bmatrix} \mathbf{c} = \begin{bmatrix} 0 \\ -50 \end{bmatrix} \tag{34}$$

for the coefficient vector $\mathbf{c} = [c_1\ c_2]^T$. This system is readily solved for

$$c_1 = \frac{1250}{(\omega^2 - 25)(\omega^2 - 100)}, \qquad c_2 = \frac{50(\omega^2 - 75)}{(\omega^2 - 25)(\omega^2 - 100)}. \tag{35}$$

For instance, if the external squared frequency is $\omega^2 = 50$, then (35) yields $c_1 = 1$, $c_2 = -1$. The resulting forced periodic oscillation is described by

$$x_1(t) = \cos \omega t, \qquad x_2(t) = -\cos \omega t.$$

Thus the two masses oscillate with equal amplitudes but in opposite directions.

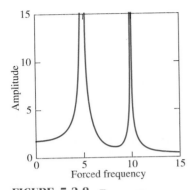

FIGURE 5.3.8. Frequency-amplitude plot for Example 3

If the external squared frequency is $\omega^2 = 125$, then (35) yields $c_1 = \frac{1}{2}$, $c_2 = 1$. The resulting forced periodic oscillation, is described by

$$x_1(t) = \frac{1}{2}\cos\omega t, \qquad x_2(t) = \cos\omega t,$$

and now the two masses oscillate in the same direction, but with the amplitude of motion of m_2 twice that of m_1.

It is evident from the denominators in (35) that c_1 and c_2 approach $+\infty$ as ω approaches either of the two natural frequencies $\omega_1 = 5$ and $\omega_2 = 10$ (found in Example 1). Figure 5.3.8 shows a plot of the amplitude $\sqrt{c_1^2 + c_2^2}$ of the forced periodic solution $\mathbf{x}(t) = \mathbf{c}\cos\omega t$ as a function of the forced frequency ω. The peaks at $\omega_2 = 5$ and $\omega_2 = 10$ exhibit visually the phenomenon of resonance. ∎

It follows from Theorem 4 of Section 5.1 that a particular solution of the forced system

$$\mathbf{x}'' = \mathbf{Ax} + \mathbf{F}_0 \cos\omega t \tag{36}$$

will be of the form

▶ $$\mathbf{x}(t) = \mathbf{x}_c(t) + \mathbf{x}_p(t), \tag{37}$$

where $\mathbf{x}_p(t)$ is a particular solution of the nonhomogeneous system and $\mathbf{x}_c(t)$ is a solution of the corresponding homogeneous system. It is typical for the effect of frictional resistance in mechanical systems to damp out the complementary function solution $\mathbf{x}_c(t)$, so that

$$\mathbf{x}_c(t) \to \mathbf{0} \qquad \text{as } t \to +\infty. \tag{38}$$

Hence $\mathbf{x}_c(t)$ is a **transient solution** that depends only upon the initial conditions; it dies out with time, leaving the **steady periodic solution** $\mathbf{x}_p(t)$ resulting from the external driving force:

$$\mathbf{x}(t) \to \mathbf{x}_p(t) \qquad \text{as } t \to +\infty. \tag{39}$$

As a practical matter, every physical system includes frictional resistance (however small) that damps out transient solutions in this manner.

5.3 Problems

Problems 1 through 6 deal with the mass-and-spring system shown in Fig. 5.3.9 with stiffness matrix

$$\mathbf{K} = \begin{bmatrix} -(k_1 + k_2) & k_2 \\ k_2 & -(k_2 + k_3) \end{bmatrix}$$

and with the given fps values for the masses and spring constants. Find the two natural frequencies of the system and describe its two natural modes of oscillation.

FIGURE 5.3.9. The mass-and-spring system for Problems 1 through 6

1. $m_1 = m_2 = 1$; $k_1 = 0$, $k_2 = 2$, $k_3 = 0$ (no walls)
2. $m_1 = m_2 = 1$; $k_1 = 1$, $k_2 = 4$, $k_3 = 1$

3. $m_1 = 1$, $m_2 = 2$; $k_1 = 1$, $k_2 = k_3 = 2$

4. $m_1 = m_2 = 1$; $k_1 = 1$, $k_2 = 2$, $k_3 = 1$

5. $m_1 = m_2 = 1$; $k_1 = 2$, $k_2 = 1$, $k_3 = 2$

6. $m_1 = 1$, $m_2 = 2$; $k_1 = 2$, $k_2 = k_3 = 4$

In Problems 7 and 8, find the natural frequencies of the three-mass system of Fig. 5.3.1, using the given masses and spring constants. For each natural frequency ω, give the ratio $a_1 : a_2 : a_3$ of amplitudes for a corresponding natural mode $x_1 = a_1 \cos \omega t$, $x_2 = a_2 \cos \omega t$, $x_3 = a_3 \cos \omega t$.

7. $m_1 = m_2 = m_3 = 1$; $k_1 = k_2 = k_3 = k_4 = 1$
(*Hint:* One eigenvalue is $\lambda = -2$.)

8. $m_1 = m_2 = m_3 = 1$; $k_1 = k_2 = k_3 = k_4 = 2$
(*Hint:* One eigenvalue is $\lambda = -4$.)

Apply the method of Example 3 to find a general solution of each system in Problems 9 through 11.

9. $x_1'' = -3x_1 + 2x_2 + \cos 3t$, $\quad 2x_2'' = 2x_1 - 4x_2$

10. $x_1'' = -3x_1 + 2x_2 + 2 \sin 2t$, $\quad x_2'' = 2x_1 - 3x_2$

11. $x'' = -3x + y + \cos t$, $\quad y'' = x - 3y + 2 \cos t$

12. In the system of Fig. 5.3.10, assume that $m_1 = 1$ (slug), $k_1 = 50$ (lb/ft), $k_2 = 10$ (lb/ft), $F_0 = 5$ (lb), and $\omega = 10$ (rad/s). Then find m_2 so that in the resulting steady periodic oscillations, the mass m_1 will remain at rest (!). Thus the effect of the second mass-and-spring pair will be to neutralize the effect of the force of the first mass. This is an example of a *dynamic damper.*

$F(t) = F_0 \cos \omega t$

k_1 \quad m_1 \quad k_2 \quad m_2

x_1 \qquad x_2

FIGURE 5.3.10. The mechanical system of Problem 12

13. Suppose that $m_1 = 2$, $m_2 = \frac{1}{2}$, $k_1 = 75$, $k_2 = 25$, $F_0 = 100$, and $\omega = 10$ (all in fps units) in the forced mass-and-spring system of Fig. 5.3.7. Find the solution of the system $\mathbf{M}\mathbf{x}'' = \mathbf{K}\mathbf{x} + \mathbf{F}$ that satisfies the initial conditions $\mathbf{x}(0) = \mathbf{x}'(0) = \mathbf{0}$.

14. Figure 5.3.11 shows two railway cars with a buffer spring. We want to investigate the transfer of momentum that occurs after car 1 with initial velocity v_0 impacts car 2 at rest. The analogue of Eq. (18) in the text is

$$\mathbf{x}'' = \begin{bmatrix} -c_1 & c_1 \\ c_2 & -c_2 \end{bmatrix} \mathbf{x}$$

with $c_i = k/m_i$ ($i = 1, 2$). Show that the eigenvalues of the coefficient matrix \mathbf{A} are $\lambda_1 = 0$ and $\lambda_2 = -c_1 - c_2$, with associated eigenvectors $\mathbf{v}_1 = [1 \ 1]^T$ and $\mathbf{v}_2 = [c_1 \ -c_2]^T$.

$x_1'(0) = v_0$ \qquad $x_2'(0) = 0$

k

m_1 $\qquad\qquad$ m_2

$x_1(t)$ $\qquad\qquad$ $x_2(t)$

FIGURE 5.3.11. The two railway cars of Problems 14 through 17

15. If the two cars of Problem 14 both weigh 16 tons (so that $m_1 = m_2 = 1000$ [slugs]) and $k = 1$ ton/ft (that is, 2000 lb/ft), show that the cars separate after $\pi/2$ seconds, and that $x_1'(t) = 0$ and $x_2'(t) = v_0$ thereafter. Thus the original momentum of car 1 is completely transferred to car 2.

16. If cars 1 and 2 weigh 8 tons and 16 tons, respectively, and $k = 3000$ lb/ft, show that the two cars separate after $\pi/3$ seconds, and that

$$x_1'(t) = -\frac{1}{3} v_0 \quad \text{and} \quad x_2'(t) = +\frac{2}{3} v_0$$

thereafter. Thus the two cars rebound in opposite directions.

17. If cars 1 and 2 weigh 24 tons and 8 tons, respectively, and $k = 1500$ lb/ft, show that the cars separate after $\pi/2$ seconds, and that

$$x_1'(t) = +\frac{1}{2} v_0 \quad \text{and} \quad x_2'(t) = +\frac{3}{2} v_0$$

thereafter. Thus both cars continue in the original direction of motion, but with different velocities.

18. In the three-railway-car system of Fig. 5.3.4, suppose that cars 1 and 3 each weigh 32 tons, that car 2 weighs 8 tons, and that each spring constant is 4 tons/ft. If $x_1'(0) = v_0$ and $x_2'(0) = x_3'(0) = 0$, show that the two springs are compressed until $t = \pi/2$ and that

$$x_1' = -\frac{1}{9} v_0 \quad \text{and} \quad x_2'(t) = x_3'(t) = +\frac{8}{9} v_0$$

thereafter. Thus car 1 rebounds, but cars 2 and 3 continue with the same velocity.

The Two-Axle Automobile

In Example 4 of Section 3.6 we investigated the vertical oscillations of a one-axle car—actually a unicycle. Now we can analyze a more realistic model: a car with two axles and with separate front and rear suspension systems. Figure 5.3.12 represents the suspension system of such a car. We assume that the

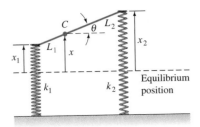

FIGURE 5.3.12. Model of the two-axle automobile

car body acts as would a solid bar of mass m and length $L = L_1 + L_2$. It has moment of inertia I about its center of mass C, which is at distance L_1 from the front end of the car. The car has front and back suspension springs with Hooke's constants k_1 and k_2, respectively. When the car is in motion, let $x(t)$ denote the vertical displacement of the center of mass of the car from equilibrium; let $\theta(t)$ denote its angular displacement (in radians) from the horizontal. Then Newton's laws of motion for linear and angular acceleration can be used to derive the equations

$$mx'' = -(k_1 + k_2)x + (k_1L_1 - k_2L_2)\theta,$$
$$I\theta'' = (k_1L_1 - k_2L_2)x - (k_1L_1^2 + k_2L_2^2)\theta. \tag{42}$$

19. Suppose that $m = 75$ slugs (the car weighs 2400 lb), $L_1 = 7$ ft, $L_2 = 3$ ft (it's a rear-engine car), $k_1 = k_2 = 2000$ lb/ft, and $I = 1000$ ft-lb-s^2. Then the equations in (42) take the form

$$75x'' + 4000x - 8000\theta = 0,$$

$$1000\theta'' - 8000x + 116{,}000\theta = 0.$$

(a) Find the two natural frequencies ω_1 and ω_2 of the car. (b) Now suppose that the car is driven at a speed of v feet per second along a washboard surface shaped like a sine curve with a wavelength of 40 ft. The result is a periodic force on the car with frequency $\omega = 2\pi v/40 = \pi v/20$. Resonance occurs when either $\omega = \omega_1$ or $\omega = \omega_2$. Find the corresponding two critical speeds of the car (in miles per hour).

20. Suppose that $k_1 = k_2 = k$ and $L_1 = L_2 = \frac{1}{2}L$ in Fig. 5.3.12 (the symmetric situation). Then show that every free oscillation is a combination of a vertical oscillation with frequency $\omega_1 = \sqrt{2k/m}$ and an angular oscillation with frequency $\omega_2 = \sqrt{kL^2/2I}$.

In Problems 21 through 23, the system of Fig. 5.3.12 is taken as a model for an undamped car with the given parameters in fps units. (a) Find the two natural frequencies of oscillation (in hertz). (b) Assume that this car is driven along a sinusoidal washboard surface with a wavelength of 40 ft. Find the two critical speeds.

21. $m = 100$, $I = 800$, $L_1 = L_2 = 5$, $k_1 = k_2 = 2000$

22. $m = 100$, $I = 1000$, $L_1 = 6$, $L_2 = 4$, $k_1 = k_2 = 2000$

23. $m = 100$, $I = 800$, $L_1 = L_2 = 5$, $k_1 = 1000$, $k_2 = 2000$

5.3 Computing Project

Earthquake-Induced Vibrations of Multistory Buildings

In this project you are to investigate the response to transverse earthquake ground oscillations of the seven-story building illustrated in Fig. 5.3.13. Suppose that each of the

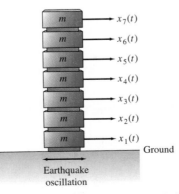

FIGURE 5.3.13. The seven-story building

seven [aboveground] floors weighs 16 tons, so the mass of each is $m = 1000$ (slugs). Also assume a horizontal restoring force of $k = 5$ (tons per foot) between adjacent floors. That is, the internal forces in response to horizontal displacements of the individual floors are those shown in Fig. 5.3.14. It follows that the free transverse oscillations indicated in Fig. 5.3.13 satisfy the equation $\mathbf{M}\mathbf{x}'' = \mathbf{K}\mathbf{x}$ with $n = 7$, $m_i = 1000$ (for each i), and $k_i = 10{,}000$ (lb/ft) for $1 \leq i \leq 7$. The system then reduces to the form $\mathbf{x}'' = \mathbf{A}\mathbf{x}$ with

$k(x_i - x_{i-1})$ m $k(x_{i+1} - x_i)$

FIGURE 5.3.14. Forces on the ith floor

$$\mathbf{A} = \begin{bmatrix} -20 & 10 & 0 & 0 & 0 & 0 & 0 \\ 10 & -20 & 10 & 0 & 0 & 0 & 0 \\ 0 & 10 & -20 & 10 & 0 & 0 & 0 \\ 0 & 0 & 10 & -20 & 10 & 0 & 0 \\ 0 & 0 & 0 & 10 & -20 & 10 & 0 \\ 0 & 0 & 0 & 0 & 10 & -20 & 10 \\ 0 & 0 & 0 & 0 & 0 & 10 & -10 \end{bmatrix}. \tag{1}$$

Once the matrix \mathbf{A} has been entered, the TI-85 command **eigVl A** takes less than 15 seconds to calculate the seven eigenvalues shown in the λ-column of the table in Fig. 5.3.15. Alternatively, you can use the *Maple* command **eigenvals(A)**, the MATLAB command **eig(A)**, or the *Mathematica* command **Eigenvalues[A]**. Then calculate the entries in the remaining columns of the table showing the natural frequencies and periods of oscillation of the seven-story building. Note that a typical earthquake producing ground oscillations with a period of 2 seconds is uncomfortably close to the fifth natural frequency (with period 1.9869 seconds) of the building.

i	Eigenvalue λ	Frequency $\omega = \sqrt{-\lambda}$	Period $P = \dfrac{2\pi}{\omega}$ (sec)
1	-38.2709	6.1863	1.0157
2	-33.3826	5.7778	1.0875
3	-26.1803	5.1167	1.2280
4	-17.9094	4.2320	1.4847
5	-10.0000	3.1623	1.9869
6	-3.8197	1.9544	3.2149
7	-0.4370	0.6611	9.5042

FIGURE 5.3.15. Frequencies and periods of natural oscillation of the seven-story building

A horizontal earthquake oscillation $E \cos \omega t$ of the ground, with amplitude E and acceleration $a = -E\omega^2 \cos \omega t$, produces an opposite inertial force $F = ma = mE\omega^2 \sin \omega t$ on each floor of the building. The resulting nonhomogeneous system is

$$\mathbf{x}'' = \mathbf{A}\mathbf{x} + (E\omega^2 \cos \omega t)\mathbf{b}, \tag{2}$$

where $\mathbf{b} = [1 \ 1 \ 1 \ 1 \ 1 \ 1 \ 1]^T$ and \mathbf{A} is the matrix of Eq. (1). Figure 5.3.16 shows a plot of *maximal amplitude* (for the forced oscillations of any single floor) versus the

period of the earthquake vibrations. The spikes correspond to the first six of the seven resonance frequencies. We see, for instance, that whereas an earthquake with period 2 (s) likely would produce destructive resonance vibrations in the building, it probably would be unharmed by an earthquake with period 2.5 (s). Different buildings have different natural frequencies of vibration, and so a given earthquake may demolish one building, but leave untouched the one next door. This type of apparent anomaly was observed in Mexico City after the devastating earthquake of September 19, 1985.

For your personal seven-story building to investigate, let the weight (in tons) of each story equal the largest digit of your student ID number and let k (in tons/ft) equal the smallest nonzero digit. Produce numerical and graphical results like those illustrated in Figs. 5.3.15 and 5.3.16. Is your building susceptible to likely damage from an earthquake with period in the 2 to 3 second range?

You might like to begin by working manually the following warm-up problems.

FIGURE 5.3.16. Resonance vibrations of a 7-story building—maximal amplitude as a function of period.

1. Find the periods of the natural vibrations of a building with two aboveground floors, with each weighing 16 tons and with each restoring force being $k = 5$ tons/ft.

2. Find the periods of the natural vibrations of a building with three aboveground floors, with each weighing 16 tons and with each restoring force being $k = 5$ tons/ft.

3. Find the natural frequencies and natural modes of vibration of a building with three aboveground floors as in Problem 2, except that the upper two floors weigh 8 tons instead of 16 tons. Give the ratios of the amplitudes A, B, and C of oscillations of the three floors in the form $A:B:C$ with $A = 1$.

4. Suppose that the building of Problem 3 is subject to an earthquake in which the ground undergoes horizontal sinusoidal oscillations with a period of 3 s and an amplitude of 3 in. Find the amplitudes of the resulting steady periodic oscillations of the three aboveground floors. Assume the fact that a motion $E \sin \omega t$ of the ground, with acceleration $a = -E\omega^2 \sin \omega t$, produces an opposite inertial force $F = -ma = mE\omega^2 \sin \omega t$ on a floor of mass m.

5.4 Multiple Eigenvalue Solutions

In Section 5.2 we saw that if the $n \times n$ matrix \mathbf{A} has n *distinct* (real or complex) eigenvalues $\lambda_1, \lambda_2, \ldots, \lambda_n$ with respective associated eigenvectors $\mathbf{v}_1, \mathbf{v}_2, \ldots, \mathbf{v}_n$, then a general solution of the system

$$\frac{d\mathbf{x}}{dt} = \mathbf{A}\mathbf{x} \tag{1}$$

is given by

$$\mathbf{x}(t) = c_1 \mathbf{v}_1 e^{\lambda_1 t} + c_2 \mathbf{v}_2 e^{\lambda_2 t} + \cdots + c_n \mathbf{v}_n e^{\lambda_n t} \tag{2}$$

with arbitrary constants c_1, c_2, \ldots, c_n. In this section we discuss the situation when the characteristic equation

$$|\mathbf{A} - \lambda \mathbf{I}| = 0 \tag{3}$$

does *not* have n distinct roots, and thus has at least one repeated root.

An eigenvalue is of **multiplicity** k if it is a k-fold root of Eq. (3). For each eigenvalue λ, the eigenvector equation

$$(\mathbf{A} - \lambda\mathbf{I})\mathbf{v} = \mathbf{0} \tag{4}$$

has at least one nonzero solution \mathbf{v}, so there is at least one eigenvector associated with λ. But an eigenvalue of multiplicity $k > 1$ may have *fewer* than k linearly independent associated eigenvectors. In this case we are unable to find a "complete set" of n linearly independent eigenvectors of \mathbf{A}, as needed to form the general solution in (2).

Let us call an eigenvalue of multiplicity k **complete** if it has k linearly independent associated eigenvectors. If every eigenvalue of the matrix \mathbf{A} is complete then — because eigenvectors associated with different eigenvalues are linearly independent — it follows that \mathbf{A} does have a complete set of n linearly independent eigenvectors \mathbf{v}_1, $\mathbf{v}_2, \ldots, \mathbf{v}_n$ associated with the eigenvalues $\lambda_1, \lambda_2, \ldots, \lambda_n$ (each repeated with its multiplicity). In this case a general solution of $\mathbf{x}' = \mathbf{A}\mathbf{x}$ is still given by the usual combination in (2).

EXAMPLE 1 Find a general solution of the system

$$\mathbf{x}' = \begin{bmatrix} 9 & 4 & 0 \\ -6 & -1 & 0 \\ 6 & 4 & 3 \end{bmatrix} \mathbf{x}. \tag{5}$$

Solution The characteristic equation of the coefficient matrix \mathbf{A} in Eq. (5) is

$$|\mathbf{A} - \lambda\mathbf{I}| = \begin{vmatrix} 9 - \lambda & 4 & 0 \\ -6 & -1 - \lambda & 0 \\ 6 & 4 & 3 - \lambda \end{vmatrix}$$

$$= (3 - \lambda)[(9 - \lambda)(-1 - \lambda) + 24]$$

$$= (3 - \lambda)(15 - 8\lambda + \lambda^2)$$

$$= (5 - \lambda)(3 - \lambda)^2 = 0.$$

Thus \mathbf{A} has the distinct eigenvalue $\lambda_1 = 5$ and the repeated eigenvalue $\lambda_2 = 3$ of multiplicity 2.

With $\lambda_1 = 5$:
The eigenvector equation $(\mathbf{A} - \lambda\mathbf{I})\mathbf{v} = \mathbf{0}$ for $\mathbf{v} = [a\ \ b\ \ c]^T$ is

$$(\mathbf{A} - 5\mathbf{I})\mathbf{v} = \begin{bmatrix} 4 & 4 & 0 \\ -6 & -6 & 0 \\ 6 & 4 & -2 \end{bmatrix} \begin{bmatrix} a \\ b \\ c \end{bmatrix} = \begin{bmatrix} 0 \\ 0 \\ 0 \end{bmatrix}.$$

Each of the first two equations, $4a + 4b = 0$ and $-6a - 6b = 0$, yields $b = -a$. Then the third equation reduces to $2a - 2c = 0$, so that $c = a$. The choice $a = 1$ then yields the eigenvector

$$\mathbf{v}_1 = [1\ \ -1\ \ 1]^T$$

associated with the eigenvalue $\lambda_1 = 5$.

With $\lambda_2 = 3$:
Now the eigenvector equation is

$$(\mathbf{A} - 3\mathbf{I})\mathbf{v} = \begin{bmatrix} 6 & 4 & 0 \\ -6 & -4 & 0 \\ 6 & 4 & 0 \end{bmatrix}\begin{bmatrix} a \\ b \\ c \end{bmatrix} = \begin{bmatrix} 0 \\ 0 \\ 0 \end{bmatrix},$$

so the nonzero vector $\mathbf{v} = [a \ b \ c]^T$ is an eigenvector if and only if

$$6a + 4b = 0; \tag{6}$$

that is, $b = -\frac{3}{2}a$. The fact that Eq. (6) does not involve c means that c is arbitrary, subject to the condition $\mathbf{v} \neq \mathbf{0}$. If $c = 1$, we may choose $a = b = 0$; this gives the eigenvector

$$\mathbf{v}_2 = [0 \ \ 0 \ \ 1]^T$$

associated with $\lambda_2 = 3$. If $c = 0$ then we must choose a to be nonzero. For instance, if $a = 2$ (to avoid fractions) then $b = -3$, so

$$\mathbf{v}_3 = [2 \ \ -3 \ \ 0]^T$$

is a second linearly independent eigenvector associated with the multiplicity 2 eigenvalue $\lambda_2 = 3$.

Thus we have found a complete set \mathbf{v}_1, \mathbf{v}_2, \mathbf{v}_3 of three eigenvectors associated with the eigenvalues 5, 3, 3. The corresponding general solution of (5) is

$$\mathbf{x}(t) = c_1\mathbf{v}_1 e^{5t} + c_2\mathbf{v}_2 e^{3t} + c_3\mathbf{v}_3 e^{3t} \tag{7}$$

$$= c_1\begin{bmatrix} 1 \\ -1 \\ 1 \end{bmatrix} e^{5t} + c_2\begin{bmatrix} 0 \\ 0 \\ 1 \end{bmatrix} e^{3t} + c_3\begin{bmatrix} 2 \\ -3 \\ 0 \end{bmatrix} e^{3t},$$

with scalar component functions given by

$$x_1(t) = c_1 e^{5t} + 2c_3 e^{3t}$$
$$x_2(t) = -c_1 e^{5t} - 3c_3 e^{3t}$$
$$x_3(t) = c_1 e^{5t} + c_2 e^{3t}. \blacksquare$$

Remark: Our choice in Example 1 of the two eigenvectors $\mathbf{v}_2 = [0 \ 0 \ 1]^T$ and $\mathbf{v}_3 = [2 \ -3 \ 0]^T$ associated with the repeated eigenvalue $\lambda_2 = 3$ bears comment. The fact that $b = -\frac{3}{2}a$ for any eigenvector associated with $\lambda_3 = 3$ means that any such eigenvector can be written as

$$\mathbf{v} = \begin{bmatrix} a \\ -\frac{3}{2}a \\ c \end{bmatrix} = c\begin{bmatrix} 0 \\ 0 \\ 1 \end{bmatrix} + \frac{1}{2}a\begin{bmatrix} 2 \\ -3 \\ 0 \end{bmatrix} = c\mathbf{v}_2 + \frac{1}{2}a\mathbf{v}_3,$$

and thus is a linear combination of \mathbf{v}_1 and \mathbf{v}_2. Therefore, given a and c not both zero, we could choose \mathbf{v} as our third eigenvector, and the new general solution

$$\mathbf{x}(t) = c_1 \mathbf{v}_1 e^{5t} + c_2 \mathbf{v}_2 e^{3t} + c_3 \mathbf{v} e^{3t}$$

would be equivalent to the one in Eq. (7). Thus we need not worry about making the "right" choice of independent eigenvectors associated with a multiple eigenvalue. Any choice will do; we generally make the simplest one we can.

Defective Eigenvalues

The following example shows that—unfortunately—not all multiple eigenvalues are complete.

EXAMPLE 2 The matrix

$$\mathbf{A} = \begin{bmatrix} 1 & -3 \\ 3 & 7 \end{bmatrix} \tag{8}$$

has characteristic equation

$$|\mathbf{A} - \lambda \mathbf{I}| = \begin{vmatrix} 1 - \lambda & -3 \\ 3 & 7 - \lambda \end{vmatrix}$$

$$= (1 - \lambda)(7 - \lambda) + 9$$

$$= \lambda^2 - 8\lambda + 16 = (\lambda - 4)^2 = 0.$$

Thus \mathbf{A} has the single eigenvalue $\lambda_1 = 4$ of multiplicity 2. The eigenvector equation

$$(\mathbf{A} - 4\mathbf{I})\mathbf{v} = \begin{bmatrix} -3 & -3 \\ 3 & 3 \end{bmatrix} \begin{bmatrix} a \\ b \end{bmatrix} = \begin{bmatrix} 0 \\ 0 \end{bmatrix}$$

then amounts to the equivalent scalar equations

$$-3a - 3b = 0, \qquad 3a + 3b = 0.$$

Hence $b = -a$ if $\mathbf{v} = [a \ b]^T$ is to be an eigenvector of \mathbf{A}. Therefore any eigenvector associated with $\lambda_1 = 4$ is a nonzero multiple of $\mathbf{v}_1 = [1 \ -1]^T$. Thus the multiplicity 2 eigenvalue $\lambda_1 = 4$ has only one independent eigenvector, and hence is incomplete. ∎

An eigenvalue λ of multiplicity $k > 1$ is called **defective** if it is not complete. If λ has only $p < k$ linearly independent eigenvectors, then the number

$$d = k - p \tag{9}$$

of "missing" eigenvectors is called the **defect** of the defective eigenvalue λ. Thus the defective eigenvalue $\lambda_1 = 4$ in Example 2 has multiplicity $k = 2$ and defect $d = 1$, because we saw that it has only $p = 1$ associated eigenvector.

If the eigenvalues of the $n \times n$ matrix \mathbf{A} are not all complete, then the eigenvalue method as yet described will produce *fewer* than the needed n linearly independent solutions of the system $\mathbf{x}' = \mathbf{A}\mathbf{x}$. We therefore need to tell how to find the "missing solutions" corresponding to a defective eigenvalue λ of multiplicity $k > 1$. Let us begin with the case $k = 2$, and suppose that we have found (as in Example 2) that there is only one eigenvector \mathbf{v}_1 associated with λ. Thus we have only the single solution

▶

$$\mathbf{x}_1(t) = \mathbf{v}_1 e^{\lambda t}. \tag{10}$$

By analogy with the case of a repeated characteristic root for a single differential equation (Section 3.3), we might expect to find a second solution of the form

$$\mathbf{x} = \mathbf{w}te^{\lambda t}. \tag{11}$$

But when we substitute (11) in $\mathbf{x}' = \mathbf{A}\mathbf{x}$, we get the equation

$$\mathbf{w}e^{\lambda t} + \mathbf{w}te^{\lambda t} = \mathbf{A}\mathbf{w}te^{\lambda t}.$$

Because the coefficients of both $e^{\lambda t}$ and $te^{\lambda t}$ must balance, it follows that $\mathbf{w} = \mathbf{0}$. Thus there is *no* nontrivial solution of the form in (11).

Still trying to make this idea work, we turn to the next most plausible possibility: a second solution of the form

$$\blacktriangleright \qquad \mathbf{x}_2(t) = \mathbf{v}te^{\lambda t} + \mathbf{w}e^{\lambda t}. \tag{12}$$

When we substitute (12) in $\mathbf{x}' = \mathbf{A}\mathbf{x}$, we get the equation

$$\mathbf{v}e^{\lambda t} + \lambda\mathbf{v}te^{\lambda t} + \lambda\mathbf{w}e^{\lambda t} = \mathbf{A}\mathbf{v}te^{\lambda t} + \mathbf{A}\mathbf{w}e^{\lambda t}. \tag{13}$$

We equate coefficients of $te^{\lambda t}$ and $e^{\lambda t}$ in Eq. (13); thus we obtain the two equations

$$\blacktriangleright \qquad (\mathbf{A} - \lambda\mathbf{I})\mathbf{v} = \mathbf{0} \tag{14}$$

and

$$\blacktriangleright \qquad (\mathbf{A} - \lambda\mathbf{I})\mathbf{w} = \mathbf{v} \tag{15}$$

that the vectors \mathbf{v} and \mathbf{w} must satisfy in order for (12) to be a solution of $\mathbf{x}' = \mathbf{A}\mathbf{x}$.

Note that Eq. (14) merely implies that $\mathbf{v}_1 = \mathbf{v}$ is an eigenvector associated with λ, and then that Eq. (15) implies that $\mathbf{v}_2 = \mathbf{w}$ satisfies the equation

$$(\mathbf{A} - \lambda\mathbf{I})^2\mathbf{v}_2 = (\mathbf{A} - \lambda\mathbf{I})\mathbf{v}_1 = \mathbf{0}.$$

Consequently we have the following method for handling a defective eigenvalue λ of multiplicity 2.

ALGORITHM: Defective Multiplicity 2 Eigenvalues

1. First find a nonzero solution \mathbf{v}_2 of the equation

$$(\mathbf{A} - \lambda\mathbf{I})^2\mathbf{v}_2 = \mathbf{0} \tag{16}$$

such that

$$(\mathbf{A} - \lambda\mathbf{I})\mathbf{v}_2 = \mathbf{v}_1 \tag{17}$$

is nonzero, and therefore is an eigenvector \mathbf{v}_1 associated with λ.

2. Then form the two independent solutions

$$\mathbf{x}_1(t) = \mathbf{v}_1 e^{\lambda t} \tag{18}$$

and

$$\mathbf{x}_2(t) = (\mathbf{v}_1 t + \mathbf{v}_2)e^{\lambda t} \tag{19}$$

of $\mathbf{x}' = \mathbf{A}\mathbf{x}$ corresponding to λ. ∎

This method always succeeds if λ is a defective multiplicity 2 eigenvalue of the matrix \mathbf{A}.

EXAMPLE 3 Find a general solution of the system

$$\mathbf{x}' = \begin{bmatrix} 1 & -3 \\ 3 & 7 \end{bmatrix} \mathbf{x}. \tag{20}$$

Solution In Example 2 we found that the coefficient matrix \mathbf{A} in Eq. (20) has the defective eigenvalue $\lambda = 4$ of multiplicity 2. We therefore begin by calculating

$$(\mathbf{A} - 4\mathbf{I})^2 = \begin{bmatrix} -3 & -3 \\ 3 & 3 \end{bmatrix}\begin{bmatrix} -3 & -3 \\ 3 & 3 \end{bmatrix} = \begin{bmatrix} 0 & 0 \\ 0 & 0 \end{bmatrix}.$$

Hence Eq. (16) is

$$\begin{bmatrix} 0 & 0 \\ 0 & 0 \end{bmatrix} \mathbf{v}_2 = \mathbf{0},$$

and therefore is satisfied by *any* choice of \mathbf{v}_2. In principle, it could happen that $(\mathbf{A} - 4\mathbf{I})\mathbf{v}_2$ is nonzero (as desired) for some choices of \mathbf{v}_2 though not for others. If we try $\mathbf{v}_2 = [1 \ 0]^T$ we find that

$$(\mathbf{A} - 4\mathbf{I})\mathbf{v}_2 = \begin{bmatrix} -3 & -3 \\ 3 & 3 \end{bmatrix}\begin{bmatrix} 1 \\ 0 \end{bmatrix} = \begin{bmatrix} -3 \\ 3 \end{bmatrix} = \mathbf{v}_1$$

is nonzero, and therefore is an eigenvector associated with $\lambda = 4$. (It is -3 times the eigenvector found in Example 2.) Therefore the two solutions of Eq. (20) given by Eqs. (18) and (19) are

$$\mathbf{x}_1(t) = \mathbf{v}_1 e^{4t} = \begin{bmatrix} -3 \\ 3 \end{bmatrix} e^{4t},$$

$$\mathbf{x}_2(t) = (\mathbf{v}_1 t + \mathbf{v}_2)e^{4t} = \begin{bmatrix} -3t + 1 \\ 3t \end{bmatrix} e^{4t}.$$

The resulting general solution

$$\mathbf{x}(t) = c_1 \mathbf{x}_1(t) + c_2 \mathbf{x}_2(t)$$

has scalar component functions

$$x_1(t) = (-3c_2 t + c_2 - 3c_1)e^{4t},$$
$$x_2(t) = (3c_2 t + 3c_1)e^{4t}.$$

Generalized Eigenvectors

The vector \mathbf{v}_2 in Eq. (16) is an example of a generalized eigenvector. If λ is an eigenvalue of the matrix \mathbf{A}, then a **rank r generalized eigenvector** associated with λ is a vector \mathbf{v} such that

$$(\mathbf{A} - \lambda\mathbf{I})^r \mathbf{v} = \mathbf{0} \qquad \text{but} \qquad (\mathbf{A} - \lambda\mathbf{I})^{r-1} \mathbf{v} \neq \mathbf{0}. \tag{21}$$

If $r = 1$ then (21) simply means that \mathbf{v} is an eigenvector associated with λ. Thus a rank 1 generalized eigenvector is an ordinary eigenvector. The vector \mathbf{v}_2 in (16) is a rank 2 generalized eigenvector (and not an ordinary eigenvector).

The multiplicity 2 method described earlier boils down to finding a pair $\{\mathbf{v}_1, \mathbf{v}_2\}$ of generalized eigenvectors, one of rank 1 and one of rank 2, such that $(\mathbf{A} - \lambda \mathbf{I})\mathbf{v}_2 = \mathbf{v}_1$. Higher multiplicity methods involve longer "chains" of generalized eigenvectors. A **length k chain of generalized eigenvectors based on the eigenvector \mathbf{v}_1** is a set $\{\mathbf{v}_1, \mathbf{v}_2, \ldots, \mathbf{v}_k\}$ of k generalized eigenvectors such that

$$
\begin{aligned}
(\mathbf{A} - \lambda \mathbf{I})\mathbf{v}_k &= \mathbf{v}_{k-1}, \\
(\mathbf{A} - \lambda \mathbf{I})\mathbf{v}_{k-1} &= \mathbf{v}_{k-2}, \\
&\;\;\vdots \\
(\mathbf{A} - \lambda \mathbf{I})\mathbf{v}_2 &= \mathbf{v}_1.
\end{aligned}
\tag{22}
$$

Because \mathbf{v}_1 is an ordinary eigenvector, $(\mathbf{A} - \lambda \mathbf{I})\mathbf{v}_1 = \mathbf{0}$. Therefore it follows from (22) that

$$
(\mathbf{A} - \lambda \mathbf{I})^k \mathbf{v}_k = \mathbf{0}.
\tag{23}
$$

If $\{\mathbf{v}_1, \mathbf{v}_2, \mathbf{v}_3\}$ is a length 3 chain of generalized eigenvectors associated with the multiple eigenvalue λ of the matrix \mathbf{A}, then it is easy to verify that three independent solutions of $\mathbf{x}' = \mathbf{A}\mathbf{x}$ are given by

$$
\begin{aligned}
\mathbf{x}_1(t) &= \mathbf{v}_1 e^{\lambda t}, \\
\mathbf{x}_2(t) &= (\mathbf{v}_1 t + \mathbf{v}_2) e^{\lambda t}, \\
\mathbf{x}_3(t) &= (\tfrac{1}{2}\mathbf{v}_1 t^2 + \mathbf{v}_2 t + \mathbf{v}_3) e^{\lambda t}.
\end{aligned}
\tag{24}
$$

For instance, the equations in (22) give

$$
\mathbf{A}\mathbf{v}_3 = \mathbf{v}_2 + \lambda \mathbf{v}_3, \qquad \mathbf{A}\mathbf{v}_2 = \mathbf{v}_1 + \lambda \mathbf{v}_2, \qquad \mathbf{A}\mathbf{v}_1 = \lambda \mathbf{v}_1,
$$

so

$$
\begin{aligned}
\mathbf{A}\mathbf{x}_3 &= \left[\frac{1}{2}\mathbf{A}\mathbf{v}_1 t^2 + \mathbf{A}\mathbf{v}_2 t + \mathbf{A}\mathbf{v}_3\right] e^{\lambda t} \\
&= \left[\frac{1}{2}\lambda\mathbf{v}_1 t^2 + (\mathbf{v}_1 + \lambda\mathbf{v}_2)t + (\mathbf{v}_2 + \lambda\mathbf{v}_3)\right] e^{\lambda t} \\
&= (\mathbf{v}_1 t + \mathbf{v}_2) e^{\lambda t} + \lambda\left(\frac{1}{2}\mathbf{v}_1 t^2 + \mathbf{v}_2 t + \mathbf{v}_3\right) e^{\lambda t} \\
&= \mathbf{x}_3'.
\end{aligned}
$$

Therefore $\mathbf{x}_3(t)$ in (24) does, indeed, define a solution of $\mathbf{x}' = \mathbf{A}\mathbf{x}$.

Consequently, in order to "handle" a multiplicity 3 eigenvalue λ, it suffices to find a length 3 chain $\{\mathbf{v}_1, \mathbf{v}_2, \mathbf{v}_3\}$ of generalized eigenvectors associated with λ. Looking at Eq. (23), we see that we need only find a solution \mathbf{v}_3 of

$$
(\mathbf{A} - \lambda \mathbf{I})^3 \mathbf{v}_3 = \mathbf{0}
$$

such that the vectors

$$
\mathbf{v}_2 = (\mathbf{A} - \lambda \mathbf{I})\mathbf{v}_3 \quad \text{and} \quad \mathbf{v}_1 = (\mathbf{A} - \lambda \mathbf{I})\mathbf{v}_2
$$

are both nonzero (though, as we will see, this is not always possible).

EXAMPLE 4 Find three linearly independent solutions of the system

$$\mathbf{x}' = \begin{bmatrix} 0 & 1 & 2 \\ -5 & -3 & -7 \\ 1 & 0 & 0 \end{bmatrix} \mathbf{x}. \tag{25}$$

Solution The characteristic equation of the coefficient matrix in Eq. (25) is

$$|\mathbf{A} - \lambda\mathbf{I}| = \begin{vmatrix} -\lambda & 1 & 2 \\ -5 & -3-\lambda & -7 \\ 1 & 0 & -\lambda \end{vmatrix}$$

$$= 1 \cdot [-7 - 2 \cdot (-3 - \lambda)] + (-\lambda)[(-\lambda)(-3-\lambda) + 5]$$

$$= -\lambda^3 - 3\lambda^2 - 3\lambda - 1 = -(\lambda + 1)^3 = 0,$$

so **A** has the eigenvalue $\lambda = -1$ of multiplicity 3. The eigenvector equation $(\mathbf{A} - \lambda\mathbf{I})\mathbf{v} = \mathbf{0}$ for an eigenvector $\mathbf{v} = [a \ b \ c]^T$ is

$$(\mathbf{A} + \mathbf{I})\mathbf{v} = \begin{bmatrix} 1 & 1 & 2 \\ -5 & -2 & -7 \\ 1 & 0 & 1 \end{bmatrix}\begin{bmatrix} a \\ b \\ c \end{bmatrix} = \begin{bmatrix} 0 \\ 0 \\ 0 \end{bmatrix}.$$

The third row $a + c = 0$ gives $c = -a$, then the first row $a + b + 2c = 0$ gives $b = a$. Thus, to within a constant multiple, the eigenvalue $\lambda = -1$ has only the single associated eigenvector $\mathbf{v} = [a \ \ a \ \ -a]^T$ with $a \neq 0$, and so the defect of $\lambda = -1$ is 2.

To apply the method described above for triple eigenvalues, we first calculate

$$(\mathbf{A} + \mathbf{I})^2 = \begin{bmatrix} 1 & 1 & 2 \\ -5 & -2 & -7 \\ 1 & 0 & 1 \end{bmatrix}\begin{bmatrix} 1 & 1 & 2 \\ -5 & -2 & -7 \\ 1 & 0 & 1 \end{bmatrix} = \begin{bmatrix} -2 & -1 & -3 \\ -2 & -1 & -3 \\ 2 & 1 & 3 \end{bmatrix}$$

and

$$(\mathbf{A} + \mathbf{I})^3 = \begin{bmatrix} 1 & 1 & 2 \\ -5 & -2 & -7 \\ 1 & 0 & 1 \end{bmatrix}\begin{bmatrix} -2 & -1 & -3 \\ -2 & -1 & -3 \\ 2 & 1 & 3 \end{bmatrix} = \begin{bmatrix} 0 & 0 & 0 \\ 0 & 0 & 0 \\ 0 & 0 & 0 \end{bmatrix}.$$

Thus *any* nonzero vector \mathbf{v}_3 will be a solution of the equation $(\mathbf{A} + \mathbf{I})^3\mathbf{v}_3 = \mathbf{0}$. Beginning with $\mathbf{v}_3 = [1 \ 0 \ 0]^T$, for instance, we calculate

$$\mathbf{v}_2 = (\mathbf{A} + \mathbf{I})\mathbf{v}_3 = \begin{bmatrix} 1 & 1 & 2 \\ -5 & -2 & -7 \\ 1 & 0 & 1 \end{bmatrix}\begin{bmatrix} 1 \\ 0 \\ 0 \end{bmatrix} = \begin{bmatrix} 1 \\ -5 \\ 1 \end{bmatrix},$$

$$\mathbf{v}_1 = (\mathbf{A} + \mathbf{I})\mathbf{v}_2 = \begin{bmatrix} 1 & 1 & 2 \\ -5 & -2 & -7 \\ 1 & 0 & 1 \end{bmatrix}\begin{bmatrix} 1 \\ -5 \\ 1 \end{bmatrix} = \begin{bmatrix} -2 \\ -2 \\ 2 \end{bmatrix}.$$

Note that \mathbf{v}_1 is the previously found eigenvector \mathbf{v} with $a = -2$; this agreement serves as a check of the accuracy of our matrix computations.

Thus we have found a length 3 chain $\{\mathbf{v}_1, \mathbf{v}_2, \mathbf{v}_3\}$ of generalized eigenvectors associated with the triple eigenvalue $\lambda = -1$. Substitution in (24) now yields the independent solutions

$$\mathbf{x}_1(t) = \mathbf{v}_1 e^{-t} = \begin{bmatrix} -2 \\ -2 \\ 2 \end{bmatrix} e^{-t},$$

$$\mathbf{x}_2(t) = (\mathbf{v}_1 t + \mathbf{v}_2)e^{-t} = \begin{bmatrix} -2t + 1 \\ -2t - 5 \\ 2t + 1 \end{bmatrix} e^{-t},$$

$$\mathbf{x}_3(t) = \left(\frac{1}{2} \mathbf{v}_1 t^2 + \mathbf{v}_2 t + \mathbf{v}_3 \right) e^{-t} = \begin{bmatrix} -t^2 + t + 1 \\ -t^2 - 5t \\ t^2 + t \end{bmatrix} e^{-t},$$

of the system $\mathbf{x}' = \mathbf{A}\mathbf{x}$.

The General Case

A fundamental theorem of linear algebra states that every $n \times n$ matrix \mathbf{A} has n linearly independent generalized eigenvectors. These n generalized eigenvectors may be arranged in chains, with the sum of the lengths of the chains associated with a given eigenvalue λ equal to the multiplicity of λ. But the structure of these chains depends upon the defect of λ, and can be quite complicated. For instance, a multiplicity 4 eigenvalue can correspond to:

- Four length 1 chains (defect 0);
- Two length 1 chains and a length 2 chain (defect 1);
- Two length 2 chains (defect 2);
- A length 1 chain and a length 3 chain (defect 2); or
- A length 4 chain (defect 3).

Note that, in each of these cases, the length of the longest chain is at most $d + 1$, where d is the defect of the eigenvalue. Consequently, once we have found all the ordinary eigenvectors associated with a multiple eigenvalue λ, and therefore know the defect d of λ, we can begin with the equation

$$(\mathbf{A} - \lambda \mathbf{I})^{d+1} \mathbf{u} = \mathbf{0} \tag{26}$$

to start building the chains of generalized eigenvectors associated with λ.

ALGORITHM: Chains of Generalized Eigenvalues

Begin with a nonzero solution \mathbf{u} of Eq. (26) and successively multiply by the matrix $\mathbf{A} - \lambda \mathbf{I}$ until the zero vector is obtained. If

$$(\mathbf{A} - \lambda\mathbf{I})\mathbf{u}_1 = \mathbf{u}_2 \neq \mathbf{0},$$
$$\vdots$$
$$(\mathbf{A} - \lambda\mathbf{I})\mathbf{u}_{k-1} = \mathbf{u}_k \neq \mathbf{0}.$$

but $(\mathbf{A} - \lambda\mathbf{I})\mathbf{u}_k = \mathbf{0}$, then the vectors

$$\{\mathbf{v}_1, \mathbf{v}_2, \ldots, \mathbf{v}_k\} = \{\mathbf{u}_k, \mathbf{u}_{k-1}, \ldots, \mathbf{u}_2, \mathbf{u}_1\}$$

(listed in reverse order to their appearance above) form a length k chain of generalized eigenvectors based on the (ordinary) eigenvector \mathbf{v}_1. ∎

Each length k chain $\{\mathbf{v}_1, \mathbf{v}_2, \ldots, \mathbf{v}_k\}$ of generalized eigenvectors (with \mathbf{v}_1 an ordinary eigenvector associated with λ) determines a set of k independent solutions of $\mathbf{x}' = \mathbf{A}\mathbf{x}$ corresponding to the eigenvalue λ:

$$\mathbf{x}_1(t) = \mathbf{v}_1 e^{\lambda t}$$
$$\mathbf{x}_2(t) = (\mathbf{v}_1 t + \mathbf{v}_2)e^{\lambda t}$$
$$\mathbf{x}_3(t) = \left(\frac{1}{2}\mathbf{v}_1 t^2 + \mathbf{v}_2 t + \mathbf{v}_3\right)e^{\lambda t} \qquad (27)$$
$$\vdots$$
$$\mathbf{x}_k(t) = \left(\frac{\mathbf{v}_1 t^{k-1}}{(k-1)!} + \cdots + \frac{\mathbf{v}_{k-2} t^2}{2!} + \mathbf{v}_{k-1} t + \mathbf{v}_k\right)e^{\lambda t}.$$

Note that (27) reduces to Eqs. (18) through (19) and (24) in the cases $k = 2$ and $k = 3$, respectively.

To ensure that we obtain n generalized eigenvectors of the $n \times n$ matrix \mathbf{A} that are actually linearly independent, and therefore produce a complete set of n linearly independent solutions of $\mathbf{x}' = \mathbf{A}\mathbf{x}$ when we amalgamate all the "chains of solutions" corresponding to different chains of generalized eigenvectors, we may rely on the following two facts:

- Any chain of generalized eigenvectors constitutes a linearly independent set of vectors.

- If two chains of generalized eigenvectors are based on linearly independent eigenvectors, then the union of these two chains is a linearly independent set of vectors (whether the two base eigenvectors are associated with different eigenvalues or with the same eigenvalue).

EXAMPLE 5 Suppose that the 6×6 matrix \mathbf{A} has two multiplicity 3 eigenvectors $\lambda_1 = -2$ and $\lambda_2 = 3$ with defects 1 and 2, respectively. Then λ_1 must have an associated eigenvector \mathbf{u}_1 and a length 2 chain $\{\mathbf{v}_1, \mathbf{v}_2\}$ of generalized eigenvectors (with the eigenvectors \mathbf{u}_1 and \mathbf{v}_1 being linearly independent), whereas λ_2 must have a length 3 chain $\{\mathbf{w}_1, \mathbf{w}_2, \mathbf{w}_3\}$ of generalized eigenvectors based on its single eigenvector \mathbf{w}_1. The six generalized eigenvectors $\mathbf{u}_1, \mathbf{v}_1, \mathbf{v}_2, \mathbf{w}_1, \mathbf{w}_2, \mathbf{w}_3$ are then linearly independent, and yield the following six independent solutions of $\mathbf{x}' = \mathbf{A}\mathbf{x}$:

$$\mathbf{x}_1(t) = \mathbf{u}_1 e^{-2t},$$

$$\mathbf{x}_2(t) = \mathbf{v}_1 e^{-2t},$$

$$\mathbf{x}_3(t) = (\mathbf{v}_1 t + \mathbf{v}_2)e^{-2t},$$

$$\mathbf{x}_4(t) = \mathbf{w}_1 e^{3t},$$

$$\mathbf{x}_5(t) = (\mathbf{w}_1 t + \mathbf{w}_2)e^{3t},$$

$$\mathbf{x}_6(t) = \left(\frac{1}{2}\mathbf{w}_1 t^2 + \mathbf{w}_2 t + \mathbf{w}_3\right)e^{3t}. \qquad \blacksquare$$

As Example 5 illustrates, the combination of independent solutions corresponding to different eigenvalues and chains of generalized eigenvectors is a routine matter. The determination of the chain structure associated with a given multiple eigenvalue can be more interesting (as in Example 6).

An Application

FIGURE 5.4.1. The railway cars of Example 6

Figure 5.4.1 shows two railway cars that are connected with a spring (permanently attached to both cars) and with a damper that exerts opposite forces on the two cars, of magnitude $c(x_1' - x_2')$ proportional to their relative velocity. The two cars also are subject to frictional resistance forces $c_1 x_1'$ and $c_2 x_2'$ proportional to their respective velocities. An application of Newton's law $ma = F$ (as in Example 1 of Section 4.1) yields the equations of motion

$$m_1 x_1'' = k(x_2 - x_1) - c_1 x_1' - c(x_1' - x_2')$$
$$m_2 x_2'' = k(x_1 - x_2) - c_2 x_2' - c(x_2' - x_1'). \qquad (28)$$

In terms of the position vector $\mathbf{x}(t) = [x_1(t)\ x_2(t)]^T$, these equations can be written in the matrix form

$$\mathbf{Mx}'' = \mathbf{Kx} + \mathbf{Rx}', \qquad (29)$$

where \mathbf{M} and \mathbf{K} are mass and stiffness matrices (as in Eqs. (2) and (3) of Section 5.3), and

$$\mathbf{R} = \begin{bmatrix} -(c + c_1) & c \\ c & -(c + c_2) \end{bmatrix}$$

is the *resistance matrix*. Unfortunately, because of the presence of the term involving \mathbf{x}', the methods of Section 5.3 cannot be used.

Instead, we write (28) as a first-order system in the four unknown functions $x_1(t)$, $x_2(t)$, $x_3(t) = x_1'(t)$, and $x_4(t) = x_2'(t)$. We get

$$\mathbf{x}' = \mathbf{Ax} \qquad (30)$$

where now $\mathbf{x} = [x_1\ x_2\ x_3\ x_4]^T$ and

$$\mathbf{A} = \begin{bmatrix} 0 & 0 & 1 & 0 \\ 0 & 0 & 0 & 1 \\ -k & k & -(c + c_1) & c \\ k & -k & c & -(c + c_2) \end{bmatrix}. \qquad (31)$$

EXAMPLE 6 With $m_1 = m_2 = c = 1$ and $k = c_1 = c_2 = 2$, the system in Eq. (30) is

$$\mathbf{x}' = \begin{bmatrix} 0 & 0 & 1 & 0 \\ 0 & 0 & 0 & 1 \\ -2 & 2 & -3 & 1 \\ 2 & -2 & 1 & -3 \end{bmatrix} \mathbf{x}. \tag{32}$$

It is not too tedious to calculate manually—although a computer algebra system such as *Maple, Mathematica,* or MATLAB is useful here—the characteristic equation

$$\lambda^4 + 6\lambda^3 + 12\lambda^2 + 8\lambda = \lambda(\lambda + 2)^3 = 0$$

of the coefficient matrix \mathbf{A} in Eq. (32). Thus \mathbf{A} has the distinct eigenvalue $\lambda_0 = 0$ and the triple eigenvalue $\lambda_1 = -2$.

With $\lambda_0 = 0$:
 The eigenvalue equation $(\mathbf{A} - \lambda\mathbf{I})\mathbf{v} = \mathbf{0}$ for the eigenvector $\mathbf{v} = [a \ b \ c \ d]^T$ is

$$\mathbf{Av} = \begin{bmatrix} 0 & 0 & 1 & 0 \\ 0 & 0 & 0 & 1 \\ -2 & 2 & -3 & 1 \\ 2 & -2 & 1 & -3 \end{bmatrix} \begin{bmatrix} a \\ b \\ c \\ d \end{bmatrix} = \begin{bmatrix} 0 \\ 0 \\ 0 \\ 0 \end{bmatrix}.$$

The first two rows give $c = d = 0$, then the last two rows yield $a = b$. Thus

$$\mathbf{v}_0 = [1 \quad 1 \quad 0 \quad 0]^T$$

is an eigenvector associated with $\lambda_0 = 0$.

With $\lambda_1 = -2$:
 The eigenvector equation $(\mathbf{A} - \lambda\mathbf{I})\mathbf{v} = \mathbf{0}$ is

$$(\mathbf{A} + 2\mathbf{I})\mathbf{v} = \begin{bmatrix} 2 & 0 & 1 & 0 \\ 0 & 2 & 0 & 1 \\ -2 & 2 & -1 & 1 \\ 2 & -2 & 1 & -1 \end{bmatrix} \begin{bmatrix} a \\ b \\ c \\ d \end{bmatrix} = \begin{bmatrix} 0 \\ 0 \\ 0 \\ 0 \end{bmatrix}.$$

The third and fourth scalar equations here are the differences of the first and second equations, and therefore are redundant. Hence \mathbf{v} is determined by the first two equations,

$$2a + c = 0 \quad \text{and} \quad 2b + d = 0.$$

We can choose a and b independently, then solve for c and d. Thereby we obtain *two* eigenvectors associated with the triple eigenvalue $\lambda_1 = -2$. The choice $a = 1$, $b = 0$ yields $c = -2$, $d = 0$ and the eigenvector

$$\mathbf{u}_1 = [1 \quad 0 \quad -2 \quad 0]^T.$$

The choice $a = 0$, $b = 1$ yields $c = 0$, $d = -2$ and the eigenvector

$$\mathbf{u}_2 = [0 \quad 1 \quad 0 \quad -2]^T.$$

Because $\lambda_1 = -2$ has defect 1, we need a generalized eigenvector of rank 2, and hence a nonzero solution \mathbf{v}_2 of the equation

$$(\mathbf{A} + 2\mathbf{I})^2 \mathbf{v}_2 = \begin{bmatrix} 2 & 2 & 1 & 1 \\ 2 & 2 & 1 & 1 \\ 0 & 0 & 0 & 0 \\ 0 & 0 & 0 & 0 \end{bmatrix} \mathbf{v}_2 = \mathbf{0}.$$

Obviously,

$$\mathbf{v}_2 = [0 \quad 0 \quad 1 \quad -1]^T$$

is such a vector, and we find that

$$(\mathbf{A} + 2\mathbf{I})\mathbf{v}_2 = \begin{bmatrix} 2 & 0 & 1 & 0 \\ 0 & 2 & 0 & 1 \\ -2 & 2 & -1 & 1 \\ 2 & -2 & 1 & -1 \end{bmatrix} \begin{bmatrix} 0 \\ 0 \\ 1 \\ -1 \end{bmatrix} = \begin{bmatrix} 1 \\ -1 \\ -2 \\ 2 \end{bmatrix} = \mathbf{v}_1$$

is nonzero, and therefore is an eigenvector associated with $\lambda_1 = -2$. Then $\{\mathbf{v}_1, \mathbf{v}_2\}$ is the length 2 chain we need.

The eigenvector \mathbf{v}_1 is neither of the two eigenvectors previously found, but we observe that $\mathbf{v}_1 = \mathbf{u}_1 - \mathbf{u}_2$. For a length 1 chain $\{\mathbf{w}_1\}$ to complete the picture, we can choose any combination of \mathbf{u}_1 and \mathbf{u}_2 that is independent of \mathbf{v}_1; for instance,

$$\mathbf{w}_1 = \mathbf{u}_1 + \mathbf{u}_2 = [1 \quad 1 \quad -2 \quad -2]^T.$$

Finally, the chains $\{\mathbf{v}_0\}$, $\{\mathbf{w}_1\}$, and $\{\mathbf{v}_1, \mathbf{v}_2\}$ yields the four independent solutions

$$\mathbf{x}_1(t) = \mathbf{v}_0 e^{0 \cdot t} = [1 \quad 1 \quad 0 \quad 0]^T,$$

$$\mathbf{x}_2(t) = \mathbf{w}_1 e^{-2t} = [1 \quad 1 \quad -2 \quad -2]^T e^{-2t},$$

$$\mathbf{x}_3(t) = \mathbf{v}_1 e^{-2t} = [1 \quad -1 \quad -2 \quad 2]^T e^{-2t}, \tag{33}$$

$$\mathbf{x}_4(t) = (\mathbf{v}_1 t + \mathbf{v}_2) e^{-2t}$$

$$= [t \quad -t \quad -2t + 1 \quad 2t - 1]^T e^{-2t}$$

of the system $\mathbf{x}' = \mathbf{A}\mathbf{x}$ in (32).

The four scalar components of the general solution

$$\mathbf{x}(t) = c_1 \mathbf{x}_1(t) + c_2 \mathbf{x}_2(t) + c_3 \mathbf{x}_3(t) + c_4 \mathbf{x}_4(t)$$

are described by the equations

$$x_1(t) = c_1 + e^{-2t}(c_2 + c_3 + c_4 t)$$

$$x_2(t) = c_1 + e^{-2t}(c_2 - c_3 - c_4 t)$$

$$x_3(t) = e^{-2t}(-2c_2 - 2c_3 + c_4 - 2c_4 t) \tag{34}$$

$$x_4(t) = e^{-2t}(-2c_2 + 2c_3 - c_4 + 2c_4 t).$$

Recall that $x_1(t)$ and $x_2(t)$ are the position functions of the equal masses, whereas $x_3(t) = x_1'(t)$ and $x_4(t) = x_2'(t)$ are their respective velocity functions.

For instance, suppose that $x_1(0) = x_2(0) = 0$ and that $x_1'(0) = x_2'(0) = v_0$. Then the equations

$$x_1(0) = c_1 + c_2 + c_3 \qquad = 0$$
$$x_2(0) = c_1 + c_2 - c_3 \qquad = 0$$
$$x_1'(0) = \qquad -2c_2 - 2c_3 + c_4 = v_0$$
$$x_2'(0) = \qquad -2c_2 + 2c_3 - c_4 = v_0$$

are readily solved for $c_1 = \frac{1}{2}v_0$, $c_2 = -\frac{1}{2}v_0$, and $c_3 = c_4 = 0$, so

$$x_1(t) = x_2(t) = \frac{1}{2} v_0(1 + e^{-2t}),$$

$$x_1'(t) = x_2'(t) = v_0 e^{-2t}.$$

In this case the two railway cars continue in the same direction with equal but exponentially damped velocities, approaching the displacements $x_1 = x_2 = \frac{1}{2}v_0$ as $t \rightarrow +\infty$.

It is of interest to interpret physically the individual generalized eigenvector solutions given in (33). The degenerate ($\lambda_0 = 0$) solution

$$\mathbf{x}_1(t) = [1 \quad 1 \quad 0 \quad 0]^T$$

describes the two masses at rest. The solution

$$\mathbf{x}_2(t) = [1 \quad 1 \quad -2 \quad -2]^T e^{-2t}$$

describes damped motions of the two masses with equal velocities in the same direction. The solutions $\mathbf{x}_3(t)$ and $\mathbf{x}_4(t)$ resulting from the length 2 chain $\{\mathbf{v}_1, \mathbf{v}_2\}$ both describe damped motion with the two masses moving in opposite directions. ∎

The methods of this section apply to complex multiple eigenvalues just as to real multiple eigenvalues (although the necessary computations tend to be somewhat lengthy). Given a complex conjugate pair $\alpha \pm \beta i$ of eigenvalues of multiplicity k, we work with one of them (say, $\lambda = \alpha - \beta i$) as if it were real to find k independent complex-valued solutions. The real and imaginary parts of these complex-valued solutions then provide $2k$ real-valued solutions associated with the two eigenvalues $\lambda = \alpha - \beta i$ and $\bar{\lambda} = \alpha + \beta i$ each of multiplicity k. See Problems 33 and 34.

5.4 Problems

Find general solutions of the systems in Problems 1 through 22.

1. $\mathbf{x}' = \begin{bmatrix} -2 & 1 \\ -1 & -4 \end{bmatrix} \mathbf{x}$

2. $\mathbf{x}' = \begin{bmatrix} 3 & -1 \\ 1 & 1 \end{bmatrix} \mathbf{x}$

3. $\mathbf{x}' = \begin{bmatrix} 1 & -2 \\ 2 & 5 \end{bmatrix} \mathbf{x}$

4. $\mathbf{x}' = \begin{bmatrix} 3 & -1 \\ 1 & 5 \end{bmatrix} \mathbf{x}$

5. $\mathbf{x}' = \begin{bmatrix} 7 & 1 \\ -4 & 3 \end{bmatrix} \mathbf{x}$

6. $\mathbf{x}' = \begin{bmatrix} 1 & -4 \\ 4 & 9 \end{bmatrix} \mathbf{x}$

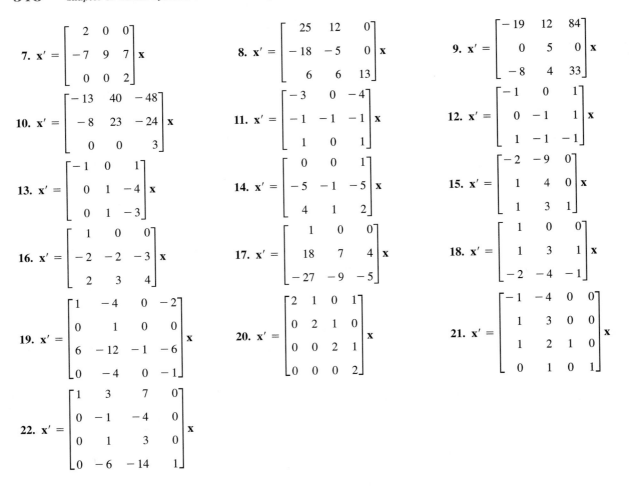

7. $\mathbf{x}' = \begin{bmatrix} 2 & 0 & 0 \\ -7 & 9 & 7 \\ 0 & 0 & 2 \end{bmatrix} \mathbf{x}$

8. $\mathbf{x}' = \begin{bmatrix} 25 & 12 & 0 \\ -18 & -5 & 0 \\ 6 & 6 & 13 \end{bmatrix} \mathbf{x}$

9. $\mathbf{x}' = \begin{bmatrix} -19 & 12 & 84 \\ 0 & 5 & 0 \\ -8 & 4 & 33 \end{bmatrix} \mathbf{x}$

10. $\mathbf{x}' = \begin{bmatrix} -13 & 40 & -48 \\ -8 & 23 & -24 \\ 0 & 0 & 3 \end{bmatrix} \mathbf{x}$

11. $\mathbf{x}' = \begin{bmatrix} -3 & 0 & -4 \\ -1 & -1 & -1 \\ 1 & 0 & 1 \end{bmatrix} \mathbf{x}$

12. $\mathbf{x}' = \begin{bmatrix} -1 & 0 & 1 \\ 0 & -1 & 1 \\ 1 & -1 & -1 \end{bmatrix} \mathbf{x}$

13. $\mathbf{x}' = \begin{bmatrix} -1 & 0 & 1 \\ 0 & 1 & -4 \\ 0 & 1 & -3 \end{bmatrix} \mathbf{x}$

14. $\mathbf{x}' = \begin{bmatrix} 0 & 0 & 1 \\ -5 & -1 & -5 \\ 4 & 1 & 2 \end{bmatrix} \mathbf{x}$

15. $\mathbf{x}' = \begin{bmatrix} -2 & -9 & 0 \\ 1 & 4 & 0 \\ 1 & 3 & 1 \end{bmatrix} \mathbf{x}$

16. $\mathbf{x}' = \begin{bmatrix} 1 & 0 & 0 \\ -2 & -2 & -3 \\ 2 & 3 & 4 \end{bmatrix} \mathbf{x}$

17. $\mathbf{x}' = \begin{bmatrix} 1 & 0 & 0 \\ 18 & 7 & 4 \\ -27 & -9 & -5 \end{bmatrix} \mathbf{x}$

18. $\mathbf{x}' = \begin{bmatrix} 1 & 0 & 0 \\ 1 & 3 & 1 \\ -2 & -4 & -1 \end{bmatrix} \mathbf{x}$

19. $\mathbf{x}' = \begin{bmatrix} 1 & -4 & 0 & -2 \\ 0 & 1 & 0 & 0 \\ 6 & -12 & -1 & -6 \\ 0 & -4 & 0 & -1 \end{bmatrix} \mathbf{x}$

20. $\mathbf{x}' = \begin{bmatrix} 2 & 1 & 0 & 1 \\ 0 & 2 & 1 & 0 \\ 0 & 0 & 2 & 1 \\ 0 & 0 & 0 & 2 \end{bmatrix} \mathbf{x}$

21. $\mathbf{x}' = \begin{bmatrix} -1 & -4 & 0 & 0 \\ 1 & 3 & 0 & 0 \\ 1 & 2 & 1 & 0 \\ 0 & 1 & 0 & 1 \end{bmatrix} \mathbf{x}$

22. $\mathbf{x}' = \begin{bmatrix} 1 & 3 & 7 & 0 \\ 0 & -1 & -4 & 0 \\ 0 & 1 & 3 & 0 \\ 0 & -6 & -14 & 1 \end{bmatrix} \mathbf{x}$

In Problems 23 through 32 the eigenvalues of the coefficient matrix \mathbf{A} are given. Find a general solution of the indicated system $\mathbf{x}' = \mathbf{A}\mathbf{x}$. In Problems 29 through 32 linear algebra software will be useful.

23. $\mathbf{x}' = \begin{bmatrix} 39 & 8 & -16 \\ -36 & -5 & 16 \\ 72 & 16 & -29 \end{bmatrix} \mathbf{x}; \quad \lambda = -1, 3, 3$

24. $\mathbf{x}' = \begin{bmatrix} 28 & 50 & 100 \\ 15 & 33 & 60 \\ -15 & -30 & -57 \end{bmatrix} \mathbf{x}; \quad \lambda = -2, 3, 3$

25. $\mathbf{x}' = \begin{bmatrix} -2 & 17 & 4 \\ -1 & 6 & 1 \\ 0 & 1 & 2 \end{bmatrix} \mathbf{x}; \quad \lambda = 2, 2, 2$

26. $\mathbf{x}' = \begin{bmatrix} 5 & -1 & 1 \\ 1 & 3 & 0 \\ -3 & 2 & 1 \end{bmatrix} \mathbf{x}; \quad \lambda = 3, 3, 3$

27. $\mathbf{x}' = \begin{bmatrix} -3 & 5 & -5 \\ 3 & -1 & 3 \\ 8 & -8 & 10 \end{bmatrix} \mathbf{x}; \quad \lambda = 2, 2, 2$

28. $\mathbf{x}' = \begin{bmatrix} -15 & -7 & 4 \\ 34 & 16 & -11 \\ 17 & 7 & 5 \end{bmatrix} \mathbf{x}; \quad \lambda = 2, 2, 2$

29. $\mathbf{x}' = \begin{bmatrix} -1 & 1 & 1 & -2 \\ 7 & -4 & -6 & 11 \\ 5 & -1 & 1 & 3 \\ 6 & -2 & -2 & 6 \end{bmatrix} \mathbf{x}; \quad \lambda = -1, -1, 2, 2$

30. $\mathbf{x}' = \begin{bmatrix} 2 & 1 & -2 & 1 \\ 0 & 3 & -5 & 3 \\ 0 & -13 & 22 & -12 \\ 0 & -27 & 45 & -25 \end{bmatrix} \mathbf{x}; \quad \lambda = -1, -1, 2, 2$

31. $\mathbf{x}' = \begin{bmatrix} 35 & -12 & 4 & 30 \\ 22 & -8 & 3 & 19 \\ -10 & 3 & 0 & -9 \\ -27 & 9 & -3 & -23 \end{bmatrix} \mathbf{x}; \quad \lambda = 1, 1, 1, 1$

32. $\mathbf{x}' = \begin{bmatrix} 11 & -1 & 26 & 6 & -3 \\ 0 & 3 & 0 & 0 & 0 \\ -9 & 0 & -24 & -6 & 3 \\ 3 & 0 & 9 & 5 & -1 \\ -48 & -3 & -138 & -30 & 18 \end{bmatrix} \mathbf{x}; \quad \lambda = 2, 2, 3, 3, 3$

33. The characteristic equation of the coefficient matrix \mathbf{A} of the system

$$\mathbf{x}' = \begin{bmatrix} 3 & -4 & 1 & 0 \\ 4 & 3 & 0 & 1 \\ 0 & 0 & 3 & -4 \\ 0 & 0 & 4 & 3 \end{bmatrix} \mathbf{x}$$

is

$$\phi(\lambda) = (\lambda^2 - 6\lambda + 25)^2 = 0.$$

Therefore \mathbf{A} has the repeated complex conjugate pair $3 \pm 4i$ of eigenvalues. First show that the complex vectors

$$\mathbf{v}_1 = [1 \quad i \quad 0 \quad 0]^T \quad \text{and} \quad \mathbf{v}_2 = [0 \quad 0 \quad 1 \quad i]^T$$

form a length 2 chain $\{\mathbf{v}_1, \mathbf{v}_2\}$ associated with the eigenvalue $\lambda = 3 - 4i$. Then calculate the real and imaginary parts of the complex-valued solutions

$$\mathbf{v}_1 e^{\lambda t} \quad \text{and} \quad (\mathbf{v}_1 t + \mathbf{v}_2) e^{\lambda t}$$

to find four independent real-valued solutions of $\mathbf{x}' = \mathbf{Ax}$.

34. The characteristic equation of the coefficient matrix \mathbf{A} of the system

$$\mathbf{x}' = \begin{bmatrix} 2 & 0 & -8 & -3 \\ -18 & -1 & 0 & 0 \\ -9 & -3 & -25 & -9 \\ 33 & 10 & 90 & 32 \end{bmatrix} \mathbf{x}$$

is

$$\phi(\lambda) = (\lambda^2 - 4\lambda + 13)^2 = 0.$$

Therefore \mathbf{A} has the repeated complex conjugate pair $2 \pm 3i$ of eigenvalues. First show that the complex vectors

$$\mathbf{v}_1 = [-i \quad 3 + 3i \quad 0 \quad -i]^T,$$
$$\mathbf{v}_2 = [3 \quad -10 + 9i \quad -i \quad 0]^T$$

form a length 2 chain $\{\mathbf{v}_1, \mathbf{v}_2\}$ associated with the eigenvalue $\lambda = 2 + 3i$. Then calculate (as in Problem 33) four independent real-valued solutions of $\mathbf{x}' = \mathbf{Ax}$.

35. Find the position functions $x_1(t)$ and $x_2(t)$ of the railway cars of Fig. 5.4.1 if the physical parameters are given by

$$m_1 = m_2 = c_1 = c_2 = c = k = 1$$

and the initial conditions are

$$x_1(0) = x_2(0) = 0, \quad x_1'(0) = x_2'(0) = v_0.$$

How far do the cars travel before stopping?

36. Repeat Problem 35 under the assumption that Car 1 is shielded from air resistance by Car 2, so now $c_1 = 0$. Show that, before stopping, the cars travel twice as far as those of Problem 35.

5.4 Computing Project

The MATLAB command **gallery(5)** produces the 5×5 example matrix

$$\mathbf{A} = \begin{bmatrix} -9 & 11 & -21 & 63 & -252 \\ 70 & -69 & 141 & -421 & 1684 \\ -575 & 575 & -1149 & 3451 & -13801 \\ 3891 & -3891 & 7782 & -23345 & 93365 \\ 1024 & -1024 & 2048 & -6144 & 24572 \end{bmatrix}.$$

Enter this matrix in whatever calculator or computer system is available, then use appropriate commands to show:

- First, the characteristic equation of A is $\lambda^5 = 0$, so A has the single eigenvalue $\lambda = 0$ of multiplicity 5.
- Second, there is only a single eigenvector associated with this eigenvalue, which thus has defect 4.

To seek a chain of generalized eigenvectors, show that $A^4 \neq 0$ but $A^5 = 0$ (the 5×5 zero matrix). Hence *any* nonzero 5-vector u_1 satisfies the equation

$$(A - \lambda I)^5 u_1 = A^5 u_1 = 0.$$

Calculate the vectors $u_2 = Au_1$, $u_3 = Au_2$, $u_4 = Au_3$, and $u_5 = Au_4$ in turn. You should find that u_5 is nonzero, and is therefore (to within a constant multiple) the unique eigenvector v of the matrix A. But can the eigenvector v you find possibly be independent of your original choice of the starting vector $u_1 \neq 0$? Investigate this question by repeating the process with several different choices of u_1.

Finally, having found a length 5 chain $\{u_5, u_4, u_3, u_2, u_1\}$ of generalized eigenvectors based on the eigenvector u_5 associated with the eigenvalue $\lambda = 0$ of the matrix A, write five linearly independent solutions of the 5-dimensional homogeneous linear system $x' = Ax$.

*5.5 Matrix Exponentials and Linear Systems

The solution vectors of a homogeneous linear system $x' = Px$ can be used to construct a matrix X that satisfies the *matrix differential equation* $X' = PX$. Suppose that $x_1(t)$, $x_2(t), \ldots, x_n(t)$ are n linearly independent solutions on some open interval of the homogeneous system

$$\blacktriangleright \qquad x' = P(t)x \qquad (1)$$

of n linear equations. Then the $n \times n$ matrix

$$\Phi(t) = \begin{bmatrix} x_{11}(t) & x_{12}(t) & \cdots & x_{1n}(t) \\ x_{21}(t) & x_{22}(t) & \cdots & x_{2n}(t) \\ \cdot & \cdot & \cdot & \cdot \\ \cdot & \cdot & \cdot & \cdot \\ \cdot & \cdot & \cdot & \cdot \\ x_{n1}(t) & x_{n2}(t) & \cdots & x_{nn}(t) \end{bmatrix}, \qquad (2)$$

having as *column* vectors the solution vectors x_1, x_2, \ldots, x_n is called a **fundamental matrix** for the system. Because its column vectors are linearly independent, it follows that the matrix $\Phi(t)$ is nonsingular and therefore has an inverse matrix $\Phi(t)^{-1}$. Because each column vector of $\Phi(t)$ satisfies Eq. (1), it follows by column-wise calculation that $\Phi'(t) = P(t)\Phi(t)$. Thus $X = \Phi(t)$ satisfies the equation $X' = PX$.

In terms of the fundamental matrix $\Phi(t)$, the general solution

$$\blacktriangleright \qquad x(t) = c_1 x_1(t) + c_2 x_2(t) + \cdots + c_n x_n(t) \qquad (3)$$

of the system $\mathbf{x}' = \mathbf{P}(t)\mathbf{x}$ can be written in the form

$$\mathbf{x}(t) = \mathbf{\Phi}(t)\mathbf{c}, \tag{4}$$

where

$$\mathbf{c} = \begin{bmatrix} c_1 \\ c_2 \\ c_3 \\ \cdot \\ \cdot \\ \cdot \\ c_n \end{bmatrix}$$

is an *arbitrary constant vector.* In order that the solution $\mathbf{x}(t)$ satisfy the initial condition

$$\mathbf{x}(a) = \mathbf{b}, \tag{5}$$

where b_1, b_2, \ldots, b_n are given, it therefore will suffice for the coefficient vector \mathbf{c} in Eq. (4) to satisfy $\mathbf{\Phi}(a)\mathbf{c} = \mathbf{b}$; that is,

$$\mathbf{c} = \mathbf{\Phi}(a)^{-1}\mathbf{b}. \tag{6}$$

When we substitute (6) in (4) we get the conclusion of the following theorem.

THEOREM 1: Fundamental Matrix Solutions

Let $\mathbf{\Phi}(t)$ be a fundamental matrix for the homogeneous linear system $\mathbf{x}' = \mathbf{P}(t)\mathbf{x}$ on an open interval containing the point $t = a$. Then the [unique] solution of the initial value problem

$$\mathbf{x}' = \mathbf{P}(t)\mathbf{x}, \qquad \mathbf{x}(a) = \mathbf{b} \tag{7}$$

is given by

$$\mathbf{x}(t) = \mathbf{\Phi}(t)\mathbf{\Phi}(a)^{-1}\mathbf{b} = \mathbf{\Phi}(t)\mathbf{\Phi}(a)^{-1}\mathbf{x}(a). \tag{8}$$

∎

Section 5.2 tells us how to find a fundamental matrix for the system

$$\mathbf{x}' = \mathbf{A}\mathbf{x} \tag{9}$$

with constant $n \times n$ coefficient matrix \mathbf{A}, at least in the case where \mathbf{A} has a complete set of n linearly independent eigenvectors $\mathbf{v}_1, \mathbf{v}_1, \ldots, \mathbf{v}_n$ associated with the [not necessarily distinct] eigenvalues $\lambda_1, \lambda_2, \ldots, \lambda_n$, respectively. In this event the corresponding solution vectors of (9) are given by

$$\mathbf{x}_i(t) = \mathbf{v}_i e^{\lambda_i t}$$

for $i = 1, 2, \ldots, n$. Therefore, the $n \times n$ matrix

$$\mathbf{\Phi}(t) = \begin{bmatrix} | & | & & | \\ \mathbf{v}_1 e^{\lambda_1 t} & \mathbf{v}_2 e^{\lambda_2 t} & \cdots & \mathbf{v}_n e^{\lambda_n t} \\ | & | & & | \end{bmatrix} \tag{10}$$

having the solutions $\mathbf{x}_1, \mathbf{x}_2, \ldots, \mathbf{x}_n$ as column vectors is a fundamental matrix for the system $\mathbf{x}' = \mathbf{A}\mathbf{x}$ (on the entire real line).

In order to apply Eq. (8), we must be able to compute the inverse matrix $\mathbf{\Phi}(a)^{-1}$. The inverse of the nonsingular 2×2 matrix

$$\mathbf{A} = \begin{bmatrix} a & b \\ c & d \end{bmatrix}$$

is

$$\mathbf{A}^{-1} = \frac{1}{\Delta} \begin{bmatrix} d & -b \\ -c & a \end{bmatrix}, \tag{11}$$

where $\Delta = \det(\mathbf{A}) = ad - bc \neq 0$. The inverse of the nonsingular 3×3 matrix $\mathbf{A} = [a_{ij}]$ is given by

$$A^{-1} = \frac{1}{\Delta} \begin{bmatrix} +A_{11} & -A_{12} & +A_{13} \\ -A_{21} & +A_{22} & -A_{23} \\ +A_{31} & -A_{32} & +A_{33} \end{bmatrix}^T, \tag{12}$$

where $\Delta = \det(\mathbf{A}) \neq 0$ and A_{ij} denotes the determinant of the 2×2 submatrix of \mathbf{A} obtained by deleting the ith row and jth column of \mathbf{A}. (Do not overlook the symbol T for *transpose* in Eq. (12).) The formula in (12) is also valid upon generalization to $n \times n$ matrices, but in practice inverses of larger matrices are usually computed instead by row reduction methods (see any linear algebra text).

EXAMPLE 1 Find a fundamental matrix for the system

$$\begin{aligned} x' &= 4x + 2y, \\ y' &= 3x - y \end{aligned} \tag{13}$$

and use it to find the solution of (13) that satisfies the initial conditions $x(0) = 1$, $y(0) = -1$.

Solution The linearly independent solutions

$$\mathbf{x}_1(t) = \begin{bmatrix} e^{-2t} \\ -3e^{-2t} \end{bmatrix} \quad \text{and} \quad \mathbf{x}_2(t) = \begin{bmatrix} 2e^{5t} \\ e^{5t} \end{bmatrix}$$

found in Example 1 of Section 5.2 yield the fundamental matrix

$$\mathbf{\Phi}(t) = \begin{bmatrix} e^{-2t} & 2e^{5t} \\ -3e^{-2t} & e^{5t} \end{bmatrix}. \tag{14}$$

Then

$$\mathbf{\Phi}(0) = \begin{bmatrix} 1 & 2 \\ -3 & 1 \end{bmatrix},$$

and the formula in (11) gives the inverse matrix

$$\mathbf{\Phi}(0)^{-1} = \frac{1}{7} \begin{bmatrix} 1 & -2 \\ 3 & 1 \end{bmatrix}. \tag{15}$$

Hence the formula in (8) gives the solution

$$\mathbf{x}(t) = \begin{bmatrix} e^{-2t} & 2e^{5t} \\ -3e^{-2t} & e^{5t} \end{bmatrix} \left(\frac{1}{7}\right) \begin{bmatrix} 1 & -2 \\ 3 & 1 \end{bmatrix} \begin{bmatrix} 1 \\ -1 \end{bmatrix} = \left(\frac{1}{7}\right) \begin{bmatrix} e^{-2t} & 2e^{5t} \\ -3e^{-2t} & e^{5t} \end{bmatrix} \begin{bmatrix} 3 \\ 2 \end{bmatrix},$$

and so

$$\mathbf{x}(t) = \frac{1}{7} \begin{bmatrix} 3e^{-2t} + 4e^{5t} \\ -9e^{-2t} + 2e^{5t} \end{bmatrix}.$$

Thus the solution of the original initial value problem is given by

$$x(t) = \frac{3}{7} e^{-2t} + \frac{4}{7} e^{5t}, \qquad y(t) = -\frac{9}{7} e^{-2t} + \frac{2}{7} e^{5t}. \qquad \blacksquare$$

Remark: An advantage of the fundamental matrix approach is this: Once we know the fundamental matrix $\mathbf{\Phi}(t)$ and the inverse matrix $\mathbf{\Phi}(a)^{-1}$, we can calculate rapidly by matrix multiplication the solutions corresponding to different initial conditions. For example, suppose that we seek the solution of the system in (13) satisfying the new initial conditions $x(0) = 77$, $y(0) = 49$. Then substitution of (14) and (15) in (8) gives the new solution

$$\mathbf{x}(t) = \frac{1}{7} \begin{bmatrix} e^{-2t} & 2e^{5t} \\ -3e^{-2t} & e^{5t} \end{bmatrix} \begin{bmatrix} 1 & -2 \\ 3 & 1 \end{bmatrix} \begin{bmatrix} 77 \\ 49 \end{bmatrix}$$

$$= \frac{1}{7} \begin{bmatrix} e^{-2t} & 2e^{5t} \\ -3e^{-2t} & e^{5t} \end{bmatrix} \begin{bmatrix} -21 \\ 280 \end{bmatrix} = \begin{bmatrix} -3e^{-2t} + 80e^{5t} \\ 9e^{-2t} + 40e^{5t} \end{bmatrix}.$$

Matrix Exponentials

We now discuss the possibility of constructing a fundamental matrix for the constant-coefficient linear system $\mathbf{x}' = \mathbf{Ax}$ directly from the coefficient matrix \mathbf{A}—that is, without first applying the methods of earlier sections to find a linearly independent set of solution vectors.

We have seen that exponential functions play a central role in the solution of linear differential equations and systems, ranging from the scalar equation $x' = kx$ with solution $x(t) = x_0 e^{kt}$ to the vector solution $\mathbf{x}(t) = \mathbf{v}e^{kt}$ of the linear system $\mathbf{x}' = \mathbf{Ax}$ whose coefficient matrix \mathbf{A} has eigenvalue λ with associated eigenvector \mathbf{v}. Now we define exponentials of matrices in such a way that

$$\mathbf{X}(t) = e^{\mathbf{A}t}$$

is a matrix solution of the matrix differential equation

$$\mathbf{X}' = \mathbf{AX}$$

with $n \times n$ coefficient matrix \mathbf{A}.

The exponential e^z of a complex number z may be defined (as in Section 3.3) by means of the exponential series

$$e^z = 1 + z + \frac{z^2}{2!} + \cdots + \frac{z^n}{n!} + \cdots. \tag{16}$$

Similarly, if \mathbf{A} is a $n \times n$ matrix, then the **exponential matrix** $e^{\mathbf{A}}$ is the $n \times n$ matrix defined by the series

$$\blacktriangleright \qquad e^{\mathbf{A}} = \mathbf{I} + \mathbf{A} + \frac{\mathbf{A}^2}{2!} + \cdots + \frac{\mathbf{A}^n}{n!} + \cdots, \qquad (17)$$

where \mathbf{I} is the identity matrix. The meaning of the infinite series on the right in (17) is given by

$$\sum_{n=0}^{\infty} \frac{\mathbf{A}^n}{n!} = \lim_{k \to \infty} \left(\sum_{n=0}^{k} \frac{\mathbf{A}^n}{n!} \right) \qquad (18)$$

where $\mathbf{A}^0 = \mathbf{I}$, $\mathbf{A}^2 = \mathbf{A}\mathbf{A}$, $\mathbf{A}^3 = \mathbf{A}\mathbf{A}^2$, and so on; inductively, $\mathbf{A}^{n+1} = \mathbf{A}\mathbf{A}^n$ if $n \geqq 0$. It can be shown that the limit in (18) exists for every $n \times n$ matrix \mathbf{A}. That is, the exponential matrix $e^{\mathbf{A}}$ is defined (by Eq. (17)) for every square matrix \mathbf{A}.

EXAMPLE 2 Consider the 2×2 diagonal matrix

$$\mathbf{A} = \begin{bmatrix} a & 0 \\ 0 & b \end{bmatrix}.$$

Then it is apparent that

$$\mathbf{A}^n = \begin{bmatrix} a^n & 0 \\ 0 & b^n \end{bmatrix}$$

for each integer $n \geqq 1$. It therefore follows that

$$e^{\mathbf{A}} = \mathbf{I} + \mathbf{A} + \frac{\mathbf{A}^2}{2!} + \cdots$$

$$= \begin{bmatrix} 1 & 0 \\ 0 & 1 \end{bmatrix} + \begin{bmatrix} a & 0 \\ 0 & b \end{bmatrix} + \begin{bmatrix} a^2/2! & 0 \\ 0 & b^2/2! \end{bmatrix} + \cdots$$

$$= \begin{bmatrix} 1 + a + a^2/2! + \cdots & 0 \\ 0 & 1 + b + b^2/2! + \cdots \end{bmatrix}.$$

Thus

$$e^{\mathbf{A}} = \begin{bmatrix} e^a & 0 \\ 0 & e^b \end{bmatrix},$$

so the exponential of the *diagonal* 2×2 matrix \mathbf{A} is obtained simply by exponentiating each diagonal element of \mathbf{A}. ∎

The $n \times n$ analogue of the 2×2 result in Example 2 is established in the same way. The exponential of the $n \times n$ diagonal matrix

$$\mathbf{D} = \begin{bmatrix} a_1 & 0 & \cdots & 0 \\ 0 & a_2 & \cdots & 0 \\ \vdots & \vdots & & \vdots \\ 0 & 0 & \cdots & a_n \end{bmatrix} \qquad (19)$$

is the $n \times n$ diagonal matrix

$$
e^{\mathbf{D}} = \begin{bmatrix} e^{a_1} & 0 & \cdots & 0 \\ 0 & e^{a_2} & \cdots & 0 \\ \vdots & \vdots & & \vdots \\ 0 & 0 & \cdots & e^{a_n} \end{bmatrix}
\tag{20}
$$

obtained by exponentiating each diagonal element of \mathbf{D}.

The matrix exponential $e^{\mathbf{A}}$ satisfies most of the exponential relations that are familiar in the case of scalar exponents. For instance, if $\mathbf{0}$ is the $n \times n$ zero matrix, then (7) yields

$$
e^{\mathbf{0}} = \mathbf{I}.
\tag{21}
$$

In Problem 25 we ask you to show that a useful law of exponents holds for $n \times n$ matrices that commute:

$$
\text{If } \mathbf{AB} = \mathbf{BA}, \quad \text{then} \quad e^{\mathbf{A}+\mathbf{B}} = e^{\mathbf{A}}e^{\mathbf{B}}.
\tag{22}
$$

In Problem 26 we ask you to conclude that

$$
(e^{\mathbf{A}})^{-1} = e^{-\mathbf{A}}.
\tag{23}
$$

In particular, the matrix $e^{\mathbf{A}}$ is nonsingular for every $n \times n$ matrix \mathbf{A} (reminiscent of the fact that $e^t \neq 0$ for all t). It follows by elementary linear algebra that the column vectors of $e^{\mathbf{A}}$ are always linearly independent.

If t is a scalar variable, then substitution of $\mathbf{A}t$ for \mathbf{A} in Eq. (17) gives

$$
e^{\mathbf{A}t} = \mathbf{I} + \mathbf{A}t + \mathbf{A}^2\frac{t^2}{2!} + \cdots + \mathbf{A}^n\frac{t^n}{n!} + \cdots.
\tag{24}
$$

(Of course, $\mathbf{A}t$ is obtained simply by multiplying each element of \mathbf{A} by t.) It happens that term-by-term differentiation of the series in (24) is valid, with the result

$$
\frac{d}{dt}(e^{\mathbf{A}t}) = \mathbf{A} + \mathbf{A}^2t + \mathbf{A}^3\frac{t^2}{2!} + \cdots = \mathbf{A}\left(\mathbf{I} + \mathbf{A}t + \mathbf{A}^2\frac{t^2}{2!} + \cdots\right);
$$

that is,

$$
\frac{d}{dt}(e^{\mathbf{A}t}) = \mathbf{A}e^{\mathbf{A}t},
\tag{25}
$$

in analogy to the formula $D_t(e^{kt}) = ke^{kt}$ from elementary calculus. Thus the matrix-valued function

$$
\mathbf{X}(t) = e^{\mathbf{A}t}
\tag{26}
$$

satisfies the matrix differential equation

$$
\mathbf{X}' = \mathbf{A}\mathbf{X}.
\tag{27}
$$

It follows from Eqs. (26) and (27) that each column vector of $e^{\mathbf{A}t}$ is a solution vector for the linear system

$$
\mathbf{x}' = \mathbf{A}\mathbf{x}.
\tag{28}
$$

Because the n column vectors of $e^{\mathbf{A}t}$ are automatically linearly independent, it also follows that the $n \times n$ matrix

$$\boldsymbol{\Phi}(t) = e^{\mathbf{A}t} \tag{29}$$

is a *fundamental matrix* for the linear system in Eq. (28). Therefore, Theorem 1 implies the following result.

THEOREM 2: Exponential Matrix Solutions

If \mathbf{A} is an $n \times n$ matrix, then the [unique] solution of the initial value problem

$$\mathbf{x}' = \mathbf{A}\mathbf{x}, \qquad \mathbf{x}(0) = \mathbf{x}_0 \tag{30}$$

is given by

$$\mathbf{x}(t) = e^{\mathbf{A}t}\mathbf{x}_0. \tag{31}$$

∎

Thus the solution of homogeneous linear systems of differential equations reduces to the task of computing exponential matrices. This task is easiest in the case of an $n \times n$ matrix \mathbf{A} having a complete set $\mathbf{v}_1, \mathbf{v}_2, \ldots, \mathbf{v}_n$ of n linearly independent eigenvectors corresponding (in order) to the n eigenvalues $\lambda_1, \lambda_2, \ldots, \lambda_n$ (not necessarily distinct). In this event we define the **eigenvector matrix P** and the diagonal **eigenvalue matrix D** of \mathbf{A} by

$$\mathbf{P} = \begin{bmatrix} | & | & & | \\ \mathbf{v}_1 & \mathbf{v}_2 & \cdots & \mathbf{v}_n \\ | & | & & | \end{bmatrix} \quad \text{and} \quad \mathbf{D} = \begin{bmatrix} \lambda_1 & 0 & \cdots & 0 \\ 0 & \lambda_2 & \cdots & 0 \\ \cdot & \cdot & & \cdot \\ \cdot & \cdot & & \cdot \\ 0 & 0 & \cdots & \lambda_n \end{bmatrix}. \tag{32}$$

Then it is not difficult to show by direct computation (for instance, see Section 6.2 of Edwards and Penney, *Elementary Linear Algebra* (Englewood Cliffs, N.J.: Prentice Hall, 1988)) that

$$\mathbf{A} = \mathbf{PDP}^{-1}. \tag{33}$$

The matrix factorization in (33) facilitates the calculation of $e^{\mathbf{A}t}$. If we substitute $\mathbf{A} = \mathbf{PDP}^{-1}$ in the series in (24), then a formal computation gives

$$e^{\mathbf{A}t} = e^{(\mathbf{PDP}^{-1})t} = e^{\mathbf{P}(\mathbf{D}t)\mathbf{P}^{-1}}$$

$$= \mathbf{I} + \mathbf{P}(\mathbf{D}t)\mathbf{P}^{-1} + \frac{1}{2!}\mathbf{P}(\mathbf{D}t)\mathbf{P}^{-1} \cdot \mathbf{P}(\mathbf{D}t)\mathbf{P}^{-1} + \cdots$$

$$= \mathbf{I} + \mathbf{P}(\mathbf{D}t)\mathbf{P}^{-1} + \frac{1}{2!}\mathbf{P}(\mathbf{D}t)^2\mathbf{P}^{-1} + \cdots$$

$$= \mathbf{P}\left[\mathbf{I} + (\mathbf{D}t) + \frac{1}{2!}(\mathbf{D}t)^2 + \cdots\right]\mathbf{P}^{-1}.$$

Thus

$$e^{\mathbf{A}t} = \mathbf{P}e^{\mathbf{D}t}\mathbf{P}^{-1}. \tag{34}$$

If we define

$$\mathbf{\Lambda}_t = e^{\mathbf{D}t} = \begin{bmatrix} e^{\lambda_1 t} & 0 & \cdots & 0 \\ 0 & e^{\lambda_2 t} & \cdots & 0 \\ \cdot & \cdot & & \cdot \\ \cdot & \cdot & & \cdot \\ \cdot & \cdot & & \cdot \\ 0 & 0 & \cdots & e^{\lambda_n t} \end{bmatrix} \tag{35}$$

using Eq. (20), then we have the following result.

THEOREM 3: Computation of $e^{\mathbf{A}t}$

Suppose that the $n \times n$ matrix \mathbf{A} has n linearly independent eigenvectors \mathbf{v}_1, \mathbf{v}_2, . . ., \mathbf{v}_n corresponding (in order) to the eigenvalues λ_1, λ_2, . . ., λ_n. If the eigenvector matrix \mathbf{P} and the diagonal matrix $\mathbf{\Lambda}_t$ are defined as in Eqs. (32) and (35), respectively (so $\mathbf{A} = \mathbf{P}\mathbf{D}\mathbf{P}^{-1}$), then

$$e^{\mathbf{A}t} = \mathbf{P}\mathbf{\Lambda}_t\mathbf{P}^{-1}. \tag{36}$$

∎

EXAMPLE 3 Find the fundamental matrix $\mathbf{\Phi}(t) = e^{\mathbf{A}t}$ and the general solution $\mathbf{x}(t) = \mathbf{\Phi}(t)\mathbf{c}$ for the linear system

$$\begin{aligned} x_1' &= 4x_1 + 2x_2, \\ x_2' &= 3x_1 - x_2. \end{aligned} \tag{37}$$

Solution In Example 1 we saw that the coefficient matrix

$$\mathbf{A} = \begin{bmatrix} 4 & 2 \\ 3 & -1 \end{bmatrix}$$

has eigenvalues $\lambda_1 = -2$ and $\lambda_2 = 5$ with associated eigenvectors

$$\mathbf{v}_1 = \begin{bmatrix} 1 \\ -3 \end{bmatrix} \quad \text{and} \quad \mathbf{v}_2 = \begin{bmatrix} 2 \\ 1 \end{bmatrix},$$

so

$$\mathbf{P} = \begin{bmatrix} 1 & 2 \\ -3 & 1 \end{bmatrix} \quad \text{and} \quad \mathbf{\Lambda}_t = \begin{bmatrix} e^{-2t} & 0 \\ 0 & e^{5t} \end{bmatrix}.$$

Because

$$\mathbf{P}^{-1} = \frac{1}{7}\begin{bmatrix} 1 & -2 \\ 3 & 1 \end{bmatrix},$$

it follows from Eq. (36) that

$$\mathbf{\Phi}(t) = e^{\mathbf{A}t} = \frac{1}{7} \begin{bmatrix} 1 & 2 \\ -3 & 1 \end{bmatrix} \begin{bmatrix} e^{-2t} & 0 \\ 0 & e^{5t} \end{bmatrix} \begin{bmatrix} 1 & -2 \\ 3 & 1 \end{bmatrix}$$

$$= \frac{1}{7} \begin{bmatrix} 1 & 2 \\ -3 & 1 \end{bmatrix} \begin{bmatrix} e^{-2t} & -2e^{-2t} \\ 3e^{5t} & e^{5t} \end{bmatrix}$$

$$= \frac{1}{7} \begin{bmatrix} e^{-2t} + 6e^{5t} & -2e^{-2t} + 2e^{5t} \\ -3e^{-2t} + 3e^{5t} & 6e^{-2t} + e^{5t} \end{bmatrix}.$$

Note that the column vectors $\mathbf{x}_1(t)$ and $\mathbf{x}_2(t)$ of the fundamental matrix $\mathbf{\Phi}(t)$ satisfy the initial conditions

$$\mathbf{x}_1(0) = \begin{bmatrix} 1 \\ 0 \end{bmatrix} \quad \text{and} \quad \mathbf{x}_2(0) = \begin{bmatrix} 0 \\ 1 \end{bmatrix}.$$

The general solution $\mathbf{x}(t) = \mathbf{\Phi}(t)\mathbf{c} = c_1\mathbf{x}_1 + c_2\mathbf{x}_2$ is

$$\mathbf{x}(t) = \frac{1}{7} \begin{bmatrix} (c_1 - 2c_2)e^{-2t} + (6c_1 + 2c_2)e^{5t} \\ (-3c_1 + 6c_2)e^{-2t} + (3c_1 + c_2)e^{5t} \end{bmatrix}.$$

EXAMPLE 4 Use the exponential matrix to find a general solution of

$$\mathbf{x}' = \begin{bmatrix} 2 & 1 \\ 0 & 2 \end{bmatrix} \mathbf{x}. \tag{38}$$

Solution The 2×2 coefficient matrix \mathbf{A} in (38) has only the single repeated eigenvalue $\lambda = 2$ and the single associated eigenvector

$$\mathbf{v} = \begin{bmatrix} 1 \\ 0 \end{bmatrix},$$

so Theorem 3 does not apply for the computation of $e^{\mathbf{A}t}$. We instead note that $\mathbf{A} = 2\mathbf{I} + \mathbf{B}$, where

$$\mathbf{B} = \begin{bmatrix} 0 & 1 \\ 0 & 0 \end{bmatrix},$$

so $e^{\mathbf{A}t} = e^{2\mathbf{I}t}e^{\mathbf{B}t}$ by (22). Now

$$e^{2\mathbf{I}t} = \begin{bmatrix} e^{2t} & 0 \\ 0 & e^{2t} \end{bmatrix}$$

by (20), and $\mathbf{B}^2 = \mathbf{0}$ by direct multiplication, so it follows from the series in (24) that

$$e^{\mathbf{B}t} = \mathbf{I} + \mathbf{B}t = \begin{bmatrix} 1 & t \\ 0 & 1 \end{bmatrix}.$$

Hence the fundamental matrix $\Phi(t) = e^{At}$ of the system in (38) is given by

$$\Phi(t) = \begin{bmatrix} e^{2t} & 0 \\ 0 & e^{2t} \end{bmatrix} \begin{bmatrix} 1 & t \\ 0 & 1 \end{bmatrix} = \begin{bmatrix} e^{2t} & te^{2t} \\ 0 & e^{2t} \end{bmatrix},$$

and so a general solution is

$$\mathbf{x}(t) = \Phi(t)\mathbf{c} = c_1 \begin{bmatrix} e^{2t} \\ 0 \end{bmatrix} + c_2 \begin{bmatrix} te^{2t} \\ e^{2t} \end{bmatrix}. \qquad \blacksquare$$

Remark: The simplicity of the computations in Example 4 may be a bit misleading. Only because of the special (so-called *upper triangular*) form of the matrix **A** was the computation of e^{At} relatively easy. For a general $n \times n$ matrix **A** not having a complete set of n linearly independent eigenvalues, the computation of the exponential matrix e^{At} can be a formidable task, one that involves the *canonical forms* of matrices that are studied in advanced linear algebra. Alternatively, a computer algebra system can be used as indicated in the project material for this section.

5.5 Problems

Find a fundamental matrix of each of the systems in Problems 1 through 8, and then apply Eq. (8) to find a solution satisfying the given initial conditions.

1. $\mathbf{x}' = \begin{bmatrix} 2 & 1 \\ 1 & 2 \end{bmatrix} \mathbf{x}, \quad \mathbf{x}(0) = \begin{bmatrix} 3 \\ -2 \end{bmatrix}$

2. $\mathbf{x}' = \begin{bmatrix} 2 & -1 \\ -4 & 2 \end{bmatrix} \mathbf{x}, \quad \mathbf{x}(0) = \begin{bmatrix} 2 \\ -1 \end{bmatrix}$

3. $\mathbf{x}' = \begin{bmatrix} 2 & -5 \\ 4 & -2 \end{bmatrix} \mathbf{x}, \quad \mathbf{x}(0) = \begin{bmatrix} 0 \\ 1 \end{bmatrix}$

4. $\mathbf{x}' = \begin{bmatrix} 3 & -1 \\ 1 & 1 \end{bmatrix} \mathbf{x}, \quad \mathbf{x}(0) = \begin{bmatrix} 1 \\ 0 \end{bmatrix}$

5. $\mathbf{x}' = \begin{bmatrix} -3 & -2 \\ 9 & 3 \end{bmatrix} \mathbf{x}, \quad \mathbf{x}(0) = \begin{bmatrix} 1 \\ -1 \end{bmatrix}$

6. $\mathbf{x}' = \begin{bmatrix} 7 & -5 \\ 4 & 3 \end{bmatrix} \mathbf{x}, \quad \mathbf{x}(0) = \begin{bmatrix} 2 \\ 0 \end{bmatrix}$

7. $\mathbf{x}' = \begin{bmatrix} 5 & 0 & -6 \\ 2 & -1 & -2 \\ 4 & -2 & -4 \end{bmatrix} \mathbf{x}, \quad \mathbf{x}(0) = \begin{bmatrix} 2 \\ 1 \\ 0 \end{bmatrix}$

8. $\mathbf{x}' = \begin{bmatrix} 3 & 2 & 2 \\ -5 & -4 & -2 \\ -5 & 5 & 3 \end{bmatrix} \mathbf{x}, \quad \mathbf{x}(0) = \begin{bmatrix} 1 \\ 0 \\ -1 \end{bmatrix}$

Compute the fundamental matrix $\Phi(t) = e^{At}$ for each system $\mathbf{x}' = \mathbf{A}\mathbf{x}$ given in Problems 9 through 20.

9. $\begin{aligned} x_1' &= 5x_1 - 4x_2 \\ x_2' &= 2x_1 - x_2 \end{aligned}$

10. $\begin{aligned} x_1' &= 6x_1 - 6x_2 \\ x_2' &= 4x_1 - x_2 \end{aligned}$

11. $\begin{aligned} x_1' &= 5x_1 - 3x_2 \\ x_2' &= 2x_1 \end{aligned}$

12. $\begin{aligned} x_1' &= 5x_1 - 4x_2 \\ x_2' &= 3x_1 - 2x_2 \end{aligned}$

13. $\begin{aligned} x_1' &= 9x_1 - 8x_2 \\ x_2' &= 6x_1 - 5x_2 \end{aligned}$

14. $\begin{aligned} x_1' &= 10x_1 - 6x_2 \\ x_2' &= 12x_1 - 7x_2 \end{aligned}$

15. $\begin{aligned} x_1' &= 6x_1 - 10x_2 \\ x_2' &= 2x_1 - 3x_2 \end{aligned}$

16. $\begin{aligned} x_1' &= 11x_1 - 15x_2 \\ x_2' &= 6x_1 - 8x_2 \end{aligned}$

17. $\begin{aligned} x_1' &= 3x_1 + x_2 \\ x_2' &= x_1 + 3x_2 \end{aligned}$

18. $\begin{aligned} x_1' &= 4x_1 + 2x_2 \\ x_2' &= 2x_1 + 4x_2 \end{aligned}$

19. $\begin{aligned} x_1' &= 9x_1 + 2x_2 \\ x_2' &= 2x_1 + 6x_2 \end{aligned}$

20. $\begin{aligned} x_1' &= 13x_1 + 4x_2 \\ x_2' &= 4x_1 + 7x_2 \end{aligned}$

Apply the method of Example 4 to find the fundamental matrix $\Phi(t) = e^{At}$ for each system $\mathbf{x}' = \mathbf{A}\mathbf{x}$ given in Problems 21 through 24.

21. $\mathbf{x}' = \begin{bmatrix} 1 & 2 \\ 0 & 1 \end{bmatrix} \mathbf{x}$ **22.** $\mathbf{x}' = \begin{bmatrix} 3 & 5 \\ 0 & 3 \end{bmatrix} \mathbf{x}$

23. $\mathbf{x}' = \begin{bmatrix} 1 & 1 & 0 \\ 0 & 1 & 1 \\ 0 & 0 & 1 \end{bmatrix} \mathbf{x}$ **24.** $\mathbf{x}' = \begin{bmatrix} 2 & 3 & 4 \\ 0 & 2 & 3 \\ 0 & 0 & 2 \end{bmatrix} \mathbf{x}$

25. Suppose that the matrices \mathbf{A} and \mathbf{B} commute; that is, that $\mathbf{AB} = \mathbf{BA}$. Prove that $e^{\mathbf{A}+\mathbf{B}} = e^{\mathbf{A}}e^{\mathbf{B}}$. *Suggestion:* Group the terms in the product of the two series on the right-hand side to obtain the series on the left.)

26. Deduce from the result of Problem 25 that, for every square matrix \mathbf{A}, the matrix $e^{\mathbf{A}}$ is nonsingular with $(e^{\mathbf{A}})^{-1} = e^{-\mathbf{A}}$.

27. Suppose that

$$\mathbf{A} = \begin{bmatrix} 0 & 1 \\ 1 & 0 \end{bmatrix}.$$

Show that $\mathbf{A}^{2n} = \mathbf{I}$ and that $\mathbf{A}^{2n+1} = \mathbf{A}$ if n is a positive integer. Conclude that

$$e^{\mathbf{A}t} = \mathbf{I} \cosh t + \mathbf{A} \sinh t,$$

and apply this fact to find a general solution of $\mathbf{x}' = \mathbf{Ax}$. Verify that it is equivalent to the general solution found by the eigenvalue method.

28. Suppose that

$$\mathbf{A} = \begin{bmatrix} 0 & 2 \\ -2 & 0 \end{bmatrix}.$$

Show that $e^{\mathbf{A}t} = \mathbf{I} \cos 2t + \frac{1}{2}\mathbf{A} \sin 2t$. Apply this fact to find a general solution of $\mathbf{x}' = \mathbf{Ax}$, and verify that it is equivalent to the solution found by the eigenvalue method.

29. Apply the technique of Example 4 to find a general solution of

$$\mathbf{x}' = \begin{bmatrix} 1 & 2 & 0 \\ 0 & 1 & 2 \\ 0 & 0 & 1 \end{bmatrix} \mathbf{x}.$$

5.5 Computing Project

If \mathbf{A} is an $n \times n$ matrix, then the *Mathematica* command **MatrixExp[A t]** or the **with(linalg)** *Maple* command **exponential(A,t)** can be used to compute the fundamental matrix $e^{\mathbf{A}t}$ for the system $\mathbf{x}' = \mathbf{Ax}$. (The success of these commands and the usefulness of the results may depend upon whether sufficiently simple expressions for eigenvalues and eigenvectors of \mathbf{A} can be found.) For example, suppose that we need to solve the initial value problem

$$x_1' = 13x_1 + 4x_2$$
$$x_2' = 4x_1 + 7x_2,$$
$$x_1(0) = 11, \quad x_2(0) = 23.$$

Using *Mathematica* we define the coefficient matrix

```
A = { {13, 4}, {4, 7} };
```

and the initial vector

```
x0 = { {11}, {23} };
```

Then a fundamental matrix for the system $\mathbf{x}' = \mathbf{Ax}$ is given by

```
fundamental = MatrixExp[ A t ]
```

$$\left\{ \left\{ \frac{E^5\ t}{5} + \frac{4\ E^{15}\ t}{5},\ \frac{-2\ E^5\ t}{5} + \frac{2\ E^{15}\ t}{5} \right\},\right.$$

$$\left.\left\{ \frac{-2\ E^5\ t}{5} + \frac{2\ E^{15}\ t}{5},\ \frac{4\ E^5\ t}{5} + \frac{E^{15}\ t}{5} \right\}\right\}$$

Hence Theorem 1 in this section gives the particular solution

```
solution = fundamental . x0;
Simplify[ solution ]
```

$$\{\{-7 \; E^{5 \; t} + 18 \; E^{15 \; t}\}, \; \{14 \; E^{5 \; t} + 9 \; E^{15 \; t}\}\}$$

Thus the desired particular solution is given in scalar form by

$$x_1(t) = -7e^{5t} + 18e^{15t}$$
$$x_2(t) = \;\;\; 14e^{5t} + \;\; 9e^{15t}.$$

Obviously this, finally, is the way to do it!

For a three-dimensional example, solve the initial value problem

$$x_1' = -149x_1 - \;\;\; 50x_2 - 154x_3$$
$$x_2' = \;\;\; 537x_1 + 180x_2 + 546x_3$$
$$x_3' = \;\; -27x_1 - \;\;\;\; 9x_2 - \;\; 25x_3,$$
$$x_1(0) = 17, \quad x_2(0) = 43, \quad x_3(0) = 79.$$

And here's a four-dimensional problem:

$$x_1' = 4x_1 + \;\;\; x_2 + \;\;\; x_3 + 7x_4$$
$$x_2' = \;\; x_1 + \;\; 4x_2 + 10x_3 + \;\;\; x_4$$
$$x_3' = \;\; x_1 + 10x_2 + \;\; 4x_3 + \;\;\; x_4$$
$$x_4' = 7x_1 + \;\;\; x_2 + \;\;\; x_3 + 4x_4,$$
$$x_1(0) = 15, \quad x_2(0) = 35, \quad x_3(0) = 55, \quad x_4(0) = 75.$$

If at this point you're having too much fun with matrix exponentials to stop, make up some problems of your own. For instance, choose any homogeneous linear system appearing in this chapter and experiment with differential initial conditions. The exotic 5×5 matrix **A** of the Section 5.4 project may suggest some interesting possibilities.

6 Nonlinear Systems and Phenomena

6.1 Stability and the Phase Plane

A wide variety of natural phenomena are modeled by two-dimensional first-order systems of the form

$$\frac{dx}{dt} = F(x, y)$$

$$\frac{dy}{dt} = G(x, y)$$

(1)

in which the independent variable t does *not* appear explicitly. Such a system is called an **autonomous system.** The absence of t on the right-hand sides in (1) makes the system easier to analyze and its solutions easier to visualize. We assume that the functions F and G are continuously differentiable in some region R in the xy-plane, which is called the **phase plane** for the system in (1). Then, according to the existence and uniqueness theorems of the Appendix, given t_0 and any point (x_0, y_0) of R, there is a *unique* solution $x = x(t)$, $y = y(t)$ of (1) that is defined on some open interval (a, b) containing t_0 and satisfies the initial conditions

$$x(t_0) = x_0, \qquad y(t_0) = y_0.$$

(2)

The equations $x = x(t)$, $y = y(t)$ then describe a parametrized solution curve in the phase plane. Any such solution curve is called a **trajectory** of the system in (1),

and precisely one trajectory passes through each point of the region R (Problem 29). A **critical point** of the system in (1) is a point (x_*, y_*) such that

$$F(x_*, y_*) = G(x_*, y_*) = 0. \tag{3}$$

If (x_*, y_*) is a critical point of the system, then the constant-valued functions

$$x(t) \equiv x_*, \qquad y(t) \equiv y_* \tag{4}$$

satisfy the equations in (1). Such a constant-valued solution is called an **equilibrium solution** of the system. Note that the trajectory of the equilibrium solution in (4) consists of the single point (x_*, y_*).

In some practical situations these very simple solutions and trajectories are the ones of most interest. For example, suppose that the system $x' = F(x, y)$, $y' = G(x, y)$ models two populations $x(t)$ and $y(t)$ of animals that cohabit the same environment, and perhaps compete for the same food or prey on one another; $x(t)$ might denote the number of foxes and $y(t)$ the number of rabbits present at time t. Then a critical point (x_*, y_*) of the system specifies a *constant* population x_* of foxes and a *constant* population y_* of rabbits that can coexist with one another in the environment. If (x_0, y_0) is *not* a critical point of the system, then it is *not* possible for constant populations of x_0 foxes and y_0 rabbits to coexist; one or both must change with time.

EXAMPLE 1 Find the critical points of the system

$$\frac{dx}{dt} = 60x - 3x^2 - 4xy,$$

$$\frac{dy}{dt} = 42y - 3y^2 - 2xy. \tag{5}$$

Solution When we look at the equations

$$60x - 3x^2 - 4xy = x(60 - 3x - 4y) = 0,$$

$$42y - 3y^2 - 2xy = y(42 - 3y - 2x) = 0$$

that a critical point (x, y) must satisfy, we see that either

$$x = 0 \quad \text{or} \quad 60 - 3x - 4y = 0, \tag{6a}$$

and either

$$y = 0 \quad \text{or} \quad 42 - 3y - 2x = 0. \tag{6b}$$

If $x = 0$ and $y \neq 0$, then the second equation in (6b) gives $y = 14$. If $y = 0$ and $x \neq 0$, then the second equation in (6a) gives $x = 20$. If x and y are each nonzero, then we solve the simultaneous equations

$$3x + 4y = 60, \qquad 2x + 3y = 42$$

for $x = 12$, $y = 6$. Thus the system in (5) has the four critical points $(0, 0)$, $(0, 14)$, $(20, 0)$, and $(12, 6)$. If $x(t)$ and $y(t)$ denote the number of foxes and the number of rabbits, respectively, and if both populations are *constant*, it follows that the equations in (5) allow only three nontrivial possibilities: either no foxes and 14 rabbits, or 20 foxes and no rabbits, or 12 foxes and 6 rabbits. In particular, the critical point $(12, 6)$ de-

scribes the *only* possibility for the coexistence of constant nonzero populations of both species. ■

Phase Portraits

If the initial point (x_0, y_0) is not a critical point, the corresponding trajectory is a curve in the *xy*-plane along which the point $(x(t), y(t))$ moves as t increases. It turns out that any trajectory not consisting of a single point is a nondegenerate curve with no self-intersections (Problem 30). We can demonstrate qualitatively the behavior of solutions of the system in (1) by constructing its **phase portrait**—a phase plane picture of its critical points and typical nondegenerate trajectories. We may construct a **slope field** by drawing typical line segments having slope

$$\frac{dy}{dx} = \frac{y'}{x'} = \frac{G(x, y)}{F(x, y)},$$

or a **direction field** by drawing typical vectors pointing in the same direction at each point as the vector $(F(x, y), G(x, y))$. Such a vector field then indicates which direction along a trajectory to travel in order to "go with the flow" described by the system.

EXAMPLE 2 For the system

$$\begin{aligned} x' &= x - y \\ y' &= 1 - x^2 \end{aligned} \tag{7}$$

we see from the first equation that $x = y$ and from the second that $x = \pm 1$ at each critical point. Thus this system has the two critical points $(-1, -1)$ and $(1, 1)$. The direction field in Fig. 6.1.1 suggests that trajectories somehow "circulate" counterclockwise around the critical point $(-1, -1)$, whereas it appears that some trajectories may approach, while others recede from, the critical point $(1, 1)$. These observations are corroborated by the phase portrait in Fig. 6.1.2 for the system in (7). ■

FIGURE 6.1.1. Direction field for the system in (7)

FIGURE 6.1.2. Phase portrait for the system in (7)

Critical Point Behavior

The behavior of the trajectories near an isolated critical point of an autonomous system is of particular interest. In the remainder of this section we illustrate with some simple examples some of the most common possibilities.

EXAMPLE 3 Consider the autonomous linear system

$$\frac{dx}{dt} = -x$$

$$\frac{dy}{dt} = -ky \quad (k \text{ constant}),$$

(8)

which has the origin $(0, 0)$ as its only critical point. The solution with initial point (x_0, y_0) is

$$x(t) = x_0 e^{-t}, \qquad y(t) = y_0 e^{-kt}.$$

(9)

If $x_0 \neq 0$, we can write

$$y = y_0 e^{-kt} = \frac{y_0}{x_0^k} (x_0 e^{-t})^k = bx^k,$$

(10)

where $b = y_0 / x_0^k$.

If $k = 1$, then each curve in Eq. (10) is a straight line through the origin. Each trajectory is an open ray along which the point

$$(x(t), y(t)) = (x_0 e^{-t}, y_0 e^{-t})$$

approaches the origin as $t \to +\infty$. This type of critical point, shown in Fig. 6.1.3, is called a **proper node.** Note the arrows that indicate the orientations of the trajectories; they indicate the direction of motion of $(x(t), y(t))$ with increasing t.

In general, the critical point (x_0, y_0) of the autonomous system in (1) is called a **node** provided that *either* every trajectory approaches (x_0, y_0) as $t \to +\infty$ *or* every trajectory recedes from (x_0, y_0) as $t \to +\infty$, *and* every trajectory is tangent at (x_0, y_0) to some straight line through the critical point. Note that the critical point $(0, 0)$ in Fig. 6.1.3—where the trajectories *are* straight lines, not merely tangents to straight lines—would remain a node if all the arrows were reversed to make the trajectories recede from the critical point rather than approach it. This node is said to be **proper** because no two different pairs of "opposite" trajectories are tangent to the same straight line. In the next paragraph we consider a case in which the critical point is a node that is not proper.

If $k = 2$ and neither x_0 nor y_0 is zero in Eq. (10), then each curve is a parabola $y = bx^2$ tangent to the x-axis at the origin. The solution curve in (9) is half of the x-axis if $y_0 = 0$, and half of the y-axis if $x_0 = 0$. The trajectories are the semiaxes and the right and left halves of the parabolas shown in Fig. 6.1.4. Along each trajectory the point $(x(t), y(t))$ approaches the origin as $t \to +\infty$. Thus all trajectories except for a single pair approach the origin tangent to the same line—the x-axis. This sort of critical point is called an **improper node.**

If $k = -1$, then $x(t) = x_0 e^{-t}$ and $y(t) = y_0 e^{t}$, so $xy = x_0 y_0 = b$. If neither x_0 nor y_0 is zero, then the trajectory is one branch of the rectangular hyperbola $xy = b$, and $y \to \pm\infty$ as $t \to +\infty$. If $x_0 = 0$ or $y_0 = 0$, the trajectory is a semiaxis of the hyperbola. The point $(x(t), y(t))$ approaches the origin along the x-axis, but recedes from it along the y-axis as $t \to +\infty$. Thus there are two trajectories that approach the critical point

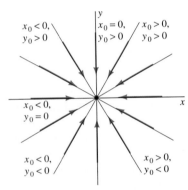

$x_0 < 0,$ $x_0 = 0,$ $x_0 > 0,$
$y_0 > 0$ $y_0 > 0$ $y_0 > 0$

$x_0 < 0,$
$y_0 = 0$

x

$x_0 < 0,$ $x_0 > 0,$
$y_0 < 0$ $y_0 < 0$

FIGURE 6.1.3. A stable proper node

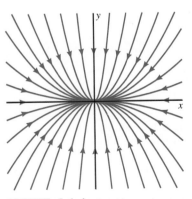

FIGURE 6.1.4. A stable improper node

(0, 0) and all others are unbounded as $t \to +\infty$. This type of critical point, shown in Fig. 6.1.5, is called a **saddle point.**

Stability

A critical point (x_*, y_*) of the autonomous system in (1) is said to be *stable* provided that if the initial point (x_0, y_0) is sufficiently close to (x_*, y_*), then $(x(t), y(t))$ remains close to (x_*, y_*) for all $t > 0$. In vector notation, with $\mathbf{x}(t) = (x(t), y(t))$, the distance between the initial point $\mathbf{x}_0 = (x_0, y_0)$ and the critical point $\mathbf{x}_* = (x_*, y_*)$ is

$$|\mathbf{x}_0 - \mathbf{x}_*| = \sqrt{(x_0 - x_*)^2 + (y_0 - y_*)^2}.$$

Thus the critical point \mathbf{x}_* is **stable** provided that, for each $\epsilon > 0$, there exists $\delta > 0$ such that

▶ $$|\mathbf{x}_0 - \mathbf{x}_*| < \delta \quad \text{implies that} \quad |\mathbf{x}(t) - \mathbf{x}_*| < \epsilon \qquad (11)$$

for all $t > 0$. The critical point (x_*, y_*) is called **unstable** if it is not stable. In each of Figs. 6.1.3 and 6.1.4, the origin (0, 0) is a stable critical point. The saddle point at (0, 0) shown in Fig. 6.1.5 is an unstable critical point.

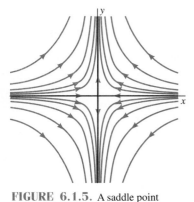

FIGURE 6.1.5. A saddle point

EXAMPLE 3
Continued

If the signs on the right-hand side in (8) are changed to obtain the system

$$\frac{dx}{dt} = x$$

$$\frac{dy}{dt} = ky, \qquad (12)$$

the solution is $x(t) = x_0 e^t$, $y(t) = y_0 e^{kt}$. Then with $k = 1$ and $k = 2$, the trajectories are the same as those shown in Figs. 6.1.3 and 6.1.4, respectively, but with the arrows reversed. In Fig. 6.1.3 with the arrows reversed, the origin is an unstable proper node; in Fig. 6.1.4 with the arrows reversed, the origin is an unstable improper node. ∎

If (x_*, y_*) is a critical point, the equilibrium solution $x(t) \equiv x_*$, $y(t) \equiv y_*$ is called **stable** or **unstable** depending upon the nature of the critical point. In applications the stability of an equilibrium solution is often a crucial matter. For instance, suppose in Example 1 that $x(t)$ and $y(t)$ denote the fox and rabbit populations, respectively, *in hundreds*. We will see in Section 6.3 that the critical point (12, 6) is stable. It follows that if we begin with *close to* 1200 foxes and 600 rabbits—rather than exactly these equilibrium values—then for all future time there will remain close to 1200 foxes and close to 600 rabbits. Thus the practical consequence of stability is that slight changes (perhaps due to random births and deaths) in the equilibrium populations will not so upset the equilibrium as to result in large deviations from the equilibrium solution.

It is possible for trajectories to remain near a stable critical point without approaching it, as Example 4 shows.

EXAMPLE 4

Consider a mass m that oscillates without damping on a spring with Hooke's constant k, so that its position function $x(t)$ satisfies the differential equation $x'' + \omega^2 x = 0$

(where $\omega^2 = k/m$). If we introduce the velocity $y = dx/dt$ of the mass, we get the system

$$\frac{dx}{dt} = y$$

$$\frac{dy}{dt} = -\omega^2 x \tag{13}$$

with general solution

$$x(t) = \quad A \cos \omega t + \quad B \sin \omega t, \tag{14a}$$

$$y(t) = -A\omega \sin \omega t + B\omega \cos \omega t. \tag{14b}$$

With $C = \sqrt{A^2 + B^2}$ and $\alpha = \tan^{-1}(B/A)$, we can rewrite the solution in (14) in the form

$$x(t) = \quad C \cos(\omega t - \alpha), \tag{15a}$$

$$y(t) = -\omega C \sin(\omega t - \alpha), \tag{15b}$$

so it becomes clear that each trajectory other than the critical point $(0, 0)$ is an ellipse with equation of the form

$$\frac{x^2}{C^2} + \frac{y^2}{\omega^2 C^2} = 1. \tag{16}$$

Each point $(x_0, y_0) \neq (0, 0)$ in the xy-plane lies on exactly one of these ellipses, and a solution $(x(t), y(t))$ with initial point (x_0, y_0) traverses the ellipse containing (x_0, y_0) in the clockwise direction with *period* $T = 2\pi/\omega$. (It is clear from (15) that $x(t + T) = x(t)$ and $y(t + T) = y(t)$ for all t.) Thus each nontrivial solution of the system in (13) is periodic and its trajectory is a simple closed curve. ■

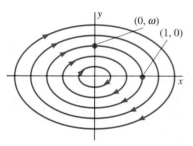

FIGURE 6.1.6. A [stable] center surrounded by closed trajectories

It is clear in Fig. 6.1.6, in which $\omega < 1$, that if the distance from (x_0, y_0) to $(0, 0)$ is less than $\delta = \omega \epsilon$, then for all t the distance from $(x(t), y(t))$ is less than ϵ. Hence $(0, 0)$ is a stable critical point of the system $x' = y$, $y' = -\omega^2 x$. Unlike the situation shown in Figs. 6.1.3 and 6.1.4, though, no single trajectory approaches $(0, 0)$. A critical point surrounded by simple closed trajectories representing periodic solutions is called a **[stable] center.**

Asymptotic Stability

The critical point (x_*, y_*) is called **asymptotically stable** if it is stable and, moreover, every trajectory that begins sufficiently close to (x_*, y_*) also approaches (x_*, y_*) as $t \to +\infty$. That is, there exists $\delta > 0$ such that

$$▶ \qquad |x_0 - x_*| < \delta \quad \text{implies that} \quad \lim_{t \to \infty} \mathbf{x}(t) = \mathbf{x}_*, \tag{17}$$

where $\mathbf{x}_0 = (x_0, y_0)$, $\mathbf{x}_* = (x_*, y_*)$, and $\mathbf{x}(t) = (x(t), y(t))$ is a solution with $\mathbf{x}(0) = \mathbf{x}_0$.

Remark The stable nodes shown in Figs. 6.1.3 and 6.1.4 are asymptotically stable because every trajectory approaches the critical point $(0, 0)$ as $t \to +\infty$. The center $(0, 0)$ in Fig. 6.1.6 is stable but not asymptotically stable, because however small an elliptical trajectory we consider, a point moving around this ellipse does not approach the origin. Thus asymptotic stability is a stronger condition than mere stability.

Now suppose that $x(t)$ and $y(t)$ denote coexisting populations for which (x_*, y_*) is an asymptotically stable critical point. Then if the initial populations x_0 and y_0 are sufficiently close to x_* and y_*, respectively, it follows that both

$$\lim_{t \to \infty} x(t) = x_* \quad \text{and} \quad \lim_{t \to \infty} y(t) = y_*. \tag{18}$$

That is, $x(t)$ and $y(t)$ actually approach the equilibrium populations x_* and y_* as $t \to +\infty$, rather than merely remaining close to those values.

For a mechanical system as in Example 4, a critical point represents an *equilibrium state* of the system—if the velocity $y = x'$ and the acceleration $y' = x''$ vanish simultaneously, then the mass remains at rest with no net force acting on it. Stability of a critical point concerns the question whether, when the mass is displaced slightly from its equilibrium, it

1. Moves back toward the equilibrium point as $t \to +\infty$,
2. Merely remains near the equilibrium point without approaching it, or
3. Moves farther away from equilibrium.

In Case 1 the critical [equilibrium] point is asymptotically stable; in Case 2 it is stable but not asymptotically so; in Case 3 it is an unstable critical point. A marble balanced on the top of a basketball is an example of an unstable critical point. A mass on a spring with damping illustrates the case of asymptotic stability of a mechanical system. The mass-and-spring without damping in Example 4 is an example of a system that is stable but not asymptotically stable.

EXAMPLE 5 Suppose that $m = 1$ and $k = 2$ for the mass and spring of Example 4 and that the mass is attached also to a dashpot with damping constant $c = 2$. Then its displacement function $x(t)$ satisfies the second-order equation

$$x''(t) + 2x'(t) + 2x(t) = 0. \tag{19}$$

With $y = x'$ we obtain the equivalent first-order system

$$\frac{dx}{dt} = y$$

$$\frac{dy}{dt} = -2x - 2y \tag{20}$$

with critical point $(0, 0)$. The characteristic equation $r^2 + 2r + 2 = 0$ of Eq. (19) has roots $-1 + i$ and $-1 - i$, so the general solution of the system in (20) is given by

$$x(t) = e^{-t}(A\cos t + B\sin t) = Ce^{-t}\cos(t - \alpha), \tag{21a}$$

$$y(t) = e^{-t}[(B - A)\cos t - (A + B)\sin t] = -C\sqrt{2}\,e^{-t}\sin\left(t - \alpha + \frac{\pi}{4}\right), \tag{21b}$$

where $C = \sqrt{A^2 + B^2}$ and $\alpha = \tan^{-1}(B/A)$. We see that $x(t)$ and $y(t)$ oscillate between positive and negative values and that each approaches zero as $t \to +\infty$. Consequently, a typical trajectory spirals toward the origin, as indicated in Fig. 6.1.7. It is clear that the critical point $(0, 0)$ is asymptotically stable; this type of critical point is called a

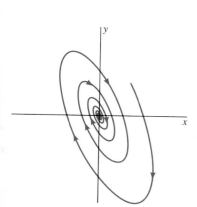

FIGURE 6.1.7. A stable spiral point and one nearby trajectory

[stable] spiral point. In the case of the mass-spring-dashpot system, a spiral point is the manifestation in the phase plane of the damped oscillations that occur because of resistance. ∎

The trajectory illustrated in Fig. 6.1.7 spirals *into* the critical point as $t \to +\infty$. In Fig. 6.1.2 we see trajectories spiraling *away from* the critical point $(-1, -1)$, which is therefore an *unstable* spiral point. Example 6 shows that it is also possible for a trajectory to spiral into a closed trajectory. A **closed** trajectory is a simple closed solution curve representing a periodic solution (like the ellipses in Fig. 6.1.6).

EXAMPLE 6 Consider the system

$$\frac{dx}{dt} = -ky + x(1 - x^2 - y^2),$$

$$\frac{dy}{dt} = kx + y(1 - x^2 - y^2). \tag{22}$$

In Problem 21 we ask you to show that $(0, 0)$ is its only critical point. This system can be solved explicitly by introducing polar coordinates $x = r \cos\theta$, $y = r \sin\theta$, as follows. First note that

$$\frac{d\theta}{dt} = \frac{d}{dt}\left(\arctan\frac{y}{x}\right) = \frac{xy' - yx'}{x^2 + y^2}.$$

Then substitute the expressions given in (22) for x' and y' to obtain

$$\frac{d\theta}{dt} = \frac{k(x^2 + y^2)}{x^2 + y^2} = k.$$

It follows that

$$\theta(t) = kt + \theta_0, \qquad \text{where } \theta_0 = \theta(0). \tag{23}$$

Then differentiation of $r^2 = x^2 + y^2$ yields

$$2r\frac{dr}{dt} = 2x\frac{dx}{dt} + 2y\frac{dy}{dt}$$

$$= 2(x^2 + y^2)(1 - x^2 - y^2) = 2r^2(1 - r^2),$$

so $r = r(t)$ satisfies the differential equation

$$\frac{dr}{dt} = r(1 - r^2). \tag{24}$$

In Problem 22 we ask you to derive the solution

$$r(t) = \frac{r_0}{\sqrt{r_0^2 + (1 - r_0^2)e^{-2t}}}, \tag{25}$$

where $r_0 = r(0)$. Thus the typical solution of Eq. (22) may be expressed in the form

$$x(t) = r(t)\cos(kt + \theta_0),$$

$$y(t) = r(t)\sin(kt + \theta_0). \tag{26}$$

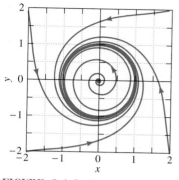

FIGURE 6.1.8. Spiral trajectories of the system in (22) with $k = 5$.

If $r_0 = 1$, then Eq. (25) gives $r(t) \equiv 1$ (the unit circle). Otherwise, if $r_0 > 0$, then Eq. (25) implies that $r(t) \to 1$ as $t \to +\infty$. Hence the trajectory defined in (26) spirals in toward the unit circle if $r_0 > 1$ and spirals out toward this closed trajectory if $0 < r_0 < 1$. Figure 6.1.8 shows a trajectory spiraling outward from the origin and four trajectories spiraling inward, all approaching the closed trajectory $r(t) \equiv 1$. ∎

Under rather general hypotheses it can be shown that there are four possibilities for a nondegenerate trajectory of the autonomous system

$$\frac{dx}{dt} = F(x, y), \qquad \frac{dy}{dt} = G(x, y).$$

The four possibilities are these:

1. $(x(t), y(t))$ approaches a critical point as $t \to +\infty$.
2. $(x(t), y(t))$ is unbounded with increasing t.
3. $(x(t), y(t))$ is a periodic solution with a closed trajectory.
4. $(x(t), y(t))$ spirals toward a closed trajectory as $t \to +\infty$.

As a consequence, the qualitative nature of the phase plane picture of the trajectories of an autonomous system is determined largely by the locations of its critical points and by the behavior of its trajectories near its critical points. We will see in Section 6.2 that, subject to mild restrictions on the functions F and G, each isolated critical point of the system $x' = F(x, y)$, $y' = G(x, y)$ resembles qualitatively one of the examples of this section—it is either a node (proper or improper), a saddle point, a center, or a spiral point.

6.1 Problems

In Problems 1 through 8, find the critical point or points of the given autonomous system, and thereby match each system with its phase portrait among Figs. 6.1.9 through 6.1.16.

1. $\dfrac{dx}{dt} = 2x - y, \qquad \dfrac{dy}{dt} = x - 3y$

2. $\dfrac{dx}{dt} = x - y, \qquad \dfrac{dy}{dt} = x + 3y - 4$

3. $\dfrac{dx}{dt} = x - 2y + 3, \qquad \dfrac{dy}{dt} = x - y + 2$

4. $\dfrac{dx}{dt} = 2x - 2y - 4, \qquad \dfrac{dy}{dt} = x + 4y + 3$

5. $\dfrac{dx}{dt} = 1 - y^2, \qquad \dfrac{dy}{dt} = x + 2y$

6. $\dfrac{dx}{dt} = x^2 + 4xy + 2y^2, \qquad \dfrac{dy}{dt} = 4 - x^2$

7. $\dfrac{dx}{dt} = x - 2y, \qquad \dfrac{dy}{dt} = 4x - x^3$

8. $\dfrac{dx}{dt} = x - y - x^2 + xy, \qquad \dfrac{dy}{dt} = -y - x^2$

FIGURE 6.1.9. Spiral point $(-2, 1)$ and saddle point $(2, -1)$.

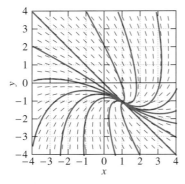

FIGURE 6.1.10. Spiral point $(1, -1)$

FIGURE 6.1.11. Saddle point $(0, 0)$

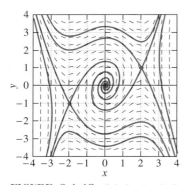

FIGURE 6.1.12. Spiral point $(0, 0)$; saddle points $(-2, -1)$ and $(2, 1)$

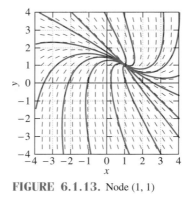

FIGURE 6.1.13. Node $(1, 1)$

FIGURE 6.1.14. Spiral point $(-1, -1)$; saddle point $(0, 0)$ and node $(1, -1)$

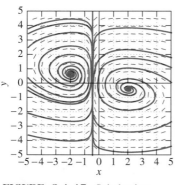

FIGURE 6.1.15. Spiral points $(-2, 2/3)$ and $(2, -2/5)$

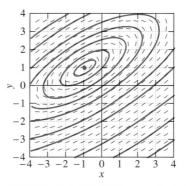

FIGURE 6.1.16. Stable center $(-1, 1)$

In Problems 9 through 12, find all equilibrium solutions (of the form $x(t) \equiv x_0$, a constant) of the given second-order differential equation.

9. $x'' + 4x - x^3 = 0$

10. $x'' + 2x' + x + 4x^3 = 0$

11. $x'' + 3x' + 4 \sin x = 0$

12. $x'' + (x^2 - 1)x' + x = 0$

Solve each of the linear systems in Problems 13 through 20 to determine whether the critical point $(0, 0)$ is stable, asymptotically stable, or unstable. Sketch typical trajectories and indicate the direction of motion with increasing t. Identify the critical point as a node, a saddle point, a center, or a spiral point.

13. $\dfrac{dx}{dt} = -2x, \quad \dfrac{dy}{dt} = -2y$

14. $\dfrac{dx}{dt} = 2x, \quad \dfrac{dy}{dt} = -2y$

15. $\dfrac{dx}{dt} = -2x, \quad \dfrac{dy}{dt} = -y$

16. $\dfrac{dx}{dt} = x, \quad \dfrac{dy}{dt} = 3y$

17. $\dfrac{dx}{dt} = y, \quad \dfrac{dy}{dt} = -x$

18. $\dfrac{dx}{dt} = -y, \quad \dfrac{dy}{dt} = 4x$

19. $\dfrac{dx}{dt} = 2y, \quad \dfrac{dy}{dt} = -2x$

20. $\dfrac{dx}{dt} = y, \quad \dfrac{dy}{dt} = -5x - 4y$

21. Verify that $(0, 0)$ is the only critical point of the system in Example 6.

22. Separate variables in (24) to derive the solution given in (25).

In Problems 23 through 26, a system $dx/dt = F(x, y)$, $dy/dt = G(x, y)$ is given. Solve the equation

$$\frac{dy}{dx} = \frac{G(x, y)}{F(x, y)}$$

to find the trajectories of the given system.

23. $\dfrac{dx}{dt} = y, \quad \dfrac{dy}{dt} = -x$

24. $\dfrac{dx}{dt} = y\,(1 + x^2 + y^2), \quad \dfrac{dy}{dt} = x\,(1 + x^2 + y^2)$

25. $\dfrac{dx}{dt} = 4y\,(1 + x^2 + y^2), \quad \dfrac{dy}{dt} = -x\,(1 + x^2 + y^2)$

26. $\dfrac{dx}{dt} = y^3 e^{x+y}, \quad \dfrac{dy}{dt} = -x^3 e^{x+y}$

27. Let $(x(t), y(t))$ be a nontrivial solution of the nonautonomous system

$$\frac{dx}{dt} = y, \qquad \frac{dy}{dt} = tx.$$

Suppose that $\phi(t) = x(t + \gamma)$ and $\psi(t) = y(t + \gamma)$, where $\gamma \neq 0$. Show that $(\phi(t), \psi(t))$ is *not* a solution of the system.

Problems 28 through 30 deal with the system

$$\frac{dx}{dt} = F(x, y), \qquad \frac{dy}{dt} = G(x, y)$$

in a region where the functions F and G are continuously differentiable, so for each number a and point (x_0, y_0), there is a unique solution with $x(a) = x_0$ and $y(a) = y_0$.

28. Suppose that $(x(t), y(t))$ is a solution of the autonomous system and that $\gamma \neq 0$. Define $\phi(t) = x(t + \gamma)$ and $\psi(t) = y(t + \gamma)$. Then show (in contrast with the situation in Problem 27) that $(\phi(t), \psi(t))$ is also a solution of the system. Thus autonomous systems have the simple but important property that a "t-translate" of a solution is again a solution.

29. Let $(x_1(t), y_1(t))$ and $(x_2(t), y_2(t))$ be two solutions having trajectories that meet at the point (x_0, y_0); thus $x_1(a) = x_2(b) = x_0$ and $y_1(a) = y_2(b) = y_0$ for some values a and b of t. Define

$$x_3(t) = x_2(t + \gamma) \qquad \text{and} \qquad y_3(t) = y_2(t + \gamma)$$

where $\gamma = b - a$, so $(x_2(t), y_2(t))$ and $(x_3(t), y_3(t))$ have the same trajectory. Apply the uniqueness theorem to show that $(x_1(t), y_1(t))$ and $(x_3(t), y_3(t))$ are identical solutions. Hence the original two trajectories are identical. Thus no two different trajectories of an autonomous system can intersect.

30. Suppose that the solution $(x_1(t), y_1(t))$ is defined for all t and that its trajectory has an apparent self-intersection:

$$x_1(a) = x_1(a + T) = x_0, \qquad y_1(a) = y_1(a + T) = y_0$$

for some $T > 0$. Introduce the solution

$$x_2(t) = x_1(t + T), \qquad y_2(t) = y_1(t + T)$$

and then apply the uniqueness theorem to show that

$$x_1(t) = x_1(t + T) \qquad \text{and} \qquad y_1(t) = y_1(t + T)$$

for *all* t. Thus the solution $(x_1(t), y_1(t))$ is periodic with period T and has a closed trajectory. Consequently a solution of an autonomous system either is periodic with a closed trajectory, or else its trajectory never passes through the same point twice.

6.1 Computing Project

Consider a first-order differential equation of the form

$$\frac{dy}{dx} = \frac{G(x, y)}{F(x, y)},\tag{1}$$

which may be difficult or impossible to solve explicitly. Its solution curves can nevertheless be plotted as trajectories of the corresponding autonomous two-dimensional system

$$\frac{dx}{dt} = F(x, y),\qquad \frac{dy}{dt} = G(x, y).\tag{2}$$

Most ODE plotters can routinely generate phase portraits for autonomous systems. (Those appearing in this chapter were plotted using the program **pplane** accompanying John Polking's *MATLAB Manual for Ordinary Differential Equations,* Prentice Hall, 1995.)

For example, to plot solution curves for the differential equation

$$\frac{dy}{dx} = \frac{2xy - y^2}{x^2 - 2xy},\tag{3}$$

we plot trajectories of the system

$$\frac{dx}{dt} = x^2 - 2xy,\qquad \frac{dy}{dt} = 2xy - y^2.\tag{4}$$

The result is shown in Fig. 6.1.17.

Plot similarly some solution curves for the following differential equations.

1. $\dfrac{dy}{dx} = \dfrac{4x - 5y}{2x + 3y}$

2. $\dfrac{dy}{dx} = \dfrac{4x - 5y}{2x - 3y}$

3. $\dfrac{dy}{dx} = \dfrac{4x - 3y}{2x - 5y}$

4. $\dfrac{dy}{dx} = \dfrac{2xy}{x^2 - y^2}$

5. $\dfrac{dy}{dx} = \dfrac{x^2 + 2xy}{y^2 + 2xy}$

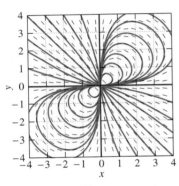

FIGURE 6.1.17. Phase portrait for the system in (4)

FIGURE 6.1.18. Phase portrait for the system corresponding to (5)

Now construct some examples of your own. Homogeneous functions like those in Problems 1 through 5—rational functions with numerator and denominator of the same degree in x and y—work well. The differential equation

$$\frac{dy}{dx} = \frac{25x + y(1 - x^2 - y^2)(4 - x^2 - y^2)}{-25y + x(1 - x^2 - y^2)(4 - x^2 - y^2)}\tag{5}$$

of this form generalizes Example 6 in this section, but would be inconvenient to solve explicitly. Its phase portrait (Fig. 6.1.18) shows two periodic closed trajectories—the circles $r = 1$ and $r = 2$. Anyone want to try for three circles?

6.2 Linear and Almost Linear Systems

We now discuss the behavior of solutions of the autonomous system

$$\frac{dx}{dt} = F(x, y), \qquad \frac{dy}{dt} = G(x, y) \tag{1}$$

near an isolated critical point (x_0, y_0) at which $F(x_0, y_0) = G(x_0, y_0) = 0$. A critical point is called **isolated** if some neighborhood of it contains no other critical point. We assume throughout that the functions F and G are continuously differentiable in a neighborhood of (x_0, y_0).

We can assume without loss of generality that $x_0 = y_0 = 0$. Otherwise, we make the substitutions $u = x - x_0$, $v = y - y_0$. Then $dx/dt = du/dt$ and $dy/dt = dv/dt$, so (1) is equivalent to the system

$$\frac{du}{dt} = F(u + x_0, v + y_0) = F_1(u, v)$$
$$\frac{dv}{dt} = G(u + x_0, v + y_0) = G_1(u, v) \tag{2}$$

that has $(0, 0)$ as an isolated critical point.

EXAMPLE 1 The system

$$\frac{dx}{dy} = 3x - x^2 - xy = x(3 - x - y)$$
$$\frac{dy}{dt} = y + y^2 - 3xy = y(1 - 3x + y) \tag{3}$$

has $(1, 2)$ as one of its critical points. We substitute $u = x - 1$, $v = y - 2$; that is, $x = u + 1$, $y = v + 2$. Then

$$3 - x - y = 3 - (u + 1) - (v + 2) = -u - v$$

and

$$1 - 3x + y = 1 - 3(u + 1) + (v + 2) = -3u + v,$$

so the system in (3) takes the form

$$\frac{du}{dt} = (u + 1)(-u - v) = -u - v - u^2 - uv$$
$$\frac{dv}{dt} = (v + 2)(-3u + v) = -6u + 2v + v^2 - 3uv \tag{4}$$

and has $(0, 0)$ as a critical point. If we can determine the trajectories of the system in (4) near $(0, 0)$, then their translations under the rigid motion that carries $(0, 0)$ to $(1, 2)$ will be the trajectories near $(1, 2)$ of the original system in (3). ∎

We therefore assume hereafter that $(0, 0)$ is an *isolated* critical point of the autonomous system in (1). It then follows from Taylor's formula for functions of two

variables that (1) can be written in the form

$$\frac{dx}{dt} = ax + by + f(x, y)$$

$$\frac{dy}{dt} = cx + dy + g(x, y),$$

(5)

where $a = F_x(0, 0)$, $b = F_y(0, 0)$, $c = G_x(0, 0)$, and $d = G_y(0, 0)$, and the functions $f(x, y)$ and $g(x, y)$ have the property that

$$\lim_{(x, y) \to (0, 0)} \frac{f(x, y)}{\sqrt{x^2 + y^2}} = \lim_{(x, y) \to (0, 0)} \frac{g(x, y)}{\sqrt{x^2 + y^2}} = 0.$$

(6)

That is, when (x, y) is near $(0, 0)$, the quantities $f(x, y)$ and $g(x, y)$ are small in comparison with $r = \sqrt{x^2 + y^2}$, which itself is small. Thus, when (x, y) is near $(0, 0)$, the nonlinear system in (5) is in some sense "near" the **linearized** system

$$\frac{dx}{dt} = ax + by$$

$$\frac{dy}{dt} = cx + dy.$$

(7)

Under the assumption that $(0, 0)$ is also an isolated critical point of this linear system, the autonomous system in (5) is therefore called **almost linear** provided that f and g satisfy the conditions in (6). It turns out that in most (but not all) cases, the trajectories near $(0, 0)$ of the almost linear system in (5) strongly resemble — qualitatively — those of its "linearization" in (7). Consequently, the first step toward understanding general autonomous systems is to characterize the critical points of linear systems.

Linear Systems

The linear system in (7) is readily solved by the elimination method of Section 4.2 or by the eigenvalue method of Section 5.2. Using the latter method, we substitute $x = Ae^{\lambda t}$ and $y = Be^{\lambda t}$ in (7). Upon dividing the resulting equations by $e^{\lambda t}$, we get the two homogeneous linear equations

$$(a - \lambda)A + \qquad bB = 0,$$

$$cA + (d - \lambda)B = 0$$

(8)

that the coefficients A and B must satisfy. In order for these equations to have a nontrivial solution, the determinant of coefficients must vanish:

$$\Delta = (a - \lambda)(d - \lambda) - bc = \lambda^2 - (a + d)\lambda + (ad - bc) = 0.$$

(9)

The nature of the solution of the system in (7) is determined by the nature of the roots of the quadratic **characteristic equation** in Eq. (9). Note that this equation is simply the characteristic equation of the coefficient matrix

$$\begin{bmatrix} a & b \\ c & d \end{bmatrix}$$

of the linear system in (7).

We assume that $(0, 0)$ is an isolated critical point of the system in (7). It follows that $ad - bc \neq 0$, so $\lambda = 0$ cannot be a root of Eq. (9). The reason is that the constant term $ad - bc$ in (9) is the determinant of the system of linear equations

$$ax + by = 0$$
$$cx + dy = 0. \tag{10}$$

If $ad - bc = 0$, then the equations in (10) are the equations of the same line through $(0, 0)$, so the system has a whole line of critical points rather than an isolated critical point at $(0, 0)$.

Consequently the characteristic equation in (9) has either:

1. Real unequal roots of the same sign;
2. Real unequal roots of opposite sign;
3. Real nonzero equal roots;
4. Complex conjugate roots; or
5. Pure imaginary roots.

These five cases are discussed separately below. In each case the critical point $(0, 0)$ resembles one of those we saw in the examples of Section 6.1—a node (proper or improper), a saddle point, a center, or a spiral point.

Real Unequal Roots of the Same Sign. In this case the general solution of (7) is of the form

$$x(t) = A_1 e^{\lambda_1 t} + A_2 e^{\lambda_2 t}$$
$$y(t) = B_1 e^{\lambda_1 t} + B_2 e^{\lambda_2 t} \tag{11}$$

where only two of the four coefficients are arbitrary. If both roots are negative $(\lambda_2 < \lambda_1 < 0)$, it is clear from (11) that x and y approach zero as $t \to +\infty$, so the critical point $(0, 0)$ is asymptotically stable. But if both roots are positive $(0 < \lambda_2 < \lambda_1)$, then x and y are unbounded as $t \to +\infty$, so the critical point $(0, 0)$ is unstable.

The system $x' = -x$, $y' = -2y$ considered in Example 3 of Section 6.1, and the improper node shown in Fig. 6.1.5 there, are typical of this case. In general, there is a linear change of coordinates $(u = a_1 x + a_2 y, \; v = b_1 x + b_2 y)$ that transforms (11) into

$$u = A e^{\lambda_1 t}, \qquad v = B e^{\lambda_2 t}. \tag{12}$$

In the [oblique] uv-coordinate system, the trajectories of the system in (12) are the straight lines $u = 0$ and $v = 0$ and curves of the form $v = Cu^k$, where $k = \lambda_2/\lambda_1 > 0$. The trajectories in the xy-coordinate system are the images of these curves under the inverse transformation from uv- to xy-coordinates. Thus $(0, 0)$ is an **improper node** like the one shown in Fig. 6.2.1, where $k = 2$, so the trajectories are parabolas in the oblique uv-system. The distinguishing feature of an improper node is that one pair of trajectories lies on the line $u = 0$, whereas all other trajectories are tangent to the line $v = 0$ at $(0, 0)$. If λ_1 and λ_2 are negative, then all trajectories approach $(0, 0)$ as $t \to +\infty$, while if λ_1 and λ_2 are positive, then the arrows in Fig. 6.2.1 would be reversed.

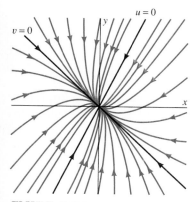

FIGURE 6.2.1. An improper node; both roots of the characteristic equation are negative.

u = 0

v = 0

FIGURE 6.2.2. A saddle point; the roots of the characteristic equation are real and of opposite sign.

Real Unequal Roots of Opposite Sign. In this case the situation is the same as in the previous case, except that $\lambda_2 < 0 < \lambda_1$ in (12). In the oblique uv-coordinate system, the trajectories determined by (12) are the straight lines $u = 0$ and $v = 0$ and curves of the form $uv^k = C$, where $k = -\lambda_1/\lambda_2 > 0$. The general situation resembles that shown in Fig. 6.2.2, where $k = 1$, so the nonlinear trajectories are hyperbolas in the uv-system. As $t \to +\infty$, the trajectories $u = Ae^{\lambda_1 t}$, $v = 0$ go to infinity because $\lambda_1 > 0$, whereas the trajectories $u = 0$, $v = Be^{\lambda_2 t}$ approach the origin because $\lambda_2 < 0$. The critical point $(0, 0)$ is therefore an unstable **saddle point** in this case.

Real Equal Roots. In this case, with $\lambda_1 = \lambda_2 = \lambda$, the general solution of the system in (7) has the form

$$x(t) = (A_1 + A_2 t)e^{\lambda t}, \qquad y(t) = (B_1 + B_2 t)e^{\lambda t} \tag{13}$$

where only two of the four coefficients are arbitrary. If $\lambda < 0$, then it is clear from (13) that $x \to 0$ and $y \to 0$ as $t \to +\infty$, so the critical point $(0, 0)$ is asymptotically stable. But if $\lambda > 0$, then x and y increase without bound as $t \to +\infty$, so $(0, 0)$ is an unstable critical point.

The nature of the trajectories depends upon whether the term $te^{\lambda t}$ is actually present in (13). The system $x' = -x$, $y' = -y$ considered in Example 3 of Section 6.1 illustrates the case in which $A_2 = B_2 = 0$, so (13) reduces to

$$x = Ae^{\lambda t}, \qquad y = Be^{\lambda t}. \tag{14}$$

Then $y = (B/A)x$ if $A \neq 0$, so all trajectories lie on straight lines through the critical point $(0, 0)$, which is therefore a **proper node** (Fig. 6.2.3).

The situation when the term $te^{\lambda t}$ is present is illustrated by the system $x' = -x$, $y' = x - y$, which has the general solution

$$x = Ae^{-t}, \qquad y = Be^{-t} + Ate^{-t}. \tag{15}$$

After we solve the first equation for $t = -\ln(x/A)$ and substitute this in the second equation, we find that

$$y = \frac{B}{A}x - x\ln\frac{x}{A} \tag{16}$$

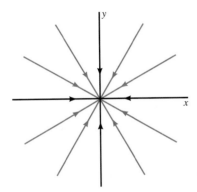

FIGURE 6.2.3. The roots of the characteristic equation are real and equal, resulting in a proper node.

and

$$\frac{dy}{dx} = \frac{y'}{x'} = \frac{-Be^{-t} + Ae^{-t} - Ate^{-t}}{-Ae^{-t}} = \frac{1}{A}(B - A + At) \tag{17}$$

if $A \neq 0$. It is clear from Eq. (17) that $dy/dx \to +\infty$ as $t \to +\infty$, so all the trajectories are tangent to the y-axis at $(0, 0)$. In this case the critical point $(0, 0)$ is an **improper node** as in Fig. 6.2.4. For a more general improper node, all trajectories are tangent to an arbitrary fixed line through the critical point, as in Fig. 6.2.5.

Complex Conjugate Roots. In this case, with $\lambda_1 = p + qi$ and $\lambda_2 = p - qi$ with p and q nonzero, the general solution has the form

$$x(t) = e^{pt}(A_1 \cos qt + A_2 \sin qt),$$
$$y(t) = e^{pt}(B_1 \cos qt + B_2 \sin qt). \tag{18}$$

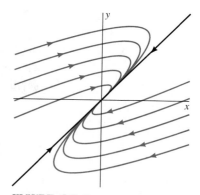

FIGURE 6.2.4. An improper node with all trajectories tangent to the y-axis

FIGURE 6.2.5. An improper node with all trajectories tangent to the graph of $y = x$

Thus $x(t)$ and $y(t)$ oscillate between positive and negative values as t increases, and the critical point $(0, 0)$ is a **spiral point** as in Example 5 of Section 6.1. If the real part p of λ_1 and λ_2 is negative, then it is clear from (18) that (x, y) approaches $(0, 0)$ as $t \to +\infty$, so $(0, 0)$ is an asymptotically stable critical point, as shown in Fig. 6.2.6. But if $p > 0$, then the critical point is unstable.

Pure Imaginary Roots. If $\lambda_1 = qi$ and $\lambda_2 = -qi$ with $q \neq 0$, then the general solution is of the form

$$x(t) = A_1 \cos qt + A_2 \sin qt, \qquad y(t) = B_1 \cos qt + B_2 \sin qt. \qquad (19)$$

As in Example 4 of Section 6.1, the trajectories are [rotated] ellipses (Fig. 6.2.7), so the critical point $(0, 0)$ is a **center:** stable but not asymptotically stable.

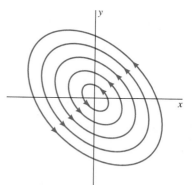

FIGURE 6.2.6. A spiral point; the roots of the characteristic equation are complex conjugates.

FIGURE 6.2.7. A center; the roots of the characteristic equation are pure imaginary.

For the linear system in (7) with $ad - bc \neq 0$, the table in Fig. 6.2.8 lists the type of critical point at $(0, 0)$ found in the five cases discussed above, according to the nature of the roots λ_1 and λ_2 of the characteristic equation in (9). Our discussion of these cases shows also that the stability of the critical point $(0, 0)$ is determined by the real parts of the characteristic roots λ_1 and λ_2, as summarized in Theorem 1. If λ_1 and λ_2 are real, then they are themselves their real parts.

Roots of Characteristic Equation	Type of Critical Point
Real, unequal, same sign	Improper node
Real, unequal, opposite sign	Saddle point
Real and equal	Proper or improper node
Complex conjugate	Spiral point
Pure imaginary	Center

FIGURE 6.2.8. Type of critical point (0,0) of the linear system in Eq. (7)

THEOREM 1: Stability of Linear Systems

Let λ_1 and λ_2 be the roots of the characteristic equation

$$\lambda^2 - (a + d)\lambda + (ad - bc) = 0 \tag{9}$$

of the linear system

$$\frac{dx}{dt} = ax + by$$

$$\frac{dy}{dt} = cx + dy \tag{7}$$

with $ad - bc \neq 0$. Then the critical point $(0, 0)$ is:

(a) asymptotically stable if the real parts of λ_1 and λ_2 are both negative;

(b) stable but not asymptotically stable if the real parts of λ_1 and λ_2 are both zero (so that $\lambda_1, \lambda_2 = \pm qi$);

(c) unstable if either λ_1 or λ_2 has a positive real part. ■

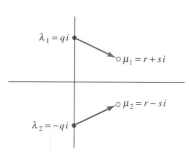

FIGURE 6.2.9. The effects of perturbation of pure imaginary roots

It is worthwhile to consider the effect of small perturbations in the coefficients a, b, c, and d of the linear system in (7), which result in small perturbations of the characteristic roots λ_1 and λ_2. If these perturbations are sufficiently small, then positive real parts (of λ_1 and λ_2) remain positive, and negative real parts remain negative. Hence an asymptotically stable critical point remains asymptotically stable, and an unstable critical point remains unstable. Part (b) of Theorem 1 is therefore the only case in which arbitrarily small perturbations can affect the stability of the critical point $(0, 0)$. In this case pure imaginary roots $\lambda_1, \lambda_2 = \pm qi$ can be changed to nearby complex roots $\mu_1, \mu_2 = r \pm si$, with r either positive or negative (see Fig. 6.2.9). Consequently, a small perturbation of the coefficients of the linear system in (7) can change a stable center to a spiral point that is either unstable or asymptotically stable.

FIGURE 6.2.10. The effects of perturbation of real equal roots

There is one other exceptional case in which the type, though not the stability, of the critical point $(0, 0)$ can be altered by a small perturbation of its coefficients. This is the case with $\lambda_1 = \lambda_2$, equal roots that (under a small perturbation of the coefficients) can split into two roots μ_1 and μ_2, which are either complex conjugates or unequal real roots (See Fig. 6.2.10). In either case, the sign of the real parts of the roots is preserved, so the stability of the critical point is unaltered. Its nature may change, how-

ever; the table in Fig. 6.2.8 shows that a node with $\lambda_1 = \lambda_2$ can either remain a node (if μ_1 and μ_2 are real) or change to a spiral point (if μ_1 and μ_2 are complex conjugates).

Suppose that the linear system in (7) is used to model a physical situation. It is unlikely that the coefficients in (7) can be measured with total accuracy, so let the unknown precise linear model be

$$\frac{dx}{dt} = a*x + b*y$$
$$\frac{dy}{dt} = c*x + d*y. \tag{7*}$$

If the coefficients in (7) are sufficiently close to those in (7*), it then follows from the discussion in the preceding paragraph that the origin (0, 0) is an asymptotically stable critical point for (7) if it is an asymptotically stable critical point for (7*), and is an unstable critical point for (7) if it is an unstable critical point for (7*). Thus in this case the approximate model in (7) and the precise model in (7*) predict the same qualitative behavior (with regard to asymptotic stability versus instability).

Almost Linear Systems

We now return to the almost linear system

$$\frac{dx}{dt} = ax + by + f(x, y)$$
$$\frac{dy}{dt} = cx + dy + g(x, y) \tag{5}$$

having (0, 0) as an isolated critical point with $ad - bc \neq 0$. Theorem 2, which we state without proof, essentially implies that—with regard to the type and stability of the critical point (0, 0)—the effect of the small nonlinear terms $f(x, y)$ and $g(x, y)$ is equivalent to the effect of a small perturbation in the coefficients of the associated *linear* system in (7).

THEOREM 2: Stability of Almost Linear Systems

Let λ_1 and λ_2 be the characteristic roots of the linear system in (7) associated with the almost linear system in (5). Then:

(a) If $\lambda_1 = \lambda_2$ are real equal roots, then the critical point (0, 0) of (5) is either a node or a spiral point, and is asymptotically stable if $\lambda_1 = \lambda_2 < 0$, unstable if $\lambda_1 = \lambda_2 > 0$.

(b) If λ_1 and λ_2 are pure imaginary, then (0, 0) is either a center or a spiral point, and may be either asymptotically stable, stable, or unstable.

(c) Otherwise—that is, unless λ_1 and λ_2 are either real equal or pure imaginary—the critical point (0, 0) of the almost linear system in (5) is of the same type and stability as the critical point (0, 0) of the associated linear system in (7).

Characteristic Roots λ_1, λ_2 of the Linearized System	Type of Critical Point of the Almost Linear System
$\lambda_1 < \lambda_2 < 0$	Stable improper node
$\lambda_1 = \lambda_2 < 0$	Stable node or spiral point
$\lambda_1 < 0 < \lambda_2$	Unstable saddle point
$\lambda_1 = \lambda_2 > 0$	Unstable node or spiral point
$\lambda_1 > \lambda_2 > 0$	Unstable improper node
$\lambda_1, \lambda_2 = a \pm bi \quad (a < 0)$	Stable spiral point
$\lambda_1, \lambda_2 = a \pm bi \quad (a > 0)$	Unstable spiral point
$\lambda_1, \lambda_2 = \pm bi$	Stable or unstable, center or spiral point

FIGURE 6.2.11. Classification of critical points of an almost linear system

Thus, if $\lambda_1 \neq \lambda_2$ and $\mathrm{Re}(\lambda_1) \neq 0$, then the type and stability of the critical point of the almost linear system in (5) can be determined by analysis of its associated linear system in (7), and only in the case of pure imaginary characteristic roots is the stability of $(0, 0)$ not determined by the linear system. Except in the sensitive cases $\lambda_1 = \lambda_2$ and $\mathrm{Re}(\lambda_i) = 0$, the trajectories near $(0, 0)$ will resemble qualitatively those of the associated linear system—they enter or leave the critical point in the same way, but may be "deformed" in a nonlinear manner. The table in Fig. 6.2.11 summarizes the situation.

An important consequence of the classification of cases in Theorem 2 is that a *critical point of an almost linear system is asymptotically stable if it is an asymptotically stable critical point of the linearization of the system.* Moreover, a critical point of the almost linear system is unstable if it is an unstable critical point of the linearized system. If an almost linear system is used to model a physical situation, then—apart from the sensitive cases mentioned in the preceding paragraph—it follows that the qualitative behavior of the system near a critical point can be determined by examining its linearization.

EXAMPLE 2 Determine the type and stability of the critical point $(0, 0)$ of the almost linear system

$$\frac{dx}{dt} = 4x + 2y + 2x^2 - 3y^2$$

$$\frac{dy}{dt} = 4x - 3y + 7xy. \tag{20}$$

Solution The characteristic equation of the associated linear system (obtained simply by deleting the quadratic terms in (20)) is

$$(4 - \lambda)(-3 - \lambda) - 8 = (\lambda - 5)(\lambda + 4) = 0,$$

so the roots $\lambda_1 = 5$ and $\lambda_2 = -4$ are real, unequal, and have opposite signs. By our discussion of this case we know that $(0, 0)$ is an unstable saddle point of the linear system, and hence by Part (c) of Theorem 2, it is also an unstable saddle point of the almost linear system in (20). The trajectories of the linear system near $(0, 0)$ are shown in Fig. 6.2.12, and those of the nonlinear system in (20) are shown in Fig. 6.2.13.

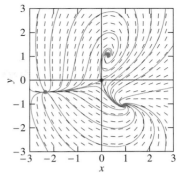

FIGURE 6.2.12. Trajectories of the linearized system of Example 2

FIGURE 6.2.13. Trajectories of the original almost linear system of Example 2

FIGURE 6.2.14. Phase portrait for the almost linear system in (20)

Figure 6.2.14 shows a phase portrait of the nonlinear system in (20) from a "wider view." In addition to the saddle point at $(0, 0)$, there are spiral points near the points $(0.279, 1.065)$ and $(0.933, -1.057)$, and a node near $(-2.354, -0.483)$.

EXAMPLE 3 Determine the type and stability of the critical point $(4, 3)$ of the almost linear system

$$\frac{dx}{dt} = 33 - 10x - 3y + x^2$$

$$\frac{dy}{dt} = -18 + 6x + 2y - xy. \tag{21}$$

Solution The substitution $u = x - 4$, $v = y - 3$ (that is, $x = u + 4$, $y = v + 3$) in (21) yields the almost linear system

$$\frac{du}{dt} = -2u - 3v + u^2$$

$$\frac{dv}{dt} = 3u - 2v - uv \tag{22}$$

having $(0, 0)$ as the corresponding critical point. The associated linear system

$$\frac{du}{dt} = -2u - 3v$$

$$\frac{dv}{dt} = 3u - 2v \tag{23}$$

has characteristic equation $(\lambda + 2)^2 + 9 = 0$, with complex conjugate roots $\lambda = -2 \pm 3i$. Hence $(0, 0)$ is an asymptotically stable spiral point of the linear system in (23), so Theorem 2 implies that $(4, 3)$ is an asymptotically stable spiral point of the original almost linear system in (21). Figure 6.2.15 shows a typical trajectory of the linear system in (23), and Fig. 6.2.16 shows how this spiral point fits into the phase portrait for the original almost linear system in (21).

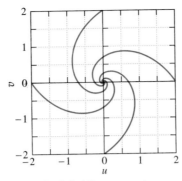

FIGURE 6.2.15. Spiral trajectories of the linear system in (23)

FIGURE 6.2.16. Phase portrait for the almost linear system in (21)

6.2 Problems

In Problems 1 through 10, determine the type of the critical point $(0, 0)$ and whether it is asymptotically stable, stable, or unstable.

1. $\dfrac{dx}{dt} = -2x + y, \quad \dfrac{dy}{dt} = x - 2y$

2. $\dfrac{dx}{dt} = 4x - y, \quad \dfrac{dy}{dt} = 2x + y$

3. $\dfrac{dx}{dt} = x + 2y, \quad \dfrac{dy}{dt} = 2x + y$

4. $\dfrac{dx}{dt} = 3x + y, \quad \dfrac{dy}{dt} = 5x - y$

5. $\dfrac{dx}{dt} = x - 2y, \quad \dfrac{dy}{dt} = 2x - 3y$

6. $\dfrac{dx}{dt} = 5x - 3y, \quad \dfrac{dy}{dt} = 3x - y$

7. $\dfrac{dx}{dt} = 3x - 2y, \quad \dfrac{dy}{dt} = 4x - y$

8. $\dfrac{dx}{dt} = x - 3y, \quad \dfrac{dy}{dt} = 6x - 5y$

9. $\dfrac{dx}{dt} = 2x - 2y, \quad \dfrac{dy}{dt} = 4x - 2y$

10. $\dfrac{dx}{dt} = x - 2y, \quad \dfrac{dy}{dt} = 5x - y$

Each of the systems in Problems 11 through 18 has a single critical point (x_0, y_0). Classify it as to type and stability. Begin by making substitutions of the form $u = x - x_0, v = y - y_0$, as in Example 1.

11. $\dfrac{dx}{dt} = x - 2y, \quad \dfrac{dy}{dt} = 3x - 4y - 2$

12. $\dfrac{dx}{dt} = x - 2y - 8, \quad \dfrac{dy}{dt} = x + 4y + 10$

13. $\dfrac{dx}{dt} = 2x - y - 2, \quad \dfrac{dy}{dt} = 3x - 2y - 2$

14. $\dfrac{dx}{dt} = x + y - 7, \quad \dfrac{dy}{dt} = 3x - y - 5$

15. $\dfrac{dx}{dt} = x - y, \quad \dfrac{dy}{dt} = 5x - 3y - 2$

16. $\dfrac{dx}{dt} = x - 2y + 1, \quad \dfrac{dy}{dt} = x + 3y - 9$

17. $\dfrac{dx}{dt} = x - 5y - 5, \quad \dfrac{dy}{dt} = x - y - 3$

18. $\dfrac{dx}{dt} = 4x - 5y + 3, \quad \dfrac{dy}{dt} = 5x - 4y + 6$

In Problems 19 through 28, investigate the type and stability of the critical point $(0, 0)$ of the given almost linear system.

19. $\dfrac{dx}{dt} = x - 3y + 2xy, \quad \dfrac{dy}{dt} = 4x - 6y - xy$

20. $\dfrac{dx}{dt} = 6x - 5y + x^2, \quad \dfrac{dy}{dt} = 2x - y + y^2$

21. $\dfrac{dx}{dt} = x + 2y + x^2 + y^2, \quad \dfrac{dy}{dt} = 2x - 2y - 3xy$

22. $\dfrac{dx}{dt} = x + 4y - xy^2, \quad \dfrac{dy}{dt} = 2x - y + x^2y$

23. $\dfrac{dx}{dt} = 2x - 5y + x^3$, $\dfrac{dy}{dt} = 4x - 6y + y^4$

24. $\dfrac{dx}{dt} = 5x - 5y + x(x^2 + y^2)$,

$\dfrac{dy}{dt} = 5x - 3y + y(x^2 + y^2)$

25. $\dfrac{dx}{dt} = x - 2y + 3xy$, $\dfrac{dy}{dt} = 2x - 3y - x^2 - y^2$

26. $\dfrac{dx}{dt} = 3x - 2y - x^2 - y^2$, $\dfrac{dy}{dt} = 2x - y + 3xy$

27. $\dfrac{dx}{dt} = x - y + x^4 - y^2$, $\dfrac{dy}{dt} = 2x - y + y^4 - x^2$

28. $\dfrac{dx}{dt} = 3x - y + x^3 + y^3$, $\dfrac{dy}{dt} = 13x - 3y + 3xy$

In Problems 29 through 32, find all critical points of the given system and investigate the type and stability of each.

29. $\dfrac{dx}{dt} = x - y$, $\dfrac{dy}{dt} = x^2 - y$

30. $\dfrac{dx}{dt} = y - 1$, $\dfrac{dy}{dt} = x^2 - y$

31. $\dfrac{dx}{dt} = y^2 - 1$, $\dfrac{dy}{dt} = x^3 - y$

32. $\dfrac{dx}{dt} = xy - 2$, $\dfrac{dy}{dt} = x - 2y$

Bifurcations

The term "bifurcation" generally refers to something "splitting apart." With regard to differential equations or systems involving a parameter, it refers to abrupt changes in the character of the solutions as the parameter is changed continuously. Problems 33 through 36 illustrate sensitive cases in which small perturbations in the coefficients of a linear or almost linear system can change the type or stability (or both) of a critical point.

33. Consider the linear system

$$\frac{dx}{dt} = \epsilon x - y, \qquad \frac{dy}{dt} = x + \epsilon y.$$

Show that the critical point $(0, 0)$ is (a) a stable spiral point if $\epsilon < 0$; (b) a center if $\epsilon = 0$; (c) an unstable spiral point if $\epsilon > 0$. Thus small perturbations of the system $x' = -y$, $y' = x$ can change both the type and stability of the critical point. Figure 6.2.17 (a)–(e) illustrate the loss of stability that occurs at $\epsilon = 0$ as the parameter increases from $\epsilon < 0$ to $\epsilon > 0$.

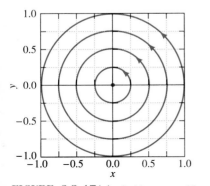

FIGURE 6.2.17(a). Stable spiral with $\epsilon = -0.2$

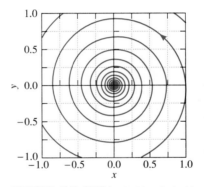

FIGURE 6.2.17(b). Stable spiral with $\epsilon = -0.05$

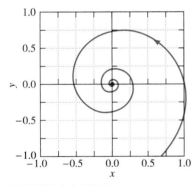

FIGURE 6.2.17(c). Stable center with $\epsilon = 0$

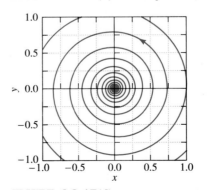

FIGURE 6.2.17(d). Unstable spiral with $\epsilon = 0.05$

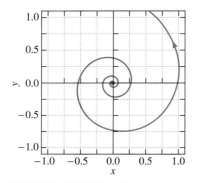

FIGURE 6.2.17(e). Unstable spiral with $\epsilon = 0.2$

34. Consider the linear system

$$\frac{dx}{dt} = -x + \epsilon y, \qquad \frac{dy}{dt} = x - y.$$

Show that the critical point $(0, 0)$ is (a) a stable spiral point if $\epsilon < 0$; (b) a stable node if $0 \le \epsilon < 1$. Thus small perturbations of the system $x' = -x$, $y' = x - y$ can change the type of the critical point $(0, 0)$ without changing its stability.

35. This problem deals with the almost linear system

$$\frac{dx}{dt} = y + hx(x^2 + y^2), \qquad \frac{dy}{dt} = -x + hy(x^2 + y^2),$$

in illustration of the sensitive case of Theorem 2, in which the theorem provides no information about the stability of the critical point $(0, 0)$. (a) Show that $(0, 0)$ is a center of the linear system obtained by setting $h = 0$. (b) Suppose that $h \ne 0$. Let $r^2 = x^2 + y^2$, and then apply the fact that

$$x\frac{dx}{dt} + y\frac{dy}{dt} = r\frac{dr}{dt}$$

to show that $dr/dt = hr^3$. (c) Suppose that $h = -1$. Integrate the differential equation in (b); then show that $r \to 0$ as $t \to +\infty$. Thus $(0, 0)$ is an asymptotically stable critical point of the almost linear system in this case. (d) Suppose that $h = +1$. Show that $r \to +\infty$ as t increases, so $(0, 0)$ is an unstable critical point in this case.

36. This problem presents the famous *Hopf bifurcation* for the almost linear system

$$\frac{dx}{dt} = \epsilon x + y - x(x^2 + y^2)$$

$$\frac{dy}{dt} = -x + \epsilon y - y(x^2 + y^2),$$

which has imaginary characteristic roots $\lambda = \pm i$ if $\epsilon = 0$. (a) Change to polar coordinates as in Example 6 of Section 6.1 to obtain the system $r' = r(\epsilon - r^2)$, $\theta' = -1$. (b) Separate variables and integrate directly to show that if $\epsilon \le 0$ then $r(t) \to 0$ as $t \to +\infty$, so in this case the origin is a stable spiral point. (c) Show similarly that if $\epsilon > 0$ then $r(t) \to \sqrt{\epsilon}$ as $t \to +\infty$, so in this case the origin is an unstable spiral point. The circle $r(t) \equiv \sqrt{\epsilon}$ itself is a closed periodic solution or *limit cycle*. Thus a limit cycle of increasing size is spawned as the parameter ϵ increases through the critical value 0.

37. In the case of a two-dimensional system that is *not* almost linear, the trajectories near an isolated critical point can exhibit a considerably more complicated structure than those near the nodes, centers, saddle points, and spiral points discussed in this section. For example, consider the system

$$\frac{dx}{dt} = x(x^3 - 2y^3)$$

$$\frac{dy}{dt} = y(2x^3 - y^3) \tag{24}$$

having $(0, 0)$ as an isolated critical point. This system is not almost linear because $(0, 0)$ is not an *isolated* critical point of the trivial associated linear system $x' = 0$, $y' = 0$. Solve the homogeneous first-order equation

$$\frac{dy}{dx} = \frac{y(2x^3 - y^3)}{x(x^3 - 2y^3)}$$

to show that the trajectories of the system in (24) are *folia of Descartes* of the form

$$x^3 + y^3 = 3cxy$$

where c is an arbitrary constant (Fig. 6.2.18).

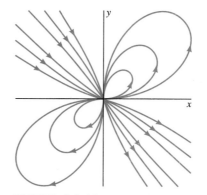

FIGURE 6.2.18. Trajectories of the system in (24)

6.2 Computing Project

FIGURE 6.2.19. Phase portrait for the system in (1)

Interesting and complicated phase portraits often result from simple nonlinear perturbations of linear systems. For instance, Fig. 6.2.19 shows a phase portrait for the system

$$\frac{dx}{dt} = -x - y^2 \cos(x + y)$$

$$\frac{dy}{dt} = y + x^2 \cos(x - y). \tag{1}$$

A dozen critical points are marked with small dots.

Suppose that we want to locate accurately the apparent spiral point near $(-1, 1)$. Our problem is to solve numerically two equations in two unknowns. Using *Mathematica*, for instance, we could proceed as follows. First we define the right-hand sides of the differential equations in (1), writing **xp** for dx/dt and **yp** for dy/dt:

```
xp = -x - y^2 Cos[x + y];

yp =  y + x^2 Cos[x - y];
```

and then solve for the desired numerical solution.

```
soln = FindRoot[ { xp == 0, yp == 0 }, {x,-1}, {y,1} ];

a = x /. soln;   b = y /. soln;

{a, b}

{-1.24992, 1.12255}
```

Thus our critical point is approximately $(-1.24992, 1.12255)$. To investigate the precise nature of this critical point, we need to substitute $u = x - a$, $v = y - b$ so that $x = a$, $y = b$ corresponds to $u = 0$, $v = 0$. The right-hand sides of the resulting equations for du/dt and dv/dt will be given by

```
subs = {x -> u + a, y -> v + b};

up = xp /. subs

vp = yp /. subs

1.24992 - u - (1.12255 + v)^2 Cos[0.127367 - u - v]

1.12255 + v + (-1.24992 + u)^2 Cos[2.37248 - u + v]
```

We can extract the coefficients of the u- and v-terms by computing partial derivatives of **up** and **vp** at the origin.

```
A = {{D[up,u], D[up,v]},

       {D[vp,u], D[vp,v]}} /. {u -> 0, v -> 0}

{{-1.16007, -2.38699}, {2.88278, -0.0865834}}
```

FIGURE 6.2.20. Phase portrait for the system in (2)

We need the eigenvalues of this matrix **A**.

Eigenvalues[A]

{-0.623324 + 2.5677 I, -0.623324 - 2.5677 I}

The fact that these eigenvalues are complex conjugates with negative real parts shows that our selected critical point is a stable spiral point.

If *Mathematica, Maple*, or another computer algebra system is available, you can proceed to investigate similarly any of the other critical points shown in Fig. 6.2.19. For a second problem, investigate some of the critical points indicated in the Fig. 6.2.20 phase portrait for the system

$$\frac{dx}{dt} = -x + y \sin y$$

$$\frac{dy}{dt} = y - x^2 \cos x. \tag{2}$$

Then investigate your own nonlinear perturbation of some simple almost linear system.

6.3 Ecological Models: Predators and Competitors

Some of the most interesting and important applications of stability theory involve the interactions between two or more biological populations occupying the same environment. We consider first a **predator–prey** situation involving two species. One species—the **predators**—feeds on the other species—the **prey**—which in turn feeds on some third food item readily available in the environment. A standard example is a population of foxes and rabbits in a woodland; the foxes (predators) eat rabbits (the prey), while the rabbits eat certain vegetation in the woodland. Other examples are sharks (predators) and food fish (prey), bass (predators) and sunfish (prey), ladybugs (predators) and aphids (prey), and beetles (predators) and scale insects (prey).

The classical mathematical model of a predator–prey situation was developed in the 1920s by the Italian mathematician Vito Volterra (1860–1940) in order to analyze the cyclic variations observed in the shark and food fish populations in the Adriatic Sea. To construct such a model, we denote the number of prey at time t by $x(t)$ and the number of predators by $y(t)$, and make the following simplifying assumptions.

1. In the absence of predators, the prey population would grow at a natural rate, with $dx/dt = ax, a > 0$.

2. In the absence of prey, the predator population would decline at a natural rate, with $dy/dt = -cy, c > 0$.

3. When both predator and prey are present, there occur, in combination with these natural rates of growth and decline, a decline in the prey population and a growth in the predator population, each at a rate proportional to the frequency of encounters between individuals of the two species. We assume further that the frequency of such encounters is proportional to the product xy, reasoning that doubling either population alone should double the frequency of encoun-

ters, while doubling both populations ought to quadruple the frequency of encounters. Consequently, the effect of predators eating prey is an *interaction rate* of decline $-bxy$ in the prey population x, and an interaction rate of growth dxy of the predator population y, with b and d positive constants.

When we adjoin the interaction rates described above to the natural rates, we obtain the **predator–prey equations**

▶

$$\frac{dx}{dt} = ax - bxy = x(a - by)$$

$$\frac{dy}{dt} = -cy + dxy = y(-c + dx), \tag{1}$$

with the constants a, b, c, and d all positive. This is an almost linear system with two critical points, $(0, 0)$ and $(c/d, a/b)$. The point $(0, 0)$ is a saddle point, but the corresponding equilibrium solution $x(t) \equiv 0$, $y(t) \equiv 0$ merely describes simultaneous extinction of both species.

The critical point $(c/d, a/b)$ is of greater interest; $x(t) \equiv c/d$ and $y(t) \equiv a/b$ are the nonzero constant prey and predator populations, respectively, that can coexist in equilibrium. We would like to know, if the initial populations x_0 and y_0 are near these critical populations, whether $(x(t), y(t))$ remains near $(c/d, a/b)$ for all $t > 0$. That is, is the critical point $(c/d, a/b)$ stable? To attempt to answer this question, we substitute $u = x - c/d, v = y - a/b$ in (1). We thereby obtain the almost linear system

$$\frac{du}{dt} = -\frac{bc}{d}v - buv$$

$$\frac{dv}{dt} = \frac{ad}{b}u + duv, \tag{2}$$

which has $(0,0)$ as its critical point corresponding to the critical point $(c/d, a/b)$ of the system in (1). The corresponding linear system

$$\frac{du}{dt} = -\frac{bc}{d}v$$

$$\frac{dv}{dt} = \frac{ad}{b}u \tag{3}$$

has characteristic equation $\lambda^2 + ac = 0$ with pure imaginary roots $\lambda_1, \lambda_2 = \pm i\sqrt{ac}$. Hence $(0, 0)$ is a stable center of (3), and the trajectories are ellipses centered at $(0, 0)$. In fact, if we divide the second equation in (3) by the first, we obtain

$$\frac{dv}{du} = -\frac{ad/b}{bc/d} \cdot \frac{u}{v} = -\frac{ad^2u}{cb^2v},$$

$$ad^2u\,du + cb^2v\,dv = 0,$$

$$ad^2u^2 + cb^2v^2 = C \tag{4}$$

$$\frac{u^2}{A^2} + \frac{v^2}{B^2} = 1,$$

FIGURE 6.3.1. Linearized trajectories of the system in (2); the directions indicated by the arrows are determined by the signs in Eq. (3).

where C is a constant of integration, $A^2 = C/ad^2$, and $B^2 = C/cb^2$. In terms of x and y, the trajectories of the linearized system are, therefore, ellipses of the form

$$\frac{1}{A^2}\left(x - \frac{c}{d}\right)^2 + \frac{1}{B^2}\left(y - \frac{a}{b}\right)^2 = 1 \tag{5}$$

centered at the critical point $(c/d, a/b)$. Some of these ellipses are shown in Fig. 6.3.1.

Unfortunately, this analysis does not settle the question of the stability of the critical point $(c/d, a/b)$ of the original nonlinear system in (1), because a stable center represents the indeterminate case of Theorem 2 of Section 6.2, in which the critical point can (aside from a center) be either an unstable or an asymptotically stable spiral point. We can in this case, however, find the trajectories explicitly by dividing the second equation in (1) by the first to obtain

$$\frac{dy}{dx} = \frac{y(-c + dx)}{x(a - by)} \qquad (Note:\ d\ times\ x\ on\ the\ right).$$

We separate the variables to get

$$\frac{c - dx}{x}\,dx + \frac{a - by}{y}\,dy = 0,$$

and thus

$$c\ln x - dx + a\ln y - by = C, \tag{6}$$

where C is a constant of integration (and dx in Eq. (6) is not a differential, but the product of the positive constant d with x). In any case, the trajectories of the system in (1) near the critical point $(c/d, a/b)$ are the level curves of the function $f(x, y)$ that appears on the left-hand side in Eq. (6). It can be shown that these trajectories are simple closed curves enclosing $(c/d, a/b)$, which is therefore a stable center. Figure 6.3.2 shows a phase plane portrait of these trajectories for the case $a = b = c = d = 1$. It follows from Problem 30 of Section 6.1 that $x(t)$ and $y(t)$ are both periodic functions of t; this explains the fluctuations that are experimentally observed in predator–prey populations. If we follow a single trajectory in Fig. 6.3.2, beginning at a point where the prey population x is maximal and $y = a/b$ (Why is $y = a/b$ when x is maximal?), we see that x decreases and y increases until $x = c/d$ and the predator population y is maximal. Then both decrease until x is minimal and $y = a/b$ again. And so on around the trajectory back to the initial point. In particular, we see that if both $x_0 > 0$ and $y_0 > 0$, then both $x(t) > 0$ and $y(t) > 0$ for all t, so both populations survive in coexistence with each other. Exception: If the fluctuations are so wide that $x(t)$ is nearly zero, there is a significant possibility that the last few prey will be devoured, resulting in their immediate extinction and the consequent eventual extinction of the predators.

FIGURE 6.3.2. Actual trajectories of the predator-prey system $x' = x - xy, \quad y' = -y + xy$

A Predator–Prey Bifurcation

Figure 6.3.3 illustrates trajectories of the predator-prey system

$$\frac{dx}{dt} = x - xy + \epsilon x(1 - x)$$

$$\frac{dy}{dt} = -y + xy \tag{7}$$

FIGURE 6.3.3. Periodic predator-prey orbits and spiral trajectories of the system in (7) with $\epsilon = 0.2$

near the critical point $(1, 1)$ for different values of the parameter ϵ. For $\epsilon = 0$ this system is of the standard form in (1), so the point $(1, 1)$ is a stable center surrounded by simple closed trajectories, as in Fig. 6.3.2. But with $\epsilon > 0$ the prey population $x(t)$ would, in the absence of predators, exhibit logistic rather than natural growth. In this case a *bifurcation* occurs and $(1, 1)$ becomes a stable spiral point. Figure 6.3.3 shows also some spiral trajectories with $\epsilon = 0.2$. (The figure is printed with aspect ratio 0.65, so that a unit square in the xy-plane is printed as a rectangle with base $x = 1$ and height $y = 0.65$.) Each trajectory was computed numerically with a *Mathematica* command of the form

```
NDSolve[ {x'[t] ==  x[t](1 - y[y]) + eps x[t](1 - x[t]),
          y'[t] == -y[t](1 - x[t]),
          x[0] == a,
          y[0] == b}, {x,y}, {t, 0, t1} ]
```

to solve the predator-prey system on the interval $0 \leq t \leq t_1$ with initial point (a, b).

Competing Species

Now we consider two species (of animals, plants, or bacteria, for instance) with populations $x(t)$ and $y(t)$ at time t and which compete with each other for the food available in their common environment. This is in marked contrast to the case in which one species preys upon the other. To construct a mathematical model that is as realistic as possible, let us assume that in the absence of either species, the other would have a bounded [logistic] population like that considered in Section 2.1. In the absence of any interaction or competition between the two species, their populations would then satisfy the differential equations

$$\frac{dx}{dt} = a_1 x - b_1 x^2$$

$$\frac{dy}{dt} = a_2 y - b_2 y^2, \tag{8}$$

each of the form of Eq. (3) of Section 2.1. But in addition, we assume that competition has the effect of a rate of decline in each population that is proportional to their product xy. We insert such terms with *negative* proportionality constants $-c_1$ and $-c_2$ in the equations in (8) to obtain the **competition equations**

$$\frac{dx}{dt} = a_1 x - b_1 x^2 - c_1 xy = x(a_1 - b_1 x - c_1 y)$$

$$\frac{dy}{dt} = a_2 y - b_2 y^2 - c_2 xy = y(a_2 - b_2 y - c_2 x), \tag{9}$$

where the coefficients a_1, a_2, b_1, b_2, c_1, and c_2 are all positive.

The almost linear system in (9) has four critical points. Upon setting the right-hand sides of the two equations equal to zero, we see that if $x = 0$, then either $y = 0$ or $y = a_2/b_2$, whereas if $y = 0$, then either $x = 0$ or $x = a_1/b_1$. This gives the three critical points $(0, 0)$, $(0, a_2/b_2)$, and $(a_1/b_1, 0)$. The fourth is at the intersection of the

two lines with equations

$$b_1 x + c_1 y = a_1,$$
$$c_2 x + b_2 y = a_2. \tag{10}$$

We assume that these two lines are not parallel and that they intersect at a point in the first quadrant. (The other cases will be explored in the exercises.) Then this point (x_E, y_E) is the fourth critical point, and it represents the possibility of peaceful coexistence of the two species, with stable populations $x(t) \equiv x_E$ and $y(t) \equiv y_E$.

We are interested in the stability of the critical point (x_E, y_E). This turns out to depend upon the relative orientation of the two lines in (10). The two possibilities are shown in Fig. 6.3.4, with the first line in (10) blue and the second black. Comparing the slopes of the two lines, we see that Fig. 6.3.4(a) corresponds to the condition that

$$\frac{a_2/b_2}{a_2/c_2} < \frac{a_1/c_1}{a_1/b_1}; \qquad \text{that is,} \quad c_1 c_2 < b_1 b_2. \tag{11}$$

Similarly, Fig. 6.3.4(b) corresponds to the condition that

$$\frac{a_2/b_2}{a_2/c_2} > \frac{a_1/c_1}{a_1/b_1}; \qquad \text{that is,} \quad c_1 c_2 > b_1 b_2. \tag{12}$$

The conditions in (11) and (12) have a natural interpretation. In the equations in (8), we see that b_1 and b_2 represent the inhibiting effect of each population on its own growth (possibly due to limitations of food or space). On the other hand, c_1 and c_2 represent the effect of competition between the two populations. Thus $b_1 b_2$ is a measure of *inhibition* while $c_1 c_2$ is a measure of *competition*. A general analysis of the system in (9) shows the following:

1. If $c_1 c_2 < b_1 b_2$, so that competition is small in comparison with inhibition, then (x_E, y_E) is an asymptotically stable critical point that is approached by each solution as $t \to +\infty$. Thus the two species can and do coexist in this case.

2. If $c_1 c_2 > b_1 b_2$, so that competition is large in comparison with inhibition, then (x_E, y_E) is an unstable critical point, and either $x(t)$ or $y(t)$ approaches zero as $t \to +\infty$. Thus the two species cannot coexist in this case; one survives and the other becomes locally extinct.

Rather than carrying out the general analysis that leads to the conclusions stated above, we present two examples that illustrate these two possibilities.

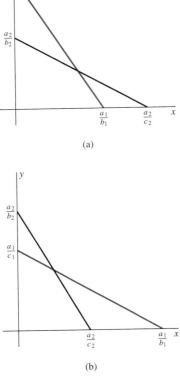

(a)

(b)

FIGURE 6.3.4. Stability of the critical point (x_E, y_E)

EXAMPLE 1 Survival of a Single Species

Suppose that the populations $x(t)$ and $y(t)$ satisfy the equations

$$\frac{dx}{dt} = 60x - 4x^2 - 3xy = x(60 - 4x - 3y),$$

$$\frac{dy}{dt} = 42y - 2y^2 - 3xy = y(42 - 3x - 2y). \tag{13}$$

These are the competition equations with $a_1 = 60$, $a_2 = 42$, $b_1 = 4$, $b_2 = 2$, and $c_1 = c_2 = 3$. Note that $c_1 c_2 = 9 > 8 = b_1 b_2$, so we should expect the results in Case 2. The four critical points are $(0, 0)$, $(0, 21)$, $(15, 0)$, and $(6, 12)$. We will analyze them individually.

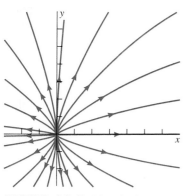

FIGURE 6.3.5. Linearized trajectories of (13) near $(0, 0)$; the common tangent is the y-axis.

The Critical Point (0, 0). We linearize the system in (13) by dropping the quadratic terms; the result is the linear system

$$\frac{dx}{dt} = 60x, \qquad \frac{dy}{dt} = 42y. \tag{14}$$

The general solution of this system is

$$x(t) = Ae^{60t}, \qquad y(t) = Be^{42t}, \tag{15}$$

so $(0, 0)$ is an unstable node for the linearized system in (14). Because the equations in (14) yield $y = Cx^{7/10}$, all the trajectories other than the x-axis are tangent to the y-axis at the origin. Figure 6.3.5 shows some of these trajectories near the critical point $(0, 0)$.

The Critical Point (0, 21). To linearize the equations in (13) near the critical point $(0, 21)$, we substitute $u = x$ and $v = y - 21$. The result is the almost linear system

$$\frac{du}{dt} = -3u - 4u^2 - 3uv$$

$$\frac{dv}{dt} = -63u - 42v - 3uv - 2v^2 \tag{16}$$

with critical point $(0, 0)$. The corresponding linear system

$$\frac{du}{dt} = -3u, \qquad \frac{dv}{dt} = -63u - 42v \tag{17}$$

has characteristic roots $\lambda_1 = -3$ and $\lambda_2 = -42$. So $(0, 21)$ is an asymptotically stable node. The general solution of (17) has the form

$$u(t) = Ae^{-3t}, \qquad v(t) = -\frac{21}{13}Ae^{-3t} + Be^{-42t}, \tag{18}$$

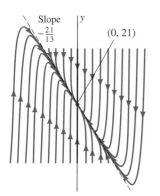

FIGURE 6.3.6. Linearized trajectories of (13) near the improper node $(0, 21)$; the trajectories are drawn accurately by computer. Although they appear to "enter" the line with slope $-21/13$, they actually are all tangent to it at the single point $(0, 21)$.

where A and B are arbitrary constants. As $t \to +\infty$, (u, v) approaches $(0, 0)$, so (x, y) approaches $(0, 21)$. With $A = 0$, Eq. (18) gives the vertical line through the critical point. The slope of any trajectory with $A \neq 0$ is

$$\frac{dy}{dx} = \frac{dy/dt}{dx/dt} = \frac{dv/dt}{du/dt} = \frac{\frac{63}{13}Ae^{-3t} - 42Be^{-42t}}{-3Ae^{-3t}} = -\frac{21}{13} + \frac{14B}{A}e^{-39t}.$$

Hence $dy/dx \to -\frac{21}{13}$ as $t \to +\infty$ and (x, y) approaches $(0, 21)$. Consequently the trajectories near the critical point $(0, 21)$ resemble those shown in Fig. 6.3.6.

The Critical Point (15, 0). The substitution $u = x - 15$, $v = y$ in the equations in (13) yields

$$\frac{du}{dt} = -60u - 45v - 4u^2 - 3uv$$

$$\frac{dv}{dt} = -3v - 3uv - 2v^2. \tag{19}$$

The corresponding linear system

$$\frac{du}{dt} = -60u - 45v, \qquad \frac{dv}{dt} = -3v \tag{20}$$

has characteristic roots $\lambda_1 = -3$ and $\lambda_2 = -60$, so this critical point is also an asymptotically stable node. The general solution is of the form

$$u(t) = -\frac{15}{19} Ae^{-3t}, \qquad v(t) = Ae^{-3t}. \tag{21}$$

As $t \to +\infty$, $(u, v) \to (0, 0)$ and so $(x, y) \to (15, 0)$. With $A = 0$ we get the horizontal line through the critical point. The slope of any trajectory with $A \neq 0$ is

$$\frac{dy}{dx} = \frac{dy/dt}{dx/dt} = \frac{dv/dt}{du/dt} = \frac{-3Ae^{-3t}}{\frac{45}{19}Ae^{-3t} - 60Be^{-60t}} = \frac{-A}{\frac{15}{19}A - 20Be^{-57t}}.$$

Hence $dy/dx \to -\frac{19}{15}$ as $t \to +\infty$ and $(x, y) \to (15, 0)$. The trajectories near $(15, 0)$ therefore resemble those shown in Fig. 6.3.7.

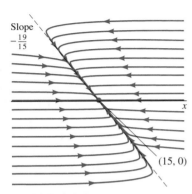

FIGURE 6.3.7. Linearized trajectories of (31) near the improper node (15, 0); the trajectories are drawn accurately by computer. Although they appear to "enter" the line with slope $-19/15$, they actually are all tangent to it at the single point (15, 0).

The Critical Point (6, 12). To linearize the equations in (13) near the critical point (6, 12) (the one representing the possibility of coexistence of the two species), we substitute $u = x - 6$ and $v = y - 12$. The result is the almost linear system

$$\frac{du}{dt} = -24u - 18v - 4u^2 - 3uv$$

$$\frac{dv}{dt} = -36u - 24v - uv - 2v^2. \tag{22}$$

The associated linear system is

$$\frac{du}{dt} = -24u - 18v, \qquad \frac{dv}{dt} = -36u - 24v. \tag{23}$$

The characteristic equation associated with Eq. (23) is

$$(-24 - \lambda)^2 - (-36) \cdot (-18) = (\lambda + 24)^2 - 2 \cdot (18)^2 = 0$$

with roots $\lambda_1 = -24 + 18\sqrt{2} > 0$ and $\lambda_2 = -24 - 18\sqrt{2} < 0$. Thus this critical point is an unstable saddle point. We find that the general solution of (23) is

$$u(t) = Ae^{\lambda_1 t} + Be^{\lambda_2 t}, \qquad v(t) = -\sqrt{2}Ae^{\lambda_1 t} + \sqrt{2}Be^{\lambda_2 t}, \tag{24}$$

where A and B are arbitrary constants. The slope of a trajectory in the linearized system is given by

$$\frac{dy}{dx} = \frac{dv/dt}{du/dt} = \sqrt{2}\left(\frac{-\lambda_1 Ae^{\lambda_1 t} + \lambda_2 Be^{\lambda_2 t}}{\lambda_1 Ae^{\lambda_1 t} + \lambda_2 Be^{\lambda_2 t}}\right). \tag{25}$$

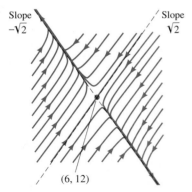

FIGURE 6.3.8. Linearized trajectories of (13) near the point (6, 12); the trajectories are drawn accurately by computer. Although they appear to "enter" the line with slope $-\sqrt{2}$, they actually have the two lines with slopes $\pm\sqrt{2}$ as asymptotes.

If $A = 0$, then $(u, v) \to (0, 0)$ and so $(x, y) \to (6, 12)$ as $t \to + \infty$ because $\lambda_2 < 0$. From (24) and (25) we see that (x, y) then approaches the critical point $(6, 12)$ along the straight line of slope $\sqrt{2}$. If $A \neq 0$ then from (25) we find that

$$\frac{dy}{dx} = \sqrt{2} \left(\frac{-\lambda_1 A + \lambda_2 B e^{-36t\sqrt{2}}}{\lambda_1 A + \lambda_2 B e^{-36t\sqrt{2}}} \right). \qquad (26)$$

With $B = 0$ we have the straight line of slope $-\sqrt{2}$ along which (x, y) leaves the saddle point as t increases, and from (26) we see that $dy/dx \to -\sqrt{2}$ along any other trajectory as $t \to + \infty$. Hence the trajectories near the critical point $(6, 12)$ resemble those shown in Fig. 6.3.8.

Now that we have completed our local analysis of the four critical points of the almost linear system in (13), we want to assemble this information into a coherent whole—to construct a phase plane picture (phase portrait) of the global behavior of the trajectories in the first quadrant (where both populations are nonnegative). If we accept the facts that

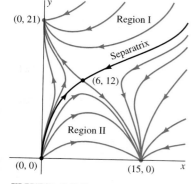

FIGURE 6.3.9. Artist's conception of trajectories consistent with the analysis in Example 1

1. Near each critical point the trajectories look qualitatively like the linearized trajectories shown in Figs. 6.3.5 through 6.3.8, and

2. As $t \to + \infty$, each trajectory either approaches a critical point or diverges toward infinity somewhere in the first quadrant,

then it follows that the phase plane picture should look qualitatively similar to the linearized trajectories shown in the schematic Fig. 6.3.9.

The two trajectories that approach the saddle point $(6, 12)$, together with that saddle point, form a **separatrix** that separates regions I and II in the figure. It plays a crucial role in determining the long-term behavior of the two populations. If the initial point (x_0, y_0) lies precisely on the separatrix, then $(x(t), y(t))$ approaches $(6, 12)$ as $t \to + \infty$. Of course, random events make it extremely unlikely that $(x(t), y(t))$ will remain on the separatrix. If not, peaceful coexistence of the two species is impossible. If (x_0, y_0) lies in Region I above the separatrix, then $(x(t), y(t))$ approaches $(0, 21)$ as $t \to + \infty$, so the population $x(t)$ decreases to zero. Alternatively, if (x_0, y_0) lies in Region II below the separatrix, then $(x(t), y(t))$ approaches $(15, 0)$ as $t \to + \infty$, so the population $y(t)$ dies out. In short, whichever population has the initial competitive advantage survives, while the other faces extinction. ∎

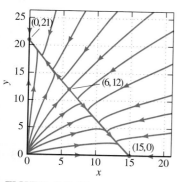

FIGURE 6.3.10. Computer-generated phase plane portrait for the system in (13)

The schematic diagram in Fig. 6.3.9 was drawn by an artist on the basis of our mathematical analysis in Example 1, before the computer-generated phase plane portrait in Fig. 6.3.10 was available. Which do you prefer—the artist's license or the computer's precision?

EXAMPLE 2 **Peaceful Coexistence**

Now suppose that the two populations satisfy the equations

$$\frac{dx}{dt} = 60x - 3x^2 - 4xy = x(60 - 3x - 4y),$$

$$\frac{dy}{dt} = 42y - 3y^2 - 2xy = y(42 - 2x - 3y). \qquad (27)$$

Here $a_1 = 60$, $a_2 = 42$, $b_1 = b_2 = 3$, $c_1 = 4$, and $c_2 = 2$. So $c_1 c_1 = 8 < 9 = b_1 b_2$: Competition is smaller than inhibition. The analysis of the system in (27) follows step by step that of the system in (13) of Example 1. We will present only the results of this analysis, leaving the details to Problems 2 through 6. There are four critical points: (0, 0), (0, 14), (20, 0), and (12, 6).

The critical point (0, 0) is an unstable node of the linearized system, just as in Example 1.

The critical point (0, 14) is an unstable saddle point of the linearized system. The entering trajectories lie along the y-axis, while the departing trajectories lie along the line through (0, 14) with slope $-\frac{14}{23}$.

The critical point (20, 0) is also an unstable saddle point of the linearized system. The entering trajectories lie along the x-axis, while the departing trajectories lie along the straight lie through (20, 0) with slope $-\frac{31}{40}$.

The critical point (12, 6) represents the possibility of peaceful coexistence because it is an asymptotically stable node. One pair of trajectories lies along the line through (12, 6) with slope $\left(-3 + \sqrt{73}\right)/16 \approx 0.35$. All other trajectories of the linearized system enter the node and are tangent to the line with slope $\left(-3 - \sqrt{73}\right)/16 \approx -0.72$. ■

Figure 6.3.11 shows an artist-drawn schematic diagram illustrating the results outlined above, whereas Fig. 6.3.12 is a computer-generated phase plane portrait for the system in (27). One especially notable feature of this system is that for *any* positive initial values x_0 and y_0, $(x(t), y(t))$ approaches (12, 6) as $t \to +\infty$, so the two species both survive in stable (peaceful) coexistence.

Examples 1 and 2 illustrate the power of elementary critical point analysis. But we must conclude with a word of caution. Ecological systems in nature are never so simple as in these examples; they normally involve far more than two species, and the rates of growth of these populations and their interactions are always more complex than those discussed in this section.

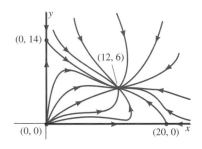

FIGURE 6.3.11. Artist's conception of trajectories consistent with the analysis in Example 2

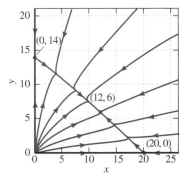

FIGURE 6.3.12. Computer-generated phase plane portrait for the system in (27)

6.3 Problems

1. Let $x(t)$ be a harmful insect population (aphids?) that under natural conditions is held somewhat in check by a benign predator insect population $y(t)$ (ladybugs?). Assume that $x(t)$ and $y(t)$ satisfy the predator–prey equations in (1), so that the stable equilibrium populations are $x_E = c/d$ and $y_E = a/b$ Now suppose that an insecticide is employed that kills (per unit time) the same fraction $f < a$ of each species of insect. Show that the harmful population x_E is increased, while the benign population y_E is decreased, so the use of the insecticide is counterproductive. This is an instance in which mathematical analysis reveals undesirable consequences of a well-intentioned interference with nature.

Problems 2 through 6 provide the details cited in Example 2 for the two competing populations $x(t)$ and $y(t)$ that satisfy the equations

$$\frac{dx}{dt} = 60x - 3x^2 - 4xy = x(60 - 3x - 4y)$$

$$\frac{dy}{dt} = 42y - 3y^2 - 2xy = y(42 - 2x - 3y). \tag{27}$$

2. Show that the critical points of the system in (27) are $(0, 0)$, $(0, 14)$, $(20, 0)$, and $(12, 6)$.

3. Show that the critical point $(0, 0)$ is an unstable node at which all but two trajectories are tangent to the y-axis.

4. (a) To investigate the critical point $(0, 14)$, substitute $u = x$, $v = y - 14$; then show that the corresponding linear system is

$$\frac{du}{dt} = 4u, \qquad \frac{dv}{dt} = -28u - 42v.$$

(b) Show that the general solution of this linear system is

$$u(t) = Ae^{4t}, \qquad v(t) = -\frac{14}{23}Ae^{4t} + Be^{-24t}.$$

(c) Then conclude that $(0, 14)$ is an unstable saddle point at which the entering and departing trajectories lie on the y-axis and on the line through $(0, 14)$ with slope $-\frac{14}{23}$.

5. (a) To investigate the critical point $(20, 0)$, substitute $u = x - 20$, $v = y$; then show that the corresponding linear system is

$$\frac{du}{dt} = -60u - 80v, \qquad \frac{dv}{dt} = 2v.$$

(b) Show that the general solution of this linear system is

$$u(t) = Ae^{-60t} - \frac{40}{31}Be^{2t}, \qquad v(t) = Be^{2t}.$$

(c) Then conclude that $(20, 0)$ is an unstable saddle point at which entering and departing trajectories lie on the x-axis and on the line through $(20, 0)$ with slope $-\frac{31}{40}$.

6. (a) To investigate the critical point $(12, 6)$, substitute $u = x - 12$, $v = y - 6$; then show that the corresponding linear system is

$$\frac{du}{dt} = -36u - 48v, \qquad \frac{dv}{dt} = -12u - 18v.$$

(b) Show that the characteristic roots of this linear system are

$$\lambda_1 = -27 + 3\sqrt{73} < 0 \quad \text{and} \quad \lambda_2 = -27 + 3\sqrt{73} < 0,$$

and that its general solution is

$$u(t) = Ae^{\lambda_1 t} + Be^{\lambda_2 t}, \qquad v(t) = Ce^{\lambda_1 t} + De^{\lambda_2 t},$$

where $C = \left(-3 + \sqrt{73}\right)A/16$ and $D = \left(-3 + \sqrt{73}\right)B/16$.
(c) Hence conclude that $(12, 6)$ is an asymptotically stable node, where two trajectories lie on the line through $(12, 6)$ with slope $\left(-3 + \sqrt{73}\right)/16$ and the others are tangent to the line through $(12, 6)$ with slope $\left(-3 - \sqrt{73}\right)/16$.

Problems 7 through 11 deal with the predator–prey system that is modeled by the equations

$$\frac{dx}{dt} = 5x - x^2 - xy = x(5 - x - y)$$

$$\frac{dy}{dt} = xy - 2y = y(x - 2). \tag{28}$$

In contrast with the system in (1) discussed in the text, the prey population $x(t)$ would—in the absence of any predators—be a bounded population described by the logistic equation $dx/dt = 5x - x^2$.

7. Show that the critical points of the system in (28) are $(0, 0)$, $(5, 0)$, and $(2, 3)$.

8. Show that the critical point $(0, 0)$ is an unstable saddle point of the linearized system, with trajectories entering along the y-axis and departing along the x-axis.

9. Show that the critical point $(5, 0)$ is an unstable saddle point of the linearized system, with trajectories entering along the x-axis and departing along the line through $(5, 0)$ with slope $-\frac{8}{5}$.

10. Show that the critical point $(2, 3)$ is an asymptotically stable spiral point of the linearized system.

11. Show that the results of Problems 7 through 10 are consistent with the global phase portrait for the original nonlinear sys-

FIGURE 6.3.13. Phase plane portrait for the system in (28)

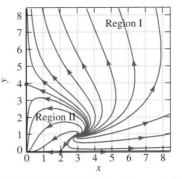

FIGURE 6.3.14. Phase plane portrait for the system in (29)

tem in (28) shown in Fig. 6.3.13. Conclude that the prey and predators coexist with stable equilibrium populations $x_E = 2$ and $y_E = 3$.

Problems 12 through 17 deal with the predator–prey system modeled by the equations

$$\frac{dx}{dt} = x^2 - 2x - xy = x(x - y - 2)$$

$$\frac{dy}{dt} = y^2 - 4y + xy = y(x + y - 4).$$

(29)

In this system, each population—the prey population $x(t)$ and the predator population $y(t)$—is an unsophisticated population (similar to the one considered in Problem 15 of Section 2.1) for each of which the only alternatives (in the absence of the other) are doomsday and extinction.

12. Show that the critical points of the system in (29) are $(0, 0)$, $(0, 4)$, $(2, 0)$, and $(3, 1)$.

13. Show that the critical point $(0, 0)$ is an asymptotically stable node of the linearized system, at which one pair of trajectories lie along the y-axis and the others are tangent to the x-axis.

14. Show that the critical point $(0, 4)$ is an unstable saddle point of the linearized system, with trajectories departing along the y-axis and entering along the line through $(0, 4)$ with slope $-\frac{2}{5}$.

15. Show that the critical point $(2, 0)$ is an unstable saddle point of the linearized system, with trajectories departing along the x-axis and entering along the line through $(2, 0)$ with slope 2.

16. Show that the critical point $(3, 1)$ is an unstable spiral point of the linearized system.

17. Verify that the results of Problems 12 through 16 are consistent with the global phase portrait for the original nonlinear system in (29) shown in Fig. 6.3.14. This is a two-dimensional version of doomsday versus extinction. If the initial point (x_0, y_0) lies in Region I, then both populations increase without bound (until doomsday), whereas if it lies in Region II, then both populations will decrease to zero.

The next two problems deal with the competition equations in (9) and the associated linearized system. The discussion in the text covered only the case in which the critical point of interest (x_E, y_E) lay in the first quadrant. You may now explore the other possibilities.

18. Determine the behavior of the linearized system associated with the system in (9) in the case that (x_E, y_E) exists but does not lie in the first quadrant. Because the populations are never negative, there are only three critical points to examine. There are two cases, depending upon whether (x_E, y_E) lies in the second quadrant or the fourth quadrant.

19. Determine the behavior of the linearized system associated with the system in (9) in the case that (x_E, y_E) does not exist because the two lines having the equations in (10) are parallel. There will be two cases, depending upon which line is above the other. (You may take for granted that the improbable—coincidence of the two lines—does not occur.)

20. A lake is initially stocked with 100 bass and 600 redear. There is ample food for the redear. Because bass prey on redear, the population of bass will increase at a rate proportional to the number of encounters between the two species; bass will also die at a rate proportional to the bass population. The redear multiply at a rate proportional to their population and die off at a rate proportional to the number of encounters between the two species. This implies that the populations $B(t)$ of bass and $R(t)$ of redear satisfy a system of differential equations of the following form:

$$B'(t) = pBR - qB, \qquad R'(t) = uR - vBR.$$

Suppose it is known that $p = 0.00004$, $q = 0.02$, $u = 0.05$, and $v = 0.0004$, with t measured in days. Then we have a predator–prey system as in Eq. (1) of this section, and the populations of the two species oscillate periodically with the same period. Approximate this period by solving the system numerically with the given initial conditions, using the Runge–Kutta method of Section 4.3.

6.3 Computing Project

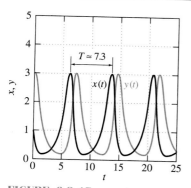

FIGURE 6.3.15. x- and y-solution curves for the predator-prey system (1) with $x(0) = 1$, $y(0) = 3$

The closed trajectories in Fig. 6.3.2 represent periodic solutions of the predator–prey system

$$\frac{dx}{dt} = x - xy, \qquad \frac{dy}{dt} = -y + xy, \tag{1}$$

but provide no information as to the actual periods of the oscillations these solutions describe. The period of a particular solution $(x(t), y(t))$ can be gleaned from the graphs of x and y as functions of t. Figure 6.3.15 shows these graphs for the solution of (1) with initial conditions $x(0) = 1$, $y(0) = 3$. The indicated measurement on the figure indicates that the (equal) periods of oscillation of $x(t)$ and $y(t)$ are given approximately by $T \approx 7.3$.

For your own predator–prey system

$$\frac{dx}{dt} = ax - bxy, \qquad \frac{dy}{dt} = -cy + dxy, \tag{2}$$

let a, b, c, and d be the last four nonzero digits of your student I.D. number. Use whatever software is available to plot typical $x(t)$- and $y(t)$-solution curves and measure the periods of oscillation of the two populations.

6.4 Nonlinear Mechanical Systems

FIGURE 6.4.1. The mass on a spring

Now we apply the qualitative methods of Sections 6.1 and 6.2 to the analysis of simple mechanical systems like the mass-on-a-spring system shown in Fig. 6.4.1. Let m denote the mass in a suitable system of units and let $x(t)$ denote the displacement of the mass at time t from its equilibrium position (where the spring is unstretched). Previously, we have always assumed that the force $F(x)$ exerted by the spring on the mass is a *linear* function of x: $F(x) = -kx$ (Hooke's law). In reality, however, every spring in nature actually is nonlinear (even if only slightly so). Moreover, springs in some automobile suspension systems deliberately are designed to be nonlinear. Here, then, we are interested specifically in the effects of nonlinearity.

So now we allow the force function $F(x)$ to be nonlinear. Because $F(0) = 0$ at the equilibrium position $x = 0$, we may assume that F has a power series expansion of the form

$$F(x) = -kx + \alpha x^2 + \beta x^3 + \cdots. \tag{1}$$

We take $k > 0$ so that the reaction of the spring is directed opposite to the displacement when x is sufficiently small. If we assume also that the reaction of the spring is symmetric with respect to positive and negative displacements by the same distance, then $F(-x) = -F(x)$, so F is an *odd* function. In this case it follows that the coefficient of x^n in (1) is zero if n is even, so the first nonlinear term is the one involving x^3.

For a simple mathematical model of a nonlinear spring we therefore take

$$F(x) = -kx + \beta x^3, \tag{2}$$

ignoring all terms in (1) of degree greater than 3. The equation of motion of the mass m is then

$$\blacktriangleright \qquad mx'' = -kx + \beta x^3. \qquad (3)$$

Introducing the velocity

$$y = \frac{dx}{dt}, \qquad (4)$$

we get the equivalent first-order system

$$\frac{dx}{dt} = y$$

$$\qquad\qquad\qquad (5)$$

$$m\frac{dy}{dt} = -kx + \beta x^3.$$

We can solve explicitly for the phase plane trajectories of this system by writing

$$\frac{dy}{dx} = \frac{dy/dt}{dx/dt} = \frac{-kx + \beta x^3}{my},$$

whence

$$my\, dy + (kx - \beta x^3)\, dx = 0.$$

Integration then yields

$$\frac{1}{2}my^2 + \frac{1}{2}kx^2 - \frac{1}{4}\beta x^4 = E \qquad (6)$$

for the equation of a typical trajectory. We write E for the arbitrary constant of integration because $\frac{1}{2}my^2$ is the kinetic energy of the mass, and it is natural to define

$$V(x) = \frac{1}{2}kx^2 - \frac{1}{4}\beta x^4 \qquad (7)$$

as the potential energy of the spring. Then Eq. (6) expresses conservation of energy for the [undamped] motion of a mass on a spring.

There are two cases to consider. The spring is called *hard* if $\beta < 0$, *soft* if $\beta > 0$. If $\beta < 0$, then the only critical point of the system in (5) is the origin $(0, 0)$, and each trajectory

$$\frac{1}{2}my^2 + \frac{1}{2}kx^2 + \frac{1}{4}|\beta|x^4 = E > 0 \qquad (8)$$

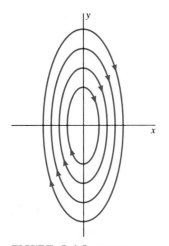

is an oval like those shown in Fig. 6.4.2. Each of these oval trajectories represents a periodic oscillation of the mass back and forth about its equilibrium position, and the critical point $(0, 0)$ is a stable center. Thus the behavior of a mass on a hard spring resembles qualitatively that of a mass on a linear spring with $\beta = 0$ (as in Example 4 of Section 6.1); the phase plane trajectories in Fig. 6.4.2 resemble the elliptical trajectories in Fig. 6.1.6. But one difference between the linear and nonlinear situations is that, whereas the period $T = 2\pi\sqrt{m/k}$ of oscillation of a mass on a linear spring is independent of the initial conditions, the period of a mass on a nonlinear spring depends upon its initial position $x(0)$ and initial velocity $y(0)$ (Problem 15).

FIGURE 6.4.2. Trajectories for a mass on a hard spring with $\beta < 0$

As the following example illustrates, there is a greater range of possible behavior for a mass on a soft spring with $\beta > 0$.

EXAMPLE 1 If $m = 1$, $k = 4$, and $\beta = 1$, then the equation of motion of the mass is

$$\frac{d^2x}{dt^2} + 4x - x^3 = 0, \tag{9}$$

and Eq. (6) gives the trajectories in the form

$$\frac{1}{2}y^2 + 2x^2 - \frac{1}{4}x^4 = E. \tag{10}$$

After solving for

$$y = \pm\sqrt{2E - 4x^2 + \tfrac{1}{2}x^4}, \tag{10'}$$

we can plot for various values of the [constant] energy E the trajectories shown in Fig. 6.4.3.

The two black curves obtained with $E = 4$ are called *separatrices*—they separate regions of different behavior—and intersect the x-axis at the critical points $(-2, 0)$ and $(2, 0)$. These, together with the other critical point $(0, 0)$, are the only points at which the mass can remain at rest.

The nature of the motion of the mass is determined by which type of trajectory its initial conditions place it on. The simple closed trajectories encircling $(0, 0)$ in the region bounded by the separatrices correspond to energies in the range $0 < E < 4$. These closed trajectories represent *periodic* oscillations of the mass back and forth around the equilibrium point $x = 0$.

The unbounded trajectories lying in the regions above and below the separatrices correspond to values of E greater than 4. These represent motions in which the mass approaches $x = 0$ with sufficient energy that it continues on through the equilibrium point, never to return again.

FIGURE 6.4.3. Trajectories for a mass on the soft spring of Example 1

The unbounded trajectories opening to the right and left correspond to negative values of E. These represent motions in which the mass initially is headed toward the equilibrium point $x = 0$, but with insufficient energy to reach it. At some point the mass reverses direction and heads back whence it came.

Although in this example Eq. (10') makes it possible to construct the phase portrait in Fig. 6.4.3, it is nevertheless instructive to examine the critical points $(0, 0)$, $(-2, 0)$, and $(2, 0)$ of the equivalent first-order system

$$\frac{dx}{dt} = y$$

$$\frac{dy}{dt} = -4x + x^3. \tag{11}$$

At $(0, 0)$ we find that the linearized system

$$\frac{dx}{dt} = y$$

$$\frac{dy}{dt} = -4x$$

has a stable center and elliptical trajectories given by

$$x(t) = A \cos 2t + B \sin 2t,$$
$$y(t) = 2B \cos 2t - 2A \sin 2t.$$

(12)

Notice that the direction of motion along these ellipses is consistent with the clockwise orientation of the closed trajectories in Fig. 6.4.3.

At $(2, 0)$ the substitution $u = x - 2$, $v = y$ in (11) yields the system

$$\frac{du}{dt} = v$$
$$\frac{dv}{dt} = 8u + 6u^2 + u^3$$

(13)

having $(0, 0)$ as the corresponding critical point. We find that the linearized system

$$\frac{du}{dt} = v$$
$$\frac{dv}{dt} = 8u$$

has a saddle point at $(0, 0)$, with hyperbolic trajectories given by

$$u(t) = A \cosh t\sqrt{8} + B \sinh t\sqrt{8},$$
$$v(t) = B\sqrt{8} \cosh t\sqrt{8} + A\sqrt{8} \sinh t\sqrt{8}.$$

(14)

These equations yield the trajectories shown in Fig. 6.4.4. Note that in appearance and direction they are consistent with the picture in Fig. 7.5.3 near $(2, 0)$. The analysis of the critical point $(-2, 0)$ is similar.

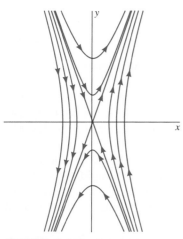

FIGURE 6.4.4. Linearized trajectories of the system in Eq. (13)

Damped Nonlinear Vibrations

Suppose now that the mass on a spring is connected also to a dashpot that provides a force of resistance proportional to the velocity $y = dx/dt$ of the mass. If the spring is still assumed nonlinear as in (2), then the equation of motion of the mass is

▶
$$mx'' = -cx' - kx + \beta x^3,$$

(15)

where $c > 0$ is the dashpot constant. If $\beta > 0$, then the equivalent first-order system

$$\frac{dx}{dt} = y$$
$$m\frac{dy}{dt} = -kx - cy + \beta x^3$$

(16)

has critical points $(0, 0)$ and $(\pm\sqrt{k/\beta}, 0)$. If we take $m = 1$ for convenience, then at $(0, 0)$ the characteristic equation of the corresponding linear system is

$$\lambda(\lambda + c) + k = \lambda^2 + c\lambda + k = 0.$$

(17)

It follows that $(0, 0)$ is a stable node if $c^2 > 4k$, a stable spiral point if $c^2 < 4k$. Example 2 illustrates the latter case.

EXAMPLE 2 Suppose that $m = 1$, $k = 5$, $\beta = \frac{5}{4}$, and $c = 2$. Then the nonlinear system in (16) is

$$\frac{dx}{dt} = y$$

$$\frac{dy}{dt} = -5x - 2y + \frac{5}{4}x^3. \tag{18}$$

In this example no explicit solution for the phase plane trajectories is available, so we proceed to investigate the critical points $(0, 0)$, $(2, 0)$, and $(-2, 0)$.

At $(0, 0)$ the linearized system

$$\frac{dx}{dt} = y$$

$$\frac{dy}{dt} = -5y - 2y$$

has characteristic equation $\lambda^2 + 2\lambda - 5 = 0$ with roots $\lambda = -1 \pm 2i$. Hence $(0, 0)$ is a stable spiral point of (18), and the linearized position function of the mass is of the form

$$x(t) = e^{-t}(A \cos 2t + B \sin 2t),$$

an exponentially damped oscillation about $x = 0$.

At $(2, 0)$ the substitution $u = x - 2$, $v = y$ in (18) yields the system

$$\frac{du}{dt} = v$$

$$\frac{dv}{dt} = 10u - 2v + \frac{15}{2}u^2 + \frac{5}{4}u^3 \tag{19}$$

with corresponding critical point $(0, 0)$. The linearized system

$$\frac{du}{dt} = v$$

$$\frac{dv}{dt} = 10u - 2v$$

has characteristic equation $\lambda^2 + 2\lambda - 10 = 0$ with roots $\lambda_1 = -1 - \sqrt{11} < 0$ and $\lambda_2 = -1 + \sqrt{11} > 0$. It follows that $(2, 0)$ is an unstable saddle point of the original system in (18). A similar analysis shows that $(-2, 0)$ is also an unstable saddle point.

The phase portrait in Fig. 6.4.5 shows trajectories of (18) plotted using the numerical methods of Section 4.3, and exhibits a stable spiral point at $(0, 0)$ and unstable saddle points at $(-2, 0)$ and $(2, 0)$. The periodic oscillations of the undamped case (Fig. 6.4.3) are now replaced by damped oscillations around the equilibrium point $x = 0$. The emphasized branches of the separatrices divide the phase plane into regions of stability and instability. Every trajectory whose initial point lies in the region between the separatrices must spiral into the origin as $t \rightarrow +\infty$, and is therefore a "sta-

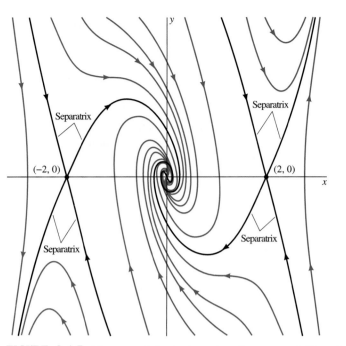

FIGURE 6.4.5. Phase portrait for the damped nonlinear system in Example 2

ble trajectory" representing a damped oscillation. The trajectories that start outside this region are unstable ones along which $x(t) \to \pm\infty$ as $t \to +\infty$. ■

The Nonlinear Pendulum

In Section 3.4 we derived the equation

▶
$$\frac{d^2\theta}{dt^2} + \frac{g}{L} \sin\theta = 0 \tag{20}$$

for the undamped oscillations of the simple pendulum shown in Fig. 6.4.6. There we used the approximation $\sin\theta \approx \theta$ for θ small to replace Eq. (20) with the linear model

$$\frac{d^2\theta}{dt^2} + \omega^2\theta = 0 \tag{21}$$

where $\omega^2 = g/L$. The general solution

$$\theta(t) = A\cos\omega t + B\sin\omega t \tag{22}$$

of Eq. (21) describes oscillations about the equilibrium position $\theta = 0$ with circular frequency ω and amplitude $C = \sqrt{A^2 + B^2}$.

The linear model does not adequately describe the possible motions of the pendulum for large values of θ. For instance, the equilibrium solution $\theta(t) = \pi$ of Eq. (20), with the pendulum standing straight up, does not satisfy the linear equation in (21). Nor does Eq. (22) include the situation in which the pendulum "goes over the top" repeatedly, so that $\theta(t)$ is a steadily increasing rather than an oscillatory function of t. To investigate these phenomena we must analyze the nonlinear equation

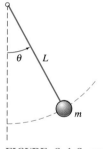

FIGURE 6.4.6. The simple pendulum

$\theta'' + \omega^2 \sin \theta = 0$ rather than merely its linearization. We also want to include the possibility of resistance proportional to velocity, so we consider the general nonlinear pendulum equation

$$\frac{d^2\theta}{dt^2} + c\frac{d\theta}{dt} + \omega^2 \sin \theta = 0. \tag{23}$$

We examine first the undamped case, in which $c = 0$. With $x(t) = \theta(t)$ and $y(t) = \theta'(t)$ the equivalent first-order system is

$$\frac{dx}{dt} = y$$

$$\frac{dy}{dt} = -\omega^2 \sin x. \tag{24}$$

Upon substituting the Taylor series for $\sin x$ we get

$$\frac{dx}{dt} = y$$

$$\frac{dy}{dt} = -\omega^2 x + \frac{\omega^2 x^3}{3!} - \frac{\omega^2 x^5}{5!} + \cdots. \tag{25}$$

Thus (24) is an almost linear system of the form

$$\frac{dx}{dt} = ax + by + f(x, y)$$

$$\frac{dy}{dt} = cx + dy + g(x, y)$$

with $f(x, y) = 0$ and $g(x, y) = \omega^2(x^3/3! - x^5/5! + \cdots)$.

The critical points of the system in (24) are the points $(n\pi, 0)$ with n as an integer. The nature of the critical point $(n\pi, 0)$ depends upon whether n is even or odd.

If $n = 2m$ is *even* then, because

$$\sin(u + 2m\pi) = \sin u,$$

the substitution $u = x - 2m\pi$, $v = y$ in (24) yields the system

$$\frac{du}{dt} = v$$

$$\frac{dv}{dt} = -\omega^2 \sin u \tag{26}$$

having $(0, 0)$ as the corresponding critical point. Just as in (25), the linearization of (26) is the system

$$\frac{du}{dt} = v$$

$$\frac{dv}{dt} = -\omega^2 u \tag{27}$$

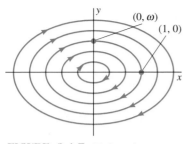

FIGURE 6.4.7. Trajectories of the system in Eq. (27)

for which $(0, 0)$ is the familiar stable center with elliptical trajectories shown in Fig. 6.4.7 (see Example 4 of Section 6.1). Although this is the delicate case in which Theorem 2 of Section 6.2 does not settle the matter, we will soon see that $(2m\pi, 0)$ is also a stable center for the original system in (24).

If $n = 2m + 1$ is *odd*, then, because

$$\sin(u + [2m + 1]\pi) = -\sin u,$$

the substitution $u = x - (2m + 1)\pi$, $v = y$ in (24) yields the system

$$\frac{du}{dt} = v$$

$$\frac{dv}{dt} = +\omega^2 \sin u \tag{28}$$

having $(0, 0)$ as the corresponding critical point. The linearization

$$\frac{du}{dt} = v$$

$$\frac{dv}{dt} = +\omega^2 u \tag{29}$$

of (28) has general solution

$$u(t) = A \cosh \omega t + B \sinh \omega t,$$

$$v(t) = B\omega \cosh \omega t + A\omega \sinh \omega t,$$

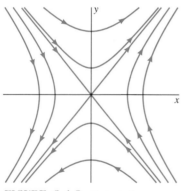

FIGURE 6.4.8. Trajectories of the system in Eq. (29)

so we see that $(0, 0)$ is the unstable saddle point shown in Fig. 6.4.8. It follows from Theorem 2 of Section 6.2 that $([2m + 1]\pi, 0)$ is a similar unstable saddle point for the original almost linear system in (24).

In the undamped case we can see how these centers and saddle points fit together by solving explicitly for the trajectories of (24). If we write

$$\frac{dy}{dx} = \frac{dy/dt}{dx/dt} = -\frac{\omega^2 \sin x}{y}$$

and separate the variables,

$$y \, dy + \omega^2 \sin x \, dx = 0,$$

then integration from $x = 0$ to $x = x$ yields

$$\frac{1}{2} y^2 + \omega^2 (1 - \cos x) = E. \tag{30}$$

We write E for the arbitrary constant of integration because, if physical units are so chosen that $m = L = 1$, then the first term on the left is the kinetic energy and the second term the potential energy of the mass on the end of the pendulum. Then E is the total mechanical energy; Eq. (30) thus expresses conservation of mechanical energy for the undamped pendulum.

If we solve Eq. (30) for y and use a half-angle identity, we get the equation

$$y = \pm \sqrt{2E - 4\omega^2 \sin^2 \tfrac{1}{2} x} \tag{31}$$

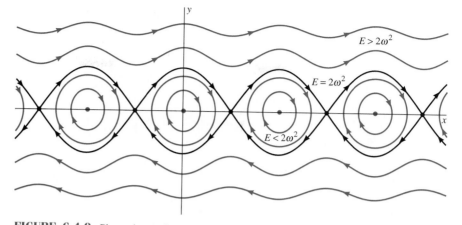

FIGURE 6.4.9. Phase plane trajectories for the undamped nonlinear pendulum. There are unstable saddles at the odd integral multiples of π and stable centers at the even integral multiples of π.

for the trajectories. Figure 6.4.9 shows the results of plotting these trajectories for various values of E. Arrows have been inserted consistent with the critical point analysis given above.

The separatrices, which are shown black in Fig. 6.4.9, correspond to the critical value $E = 2\omega^2$ of the energy; they enter and leave the unstable critical points $(n\pi, 0)$ with n an odd integer. Following the arrows along a separatrix, the pendulum theoretically approaches a balanced vertical position $\theta = x = (2m + 1)\pi$ with just enough energy to reach it but not enough to "go over the top." The instability of this equilibrium position indicates that this behavior will never be observed in practice!

The simple closed trajectories encircling the stable critical points—all of which correspond to the downward position $\theta = 2m\pi$ of the pendulum—represent periodic oscillations of the pendulum back and forth about the stable equilibrium position $\theta = 0$. These correspond to energies $E < 2\omega^2$ that are insufficient for the pendulum to ascend to the vertical upward position. The unbounded trajectories with $E > 2\omega^2$ represent whirling motions of the pendulum in which it goes over the top repeatedly.

If the pendulum is released from rest with initial conditions

$$x(0) = \theta(0) = \alpha, \qquad y(0) = \theta'(0) = 0, \tag{32}$$

then Eq. (30) with $t = 0$ reduces to

$$\omega^2(1 - \cos \alpha) = E. \tag{33}$$

Hence $E < 2\omega^2$ if $0 < \alpha < \pi$, so a periodic oscillation of the pendulum ensues. To determine the *period* of this oscillation, we subtract Eq. (33) from Eq. (30) and write the result (with $x = \theta$ and $y = d\theta/dt$) in the form

$$\frac{1}{2}\left(\frac{d\theta}{dt}\right)^2 = \omega^2(\cos \theta - \cos \alpha). \tag{34}$$

The period T of time required for one complete oscillation is four times the amount of time required for θ to decrease from $\theta = \alpha$ to $\theta = 0$, one-fourth of an oscil-

lation. Hence we solve (34) for $dt/d\theta$ and integrate to get

$$T = \frac{4}{\omega\sqrt{2}} \int_0^\alpha \frac{d\theta}{\sqrt{\cos\theta - \cos\alpha}}. \tag{35}$$

To attempt to evaluate this integral we first use the identity $\cos\theta = 1 - 2\sin^2(\theta/2)$ and get

$$T = \frac{2}{\omega} \int_0^\alpha \frac{d\theta}{\sqrt{k^2 - \sin^2(\theta/2)}}, \tag{36}$$

where

$$k = \sin\frac{\alpha}{2}. \tag{37}$$

Next, the substitution $u = (1/k)\sin(\theta/2)$ yields

$$T = \frac{4}{\omega} \int_0^1 \frac{du}{\sqrt{(1 - u^2)(1 - k^2 u^2)}}. \tag{38}$$

Finally, the substitution $u = \sin\phi$ gives

$$T = \frac{4}{\omega} \int_0^{\pi/2} \frac{d\phi}{\sqrt{1 - k^2 \sin^2\phi}}. \tag{39}$$

The integral in (39) is the *elliptic integral of the first kind* that is often denoted by $F(k, \pi/2)$. It can be evaluated numerically as follows. First we use the binomial series

$$\frac{1}{\sqrt{1-x}} = 1 + \sum_{n=1}^\infty \frac{1\cdot3\cdots(2n-1)}{2\cdot4\cdots(2n)} x^n \tag{40}$$

with $x = k^2\sin^2\phi < 1$ to expand the integrand in (39). Then we integrate termwise using the tabulated integral formula

$$\int_0^{\pi/2} \sin^{2n}\phi \, d\phi = \frac{\pi}{2} \cdot \frac{1\cdot3\cdots(2n-1)}{2\cdot4\cdots(2n)}. \tag{41}$$

The final result is the formula

$$T = \frac{2\pi}{\omega}\left[1 + \sum_{n=1}^\infty \left(\frac{1\cdot3\cdots(2n-1)}{2\cdot4\cdots(2n)}\right)^2 k^{2n} \right]$$

$$= T_0\left[1 + \left(\frac{1}{2}\right)^2 k^2 + \left(\frac{1\cdot3}{2\cdot4}\right)^2 k^4 + \left(\frac{1\cdot3\cdot5}{2\cdot4\cdot6}\right)^2 k^6 + \cdots \right] \tag{42}$$

for the period T of the nonlinear pendulum released from rest with initial angle $\theta(0) = \alpha$, in terms of the linearized period $T_0 = 2\pi/\omega$ and $k = \sin(\alpha/2)$.

The infinite series within the brackets in (42) gives the factor T/T_0 by which the nonlinear period T is longer than the linearized period. The table in Fig. 6.4.10, obtained by summing this series numerically, shows how T/T_0 increases as α is increased. Thus T is 0.19% greater than T_0 if $\alpha = 10°$, whereas T is 18.03% greater than T_0 if $\alpha = 90°$. But even a 0.19% discrepancy is significant—the calculation

$$(0.0019) \times 3600 \frac{\text{seconds}}{\text{hour}} \times 24 \frac{\text{hours}}{\text{day}} \times 7 \frac{\text{days}}{\text{week}} \approx 1149 \quad [\text{seconds}]$$

α	T/T_0
10°	1.0019
20°	1.0077
30°	1.0174
40°	1.0313
50°	1.0498
60°	1.0732
70°	1.1021
80°	1.1375
90°	1.1803

FIGURE 6.4.10. Dependence of the period T of a nonlinear pendulum on its initial angle α

shows that the linearized model is quite inadequate for a pendulum clock; a discrepancy of 19 min 9 s after only one week is unacceptable.

Damped Pendulum Oscillations

Finally, we discuss briefly the *damped* nonlinear pendulum. The almost linear first-order system equivalent to Eq. (23) is

$$\frac{dx}{dt} = y$$

$$\frac{dy}{dt} = -\omega^2 \sin x - cy, \tag{43}$$

and again the critical points are of the form $(n\pi, 0)$ with n an integer. In Problem 9 we ask you to verify that:

- If n is odd, then $(n\pi, 0)$ is an unstable saddle point of (43), just as in the undamped case; but
- If n is even and $c^2 > 4\omega^2$, then $(n\pi, 0)$ is a stable node; whereas
- If n is even and $c^2 < 4\omega^2$, then $(n\pi, 0)$ is a stable spiral point.

Figure 6.4.11 shows the phase plane trajectories for the most interesting underdamped case, $c^2 < 4\omega^2$. Other than the physically unattainable separatrix trajectories that enter unstable saddle points, every trajectory eventually is "trapped" by one of the stable spiral points $(n\pi, 0)$ with n an even integer. What this means is that even if the pendulum starts with enough energy to go over the top, after a certain (finite) number of revolutions it has lost enough energy that thereafter it undergoes damped oscillations about its stable (lower) equilibrium position.

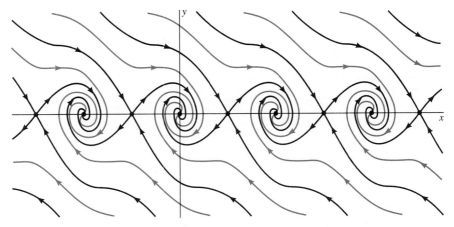

FIGURE 6.4.11. Phase plane trajectories for the underdamped nonlinear pendulum. There are unstable saddles at the odd integral multiples of π and spiral points at the even integral multiples of π.

6.4 Problems

In Problems 1 through 4, show that the given system is almost linear with $(0, 0)$ as a critical point, and classify this critical point as to type and stability.

1. $\dfrac{dx}{dt} = 1 - e^x + 2y$
$\dfrac{dy}{dt} = -x - 4\sin y$

2. $\dfrac{dx}{dt} = 2\sin x + \sin y$
$\dfrac{dy}{dt} = \sin x + 2\sin y$

3. $\dfrac{dx}{dt} = e^x + 2y - 1$
$\dfrac{dy}{dt} = 8x + e^y - 1$

4. $\dfrac{dx}{dt} = \sin x \cos y - 2y$
$\dfrac{dy}{dt} = 4x - 3\cos x \sin y$

Find and classify each of the critical points of the almost linear systems in Problems 5 through 8.

5. $\dfrac{dx}{dt} = -x + \sin y$
$\dfrac{dy}{dt} = 2x$

6. $\dfrac{dx}{dt} = y$
$\dfrac{dy}{dt} = \sin \pi x - y$

7. $\dfrac{dx}{dt} = 1 + e^{x-y}$
$\dfrac{dy}{dt} = 2\sin x$

8. $\dfrac{dx}{dt} = 3\sin x + y$
$\dfrac{dy}{dt} = \sin x + 2y$

9. For the damped pendulum system in (43), verify the classification of critical points of the form $(n\pi, 0)$ that is stated in the text.

In Problems 10 through 14, a second-order equation of the form

$$\frac{d^2x}{dt^2} + f(x, x') = 0,$$

corresponding to a certain mass-and-spring system, is given. Find and classify the critical points of the equivalent first-order system.

10. $x'' + 20x - 5x^3 = 0$: Verify that the critical points resemble those shown in Fig. 6.4.3.

11. $x'' + 2x' + 20x - 5x^3 = 0$: Verify that the critical points resemble those shown in Fig. 6.4.5.

12. $x'' - 8x + 2x^3 = 0$: Here the linear part of the force is repulsive rather than attractive (as for an ordinary spring). Verify that the critical points resemble those shown in Fig. 6.4.13. Thus there are two stable equilibrium points and three types of periodic oscillations.

13. $x'' + 4x - x^2 = 0$: Here the force function is nonsymmetric. Verify that the critical points resemble those shown in Fig. 6.4.14.

14. $x'' + 4x - 5x^3 + x^5 = 0$: The idea here is that terms through the fifth degree in an odd force function have been retained. Verify that the critical points resemble those shown in Fig. 6.4.15.

15. This problem outlines an investigation of the period T of oscillation of a mass on a nonlinear spring with equation of motion

$$\frac{d^2x}{dt^2} + \phi(x) = 0. \tag{44}$$

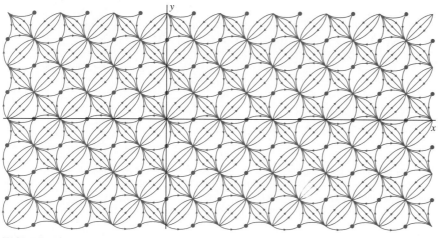

FIGURE 6.4.12. Trajectories of the system in Problem 2

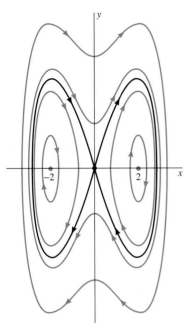

FIGURE 6.4.13. The phrase portrait for Problem 12

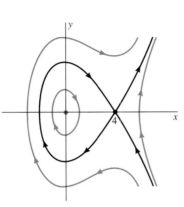

FIGURE 6.4.14. The phase portrait for Problem 13

FIGURE 6.4.15. The phase portrait for Problem 14

If $\phi(x) = kx$ with $k > 0$, then the spring actually is linear with period $T_0 = 2\pi/\sqrt{k}$. (a) Integrate once (as in Eq. (6)) to derive the energy equation

$$\frac{1}{2} y^2 + V(x) = E \tag{45}$$

where $y = dx/dt$ and

$$V(x) = \int_0^x \phi(u)\, du. \tag{46}$$

(b) If the mass is released from rest with initial conditions $x(0) = x_0$, $y(0) = 0$ and periodic oscillations ensue, conclude from Eq. (45) that $E = V(x_0)$ and that the time T required for one complete oscillation is

$$T = \frac{4}{\sqrt{2}} \int_0^{x_0} \frac{du}{\sqrt{V(x_0) - V(u)}}. \tag{47}$$

(c) If $\phi(x) = kx - \beta x^3$ as in the text, deduce from Eqs. (46) and (47) that

$$T = 4\sqrt{2} \int_0^{x_0} \frac{dx}{\sqrt{(x_0^2 - u^2)(2k - \beta x_0^2 - \beta u^2)}}. \tag{48}$$

(d) Substitute $u = x_0 \cos \phi$ in (48) to show that

$$T = \frac{2T_0}{\pi\sqrt{1 - \epsilon}} \int_0^{\pi/2} \frac{d\phi}{\sqrt{1 - \mu \sin^2 \phi}}, \tag{49}$$

where $T_0 = 2\pi/\sqrt{k}$ is the linear period,

$$\epsilon = \frac{\beta}{k} x_0^2, \quad \text{and} \quad \mu = -\frac{1}{2} \cdot \frac{\epsilon}{1 - \epsilon}. \tag{50}$$

(e) Finally, use the binomial series in (40) and the integral formula in (41) to evaluate the elliptic integral in (49) and thereby show that the period T of oscillation is given by

$$T = \frac{T_0}{\sqrt{1 - \epsilon}} \left(1 + \frac{1}{4} \mu + \frac{9}{64} \mu^2 + \frac{25}{256} \mu^3 + \cdots \right). \tag{51}$$

(f) If $\epsilon = \beta x_0^2/k$ is sufficiently small that ϵ^2 is negligible, deduce from Eqs. (50) and (51) that

$$T \approx T_0 \left(1 + \frac{3}{8} \epsilon \right) = T_0 \left(1 + \frac{3\beta}{8k} x_0^2 \right). \tag{52}$$

It follows that:

- If $\beta > 0$, so the spring is *soft*, then $T > T_0$, and increasing x_0 increases T, so the larger ovals in Fig. 6.4.3 correspond to smaller frequencies.

- If $\beta < 0$, so the spring is *hard*, then $T < T_0$, and increasing x_0 decreases T, so the larger ovals in Fig. 6.4.2 correspond to larger frequencies.

6.4 Computing Projects

Rayleigh's Equation

The British mathematical physicist Lord Rayleigh (John William Strutt, 1842–1919) introduced an equation of the form

$$mx'' + kx = ax' - b(x')^3 \qquad (1)$$

to model the oscillations of a clarinet reed. With $y = x'$ we get the autonomous system

$$x' = y$$

$$y' = \frac{-kx + ay - by^3}{m} \qquad (2)$$

whose phase plane portrait is shown in Fig. 6.4.16 (for the case $m = k = a = b = 1$). The outward and inward spiral trajectories converge to a "limit cycle" solution that corresponds to periodic oscillations of the reed. The period T (and hence the frequency) of these oscillations can be measured on a *tx*-solution curve plotted as in Fig. 6.4.17. This period of oscillation depends only on the parameters m, k, a, and b in Eq. (1), and is independent of the initial conditions (why?).

FIGURE 6.4.16. Phase plane portrait for the Rayleigh system in (2) with $m = k = a = b = 1$

FIGURE 6.4.17. *tx*-solution curve with initial conditions $x(0) = 0.01$, $x'(0) = 0$

Choose your own parameters m, k, a, and b (perhaps the least four nonzero digits in your student I.D. number), and use an available ODE plotting utility to plot trajectories and solution curves as in Figs. 6.4.16 and 6.4.17. Change *one* of your parameters to see how the amplitude and frequency of the resulting periodic oscillations are altered.

Van der Pol's Equation

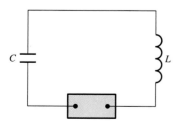

FIGURE 6.4.18. A simple circuit with an active element

Figure 6.4.18 shows a simple RLC circuit in which the usual (passive) resistance R been replaced by an active element (such as a vacuum tube or semiconductor) across which the voltage drop V is given by a known function $f(I)$ of the current. Of course, $V = f(I) = IR$ for a resistor. If we substitute $f(I)$ for IR in the familiar RLC-circuit

equation $LI'' + RI' + I/C = 0$ of Section 3.7, we get the second-order equation

$$LI'' + f'(I) + \frac{I}{C} = 0. \tag{3}$$

In a 1924 study of oscillator circuits in early commercial radios, Balthasar van der Pol (1889–1959) assumed the voltage drop to be given by a nonlinear function of the form $f(I) = bI^3 - aI$, which with Eq. (3) becomes

$$LI'' + (3bI^2 - a)I' + \frac{I}{C} = 0. \tag{4}$$

This equation is closely related to Rayleigh's equation, and has phase portraits resembling Fig. 6.4.16. Indeed, differentiation of the second equation in (2) and the substitution $x' = y$ yield the equation

$$my'' + (3by^2 - a)y' + ky = 0, \tag{5}$$

which has the same form as Eq. (4).

If we denote by τ the time variable in Eq. (4) and make the substitutions $x = I\sqrt{L}$, $t = \tau/\sqrt{LC}$, the result is

$$\frac{d^2x}{dt^2} + \left(\frac{3bx^2}{L} - a \right) \frac{dx}{dt} + x = 0.$$

With $\mu = a$ and $2b/aL = 1$ this gives the standard form

$$x'' + \mu(x^2 - 1)x' + x = 0 \tag{6}$$

of *van der Pol's equation*. Plot phase portraits with several different values of the parameter μ to see how it appears to affect the frequency of the oscillations corresponding to the limit cycle.

6.5 Chaos in Dynamical Systems

In preceding sections we have looked at population growth and mechanical systems from a deterministic point of view—with the expectation that the initial state of a physical system fully determines its future evolution. But many common systems exhibit behavior that sometimes appears chaotic, in the sense that future states may not seem reliably predictable from a knowledge of initial conditions. This section includes project material illustrating the phenomenon of *chaos,* which is a topic of much current interest in science and engineering.

Population Growth and Period-Doubling

In Section 2.1 we introduced the logistic differential equation

$$\frac{dP}{dt} = aP - bP^2 \qquad (a, b > 0) \tag{1}$$

that models a bounded (rather than exponentially growing) population. Indeed, if the population $P(t)$ satisfies Eq. (1), then as $t \to +\infty$, $P(t)$ approaches the [finite] limiting

population $M = a/b$. We discuss here a "discrete" version of the logistic equation that has long been familiar to scientists, but only recently has been discovered to predict quite exotic and unexpected patterns of behavior for certain populations.

In order to solve Eq. (1) numerically as in Section 2.4, we first choose a fixed step size $h > 0$ and consider the sequence of discrete times

$$t_0, \quad t_1, \quad t_2, \ldots, \quad t_n, \quad t_{n+1}, \quad \ldots, \tag{2}$$

where $t_{n+1} = t_n + h$ for each n. Beginning with the initial value $P_0 = P(t_0)$, we then calculate approximations

$$P_1, \quad P_2, \ldots, \quad P_n, \quad P_{n+1}, \quad \ldots \tag{3}$$

to the true values $P(t_1)$, $P(t_2)$, $P(t_3)$, \ldots of the actual population $P(t)$. For instance, Euler's method for the logistic equation in (1) consists of calculating the approximations in (3) iteratively by means of the formula

$$P_{n+1} = P_n + (aP_n - bP_n^2) \cdot h. \tag{4}$$

Now suppose that the population is one for which the step size h can be chosen so that the approximations calculated using Eq. (4) agree to acceptable accuracy with the actual population values. This might be the case, for instance, for an animal or insect population in which all reproduction takes place within short-duration breeding seasons that recur at regular intervals. If h is the interval between successive breeding seasons, then the population P_n during one breeding season may depend only upon the population P_{n-1} during the previous season, and P_n may completely determine the population P_{n+1} during the next breeding season.

So let us assume for the sake of discussion that the successive values $P_n = P(t_n)$ of the population are given by the equation

$$P_{n+1} = P_n + (aP_n - bP_n^2) \cdot h. \tag{4}$$

Thus we replace the original differential equation in (1) with a "discrete" *difference equation*

$$\Delta P_n = (aP_n - bP_n^2)\Delta t \tag{5}$$

that gives the population difference $\Delta P_n = P_{n+1} - P_n$ in terms of the time difference $h = \Delta t$ and the preceding population P_n.

Equation (4) can be rewritten as the *logistic difference equation*

$$P_{n+1} = rP_n - sP_n^2, \tag{6}$$

where

$$r = 1 + ah \qquad \text{and} \qquad s = bh. \tag{7}$$

The substitution

$$P_n = \frac{r}{s} x_n \tag{8}$$

in Eq. (6) simplifies it still further to

$$x_{n+1} = rx_n(1 - x_n). \tag{9}$$

At this point we focus our attention on the final iterative formula in Eq. (9). Beginning with given values of x_0 and r, this formula generates a sequence x_1, x_2,

x_3, \ldots of values corresponding to the successive times t_1, t_2, t_3, \ldots . We may think of x_n, the value at time t_n, as the *fraction* of the maximum population that the environment can support. Assuming that the limiting fractional population

$$x_\infty = \lim_{n \to \infty} x_n \qquad (10)$$

exists, we want to investigate the way in which x_∞ depends upon the *growth parameter* r in Eq. (9). That is, if we regard r as the *input* to the process and x_∞ as the *output*, we ask how the output depends upon the input.

TI-85	BASIC
:1.5->R	R = 1.5
:0.5->X	X = 0.5
:For(N,1,200)	FOR N=1 TO 200
:R*X*(1-X)->X	X = R*X*(1-X)
:Disp X	PRINT X
:End	NEXT

FIGURE 6.5.1. TI-85 and BASIC versions of a simple iteration program

The iteration in Eq. (9) is readily implemented in any available calculator or computer language. Figure 6.5.1 shows illustrative TI-85 and BASIC code for a simple program that calculates the first couple of hundred iterates. The corresponding *Maple* or MATLAB code would be virtually identical. *Mathematica* has a convenient iteration command **NestList[g, x0, k]** that displays the list $\{x_0, x_1, x_2, \ldots, x_k\}$ obtained by beginning with x_0 and applying the iteration $x_{n+1} = g(x_n)$ the preassigned number k times in succession. [In Eq. (9) we have $g(x) = rx(1 - x)$.] For instance, the commands

```
g[x_] := r x (1 - x)
r = 1.5;
NestList[g, 0.5, 200];
Partition[ Drop[ %, 195 ], 5] // TableForm
0.333333  0.333333  0.333333  0.333333  0.333333
```

carry out the iteration in (9) with $r = 1.5$ and $x_0 = 0.5$. The last command simply drops the first 195 iterates and displays the next five.

Because $r = 1 + ah$ in (7), only values of r greater than 1 are pertinent to our idealized model of discrete population growth. It turns out that, for a typical such value of the growth parameter r entered at the first line, the results do not depend materially on the starting value x_0. After a reasonable number of iterations — the number required depends on the value of r — the value of x_n generally appears to "stabilize" on a limiting value x_∞ as in (10). For example, Fig. 6.5.2 shows results of runs of our simple iteration program with the values $r = 1.5$, 2.0, and 2.5 of the growth rate parameter, yielding limiting (fractional) populations

$$x_\infty = 0.333333, \qquad 0.500000, \qquad \text{and} \qquad 0.600000,$$

respectively. Thus it appears that x_∞ exists and that its value grows moderately as r increases.

With	r = 1.5	r = 2.0	r = 2.5
x_0	0.5	0.5	0.5
x_1	0.3750	0.5000	0.6250
x_2	0.3516	0.5000	0.5859
.	.	.	.
.	.	.	.
.	.	.	.
x_{197}	0.3333	0.5000	0.6000
x_{198}	0.3333	0.5000	0.6000
x_{199}	0.3333	0.5000	0.6000
x_{200}	0.3333	0.5000	0.6000

FIGURE 6.5.2. Iterates with growth parameters $r = 1.5, 2.0, 2.5$

Exercise 1. Try several other values of the growth rate parameter in the range $1 < r < 3$. Do your results support the conjecture that the limiting population always exists and is an increasing function of r?

The results in Fig. 6.5.3 show that the conjecture stated in Exercise 1 is false! With growth rate parameters $r = 3$ and $r = 3.25$, the [fractional] population fails to stabilize on a single limiting population. Instead, it oscillates between two different populations in alternate months (thinking of a month as our unit of time). For instance, with $r = 3.25$ we see that

$$x_{1000} = x_{1002} = x_{1004} = \cdots = 0.4953,$$

```
g[x_] := r x (1 -x)
r = 3;
NestList[g, 0.5, 1006];
Partition[Drop[%, 1000],2] // TableForm
0.6592   0.6740
0.6592   0.6740
0.6592   0.6740

r = 3.25;
NestList[g, 0.5, 1006];
Partition[Drop[%, 1000],2] // TableForm
0.4953   0.8124
0.4953   0.8124
0.4953   0.8124

r = 3.5;
NestList[g, 0.5, 1012];
Partition[Drop[%, 1000],4] // TableForm
0.5009   0.8750   0.3828   0.8269
0.5009   0.8750   0.3828   0.8269
0.5009   0.8750   0.3828   0.8269
```

FIGURE 6.5.3. Cycles with periods 2 and 4

whereas

$$x_{1001} = x_{1003} = x_{1005} = \cdots = 0.8124.$$

Thus we have not a single limiting population, but rather a "limiting cycle" consisting of two distinct populations. Furthermore, when the growth rate is increased to $r = 3.5$, the period of the cycle *doubles,* and now we have a limiting cycle with a *period* of 4—the population cycles repeatedly through the four distinct values 0.5009, 0.8750, 0.3828, and 0.8269.

Exercise 2. Try values of the growth rate parameter in the range $2.9 < r < 3.0$ to determine as closely as possible just where the single limiting population splits (as r increases) into a cycle of period 2. This should happen just a bit short of $r = 3$.

Figure 6.5.4 shows cycles with periods 8 and 16 obtained with parameter values $r = 3.55$ and $r = 3.565$, respectively. Obviously events are now changing quite rapidly. This is the phenomenon of *period doubling* for which the innocuous (in appearance) iteration $x_{n+1} = rx_n(1 - x_n)$ has become famous in recent years.

```
r = 3.55;
NestList[g, 0.5, 1025];
Partition[Drop[%, 1000],8] // TableForm
```

0.5060	0.8874	0.3548	0.8127	0.5405	0.8817	0.3703	0.8278
0.5060	0.8874	0.3548	0.8127	0.5405	0.8817	0.3703	0.8278
0.5060	0.8874	0.3548	0.8127	0.5405	0.8817	0.3703	0.8278

```
r = 3.565;
NestList[g, 0.5, 1035];
Partition[Drop[%, 1000],16] // TableForm
```

0.4860	0.8905	0.3475	0.8083	0.5523	0.8815	0.3724	0.8332
0.4954	0.8912	0.3457	0.8064	0.5565	0.8799	0.3768	0.8372
0.4860	0.8905	0.3475	0.8083	0.5523	0.8815	0.3724	0.8332
0.4954	0.8912	0.3457	0.8064	0.5565	0.8799	0.3768	0.8372

FIGURE 6.5.4. Cycles with periods 8 and 16

Exercise 3. See if you can find a cycle of period 32 somewhere between $r = 3.565$ and $r = 3.57$.

As the growth rate parameter is increased beyond $r = 3.56$, period doubling occurs so rapidly that utter chaos appears to break out somewhere near $r = 3.57$. The iterations shown in Fig. 6.5.5 indicate that, with $r = 3.57$ and with $r = 3.60$, the earlier periodicity seems to have disappeared. No periodic cycles are evident, and the population appears to be changing (from one month to the next) in some essentially random fashion. Indeed, the deterministic population growth that is observed with smaller growth parameters seems now to have degenerated into a non-deterministic process of seemingly random change.

```
r = 3.57;
NestList[g, 0.5, 1035];
Partition[Drop[%, 1000],8] // TableForm
```

0.4751	0.8903	0.3487	0.8108	0.5477	0.8844	0.3650	0.8275
0.5096	0.8922	0.3434	0.8050	0.5604	0.8795	0.3784	0.8397
0.4805	0.8911	0.3463	0.8082	0.5534	0.8823	0.3707	0.8328
0.4970	0.8925	0.3426	0.8041	0.5624	0.8786	0.3808	0.8418

```
r = 3.6;
NestList[g, 0.5, 1035];
Partition[Drop[%, 1000],8] // TableForm
```

0.4345	0.8846	0.3676	0.8369	0.4914	0.8997	0.3248	0.7895
0.5984	0.8652	0.4199	0.8769	0.3885	0.8553	0.4456	0.8893
0.3543	0.8236	0.5231	0.8981	0.3295	0.7954	0.5859	0.8734
0.3980	0.8626	0.4268	0.8807	0.3782	0.8466	0.4675	0.8962

FIGURE 6.5.5. Chaos!

The solutions and computer lab manuals accompanying this text include BASIC, *Mathematica,* and other versions of a program called PICHFORK. This program produces a visual presentation of the way in which the behavior of our iteration depends upon the value of the growth parameter r. For each value of r in the input interval $a \leqq r \leqq b$ (the horizontal axis in the resulting diagram), 1000 iterations are first carried out to achieve "stability." Then the next 250 values of x generated by the iteration are plotted on the vertical axis—that is, the screen pixel at (r, x) is "turned on." The descriptively named "pitchfork diagram" that results then shows at a glance whether a given value of r corresponds to a cycle (with finite period) or to chaos. If the resolution in the picture suffices to make it clear that only finitely many values of x are plotted above a given value of r, then we see that the iteration is "eventually periodic" for that specific value of the growth rate parameter.

Figure 6.5.6 shows the pitchfork diagram for the range $2.8 \leqq r \leqq 4.0$. Scanning from left to right, we see a single limiting population until $r \approx 3$, then a cycle with period 2 until $r \approx 3.45$, then a cycle of period 4, then one of period 8, and so forth, rapidly approaching the darkness of chaos. But note the vertical bands of "white space" that appear in the diagram between $r = 3.6$ and $r = 3.7$, between $r = 3.7$ and $r = 3.8$, and again between $r = 3.8$ and $r = 3.9$. These represent regions where [periodic] order returns from the preceding chaos.

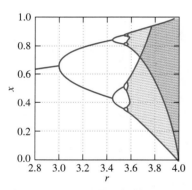

FIGURE 6.5.6. The pitchfork diagram with $2.8 \leqq r \leqq 4$, $0 \leqq x \leqq 1$

For instance, Fig. 6.5.7 shows the interval $3.8 \leqq r \leqq 3.9$, where we observe a cycle of period 3 that emerges suddenly from the chaos near $r = 3.83$, and then splits successively into cycles of orders 6, 12, 24, . . . (Fig. 6.5.8). This period-doubling beginning with a cycle of period 3 is especially significant—a fundamental article by James Yorke and T.-Y. Li in the 1975 *American Mathematical Monthly* was entitled "Period Three Implies Chaos." According to this article, the existence of a cycle of period 3 (for an appropriate iteration) implies the existence of cycles of every other [finite] period, as well as chaotic "cycles" with no period at all.

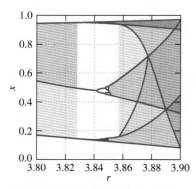

FIGURE 6.5.7. The pitchfork diagram with $3.8 \leqq r \leqq 3.9$, $0 \leqq x \leqq 1$

Project 1. Use Program PICHFORK to search for other interesting cycles, and verify their apparent periods by appropriate iterative computations. For instance, you should find a cycle with period 10 between $r = 3.60$ and $r = 3.61$, and one with pe-

```
r = 3.84;
NestList[g, 0.5, 1010];
Partition[Drop[%, 1000],3] // TableForm
```

0.9594	0.1494	0.4880
0.9594	0.1494	0.4880
0.9594	0.1494	0.4880

```
r = 3.845;
NestList[g, 0.5, 1020];
Partition[Drop[%, 1000],6] // TableForm
```

0.9582	0.1540	0.5009	0.9612	0.1432	0.4718
0.9582	0.1540	0.5009	0.9612	0.1432	0.4718
0.9582	0.1540	0.5009	0.9612	0.1432	0.4718

```
r = 3.848;
NestList[g, 0.5, 1040];
Partition[Drop[%, 1000],12] // TableForm
```

0.9573	0.1571	0.5096	0.9616	0.1419	0.4686
0.9582	0.1541	0.5015	0.9620	0.1407	0.4652
0.9573	0.1571	0.5096	0.9616	0.1419	0.4686
0.9582	0.1541	0.5015	0.9620	0.1407	0.4652
0.9573	0.1571	0.5096	0.9616	0.1419	0.4686
0.9582	0.1541	0.5015	0.9620	0.1407	0.4652

FIGURE 6.5.8. Cycles with periods 3, 6, and 12

riod 14 between $r = 3.59$ and $r = 3.60$. Can you find cycles with period 5 and 7? If so, look for subsequent period-doubling. A run of PICHFORK requires several hundred thousand iterations, so it will help if you have a fast computer (or one you can leave running overnight).

As we scan the pitchfork diagram (Fig. 6.5.6) from left to right, we spot the successive values r_1, r_2, r_3, \ldots of the growth rate parameter at which a *bifurcation* or qualitative change in the iteration $x_{n+1} = rx_n(1 - x_n)$ occurs as the value of r is increased further. These are the discrete values of r at which any sufficiently small increase in the growth parameter doubles the period of the iteration. In the 1970s the Los Alamos physicist Mitchell Feigenbaum discovered that a certain order underlies this period-doubling toward chaos:

$$\lim_{k \to \infty} \frac{r_k - r_{k-1}}{r_{k+1} - r_k} = 4.6692016091 \ldots . \tag{11}$$

The fraction on the left in Eq. (11) is the ratio of the lengths of successive constant-period "windows" in the pitchfork diagram. It is the fact that this ratio approaches a limit as $k \to \infty$, rather than the specific value of this limit, that demonstrates a sort of "order" underlying the period-doubling observed with the particular iteration $x_{n+1} = rx_n(1 - x_n)$. On the other hand, it is now known that precisely the same *Feigenbaum*

constant 4.6692016901 . . . plays exactly the same role for a wide variety of period-doubling phenomena arising in many different areas of science.

Project 2. Feigenbaum used an HP-65 pocket calculator (rather than a powerful computer) to carry out the computations leading to the discovery of his famous constant. Perhaps you would like to use iterative computations and/or PICHFORK to isolate the first few bifurcation values r_1, r_2, r_3, \ldots with sufficient accuracy to verify that the limit in (11) is approximately 4.67. You can consult pages 124–126 of T. Gray and J. Glynn, *Exploring Mathematics with Mathematica* (Addison-Wesley, 1991) for a fancier approach.

Period-Doubling in Mechanical Systems

In Section 6.4 we introduced the second-order differential equation

$$mx'' + cx' + kx + \beta x^3 = 0 \tag{12}$$

to model the free velocity-damped vibrations of a mass m on a nonlinear spring. Recall that the term kx in Eq. (12) represents the force exerted on the mass by a *linear* spring, whereas the term βx^3 represents the nonlinearity of an actual spring.

We want now to discuss the *forced vibrations* that result when an external force $F(t) = F_0 \cos \omega t$ acts on the mass. With such a force adjoined to the system in Eq. (12), we obtain the **forced Duffing equation**

$$\blacktriangleright \qquad mx'' + cx' + kx + \beta x^3 = F_0 \cos \omega t \tag{13}$$

for the displacement $x(t)$ of the mass from its equilibrium position. For most values of the parameters it is impossible to solve Eq. (13) explicitly for $x(t)$. Nevertheless, its solutions can be portrayed qualitatively by means of [numerically approximated] phase plane trajectories like those we used in Section 6.4 to describe free vibrations of nonlinear mechanical systems.

The Hooke's constant k is positive for a typical spring that resists displacement from equilibrium. But there do exist simple physical systems that emulate a spring having a negative Hooke's constant. For example, Fig. 6.5.9 shows a mass m atop a vertical metal filament. We assume that the thin metal filament can oscillate only in a vertical plane, and behaves like a flexible column that "buckles" or bends when the mass is displaced to either side of the vertical position. Then there is one stable equilibrium point to the left ($x < 0$) and another to the right ($x > 0$), but the vertical equilibrium position ($x = 0$) is unstable. When the mass is displaced slightly from this unstable equilibrium position, the internal force exerted on it is *repulsive* rather than attractive; this corresponds to a *negative* value of k in Eq. (13). If a periodic force is exerted on the mass by an oscillating electromagnetic field, and air resistance damps its oscillations, then Eq. (13) with $k < 0$ but with $c, \beta > 0$ is a reasonable mathematical model for its horizontal displacement function $x(t)$.

In the absence of both damping and the external force, the phase plane trajectories of the free oscillations of the mass would resemble those shown in Fig. 6.4.13 (with Problem 12 in Section 6.4). The mass behaves as though it is repelled by the unstable critical point at $x = 0$ but is attracted by each of the two stable critical points symmetrically located on either side of the origin.

We saw in Section 3.6 that in the *linear* case a periodic external force $F(t) = F_0 \cos \omega t$ causes a steady periodic response $x(t) = C \cos(\omega t - \alpha)$ with the *same* fre-

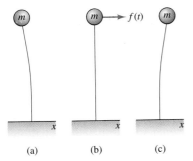

FIGURE 6.5.9. Equilibrium positions of a mass on a filament: (a) stable equilibrium with $x < 0$; (b) unstable equilibrium at $x = 0$; (c) stable equilibrium with $x > 0$.

quency ω. The amplitude C of the steady periodic response is proportional to the amplitude F_0 of the external force. For instance, if the periodic external force is doubled in amplitude, then the only change in the response is that its amplitude is doubled also.

To illustrate the quite different behavior of a nonlinear system, we take $k = -1$ and $m = c = \beta = \omega = 1$ in Eq. (13) so the differential equation is

$$x'' + x' - x + x^3 = F_0 \cos t. \tag{14}$$

As an exercise you may verify that the two stable critical points are $(-1, 0)$ and $(1, 0)$. We want to examine the dependence of the (presumably steady periodic) response $x(t)$ upon the amplitude F_0 of the periodic external force of period $2\pi/\omega = 2\pi$.

Figures 6.5.10 through 6.5.13 show the solutions of Eq. (14) obtained with the successive values $F_0 = 0.60$, 0.70, 0.75, and 0.80 of the amplitude of the external force. In each case the equation was solved numerically with initial conditions

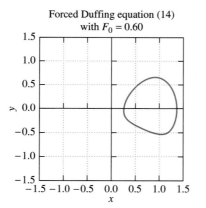

FIGURE 6.5.10(a). Period 2π response with $F_0 = 0.60$: (a) phase plane trajectory

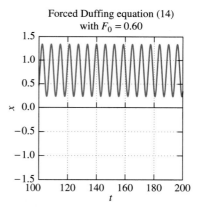

FIGURE 6.5.10(b). Period 2π response with $F_0 = 0.60$: (b) solution $x(t)$

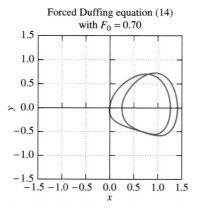

FIGURE 6.5.11(a). Period 4π response with $F_0 = 0.70$: (a) phase plane trajectory

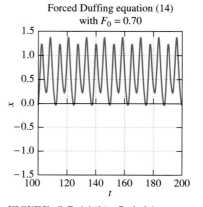

FIGURE 6.5.11(b). Period 4π response with $F_0 = 0.70$: (b) solution $x(t)$

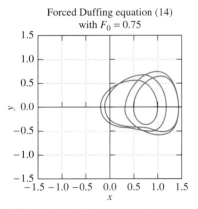

FIGURE 6.5.12(a). Period 8π response with $F_0 = 0.75$: (a) phase plane trajectory

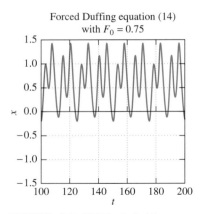

FIGURE 6.5.12(b). Period 8π response with $F_0 = 0.75$: (b) solution $x(t)$

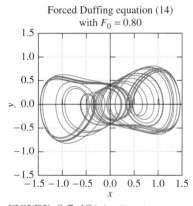

FIGURE 6.5.13(a). Chaotic response with $F_0 = 0.80$: (a) phase plane trajectory

FIGURE 6.5.13(b). Chaotic response with $F_0 = 0.80$: (b) solution $x(t)$

$x(0) = 1$, $x'(0) = 0$ and the resulting solution plotted for the range $100 \leqq t \leqq 200$ (to show the steady periodic response remaining after the initial transient response has died out). Part (a) of each figure shows the phase plane trajectory $x = x(t)$, $y = x'(t)$, and part (b) shows the actual solution curve $x = x(t)$ in the tx-plane. Part (a) exhibits the qualitative character of the solution more vividly, but part (b) is required to determine the period and frequency of the solution.

Figure 6.5.10 shows a simple oscillation of period 2π of the mass about the right-hand critical point. In the ensuing sequence of figures we see successive *period-doubling* and finally *chaos* as the amplitude of the external force is increased in the range from $F_0 = 0.6$ to $F_0 = 0.8$. This *period-doubling toward chaos* is a common characteristic of the behavior of a *nonlinear* mechanical system as an appropriate physical parameter (such as m, c, k, β, F_0, or ω in Eq. (13)) is increased or decreased. No such phenomenon occurs in linear systems.

Project 3. Use an ODE plotting utility to see whether you can reproduce Figs. 6.5.10–6.5.13. Then investigate the parameter range $1.00 \leqq F_0 \leqq 1.10$ for the force

constant in Eq. (14). With $F_0 = 1.00$ you should see a period 6π phase plane trajectory that encircles *both* stable critical points (as well as the unstable one). The period doubles around $F_0 = 1.07$ and chaos sets in around $F_0 = 1.10$. See whether you can spot a second period-doubling somewhere between $F_0 = 1.07$ and $F_0 = 1.10$. Produce both phase plane trajectories and *tx*-solution curves on which you can measure the periods.

The Lorenz Strange Attractor

The substitution of $x_1 = x$, $x_2 = x'$ in the forced Duffing equation (Eq. (13)) yields a two-dimensional nonlinear system of first-order differential equations, and period-doubling phenomena are characteristic of such systems. But in higher dimensions even more exotic phenomena occur, and are currently the subject of much active investigation. All this work stems ultimately from the original investigation of an extraordinary three-dimensional nonlinear system by the mathematical meteorologist E. N. Lorenz, who later described its discovery as follows.

> By the middle 1950s "numerical weather prediction;" i.e., forecasting by numerically integrating such approximations to the atmospheric equations as could feasibly be handled, was very much in vogue, despite the rather mediocre results which it was then yielding. A smaller but determined group favored statistical prediction . . . I was skeptical, and decided to test the idea by applying the statistical method to a set of artificial data, generated by solving a system of equations numerically . . . The first task was to find a suitable system of equations to solve . . . The system would have to be simple enough . . . and the general solution would have to be aperiodic, since the statistical prediction of a periodic series would be a trivial matter, once the periodicity had been detected . . . [In the course of talks with Dr. Barry Saltzman] he showed me some work on thermal convections, in which he used a system of seven ordinary differential equations. Most of his solutions soon acquired periodic behavior, but one solution refused to settle down. Moreover, in this solution four of the variables appeared to approach zero. Presumably the equations governing the remaining three variables, with the terms containing the four variables eliminated, would also possess aperiodic solutions. Upon my return I put the three equations on our computer, and confirmed the aperiodicity which Saltzman had noted. We were finally in business. [Quoted in E. Hairer, S. P. Norsett, and G. Wanner, *Solving Ordinary Differential Equations I* (New York: Springer–Verlag, 1987).]

The famous *Lorenz system* of differential equations is given by

$$\frac{dx}{dt} = -sx + sy$$

$$\frac{dy}{dt} = -xz + rx - y \qquad (15)$$

$$\frac{dz}{dt} = xy - bz.$$

FIGURE 6.5.14. The *xz*-projection of the Lorenz trajectory with $-20 \le x \le 20, 0 \le z \le 50$

A solution curve in *xyz*-space is best visualized by looking at its projection into some *plane*, typically one of the three coordinate planes. Fig. 6.5.14 shows the projection into the *xz*-plane of the solution obtained by numerical integration with the parameter values $b = \frac{8}{3}, s = 10, r = 28$ and the initial values $x(0) = -8, y(0) = 8, z(0) = 27$.

As the projection in Fig. 6.5.14 is traced in "real time," the moving solution point $P(x(t), y(t), x(t))$ appears to undergo a random number of oscillations on the right followed by a random number of oscillations on the left, then a random number on the right followed by a random number on the left, and so on. Given the meteorological origin of the Lorenz system, one naturally thinks of a random number of clear days followed by a random number of rainy days, then a random number of clear days followed by a random number of rainy days, and so on.

A close examination of such projections of the Lorenz trajectory shows that it is *not* simply oscillating back and forth around a pair of critical points (as Fig. 6.5.14 may initially suggest). Instead, as $t \to +\infty$, the solution point $P(t)$ on the trajectory wanders back in forth in space approaching closer and closer to a certain complicated set of points whose detailed structure is not yet fully understood. This elusive set that appears somehow to "attract" the solution point is the famous *Lorenz strange attractor.*

Project 4. First use an ODE plotting utility to reproduce the *xz*-projection of the Lorenz trajectory shown in Fig. 6.5.14. Use the parameter values and initial conditions listed immediately after Eq. (15) and numerically integrate the Lorenz system on the interval $0 \le t \le 50$. Plot also the *xy*- and *yz*-projections of this same solution. Next, experiment with different parameter values and initial conditions. For instance, see if you can find a periodic solution with $r = 70$ (and $b = \frac{8}{3}, s = 10$ as before) and initial values $x_0 = -4$ and $z_0 = 64$. To get a trajectory that almost repeats itself, you will need to try different values of y_0 in the range $0 < y_0 < 10$ and look at *xz*-projections as in Fig. 6.5.14.

Project 5. Another much-studied nonlinear three-dimensional system is the Rossler system

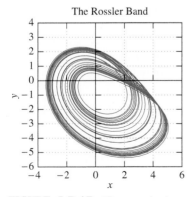

FIGURE 6.5.15. The *xy*-projection of the Rossler band

$$\frac{dx}{dt} = -y - z$$

$$\frac{dy}{dt} = x + ay \tag{16}$$

$$\frac{dz}{dt} = b + z(x - c).$$

Figure 6.5.15 shows an *xy*-projection of the *Rossler band*, a chaotic attractor obtained with the values $a = 0.398, b = 2$, and $c = 4$ of the parameters in (16). In the *xy*-plane the Rossler band looks "folded," but in space it appears twisted like a Möbius strip. Investigate the period-doubling toward chaos that occurs with the Rossler system as the parameter a is increased, beginning with $a = 0.3, a = 0.35$, and $a = 0.375$ (take $b = 2$ and $c = 4$ in all cases).

In this section we have given just a taste of the ideas that are the focus of contemporary applications of nonlinear systems. To see how these ideas come full circle, consult the discussion of the Lorenz system in pages 117–123 of the book by Hairer *et al.* referenced above. There you will see a certain aspect of the Lorenz trajectory described visually by means of a picture that looks very much like the pitchfork diagram shown in Fig. 6.5.6, together with the very same Feigenbaum constant 4.6692 . . . !

For an engaging account of the historical background to this final section of Chapter 6, see James Gleick, *Chaos: Making a New Science* (New York: Viking Press, 1987). For more detailed discussions of the forced Duffing, Lorenz, and Rossler equations, see J. M. T. Thompson and H. B. Stewart, *Nonlinear Dynamics and Chaos* (New York: John Wiley, 1986).

7 Laplace Transform Methods

7.1 Laplace Transforms and Inverse Transforms

In Chapter 3 we saw that linear differential equations with constant coefficients have numerous applications and can be solved systematically. There are common situations, however, in which the alternative method of this chapter is preferable. For example, recall the differential equations

$$mx'' + cx' + kx = F(t) \qquad \text{and} \qquad LI'' + RI' + \frac{1}{C}I = E'(t)$$

corresponding to a mass-spring-dashpot system and a series RLC circuit, respectively. It often happens in practice that the forcing term, $F(t)$ or $E'(t)$, has discontinuities — for example, when the voltage supplied to an electrical circuit is turned off and on periodically. In this case the methods of Chapter 3 can be quite awkward, and the Laplace transform method is more convenient.

The differentiation operator D can be viewed as a transformation which when applied to the function $f(t)$ yields the new function $D\{f(t)\} = f'(t)$. The Laplace transformation \mathcal{L} involves the operation of integration and yields the new function $\mathcal{L}\{f(t)\} = F(s)$ of a new independent variable s. The situation is diagrammed in Fig.

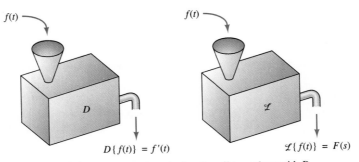

FIGURE 7.1.1. Transformation of a function: \mathcal{L} in analogy with D

7.1.1. After learning in this section how to compute the Laplace transform $F(s)$ of a function $f(t)$, we will see in Section 7.2 that the Laplace transform converts a *differential* equation in the unknown function $f(t)$ into an *algebraic* equation in $F(s)$. Because algebraic equations are generally easier to solve than differential equations, this is one method that simplifies the problem of finding the solution $f(t)$.

DEFINITION: The Laplace Transform

Given a function $f(t)$ defined for all $t \geqq 0$, the **Laplace transform** of f is the function F defined as follows:

$$F(s) = \mathcal{L}\{f(t)\} = \int_0^\infty e^{-st} f(t)\, dt \tag{1}$$

for all values of s for which the improper integral converges.

Recall that an **improper integral** over an infinite interval is defined as a limit of integrals over bounded intervals; that is,

$$\int_a^\infty g(t)\, dt = \lim_{b \to \infty} \int_a^b g(t)\, dt. \tag{2}$$

If the limit in (2) exists, then we say that the improper integral **converges;** otherwise, it **diverges** or fails to exist. Note that the integrand of the improper integral in (1) contains the parameter s in addition to the variable of integration t. Therefore, when the integral in (1) converges, it converges not merely to a number, but to a *function F of s*. As in the following examples, it is typical for the improper integral in the definition of $\mathcal{L}\{f(t)\}$ to converge for some values of s and diverge for others.

EXAMPLE 1 With $f(t) \equiv 1$ for $t \geqq 0$, the definition of the Laplace transform in (1) gives

$$\mathcal{L}\{1\} = \int_0^\infty e^{-st}\, dt = \left[-\frac{1}{s} e^{-st} \right]_0^\infty = \lim_{b \to \infty} \left[-\frac{1}{s} e^{-bs} + \frac{1}{s} \right],$$

and therefore

$$\mathcal{L}\{1\} = \frac{1}{s} \quad \text{for } s > 0. \tag{3}$$

As in (3), it's good practice to specify the domain of the Laplace transform—in problems as well as in examples. Also, in this computation we have used the common abbreviation

$$\left[g(t)\right]_a^\infty = \lim_{b \to \infty} \left[g(t)\right]_a^b.$$ (4)

∎

Remark: The limit we computed in Example 1 would not exist if $s < 0$, for then $(1/s)e^{-bs}$ would become unbounded as $b \to +\infty$. Hence $\mathcal{L}\{1\}$ is defined only for $s > 0$. This is typical of Laplace transforms; the domain of a transform is normally of the form $s > a$ for some number a.

EXAMPLE 2 With $f(t) = e^{at}$ for $t \geq 0$, we obtain

$$\mathcal{L}\{e^{at}\} = \int_0^\infty e^{-st} e^{at}\, dt = \int_0^\infty e^{-(s-a)t}\, dt = \left[-\frac{e^{-(s-a)t}}{s-a}\right]_{t=0}^\infty.$$

If $s - a > 0$, then $e^{-(s-a)t} \to 0$ as $t \to +\infty$, so it follows that

▶
$$\mathcal{L}\{e^{at}\} = \frac{1}{s-a} \quad \text{for } s > a.$$ (5)

Note here that the improper integral giving $\mathcal{L}\{e^{at}\}$ diverges if $s \leq a$. It is worth noting also that the formula in (5) holds if a is a complex number. For then, with $a = \alpha + i\beta$,

$$e^{-(s-a)t} = e^{i\beta t} e^{-(s-\alpha)t} \to 0$$

as $t \to +\infty$, provided that $s > \alpha = \mathrm{Re}\,(a)$; recall that $e^{i\beta t} = \cos \beta t + i \sin \beta t$. ∎

The Laplace transform $\mathcal{L}\{t^a\}$ of a power function is most conveniently expressed in terms of the **gamma function** $\Gamma(x)$, which is defined for $x > 0$ by the formula

▶
$$\Gamma(x) = \int_0^\infty e^{-t} t^{x-1}\, dt.$$ (6)

For an elementary discussion of $\Gamma(x)$, see the subsection on the gamma function in Section 8.5, where it is shown that

$$\Gamma(1) = 1$$ (7)

and that

$$\Gamma(x + 1) = x\Gamma(x)$$ (8)

for $x > 0$. It then follows that if n is a positive integer, then

$$\Gamma(n + 1) = n\Gamma(n)$$

$$= n \cdot (n - 1)\Gamma(n - 1)$$

$$= n \cdot (n - 1) \cdot (n - 2)\Gamma(n - 2)$$

$$\vdots$$

$$= n(n - 1)(n - 2) \cdots 2\Gamma(2)$$

$$= n(n - 1)(n - 2) \cdots 2 \cdot 1 \cdot \Gamma(1);$$

thus

$$\Gamma(n + 1) = n! \tag{9}$$

if n is a positive integer. Therefore the function $\Gamma(x + 1)$, which is defined and continuous for all $x > -1$, agrees with the factorial function for $x = n$, a positive integer.

EXAMPLE 3 Suppose that $f(t) = t^a$ for $t \geq 0$, where a is real and $a > -1$. Then

$$\mathcal{L}\{t^a\} = \int_0^\infty e^{-st}t^a\, dt.$$

If we substitute $u = st$, $t = u/s$, and $dt = du/s$ in this integral, we get

$$\mathcal{L}\{t^a\} = \frac{1}{s^{a+1}} \int_0^\infty e^{-u}u^a\, du = \frac{\Gamma(a + 1)}{s^{a+1}} \tag{10}$$

for all $s > 0$ (so that $u = st > 0$). Because $\Gamma(n + 1) = n!$ if n is a nonnegative integer, we see that

$$\mathcal{L}\{t^n\} = \frac{n!}{s^{n+1}} \quad \text{for } s > 0. \tag{11}$$

For instance,

$$\mathcal{L}\{t\} = \frac{1}{s^2}, \qquad \mathcal{L}\{t^2\} = \frac{2}{s^3}, \qquad \text{and} \qquad \mathcal{L}\{t^3\} = \frac{6}{s^4}.$$

As in Problems 1 and 2, these formulas can be derived immediately from the definition, without use of the gamma function.

Linearity of Transforms

It is not necessary for us to proceed much further in the computation of Laplace transforms directly from the definition. Once we know the Laplace transforms of several functions, we can combine them to obtain transforms of other functions. The reason is that the Laplace transformation is a *linear* operation.

THEOREM 1: Linearity of the Laplace Transformation

If a and b are constants, then

$$\mathcal{L}\{af(t) + bg(t)\} = a\mathcal{L}\{f(t)\} + b\mathcal{L}\{g(t)\} \tag{12}$$

for all s such that the Laplace transforms of the functions f and g both exist. ∎

The proof of Theorem 1 follows immediately from the linearity of the operations of taking limits and of integration:

$$\mathcal{L}\{af(t) + bg(t)\} = \int_0^\infty e^{-st}[af(t) + bg(t)]\, dt$$

$$= \lim_{c \to \infty} \int_0^c e^{-st}[af(t) + bg(t)]\, dt$$

$$= a\left(\lim_{c \to \infty} \int_0^c e^{-st}f(t)\, dt\right) + b\left(\lim_{c \to \infty} \int_0^c e^{-st}g(t)\, dt\right)$$

$$= a\mathcal{L}\{f(t)\} + b\mathcal{L}\{g(t)\}.$$

EXAMPLE 4 The computation of $\mathcal{L}\{t^{n/2}\}$ is based on the known special value

$$\Gamma\left(\frac{1}{2}\right) = \sqrt{\pi} \tag{13}$$

of the gamma function. For instance, it follows that

$$\Gamma\left(\frac{5}{2}\right) = \frac{3}{2}\Gamma\left(\frac{3}{2}\right) = \frac{3}{2} \cdot \frac{1}{2}\Gamma\left(\frac{1}{2}\right) = \frac{3}{4}\sqrt{\pi},$$

using the formula $\Gamma(x + 1) = x\Gamma(x)$ in (9), first with $x = \frac{3}{2}$ and then with $x = \frac{1}{2}$. Now the formulas in (10) through (12) yield

$$\mathcal{L}\{3t^2 + 4t^{3/2}\} = 3\frac{2!}{s^3} + \frac{4\Gamma(\frac{5}{2})}{s^{5/2}} = \frac{6}{s^3} + 3\sqrt{\frac{\pi}{s^5}}.$$

EXAMPLE 5 Recall that $\cosh kt = (e^{kt} + e^{-kt})/2$. If $k > 0$, then Theorem 1 and Example 2 together give

$$\mathcal{L}\{\cosh kt\} = \frac{1}{2}\mathcal{L}\{e^{kt}\} + \frac{1}{2}\mathcal{L}\{e^{-kt}\} = \frac{1}{2}\left(\frac{1}{s-k} + \frac{1}{s+k}\right);$$

that is,

$$\mathcal{L}\{\cosh kt\} = \frac{s}{s^2 - k^2} \quad \text{for } s > k > 0. \tag{14}$$

Similarly,

$$\mathcal{L}\{\sinh kt\} = \frac{k}{s^2 - k^2} \quad \text{for } s > k > 0. \tag{15}$$

Because $\cos kt = (e^{ikt} + e^{-ikt})/2$, the formula in (5) (with $a = ik$) yields

$$\mathcal{L}\{\cos kt\} = \frac{1}{2}\left(\frac{1}{s-ik} + \frac{1}{s+ik}\right) = \frac{1}{2} \cdot \frac{2s}{s^2 - (ik)^2},$$

and thus

$$\mathcal{L}\{\cos kt\} = \frac{s}{s^2 + k^2} \quad \text{for } s > 0. \tag{16}$$

(The domain follows from $s > \text{Re}(ik) = 0$.) Similarly,

$$\mathcal{L}\{\sin kt\} = \frac{k}{s^2 + k^2} \quad \text{for } s > 0. \tag{17}$$

EXAMPLE 6 Applying linearity, the formula in (16), and a familiar trigonometric identity, we get

$$\mathcal{L}\{3e^{2t} + 2\sin^2 3t\} = \mathcal{L}\{3e^{2t} + 1 - \cos 6t\}$$

$$= \frac{3}{s-2} + \frac{1}{s} - \frac{s}{s^2 + 36}$$

$$= \frac{3s^3 + 144s - 72}{s(s-2)(s^2 + 36)} \quad \text{for } s > 0. \quad \blacksquare$$

Inverse Transforms

According to Theorem 3 of this section, no two different functions that are both continuous for all $t \geq 0$ can have the same Laplace transform. Thus if $F(s)$ is the transform of some continuous function $f(t)$, then $f(t)$ is uniquely determined. This observation allows us to make the following definition: If $F(s) = \mathcal{L}\{f(t)\}$, then we call $f(t)$ the **inverse Laplace transform** of $F(s)$ and write

▶
$$f(t) = \mathcal{L}^{-1}\{F(s)\}. \tag{18}$$

EXAMPLE 7
$$\mathcal{L}^{-1}\left\{\frac{1}{s^3}\right\} = \frac{1}{2}t^2, \qquad \mathcal{L}^{-1}\left\{\frac{1}{s+2}\right\} = e^{-2t}, \qquad \mathcal{L}^{-1}\left\{\frac{2}{s^2+9}\right\} = \frac{2}{3}\sin 3t,$$

and so on. ∎

Notation: Functions and Their Transforms. Throughout this chapter we denote functions of t by lowercase letters. The transform of a function will always be denoted by that same letter capitalized. Thus $F(s)$ is the Laplace transform of $f(t)$, and $x(t)$ is the inverse Laplace transform of $X(s)$.

A table of Laplace transforms serves a purpose similar to that of a table of integrals. The table in Fig. 7.1.2 lists the transforms derived in this section; many addi-

$f(t)$	$F(s)$			
1	$\dfrac{1}{s}$	$(s > 0)$		
t	$\dfrac{1}{s^2}$	$(s > 0)$		
$t^n \quad (n \geq 0)$	$\dfrac{n!}{s^{n+1}}$	$(s > 0)$		
$t^a \quad (a > -1)$	$\dfrac{\Gamma(a+1)}{s^{a+1}}$	$(s > 0)$		
e^{at}	$\dfrac{1}{s-a}$	$(s > a)$		
$\cos kt$	$\dfrac{s}{s^2+k^2}$	$(s > 0)$		
$\sin kt$	$\dfrac{k}{s^2+k^2}$	$(s > 0)$		
$\cosh kt$	$\dfrac{s}{s^2-k^2}$	$(s >	k)$
$\sinh kt$	$\dfrac{k}{s^2-k^2}$	$(s >	k)$
$u(t-a)$	$\dfrac{e^{-as}}{s}$	$(s > 0)$		

FIGURE 7.1.2. A short table of Laplace transforms

tional transforms can be derived from these few, using various general properties of the Laplace transformation (which we will discuss in subsequent sections).

Piecewise Continuous Functions

As we remarked at the beginning of this section, we need to be able to handle certain types of discontinuous functions. The function $f(t)$ is said to be **piecewise continuous** on the bounded interval $a \leq t \leq b$ provided that $[a, b]$ can be subdivided into finitely many abutting subintervals so that:

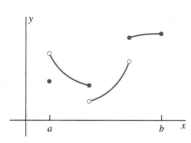

1. f is continuous in the interior of each of these subintervals; and

2. $f(t)$ has a finite limit as t approaches each endpoint of each subinterval from its interior.

FIGURE 7.1.3. The graph of a piecewise continuous function; the solid dots indicate values of the function at discontinuities.

We say that f is piecewise continuous for $t \geq 0$ if it is piecewise continuous on every bounded subinterval of $[0, +\infty)$. Thus a piecewise continuous function has only simple discontinuities (if any) and only at isolated points. At such points the value of the function experiences a finite jump, as indicated in Fig. 7.1.3. The **jump in $f(t)$ at the point** c is defined to be $f(c+) - f(c-)$, where

$$f(c+) = \lim_{\epsilon \to 0^+} f(c + \epsilon) \qquad \text{and} \qquad f(c-) = \lim_{\epsilon \to 0^+} f(c - \epsilon).$$

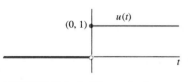

FIGURE 7.1.4. The graph of the unit step function

Perhaps the simplest piecewise continuous (but discontinuous) function is the unit step function, whose graph appears in Fig. 7.1.4. It is defined as follows:

$$u(t) = \begin{cases} 0 & \text{for } t < 0, \\ 1 & \text{for } t \geq 0. \end{cases} \tag{19}$$

Because $u(t) = 1$ for $t \geq 0$ and because the Laplace transform involves only the values of a function for $t \geq 0$, we see immediately that

$$\mathcal{L}\{u(t)\} = \frac{1}{s} \qquad (s > 0). \tag{20}$$

FIGURE 7.1.5. The unit step function $u_a(t)$ has a jump at $t = a$.

The graph of the unit step function $u_a(t) = u(t - a)$ appears in Fig. 7.1.5. Its jump occurs at $t = a$ rather than at $t = 0$; equivalently,

$$u_a(t) = u(t - a) = \begin{cases} 0 & \text{for } t < a, \\ 1 & \text{for } t \geq a. \end{cases} \tag{21}$$

EXAMPLE 8 Find $\mathcal{L}\{u_a(t)\}$ if $a > 0$.

Solution We begin with the definition of the Laplace transform. We obtain

$$\mathcal{L}\{u_a(t)\} = \int_0^\infty e^{-st} u_a(t)\, dt = \int_a^\infty e^{-st}\, dt = \lim_{b \to \infty} \left[-\frac{e^{-st}}{s} \right]_{t=a}^{b};$$

consesequently,

$$\mathcal{L}\{u_a(t)\} = \frac{e^{-as}}{s} \qquad (s > 0, \quad a > 0). \tag{22}$$

General Properties of Transforms

It is a familiar fact from calculus that the integral

$$\int_a^b g(t)\,dt$$

exists if g is piecewise continuous on the bounded interval $[a, b]$. Hence if f is piecewise continuous for $t \geq 0$, it follows that the integral

$$\int_0^b e^{-st}f(t)\,dt$$

exists for all $b < +\infty$. But in order for $F(s)$—the limit of this last integral as $b \to +\infty$—to exist, we need some condition to limit the rate of growth of $f(t)$ as $t \to +\infty$. The function f is said to be **of exponential order** as $t \to +\infty$ if there exist nonnegative constants M, c, and T such that

$$|f(t)| \leq Me^{ct} \quad \text{for } t \geq T. \tag{23}$$

Thus a function is of exponential order provided that it grows no more rapidly (as $t \to +\infty$) than a constant multiple of some exponential function with a linear exponent. The particular values of M, c, and T are not so important. What is important is that some such values exist so that the condition in (23) is satisfied.

Every polynomial $p(t)$ is of exponential order, with $M = c = 1$ in (23); this follows from the fact that $p(t)/e^t \to 0$ as $t \to +\infty$. The function $g(t) = e^{t^2}$ is an example of one that is *not* of exponential order: Because

$$\lim_{t \to \infty} \frac{e^{t^2}}{e^{ct}} = \lim_{t \to \infty} e^{t^2 - ct} = +\infty,$$

the condition in (23) cannot hold for any (finite) value of M. The condition in (23) merely says that $f(t)/e^{ct}$ is *bounded* for t sufficiently large. In particular, any bounded function—such as $\cos kt$ or $\sin kt$—is of exponential order.

THEOREM 2: Existence of Laplace Transforms

If the function f is piecewise continuous for $t \geq 0$ and is of exponential order as $t \to +\infty$, then its Laplace transform $F(s) = \mathcal{L}\{f(t)\}$ exists. More precisely, if f is piecewise continuous and satisfies the condition in (23), then $F(s)$ exists for all $s > c$.

Proof: First we note that we can take $T = 0$ in (19). For by piecewise continuity, $|f(t)|$ is bounded on $[0, T]$. Increasing M in (19) if necessary, we can therefore assume that $|f(t)| \leq M$ if $0 \leq t \leq T$. Because $e^{ct} \geq 1$ for $t \geq 0$, it then follows that $|f(t)| \leq Me^{ct}$ for all $t \geq 0$.

By a standard theorem on convergence of improper integrals—the fact that absolute convergence implies convergence—it suffices for us to prove that the integral

$$\int_0^\infty |e^{-st}f(t)|\,dt$$

exists for $s > c$. To do this, it suffices in turn to show that the value of the integral

$$\int_0^b \left| e^{-st} f(t) \right| dt$$

remains bounded as $b \to +\infty$. But the fact that $|f(t)| \leq M e^{ct}$ for all $t \geq 0$ implies that

$$\int_0^b \left| e^{-st} f(t) \right| dt \leq \int_0^b \left| e^{-st} M e^{ct} \right| dt = M \int_0^b e^{-(s-c)t} dt$$

$$\leq M \int_0^\infty e^{-(s-c)t} dt = \frac{M}{s - c}$$

if $s > c$. This proves Theorem 2. ∎

We have shown, moreover, that

$$|F(s)| \leq \int_0^\infty \left| e^{-st} f(t) \right| dt \leq \frac{M}{s - c} \tag{24}$$

if $s > c$. When we take limits as $s \to +\infty$, we get the following additional result.

COROLLARY: F(s) for s Large

If $f(t)$ satisfies the hypotheses of Theorem 2, then

$$\lim_{s \to \infty} F(s) = 0. \tag{25}$$

∎

The condition in (25) severely limits the functions that can be Laplace transforms. For instance, the function $G(s) = s/(s + 1)$ cannot be the Laplace transform of any "reasonable" function because its limit as $s \to +\infty$ is 1, not 0. More generally, a rational function—a quotient of two polynomials—can be (and is, as we shall see) a Laplace transform only if the degree of its numerator is less than the degree of its denominator.

On the other hand, the hypotheses of Theorem 2 are sufficient, but not necessary, conditions for existence of the Laplace transform of $f(t)$. For example, the function $f(t) = 1/\sqrt{t}$ fails to be piecewise continuous (at $t = 0$), but nevertheless (Example 3 with $a = -\frac{1}{2} > -1$) its Laplace transform

$$\mathcal{L}\{t^{-1/2}\} = \frac{\Gamma\left(\frac{1}{2}\right)}{s^{1/2}} = \sqrt{\frac{\pi}{s}}$$

both exists and violates the condition in (24), which would imply that $sF(s)$ remains bounded as $s \to +\infty$.

The remainder of this chapter is devoted largely to techniques for solving a differential equation by first finding the Laplace transform of its solution. It is then vital for us to know that this uniquely determines the solution of the differential equation; that is, that the function of s we have found has only one inverse Laplace transform that

could be the desired solution. The following theorem is proved in Chapter 6 of Churchill's *Operational Mathematics,* 3rd ed. (New York: McGraw-Hill, 1972).

THEOREM 3: Uniqueness of Inverse Laplace Transforms

Suppose that the functions $f(t)$ and $g(t)$ satisfy the hypotheses of Theorem 2, so that their Laplace transforms $F(s)$ and $G(s)$ both exist. If $F(s) = G(s)$ for all $s > c$ (for some c), then $f(t) = g(t)$ wherever f and g are both continuous. ∎

Thus two piecewise continuous functions of exponential order with the same Laplace transform can differ only at their isolated points of discontinuity. This is of no importance in most practical applications, so we may regard inverse Laplace transforms as being essentially unique. In particular, two solutions of a differential equation must both be continuous, and hence must be the same solution if they have the same Laplace transform.

Historical Remark. Laplace transforms have an interesting history. The integral in the definition of the Laplace transform probably appeared first in the work of Euler. It is customary in mathematics to name a technique or theorem for the next person after Euler to discover it (else there will be several hundred different examples of "Euler's theorem"). In this case, the next person was the French mathematician Pierre Simon de Laplace (1749–1827), who employed such integrals in his work on probability theory. The so-called operational techniques for solving differential equations, which are based on Laplace transforms, were not exploited by Laplace. Indeed, they were discovered and popularized by practicing engineers—notably the English electrical engineer Oliver Heaviside (1850–1925). These techniques were successfully and widely applied before they had been rigorously justified, and around the beginning of this century their validity was the subject of considerable controversy.

7.1 Problems

Apply the definition in (1) to find directly the Laplace transforms of the functions described (by formula or graph) in Problems 1 through 10.

1. $f(t) = t$ **2.** $f(t) = t^2$

3. $f(t) = e^{3t+1}$ **4.** $f(t) = \cos t$

5. $f(t) = \sinh t$ **6.** $f(t) = \sin^2 t$

7.

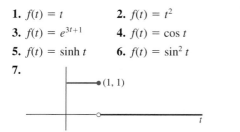

FIGURE 7.1.6. The graph of the function of Problem 7

8.

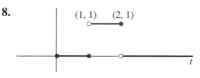

FIGURE 7.1.7. The graph of the function of Problem 8

9.

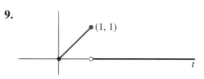

FIGURE 7.1.8. The graph of the function of Problem 9

10.

FIGURE 7.1.9. The graph of the function of Problem 10

Use the transforms in Fig. 7.1.2 to find the Laplace transforms of the functions in Problems 11 through 22. A preliminary integration by parts may be necessary.

11. $f(t) = \sqrt{t} + 3t$

12. $f(t) = 3t^{5/2} - 4t^3$

13. $f(t) = t - 2e^{3t}$

14. $f(t) = t^{3/2} + e^{-10t}$

15. $f(t) = 1 + \cosh 5t$

16. $f(t) = \sin 2t + \cos 2t$

17. $f(t) = \cos^2 2t$

18. $f(t) = \sin 3t \cos 3t$

19. $f(t) = (1 + t)^3$

20. $f(t) = te^t$

21. $f(t) = t \cos 2t$

22. $f(t) = \sinh^2 3t$

Use the transforms in Fig. 7.1.2 to find the inverse Laplace transforms of the functions in Problems 23 through 32.

23. $F(s) = \dfrac{3}{s^4}$

24. $F(s) = s^{-3/2}$

25. $F(s) = \dfrac{1}{s} - \dfrac{2}{s^{5/2}}$

26. $F(s) = \dfrac{1}{s + 5}$

27. $F(s) = \dfrac{3}{s - 4}$

28. $F(s) = \dfrac{3s + 1}{s^2 + 4}$

29. $F(x) = \dfrac{5 - 3s}{s^2 + 9}$

30. $F(s) = \dfrac{9 + s}{4 - s^2}$

31. $F(s) = \dfrac{10s - 3}{25 - s^2}$

32. $F(s) = 2s^{-1}e^{-3s}$

33. Derive the transform of $\sin kt$ by the method used in the text to derive the formula in (16).

34. Derive the transform of $\sinh kt$ by the method used in the text to derive the formula in (14).

35. Use the tabulated integral $\int e^{ax} \cos bx \, dx$ to obtain $\mathcal{L}\{\cos kt\}$ directly from the definition of the Laplace transform.

36. Show that the function $f(t) = \sin(e^{t^2})$ is of exponential order as $t \to +\infty$, but that its derivative is not.

37. Let $f(t) = 1$ for $0 \leq t \leq a$, $f(t) = 0$ for $t > a$ (where $a > 0$). Express f in terms of unit step functions to show that $\mathcal{L}\{f(t)\} = s^{-1}(1 - e^{-as})$.

38. Let $f(t) = 1$ if $a \leq t \leq b$, $f(t) = 0$ if either $t < a$ or $t > b$ (where $0 < a < b$). Express f in terms of unit step functions to show that
$$\mathcal{L}\{f(t)\} = s^{-1}(e^{-as} - e^{-bs}).$$

39. The unit staircase function is defined as follows:
$$f(t) = n \quad \text{if } n - 1 < t \leq n, \quad n = 1, 2, 3, \ldots .$$

(a) Sketch the graph of f to see why its name is appropriate.
(b) Show that
$$f(t) = \sum_{n=0}^{\infty} u(t - n)$$
for all $t > 0$. (c) Assume that the Laplace transform of the infinite series in part (b) can be taken termwise. Apply the geometric series to obtain the result
$$\mathcal{L}\{f(t)\} = \frac{1}{s(1 - e^{-s})}.$$

40. (a) The graph of the function f is shown in Fig. 7.1.10. Show that f can be written in the form
$$f(t) = \sum_{n=0}^{\infty} (-1)^n u(t - n).$$

(b) Use the method of Problem 39 to show that
$$\mathcal{L}\{f(t)\} = \frac{1}{s(1 + e^{-s})}$$

FIGURE 7.1.10. The graph of the function of Problem 40

41. The graph of the square wave function $g(t)$ is shown in Fig. 7.1.11. Express g in terms of the function f of Problem 40 and hence deduce that
$$\mathcal{L}\{g(t)\} = \frac{1 - e^{-s}}{s(1 + e^{-s})} = \frac{1}{s} \tanh \frac{s}{2}.$$

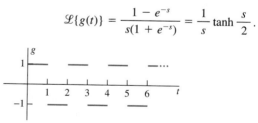

FIGURE 7.1.11. The graph of the function of Problem 41

42. Consider the function $f(t) \equiv 0$. (a) Compute $f'(t) = D_t\{f(t)\}$ and sketch its graph. (b) Now modify f to obtain the new function
$$g(t) = \begin{cases} 1 & \text{if } 0 \leq t \leq 1; \\ 0 & \text{otherwise.} \end{cases}$$

Compute $g'(t) = D_t\{g(t)\}$ and sketch its graph. Note that g is obtained from f by modifying f only on the interval $[0, 1]$. Where do the functions $f'(t)$ and $g'(t)$ agree?

43. Consider the function $f(t) \equiv 0$. (a) Compute $F(s) = \mathcal{L}\{f(t)\}$ and sketch its graph. (b) Now modify f to obtain the new function

$$g(t) = \begin{cases} 1 & \text{if } 0 \leq t \leq 1; \\ 0 & \text{otherwise.} \end{cases}$$

Compute $G(s) = \mathcal{L}\{g(t)\}$ and sketch its graph. Note that g is obtained from f by modifying f *only* on the interval $[0, 1]$. Where do the functions $F(s)$ and $G(s)$ agree? (c) Comment on the difference between the operators D_t and \mathcal{L} illustrated by Problems 42 and 43.

7.2 Transformation of Initial Value Problems

We now discuss the application of Laplace transforms to solve a linear differential equation with constant coefficients such as

$$ax''(t) + bx'(t) + cx(t) = f(t), \tag{1}$$

with given initial conditions $x(0) = x_0$ and $x'(0) = x_0'$. By the linearity of the Laplace transformation, we can transform Eq. (1) by separately taking the Laplace transform of each term in the equation. The transformed equation is

$$a\mathcal{L}\{x''(t)\} + b\mathcal{L}\{x'(t)\} + c\mathcal{L}\{x(t)\} = \mathcal{L}\{f(t)\}; \tag{2}$$

it involves the transforms of the derivatives x' and x'' of the unknown function $x(t)$. The key to the method is Theorem 1, which tells us how to express the transform of the *derivative* of a function in terms of the transform of the function itself.

THEOREM 1: Transforms of Derivatives

Suppose that the function $f(t)$ is continuous and piecewise smooth for $t \geq 0$ and is of exponential order as $t \to +\infty$, so that there exist nonnegative constants M, c, and T such that

$$|f(t)| \leq Me^{ct} \quad \text{for } t \geq T. \tag{3}$$

Then $\mathcal{L}\{f'(t)\}$ exists for $s > c$, and

$$\mathcal{L}\{f'(t)\} = s\mathcal{L}\{f(t)\} - f(0) = sF(s) - f(0). \tag{4}$$

The function f is called **piecewise smooth** on the bounded interval $[a, b]$ if it is piecewise continuous on $[a, b]$ and differentiable except at finitely many points, with $f'(t)$ being piecewise continuous on $[a, b]$. We may assign arbitrary values to $f'(t)$ at the isolated points at which f is not differentiable. We say that f is piecewise smooth for $t \geq 0$ if it is piecewise smooth on every bounded subinterval of $[0, +\infty)$. Figure 7.2.1 indicates how "corners" on the graph of f correspond to discontinuities in its derivative f'.

The main idea of the proof of Theorem 1 is exhibited best by the case in which $f'(t)$ is continuous (not merely piecewise continuous) for $t \geq 0$. Then, beginning with the definition of $\mathcal{L}\{f'(t)\}$ and integrating by parts, we get

$$\mathcal{L}\{f'(t)\} = \int_0^\infty e^{-st}f'(t)\, dt = \left[e^{-st}f(t) \right]_{t=0}^\infty + s\int_0^\infty e^{-st}f(t)\, dt.$$

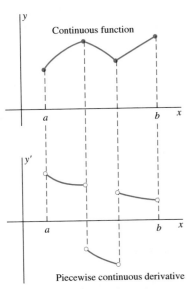

Continuous function

Piecewise continuous derivative

FIGURE 7.2.1. The discontinuities of f' correspond to "corners" on the graph of f.

Because of (3), the integrated term $e^{-st}f(t)$ approaches 0 (when $s > c$) as $t \to +\infty$, and its value at the lower limit $t = 0$ contributes $-f(0)$ to the evaluation of the expression above. The integral that remains above is simply $\mathscr{L}\{f(t)\}$; by Theorem 2 of Section 7.1, the integral converges when $s > c$. Then $\mathscr{L}\{f'(t)\}$ exists when $s > c$, and its value is that given in Eq. (4). We will defer the case in which $f'(t)$ has isolated discontinuities to the end of this section.

Solution of Initial Value Problems

In order to transform Eq. (1), we need the transform of the second derivative as well. If we assume that $g(t) = f'(t)$ satisfies the hypotheses of Theorem 1, then that theorem yields

$$\mathscr{L}\{f''(t)\} = \mathscr{L}\{g'(t)\} = s\mathscr{L}\{g(t)\} - g(0)$$
$$= s\mathscr{L}\{f'(t)\} - f'(0)$$
$$= s[s\mathscr{L}\{f(t)\} - f(0)] - f'(0),$$

and thus

▶ $$\mathscr{L}\{f''(t)\} = s^2 F(s) - sf(0) - f'(0). \tag{5}$$

A repetition of this calculation gives

$$\mathscr{L}\{f'''(t)\} = s\mathscr{L}\{f''(t)\} - f''(0) = s^3 F(s) - s^2 f(0) - sf'(0) - f''(0). \tag{6}$$

After finitely many such steps we obtain the following extension of Theorem 1.

COROLLARY: Transforms of Higher Derivatives

Suppose that the functions $f, f', f'', \ldots, f^{(n-1)}$ are continuous and piecewise smooth for $t \geq 0$, and that each of these functions satisfies the condition in (3) with the same values of M and c. Then $\mathscr{L}\{f^{(n)}(t)\}$ exists when $s > c$, and

$$\mathscr{L}\{f^{(n)}(t)\} = s^n \mathscr{L}\{f(t)\} - s^{n-1}f(0) - s^{n-2}f'(0) - \cdots - f^{(n-1)}(0)$$
$$= s^n F(s) - s^{n-1}f(0) - \cdots - sf^{(n-2)}(0) - f^{(n-1)}(0). \tag{7}$$

∎

EXAMPLE 1 Solve the initial value problem

$$x'' - x' - 6x = 0; \qquad x(0) = 2, \quad x'(0) = -1.$$

Solution With the given initial values, Eqs. (4) and (5) yield

$$\mathscr{L}\{x'(t)\} = s\mathscr{L}\{x(t)\} - x(0) = sX(s) - 2$$

and

$$\mathscr{L}\{x''(t)\} = s^2\mathscr{L}\{x(t)\} - sx(0) - x'(0) = s^2 X(s) - 2s + 1,$$

where (according to our convention about notation) $X(s)$ denotes the Laplace transform of the (unknown) function $x(t)$. Hence the transformed equation is

$$[s^2 X(s) - 2s + 1] - [sX(s) - 2] - 6[X(s)] = 0,$$

which we quickly simplify to

$$(s^2 - s - 6)X(s) - 2s + 3 = 0.$$

Thus

$$X(s) = \frac{2s - 3}{s^2 - s - 6} = \frac{2s - 3}{(s - 3)(s + 2)}.$$

By the method of partial fractions (of integral calculus), there exist constants A and B such that

$$\frac{2s - 3}{(s - 3)(s + 2)} = \frac{A}{s - 3} + \frac{B}{s + 2},$$

and multiplication of both sides of this equation by $(s - 3)(s + 2)$ yields the identity

$$2s - 3 = A(s + 2) + B(s - 3).$$

If we substitute $s = 3$, we find that $A = \frac{3}{5}$; substitution of $s = -2$ shows that $B = \frac{7}{5}$. Hence

$$\mathcal{L}\{x(t)\} = \frac{\frac{3}{5}}{s - 3} + \frac{\frac{7}{5}}{s + 2}.$$

Because $\mathcal{L}^{-1}\{1/(s - a)\} = e^{at}$, it follows that

$$x(t) = \tfrac{3}{5}e^{3t} + \tfrac{7}{5}e^{-2t}$$

is the solution of the original initial value problem. Note that we did not first find the general solution of the differential equation. The Laplace transform method directly yields the desired particular solution, automatically taking into account—via Theorem 1 and its corollary—the given initial conditions.

EXAMPLE 2 Solve the initial value problem

$$x'' + 4x = \sin 3t; \qquad x(0) = x'(0) = 0.$$

$k = 4$ $f(t) = \sin 3t$
$m = 1$
$x(t)$

FIGURE 7.2.2. A mass-spring system satisfying the initial value problem of Example 2. The mass is initially at rest in its equilibrium position.

Such a problem arises in the motion of a mass-spring system with external force, as shown in Fig. 7.2.2.

Solution Because both initial values are zero, Eq. (5) yields $\mathcal{L}\{x''(t)\} = s^2X(s)$. We read the transform of $\sin 3t$ from the table on page 402, and thereby get the transformed equation

$$s^2X(s) + 4X(s) = \frac{3}{s^2 + 9}.$$

Therefore

$$X(s) = \frac{3}{(s^2 + 4)(s^2 + 9)}.$$

The method of partial fractions calls for

$$\frac{3}{(s^2 + 4)(s^2 + 9)} = \frac{As + B}{s^2 + 4} + \frac{Cs + D}{s^2 + 9}.$$

The fact that there are no terms of odd degree on the left-hand side suggests that we set $A = C = 0$, because nonzero values for A or C would lead to terms of odd degree—but no such terms are present in the numerator on the left. So we replace A and C with zero, then multiply both sides by $(s^2 + 4)(s^2 + 9)$. The result is the identity

$$3 = B(s^2 + 9) + D(s^2 + 4) = (B + D)s^2 + (9B + 4D).$$

When we equate coefficients of like powers of s we get the linear equations

$$B + D = 0$$

$$9B + 4D = 3$$

that are readily solved for $B = \frac{3}{5}$ and $D = -\frac{3}{5}$. Hence

$$\mathcal{L}\{x(t)\} = \frac{3}{10} \cdot \frac{2}{s^2 + 4} - \frac{1}{5} \cdot \frac{3}{s^2 + 9}.$$

Because $\mathcal{L}\{\sin 2t\} = 2/(s^2 + 4)$ and $\mathcal{L}\{\sin 3t\} = 3/(s^2 + 9)$, it follows that

$$x(t) = \frac{3}{10} \sin 2t - \frac{1}{5} \sin 3t.$$

Note that the Laplace transform method again gives the solution directly, without the necessity of first finding the complementary function and a particular solution of the original nonhomogeneous differential equation. Thus nonhomogeneous equations are solved in exactly the same manner as are homogeneous equations. ∎

Linear Systems

Laplace transforms are used frequently in engineering problems to solve linear systems in which the coefficients are all constants. When initial conditions are specified, the Laplace transform reduces such a linear system of differential equations to a linear system of algebraic equations in which the unknowns are the transforms of the solution functions. As Example 3 illustrates, the technique for a system is essentially the same as for a single linear differential equation with constant coefficients.

EXAMPLE 3 Solve the system

$$2x'' = -6x + 2y,$$
$$y'' = 2x - 2y + 40 \sin 3t \tag{8}$$

subject to the initial conditions

$$x(0) = x'(0) = y(0) = y'(0) = 0. \tag{9}$$

Thus the force $f(t) = 40 \sin 3t$ is suddenly applied to the second mass of Fig. 7.2.3 at time $t = 0$ when the system is at rest in its equilibrium position.

Solution We write $X(s) = \mathcal{L}\{x(t)\}$ and $Y(s) = \mathcal{L}\{y(t)\}$. Then the initial conditions in (9) imply that

$$\mathcal{L}\{x''(t)\} = s^2 X(s) \qquad \text{and} \qquad \mathcal{L}\{y''(t)\} = s^2 Y(s).$$

FIGURE 7.2.3. A mass-spring system satisfying the initial value problem of Example 3. Both masses are initially at rest in their equilibrium positions.

Because $\mathcal{L}\{\sin 3t\} = 3/(s^2 + 9)$, the transforms of the equations in (8) are the equations

$$2s^2 X(s) = -6X(s) + 2Y(s),$$

$$s^2 Y(s) = 2X(s) - 2Y(s) + \frac{120}{s^2 + 9}.$$

Thus the transformed system is

$$(s^2 + 3)X(s) \qquad - Y(s) = 0,$$

$$-2X(s) + (s^2 + 2)Y(s) = \frac{120}{s^2 + 9}. \tag{10}$$

The determinant of this pair of linear equations in $X(s)$ and $Y(s)$ is

$$\begin{vmatrix} s^2 + 3 & -1 \\ -2 & s^2 + 2 \end{vmatrix} = (s^2 + 3)(s^2 + 2) - 2 = (s^2 + 1)(s^2 + 4),$$

and we readily solve—using Cramer's rule, for instance—the system in (10) for

$$X(s) = \frac{120}{(s^2 + 1)(s^2 + 4)(s^2 + 9)} = \frac{5}{s^2 + 1} - \frac{8}{s^2 + 4} + \frac{3}{s^2 + 9} \tag{11a}$$

and

$$Y(s) = \frac{120(s^2 + 3)}{(s^2 + 1)(s^2 + 4)(s^2 + 9)} = \frac{10}{s^2 + 1} + \frac{8}{s^2 + 4} - \frac{18}{s^2 + 9}. \tag{11b}$$

The partial fraction decompositions in Eqs. (11a) and (11b) are readily found using the method of Example 2. For instance, noting that the denominator factors are linear in s^2, we can write

$$\frac{120}{(s^2 + 1)(s^2 + 4)(s^2 + 9)} = \frac{A}{s^2 + 1} + \frac{B}{s^2 + 4} + \frac{C}{s^2 + 9},$$

and it follows that

$$120 = A(s^2 + 4)(s^2 + 9) + B(s^2 + 1)(s^2 + 9) + C(s^2 + 1)(s^2 + 4). \tag{12}$$

Substitution of $s^2 = -1$ (that is, $s = i$, a zero of the factor $s^2 + 1$) in Eq. (12) gives $120 = A \cdot 3 \cdot 8$, so $A = 5$. Similarly, substitution of $s^2 = -4$ in Eq. (12) yields $B = -8$, and substitution of $s^2 = -9$ yields $C = 3$. Thus we obtain the partial fraction decomposition shown in Eq. (11a).

At any rate, the inverse Laplace transforms of the expressions in Eqs. (11a) and (11b) give the solution

$$x(t) = 5 \sin t - 4 \sin 2t + \sin 3t,$$

$$y(t) = 10 \sin t + 4 \sin 2t - 6 \sin 3t.$$

The Transform Perspective

Let us regard the general constant-coefficient second-order equation as the equation of motion

$$mx'' + cx' + kx = f(t)$$

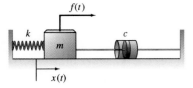

FIGURE 7.2.4. A mass-spring-dashpot system with external force $f(t)$

of the familiar mass-spring-dashpot system (Fig. 7.2.4). Then the transformed equation is

$$m[s^2X(s) - sx(0) - x'(0)] + c[sX(s) - x(0)] + kX(s) = F(s). \tag{13}$$

Note that Eq. (13) is an *algebraic* equation—indeed, a linear equation—in the "unknown" $X(s)$. This is the source of the power of the Laplace transform method:

> Linear **differential** equations are transformed
> into readily solved **algebraic** equations.

If we solve Eq. (13) for $X(s)$, we get

$$X(s) = \frac{F(s)}{Z(s)} + \frac{I(s)}{Z(s)} \tag{14}$$

where

$$Z(s) = ms^2 + cs + k \quad \text{and} \quad I(s) = mx(0)s + mx'(0) + cx(0).$$

Note that $Z(s)$ depends only on the physical system itself. Thus Eq. (14) presents $X(s) = \mathcal{L}\{x(t)\}$ as the sum of a term depending only on the external force and one depending only on the initial conditions. In the case of an underdamped system, these two terms are the transforms

$$\mathcal{L}\{x_{sp}(t)\} = \frac{F(s)}{Z(s)} \quad \text{and} \quad \mathcal{L}\{x_{tr}(t)\} = \frac{I(s)}{Z(s)}$$

of the steady periodic solution and the transient solution, respectively. The only potential difficulty in finding these solutions is in finding the inverse Laplace transform of the right-hand side in Eq. (14). Much of the remainder of this chapter is devoted to finding Laplace transforms and inverse transforms. In particular, we seek those methods that are sufficiently powerful to enable us to solve problems that—unlike those in Examples 1 and 2—cannot be solved readily by the methods of Chapter 1.

Additional Transform Techniques

EXAMPLE 4 Show that

$$\mathcal{L}\{te^{at}\} = \frac{1}{(s-a)^2}.$$

Solution If $f(t) = te^{at}$, then $f(0) = 0$ and $f'(t) = e^{at} + ate^{at}$. Hence Theorem 1 gives

$$\mathcal{L}\{e^{at} + ate^{at}\} = \mathcal{L}\{f'(t)\} = s\mathcal{L}\{f(t)\} = s\mathcal{L}\{te^{at}\}.$$

It follows from the linearity of the transform that

$$\mathcal{L}\{e^{at}\} + a\mathcal{L}\{te^{at}\} = s\mathcal{L}\{te^{at}\}.$$

Hence

$$\mathcal{L}\{te^{at}\} = \frac{\mathcal{L}\{e^{at}\}}{s-a} = \frac{1}{(s-a)^2} \tag{15}$$

because $\mathcal{L}\{e^{at}\} = 1/(s-a)$.

EXAMPLE 5 Find $\mathcal{L}\{t \sin kt\}$.

> **Solution** Let $f(t) = t \sin kt$. Then $f(0) = 0$ and
>
> $$f'(t) = \sin kt + kt \cos kt.$$
>
> The derivative involves the new function $t \cos kt$, so we note that $f'(0) = 0$ and differentiate again. The result is
>
> $$f''(t) = 2k \cos kt - k^2 t \sin kt.$$
>
> But $\mathcal{L}\{f''(t)\} = s^2 \mathcal{L}\{f(t)\}$ by the formula in (5) for the transform of the second derivative, and $\mathcal{L}\{\cos kt\} = s/(s^2 + k^2)$, so we have
>
> $$\frac{2ks}{s^2 + k^2} - k^2 \mathcal{L}\{t \sin kt\} = s^2 \mathcal{L}\{t \sin kt\}.$$
>
> Finally, we solve this equation for
>
> $$\mathcal{L}\{t \sin kt\} = \frac{2ks}{(s^2 + k^2)^2}. \tag{16}$$
>
> This procedure is considerably more pleasant than the alternative of evaluating the integral
>
> $$\mathcal{L}\{t \sin kt\} = \int_0^\infty t e^{-st} \sin kt \, dt. \qquad \blacksquare$$

Examples 4 and 5 exploit the fact that if $f(0) = 0$, then differentiation of f corresponds to multiplication of its transform by s. It is reasonable to expect the inverse operation of integration (antidifferentiation) to correspond to division of the transform by s.

THEOREM 2: Transforms of Integrals

If $f(t)$ is a piecewise continuous function for $t \geq 0$ and satisfies the condition of exponential order $|f(t)| \leq Me^{ct}$ for $t \geq T$, then

$$\mathcal{L}\left\{ \int_0^t f(\tau) \, d\tau \right\} = \frac{1}{s} \mathcal{L}\{f(t)\} = \frac{F(s)}{s} \tag{17}$$

for $s > c$. Equivalently,

$$\mathcal{L}^{-1}\left\{ \frac{F(s)}{s} \right\} = \int_0^t f(\tau) \, d\tau. \tag{18}$$

Proof: Because f is piecewise continuous, the fundamental theorem of calculus implies that

$$g(t) = \int_0^t f(\tau) \, d\tau$$

is continuous and that $g'(t) = f(t)$ where f is continuous; thus g is continuous and piecewise smooth for $t \geq 0$. Furthermore,

$$|g(t)| \leq \int_0^t |f(\tau)| \, d\tau \leq M \int_0^t e^{c\tau} \, d\tau = \frac{M}{c}(e^{ct} - 1) < \frac{M}{c} e^{ct},$$

so $g(t)$ is of exponential order as $t \to +\infty$. Hence we can apply Theorem 1 to g; this gives

$$\mathcal{L}\{f(t)\} = \mathcal{L}\{g'(t)\} = s\mathcal{L}\{g(t)\} - g(0).$$

Now $g(0) = 0$, so division by s yields

$$\mathcal{L}\left\{ \int_0^t f(\tau)\, d\tau \right\} = \mathcal{L}\{g(t)\} = \frac{\mathcal{L}\{f(t)\}}{s},$$

which completes the proof. ∎

EXAMPLE 6 Find the inverse Laplace transform of

$$\frac{1}{s^2(s-a)}.$$

Solution In effect, Eq. (18) means that we can delete a factor of s from the denominator, find the inverse transform of the resulting simpler expression, and finally integrate from 0 to t (to "correct" for the missing factor s). Thus

$$\mathcal{L}^{-1}\left\{ \frac{1}{s(s-a)} \right\} = \int_0^t \mathcal{L}^{-1}\left\{ \frac{1}{s-a} \right\} d\tau = \int_0^t e^{a\tau}\, d\tau = \frac{1}{a}(e^{at} - 1).$$

We now repeat the technique to obtain

$$\mathcal{L}^{-1}\left\{ \frac{1}{s^2(s-a)} \right\} = \int_0^t \mathcal{L}^{-1}\left\{ \frac{1}{s(s-a)} \right\} d\tau = \int_0^t \frac{1}{a}(e^{a\tau} - 1)\, d\tau$$

$$= \left[\frac{1}{a}\left(\frac{1}{a}e^{a\tau} - \tau \right) \right]_0^t = \frac{1}{a^2}(e^{at} - at - 1).$$

This technique is often a more convenient way than the method of partial fractions for finding an inverse transform of a fraction of the form $P(s)/[s^n Q(s)]$.

Proof of Theorem 1: We conclude this section with the proof of Theorem 1 in the general case in which f' is merely piecewise continuous. We need to prove that the limit

$$\lim_{b \to \infty} \int_0^b e^{-st} f'(t)\, dt$$

exists and also need to find its value. With b fixed, let $t_1, t_2, \ldots, t_{k-1}$ be the points interior to the interval $[0, b]$ at which f' is discontinuous. Let $t_0 = 0$ and $t_k = b$. Then we can integrate by parts on each interval (t_{n-1}, t_n) where f' is continuous. This yields

$$\int_0^b e^{-st} f'(t)\, dt = \sum_{n=1}^k \int_{t_{n-1}}^{t_n} e^{-st} f'(t)\, dt$$

$$= \sum_{n=1}^k \left(\left[e^{-st} f(t) \right]_{t_{n-1}}^{t_n} + s \int_{t_{n-1}}^{t_n} e^{-st} f(t)\, dt \right)$$

$$= -f(0) - \sum_{n=1}^{k-1} e^{-st_n} j_f(t_n) + e^{-sb} f(b) + s \int_0^b e^{-st} f(t)\, dt, \quad (19)$$

where

$$j_f(t_n) = f(t_n^+) - f(t_n^-) \tag{20}$$

is the jump in $f(t)$ at $t = t_n$. But because f is continuous, each jump is zero: $j_f(t_n) = 0$ for all n. Moreover, if $b > c$, then $e^{-sb}f(b) \to 0$ as $b \to +\infty$. Therefore when we take the limit in (16) as $b \to +\infty$, we get the desired result:

$$\mathcal{L}\{f'(t)\} = s\mathcal{L}\{f(t)\} - f(0). \qquad \blacksquare$$

Extension of Theorem 1. Suppose that the original function $f(t)$ is itself only piecewise continuous (instead of continuous), with its (finite jump) discontinuities located at the points t_1, t_2, t_3, \ldots. Assuming that $\mathcal{L}\{f'(t)\}$ exists, when we take the limit in (19) as $b \to +\infty$, we get

$$\mathcal{L}\{f'(t)\} = sF(s) - f(0) - \sum_{n=1}^{\infty} e^{-st_n} j_f(t_n). \tag{21}$$

EXAMPLE 7 Let $f(t) = 1 + [\![t]\!]$ be the unit staircase function; its graph is shown in Fig. 7.2.5. Then $f(0) = 1$, $f'(t) \equiv 0$, and $j_f(n) = 1$ for each integer $n = 1, 2, 3, \ldots$ Hence Eq. (21) yields

$$0 = sF(s) - 1 - \sum_{n=1}^{\infty} e^{-ns},$$

so the Laplace transform of $f(t)$ is

$$F(s) = \frac{1}{s} \sum_{n=0}^{\infty} e^{-ns} = \frac{1}{s(1 - e^{-s})}.$$

In the last step, we used the formula for the sum of a geometric series,

$$\sum_{n=0}^{\infty} x^n = \frac{1}{1 - x},$$

with $x = e^{-s} < 1$.

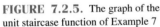

FIGURE 7.2.5. The graph of the unit staircase function of Example 7

7.2 Problems

Use Laplace transforms to solve the initial value problems in Problems 1 through 16.

1. $x'' + 4x = 0$; $x(0) = 5$, $x'(0) = 0$

2. $x'' + 9x = 0$; $x(0) = 3$, $x'(0) = 4$

3. $x'' - x' - 2x = 0$; $x(0) = 0$, $x'(0) = 2$

4. $x'' + 8x' + 15x = 0$; $x(0) = 2$, $x'(0) = -3$

5. $x'' + x = \sin 2t$; $x(0) = 0 = x'(0)$

6. $x'' + 4x = \cos t$; $x(0) = 0 = x'(0)$

7. $x'' + x = \cos 3t$; $x(0) = 1$, $x'(0) = 0$

8. $x'' + 9x = 1$; $x(0) = 0 = x'(0)$

9. $x'' + 4x' + 3x = 1$; $x(0) = x'(0) = 0$

10. $x'' + 3x' + 2x = t$; $x(0) = 0$, $x'(0) = 2$

11. $x' = 2x + y$, $y' = 6x + 3y$; $x(0) = 1$, $y(0) = -2$

12. $x' = x + 2y$, $y' = x + e^{-t}$; $x(0) = y(0) = 0$

13. $x' + 2y' + x = 0$, $x' - y' + y = 0$; $x(0) = 0$, $y(0) = 1$

14. $x'' + 2x + 4y = 0$, $y'' + x + 2y = 0$; $x(0) = y(0) = 0$, $x'(0) = y'(0) = -1$

15. $x'' + x' + y' + 2x - y = 0$, $y'' + x' + y' + 4x - 2y = 0$; $x(0) = y(0) = 1$, $x'(0) = y'(0) = 0$

16. $x' = x + z$, $y' = x + y$, $z' = -2x - z$; $x(0) = 1$, $y(0) = 0$, $z(0) = 0$

Apply Theorem 2 to find the inverse Laplace transforms of the functions in Problems 17 through 24.

17. $F(s) = \dfrac{1}{s(s-3)}$

18. $F(s) = \dfrac{3}{s(s+5)}$

19. $F(s) = \dfrac{1}{s(s^2+4)}$

20. $F(s) = \dfrac{2s+1}{s(s^2+9)}$

21. $F(s) = \dfrac{1}{s^2(s^2+1)}$

22. $F(s) = \dfrac{1}{s(s^2-9)}$

23. $F(s) = \dfrac{1}{s^2(s^2-1)}$

24. $F(s) = \dfrac{1}{s(s+1)(s+2)}$

25. Apply Theorem 1 to derive $\mathcal{L}\{\sin kt\}$ from the formula for $\mathcal{L}\{\cos kt\}$.

26. Apply Theorem 1 to derive $\mathcal{L}\{\cosh kt\}$ from the formula for $\mathcal{L}\{\sinh kt\}$.

27. (a) Apply Theorem 1 to show that

$$\mathcal{L}\{t^n e^{at}\} = \frac{n}{s-a}\,\mathcal{L}\{t^{n-1}e^{at}\}.$$

(b) Deduce that $\mathcal{L}\{t^n e^{at}\} = n!/(s-a)^{n+1}$ for $n = 1, 2, 3, \ldots$.

Apply Theorem 1 as in Example 5 to derive the Laplace transforms in Problems 28 through 30.

28. $\mathcal{L}\{t \cos kt\} = \dfrac{s^2 - k^2}{(s^2+k^2)^2}$

29. $\mathcal{L}\{t \sinh kt\} = \dfrac{2ks}{(s^2-k^2)^2}$

30. $\mathcal{L}\{t \cosh kt\} = \dfrac{s^2 + k^2}{(s^2-k^2)^2}$

31. Apply the results in Example 5 and Problem 28 to show that

$$\mathcal{L}^{-1}\left\{\frac{1}{(s^2+k^2)^2}\right\} = \frac{1}{2k^3}(\sin kt - kt \cos kt).$$

Apply the extension of Theorem 1 in Eq. (21) to derive the Laplace transforms given in Problems 32 through 37.

32. $\mathcal{L}\{u(t-a)\} = s^{-1}e^{-as}$ for $a > 0$.

33. If $f(t) = 1$ on the interval $[a, b]$ (where $0 < a < b$) and $f(t) = 0$ otherwise, then

$$\mathcal{L}\{f(t)\} = \frac{e^{-as} - e^{-bs}}{s}.$$

34. If $f(t) = (-1)^{[\![t]\!]}$ is the square wave function whose graph is shown in Fig. 7.2.6, then

$$\mathcal{L}\{f(t)\} = \frac{1}{s} \tanh \frac{s}{2}.$$

(*Suggestion:* Use the geometric series.)

FIGURE 7.2.6. The graph of the square wave function of Problem 34

35. If $f(t)$ is the unit on-off function whose graph is shown in Fig. 7.2.7, then

$$\mathcal{L}\{f(t)\} = \frac{1}{s(1 + e^{-s})}.$$

FIGURE 7.2.7. The graph of the off-on function of Problem 35

36. If $g(t)$ is the triangular wave function whose graph is shown in Fig. 7.2.8, then

$$\mathcal{L}\{g(t)\} = \frac{1}{s^2} \tanh \frac{s}{2}.$$

FIGURE 7.2.8. The graph of the triangular wave function of Problem 36

37. If $f(t)$ is the sawtooth function whose graph is shown in Fig. 7.2.9, then

$$\mathcal{L}\{f(t)\} = \frac{1}{s^2} - \frac{e^{-s}}{s(1 - e^{-s})}.$$

(*Suggestion:* Note that $f'(t) \equiv 1$ where it is defined.)

FIGURE 7.2.9. The graph of the sawtooth function of Problem 37

7.3 Translation and Partial Fractions

As illustrated by Examples 1 and 2 of Section 7.2, the solution of a linear differential equation with constant coefficents can often be reduced to the matter of finding the inverse Laplace transform of a rational function of the form

$$R(s) = \frac{P(s)}{Q(s)} \tag{1}$$

where the degree of $P(s)$ is less than that of $Q(s)$. The technique for finding $\mathcal{L}^{-1}\{R(s)\}$ is based on the same method of partial fractions that we use in elementary calculus to integrate rational functions. The following two rules describe the **partial fraction decomposition** of $R(s)$, in terms of the factorization of the denominator $Q(s)$ into linear factors and irreducible quadratic factors corresponding to the real and complex zeros, respectively, of $Q(s)$.

RULE 1: Linear Factor Partial Fractions

The part of the partial fraction decomposition of $R(s)$ corresponding to the linear factor $s - a$ of multiplicity n is a sum of n partial fractions, having the form

$$\frac{A_1}{s - a} + \frac{A_2}{(s - a)^2} + \cdots + \frac{A_n}{(s - a)^n}, \tag{2}$$

where $A_1, A_2, \ldots,$ and A_n are constants. ■

RULE 2: Quadratic Factor Partial Fractions

The part of the partial fraction decomposition corresponding to the irreducible quadratic factor $(s - a)^2 + b^2$ of multiplicity n is a sum of n partial fractions, having the form

$$\frac{A_1 s + B_1}{(s - a)^2 + b^2} + \cdots + \frac{A_n s + B_n}{[(s - a)^2 + b^2]^n}, \tag{3}$$

where $A_1, A_2, \ldots, A_n, B_1, B_2, \ldots, B_n$ are constants. ■

Finding $\mathcal{L}^{-1}\{R(s)\}$ involves two steps: First we must find the partial fraction decomposition of $R(s)$, and then we must find the inverse Laplace transform of each of the individual partial fractions of the types that appear in (2) and (3). The latter step is based on the following elementary property of Laplace transforms.

THEOREM 1: Translation on the s-Axis

If $F(s) = \mathcal{L}\{f(t)\}$ exists for $s > c$, then $\mathcal{L}\{e^{at}f(t)\}$ exists for $s > a + c$, and

$$\mathcal{L}\{e^{at}f(t)\} = F(s - a). \tag{4}$$

Equivalently,

$$\mathcal{L}^{-1}\{F(s - a)\} = e^{at}f(t). \tag{5}$$

Thus the translation $s \to s - a$ in the transform corresponds to multiplication of the original function of t by e^{at}.

Proof: If we simply replace s with $s - a$ in the definition of $F(s) = \mathcal{L}\{f(t)\}$, we obtain

$$F(s - a) = \int_0^\infty e^{-(s-a)t} f(t) \, dt = \int_0^\infty e^{-st}[e^{at}f(t)] \, dt = \mathcal{L}\{e^{at}f(t)\}.$$

This is Eq. (4), and it is clear that Eq. (5) is the same. ∎

If we apply the translation theorem to the formulas for the Laplace transforms of t^n, $\cos kt$, and $\sin kt$ that we already know—multiplying each of these functions by e^{at} and replacing s with $s - a$ in the transforms—we get the following additions to the table of Fig. 7.1.2.

$f(t)$	$F(s)$		
$e^{at}t^n$	$\dfrac{n!}{(s-a)^{n+1}}$,	$s > a$	(6)
$e^{at}\cos kt$	$\dfrac{s-a}{(s-a)^2 + k^2}$,	$s > a$	(7)
$e^{at}\sin kt$	$\dfrac{k}{(s-a)^2 + k^2}$,	$s > a$	(8)

For ready reference, all the Laplace transforms derived in this chapter are listed in the table of transforms that appears in the endpapers.

EXAMPLE 1 Consider a mass-and-spring system with $m = \frac{1}{2}$, $k = 17$, and $c = 3$ in mks units (Fig. 7.3.1). As usual, let $x(t)$ denote the displacement of the mass m from its equilibrium position. If the mass is set in motion with $x(0) = 3$ and $x'(0) = 1$, find $x(t)$ for the resulting damped free oscillations.

FIGURE 7.3.1. The mass-spring-dashpot system of Example 1

Solution The differential equation is $\frac{1}{2}x'' + 3x' + 17x = 0$, so we need to solve the initial value problem

$$x'' + 6x' + 34x = 0; \qquad x(0) = 3, \qquad x'(0) = 1.$$

We take the Laplace transform of each term of the differential equation; because (obviously) $\mathcal{L}\{0\} \equiv 0$, we get the equation

$$[s^2 X(s) - 3s - 1] + 6[sX(s) - 3] + 34X(s) = 0,$$

which we solve for

$$X(s) = \frac{3s + 19}{s^2 + 6s + 34} = 3\frac{s + 3}{(s + 3)^2 + 25} + 2\frac{5}{(s + 3)^2 + 25}.$$

Applying the formulas in (7) and (8) with $a = -3$ and $k = 5$, we now see that

$$x(t) = e^{-3t}(3\cos 5t + 2\sin 5t).$$
∎

Example 2 illustrates a useful technique for finding the partial fraction coefficients in the case of nonrepeated linear factors.

EXAMPLE 2 Find the inverse Laplace transform of

$$R(s) = \frac{s^2 + 1}{s^3 - 2s^2 - 8s}.$$

Solution Note that the denominator of $R(s)$ factors as $Q(s) = s(s + 2)(s - 4)$. Hence

$$\frac{s^2 + 1}{s^3 - 2s^2 - 8s} = \frac{A}{s} + \frac{B}{s + 2} + \frac{C}{s - 4}.$$

Multiplication of each term of this equation by $Q(s)$ yields

$$s^2 + 1 = A(s + 2)(s - 4) + Bs(s - 4) + Cs(s + 2).$$

When we successively substitute the three zeros $s = 0$, $s = -2$, and $s = 4$ of the denominator $Q(s)$ in this equation, we get the results

$$-8A = 1, \qquad 12B = 5, \qquad \text{and} \qquad 24C = 17.$$

Thus $A = -\frac{1}{8}$, $B = \frac{5}{12}$, and $C = \frac{17}{24}$, so

$$\frac{s^2 + 1}{s^3 - 2s^2 - 8s} = -\frac{\frac{1}{8}}{s} + \frac{\frac{5}{12}}{s + 2} + \frac{\frac{17}{24}}{s - 4},$$

and hence

$$\mathcal{L}^{-1}\left\{ \frac{s^2 + 1}{s^3 - 2s^2 - 8s} \right\} = -\frac{1}{8} + \frac{5}{12} e^{-2t} + \frac{17}{24} e^{4t}. \qquad ■$$

Example 3 illustrates a differentiation technique for finding the partial fraction coefficients in the case of repeated linear factors.

EXAMPLE 3 Solve the initial value problem

$$y'' + 4y' + 4y = t^2; \qquad y(0) = y'(0) = 0.$$

Solution The transformed equation is

$$s^2 Y(s) + 4s Y(s) + 4Y(s) = \frac{2}{s^3}.$$

Thus

$$Y(s) = \frac{2}{s^3(s + 2)^2} = \frac{A}{s^3} + \frac{B}{s^2} + \frac{C}{s} + \frac{D}{(s + 2)^2} + \frac{E}{s + 2}. \qquad (9)$$

To find A, B, and C, we multiply both sides by s^3 to obtain

$$\frac{2}{(s + 2)^2} = A + Bs + Cs^2 + s^3 F(s), \qquad (10)$$

where $F(s) = D(s + 2)^{-2} + E(s + 2)^{-1}$ is the sum of the two partial fractions corresponding to $(s + 2)^2$. Substitution of $s = 0$ in Eq. (10) yields $A = \frac{1}{2}$. To find B and C, we differentiate Eq. (10) twice to obtain

$$\frac{-4}{(s + 2)^3} = B + 2Cs + 3s^2F(s) + s^3F'(s) \tag{11}$$

and

$$\frac{12}{(s + 2)^4} = 2C + 6sF(s) + 6s^2F'(s) + s^3F''(s). \tag{12}$$

Now substitution of $s = 0$ in Eq. (11) yields $B = -\frac{1}{2}$, and substitution of $s = 0$ in Eq. (12) yields $C = \frac{3}{8}$.

To find D and E, we multiply each side in Eq. (9) by $(s + 2)^2$ to get

$$\frac{2}{s^3} = D + E(s + 2) + (s + 2)^2G(s), \tag{13}$$

where $G(s) = As^{-3} + Bs^{-2} + Cs^{-1}$, and then differentiate to obtain

$$-\frac{6}{s^4} = E + 2(s + 2)G(s) + (s + 2)^2G'(s). \tag{14}$$

Substitution of $s = -2$ in Eqs. (13) and (14) now yields $D = -\frac{1}{4}$ and $E = -\frac{3}{8}$. Thus

$$Y(s) = \frac{\frac{1}{2}}{s^3} - \frac{\frac{1}{2}}{s^2} + \frac{\frac{3}{8}}{s} - \frac{\frac{1}{4}}{(s + 2)^2} - \frac{\frac{3}{8}}{s + 2},$$

so the solution of the given initial value problem is

$$y(t) = \frac{1}{4}t^2 - \frac{1}{2}t + \frac{3}{8} - \frac{1}{4}te^{-2t} - \frac{3}{8}e^{-2t}. \qquad \blacksquare$$

Examples 4, 5, and 6 illustrate techniques for dealing with quadratic factors in partial fraction decompositions.

EXAMPLE 4 Consider the mass-spring-dashpot system as in Example 1, but with initial conditions $x(0) = x'(0) = 0$ and with the imposed external force $F(t) = 15 \sin 2t$. Find the resulting transient motion and steady periodic motion of the mass.

Solution The initial value problem we need to solve is

$$x'' + 6x' + 34x = 30 \sin 2t; \qquad x(0) = x'(0) = 0.$$

The transformed equation is

$$s^2X(s) + 6sX(s) + 34X(s) = \frac{60}{s^2 + 4}.$$

Hence

$$X(s) = \frac{60}{(s^2 + 4)[(s + 3)^2 + 25]} = \frac{As + B}{s^2 + 4} + \frac{Cs + D}{[(s + 3)^2 + 25]}.$$

When we multiply both sides by the common denominator, we get

$$60 = (As + B)[(s + 3)^2 + 25] + (Cs + D)(s^2 + 4). \qquad (15)$$

To find A and B, we substitute the zero $s = 2i$ of the quadratic factor $s^2 + 4$ in Eq. (15); the result is

$$60 = (2iA + B)[(2i + 3)^2 + 25],$$

which we simplify to

$$60 = (-24A + 30B) + (60A + 12B)i.$$

We now equate real parts and imaginary parts on each side of this equation to obtain the two linear equations

$$-24A + 30B = 60 \qquad \text{and} \qquad 60A + 12B = 0,$$

which are readily solved for $A = -\frac{10}{29}$ and $B = \frac{50}{29}$.

To find C and D, we substitute the zero $s = -3 + 5i$ of the quadratic factor $(s + 3)^2 + 25$ in Eq. (15) and get

$$60 = [C(-3 + 5i) + D][(-3 + 5i)^2 + 4],$$

which we simplify to

$$60 = (186C - 12D) + (30C - 30D)i.$$

Again we equate real parts and imaginary parts; this yields the two linear equations

$$186C - 12D = 60 \qquad \text{and} \qquad 30C - 30D = 0,$$

and we readily find their solution to be $C = D = \frac{10}{29}$.

With these values of the coefficients A, B, C, and D, our partial fraction decomposition of $X(s)$ is

$$X(s) = \frac{1}{29}\left(\frac{-10s + 50}{s^2 + 4} + \frac{10s + 10}{(s + 3)^2 + 25}\right)$$

$$= \frac{1}{29}\left(\frac{-10(s) + (25)(2)}{s^2 + 4} + \frac{10(s + 3) - (4)(5)}{(s + 3)^2 + 25}\right).$$

After we compute the inverse Laplace transforms, we get the position function

$$x(t) = \frac{5}{29}(-2\cos 2t + 5\sin 2t) + \frac{2}{29}e^{-3t}(5\cos 5t - 2\sin 5t).$$

The terms of circular frequency 2 constitute the steady periodic forced oscillations of the mass, whereas the exponentially damped terms of circular frequency 5 constitute its transient motion. Note that the transient motion is nonzero even though both initial conditions are zero. ∎

The following two inverse Laplace transforms are used in inverting partial fractions that correspond to the case of repeated quadratic factors:

$$\mathcal{L}^{-1}\left\{\frac{s}{(s^2 + k^2)^2}\right\} = \frac{1}{2k}\, t \sin kt \qquad (16)$$

and

$$\mathcal{L}^{-1}\left\{\frac{1}{(s^2 + k^2)^2}\right\} = \frac{1}{2k^3}(\sin kt - kt \cos kt). \tag{17}$$

These follow from Example 5 and Problem 31 of Section 7.2, respectively. Because of the presence in Eqs. (16) and (17) of the terms $t \sin kt$ and $t \cos kt$, a repeated quadratic factor ordinarily signals the phenomenon of resonance in an undamped mechanical or electrical system.

EXAMPLE 5 Use Laplace transforms to solve the initial value problem

$$x'' + \omega_0^2 x = F_0 \sin \omega t; \qquad x(0) = 0 = x'(0)$$

that determines the undamped forced oscillations of a mass on a spring.

Solution When we transform the differential equation, we get the equation

$$s^2 X(s) + \omega_0^2 X(s) = \frac{F_0 \omega}{s^2 + \omega^2}, \qquad \text{so} \qquad X(s) = \frac{F_0 \omega}{(s^2 + \omega^2)(s^2 + \omega_0^2)}.$$

If $\omega \neq \omega_0$, we find without difficulty that

$$X(s) = \frac{F_0 \omega}{\omega^2 - \omega_0^2}\left(\frac{1}{s^2 + \omega_0^2} - \frac{1}{s^2 + \omega^2}\right),$$

so it follows that

$$x(t) = \frac{F_0 \omega}{\omega^2 - \omega_0^2}\left(\frac{1}{\omega_0}\sin \omega_0 t - \frac{1}{\omega}\sin \omega t\right).$$

But if $\omega = \omega_0$, we have

$$X(s) = \frac{F_0 \omega_0}{(s^2 + \omega_0^2)^2},$$

so Eq. (17) yields the resonance solution

$$x(t) = \frac{F_0}{2\omega_0^2}(\sin \omega_0 t - \omega_0 t \cos \omega_0 t).$$

EXAMPLE 6 Solve the initial value problem

$$y^{(4)} + 2y'' + y = 4te^t;$$
$$y(0) = y'(0) = y''(0) = y^{(3)}(0) = 0.$$

Solution First we observe that

$$\mathcal{L}\{y''(t)\} = s^2 Y(s), \quad \mathcal{L}\{y^{(4)}(t)\} = s^4 Y(s), \qquad \text{and} \qquad \mathcal{L}\{te^t\} = \frac{1}{(s-1)^2}.$$

Hence the transformed equation is

$$(s^4 + 2s^2 + 1)Y(s) = \frac{4}{(s-1)^2}.$$

Thus our problem is to find the inverse transform of

$$Y(s) = \frac{4}{(s-1)^2(s^2+1)^2}$$
$$= \frac{A}{(s-1)^2} + \frac{B}{s-1} + \frac{Cs+D}{(s^2+1)^2} + \frac{Es+F}{s^2+1}. \tag{18}$$

If we multiply by the common denominator $(s - 1)^2(s^2 + 1)^2$ we get the equation

$$A(s^2 + 1)^2 + B(s - 1)(s^2 + 1)^2 + Cs(s - 1)^2$$
$$+ D(s - 1)^2 + Es(s - 1)^2(s^2 + 1) + F(s - 1)^2(s^2 + 1) = 4. \quad (19)$$

Upon substituting $s = 1$ we find that $A = 1$.

Equation (19) is an identity that holds for all values of s. To find the values of the remaining coefficients, we substitute successively the values $s = 0$, $s = -1$, $s = -2$, and $s = 3$ in Eq. (19). This yields the system

$$-B \qquad + D \qquad + \quad F = 3,$$
$$-8B - 4C + 4D - 8E + 8F = 0,$$
$$25B + 2C + D + 10E + 5F = -21, \quad (20)$$
$$-75B - 18C + 9D - 90E + 45F = -21,$$
$$200B + 12C + 4D + 120E + 40F = -96$$

of five linear equations in B, C, D, E, and F. With the aid of a calculator programmed to solve linear systems, we find that $B = -2$, $C = 2$, $D = 0$, $E = 2$, and $F = 1$. We now substitute the coefficients we have found in Eq. (18), and thus obtain

$$Y(s) = \frac{1}{(s - 1)^2} - \frac{2}{s - 1} + \frac{2s}{(s^2 + 1)^2} + \frac{2s + 1}{s^2 + 1}.$$

Recalling Eq. (16), the translation property, and the familiar transforms of $\cos t$ and $\sin t$, we see finally that the solution of the given initial value problem is

$$y(t) = (t - 2)e^t + (t + 1)\sin t + 2\cos t.$$

7.3 Problems

Apply the translation theorem to find the Laplace transforms of the functions in Problems 1 through 4.

1. $f(t) = t^4 e^{\pi t}$

2. $f(t) = t^{3/2}e^{-4t}$

3. $f(t) = e^{-2t}\sin 3\pi t$

4. $f(t) = e^{-t/2}\cos 2\left(t - \frac{\pi}{8}\right)$

Apply the translation theorem to find the inverse Laplace transforms of the functions in Problems 5 through 10.

5. $F(s) = \dfrac{3}{2s - 4}$

6. $F(s) = \dfrac{s - 1}{(s + 1)^3}$

7. $F(s) = \dfrac{1}{s^2 + 4s + 4}$

8. $F(s) = \dfrac{s + 2}{s^2 + 4s + 5}$

9. $F(s) = \dfrac{3s + 5}{s^2 - 6s + 25}$

10. $F(s) = \dfrac{2s - 3}{9s^2 - 12s + 20}$

Use partial fractions to find the inverse Laplace transforms of the functions in Problems 11 through 22.

11. $F(s) = \dfrac{1}{s^2 - 4}$

12. $F(s) = \dfrac{5s - 6}{s^2 - 3s}$

13. $F(s) = \dfrac{5 - 2s}{s^2 + 7s + 10}$

14. $F(s) = \dfrac{5s - 4}{s^3 - s^2 - 2s}$

15. $F(s) = \dfrac{1}{s^3 - 5s^2}$

16. $F(s) = \dfrac{1}{(s^2 + s - 6)^2}$

17. $F(s) = \dfrac{1}{s^4 - 16}$

18. $F(s) = \dfrac{s^3}{(s - 4)^4}$

19. $F(s) = \dfrac{s^2 - 2s}{s^4 + 5s^2 + 4}$

20. $F(s) = \dfrac{1}{s^4 - 8s^2 + 16}$

21. $F(s) = \dfrac{s^2 + 3}{(s^2 + 2s + 2)^2}$

22. $F(s) = \dfrac{2s^3 - s^2}{(4s^2 - 4s + 5)^2}$

Use the factorization

$$s^4 + 4a^4 = (s^2 - 2as + 2a^2)(s^2 + 2as + 2a^2)$$

to derive the inverse Laplace transforms listed in Problems 23 through 26.

23. $\mathcal{L}^{-1}\left\{\dfrac{s^3}{s^4 + 4a^4}\right\} = \cosh at \cos at$

24. $\mathcal{L}^{-1}\left\{\dfrac{s}{s^4 + 4a^4}\right\} = \dfrac{1}{2a^2} \sinh at \sin at$

25. $\mathcal{L}^{-1}\left\{\dfrac{s^2}{s^4 + 4a^4}\right\} = \dfrac{1}{2a} (\cosh at \sin at + \sinh at \cos at)$

26. $\mathcal{L}^{-1}\left\{\dfrac{1}{s^4 + 4a^4}\right\} = \dfrac{1}{4a^3} (\cosh at \sin at - \sinh at \cos at)$

Use Laplace transforms to solve the initial value problems in Problems 27 through 38.

27. $x'' + 6x' + 25x = 0$; $x(0) = 2$, $x'(0) = 3$

28. $x'' - 6x' + 8x = 2$; $x(0) = x'(0) = 0$

29. $x'' - 4x = 3t$; $x(0) = x'(0) = 0$

30. $x'' + 4x' + 8x = e^{-t}$; $x(0) = x'(0) = 0$

31. $x^{(3)} + x'' - 6x' = 0$; $x(0) = 0$, $x'(0) = x''(0) = 1$

32. $x^{(4)} - x = 0$; $x(0) = 1$, $x'(0) = x''(0) = x^{(3)}(0) = 0$

33. $x^{(4)} + x = 0$; $x(0) = x'(0) = x''(0) = 0$, $x^{(3)}(0) = 1$

34. $x^{(4)} + 13x'' + 36x = 0$; $x(0) = x''(0) = 0$, $x'(0) = 2$, $x^{(3)}(0) = -13$

35. $x^{(4)} + 8x'' + 16x = 0$; $x(0) = x'(0) = x''(0) = 0$, $x^{(3)}(0) = 1$

36. $x^{(4)} + 2x'' + x = e^{2t}$; $x(0) = x'(0) = x''(0) = x^{(3)}(0) = 0$

37. $x'' + 4x' + 13x = te^{-t}$; $x(0) = 0$, $x'(0) = 2$

38. $x'' + 6x' + 18x = \cos 2t$; $x(0) = 1$, $x'(0) = -1$

Problems 39 and 40 illustrate two types of resonance in a mass-spring-dashpot system with given external force $F(t)$ and with the initial conditions $x(0) = x'(0) = 0$.

39. Suppose that $m = 1$, $k = 9$, $c = 0$, and $F(t) = 6 \cos 3t$. Use the inverse transform given in Eq. (16) to derive the solution $x(t) = t \sin 3t$.

40. Suppose that

$$m = 1, k = 9.04, c = 0.4, \quad \text{and} \quad F(t) = 6e^{-t/5} \cos 3t.$$

Derive the solution

$$x(t) = te^{-t/5} \sin 3t.$$

Show that the maximum value of the amplitude function $A(t) = te^{-t/5}$ is $A(5) = 5/e$. Thus (as indicated in Fig. 7.3.2) the oscillations of the mass increase in amplitude during the first 5 s before being damped out as $t \to +\infty$.

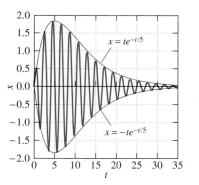

FIGURE 7.3.2. Graph of the amplitude function in Problem 40

7.3 Computing Project

Computer algebra systems can work directly with Laplace transforms. *Maple*, for instance, has the built-in functions **laplace** and **invlaplace**:

```
> laplace(t*sin(t), t, s);
```

$$2\dfrac{s}{(s^2 + 1)^2}$$

```
> invlaplace(s/(s^2 + 1)^4, s, t);
```

$$-\dfrac{1}{48} t^3 \sin(t) - \dfrac{1}{16} t^2 \cos(t) + \dfrac{1}{16} t \sin(t)$$

The corresponding *Mathematica* commands

```
LaplaceTransform[ x[t], t, s ]

InverseLaplaceTransform[ X(s), s, t ]
```

are available in the **Calculus:LaplaceTransform** package.

To illustrate the semi-automated solution of initial value problems, begin with the mass-spring-dashpot equation

```
> diffEq := m*diff(x(t),t,t) + c*diff(x(t),t) + k*x(t) = f;
```

$$diffEq := m \left(\frac{\partial^2}{\partial t^2} x(t) \right) + c \left(\frac{\partial}{\partial t} x(t) \right) + kx(t) = f$$

and introduce the parameters and force function of Problem 40 in this section:

```
> m := 1: c := 4/10: k := 904/100:
```

(The Laplace transforms in both *Maple* and *Mathematica* yield simpler expressions when rational rather than decimal number coefficients are used.)

```
> f := 6*exp(-t/5)*cos(3*t):
```

We now transform the differential equation,

```
> algEq := laplace(diffEq, t, s):
```

and substitute the zero initial conditions:

```
> algEq := subs(x(0)=0, D(x)(0)=0, algEq);
```

$$algEq := laplace(x(t),t,s)\ s^2 + \frac{2}{5} laplace(x(t),t,s)\ s$$

$$+ \frac{226}{25} laplace(x(t),t,s) = 6\ \frac{s + \dfrac{1}{5}}{\left(s + \dfrac{1}{5}\right)^2 + 9}$$

Then we solve this algebraic equation for the Laplace transform:

```
> X := simplify(solve(algEq, laplace(x(t),t,s) ));
```

$$X := 750\ \frac{5s + 1}{(25s^2 + 10s + 226)^2}$$

and ask *Maple* to invert it.

```
> x := invlaplace(X, s, t);
```

$$x := t\ e^{(-1/5\,t)}\ \sin(3t)$$

The plot command

```
> plot(x, t=0..35);
```

finally displays a solution curve like the one shown in Fig. 7.3.2.

You can apply this method to solve Problems 27 through 38 in this section. Better, solve some problems of your own construction. Damped oscillatory force functions il-

lustrate well the advantages of Laplace transforms. For instance, carry out the preceding program of calculation beginning with the external force function

$$f(t) = 2e^{-t/5}(6t \cos 3t + \sin 3t).$$

Graph both the force function $f(t)$ and the response function $x(t)$. *Question:* What force function $f(t)$ leads (with the same mass-spring-dashpot parameters and initial conditions as above) to the solution function $x(t) = t^3 e^{-t/5} \sin 3t$?

7.4 Derivatives, Integrals, and Products of Transforms

The Laplace transform of the (initially unknown) solution of a differential equation is sometimes recognizable as the product of the transforms of two *known* functions. For example, when we transform the initial value problem

$$x'' + x = \cos t; \qquad x(0) = x'(0) = 0,$$

we get

$$X(s) = \frac{s}{(s^2 + 1)^2} = \frac{s}{s^2 + 1} \cdot \frac{1}{s^2 + 1} = \mathcal{L}\{\cos t\} \cdot \mathcal{L}\{\sin t\}.$$

This strongly suggests that there ought to be a way of combining the two functions $\sin t$ and $\cos t$ to obtain a function $x(t)$ whose transform is the *product* of *their* transforms. But obviously $x(t)$ is *not* simply the product of $\cos t$ and $\sin t$, because

$$\mathcal{L}\{\cos t \sin t\} = \mathcal{L}\left\{\frac{1}{2} \sin 2t\right\} = \frac{1}{s^2 + 4} \neq \frac{s}{(s^2 + 1)^2}.$$

Thus $\mathcal{L}\{\cos t \sin t\} \neq \mathcal{L}\{\cos t\} \cdot \mathcal{L}\{\sin t\}$.

Theorem 1 of this section will tell us that the function

$$h(t) = \int_0^t f(\tau)g(t - \tau) \, d\tau \tag{1}$$

has the desired property that

$$\mathcal{L}\{h(t)\} = H(s) = F(s) \cdot G(s). \tag{2}$$

The new function of t defined as the integral in (1) depends only on f and g and is called the *convolution* of f and g. It is denoted by $f * g$, the idea being that it is a new type of product of f and g, so tailored that its transform is the product of the transforms of f and g.

DEFINITION: The Convolution of Two Functions

The **convolution** $f * g$ of the piecewise continuous functions f and g is defined for $t \geq 0$ as follows:

$$(f * g)(t) = \int_0^t f(\tau)g(t - \tau) \, d\tau. \tag{3}$$

We also write $f(t) * g(t)$ when convenient. In terms of the convolution product, Theorem 1 of this section says that

▶
$$\mathcal{L}\{f * g\} = \mathcal{L}\{f\} \cdot \mathcal{L}\{g\}.$$

If we make the substitution $u = t - \tau$ in the integral in (3), we see that

$$f(t) * g(t) = \int_0^t f(\tau)g(t - \tau) \, d\tau = \int_t^0 f(t - u)g(u)(-\, du)$$

$$= \int_0^t g(u)f(t - u) \, du = g(t) * f(t).$$

Thus the convolution is *commutative:* $f * g = g * f$.

EXAMPLE 1 The convolution of $\cos t$ and $\sin t$ is

$$(\cos t) * (\sin t) = \int_0^t \cos \tau \sin (t - \tau) \, d\tau.$$

We apply the trigonometric identity

$$\cos A \sin B = \frac{1}{2} [\sin (A + B) - \sin (A - B)]$$

to obtain

$$(\cos t) * (\sin t) = \int_0^t \frac{1}{2} [\sin t - \sin (2\tau - t)] \, d\tau$$

$$= \frac{1}{2} \left[\tau \sin t + \frac{1}{2} \cos (2\tau - t) \right]_{\tau = 0}^t ;$$

that is,

$$(\cos t) * (\sin t) = \frac{1}{2} t \sin t.$$

And we recall from Example 5 of Section 7.2 that the Laplace transform of $\frac{1}{2} t \sin t$ is indeed $s/(s^2 + 1)^2$. ∎

Theorem 1 is proved at the end of this section.

THEOREM 1: The Convolution Property

Suppose that $f(t)$ and $g(t)$ are piecewise continuous for $t \geq 0$ and that $|f(t)|$ and $|g(t)|$ are bounded by Me^{ct} as $t \to +\infty$. Then the Laplace transform of the convolution $f(t) * g(t)$ exists when $s > c$; moreover,

$$\mathcal{L}\{f(t) * g(t)\} = \mathcal{L}\{f(t)\} \cdot \mathcal{L}\{g(t)\} \tag{4}$$

and

$$\mathcal{L}^{-1}\{F(s) \cdot G(s)\} = f(t) * g(t). \tag{5}$$

∎

Thus we can find the inverse transform of the product $F(s) \cdot G(s)$, provided that we

can evaluate the integral

$$\mathcal{L}^{-1}\{F(s)\cdot G(s)\} = \int_0^t f(\tau)\, g(t - \tau)\, d\tau. \tag{5'}$$

Example 2 illustrates the fact that convolution often provides a convenient alternative to the use of partial fractions for finding inverse transforms.

EXAMPLE 2 With $f(t) = \sin 2t$ and $g(t) = e^t$, convolution yields

$$\mathcal{L}^{-1}\left\{\frac{2}{(s - 1)(s^2 + 4)}\right\} = (\sin 2t) * e^t = \int_0^t e^{t-\tau} \sin 2\tau\, d\tau = e^t \int_0^t e^{-\tau} \sin 2\tau\, d\tau$$

$$= e^t \left[\frac{e^{-\tau}}{5}\, (-\sin 2\tau - 2\cos 2\tau)\right]_0^t,$$

so

$$\mathcal{L}^{-1}\left\{\frac{2}{(s - 1)(s^2 + 4)}\right\} = \frac{2}{5}\, e^t - \frac{1}{5}\, \sin\, 2t - \frac{2}{5}\, \cos\, 2t.$$

Differentiation of Transforms

According to Theorem 1 of Section 7.2, if $f(0) = 0$ then differentiation of $f(t)$ corresponds to multiplication of its transform by s. Theorem 2, proved at the end of this section, tells us that differentiation of the transform $F(s)$ corresponds to multiplication of the original function $f(t)$ by $-t$.

THEOREM 2: Differentiation of Transforms

If $f(t)$ is piecewise continuous for $t \geq 0$ and $|f(t)| \leq Me^{ct}$ as $t \to +\infty$, then

$$\mathcal{L}\{-tf(t)\} = F'(s) \tag{6}$$

for $s > c$. Equivalently,

$$f(t) = \mathcal{L}^{-1}\{F(s)\} = -\frac{1}{t}\, \mathcal{L}^{-1}\{F'(s)\}. \tag{7}$$

Repeated application of Eq. (6) gives

$$\mathcal{L}\{t^n f(t)\} = (-1)^n F^{(n)}(s) \tag{8}$$

for $n = 1, 2, 3, \ldots$. ∎

EXAMPLE 3 Find $\mathcal{L}\{t^2 \sin kt\}$.

 Solution Equation (8) gives

$$\mathcal{L}\{t^2 \sin kt\} = (-1)^2\, \frac{d^2}{ds^2}\left(\frac{k}{s^2 + k^2}\right)$$

$$= \frac{d}{ds}\left[\frac{-2ks}{(s^2 + k^2)^2}\right] = \frac{6ks^2 - 2k^3}{(s^2 + k^2)^3}. \tag{9}$$

∎

The form of the differentiation property in Eq. (7) is often helpful in finding an inverse transform when the *derivative* of the transform is easier to work with than the transform itself.

EXAMPLE 4 Find $\mathcal{L}^{-1}\{\tan^{-1}(1/s)\}$.

Solution The derivative of $\tan^{-1}(1/s)$ is a simple rational function, so we apply Eq. (7):

$$\mathcal{L}^{-1}\left\{\tan^{-1}\frac{1}{s}\right\} = -\frac{1}{t}\mathcal{L}^{-1}\left\{\frac{d}{ds}\tan^{-1}\frac{1}{s}\right\} = -\frac{1}{t}\mathcal{L}^{-1}\left\{\frac{-1/s^2}{1+(1/s)^2}\right\}$$

$$= -\frac{1}{t}\mathcal{L}^{-1}\left\{\frac{-1}{s^2+1}\right\} = -\frac{1}{t}(-\sin t).$$

Therefore

$$\mathcal{L}^{-1}\left\{\tan^{-1}\frac{1}{s}\right\} = \frac{\sin t}{t}. \qquad\blacksquare$$

Equation (8) can be applied to transform a linear differential equation having polynomial, rather than constant, coefficients. The result will be a differential equation involving the transform; whether this procedure leads to success depends, of course, on whether we can solve the new equation more readily than the old one.

EXAMPLE 5 Let $x(t)$ be the solution of Bessel's equation of order zero,

$$tx'' + x' + tx = 0,$$

such that $x(0) = 1$ and $x'(0) = 0$. This solution of Bessel's equation is customarily denoted by $J_0(t)$. Because

$$\mathcal{L}\{x'(t)\} = sX(s) - 1 \qquad \text{and} \qquad \mathcal{L}\{x''(t)\} = s^2X(s) - s,$$

and because x and x'' are each multiplied by t, application of Eq. (7) yields the transformed equation

$$-\frac{d}{ds}[s^2X(s) - s] + [sX(s) - 1] - \frac{d}{ds}[X(s)] = 0.$$

The result of differentiation and simplification is the differential equation $(s^2 + 1)X'(s) + sX(s) = 0$. This equation is separable—

$$\frac{X'(s)}{X(s)} = -\frac{s}{s^2+1};$$

its general solution is

$$X(s) = \frac{C}{\sqrt{s^2+1}}.$$

In Problem 39 we outline the argument that $C = 1$. Because $X(s) = \mathcal{L}\{J_0(t)\}$, it follows that

$$\mathcal{L}\{J_0(t)\} = \frac{1}{\sqrt{s^2+1}}. \tag{10}$$

\blacksquare

Integration of Transforms

Differentiation of $F(s)$ corresponds to multiplication of $f(t)$ by t (together with a change of sign). It is therefore natural to expect that integration of $F(s)$ will correspond to division of $f(t)$ by t. Theorem 3, proved at the end of this section, confirms this, provided that the resulting quotient $f(t)/t$ remains "nice" as $t \to 0$; that is, provided that

$$\lim_{t \to 0^+} \frac{f(t)}{t} \quad \text{exists and is finite.} \tag{11}$$

THEOREM 3: Integration of Transforms

Suppose that $f(t)$ is piecewise continuous for $t \geq 0$, that $f(t)$ satisfies the condition in (11), and that $|f(t)| \leq Me^{ct}$ as $t \to +\infty$. Then

$$\mathscr{L}\left\{\frac{f(t)}{t}\right\} = \int_s^\infty F(\sigma)\,d\sigma \tag{12}$$

when $s > c$. Equivalently,

$$f(t) = \mathscr{L}^{-1}\{F(s)\} = t\mathscr{L}^{-1}\left\{\int_s^\infty F(\sigma)\,d\sigma\right\}. \tag{13}$$

∎

EXAMPLE 6 Find $\mathscr{L}\{(\sinh t)/t\}$.

 Solution We first verify that the condition in (11) holds:

$$\lim_{t \to 0} \frac{\sinh t}{t} = \lim_{t \to 0} \frac{e^t - e^{-t}}{2t} = \lim_{t \to 0} \frac{e^t + e^{-t}}{2} = 1,$$

with the aid of l'Hôpital's rule. Then Eq. (12), with $f(t) = \sinh t$, yields

$$\mathscr{L}\left\{\frac{\sinh t}{t}\right\} = \int_s^\infty \mathscr{L}\{\sinh t\}\,d\sigma = \int_s^\infty \frac{d\sigma}{\sigma^2 - 1}$$

$$= \frac{1}{2}\int_s^\infty \left(\frac{1}{\sigma - 1} - \frac{1}{\sigma + 1}\right)d\sigma = \frac{1}{2}\left[\ln \frac{\sigma - 1}{\sigma + 1}\right]_s^\infty.$$

Therefore

$$\mathscr{L}\left\{\frac{\sinh t}{t}\right\} = \frac{1}{2}\ln \frac{s + 1}{s - 1},$$

because $\ln 1 = 0$.

∎

 The form of the integration property in Eq.(13) is often helpful in finding an inverse transform when the indefinite *integral* of the transform is easier to handle than the transform itself.

EXAMPLE 7 Find $\mathscr{L}^{-1}\{2s/(s^2 - 1)^2\}$.

Solution We could use partial fractions, but it is much simpler to apply Eq. (13). This gives

$$\mathscr{L}^{-1}\left\{\frac{2s}{(s^2-1)^2}\right\} = t\mathscr{L}^{-1}\left\{\int_s^{\infty}\frac{2\sigma\,d\sigma}{(\sigma^2-1)^2}\right\}$$

$$= t\mathscr{L}^{-1}\left\{\left[\frac{-1}{\sigma^2-1}\right]_s^{\infty}\right\} = t\mathscr{L}^{-1}\left\{\frac{1}{s^2-1}\right\},$$

and therefore

$$\mathscr{L}^{-1}\left\{\frac{2s}{(s^2-1)^2}\right\} = t\sinh t.$$

*Proofs of Theorems

Proof of Theorem 1: The transforms $F(s)$ and $G(s)$ exist when $s > c$ by Theorem 2 of Section 7.1. The definition of the Laplace transform gives

$$G(s) = \int_0^{\infty} e^{-su}g(u)\,du = \int_{-\tau}^{\infty} e^{s(t-\tau)}g(t-\tau)\,dt \quad (u = t - \tau),$$

and therefore

$$G(s) = e^{s\tau}\int_0^{\infty} e^{-st}g(t-\tau)\,dt,$$

because we may *define $f(t)$ and $g(t)$ to be zero for $t < 0$.* Then

$$F(s)\,G(s) = G(s)\int_0^{\infty} e^{-s\tau}f(\tau)\,d\tau = \int_0^{\infty} e^{-s\tau}f(\tau)\,G(s)\,d\tau$$

$$= \int_0^{\infty} e^{-s\tau}f(\tau)\left(e^{s\tau}\int_0^{\infty} e^{-st}g(t-\tau)\,dt\right)d\tau$$

$$= \int_0^{\infty}\left(\int_0^{\infty} e^{-st}f(\tau)g(t-\tau)\,dt\right)d\tau.$$

Now our hypotheses on f and g imply that the order of integration may be reversed. (The proof of this requires a discussion of uniform convergence of improper integrals, and can be found in Chapter 2 of Churchill's *Operational Mathematics,* 3rd ed. (New York: McGraw-Hill, 1972).) Hence

$$F(s)\,G(s) = \int_0^{\infty}\left(\int_0^{\infty} e^{-st}f(\tau)g(t-\tau)\,d\tau\right)dt$$

$$= \int_0^{\infty} e^{-st}\left(\int_0^t f(\tau)g(t-\tau)\,d\tau\right)dt$$

$$= \int_0^{\infty} e^{-st}[f(t)*g(t)]\,dt,$$

and therefore,

$$F(s)\,G(s) = \mathscr{L}\{f(t)*g(t)\}.$$

We replaced the upper limit of the inner integral with t because $g(t - \tau) = 0$ whenever $\tau > t$. This completes the proof of Theorem 1. ∎

Proof of Theorem 2: Because

$$F(s) = \int_0^\infty e^{-st} f(t)\, dt,$$

differentiation under the integral sign yields

$$F'(s) = \frac{d}{ds} \int_0^\infty e^{-st} f(t)\, dt$$

$$= \int_0^\infty \frac{d}{ds} [e^{-st} f(t)]\, dt = \int_0^\infty e^{-st} [-tf(t)]\, dt;$$

thus

$$F'(s) = \mathcal{L}\{-tf(t)\},$$

which is Eq. (6). We obtain Eq. (7) by applying \mathcal{L}^{-1} and then dividing by $-t$. The validity of differentiation under the integral sign depends upon uniform convergence of the resulting integral; this is discussed in Chapter 2 of the book by Churchill just mentioned. ∎

Proof of Theorem 3: By definition,

$$F(\sigma) = \int_0^\infty e^{-\sigma t} f(t)\, dt.$$

So integration of $F(\sigma)$ from s to $+\infty$ gives

$$\int_s^\infty F(\sigma)\, d\sigma = \int_s^\infty \left(\int_0^\infty e^{-\sigma t} f(t)\, dt \right) d\sigma.$$

Under the hypotheses of the theorem, the order of integration may be reversed (see Churchill's book again); it follows that

$$\int_s^\infty F(\sigma)\, d\sigma = \int_0^\infty \left(\int_s^\infty e^{-\sigma t} f(t)\, d\sigma \right) dt$$

$$= \int_0^\infty \left[\frac{e^{-\sigma t}}{-t} \right]_{\sigma=s}^\infty f(t)\, dt$$

$$= \int_0^\infty e^{-st} \frac{f(t)}{t}\, dt = \mathcal{L}\left\{ \frac{f(t)}{t} \right\}.$$

This verifies Eq. (12), and Eq. (13) follows upon first applying \mathcal{L}^{-1} and then multiplying by t. ∎

7.4 Problems

Find the convolution $f(t) * g(t)$ in Problems 1 through 6.

1. $f(t) = t$, $g(t) \equiv 1$ **2.** $f(t) = t$, $g(t) = e^{at}$

3. $f(t) = g(t) = \sin t$ **4.** $f(t) = t^2$, $g(t) = \cos t$

5. $f(t) = g(t) = e^{at}$

6. $f(t) = e^{at}$, $g(t) = e^{bt}$ $(a \neq b)$

Apply the convolution theorem to find the inverse Laplace transforms of the functions in Problems 7 through 14.

7. $F(s) = \dfrac{1}{s(s-3)}$ **8.** $F(s) = \dfrac{1}{s(s^2+4)}$

9. $F(s) = \dfrac{1}{(s^2+9)^2}$ **10.** $F(s) = \dfrac{1}{s^2(s^2+k^2)}$

11. $F(s) = \dfrac{s^2}{(s^2+4)^2}$ **12.** $F(s) = \dfrac{1}{s(s^2+4s+5)}$

13. $F(s) = \dfrac{s}{(s-3)(s^2+1)}$ **14.** $F(s) = \dfrac{s}{s^4+5s^2+4}$

In Problems 15 through 22, apply either Theorem 2 or Theorem 3 to find the Laplace transform of $f(t)$.

15. $f(t) = t \sin 3t$ **16.** $f(t) = t^2 \cos 2t$

17. $f(t) = te^{2t} \cos 3t$ **18.** $f(t) = te^{-t} \sin^2 t$

19. $f(t) = \dfrac{\sin t}{t}$ **20.** $f(t) = \dfrac{1 - \cos 2t}{t}$

21. $f(t) = \dfrac{e^{3t} - 1}{t}$ **22.** $f(t) = \dfrac{e^t - e^{-t}}{t}$

Find the inverse transforms of the functions in Problems 23 through 28.

23. $F(s) = \ln \dfrac{s-2}{s+2}$ **24.** $F(s) = \ln \dfrac{s^2+1}{s^2+4}$

25. $F(s) = \ln \dfrac{s^2+1}{(s+2)(s-3)}$ **26.** $F(s) = \tan^{-1} \dfrac{3}{s+2}$

27. $F(s) = \ln\left(1 + \dfrac{1}{s^2}\right)$ **28.** $F(s) = \dfrac{s}{(s^2+1)^3}$

In Problems 29 through 34, transform the given differential equation to find a nontrivial solution such that $x(0) = 0$.

29. $tx'' + (t-2)x' + x = 0$

30. $tx'' + (3t-1)x' + 3x = 0$

31. $tx'' - (4t+1)x' + 2(2t+1)x = 0$

32. $tx'' + 2(t-1)x' - 2x = 0$

33. $tx'' - 2x' + tx = 0$

34. $tx'' + (4t-2)x' + (13t-4)x = 0$

35. Apply the convolution theorem to show that

$$\mathcal{L}^{-1}\left\{\frac{1}{(s-1)\sqrt{s}}\right\} = \frac{2e^t}{\sqrt{\pi}} \int_0^{\sqrt{t}} e^{-u^2}\, du = e^t \operatorname{erf} \sqrt{t}.$$

(*Suggestion:* Substitute $u = \sqrt{t}$.)

In Problems 36 through 38, apply the convolution theorem to derive the indicated solution $x(t)$ of the given differential equation with initial conditions $x(0) = x'(0) = 0$.

36. $x'' + 4x = f(t)$; $x(t) = \dfrac{1}{2} \displaystyle\int_0^t f(t-\tau) \sin 2\tau \, d\tau$

37. $x'' + 2x' + x = f(t)$; $x(t) = \displaystyle\int_0^t \tau e^{-\tau} f(t-\tau)\, d\tau$

38. $x'' + 4x' + 13x = f(t)$;

$$x(t) = \frac{1}{3}\int_0^t f(t-\tau)e^{-2\tau}\sin 3\tau \, d\tau$$

Termwise Inverse Transformation of Series

In Chapter 2 of Churchill's *Operational Mathematics,* the following theorem is proved. Suppose that $f(t)$ is continuous for $t \geq 0$, that $f(t)$ is of exponential order at $t \to +\infty$, and that

$$F(s) = \sum_{n=0}^{\infty} \frac{a_n}{s^{n+k+1}}$$

where $0 \leq k < 1$ and the series converges absolutely for $s > c$. Then

$$f(t) = \sum_{n=0}^{\infty} \frac{a_n t^{n+k}}{\Gamma(n+k+1)}.$$

Apply this result in Problems 39 through 41.

39. In Example 5 it was shown that

$$\mathcal{L}\{J_0(t)\} = \frac{C}{\sqrt{s^2+1}} = \frac{C}{s}\left(1 + \frac{1}{s^2}\right)^{-1/2}.$$

Expand with the aid of the binomial series and then compute the inverse transformation term by term to obtain

$$J_0(t) = C \sum_{n=0}^{\infty} \frac{(-1)^n t^{2n}}{2^{2n} (n!)^2}.$$

Finally note that $J_0(0) = 1$ implies that $C = 1$.

40. Expand the function $F(s) = s^{-1/2}e^{-1/s}$ in powers of s^{-1} to show that

$$\mathcal{L}^{-1}\left\{\frac{1}{\sqrt{s}}e^{-1/s}\right\} = \frac{1}{\sqrt{\pi t}}\cos 2\sqrt{t}.$$

41. Show that

$$\mathcal{L}^{-1}\left\{\frac{1}{s}e^{-1/s}\right\} = J_0(2\sqrt{t}).$$

*7.5 Periodic and Piecewise Continuous Input Functions

FIGURE 7.5.1. Graph of the unit step function at $t = a$

Mathematical models of mechanical or electrical systems often involve functions with discontinuities corresponding to external forces that are turned abruptly on or off. One such simple off-on function is the **unit step function** at $t = a$; its formula is

$$u_a(t) = u(t - a) = \begin{cases} 0 & \text{if } t < a, \\ 1 & \text{if } t \geq a, \end{cases} \tag{1}$$

and its graph appears in Fig. 7.5.1.

In Example 8 of Section 7.1 we saw that if $a \geq 0$, then

$$\mathcal{L}\{u(t - a)\} = \frac{e^{-as}}{s}. \tag{2}$$

Because $\mathcal{L}\{u(t)\} = 1/s$, Eq. (2) implies that multiplication of the transform of $u(t)$ by e^{-as} corresponds to the translation $t \to t - a$ in the original independent variable. Theorem 1 tells us that this fact, when properly interpreted, is a general property of the Laplace transformation.

THEOREM 1: Translation on the t-Axis

If $\mathcal{L}\{f(t)\}$ exists for $s > c$, then

$$\mathcal{L}\{u(t - a)f(t - a)\} = e^{-as}F(s) \tag{3a}$$

and

$$\mathcal{L}^{-1}\{e^{-as}F(s)\} = u(t - a)f(t - a) \tag{3b}$$

when $s > c + a$. ∎

Note that

$$u(t - a)f(t - a) = \begin{cases} 0 & \text{if } t < a, \\ f(t - a) & \text{if } t \geq a. \end{cases} \tag{4}$$

Thus Theorem 1 implies that $\mathcal{L}^{-1}\{e^{-as}F(s)\}$ is the function whose graph for $t \geq a$ is the translation a units to the right of the graph of $f(t)$. Note that the part of the graph of $f(t)$ to the left of $t = 0$ is cut off and not translated (Fig. 7.5.2).

Proof of Theorem 1: From the definition of $\mathcal{L}\{f(t)\}$, we get

$$e^{-as}F(s) = e^{-as}\int_0^\infty e^{-s\tau}f(\tau)\,d\tau = \int_0^\infty e^{-s(\tau + a)}f(\tau)\,d\tau.$$

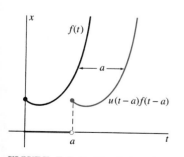

FIGURE 7.5.2. Translation of $f(t)$ a units to the right

The substitution $t = \tau + a$ then yields

$$e^{-as} F(s) = \int_a^\infty e^{-st} f(t - a)\, dt.$$

From Eq. (4) we see that this is the same as

$$e^{-as} F(s) = \int_a^\infty e^{-st} u(t - a) f(t - a)\, dt = \mathcal{L}\{u(t - a) f(t - a)\},$$

because $u(t - a) f(t - a) = 0$ for $t < a$. We have therefore completed the proof of Theorem 1. ∎

EXAMPLE 1 With $f(t) = \frac{1}{2} t^2$, Theorem 1 gives

$$\mathcal{L}^{-1}\left\{\frac{e^{-as}}{s^3}\right\} = u(t - a)\frac{1}{2}(t - a)^2 = \begin{cases} 0 & \text{if } t < a, \\ \frac{1}{2}(t - a)^2 & \text{if } t \le a \end{cases} \qquad \text{(Fig. 7.5.3)}.$$

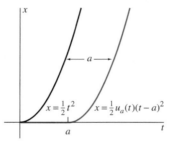

FIGURE 7.5.3. The graph of the inverse transform of Example 1

EXAMPLE 2 Find $\mathcal{L}\{g(t)\}$ if

$$g(t) = \begin{cases} 0 & \text{if } t < 3, \\ t^2 & \text{if } t \ge 3 \end{cases} \qquad \text{(Fig. 7.5.4)}.$$

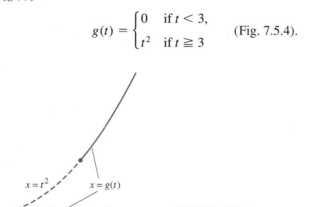

FIGURE 7.5.4. The graph of the function $g(t)$ of Example 2

Solution Before applying Theorem 1, we must first write $g(t)$ in the form $u(t - 3)f(t - 3)$. The function $f(t)$ whose translation 3 units to the right agrees (for $t \ge 3$) with $g(t) = t^2$ is $f(t) = (t + 3)^2$ because $f(t - 3) = t^2$. But then

$$F(s) = \mathcal{L}\{t^2 + 6t + 9\} = \frac{2}{s^3} + \frac{6}{s^2} + \frac{9}{s},$$

so now Theorem 1 yields

$$\mathcal{L}\{g(t)\} = \mathcal{L}\{u(t-3)f(t-3)\} = e^{-3s}F(s) = e^{-3s}\left(\frac{2}{s^3} + \frac{6}{s^2} + \frac{9}{s}\right).$$

EXAMPLE 3 Find $\mathcal{L}\{f(t)\}$ if

$$f(t) = \begin{cases} \cos 2t & \text{if } 0 \le t < 2\pi, \\ 0 & \text{if } t \ge 2\pi. \end{cases} \qquad \text{(Fig. 7.5.5)}.$$

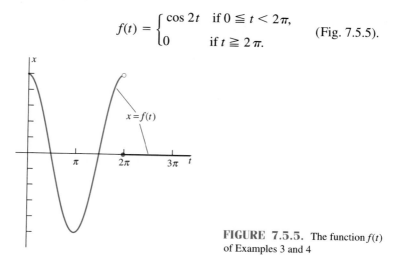

FIGURE 7.5.5. The function $f(t)$ of Examples 3 and 4

Solution We note first that

$$f(t) = [1 - u(t - 2\pi)]\cos 2t = \cos 2t - u(t - 2\pi)\cos 2(t - 2\pi)$$

because of the periodicity of the cosine function. Hence Theorem 1 gives

$$\mathcal{L}\{f(t)\} = \mathcal{L}\{\cos 2t\} - e^{-2\pi s}\mathcal{L}\{\cos 2t\} = \frac{s(1 - e^{-2\pi s})}{s^2 + 4}.$$

EXAMPLE 4 A mass that weighs 32 lb (mass $m = 1$ slug) is attached to the free end of a long light spring that is stretched 1 ft by a force of 4 lb ($k = 4$ lb/ft). The mass is initially at rest in its equilibrium position. Beginning at time $t = 0$ (seconds), an external force $F(t) = \cos 2t$ is applied to the mass, but at time $t = 2\pi$ this force is turned off (abruptly discontinued) and the mass is allowed to continue its motion unimpeded. Find the resulting position function $x(t)$ of the mass.

Solution We need to solve the initial value problem

$$x'' + 4x = f(t); \qquad x(0) = x'(0) = 0,$$

where $f(t)$ is the function of Example 3. The transformed equation is

$$(s^2 + 4)X(s) = F(s) = \frac{s(1 - e^{-2\pi s})}{s^2 + 4},$$

so

$$X(s) = \frac{s}{(s^2 + 4)^2} - e^{-2\pi s}\frac{s}{(s^2 + 4)^2}.$$

Because

$$\mathcal{L}^{-1}\left\{\frac{2}{(s^2 + 4)^2}\right\} = \frac{1}{4} t \sin 2t$$

by Eq. (16) of Section 7.3, it follows from Theorem 1 that

$$x(t) = \frac{1}{4} t \sin 2t - u(t - 2\pi) \cdot \frac{1}{4}(t - 2\pi) \sin 2(t - 2\pi)$$

$$= \frac{1}{4} [t - u(t - 2\pi) \cdot (t - 2\pi)] \sin 2t.$$

If we separate the cases $t < 2\pi$ and $t \geqq 2\pi$, we find that the position function may be written in the form

$$x(t) = \begin{cases} \frac{1}{4} t \sin 2t & \text{if } t < 2\pi, \\ \frac{1}{2}\pi \sin 2t & \text{if } t \geqq 2\pi. \end{cases}$$

As indicated by the graph of $x(t)$ shown in Fig. 7.5.6, the mass oscillates with circular frequency $\omega = 2$ and with linearly increasing amplitude until the force is removed at time $t = 2\pi$. Thereafter, the mass continues to oscillate with the same frequency but with constant amplitude $\pi/2$. The force $F(t) = \cos 2t$ would produce pure resonance if continued indefinitely, but we see that its effect ceases immediately when it is turned off. ∎

FIGURE 7.5.6. The graph of the function $x(t)$ of Example 4.

If we were to attack Example 4 with the methods of Chapter 3, we would need to solve one problem for the interval $0 \leqq t < 2\pi$ and then solve a new problem with different initial conditions for the interval $t \geqq 2\pi$. In such a situation the Laplace transform method enjoys the distinct advantage of not requiring the solution of different problems on different intervals.

EXAMPLE 5 Consider the RLC circuit shown in Fig. 7.5.7, with $R = 110\ \Omega$, $L = 1$ H, $C = 0.001$ F, and a battery supplying $E_0 = 90$ V. Initially there is no current in the circuit and no charge on the capacitor. At time $t = 0$ the switch is closed and left closed for 1 second. At time $t = 1$ it is opened and left open. Find the resulting current in the circuit.

Solution We recall from Section 3.7 the basic series circuit equation

$$L\frac{di}{dt} + Ri + \frac{1}{C}q = e(t); \tag{5}$$

we use lowercase letters for current, charge, and voltage and reserve uppercase letters for their transforms. With the given circuit elements, Eq. (5) is

$$\frac{di}{dt} + 110i + 1000q = e(t), \tag{6}$$

FIGURE 7.5.7. The series RLC circuit of Example 5

where $e(t) = 90[1 - u(t - 1)]$, corresponding to the opening and closing of the switch.

In Section 3.7 our strategy was to differentiate both sides of Eq. (5), then apply the relation

$$i = \frac{dq}{dt} \tag{7}$$

to obtain the second-order equation

$$L\frac{d^2i}{dt^2} + R\frac{di}{dt} + \frac{1}{C}i = e'(t).$$

Here we do not use that method, because $e'(t) = 0$ except at $t = 1$, whereas the jump from $e(t) = 90$ when $t < 1$ to $e(t) = 0$ when $t > 1$ would seem to require that $e'(1) = -\infty$. Thus $e'(t)$ seems to have an infinite discontinuity at $t = 1$. This phenomenon will be discussed in Section 7.6. For now, we will simply note that it is an odd situation and circumvent it rather than attempt to deal with it here.

In order to avoid the possible problem at $t = 1$, we observe that the initial value $q(0) = 0$ and Eq. (7) yield, upon integration,

$$q(t) = \int_0^t i(\tau)\,d\tau. \tag{8}$$

We substitute Eq. (8) in Eq. (5) to obtain

$$L\frac{di}{dt} + Ri + \frac{1}{C}\int_0^t i(\tau)\,d\tau = e(t). \tag{9}$$

This is the **integrodifferential equation** of a series RLC circuit; it involves both the integral and the derivative of the unknown function $i(t)$. The Laplace transform method works well with such an equation.

In the present example, Eq. (9) is

$$\frac{di}{dt} + 110i + 1000\int_0^t i(\tau)\,d\tau = 90[1 - u(t - 1)]. \tag{10}$$

Because

$$\mathcal{L}\left\{\int_0^t i(\tau)\,d\tau\right\} = \frac{I(s)}{s}$$

by Theorem 2 of Section 7.2 on transforms of integrals, the transformed equation is

$$sI(s) + 110I(s) + 1000\frac{I(s)}{s} = \frac{90}{s}(1 - e^{-s}).$$

We solve this equation for $I(s)$ to obtain

$$I(s) = \frac{90(1 - e^{-s})}{s^2 + 110s + 1000}.$$

But

$$\frac{90}{s^2 + 110s + 1000} = \frac{1}{s + 10} - \frac{1}{s + 100},$$

so we have

$$I(s) = \frac{1}{s + 10} - \frac{1}{s + 100} - e^{-s}\left(\frac{1}{s + 10} - \frac{1}{s + 100}\right).$$

We now apply Theorem 1 with $f(t) = e^{-10t} - e^{-100t}$; thus the inverse transform is

$$i(t) = e^{-10t} - e^{-100t} - u(t-1)[e^{-10(t-1)} - e^{-100(t-1)}].$$

After we separate the cases $t < 1$ and $t \geq 1$, we find that the current in the circuit is given by

$$i(t) = \begin{cases} e^{-10t} - e^{-100t} & \text{if } t < 1, \\ e^{-10t} - e^{-10(t-1)} - e^{-100t} + e^{-100(t-1)} & \text{if } t \geq 1. \end{cases}$$

The portion $e^{-10t} - e^{-100t}$ of the solution would describe the current if the switch were left closed for all t rather than being open for $t \geq 1$.

Transforms of Periodic Functions

FIGURE 7.5.8. The graph of a function with period p

Periodic forcing functions in practical mechanical or electrical systems often are more complicated than pure sines or cosines. The nonconstant function $f(t)$ defined for $t \geq 0$ is said to be **periodic** if there is a number $p > 0$ such that

$$f(t + p) = f(t) \tag{11}$$

for all $t \geq 0$. The least positive value of p (if any) for which Eq. (11) holds is called the **period** of f. Such a function is shown in Fig. 7.5.8. Theorem 2 simplifies the computation of the Laplace transform of a periodic function.

■ **THEOREM 2: Transforms of Periodic Functions**

Let $f(t)$ be periodic with period p and piecewise continuous for $t \geq 0$. Then the transform $F(s) = \mathcal{L}\{f(t)\}$ exists for $s > 0$, and is given by

$$F(s) = \frac{1}{1 - e^{-ps}} \int_0^p e^{-st} f(t)\, dt. \tag{12}$$

Proof: The definition of the Laplace transform gives

$$F(s) = \int_0^\infty e^{-st} f(t)\, dt = \sum_{n=0}^\infty \int_{np}^{(n+1)p} e^{-st} f(t)\, dt.$$

The substitution $t = \tau + np$ in the nth integral following the summation sign yields

$$\int_{np}^{(n+1)p} e^{-st} f(t)\, dt = \int_0^p e^{-s(\tau + np)} f(\tau + np)\, d\tau = e^{-nps} \int_0^p e^{-s\tau} f(\tau)\, d\tau$$

because $f(\tau + np) = f(\tau)$ by periodicity. Thus

$$F(s) = \sum_{n=0}^\infty \left(e^{-nps} \int_0^p e^{-s\tau} f(\tau)\, d\tau \right) = (1 + e^{-ps} + e^{-2ps} + \cdots) \int_0^p e^{-s\tau} f(\tau)\, d\tau.$$

Consequently,

$$F(s) = \frac{1}{1 - e^{-ps}} \int_0^p e^{-s\tau} f(\tau)\, d\tau.$$

We used the geometric series

$$\frac{1}{1-x} = 1 + x + x^2 + x^3 + \cdots,$$

with $x = e^{-ps} < 1$ (for $s > 0$) to sum the series in the final step. Thus we have derived Eq. (12). ∎

The principal advantage of Theorem 2 is that it enables us to find the Laplace transform of a periodic function without the necessity of an explicit evaluation of an improper integral.

EXAMPLE 6 Figure 7.5.9 shows the graph of the square wave function $f(t) = (-1)^{\llbracket a t \rrbracket}$ of period $p = 2a$; $\llbracket x \rrbracket$ denotes the greatest integer not exceeding x. By Theorem 2 the Laplace transform of $f(t)$ is

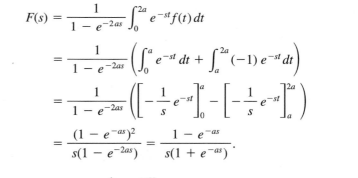

$$F(s) = \frac{1}{1 - e^{-2as}} \int_0^{2a} e^{-st} f(t)\, dt$$

$$= \frac{1}{1 - e^{-2as}} \left(\int_0^a e^{-st}\, dt + \int_a^{2a} (-1) e^{-st}\, dt \right)$$

$$= \frac{1}{1 - e^{-2as}} \left(\left[-\frac{1}{s} e^{-st} \right]_0^a - \left[-\frac{1}{s} e^{-st} \right]_a^{2a} \right)$$

$$= \frac{(1 - e^{-as})^2}{s(1 - e^{-2as})} = \frac{1 - e^{-as}}{s(1 + e^{-as})}.$$

$f(t)$	

FIGURE **7.5.9.** The graph of the square wave function of Example 6

Therefore,

$$F(s) = \frac{1 - e^{-as}}{s(1 + e^{-as})} \tag{13a}$$

$$= \frac{e^{as/2} - e^{-as/2}}{s(e^{as/2} + e^{-as/2})} = \frac{1}{s} \tanh \frac{as}{2}. \tag{13b}$$

EXAMPLE 7 Figure 7.5.10 shows the graph of a triangular wave function $g(t)$ of period $p = 2a$. Because the derivative $g'(t)$ is the square wave function of Example 6, it follows from the formula in (13b) and Theorem 2 of Section 7.2 that the transform of this triangular wave function is

$$G(s) = \frac{F(s)}{s} = \frac{1}{s^2} \tanh \frac{as}{2}. \tag{14}$$

FIGURE **7.5.10.** The graph of the triangular wave function of Example 7

EXAMPLE 8 Consider a mass-spring-dashpot system with $m = 1$, $c = 4$, and $k = 20$ in appropriate units. Suppose that the system is initially at rest at equilibrium ($x(0) = x'(0) = 0$) and that the mass is acted on beginning at time $t = 0$ by the external force $f(t)$ whose

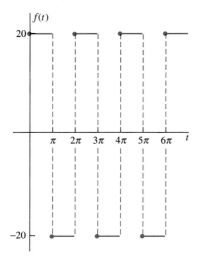

FIGURE 7.5.11. The graph of the external force function of Example 8

graph is shown in Fig. 7.5.11: the square wave with amplitude 20 and period 2π. Find the position function $x(t)$.

Solution The initial value problem is

$$x'' + 4x' + 20x = f(t); \qquad x(0) = x'(0) = 0.$$

The transformed equation is

$$s^2 X(s) + 4sX(s) + 20X(s) = F(s). \qquad (15)$$

From Example 6 with $a = \pi$ we see that the transform of $f(t)$ is

$$\begin{aligned} F(s) &= \frac{20}{s} \cdot \frac{1 - e^{-\pi s}}{1 + e^{-\pi s}} \\ &= \frac{20}{s}(1 - e^{-\pi s})(1 - e^{-\pi s} + e^{-2\pi s} - e^{-3\pi s} + \cdots) \\ &= \frac{20}{s}(1 - 2e^{-\pi s} + 2e^{-2\pi s} - 2e^{-3\pi s} + \cdots), \end{aligned}$$

so that

$$F(s) = \frac{20}{s} + \frac{40}{s} \sum_{n=1}^{\infty} (-1)^n e^{-n\pi s}. \qquad (16)$$

Substitution of Eq. (16) in Eq. (15) yields

$$\begin{aligned} X(s) &= \frac{F(s)}{s^2 + 4s + 16} \\ &= \frac{20}{s[(s + 2)^2 + 16]} + 2 \sum_{n=1}^{\infty} (-1)^n \frac{20 e^{-n\pi s}}{s[(s + 2)^2 + 16]}. \end{aligned} \qquad (17)$$

From the transform in Eq. (8) of Section 7.3, we get

$$\mathcal{L}^{-1}\left\{\frac{20}{(s + 2)^2 + 16}\right\} = 5e^{-2t} \sin 4t,$$

so by Theorem 2 of Section 7.2 we have

$$g(t) = \mathcal{L}^{-1}\left\{\frac{20}{s[(s + 2)^2 + 16]}\right\} = \int_0^t 5e^{-2\tau} \sin 4\tau \, d\tau.$$

Using a tabulated formula for $\int e^{at} \sin bt \, dt$, we get

$$g(t) = 1 - e^{-2t}(\cos 4t + \tfrac{1}{2} \sin 4t) = 1 - h(t), \qquad (18)$$

where

$$h(t) = e^{-2t}(\cos 4t + \tfrac{1}{2} \sin 4t). \qquad (19)$$

Now we apply Theorem 1 to find the inverse transform of the right-hand term in Eq. (17). The result is

$$x(t) = g(t) + 2 \sum_{n=1}^{\infty} (-1)^n u(t - n\pi) g(t - n\pi), \qquad (20)$$

and we note that for any fixed value of t the sum in Eq. (20) is finite. Moreover,

$$g(t - n\pi) = 1 - e^{-2(t - n\pi)}\left[\cos 4(t - n\pi) + \frac{1}{2}\sin 4(t - n\pi)\right]$$

$$= 1 - e^{2n\pi}e^{-2t}(\cos 4t + \frac{1}{2}\sin 4t).$$

Therefore,

$$g(t - n\pi) = 1 - e^{2n\pi}h(t). \tag{21}$$

Hence if $0 < t < \pi$, then

$$x(t) = 1 - h(t).$$

If $\pi < t < 2\pi$, then

$$x(t) = [1 - h(t)] - 2[1 - e^{2\pi}h(t)] = -1 + h(t) - 2h(t)[1 - e^{2\pi}].$$

If $2\pi < t < 3\pi$, then

$$x(t) = [1 - h(t)] - 2[1 - e^{2\pi}h(t)] + 2[1 - e^{4\pi}h(t)]$$

$$= 1 + h(t) - 2h(t)[1 - e^{2\pi} + e^{4\pi}].$$

The general expression for $n\pi < t < (n + 1)\pi$ is

$$x(t) = h(t) + (-1)^n - 2h(t)[1 - e^{2\pi} + \cdots + (-1)^n e^{2n\pi}]$$

$$= h(t) + (-1)^n - 2h(t)\frac{1 + (-1)^n e^{2(n+1)\pi}}{1 + e^{2\pi}}, \tag{22}$$

which we obtained with the aid of the familiar formula for the sum of a finite geometric progression. A rearrangement of Eq. (22) finally gives, with the aid of Eq. (19)

$$x(t) = \frac{e^{2\pi} - 1}{e^{2\pi} + 1} e^{-2t}\left(\cos 4t + \frac{1}{2}\sin 4t\right) + (-1)^n$$

$$- \frac{2 \cdot (-1)^n e^{2\pi}}{e^{2\pi} + 1} e^{-2(t - n\pi)}\left(\cos 4t + \frac{1}{2}\sin 4t\right) \tag{23}$$

for $n\pi < t < (n + 1)\pi$. The first term in Eq. (23) is the transient solution

$$x_{tr}(t) \approx (0.9963) e^{-2t}\left(\cos 4t + \frac{1}{2}\sin 4t\right) \approx (1.1139) e^{-2t}\cos(4t - 0.4636). \tag{24}$$

The last two terms in Eq. (23) give the steady periodic solution x_{sp}. To investigate it, we write $\tau = t - n\pi$ for t in the interval $n\pi < t < (n + 1)\pi$. Then

$$x_{sp}(t) = (-1)^n\left[1 - \frac{2e^{2\pi}}{e^{2\pi} + 1} e^{-2\tau}\left(\cos 4\tau + \frac{1}{2}\sin 4\tau\right)\right] \tag{25}$$

$$\approx (-1)^n[1 - (2.2319) e^{-2\tau}\cos(4\tau - 0.4636)].$$

Figure 7.5.12 shows that graph of $x_{sp}(t)$. Its most interesting feature is the appearance of periodically damped oscillations with a frequency *four times* that of the imposed

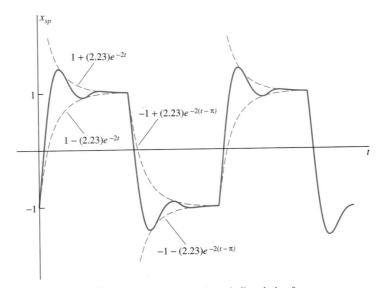

FIGURE 7.5.12. The graph of the steady periodic solution for Example 8; note the "periodically damped" oscillations with frequency four times that of the imposed force.

force $f(t)$. In Chapter 9 (Fourier Series) we will see why a periodic external force sometimes excites oscillations at a higher frequency than the imposed frequency. ■

7.5 Problems

Find the inverse Laplace transform $f(t)$ of the functions given in Problems 1 through 10, and sketch the graph of $f(t)$.

1. $F(s) = \dfrac{e^{-3s}}{s^2}$

2. $F(s) = \dfrac{e^{-s} - e^{-3s}}{s^2}$

3. $F(s) = \dfrac{e^{-s}}{s + 2}$

4. $F(s) = \dfrac{e^{-s} - e^{2-2s}}{s - 1}$

5. $F(s) = \dfrac{e^{-\pi s}}{s^2 + 1}$

6. $F(s) = \dfrac{se^{-s}}{s^2 + \pi^2}$

7. $F(s) = \dfrac{1 - e^{-2\pi s}}{s^2 + 1}$

8. $F(s) = \dfrac{s(1 - e^{-2s})}{s^2 + \pi^2}$

9. $F(s) = \dfrac{s(1 + e^{-3s})}{s^2 + \pi^2}$

10. $F(s) = \dfrac{2s(e^{-\pi s} - e^{-2\pi s})}{s^2 + 4}$

Find the Laplace transform of the functions given in Problems 11 through 22.

11. $f(t) = 2$ if $0 \le t < 3$; $f(t) = 0$ if $t \ge 3$

12. $f(t) = 3$ if $1 \le t \le 4$; $f(t) = 0$ if $t < 1$ or if $t > 4$

13. $f(t) = \sin t$ if $0 \le t \le 2\pi$; $f(t) = 0$ if $t > 2\pi$

14. $f(t) = \cos \pi t$ if $0 \le t \le 2$; $f(t) = 0$ if $t > 2$

15. $f(t) = \sin t$ if $0 \le t \le 3\pi$; $f(t) = 0$ if $t > 3\pi$

16. $f(t) = \sin 2t$ if $\pi \le t \le 2\pi$; $f(t) = 0$ if $t < \pi$ or if $t > 2\pi$

17. $f(t) = \sin \pi t$ if $2 \le t \le 3$; $f(t) = 0$ if $t < 2$ or if $t > 3$

18. $f(t) = \cos \frac{1}{2}\pi t$ if $3 \le t \le 5$; $f(t) = 0$ if $t < 3$ or if $t > 5$

19. $f(t) = 0$ if $t < 1$; $f(t) = t$ if $t \ge 1$

20. $f(t) = t$ if $t \le 1$; $f(t) = 1$ if $t > 1$

21. $f(t) = t$ if $t \le 1$; $f(t) = 2 - t$ if $1 \le t \le 2$; $f(t) = 0$ if $t > 2$

22. $f(t) = t^3$ if $1 \le t \le 2$; $f(t) = 0$ if $t < 1$ or if $t > 2$

23. Apply Theorem 2 with $p = 1$ to verify that $\mathcal{L}\{1\} = 1/s$.

24. Apply Theorem 2 to verify that $\mathcal{L}\{\cos kt\} = s/(s^2 + k^2)$.

25. Apply Theorem 2 to show that the Laplace transform of the square wave function of Fig. 7.5.13 is

$$\mathscr{L}\{f(t)\} = \frac{1}{s(1 + e^{-as})}.$$

FIGURE 7.5.13. The graph of the square wave function of Problem 25

26. Apply Theorem 2 to show that the Laplace transform of the sawtooth function $f(t)$ of Fig. 7.5.14 is

$$F(s) = \frac{1}{as^2} - \frac{e^{-as}}{s(1 - e^{-as})}.$$

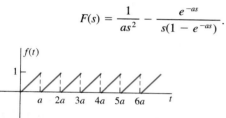

FIGURE 7.5.14. The graph of the sawtooth function of Problem 26

27. Let $g(t)$ be the staircase function of Fig. 7.5.15. Show that $g(t) = (t/a) - f(t)$, where $f(t)$ is the sawtooth function of Fig. 7.5.14, and hence deduce that

$$\mathscr{L}\{g(t)\} = \frac{e^{-as}}{s(1 - e^{-as})}.$$

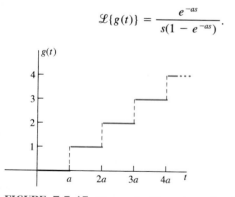

FIGURE 7.5.15. The graph of the staircase function of Problem 27

28. Suppose that $f(t)$ is a periodic function of period $2a$ with $f(t) = t$ if $0 \leq t < a$ and $f(t) = 0$ if $a \leq t < 2a$. Find $\mathscr{L}\{f(t)\}$.

29. Suppose that $f(t)$ is the half-wave rectification of $\sin kt$, shown in Fig. 7.5.16. Show that

$$\mathscr{L}\{f(t)\} = \frac{k}{(s^2 + k^2)(1 - e^{-\pi s/k})}.$$

FIGURE 7.5.16. The half-wave rectification of $\sin kt$

30. Let $g(t) = u(t - \pi/k)f(t - \pi/k)$, where $f(t)$ is the function of Problem 29. Note that $h(t) = f(t) + g(t)$ is the full-wave rectification of $\sin kt$ shown in Fig. 7.5.17. Hence deduce from Problem 29 that

$$\mathscr{L}\{h(t)\} = \frac{k}{s^2 + k^2} \coth \frac{\pi s}{2k}.$$

FIGURE 7.5.17. The full-wave rectification of $\sin kt$

In Problems 31 through 35, the values of mass m, spring constant k, dashpot resistance c, and force $f(t)$ are given for a mass-spring-dashpot system with external forcing function. Solve the initial value problem

$$mx'' + cx' + kx = f(t);$$

$$x(0) = 0 = x'(0)$$

with the given data.

31. $m = 1$, $k = 4$, $c = 0$; $f(t) = 1$ if $0 \leq t < \pi$, $f(t) = 0$ if $t > \pi$

32. $m = 1$, $k = 4$, $c = 5$; $f(t) = 1$ if $0 \leq t < 2$, $f(t) = 0$ if $t > 2$

33. $m = 1$, $k = 9$, $c = 0$; $f(t) = \sin t$ if $0 \leq t \leq 2\pi$, $f(t) = 0$ if $t > 2\pi$

34. $m = 1$, $k = 1$, $c = 0$; $f(t) = t$ if $0 \leq t < 1$, $f(t) = 0$ if $t \geq 1$

35. $m = 1$, $k = 4$, $c = 4$; $f(t) = t$ if $0 \leq t \leq 2$, $f(t) = 0$ if $t \geq 2$

In Problems 36 through 40, the values of the elements of an RLC circuit are given. Solve the initial value problem

$$L\frac{di}{dt} + Ri + \frac{1}{C}\int_0^t i(\tau)\,d\tau = e(t); \qquad i(0) = 0$$

with the given impressed voltage $e(t)$.

36. $L = 0$, $R = 100$, $C = 10^{-3}$; $e(t) = 100$ if $0 \leq t < 1$; $e(t) = 0$ if $t \geq 1$

37. $L = 1$, $R = 0$, $C = 10^{-4}$; $e(t) = 100$ if
$0 \le t < 2\pi$; $e(t) = 0$ if $t \ge 2\pi$

38. $L = 1$, $R = 0$, $C = 10^{-4}$; $e(t) = 100 \sin 10t$ if
$0 \le t < \pi$; $e(t) = 0$ if $t \ge \pi$

39. $L = 1$, $R = 150$, $C = 2 \times 10^{-4}$; $e(t) = 100t$ if
$0 \le t < 1$; $e(t) = 0$ if $t \ge 1$

40. $L = 1$, $R = 100$, $C = 4 \times 10^{-4}$; $e(t) = 50t$ if
$0 \le t < 1$; $e(t) = 0$ if $t \ge 1$

In Problems 41 and 42, a mass-spring-dashpot system with external force $f(t)$ is described. Under the assumption that $x(0) = x'(0) = 0$, use the method of Example 8 to find the transient and steady periodic motions of the mass.

41. $m = 1$, $k = 4$, $c = 0$; $f(t)$ is a square wave function with amplitude 4 and period 2π.

42. $m = 1$, $k = 10$, $c = 2$; $f(t)$ is a square wave function with amplitude 10 and period 2π.

7.5 Computing Project

Periodic piecewise linear functions occur so frequently as input functions in engineering applications that they are sometimes called **engineering functions.** Computations with such functions are readily handled by computer algebra systems. In *Mathematica*, for instance, we can define

```
SawTooth[t_] := 2 t - 2 Floor[t] - 1

TriangularWave[t_] := Abs[2 SawTooth[(2 t - 1)/4]] - 1

SquareWave[t_] := Sign[ TriangularWave[t] ]
```

Plot each of the functions to verify that it has period 2 and that its name is aptly chosen. For instance, the result of

```
Plot[ SquareWave[t], {t, 0, 6} ];
```

should look like Fig. 7.5.9. If $f(t)$ is one of these engineering functions, then the function $f(2t/p)$ will have period p. To illustrate this, try

```
Plot[ TriangularWave[ 2 t/p ], {t, 0, 3 p} ];
```

with various values of p.

Now let's consider the mass-spring-dashpot equation

```
diffEq = m x''[t] + c x'[t] + k x[t] == input
```

with selected parameter values and an input forcing function with period p and amplitude F_0.

```
m = 4; c = 8; k = 5; p = 1; F0 = 4;

input = F0 SquareWave[2 t/p];
```

You can plot this **input** function to verify that it has period 1:

```
Plot[ input, {t, 0, 10} ];
```

Next, let's suppose that the mass is initially at rest in its equilibrium position and solve numerically the resulting initial value problem.

```
response = NDSolve[ {diffEq, x[0] == 0, x'[0] == 0},
                    x, {t, 0, 10}, MaxSteps -> 1000 ]

Plot[ x[t] /. response, {t, 0, 10} ];
```

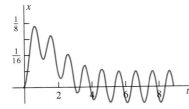

FIGURE 7.5.18. Response $x(t)$ to period 1 square wave input

In the resulting Fig. 7.5.18 we see that after an initial transient dies out, the response function $x(t)$ settles down (as expected?) to a periodic oscillation with the same period as the input.

Investigate this initial value problem with various mass-spring-dashpot parameters—for instance, selected digits of your student I.D. number—and with input engineering functions having various amplitudes and periods.

7.6 Impulses and Delta Functions

Consider a force $f(t)$ that acts only during a very short time interval $a \leq t \leq b$, with $f(t) = 0$ outside this interval. A typical example would be the *impulsive force* of a bat striking a ball—the impact is almost instantaneous. A quick surge of voltage (resulting from a lightning bolt, for instance) is an analogous electrical phenomenon. In such a situation it often happens that the principal effect of the force depends only on the value of the integral

$$p = \int_a^b f(t)\, dt \tag{1}$$

and does not depend otherwise on precisely how $f(t)$ varies with time t. The number p in Eq. (1) is called the **impulse** of the force $f(t)$ over the interval $[a, b]$.

In the case of a force $f(t)$ that acts on a particle of mass m in linear motion, integration of Newton's law

$$f(t) = mv'(t) = \frac{d}{dt}[mv(t)]$$

yields

$$p = \int_a^b \frac{d}{dt}[mv(t)]\, dt = mv(b) - mv(a). \tag{2}$$

Thus the impulse of the force is equal to the change in momentum of the particle. So if change in momentum is the only effect with which we are concerned, we need know only the impulse of the force; we need know neither the precise function $f(t)$ nor even the precise time interval during which it acts. This is fortunate, because in a situation such as that of a batted ball, we are unlikely to have such detailed information about the impulsive force that acts on the ball.

Our strategy for handling such a situation is to set up a reasonable mathematical model in which the unknown force $f(t)$ is replaced with a simple and explicit force that has the same impulse. Suppose for simplicity that $f(t)$ has impulse 1 and acts during some brief time interval beginning at time $t = a \geq 0$. Then we can select a fixed number $\epsilon > 0$ that approximates the length of this time interval and replace $f(t)$ with the specific function

$$d_{a,\epsilon}(t) = \begin{cases} \dfrac{1}{\epsilon} & \text{if } a \leq t < a + \epsilon, \\ 0 & \text{otherwise.} \end{cases} \tag{3}$$

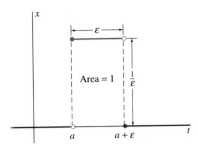

FIGURE 7.6.1. The graph of the impulse function $d_{a,\epsilon}(t)$

This is a function of t, with a and ϵ being parameters that specify the time interval $[a, a + \epsilon]$. If $b \geqq a + \epsilon$, then we see (Fig. 7.6.1) that the impulse of $d_{a,\epsilon}$ over $[a, b]$ is

$$p = \int_a^b d_{a,\epsilon}(t)\,dt = \int_a^{a+\epsilon} \frac{1}{\epsilon}\,dt = 1.$$

Thus $d_{a,\epsilon}$ has a *unit* impulse, whatever the number ϵ may be. Essentially the same computation gives

$$\int_0^\infty d_{a,\epsilon}(t)\,dt = 1. \tag{4}$$

Because the precise time interval during which the force acts seems unimportant, it is tempting to think of an *instantaneous impulse* that occurs precisely at the instant $t = a$. We might try to model such an instantaneous unit impulse by taking the limit as $\epsilon \to 0$, thereby defining

$$\delta_a(t) = \lim_{\epsilon \to 0} d_{a,\epsilon}(t), \tag{5}$$

where $a \geqq 0$. It we could also take the limit under the integral sign in Eq. (4), then it would follow that

$$\int_0^\infty \delta_a(t)\,dt = 1. \tag{6}$$

But the limit in Eq. (5) gives

$$\delta_a(t) = \begin{cases} +\infty & \text{if } t = a, \\ 0 & \text{if } t \neq a. \end{cases} \tag{7}$$

Obviously, no function can satisfy both (6) and (7)—if a function is zero except at a single point, then its integral is not 1 but zero. Nevertheless, the symbol $\delta_a(t)$ is very useful. However interpreted, it is called the **Dirac delta function** at a after the British theoretical physicist P. A. M. Dirac (1902–1984), who in the early 1930s introduced a "function" allegedly enjoying the properties in Eqs. (6) and (7).

Delta Functions as Operators

The following computation motivates the meaning that we will attach here to the symbol $\delta_a(t)$. If $g(t)$ is a continuous function, then the mean value theorem for integrals implies that

$$\int_a^{a+\epsilon} g(t)\,dt = \epsilon g(\bar{t})$$

for some point \bar{t} in $[a, a + \epsilon]$. It follows that

$$\lim_{\epsilon \to 0} \int_0^\infty g(t)\,d_{a,\epsilon}(t)\,dt = \lim_{\epsilon \to 0} \int_a^{a+\epsilon} g(t) \cdot \frac{1}{\epsilon}\,dt = \lim_{\epsilon \to 0} g(\bar{t}) = g(a) \tag{8}$$

by continuity of g at $t = a$. If $\delta_a(t)$ *were* a function in the strictest sense of the definition, and if we could interchange the limit and the integral in Eq. (8), we therefore

could conclude that

$$\int_0^\infty g(t)\,\delta_a(t)\,dt = g(a). \qquad (9)$$

We take Eq. (9) as the *definition* (!) of the symbol $\delta_a(t)$. Although we call it the delta function, it is not a genuine function; instead, it specifies the *operation*

$$\int_0^\infty \cdots \delta_a(t)\,dt$$

which—when applied to a continuous function $g(t)$—sifts out or selects the value $g(a)$ of this function at the point $a \geqq 0$. This idea is shown schematically in Fig. 7.6.2. Note that we will use the symbol $\delta_a(t)$ only in the context of integrals such as that in Eq. (9), or when it will appear subsequently in such an integral.

For instance, if we take $g(t) = e^{-st}$ in Eq. (9), the result is

$$\int_0^\infty e^{-st}\,\delta_a(t)\,dt = e^{-as}. \qquad (10)$$

We therefore *define* the Laplace transform of the delta function to be

$$\mathcal{L}\{\delta_a(t)\} = e^{-as} \qquad (a \geqq 0). \qquad (11)$$

If we write

$$\delta(t) = \delta_0(t) \qquad \text{and} \qquad \delta(t - a) = \delta_a(t), \qquad (12)$$

then (11) with $a = 0$ gives

$$\mathcal{L}\{\delta(t)\} = 1. \qquad (13)$$

Note that if $\delta(t)$ were an actual function, then Eq. (13) would contradict the corollary to Theorem 2 of Section 7.1. There is no problem here; $\delta(t)$ is not a function, and Eq. (13) is our *definition* of $\mathcal{L}\{\delta(t)\}$.

Delta Function Inputs

Now, finally, suppose that we are given a mechanical system whose response $x(t)$ to the external force $f(t)$ is determined by the differential equation

$$Ax'' + Bx' + Cx = f(t). \qquad (14)$$

To investigate the response of this system to a unit impulse at the instant $t = a$, it seems reasonable to replace $f(t)$ with $\delta_a(t)$ and begin with the equation

$$Ax'' + Bx' + Cx = \delta_a(t). \qquad (15)$$

But what is meant by the solution of such an equation? We will call $x(t)$ a solution of Eq. (15) provided that

$$x(t) = \lim_{\epsilon \to 0} x_\epsilon(t), \qquad (16)$$

where $x_\epsilon(t)$ is a solution of

$$Ax'' + Bx' + Cx = d_{a,\,\epsilon}(t). \qquad (17)$$

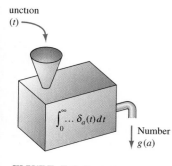

unction
(t)

$$\int_0^\infty \cdots \delta_a(t)\,dt$$

Number
$g(a)$

FIGURE 7.6.2. A diagram illustrating how the delta function "sifts out" the value $g(a)$

Because

$$d_{a,\epsilon}(t) = \frac{1}{\epsilon}[u_a(t) - u_{a+\epsilon}(t)] \tag{18}$$

is an ordinary function, Eq. (17) makes sense. For simplicity suppose the initial conditions to be $x(0) = x'(0) = 0$. When we transform Eq. (17), writing $X_\epsilon = \mathcal{L}\{x_\epsilon\}$, we get the equation

$$(As^2 + Bs + C)X_\epsilon(s) = \frac{1}{\epsilon}\left(\frac{e^{-as}}{s} - \frac{e^{-(a+\epsilon)s}}{s}\right) = (e^{-as})\frac{1 - e^{-s\epsilon}}{s\epsilon}.$$

If we take the limit in the last equation as $\epsilon \to 0$, and note that

$$\lim_{\epsilon \to 0} \frac{1 - e^{-s\epsilon}}{s\epsilon} = 1$$

by l'Hôpital's rule, we get the equation

$$(As^2 + Bs + C)X_\epsilon(s) = e^{-as}. \tag{19}$$

Note that this is precisely the same result that we would obtain if we transformed Eq. (15) directly, using the fact that $\mathcal{L}\{\delta_a(t)\} = e^{-as}$.

On this basis it is reasonable to solve a differential equation involving a delta function by employing the Laplace transform method exactly as if $\delta_a(t)$ were an ordinary function. It is important to verify that the solution so obtained agrees with the one defined in Eq. (16), but this depends on a highly technical analysis of the limiting procedures involved; we consider it beyond the scope of the present discussion. The formal method is valid in all the examples of this section and will produce correct results in the subsequent problem set.

EXAMPLE 1 A mass $m = 1$ is attached to a spring with constant $k = 4$; there is no dashpot. The mass is released from rest with $x(0) = 3$. At the instant $t = 2\pi$ the mass is struck with a hammer, providing an impulse $p = 8$. Determine the motion of the mass.

Solution We need to solve the initial value problem

$$x'' + 4x = 8\delta_{2\pi}(t); \qquad x(0) = 3, \qquad x'(0) = 0.$$

We apply the Laplace transform to get

$$s^2 X(s) - 3s + 4X(s) = 8e^{-2\pi s},$$

so

$$X(s) = \frac{3s}{s^2 + 4} + \frac{8e^{-2\pi s}}{s^2 + 4}.$$

Recalling the transforms of sine and cosine, as well as the theorem on translations on the t-axis (Theorem 1 of Section 7.5), we see that the inverse transform is

$$x(t) = 3\cos 2t + 4u(t - 2\pi)\sin 2(t - 2\pi)$$

$$= 3\cos 2t + 4u_{2\pi}(t)\sin 2t.$$

Because $3\cos 2t + 4\sin 2t = 5\cos(2t - \alpha)$ with $\alpha = \tan^{-1}(4/3) \approx 0.9273$, separa-

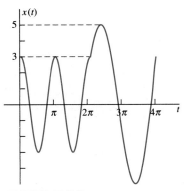

tion of the cases $t < 2\pi$ and $t > 2\pi$ gives

$$x(t) \approx \begin{cases} 3 \cos 2t & \text{if } t \le 2\pi, \\ 5 \cos(2t - 0.9273) & \text{if } t \ge 2\pi. \end{cases}$$

The resulting motion is shown in Fig. 7.6.3. Note that the impulse at $t = 2\pi$ results in a discontinuity in the velocity at $t = 2\pi$, as it instantaneously increases the amplitude of the oscillations of the mass from 3 to 5. ∎

FIGURE 7.6.3. The motion of the mass of Example 1

Delta Functions and Step Functions

It is useful to regard the delta function $\delta_a(t)$ as the derivative of the unit step function $u_a(t)$. To see why this is reasonable, consider the continuous approximation $u_{a,\epsilon}(t)$ to $u_a(t)$ shown in Fig. 7.6.4. We readily verify that

$$\frac{d}{dt} u_{a,\epsilon}(t) = d_{a,\epsilon}(t).$$

Because

$$u_a(t) = \lim_{\epsilon \to 0} u_{a,\epsilon}(t) \qquad \text{and} \qquad \delta_a(t) = \lim_{\epsilon \to 0} d_{a,\epsilon}(t),$$

an interchange of limits and derivatives yields

$$\frac{d}{dt} u_a(t) = \lim_{\epsilon \to 0} \frac{d}{dt} u_{a,\epsilon}(t) = \lim_{\epsilon \to 0} d_{a,\epsilon}(t),$$

and therefore

$$\frac{d}{dt} u_a(t) = \delta_a(t) = \delta(t - a). \tag{20}$$

FIGURE 7.6.4. Approximation of $u_a(t)$ by $u_{a,\epsilon}(t)$

We may regard this as the *formal definition* of the derivative of the unit step function, although $u_a(t)$ is not differentiable in the ordinary sense at $t = a$.

EXAMPLE 2 We return to the RLC circuit of Example 5 of Section 7.5, with $R = 110 \ \Omega$, $L = 1$ H, $C = 0.001$ F, and a battery supplying $e_0 = 90$ V. Suppose that the circuit is initially passive—no current and no charge. At time $t = 0$ the switch is closed and at time $t = 1$ it is opened and left open. Find the resulting current $i(t)$ in the circuit.

Solution In Section 7.5 we circumvented the discontinuity in the voltage by employing the integrodifferential form of the circuit equation. Now that delta functions are available, we may begin with the ordinary circuit equation

$$Li'' + Ri' + \frac{1}{C} i = e'(t).$$

In this example we have

$$e(t) = 90 - 90u(t - 1) = 90 - 90u_1(t).$$

so $e'(t) = -90\delta(t - 1)$ by Eq. (20). Hence we want to solve the initial value problem

$$i'' + 110i' + 1000i = -90\delta(t - 1); \tag{21}$$
$$i(0) = 0, \qquad i'(0) = 90.$$

The fact that $i'(0) = 90$ comes from substitution of $t = 0$ in the equation

$$Li'(t) + Ri(t) + \frac{1}{C} q(t) = e(t)$$

with the numerical values $i(0) = q(0) = 0$ and $e(0) = 90$.

When we transform the problem in (21), we get the equation

$$s^2 I(s) - 90 + 110s I(s) + 1000 I(s) = -90 e^{-s}.$$

Hence

$$I(s) = \frac{90(1 - e^{-s})}{s^2 + 110s + 1000}.$$

This is precisely the same transform $I(s)$ we found in Example 5 of Section 7.5, so inversion of $I(s)$ yields the same solution $i(t)$ recorded there.

EXAMPLE 3 Consider a mass on a spring with $m = k = 1$ and $x(0) = x'(0) = 0$. At each of the instants $t = 0, \pi, 2\pi, 3\pi, \ldots, n\pi, \ldots$, the mass is struck a hammer blow with a unit impulse. Determine the resulting motion.

Solution We need to solve the initial value problem

$$x'' + x = \sum_{n=0}^{\infty} \delta_{n\pi}(t); \qquad x(0) = 0 = x'(0).$$

Because $\mathcal{L}\{\delta_{n\pi}(t)\} = e^{-n\pi s}$, the transformed equation is

$$s^2 X(s) + X(s) = \sum_{n=0}^{\infty} e^{-n\pi s},$$

so

$$X(s) = \sum_{n=0}^{\infty} \frac{e^{-n\pi s}}{s^2 + 1}.$$

We compute the inverse Laplace transform term by term; the result is

$$x(t) = \sum_{n=0}^{\infty} u(t - n\pi) \sin(t - n\pi).$$

Because $\sin(t - n\pi) = (-1)^n \sin t$ and $u(t - n\pi) = 0$ for $t < n\pi$, we see that if $n\pi < t < (n + 1)\pi$, then

$$x(t) = \sin t - \sin t + \sin t - \cdots + (-1)^n \sin t;$$

that is,

$$x(t) = \begin{cases} \sin t & \text{if } n \text{ is even,} \\ 0 & \text{if } n \text{ is odd.} \end{cases}$$

FIGURE 7.6.5. The half-wave rectification of $\sin t$

Hence $x(t)$ is the half-wave rectification of $\sin t$ shown in Fig. 7.6.5. The physical explanation is that the first hammer blow (at time $t = 0$) starts the mass moving to the right; just as it returns to the origin, the second hammer blow stops it dead; it remains motionless until the third hammer blow starts it moving again, and so on. Of course, if

the hammer blows are not perfectly synchronized then the motion of the mass will be quite different. ∎

Systems Analysis and Duhamel's Principle

Consider a physical system in which the *output* or *response* $x(t)$ to the *input* function $f(t)$ is described by the differential equation

$$ax'' + bx' + cx = f(t), \tag{22}$$

where the constant coefficients a, b, and c are determined by the physical parameters of the system and are independent of $f(t)$. The mass-spring-dashpot system and the series RLC circuit are familiar examples of this general situation.

For simplicity we assume that the system is initially passive: $x(0) = x'(0) = 0$. Then the transform of Eq. (22) is

$$as^2X(s) + bsX(s) + cX(s) = F(s),$$

so

$$X(s) = \frac{F(s)}{as^2 + bs + c} = W(s)\,F(s). \tag{23}$$

The function

$$W(s) = \frac{1}{as^2 + bs + c} \tag{24}$$

is called the **transfer function** of the system. Thus the transform of the response to the input $f(t)$ is the product of $W(s)$ and the transform $F(s)$.

The function

$$w(t) = \mathcal{L}^{-1}\{W(s)\} \tag{25}$$

is called the **weight function** of the system. From Eq. (24) we see by convolution that

$$x(t) = \int_0^t w(\tau)\,f(t - \tau)\,d\tau. \tag{26}$$

This formula is **Duhamel's principle** for the system. What is important is that the weight function $w(t)$ is determined completely by the parameters of the system. Once $w(t)$ has been determined, the integral in (26) gives the response of the system to an arbitrary input function $f(t)$.

EXAMPLE 4 Consider a mass-spring-dashpot system (initially passive) which responds to the external force $f(t)$ in accord with the equation $x'' + 6x' + 10x = f(t)$. Then

$$W(s) = \frac{1}{s^2 + 6s + 10} = \frac{1}{(s + 3)^2 + 1},$$

so the weight function is $w(t) = e^{-3t}\sin t$. Then Duhamel's principle implies that the response $x(t)$ to the force $f(t)$ is

$$x(t) = \int_0^t e^{-3\tau}(\sin \tau)f(t - \tau)\,d\tau. \quad\blacksquare$$

Note that

$$W(s) = \frac{1}{as^2 + bs + c} = \frac{\mathcal{L}\{\delta(t)\}}{as^2 + bs + c}.$$

Consequently, it follows from Eq. (23) that the weight function is simply the response of the system to the delta function input $\delta(t)$. For this reason $w(t)$ is sometimes called the **unit impulse response.** A response that is usually easier to measure in practice is the response $h(t)$ to the unit step function $u(t)$; $h(t)$ is the **unit step response.** Because $\mathcal{L}\{u(t)\} = 1/s$, we see from Eq. (23) that the transform of $h(t)$ is

$$H(s) = \frac{W(s)}{s}.$$

It follows from the formula for transforms of integrals that

$$h(t) = \int_0^t w(\tau)\,d\tau, \qquad \text{so that} \quad w(t) = h'(t). \tag{27}$$

Thus the weight function, or unit impulse response, is the derivative of the unit step response. Substitution of (27) in Duhamel's principle gives

$$x(t) = \int_0^t h'(\tau)f(t - \tau)\,d\tau \tag{28}$$

for the response of the system to the input $f(t)$.

Applications. To describe a typical application of Eq. (28), suppose that we are given a complex series circuit containing many inductors, resistors, and capacitors. Assume that its circuit equation is a linear equation of the form in (22), though with i in place of x. What if the coefficients a, b, and c are unknown, perhaps only because they are too difficult to compute? We would still want to know the current $i(t)$ corresponding to any input $f(t) = e'(t)$. We connect the circuit to a linearly increasing voltage $e(t) = t$, so that $f(t) = e'(t) = 1 = u(t)$, and measure the response $h(t)$ with an ammeter. We then compute the derivative $h'(t)$, either numerically or graphically. Then according to Eq. (28), the output current $i(t)$ corresponding to the input voltage $e(t)$ will be given by

$$i(t) = \int_0^t h'(\tau)\,e'(t - \tau)\,d\tau$$

(using the fact that $f(t) = e'(t)$).

Historical Remark: In conclusion we remark that around 1950, after engineers and physicists had been using delta functions widely and fruitfully for about 20 years without rigorous justification, the French mathematician Laurent Schwartz developed a rigorous mathematical theory of *generalized functions* that supplied the missing logical foundation for delta function techniques. Every piecewise continuous ordinary function is a generalized function, but the delta function is an example of a generalized function that is not an ordinary function.

7.6 Problems

Solve the initial value problems in Problems 1 through 8.

1. $x'' + 4x = \delta(t)$; $x(0) = x'(0) = 0$

2. $x'' + 4x = \delta(t) + \delta(t - \pi)$; $x(0) = x'(0) = 0$

3. $x'' + 4x' + 4x = 1 + \delta(t - 2)$; $x(0) = x'(0) = 0$

4. $x'' + 2x' + x = t + \delta(t)$; $x(0) = 0$, $x'(0) = 1$

5. $x'' + 2x' + 2x = 2\delta(t - \pi)$; $x(0) = x'(0) = 0$

6. $x'' + 9x = \delta(t - 3\pi) + \cos 3t$; $x(0) = x'(0) = 0$

7. $x'' + 4x' + 5x = \delta(t - \pi) + \delta(t - 2\pi)$; $x(0) = 0$, $x'(0) = 2$

8. $x'' + 2x' + x = \delta(t) - \delta(t - 2)$; $x(0) = 2 = x'(0)$

Apply Duhamel's principle to write an integral formula for the solution of the initial value problems in Problems 9 through 12.

9. $x'' + 4x = f(t)$; $x(0) = x'(0) = 0$

10. $x'' + 6x' + 9x = f(t)$; $x(0) = x'(0) = 0$

11. $x'' + 6x' + 8x = f(t)$; $x(0) = x'(0) = 0$

12. $x'' + 4x' + 8x = f(t)$; $x(0) = x'(0) = 0$

13. This problem deals with a mass m, initially at rest at the origin, that receives an impulse p at time $t = 0$. (a) Find the solution $x_\epsilon(t)$ of the problem

$$mx'' = pd_{0,\epsilon}(t); \qquad x(0) = x'(0) = 0.$$

(b) Show that $\lim_{\epsilon \to 0} x_\epsilon(t)$ agrees with the solution of the problem

$$mx'' = p\delta(t); \qquad x(0) = x'(0) = 0.$$

(c) Show that $mv = p$ for $t > 0$ ($v = dx/dt$).

14. Verify that $u'(t - a) = \delta(t - a)$ by solving the problem

$$x' = \delta(t - a); \qquad x(0) = 0$$

to obtain $x(t) = u(t - a)$.

15. This problem deals with a mass m on a spring (with constant k) that receives an impulse $p_0 = mv_0$ at time $t = 0$. Show that the initial value problems

$$mx'' + kx = 0; \qquad x(0) = 0, \qquad x'(0) = v_0$$

and

$$mx'' + kx = p_0\delta(t); \qquad x(0) = 0, \qquad x'(0) = 0$$

have the same solution. Thus the effect of $p_0\delta(t)$ is, indeed, to impart to the particle an initial momentum p_0.

16. This is a generalization of Problem 15. Show that the problems

$$ax'' + bx' + cx = f(t); \qquad x(0) = 0, \qquad x'(0) = v_0$$

and

$$ax'' + bx' + cx = f(t) + av_0\delta(t); \qquad x(0) = x'(0) = 0$$

have the same solution for $t > 0$. Thus the effect of the term $av_0\delta(t)$ is to supply the initial condition $x'(0) = v_0$.

17. Consider an initially passive RC circuit (no inductance) with a battery supplying e_0 volts. (a) If the switch to the battery is closed at time $t = a$ and opened at time $t = b > a$ (and left open thereafter), show that the current in the circuit satisfies the initial value problem

$$Ri' + \frac{1}{C}i = e_0\delta(t - a) - e_0\delta(t - b); \qquad i(0) = 0.$$

(b) Solve this problem if $R = 100\ \Omega$, $C = 10^{-4}$ F, $e_0 = 100$ V, $a = 1$ (s), and $b = 2$ (s). Show that $i(t) > 0$ if $1 < t < 2$ and that $i(t) < 0$ if $t > 2$.

18. Consider an initially passive LC circuit (no resistance) with a battery supplying e_0 volts. (a) If the switch is closed at time $t = 0$ and opened at time $t = a > 0$, show that the current in the circuit satisfies the initial value problem

$$Li'' + \frac{1}{C}i = e_0\delta(t) - e_0\delta(t - a);$$

$$i(0) = i'(0) = 0.$$

(b) If $L = 1$ H, $C = 10^{-2}$ F, $e_0 = 10$ V, and $a = \pi$ (s), show that

$$i(t) = \begin{cases} \sin 10t & \text{if } t < \pi, \\ 0 & \text{if } t > \pi. \end{cases}$$

Thus the current oscillates through five cycles and then stops abruptly when the switch is opened.

19. Consider the LC circuit of Problem 18(b), except suppose that the switch is alternately closed and opened at time $t = 0$, $\pi/10$, $2\pi/10$, (a) Show that $i(t)$ satisfies the initial value problem

$$i'' + 100i = 10 \sum_{n=0}^{\infty} (-1)^n \delta\left(t - \frac{n\pi}{10}\right); \qquad i(0) = i'(0) = 0.$$

(b) Solve this initial value problem to show that

$$i(t) = (n + 1) \sin 10t \quad \text{if} \quad \frac{n\pi}{10} < t < \frac{(n + 1)\pi}{10}.$$

Thus a resonance phenomenon occurs.

20. Repeat Problem 19, except suppose that the switch is alternately closed and opened at times $t = 0$, $\pi/5$, $2\pi/5$, . . . ,

$n\pi/5$, Now show that if

$$\frac{n\pi}{5} < t < \frac{(n+1)\pi}{5},$$

then

$$i(t) = \begin{cases} \sin 10t & \text{if } n \text{ is even;} \\ 0 & \text{if } n \text{ is odd.} \end{cases}$$

Thus the current in alternate cycles of length $\pi/5$ first executes a sine oscillation during one cycle, then is dormant during the next cycle, and so on.

21. Consider an RLC circuit in series with a battery, with $L = 1$ H, $R = 60$ Ω, $C = 10^{-3}$ F, and $e_0 = 10$ V. (a) Suppose that the switch is alternately closed and opened at times $t = 0$, $\pi/10$, $2\pi/10$, Show that $i(t)$ satisfies the initial value problem

$$i'' + 60i' + 1000i = 10 \sum_{n=0}^{\infty} (-1)^n \delta\left(t - \frac{n\pi}{10}\right);$$

$$i(0) = i'(0) = 0.$$

(b) Solve this problem to show that if

$$\frac{n\pi}{10} < t < \frac{(n+1)\pi}{10},$$

then

$$i(t) = \frac{e^{3n\pi+3\pi} - 1}{e^{3\pi} - 1} e^{-30t} \sin 10t.$$

22. Consider a mass $m = 1$ on a spring with constant $k = 1$, initially at rest, but struck with a hammer at each of the instants $t = 0, 2\pi, 4\pi$ Suppose that each hammer blow imparts an impulse of $+1$. Show that the position function $x(t)$ of the mass satisfies the initial value problem

$$x'' + x = \sum_{n=0}^{\infty} \delta(t - 2n\pi); \qquad x(0) = x'(0) = 0.$$

Solve this problem to show that if $2n\pi < t < 2(n+1)\pi$, then $x(t) = (n+1)\sin t$. Thus resonance occurs because the mass is struck each time it passes through the origin moving to the right—in contrast with Example 3, in which the mass was struck each time it returned to the origin.

8 Power Series Methods

In Section 3.3 we saw that solving a homogeneous linear differential equation with constant coefficients can be reduced to the algebraic problem of finding the roots of its characteristic equation. There is no similar procedure for solving linear differential equations with *variable* coefficients, at least not routinely and in finitely many steps. With the exception of special types, such as the occasional equation that can be solved by inspection, linear equations with variable coefficients generally require the power series techniques of this chapter.

These techniques suffice for many of the nonelementary differential equations that appear most frequently in applications. Perhaps the most important (because of its applications in such areas as acoustics, heat flow, and electromagnetic radiation) is **Bessel's equation** of order n:

$$x^2 y'' + xy' + (x^2 - n^2)y = 0.$$

Legendre's equation of order n is important in many applications; it has the form

$$(1 - x^2)y'' - 2xy' + n(n + 1)y = 0.$$

In this section we introduce the **power series method** in its simplest form and, along the way, state (without proof) several theorems that constitute a review of the

457

basic facts about power series. Recall first that a **power series** in (powers of) $x - a$ is an infinite series of the form

$$\sum_{n=0}^{\infty} c_n(x - a)^n = c_0 + c_1(x - a) + c_2(x - a)^2 + \cdots + c_n(x - a)^n + \cdots. \quad (1)$$

If $a = 0$, this is a power series in x:

$$\sum_{n=0}^{\infty} c_n x^n = c_0 + c_1 x + c_2 x^2 + \cdots + c_n x^n + \cdots. \quad (2)$$

We will confine our review mainly to power series in x, but every general property of power series in x can be converted to a general property of power series in $x - a$ by replacement of x with $x - a$.

The power series in (2) **converges** on the interval I provided that the limit

$$\sum_{n=0}^{\infty} c_n x^n = \lim_{N \to \infty} \sum_{n=0}^{N} c_n x^n \quad (3)$$

exists for all x in I. In this case the sum

$$f(x) = \sum_{n=0}^{\infty} c_n x^n \quad (4)$$

is defined on I, and we call the series $\sum c_n x^n$ a **power series representation** of the function f on I. The following power series representations of elementary functions should be familiar to you from introductory calculus.

$$e^x = \sum_{n=0}^{\infty} \frac{x^n}{n!} = 1 + x + \frac{x^2}{2!} + \frac{x^3}{3!} + \cdots; \quad (5)$$

$$\cos x = \sum_{n=0}^{\infty} \frac{(-1)^n x^{2n}}{(2n)!} = 1 - \frac{x^2}{2!} + \frac{x^4}{4!} - \cdots; \quad (6)$$

$$\sin x = \sum_{n=0}^{\infty} \frac{(-1)^n x^{2n+1}}{(2n+1)!} = x - \frac{x^3}{3!} + \frac{x^5}{5!} - \cdots; \quad (7)$$

$$\cosh x = \sum_{n=0}^{\infty} \frac{x^{2n}}{(2n)!} = 1 + \frac{x^2}{2!} + \frac{x^4}{4!} + \cdots; \quad (8)$$

$$\sinh x = \sum_{n=0}^{\infty} \frac{x^{2n+1}}{(2n+1)!} = x + \frac{x^3}{3!} + \frac{x^5}{5!} + \cdots; \quad (9)$$

$$\ln(1 + x) = \sum_{n=1}^{\infty} \frac{(-1)^{n+1} x^n}{n} = x - \frac{x^2}{2} + \frac{x^3}{3} - \cdots; \quad (10)$$

$$\frac{1}{1 - x} = \sum_{n=0}^{\infty} x^n = 1 + x + x^2 + x^3 + \cdots; \quad (11)$$

and

$$(1 + x)^\alpha = 1 + \alpha x + \frac{\alpha(\alpha - 1)x^2}{2!} + \frac{\alpha(\alpha - 1)(\alpha - 2)x^3}{3!} + \cdots. \quad (12)$$

In compact summation notation, we observe the usual conventions that $0! = 1$ and that $x^0 = 1$ for all x, including $x = 0$. The series in (5) through (9) converge to the indicated functions for all x. In contrast, the series in (10) and (11) converge if $|x| < 1$ but diverge if $|x| > 1$. (What if $|x| = 1$?) The series in (11) is the **geometric series.** The series in (12), with α an arbitrary real number, is the **binomial series.** If α is a nonnegative integer, then the binomial series converges for all x. Otherwise it converges if $|x| < 1$ and diverges if $|x| > 1$; its behavior for $|x| = 1$ depends on the value of α.

Power series such as those listed in (5) through (12) are often derived as Taylor series. The **Taylor series** with **center** $x = a$ of the function f is the power series

$$\sum_{n=0}^{\infty} \frac{f^{(n)}(a)}{n!} (x - a)^n = f(a) + f'(a)(x - a) + \frac{f''(a)}{2!}(x - a)^2 + \cdots \quad (13)$$

in powers of $x - a$, under the hypothesis that f is infinitely differentiable at $x = a$ (so that the coefficients in (13) are all defined). If the Taylor series of f converges to $f(x)$ for all x in some open interval containing a, then we say that the function f is **analytic** at $x = a$. For example, every polynomial is analytic everywhere and every rational function is analytic wherever its denominator is nonzero. More generally, if the two functions f and g are both analytic at $x = a$, then so are their sum $f + g$ and their product $f \cdot g$, as is their quotient f/g wherever g is nonzero.

For instance, the function $\tan x = (\sin x)/(\cos x)$ is analytic at $x = 0$ because $\cos 0 = 1 \neq 0$ and the sine and cosine functions are analytic (by virtue of their convergent power series representations in Eqs. (6) and (7)). It is rather awkward to compute the Taylor series of the tangent function using (13) because of the way in which its successive derivatives grow in complexity (try it!). Fortunately, power series may be manipulated algebraically in much the same way as polynomials. For example, if

$$f(x) = \sum_{n=0}^{\infty} a_n x^n \quad \text{and} \quad g(x) = \sum_{n=0}^{\infty} b_n x^n, \quad (14)$$

then

$$f(x) + g(x) = \sum_{n=0}^{\infty} (a_n + b_n) x^n \quad (15)$$

and

$$f(x)g(x) = \sum_{n=0}^{\infty} c_n x^n$$
$$= a_0 b_0 + (a_0 b_1 + a_1 b_0)x + (a_0 b_2 + a_1 b_1 + a_2 b_0)x^2 + \cdots \quad (16)$$

where $c_n = a_0 b_n + a_1 b_{n-1} + \cdots + a_n b_0$. The series in (15) is the result of **termwise addition** and the series in (16) is the result of **formal multiplication**—multiplying each term of the first series by each term of the second and then collecting coefficients of like powers of x. (Thus the processes strongly resemble addition and multiplication of ordinary polynomials.) The series in (15) and (16) converge to $f(x) + g(x)$ and $f(x)g(x)$, respectively, on any open interval on which both the series in (14) converge.

For example,

$$\sin x \cos x = \left(x - \frac{1}{6}x^3 + \frac{1}{120}x^5 - \cdots \right)\left(1 - \frac{1}{2}x^2 + \frac{1}{24}x^4 - \cdots \right)$$

$$= x + \left(-\frac{1}{6} - \frac{1}{2} \right)x^3 + \left(\frac{1}{24} + \frac{1}{12} + \frac{1}{120} \right)x^5 + \cdots$$

$$= x - \frac{4}{6}x^3 + \frac{16}{120}x^5 - \cdots$$

$$= \frac{1}{2}\left[(2x) - \frac{(2x)^3}{3!} + \frac{(2x)^5}{5!} - \cdots \right] = \frac{1}{2}\sin 2x$$

for all x.

Similarly, the quotient of two power series can be computed by long division, as illustrated by the computation shown in Fig. 8.1.1. This division of the Taylor series

FIGURE 8.1.1 Obtaining the series for $\tan x$ by division of series

for cos x into that for sin x yields the first few terms of the series

$$\tan x = x + \frac{1}{3} x^3 + \frac{2}{15} x^5 + \frac{17}{315} x^7 + \cdots. \tag{17}$$

Division of power series is more treacherous than multiplication; the series thus obtained for f/g may fail to converge at some points where the series for f and g both converge. For example, the sine and cosine series converge for all x, but the tangent series in (17) converges only if $|x| < \pi/2$.

The Power Series Method

The **power series method** for solving a differential equation consists of substituting the power series

$$y = \sum_{n=0}^{\infty} c_n x^n \tag{18}$$

in the differential equation and then attempting to determine what the coefficients c_0, c_1, c_2, . . . must be in order that the power series will satisfy the differential equation. This is reminiscent of the method of undetermined coefficients, but now we have infinitely many coefficients somehow to determine. This method is not always successful, but when it is we obtain an infinite series representation of a solution, in contrast to the "closed form" solutions that our previous methods have yielded.

Before we can substitute the power series in (18) in a differential equation, we must first know what to substitute for the derivatives y', y'' The following theorem (stated without proof) tells us that the derivative y' of $y = \sum c_n x^n$ is obtained by the simple procedure of writing the sum of the derivatives of the individual terms in the series for y.

THEOREM 1: Termwise Differentiation of Power Series

If the power series representation

$$f(x) = \sum_{n=0}^{\infty} c_n x^n = c_0 + c_1 x + c_2 x^2 + c_3 x^3 + \cdots \tag{19}$$

of the function f converges on the open interval I, then f is differentiable on I, and

$$f'(x) = \sum_{n=1}^{\infty} n c_n x^{n-1} = c_1 + 2c_2 x + 3c_3 x^2 + \cdots \tag{20}$$

at each point of I.

∎

For example, differentiation of the geometric series

$$\frac{1}{1 - x} = \sum_{n=0}^{\infty} x^n = 1 + x + x^2 + x^3 + \cdots \tag{11}$$

gives

$$\frac{1}{(1-x)^2} = \sum_{n=1}^{\infty} nx^{n-1} = 1 + 2x + 3x^2 + 4x^3 + \cdots.$$

The process of determining the coefficients in the series $y = \sum c_n x^n$ so that it will satisfy a given differential equation depends also on Theorem 2. This theorem—stated without proof—tells us that if two power series represent the same function, then they are the same series. In particular, the Taylor series in (13) is the only power series (in powers of $x - a$) that represents the function f.

THEOREM 2: Identity Principle

If

$$\sum_{n=0}^{\infty} a_n x^n = \sum_{n=0}^{\infty} b_n x^n$$

for every point x in some open interval I, then $a_n = b_n$ for all $n \geq 0$. ∎

In particular, if $\sum a_n x^n = 0$ for all x in some open interval, it follows from Theorem 2 that $a_n = 0$ for all $n \geq 0$.

EXAMPLE 1 Solve the equation $y' + 2y = 0$.

Solution We substitute the series

$$y = \sum_{n=0}^{\infty} c_n x^n \qquad \text{and} \qquad y' = \sum_{n=1}^{\infty} nc_n x^{n-1},$$

and obtain

$$\sum_{n=1}^{\infty} nc_n x^{n-1} + 2 \sum_{n=0}^{\infty} c_n x^n = 0. \tag{21}$$

To compare coefficients here, we need the general term in each sum to be the term containing x^n. To accomplish this, we shift the index of summation in the first sum. To see how to do this, note that

$$\sum_{n=1}^{\infty} nc_n x^{n-1} = c_1 + 2c_2 x + 3c_3 x^2 + \cdots = \sum_{n=0}^{\infty} (n+1)c_{n+1} x^n.$$

Thus we can replace n with $n + 1$ if, at the same time, we start counting one step lower; that is, at $n = 0$ rather than at $n = 1$. This is a shift of $+1$ in the index of summation. The result of making this shift in (21) is the identity

$$\sum_{n=0}^{\infty} (n+1)c_{n+1} x^n + 2 \sum_{n=0}^{\infty} c_n x^n = 0;$$

that is,

$$\sum_{n=0}^{\infty} [(n+1)c_{n+1} + 2c_n] x^n = 0.$$

If this is true on some open interval, then it follows from the identity principle that $(n + 1)c_{n+1} + 2c_n = 0$ for all $n \geq 0$; consequently,

▶
$$c_{n+1} = -\frac{2c_n}{n + 1} \tag{22}$$

for all $n \geq 0$. Equation (22) is a **recurrence relation** from which we can successively compute c_1, c_2, c_3, \ldots in terms of c_0; the latter will turn out to be the arbitrary constant that we expect to find in a general solution of a first-order differential equation.

With $n = 0$, Eq. (22) gives

$$c_1 = -\frac{2c_0}{1}.$$

With $n = 1$, Eq. (22) gives

$$c_2 = -\frac{2c_1}{2} = +\frac{2^2 c_0}{1 \cdot 2} = +\frac{2^2 c_0}{2!}.$$

With $n = 2$, Eq. (22) gives

$$c_3 = -\frac{2c_2}{3} = -\frac{2^3 c_0}{1 \cdot 2 \cdot 3} = -\frac{2^3 c_0}{3!}.$$

By now it should be clear that after n such steps, we will have

▶
$$c_n = (-1)^n \frac{2^n c_0}{n!}, \qquad n \geq 1.$$

(This is easy to prove by induction on n.) Consequently, our solution takes the form

$$y(x) = \sum_{n=0}^{\infty} c_n x^n = \sum_{n=0}^{\infty} (-1)^n \frac{2^n c_0}{n!} x^n = c_0 \sum_{n=0}^{\infty} \frac{(-2x)^n}{n!} = c_0 e^{-2x}.$$

In the final step we have used the familiar exponential series in (5) to identify our power series solution as the same solution $y(x) = c_0 e^{-2x}$ we could have obtained by the method of separation of variables.

Shift of Index of Summation

In the solution of Example 1 we wrote

$$\sum_{n=1}^{\infty} n c_n x^{n-1} = \sum_{n=0}^{\infty} (n + 1)c_{n+1} x^n \tag{23}$$

by shifting the index of summation by $+1$ in the series on the left. That is, we simultaneously *increased* the index of summation by 1 (replacing n with $n + 1$, $n \to n + 1$) and *decreased* the starting point by 1, from $n = 1$ to $n = 0$, thereby obtaining the series on the right. This procedure is valid because each infinite series in (23) is simply a compact notation for the single series

$$c_1 + 2c_2 x + 3c_3 x^2 + 4c_4 x^3 + \cdots. \tag{24}$$

More generally, we can shift the index of summation by k in an infinite series by simultaneously *increasing* the summation index by k ($n \to n + k$) and *decreasing* the

starting point by k. For instance, a shift by $+2$ ($n \rightarrow n + 2$) yields

$$\sum_{n=3}^{\infty} a_n x^{n-1} = \sum_{n=1}^{\infty} a_{n+2} x^{n+1}.$$

If k is negative we interpret a "decrease by k" as an increase by $-k = |k|$. Thus a shift by -2 ($n \rightarrow n - 2$) in the index of summation yields

$$\sum_{n=1}^{\infty} nc_n x^{n-1} = \sum_{n=3}^{\infty} (n - 2)c_{n-2} x^{n-3} \, ;$$

we have *decreased* the index of summation by 2, but *increased* the starting point by 2, from $n = 1$ to $n = 3$. You should check that the summation on the right is merely another representation of the series in (24).

We know that the power series obtained in Example 1 converges for all x because it is an exponential series. More commonly, a power series solution is not recognizable in terms of the familiar elementary functions. When we get an unfamiliar power series solution, we need a way of finding where it converges. After all, $y = \sum c_n x^n$ is merely an *assumed* form of the solution. The procedure illustrated in Example 1 for finding the coefficients $\{c_n\}$ is merely a formal process and may or may not be valid. Its validity—in applying Theorem 1 to compute y' and applying Theorem 2 to obtain a recurrence relation for the coefficients—depends on the convergence of the initially *unknown* series $y = \sum c_n x^n$. Hence this formal process is justified only if in the end we can show that the power series we obtain converges on some open interval. If so, it then represents a solution of the differential equation on that interval. The following theorem (which we state without proof) may be used for this purpose.

THEOREM 3: Radius of Convergence

Given the power series $\sum c_n x^n$, suppose that the limit

$$\rho = \lim_{n \rightarrow \infty} \left| \frac{c_n}{c_{n+1}} \right| \tag{25}$$

exists (ρ is finite) or is infinite (in this case we will write $\rho = \infty$). Then:

(a) If $\rho = 0$, then the series diverges for all $x \neq 0$.
(b) If $0 < \rho < \infty$, then $\sum c_n x^n$ converges if $|x| < \rho$ and diverges if $|x| > \rho$.
(c) If $\rho = \infty$, then the series converges for all x. ∎

The number ρ in (25) is called the **radius of convergence** of the power series $\sum c_n x^n$. For instance, for the power series obtained in Example 1, we have

$$\rho = \lim_{n \rightarrow \infty} \left| \frac{(-1)^n 2^n c_0 / n!}{(-1)^{n+1} 2^{n+1} c_0 / (n+1)!} \right| = \lim_{n \rightarrow \infty} \frac{n+1}{2} = \infty,$$

and consequently the series we obtained in Example 1 converges for all x. Even if the limit in (25) fails to exist, there always will exist a number ρ such that exactly one of the alternatives (a), (b), or (c) in Theorem 3 holds. This number may be difficult to

find, but for the power series we will consider in this chapter, Eq. (25) will be quite sufficient for computing the radius of convergence.

EXAMPLE 2 Solve the equation $(x - 3)y' + 2y = 0$.

Solution As before, we substitute

$$y = \sum_{n=0}^{\infty} c_n x^n \quad \text{and} \quad y' = \sum_{n=1}^{\infty} n c_n x^{n-1}$$

to obtain

$$(x - 3) \sum_{n=1}^{\infty} n c_n x^{n-1} + 2 \sum_{n=0}^{\infty} c_n x^n = 0,$$

so that

$$\sum_{n=1}^{\infty} n c_n x^n - 3 \sum_{n=1}^{\infty} n c_n x^{n-1} + 2 \sum_{n=0}^{\infty} c_n x^n = 0.$$

In the first sum we can replace $n = 1$ with $n = 0$ with no effect on the sum. In the second sum we shift the index of summation by $+1$. This yields

$$\sum_{n=0}^{\infty} n c_n x^n - 3 \sum_{n=0}^{\infty} (n + 1) c_{n+1} x^n + 2 \sum_{n=0}^{\infty} c_n x^n = 0;$$

that is,

$$\sum_{n=0}^{\infty} [n c_n - 3 (n + 1) c_{n+1} + 2 c_n] x^n = 0.$$

The identity principle then gives

$$n c_n - 3 (n + 1) c_{n+1} + 2 c_n = 0,$$

from which we obtain the recurrence relation

$$c_{n+1} = \frac{n + 2}{3 (n + 1)} c_n \quad \text{for } n \geq 0.$$

We apply this formula with $n = 0$, $n = 1$, and $n = 2$ in turn, and find that

$$c_1 = \frac{2}{3} c_0, \qquad c_2 = \frac{3}{3 \cdot 2} c_2 = \frac{3}{3^2} c_0, \qquad \text{and} \qquad c_3 = \frac{4}{3 \cdot 3} c_2 = \frac{4}{3^3} c_0.$$

This is almost enough to make the pattern evident; it is not difficult to show by induction on n that

$$c_n = \frac{n + 1}{3^n} c_0 \quad \text{if } n \geq 1.$$

Hence our proposed power series solution is

$$y(x) = c_0 \sum_{n=0}^{\infty} \frac{n + 1}{3^n} x^n. \tag{26}$$

Its radius of convergence is

$$\rho = \lim_{n \to \infty} \left| \frac{c_n}{c_{n+1}} \right| = \lim_{n \to \infty} \frac{3n + 3}{n + 2} = 3.$$

Thus the series in (26) converges if $-3 < x < 3$ but diverges if $|x| > 3$. In this particular example we can explain why. An elementary solution (obtained by separation of variables) of our differential equation is $y = 1/(3 - x)^2$. If we differentiate termwise the geometric series

$$\frac{1}{3 - x} = \frac{\dfrac{1}{3}}{1 - \dfrac{x}{3}} = \frac{1}{3} \sum_{n=0}^{\infty} \frac{x^n}{3^n},$$

we get a constant multiple of the series in (26). Thus this series (with the arbitrary constant c_0 appropriately chosen) represents the solution

$$y(x) = \frac{1}{(3 - x)^2}$$

on the interval $-3 < x < 3$, and the singularity at $x = 3$ is the reason why the radius of convergence of our power series solution turned out to be $\rho = 3$.

EXAMPLE 3 Solve the equation $x^2 y' = y - x - 1$.

 Solution We make the usual substitutions $y = \sum c_n x^n$ and $y' = \sum n c_n x^{n-1}$, which yield

$$x^2 \sum_{n=1}^{\infty} n c_n x^{n-1} = -1 - x + \sum_{n=0}^{\infty} c_n x^n,$$

so that

$$\sum_{n=1}^{\infty} n c_n x^{n+1} = -1 - x + \sum_{n=0}^{\infty} c_n x^n.$$

Because of the presence of the two terms -1 and $-x$ on the right-hand side, we need to split off the first two terms, $c_0 + c_1 x$, of the series on the right for comparison. If we also shift the index of summation on the left by -1 (replace $n = 1$ with $n = 2$ and n with $n - 1$), we get

$$\sum_{n=2}^{\infty} (n - 1) c_{n-1} x^n = -1 - x + c_0 + c_1 x + \sum_{n=2}^{\infty} c_n x^n.$$

Because the left-hand side contains neither a constant term nor a term containing x to the first power, the identity principle now yields $c_0 = 1$, $c_1 = 1$, and $c_n = (n - 1)c_{n-1}$ for $n \geq 2$. It follows that

$$c_2 = 1 \cdot c_1 = 1!, \qquad c_3 = 2 \cdot c_2 = 2!, \qquad c_4 = 3 \cdot c_3 = 3!,$$

and, in general, that

▶ $$c_n = (n - 1)! \quad \text{for } n \geq 2.$$

Thus we obtain the power series

$$y(x) = 1 + x + \sum_{n=2}^{\infty} (n - 1)!x^n.$$

But the radius of convergence of this series is

$$\rho = \lim_{n \to \infty} \frac{(n - 1)!}{n!} = \lim_{n \to \infty} \frac{1}{n} = 0,$$

so the series converges only for $x = 0$. What does this mean? Simply that the given differential equation does not have a (convergent) power series solution of the assumed form $y = \sum c_n x^n$. This example serves as a warning that the simple act of writing $y = \sum c_n x^n$ involves an assumption that may be false.

EXAMPLE 4 Solve the equation $y'' + y = 0$.

Solution If we assume a solution of the form

$$\blacktriangleright \qquad y = \sum_{n=0}^{\infty} c_n x^n,$$

we find that

$$\blacktriangleright \qquad y' = \sum_{n=1}^{\infty} n c_n x^{n-1} \qquad \text{and} \qquad y'' = \sum_{n=2}^{\infty} n(n - 1)c_n x^{n-2}.$$

Substitution for y and y'' in the differential equation then yields

$$\sum_{n=2}^{\infty} n(n - 1)c_n x^{n-2} + \sum_{n=0}^{\infty} c_n x^n = 0.$$

We shift the index of summation in the first sum by $+2$ (replace $n = 2$ with $n = 0$ and n with $n + 2$). This gives

$$\sum_{n=0}^{\infty} (n + 2)(n + 1)c_{n+2} x^n + \sum_{n=0}^{\infty} c_n x^n = 0.$$

The identity $(n + 2)(n + 1)c_{n+2} + c_n = 0$ now follows from the identity principle, and thus we obtain the recurrence relation

$$\blacktriangleright \qquad c_{n+2} = -\frac{c_n}{(n + 1)(n + 2)} \qquad (27)$$

for $n \geqq 0$. It is evident that this formula will determine the coefficients c_n with even subscript in terms of c_0 and those of odd subscript in terms of c_1; c_0 and c_1 are not predetermined, and thus will be the two arbitrary constants we expect to find in a general solution of a second-order equation.

When we apply the recurrence relation in (27) with $n = 0, 2$, and 4 in turn, we get

$$c_2 = -\frac{c_0}{2!}, \qquad c_4 = \frac{c_0}{4!}, \qquad \text{and} \qquad c_6 = -\frac{c_0}{6!}.$$

Taking $n = 1, 3$, and 5 in turn, we find that

$$c_3 = -\frac{c_1}{3!}, \qquad c_5 = \frac{c_1}{5!}, \qquad \text{and} \qquad c_7 = -\frac{c_1}{7!}.$$

Again, the pattern is clear; we leave it for you to show (by induction) that for $k \geq 1$,

▶ $$c_{2k} = \frac{(-1)^k c_0}{(2k)!} \qquad \text{and} \qquad c_{2k+1} = \frac{(-1)^k c_1}{(2k+1)!}.$$

Thus we get the power series solution

$$y(x) = c_0\left(1 - \frac{x^2}{2!} + \frac{x^4}{4!} - \frac{x^6}{6!} + \cdots\right) + c_1\left(x - \frac{x^3}{3!} + \frac{x^5}{5!} - \frac{x^7}{7!} + \cdots\right);$$

that is, $y(x) = c_0 \cos x + c_1 \sin x$. Note that we have no problem with the radius of convergence here; the Taylor series for the sine and cosine functions converge for all x. ∎

The solution of Example 4 can bear further comment. Suppose that we had never heard of the sine and cosine functions, let alone their Taylor series. We would then have discovered the two power series solutions

$$C(x) = \sum_{n=0}^{\infty} \frac{(-1)^n x^{2n}}{(2n)!} = 1 - \frac{x^2}{2!} + \frac{x^4}{4!} - \cdots \tag{28}$$

and

$$S(x) = \sum_{n=0}^{\infty} \frac{(-1)^n x^{2n+1}}{(2n+1)!} = x - \frac{x^3}{3!} + \frac{x^5}{5!} - \cdots \tag{29}$$

of the differential equation $y'' + y = 0$. It is clear that $C(0) = 1$ and that $S(0) = 0$. After verifying that the two series in (28) and (29) converge for all x, we can differentiate them term by term to find that

$$C'(x) = -S(x) \qquad \text{and} \qquad S'(x) = C(x). \tag{30}$$

Consequently $C'(0) = 0$ and $S'(0) = 1$. Thus with the aid of the power series method (all the while knowing nothing about the sine and cosine functions), we have discovered that $y = C(x)$ is the unique solution of

$$y'' + y = 0$$

that satisfies the initial conditions $y(0) = 1$ and $y'(0) = 0$, and that $y = S(x)$ is the unique solution that satisfies the initial conditions $y(0) = 0$ and $y'(0) = 1$. It follows that $C(x)$ and $S(x)$ are linearly independent, and—recognizing the importance of the differential equation $y'' + y = 0$—we can agree to call C the *cosine* function and S the *sine* function. Indeed, all the usual properties of these two functions can be established, using only their initial values (at $x = 0$) and the derivatives in (30); there is no need to refer to triangles or even to angles. (Can you use the series in (28) and (29) to show that $[C(x)]^2 + [S(x)]^2 = 1$ for all x?) This demonstrates that the cosine and sine functions are fully determined by the differential equation $y'' + y = 0$ of which they are the natural linearly independent solutions. Figures 8.1.2 and 8.1.3 show how the geometric character of the graphs of $\cos x$ and $\sin x$ is revealed by the graphs of the

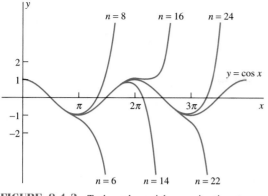

FIGURE 8.1.2. Taylor polynomial approximations to $\cos x$

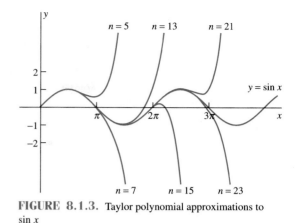

FIGURE 8.1.3. Taylor polynomial approximations to $\sin x$

Taylor polynomial approximations that we get by truncating the infinite series in (28) and (29).

This is by no means an uncommon situation. Many important special functions of mathematics occur in the first instance as power series solutions of differential equations, and thus are in practice *defined* by means of these power series. In the remaining sections of this chapter we will see numerous examples of such functions.

8.1 Problems

In Problems 1 through 10, find a power series solution of the given differential equation. Determine the radius of convergence of the resulting series, and use the series in Eqs. (5) through (12) to identify the series solution in terms of familiar elementary functions. (Of course, no one can prevent you from checking your work by also solving the equations by the methods of earlier chapters!)

1. $y' = y$

2. $y' = 4y$

3. $2y' + 3y = 0$

4. $y' + 2xy = 0$

5. $y' = x^2 y$

6. $(x - 2)y' + y = 0$

7. $(2x - 1)y' + 2y = 0$

8. $2(x + 1)y' = y$

9. $(x - 1)y' + 2y = 0$

10. $2(x - 1)y' = 3y$

In Problems 11 through 14, use the method of Example 4 to find two linearly independent power series solutions of the given differential equation. Determine the radius of convergence of each series, and identify the general solution in terms of familiar elementary functions.

11. $y'' = y$

12. $y'' = 4y$

13. $y'' + 9y = 0$

14. $y'' + y = x$

Show (as in Example 3) that the power series method fails to yield a power series solution of the form $y = \sum c_n x^n$ for the differential equations in Problems 15 through 18.

15. $xy' + y = 0$

16. $2xy' = y$

17. $x^2 y' + y = 0$

18. $x^3 y' = 2y$

In Problems 19 through 22, first derive a recurrence relation giving c_n for $n \geq 2$ in terms of c_0 or c_1 (or both). Then apply the given initial conditions to find the values of c_0 and c_1. Next determine c_n (in terms of n, as in the text) and, finally, identify the particular solution in terms of familiar elementary functions.

19. $y'' + 4y = 0;\quad y(0) = 0,\quad y'(0) = 3$

20. $y'' - 4y = 0;\quad y(0) = 2,\quad y'(0) = 0$

21. $y'' - 2y + y = 0;\quad y(0) = 0,\quad y'(0) = 1$

22. $y'' + y' - 2y = 0;\quad y(0) = 1,\quad y'(0) = -2$

23. Show that the equation

$$x^2 y'' + x^2 y' + y = 0$$

has no power series solution of the form $y = \sum c_n x^n$.

24. Establish the binomial series in (12) by means of the following steps. (a) Show that $y = (1 + x)^\alpha$ satisfies the initial value problem $(1 + x)y' = \alpha y$, $y(0) = 1$. (b) Show that the power series method gives the binomial series in (12) as the solution of the initial value problem in part (a), and that this series converges if $|x| < 1$. (c) Explain why the validity of the binomial series given in (12) follows from parts (a) and (b).

25. (a) Show that the solution of the initial value problem

$$y' = 1 + y^2, \qquad y(0) = 0$$

is $y(x) = \tan x$. (b) Because $y(x) = \tan x$ is an odd function with $y'(0) = 1$, its Taylor series is of the form

$$y = x + c_3 x^3 + c_5 x^5 + c_7 x^7 + \cdots.$$

Substitute this series in $y' = 1 + y^2$ and equate like powers of x to derive the following relations.

$$3c_3 = 1 \qquad\qquad 5c_5 = 2c_3$$

$$7c_7 = 2c_5 + (c_3)^2 \qquad 9c_9 = 2c_7 + 2c_3 c_5$$

$$11c_{11} = 2c_9 + 2c_3 c_7 + (c_5)^2$$

(c) Conclude that

$$\tan x = x + \frac{1}{3} x^3 + \frac{2}{15} x^5 + \frac{17}{315} x^7$$

$$+ \frac{62}{2835} x^9 + \frac{1382}{155925} x^{11} + \cdots.$$

26. This section introduces the use of infinite series to solve differential equations. Conversely, differential equations can sometimes be used to sum infinite series. For example, consider the infinite series

$$1 + \frac{1}{1!} - \frac{1}{2!} + \frac{1}{3!} + \frac{1}{4!} - \frac{1}{5!} + \cdots;$$

note the $+ + - + + -$ pattern of signs superimposed on the terms of the series for the number e. We could evaluate this series if we could obtain a formula for the function

$$f(x) = 1 + x - \frac{1}{2!} x^2 + \frac{1}{3!} x^3 + \frac{1}{4!} x^4 - \frac{1}{5!} x^5 + \cdots,$$

because the sum of the numerical series in question is simply $f(1)$. (a) It's possible to show that the power series given here converges for all x and is termwise differentiable. Given these facts, show that $y = f(x)$ satisfies the initial value problem

$$y^{(3)} = y; \qquad y(0) = y'(0) = 1, \qquad y''(0) = -1.$$

(b) Solve this initial value problem to show that

$$f(x) = \frac{1}{3} e^x + \frac{2}{3} e^{-x/2} \left(\cos \frac{\sqrt{3}}{2} x + \sqrt{3} \sin \frac{\sqrt{3}}{2} x \right).$$

For a suggestion, see Problem 42 of Section 3.3. (c) Evaluate $f(1)$ to find the sum of the numerical series given here.

8.2 Series Solutions Near Ordinary Points

The power series method introduced in Section 8.1 can be applied to linear equations of any order, but its most important applications are to homogeneous second-order linear differential equations of the form

$$A(x)y'' + B(x)y' + C(x)y = 0, \tag{1}$$

where the coefficients A, B, and C are analytic functions of x. Indeed, in most applications these coefficient functions are simple polynomials.

We saw in Example 3 of Section 8.1 that the series method does not always yield a series solution. To discover when it does succeed, we rewrite Eq. (1) in the form

$$\blacktriangleright \qquad y'' + P(x)y' + Q(x)y = 0 \tag{2}$$

with leading coefficient 1, and with $P = B/A$ and $Q = C/A$. Note that $P(x)$ and $Q(x)$ will generally fail to be analytic at points where $A(x)$ vanishes. For instance, consider the equation

$$xy'' + y' + xy = 0. \tag{3}$$

The coefficient functions in (3) are continuous everywhere. But in the form of (2) it is

the equation

$$y'' + \frac{1}{x}y' + y = 0 \tag{4}$$

with $P(x) = 1/x$ not analytic at $x = 0$.

The point $x = a$ is called an **ordinary point** of Eq. (2)—and of the equivalent Eq. (1)—provided that the functions $P(x)$ and $Q(x)$ are both analytic at $x = a$. Otherwise, $x = a$ is a **singular point.** Thus the only singular point of Eqs. (3) and (4) is $x = 0$. Recall that a quotient of analytic functions is analytic wherever the denominator is nonzero. It follows that, if $A(a) \neq 0$ in Eq. (1) with analytic coefficients, then $x = a$ is an ordinary point. If $A(x)$, $B(x)$, and $C(x)$ are *polynomials* with no common factors, then $x = a$ is an ordinary point if and only if $A(a) \neq 0$.

EXAMPLE 1 The point $x = 0$ is an ordinary point of the equation

$$xy'' + (\sin x)y' + x^2 y = 0,$$

despite the fact that $A(x) = x$ vanishes at $x = 0$. The reason is that

$$P(x) = \frac{\sin x}{x} = \frac{1}{x}\left(x - \frac{x^3}{3!} + \frac{x^5}{5!} - \cdots\right) = 1 - \frac{x^2}{3!} + \frac{x^4}{5!} - \cdots$$

is nevertheless analytic at $x = 0$ because the division by x yields a convergent power series.

EXAMPLE 2 The point $x = 0$ is *not* an ordinary point of the equation

$$y'' + x^2 y' + x^{1/2} y = 0.$$

For while $P(x) = x^2$ is analytic at the origin, $Q(x) = x^{1/2}$ is not. The reason is that $Q(x)$ is not differentiable at $x = 0$ and hence is not analytic there. (Theorem 1 of Section 8.1 implies that an analytic function must be differentiable.)

EXAMPLE 3 The point $x = 0$ is an ordinary point of the equation

$$(1 - x^3)y'' + (7x^2 + 3x^5)y' + (5x - 13x^4)y = 0$$

because the coefficient functions $A(x)$, $B(x)$, and $C(x)$ are polynomials with $A(0) \neq 0$. ∎

Theorem 2 of Section 3.1 implies that Eq. (2) has two linearly independent solutions on any open interval where the coefficient functions $P(x)$ and $Q(x)$ are continuous. The basic fact for our present purpose is that near an *ordinary* point a, these solutions will be power series in powers of $x - a$. A proof of the following theorem can be found in Chapter 3 of Coddington, *An Introduction to Ordinary Differential Equations* (Englewood Cliffs, N.J.: Prentice Hall, 1961).

THEOREM 1: Solutions Near an Ordinary Point

Suppose that a is an ordinary point of the equation

$$A(x)y'' + B(x)y' + C(x)y = 0; \tag{1}$$

that is, the functions $P = B/A$ and $Q = C/A$ are analytic at $x = a$. Then Eq. (1) has two linearly independent solutions, each of the form

$$\blacktriangleright \qquad y(x) = \sum_{n=0}^{\infty} c_n(x - a)^n. \qquad (5)$$

The radius of convergence of any such series solution is at least as large as the distance from a to the nearest (real or complex) singular point of Eq. (1). The coefficients in the series in (5) can be determined by its substitution in Eq. (1). ■

EXAMPLE 4 Determine the radius of convergence guaranteed by Theorem 1 of a series solution of

$$(x^2 + 9)y'' + xy' + x^2 y = 0 \qquad (6)$$

in powers of x. Repeat for a series in powers of $x - 4$.

Solution This example illustrates the fact that we must take into account complex singular points as well as real ones. Because

$$P(x) = \frac{x}{x^2 + 9} \qquad \text{and} \qquad Q(x) = \frac{x^2}{x^2 + 9},$$

the only singular points of Eq. (6) are $\pm 3i$. The distance (in the complex plane) of each of these from 0 is 3, so a series solution of the form $\sum c_n x^n$ has the radius of convergence at least 3. The distance of each singular point from 4 is 5, so a series solution of the form $\sum c_n(x - 4)^n$ has radius of convergence at least 5 (see Fig. 8.2.1).

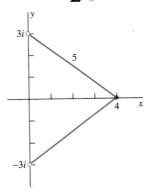

FIGURE 8.2.1. Radius of convergence as distance to nearest singularity

EXAMPLE 5 Find the general solution in powers of x of

$$(x^2 - 4)y'' + 3xy' + y = 0. \qquad (7)$$

Then find the particular solution with $y(0) = 4$, $y'(0) = 1$.

Solution The only singular points of Eq. (7) are ± 2, so the series we get will have radius of convergence at least 2. Substitution of

$$\blacktriangleright \qquad y = \sum_{n=0}^{\infty} c_n x^n, \qquad y' = \sum_{n=1}^{\infty} n c_n x^{n-1}, \qquad \text{and} \qquad y'' = \sum_{n=2}^{\infty} n(n-1) c_n x^{n-2}$$

in Eq. (7) yields

$$\sum_{n=2}^{\infty} n(n-1)c_n x^n - 4 \sum_{n=2}^{\infty} n(n-1)c_n x^{n-2} + 3 \sum_{n=1}^{\infty} nc_n x^n + \sum_{n=0}^{\infty} c_n x^n = 0.$$

We can begin the first and third summations at $n = 0$ as well, because no nonzero terms are thereby introduced. We shift the index of summation in the second sum by $+2$, replacing n with $n + 2$ and using the initial value $n = 0$. This gives

$$\sum_{n=0}^{\infty} n(n-1)c_n x^n - 4 \sum_{n=0}^{\infty} (n+2)(n+1)c_{n+2} x^n + 3 \sum_{n=0}^{\infty} nc_n x^n + \sum_{n=0}^{\infty} c_n x^n = 0.$$

After collecting coefficients of c_n and c_{n+2}, we obtain

$$\sum_{n=0}^{\infty} [(n^2 + 2n + 1)c_n - 4(n+2)(n+1)c_{n+2}]x^n = 0.$$

The identity principle yields

$$(n+1)^2 c_n - 4(n+2)(n+1)c_{n+2} = 0,$$

which leads to the recurrence relation

$$\blacktriangleright \qquad c_{n+2} = \frac{(n+1)c_n}{4(n+2)} \qquad (8)$$

for $n \geq 0$. With $n = 0, 2$, and 4 in turn, we get

$$c_2 = \frac{c_0}{4 \cdot 2}, \quad c_4 = \frac{3c_2}{4 \cdot 4} = \frac{3c_0}{4^2 \cdot 2 \cdot 4}, \quad \text{and} \quad c_6 = \frac{5c_4}{4 \cdot 6} = \frac{3 \cdot 5 c_0}{4^3 \cdot 2 \cdot 4 \cdot 6}.$$

Continuing in this fashion, we evidently would find that

$$c_{2n} = \frac{3 \cdot 5 \cdots (2n-1)}{4^n \cdot 2 \cdot 4 \cdots (2n)} c_0.$$

With the common notation

$$(2n+1)!! = 1 \cdot 3 \cdot 5 \cdots (2n+1) = \frac{(2n+1)!}{2^n \cdot n!}$$

and the observation that $2 \cdot 4 \cdot 6 \cdots (2n) = 2^n \cdot n!$, we finally obtain

$$\blacktriangleright \qquad c_{2n} = \frac{(2n-1)!!}{2^{3n} \cdot n!} c_0. \qquad (9)$$

(We also used the fact that $4^n \cdot 2^n = 2^{3n}$.)

With $n = 1, 3$, and 5 in Eq. (8), we get

$$c_3 = \frac{2c_1}{4 \cdot 3}, \quad c_5 = \frac{4c_3}{4 \cdot 5} = \frac{2 \cdot 4 c_1}{4^2 \cdot 3 \cdot 5}, \quad \text{and} \quad c_7 = \frac{6c_5}{4 \cdot 7} = \frac{2 \cdot 4 \cdot 6 c_1}{4^3 \cdot 3 \cdot 5 \cdot 7}.$$

It is apparent that the pattern is

$$\blacktriangleright \qquad c_{2n+1} = \frac{2 \cdot 4 \cdot 6 \cdots (2n)}{4^n \cdot 3 \cdot 5 \cdots (2n+1)} c_1 = \frac{n!}{2^n \cdot (2n+1)!!} c_1. \qquad (10)$$

The formula in (9) gives the coefficients of even subscript in terms of c_0, and the formula in (10) gives the coefficients of odd subscript in terms of c_1. After we separately collect the terms of the series of even and odd degree, we get the general solution

$$y(x) = c_0 \left(1 + \sum_{n=1}^{\infty} \frac{(2n-1)!!}{2^{3n}n!} x^{2n} \right) + c_1 \left(x + \sum_{n=1}^{\infty} \frac{n!}{2^n(2n+1)!!} x^{2n+1} \right). \quad (11)$$

Alternatively,

$$y(x) = c_0 \left(1 + \frac{1}{8} x^2 + \frac{3}{128} x^4 + \frac{5}{1024} x^6 + \cdots \right)$$
$$+ c_1 \left(x + \frac{1}{6} x^3 + \frac{1}{30} x^5 + \frac{1}{140} x^7 + \cdots \right). \quad (11')$$

Because $y(0) = c_0$ and $y'(0) = c_1$, the given initial conditions imply that $c_0 = 4$ and $c_1 = 1$. Using these values in Eq. (11'), the first few terms of the particular solution satisfying $y(0) = 4$ and $y'(0) = 1$ are

$$y(x) = 4 + x + \frac{1}{2} x^2 + \frac{1}{6} x^3 + \frac{3}{32} x^4 + \frac{1}{30} x^5 + \cdots. \quad (12)$$

∎

Remark: As in Example 5, substitution of $y = \sum c_n x^n$ in a linear second-order equation with $x = 0$ an ordinary point typically leads to a recurrence relation that can be used to express each of the successive coefficients c_2, c_3, c_4, \ldots in terms of the first two, c_0 and c_1. In this event two linearly independent solutions are obtained as follows. Let $y_0(x)$ be the solution obtained with $c_0 = 1$ and $c_1 = 0$, and let $y_1(x)$ be the solution obtained with $c_0 = 0$ and $c_1 = 1$. Then

$$y_0(0) = 1, \quad y_0'(0) = 0 \quad \text{and} \quad y_1(0) = 0, \quad y_1'(0) = 1,$$

so it is clear that y_0 and y_1 are linearly independent. In Example 5, $y_0(x)$ and $y_1(x)$ are defined by the two series that appear on the right-hand side in Eq. (11), which expresses the general solution in the form $y = c_0 y_0 + c_1 y_1$.

Translated Series Solutions

If in Example 5 we had sought a particular solution with given initial values $y(a)$ and $y'(a)$, we would have needed the general solution in the form

$$y(x) = \sum_{n=0}^{\infty} c_n(x-a)^n ; \quad (13)$$

that is, in powers $x - a$ rather than in powers of x. For only with a solution of the form in (13) is it true that the initial conditions

$$y(a) = c_0 \quad \text{and} \quad y'(a) = c_1$$

determine the arbitrary constants c_0 and c_1 in terms of the initial values of y and y'. Consequently, in order to solve an initial value problem, we need a series expansion of the general solution centered at the point where the initial conditions are specified.

EXAMPLE 6 Solve the initial value problem

$$(t^2 - 2t - 3)\frac{d^2y}{dt^2} + 3(t - 1)\frac{dy}{dt} + y = 0; \qquad y(1) = 4, \quad y'(1) = 1. \qquad (14)$$

Solution We need a general solution of the form $\sum c_n(t - 1)^n$. But instead of substituting this series in (14) to determine the coefficients, it simplifies the computations if we first make the substitution $x = t - 1$, so that we wind up looking for a series of the form $\sum c_n x^n$ after all. To transform Eq. (14) into one with the new independent variable x, we note that

$$t^2 - 2t - 3 = (x + 1)^2 - 2(x + 1) - 3 = x^2 - 4,$$

$$\frac{dy}{dt} = \frac{dy}{dx}\frac{dx}{dt} = \frac{dy}{dx} = y',$$

and

$$\frac{d^2y}{dt^2} = \left[\frac{d}{dx}\left(\frac{dy}{dt}\right)\right]\frac{dx}{dt} = \frac{d}{dx}(y') = y'',$$

where primes denote differentiation with respect to x. Hence we transform Eq. (14) into

$$(x^2 - 4)y'' + 3xy' + y = 0$$

with initial conditions $y = 4$ and $y' = 1$ at $x = 0$ (corresponding to $t = 1$). This is the initial value problem we solved in Example 5, so the particular solution in (12) is available. We substitute $t - 1$ for x in Eq. (12), and thereby obtain the desired particular solution

$$y(t) = 4 + (t - 1) + \frac{1}{2}(t - 1)^2 + \frac{1}{6}(t - 1)^3$$

$$+ \frac{3}{32}(t - 1)^4 + \frac{1}{30}(t - 1)^5 + \cdots.$$

This series converges if $-1 < t < 3$. (Why?) A series such as this can be used to estimate numerical values of the solution. For instance,

$$y(0.8) = 4 + (-0.2) + \frac{1}{2}(-0.2)^2 + \frac{1}{6}(-0.2)^3$$

$$+ \frac{3}{32}(-0.2)^4 + \frac{1}{30}(-0.2)^5 + \cdots,$$

so that $y(0.8) \approx 3.8188$. ∎

The last computation of Example 6 illustrates the fact that series solutions of differential equations are useful not only for establishing general properties of a solution, but also for **numerical computations** when an expression of the solution in terms of elementary functions is unavailable.

Types of Recurrence Relations

The formula in Eq. (8) is an example of a **two-term** recurrence relation; it expresses each coefficient in the series in terms of *one* of the preceding coefficients. A **many-**

term recurrence relation expresses each coefficient in the series in terms of two or more preceding coefficients. In the case of a many-term recurrence relation, it is generally inconvenient or even impossible to find a formula that gives the typical c_n in terms of n. The next example shows what we sometimes can do with a three-term recurrence relation.

EXAMPLE 7 Find two linearly independent solutions of

$$y'' - xy' - x^2y = 0. \tag{15}$$

Solution We make the usual substitution of the power series $y = \sum c_n x^n$. This results in the equation

$$\sum_{n=2}^{\infty} n(n-1)c_n x^{n-2} - \sum_{n=1}^{\infty} nc_n x^n - \sum_{n=0}^{\infty} c_n x^{n+2} = 0.$$

We can start the second sum at $n = 0$ without changing anything else. To make each sum include x^n in its general term, we shift the index of summation in the first sum by $+2$ (replace n with $n + 2$), and we shift it by -2 in the third sum (replace n with $n - 2$). These shifts yield

$$\sum_{n=0}^{\infty} (n+2)(n+1)c_{n+2} x^n - \sum_{n=0}^{\infty} nc_n x^n - \sum_{n=2}^{\infty} c_{n-2} x^n = 0.$$

The common range of these three summations is $n \geq 2$, so we must separate the terms corresponding to $n = 0$ and $n = 1$ in the first two sums before collecting coefficients of x^n. This gives

$$2c_2 + 6c_3 x - c_1 x + \sum_{n=2}^{\infty} [(n+2)(n+1)c_{n+2} - nc_n - c_{n-2}]x^n = 0.$$

The identity principle now implies that $2c_2 = 0$, $6c_3 - c_1 = 0$, and

$$(n+2)(n+1)c_{n+2} - nc_n - c_{n-2} = 0$$

for $n \geq 2$. Hence we get $c_2 = 0$, $c_3 = \frac{1}{6}c_1$, and the three-term recurrence relation

▶ $$c_{n+2} = \frac{nc_n + c_{n-2}}{(n+2)(n+1)} \tag{16}$$

for $n \geq 2$. In particular,

$$c_4 = \frac{2c_2 + c_0}{12}, \qquad c_5 = \frac{3c_3 + c_1}{20}, \qquad c_6 = \frac{4c_4 + c_2}{30},$$

$$c_7 = \frac{5c_5 + c_3}{42}, \qquad c_8 = \frac{6c_6 + c_4}{56}. \tag{17}$$

Thus all values of c_n for $n \geq 4$ are given in terms of the arbitrary constants c_0 and c_1 because $c_2 = 0$ and $c_3 = \frac{1}{6}c_1$.

To get our first solution y_1 of Eq. (15), we choose $c_0 = 1$ and $c_1 = 0$, so that $c_2 = c_3 = 0$. Then the formulas in (17) yield

$$c_4 = \frac{1}{12}, \quad c_5 = 0, \quad c_6 = \frac{1}{90}, \quad c_7 = 0, \quad c_8 = \frac{3}{1120};$$

thus

$$y_1(x) = 1 + \frac{1}{12}x^4 + \frac{1}{90}x^6 + \frac{3}{1120}x^8 + \cdots. \tag{18}$$

Because $c_1 = c_3 = 0$, it is clear from Eq. (16) that this series contains only terms of even degree.

To obtain our second linearly independent solution y_2 of Eq. (15), we take $c_0 = 0$ and $c_1 = 1$, so that $c_2 = 0$ and $c_3 = \frac{1}{6}$. Then the formulas in (17) yield

$$c_4 = 0, \quad c_5 = \frac{3}{40}, \quad c_6 = 0, \quad c_7 = \frac{13}{1008},$$

so that

$$y_2(x) = x + \frac{1}{6}x^3 + \frac{3}{40}x^5 + \frac{13}{1008}x^7 + \cdots. \tag{19}$$

Because $c_0 = c_2 = 0$, it is clear from Eq. (16) that this series contains only terms of odd degree. The solutions $y_1(x)$ and $y_2(x)$ are linearly independent because $y_1(0) = 1$ and $y_1'(0) = 0$, whereas $y_2(0) = 0$ and $y_2'(0) = 1$. The general solution of Eq. (15) is a linear combination of the power series in (18) and (19). Equation (15) has no singular points, so the power series representing $y_1(x)$ and $y_2(x)$ converge for all x. ∎

*The Legendre Equation

The **Legendre equation** of order α is the second-order linear differential equation

$$\blacktriangleright \qquad (1 - x^2)y'' - 2xy' + \alpha(\alpha + 1)y = 0, \tag{20}$$

where the real number α satisfies the inequality $\alpha > -1$. This differential equation has extensive applications, ranging from numerical integration formulas (such as Gaussian quadrature) to the problem of determining the steady state temperature within a solid spherical ball when the temperatures at points of its boundary are known. The only singular points of the Legendre equation are at $+1$ and -1, so it has two linearly independent solutions that can be expressed as power series in powers of x with radius of convergence at least 1. The substitution $y = \sum c_n x^n$ in Eq. (20) leads (see Problem 31) to the recurrence relation

$$\blacktriangleright \qquad c_{m+2} = -\frac{(\alpha - m)(\alpha + m + 1)}{(m + 1)(m + 2)} c_m \tag{21}$$

for $m \geq 0$. We are using m as the index of summation because we have another role for n to play.

In terms of the arbitrary constants c_0 and c_1, Eq. (21) yields

$$c_2 = -\frac{\alpha(\alpha + 1)}{2!} c_0,$$

$$c_3 = -\frac{(\alpha - 1)(\alpha + 2)}{3!} c_1,$$

$$c_4 = \frac{\alpha(\alpha - 2)(\alpha + 1)(\alpha + 3)}{4!} c_0,$$

$$c_5 = \frac{(\alpha - 1)(\alpha - 3)(\alpha + 2)(\alpha + 4)}{5!} c_1.$$

One can show without much trouble that for $m > 0$,

$$c_{2m} = (-1)^m \frac{\alpha(\alpha - 2)(\alpha - 4) \cdots (\alpha - 2m + 2)(\alpha + 1)(\alpha + 3) \cdots (\alpha + 2m - 1)}{(2m)!} c_0 \tag{22}$$

and

$$c_{2m+1} = (-1)^m \frac{(\alpha - 1)(\alpha - 3) \cdots (\alpha - 2m + 1)(\alpha + 2)(\alpha + 4) \cdots (\alpha + 2m)}{(2m + 1)!} c_1. \tag{23}$$

Alternatively,

$$c_{2m} = (-1)^m a_{2m} c_0 \quad \text{and} \quad c_{2m+1} = (-1)^m a_{2m+1} c_1,$$

where a_{2m} and a_{2m+1} denote the fractions in Eqs. (22) and (23), respectively. With this notation, we get two linearly independent power series solutions

$$y_1(x) = c_0 \sum_{m=0}^{\infty} (-1)^m a_{2m} x^{2m} \quad \text{and} \quad y_2(x) = c_1 \sum_{m=0}^{\infty} (-1)^m a_{2m+1} x^{2m+1} \tag{24}$$

of Legendre's equation of order α.

Now suppose that $\alpha = n$, a nonnegative *integer*. If $\alpha = n$ is even, we see from (22) that $a_{2m} = 0$ when $2m > n$. In this case $y_1(x)$ is a *polynomial* of degree n and y_2 is a (nonterminating) infinite series. If $\alpha = n$ is odd, we see from (23) that $a_{2m+1} = 0$ when $2m + 1 > n$. In this case, $y_2(x)$ is a *polynomial* of degree n and y_1 is a (nonterminating) infinite series. Thus in either case, one of the two solutions in (24) is a polynomial and the other is a nonterminating series.

With an appropriate choice (made separately for each n) of the arbitrary constants c_0 (n even) or c_1 (n odd), the nth-degree polynomial solution of Legendre's equation of order n,

$$\blacktriangleright \qquad\qquad (1 - x^2)y'' - 2xy' + n(n + 1) = 0, \tag{25}$$

is denoted by $P_n(x)$ and is called the **Legendre polynomial** of degree n. It is customary (for a reason indicated in Problem 32) to choose the arbitrary constant so that the coefficient of x^n in $P_n(x)$ is $(2n)!/[2^n(n!)^2]$. It then turns out that

$$\blacktriangleright \qquad\qquad P_n(x) = \sum_{k=0}^{N} \frac{(-1)^k (2n - 2k)!}{2^n k! (n - k)! (n - 2k)!} x^{n-2k}, \tag{26}$$

where $N = [\![n/2]\!]$, the integral part of $n/2$. The first six Legendre polynomials are

$$P_0(x) \equiv 1, \qquad\qquad P_1(x) = x,$$

$$P_2(x) = \frac{1}{2} (3x^2 - 1), \qquad\qquad P_3(x) = \frac{1}{2} (5x^3 - 3x),$$

$$P_4(x) = \frac{1}{8} (35x^4 - 30x^2 + 3), \qquad P_5(x) = \frac{1}{8} (63x^5 - 70x^3 + 15x).$$

8.2 Problems

Find general solutions in powers of x of the differential equations in Problems 1 through 15. State the recurrence relation and the guaranteed radius of convergence in each case.

1. $(x^2 - 1)y'' + 4xy' + 2y = 0$

2. $(x^2 + 2)y'' + 4xy' + 2y = 0$

3. $y'' + xy' + y = 0$

4. $(x^2 + 1)y'' + 6xy' + 4y = 0$

5. $(x^2 - 3)y'' + 2xy' = 0$

6. $(x^2 - 1)y'' - 6xy' + 12y = 0$

7. $(x^2 + 3)y'' - 7xy' + 16y = 0$

8. $(2 - x^2)y'' - xy' + 16y = 0$

9. $(x^2 - 1)y'' + 8xy' + 12y = 0$

10. $3y'' + xy' - 4y = 0$

11. $5y'' - 2xy' + 10y = 0$

12. $y'' - x^2y' - 3xy = 0$

13. $y'' + x^2y' + 2xy = 0$

14. $y'' + xy = 0$ (an *Airy equation*)

15. $y'' + x^2y = 0$

Use power series to solve the initial value problems in Problems 16 and 17.

16. $(1 + x^2)y'' + 2xy' - 2y = 0$; $y(0) = 0$ $y'(0) = 1$

17. $y'' + xy' - 2y = 0$; $y(0) = 1$, $y'(0) = 0$

Solve the initial value problems in Problems 18 through 22. First make a substitution of the form $t = x - a$, and then find a solution $\sum c_n t^n$ of the transformed differential equation. State the interval of values of x for which Theorem 1 of this section guarantees convergence.

18. $y'' + (x - 1)y' + y = 0$; $y(1) = 2$, $y'(1) = 0$

19. $(2x - x^2)y'' - 6(x - 1)y' - 4y = 0$; $y(1) = 0$, $y'(1) = 1$

20. $(x^2 - 6x + 10)y'' - 4(x - 3)y' + 6y = 0$; $y(3) = 2$, $y'(3) = 0$

21. $(4x^2 + 16x + 17)y'' = 8y$; $y(-2) = 1$, $y'(-2) = 0$

22. $(x^2 + 6x)y'' + (3x + 9)y' - 3y = 0$; $y(-3) = 0$, $y'(-3) = 2$

In Problems 23 through 26, find a three-term recurrence relation for solutions of the form $y = \sum c_n x^n$. Then find the first three nonzero terms in each of two linearly independent solutions.

23. $y'' + (1 + x)y = 0$

24. $(x^2 - 1)y'' + 2xy' + 2xy = 0$

25. $y'' + x^2y' + x^2y = 0$

26. $(1 + x^3)y'' + x^4y = 0$

27. Solve the initial value problem

$$y'' + xy' + (2x^2 + 1)y = 0; \qquad y(0) = 1, \qquad y'(0) = -1.$$

Determine sufficiently many terms to compute $y(1/2)$ accurate to four decimal places.

In Problems 28 through 30, find the first three nonzero terms in each of two linearly independent solutions of the form $y = \sum c_n x^n$. Substitute known Taylor series for the analytic functions and retain enough terms to compute the necessary coefficients.

28. $y'' + e^{-x}y = 0$

29. $(\cos x)y'' + y = 0$

30. $xy'' = (\sin x)y' + xy = 0$

31. Derive the recurrence relation in (21) for the Legendre equation.

32. Follow the steps outlined below to establish **Rodrigues' formula**

$$P_n(x) = \frac{1}{n!\, 2^n} \frac{d^n}{dx^n} (x^2 - 1)^n$$

for the nth-degree Legendre polynomial. (a) Show that $v = (x^2 - 1)^n$ satisfies the differential equation

$$(1 - x^2)v' + 2nxv = 0.$$

Differentiate each side of this equation to obtain

$$(1 - x^2)v'' + 2(n - 1)xv' + 2nv = 0.$$

(b) Differentiate each side of the last equation n times in succession to obtain

$$(1 - x^2)v^{(n+2)} - 2xv^{(n+1)} + n(n + 1)v^{(n)} = 0.$$

Thus $u = v^{(n)} = D^n(x^2 - 1)^n$ satisfies Legendre's equation of order n. (c) Show that the coefficient of x^n in u is $(2n)!/n!$; then state why this proves Rodrigues' formula. (Note that the coefficient of x^n in $P_n(x)$ is $(2n)!/[2^n(n!)^2]$.)

33. The **Hermite equation** of order α is

$$y'' - 2xy' + 2\alpha y = 0.$$

(a) Derive the two power series solutions

$$y_1 = 1 + \sum_{n=1}^{\infty} (-1)^m \frac{2^m \alpha(\alpha - 2) \cdots (\alpha - 2m + 2)}{(2m)!} x^{2m}$$

and

$$y_2 = x +$$
$$\sum_{m=1}^{\infty} (-1)^m \frac{2^m (\alpha - 1)(\alpha - 3) \cdots (\alpha - 2m + 1)}{(2m + 1)!} x^{2m+1}.$$

Show that y_1 is a polynomial if α is an even integer, whereas y_2 is a polynomial if α is an odd integer. (b) The **Hermite polynomial** of degree n is denoted by $H_n(x)$. It is the nth-degree polynomial solution of Hermite's equation, multiplied by a suitable constant so that the coefficient of x^n is 2^n. Show that the

first six Hermite polynomials are

$$H_0(x) \equiv 1, \qquad H_1(x) = 2x,$$

$$H_2(x) = 4x^2 - 2, \quad H_3(x) = 8x^3 - 12x,$$

$$H_4(x) = 16x^4 - 48x^2 + 12,$$

$$H_5(x) = 32x^5 - 160x^3 + 120x.$$

(c) A general formula for the Hermite polynomials is

$$H_n(x) = (-1)^n e^{x^2} \frac{d^n}{dx^n} \left(e^{-x^2} \right).$$

Verify that this formula does in fact give an nth-degree polynomial.

8.2 Computing Project

Here we illustrate the use of a computer algebra system to apply the power series method. As a first example, follow along with us in solving the differential equation $y'' + y = 0$ of Example 4 in Section 8.1. Using *Mathematica,* we first write the initial 10 terms of a proposed series solution:

```
y = Sum[ c[n] x^n, {n, 0, 9} ] + O[x]^10
```

$$c[0] + c[1]\ x + c[2]\ x^2 + c[3]\ x^3 + c[4]\ x^4 + c[5]\ x^5 +$$
$$c[6]\ x^6 + c[7]\ x^7 + c[8]\ x^8 + c[9]\ x^9 + O[x]^{10}$$

Then we substitute this series into the differential equation

```
deq1 = D[ y, x, x ] + y == 0
```

$$(c[0] + 2\ c[2]) + (c[1] + 6\ c[3])\ x + (c[2] + 12\ c[4])\ x^2$$
$$(c[3] + 20\ c[5])\ x^3 + (c[4] + 30\ c[6])\ x^4 +$$
$$(c[5] + 42\ c[7])\ x^5 + (c[6] + 56\ c[8])\ x^6 +$$
$$(c[7] + 72\ c[9])\ x^7 + O[x]^8 == 0$$

Note that *Mathematica* has automatically collected coefficients of like powers for us! In fact, we can ask it to extract the equations the successive coefficients satisfy, using the command **LogicalExpand[series == 0]** that equates each of the series coefficients to zero.

```
coeffEqns = LogicalExpand[ deq1 ]
```

$$c[0] + 2\ c[2] == 0\ \&\&\ c[1] + 6\ c[3] == 0\ \&\&$$
$$c[2] + 12\ c[4] == 0\ \&\&\ c[3] + 20\ c[5] == 0\ \&\&$$
$$c[4] + 30\ c[6] == 0\ \&\&\ c[5] + 42\ c[7] == 0\ \&\&$$
$$c[6] + 56\ c[8] == 0\ \&\&\ c[7] + 72\ c[9] == 0$$

The double ampersand **&&** is just "and" in *Mathematica,* so we have here a collection of eight linear equations relating the ten coefficients (**c[0]** through **c[9]**). We therefore should be able to solve for the successive coefficients

> **succCoeffs = Table[c[n], {n, 2, 9}]**

> {c[2], c[3], c[4], c[5], c[6], c[7], c[8], c[9]}

in terms of **c[0]** and **c[1]**.

> **coeffs = Solve[coeffEqns, succCoeffs]**

$$\{\{c[8] \rightarrow \frac{c[0]}{40320}, \quad c[9] \rightarrow \frac{c[1]}{362880},$$

$$c[2] \rightarrow \frac{-c[0]}{2}, \quad c[3] \rightarrow \frac{-c[1]}{6},$$

$$c[4] \rightarrow \frac{c[0]}{24}, \quad c[5] \rightarrow \frac{c[1]}{120},$$

$$c[6] \rightarrow \frac{-c[0]}{720}, \quad c[7] \rightarrow \frac{-c[1]}{5040}\}\}$$

Now substitute all these coefficients back into the series.

> **genSoln = y /. coeffs**

$$\{c[0] + c[1] \ x - \frac{c[0] \ x^2}{2} - \frac{c[1] \ x^3}{6} + \frac{c[0] \ x^4}{24} + \frac{c[1] \ x^5}{120} -$$

$$\frac{c[0] \ x^6}{720} - \frac{c[1] \ x^7}{5040} + \frac{c[0] \ x^8}{40320} + \frac{c[1] \ x^9}{362880} + O[x]^{10}\}$$

We can finally extract our two linearly independent solutions by picking out the coefficients of **c[0]** and **c[1]**.

> **ourCos = Coefficient[genSoln, c[0]]**

$$\{1 - \frac{x^2}{2} + \frac{x^4}{24} - \frac{x^6}{720} + \frac{x^8}{40320}\}$$

> **ourSin = Coefficient[genSoln, c[1]]**

$$\{x - \frac{x^3}{6} + \frac{x^5}{120} - \frac{x^7}{5040} + \frac{x^9}{362880}\}$$

Of course, we recognize the initial terms of the cosine and sine series, respectively.

You can assemble the preceding commands in a "template" for application to differential equations such as those in Problems 1 through 15 of this section.

An interesting application is to derive in this way Legendre polynomials like those listed at the end of this section. For instance, try substituting the series **y** above in the Legendre equation $(1 - x^2)y'' - 2xy' + 30y = 0$ of order $n = 5$. One of the two linearly independent solutions you obtain should be a constant multiple of $P_5(x)$. The Hermite polynomials of Problem 33 can be derived similarly.

Maple users can use the built-in **dsolve** procedure with the **series** option to solve directly for power series solutions of a linear differential equation having $x = 0$

as an ordinary point. For example, with the Legendre equation

```
> deq2 := (1 - x^2)*diff(y(x),x,x) - 2*x*diff(y(x),x) + 30*y(x) = 0:
```

mentioned earlier, we obtain two (truncated) linearly independent series solutions by specifying the initial conditions as follows:

```
> Order := 12:
```

```
> dsolve({deq2, y(0)=0, D(y)(0)=1}, y(x), series);
```

$$y(x) = x - \frac{14}{3} x^3 + \frac{21}{5} x^5 + O(x^{12})$$

```
> dsolve({deq2, y(0)=1, D(y)(0)=0}, y(x), series);
```

$$y(x) = 1 - 15x^2 + 30x^4 - 10x^6 - \frac{15}{7} x^8 - x^{10} + O(x^{12})$$

The first of these provides a constant multiple of the standard fifth-order Legendre polynomial $P_5(x)$.

8.3 Regular Singular Points

We now investigate the solution of the homogeneous second-order linear equation

$$A(x)y'' + B(x)y' + C(x)y = 0 \tag{1}$$

near a singular point. Recall that if the functions A, B, and C are polynomials having no common factors, then the singular points of Eq. (1) are simply those points where $A(x)$ vanishes. For instance, $x = 0$ is the only singular point of the Bessel equation of order n,

$$x^2y'' + xy' + (x^2 - n^2)y = 0,$$

whereas the Legendre equation of order n,

$$(1 - x^2)y'' - 2xy' + n(n + 1)y = 0,$$

has the two singular points $x = -1$ and $x = 1$. It turns out that some of the features of the solutions of such equations of the most importance for applications are largely determined by their behavior near their singular points.

We will restrict our attention to the case in which $x = 0$ is a singular point of Eq. (1). A differential equation having $x = a$ as a singular point is easily transformed by the substitution $t = x - a$ into one having a corresponding singular point at 0. For example, let us substitute $t = x - 1$ in the Legendre equation of order n. Because

$$y' = \frac{dy}{dx} = \frac{dy}{dt} \frac{dt}{dx} = \frac{dy}{dt},$$

$$y'' = \frac{d^2y}{dx^2} = \left[\frac{d}{dt} \left(\frac{dy}{dt} \right) \right] \frac{dt}{dx} = \frac{d^2y}{dt^2},$$

and $1 - x^2 = 1 - (t + 1)^2 = -2t - t^2$, we get the equation

$$-t(t + 2)\frac{d^2 y}{dt^2} - 2(t + 1)\frac{dy}{dt} + n(n + 1)y = 0.$$

This new equation has the singular point $t = 0$ corresponding to $x = 1$ in the original equation; it has also the singular point $t = -2$ corresponding to $x = -1$.

Types of Singular Points

A differential equation having a singular point at 0 ordinarily will *not* have power series solutions of the form $y(x) = \sum c_n x^n$, so the straightforward methods of Section 8.2 fail in this case. To investigate the form that a solution of such an equation might take, we assume that Eq. (1) has analytic coefficient functions and rewrite it in the standard form

$$\blacktriangleright \qquad y'' + P(x)y' + Q(x)y = 0, \qquad\qquad (2)$$

where $P = B/A$ and $Q = C/A$. Recall that $x = 0$ is an ordinary point (as opposed to a singular point) of Eq. (2) if the functions $P(x)$ and $Q(x)$ are analytic at $x = 0$; that is, if $P(x)$ and $Q(x)$ have convergent power series expansions in powers of x on some open interval containing $x = 0$. Now it can be proved that each of the functions $P(x)$ and $Q(x)$ *either* is analytic *or* approaches $\pm\infty$ as $x \to 0$. Consequently, $x = 0$ is a singular point of Eq. (2) provided that either $P(x)$ or $Q(x)$ (or both) approaches $\pm\infty$ as $x \to 0$. For instance, if we rewrite the Bessel equation of order n in the form

$$y'' + \frac{1}{x}y + \left(1 - \frac{n^2}{x^2}\right)y = 0,$$

we see that $P(x) = 1/x$ and $Q(x) = 1 - (n/x)^2$ both approach infinity as $x \to 0$.

We will see presently that the power series method can be generalized to apply near the singular point $x = 0$ of Eq. (2), provided that $P(x)$ approaches infinity no more rapidly that $1/x$, and $Q(x)$ no more rapidly that $1/x^2$, as $x \to 0$. This is a way of saying that $P(x)$ and $Q(x)$ have only "weak" singularities at $x = 0$. To state this more precisely, we rewrite Eq. (2) in the form

$$\blacktriangleright \qquad y'' + \frac{p(x)}{x}y' + \frac{q(x)}{x^2}y = 0, \qquad\qquad (3)$$

where

$$\blacktriangleright \qquad p(x) = xP(x) \qquad \text{and} \qquad q(x) = x^2 Q(x). \qquad\qquad (4)$$

DEFINITION: Regular Singular Point

The singular point $x = 0$ of Eq. (3) is a **regular singular point** if the functions $p(x)$ and $q(x)$ are both analytic at $x = 0$. Otherwise it is an **irregular singular point.** ■

In particular, the singular point $x = 0$ is a *regular* singular point if $p(x)$ and $q(x)$ are both polynomials. For instance, we see that $x = 0$ is a regular singular point of

Bessel's equation of order n by writing that equation in the form

$$y'' + \frac{1}{x} y' + \frac{x^2 - n^2}{x^2} y = 0,$$

noting that $p(x) \equiv 1$ and $q(x) = x^2 - n^2$ are both polynomials in x.

By contrast, consider the equation

$$2x^3 y'' + (1 + x)y' + 3xy = 9,$$

which has the singular point $x = 0$. If we write this equation in the form of (3), we get

$$y'' + \frac{(1 + x)/(2x^2)}{x} y' + \frac{\frac{3}{2}}{x^2} y = 0.$$

Because

$$p(x) = \frac{1 + x}{2x^2} = \frac{1}{2x^2} + \frac{1}{2x} \to \infty$$

as $x \to 0$ (although $q(x) \equiv \frac{3}{2}$ is a polynomial), we see that $x = 0$ is an irregular singular point. We will not discuss the solution of differential equations near irregular singular points; this is a considerably more advanced topic than the solution of differential equations near regular singular points.

EXAMPLE 1 Consider the differential equation

$$x^2(1 + x)y'' + x(4 - x^2)y' + (2 + 3x)y = 0.$$

In the standard form $y'' + Py' + Qy = 0$ it is

$$y'' + \frac{4 - x^2}{x(1 + x)} y' + \frac{2 + 3x}{x^2(1 + x)} y = 0.$$

Because

$$P(x) = \frac{4 - x^2}{x(1 + x)} \qquad \text{and} \qquad Q(x) = \frac{2 + 3x}{x^2(1 + x)}$$

both approach ∞ as $x \to 0$, we see that $x = 0$ is a singular point. To determine the nature of this singular point we write the differential equation in the form of Eq. (3):

$$y'' + \frac{(4 - x^2)/(1 + x)}{x} y' + \frac{(2 + 3x)/(1 + x)}{x^2} y = 0.$$

Thus

$$p(x) = \frac{4 - x^2}{1 + x} \qquad \text{and} \qquad q(x) = \frac{2 + 3x}{1 + x}.$$

Because a quotient of polynomials is analytic wherever the denominator is nonzero, we see that $p(x)$ and $q(x)$ are both analytic at $x = 0$. Hence $x = 0$ is a *regular* singular point of the given differential equation. ∎

It may happen that when we begin with a differential equation in the general form in Eq. (1) and rewrite it in the form in (3), the functions $p(x)$ and $q(x)$ as given in (4) are indeterminate forms at $x = 0$. In this case the situation is determined by the limits

$$p_0 = p(0) = \lim_{x \to 0} p(x) = \lim_{x \to 0} xP(x) \tag{5}$$

and

$$q_0 = q(0) = \lim_{x \to 0} q(x) = \lim_{x \to 0} x^2 Q(x). \tag{6}$$

If $p_0 = 0 = q_0$ then $x = 0$ may be an ordinary point. Otherwise, if the limits in both (5) and (6) exist and are *finite*, then $x = 0$ is a regular singular point. If either limit fails to exist or is infinite, then $x = 0$ is an irregular singular point.

Remark: The most common case in applications, for the differential equation written in the form

$$y'' + \frac{p(x)}{x} y' + \frac{q(x)}{x^2} y = 0, \tag{3}$$

is that the functions $p(x)$ and $q(x)$ are *polynomials*. In this case $p_0 = p(0)$ and $q_0 = q(0)$ are simply the constant terms of these polynomials, so there is no need to evaluate the limits in Eqs. (5) and (6).

EXAMPLE 2 To investigate the nature of the point $x = 0$ for the differential equation

$$x^4 y'' + (x^2 \sin x) y' + (1 - \cos x) y = 0,$$

we first write it in the form in (3):

$$y'' + \frac{(\sin x)/x}{x} y' + \frac{(1 - \cos x)/x^2}{x^2} y = 0.$$

Then l'Hôpital's rule gives the values

$$p_0 = \lim_{x \to 0} \frac{\sin x}{x} = \lim_{x \to 0} \frac{\cos x}{1} = 1$$

and

$$q_0 = \lim_{x \to 0} \frac{1 - \cos x}{x^2} = \lim_{x \to 0} \frac{\sin x}{2x} = \frac{1}{2}$$

for the limits in Eqs. (5) and (6). While not both are zero, we see that $x = 0$ is a regular singular point because each limit is finite. Alternatively, we could write

$$p(x) = \frac{\sin x}{x} = \frac{1}{x}\left(x - \frac{x^3}{3!} + \frac{x^5}{5!} - \cdots\right) = 1 - \frac{x^2}{3!} + \frac{x^4}{5!} - \cdots$$

and

$$q(x) = \frac{1 - \cos x}{x^2} = \frac{1}{x^2}\left[1 - \left(1 - \frac{x^2}{2!} + \frac{x^4}{4!} - \frac{x^6}{6!} + \cdots\right)\right]$$

$$= \frac{1}{2!} - \frac{x^2}{4!} + \frac{x^4}{6!} - \cdots.$$

These (convergent) power series show explicitly that $p(x)$ and $q(x)$ are analytic and moreover that $p_0 = p(0) = 1$ and $q_0 = q(0) = \frac{1}{2}$. ∎

The Method of Frobenius

We now approach the task of actually finding solutions of a second-order linear differential equation near the regular singular point $x = 0$. The simplest such equation is the

constant-coefficient *equidimensional equation*

$$x^2 y'' + p_0 x y' + q_0 y = 0 \tag{7}$$

to which Eq. (3) reduces when $p(x) \equiv p_0$ and $q(x) \equiv q_0$ are constants. In this case we can verify by direct substitution that the simple power function $y(x) = x^r$ is a solution of Eq. (7) if and only if r is a root of the quadratic equation

$$r(r - 1) + p_0 r + q_0 = 0. \tag{8}$$

In the general case, in which $p(x)$ and $q(x)$ are power series rather than constants, it is a reasonable conjecture that our differential equation might have a solution of the form

$$y(x) = x^r \sum_{n=0}^{\infty} c_n x^n = \sum_{n=0}^{\infty} c_n x^{n+r} = c_0 x^r + c_1 x^{r+1} + c_2 x^{r+2} + \cdots \tag{9}$$

—the product of x^r and a power series. This turns out to be a very fruitful conjecture; according to Theorem 1 (soon to be stated formally), every equation of the form in (1) having $x = 0$ as a regular singular point does, indeed, have at least one such solution. This fact is the basis for the **method of Frobenius,** named for the German mathematician Georg Frobenius (1848–1917), who discovered the method in the 1870s.

An infinite series of the form in (9) is called a **Frobenius series.** Note that a Frobenius series is generally *not* a power series. For instance, with $r = -\frac{1}{2}$ the series in (9) takes the form

$$y = c_0 x^{-1/2} + c_1 x^{1/2} + c_2 x^{3/2} + \cdots ;$$

it is not a series in *integral* powers of x.

To investigate the possible existence of Frobenius series solutions, we begin with the equation

$$x^2 y'' + x p(x) y' + q(x) y = 0 \tag{10}$$

obtained by multiplying the equation in (3) by x^2. If $x = 0$ is a regular singular point, then $p(x)$ and $q(x)$ are analytic at $x = 0$, so

$$\begin{aligned} p(x) &= p_0 + p_1 x + p_2 x^2 + \cdots , \\ q(x) &= q_0 + q_1 x + q_2 x^2 + \cdots . \end{aligned} \tag{11}$$

Suppose that Eq. (10) has the Frobenius series solution

$$y = \sum_{n=0}^{\infty} c_n x^{n+r}. \tag{12}$$

We may (and always do) assume that $c_0 \neq 0$ because the series must have a first nonzero term. Termwise differentiation in (12) leads to

$$y' = \sum_{n=0}^{\infty} c_n (n + r) x^{n+r-1} \tag{13}$$

and

$$y'' = \sum_{n=0}^{\infty} c_n (n + r)(n + r - 1) x^{n+r-2}. \tag{14}$$

Substitution of the series in Eqs. (11) through (14) in Eq. (10) now yields

$$[r(r-1)c_0x^r + (r+1)rc_1x^{r+1} + \cdots]$$
$$+ [p_0x + p_1x^2 + \cdots][rc_0x^{r-1} + (r+1)c_1x^r + \cdots]$$
$$+ [q_0 + q_1x + \cdots][c_0x^r + c_1x^{r+1} + \cdots] = 0. \tag{15}$$

The lowest power of x that appears in Eq. (15) is x^r. If Eq. (15) is to be satisfied identically, the coefficient $r(r-1)c_0 + p_0rc_0 + q_0c_0$ of x^r must vanish. Because $c_0 \neq 0$, it follows that r must satisfy the quadratic equation

▶
$$r(r-1) + p_0r + q_0 = 0 \tag{16}$$

of precisely the same form as that obtained with the equidimensional equation in (7). Equation (16) is called the **indicial equation** of the differential equation in (10), and its two roots (possibly equal) are the **exponents** of the differential equation (at the regular singular point $x = 0$).

 Our derivation of Eq. (16) shows that *if* the Frobenius series $y = x^r \sum c_n x^n$ is to be a solution of the differential equation in (10), *then* the exponent r must be one of the roots r_1 and r_2 of the indicial equation in (16). If $r_1 \neq r_2$ it follows that there are two possible Frobenius series solutions, whereas if $r_1 = r_2$ there is only one possible Frobenius series solution; the second solution cannot be a Frobenius series. The exponents r_1 and r_2 in the possible Frobenius series solutions are determined (using the indicial equation) by the values $p_0 = p(0)$ and $q_0 = q(0)$ that we have discussed. In practice, particularly when the coefficients in the differential equation in the original form in (1) are polynomials, the simplest way of finding p_0 and q_0 is often to write the equation in the form

$$y'' + \frac{p_0 + p_1x + \cdots}{x}y' + \frac{q_0 + q_1x + \cdots}{x^2}y = 0. \tag{17}$$

Then inspection of the series that appear in the two numerators reveals the constants p_0 and q_0.

EXAMPLE 3 Find the exponents in the possible Frobenius series solutions of the equation

$$2x^2(1+x)y'' + 3x(1+x)^3y' - (1-x^2)y = 0.$$

 Solution We divide each term by $2x^2(1+x)$ to recast the differential equation in the form

$$y'' + \frac{\frac{3}{2}(1 + 2x + x^2)}{x}y' + \frac{-\frac{1}{2}(1-x)}{x^2}y = 0,$$

and thus see that $p_0 = \frac{3}{2}$ and $q_0 = -\frac{1}{2}$. Hence the indicial equation is

$$r(r-1) + \frac{3}{2}r - \frac{1}{2} = r^2 + \frac{1}{2}r - \frac{1}{2} = (r+1)\left(r - \frac{1}{2}\right) = 0,$$

with roots $r_1 = \frac{1}{2}$ and $r_2 = -1$. The two possible Frobenius series solutions are then of the forms

$$y_1(x) = x^{1/2}\sum_{n=0}^{\infty} a_n x^n \qquad \text{and} \qquad y_2(x) = x^{-1}\sum_{n=0}^{\infty} b_n x^n.$$

Frobenius Series Solutions

Once the exponents r_1 and r_2 are known, the coefficients in a Frobenius series solution are determined by substitution of the series in Eqs. (12) through (14) in the differential equation, essentially the same method as was used to determine coefficients in power series solutions in Section 8.2. If the exponents r_1 and r_2 are complex conjugates, then there always exist two linearly independent Frobenius series solutions. We will restrict our attention here to the case in which r_1 and r_2 are both real. We also will seek solutions only for $x > 0$. Once such a solution has been found, we need only replace x^{r_1} with $|x|^{r_1}$ to obtain a solution for $x < 0$. The following theorem is proved in Chapter 4 of Coddington's *An Introduction to Ordinary Differential Equations*.

THEOREM 1: Frobenius Series Solutions

Suppose that $x = 0$ is a regular singular point of the equation

$$x^2 y'' + x p(x) y' + q(x) y = 0. \tag{10}$$

Let $\rho > 0$ denote the minimum of the radii of convergence of the power series

$$p(x) = \sum_{n=0}^{\infty} p_n x^n \quad \text{and} \quad q(x) = \sum_{n=0}^{\infty} q_n x^n.$$

Let r_1 and r_2 be the roots, with $r_1 \geqq r_2$, of the indicial equation $r(r-1) + p_0 r + q_0 = 0$. Then:

(a) For $x > 0$, there exists a solution of Eq. (10) of the form

$$y_1(x) = x^{r_1} \sum_{n=0}^{\infty} a_n x^n \quad (a_0 \neq 0) \tag{18}$$

corresponding to the larger root r_1.

(b) If $r_1 - r_2$ is neither zero nor a positive integer, then there exists a second linearly independent solution for $x > 0$ of the form

$$y_2(x) = x^{r_2} \sum_{n=0}^{\infty} b_n x^n \quad (b_0 \neq 0) \tag{19}$$

corresponding to the smaller root r_2.

The radii of convergence of the power series in Eqs. (18) and (19) are each at least ρ. The coefficients in these series can be determined by substituting the series in the differential equation

$$x^2 y'' + x p(x) y' + q(x) y = 0. \tag{10}$$

∎

We have already seen that if $r_1 = r_2$, then there can exist only one Frobenius series solution. It turns out that, if $r_1 - r_2$ is a positive integer, there may or may not exist a second Frobenius series solution of the form in Eq. (19) corresponding to the smaller root r_2. These exceptional cases are discussed in Section 8.4. Examples 4 through 6 illustrate the process of determining the coefficients in those Frobenius series solutions that are guaranteed by Theorem 1.

EXAMPLE 4 Find the Frobenius series solutions of

$$2x^2 y'' + 3xy' - (x^2 + 1)y = 0. \tag{20}$$

Solution First we divide each term by $2x^2$ to put the equation in the form in (17):

$$y'' + \frac{\frac{3}{2}}{x} y' + \frac{-\frac{1}{2} - \frac{1}{2} x^2}{x^2} y = 0. \tag{21}$$

We now see that $x = 0$ is a regular singular point, and that $p_0 = \frac{3}{2}$ and $q_0 = -\frac{1}{2}$. Because $p(x) \equiv \frac{3}{2}$ and $q(x) = -\frac{1}{2} - \frac{1}{2} x^2$ are polynomials, the Frobenius series we obtain will converge for all $x > 0$. The indicial equation is

$$r(r - 1) + \frac{3}{2} r - \frac{1}{2} = \left(r - \frac{1}{2} \right)(r + 1) = 0,$$

so the exponents are $r_1 = \frac{1}{2}$ and $r_2 = -1$. They do not differ by an integer, so the theorem guarantees the existence of two linearly independent Frobenius series solutions. Rather than separately substituting

$$y_1 = x^{1/2} \sum a_n x^n \quad \text{and} \quad y_2 = x^{-1} \sum b_n x^n$$

in Eq. (20), it is more efficient to begin by substituting $y = x^r \sum c_n x^n$. We will then get a recurrence relation that depends on r. With the value $r_1 = \frac{1}{2}$ it becomes a recurrence relation for the series for y_1, whereas with $r_2 = -1$ it becomes a recurrence relation for the series for y_2.

When we substitute

▶
$$y = \sum_{n=0}^{\infty} c_n x^{n+r}, \qquad y' = \sum_{n=0}^{\infty} (n + r)c_n x^{n+r-1},$$

and

▶
$$y'' = \sum_{n=0}^{\infty} (n + r)(n + r - 1)c_n x^{n+r-2}$$

in Eq. (20)—the original differential equation, rather than Eq. (21)—we get

$$2 \sum_{n=0}^{\infty} (n + r)(n + r - 1)c_n x^{n+r} + 3 \sum_{n=0}^{\infty} (n + r)c_n x^{n+r}$$

$$- \sum_{n=0}^{\infty} c_n x^{n+r+2} - \sum_{n=0}^{\infty} c_n x^{n+r} = 0. \tag{22}$$

At this stage there are several ways to proceed. A good standard practice is to shift indices so that each exponent will be the same as the smallest one present. In this example, we shift the index of summation in the third sum by -2 to bring its exponent down from $n + r + 2$ to $n + r$. This gives

$$2 \sum_{n=0}^{\infty} (n + r)(n + r - 1)c_n x^{n+r} + 3 \sum_{n=0}^{\infty} (n + r)c_n x^{n+r}$$

$$- \sum_{n=2}^{\infty} c_{n-2} x^{n+r} - \sum_{n=0}^{\infty} c_n x^{n+r} = 0. \tag{23}$$

The common range of summation is $n \geq 2$, so we must treat $n = 0$ and $n = 1$ separately. Following our standard practice, the terms corresponding to $n = 0$ will always give the indicial equation

$$[2r(r-1) + 3r - 1]c_0 = 2\left(r^2 + \frac{1}{2}r - \frac{1}{2}\right)c_0 = 0.$$

The terms corresponding to $n = 1$ yield

$$[2(r+1)r + 3(r+1) - 1]c_1 = (2r^2 + 5r + 2)c_1 = 0.$$

Because the coefficient $2r^2 + 5r + 2$ of c_1 is nonzero whether $r = \frac{1}{2}$ or $r = -1$, it follows that

$$c_1 = 0 \tag{24}$$

in either case.

The coefficient of x^{n+r} in Eq. (23) is

$$2(n+r)(n+r-1)c_n + 3(n+r)c_n - c_{n-2} - c_n = 0.$$

We solve for c_n and simplify to obtain the recurrence relation

$$\blacktriangleright \qquad c_n = \frac{c_{n-2}}{2(n+r)^2 + (n+r) - 1} \qquad \text{for } n \geq 2. \tag{25}$$

The case $r_1 = \frac{1}{2}$: We now write a_n in place of c_n and substitute $r = \frac{1}{2}$ in Eq. (25). This gives the recurrence relation

$$\blacktriangleright \qquad a_n = \frac{a_{n-2}}{2n^2 + 3n} \qquad \text{for } n \geq 2. \tag{26}$$

With this formula we can determine the coefficients in the first Frobenius solution y_1. In view of Eq. (24) we see that $a_n = 0$ whenever n is odd. With $n = 2, 4,$ and 6 in Eq. (26), we get

$$a_2 = \frac{a_0}{14}, \qquad a_4 = \frac{a_2}{44} = \frac{a_0}{616}, \qquad \text{and} \qquad a_6 = \frac{a_4}{90} = \frac{a_0}{55440}.$$

Hence our first Frobenius series solution is

$$y_1(x) = a_0 x^{1/2}\left(1 + \frac{x^2}{14} + \frac{x^4}{616} + \frac{x^6}{55440} + \cdots\right).$$

The case $r_2 = -1$: We may now write b_n in place of c_n and substitute $r = -1$ in (25). This gives the recurrence relation

$$\blacktriangleright \qquad b_n = \frac{b_{n-2}}{2n^2 - 3n} \qquad \text{for } n \geq 2. \tag{27}$$

Again, Eq. (24) implies that $b_n = 0$ for n odd. With $n = 2, 4,$ and 6 in (27), we get

$$b_2 = \frac{b_0}{2}, \qquad b_4 = \frac{b_2}{20} = \frac{b_0}{40}, \qquad \text{and} \qquad b_6 = \frac{b_4}{54} = \frac{b_0}{2160}.$$

Hence our second Frobenius series solution is

$$y_2(x) = b_0 x^{-1}\left(1 + \frac{1}{2}x^2 + \frac{x^4}{40} + \frac{x^6}{2160} + \cdots\right).$$

EXAMPLE 5 Find a Frobenius solution of Bessel's equation of order zero,

▶
$$x^2 y'' + xy' + x^2 y = 0. \tag{28}$$

Solution In the form of (17), Eq. (28) becomes

$$y'' + \frac{1}{x} y + \frac{x^2}{x^2} y = 0.$$

Hence $x = 0$ is a regular singular point with $p(x) \equiv 1$ and $q(x) = x^2$, so our series will converge for all $x > 0$. Because $p_0 = 1$ and $q_0 = 0$, the indicial equation is

$$r(r - 1) + r = r^2 = 0.$$

Thus we obtain only the single exponent $r = 0$, and so there is only one Frobenius series solution

$$y(x) = x^0 \sum_{n=0}^{\infty} c_n x^n$$

of Eq. (28); it is in fact a power series.

Thus we substitute $y = \sum c_n x^n$ in (28); the result is

$$\sum_{n=0}^{\infty} n(n-1)c_n x^n + \sum_{n=0}^{\infty} nc_n x^n + \sum_{n=0}^{\infty} c_n x^{n+2} = 0.$$

We combine the first two sums and shift the index of summation in the third by -2 to obtain

$$\sum_{n=0}^{\infty} n^2 c_n x^n + \sum_{n=2}^{\infty} c_{n-2} x^n = 0.$$

The term corresponding to x^0 gives $0 = 0$: no information. The term corresponding to x^1 gives $c_1 = 0$, and the term for x^n yields the recurrence relation

▶
$$c_n = -\frac{c_{n-2}}{n^2} \qquad \text{for } n \geq 2. \tag{29}$$

Because $c_1 = 0$, we see that $c_n = 0$ whenever n is odd. Substituting $n = 2, 4,$ and 6 in Eq. (29), we get

$$c_2 = -\frac{c_0}{2^2}, \qquad c_4 = -\frac{c_2}{4^2} = \frac{c_0}{2^2 4^2}, \qquad \text{and} \qquad c_6 = -\frac{c_4}{6^2} = -\frac{c_0}{2^2 4^2 6^2}.$$

Evidently, the pattern is

▶
$$c_{2n} = \frac{(-1)^n c_0}{2^2 \cdot 4^2 \cdots (2n)^2} = \frac{(-1)^n c_0}{2^{2n}(n!)^2}.$$

The choice $c_0 = 0$ gives us one of the most important special functions in mathematics, the **Bessel function of order zero of the first kind,** denoted by $J_0(x)$. Thus

▶
$$J_0(x) = \sum_{n=0}^{\infty} \frac{(-1)^n x^{2n}}{2^{2n}(n!)^2} = 1 - \frac{x^2}{4} + \frac{x^4}{64} - \frac{x^6}{2304} + \cdots. \tag{30}$$

In this example we have not been able to find a second linearly independent solution of Bessel's equation of order zero. We will derive that solution in Section 8.4; it will not be a Frobenius series.

When $r_1 - r_2$ is an Integer

Recall that, if $r_1 - r_2$ is a positive integer, then Theorem 1 guarantees only the existence of the Frobenius series solution corresponding to the larger exponent r_1. Example 6 illustrates the fortunate case in which the series method nevertheless yields a second Frobenius series solution. The case in which the second solution is not a Frobenius series will be discussed in Section 8.4.

EXAMPLE 6 Find the Frobenius series solutions of

$$xy'' + 2y' + xy = 0. \qquad (31)$$

Solution In standard form the equation becomes

$$y'' + \frac{2}{x}y' + \frac{x^2}{x^2}y = 0,$$

so we see that $x = 0$ is a regular singular point with $p_0 = 2$ and $q_0 = 0$. The indicial equation

$$r(r - 1) + 2r = r(r + 1) = 0$$

has roots $r_1 = 0$ and $r_2 = -1$, which differ by an integer. In this case when $r_1 - r_2$ is an integer, it is better to depart from the standard procedure of Example 4 and begin our work with the *smaller* exponent. As you will see, the recurrence relation will then tell us whether or not a second Frobenius series solution exists. If it does exist, our computations will simultaneously yield *both* Frobenius series solutions. If the second solution does not exist, we begin anew with the larger exponent $r = r_1$ to obtain the one Frobenius series solution guaranteed by Theorem 1.

Hence we begin by substituting

$$y = x^{-1} \sum_{n=0}^{\infty} c_n x^n = \sum_{n=0}^{\infty} c_n x^{n-1}$$

in (31). This gives

$$\sum_{n=0}^{\infty} (n-1)(n-2)c_n x^{n-2} + 2\sum_{n=0}^{\infty} (n-1)c_n x^{n-2} + \sum_{n=0}^{\infty} c_n x^n = 0.$$

We combine the first two sums and shift the index by -2 in the third to obtain

$$\sum_{n=0}^{\infty} n(n-1)c_n x^{n-2} + \sum_{n=2}^{\infty} c_{n-2} x^{n-2} = 0. \qquad (32)$$

The cases $n = 0$ and $n = 1$ reduce to

$$0 \cdot c_0 = 0 \quad \text{and} \quad 0 \cdot c_1 = 0.$$

Hence we have *two* arbitrary constants c_0 and c_1, and therefore can expect to find a general solution incorporating two linearly independent Frobenius series solutions. If, for $n = 1$, we had obtained an equation such as $0 \cdot c_1 = 3$, which can be satisfied for *no* choice of c_1, this would have told us that no second Frobenius series solution could exist.

Now knowing that all is well, from (32) we read the recurrence relation

$$c_n = -\frac{c_{n-2}}{n(n-1)} \qquad \text{for } n \geq 2. \tag{33}$$

The first few values of n give

$$c_2 = -\frac{1}{2 \cdot 1} c_0, \qquad\qquad c_3 = -\frac{1}{3 \cdot 2} c_1,$$

$$c_4 = -\frac{1}{4 \cdot 3} c_2 = \frac{c_0}{4!}, \qquad c_5 = -\frac{1}{5 \cdot 4} c_3, = \frac{c_1}{5!},$$

$$c_6 = -\frac{1}{6 \cdot 5} c_4 = -\frac{c_0}{6!}, \qquad c_7 = -\frac{1}{7 \cdot 6} c_5, = -\frac{c_1}{7!};$$

evidently the pattern is

$$c_{2n} = \frac{(-1)^n c_0}{(2n)!}, \qquad c_{2n+1} = \frac{(-1)^n c_1}{(2n+1)!}$$

for $n \geq 1$. Therefore our solution is

$$y(x) = x^{-1} \sum_{n=0}^{\infty} c_n x^n$$

$$= \frac{c_0}{x}\left(1 - \frac{x^2}{2!} + \frac{x^4}{4!} - \cdots\right) + \frac{c_1}{x}\left(x - \frac{x^3}{3!} + \frac{x^5}{5!} - \cdots\right)$$

$$= \frac{c_0}{x} \sum_{n=0}^{\infty} \frac{(-1)^n x^{2n}}{(2n)!} + \frac{c_1}{x} \sum_{n=0}^{\infty} \frac{(-1)^n x^{2n+1}}{(2n+1)!}.$$

Thus

$$y(x) = \frac{1}{x}(c_0 \cos x + c_1 \sin x).$$

We have thus found a general solution expressed as a linear combination of the two Frobenius series solutions

$$y_1(x) = \frac{\cos x}{x} \qquad \text{and} \qquad y_2(x) = \frac{\sin x}{x}.$$

Summary

When confronted with a linear second-order differential equation

$$A(x)y'' + B(x)y' + C(x)y = 0$$

with analytic coefficient functions, in order to investigate the possible existence of series solutions we first write the equation in standard form

$$y'' + P(x)y' + Q(x)y = 0.$$

If $P(x)$ and $Q(x)$ are both analytic at $x = 0$ then $x = 0$ is an ordinary point, and the equation has two linearly independent power series solutions.

Otherwise, $x = 0$ is a singular point, and we next write the differential equation in the form

$$\blacktriangleright \qquad y'' + \frac{p(x)}{x} y' + \frac{q(x)}{x^2} y = 0.$$

If $p(x)$ and $q(x)$ are both analytic at $x = 0$, then $x = 0$ is a regular singular point. In this case we find the two exponents r_1 and r_2 (assumed real, and with $r_1 \geq r_2$) by solving the indicial equation

$$\blacktriangleright \qquad r(r - 1) + p_0 r + q_0 = 0,$$

where $p_0 = p(0)$ and $q_0 = q(0)$. There always exists a Frobenius series solution $y_1 = x^{r_1} \sum a_n x^n$ associated with the larger exponent r_1, and if $r_1 - r_2$ is not an integer, the existence of a second Frobenius series solution $y_2 = x^{r_2} \sum b_n x^n$ is also guaranteed.

8.3 Problems

In Problems 1 through 8, determine whether $x = 0$ is an ordinary point, a regular singular point, or an irregular singular point. If it is a regular singular point, find the exponents of the differential equation at $x = 0$.

1. $xy'' + (x - x^3)y' + (\sin x)y = 0$

2. $xy'' + x^2 y' + (e^x - 1)y = 0$

3. $x^2 y'' + (\cos x)y' + xy = 0$

4. $3x^3 y'' + 2x^2 y' + (1 - x^2)y = 0$

5. $x(1 + x)y'' + 2y' + 3xy = 0$

6. $x^2(1 - x^2)y'' + 2xy' - 2y = 0$

7. $x^2 y'' + (6 \sin x)y' + 6y = 0$

8. $(6x + 2x^3)y'' + 21xy' + 9(x^2 - 1)y = 0$

If $x = a \neq 0$ is a singular point of a second-order linear differential equation, then the substitution $t = x - a$ transforms it into a differential equation having $t = 0$ as a singular point. We then attribute to the original equation at $x = a$ the behavior of the new equation at $t = 0$. Classify (as regular or irregular) the singular points of the differential equations in Problems 9 through 16.

9. $(1 - x)y'' + xy' + x^2 y = 0$

10. $(1 - x)^2 y'' + (2x - 2)y' + y = 0$

11. $(1 - x^2)y'' - 2xy' + 12y = 0$

12. $(x - 2)^3 y'' + 3(x - 2)^2 y' + x^3 y = 0$

13. $(x^2 - 4)y'' + (x - 2)y' + (x + 2)y = 0$

14. $(x^2 - 9)^2 y'' + (x^2 + 9)y' + (x^2 + 4)y = 0$

15. $(x - 2)^2 y'' - (x^2 - 4)y' + (x + 2)y = 0$

16. $x^3(1 - x)y'' + (3x + 2)y' + xy = 0$

Find two linearly independent Frobenius series solutions (for $x > 0$) of each of the differential equations in Problems 17 through 26.

17. $4xy'' + 2y' + y = 0$

18. $2xy'' + 3y' - y = 0$

19. $2xy'' - y' - y = 0$

20. $3xy'' + 2y' + 2y = 0$

21. $2x^2 y'' + xy' - (1 + 2x^2)y = 0$

22. $2x^2 y'' + xy' - (3 - 2x^2)y = 0$

23. $6x^2 y'' + 7xy' - (x^2 + 2)y = 0$

24. $3x^2 y'' + 2xy' + x^2 y = 0$

25. $2xy'' + (1 + x)y' + y = 0$

26. $2xy'' + (1 - 2x^2)y' - 4xy = 0$

Use the method of Example 6 to find two linearly independent Frobenius series solutions of the differential equations in Problems 27 through 31.

27. $xy'' + 2y' + 9xy = 0$

28. $xy'' + 2y' - 4xy = 0$

29. $4xy'' + 8y' + xy = 0$

30. $xy'' - y' + 4x^3 y = 0$

31. $4x^2 y'' - 4xy' + (3 - 4x^2)y = 0$

In Problems 32 through 34, find the first three nonzero terms of each of two linearly independent Frobenius series solutions.

32. $2x^2 y'' + x(x + 1)y' - (2x + 1)y = 0$

33. $(2x^2 + 5x^3)y'' + (3x - x^2)y' - (1 + x)y = 0$

34. $2x^2y'' + (\sin x)y' - (\cos x)y = 0$

35. Note that $x = 0$ is an irregular point of the equation

$$x^2y'' + (3x - 1)y' + y = 0.$$

(a) Show that $y = x^r \sum c_n x^n$ can satisfy this equation only if $r = 0$. (b) Substitute $y = \sum c_n x^n$ to derive the "formal" solution $y = \sum n! x^n$. What is the radius of convergence of this series?

36. (a) Suppose that A and B are nonzero constants. Show that the equation $x^2y'' + Ay' + By = 0$ has at most one solution of the form $y = x^r \sum c_n x^n$. (b) Repeat part (a) with the equation $x^3y'' + Axy' + By = 0$. (c) Show that the equation $x^3y'' + Ax^2y' + By = 0$ has no Frobenius series solution. (*Suggestion:* In each case substitute $y = x^r \sum c_n x^n$ in the given equation to determine the possible values of r.)

37. (a) Use the method of Frobenius to derive the solution $y_1 = x$ of the equation $x^3y'' - xy' + y = 0$. (b) Verify by substitution the second solution $y_2 = xe^{-1/x}$. Does y_2 have a Frobenius series representation?

38. Apply the method of Frobenius to Bessel's equation of order $\frac{1}{2}$,

$$x^2y'' + xy' + \left(x^2 - \frac{1}{4}\right)y = 0,$$

to derive its general solution for $x > 0$,

$$y(x) = c_0 \frac{\cos x}{\sqrt{x}} + c_1 \frac{\sin x}{\sqrt{x}}.$$

39. (a) Show that Bessel's equation of order 1,

$$x^2y'' + xy' + (x^2 - 1)y = 0,$$

has exponents $r_1 = 1$ and $r_2 = -1$ at $x = 0$, and that the Frobenius series solution corresponding to $r_1 = 1$ is

$$J_1(x) = \frac{x}{2} \sum_{n=0}^{\infty} \frac{(-1)^n x^{2n}}{n!(n+1)!2^{2n}}.$$

(b) Show that there is no Frobenius solution corresponding to the smaller exponent $r_2 = -1$; that is, show that it is impossible to determine the coefficients in

$$y_2(x) = x^{-1} \sum_{n=0}^{\infty} c_n x^n.$$

40. Consider the equation $x^2y'' + xy' + (1 - x)y = 0$. (a) Show that its exponents are $\pm i$, so it has complex-valued Frobenius series solutions

$$y_+ = x^i \sum_{n=0}^{\infty} p_n x^n \quad \text{and} \quad y_- = x^{-i} \sum_{n=0}^{\infty} q_n x^n$$

with $p_0 = q_0 = 1$. (b) Show that the recursion formula is

$$c_n = \frac{c_{n-1}}{n^2 + 2rn}.$$

Apply it with $r = i$ to obtain $p_n = c_n$, $r = -i$ to obtain $q_n = c_n$. Conclude that p_n and q_n are complex conjugates: $p_n = a_n + ib_n$ and $q_n = a_n - ib_n$, where the numbers $\{a_n\}$ and $\{b_n\}$ are real. (c) Deduce from part (b) that the differential equation of this problem has real-valued solutions of the form

$$y_1(x) = A(x) \cos(\ln x) - B(x) \sin(\ln x),$$

$$y_2(x) = A(x) \sin(\ln x) + B(x) \cos(\ln x),$$

where $A(x) = \sum a_n x^n$ and $B(x) = \sum b_n x^n$.

41. Consider the differential equation

$$x(x - 1)(x + 1)^2 y'' + 2x(x - 3)(x + 1)y' - 2(x - 1)y = 0$$

that appeared in an advertisement for a symbolic algebra program in the March 1984 issue of the *American Mathematical Monthly*. (a) Show that $x = 0$ is a regular singular point with exponents $r_1 = 1$ and $r_2 = 0$. (b) It follows from Theorem 1 that this differential equation has a power series solution of the form

$$y_1(x) = x + c_2 x^2 + c_3 x^3 + \cdots.$$

Substitute this series (with $c_1 = 1$) in the differential equation to show that $c_2 = -2$, $c_3 = 3$, and

$$c_{n+2}$$
$$= \frac{n(n-1)c_{n-1} + (n^2 - 5n - 2)c_n - (n^2 + 7n + 4)c_{n+1}}{(n+1)(n+2)}$$

for $n \geq 2$. (c) Use the recurrence relation in part (b) to prove by induction that $c_n = (-1)^{n+1} n$ for $n \geq 1$ (!). Hence deduce (using the geometric series) that

$$y_1(x) = \frac{x}{(1 + x)^2}$$

for $0 < x < 1$.

42. This problem is a brief introduction to Gauss's **hypergeometric equation**

$$x(1 - x)y'' + [\gamma - (\alpha + \beta + 1)x]y' - \alpha\beta y = 0, \quad (34)$$

where α, β, and γ are constants. This famous equation has wide-ranging applications in mathematics and physics. (a) Show that $x = 0$ is a regular singular point of Eq. (34), with exponents 0 and $1 - \gamma$. (b) If γ is not zero or a negative integer, it follows (Why?) that Eq. (34) has a power series solution

$$y(x) = x^0 \sum_{n=0}^{\infty} c_n x^n = \sum_{n=0}^{\infty} c_n x^n$$

with $c_0 \neq 0$. Show that the recurrence relation for this series is

$$c_{n+1} = \frac{(\alpha + n)(\beta + n)}{(\gamma + n)(1 + n)} c_n$$

for $n \geq 0$. (c) Conclude that with $c_0 = 1$ the series in part (b) is

$$y(x) = 1 + \sum_{n=0}^{\infty} \frac{\alpha_n \beta_n}{n! \gamma_n} x^n \qquad (35)$$

where $\alpha_n = \alpha(\alpha + 1)(\alpha + 2) \cdots (\alpha + n - 1)$ for $n \geq 1$, and

β_n and γ_n are defined similarly. (d) The series in (35) is known as the **hypergeometric series,** and is commonly denoted by $F(\alpha, \beta, \gamma, x)$. Show that:

(i) $F(1, 1, 1, x) = \dfrac{1}{1 - x}$ (the geometric series)

(ii) $xF(1, 1, 2, -x) = \ln(1 + x)$

(iii) $xF(\frac{1}{2}, 1, \frac{3}{2}, -x^2) = \tan^{-1} x$

(iv) $F(-k, 1, 1, -x) = (1 + x)^k$ (the binomial series)

8.3 Computing Project

Here we illustrate the use of a computer algebra system to apply the method of Frobenius. As a first example, we consider the differential equation

$$2x^2 y'' + 3xy' - (x^2 + 1)y = 0$$

of Example 4, where we found the two indicial roots $r_1 = \frac{1}{2}$ and $r_2 = -1$. Using *Mathematica* to begin with $r = \frac{1}{2}$, we first write the initial seven terms of a proposed Frobenius series solution:

```
y = x^(1/2) Sum[ a[n] x^n, {n, 0, 6} + O[x]^7
```
$a[0]$ Sqrt$[x]$ + $a[1]$ $x^{3/2}$ + $a[2]$ $x^{5/2}$ + $a[3]$ $x^{7/2}$ + $a[4]$ $x^{9/2}$ + $a[5]$ $x^{11/2}$ + $a[6]$ $x^{13/2}$ + O$[x]7$

Then we substitute this series into the differential equation.

```
deq1 = 2 x^2 D[y,x,x] + 3 x D[y,x] - (x^2 + 1)y == 0
```
5 $a[1]$ $x^{3/2}$ + $(-a[0]$ + 14 $a[2])$ $x^{5/2}$ + $(-a[1]$ + 27 $a[3])$ $x^{7/2}$ + $(-a[2]$ + 44 $a[4])$ $x^{9/2}$ + $(-a[3]$ + 65 $a[5])$ $x^{11/2}$ + $(-a[4]$ + 90 $a[6])$ $x^{13/2}$ + O$[x]^7$ == 0

Mathematica has automatically collected like powers for us, and we can use the **LogicalExpand** command to extract the equations that the successive coefficients satisfy.

```
coeffEqns  =  LogicalExpand [ deq1 ]
```
5 $a[1]$ == 0 && $-a[0]$ + 14 $a[2]$ == 0 && $-a[1]$ + 27 $a[3]$ == 0 &&

$-a[2]$ + 44 $a[4]$ == 0 && $-a[3]$ + 65 $a[5]$ == 0 &&

$-a[4]$ + 90 $a[6]$ == 0

We have here a collection of six linear equations relating the seven coefficients (**a[0]** through **a[6]**). Hence we should be able to solve for the successive coefficients

```
succCoeffs  =  Table[ a[n], {n, 1, 6} ]
```
$\{a[1], a[2], a[3], a[4], a[5], a[6]\}$

in terms of **a[0]**.

 coeffs = Solve[coeffEqns, succCoeffs]

$$\{\{a[5] \rightarrow 0, \; a[6] \rightarrow \frac{a[0]}{55440}, \; a[1] \rightarrow 0, \; a[2] \rightarrow \frac{a[0]}{14},$$
$$a[3] \rightarrow 0, \; a[4] \rightarrow \frac{a[0]}{616}\}\}$$

Finally we substitute all these coefficients back into the original series.

 partSoln = y /. coeffs

$$\{a[0] \; \text{Sqrt}[x] + \frac{a[0] \; x^{5/2}}{14} + \frac{a[0] \; x^{9/2}}{616} + \frac{a[0] \; x^{13/2}}{55440} + O[x]^7\}$$

Note that (after factoring out $a_0 x^{1/2}$) this result agrees with the first particular solution $y_1(x)$ found in the text.

 Now repeat the process, beginning with the indicial root $r_1 = -1$, to derive the second particular solution found previously.

 In the following examples, use this method to derive Frobenius series solutions that can be checked against the given known general solutions.

1. $xy'' - y' + 4x^3 y = 0$, $y(x) = A \cos x^2 + B \sin x^2$

2. $xy'' - 2y' + 9x^5 y = 0$, $y(x) = A \cos x^3 + B \sin x^3$

3. $4xy'' - 2y' + y = 0$, $y(x) = A \cos \sqrt{x} + B \sin \sqrt{x}$

4. $xy'' + 2y' + xy = 0$, $y(x) = \dfrac{1}{x} (A \cos x + B \sin x)$

5. $4xy'' + 6y' + y = 0$, $y(x) = \dfrac{1}{\sqrt{x}} (A \cos \sqrt{x} + B \sin \sqrt{x})$

6. $x^2 y'' + xy' + (4x^4 - 1)y = 0$, $y(x) = \dfrac{1}{x} (A \cos x^2 + B \sin x^2)$

7. $xy'' + 3y' + 4x^3 y = 0$, $y(x) = \dfrac{1}{x^2}(A \cos x^2 + B \sin x^2)$

8. $x^2 y'' + x^2 y' - 2y = 0$, $y(x) = \dfrac{1}{x} [A(2 - x) + B(2 + x)e^{-x}]$

The following three problems involve the arctangent series

$$\tan^{-1} x = x - \frac{x^3}{3} + \frac{x^5}{5} - \frac{x^7}{7} + \cdots .$$

9. $(x + x^3)y'' + (2 + 4x^2)y' + 2xy = 0$, $y(x) = \dfrac{1}{x} (A + B \tan^{-1} x)$

10. $(2x + 2x^2)y'' + (3 + 5x)y' + y = 0$, $y(x) = \dfrac{1}{\sqrt{x}} (A + B \tan^{-1} \sqrt{x})$

11. $(x + x^5)y'' + (3 + 7x^4)y' + 8x^3 y = 0$, $y(x) = \dfrac{1}{x^2}(A + B \tan^{-1} x^2)$

8.4 Method of Frobenius: The Exceptional Cases

We continue our discussion of the equation

$$\blacktriangleright \qquad y'' + \frac{p(x)}{x} y' + \frac{q(x)}{x^2} y = 0 \tag{1}$$

where $p(x)$ and $q(x)$ are analytic at $x = 0$, and $x = 0$ is a regular singular point. If the roots r_1 and r_2 of the indicial equation

$$\blacktriangleright \qquad \phi(r) = r(r-1) + p_0 r + q_0 = 0 \tag{2}$$

do not differ by an integer, then Theorem 1 of Section 8.3 guarantees that Eq. (1) has two linearly independent Frobenius series solutions. We consider now the more complex situation in which $r_1 - r_2$ is an integer. If $r_1 = r_2$, then there is only one exponent available, and thus there can be only one Frobenius series solution. But we saw in Example 6 of Section 8.3 that if $r_1 = r_2 + N$, with N a positive integer, then it is possible that a second Frobenius series solution exists. We will also see that it is possible that such a solution does not exist. In fact, the second solution involves $\ln x$ when it is not a Frobenius series. As you will see in Examples 3 and 4, these exceptional cases occur in the solution of Bessel's equation. For applications, this is the most important second-order linear differential equation with variable coefficients.

The Nonlogarithmic Case with $r_1 = r_2 + N$

In Section 8.3 we derived the indicial equation by substituting the power series $p(x) = \sum p_n x^n$ and $q(x) = \sum q_n x^n$ and the Frobenius series

$$y(x) = x^r \sum_{n=0}^{\infty} c_n x^n = \sum_{n=0}^{\infty} c_n x^{n+r} \qquad (c_0 \neq 0) \tag{3}$$

in the differential equation in the form

$$x^2 y'' + x p(x) y' + q(x) y = 0. \tag{4}$$

The result of this substitution, after collection of the coefficients of like powers of x, is an equation of the form

$$\sum_{n=0}^{\infty} F_n(r) x^{n+r} = 0 \tag{5}$$

in which the coefficients depend on r. It turns out that the coefficient of x^r is

$$F_0(r) = [r(r-1) + p_0 r + q_0] c_0 = \phi(r) c_0, \tag{6}$$

which gives the indicial equation because $c_0 \neq 0$ by assumption; also, for $n \geq 1$, the coefficient of x^{n+r} has the form

$$F_n(r) = \phi(r+n) c_n + L_n(r; c_0, c_1, \cdots, c_{n-1}). \tag{7}$$

Here L_n is a certain linear combination of $c_0, c_1, \cdots, c_{n-1}$. Although the exact formula is not necessary for our purposes, it happens that

$$L_n = \sum_{k=0}^{n-1} [(r+k) p_{n-k} + q_{n-k}] c_k. \tag{8}$$

Because all the coefficients in (5) must vanish for the Frobenius series to be a solution of Eq. (4), it follows that the exponent r and the coefficients c_0, c_1, \ldots, c_n must satisfy the equation

$$\phi(r + n)c_n + L_n(r; c_0, c_1, \ldots, c_{n-1}) = 0. \tag{9}$$

This is a *recurrence relation* for c_n in terms of $c_0, c_1, \ldots, c_{n-1}$.

Now suppose that $r_1 = r_2 + N$ with N a positive integer. If we use the larger exponent r_1 in Eq. (9), then the coefficient $\phi(r_1 + n)$ of c_n will be nonzero for every $n \geqq 1$ because $\phi(r) = 0$ only when $r = r_1$ and when $r = r_2 < r_1$. Once $c_0, c_1, \ldots, c_{n-1}$ have been determined, we therefore can solve Eq. (9) for c_n and continue to compute successive coefficients in the Frobenius series solution corresponding to the exponent r_1.

But when we use the smaller exponent r_2, there is a potential difficulty in computing c_n. For in this case $\phi(r_2 + N) = 0$, so Eq. (9) becomes

$$0 \cdot c_N + L_N(r_2; c_0, c_1, \ldots, c_{N-1}) = 0. \tag{10}$$

At this stage $c_0, c_1, \ldots, c_{N-1}$ have already been determined. If it happens that

$$L_N(r_2; c_0, c_1, \ldots, c_{N-1}) = 0,$$

then we can choose c_N arbitrarily and continue to determine the remaining coefficients in a second Frobenius series solution. But if it happens that

$$L_N(r_2; c_0, c_1, \ldots, c_{N-1}) \neq 0,$$

then Eq. (10) is not satisfied with any choice of c_N; in this case there cannot exist a second Frobenius series solution corresponding to the smaller exponent r_2. Examples 1 and 2 illustrate these two possibilities.

EXAMPLE 1 Consider the equation

$$x^2 y'' + (6x + x^2)y' + xy = 0. \tag{11}$$

Here $p_0 = 6$ and $q_0 = 0$, so the indicial equation is

$$\phi(r) = r(r - 1) + 6r = r^2 + 5r = 0 \tag{12}$$

with roots $r_1 = 0$ and $r_2 = -5$; the roots differ by the integer $N = 5$. We substitute the Frobenius series $y = \sum c_n x^{n+r}$ and get

$$\sum_{n=0}^{\infty} (n + r)(n + r - 1)c_n x^{n+r} + 6 \sum_{n=0}^{\infty} (n + r)c_n x^{n+r}$$

$$+ \sum_{n=0}^{\infty} (n + r)c_n x^{n+r+1} + \sum_{n=0}^{\infty} c_n x^{n+r+1} = 0.$$

When we combine the first two and also the last two sums, and in the latter shift the index by -1, the result is

$$\sum_{n=0}^{\infty} [(n + r)^2 + 5(n + r)]c_n x^{n+r} + \sum_{n=1}^{\infty} (n + r)c_{n-1} x^{n+r} = 0.$$

The terms corresponding to $n = 0$ give the indicial equation in (12), whereas for

$n \geq 1$ we get the equation

$$[(n + r)^2 + 5(n + r)]c_n + (n + r)c_{n-1} = 0, \tag{13}$$

which in this example corresponds to the general equation in (9). Note that the coefficient of c_n is $\phi(n + r)$.

We now follow the recommendation in Section 8.3 for the case $r_1 = r_2 + N$: We begin with the smaller root $r_2 = -5$. With $r_2 = -5$, Eq. (13) reduces to

$$\blacktriangleright \qquad\qquad n(n - r)c_n + (n - 5)c_{n-1} = 0. \tag{14}$$

If $n \neq 5$, we can solve this equation for c_n to obtain the recurrence relation

$$\blacktriangleright \qquad\qquad c_n = -\frac{c_{n-1}}{n} \quad \text{for } n \neq 5. \tag{15}$$

This yields

$$c_1 = -c_0, \qquad\qquad\qquad c_2 = -\frac{c_1}{2} = \frac{c_0}{2},$$
$$\tag{16}$$
$$c_3 = -\frac{c_2}{3} = -\frac{c_0}{6}, \quad \text{and} \quad c_4 = -\frac{c_3}{4} = \frac{c_0}{24}.$$

In the case $r_1 = r_2 + N$, it is always the coefficient c_N that requires special consideration. Here $N = 5$, and for $n = 5$ Eq. (14) takes the form $0 \cdot c_5 + 0 = 0$. Hence c_5 is a second arbitrary constant, and we can compute additional coefficients, still using the recursion formula in (15):

$$c_6 = -\frac{c_5}{6}, \quad c_7 = -\frac{c_6}{7} = \frac{c_5}{6 \cdot 7}, \quad c_8 = -\frac{c_7}{8} = -\frac{c_5}{6 \cdot 7 \cdot 8}, \tag{17}$$

and so on.

When we combine the results in (16) and (17), we get

$$y = x^{-5} \sum_{n=0}^{\infty} c_n x^n$$

$$= c_0 x^{-5} \left(1 - x + \frac{x^2}{2} - \frac{x^3}{6} + \frac{x^4}{24} \right)$$

$$+ c_5 x^{-5} \left(x^5 - \frac{x^5}{6} + \frac{x^7}{6 \cdot 7} - \frac{x^8}{6 \cdot 7 \cdot 8} + \cdots \right)$$

in terms of the two arbitrary constants c_0 and c_5. Thus we have found the two Frobenius series solutions

$$y_1(x) = x^{-5} \left(1 - x + \frac{x^2}{2} - \frac{x^3}{6} + \frac{x^4}{24} \right)$$

and

$$y_2(x) = 1 + \sum_{n=1}^{\infty} \frac{(-1)^n x^n}{6 \cdot 7 \cdots (n + 5)} = 1 + 120 \sum_{n=1}^{\infty} \frac{(-1)^n x^n}{(n + 5)!}$$

of Eq. (11).

EXAMPLE 2 Determine whether or not the equation

$$x^2 y'' - xy' + (x^2 - 8)y = 0 \tag{18}$$

has two linearly independent Frobenius series solutions.

Solution Here $p_0 = -1$ and $q_0 = -8$, so the indicial equation is

$$\phi(r) = r(r - 1) - r - 8 = r^2 - 2r - 8 = 0$$

with roots $r_1 = 4$ and $r_2 = -2$ differing by $N = 6$. On substitution of $y = \sum c_n x^{n+r}$ in Eq. (18), we get

$$\sum_{n=0}^{\infty} (n + r)(n + r - 1)c_n x^{n+r} - \sum_{n=0}^{\infty} (n + r)c_n x^{n+r}$$

$$+ \sum_{n=0}^{\infty} c_n x^{n+r+2} - 8 \sum_{n=0}^{\infty} c_n x^{n+r} = 0.$$

If we shift the index by -2 in the third sum and combine the other three sums, we get

$$\sum_{n=0}^{\infty} [(n + r)^2 - 2(n + r) - 8]c_n x^{n+r} + \sum_{n=2}^{\infty} c_{n-2} x^{n+r} = 0.$$

The coefficient of x^r gives the indicial equation, and the coefficient of x^{r+1} gives

$$[(r + 1)^2 - 2(r + 1) - 8]c_1 = 0.$$

Because the coefficient of c_1 is nonzero both for $r = 4$ and for $r = -2$, it follows that $c_1 = 0$ in each case. For $n \geq 2$ we get the equation

▶ $$[(n + r)^2 - 2(n + r) - 8]c_n + c_{n-2} = 0, \tag{19}$$

which corresponds in this example to the general equation in (9); note that the coefficient of c_n is $\phi(n + r)$.

We work first with the smaller root $r = r_2 = -2$. Then Eq. (19) becomes

▶ $$n(n - 6)c_n + c_{n-2} = 0 \tag{20}$$

for $n \geq 2$. For $n \neq 6$ we can solve for the recurrence relation

▶ $$c_n = -\frac{c_{n-2}}{n(n - 6)} \qquad (n \geq 2, n \neq 6). \tag{21}$$

Because $c_1 = 0$, this formula gives

$$c_2 = \frac{c_0}{8}, \qquad\qquad c_3 = 0,$$

$$c_4 = \frac{c_2}{8} = \frac{c_0}{64}, \qquad \text{and} \qquad c_5 = 0.$$

Now Eq. (20) with $n = 6$ reduces to

$$0 \cdot c_6 + \frac{c_0}{64} = 0.$$

But $c_0 \neq 0$ by assumption, and hence there is no way to choose c_6 so that this equation

holds. Thus there is *no* Frobenius series solution corresponding to the smaller root $r_2 = -2$.

To find the single Frobenius series solution corresponding to the larger root $r_1 = 4$, we substitute $r = 4$ in Eq. (19) to obtain the recurrence relation

$$\blacktriangleright \qquad c_n = -\frac{c_{n-2}}{n(n+6)} \qquad (n \geqq 2). \qquad (22)$$

This gives

$$c_2 = -\frac{c_0}{2 \cdot 8}, \qquad c_4 = -\frac{c_2}{4 \cdot 10} = \frac{c_0}{2 \cdot 4 \cdot 8 \cdot 10}.$$

The general pattern is

$$c_{2n} = \frac{(-1)^n c_0}{2 \cdot 4 \cdots (2n) \cdot 8 \cdot 10 \cdots (2n+6)} = \frac{(-1)^n 48 c_0}{2^{2n+3} n!(n+3)!}.$$

This yields the Frobenius series solution

$$y_1(x) = x^4 \left(1 + 48 \sum_{n=1}^{\infty} \frac{(-1)^n x^{2n}}{2^{2n+3} n!(n+3)!} \right)$$

of Eq. (18).

Reduction of Order

When only a single Frobenius series solution exists, we need another technique. We discuss here the method of **reduction of order,** which enables us to use one known solution y_1 of a second-order homogeneous linear differential equation to find a second linearly independent solution y_2. Consider the second-order equation

$$y'' + P(x)y' + Q(x)y = 0 \qquad (23)$$

on an open interval I on which P and Q are continuous. Suppose that we know one solution y_1 of (23). By Theorem 2 of Section 3.1, there exists a second linearly independent solution y_2; our problem is to find y_2. Equivalently, we would like to find the quotient

$$v(x) = \frac{y_2(x)}{y_1(x)}. \qquad (24)$$

Once we know $v(x)$, y_2 will then be given by

$$y_2(x) = v(x)y_1(x). \qquad (25)$$

We begin by substituting the expression in (25) in Eq. (23), using the derivatives

$$y_2' = vy_1' + v'y_1 \qquad \text{and} \qquad y_2'' = vy_1'' + 2v'y_1' + v''y_1.$$

We get

$$[vy_1'' + 2v'y_1' + v''y_1] + P[vy_1' + v'y_1] + Qvy_1 = 0,$$

and rearrangement gives

$$v[y_1'' + Py_1' + Qy_1] + v''y_1 + 2v'y_1' + Pv'y_1 = 0.$$

But the bracketed terms in this last equation vanish because $y_1(x)$ is a solution of Eq. (23). This leaves the equation

$$y_1 v'' + (2y_1' + Py_1)v' = 0. \tag{26}$$

The key to the success of this method is that Eq. (26) is *linear* in v'. Thus the substitution in (25) has reduced the second-order linear equation in (23) to the first-order (in v') linear equation in (26). If we write $u = v'$ and assume that $y_1(x)$ never vanishes on I, then (26) yields

$$u' + \left(2\frac{y_1'}{y_1} + P(x)\right)u = 0. \tag{27}$$

An integrating factor for Eq. (27) is

$$\rho = \exp\left(\int\left(2\frac{y_1'}{y_1} + P(x)\right)dx\right) = \exp\left(2\ln|y_1| + \int P(x)dx\right);$$

thus

$$\rho(x) = y_1^2 e^{\int P(x)\,dx}.$$

We now integrate the equation in (27) to obtain

$$uy_1^2 e^{\int P(x)\,dx} = C, \qquad \text{so} \qquad v' = u = \frac{C}{y_1^2}e^{-\int P(x)\,dx}.$$

Another integration now gives

$$\frac{y_2}{y_1} = v = C\int\frac{e^{-\int P(x)\,dx}}{y_1^2}dx + K.$$

With the particular choices $C = 1$ and $K = 0$, we get

$$y_2 = y_1\int\frac{e^{-\int P(x)\,dx}}{y_1^2}dx. \tag{28}$$

This formula provides a second solution $y_2(x)$ of Eq. (23) on any interval where $y_1(x)$ is never zero. Note that because an exponential function never vanishes, $y_2(x)$ is a non-constant multiple of $y_1(x)$, so y_1 and y_2 are linearly independent solutions.

The Logarithmic Cases

We now investigate the general form of the second solution of the equation

$$y'' + \frac{p(x)}{x}y' + \frac{q(x)}{x^2}y = 0, \tag{1}$$

under the assumption that its exponents r_1 and $r_2 = r_1 - N$ differ by the integer $N \geq 0$. We assume that we have already found the Frobenius series solution

$$y_1(x) = x^{r_1}\sum_{n=0}^{\infty}a_n x^n \qquad (a_0 \neq 0) \tag{29}$$

for $x > 0$ corresponding to the larger exponent r_1. Let us write $P(x)$ for $p(x)/x$ and $Q(x)$ for $q(x)/x^2$. Thus we can rewrite Eq. (1) in the form $y'' + Py' + Qy = 0$ of Eq. (23).

Because the indicial equation has roots r_1 and $r_2 = r_1 - N$, it can be factored easily:

$$r^2 + (p_0 - 1)r + q_0 = (r - r_1)(r - r_1 + N)$$

$$= r^2 + (N - 2r_1)r + (r_1^2 - r_1 N) = 0,$$

so we see that

$$p_0 - 1 = N - 2r_1;$$

that is,

$$-p_0 - 2r_1 = -1 - N. \tag{30}$$

In preparation for use of the reduction of order formula in (28), we write

$$P(x) = \frac{p_0 + p_1 x + p_2 x^2 + \cdots}{x} = \frac{p_0}{x} + p_1 + p_2 x + \cdots.$$

Then

$$e^{-\int P(x)\,dx} = \exp\left[-\int\left(\frac{p_0}{x} + p_1 + p_2 x^2 + \cdots\right) dx\right]$$

$$= \exp\left(-p_0 \ln x - p_1 x - \frac{1}{2} p_2 x^2 - \cdots\right)$$

$$= x^{-p_0} \exp\left(-p_1 x - \frac{1}{2} p_2 x^2 - \cdots\right),$$

so that

$$e^{-\int P(x)\,dx} = x^{-p_0}(1 + A_1 x + A_2 x^2 + \cdots). \tag{31}$$

In the last step we have used the fact that a composition of analytic functions is analytic and therefore has a power series representation; the initial coefficient of that series in (31) is 1 because $e^0 = 1$.

We now substitute (29) and (31) in (28); with the choice $a_0 = 1$ in (29), this yields

$$y_2 = y_1 \int \frac{x^{-p_0}(1 + A_1 x + A_2 x^2 + \cdots)}{x^{2r_1}(1 + a_1 x + a_2 x^2 + \cdots)^2}\,dx.$$

We square the denominator and simplify:

$$y_2 = y_1 \int \frac{x^{-p_0 - 2r_1}(1 + A_1 x + A_2 x^2 + \cdots)}{1 + B_1 x + B_2 x^2 + \cdots}\,dx$$

$$= y_1 \int x^{-1-N}(1 + C_1 x + C_2 x^2 + \cdots)\,dx \tag{32}$$

(we used long division and (30) in the last step). We now consider separately the cases $N = 0$ and $N > 0$. We want to ascertain the general form of y_2 without keeping track of specific coefficients.

Equal Exponents: $r_1 = r_2$

With $N = 0$, Eq. (32) gives

$$y_2 = y_1 \int \left(\frac{1}{x} + C_1 + C_2 x^2 + \cdots \right) dx$$

$$= y_1 \ln x + y_1 \left(C_1 x + \frac{1}{2} C_2 x^2 + \cdots \right)$$

$$= y_1 \ln x + x^{r_1}(1 + a_1 x + \cdots) \left(C_1 x + \frac{1}{2} C_2 x^2 + \cdots \right)$$

$$= y_1 \ln x + x^{r_1}(b_0 x + b_1 x^2 + b_2 x^3 + \cdots).$$

Consequently, in the case of equal exponents, the general form of y_2 is

$$y_2(x) = y_1(x) \ln x + x^{1+r_1} \sum_{n=0}^{\infty} b_n x^n. \tag{33}$$

Note the logarithmic term; it is always present when $r_1 = r_2$.

Positive Integral Difference: $r_1 = r_2 + N$

With $N > 0$, Eq. (32) gives

$$y_2 = y_1 \int x^{-1-N}(1 + C_1 x + C_2 x^2 + \cdots + C_N x^N + \cdots) \, dx$$

$$= y_1 \int \left(\frac{C_N}{x} + \frac{1}{x^{N+1}} + \frac{C_1}{x^N} + \cdots \right) dx$$

$$= C_N y_1 \ln x + y_1 \left(\frac{x^{-N}}{-N} + \frac{C_1 x^{-N+1}}{-N+1} + \cdots \right)$$

$$= C_N y_1 \ln x + x^{r_2+N} \left(\sum_{n=0}^{\infty} a_n x^n \right) x^{-N} \left(-\frac{1}{N} + \frac{C_1 x}{-N+1} + \cdots \right),$$

so that

$$y_2(x) = C_N y_1(x) \ln x + x^{r_2} \sum_{n=0}^{\infty} b_n x^n, \tag{34}$$

where $b_0 = -a_0/N \neq 0$. This gives the general form of y_2 in the case of exponents differing by a positive integer. Note the coefficient C_N that appears in (34) but not in (33). If it happens that $C_N = 0$, then there is no logarithmic term; if so, Eq. (1) has a second Frobenius series solution (as in Example 1).

In our derivation of Eqs. (33) and (34)—which exhibit the general form of the second solution in the cases $r_1 = r_2$ and $r_1 - r_2 = N$, respectively—we have said nothing about the radii of convergence of the various power series that appear. Theorem 1 (next) is a summation of the preceding discussion, and also tells where the series in (33) and (34) converge. As in Theorem 1 of Section 8.3, we restrict our attention to solutions for $x > 0$.

THEOREM 1: The Exceptional Cases

Suppose that $x = 0$ is a regular singular point of the equation

$$x^2 y'' + x p(x) y' + q(x) y = 0 \tag{4}$$

Let $\rho > 0$ denote the minimum of the radii of convergence of the power series

$$p(x) = \sum_{n=0}^{\infty} p_n x^n \qquad \text{and} \qquad q(x) = \sum_{n=0}^{\infty} q_n x^n.$$

Let r_1 and r_2 be the roots, with $r_1 \geq r_2$, of the indicial equation

$$r(r - 1) + p_0 r + q_0 = 0.$$

(a) If $r_1 = r_2$, then Eq. (4) has two solutions y_1 and y_2 of the forms

$$y_1(x) = x^{r_1} \sum_{n=0}^{\infty} a_n x^n \qquad (a_0 \neq 0) \tag{35a}$$

and

▶
$$y_2(x) = y_1(x) \ln x + x^{r_1 + 1} \sum_{n=0}^{\infty} b_n x^n. \tag{35b}$$

(b) If $r_1 - r_2 = N$, a positive integer, then Eq. (4) has two solutions y_1 and y_2 of the forms

$$y_1(x) = x^{r_1} \sum_{n=0}^{\infty} a_n x^n \qquad (a_0 \neq 0) \tag{36a}$$

and

▶
$$y_2(x) = C y_1(x) \ln x + x^{r_2} \sum_{n=0}^{\infty} b_n x^n. \tag{36b}$$

In Eq. (36b), $b_0 \neq 0$ but C may be either zero or nonzero, so the logarithmic term may or may not actually be present in this case. The radii of convergence of the power series of this theorem are all at least ρ. The coefficients in these series (and the constant C in Eq. (36b)) may be determined by direct substitution of the series in the differential equation in (4). ∎

EXAMPLE 3 We will illustrate the case $r_1 = r_2$ by deriving the second solution of Bessel's equation of order zero,

$$x^2 y'' + x y' + x^2 y + 0, \tag{37}$$

for which $r_1 = r_2 = 0$. In Example 5 of Section 8.3 we found the first solution,

$$y_1(x) = J_0(x) = \sum_{n=0}^{\infty} \frac{(-1)^n x^{2n}}{2^{2n}(n!)^2}. \tag{38}$$

According to Eq. (35b) the second solution will have the form

$$y_2 = y_1 \ln x + \sum_{n=1}^{\infty} b_n x^n. \tag{39}$$

The first two derivatives of y_2 are

$$y_2' = y_1' \ln x + \frac{y_1}{x} + \sum_{n=1}^{\infty} n b_n x^{n-1}$$

and

$$y_2'' = y_1'' \ln x + \frac{2y_1'}{x} - \frac{y_1}{x^2} + \sum_{n=2}^{\infty} n(n-1) b_n x^{n-2}.$$

We substitute these in Eq. (37) and use the fact that $J_0(x)$ also satisfies this equation to obtain

$$0 = x^2 y_2'' + xy_2' + x^2 y_2$$

$$= [x^2 y_1'' + xy_1' + x^2 y_1] \ln x + 2xy_1'$$

$$+ \sum_{n=2}^{\infty} n(n-1) b_n x^n + \sum_{n=1}^{\infty} n b_n x^n + \sum_{n=1}^{\infty} b_n x^{n+2},$$

and it follows that

$$0 = 2 \sum_{n=1}^{\infty} \frac{(-1)^n 2n x^{2n}}{2^{2n}(n!)^2} + b_1 x + 2^2 b_2 x^2 + \sum_{n=3}^{\infty} (n^2 b_n + b_{n-2}) x^n. \tag{40}$$

The only term involving x in Eq. (405) is $b_1 x$, so $b_1 = 0$. But $n^2 b_n + b_{n-2} = 0$ if n is odd, and it follows that all the coefficients of odd subscript in y_2 vanish.

Now we examine the coefficients with even subscript in Eq. (40). First we see that

$$b_2 = -2 \frac{(-1)(2)}{2^2 2^2 (1!)^2} = \frac{1}{4}. \tag{41}$$

For $n \geq 2$, we read the recurrence relation

$$(2n)^2 b_{2n} + b_{2n-2} = -\frac{(2)(-1)^n (2n)}{2^{2n}(n!)^2} \tag{42}$$

from (40). Nonhomogeneous recurrence relations such as (42) are typical of the exceptional cases of the method of Frobenius, and their solution often requires a bit of ingenuity. The usual strategy depends on detecting the most conspicuous dependence of b_{2n} on n. We note the presence of $2^{2n}(n!)^2$ on the right-hand side in (42); in conjunction with the coefficient $(2n)^2$ on the left-hand side, we are induced to think of b_{2n} as *something* divided by $2^{2n}(n!)^2$. Noting also the alternation of sign, we make the substitution

$$b_{2n} = \frac{(-1)^{n+1} c_{2n}}{2^{2n}(n!)^2}, \tag{43}$$

in the expectation that the recurrence relation for c_{2n} will be simpler than the one for b_{2n}. We chose $(-1)^{n+1}$ rather than $(-1)^n$ because $b_2 = \frac{1}{4} > 0$; with $n = 1$ in (43), we get $c_2 = 1$. Substitution of (43) in (42) gives

$$(2n)^2 \frac{(-1)^{n+1} c_{2n}}{2^{2n}(n!)^2} + \frac{(-1)^n c_{2n-2}}{2^{2n-2}[(n-1)!]^2} = \frac{(-2)(-2)^n (2n)}{2^{2n}(n!)^2},$$

which boils down to the extremely simple recurrence relation

$$c_{2n} = c_{2n-2} + \frac{1}{n}.$$

Thus

$$c_4 = c_2 + \frac{1}{2} = 1 + \frac{1}{2},$$

$$c_6 = c_4 + \frac{1}{3} = 1 + \frac{1}{2} + \frac{1}{3},$$

$$c_8 = c_6 + \frac{1}{4} = 1 + \frac{1}{2} + \frac{1}{3} + \frac{1}{4},$$

and so on. Evidently

$$c_{2n} = 1 + \frac{1}{2} + \frac{1}{3} + \cdots + \frac{1}{n} = H_n, \tag{44}$$

where we denote by H_n the nth partial sum of the harmonic series $\sum(1/n)$.

Finally, keeping in mind that the coefficient of odd subscript are all zero, we substitute (43) and (44) in (39) to obtain the second solution

$$
\begin{aligned}
y_2(x) &= J_0(x) \ln x + \sum_{n=1}^{\infty} \frac{(-1)^{n+1} H_n x^{2n}}{2^{2n}(n!)^2} \\
&= J_0(x) \ln x + \frac{x^2}{4} - \frac{3x^4}{128} + \frac{11x^6}{13824} - \cdots \tag{45}
\end{aligned}
$$

of Bessel's equation of order zero. The power series in (45) converges for all x. The most commonly used linearly independent [of $J_0(x)$] second solution is

$$Y_0(x) = \frac{2}{\pi}(\gamma - \ln 2)y_1 + \frac{2}{\pi} y_2;$$

that is,

$$Y_0(x) = \frac{2}{\pi}\left[\left(\gamma + \ln \frac{x}{2}\right)J_0(x) + \sum_{n=1}^{\infty} \frac{(-1)^{n+1} H_n x^{2n}}{2^{2n}(n!)^2}\right], \tag{46}$$

where γ denotes *Euler's constant:*

$$\gamma = \lim_{n \to \infty}(H_n - \ln n) \approx 0.57722. \tag{47}$$

This particular combination $Y_0(x)$ is chosen because of its nice behavior as $x \to +\infty$; it is called the **Bessel function of order zero of the second kind.**

EXAMPLE 4 As an alternative to the method of substitution, we illustrate the case $r_1 - r_2 = N$ by employing the technique of reduction of order to derive a second solution of Bessel's equation of order 1,

$$x^2 y'' + xy' + (x^2 - 1)y = 0; \tag{48}$$

the associated indicial equation has roots $r_1 = 1$ and $r_2 = -1$. According to Problem 39 of Section 8.3, one solution of Eq. (48) is

$$y_1(x) = J_1(x) = \frac{x}{2} \sum_{n=0}^{\infty} \frac{(-1)^n x^{2n}}{2^{2n} n!(n+1)!} = \frac{x}{2} - \frac{x^3}{16} + \frac{x^5}{384} - \frac{x^7}{18432} + \cdots. \tag{49}$$

With $P(x) = 1/x$ from (48), the reduction of order formula in (28) yields

$$y_2 = y_1 \int \frac{dx}{xy_1^2}$$

$$= y_1 \int \frac{dx}{x(x/2 - x^3/16 + x^5/384 - x^7/18432 + \cdots)^2}$$

$$= y_1 \int \frac{4\,dx}{x^3(1 - x^2/8 + x^4/192 - x^6/9216 + \cdots)^2}$$

$$= 4y_1 \int \frac{dx}{x^3(1 - x^2/4 + 5x^4/192 - 7x^6/4608 + \cdots)}$$

$$= 4y_1 \int \frac{1}{x^3}\left(1 + \frac{x^2}{4} + \frac{7x^4}{192} + \frac{19x^6}{4608} + \cdots\right)dx$$

$$= 4y_1 \int \left(\frac{1}{4x} + \frac{1}{x^3} + \frac{7x}{192} + \frac{19x^3}{4608} + \cdots\right)dx$$

$$= y_1 \ln x + 4y_1\left(-\frac{1}{2x^2} + \frac{7x^2}{384} + \frac{19x^4}{18432} + \cdots\right).$$

Thus

$$y_2(x) = y_1(x)\ln x - \frac{1}{x} + \frac{x}{8} + \frac{x^3}{32} - \frac{11x^5}{4608} + \cdots. \tag{50}$$

Note that the technique of reduction of order readily yields the first several terms of the series, but does not provide a recurrence relation that can be used to determine the general term of the series.

With a computation similar to that shown in Example 3 (but more complicated — see Problem 21), the method of substitution can be used to derive the solution

$$y_3(x) = y_1(x)\ln x - \frac{1}{x} + \sum_{n=1}^{\infty} \frac{(-1)^n(H_n + H_{n-1})x^{2n-1}}{2^{2n}n!(n-1)!}, \tag{51}$$

where H_n is defined in (44) for $n \geqq 1$; $H_0 = 0$. The reader can verify that the terms shown in (50) agree with

$$y_2(x) = \frac{3}{4}J_1(x) + y_3(x). \tag{52}$$

The most commonly used linearly independent (of J_1) solution of Bessel's equation of order 1 is the combination

$$Y_1(x) = \frac{2}{\pi}(\gamma - \ln 2)y_1 + \frac{2}{\pi}y_3$$

$$= \frac{2}{\pi}\left[\left(\gamma + \ln \frac{x}{2}\right)J_1(x) - \frac{1}{x} + \sum_{n=1}^{\infty} \frac{(-1)^n(H_n + H_{n-1})x^{2n-1}}{2^{2n}n!(n-1)!}\right]. \tag{53}$$

∎

Examples 3 and 4 illustrate two methods of finding the solution in the logarithmic cases — direct substitution and reduction of order. A third alternative is outlined in Problem 19.

8.4 Problems

In Problems 1 through 8, either apply the method of Example 1 to find two linearly independent Frobenius series solutions, or find one such solution and show (as in Example 2) that a second such solution does not exist.

1. $xy'' + (3 - x)y' - y = 0$

2. $xy'' + (5 - x)y' - y = 0$

3. $xy'' + (5 + 3x)y' + 3y = 0$

4. $5xy'' + (30 + 3x)y' + 3y = 0$

5. $xy'' - (4 + x)y' + 3y = 0$

6. $2xy'' - (6 + 2x)y' + y = 0$

7. $x^2y'' + (2x + 3x^2)y' - 2y = 0$

8. $x(1 - x)y'' - 3y' + 2y = 0$

In Problems 9 through 14, first find the first four nonzero terms in a Frobenius series solution of the given differential equation. Then use the reduction of order technique (as in Example 4) to find the logarithmic term and the first three nonzero terms in a second linearly independent series solution.

9. $xy'' + y' - xy = 0$

10. $x^2y'' - xy' + (x^2 + 1)y = 0$

11. $x^2y'' + (x^2 - 3x)y' + 4y = 0$

12. $x^2y'' + x^2y' - 2y = 0$

13. $x^2y'' + (2x^2 - 3x)y' + 3y = 0$

14. $x^2y'' + x(1 + x)y' - 4y = 0$

15. Begin with

$$J_0(x) = 1 - \frac{x^2}{4} + \frac{x^4}{64} - \frac{x^6}{2304} + \cdots.$$

Using the method of reduction of order, derive the second linearly independent solution

$$y_2(x) = J_0(x) \ln x + \frac{x^2}{4} - \frac{3x^4}{128} + \frac{11x^6}{13824} - \cdots$$

of Bessel's equation of order zero.

16. Find two linearly independent Frobenius series solutions of Bessel's equation of order $\frac{3}{2}$,

$$x^2y'' + xy' + \left(x^2 - \frac{9}{4}\right)y = 0.$$

17. (a) Verify that $y_1(x) = xe^x$ is one solution of

$$x^2y'' - x(1 + x)y' + y = 0.$$

(b) Note that $r_1 = r_2 = 1$. Substitute

$$y_2 = y_1 \ln x + \sum_{n=1}^{\infty} b_n x^{n+1}$$

in the differential equation to deduce that $b_1 = -1$ and that

$$nb_n - b_{n-1} = -\frac{1}{n!} \quad \text{for } n \geq 2.$$

(c) Substitute $b_n = +c_n/n!$ in this recurrence relation and conclude from the result that $c_n = -H_n$. Thus the second solution is

$$y_2(x) = xe^x \ln x - \sum_{n=1}^{\infty} \frac{H_n x^{n+1}}{n!}.$$

18. Consider the equation $xy'' - y = 0$, which has exponents $r_1 = 1$ and $r_2 = 0$ at $x = 0$. (a) Derive the Frobenius series solution

$$y_1(x) = \sum_{n=1}^{\infty} \frac{x^n}{n!(n-1)!}.$$

(b) Substitute

$$y_2 = Cy_1 \ln x + \sum_{n=0}^{\infty} b_n x^n$$

in the equation $xy'' - y = 0$ to derive the recurrence relation

$$n(n+1)b_{n+1} - b_n = -\frac{2n+1}{(n+1)!n!}C.$$

Conclude from this result that a second solution is

$$y_2(x) = y_1(x) \ln x + 1 - \sum_{n=1}^{\infty} \frac{H_n + H_{n-1}}{n!(n-1)!} x^n.$$

19. Suppose that the differential equation

$$L[y] = x^2y'' + xp(x)y' + q(x)y = 0 \tag{54}$$

has equal exponents $r_1 = r_2$ at the regular singular point $x = 0$, so that its indicial equation is

$$\phi(r) = (r - r_1)^2 = 0.$$

Let $c_0 = 1$ and define $c_n(r)$ for $n \geq 1$ by using Eq. (9); that is,

$$c_n(r) = -\frac{L_n(r; c_0, c_1, \ldots, c_{n-1})}{\phi(r+n)}. \tag{55}$$

Then define the function $y(x, r)$ of x and r to be

$$y(x, r) = \sum_{n=0}^{\infty} c_n(r) x^{n+r}. \tag{56}$$

(a) Deduce from the discussion preceding Eq. (9) that

$$L[y(x, r)] = x^r(r - r_1)^2. \tag{57}$$

Hence deduce that

$$y_1 = y(x, r_1) = \sum_{n=0}^{\infty} c_n(r_1)x^{n+r_1} \qquad (58)$$

is one solution of Eq. (54). (b) Differentiate Eq. (57) with respect to r to show that

$$L[y_r(x, r_1)] = \frac{\partial}{\partial r}[x^r(r - r_1)^2]\Big|_{r=r_1} = 0.$$

Deduce that $y_2 = y_r(x, r_1)$ is a second solution of Eq. (54). (c) Differentiate Eq. (58) with respect to r to show that

$$y_2 = y_1 \ln x + x^{r_1} \sum_{n=1}^{\infty} c_n'(r_1)x^n. \qquad (59)$$

20. Use the method of Problem 19 to derive both the solutions in (38) and (45) of Bessel's equation of order zero. The following steps outline this computation. (a) Take $c_0 = 1$; show that Eq. (55) reduces in this case to

$$(r + 1)^2 c_1(r) = 0 \qquad \text{and}$$

$$c_n(r) = -\frac{c_{n-2}(r)}{(n + r)^2} \quad \text{for } n \geq 2. \qquad (60)$$

(b) Next show that $c_1(0) = c_1'(0) = 0$, and then deduce from (60) that $c_n(0) = c_n'(0) = 0$ for n odd. Hence you need to compute $c_n(0)$ and $c_n'(0)$ only for n even. (c) Deduce from (60) that

$$c_{2n}(r) = \frac{(-1)^n}{(r + 2)^2(r + 4)^2 \cdots (r + 2n)^2}. \qquad (61)$$

With $r = r_1 = 0$ in (58), this gives $J_0(x)$. (d) Differentiate (61) to show that

$$c_{2n}'(0) = \frac{(-1)^{n+1}H_n}{2^{2n}(n!)^2}.$$

Substitution of this result in (59) gives the second solution in (45).

21. Derive the logarithmic solution in (51) of Bessel's equation of order 1 by the method of substitution. The following steps outline this computation. (a) Substitute

$$y_2 = CJ_1(x) \ln x + x^{-1}\left(1 + \sum_{n=1}^{\infty} b_n x^n\right)$$

in Bessel's equation to obtain

$$-b_1 + x + \sum_{n=2}^{\infty} [(n^2 - 1)b_{n+1} + b_{n-1}]x^n$$

$$+ C\left[x + \sum_{n=1}^{\infty} \frac{(-1)^n(2n + 1)x^{2n+1}}{2^{2n}(n + 1)!n!}\right] = 0. \qquad (62)$$

(b) Deduce from Eq. (62) that $C = -1$ and that $b_n = 0$ for n odd. (c) Next deduce the recurrence relation

$$[(2n + 1)^2 - 1]b_{2n+2} + b_{2n} = \frac{(-1)^n(2n + 1)}{2^{2n}(n + 1)!n!} \qquad (62)$$

for $n \geq 1$. Note that if b_2 is chosen arbitrarily, then b_{2n} is determined for all $n > 1$. (d) Take $b_2 = \frac{1}{4}$ and substitute

$$b_{2n} = \frac{(-1)^n c_{2n}}{2^{2n}(n - 1)!n!}$$

in Eq. (63) to obtain

$$c_{2n+2} - c_{2n} = \frac{1}{n + 1} + \frac{1}{n}.$$

(e) Note that $c_2 = 1 = H_1 + H_0$ and deduce that

$$c_{2n} = H_n + H_{n-1}.$$

8.4 Computing Project

The reduction of order formula in Eq. (28) of this section is readily implemented with a computer algebra system such as *Mathematica*. Here we illustrate its use to derive a second solution of Bessel's equation of order zero, beginning with the known power series solution $J_0(x)$:

```
y1 = Sum[ (-x^2/4)^n / (n!)^2, {n, 0, 4} ] + O[x]^9
```

$$1 - \frac{x^2}{4} + \frac{x^4}{64} - \frac{x^6}{2304} + \frac{x^8}{147456} + O[x]^9$$

Then with

```
P = 1/x;
```

we need only substitute in the integral of Eq. (28):

```
integral = Integrate[ Exp[ -Integrate[P,x]]/y1^2, x ]
```

$$\text{Log}[x] + \frac{x^2}{4} + \frac{5 \ x^4}{128} + \frac{23 \ x^6}{2345} + \frac{677 \ x^8}{589824} + O[x]^9$$

Then the computation

```
y1 (integral - Log[x])
```

$$\frac{x^2}{4} - \frac{3 \ x^4}{128} + \frac{11 \ x^6}{13824} - \frac{25 \ x^8}{1769472} + O[x]^9$$

gives the power series terms that we see in Eq. (45) of the text.

After verifying these computations using an available computer algebra system, begin with the power series for $J_1(x)$ in Eq. (49) and derive similarly the second solution in (50) of Bessel's equation of order 1. Problems 9 through 14 in this section can also be automated in this way.

8.5 Bessel's Equation

We have already seen several cases of Bessel's equation of order $p \geqq 0$,

$$x^2 y'' + xy' + (x^2 - p^2)y = 0. \tag{1}$$

Its solutions are now called Bessel functions of order p. Such functions first appeared in the 1730s in the work of Daniel Bernoulli and Euler on the oscillations of a vertically suspended chain. The equation itself appears in a 1764 article by Euler on the vibrations of a circular drumhead, and Fourier used Bessel functions in his classical treatise on heat (1822). But their general properties were first studied systematically in an 1824 memoir by F. W. Bessel, who was investigating the motion of planets. The standard source of information on Bessel functions is G. N. Watson's *A Treatise on the Theory of Bessel Functions,* 2nd ed. (Cambridge: Cambridge University Press, 1944). Its 36 pages of references, which cover only the period up to 1922, give some idea of the vast literature of this subject.

Bessel's equation in (1) has indicial equation $r^2 - p^2 = 0$, with roots $r = \pm p$. If we substitute $y = \sum c_m x^{m+r}$ in (1), we find in the usual manner that $c_1 = 0$ and that

$$[(m + r)^2 - p^2]c_m + c_{m-2} = 0 \tag{2}$$

for $m \geqq 2$. The verification of Eq. (2) is left to the reader (Problem 6).

The Case $r = p > 0$

If we use $r = p$ and write a_m in place of c_m, then Eq. (2) yields the recursion formula

$$a_m = - \frac{a_{m-2}}{m(2p + m)}. \tag{3}$$

Because $a_1 = 0$, it follows that $a_m = 0$ for all odd m. The first few even coefficients

are

$$a_2 = -\frac{a_0}{2(2p + 2)} = -\frac{a_0}{2^2(p + 1)},$$

$$a_4 = -\frac{a_2}{4(2p + 4)} = \frac{a_0}{2^4 \cdot 2(p + 1)(p + 2)},$$

$$a_6 = -\frac{a_4}{6(2p + 6)} = -\frac{a_0}{2^6 \cdot 2 \cdot 3(p + 1)(p + 2)(p + 3)}.$$

The general pattern is

$$a_{2m} = \frac{(-1)^m a_0}{2^{2m} m!(p + 1)(p + 2) \cdots (p + m)},$$

so with the larger root $r = p$ we get the solution

$$\blacktriangleright \qquad y_1(x) = a_0 \sum_{m=1}^{\infty} \frac{(-1)^m x^{2m+p}}{2^{2m} m!(p + 1)(p + 2) \cdots (p + m)}. \qquad (4)$$

If $p = 0$ this is the only Frobenius series solution; with $a_0 = 1$ as well, it is the function $J_0(x)$ we have seen before.

The Case $r = -p < 0$

If we use $r = -p$ and write b_m in place of c_m, Eq. (2) takes the form

$$\blacktriangleright \qquad m(m - 2p)b_m + b_{m-2} = 0 \qquad (5)$$

for $m \geq 2$, whereas $b_1 = 0$. We see that there is a potential difficulty if it happens that $2p$ is a positive integer—that is, if p is either a positive integer or an odd integral multiple of $\frac{1}{2}$. For then when $m = 2p$, Eq. (5) is simply $0 \cdot b_m + b_{m-2} = 0$. Thus if $b_{m-2} \neq 0$, no value of b_m can satisfy this equation.

But if p is an odd integral multiple of $\frac{1}{2}$, we can circumvent this difficulty. For suppose that $p = k/2$ where k is an odd positive integer. Then we need only choose $b_m = 0$ for all odd values of m. The crucial step is the kth step,

$$k(k - k)b_k + b_{k-2} = 0;$$

and this equation will hold because $b_k = b_{k-2} = 0$.

Hence if p is *not* a positive integer, we take $b_m = 0$ for m odd and define the coefficients of even subscript in terms of b_0 by means of the recursion formula

$$b_m = -\frac{b_{m-2}}{m(m - 2p)}, \qquad m \geq 2. \qquad (6)$$

In comparing (6) with (3), we see that (6) will lead to the same result as that in (4), except with p replaced with $-p$. Thus in this case we obtain the second solution

$$\blacktriangleright \qquad y_2(x) = b_0 \sum_{m=1}^{\infty} \frac{(-1)^m x^{2m-p}}{2^{2m} m!(-p + 1)(-p + 2) \cdots (-p + m)}. \qquad (7)$$

The series in (4) and (7) converge for all $x > 0$ because $x = 0$ is the only singular point of Bessel's equation. If $p > 0$, the leading term in y_1 is $a_0 x^p$, whereas the leading

term in y_2 is $b_0 x^{-p}$. Hence $y_1(0) = 0$, but $y_2(x) \to \pm\infty$ as $x \to 0$, so it is clear that y_1 and y_2 are linearly independent solutions of Bessel's equation of order $p > 0$.

The Gamma Function

The formulas in (4) and (7) can be simplified by use of the **gamma function** $\Gamma(x)$, which is defined for $x > 0$ by

$$\Gamma(x) = \int_0^\infty e^{-t} t^{x-1} \, dt. \tag{8}$$

It is not difficult to show that this improper integral converges for each $x > 0$. The gamma function is a generalization for $x > 0$ of the factorial function $n!$, which is defined only if n is a nonnegative integer. To see the way in which $\Gamma(x)$ is a generalization of $n!$, we note first that

$$\Gamma(1) = \int_0^\infty e^{-t} \, dt = \lim_{b \to \infty} \left[-e^{-t} \right]_0^b = 1. \tag{9}$$

Then we integrate by parts:

$$\Gamma(x+1) = \sum_{b \to \infty} \int_0^b e^{-t} t^x \, dt = \lim_{b \to \infty} \left(\left[-e^{-t} t^x \right]_0^b + \int_0^b x e^{-t} t^{x-1} \, dt \right)$$

$$= x \left(\lim_{b \to \infty} \int_0^b e^{-t} t^{x-1} \, dt \right);$$

that is,

$$\blacktriangleright \qquad\qquad \Gamma(x+1) = x\Gamma(x). \tag{10}$$

This is the most important property of the gamma function.

If we combine Eqs. (9) and (10), we see that

$$\Gamma(2) = 1 \cdot \Gamma(1) = 1!, \qquad \Gamma(3) = 2 \cdot \Gamma(2) = 2!, \qquad \Gamma(4) = 3 \cdot \Gamma(3) = 3!,$$

and in general that

$$\blacktriangleright \qquad\qquad \Gamma(n+1) = n! \quad \text{for } n \geqq 0. \tag{11}$$

An important special value of the gamma function is

$$\Gamma\left(\frac{1}{2}\right) = \int_0^\infty e^{-t} t^{-1/2} \, dt = 2 \int_0^\infty e^{-u^2} \, du = \sqrt{\pi}, \tag{12}$$

where we have substituted u^2 for t in the first integral; the fact that

$$\int_0^\infty e^{-u^2} \, du = \frac{\sqrt{\pi}}{2}$$

is known, but is far from obvious.

Although $\Gamma(x)$ is defined in (8) only for $x > 0$, we can use the recursion formula in (10) to define $\Gamma(x)$ whenever x is neither zero nor a negative integer. If $-1 < x < 0$, then

$$\Gamma(x) = \frac{\Gamma(x+1)}{x};$$

FIGURE 8.5.1. Graph of the extended gamma function

the right-hand side is defined because $0 < x + 1 < 1$. The same formula may then be used to extend the defnition of $\Gamma(x)$ to the open interval $(-2, -1)$, then to the open interval $(-3, -2)$, and so on. The graph of the gamma function thus extended is shown in Fig. 8.5.1. The student who would like to pursue this fascinating topic further should consult Artin's *The Gamma Function* (New York: Holt, Rinehart and Winston, 1964). In only 39 pages, this is one of the finest expositions in the entire literature of mathematics.

Bessel Functions of the First Kind

If we choose $a_0 = 1/[2^p \Gamma(p + 1)]$ in (4), where $p > 0$, and note that

$$\Gamma(p + m + 1) = (p + m)(p + m - 1) \cdots (p + 2)(p + 1)\Gamma(p + 1)$$

by repeated application of Eq. (10), we can write the **Bessel function of the first kind of order** p very concisely with the aid of the gamma function:

▶
$$J_p(x) = \sum_{m=0}^{\infty} \frac{(-1)^m}{m!\,\Gamma(p + m + 1)} \left(\frac{x}{2}\right)^{2m+p}. \tag{13}$$

Similarly, if $p > 0$ is not an integer, we choose $b_0 = 1/[2^{-p}\Gamma(-p + 1)]$ in (7) to obtain the linearly independent second solution

▶
$$J_{-p}(x) = \sum_{m=0}^{\infty} \frac{(-1)^m}{m!\,\Gamma(-p + m + 1)} \left(\frac{x}{2}\right)^{2m-p} \tag{14}$$

of Bessel's equation of order p. If p is not an integer, we have the general solution

$$y(x) = c_1 J_p(x) + c_2 J_{-p}(x) \tag{15}$$

for $x > 0$; x^p must be replaced by $|x|^p$ in Eqs. (13) through (15) to get the correct solutions for $x < 0$.

If $p = n$, a nonnegative integer, then Eq. (13) gives

▶
$$J_n(x) = \sum_{m=0}^{\infty} \frac{(-1)^m}{m!\,(m + n)!} \left(\frac{x}{2}\right)^{2m+n} \tag{16}$$

for the Bessel functions of the first kind of integral order. Thus

$$J_0(x) = \sum_{m=0}^{\infty} \frac{(-1)^m x^{2m}}{2^{2m}(m!)^2} = 1 - \frac{x^2}{2^2} + \frac{x^4}{2^2 4^2} - \frac{x^6}{2^2 4^2 6^2} + \cdots \tag{17}$$

and

$$J_1(x) = \sum_{m=0}^{\infty} \frac{(-1)^m x^{2m+1}}{2^{2m+1} m!(m + 1)!} = \frac{x}{2} - \frac{1}{2!}\left(\frac{x}{2}\right)^3 + \frac{1}{2!3!}\left(\frac{x}{2}\right)^5 - \cdots. \tag{18}$$

The graphs of $J_0(x)$ and $J_1(x)$ are shown in Fig. 8.5.2. In a general way they resemble damped cosine and sine oscillations, respectively (see Problem 27). Indeed, if you examine the series in (17), you can see part of the reason why $J_0(x)$ and $\cos x$ *might* be similar—only minor changes in the denominators in (17) are needed to produce the Taylor series for $\cos x$. As suggested by Fig. 8.5.2, the zeros of the functions $J_0(x)$ and $J_1(x)$ are *interlaced*—between any two consecutive zeros of $J_0(x)$ there is precisely one zero of $J_1(x)$ (Problem 26) and vice versa. The first four zeros of $J_0(x)$ are approxi-

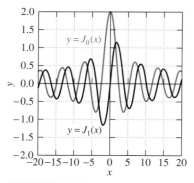

FIGURE 8.5.2. Graphs of the Bessel functions $J_0(x)$ and $J_1(x)$

n	nth zero of $J_0(x)$	$\left(n - \dfrac{1}{4}\right)\pi$	nth zero of $J_1(x)$	$\left(n + \dfrac{1}{4}\right)\pi$
1	2.4048	2.3562	3.8317	3.9270
2	5.5201	5.4978	7.0156	7.0686
3	8.6537	8.6394	10.1735	10.2102
4	11.7915	11.7810	13.3237	13.3518
5	14.9309	14.9226	16.4706	16.4934

FIGURE 8.5.3 Zeros of $J_0(x)$ and $J_1(x)$

mately 2.4048, 5.5201, 8.6537, and 11.7915. For n large, the nth zero of $J_0(x)$ is approximately $(n - \frac{1}{4})\pi$; the nth zero of $J_1(x)$ is approximately $(n + \frac{1}{4})\pi$. Thus the interval between consecutive zeros of either $J_0(x)$ or $J_1(x)$ is approximately π—another similarity with $\cos x$ and $\sin x$. You can see the way the accuracy of these approximations increases with increasing n by rounding the entries in the table in Fig. 8.5.3 to two decimal places.

It turns out that $J_p(x)$ is an elementary function if the order p is half an odd integer. For instance, on substitution of $p = \frac{1}{2}$ and $p = -\frac{1}{2}$ in Eqs. (13) and (14), respectively, the results can be recognized (Problem 2) as

$$J_{1/2}(x) = \sqrt{\frac{2}{\pi x}} \sin x \quad \text{and} \quad J_{-1/2}(x) = \sqrt{\frac{2}{\pi x}} \cos x. \quad (19)$$

Bessel Functions of the Second Kind

The methods of Section 8.4 must be used to find linearly independent second solutions of integral order. A very complicated generalization of Example 3 in that section gives the formula

$$Y_n(x) = \frac{2}{\pi}\left(\gamma + \ln\frac{x}{2}\right)J_n(x) - \frac{1}{\pi}\sum_{m=0}^{n-1}\frac{2^{n-2m}(n-m-1)!}{m!x^{n-2m}}$$

$$- \frac{1}{\pi}\sum_{m=0}^{\infty}\frac{(-1)^m(H_m + H_{m+n})}{m!(m+n)!}\left(\frac{x}{2}\right)^{n+2m}, \quad (20)$$

with the notation used there. If $n = 0$ the first sum in (20) is taken to be zero. Here, $Y_n(x)$ is called the **Bessel function of the second kind of integral order** $n \geq 0$.

The general solution of Bessel's equation of integral order n is

$$y(x) = c_1 J_n(x) + c_2 Y_n(x). \quad (21)$$

It is important to note that $Y_n(x) \to -\infty$ as $x \to 0$ (Fig. 8.5.4). Hence $c_2 = 0$ in Eq. (21) if $y(x)$ is continuous at $x = 0$. Thus if $y(x)$ is a *continuous* solution of Bessel's equation of order n, it follows that

$$y(x) = cJ_n(x)$$

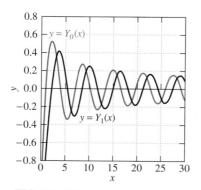

FIGURE 8.5.4. Graphs of the Bessel functions $Y_0(x)$ and $Y_1(x)$

for some constant c. Because $J_0(0) = 1$, we see in addition that if $n = 0$, then $c = y(0)$. In Section 10.4 we will see that this single fact regarding Bessel functions has numerous physical applications.

Bessel Function Identities

Bessel functions are analogous to trigonometric functions in that they satisfy a large number of standard identities of frequent utility, especially in the evaluation of integrals involving Bessel functions. Differentiation of

$$J_p(x) = \sum_{m=0}^{\infty} \frac{(-1)^m}{m!\Gamma(p+m+1)} \left(\frac{x}{2}\right)^{2m+p} \tag{13}$$

in the case that p is a nonnegative integer gives

$$\frac{d}{dx}[x^p J_p(x)] = \frac{d}{dx} \sum_{m=0}^{\infty} \frac{(-1)^m x^{2m+2p}}{2^{2m+p} m!(p+m)!}$$

$$= \sum_{m=0}^{\infty} \frac{(-1)^m x^{2m+2p-1}}{2^{2m+p-1} m!(p+m-1)!}$$

$$= x^p \sum_{m=0}^{\infty} \frac{(-1)^m x^{2m+p-1}}{2^{2m+p-1} m!(p+m-1)!},$$

and thus we have shown that

$$\frac{d}{dx}[x^p J_p(x)] = x^p J_{p-1}(x). \tag{22}$$

Similarly,

$$\frac{d}{dx}[x^{-p} J_p(x)] = -x^{-p} J_{p+1}(x). \tag{23}$$

If we carry out the differentiations in Eqs. (22) and (23) and then divide the resulting identities by x^p and x^{-p}, respectively, we obtain (Problem 8) the identities

$$J_p'(x) = J_{p-1}(x) - \frac{p}{x} J_p(x) \tag{24}$$

and

$$J_p'(x) = \frac{p}{x} J_p(x) - J_{p+1}(x). \tag{25}$$

Thus we may express the derivatives of Bessel functions in terms of Bessel functions themselves. Subtraction of Eq. (25) from Eq. (24) gives the recursion formula

$$J_{p+1}(x) = \frac{2p}{x} J_p(x) - J_{p-1}(x), \tag{26}$$

which can be used to express Bessel functions of high order in terms of Bessel functions of lower orders. In the form

$$J_{p-1}(x) = \frac{2p}{x} J_p(x) - J_{p+1}(x), \tag{27}$$

it can be used to express Bessel functions of large negative order in terms of Bessel functions of numerically smaller negative orders.

The identities in Eqs. (22) through (27) hold wherever they are meaningful—that is, whenever no Bessel functions of negative integral order appear. In particular, they hold for all nonintegral values of p.

EXAMPLE 1 With $p = 0$, Eq. (22) gives

$$\int x J_0(x)\, dx = x J_1(x) + C.$$

Similarly, with $p = 0$, Eq. (23) gives

$$\int J_1(x)\, dx = - J_0(x) + C.$$

EXAMPLE 2 Using first $p = 2$ and then $p = 1$ in Eq. (26), we get

$$J_3(x) = \frac{4}{x} J_2(x) - J_1(x) = \frac{4}{x} \left[\frac{2}{x} J_1(x) - J_0(x) \right] - J_1(x),$$

so that

$$J_3(x) = - \frac{4}{x} J_0(x) + \left(\frac{8}{x^2} - 1 \right) J_1(x).$$

With similar manipulations every Bessel function of positive integral order can be expressed in terms of $J_0(x)$ and $J_1(x)$.

EXAMPLE 3 To evaluate $\int x J_2(x)\, dx$, we first note that

$$\int x^{-1} J_2(x)\, dx = - x^{-1} J_1(x) + C$$

by Eq. (23) with $p = 1$. We therefore write

$$\int x J_2(x)\, dx = \int x^2 [x^{-1} J_2(x)]\, dx$$

and integrate by parts with

$$u = x^2, \qquad\qquad dv = x^{-1} J_2(x)\, dx,$$
$$du = 2x\, dx, \qquad \text{and} \qquad v = - x^{-1} J_1(x).$$

This gives

$$\int x J_2(x)\, dx = - x J_1(x) + 2 \int J_1(x)\, dx = - x J_1(x) - 2 J_0(x) + C,$$

with the aid of the second result of Example 1. ∎

The Parametric Bessel Equation

The **parametric Bessel equation of order** n is

$$x^2 y'' + x y' + (\alpha^2 x^2 - n^2) y = 0, \tag{28}$$

with α a positive parameter. As we will see in Chapter 10, this equation appears in the solution of Laplace's equation in polar coordinates. It is easy to see (Problem 9) that

the substitution $t = \alpha x$ transforms Eq. (28) into the (standard) Bessel equation

$$t^2 \frac{d^2 y}{dt^2} + t \frac{dy}{dt} + (t^2 - n^2)y = 0 \tag{29}$$

with general solution $y(t) = c_1 J_n(t) + c_2 Y_n(t)$. Hence the general solution of Eq. (28) is

$$y(x) = c_1 J_n(\alpha x) + c_2 Y_n(\alpha x). \tag{30}$$

Now consider the eigenvalue problem

$$x^2 y'' + xy' + (\lambda x^2 - n^2) = 0,$$
$$y(L) = 0 \tag{31}$$

on the interval $[0, L]$. We seek the *positive* values of λ for which there exists a non-trivial solution of (31) that is *continuous* on $[0, L]$. If we write $\lambda = \alpha^2$, then the differential equation in (31) is that in Eq. (28), so its general solution is given in Eq. (30). Because $Y_n(x) \to -\infty$ as $x \to 0$ but $J_n(0)$ is finite, the continuity of $y(x)$ requires that $c_2 = 0$. Thus $y(x) = c_1 J_n(\alpha x)$. The endpoint condition $y(L) = 0$ now implies that $z = \alpha L$ must be a (positive) root of the equation

$$J_n(z) = 0. \tag{32}$$

For $n > 1$, $J_n(x)$ oscillates rather like $J_1(x)$ in Fig. 8.5.2 and hence has an infinite sequence of positive roots $\gamma_{n1}, \gamma_{n2}, \gamma_{n3}, \dots$. It follows that the kth positive eigenvalue of the problem in (31) is

$$\lambda_k = (\alpha_k)^2 = \frac{(\gamma_{nk})^2}{L^2}, \tag{33}$$

and that its associated eigenfunction is

$$y_k(x) = J_n\left(\frac{\gamma_{nk} x}{L}\right). \tag{34}$$

The roots γ_{nk} of Eq. (32) for $n \leq 8$ and $k \leq 20$ are tabulated in Table 9.5 of M. Abramowitz and I. A. Stegun, *Handbook of Mathematical Functions* (New York: Dover, 1965).

8.5 Problems

1. Differentiate termwise the series for $J_0(x)$ to show directly that $J_0'(x) = -J_1(x)$ (another analogy with the cosine and sine functions).

2. (a) Deduce from Eqs. (10) and (12) that

$$\Gamma\left(n + \frac{1}{2}\right) = \frac{1 \cdot 3 \cdots (2n - 1)}{2^n} \sqrt{\pi}.$$

(b) Use the result of part (a) to verify the formulas in Eq. (19) for $J_{1/2}(x)$ and $J_{-1/2}(x)$.

3. (a) Suppose that m is a positive integer. Show that

$$\Gamma\left(m + \frac{2}{3}\right) = \frac{2 \cdot 5 \cdots (3m - 1)}{3^m} \Gamma\left(\frac{2}{3}\right).$$

(b) Conclude from part (a) and Eq. (13) that

$$J_{-1/3}(x) = \frac{(x/2)^{-1/3}}{\Gamma\left(\frac{2}{3}\right)} \left(1 + \sum_{m=1}^{\infty} \frac{(-1)^m 3^m x^{2m}}{2^{2m} m! \cdot 2 \cdot 5 \cdots (3m - 1)}\right).$$

4. Apply Eqs. (19), (26), and (27) to show that

$$J_{3/2}(x) = \sqrt{\frac{2}{\pi x^3}} \, (\sin x - x \cos x)$$

and

$$J_{-3/2}(x) = -\sqrt{\frac{2}{\pi x^3}} \, (\cos x + x \sin x).$$

5. Express $J_4(x)$ in terms of $J_0(x)$ and $J_1(x)$.

6. Derive the recursion formula in Eq. (2) for Bessel's equation.

7. Verify the identity in Eq. (23) by termwise differentiation.

8. Deduce the identities in Eqs. (24) and (25) from those in Eqs. (22) and (23).

9. Verify that the substitution $t = \alpha x$ transforms the parametric Bessel equation in (28) into the equation in (29).

10. Show that

$$4J_p''(x) = J_{p-2}(x) - 2J_p(x) + J_{p+2}(x).$$

11. Use the relation $\Gamma(x + 1) = x\Gamma(x)$ to deduce from Eqs. (13) and (14) that if p is not a negative integer then

$$J_p(x) =$$

$$\frac{(x/2)^p}{\Gamma(p + 1)} \left[1 + \sum_{m=1}^{\infty} \frac{(-1)^m (x/2)^{2m}}{m!(p + 1)(p + 2) \cdots (p + m)} \right].$$

This form is more convenient for the computation of $J_p(x)$ because only the single value $\Gamma(p + 1)$ of the gamma function is required.

12. Use the series of Problem 11 to find $y(0) = \lim_{x \to 0} y(x)$ if

$$y(x) = x^2 \left[\frac{J_{5/2}(x) + J_{-5/2}(x)}{J_{1/2}(x) + J_{-1/2}(x)} \right].$$

Any integral of the form $\int x^m J_n(x) \, dx$ can be evaluated in terms of Bessel functions and the indefinite integral $\int J_0(x) \, dx$. The latter integral cannot be simplified further, but the function $\int_0^x J_0(t) \, dt$ is tabulated in Table 11.1 of Abramowitz and Stegun. Use the identities in Eqs. (22) and (23) to evaluate the integrals in Problems 13 through 21.

13. $\int x^2 J_0(x) \, dx$ **14.** $\int x^3 J_0(x) \, dx$

15. $\int x^4 J_0(x) \, dx$ **16.** $\int x J_1(x) \, dx$

17. $\int x^2 J_1(x) \, dx$ **18.** $\int x^3 J_1(x) \, dx$

19. $\int x^4 J_1(x) \, dx$ **20.** $\int J_2(x) \, dx$

21. $\int J_3(x) \, dx$

22. Prove that

$$J_0(x) = \frac{1}{\pi} \int_0^{\pi} \cos(x \sin \theta) \, d\theta$$

by showing that the right-hand side satisfies Bessel's equation of order zero and has the value $J_0(0)$ when $x = 0$. Explain why this constitutes a proof.

23. Prove that

$$J_1(x) = \frac{1}{\pi} \int_0^{\pi} \cos(\theta - x \sin \theta) \, d\theta$$

by showing that the right-hand side satisfies Bessel's equation of order 1 and that its derivative has the value $J_1'(0)$ when $x = 0$. Explain why this constitutes a proof.

24. It can be shown that

$$J_n(x) = \frac{1}{\pi} \int_0^{\pi} \cos(n\theta - x \sin \theta) \, d\theta.$$

With $n \geq 2$, show that the right-hand side satisfies Bessel's equation of order n and also agrees with the values $J_n(0)$ and $J_n'(0)$. Explain why this does *not* suffice to prove the assertion above.

25. Deduce from Problem 22 that

$$J_0(x) = \frac{1}{2\pi} \int_0^{2\pi} e^{ix \sin \theta} \, d\theta.$$

(*Suggestion:* Show first that

$$\int_0^{2\pi} e^{ix \sin \theta} \, d\theta = \int_0^{\pi} (e^{ix \sin \theta} + e^{-ix \sin \theta}) \, d\theta;$$

then use Euler's formula.)

26. Use Eqs. (22) and (23) and Rolle's theorem to prove that between any two consecutive zeros of $J_n(x)$ there is precisely one zero of $J_{n+1}(x)$.

27. (a) Show that the substitution $y = x^{-1/2} z$ in Bessel's equation of order p,

$$x^2 y'' + xy' + (x^2 - p^2)y = 0,$$

yields

$$z'' + \left(1 - \frac{p^2 - \frac{1}{4}}{x^2} \right) z = 0.$$

(b) If x is so large that $\left(p^2 - \frac{1}{4} \right)/x^2$ is negligible, then the latter equation reduces to $z'' + z \approx 0$. Explain why this suggests (without proving it) that if $y(x)$ is a solution of Bessel's equation, then

$$y(x) \approx x^{-1/2}(A \cos x + B \sin x) = Cx^{-1/2} \cos(x - \alpha)$$

with C and α constants, and x large.

Asymptotic Approximations

It is known that the choices $C = \sqrt{2/\pi}$ and $\alpha = (2n + 1)\pi/4$ yield the best approximation to $J_n(x)$ for x large:

$$J_n(x) \approx \sqrt{\frac{2}{\pi x}} \cos\left(x - (2n + 1)\frac{\pi}{4}\right). \quad (35)$$

Similarly,

$$Y_n(x) \approx \sqrt{\frac{2}{\pi x}} \sin\left(x - (2n + 1)\frac{\pi}{4}\right). \quad (36)$$

In particular,

$$J_0(x) \approx \sqrt{\frac{2}{\pi x}} \cos\left(x - \frac{\pi}{4}\right)$$

and

$$Y_0(x) \approx \sqrt{\frac{2}{\pi x}} \sin\left(x - \frac{\pi}{4}\right)$$

if x is large. These are *asymptotic approximations* in that the ratio of the two sides approaches unity at $x \to +\infty$.

*8.6 Applications of Bessel Functions

The importance of Bessel functions stems not only from the frequent appearance of Bessel's equation in applications, but also from the fact that the solutions of many other second-order linear differential equations can be expressed in terms of Bessel functions. To see how this comes about, we begin with Bessel's equation of order p in the form

$$z^2 \frac{d^2 w}{dz^2} + z \frac{dw}{dz} + (z^2 - p^2)w = 0, \quad (1)$$

and substitute

$$w = x^{-\alpha}y, \qquad z = kx^\beta. \quad (2)$$

Then a routine (though lengthy) transformation of Eq. (1) yields

$$x^2 y'' + (1 - 2\alpha)xy' + (\alpha^2 - \beta^2 p^2 + \beta^2 k^2 x^{2\beta})y = 0;$$

that is,

$$x^2 y'' + Axy' + (B + Cx^q)y = 0, \quad (3)$$

where the constants A, B, C, and q are given by

$$A = 1 - 2\alpha, \qquad B = \alpha^2 - \beta^2 p^2, \qquad C = \beta^2 k^2, \qquad \text{and} \qquad q = 2\beta. \quad (4)$$

It is a simple matter to solve the equations in (4) for

$$\alpha = \frac{1 - A}{2}, \qquad \beta = \frac{q}{2},$$

$$k = \frac{2\sqrt{C}}{q}, \qquad \text{and} \qquad p = \frac{\sqrt{(1 - A)^2 - 4B}}{q}. \quad (5)$$

Under the assumption that the square roots in (5) are real, it follows that the general solution of Eq. (3) is

$$y(x) = x^\alpha w(z) = x^\alpha w(kx^\beta),$$

where

$$w(z) = c_1 J_p(z) + c_2 J_{-p}(z)$$

(assuming p not an integer) is the general solution of the Bessel equation in (1). This establishes the following result.

THEOREM 1: Solutions in Bessel Functions

If $C > 0$, $q \neq 0$, and $(1 - A)^2 \geq 4B$, then the general solution (for $x > 0$) of Eq. (3) is

$$y(x) = x^\alpha [c_1 J_p(kx^\beta) + c_2 J_{-p}(kx^\beta)], \tag{6}$$

where α, β, k, and p are given by the equations in (5). If p is an integer, then J_{-p} is to be replaced with Y_p. ■

EXAMPLE 1 Solve the equation

$$4x^2 y'' + 8xy' + (x^4 - 3)y = 0. \tag{7}$$

Solution To compare Eq. (7) with Eq. (3), we rewrite the former as

$$x^2 y'' + 2xy' + \left(-\frac{3}{4} + \frac{1}{4}x^4\right)y = 0$$

and see that $A = 2$, $B = -\frac{3}{4}$, $C = \frac{1}{4}$, and $q = 4$. Then the equations in (5) give $\alpha = -\frac{1}{2}$, $\beta = 2$, $k = \frac{1}{4}$, and $p = \frac{1}{2}$. Thus the general solution in (6) of Eq. (7) is

$$y(x) = x^{-1/2}\left[c_1 J_{1/2}\left(\frac{1}{4}x^2\right) + c_2 J_{-1/2}\left(\frac{1}{4}x^2\right)\right].$$

If we recall from Eq. (19) of Section 8.5 that

$$J_{1/2}(z) = \sqrt{\frac{2}{\pi z}} \sin z \quad \text{and} \quad J_{-1/2}(z) = \sqrt{\frac{2}{\pi z}} \cos z,$$

we see that a general solution of Eq. (7) can be written in the elementary form

$$y(x) = x^{-3/2}\left(A \cos \frac{x^2}{4} + B \sin \frac{x^2}{4}\right). \qquad ■$$

EXAMPLE 2 Solve the Airy equation

$$y'' + 9xy = 0. \tag{8}$$

Solution First we rewrite the equation in the form

$$x^2 y'' + 9x^3 y = 0.$$

This is the special case of Eq. (3) with $A = B = 0$, $C = 9$, and $q = 3$. It follows from the equations in (5) that $\alpha = \frac{1}{2}$, $\beta = \frac{3}{2}$, $k = 2$, and $p = \frac{1}{3}$. Thus the general solution of Eq. (8) is

$$y(x) = x^{1/2}[c_1 J_{1/3}(2x^{3/2}) + c_2 J_{-1/3}(2x^{3/2})]. \qquad ■$$

Buckling of a Vertical Column

For a practical application, we now consider the problem of determining when a uniform vertical column will buckle under its own weight. We take $x = 0$ at the free top

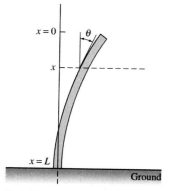

$x = 0$

θ

x

$x = L$

Ground

FIGURE 8.6.1. The buckling column

end of the column and $x = L > 0$ at its bottom; we assume that the bottom is rigidly imbedded in the ground (or in concrete; see Fig. 8.6.1). Denote the angular deflection of the column at the point x by $\theta(x)$. From the theory of elasticity it follows that

$$EI \frac{d^2\theta}{dx^2} + g\rho x\theta = 0, \tag{9}$$

where E is the Young's modulus of the material of the column, I is its cross-sectional moment of inertia, ρ is the linear density of the column, and g is gravitational acceleration. The boundary conditions are

$$\theta'(0) = 0, \qquad \theta(L) = 0. \tag{10}$$

We will accept (9) and (10) as an appropriate statement of the problem and attempt to solve it in this form. With

$$\lambda = \gamma^2 = \frac{g\rho}{EI}, \tag{11}$$

we have the eigenvalue problem

$$\theta'' + \gamma^2 x\theta = 0; \qquad \theta'(0) = 0, \qquad \theta(L) = 0. \tag{12}$$

The column can buckle only if there is a nontrivial solution of (12); otherwise the column will remain in its undeflected vertical position.

The differential equation in (12) is an Airy equation similar to the one in Example 2. It has the form of Eq. (3) with $A = 0$, $B = 0$, $C = \gamma^2$, and $q = 3$. The equations in (5) give $\alpha = \frac{1}{2}$, $\beta = \frac{3}{2}$, $k = \frac{2}{3}\gamma$, and $p = \frac{1}{3}$. So the general solution is

$$\theta(x) = x^{1/2}\left[c_1 J_{1/3}\left(\frac{2}{3}\gamma x^{3/2} \right) + c_2 J_{-1/3}\left(\frac{2}{3}\gamma x^{3/2} \right) \right]. \tag{13}$$

In order to apply the initial conditions, we substitute $p = \pm\frac{1}{3}$ in

$$J_p(x) = \sum_{m=0}^{\infty} \frac{(-1)^m}{m!\Gamma(p + m + 1)}\left(\frac{x}{2} \right)^{2m+p},$$

and find after some simplifications that

$$\theta(x) = \frac{c_1 \gamma^{1/3}}{3^{1/3}\Gamma(\frac{4}{3})}\left(x - \frac{\gamma^2 x^4}{12} + \frac{\gamma^4 x^7}{504} - \cdots \right)$$

$$+ \frac{c_2 3^{1/3}}{\gamma^{1/3}\Gamma(\frac{2}{3})}\left(1 - \frac{\gamma^2 x^3}{6} + \frac{\gamma^4 x^6}{180} - \cdots \right).$$

From this it is clear that the endpoint condition $\theta'(0) = 0$ implies that $c_1 = 0$, so

$$\theta(x) = c_2 x^{1/2} J_{-1/3}\left(\frac{2}{3}\gamma x^{3/2} \right). \tag{14}$$

The endpoint condition $\theta(L) = 0$ now gives

$$J_{-1/3}\left(\frac{2}{3}\gamma L^{3/2} \right) = 0. \tag{15}$$

Thus the column will buckle only if $z = \frac{2}{3}\gamma L^{3/2}$ is a root of the equation

FIGURE 8.6.2. Graph of $J_{-1/3}(x)$

$J_{-1/3}(z) = 0$. The graph of

$$J_{-1/3}(z) = \frac{(z/2)^{-1/3}}{\Gamma\left(\frac{2}{3}\right)}\left(1 + \sum_{m=1}^{\infty} \frac{(-1)^m 3^m z^{2m}}{2^{2m}(m!) \cdot 2 \cdot 5 \cdots (3m-1)}\right) \tag{16}$$

(see Problem 3 of Section 8.5) is shown in Fig. 8.6.2, where we see that the smallest positive zero z_1 is a bit less than 2. Most technical computing systems can find roots like this one. For instance, the *Mathematica* command

```
FindRoot[ BesselJ[ -1/3, z ] == 0, {z,2} ]
```

or the *Maple* command

```
fsolve( BesselJ(-1/3,z) = 0, z)
```

yields $z_1 = 1.86635$ (accurate to five decimal places).

The shortest length L_1 for which the column will buckle under its own weight is

$$L_1 = \left(\frac{3z_1}{2\gamma}\right)^{2/3} = \left[\frac{3z_1}{2}\left(\frac{EI}{\rho g}\right)^{1/2}\right]^{2/3}.$$

If we substitute $z_1 \approx 1.86635$ and $\rho = \delta A$, where δ is the volumetric density of the material of the column and A is its cross-sectional area, we finally get

$$L_1 \approx (1.986)\left(\frac{EI}{g\delta A}\right)^{1/3} \tag{17}$$

for the critical buckling length. For example, with a steel column or rod for which $E = 2.8 \times 10^7$ lb/in.2 and $g\delta = 0.28$ lb/in.3, the formula in (17) gives the results shown in the table in Fig. 8.6.3.

Cross Section of Rod	Shortest Buckling Length L_1
Circular with $r = 0.5$ in.	30 ft 6 in.
Circular with $r = 1.5$ in.	63 ft 5 in.
Annular with $r_{inner} = 1.25$ in. and $r_{outer} = 1.5$ in.	75 ft 7 in.

FIGURE 8.6.3

We have used the familiar formulas $A = \pi r^2$ and $I = \frac{1}{4}\pi r^4$ for a circular disk. The data in the table show why flagpoles are hollow.

8.6 Problems

In Problems 1 through 12, express the general solution of the given differential equation in terms of Bessel functions.

1. $x^2 y'' - xy' + (1 + x^2)y = 0$

2. $xy'' + 3y' + xy = 0$

3. $xy'' - y' + 36x^3 y = 0$

4. $x^2 y'' - 5xy' + (8 + x)y = 0$

5. $36x^2 y'' + 60xy' + (9x^3 - 5)y = 0$

6. $16x^2 y'' + 24xy' + (1 + 144x^3)y = 0$

7. $x^2 y'' + 3xy' + (1 + x^2)y = 0$

8. $4x^2 y'' - 12xy' + (15 + 16x)y = 0$

9. $16x^2 y'' - (5 - 144x^3)y = 0$

10. $2x^2 y'' - 3xy' - 2(14 - x^5)y = 0$

11. $y'' + x^4 y = 0$

12. $y'' + 4x^3 = 0$

13. Apply Theorem 1 to show that the general solution of

$$xy'' + 2y' + xy = 0$$

is $y(x) = x^{-1}(A \cos x + B \sin x)$.

14. Verify that the substitutions in (2) in Bessel's equation (Eq. (1)) yield Eq. (3).

15. (a) Show that the substitution

$$y = -\frac{1}{u}\frac{du}{dx}$$

transforms the Ricatti equation $dy/dx = x^2 + y^2$ into $u'' + x^2 u = 0$. (b) Show that the general solution of $dy/dx = x^2 + y^2$ is

$$y(x) = x \frac{J_{3/4}\left(\frac{1}{2}x^2\right) - cJ_{-3/4}\left(\frac{1}{2}x^2\right)}{cJ_{1/4}\left(\frac{1}{2}x^2\right) + J_{-1/4}\left(\frac{1}{2}x^2\right)}.$$

(*Suggestion:* Apply the identities in Eqs. (22) and (23) of Section 8.5.)

16. (a) Substitute the series of Problem 11 of Section 8.5 in the result of Problem 15 here to show that the solution of the initial value problem

$$\frac{dy}{dx} = x^2 + y^2, \qquad y(0) = 0$$

is

$$y(x) = x\frac{J_{3/4}\left(\frac{1}{2}x^2\right)}{J_{-1/4}\left(\frac{1}{2}x^2\right)}.$$

(b) Deduce similarly that the solution of the initial value problem

$$\frac{dy}{dx} = x^2 + y^2, \qquad y(0) = 1$$

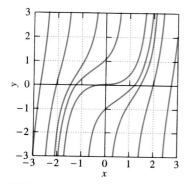

FIGURE 8.6.4. Solution curves of $y' = x^2 + y^2$

is

$$y(x) = x\frac{2\Gamma\left(\frac{3}{4}\right)J_{3/4}\left(\frac{1}{2}x^2\right) + \Gamma\left(\frac{1}{4}\right)J_{-3/4}\left(\frac{1}{2}x^2\right)}{2\Gamma\left(\frac{3}{4}\right)J_{-1/4}\left(\frac{1}{2}x^2\right) - \Gamma\left(\frac{1}{4}\right)J_{1/4}\left(\frac{1}{2}x^2\right)}.$$

Some solutions curves of the equation $dy/dx = x^2 + y^2$ are shown in Fig. 8.6.4. The location of the asymptotes where $y(x) \to +\infty$ can be found by using Newton's method to find the zeros of the denominators in the formula for the solutions as listed here.

17. Figure 8.6.5 shows a linearly tapered rod with circular cross section, subject to an axial force P of compression. As in Section 3.8, its deflection curve $y = y(x)$ satisfies the endpoint value problem

$$EIy'' + Py = 0; \qquad y(a) = y(b) = 0. \tag{18}$$

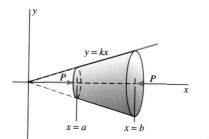

FIGURE 8.6.5. The tapered rod of Problem 17

Here, however, the moment of inertia $I = I(x)$ of the cross section at x is given by

$$I(x) = \frac{1}{4}\pi(kx)^4 = I_0 \cdot \left(\frac{x}{b}\right)^4,$$

where $I_0 = I(b)$, the value of I at $x = b$. Substitution of $I(x)$ in the differential equation in (18) yields the eigenvalue problem

$$x^4 y'' + \lambda y = 0, \qquad y(a) = y(b) = 0,$$

where $\lambda = \mu^2 = Pb^4/EI_0$. (a) Apply the theorem of this section to show that the general solution of $x^4 y'' + \mu^2 y = 0$ is

$$y(x) = x\left(A\cos\frac{\mu}{x} + B\sin\frac{\mu}{x}\right).$$

(b) Conclude that the nth eigenvalue is given by $\mu_n = n\pi ab/L$, where $L = b - a$ is the length of the rod, and hence that the nth buckling force is

$$P_n = \frac{n^2\pi^2}{L^2}\left(\frac{a}{b}\right)^2 EI_0.$$

Note that if $a = b$, this result reduces to Eq. (28) of Section 3.8.

18. Consider a variable length pendulum as indicated in Fig. 8.6.6. Assume that its length is increasing linearly with time, $L(t) = a + bt$. It can be shown that the oscillations of this pendulum satisfy the differential equation

$$L\theta'' + 2L'\theta' + g\theta = 0$$

under the usual condition that θ is so small that $\sin\theta$ is very well approximated by θ: $\theta \approx \sin\theta$. Substitute $L = a + bt$ to derive the general solution

$$\theta(t) = \frac{1}{\sqrt{L}}\left[AJ_1\left(\frac{2}{b}\sqrt{gL}\right) + BY_1\left(\frac{2}{b}\sqrt{gL}\right)\right].$$

For the application of this solution to a discussion of the steadily descending pendulum ("its nether extremity was formed of a crescent of glittering steel, about a foot in length from horn to horn; the horns upward, and the under edge as keen as that of a razor . . . and the whole hissed as it swung through the air . . . down and still down it came") of Edgar Allan Poe's macabre classic "The Pit and the Pendulum," see the article by Borrelli, Coleman, and Hobson in the March 1985 issue of *Mathematics Magazine* (Vol. 58, pp. 78–83).

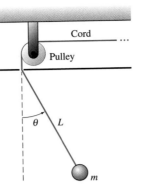

FIGURE 8.6.6. A variable length pendulum

8.6 Computing Project

A Riccati equation is one of the form

$$\frac{dy}{dx} = A(x)y^2 + B(x)y + C(x).$$

Many Riccati equations like the ones listed next can be solved explicitly in terms of Bessel functions.

$$\frac{dy}{dx} = x^2 + y^2; \tag{1}$$

$$\frac{dy}{dx} = x^2 - y^2; \tag{2}$$

$$\frac{dy}{dx} = y^2 - x^2; \tag{3}$$

$$\frac{dy}{dx} = x + y^2; \tag{4}$$

$$\frac{dy}{dx} = x - y^2; \tag{5}$$

$$\frac{dy}{dx} = y^2 - x. \tag{6}$$

For example, Problem 15 in this section says that the general solution of Eq. (1) is given by

$$y(x) = x\frac{J_{3/4}\left(\frac{1}{2}x^2\right) - cJ_{-3/4}\left(\frac{1}{2}x^2\right)}{cJ_{1/4}\left(\frac{1}{2}x^2\right) + J_{-1/4}\left(\frac{1}{2}x^2\right)}. \tag{7}$$

See whether the symbolic DE solver command in your computer algebra system, such as *Maple's*

```
dsolve(diff(y(x),x) = x^2 + y(x)^2, y(x))
```

or *Mathematica's*

```
DSolve[ y'[x] == x^2 + y[x]^2, y[x], x ]
```

agrees with Eq. (7). If Bessel functions other than those appearing in Eq. (7) are involved, you may need to apply the identities in (26) and (27) of Section 8.5 to transform the computer's "answer" to (7). Then see whether your system can take the limit as $x \to 0$ in (7) to show that the arbitrary constant c is given in terms of the initial value $y(0)$ by

$$c = -\frac{y(0)\Gamma\left(\frac{1}{4}\right)}{2\Gamma\left(\frac{3}{4}\right)}. \tag{8}$$

Now you should be able to use built-in Bessel functions to plot typical solution curves like those shown in Fig. 8.6.4.

Next, investigate similarly one of the other equations in (2) through (6). Each has a general solution of the same general form in (7)—a quotient of linear combinations of Bessel functions. In addition to $J_p(x)$ and $Y_p(x)$, these solutions may involve the *modified Bessel functions*

$$I_p(x) = i^{-p}J_p(ix)$$

and

$$K_p(x) = \frac{\pi}{2}i^{-p}[J_p(ix) + Y_p(ix)]$$

that satisfy the *modified Bessel equation*

$$x^2 y'' + xy' - (x^2 + p^2)y = 0$$

of order p. For instance, the general solution of Eq. (5) is given for $x > 0$ by

$$y(x) = \sqrt{x}\,\frac{I_{2/3}\left(\frac{2}{3}x^{3/2}\right) - cI_{-2/3}\left(\frac{2}{3}x^{3/2}\right)}{I_{-1/3}\left(\frac{2}{3}x^{3/2}\right) - cI_{1/3}\left(\frac{2}{3}x^{3/2}\right)}, \tag{9}$$

where

$$c = -\frac{y(0)\Gamma\left(\frac{1}{3}\right)}{\sqrt[3]{3}\,\Gamma\left(\frac{2}{3}\right)}. \tag{10}$$

Figure 8.6.7 shows some typical solution curves, together with the parabola $y^2 = x$ that appears to bear an interesting relation to Eq. (6)—we see a funnel near $y = +\sqrt{x}$ and a spout near $y = -\sqrt{x}$.

The Bessel functions with imaginary argument that appear in the definition of $I_p(x)$ and $K_p(x)$ may look exotic, but the power series of the modified function $I_n(x)$ is simply that of the unmodified function $J_n(x)$ except without the alternating minus signs. For instance,

$$I_0(x) = 1 + \frac{x^2}{4} + \frac{x^4}{64} + \frac{x^6}{2304} + \cdots$$

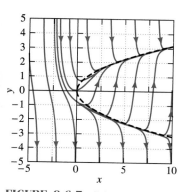

FIGURE 8.6.7. Solution curves for $y' = x - y^2$

and

$$I_1(x) = \frac{x}{2} + \frac{x^3}{16} + \frac{x^5}{384} + \frac{x^7}{18432} + \cdots.$$

Check these power series expansions using your computer algebra system—look at **BesselI** in either *Maple* of *Mathematica*—and compare them with Eqs. (17) and (18) in Section 8.5.

The second-order differential equations with the same right-hand sides as in Eqs. (1) through (6) have interesting solutions which, however, cannot be expressed in terms of elementary functions and/or "known" special functions such as Bessel functions. Nevertheless, they can be investigated using an ODE plotter. For instance, the interesting pattern in Fig. 8.6.8 shows solution curves of the second-order equation

$$y'' = y^2 - x \tag{11}$$

with the same initial value $y(0) = 0$ but different slopes $y'(0) = -3.3, -3.1, \ldots,$ 0.7. Equation (11) is a form of the *first Painlevé transcendant,* an equation that arose historically in the classification of nonlinear second-order differential equations in terms of their critical points (see Chapter 14 of E. L. Ince, *Ordinary Differential Equations,* New York: Dover Publications, 1956). Figure 8.6.8 was suggested by an article by Anne Noonburg containing a similar figure in the Spring 1993 issue of the *C•ODE•E Newsletter.*

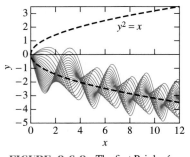

FIGURE 8.6.8. The first Painlevé transcendant $y'' = y^2 - x$, $y(0) = 0$, $y'(0) = -3.3, -3.1, \ldots, 0.7$

9 Fourier Series Methods

9.1 Periodic Functions and Trigonometric Series

As motivation for the subject of Fourier series, we consider the differential equation

$$\frac{d^2x}{dt^2} + \omega_0^2 x = f(t) \tag{1}$$

that models the behavior of a mass-and-spring system with natural [circular] frequency ω_0, moving under the influence of an external force of magnitude $f(t)$ per unit mass. As we saw in Section 3.6, a particular solution of Eq. (1) can easily be found by the method of undetermined coefficients if $f(t)$ is a simple harmonic function—a sine or cosine function. For instance, the equation

$$\frac{d^2x}{dt^2} + \omega_0^2 x = A \cos \omega t \tag{2}$$

with $\omega^2 \neq \omega_0^2$ has the particular solution

$$x_p(t) = \frac{A}{\omega_0^2 - \omega^2} \cos \omega t, \tag{3}$$

which is readily found by beginning with the trial solution $x_p(t) = a \cos \omega t$.

Now suppose, more generally, that the force function $f(t)$ in Eq. (1) is a linear combination of simple harmonic functions. Then, on the basis of Eq. (3) and the analogous formula with sine in place of cosine, we can apply the principle of superposition to construct a particular solution of Eq. (1). For example, consider the equation

$$\frac{d^2x}{dt^2} + \omega_0^2 x = \sum_{n=1}^{N} A_n \cos \omega_n t, \tag{4}$$

in which ω_0^2 is equal to none of the ω_n^2. Equation (4) has the particular solution

$$x_p(t) = \sum_{n=1}^{N} \frac{A_n}{\omega_0^2 - \omega_n^2} \cos \omega_n t, \tag{5}$$

obtained by adding the solutions given in Eq. (3) corresponding to the N terms on the right-hand side in Eq. (4).

Mechanical (and electrical) systems often involve periodic forcing functions that are not [simply] finite linear combinations of sines and cosines. Nevertheless, as we will soon see, any reasonably nice periodic function $f(t)$ has a representation as an *infinite series* of trigonometric terms. This fact opens the way toward solving Eq. (1) by superposition of trigonometric "building blocks," with the finite sum in Eq. (5) replaced with an infinite series.

DEFINITION: Periodic Function

The function $f(t)$ defined for all t is said to be **periodic** provided that there exists a positive number p such that

$$f(t + p) = f(t) \tag{6}$$

for all t. The number p is then called a **period** of the function f. ∎

Note that the period of a periodic function is not unique; for example, if p is a period of $f(t)$, then so are the numbers $2p$, $3p$, and so on. Indeed, every positive number is a period of any constant function.

If there exists a smallest positive number P such that $f(t)$ is periodic with period P, then we will call P *the* period of f. For instance, the period of the functions $g(t) = \cos nt$ and $h(t) = \sin nt$ (where n is a positive integer) is $2\pi/n$ because

$$\cos n\left(t + \frac{2\pi}{n}\right) = \cos(nt + 2\pi) = \cos nt$$

and

$$\sin n\left(t + \frac{2\pi}{n}\right) = \sin(nt + 2\pi) = \sin nt. \tag{7}$$

Moreover, 2π itself is a period of the functions $g(t)$ and $h(t)$. Ordinarily we will have no need to refer to the smallest period of a function $f(t)$ and will simply say that $f(t)$ has period p if p is a period of $f(t)$.

In Section 7.5 we saw several examples of piecewise continuous periodic functions. For instance, the square wave function having the graph shown in Fig. 9.1.1 has period 2π.

FIGURE 9.1.1. A square wave function

Because $g(t) = \cos nt$ and $h(t) = \sin nt$ each have period 2π, any linear combination of sines and cosines of integral multiples of t, such as

$$f(t) = 3 + \cos t - \sin t + 5 \cos 2t + 17 \sin 3t,$$

has period 2π. But every such linear combination is continuous, so the square wave function cannot be expressed in such manner. In his celebrated treatise *The Analytical Theory of Heat* (1822), the French scientist Joseph Fourier (1768–1830) made the remarkable assertion that every function $f(t)$ with period 2π can be represented by an *infinite* trigonometric series of the form

$$\frac{a_0}{2} + \sum_{n=1}^{\infty} (a_n \cos nt + b_n \sin nt). \tag{8}$$

We will see in Section 9.2 that under rather mild restrictions on the function $f(t)$, this is so! An infinite series of the form in (8) is called a *Fourier series,* and the representation of functions by Fourier series is one of the most widely used techniques in applied mathematics, especially for the solution of partial differential equations (see Sections 9.5 through 9.7).

Fourier Series of Period 2π Functions

In this section we will confine our attention to functions of period 2π. We want to determine what the coefficients in the Fourier series in (8) must be if it is to converge to a given function $f(t)$ of period 2π. For this purpose we need the following integrals, in which m and n denote positive integers (Problems 27 through 29):

$$\int_{-\pi}^{\pi} \cos mt \cos nt \, dt = \begin{cases} 0 & \text{if } m \neq n, \\ \pi & \text{if } m = n. \end{cases} \tag{9}$$

$$\int_{-\pi}^{\pi} \sin mt \sin nt \, dt = \begin{cases} 0 & \text{if } m \neq n, \\ \pi & \text{if } m = n. \end{cases} \tag{10}$$

$$\int_{-\pi}^{\pi} \cos mt \sin nt \, dt = 0 \quad \text{for all } m \text{ and } n. \tag{11}$$

These formulas imply that the functions $\cos nt$ and $\sin nt$ for $n = 1, 2, 3, \ldots$ constitute a *mutually orthogonal* set of functions on the interval $[-\pi, \pi]$. Two real-valued functions $u(t)$ and $v(t)$ are said to be **orthogonal** on the interval $[a, b]$ provided that

$$\int_a^b u(t) \, v(t) \, dt = 0. \tag{12}$$

Suppose now that the piecewise continuous function $f(t)$ of period 2π has a Fourier series representation

$$\blacktriangleright \qquad f(t) = \frac{a_0}{2} + \sum_{m=1}^{\infty} (a_m \cos mt + b_m \sin mt), \tag{13}$$

in the sense that the infinite series on the right converges to the value $f(t)$ for every t. We assume in addition that, when the infinite series in Eq. (13) is multiplied by any continuous function, the resulting series can be integrated term by term. Then the result of termwise integration of Eq. (13) itself from $t = -\pi$ to $t = \pi$ is

$$\int_{-\pi}^{\pi} f(t)\, dt = \frac{a_0}{2} \int_{-\pi}^{\pi} 1\, dt + \sum_{m=1}^{\infty} \left(a_m \int_{-\pi}^{\pi} \cos mt\, dt \right) + \sum_{m=1}^{\infty} \left(b_m \int_{-\pi}^{\pi} \sin mt\, dt \right) = \pi a_0$$

because all the trigonometric integrals vanish. Hence

$$a_0 = \frac{1}{\pi} \int_{-\pi}^{\pi} f(t)\, dt. \tag{14}$$

If we first multiply each side in Eq. (13) by $\cos nt$ and then integrate termwise, the result is

$$\int_{-\pi}^{\pi} f(t) \cos nt\, dt = \frac{a_0}{2} \int_{-\pi}^{\pi} \cos nt\, dt$$

$$+ \sum_{m=1}^{\infty} \left(a_m \int_{-\pi}^{\pi} \cos mt \cos nt\, dt \right) + \sum_{m=1}^{\infty} \left(b_m \int_{-\pi}^{\pi} \sin mt \cos nt\, dt \right);$$

it then follows from Eq. (11) that

$$\int_{-\pi}^{\pi} f(t) \cos nt\, dt = \sum_{m=1}^{\infty} a_m \left(\int_{-\pi}^{\pi} \cos mt \cos nt\, dt \right). \tag{15}$$

But, of all the integrals (for $m = 1, 2, 3, \ldots$) on the right-hand side in (15), only the one for which $m = n$ is nonzero. Thus Eq. (9) yields

$$\int_{-\pi}^{\pi} f(t) \cos nt\, dt = a_n \int_{-\pi}^{\pi} \cos^2 nt\, dt = \pi a_n,$$

so the value of the coefficient a_n is

$$\blacktriangleright \qquad a_n = \frac{1}{\pi} \int_{-\pi}^{\pi} f(t) \cos nt\, dt. \tag{16}$$

Note that with $n = 0$, the formula in (16) reduces to Eq. (14); this explains why we denoted the constant term in the original Fourier series by $\frac{1}{2}a_0$ (rather than simply a_0). If we multiply each side in Eq. (13) by $\sin nt$ and then integrate termwise, we find in a similar way that

$$\blacktriangleright \qquad b_n = \frac{1}{\pi} \int_{-\pi}^{\pi} f(t) \sin nt\, dt. \tag{17}$$

In short, we have found that if the series in (13) converges to $f(t)$ and if the termwise integrations carried out above are valid, then the coefficients in the series must have the values given in Eqs. (16) and (17). This motivates us to *define* the Fourier series of a periodic function by means of these formulas, whether or not the resulting series converges to the function (or even converges at all).

DEFINITION: Fourier Series and Fourier Coefficients

Let $f(t)$ be a piecewise continuous function of period 2π that is defined for all t. Then the **Fourier series** of $f(t)$ is the series

$$\blacktriangleright \qquad \frac{a_0}{2} + \sum_{n=1}^{\infty} (a_n \cos nt + b_n \sin nt), \tag{18}$$

where the **Fourier coefficients** a_n and b_n are defined by means of the formulas

$$a_n = \frac{1}{\pi} \int_{-\pi}^{\pi} f(t) \cos nt \, dt \tag{16}$$

for $n = 0, 1, 2, 3, \ldots$ and

$$b_n = \frac{1}{\pi} \int_{-\pi}^{\pi} f(t) \sin nt \, dt \tag{17}$$

for $n = 1, 2, 3, \ldots$. ∎

It can (and often does) happen that the Fourier series of a function fails to converge to the function at certain points in the domain of the function. We will therefore write

$$f(t) \sim \frac{a_0}{2} + \sum_{n=1}^{\infty} (a_n \cos nt + b_n \sin nt), \tag{19}$$

not using an equals sign between the function and its Fourier series until we have discussed convergence of Fourier series in Section 9.2.

Suppose that the piecewise continuous function $f(t)$ as given initially is defined only on the interval $[-\pi, \pi]$, and assume that $f(-\pi) = f(\pi)$. Then we can extend f so that its domain includes all real numbers by means of the periodicity condition $f(t + 2\pi) = f(t)$ for all t. We continue to denote this extension of the original function by f, and note that it automatically has period 2π. Its graph looks the same on every interval of the form

$$(2n - 1)\pi \leqq t \leqq (2n + 1)\pi$$

(Fig. 9.1.2). For instance, the square wave function of Fig. 9.1.1 can be described as the period 2π function such that

$$f(t) = \begin{cases} -1 & \text{if } -\pi < t < 0; \\ +1 & \text{if } 0 < t < \pi; \\ 0 & \text{if } t = -\pi, 0, \text{ or } \pi. \end{cases} \tag{20}$$

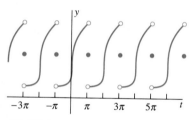

FIGURE 9.1.2. Extending a function to produce a periodic function

Thus the square wave function is the period 2π function defined on one full period by means of Eq. (20).

We need to consider Fourier series of piecewise continuous functions because many functions that appear in applications are only piecewise continuous, not continuous. Note that the integrals in Eqs. (16) and (17) exist if $f(t)$ is piecewise continuous, so every piecewise continuous function has a Fourier series.

EXAMPLE 1 Find the Fourier series of the square wave function defined in Eq. (20).

Solution It is always a good idea to calculate a_0 separately, using Eq. (14). Thus

$$a_0 = \frac{1}{\pi} \int_{-\pi}^{\pi} f(t) \, dt = \frac{1}{\pi} \int_{-\pi}^{0} (-1) \, dt + \frac{1}{\pi} \int_{0}^{\pi} (+1) \, dt = \frac{1}{\pi}(-\pi) + \frac{1}{\pi}(\pi) = 0.$$

We split the first integral into two integrals because $f(t)$ is defined by different formu-

las on the intervals $(-\pi, 0)$ and $(0, \pi)$; the values of $f(t)$ at the endpoints of these intervals do not affect the values of the integrals.

Equation (16) yields (for $n > 0$)

$$a_n = \frac{1}{\pi} \int_{-\pi}^{\pi} f(t) \cos nt \, dt = \frac{1}{\pi} \int_{-\pi}^{0} (-\cos nt) \, dt + \frac{1}{\pi} \int_{0}^{\pi} \cos nt \, dt$$

$$= \frac{1}{\pi} \left[-\frac{1}{n} \sin nt \right]_{-\pi}^{0} + \frac{1}{\pi} \left[\frac{1}{n} \sin nt \right]_{0}^{\pi} = 0.$$

And Eq. (17) yields

$$b_n = \frac{1}{\pi} \int_{-\pi}^{\pi} f(t) \sin nt \, dt = \frac{1}{\pi} \int_{-\pi}^{0} (-\sin nt) \, dt + \frac{1}{\pi} \int_{0}^{\pi} \sin nt \, dt$$

$$= \frac{1}{\pi} \left[\frac{1}{n} \cos nt \right]_{-\pi}^{0} + \frac{1}{\pi} \left[-\frac{1}{n} \cos nt \right]_{0}^{\pi}$$

$$= \frac{2}{n\pi} (1 - \cos n\pi) = \frac{2}{n\pi} [1 - (-1)^n].$$

Thus $a_n = 0$ for all $n \geqq 0$, and

$$b_n = \begin{cases} \dfrac{4}{n\pi} & \text{for } n \text{ odd;} \\ 0 & \text{for } n \text{ even.} \end{cases}$$

The last result follows because $\cos(-n\pi) = \cos(n\pi) = (-1)^n$. With these values of the Fourier coefficients, we obtain the Fourier series

$$f(t) \sim \frac{4}{\pi} \sum_{n \text{ odd}} \frac{\sin nt}{n} = \frac{4}{\pi} \left(\sin t + \frac{1}{3} \sin 3t + \frac{1}{5} \sin 5t + \cdots \right). \qquad (21)$$

Here we have introduced the useful abbreviation

$$\sum_{n \text{ odd}} \quad \text{for} \quad \sum_{\substack{n = 1 \\ n \text{ odd}}}^{\infty}$$

—for example,

$$\sum_{n \text{ odd}} \frac{1}{n} = 1 + \frac{1}{3} + \frac{1}{5} + \cdots.$$

Figure 9.1.3 shows the graphs of several of the partial sums

$$S_N(t) = \frac{4}{\pi} \sum_{n=1}^{N} \frac{\sin(2n - 1)t}{2n - 1}$$

of the Fourier series in (21). Note that as t approaches a discontinuity of $f(t)$ from either side, the value of $S_N(t)$ tends to overshoot the limiting value of $f(t)$—either $+1$ or -1 in this case. This behavior of a Fourier series near a point of discontinuity of its function is typical and is known as **Gibbs' phenomenon.** ■

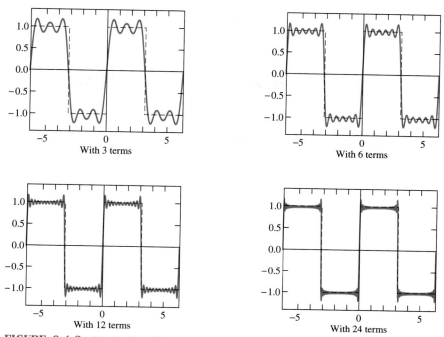

FIGURE 9.1.3. Graphs of partial sums of the Fourier series of the square wave function (Example 1) with $N = 3, 6, 12,$ and 24 terms

The following integral formulas, easily derived by integration by parts, are useful in computing Fourier series of polynomial functions:

$$\int u \cos u \, du = \cos u + u \sin u + C; \tag{22}$$

$$\int u \sin u \, du = \sin u - u \cos u + C; \tag{23}$$

$$\int u^n \cos u \, du = u^n \sin u - n \int u^{n-1} \sin u \, du; \tag{24}$$

$$\int u^n \sin u \, du = -u^n \cos u + n \int u^{n-1} \cos u \, du. \tag{25}$$

EXAMPLE 2 Find the Fourier series of the period 2π function that is defined in one period to be

$$f(t) = \begin{cases} 0 & \text{if } -\pi < t \leq 0; \\ t & \text{if } 0 \leq t < \pi; \\ \dfrac{\pi}{2} & \text{if } t = \pm \pi. \end{cases} \tag{26}$$

The graph of f is shown in Fig. 9.1.4.

FIGURE 9.1.4. The periodic function of Example 2

Solution The values of $f(\pm \pi)$ are irrelevant because they have no effect on the values of the integrals that yield the Fourier coefficients. Because $f(t) \equiv 0$ on the inter-

val $(-\pi, 0)$, each integral from $t = -\pi$ to $t = \pi$ may be replaced with an integral from $t = 0$ to $t = \pi$. Equations (14), (16), and (17) therefore give

$$a_0 = \frac{1}{\pi} \int_0^\pi t \, dt = \frac{1}{\pi} \left[\frac{1}{2} t^2 \right]_0^\pi = \frac{\pi}{2};$$

$$a_n = \frac{1}{\pi} \int_0^\pi t \cos nt \, dt = \frac{1}{n^2 \pi} \int_0^{n\pi} u \cos u \, du \qquad \left(u = nt, t = \frac{u}{n} \right)$$

$$= \frac{1}{n^2 \pi} \left[\cos u + u \sin u \right]_0^{n\pi} \qquad \text{(by Eq. (22))}$$

$$= \frac{1}{n^2 \pi} [(-1)^n - 1].$$

Consequently, $a_n = 0$ if n is even and $n \geqq 2$;

$$a_n = -\frac{2}{n^2 \pi} \quad \text{if } n \text{ is odd.}$$

Next,

$$b_n = \frac{1}{\pi} \int_0^\pi t \sin nt \, dt = \frac{1}{n^2 \pi} \int_0^{n\pi} u \sin u \, du$$

$$= \frac{1}{n^2 \pi} \left[\sin u - u \cos u \right]_0^{n\pi} \qquad \text{(by Eq. (20))}$$

$$= -\frac{1}{n} \cos n\pi.$$

Thus

$$b_n = \frac{(-1)^{n+1}}{n} \quad \text{for all } n \geqq 1.$$

Therefore, the Fourier series of $f(t)$ is

$$f(t) \sim \frac{\pi}{4} - \frac{2}{\pi} \sum_{n \text{ odd}} \frac{\cos nt}{n^2} + \sum_{n=1}^\infty \frac{(-1)^{n+1} \sin nt}{n}. \qquad (27)$$

∎

If $f(t)$ is a function of period 2π, it is readily verified (Problem 30) that

$$\int_{-\pi}^\pi f(t) \, dt = \int_a^{a+2\pi} f(t) \, dt \qquad (28)$$

for all a. That is, the integral of $f(t)$ over one interval of length 2π is equal to its integral over any other such interval. In case $f(t)$ is given explicitly on the interval $[0, 2\pi]$ rather than on $[-\pi, \pi]$, it may be more convenient to compute its Fourier coefficients as

$$a_n = \frac{1}{\pi} \int_0^{2\pi} f(t) \cos nt \, dt \qquad (29a)$$

and

$$b_n = \frac{1}{\pi} \int_0^{2\pi} f(t) \sin nt \, dt \qquad (29b)$$

9.1 Problems

In Problems 1 through 10, determine whether or not the given function is periodic. If so, find its smallest period.

1. $f(t) = \sin 3t$ **2.** $f(t) = \cos 2\pi t$

3. $f(t) = \cos \dfrac{3t}{2}$ **4.** $f(t) = \sin \dfrac{\pi t}{3}$

5. $f(t) = \tan t$ **6.** $f(t) = \cot 2\pi t$

7. $f(t) = \cosh 3t$ **8.** $f(t) = \sinh \pi t$

9. $f(t) = |\sin t|$ **10.** $f(t) = \cos^2 3t$

In Problems 11 through 26, the values of a period 2π function $f(t)$ in one full period are given. Sketch several periods of its graph and find its Fourier series.

11. $f(t) = 1, \quad -\pi \leqq t \leqq \pi$

12. $f(t) = \begin{cases} +3, & -\pi < t \leqq 0; \\ -3, & 0 < t \leqq \pi \end{cases}$

13. $f(t) = \begin{cases} 0, & -\pi < t \leqq 0; \\ 1, & 0 < t \leqq \pi \end{cases}$

14. $f(t) = \begin{cases} 3, & -\pi < t \leqq 0; \\ -2, & 0 < t \leqq \pi \end{cases}$

15. $f(t) = t, \quad -\pi < t \leqq \pi$

16. $f(t) = t, \quad 0 < t < 2\pi$

17. $f(t) = |t|, \quad -\pi \leqq t \leqq \pi$

18. $f(t) = \begin{cases} \pi + t, & -\pi < t \leqq 0; \\ \pi - t, & 0 \leqq t \leqq \pi \end{cases}$

19. $f(t) = \begin{cases} \pi + t, & -\pi \leqq t < 0; \\ 0, & 0 \leqq t \leqq \pi \end{cases}$

20. $f(t) = \begin{cases} 0, & -\pi \leqq t < -\dfrac{\pi}{2}; \\ 1, & -\dfrac{\pi}{2} \leqq t \leqq \dfrac{\pi}{2}; \\ 0, & \dfrac{\pi}{2} < t \leqq \pi \end{cases}$

21. $f(t) = t^2, \quad -\pi \leqq t \leqq \pi$

22. $f(t) = t^2, \quad 0 \leqq t < 2\pi$

23. $f(t) = \begin{cases} 0, & -\pi \leqq t \leqq 0; \\ t^2, & 0 \leqq t < \pi \end{cases}$

24. $f(t) = |\sin t|, \quad -\pi \leqq t \leqq \pi$

25. $f(t) = \cos^2 2t, \quad -\pi \leqq t \leqq \pi$

26. $f(t) = \begin{cases} 0, & -\pi \leqq t \leqq 0; \\ \sin t, & 0 \leqq t \leqq \pi \end{cases}$

27. Verify Eq. (9). (*Suggestion:* Use the trigonometric identity

$$\cos A \cos B = \frac{1}{2} [\cos (A + B) + \cos (A - B)].)$$

28. Verify Eq. (10).

29. Verify Eq. (11).

30. Let $f(t)$ be a piecewise continuous function with period P.
(a) Suppose that $0 \leqq a < P$. Substitute $u = t - P$ to show that

$$\int_P^{a+P} f(t) \, dt = \int_0^a f(t) \, dt.$$

Conclude that

$$\int_a^{a+P} f(t) \, dt = \int_0^P f(t) \, dt.$$

(b) Given A, choose n so that $A = nP + a$ with $0 \leqq a < P$. Then substitute $v = t - nP$ to show that

$$\int_A^{A+P} f(t) \, dt = \int_a^{a+P} f(t) \, dt = \int_0^P f(t) \, dt.$$

31. Multiply each side in Eq. (13) by $\sin nt$ and then integrate term by term to derive Eq. (17).

9.2 General Fourier Series and Convergence

In Section 9.1 we defined the Fourier series of a periodic function of period 2π. Now let $f(t)$ be a function that is piecewise continuous for all t and has arbitrary period $P > 0$. We write

$$P = 2L, \tag{1}$$

so L is the **half-period** of the period function f. Let us define the function g as follows:

$$g(u) = f\left(\frac{Lu}{\pi}\right) \tag{2}$$

for all u. Then

$$g(u + 2\pi) = f\left(\frac{Lu}{\pi} + 2L\right) = f\left(\frac{Lu}{\pi}\right) = g(u),$$

and hence $g(u)$ is also periodic and has period 2π. Consequently, g has the Fourier series

$$g(u) \sim \frac{a_0}{2} + \sum_{n=1}^{\infty} (a_n \cos nu + b_n \sin nu) \tag{3}$$

with Fourier coefficients

$$a_n = \frac{1}{\pi} \int_{-\pi}^{\pi} g(u) \cos nu \, du \tag{4a}$$

and

$$b_n = \frac{1}{\pi} \int_{-\pi}^{\pi} g(u) \sin nu \, du. \tag{4b}$$

If we now write

$$t = \frac{Lu}{\pi}, \qquad u = \frac{\pi t}{L}, \qquad f(t) = g(u), \tag{5}$$

then

$$f(t) = g\left(\frac{\pi t}{L}\right) \sim \frac{a_0}{2} + \sum_{n=1}^{\infty}\left(a_n \cos \frac{n\pi t}{L} + b_n \sin \frac{n\pi t}{L}\right), \tag{6}$$

and then substitution of (5) in (4) yields

$$a_n = \frac{1}{\pi} \int_{-\pi}^{\pi} g(u) \cos nu \, du \qquad \left(u = \frac{\pi t}{L}, \ du = \frac{\pi \, dt}{L}\right)$$

$$= \frac{1}{L} \int_{-L}^{L} g\left(\frac{\pi t}{L}\right) \cos \frac{n\pi t}{L} \, dt.$$

Therefore,

$$a_n = \frac{1}{L} \int_{-L}^{L} f(t) \cos \frac{n\pi t}{L} \, dt; \tag{7}$$

similarly,

$$b_n = \frac{1}{L} \int_{-L}^{L} f(t) \sin \frac{n\pi t}{L} \, dt. \tag{8}$$

This computation motivates the following definition of the Fourier series of a periodic function of period $2L$.

DEFINITION: Fourier Series and Fourier Coefficients

Let $f(t)$ be a piecewise continuous function of period $2L$ that is defined for all t. Then the **Fourier series** of $f(t)$ is the series

$$\blacktriangleright \qquad f(t) \sim \frac{a_0}{2} + \sum_{n=1}^{\infty} \left(a_n \cos \frac{n\pi t}{L} + b_n \sin \frac{n\pi t}{L} \right), \tag{6}$$

where the **Fourier coefficients** $\{a_n\}_0^{\infty}$ and $\{b_n\}_1^{\infty}$ are defined to be

$$\blacktriangleright \qquad a_n = \frac{1}{L} \int_{-L}^{L} f(t) \cos \frac{n\pi t}{L} \, dt \tag{7}$$

and

$$\blacktriangleright \qquad b_n = \frac{1}{L} \int_{-L}^{L} f(t) \sin \frac{n\pi t}{L} \, dt. \tag{8}$$

■

With $n = 0$ Eq. (7) takes the simple form

$$a_0 = \frac{1}{L} \int_{-L}^{L} f(t) \, dt, \tag{9}$$

which demonstrates that the constant term $\frac{1}{2} a_0$ in the Fourier series of f is simply the average value of $f(t)$ on the interval $[-L, L]$.

As a consequence of Problem 30 of Section 9.1, we may evaluate the integrals in (7) and (8) over any other interval of length $2L$. For instance, if $f(t)$ is given by a single formula for $0 < t < 2L$, it may be more convenient to compute the integrals

$$a_n = \frac{1}{L} \int_0^{2L} f(t) \cos \frac{n\pi t}{L} \, dt \tag{10a}$$

and

$$b_n = \frac{1}{L} \int_0^{2L} f(t) \sin \frac{n\pi t}{L} \, dt. \tag{10b}$$

EXAMPLE 1 Figure 9.2.1 shows the graph of a square wave function with period 4. Find its Fourier series.

 Solution Here $L = 2$; also, $f(t) = -1$ if $-2 < t < 0$, whereas $f(t) = 1$ if $0 < t < 2$. Hence Eqs. (7), (8), and (9) yield

FIGURE 9.2.1. The square wave function of Example 1

$$a_0 = \frac{1}{2} \int_{-2}^{2} f(t)\,dt = \frac{1}{2} \int_{-2}^{0} (-1)\,dt + \frac{1}{2} \int_{0}^{2} (+1)\,dt = 0,$$

$$a_n = \frac{1}{2} \int_{-2}^{0} (-1) \cos \frac{n\pi t}{2}\,dt + \frac{1}{2} \int_{0}^{2} (+1) \cos \frac{n\pi t}{2}\,dt$$

$$= \frac{1}{2} \left[-\frac{2}{n\pi} \sin \frac{n\pi t}{2} \right]_{-2}^{0} + \frac{1}{2} \left[\frac{2}{n\pi} \sin \frac{n\pi t}{2} \right]_{0}^{2} = 0,$$

and

$$b_n = \frac{1}{2} \int_{-2}^{0} (-1) \sin \frac{n\pi t}{2}\,dt + \frac{1}{2} \int_{0}^{2} (+1) \sin \frac{n\pi t}{2}\,dt$$

$$= \frac{1}{2} \left[\frac{2}{n\pi} \cos \frac{n\pi t}{2} \right]_{-2}^{0} + \frac{1}{2} \left[-\frac{2}{n\pi} \cos \frac{n\pi t}{2} \right]_{0}^{2}$$

$$= \frac{2}{n\pi} \left[1 - (-1)^n \right] = \begin{cases} \dfrac{4}{n\pi} & \text{if } n \text{ is odd,} \\[2mm] 0 & \text{if } n \text{ is even.} \end{cases}$$

Thus the Fourier series is

$$f(t) \sim \frac{4}{\pi} \sum_{n\ \text{odd}} \frac{1}{n} \sin \frac{n\pi t}{2} \tag{11a}$$

$$= \frac{4}{\pi} \left(\sin \frac{\pi t}{2} + \frac{1}{3} \sin \frac{3\pi t}{2} + \frac{1}{5} \sin \frac{5\pi t}{2} + \cdots \right). \tag{11b}$$

∎

The Convergence Theorem

We want to impose conditions on the periodic function f that are enough to guarantee that its Fourier series actually converges to $f(t)$ at least at those values of t at which f is continuous. Recall that the function f is said to be *piecewise continuous* on the interval $[a, b]$ provided that there is a finite partition of $[a, b]$ with endpoints

$$a = t_0 < t_1 < t_2 < \cdots < t_{n-1} < t_n = b$$

such that:

1. f is continuous on each open subinterval $t_{i-1} < t < t_i$; and
2. At each endpoint t_i of such a subinterval the limit of $f(t)$, as t approaches t_i from within the subinterval, exists and is finite.

The function f is called *piecewise continuous* for all t if it is piecewise continuous on every bounded interval. It follows that a piecewise continuous function is continuous except possibly at isolated points, and that at each such point of discontinuity, the one-sided limits

$$f(t+) = \lim_{u \to t^+} f(u) \qquad \text{and} \qquad f(t-) = \lim_{u \to t^-} f(u) \tag{12}$$

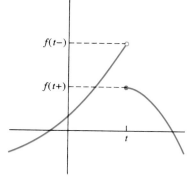

FIGURE 9.2.2. A finite jump discontinuity

both exist and are finite. Thus a piecewise continuous function has only isolated "finite jump" discontinuities like the one shown in Fig. 9.2.2.

The square wave and sawtooth functions that we saw in Chapter 7 are typical examples of periodic piecewise continuous functions. The function $f(t) = \tan t$ is a periodic function (of period π) that is not piecewise continuous because it has infinite discontinuities. The function $g(t) = \sin(1/t)$ is not piecewise continuous on $[-1, 1]$ because its one-sided limits at $t = 0$ do not exist. The function

$$h(t) = \begin{cases} t & \text{if } t = \dfrac{1}{n} \\ 0 & \text{otherwise} \end{cases} \quad (n \text{ an integer}),$$

on $[-1, 1]$ has one-sided limits everywhere, but is not piecewise continuous because its discontinuities are not isolated—it has the infinite sequence $\{1/n\}_1^\infty$ of discontinuities; a piecewise continuous function can have only finitely many discontinuities in any bounded interval.

Note that a piecewise continuous function need not be defined at its isolated points of discontinuity. Alternatively, it can be defined arbitrarily at such points. For instance, the square wave function f of Fig. 9.2.1 is piecewise continuous no matter what its values might be at the points $\{2n\}_1^\infty$ at which it is discontinuous. Its derivative f' is also piecewise continuous; $f'(t) = 0$ unless t is an even integer, in which case $f'(t)$ is undefined.

The piecewise continuous function f is said to be **piecewise smooth** provided that its derivative f' is piecewise continuous. The theorem below tells us that the Fourier series of a piecewise smooth function converges everywhere. More general Fourier convergence theorems—with weaker hypotheses on the periodic function f—are known. But the hypothesis that f is piecewise smooth is easy to check and is satisfied by most functions encountered in practical applications. A proof of the following theorem may be found in G. P. Tolstov, *Fourier Series* (New York: Dover, 1976).

THEOREM 1: Convergence of Fourier Series

Suppose that the periodic function f is piecewise smooth. Then its Fourier series in (6) converges

(a) to the value $f(t)$ at each point where f is continuous, and

(b) to the value $\frac{1}{2}[f(t+) + f(t-)]$ at each point where f is discontinuous. ∎

Note that $\frac{1}{2}[f(t+) + f(t-)]$ is the *average* of the right-hand and left-hand limits of f at the point t. If f is continuous at t, then $f(t) = f(t+) = f(t-)$, so

$$f(t) = \frac{f(t+) + f(t-)}{2}. \tag{13}$$

Hence the theorem above could be rephrased as follows: The Fourier series of a piecewise smooth function f converges for *every* t to the average value in (13). For this rea-

son it is customary to write

$$f(t) = \frac{a_0}{2} + \sum_{n=1}^{\infty} \left(a_n \cos \frac{n\pi t}{L} + b_n \sin \frac{n\pi t}{L} \right), \tag{14}$$

with the understanding that the piecewise smooth function f has been redefined (if necessary) at each of its points of discontinuity in order to satisfy the average value condition in (13).

EXAMPLE 1
Continued

Figure 9.2.1 shows us at a glance that if t_0 is an even integer, then

$$\lim_{t \to t_0^-} f(t) = -1 \quad \text{and} \quad \lim_{t \to t_0^+} f(t) = +1.$$

Hence

$$\frac{f(t_0+) + f(t_0-)}{2} = 0.$$

Note that, in accord with the theorem above, the Fourier series of $f(t)$ in (11) clearly converges to zero if t is an even integer (because $\sin n\pi = 0$).

EXAMPLE 2

Let $f(t)$ be a function of period 2 with $f(t) = t^2$ if $0 < t < 2$. We define $f(t)$ for t an even integer by the average value condition in (13); consequently, $f(t) = 2$ if t is an even integer. The graph of the function f appears in Fig. 9.2.3. Find its Fourier series.

Solution Here $L = 1$, and it is most convenient to integrate from $t = 0$ to $t = 2$. Then

$$a_0 = \frac{1}{1} \int_0^2 t^2 \, dt = \left[\frac{1}{3} t^3 \right]_0^2 = \frac{8}{3}.$$

FIGURE 9.2.3. The period 2 function of Example 2

With the aid of the integral formulas in Eqs. (22) through (25) of Section 9.1 we obtain

$$a_n = \int_0^2 t^2 \cos n\pi t \, dt$$

$$= \frac{1}{n^3 \pi^3} \int_0^{2n\pi} u^2 \cos u \, du \qquad \left(u = n\pi t, \ t = \frac{u}{n\pi} \right)$$

$$= \frac{1}{n^3 \pi^3} \left[u^2 \sin u - 2 \sin u + 2u \cos u \right]_0^{2n\pi} = \frac{4}{n^2 \pi^2};$$

$$b_n = \int_0^2 t^2 \sin n\pi t \, dt = \frac{1}{n^3 \pi^3} \int_0^{2n\pi} u^2 \sin u \, du$$

$$= \frac{1}{n^3 \pi^3} \left[-u^2 \cos u + 2 \cos u + 2u \sin u \right]_0^{2n\pi} = -\frac{4}{n\pi}.$$

Hence the Fourier series of f is

$$f(t) = \frac{4}{3} + \frac{4}{\pi^2} \sum_{n=1}^{\infty} \frac{\cos n\pi t}{n^2} - \frac{4}{\pi} \sum_{n=1}^{\infty} \frac{\sin n\pi t}{n}, \tag{15}$$

and Theorem 1 assures us that this series converges to $f(t)$ for all t. ∎

We can draw some interesting consequences from the Fourier series in (15). If we substitute $t = 0$ on each side, we find that

$$f(0) = 2 = \frac{4}{3} + \frac{4}{\pi^2} \sum_{n=1}^{\infty} \frac{1}{n^2}.$$

On solving for the series, we obtain the lovely summation

$$\blacktriangleright \qquad \sum_{n=1}^{\infty} \frac{1}{n^2} = 1 + \frac{1}{2^2} + \frac{1}{3^2} + \frac{1}{4^2} + \cdots = \frac{\pi^2}{6} \qquad (16)$$

that was discovered by Euler. If we substitute $t = 1$ in Eq. (15), we get

$$f(1) = 1 = \frac{4}{3} + \frac{4}{\pi^2} \sum_{n=1}^{\infty} \frac{(-1)^n}{n^2},$$

which yields

$$\sum_{n=1}^{\infty} \frac{(-1)^{n+1}}{n^2} = 1 - \frac{1}{2^2} + \frac{1}{3^2} - \frac{1}{4^2} + \cdots = \frac{\pi^2}{12}. \qquad (17)$$

If we add the series in Eqs. (16) and (17) and then divide by 2, the "even" terms cancel and the result is

$$\sum_{n \text{ odd}} \frac{1}{n^2} = 1 + \frac{1}{3^2} + \frac{1}{5^2} + \frac{1}{7^2} + \cdots = \frac{\pi^2}{8}. \qquad (18)$$

9.2 Problems

In Problems 1 through 14, the values of a periodic function $f(t)$ in one full period are given; at each discontinuity the value of $f(t)$ is that given by the average value condition in (13). Sketch the graph of f and find its Fourier series.

1. $f(t) = \begin{cases} -2, & -3 < t < 0; \\ 2, & 0 < t < 3 \end{cases}$

2. $f(t) = \begin{cases} 0, & -5 < t < 0; \\ 1, & 0 < t < 5 \end{cases}$

3. $f(t) = \begin{cases} 2, & -2\pi < t < 0; \\ -1, & 0 < t < 2\pi \end{cases}$

4. $f(t) = t, \quad -2 < t < 2$

5. $f(t) = t, \quad -2\pi < t < 2\pi$

6. $f(t) = t, \quad 0 < t < 3$

7. $f(t) = |t|, \quad -1 < t < 1$

8. $f(t) = \begin{cases} 0, & 0 < t < 1; \\ 1, & 1 < t < 2; \\ 0, & 2 < t < 3 \end{cases}$

9. $f(t) = t^2, \quad -1 < t < 1$

10. $f(t) = \begin{cases} 0, & -2 < t < 0; \\ t^2, & 0 < t < 2 \end{cases}$

11. $f(t) = \cos \dfrac{\pi t}{2}, \quad -1 < t < 1$

12. $f(t) = \sin \pi t, \quad 0 < t < 1$

13. $f(t) = \begin{cases} 0, & -1 < t < 0; \\ \sin \pi t, & 0 < t < 1 \end{cases}$

14. $f(t) = \begin{cases} 0, & -2\pi < t < 0; \\ \sin t, & 0 < t < 2\pi \end{cases}$

15. (a) Suppose that f is a function of period 2π with $f(t) = t^2$ for $0 < t < 2\pi$. Show that

$$f(t) = \frac{4\pi^2}{3} + 4 \sum_{n=1}^{\infty} \frac{\cos nt}{n^2} - 4\pi \sum_{n=1}^{\infty} \frac{\sin nt}{n}.$$

(b) Deduce the series summations in Eqs. (16) and (17) from the Fourier series in part (a).

16. (a) Suppose that f is a function of period 2 such that $f(t) = 0$ if $-1 < t < 0$ and $f(t) = t$ if $0 < t < 1$. Show that

$$f(t) = \frac{1}{4} - \frac{2}{\pi^2} \sum_{n \text{ odd}} \frac{\cos n\pi t}{n^2} + \frac{1}{\pi} \sum_{n=1}^{\infty} (-1)^{n+1} \frac{\sin n\pi t}{n}.$$

(b) Deduce the series summation in Eq. (18) from the Fourier series in part (a).

17. (a) Suppose that f is a function of period 2 with $f(t) = t$ for $0 < t < 2$. Show that

$$f(t) = 1 - \frac{2}{\pi} \sum_{n=1}^{\infty} \frac{\sin n\pi t}{n}.$$

(b) Substitute an appropriate value of t to deduce **Leibniz's series**

$$1 - \frac{1}{3} + \frac{1}{5} - \frac{1}{7} + \cdots = \frac{\pi}{4}.$$

Derive the Fourier series listed in Problems 18 through 21.

18. $\displaystyle\sum_{n=1}^{\infty} \frac{\sin nt}{n} = \frac{\pi - t}{2}$ $\quad(0 < t < 2\pi)$

19. $\displaystyle\sum_{n=1}^{\infty} (-1)^{n+1} \frac{\sin nt}{n} = \frac{t}{2}$ $\quad(-\pi < t < \pi)$

20. $\displaystyle\sum_{n=1}^{\infty} \frac{\cos nt}{n^2} = \frac{3t^2 - 6\pi t + 2\pi^2}{12}$ $\quad(0 < t < 2\pi)$

21. $\displaystyle\sum_{n=1}^{\infty} (-1)^{n+1} \frac{\cos nt}{n^2} = \frac{\pi^2 - 3t^2}{12}$ $\quad(-\pi < t < \pi)$

22. Suppose that $p(t)$ is a polynomial of degree n. Show by repeated integration by parts that

$$\int p(t)\, g(t)\, dt = p(t)\, G_1(t) - p'(t)\, G_2(t)$$
$$+ p''(t)\, G_3(t) - \cdots + (-1)^n p^{(n)}(t)\, G_{n+1}(t)$$

where $G_k(t)$ denotes the kth iterated antiderivative $G_k(t) = (D^{-1})^k g(t)$. This formula is useful in computing Fourier coefficients of polynomials.

23. Apply the integral formula of Problem 22 to show that

$$\int t^4 \cos t\, dt = t^4 \sin t + 4t^3 \cos t$$
$$- 12t^2 \sin t - 24t \cos t + 24 \sin t + C$$

and that

$$\int t^4 \sin t\, dt = -t^4 \cos t + 4t^3 \sin t$$
$$+ 12t^2 \cos t - 24t \sin t - 24 \cos t + C.$$

24. (a) Show that for $0 < t < 2\pi$,

$$t^4 = \frac{16\pi^4}{5} + 16 \sum_{n=1}^{\infty} \left(\frac{2\pi^2}{n^2} - \frac{3}{n^4} \right) \cos nt$$
$$+ 16\pi \sum_{n=1}^{\infty} \left(\frac{3}{n^3} - \frac{\pi^2}{n} \right) \sin nt.$$

(b) From the Fourier series in part (a), deduce the summations

$$\sum_{n=1}^{\infty} \frac{1}{n^4} = \frac{\pi^4}{90}, \qquad \sum_{n=1}^{\infty} \frac{(-1)^{n+1}}{n^4} = \frac{7\pi^4}{720},$$

and

$$\sum_{n \text{ odd}} \frac{1}{n^4} = \frac{\pi^4}{96}.$$

25. (a) Find the Fourier series of the period 2π function $f(t)$ with $f(t) = t^3$ if $-\pi < t < \pi$. (b) Use the series of part (a) to derive the summation

$$1 - \frac{1}{3^3} + \frac{1}{5^3} - \frac{1}{7^3} + \cdots = \frac{\pi^3}{32}.$$

(c) *Attempt* to evaluate the series

$$\sum_{n=1}^{\infty} \frac{1}{n^3} = 1 + \frac{1}{2^3} + \frac{1}{3^3} + \frac{1}{4^3} + \cdots$$

by substituting an appropriate value of t in the Fourier series of part (a). Is your attempt successful? Explain.

9.2 Computing Project

A computer algebra system such as *Derive, Maple,* or *Mathematica* can greatly ease the burden of calculation of the Fourier coefficients of a given function $f(t)$. In the case of a function defined "piecewise," we must take care to "split" the integral according to the different intervals of definition of the function. For instance, consider the period 2π square wave function with values -1 on $(-\pi, 0)$ and $+1$ on $(0, \pi)$. Using *Maple* we can calculate the coefficients

```
> a := n -> (1/Pi)*(int(-cos(n*t), t=-Pi..0) +
                    int(+cos(n*t), t=0..Pi)):

> a(n);

    0

> b := n -> (1/Pi)*(int(-sin(n*t), t=-Pi..0) +
                    int(+sin(n*t), t=0..Pi)):

> b(n);
```

$$\frac{2\dfrac{1}{n} - 2\dfrac{\cos(n\pi)}{n}}{\pi}$$

Then a typical partial sum of the Fourier series is given by

```
> fourierSum := sum( 'b(n)*sin(n*t)', 'n'=1..7 );
```

fourierSum :=

$$4\frac{\sin(t)}{\pi} + \frac{4}{3}\ \frac{\sin(3t)}{\pi} + \frac{4}{5}\ \frac{\sin(5t)}{\pi} + \frac{4}{7}\ \frac{\sin(7t)}{\pi}$$

and we can plot a graph like one of those in Fig. 9.1.3 using a command such as

```
> plot(fourierSum, t = -2*Pi..2*Pi);
```

The analogous *Mathematica* commands are

```
a[n_] = (1/Pi)*(Integrate[-Cos[n*t], {t,-Pi,0}] +
                Integrate[+Cos[n*t], {t,0,Pi}]);

b[n_] := (1/Pi)*(Integrate[-Sin[n*t], {t,-Pi,0}] +
                 Integrate[+Sin[n*t], {t,0,Pi}]);

fourierSum = Sum[ b[n]*Sin[n*t], {n,1,7} ]

Plot[ fourierSum, {t, -2*Pi, 2*Pi} ];
```

To practice the symbolic calculation of Fourier series in this manner, you can begin by verifying the Fourier series calculated manually in Examples 1 and 2 of this section. Then Problems 1 through 21 are fair game. Finally, the period 2π triangular wave and trapezoidal wave functions illustrated in Figs. 9.2.4 and 9.2.5 have especially interesting Fourier series that we invite you to discover for yourself.

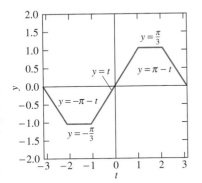

FIGURE 9.2.4. Triangular wave

FIGURE 9.2.5. Trapezoidal wave

9.3 Even-Odd Functions and Termwise Differentiation

Certain properties of functions are reflected prominently in their Fourier series. The function f defined for all t is said to be **even** if

$$f(-t) = f(t) \tag{1}$$

for all t; f is **odd** if

▶
$$f(-t) = -f(t) \tag{2}$$

for all t. The first condition implies that the graph of $y = f(t)$ is symmetric with respect to the y-axis, whereas the condition in (2) implies that the graph of an odd function is symmetric with respect to the origin (see Fig. 9.3.1). The functions $f(t) = t^{2n}$ and $g(t) = \cos t$ are even functions, whereas the functions $f(t) = t^{2n+1}$ and $g(t) = \sin t$ are odd. We will see that the Fourier series of an even periodic function has only cosine terms and that the Fourier series of an odd periodic function has only sine terms.

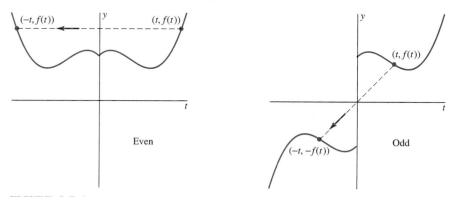

FIGURE 9.3.1. (a) An even function; (b) an odd function

Addition and cancellation of areas as indicated in Fig. 9.3.2 reminds us of the following basic facts about integrals of even and odd functions over an interval $[-a, a]$ that is symmetric about the origin.

If f is even:
$$\int_{-a}^{a} f(t)\, dt = 2 \int_{0}^{a} f(t)\, dt. \tag{3}$$

If f is odd:
$$\int_{-a}^{a} f(t)\, dt = 0. \tag{4}$$

These facts are easy to verify analytically (Problem 17).

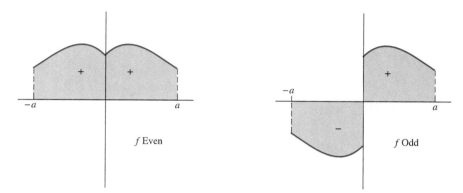

FIGURE 9.3.2. Area under the graph of (a) an even function and (b) an odd function

It follows immediately from Eqs. (1) and (2) that the product of two even functions is even, as is the product of two odd functions; the product of an even function and an odd function is odd. In particular, if $f(t)$ is an *even* periodic function of period $2L$, then $f(t) \cos(n\pi t/L)$ is even, whereas $f(t) \sin(n\pi t/L)$ is odd, because the cosine function is even and the sine function is odd. When we compute the Fourier coefficients of f, we therefore get

$$a_n = \frac{1}{L} \int_{-L}^{L} f(t) \cos \frac{n\pi t}{L} \, dt = \frac{2}{L} \int_{0}^{L} f(t) \cos \frac{n\pi t}{L} \, dt \qquad (5a)$$

and

$$b_n = \frac{1}{L} \int_{-L}^{L} f(t) \sin \frac{n\pi t}{L} \, dt = 0 \qquad (5b)$$

because of (3) and (4). Hence the Fourier series of the *even* function f of period $2L$ has only *cosine* terms:

$$f(t) = \frac{a_0}{2} + \sum_{n=1}^{\infty} a_n \cos \frac{n\pi t}{L} \qquad (f \text{ even}) \qquad (6)$$

with the values of a_n given by Eq. (5a). If $f(t)$ is *odd*, then $f(t) \cos(n\pi t/L)$ is odd, whereas $f(t) \sin(n\pi t/L)$ is even, so

$$a_n = \frac{1}{L} \int_{-L}^{L} f(t) \cos \frac{n\pi t}{L} \, dt = 0 \qquad (7a)$$

and

$$b_n = \frac{1}{L} \int_{-L}^{L} f(t) \sin \frac{n\pi t}{L} \, dt = \frac{2}{L} \int_{0}^{L} f(t) \sin \frac{n\pi t}{L} \, dt. \qquad (7b)$$

Hence the Fourier series of the *odd* function f of period $2L$ has only *sine* terms:

$$f(t) = \sum_{n=1}^{\infty} b_n \sin \frac{n\pi t}{L} \qquad (f \text{ odd}) \qquad (8)$$

with the coefficients b_n given in Eq. (7b).

Even and Odd Extensions

In all our earlier discussions and examples, we began with a periodic function defined *for all* t; the Fourier series of such a function is uniquely determined by the Fourier coefficient formulas. In many practical situations, however, we begin with a function f defined only on an interval of the form $0 < t < L$, and we want to represent its values on this interval by a Fourier series of period $2L$. The first step is the necessary extension of f to the interval $-L < t < 0$. Granted this, we may extend f to the entire real line by the periodicity condition $f(t + 2L) = f(t)$ (and use the average value property should any discontinuities arise). But *how* we define f for $-L < t < 0$ is our choice, and the Fourier series representation for $f(t)$ on $(0, L)$ that we obtain will depend upon that choice. Specifically, different choices of the extension of f to the interval $(-L, 0)$ will yield different Fourier series that converge to the same function $f(t)$ in the original interval $0 < t < L$, but which converge to the different extensions of f on the interval $-L < t < 0$.

In practice, given $f(t)$ defined for $0 < t < L$, we generally make one of two natural choices — we extend f to obtain either an even function or an odd function. The **even period 2L extension** of f is the function f_E defined as

$$f_E(t) = \begin{cases} f(t) & \text{if} \quad 0 < t < L; \\ f(-t) & \text{if} \quad -L < t < 0 \end{cases} \tag{9}$$

and by $f_E(t + 2L) = f_E(t)$ for all t. The values of $f_E(t)$ for t an integral multiple of L are not important because they cannot affect the Fourier series of f_E. The Fourier series of the even extension f_E, given by Eqs. (5) and (6), will contain only cosine terms and is called the *Fourier cosine series* of the original function f.

The **odd period 2L extension** of f is the function f_O defined as

$$f_O(t) = \begin{cases} f(t) & \text{if} \quad 0 < t < L; \\ -f(-t) & \text{if} \quad -L < t < 0 \end{cases} \tag{10}$$

and by $f_O(t + 2L) = f_O(t)$ for all t. The Fourier series of the odd extension f_O, given by Eqs. (7) and (8), will contain only sine terms and is called the *Fourier sine series* of the original function f.

◼ DEFINITION: Fourier Cosine and Sine Series

Suppose that the function $f(t)$ is piecewise continuous on the interval $[0, L]$. Then the **Fourier cosine series** of f is the series

$$f(t) = \frac{a_0}{2} + \sum_{n=1}^{\infty} a_n \cos \frac{n\pi t}{L} \tag{11}$$

with

$$a_n = \frac{2}{L} \int_0^L f(t) \cos \frac{n\pi t}{L} \, dt. \tag{12}$$

The **Fourier sine series** of f is the series

$$f(t) = \sum_{n=1}^{\infty} b_n \sin \frac{n\pi t}{L} \tag{13}$$

with

$$b_n = \frac{2}{L} \int_0^L f(t) \sin \frac{n\pi t}{L} \, dt. \tag{14}$$

◼

Assuming that f is piecewise smooth and satisfies the average value condition $f(t) = \frac{1}{2}[f(t+) + f(t-)]$ at each of its isolated discontinuities, Theorem 1 of Section 9.2 implies that each of the two series in (11) and (13) converges to $f(t)$ for all t in the interval $0 < t < L$. Outside this interval, the cosine series in (11) converges to the even period $2L$ extension of f, whereas the sine series in (13) converges to the odd period $2L$ extension of f. In many cases of interest we have no concern with the values of f outside the original interval $(0, L)$, and therefore the choice between (11) and (12) or

(13) and (14) is determined by whether we prefer to represent $f(t)$ in the interval $(0, L)$ by a cosine series or a sine series. (See Example 2 for a situation that dictates our choice between a Fourier cosine series and a Fourier sine series to represent a given function.)

EXAMPLE 1 Suppose that $f(t) = t$ for $0 < t < L$. Find both the Fourier cosine series and the Fourier sine series for f.

> **Solution** Equation (12) gives
>
> $$a_0 = \frac{2}{L} \int_0^L t \, dt = \frac{2}{L} \left[\frac{1}{2} t^2 \right]_0^L = L$$
>
> and
>
> $$a_n = \frac{2}{L} \int_0^L t \cos \frac{n\pi t}{L} \, dt = \frac{2L}{n^2\pi^2} \int_0^{n\pi} u \cos u \, du$$
>
> $$= \frac{2L}{n^2\pi^2} \Big[u \sin u + \cos u \Big]_0^{n\pi} = \begin{cases} -\dfrac{4L}{n^2\pi^2} & \text{for } n \text{ odd;} \\ 0 & \text{for } n \text{ even.} \end{cases}$$
>
>
>
> Thus the Fourier cosine series of f is
>
> $$t = \frac{L}{2} - \frac{4L}{\pi^2} \left(\cos \frac{\pi t}{L} + \frac{1}{3^2} \cos \frac{3\pi t}{L} + \frac{1}{5^2} \cos \frac{5\pi t}{L} + \cdots \right) \tag{15}$$
>
> for $0 < t < L$. Next, Eq. (14) gives
>
> $$b_n = \frac{2}{L} \int_0^L t \sin \frac{n\pi t}{L} \, dt = \frac{2L}{n^2\pi^2} \int_0^{n\pi} u \sin u \, du$$
>
> $$= \frac{2L}{n^2\pi^2} \Big[-u \cos u + \sin u \Big]_0^{n\pi} = \frac{2L}{n\pi} (-1)^{n+1}.$$
>
> Thus the Fourier sine series of f is
>
> $$t = \frac{2L}{\pi} \left(\sin \frac{\pi t}{L} - \frac{1}{2} \sin \frac{2\pi t}{L} + \frac{1}{3} \sin \frac{3\pi t}{L} - \cdots \right) \tag{16}$$
>
> for $0 < t < L$. The series in Eq. (15) converges to the even period $2L$ extension of f shown in Fig. 9.3.3; the series in Eq. (16) converges to the odd period $2L$ extension shown in Fig. 9.3.4. ∎

FIGURE 9.3.3. The even period $2L$ extension of f

FIGURE 9.3.4. The odd period $2L$ extension of f

Termwise Differentiation of Fourier Series

In this and in subsequent sections, we want to consider Fourier series as possible solutions of differential equations. In order to substitute a Fourier series for the unknown dependent variable in a differential equation to check whether it is a solution, we first need to differentiate the series in order to compute the derivatives that appear in the equation. Care is required here; term-by-term differentiation of an infinite series of variable terms is not always valid. Theorem 1 gives sufficient conditions for the validity of termwise differentiation of a Fourier series.

THEOREM 1: Termwise Differentiation of Fourier Series

Suppose that the function f is continuous for all t, periodic with period $2L$, and that its derivative f' is piecewise smooth for all t. Then the Fourier series of f' is the series

$$f'(t) = \sum_{n=1}^{\infty} \left(-\frac{n\pi}{L} a_n \sin\frac{n\pi t}{L} + \frac{n\pi}{L} b_n \cos\frac{n\pi t}{L} \right) \tag{17}$$

obtained by termwise differentiation of the Fourier series

$$f(t) = \frac{a_0}{2} + \sum_{n=1}^{\infty} \left(a_n \cos\frac{n\pi t}{L} + b_n \sin\frac{n\pi t}{L} \right). \tag{18}$$

Proof: The point of the theorem is that the differentiated series in Eq. (17) actually converges to $f'(t)$ (with the usual proviso about average values). But because f' is periodic and piecewise smooth, we know from Theorem 1 of Section 9.2 that the Fourier series of f' converges to $f'(t)$:

$$f'(t) = \frac{\alpha_0}{2} + \sum_{n=1}^{\infty} \left(\alpha_n \cos\frac{n\pi t}{L} + \beta_n \sin\frac{n\pi t}{L} \right). \tag{19}$$

In order to prove Theorem 1, it therefore suffices to show that the series in Eqs. (17) and (19) are identical. We will do so under the additional hypothesis that f' is continuous everywhere. Then

$$\alpha_0 = \frac{1}{L}\int_{-L}^{L} f'(t)\,dt = \frac{1}{L}\left[f(t) \right]_{-L}^{L} = 0$$

because $f(L) = f(-L)$ by periodicity, and

$$\alpha_n = \frac{1}{L}\int_{-L}^{L} f'(t)\cos\frac{n\pi t}{L}\,dt$$

$$= \frac{1}{L}\left[f(t)\cos\frac{n\pi t}{L} \right]_{-L}^{L} + \frac{n\pi}{L}\cdot\frac{1}{L}\int_{-L}^{L} f(t)\sin\frac{n\pi t}{L}\,dt$$

—integration by parts. It follows that

$$\alpha_n = \frac{n\pi}{L} b_n.$$

Similarly, we find that

$$\beta_n = -\frac{n\pi}{L} a_n,$$

and therefore the series in Eqs. (17) and (19) are, indeed, identical. ∎

Whereas the assumption that the derivative f' is continuous is merely a convenience — the proof of Theorem 1 can be strengthened to allow isolated discontinuities in f' — it is important to note that the conclusion of Theorem 1 generally fails when f itself is discontinuous. For example, consider the Fourier series

$$t = \frac{2L}{\pi}\left(\sin\frac{\pi t}{L} - \frac{1}{2}\sin\frac{2\pi t}{L} + \frac{1}{3}\sin\frac{3\pi t}{L} - \cdots \right), \tag{16}$$

$-L < t < L$, of the discontinuous sawtooth function having the graph shown in Fig. 9.3.4. All the hypotheses of Theorem 1 are satisfied apart from the continuity of f, and f has only isolated jump discontinuities. But the series

$$2\left(\cos\frac{\pi t}{L} - \cos\frac{2\pi t}{L} + \cos\frac{3\pi t}{L} - \cdots\right) \tag{20}$$

obtained by differentiating the series in Eq. (16) term by term diverges (for instance, when $t = 0$ and when $t = L$), and therefore termwise differentiation of the series in Eq. (16) is not valid.

By contrast, consider the [continuous] triangular wave function $f(t)$ having the graph shown in Fig. 9.3.3, with $f(t) = |t|$ for $-L < t < L$. This function satisfies all the hypotheses of Theorem 1, so its Fourier series

$$f(t) = \frac{L}{2} - \frac{4L}{\pi^2}\left(\cos\frac{\pi t}{L} + \frac{1}{3^2}\cos\frac{3\pi t}{L} + \frac{1}{5^2}\cos\frac{5\pi t}{L} + \cdots\right) \tag{15}$$

can be differentiated termwise. The result is

$$f'(t) = \frac{4}{\pi}\left(\sin\frac{\pi t}{L} + \frac{1}{3}\sin\frac{3\pi t}{L} + \frac{1}{5}\sin\frac{5\pi t}{L} + \cdots\right), \tag{21}$$

which is the Fourier series of the period $2L$ square wave function that takes the value -1 for $-L < t < 0$ and $+1$ for $0 < t < L$.

Fourier Series Solutions of Differential Equations

In the remainder of this chapter and in Chapter 10, we will frequently need to solve endpoint value problems of the general form

$$ax'' + bx' + cx = f(t) \quad (0 < t < L); \tag{22}$$

$$x(0) = x(L) = 0, \tag{23}$$

where the function $f(t)$ is given. We might consider applying the techniques of Chapter 3, solving the problem by:

1. First finding the general solution $x_c = c_1 x_1 + c_2 x_2$ of the associated homogeneous differential equation;

2. Then finding a single particular solution x_p of the nonhomogeneous equation in (22); and

3. Finally, determining the constants c_1 and c_2 so that $x = x_c + x_p$ satisfies the endpoint conditions in (23).

In many problems, the following Fourier series method is more convenient and more useful. We first extend the definition of the function $f(t)$ to the interval $-L < t < 0$ in an appropriate way, and then to the entire real line by the periodicity condition $f(t + 2L) = f(t)$. Then the function f, if piecewise smooth, has a Fourier series

$$f(t) = \frac{A_0}{2} + \sum_{n=1}^{\infty}\left(A_n\cos\frac{n\pi t}{L} + B_n\sin\frac{n\pi t}{L}\right), \tag{24}$$

which has coefficients A_n and B_n that we can and do compute. We then assume that the differential equation in (22) has a solution $x(t)$ with a Fourier series

$$x(t) = \frac{a_0}{2} + \sum_{n=1}^{\infty}\left(a_n \cos\frac{n\pi t}{L} + b_n \sin\frac{n\pi t}{L}\right) \qquad (25)$$

that may validly be differentiated twice termwise. We attempt to determine the coefficients in Eq. (25) by first substituting the series in Eqs. (24) and (25) into the differential equation in (22) and then equating coefficients of like terms. If this procedure is carried out in such a way that the resulting series in Eq. (25) also satisfies the endpoint conditions in (23), then we have a "formal Fourier series solution" of the original endpoint value problem; that is, a solution subject to verification of the assumed termwise differentiability. Example 2 illustrates this process.

EXAMPLE 2 Find a formal Fourier series solution of the endpoint value problem

$$x'' + 4x = 4t, \qquad (26)$$

$$x(0) = x(1) = 0. \qquad (27)$$

Solution Here $f(t) = 4t$ for $0 < t < 1$. A crucial first step—which we did not make explicit in the outline above—is to choose a periodic extension $f(t)$ so that each term in its Fourier series satisfies the endpoint conditions in (27). For this purpose we choose the odd period 2 extension, because each term of the form $\sin n\pi t$ satisfies (27). Then from the series in Eq. (16) with $L = 1$, we get the Fourier series

$$4t = \frac{8}{\pi}\sum_{n=1}^{\infty}\frac{(-1)^{n+1}}{n}\sin n\pi t \qquad (28)$$

for $0 < t < 1$. We therefore anticipate a sine series solution

$$x(t) = \sum_{n=1}^{\infty} b_n \sin n\pi t, \qquad (29)$$

noting that any such series will satisfy the endpoint conditions in (27). When we substitute the series in (28) and (29) in Eq. (26), the result is

$$\sum_{n=1}^{\infty}(-n^2\pi^2 + 4) b_n \sin n\pi t = \frac{8}{\pi}\sum_{n=1}^{\infty}\frac{(-1)^{n+1}}{n}\sin n\pi t. \qquad (30)$$

We next equate coefficients of like terms in Eq. (30). This yields

$$b_n = \frac{8\cdot(-1)^{n+1}}{n\pi(4 - n^2\pi^2)},$$

so our formal Fourier series solution is

$$x(t) = \frac{8}{\pi}\sum_{n=1}^{\infty}\frac{(-1)^{n+1}\sin n\pi t}{n(4 - n^2\pi^2)}. \qquad (31)$$

In Problem 16 we ask you to derive the exact solution

$$x(t) = t - \frac{\sin 2t}{\sin 2} \qquad (0 \le t \le 1), \qquad (32)$$

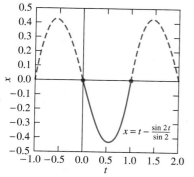

FIGURE 9.3.5. Graph of the solution in Example 2

and to verify that (31) is the Fourier series of the odd period 2 extension of this solution.

The dashed curve in Fig. 9.3.5 was plotted by summing 10 terms of the Fourier series in (31). The solid curve for $0 \leqq t \leqq 2$ is the graph of the exact solution in (32). ∎

Termwise Integration of Fourier Series

Theorem 2 guarantees that the Fourier series of a piecewise continuous periodic function can always be integrated term by term, whether or not it converges! A proof is outlined in Problem 25.

THEOREM 2: **Termwise Integration of Fourier Series**

Suppose that f is a piecewise continuous periodic function with period $2L$ and Fourier series

$$f(t) \sim \frac{a_0}{2} + \sum_{n=1}^{\infty} \left(a_n \cos \frac{n\pi t}{L} + b_n \sin \frac{n\pi t}{L} \right), \tag{33}$$

which may not converge. Then

$$\int_0^t f(s)\,ds = \frac{a_0 t}{2} + \sum_{n=1}^{\infty} \frac{L}{n\pi} \left[a_n \sin \frac{n\pi t}{L} - b_n \left(\cos \frac{n\pi t}{L} - 1 \right) \right], \tag{34}$$

with the series on the right-hand side convergent for all t. Note that the series in Eq. (34) is the result of term-by-term integration of the series in (33). ∎

EXAMPLE 3 Let us attempt to verify the conclusion of Theorem 2 in the case that $f(t)$ is the period 2π function such that

$$f(t) = \begin{cases} -1, & -\pi < t < 0; \\ +1, & 0 < t < \pi. \end{cases} \tag{35}$$

By Example 1 of Section 9.1, the Fourier series of f is

$$f(t) = \frac{4}{\pi} \left(\sin t + \frac{1}{3} \sin 3t + \frac{1}{5} \sin 5t + \cdots \right). \tag{36}$$

Theorem 2 then implies that

$$F(t) = \int_0^t f(s)\,ds$$

$$= \int_0^t \frac{4}{\pi} \left(\sin s + \frac{1}{3} \sin 3s + \frac{1}{5} \sin 5s + \cdots \right) ds$$

$$= \frac{4}{\pi} \left[(1 - \cos t) + \frac{1}{3^2} (1 - \cos 3t) + \frac{1}{5^2} (1 - \cos 5t) + \cdots \right].$$

Thus

$$F(t) = \frac{4}{\pi}\left(1 + \frac{1}{3^2} + \frac{1}{5^2} + \cdots\right) - \frac{4}{\pi}\left(\cos t + \frac{1}{3^2}\cos 3t + \frac{1}{5^2}\cos 5t + \cdots\right).$$

(37)

On the other hand, direct integration of (35) yields

$$F(t) = \int_0^t f(s)\,ds = |t| = \begin{cases} -t, & -\pi < t < 0, \\ t, & 0 < t < \pi. \end{cases}$$

We know from Example 1 in this section (with $L = \pi$) that

$$|t| = \frac{\pi}{2} - \frac{4}{\pi}\left(\cos t + \frac{1}{3^2}\cos 3t + \frac{1}{5^2}\cos 5t + \cdots\right).$$

(38)

We also know from Eq. (18) of Section 9.2 that

$$1 + \frac{1}{3^2} + \frac{1}{5^2} + \cdots = \frac{\pi^2}{8},$$

so it follows that the two series in Eqs. (37) and (38) are indeed identical. ∎

9.3 Problems

In Problems 1 through 10, a function $f(t)$ defined on an interval $0 < t < L$ is given. Find the Fourier cosine and sine series of f, and sketch the graphs of the two extensions of f to which these two series converge.

1. $f(t) = 1, \quad 0 < t < L$

2. $f(t) = 1 - t, \quad 0 < t < 1$

3. $f(t) = 1 - t, \quad 0 < t < 2$

4. $f(t) = \begin{cases} t, & 0 < t \leq 1; \\ 2 - t, & 1 \leq t < 2 \end{cases}$

5. $f(t) = \begin{cases} 0, & 0 < t < 1; \\ 1, & 1 < t < 2; \\ 0, & 2 < t < 3 \end{cases}$

6. $f(t) = t^2, \quad 0 < t < L$

7. $f(t) = t(\pi - t), \quad 0 < t < \pi$

8. $f(t) = t - t^2, \quad 0 < t < 1$

9. $f(t) = \sin t, \quad 0 < t < \pi$

10. $f(t) = \begin{cases} \sin t, & 0 < t \leq \pi \\ 0, & \pi \leq t < 2\pi \end{cases}$

Find formal Fourier series solutions of the endpoint value problems in Problems 11 through 14.

11. $x'' + 2x = 1, \quad x(0) = x(\pi) = 0$

12. $x'' - 4x = 1, \quad x(0) = x(\pi) = 0$

13. $x'' + x = t, \quad x(0) = x(1) = 0$

14. $x'' + 2x = t, \quad x(0) = x(2) = 0$

15. Find a formal Fourier series solution of the endpoint value problem

$$x'' + 2x = t, \qquad x'(0) = x'(\pi) = 0.$$

(*Suggestion:* Use a Fourier cosine series in which each term satisfies the endpoint conditions.)

16. (a) Derive the solution $x(t) = t - (\sin 2t)/(\sin 2)$ of the endpoint value problem

$$x'' + 4x = 4t, \qquad x(0) = x(1) = 0.$$

(b) Show that the series in Eq. (31) is the Fourier sine series of the solution in part (a).

17. (a) Suppose that f is an even function. Show that

$$\int_{-a}^{0} f(t)\,dt = \int_0^a f(t)\,dt.$$

(b) Suppose that f is an odd function. Show that

$$\int_{-a}^{0} f(t)\,dt = -\int_0^a f(t)\,dt.$$

18. By Example 2 of Section 9.2, the Fourier series of the pe-

riod 2 function f with $f(t) = t^2$ for $0 < t < 2$ is

$$f(t) = \frac{4}{3} + \frac{4}{\pi^2} \sum_{n=1}^{\infty} \frac{\cos n\pi t}{n^2} - \frac{4}{\pi} \sum_{n=1}^{\infty} \frac{\sin n\pi t}{n}.$$

Show that the termwise derivative of this series does not converge to $f'(t)$.

19. Begin with the Fourier series

$$t = 2 \sum_{n=1}^{\infty} \frac{(-1)^{n+1}}{n} \sin nt, \qquad -\pi < t < \pi,$$

and integrate termwise three times in succession to obtain the series

$$\frac{1}{24} t^4 = \frac{\pi^2 t^2}{12} - 2 \sum_{n=1}^{\infty} \frac{(-1)^n}{n^4} \cos nt + 2 \sum_{n=1}^{\infty} \frac{(-1)^n}{n^4}.$$

20. Substitute $t = \pi/2$ and $t = \pi$ in the series of Problem 19 to obtain the summations

$$\sum_{n=1}^{\infty} \frac{1}{n^4} = \frac{\pi^4}{90}, \qquad \sum_{n=1}^{\infty} \frac{(-1)^{n+1}}{n^4} = \frac{7\pi^4}{720},$$

and

$$1 + \frac{1}{3^4} + \frac{1}{5^4} + \frac{1}{7^4} + \cdots = \frac{\pi^4}{96}.$$

21. (Odd half-multiple sine series) Let $f(t)$ be given for $0 < t < L$, and define $F(t)$ for $0 < t < 2L$ as follows:

$$F(t) = \begin{cases} f(t), & 0 < t < L; \\ f(2L - t), & L < t < 2L. \end{cases}$$

Thus the graph of $F(t)$ is symmetric about the line $t = L$ (Fig. 9.3.6). Then the period $4L$ Fourier sine series of F is

$$F(t) = \sum_{n=1}^{\infty} b_n \sin \frac{n\pi t}{2L},$$

where

$$b_n = \frac{1}{L} \int_0^L f(t) \sin \frac{n\pi t}{2L} \, dt + \frac{1}{L} \int_L^{2L} f(2L - t) \sin \frac{n\pi t}{2L} \, dt.$$

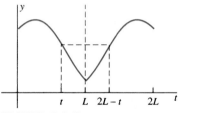

FIGURE 9.3.6. Construction of F from f in Problem 21

Substitute $s = 2L - t$ in the second integral to derive the series (for $0 < t < L$)

$$f(t) = \sum_{n \text{ odd}} b_n \sin \frac{n\pi t}{2L},$$

where

$$b_n = \frac{2}{L} \int_0^L f(t) \sin \frac{n\pi t}{2L} \, dt \qquad (n \text{ odd}).$$

22. (Odd half-multiple cosine series) Let $f(t)$ be given for $0 < t < L$, and define $G(t)$ for $0 < t < 2L$ as follows:

$$G(t) = \begin{cases} f(t), & 0 < t < L; \\ -f(2L - t), & L < t < 2L. \end{cases}$$

Use the period $4L$ Fourier cosine series of $G(t)$ to derive the series (for $0 < t < L$)

$$f(t) = \sum_{n \text{ odd}} a_n \cos \frac{n\pi t}{2L},$$

where

$$a_n = \frac{2}{L} \int_0^L f(t) \cos \frac{n\pi t}{2L} \, dt \qquad (n \text{ odd}).$$

23. Given: $f(t) = t$, $0 < t < 2\pi$. Derive the odd half-multiple sine series (Problem 21)

$$f(t) = \frac{8}{\pi} \sum_{n \text{ odd}} \frac{(-1)^{(n-1)/2}}{n^2} \sin \frac{nt}{2}.$$

24. Given the endpoint value problem

$$x'' - x = t, \qquad x(0) = 0, \qquad x'(\pi) = 0,$$

note that any constant multiple of $\sin(nt/2)$ with n odd satisfies the endpoint conditions. Hence use the odd half-multiple sine series of Problem 23 to derive the formal Fourier series solution

$$x(t) = \frac{32}{\pi} \sum_{n \text{ odd}} \frac{(-1)^{(n+1)/2}}{n^2(n^2 + 4)} \sin \frac{nt}{2}.$$

25. In this problem we outline the proof of Theorem 2. Suppose that $f(t)$ is a piecewise continuous period $2L$ function. Define

$$F(t) = \int_0^t \left[f(s) - \frac{1}{2} a_0 \right] ds,$$

where a_n and b_n denote the Fourier coefficients of $f(t)$. (a) Show directly that $F(t + 2L) = F(t)$, so that F is a continuous period $2L$ function, and therefore has a convergent Fourier series

$$F(t) = \frac{1}{2} A_0 + \sum_{n=1}^{\infty} \left(A_n \cos \frac{n\pi t}{L} + B_n \sin \frac{n\pi t}{L} \right).$$

(b) Suppose that $n \geq 1$. Show by direct computation that

$$A_n = -\frac{L}{n\pi} b_n \qquad \text{and} \qquad B_n = \frac{L}{n\pi} a_n.$$

(c) Thus

$$\int_0^t f(s)\,ds = \frac{t}{2}\,a_0 + \frac{1}{2}\,A_0$$

$$+ \sum_{n=1}^{\infty} \frac{L}{n\pi}\left(a_n \sin\frac{n\pi t}{L} - b_n \cos\frac{n\pi t}{L}\right).$$

Finally, substitute $t = 0$ to see that

$$\frac{1}{2}\,A_0 = \sum_{n=1}^{\infty} \frac{L}{n\pi}\,b_n.$$

9.3 Computing Project

This project exhibits the use of unit step functions for the efficient computation of Fourier series of "piecewise-defined" functions. The unit step function (with values 0 for $t < 0$ and 1 for $t > 0$ is available for *Mathematica* calculations if we load the delta functions package.

> `<<Calculus`DiracDelta``

The "unit function" defined by

> `unit[t_,a_,b_] := UnitStep[t - a] - UnitStep[t - b]`

then has the value 1 on the interval $a \leqq t < b$ and 0 otherwise. For instance,

> `Plot[unit[t, 1, 2], {t, 0, 3}];`

to illustrate the graph of a unit function.

We can use unit functions to define a given piecewise smooth function $f(t)$ as a "linear combination" of different unit functions corresponding to the intervals on which the function is smooth, with the unit function for each interval multiplied by the formula defining $f(t)$ on that interval.

For example, consider the even period 2π function whose graph is shown in Fig. 9.3.7. This "trapezoidal wave function" is defined for $0 < t < \pi$ by

> `f[t_] := (Pi/3)*unit[t,0,Pi/6] +`
> ` (Pi/2 - t)*unit[t,Pi/6,5*Pi/6] +`
> ` (-Pi/3)*unit[t,5*Pi/6,Pi]`

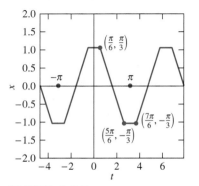

FIGURE 9.3.7. Even period 2π trapezoidal wave function

It is clear that $a_0 = 0$ (why?), as we verify with the computation

```
L = Pi;
a0 = (2/L)*Integrate[ f[t], {t, 0, L} ]

    0
```

The coefficient a_n is given for $n > 0$ by

```
a[n_] = (2/L)*Integrate[ f[t]*Cos[n*Pi*t/L], {t, 0, L}];
```

and then a typical partial sum of the Fourier cosine series of $f(t)$ is given by

```
fourierSum = a0/2 + Sum[ a[n]*Cos[n*Pi*t/L], {n,1,25}]
```

$$\frac{2\mathrm{Sqrt}[3]\ \mathrm{Cos}[t]}{\mathrm{Pi}} - \frac{2\mathrm{Sqrt}[3]\ \mathrm{Cos}[5\ t]}{25\ \mathrm{Pi}} - \frac{2\mathrm{Sqrt}[3]\ \mathrm{Cos}[7\ t]}{49\ \mathrm{Pi}} +$$

$$\frac{2\mathrm{Sqrt}[3]\ \mathrm{Cos}[11\ t]}{121\ \mathrm{Pi}} + \frac{2\mathrm{Sqrt}[3]\ \mathrm{Cos}[13\ t]}{169\ \mathrm{Pi}} - \frac{2\mathrm{Sqrt}[3]\ \mathrm{Cos}[17\ t]}{289\ \mathrm{Pi}} -$$

$$\frac{2\mathrm{Sqrt}[3]\ \mathrm{Cos}[19\ t]}{361\ \mathrm{Pi}} + \frac{2\mathrm{Sqrt}[3]\ \mathrm{Cos}[23\ t]}{529\ \mathrm{Pi}} + \frac{2\mathrm{Sqrt}[3]\ \mathrm{Cos}[25\ t]}{625\ \mathrm{Pi}}$$

Thus we discover the lovely Fourier series

$$f(t) = \frac{2\sqrt{3}}{\pi} \sum \frac{(\pm)\cos nt}{n^2}$$

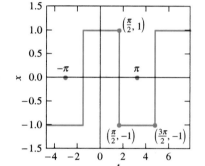

FIGURE 9.3.8. Even period 2π square wave function

with a $+ - - + + - - + +$. . . pattern of signs, the summation being taken over all odd positive integers n that are *not* multiples of 3. You can enter the command

```
Plot[ fourierSum, {t, -2*Pi, 3*Pi} ];
```

to verify that this Fourier series is consistent with Fig. 9.3.7.

Use the method illustrated here to find the Fourier series of the following period 2π functions

1. The even square wave function whose graph is shown in Fig. 9.3.8.
2. The even and odd triangular wave functions whose graphs are shown in Figs. 9.2.4 and 9.3.9.
3. The odd trapezoidal wave function whose graph is shown in Fig. 9.2.5.

Then use unit functions similarly to find Fourier series of some piecewise smooth functions of your own choice, perhaps ones that have periods other than 2π and are neither even nor odd.

FIGURE 9.3.9. Even period 2π triangular wave function

*9.4 Applications of Fourier Series

We consider first the motion of a mass m on a spring with Hooke's constant k under the influence of a *periodic* external force $F(t)$, as indicated in Fig. 9.4.1. Its displace-

Equilibrium
position

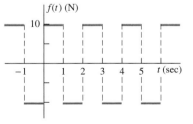

FIGURE 9.4.1. A mass-and-spring
system with external force

ment from equilibrium $x(t)$ satisfies the familiar equation

$$mx'' + kx = F(t). \tag{1}$$

The general solution of Eq. (1) is of the form

$$x(t) = c_1 \cos \omega_0 t + c_2 \sin \omega_0 t + x_p(t), \tag{2}$$

where $\omega_0 = \sqrt{k/m}$ is the natural frequency of the system and $x_p(t)$ is a particular solution of Eq. (1). The values c_1 and c_2 would be determined by the initial conditions. Here we want to use Fourier series to find a *periodic* particular solution of Eq. (1). We will denote it by $x_{sp}(t)$ and call it a **steady periodic solution.**

We assume for simplicity that $F(t)$ is an odd function with period $2L$, so its Fourier series has the form

$$F(t) = \sum_{n=1}^{\infty} B_n \sin \frac{n\pi t}{L}. \tag{3}$$

If $n\pi/L$ is not equal to ω_0 for any positive integer n, we can determine a steady periodic solution of the form

$$x_{sp}(t) = \sum_{n=1}^{\infty} b_n \sin \frac{n\pi t}{L} \tag{4}$$

by substituting the series in Eqs. (3) and (4) in Eq. (1) to find the coefficients in Eq. (4). Example 1 illustrates this procedure.

EXAMPLE 1 Suppose that $m = 2$ kg, $k = 32$ N/m, and that $F(t)$ is an odd periodic force with a period of 2 s given in one period by

$$F(t) = \begin{cases} +10 \text{ N} & \text{if } 0 < t < 1; \\ -10 \text{ N} & \text{if } 1 < t < 2. \end{cases} \tag{5}$$

Find the steady periodic motion $x_{sp}(t)$.

Solution The graph of the periodic forcing function $F(t)$ is shown in Fig. 9.4.2. By essentially the same computation as in Example 1 of Section 9.1, the Fourier series of $F(t)$ is

$$F(t) = \frac{40}{\pi} \sum_{n \text{ odd}} \frac{\sin n\pi t}{n}; \tag{6}$$

f(t) (N)

FIGURE 9.4.2. The graph of the
forcing function of Example 1

note that it contains terms corresponding only to n odd. When we substitute this series and

$$x_{sp}(t) = \sum_{n \text{ odd}} b_n \sin n\pi t, \tag{7}$$

a trial solution likewise containing only odd terms, into Eq. (1) with $m = 2$ and $k = 32$, we get

$$\sum_{n \text{ odd}} b_n(-2n^2\pi^2 + 32) \sin n\pi t = \frac{40}{\pi} \sum_{n \text{ odd}} \frac{\sin n\pi t}{n}.$$

We equate coefficients of like terms; the result is that

$$b_n = \frac{20}{n\pi (16 - n^2\pi^2)} \quad \text{for } n \text{ odd.}$$

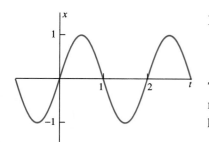

FIGURE 9.4.3. The graph of $x_{sp}(t)$

Hence

$$x_{sp}(t) = \frac{20}{\pi} \sum_{n \text{ odd}} \frac{\sin n\pi t}{n(16 - n^2\pi^2)}. \tag{8}$$

The fact that each term in Eq. (8) is symmetric about $t = \frac{1}{2}$ suggests that $x_{sp}(t)$ is maximal when $t = \frac{1}{2}$, as does the graph shown in Fig. 9.4.3. Assuming this, we find the amplitude of the steady periodic motion to be

$$x_{sp}\left(\frac{1}{2}\right) = \frac{20}{\pi} \sum_{n \text{ odd}} \frac{\sin \dfrac{n\pi}{2}}{n(16 - n^2\pi^2)}.$$

The first ten terms yield $x\left(\frac{1}{2}\right) \approx 1.063$ m. ∎

If there is a nonzero term $B_N \sin (N\pi t/L)$ in the Fourier series of $F(t)$ for which $N\pi/L = \omega_0$, then this term causes **pure resonance.** The reason is that the equation

$$mx'' + kx = B_N \sin \omega_0 t$$

has the resonance solution

$$x(t) = -\frac{B_N}{2m\omega_0} t \cos \omega_0 t.$$

The solution corresponding to Eq. (4) in this case is then

$$x(t) = -\frac{B_N}{2m\omega_0} t \cos \omega_0 t + \sum_{n \neq N} \frac{B_n \sin \dfrac{n\pi t}{L}}{m\left(\omega_0^2 - \dfrac{n^2\pi^2}{L^2}\right)}. \tag{9}$$

EXAMPLE 2 Suppose that $m = 2$ kg and $k = 32$ N/m as in Example 1. Determine whether pure resonance will occur if $F(t)$ is an odd periodic function defined in one period to be

(a) $F(t) = \begin{cases} +10, & 0 < t < \pi; \\ -10, & \pi < t < 2\pi. \end{cases}$

(b) $F(t) = 10t, \quad -\pi < t < \pi.$

Solution (a) The natural frequency is $\omega_0 = 4$, and the Fourier series of $F(t)$ is

$$F(t) = \frac{40}{\pi}\left(\sin t + \frac{1}{3}\sin 3t + \frac{1}{5}\sin 5t + \cdots\right).$$

Because this series contains no $\sin 4t$ term, no resonance occurs.

(b) In this case the Fourier series is

$$F(t) = 20 \sum_{n=1}^{\infty} \frac{(-1)^{n+1}}{n} \sin nt.$$

Pure resonance occurs because of the presence of the term containing the factor $\sin 4t$. ∎

Example 3 illustrates the *near resonance* that can occur when a single term in the solution series is magnified because its frequency is close to the natural frequency ω_0.

EXAMPLE 3 Find a steady periodic solution of

$$x'' + 10x = F(t), \tag{10}$$

where $F(t)$ is the function of period 4 with $F(t) = 5t$ for $-2 < t < 2$ and Fourier series

$$F(t) = \frac{20}{\pi} \sum_{n=1}^{\infty} \frac{(-1)^{n+1}}{n} \sin \frac{n\pi t}{2}. \tag{11}$$

Solution When we substitute Eq. (11) and

$$x_{sp}(t) = \sum_{n=1}^{\infty} b_n \sin \frac{n\pi t}{2}$$

in (10), we obtain

$$\sum_{n=1}^{\infty} b_n \left(-\frac{n^2\pi^2}{4} + 10 \right) \sin \frac{n\pi t}{2} = \frac{20}{\pi} \sum_{n=1}^{\infty} \frac{(-1)^{n+1}}{n} \sin \frac{n\pi t}{2}.$$

We equate coefficients of like terms and then solve for b_n to get the steady periodic solution

$$x_{sp}(t) = \frac{80}{\pi} \sum_{n=1}^{\infty} \frac{(-1)^{n+1}}{n(40 - n^2\pi^2)} \sin \frac{n\pi t}{2}$$

$$\approx (0.8452) \sin \frac{\pi t}{2} - (24.4111) \sin \frac{2\pi t}{2} - (0.1738) \sin \frac{3\pi t}{2} + \cdots.$$

The large magnitude of the second term results from the fact that $\omega_0 = \sqrt{10} \approx \pi = 2\pi/2$. Thus the dominant motion of a spring with the differential equation in (10) would be an oscillation with frequency π radians per second, period 2 s, and amplitude about 24, consistent with the graph of $x_{sp}(t)$ shown in Fig. 9.4.4.

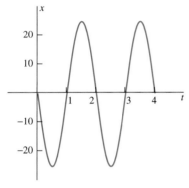

FIGURE 9.4.4. The graph of $x_{sp}(t)$

Damped Forced Oscillations

Now we consider the motion of a mass m attached both to a spring with Hooke's constant k and to a dashpot with damping constant c, under the influence of a *periodic* external force $F(t)$ (Fig. 9.4.5). The displacement $x(t)$ of the mass from equilibrium satisfies the equation

$$mx'' + cx' + kx = F(t). \tag{12}$$

We recall from Problem 21 of Section 3.6 that the steady periodic solution of Eq. (12) with $F(t) = F_0 \sin \omega t$ is

$$x(t) = \frac{F_0}{\sqrt{(k - m\omega^2)^2 + (c\omega)^2}} \sin(\omega t - \alpha), \tag{13}$$

where

$$\alpha = \tan^{-1} \frac{c\omega}{k - m\omega^2}, \qquad 0 \leq \alpha \leq \pi. \tag{14}$$

FIGURE 9.4.5. A damped mass-and-spring system with external force

If $F(t)$ is an odd period $2L$ function with Fourier series

$$F(t) = \sum_{n=1}^{\infty} B_n \sin \frac{n\pi t}{L}, \tag{15}$$

then the formulas above yield, by superposition, the steady periodic solution

$$x_{sp}(t) = \sum_{n=1}^{\infty} \frac{B_n \sin(\omega_n t - \alpha_n)}{\sqrt{(k - m\omega_n^2)^2 + (c\omega_n)^2}}, \tag{16}$$

where $\omega_n = n\pi/L$ and α_n is the angle determined by Eq. (14) with this value of ω. Example 4 illustrates the interesting fact that the dominant frequency of the steady periodic solution can be an *integral multiple* of the frequency of the force $F(t)$.

EXAMPLE 4 Suppose that $m = 3$ kg, $c = 0.02$ N/m/s, $k = 27$ N/m, and $F(t)$ is the odd period 2π function with $F(t) = \pi t - t^2$ if $0 < t < \pi$. Find the steady periodic motion $x_{sp}(t)$.

Solution We find that the Fourier series of $F(t)$ is

$$F(t) = \frac{8}{\pi}\left(\sin t + \frac{1}{3^3}\sin 3t + \frac{1}{5^3}\sin 5t + \cdots\right). \tag{17}$$

Thus $B_n = 0$ for n even, $B_n = 8/(\pi n^3)$ for n odd, and $\omega_n = n$. Equation (16) gives

$$x(t) = \frac{8}{\pi}\sum_{n \text{ odd}} \frac{\sin(nt - \alpha_n)}{n^3\sqrt{(27 - 3n^2)^2 + (0.02n)^2}} \tag{18}$$

with

$$\alpha_n = \tan^{-1}\frac{(0.02)n}{27 - 3n^2}, \qquad 0 \le \alpha_n \le \pi. \tag{19}$$

With the aid of a programmable calculator, we find that

$$x_{sp}(t) \approx (0.1061)\sin(t - 0.0008) + (1.5719)\sin\left(3t - \frac{\pi}{2}\right)$$

$$+ (0.0004)\sin(5t - 3.1395) + (0.0001)\sin(7t - 3.1404) + \cdots. \tag{20}$$

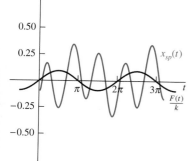

0.50
0.25
$x_{sp}(t)$
π 2π 3π t
$\frac{F(t)}{k}$
−0.25
−0.50

FIGURE 9.4.6. The imposed force and the resulting steady periodic motion in Example 4

Because the coefficient corresponding to $n = 3$ is much larger than the others, the response of this system is approximately a sinusoidal motion with frequency *three times* that of the input force. Figure 9.4.6 shows $x_{sp}(t)$ in comparison with the reduced force $F(t)/k$ that has the appropriate dimension of distance.

What is happening here is this: The mass $m = 3$ on a spring with $k = 27$ has (if we ignore the small effect of the dashpot) a natural frequency $\omega_0 = \sqrt{k/m} = 3$ rad/s. The imposed external force $F(t)$ has a [smallest] period of 2π s and hence a fundamental frequency of 1 rad/s. Consequently, the term corresponding to $n = 3$ in the Fourier series of $F(t)$ (in Eq. (17)) has the same frequency as the natural frequency of the system. Thus near resonance vibrations occur, with the mass completing essentially *three* oscillations for every single oscillation of the external force. This is the physical effect of the dominant $n = 3$ term on the right-hand side in Eq. (20). For instance, you can push a friend in a swing quite high even if you push the swing only every *third* time it returns to you. This also explains why some transformers "hum" at a frequency much higher than 60 Hz.

This is a general phenomenon that must be taken into account in the design of mechanical systems. To avoid the occurrence of abnormally large and potentially destructive near resonance vibrations, the system must be so designed that it is not subject to any external periodic force, some *integral multiple* of whose fundamental frequency is close to any natural frequency of vibration. ■

9.4 Problems

Find steady periodic solutions of the differential equations in Problems 1 through 6.

1. $x'' + 5x = F(t)$, where $F(t)$ is the function of period 2π such that $F(t) = 3$ if $0 < t < \pi$, $F(t) = -3$ if $\pi < t < 2\pi$.

2. $x'' + 10x = F(t)$, where $F(t)$ is the even function of period 4 such that $F(t) = 3$ if $0 < t < 1$, $F(t) = -3$ if $1 < t < 2$.

3. $x'' + 3x = F(t)$, where $F(t)$ is the odd function of period 2π with $F(t) = 2t$ if $0 < t < \pi$.

4. $x'' + 4x = F(t)$, where $F(t)$ is the even function of period 4 with $F(t) = 2t$ if $0 < t < 2$.

5. $x'' + 10x = F(t)$, where $F(t)$ is the odd function of period 2 with $F(t) = t - t^2$ if $0 < t < 1$.

6. $x'' + 2x = F(t)$, where $F(t)$ is the even function of period 2π with $F(t) = \sin t$ if $0 < t < \pi$.

In each of Problems 7 through 12, the mass m and Hooke's constant k for a mass-and-spring system are given. Determine whether or not pure resonance will occur under the influence of the given external periodic force $F(t)$.

7. $m = 1$, $k = 9$; $F(t)$ is the odd function of period 2π with $F(t) = 1$ for $0 < t < \pi$.

8. $m = 2$, $k = 10$; $F(t)$ is the odd function of period 2 with $F(t) = 1$ for $0 < t < 1$.

9. $m = 3$, $k = 12$; $F(t)$ is the odd function of period 2π with $F(t) = 3$ for $0 < t < \pi$.

10. $m = 1$, $k = 4\pi^2$; $F(t)$ is the odd function of period 2 with $F(t) = 2t$ if $0 < t < 1$.

11. $m = 3$, $k = 48$; $F(t)$ is the even function of period 2π with $F(t) = t$ if $0 < t < \pi$.

12. $m = 2$, $k = 50$; $F(t)$ is the odd function of period 2π with $F(t) = \pi t - t^2$ if $0 < t < \pi$.

In each of Problems 13 through 16, the values of m, c, and k for a damped mass-and-spring system are given. Find the steady periodic motions—in the form of Eq. (16)—of the mass under the influence of the given external force $F(t)$. Compute the coefficients and phase angles for the first three nonzero terms in the series for $x_{sp}(t)$.

13. $m = 1$, $c = 0.1$, $k = 4$; $F(t)$ is the force of Problem 1.

14. $m = 2$, $c = 0.1$, $k = 18$; $F(t)$ is the force of Problem 3.

15. $m = 3$, $c = 1$, $k = 30$; $F(t)$ is the force of Problem 5.

16. $m = 1$, $c = 0.01$, $k = 4$; $F(t)$ is the force of Problem 4.

17. Consider a forced damped mass-and-spring system with $m = \frac{1}{4}$ slug, $c = 0.6$ lb/ft/s, $k = 36$ lb/ft. The force $F(t)$ is the period 2 (s) function with $F(t) = 15$ if $0 < t < 1$, $F(t) = -15$ if $1 < t < 2$. (a) Find the steady periodic solution in the form

$$x_{sp}(t) = \sum_{n=1}^{\infty} b_n \sin(n\pi t - \alpha_n).$$

(b) Find the location—to the nearest tenth of an inch—of the mass when $t = 5$ s.

18. Consider a forced damped mass-and-spring system with $m = 1$, $c = 0.01$, and $k = 25$. The force $F(t)$ is the odd function of period 2π with $F(t) = t$ if $0 < t < \pi/2$, $F(t) = \pi - t$ if $\pi/2 < t < \pi$. Find the steady periodic motion; compute enough terms of its series to see that the dominant frequency of the motion is *five* times that of the external force.

9.5 Heat Conduction and Separation of Variables

The most important applications of Fourier series are to the solution of partial differential equations by means of the method of separation of variables that we introduce in this section. Recall that a *partial differential equation* is one containing one or more *partial* derivatives of a dependent variable that is a function of at least two indepen-

dent variables. An example is the **one-dimensional heat equation**

$$\frac{\partial u}{\partial t} = k\frac{\partial^2 u}{\partial x^2},\tag{1}$$

in which the dependent variable u is an unknown function of x and t, and k is a given constant.

The Heated Rod

Equation (1) models the variation of temperature u with position x and time t in a heated rod that extends along the x-axis. We assume that the rod has uniform cross section with area A perpendicular to the axis, and that it is made of a homogeneous material. We assume further that the cross section of the rod is so small that u is constant on each cross section, and that the lateral surface of the rod is insulated so that no heat can pass through it. Then u will, indeed, be a function of x and t, and heat will flow along the rod in only the x-direction. In general, we envision heat as flowing like a fluid from the warmer to the cooler parts of a body.

The **heat flux** $\phi(x, t)$ in the rod is the rate of flow of heat at time t across a unit area of the cross section at x. Typical units for ϕ are calories per second per square centimeter. The derivation of Eq. (1) is based upon the empirical principle that

$$\phi = -K\frac{\partial u}{\partial x},\tag{2}$$

where the proportionality constant K is called the **thermal conductivity** of the material of the rod. The minus sign in Eq. (2) corresponds to the fact that heat flows in the negative x-direction when $u_x > 0$, whereas ϕ is positive for heat flow in the positive x-direction; in short, heat flows from a hot place to a cold place, not vice versa.

Now consider a small segment of the rod corresponding to the interval $[x, x + \Delta x]$, as shown in Fig. 9.5.1. The rate of flow R (in calories per second) of heat *into* this segment through its two ends is

$$R = A\,\phi(x, t) - A\,\phi(x + \Delta x, t) = KA[u_x(x + \Delta x, t) - u_x(x, t)].\tag{3}$$

$A\phi(x, t)$ $A\phi(x + \Delta x, t)$

x $x + \Delta x$

FIGURE 9.5.1. Net flow of heat into a short segment of the rod

The resulting time rate of change u_t of the temperature in the segment depends upon its density δ (grams per cubic centimeter) and specific heat c (both assumed constant). The **specific heat** c is the amount of heat (in calories) required to raise by $1°$ the temperature of 1 g of material. Consequently $c\delta u$ calories of heat are required to raise 1 cm^3 of the material from temperature zero to temperature u. A short slice of the rod of length dx has volume $A\,dx$, so $c\delta uA\,dx$ calories of heat are required to raise the temperature of this slice from 0 to u. The **heat content**

$$Q(t) = \int_x^{x+\Delta x} c\,\delta Au(x, t)\,dx\tag{4}$$

of the segment $[x, x + \Delta x]$ of the rod is the amount of heat needed to raise it from zero to the given temperature $u(x, t)$. Because heat enters and leaves the segment only through its ends, we see from Eq. (3) that

$$Q'(t) = KA[u_x(x + \Delta x, t) - u_x(x, t)].\tag{5}$$

On the other hand, note that $R = dQ/dt$. Thus by differentiating Eq. (4) within the in-

tegral and applying the mean value theorem for integrals, we see that

$$Q'(t) = \int_{x}^{x + \Delta x} c\,\delta A u_t(x, t)\, dx = c\,\delta A u_t(\bar{x}, t)\,\Delta x \tag{6}$$

for some \bar{x} in $(x, x + \Delta x)$. Upon equating the values in Eqs. (5) and (6), we get

$$c\delta A u_t(\bar{x}, t)\,\Delta x = KA[u_x(x + \Delta x, t) - u_x(x, t)], \tag{7}$$

so

$$u_t(\bar{x}, t) = k\,\frac{u_x(x + \Delta x, t) - u_x(x, t)}{\Delta x}, \tag{8}$$

where

$$k = \frac{K}{c\delta} \tag{9}$$

is the **thermal diffusivity** of the material. Finally, by taking the limit in Eq. (8) as $\Delta x \to 0$ and $\bar{x} \to x$, we obtain the one-dimensional heat equation

$$\frac{\partial u}{\partial t} = k\,\frac{\partial^2 u}{\partial x^2}. \tag{1}$$

Thus the temperature $u(x, t)$ in a thin rod with insulated sides must satisfy this partial differential equation.

Boundary Conditions

Now suppose that the rod has finite length L, extending from $x = 0$ to $x = L$. Its temperature function $u(x, t)$ will be determined among all possible solutions of Eq. (1) by appropriate subsidiary conditions. In fact, whereas a solution of an ordinary differential equation involves arbitrary constants, a solution of a partial differential equation generally involves arbitrary *functions*. In the case of our rod, we can specify its temperature function $f(x)$ at time $t = 0$. This gives the *initial condition*

$$u(x, 0) = f(x). \tag{10}$$

We may also specify fixed temperatures at the two ends of the rod. For instance, if each end were clamped against a large block of ice at temperature zero, we would have the *endpoint conditions*

$$u(0, t) = u(L, t) = 0 \qquad \text{(for all } t\text{)}. \tag{11}$$

Combining all this, we get the **boundary value problem**

$$\frac{\partial u}{\partial t} = k\,\frac{\partial^2 u}{\partial x^2} \qquad (0 < x < L, \quad t > 0); \tag{12a}$$

$$u(0, t) = u(L, t) = 0, \tag{12b}$$

$$u(x, 0) = f(x). \tag{12c}$$

Figure 9.5.2 gives a geometric interpretation of the boundary value problem in (12): We are to find a function $u(x, t)$ that is continuous on the unbounded strip (including its boundary) shaded in the xt-plane. This function must satisfy the differential equation in (12a) at each interior point of the strip, and on the boundary of the strip must have the values prescribed by the boundary conditions in (12b) and (12c). Physi-

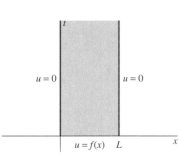

FIGURE 9.5.2. A geometric interpretation of the boundary value problem in Eqs. (12a)–(12c)

cal intuition suggests that if $f(x)$ is a reasonable function, then there will exist one and only one such function $u(x, t)$.

Instead of having fixed temperatures, the two ends of the rod might be insulated. In this case no heat would flow through either end, so we see from Eq. (2) that the conditions in (12b) would be replaced in the boundary value problem by the endpoint conditions

$$u_x(0, t) = u_x(L, t) = 0 \tag{13}$$

(for all t). Alternatively, the rod could be insulated at one end and have a fixed temperature at the other. This and other endpoint possibilities are discussed in the problems.

Superposition of Solutions

Note that the heat equation in (12a) is *linear*. That is, any linear combination $u = c_1 u_1 + c_2 u_2$ of two solutions of (12a) is also a solution of (12a); this follows immediately from the linearity of partial differentiation. It is also true that if u_1 and u_2 each satisfy the conditions in (12b), then so does any linear combination $u = c_1 u_1 + c_2 u_2$. The conditions in (12b) are therefore called **homogeneous** boundary conditions (though a more descriptive term might be *linear* boundary conditions). By contrast, the final boundary condition in (12c) is not homogeneous; it is a **nonhomogeneous** boundary condition.

Our overall strategy for solving the boundary value problem in (12a) through (12c) will be to find functions u_1, u_2, u_3, \ldots that satisfy both the partial differential equation in (12a) and the homogeneous boundary conditions in (12b), and then attempt to combine these functions by superposition, as if they were building blocks, in the hope of obtaining a solution $u = c_1 u_1 + c_2 u_2 + \cdots$ that satisfies the nonhomogeneous condition in (12c) as well. Example 1 illustrates this approach.

EXAMPLE 1 It is easy to verify by direct substitution that each of the functions

$$u_1(x, t) = e^{-t} \sin x, \quad u_2(x, t) = e^{-4t} \sin 2x, \quad \text{and} \quad u_3(x, t) = e^{-9t} \sin 3x$$

satisfies the equation $u_t = u_{xx}$. Use these functions to construct a solution of the boundary value problem

$$\frac{\partial u}{\partial t} = \frac{\partial^2 u}{\partial x^2} \qquad (0 < x < \pi, \quad t > 0); \tag{14a}$$

$$u(0, t) = u(\pi, t) = 0, \tag{14b}$$

$$u(x, 0) = 80 \sin^3 x = 60 \sin x - 20 \sin 3x. \tag{14c}$$

Solution Any linear combination of the form

$$u(x, t) = c_1 u_1(x, t) + c_2 u_2(x, t) + c_3 u_3(x, t)$$
$$= c_1 e^{-t} \sin x + c_2 e^{-4t} \sin 2x + c_3 e^{-9t} \sin 3x$$

satisfies both the differential equation in (14a) and the homogeneous conditions in (14b). Because

$$u(x, 0) = c_1 \sin x + c_2 \sin 2x + c_3 \sin 3x,$$

we see that we can also satisfy the nonhomogeneous condition in (14c) simply by choosing $c_1 = 60$, $c_2 = 0$, and $c_3 = -20$. Thus a solution of the given boundary value problem is

$$u(x, t) = 60e^{-t} \sin x - 20e^{-9t} \sin 3x. \qquad \blacksquare$$

The boundary value problem in Example 1 is exceptionally simple in that only a finite number of homogeneous solutions are needed to satisfy by superposition the nonhomogeneous boundary condition. It is more usual that an infinite sequence u_1, u_2, u_3, . . . of functions satisfying (12a) and (12b) is required. If so, we write the infinite series

$$\blacktriangleright \qquad u(x, t) = \sum_{n=1}^{\infty} c_n u_n(x, t) \qquad (15)$$

and then attempt to determine the coefficients c_1, c_2, c_3, . . . in order to satisfy (12c) as well. The following principle summarizes the properties of this infinite series that must be verified in order to ensure that we have a solution of the boundary value problem in (12a) through (12c).

PRINCIPLE: **Superposition of Solutions**

Suppose that each of the functions u_1, u_2, u_3, . . . satisfies both the differential equation in (12a) (for $0 < x < L$ and $t > 0$) and the homogeneous conditions in (12b). Suppose also that the coefficients in Eq. (15) are chosen to meet the following three criteria:

1. For $0 < x < L$ and $t > 0$, the function determined by the series in (15) is continuous and termwise differentiable (once with respect to t and twice with respect to x).

2. $\displaystyle\sum_{n=1}^{\infty} c_n u_n(x, 0) = f(x)$.

3. The function $u(x, t)$ determined by Eq. (15) interior to the strip $0 \leqq x \leqq L$ and $t \geqq 0$, and by the boundary conditions in (12b) and (12c) on its boundary, is continuous.

Then $u(x, t)$ is a solution of the boundary value problem in (12a) through (12c). \blacksquare

In the method of separation of variables described next, we concentrate on finding the solutions u_1, u_2, u_3, . . . satisfying the homogeneous conditions and on determining the coefficients so that the series in Eq. (15) satisfies the nonhomogeneous condition upon substitution of $t = 0$. At this point we have only a *formal* series solution of the boundary value problem—one that is subject to verification of the continuity and differentiability conditions given in part (1) of the theorem. If the function $f(x)$ in (12c) is piecewise smooth, it can be proved that a formal series solution always satisfies these restrictions and, moreover, is the unique solution of the boundary value problem. For this proof, see Chapter 6 of R. V. Churchill and J. W. Brown, *Fourier Series and Boundary Value Problems,* 3rd ed. (New York: McGraw-Hill, 1978).

Separation of Variables

This method of solving the boundary value problem of (12a) through (12c) for the heated rod was introduced by Fourier in his study of heat cited in Section 9.1. We first search for the *building block* functions u_1, u_2, u_3, . . . that satisfy the differential equation $u_t = ku_{xx}$ and the homogeneous conditions $u(0, t) = u(L, t) = 0$, with each of these functions being of the special form

$$u(x, t) = X(x)T(t) \tag{16}$$

in which the variables x and t are "separated." Substitution of Eq. (16) in $u_t = ku_{xx}$ yields $XT' = kX''T$, where for brevity we write T' for $T'(t)$ and X'' for $X''(x)$. Division of both sides by kXT then gives

$$\frac{X''}{X} = \frac{T'}{kT}. \tag{17}$$

The left-hand side of Eq. (17) is a function of x alone, but the right-hand side is a function of t alone. If t is held constant on the right-hand side, then the left-hand side X''/X must remain constant as x varies. Similarly, if x is held constant on the left-hand side, then the right-hand side T'/kT must remain constant as t varies. Consequently, equality can hold only if each of these two expressions is the same *constant,* which for convenience we denote by $-\lambda$. Thus Eq. (17) becomes

$$\frac{X''}{X} = \frac{T'}{kT} = -\lambda, \tag{18}$$

which consists of the two equations

$$X''(x) + \lambda X(x) = 0, \tag{19}$$

$$T'(t) + \lambda kT(t) = 0. \tag{20}$$

It follows that the product function $u(x, t) = X(x)T(t)$ satisfies the partial differential equation $u_t = ku_{xx}$ if $X(x)$ and $T(t)$ separately satisfy the ordinary differential equations in (19) and (20) for some value of the constant λ.

We focus first on $X(x)$. The homogeneous endpoint conditions are

$$u(0, t) = X(0)T(t) = 0, \qquad u(L, t) = X(L)T(t) = 0. \tag{21}$$

If $T(t)$ is to be a nontrivial function of t, then (21) can hold only if $X(0) = X(L) = 0$. Thus $X(x)$ must satisfy the endpoint value problem

$$X'' + \lambda X = 0,$$
$$X(0) = 0, \quad X(L) = 0. \tag{22}$$

This is actually an eigenvalue problem of the type we discussed in Section 3.8. Indeed, we saw in Example 3 of that section that (22) has a nontrivial solution if and only if λ is one of the eigenvalues

$$\lambda_n = \frac{n^2\pi^2}{L^2}, \qquad n = 1, 2, 3, \ldots, \tag{23}$$

and that an eigenfunction associated with λ_n is

$$X_n(x) = \sin\frac{n\pi x}{L}, \qquad n = 1, 2, 3, \ldots. \tag{24}$$

Recall that the reasoning behind (23) and (24) is as follows. If $\lambda = 0$, then (22) obviously implies that $X(x) \equiv 0$. If $\lambda = -\alpha^2 < 0$, then

$$X(x) = A \cosh \alpha x + B \sinh \alpha x,$$

and then the conditions $X(0) = 0 = X(L)$ imply that $A = B = 0$. Hence the only possibility for a nontrivial eigenfunction is that $\lambda = \alpha^2 > 0$. Then

$$X(x) = A \cos \alpha x + B \sin \alpha x,$$

and the conditions $X(0) = 0 = X(L)$ then imply that $A = 0$ and that $\alpha = n\pi/L$ for some positive integer n. Whenever separation of variables leads to an unfamiliar eigenvalue problem, we generally must consider separately the cases $\lambda = 0$, $\lambda = -\alpha^2 < 0$, and $\lambda = \alpha^2 > 0$.

Now we turn our attention to Eq. (20), knowing that the constant λ must be one of the eigenvalues listed in (23). For the nth of these possibilities we write Eq. (20) as

$$T_n' + \frac{n^2\pi^2 k}{L^2} T_n = 0, \tag{25}$$

in anticipation of a different solution $T_n(t)$ for each different integer n. A nontrivial solution of this equation is

$$T_n(t) = e^{-n^2\pi^2 kt/L^2}. \tag{26}$$

We omit the arbitrary constant because it will (in effect) be inserted later.

To summarize our progress, we have discovered the two associated sequences $\{X_n\}_1^\infty$ and $\{T_n\}_1^\infty$ of functions given in (24) and (26). Together they yield the sequence of product functions

$$u_n(x, t) = X_n(x) T_n(t) = e^{-n^2\pi^2 kt/L^2} \sin \frac{n\pi x}{L}, \tag{27}$$

$n = 1, 2, 3, \ldots$. Each of these functions satisfies both the heat equation $u_t = ku_{xx}$ and the homogeneous conditions $u(0, t) = u(L, t) = 0$. Now we combine these functions (*superposition*) to attempt to satisfy the nonhomogeneous condition $u(x, 0) = f(x)$ as well. We therefore form the infinite series

$$u(x, t) = \sum_{n=1}^{\infty} c_n u_n(x, t) = \sum_{n=1}^{\infty} c_n e^{-n^2\pi^2 kt/L^2} \sin \frac{n\pi x}{L}. \tag{28}$$

It remains only to determine the constant coefficients $\{c_n\}_1^\infty$ so that

$$u(x, 0) = \sum_{n=1}^{\infty} c_n \sin \frac{n\pi x}{L} = f(x). \tag{29}$$

But this will be the Fourier sine series of $f(x)$ on $[0, L]$ provided we choose

$$\blacktriangleright \qquad c_n = b_n = \frac{2}{L} \int_0^L f(x) \sin \frac{n\pi x}{L}\, dx \tag{30}$$

for each $n = 1, 2, 3, \ldots$. Thus we have the following result.

THEOREM 1: The Heated Rod with Zero Endpoint Temperatures

The boundary value problem in (12a)–(12c) for a heated rod with zero endpoint temperatures has the formal series solution

$$u(x, t) = \sum_{n=1}^{\infty} b_n e^{-n^2 \pi^2 kt/L^2} \sin \frac{n\pi x}{L}, \qquad (31)$$

where the $\{b_n\}$ are the Fourier sine coefficients in Eq. (30) of the rod's initial temperature function $f(x)$.

Remark: By taking the limit in (31) termwise as $t \to +\infty$, we get $u(x, \infty) \equiv 0$, as we expect because the two ends of the rod are held at temperature zero.

The series solution in Eq. (31) usually converges quite rapidly, unless t is quite small, because of the presence of the negative exponential factors. Therefore it is practical for numerical computations. For use in problems and examples, values of the thermal diffusivity constant k for some common materials are listed in the table in Fig. 9.5.3.

Material	k (cm²/s)
Silver	1.70
Copper	1.15
Aluminum	0.85
Iron	0.15
Concrete	0.005

FIGURE 9.5.3. Some thermal diffusivity constants

EXAMPLE 2 Suppose that a rod 50 cm long is immersed in steam until its temperature is 100°C throughout. At time $t = 0$, its lateral surface is insulated and its two ends embedded in ice at 0°C. Calculate the temperature at its midpoint after a half hour if the rod is made of (a) iron; (b) concrete.

Solution The boundary value problem for this rod is

$$u_t = ku_{xx};$$

$$u(0, t) = u(50, t) = 0,$$

$$u(x, 0) = 100.$$

The Fourier sine series of $f(x) \equiv 100$ is

$$f(x) = 100 = \frac{400}{\pi} \sum_{n \text{ odd}} \frac{1}{n} \sin \frac{n\pi x}{50}$$

for $0 < x < 50$. The coefficients $\{b_n\}$ in Eq. (31) are simply the Fourier sine coefficients of $f(x)$, so the solution of the boundary value problem is

$$u(x, t) = \frac{400}{\pi} \sum_{n \text{ odd}} \frac{1}{n} e^{-n^2 \pi^2 kt/2500} \sin \frac{n\pi x}{50}.$$

Hence the temperature at the midpoint $x = 25$ cm at time $t = 1800$ s is

$$u(25, 1800) = \frac{400}{\pi} \sum_{n \text{ odd}} \frac{(-1)^{n+1}}{n} e^{-18n^2 \pi^2 k/25}.$$

(a) With $k = 0.15$ for iron, this series gives

$$u \approx 43.8519 - 0.0029 + 0.0000 - \cdots \approx 43.85°C.$$

(b) With $k = 0.005$ for concrete, it gives

$$u \approx 122.8795 - 30.8257 + 10.4754 - 3.1894$$
$$+ \, 0.7958 - 0.1572 + 0.0242 - 0.0029$$
$$+ \, 0.0003 - 0.0000 + \cdots \approx 100.00°\text{C}.$$

Thus concrete is a very effective insulator. ■

Insulated Endpoint Conditions

We now consider the boundary value problem

$$\frac{\partial u}{\partial t} = k \frac{\partial^2 u}{\partial x^2} \qquad (0 < x < L, \quad t > 0); \tag{32a}$$

$$u_x(0, t) = u_x(L, t) = 0, \tag{32b}$$

$$u(x, 0) = f(x), \tag{32c}$$

which corresponds to a rod of length L with initial temperature $f(x)$, but with its two ends insulated. The separation of variables $u(x, t) = X(x)T(t)$ proceeds as in Eqs. (16) through (20) without change. But the homogeneous endpoint conditions in (32b) yield $X'(0) = X'(L) = 0$. Thus $X(t)$ must satisfy the endpoint value problem

$$X'' + \lambda X = 0,$$
$$X'(0) = 0, \qquad X'(L) = 0. \tag{33}$$

We must consider separately the possibilities $\lambda = 0$, $\lambda = -\alpha^2 < 0$, and $\lambda = +\alpha^2 > 0$ for the eigenvalues.

With $\lambda = 0$, the general solution of $X'' = 0$ is $X(x) = Ax + B$, so $X'(x) = A$. Hence the endpoint conditions in (33) require $A = 0$, but B may be nonzero. Because a constant multiple of an eigenfunction is an eigenfunction, we can choose any constant value we wish for B. Thus, with $B = 1$, we have the zero eigenvalue and associated eigenfunction

$$\lambda_0 = 0, \qquad X_0(x) \equiv 1. \tag{34}$$

With $\lambda = 0$ in Eq. (20), we get $T'(t) = 0$, so we may take $T_0(t) \equiv 1$ as well.

With $\lambda = -\alpha^2 < 0$, the general solution of the equation $X'' - \alpha^2 X = 0$ is

$$X(x) = A \cosh \alpha x + B \sinh \alpha x,$$

and we readily verify that $X'(0) = X'(L) = 0$ only if $A = B = 0$. Thus there are no negative eigenvalues.

With $\lambda = +\alpha^2 > 0$, the general solution of $X'' + \alpha^2 X = 0$ is

$$X(x) = A \cos \alpha x + B \sin \alpha x,$$

$$X'(x) = -A\alpha \sin \alpha x + B\alpha \cos \alpha x.$$

Hence $X'(0) = 0$ implies that $B = 0$, and then

$$X'(L) = -A\alpha \sin \alpha L = 0$$

requires that αL be an integral multiple of π, because $\alpha \neq 0$ and $A \neq 0$ if we are to have a nontrivial solution. Thus we have the infinite sequence of eigenvalues and asso-

ciated eigenfunctions

$$\lambda_n = \alpha_n^2 = \frac{n^2\pi^2}{L^2}, \qquad X_n(x) = \cos\frac{n\pi x}{L} \tag{35}$$

for $n = 1, 2, 3, \ldots$. Just as before, the solution of Eq. (20) with $\lambda = n^2\pi^2/L^2$ is $T_n(t) = e^{-n^2\pi^2 kt/L^2}$.

Therefore our product functions satisfying the homogeneous conditions are

$$u_0(x, t) \equiv 1; \qquad u_n(x, t) = e^{-n^2\pi^2 kt/L^2}\cos\frac{n\pi x}{L} \tag{36}$$

for $n = 1, 2, 3, \ldots$. Hence our trial solution is

$$u(x, t) = c_0 + \sum_{n=1}^{\infty} c_n e^{-n^2\pi^2 kt/L^2}\cos\frac{n\pi x}{L}. \tag{37}$$

In order to satisfy the nonhomogeneous condition $u(x, 0) = f(x)$, we obviously want Eq. (37) to reduce when $t = 0$ to the Fourier cosine series

$$f(x) = \frac{a_0}{2} + \sum_{n=1}^{\infty} a_n\cos\frac{n\pi x}{L}, \tag{38}$$

where

$$a_n = \frac{2}{L}\int_0^L f(x)\cos\frac{n\pi x}{L}\,dx \tag{39}$$

for $n = 0, 1, 2, \ldots$. Thus we have the following result.

THEOREM 2: Heated Rod with Insulated Ends

The boundary value problem in (32a)–(32c) for a heated rod with insulated ends has the formal series solution

$$u(x, t) = \frac{a_0}{2} + \sum_{n=1}^{\infty} a_n e^{-n^2\pi^2 kt/L^2}\cos\frac{n\pi x}{L} \tag{40}$$

where the $\{a_n\}$ are the Fourier cosine coefficients in (39) of the rod's initial temperature function $f(x)$. ∎

Remark: Note that

$$\lim_{t\to\infty} u(x, t) = \frac{a_0}{2} = \frac{1}{L}\int_0^L f(x)\,dx, \tag{41}$$

the average value of the initial temperature. With both the lateral surface and the ends of the rod insulated, its original heat content ultimately distributes itself uniformly throughout the rod.

Finally, we point out that, although we set up the boundary value problems (12a) through (12c) and (32a) through (32c) for a rod of length L, they also model the temperature $u(x, t)$ within the infinite slab $0 \le x \le L$ in three-dimensional space if its initial temperature $f(x)$ depends only upon x, and its two faces $x = 0$ and $x = L$ are either both insulated or both held at temperature zero.

9.5 Problems

Solve the boundary value problems in Problems 1 through 12.

1. $u_t = 3u_{xx}$, $0 < t < \pi$, $t > 0$; $u(0, t) = u(\pi, t) = 0$, $u(x, 0) = 4 \sin 2x$

2. $u_t = 10u_{xx}$, $0 < x < 5$, $t > 0$; $u_x(0, t) = u_x(5, t) = 0$, $u(x, 0) = 7$

3. $u_t = 2u_{xx}$, $0 < x < 1$, $t > 0$; $u(0, t) = u(1, t) = 0$, $u(x, 0) = 5 \sin \pi x - \frac{1}{5} \sin 3\pi x$

4. $u_t = u_{xx}$, $0 < x < \pi$, $t > 0$; $u(0, t) = u(\pi, t) = 0$, $u(x, 0) = 4 \sin 4x \cos 2x$

5. $u_t = 2u_{xx}$, $0 < x < 3$, $t > 0$; $u_x(0, t) = u_x(3, t) = 0$, $u(x, 0) = 4 \cos \frac{2}{3} \pi x - 2 \cos \frac{4}{3} \pi x$

6. $2u_t = u_{xx}$, $0 < x < 1$, $t > 0$; $u(0, t) = u(1, t) = 0$, $u(x, 0) = 4 \sin \pi x \cos^3 \pi x$

7. $3u_t = u_{xx}$, $0 < x < 2$, $t > 0$; $u_x(0, t) = u_x(2, t) = 0$, $u(x, 0) = \cos^2 2\pi x$

8. $u_t = u_{xx}$, $0 < x < 2$, $t > 0$; $u_x(0, t) = u_x(2, t) = 0$, $u(x, 0) = 10 \cos \pi x \cos 3\pi x$

9. $10u_t = u_{xx}$, $0 < x < 5$, $t > 0$; $u(0, t) = u(5, t) = 0$, $u(x, 0) = 25$

10. $5u_t = u_{xx}$, $0 < x < 10$, $t > 0$; $u(0, t) = u(10, t) = 0$, $u(x, 0) = 4x$

11. $5u_t = u_{xx}$, $0 < x < 10$, $t > 0$; $u_x(0, t) = u_x(10, t) = 0$, $u(x, 0) = 4x$

12. $u_t = u_{xx}$, $0 < x < 100$, $t > 0$; $u(0, t) = u(100, t) = 0$; $u(x, 0) = x(100 - x)$

13. Suppose that a rod 40 cm long with insulated lateral surface is heated to a uniform temperature of 100°C, and that at time $t = 0$ its two ends are embedded in ice at 0°C. (a) Find the formal series solution for the temperature $u(x, t)$ of the rod. (b) In the case the rod is made of copper, show that after 5 min the temperature at its midpoint is about 15°C. (c) In the case the rod is made of concrete, use the first term of the series to find the time required for its midpoint to cool to 15°C.

14. A copper rod 50 cm long with insulated lateral surface has initial temperature $u(x, 0) = 2x$, and at time $t = 0$ its two ends are insulated. (a) Find $u(x, t)$. (b) What will its temperature be at $x = 10$ after 1 min? (c) After approximately how long will its temperature at $x = 10$ be 45°C?

15. The two faces of the slab $0 \leq x \leq L$ are kept at temperature zero, and the initial temperature of the slab is given by $u(x, 0) = A$ (a constant) for $0 < x < L/2$, $u(x, 0) = 0$ for $L/2 < x < L$. Derive the formal series solution

$$u(x, t) = \frac{4A}{\pi} \sum_{n=1}^{\infty} \frac{\sin^2 (n\pi/4)}{n} e^{-n^2 \pi^2 kt/L^2} \sin \frac{n\pi x}{L}.$$

16. Two iron slabs are each 25 cm thick. Initially one is at temperature 100°C throughout and the other is at temperature 0°C. At time $t = 0$ they are placed face to face, and their outer faces are kept at 0°C. (a) Use the result of Problem 15 to find that after a half hour the temperature of their common face is approximately 22°C. (b) Suppose that the two slabs are instead made of concrete. How long will it be until their common face reaches a temperature of 22°C?

17. (Steady-state and transient temperatures) Let a laterally insulated rod with initial temperature $u(x, 0) = f(x)$ have fixed endpoint temperatures $u(0, t) = A$ and $u(L, t) = B$. (a) It is observed empirically that as $t \to +\infty$, $u(x, t)$ approaches a **steady-state temperature** $u_{ss}(x)$ that corresponds to setting $u_t = 0$ in the boundary value problem. Thus $u_{ss}(x)$ is the solution of the endpoint value problem

$$\frac{\partial^2 u_{ss}}{\partial x^2} = 0, \qquad u_{ss}(0) = A, \qquad u_{ss}(L) = B.$$

Find $u_{ss}(x)$. (b) The **transient temperature** $u_{tr}(x, t)$ is defined to be

$$u_{tr}(x, t) = u(x, t) - u_{ss}(x).$$

Show that u_{tr} satisfies the boundary value problem

$$\frac{\partial u_{tr}}{\partial t} = k \frac{\partial^2 u_{tr}}{\partial x^2};$$

$$u_{tr}(0, t) = u_{tr}(L, t) = 0,$$

$$u_{tr}(x, 0) = g(x) = f(x) - u_{ss}(x).$$

(c) Conclude from the formulas in (30) and (31) that

$$u(x, t) = u_{ss}(x) + u_{tr}(x, t)$$

$$= u_{ss}(x) + \sum_{n=1}^{\infty} c_n e^{-n^2 \pi^2 kt/L^2} \sin \frac{n\pi x}{L},$$

where

$$c_n = \frac{2}{L} \int_0^L [f(x) - u_{ss}(x)] \sin \frac{n\pi x}{L} dx.$$

18. Suppose that a laterally insulated rod with length $L = 50$ and thermal diffusivity $k = 1$ has initial temperature $u(x, 0) = 0$ and endpoint temperatures $u(0, t) = 0$, $u(50, t) = 100$. Apply the result of Problem 17 to show that

$$u(x, t) = 2x - \frac{200}{\pi} \sum_{n=1}^{\infty} \frac{(-1)^{n+1}}{n} e^{-n^2 \pi^2 kt/2500} \sin \frac{n\pi x}{50}.$$

19. Suppose that heat is generated within a laterally insulated rod at the rate of $q(x, t)$ calories per second per cubic centimeter. Extend the derivation of the heat equation in this section to de-

rive the equation

$$\frac{\partial u}{\partial t} = k\frac{\partial^2 u}{\partial x^2} + \frac{q(x, t)}{c\delta}.$$

20. Suppose that current flowing through a laterally insulated rod generates heat at a constant rate; then Problem 19 yields the equation

$$\frac{\partial u}{\partial t} = k\frac{\partial^2 u}{\partial x^2} + C.$$

Assume the boundary conditions $u(0, t) = u(L, t) = 0$ and $u(x, 0) = f(x)$. (a) Find the steady-state temperature $u_{ss}(x)$ determined by

$$0 = k\frac{d^2 u_{ss}}{dx^2} + C, \qquad u_{ss}(0) = u_{ss}(L) = 0.$$

(b) Show that the transient temperature

$$u_{tr}(x, t) = u(x, t) - u_{ss}(x)$$

satisfies the boundary value problem

$$\frac{\partial u_{tr}}{\partial t} = k\frac{\partial^2 u_{tr}}{\partial x^2};$$

$$u_{tr}(0, t) = u_{tr}(L, t) = 0,$$

$$u_{tr}(x, 0) = g(x) = f(x) - u_{ss}(x).$$

Hence conclude from the formulas in (34) and (35) that

$$u(x, t) = u_{ss}(x) + \sum_{n=1}^{\infty} c_n e^{-n^2\pi^2 kt/L^2} \sin\frac{n\pi x}{L},$$

where

$$c_n = \frac{2}{L}\int_0^L [f(x) - u_{ss}(x)] \sin\frac{n\pi x}{L} dx.$$

21. The answer to Problem 20(a) is $u_{ss}(x) = Cx(L - x)/2k$. If $f(x) \equiv 0$ in Problem 20, so the rod being heated is initially at temperature zero, deduce from the result of part (b) that

$$u(x, t) = \frac{Cx}{2k}(L - x) - \frac{4CL^2}{k\pi^3}\sum_{n\text{ odd}}\frac{1}{n^3} e^{-n^2\pi^2 kt/L^2} \sin\frac{n\pi x}{L}.$$

22. Consider the temperature $u(x, t)$ in a bare slender wire with

$u(0, t) = u(L, t) = 0$ and $u(x, 0) = f(x)$. Instead of being laterally insulated, the wire loses heat to a surrounding medium (at fixed temperature zero) at a rate proportional to $u(x, t)$. (a) Conclude from Problem 19 that

$$\frac{\partial u}{\partial t} = k\frac{\partial^2 u}{\partial x^2} - hu,$$

where h is a positive constant. (b) Then substitute $u(x, t) = e^{-ht}v(x, t)$ to show that $v(x, t)$ satisfies the boundary value problem having the solution given in (30) and (31). Hence conclude that

$$u(x, t) = e^{-ht}\sum_{n=1}^{\infty} c_n e^{-n^2\pi^2 kt/L^2} \sin\frac{n\pi x}{L},$$

where

$$c_n = \frac{2}{L}\int_0^L f(x) \sin\frac{n\pi x}{L} dx.$$

23. Consider a slab with thermal conductivity K occupying the region $0 \le x \le L$. Suppose that, in accord with Newton's law of cooling, each face of the slab loses heat to the surrounding medium (at temperature zero) at the rate of Hu calories per second per square centimeter. Deduce from Eq. (2) that the temperature $u(x, t)$ in the slab satisfies the boundary conditions

$$hu(0, t) - u_x(0, t) = 0 = hu(L, t) + u_x(L, t)$$

where $h = H/K$.

24. Suppose that a laterally insulated rod with length L, thermal diffusivity k, and initial temperature $u(x, 0) = f(x)$ is insulated at the end $x = L$ and held at temperature zero at $x = 0$. (a) Separate the variables to show that the eigenfunctions are

$$X_n(x) = \sin(n\pi x/2L)$$

for n odd. (b) Use the odd half-multiple sine series of Problem 21 in Section 9.3 to derive the solution

$$u(x, t) = \sum_{n\text{ odd}} c_n e^{-n^2\pi^2 kt/4L^2} \sin\frac{n\pi x}{2L},$$

where

$$c_n = \frac{2}{L}\int_0^L f(x) \sin\frac{n\pi x}{2L} dx.$$

9.5 Computing Project

First let's investigate numerically the temperature function

$$u(x, t) = \frac{4T_0}{\pi}\sum_{n\text{ odd}}\frac{1}{n}\exp\left(-\frac{n^2\pi^2 kt}{L^2}\right)\sin\frac{n\pi x}{L}$$

of the heated rod of Example 2, of length $L = 50$ cm, having constant initial temperature $T_0 = 100$ and thermal diffusivity $k = 0.15$ (for iron). The following *Mathematica* function sums the first m nonzero terms of this series.

```
L = 50; T0 = 100; k = 0.15; m = 25;

u[x_,t_] :=

Sum[ (4*T0/Pi)*Exp[-n*n*Pi*Pi*k*t/L^2]*Sin[n*Pi*x/L]/n,

    {n, 1, 2*m - 1, 2} ] // N
```

As a practical matter, $m = 25$ terms suffice to give the value $u(x, t)$ after 10 seconds (or longer) with two decimal places of accuracy throughout the interval $0 \leq x \leq 50$. (How might you check this assertion?) For instance, the midpoint temperature

```
u[ 25, 1800 ]
```

43.849

agrees with that found in the text.

The graph of $u(x, 30)$ in Fig. 9.5.4 shows that after 30 seconds the rod has cooled appreciably only near its two ends, and still has temperature near 100° for $10 \leq x \leq 40$. Figure 9.5.5 shows the graph of $u(x, 1800)$ after 30 minutes, and illustrates the fact (?) that the rod's maximum temperature is always at its midpoint, where $x = 25$.

The graph of $u(25, t)$ for a two-hour period shown in Fig. 9.5.6 indicates that the midpoint temperature takes something more than 1500 seconds (25 minutes) to fall to 50°. Figure 9.5.7 shows a magnification of the graph near its intersection point with the horizontal line $u = 50$, and indicates that this actually takes about 1578 seconds (26 min 18 s).

For your very own rod with constant initial temperature $f(x) = T_0 = 100$ to investigate in this manner, let

$$L = 100 + 10p \qquad \text{and} \qquad k = 1 + (0.1)q,$$

where p is the largest and q is the smallest nonzero digit of your student I.D. number.

FIGURE 9.5.4. Graph of $u(x, 30)$
giving rod temperatures after 30 seconds

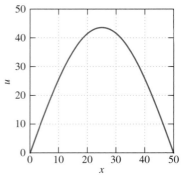

FIGURE 9.5.5. Graph of $u(x, 1800)$
giving rod temperatures after 30 minutes

FIGURE 9.5.6. Graph of $u(25, t)$ giving the rod's midpoint temperatures

FIGURE 9.5.7. Magnification of graph of $u(25, t)$ giving the rod's midpoint temperatures

1. If the two ends of the rod are both held at temperature zero, then determine how long (to the nearest second) it will take for the rod's midpoint temperature to fall to $50°$.

2. If the end $x = L$ of the rod is insulated, but the end $x = 0$ is held at temperature zero, then the temperature function $u(x, t)$ is given by the Fourier series in Problem 24 of this section. Determine how long it will be until the maximum temperature anywhere in the rod is $50°$.

9.6 Vibrating Strings and the One-Dimensional Wave Equation

Although Fourier systematized the method of separation of variables, trigonometric series solutions of partial differential equations had appeared earlier in eighteenth-century investigations of vibrating strings by Euler, d'Alembert, and Daniel Bernoulli. To derive the partial differential equation that models the vibrations of a string, we begin with a flexible uniform string with linear density ρ (in grams per centimeter or slugs per foot) stretched under a tension of T (dynes or pounds) between the fixed points $x = 0$ and $x = L$. Suppose that, as the string vibrates in the xy-plane about its equilibrium position, each point moves parallel to the y-axis, so we can denote by $y(x, t)$ the displacement at time t of the point x of the string. Then, for any fixed value of t, the shape of the string at time t is the curve $y = y(x, t)$. We assume also that the deflection of the string remains so slight that the approximation $\sin \theta \approx \tan \theta = y_x(x, t)$ is quite accurate (Fig. 9.6.1). Finally, we assume that in addition to the internal forces of tension acting tangentially to the string, it is acted on by an external vertical force with linear density $F(x)$ in such units as dynes per centimeter or pounds per foot.

We want to apply Newton's law $F = ma$ to the short segment of string of mass $\rho \, \Delta x$ corresponding to the interval $[x, x + \Delta x]$, with a being the vertical acceleration $y_{tt}(\bar{x}, t)$ of its midpoint. Reading the vertical components of the force shown in Fig. 9.6.1, we get

$$(\rho \, \Delta x) \cdot y_{tt}(\bar{x}, t) \approx T \sin(\theta + \Delta\theta) - T \sin \theta + F(\bar{x}) \, \Delta x$$

$$\approx Ty_x(x + \Delta x, t) - Ty_x(x, t) + F(\bar{x}) \, \Delta x,$$

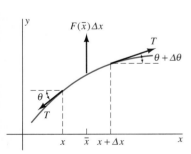

FIGURE 9.6.1. Forces on a short segment of the vibrating string

so division by Δx yields

$$\rho y_{tt}(\bar{x}, t) \approx T \frac{y_x(x + \Delta x, t) - y_x(x, t)}{\Delta x} + F(\bar{x}).$$

When we take the limit as $\Delta x \to 0$ and $\bar{x} \to x$, we obtain the partial differential equation

▶
$$\rho \frac{\partial^2 y}{\partial t^2} = T \frac{\partial^2 y}{\partial x^2} + F(x) \tag{1}$$

that describes the vertical vibrations of a flexible string with constant linear density ρ and tension T under the influence of an external vertical force with linear density $F(x)$. If we set

$$a^2 = \frac{T}{\rho} \tag{2}$$

and set $F(x) \equiv 0$ in (1), we get the **one-dimensional wave equation**

▶
$$\frac{\partial^2 y}{\partial t^2} = a^2 \frac{\partial^2 y}{\partial x^2} \tag{3}$$

that models the *free* vibrations of a uniform flexible string.

The fixed ends of the string at the points $x = 0$ and $x = L$ on the x-axis correspond to the *endpoint conditions*

$$y(0, t) = y(L, t) = 0. \tag{4}$$

Our intuition about the physics of the situation suggests that the motion of the string will be determined if we specify both its **initial position function**

$$y(x, 0) = f(x) \qquad (0 < x < L) \tag{5}$$

and its **initial velocity function**

$$y_t(x, 0) = g(x) \qquad (0 < x < L). \tag{6}$$

On combining Eqs. (3) through (6), we get the boundary value problem

$$\frac{\partial^2 y}{\partial t^2} = a^2 \frac{\partial^2 y}{\partial x^2} \qquad (0 < x < L, \quad t > 0) \tag{7a}$$

$$y(0, t) = y(L, t) = 0, \tag{7b}$$

▶
$$y(x, 0) = f(x) \qquad (0 < x < L) \tag{7c}$$

$$y_t(x, 0) = g(x) \qquad (0 < x < L) \tag{7d}$$

for the displacement function $y(x, t)$ of a freely vibrating string with fixed ends, initial position $f(x)$, and initial velocity $g(x)$.

Solution by Separation of Variables

Like the heat equation, the wave equation in (7a) is linear: Any linear combination of two solutions is again a solution. Another similarity is that the endpoint conditions in (7b) are homogeneous. Unfortunately, the conditions in both (7c) and (7d) are nonhomogeneous; we must deal with *two* nonhomogeneous boundary conditions.

As we described in Section 9.5, the method of separation of variables involves superposition of solutions satisfying the homogeneous conditions to obtain a solution that also satisfies a single nonhomogeneous boundary condition. To adapt the technique to the situation at hand, we adopt the "divide and conquer" strategy of splitting the problem in (7a) through (7d) into the following two separate boundary value problems, each involving only a single nonhomogeneous boundary condition:

Problem A	**Problem B**
$y_{tt} = a^2 y_{xx}$;	$y_{tt} = a^2 y_{xx}$;
$y(0, t) = y(L, t) = 0,$	$y(0, t) = y(L, t) = 0,$
$y(x, 0) = f(x),$	$y(x, 0) = 0,$
$y_t(x, 0) = 0.$	$y_t(x, 0) = g(x).$

If we can separately find a solution $y_A(x, t)$ of Problem A and a solution $y_B(x, t)$ of Problem B, then their sum $y(x, t) = y_A(x, t) + y_B(x, t)$ will be a solution of the original problem in (7a) through (7d) because

$$y(x, 0) = y_A(x, 0) + y_B(x, 0) = f(x) + 0 = f(x)$$

and

$$y_t(x, 0) = \{y_A\}_t(x, 0) + \{y_B\}_t(x, 0) = 0 + g(x) = g(x).$$

So let us attack Problem A with the method of separation of variables. Substitution of

$$y(x, t) = X(x)T(t) \tag{8}$$

in $y_{tt} = a^2 y_{xx}$ yields $XT'' = a^2 X''T$; that is,

$$\frac{X''}{X} = \frac{T''}{a^2 T}. \tag{9}$$

The functions X''/X of x and T''/a^2T of t can agree for all x and all t only if each is equal to the same constant. Consequently we may conclude that

$$\frac{X''}{X} = \frac{T''}{a^2 T} = -\lambda \tag{10}$$

for some constant λ; the minus sign is inserted here merely to facilitate recognition of the eigenvalue problem in (13), given below. Thus our partial differential equation separates into the two ordinary differential equations

$$X'' + \lambda X = 0, \tag{11}$$

$$T'' + \lambda a^2 T = 0. \tag{12}$$

The endpoint conditions

$$y(0, t) = X(0)T(t) = 0, \qquad y(L, t) = X(L)T(t) = 0$$

require that $X(0) = X(L) = 0$ if $T(t)$ is a nontrivial function. Hence $X(x)$ must satisfy the now familiar eigenvalue problem

$$X'' + \lambda X = 0, \qquad X(0) = X(L) = 0. \tag{13}$$

As in Eqs. (23) and (24) of Section 9.5, the eigenvalues of this problem are the numbers

$$\lambda_n = \frac{n^2\pi^2}{L^2}, \qquad n = 1, 2, 3, \cdots, \tag{14}$$

and the eigenfunction associated with λ_n is

$$X_n(x) = \sin\frac{n\pi x}{L}, \qquad n = 1, 2, 3, \cdots. \tag{15}$$

Now we turn to Eq. (12). The homogeneous initial condition

$$y_t(x, 0) = X(x)T'(0) = 0$$

implies that $T'(0) = 0$. Therefore the solution $T_n(t)$ associated with the eigenvalue $\lambda_n = n^2\pi^2/L^2$ must satisfy the conditions

$$T_n'' + \frac{n^2\pi^2a^2}{L^2}T_n = 0, \qquad T_n'(0) = 0. \tag{16}$$

The general solution of the differential equation in (16) is

$$T_n(t) = A_n\cos\frac{n\pi at}{L} + B_n\sin\frac{n\pi at}{L}. \tag{17}$$

Its derivative

$$T_n'(t) = \frac{n\pi a}{L}\left(-A_n\sin\frac{n\pi at}{L} + B_n\cos\frac{n\pi at}{L}\right)$$

satisfies the condition $T_n'(0) = 0$ if $B_n = 0$. Thus a nontrivial solution of (16) is

$$T_n(t) = \cos\frac{n\pi at}{L}. \tag{18}$$

We combine the results in Eqs. (15) and (18) to obtain the infinite sequence of product functions

$$y_n(x, t) = X_n(x)T_n(t) = \cos\frac{n\pi at}{L}\sin\frac{n\pi x}{L}, \tag{19}$$

$n = 1, 2, 3, \ldots$. Each of these *building block* functions satisfies both the wave equation $y_{tt} = a^2y_{xx}$ and the homogeneous boundary conditions in Problem A. By superposition we get the infinite series

$$y_n(x, t) = \sum_{n=1}^{\infty} A_nX_n(x)T_n(t) = \sum_{n=1}^{\infty} A_n\cos\frac{n\pi at}{L}\sin\frac{n\pi x}{L}. \tag{20}$$

It remains only to choose the coefficients $\{A_n\}$ to satisfy the nonhomogeneous boundary condition

$$y(x, 0) = \sum_{n=1}^{\infty} A_n\sin\frac{n\pi x}{L} = f(x) \tag{21}$$

for $0 \leqq x \leqq L$. But this will be the Fourier sine series of $f(x)$ on $[0, L]$ provided that we choose

$$A_n = \frac{2}{L} \int_0^L f(x) \sin \frac{n\pi x}{L} \, dx. \tag{22}$$

Thus we see finally that a formal series solution of Problem A is

$$y(x, t) = \sum_{n=1}^{\infty} A_n \cos \frac{n\pi at}{L} \sin \frac{n\pi x}{L}, \tag{23}$$

with the coefficients $\{A_n\}_1^{\infty}$ computed using Eq. (22). Note that the series in (23) is obtained from the Fourier sine series of $f(x)$ simply by inserting the factor $\cos(n\pi at/L)$ in the nth term. Note also that this term has [circular] frequency $\omega_n = n\pi a/L$.

EXAMPLE 1 It follows immediately that the solution of the boundary value problem

$$\frac{\partial^2 y}{\partial t^2} = 4 \frac{\partial^2 y}{\partial x^2} \qquad (0 < x < \pi, \quad t > 0);$$

$$y(0, \ t) = y(\pi, t) = 0,$$

$$y(x, 0) = \frac{1}{10} \sin^3 x = \frac{3}{40} \sin x - \frac{1}{40} \sin 3x,$$

$$y_t(x, 0) = 0,$$

for which $L = \pi$ and $a = 2$, is

$$y(x, t) = \frac{3}{40} \cos 2t \sin x - \frac{1}{40} \cos 6t \sin 3x.$$

The reason is that we are given explicitly the Fourier sine series of $f(x)$ with $A_1 = \frac{3}{40}, A_3 = -\frac{1}{40}$, and $A_n = 0$ otherwise.

EXAMPLE 2
(A plucked string)

Figure 9.6.2 shows the initial position function $f(x)$ for a stretched string (of length L) that is set in motion by moving its midpoint $x = L/2$ aside the distance $\frac{1}{2}bL$ and then releasing it from rest at time $t = 0$. The corresponding boundary value problem is

$$y_{tt} = a^2 y_{xx} \qquad (0 < x < L, \quad t > 0);$$

$$y(0, t) = y(L, t) = 0,$$

$$y(x, 0) = f(x),$$

$$y_t(x, 0) = 0,$$

FIGURE 9.6.2. The initial position of the plucked string of Example 2

where $f(x) = bx$ for $0 \leq x \leq L/2$ and $f(x) = b(L - x)$ for $L/2 \leq x \leq L$. Find $y(x, t)$.

Solution The nth Fourier sine coefficient of $f(x)$ is

$$A_n = \frac{2}{L} \int_0^L f(x) \sin \frac{n\pi x}{L} \, dx$$

$$= \frac{2}{L} \int_0^{L/2} bx \sin \frac{n\pi x}{L} \, dx + \frac{2}{L} \int_{L/2}^L b(L - x) \sin \frac{n\pi x}{L} \, dx;$$

it follows that

$$A_n = \frac{4bL}{n^2\pi^2}\sin\frac{n\pi}{2}.$$

Hence Eq. (23) yields the formal series solution

$$
\begin{aligned}
y(x, t) &= \frac{4bL}{\pi^2}\sum_{n=1}^{\infty}\frac{1}{n^2}\sin\frac{n\pi}{2}\cos\frac{n\pi at}{L}\sin\frac{n\pi x}{L} \\
&= \frac{4bL}{\pi^2}\left(\cos\frac{\pi at}{L}\sin\frac{\pi x}{L} - \frac{1}{3^2}\cos\frac{3\pi at}{L}\sin\frac{3\pi x}{L} + \cdots\right). \quad (24) \quad\blacksquare
\end{aligned}
$$

Music

Numerous familiar musical instruments employ vibrating strings to generate the sounds they produce. When a string vibrates with a given frequency, vibrations at this frequency are transmitted through the air—in the form of periodic variations in air density called **sound waves**—to the ear of the listener. For instance, middle C is a *tone* with a frequency of approximately 256 Hz. When several tones are heard simultaneously, the combination is perceived as harmonious if the ratios of their frequencies are nearly ratios of small whole numbers; otherwise many perceive the combinations as dissonant.

The series in Eq. (23) represents the motion of a string as a superposition of infinitely many vibrations with different frequencies. The nth term

$$A_n\cos\frac{n\pi at}{L}\sin\frac{n\pi x}{L}$$

represents a vibration with frequency

$$\nu_n = \frac{\omega_n}{2\pi} = \frac{n\pi a/L}{2\pi} = \frac{n}{2L}\sqrt{\frac{T}{\rho}}\quad\text{(Hz)}. \quad (25)$$

The lowest of these frequencies,

$$\nu_1 = \frac{1}{2L}\sqrt{\frac{T}{\rho}}\quad\text{(Hz)}, \quad (26)$$

is called the **fundamental frequency,** and it is ordinarily predominant in the sound we hear. The frequency $\nu_n = n\nu_1$ of the nth **overtone** or **harmonic** is an integral multiple of ν_1, and this is why the sound of a single vibrating string is harmonious rather than dissonant.

Note in Eq. (26) that the fundamental frequency ν_1 is proportional to \sqrt{T} and inversely proportional to L and to $\sqrt{\rho}$. Thus we can double this frequency—and hence get a fundamental tone one **octave** higher—either by halving the length L or by quadrupling the tension T. The initial conditions do *not* affect ν_1; instead, they determine the coefficients in (23) and hence the extent to which the higher harmonics contribute to the sound produced. Therefore the initial conditions affect the **timbre,** or overall frequency mixture, rather than the fundamental frequency. (Technically this is true only for relatively small displacements of the string; if you strike a piano key rather

forcefully you may be able to detect a very slight and very brief initial deviation from the usual frequency of the note.)

According to one (rather simplistic) theory of hearing, the loudness of the sound produced by a vibrating string is proportional to its total [kinetic plus potential] energy, which is given by

$$E = \frac{1}{2} \int_0^L \left[\rho \left(\frac{\partial y}{\partial t} \right)^2 + T \left(\frac{\partial y}{\partial x} \right)^2 \right] dx. \tag{27}$$

In Problem 17 we ask you to show that substitution of the series in (23) in the formula in (27) yields

$$E = \frac{\pi^2 T}{4L} \sum_{n=1}^{\infty} n^2 A_n^2. \tag{28}$$

The ratio of the nth term $n^2 A_n^2$ to the sum $\sum n^2 A_n^2$ is then the portion of the whole sound attributable to the nth harmonic.

We illustrate this theory with the series in (24), which describes the motion of the plucked string of Example 2. Note that the even harmonics are missing, and that $A_n = 4bL/\pi^2 n^2$ for n odd. Hence Eq. (28) gives

$$E = \frac{\pi^2 T}{4L} \sum_{n \text{ odd}} n^2 \frac{16 b^2 L^2}{\pi^4 n^4} = \frac{4b^2 LT}{\pi^2} \sum_{n \text{ odd}} \frac{1}{n^2},$$

so the proportion of the sound associated with the nth harmonic (for n odd) is

$$\frac{1/n^2}{\displaystyle\sum_{n \text{ odd}} 1/n^2} = \frac{1/n^2}{\pi^2/8} = \frac{8}{\pi^2 n^2}.$$

Substituting $n = 1$ and $n = 3$, we find that 81.06% of the sound of the string of Example 2 is associated with the fundamental tone and 9.01% with the harmonic corresponding to $n = 3$.

The d'Alembert Solution

In contrast to series solutions of the heat equation, formal series solutions of the wave equation ordinarily do *not* possess sufficient termwise differentiability to permit verification of the solution by application of a superposition theorem analogous to the one stated in Section 9.5. For instance, termwise differentiation of the series in (24) would yield the series

$$\frac{\partial^2 y}{\partial x^2} = -\frac{4b}{L} \sum_{n=1}^{\infty} \sin \frac{n\pi}{2} \cos \frac{n\pi a t}{L} \sin \frac{n\pi x}{L},$$

which generally fails to converge, because the "convergence factor" $1/n^2$ has disappeared after the second differentiation.

There is, however, an alternative approach that both verifies the solution in (23) and yields valuable additional information about it. If we apply the trigonometric identity

$$2 \sin A \cos B = \sin(A + B) + \sin(A - B)$$

with $A = n\pi x/L$ and $B = n\pi at/L$, then (23) gives

$$y(x, t) = \sum_{n=1}^{\infty} A_n \sin \frac{n\pi x}{L} \cos \frac{n\pi at}{L}$$

$$= \frac{1}{2} \sum_{n=1}^{\infty} A_n \sin \frac{n\pi}{L} (x + at) + \frac{1}{2} \sum_{n=1}^{\infty} A_n \sin \frac{n\pi}{L} (x - at). \qquad (29)$$

But, by definition of the coefficients,

$$\sum_{n=1}^{\infty} A_n \sin \frac{n\pi x}{L} = F(x)$$

for all x, where $F(x)$ is the *odd* extension of period $2L$ of the initial position function $f(x)$. Hence (29) means that

$$\blacktriangleright \qquad\qquad y(x, t) = \frac{1}{2} [F(x + at) + F(x - at)]. \qquad (30)$$

Therefore the series in (23) converges to the expression on the right-hand side in (30), which is known as the **d'Alembert form** of the solution of Problem A for the vibrating string. Moreover, using the chain rule it is easy to verify (Problems 13 and 14) that the function $y(x, t)$ defined in (30) does, indeed, satisfy the equation $y_{tt} = a^2 y_{xx}$ (under the assumption that F is twice differentiable), as well as the boundary conditions $y(0, t) = y(L, t) = 0$ and $y(x, 0) = f(x)$.

For any function $F(x)$, the functions $F(x + at)$ and $F(x - at)$ represent "waves" moving to the left and right, respectively, along the x-axis with speed a. This fact is illustrated in Fig. 9.6.3, which shows the graphs of these two functions for successive

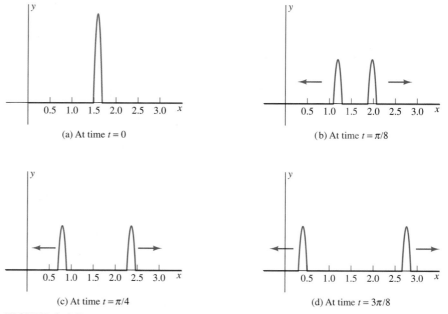

(a) At time $t = 0$

(b) At time $t = \pi/8$

(c) At time $t = \pi/4$

(d) At time $t = 3\pi/8$

FIGURE 9.6.3. The pulse $F(x)$ produces two waves—one moving to the left, one to the right

values of t, in a typical case where the initial position function $F(x)$ is a pulse function centered at the midpoint $x = \pi/2$ of a string of length $L = \pi$ with $a = 1$ (so the fundamental period of vibration is 2π). Thus the d'Alembert solution in (30) expresses $y(x, t)$ as a superposition of two waves moving in opposite directions with speed a. This is why the equation $y_{tt} = a^2 y_{xx}$ is called the *wave* equation.

Strings with Initial Velocity

The separation of variables solution of Problem B, with initial conditions $y(x, 0) = 0$ and $y_t(x, t) = g(x)$, proceeds precisely as did that of Problem A until Eq. (16) is reached. But then $y(x, 0) = X(x)T(0) = 0$ implies that $T(0) = 0$, so instead of (16) we have

$$\frac{d^2 T_n}{dt^2} + \frac{n^2 \pi^2 a^2}{L^2} T_n = 0, \qquad T_n(0) = 0. \tag{31}$$

From Eq. (17) we see that a nontrivial solution of (31) is

$$T_n(t) = \sin \frac{n \pi a t}{L}. \tag{32}$$

Our formal power series solution is therefore of the form

$$\blacktriangleright \qquad y(x, t) = \sum_{n=1}^{\infty} B_n \sin \frac{n \pi a t}{L} \sin \frac{n \pi x}{L}, \tag{33}$$

so we want to choose the coefficients $\{B_n\}$ so that

$$y_t(x, 0) = \sum_{n=1}^{\infty} B_n \frac{n \pi a}{L} \sin \frac{n \pi x}{L} = g(x). \tag{34}$$

Thus we want $B_n \cdot n \pi a/L$ to be the Fourier sine coefficient b_n of $g(x)$ on $[0, L]$:

$$B_n \frac{n \pi a}{L} = b_n = \frac{2}{L} \int_0^L g(x) \sin \frac{n \pi x}{L} \, dx.$$

Hence we choose

$$\blacktriangleright \qquad B_n = \frac{2}{n \pi a} \int_0^L g(x) \sin \frac{n \pi x}{L} \, dx \tag{35}$$

in order for $y(x, t)$ in (33) to be a formal series solution of Problem B.

EXAMPLE 3 Consider a string on a guitar lying crosswise in the back of a pickup truck that at time $t = 0$ slams into a brick wall with speed v_0. Then $g(x) \equiv v_0$, so

$$B_n = \frac{2}{n \pi a} \int_0^L v_0 \sin \frac{n \pi x}{L} \, dx = \frac{2 v_0 L}{n^2 \pi^2 a} [1 - (-1)^n].$$

Hence the series in (33) gives

$$y(x, t) = \frac{4 v_0 L}{\pi^2 a} \sum_{n \text{ odd}} \frac{1}{n^2} \sin \frac{n \pi a t}{L} \sin \frac{n \pi x}{L}. \qquad \blacksquare$$

If we differentiate the series in (33) termwise with respect to t, we get

$$y_t(x, t) = \sum_{n=1}^{\infty} b_n \sin \frac{n\pi x}{L} \cos \frac{n\pi a t}{L} = \frac{1}{2}[G(x + at) + G(x - at)], \quad (36)$$

where G is the odd period $2L$ extension of the initial velocity function $g(x)$, using the same device as in the derivation of Eq. (30). In Problem 15 we ask you to deduce that

$$y(x, t) = \frac{1}{2a}[H(x + at) + H(x - at)], \quad (37)$$

where the function $H(x)$ is defined to be

$$H(x) = \int_0^x G(s)\, ds. \quad (38)$$

If, finally, a string has both an initial position function $y(x, 0) = f(x)$ and an initial velocity $y_t(x, 0) = g(x)$, then we can obtain its displacement function $y(x, t)$ by adding the d'Alembert solutions of Problems A and B given in Eqs. (30) and (37), respectively. Hence the vibrations of this string with general initial conditions are described by

$$y(x, t) = \frac{1}{2}[F(x + at) + F(x - at)] + \frac{1}{2a}[H(x + at) + H(x - at)], \quad (39)$$

a superposition of four waves moving along the x-axis with speed a, two moving to the left and two to the right.

9.6 Problems

Solve the boundary value problems in Problems 1 through 10.

1. $y_{tt} = 4y_{xx}$, $0 < x < \pi$, $t > 0$; $y(0, t) = y(\pi, t) = 0$, $y(x, 0) = \frac{1}{10}\sin 2x$, $y_t(x, 0) = 0$

2. $y_{tt} = y_{xx}$, $0 < x < 1$, $t > 0$; $y(0, t) = y(1, t) = 0$, $y(x, 0) = \frac{1}{10}\sin \pi x - \frac{1}{20}\sin 3\pi x$, $y_t(x, 0) = 0$

3. $4y_{tt} = y_{xx}$, $0 < x < \pi$, $t > 0$; $y(0, t) = y(\pi, t) = 0$, $y(x, 0) = y_t(x, 0) = \frac{1}{10}\sin x$

4. $4y_{tt} = y_{xx}$, $0 < x < 2$, $t > 0$; $y(0, t) = y(2, t) = 0$, $y(x, 0) = \frac{1}{5}\sin \pi x \cos \pi x$, $y_t(x, 0) = 0$

5. $y_{tt} = 25y_{xx}$, $0 < x < 3$, $t > 0$; $y(0, t) = y(3, t) = 0$, $y(x, 0) = \frac{1}{4}\sin \pi x$, $y_t(x, 0) = 10\sin 2\pi x$

6. $y_{tt} = 100y_{xx}$, $0 < x < \pi$, $t > 0$; $y(0, t) = y(\pi, t) = 0$, $y(x, 0) = x(\pi - x)$, $y_t(x, 0) = 0$

7. $y_{tt} = 100y_{xx}$, $0 < x < 1$, $t > 0$; $y(0, t) = y(1, t) = 0$, $y(x, 0) = 0$, $y_t(x, 0) = x$

8. $y_{tt} = 4y_{xx}$, $0 < x < \pi$, $t > 0$; $y(0, t) = y(\pi, t) = 0$, $y(x, 0) = \sin x$, $y_t(x, 0) = 1$

9. $y_{tt} = 4y_{xx}$, $0 < x < 1$, $t > 0$; $y(0, t) = y(1, t) = 0$, $y(x, 0) = 0$, $y_t(x, 0) = x(1 - x)$

10. $y_{tt} = 25y_{xx}$, $0 < x < \pi$, $t > 0$; $y(0, t) = y(\pi, t) = 0$, $y(x, 0) = y_t(x, 0) = \sin^2 x$

11. Suppose that a string 2 ft long weighs $\frac{1}{32}$ oz and is subjected to a tension of 32 lb. Find the fundamental frequency with which it vibrates and the velocity with which the vibration waves travel along it.

12. Show that the amplitude of the oscillations of the midpoint of the string of Example 3 is

$$y\left(\frac{L}{2}, \frac{L}{2a}\right) = \frac{4v_0 L}{\pi^2 a} \sum_{n \text{ odd}} \frac{1}{n^2} = \frac{v_0 L}{2a}.$$

If the string is the string of Problem 11 and the impact speed of the pickup truck is 60 mi/h, show that this amplitude is approximately 1 in.

13. Suppose that the function $F(x)$ is twice differentiable for all x. Use the chain rule to verify that the functions

$$y(x, t) = F(x + at) \qquad \text{and} \qquad y(x, t) = F(x - at)$$

satisfy the equation $y_{tt} = a^2 y_{xx}$.

14. Given the differentiable odd period $2L$ function $F(x)$, show that the function

$$y(x, t) = \frac{1}{2}[F(x + at) + F(x - at)]$$

satisfies the conditions $y(0, t) = y(L, t) = 0$, $y(x, 0) = F(x)$, and $y_t(x, 0) = 0$.

15. If $y(x, 0) = 0$, then Eq. (36) implies (why?) that

$$y(x, t) = \frac{1}{2}\int_0^t G(x + a\tau)\, d\tau + \frac{1}{2}\int_0^t G(x - a\tau)\, d\tau.$$

Make appropriate substitutions in these integrals to derive Eqs. (37) and (38).

16. (a) Show that the substitutions $u = x + at$ and $v = x - at$ transform the equation $y_{tt} = a^2 y_{xx}$ into the equation $y_{uv} = 0$.
(b) Conclude that every solution of $y_{tt} = a^2 y_{xx}$ is of the form

$$y(x, t) = F(x + at) + G(x - at),$$

which represents two waves traveling in opposite directions, each with speed a.

17. Suppose that

$$y(x, t) = \sum A_n \cos\left(\frac{n\pi at}{L}\right) \sin\left(\frac{n\pi x}{L}\right).$$

Square the derivatives y_t and y_x and then integrate termwise— applying the orthogonality of the sine and cosine functions—to verify that

$$E = \frac{1}{2}\int_0^L (\rho y_t^2 + Ty_x^2)\, dx = \frac{\pi^2 T}{4L} \sum_{n=1}^\infty n^2 A_n^2.$$

18. Consider a stretched string, initially at rest; its end at $x = 0$ is fixed, but its end at $x = L$ is free—it is allowed to slide without friction along the vertical line $x = L$. The corresponding boundary value problem is

$$y_{tt} = a^2 y_{xx} \quad (0 < x < L, \quad t > 0);$$

$$y(0, t) = y_x(L, t) = 0,$$

$$y(x, 0) = f(x),$$

$$y_t(x, 0) = 0.$$

Separate the variables and use the odd half-multiple sine series of $f(x)$, as in Problem 24 of Section 9.5, to derive the solution

$$y(x, t) = \sum_{n\ \text{odd}} A_n \cos\frac{n\pi at}{2L} \sin\frac{n\pi x}{2L},$$

where

$$A_n = \frac{2}{L}\int_0^L f(x) \sin\frac{n\pi x}{2L}\, dx.$$

Problems 19 and 20 deal with the vibrations of a string under the influence of the downward force $F(x) = -\rho g$ of gravity.

According to Eq. (1), its displacement function satisfies the partial differential equation

$$\frac{\partial^2 y}{\partial t^2} = a^2 \frac{\partial^2 y}{\partial x^2} - g \tag{40}$$

with endpoint conditions $y(0, t) = y(L, t) = 0$.

19. Suppose first that the string hangs in a stationary position, so that $y = y(x)$ and $y_{tt} = 0$, and hence its differential equation of motion takes the simple form $a^2 y'' = g$. Derive the stationary solution

$$y(x) = \phi(x) = \frac{gx}{2a^2}(x - L).$$

20. Now suppose that the string is released from rest in equilibrium; consequently the initial conditions are $y(x, 0) = 0$ and $y_t(x, 0) = 0$. Define

$$v(x, t) = y(x, t) - \phi(x),$$

where $\phi(x)$ is the stationary solution of Problem 19. Deduce from Eq. (40) that $v(x, t)$ satisfies the boundary value problem

$$v_{tt} = a^2 v_{xx};$$

$$v(0, t) = v(L, t) = 0,$$

$$v(x, 0) = -\phi(x),$$

$$v_t(x, 0) = 0.$$

Conclude from Eqs. (22) and (23) that

$$y(x, t) - \phi(x) = \sum_{n=1}^\infty A_n \cos\frac{n\pi at}{L} \sin\frac{n\pi x}{L},$$

where the coefficients $\{A_n\}$ are the Fourier sine coefficients of $f(x) = -\phi(x)$. Finally, explain why it follows that the string oscillates between the positions $y = 0$ and $y = 2\phi(x)$.

21. For a string vibrating in air with resistance proportional to velocity, the boundary value problem is

$$y_{tt} = a^2 y_{xx} - 2hy;$$

$$y(0, t) = y(L, t) = 0,$$

$$y(x, 0) = f(x),$$

$$y_t(x, 0) = 0.$$

Assume that $0 < h < \pi a/L$. (a) Substitute

$$y(x, t) = X(x)T(t)$$

in (41) to obtain the equations

$$X'' + \lambda X = 0, \qquad X(0) = X(L) = 0 \tag{42}$$

and

$$T'' + 2hT' + a^2\lambda T = 0, \qquad T'(0) = 0. \qquad (43)$$

(b) The eigenvalues and eigenfunctions of (42) are

$$\lambda_n = \frac{n^2\pi^2}{L^2} \qquad \text{and} \qquad X_n(x) = \sin\left(\frac{n\pi x}{L}\right)$$

(as usual). Show that the general solution with $\lambda = n^2\pi^2/L^2$ of the differential equation in (43) is

$$T_n(t) = e^{-ht}(A_n \cos \omega_n t + B_n \sin \omega_n t),$$

where $\omega_n = \sqrt{(n^2\pi^2 a^2/L^2) - h^2} < n\pi a/L$. (c) Show that $T_n'(0) = 0$ implies that $B_n = hA_n/\omega_n$, and hence that to within a constant multiplicative coefficient,

$$T_n(t) = e^{-ht}\cos(\omega_n t - \alpha_n)$$

where $\alpha_n = \tan^{-1}(h/\omega_n)$. (d) Finally, conclude that

$$y(x, t) = e^{-ht}\sum_{n=1}^{\infty} c_n \cos(\omega_n t - \alpha_n)\sin\frac{n\pi x}{L},$$

where

$$c_n = \frac{2}{L\cos\alpha_n}\int_0^L f(x)\sin\frac{n\pi x}{L}\,dx.$$

From this formula we see that the air resistance has three main effects: exponential damping of amplitudes, decreased frequencies $\omega_n < n\pi a/L$, and the production of the phase delay angles α_n.

22. Rework Problem 21 as follows: First substitute $y(x, t) = e^{-ht}v(x, t)$ in Eq. (41) and then show that the boundary value problem for $v(x, t)$ is

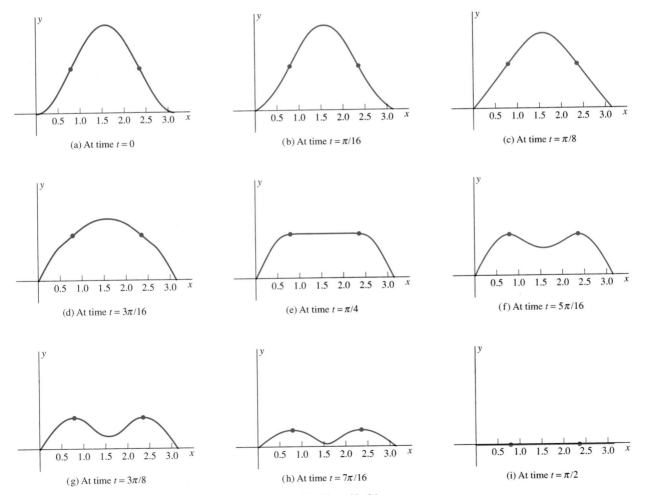

(a) At time $t = 0$ (b) At time $t = \pi/16$ (c) At time $t = \pi/8$

(d) At time $t = 3\pi/16$ (e) At time $t = \pi/4$ (f) At time $t = 5\pi/16$

(g) At time $t = 3\pi/8$ (h) At time $t = 7\pi/16$ (i) At time $t = \pi/2$

FIGURE 9.6.4. Successive snapshots of the vibrating string of Problems 23–24

$$v_{tt} = a^2 v_{xx} + h^2 v;$$

$$v(0, t) = v(L, t) = 0,$$

$$v(x, 0) = f(x),$$

$$v_t(x, 0) = hf(x).$$

Next show that the substitution $v(x, t) = X(x)T(t)$ leads to the equations

$$X'' + \lambda X = 0, \qquad X(0) = X(L) = 0,$$

$$T'' + (\lambda a^2 - h^2) T = 0.$$

Proceed in this manner to derive the solution $y(x, t)$ given in Problem 21(d).

The snapshots in Fig. 9.6.4 show successive positions of a vibrating string with length $L = \pi$ and $a = 1$ (so its period of oscillation is 2π). The string is initially at rest with fixed endpoints, and at time $t = 0$ it is set in motion with initial position function

$$f(x) = 2 \sin^2 x = 1 - \cos 2x. \tag{44}$$

23. The most interesting snapshot is the one in Fig. 9.6.4(e), where it appears that the string exhibits a momentary "flat spot" at the instant $t = \pi/4$. Indeed, apply the d'Alembert formula in (30) to prove that the string's position function $y(x, t)$ satisfies the condition

$$y(x, \pi/4) = 1 \quad \text{for} \quad \frac{\pi}{4} \leq x \leq \frac{3\pi}{4}.$$

24. (a) Show that the position function $f(x)$ defined in (44) has inflection points $[f''(x) = 0]$ at $x = \pi/4$ and at $x = 3\pi/4$. (b) In snapshots (a)–(e) of Fig. 9.6.4 it appears that these two inflection points may remain fixed during some initial portion of the string's vibration. Indeed, apply the d'Alembert formula to show that if either $x = \pi/4$ or $x = 3\pi/4$, then $y(x, t) = 1$ for $0 \leq t \leq \pi/4$.

9.6 Computing Project

The d'Alembert solution

$$y(x, t) = \frac{1}{2}[F(x + at) + F(x - at)]$$

of the vibrating string problem is readily implemented in a computer algebra system such as *Maple* or *Mathematica*. To plot the snapshots shown in Fig. 9.6.4, we started (using *Mathematica*) with the string's initial position function $f(x)$ defined by

```
f[x_] := 2*(Sin[x])^2
```

To define the odd period 2π extension $F(x)$ of $f(x)$, we need the function $s(x)$ that shifts the point x by a multiple of π into the interval $[0, \pi]$.

```
s[x_] := Block[{k}, k = Floor[ N[x/Pi] ];
            If[EvenQ[k], N[x-k*Pi], N[x-k*Pi-Pi]]]
```

Then the desired odd extension is defined by

```
F[x_] := If[ s[x] > 0, (*then*)    f[s[x]],
                       (*else*)   -f[-s[x]] ]
```

Finally, the d'Alembert solution is

```
G[x_,t_] := (F[x+t] + F[x-t])/2
```

A snapshot of the position of the string at time t is plotted by

```
stringAt[ t_ ] := Plot[ G[x,t], {x,0,Pi},
                        PlotRange -> {-2,2} ];
```

For example, the command

```
stringAt[ Pi/4 ]
```

plots the snapshot in Fig. 9.6.4(e) showing the flat spot discussed in Problem 23. We can plot a whole sequence of snapshots at once:

```
snapshots = Table[ stringAt[t], {t, 0, Pi, Pi/12} ]
```

These snapshots can be animated to show the vibrating string in motion, or we can exhibit the successive positions of the string in a single figure (Figure 9.6.5) with the command

```
Show[ snapshots ]
```

The initial position function

```
f[x_] := If[ x < Pi/2, x, Pi - x ] // N
```

corresponding to the triangular wave function of Fig. 9.2.4 generates in this way the composite picture shown in Fig. 9.6.6. Similarly, the trapezoidal wave function

```
f[x_] := Which[ 0 <= x < Pi/3, x,
               Pi/3 <= x < 2*Pi/3, Pi/3,
               2*Pi/3 <= x <= Pi, Pi - x ] // N
```

corresponding to the trapezoidal wave function of Fig. 9.2.5 produces the picture shown in Fig. 9.6.7.

The bump function defined by

```
f[x_] := If[ Abs[x - Pi/2] < 0.1,
            -200*((x - Pi/2)^2 - (0.1)^2), 0 ]
```

was used to plot the traveling waves shown in Fig. 9.6.3. The bump function defined by

```
f[x_] := (Sin[x])^200
```

produces similar waves traveling (initially) in opposite directions. The initial position function

```
f[x_] := If[ x < Pi/2, (Sin[x + 1.5])^200, 0 ]
```

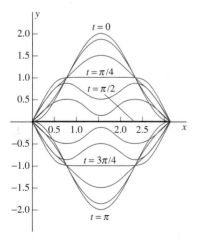

FIGURE 9.6.5. Successive positions of vibrating string with initial position $f(x) = 2 \sin^2 x$

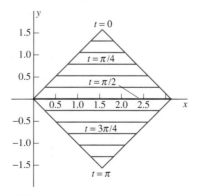

FIGURE 9.6.6. Successive positions of vibrating string with triangular initial position

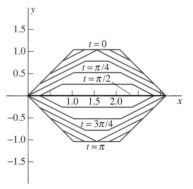

FIGURE 9.6.7. Successive positions of vibrating string with trapezoidal initial position

generates a single wave that starts at $x = 0$ and (initially) travels to the right.

After exploring some of the possibilities indicated above, try some initial position functions of your own choice. Any continuous function f such that $f(0) = f(\pi) = 0$ is fair game. The more exotic the resulting vibration of the string, the better.

If a guitar string is plucked in the middle, will the sound be different from the sound if it is plucked near one end?

9.7 Steady-State Temperature and Laplace's Equation

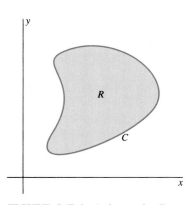

FIGURE 9.7.1. A plane region R and its bounding curve C

We now consider the temperature in a two-dimensional plate, or lamina, that occupies a region R in the xy-plane bounded by a piecewise smooth curve C, as shown in Fig. 9.7.1. We assume that the faces of the plate are insulated, and that it is so thin that the temperature within it does not vary in the direction perpendicular to the xy-plane. We want to determine, under various conditions, the temperature $u(x, y, t)$ at the point (x, y) at time t.

Let the plate consist of material with density δ (mass per unit volume), specific heat c (per unit mass), and thermal conductivity K, all assumed constant throughout the plate. Under these assumptions, it can be shown (by a generalization of the derivation of the one-dimensional heat equation in Section 9.5) that the temperature function $u(x, y, t)$ satisfies the **two-dimensional heat equation**

$$\frac{\partial u}{\partial t} = k \left(\frac{\partial^2 u}{\partial x^2} + \frac{\partial^2 u}{\partial y^2} \right). \tag{1}$$

As in Section 9.5, k denotes the thermal diffusivity,

$$k = \frac{K}{c\delta}, \tag{2}$$

of the material of the plate. The sum of second derivatives on the right-hand side in (1) is the **Laplacian** of the function u, commonly denoted by

$$\nabla^2 u = \frac{\partial^2 u}{\partial x^2} + \frac{\partial^2 u}{\partial y^2}, \tag{3}$$

so the two-dimensional heat equation may be written as

$$\frac{\partial u}{\partial t} = k \nabla^2 u. \tag{1'}$$

In comparing Eq. (1′) with the one-dimensional heat equation $u_t = ku_{xx}$, we see that in passing from one to two dimensions, the second-order space derivative u_{xx} is replaced with the Laplacian $\nabla^2 u$. This is an instance of a general phenomenon. For instance, if a flexible stretched membrane occupies in equilibrium a region in the xy-plane and vibrates in the (perpendicular) z-direction, then its displacement function $z = z(x, y, t)$ satisfies the **two-dimensional wave equation**

$$\frac{\partial^2 z}{\partial t^2} = a^2 \left(\frac{\partial^2 z}{\partial x^2} + \frac{\partial^2 z}{\partial y^2} \right) = a^2 \nabla^2 z. \tag{4}$$

This equation has the same relation to the one-dimensional wave equation $z_{tt} = a^2 z_{xx}$ (here writing $z(x, t)$ for the displacement of a string) as Eq. (1') has to the one-dimensional heat equation.

In this section we confine our attention to the steady-state situation in which the temperature u does not vary with time, and so is a function only of x and y. Thus we are interested in the *steady-state temperature* of a plate. In this case $u_t = 0$, so Eq. (1) becomes the **two-dimensional Laplace equation**

$$\blacktriangleright \qquad \nabla^2 u = \frac{\partial^2 u}{\partial x^2} + \frac{\partial^2 u}{\partial y^2} = 0. \qquad (5)$$

This important partial differential equation is known as the **potential equation.** The three-dimensional Laplace equation $u_{xx} + u_{yy} + u_{zz} = 0$ is satisfied (in empty space) by electric and gravitational potential functions. It is also satisfied by the velocity potential function for the steady irrotational flow of an incompressible and inviscid liquid.

Dirichlet Problems

A particular solution of Laplace's equation in a bounded plane region R is determined by appropriate boundary conditions. For example, it is plausible on physical grounds that the steady-state temperature $u(x, y)$ in a plate is determined if we know that $u(x, y)$ agrees with a given function $f(x, y)$ at each point of the boundary curve C of the plate. To find the steady-state temperature in a plate with assigned boundary values, we need to solve the boundary value problem

$$\blacktriangleright \qquad \begin{aligned} \frac{\partial^2 u}{\partial x^2} + \frac{\partial^2 u}{\partial y^2} &= 0 && \text{(within } R\text{);} \\ u(x, y) &= f(x, y) && \text{(if } (x, y) \text{ is on } C\text{).} \end{aligned} \qquad (6)$$

Such a problem, finding a solution of Laplace's equation in a region R with given boundary values, is called a **Dirichlet problem.** It is known that, if the boundary curve C and the boundary value function are reasonably well behaved, then there exists a unique solution of the Dirichlet problem in (6).

Figure 9.7.2 shows a rectangular plate with indicated boundary values along its four edges. The corresponding Dirichlet problem is

$$\begin{aligned} u_{xx} + u_{yy} &= 0 && \text{(in } R\text{);} \\ u(x, 0) = f_1(x), \qquad u(x, b) &= f_2(x) && (0 < x < a), \\ u(0, y) = g_1(y), \qquad u(a, y) &= g_2(y) && (0 < y < b). \end{aligned} \qquad (7)$$

FIGURE 9.7.2. A rectangular plate with given boundary values

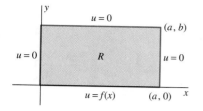

FIGURE 9.7.3. The boundary value problem of Example 1

Because there are four nonhomogeneous conditions (rather than one), this boundary value problem is not directly susceptible to the method of separation of variables. In Section 9.6, when confronted with this difficulty, we split the problem of the vibrating string with both initial position and initial velocity into two problems with a single nonhomogeneous condition each. In a similar way, the boundary value problem in (7) can be split into *four* problems, each with a single nonhomogeneous boundary condition. For each of these four problems, $u(x, y)$ will be zero along three edges of the rectangle and will have assigned values on the fourth. Each of these four boundary value problems can be solved by separation of variables, and the sum of the four solutions is the solution of the original problem in (7). In the following example we solve one of these four problems—the one illustrated in Fig. 9.7.3.

EXAMPLE 1 Solve the boundary value problem

$$u_{xx} + u_{yy} = 0;$$
$$u(0, y) = u(a, y) = u(x, b) = 0, \tag{8}$$
$$u(x, 0) = f(x)$$

for the rectangle in Fig. 9.7.3.

Solution Substitution of $u(x, y) = X(x)Y(y)$ gives $X''Y + XY'' = 0$, so

$$\frac{X''}{X} = -\frac{Y''}{Y} = -\lambda \tag{9}$$

for some constant λ. Thus $X(x)$ must satisfy the familiar eigenvalue problem

$$X'' + \lambda X'' = 0,$$
$$X(0) = X(a) = 0.$$

The eigenvalues and associated eigenfunctions are

$$\lambda_n = \frac{n^2 \pi^2}{a^2}, \qquad X_n(x) = \sin \frac{n\pi x}{a} \tag{10}$$

for $n = 1, 2, 3, \ldots$. From Eq. (9), with $\lambda = n^2\pi^2/a^2$ and the remaining homogeneous boundary condition in (8), we get

$$Y_n'' - \frac{n^2\pi^2}{a^2} Y_n = 0, \qquad Y_n(b) = 0. \tag{11}$$

The general solution of the differential equation in (11) is

$$Y_n(y) = A_n \cosh \frac{n\pi y}{a} + B_n \sinh \frac{n\pi y}{a},$$

and the condition

$$Y_n(b) = A_n \cosh \frac{n\pi b}{a} + B_n \sinh \frac{n\pi b}{a} = 0$$

implies that $B_n = -[A_n \cosh(n\pi b/a)]/[\sinh(n\pi b/a)]$, so

$$Y_n(y) = A_n \cosh \frac{n\pi y}{a} - \frac{A_n \cosh(n\pi b/a)}{\sinh(n\pi b/a)} \sinh \frac{n\pi y}{a}$$

$$= \frac{A_n}{\sinh(n\pi b/a)} \left(\sinh \frac{n\pi b}{a} \cosh \frac{n\pi y}{a} - \cosh \frac{n\pi b}{a} \sinh \frac{n\pi y}{a} \right).$$

Therefore

$$Y_n(y) = c_n \sinh \frac{n\pi}{a}(b-y) \tag{12}$$

where $c_n = A_n/\sinh(n\pi b/a)$. From (10) and (12) we obtain the formal series solution

$$\blacktriangleright \qquad u(x,y) = \sum_{n=1}^{\infty} X_n(x) Y_n(y) = \sum_{n=1}^{\infty} c_n \sin \frac{n\pi x}{a} \sinh \frac{n\pi}{a}(b-y). \tag{13}$$

It remains only to choose the coefficients $\{c_n\}$ to satisfy the nonhomogeneous condition

$$u(x,0) = \sum_{n=1}^{\infty} \left(c_n \sinh \frac{n\pi b}{a} \right) \sin \frac{n\pi x}{a} = f(x).$$

For this purpose we want

$$c_n \sinh \frac{n\pi b}{a} = b_n = \frac{2}{a} \int_0^a f(x) \sin \frac{n\pi x}{a} \, dx,$$

so

$$\blacktriangleright \qquad c_n = \frac{2}{a \sinh(n\pi b/a)} \int_0^a f(x) \sin \frac{n\pi x}{a} \, dx. \tag{14}$$

With this choice of coefficients, the series in (13) is a formal series solution of the Dirichlet problem in (8). ∎

For instance, suppose that

$$f(x) = T_0 = \frac{4T_0}{\pi} \sum_{n \text{ odd}} \frac{1}{n} \sin \frac{n\pi x}{a}$$

if $0 < x < a$, so that $b_n = 4T_0/(\pi n)$ for n odd and $b_n = 0$ for n even. Then the formulas in (13) and (14) yield

$$u(x,y) = \frac{4T_0}{\pi} \sum_{n \text{ odd}} \frac{\sin(n\pi x/a) \sinh(n\pi[b-y]/a)}{n \sinh(n\pi b/a)} \tag{15}$$

for the steady-state temperature in a rectangular plate with its base held at temperature T_0 and its other three edges at temperature zero. In particular, suppose that $T_0 = 100$ and that $a = b = 10$. Then from Eq. (15) we find that the temperature at the center of the plate is

$$u(5,5) = \frac{400}{\pi} \sum_{n \text{ odd}} \frac{\sin(n\pi/2) \sinh(n\pi/2)}{n \sinh n\pi}$$

$$\approx 25.3716 - 0.3812 + 0.0099 - 0.0003;$$

thus $u(5,5)$ is approximately 25.00.

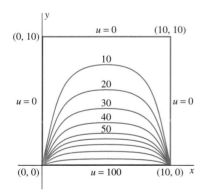

FIGURE 9.7.4. Typical level curve of the function $u(x,y)$ in Eq. (15)

Question. Can you think of an argument—perhaps using symmetry—that proves (without using the series solution) that $u(5, 5)$ is exactly 25?

Remark: In practice, engineers use solutions like the one in Eq. (15) to plot the variation of temperature within a plate or piece of machinery; they are particularly interested in any "hot spots" that may appear. Such information is often presented by constructing *level curves* on which the temperature function $u(x, y)$ is constant. Figure 9.7.4 shows typical level curves for the function $u(x, y)$ in (15) with $a = b = 10$ and $T_0 = 100$.

EXAMPLE 2 Let R be the "semi-infinite" strip shown in Fig. 9.7.5. Solve the boundary value problem

$$u_{xx} + u_{yy} = 0 \qquad \text{(in } R\text{)};$$
$$u(x, 0) = u(x, b) = 0 \qquad (0 < x < \infty),$$
$$u(x, y) \text{ is bounded as } x \to +\infty,$$
$$u(0, y) = g(y). \qquad (16)$$

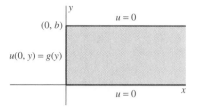

FIGURE 9.7.5. "Semi-infinite" strip of Example 2

Solution The condition that $u(x, y)$ is bounded as $x \to +\infty$ plays the role of a homogeneous boundary condition associated with the "missing" right edge of the "rectangle;" this is typical of Dirichlet problems for unbounded regions. With $u(x, y) = X(x)Y(y)$, the actual homogeneous conditions give $Y(0) = Y(b) = 0$. Hence it is $Y(y)$ that will satisfy an eigenvalue problem. We therefore write the separation in (9) as

$$\frac{Y''}{Y} = -\frac{X''}{X} = -\lambda, \qquad (17)$$

changing the sign of λ to get the familiar eigenvalue problem

$$Y'' + \lambda Y = 0, \qquad Y(0) = Y(b) = 0$$

with eigenvalues and associated eigenfunctions

$$\lambda_n = \frac{n^2 \pi^2}{b^2}, \qquad Y_n(y) = \sin \frac{n \pi y}{b}. \qquad (18)$$

The general solution of

$$X_n'' - \frac{n^2 \pi^2}{b^2} X_n = 0$$

is $X_n(x) = A_n e^{n\pi x/b} + B_n e^{-n\pi x/b}$. We write the solution in exponential form because then the condition that $u(x, y)$, and hence $X(x)$, is bounded as $x \to +\infty$ immediately implies that $A_n = 0$ for all n. Suppressing the constant, this leaves

$$X_n(x) = e^{-n\pi x/b}. \qquad (19)$$

From Eqs. (18) and (19) we get the formal series solution

$$\blacktriangleright \qquad u(x, y) = \sum_{n=1}^{\infty} b_n X_n(x) Y_n(y) = \sum_{n=1}^{\infty} b_n e^{-n\pi x/b} \sin \frac{n \pi y}{b} \qquad (20)$$

that satisfies the homogeneous boundary conditions and the boundedness condition. In

order also to satisfy the nonhomogeneous condition

$$u(0, y) = \sum_{n=1}^{\infty} b_n \sin \frac{n\pi y}{b} = g(y),$$

we choose b_n to be the Fourier sine coefficient

$$b_n = \frac{2}{b} \int_0^b g(y) \sin \frac{n\pi y}{b} \, dy \qquad (21)$$

of the function $g(y)$ on $[0, b]$.

For instance, if

$$g(y) = T_0 = \frac{4T_0}{\pi} \sum_{n \text{ odd}} \frac{1}{n} \sin \frac{n\pi y}{b}$$

for $0 < y < b$, then Eqs. (20) and (21) yield

$$u(x, y) = \frac{4T_0}{\pi} \sum_{n \text{ odd}} \frac{1}{n} e^{-n\pi x/b} \sin \frac{n\pi y}{b}.$$

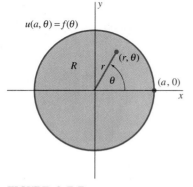

FIGURE 9.7.6. Typical level curve of the function $u(x, y)$ of Example 2

Figure 9.7.6 shows some typical level curves of the temperature function defined by this formula with $b = 10$ and $T_0 = 100$.

The Dirichlet Problem for a Circular Disk

We now investigate the steady-state temperature in a circular disk of radius a with insulated faces and with given boundary temperatures. Obviously we should accommodate the geometry of the circle by expressing $u = u(r, \theta)$ in terms of polar coordinates r and θ, with $x = r \cos \theta$ and $y = r \sin \theta$. When these equations are used to transform the Laplacian, the result is **Laplace's equation in polar coordinates:**

$$\nabla^2 u = \frac{\partial^2 u}{\partial r^2} + \frac{1}{r}\frac{\partial u}{\partial r} + \frac{1}{r^2}\frac{\partial^2 u}{\partial \theta^2} = 0. \qquad (22)$$

We prescribe assigned boundary temperatures (as indicated in Fig.9.7.7) by requiring that

$$u(a, \theta) = f(\theta), \qquad (23)$$

where the function $f(\theta)$ of period 2π is given. In addition, because (r, θ) and $(r, \theta + 2\pi)$ are the polar coordinates of the same point, we impose upon u the periodicity condition

$$u(r, \theta) = u(r, \theta + 2\pi) \qquad (24)$$

for $r < a$ and all θ; this will play the role of a homogeneous boundary condition.

To solve the boundary value problem in (22)–(24), we substitute $u(r, \theta) = R(t)\,\Theta(\theta)$ in Eq. (22); the result is

FIGURE 9.7.7. The Dirichlet problem for a circular disk

$$R''\Theta + \frac{1}{r}R'\Theta + \frac{1}{r^2}R\Theta'' = 0.$$

Division by $R\Theta/r^2$ gives

$$\frac{r^2 R'' + r R'}{R} + \frac{\Theta''}{\Theta} = 0,$$

so it follows that

$$\frac{r^2R'' + rR'}{R} = -\frac{\Theta''}{\Theta} = \lambda$$

for some constant λ. This yields the two ordinary differential equations

$$r^2R'' + rR' - \lambda R = 0 \tag{25}$$

and

$$\Theta'' + \lambda\Theta = 0. \tag{26}$$

The general solution of Eq. (26) is

$$\Theta(\theta) = A\cos\alpha\theta + B\sin\alpha\theta \quad \text{if } \lambda = \alpha^2 > 0, \tag{27a}$$

$$\Theta(\theta) = A + B\theta \qquad\qquad \text{if } \lambda = 0, \tag{27b}$$

$$\Theta(\theta) = Ae^{\alpha\theta} + Be^{-\alpha\theta} \qquad \text{if } \lambda = -\alpha^2 < 0. \tag{27c}$$

Now we apply the condition in (24), which implies that $\Theta(\theta) = \Theta(\theta + 2\pi)$; that is, that $\Theta(\theta)$ has period 2π. In Problems 22 and 23 we ask you to show that this is so only if $\lambda = n^2$ (n an integer) in (27a) or if $\lambda = 0$ and $B = 0$ in (27b). Thus we have the eigenvalues and associated eigenfunctions

$$\lambda_0 = 0, \qquad \Theta_0(\theta) = 1; \tag{28a}$$

$$\lambda_n = n^2, \qquad \Theta_n(\theta) = A_n\cos n\theta + B_n\sin n\theta \tag{28b}$$

for $n = 1, 2, 3, \ldots$.

Next we turn our attention to Eq. (25). With $\lambda_0 = 0$ it reduces to the equation $r^2R_0'' + rR_0' = 0$ with general solution

$$R_0(r) = C_0 + D_0\ln r. \tag{29}$$

Of course we want $u(r, \theta)$, and hence $R(r)$, to be continuous at $r = 0$; this requires that $D_0 = 0$ in (29), so $R_0(r) = C_0$. With $\lambda = \lambda_n = n^2$, Eq. (25) is the equation

$$r^2R_n'' + rR_n' - n^2R_n = 0.$$

Upon substituting the trial solution $R(r) = r^k$, we find that $k = \pm n$, so the general solution of the previous equation is

$$R_n(r) = C_n r^n + \frac{D_n}{r^n}. \tag{30}$$

Continuity at $r = 0$ then requires that $D_n = 0$, so $R_n(r) = C_n r^n$.

Finally we combine the results in Eqs. (28) through (30) with $D_n \equiv 0$ to obtain a formal series solution of the form

$$u(r, \theta) = \sum_{n=0}^{\infty} R_n(r)\Theta_n(\theta);$$

that is,

$$u(r, \theta) = \frac{a_0}{2} + \sum_{n=1}^{\infty} (a_n\cos n\theta + b_n\sin n\theta)r^n. \tag{31}$$

In order that the boundary condition $u(a, \theta) = f(\theta)$ be satisfied, we want

$$u(a, \theta) = \frac{a_0}{2} + \sum_{n=1}^{\infty} (a_n a^n \cos n\theta + b_n a^n \sin n\theta)$$

to be the Fourier series of $f(\theta)$ on $[0, 2\pi]$. Hence we choose

$$\blacktriangleright \qquad a_n = \frac{1}{\pi a^n} \int_0^{2\pi} f(\theta) \cos n\theta \, d\theta \qquad (n = 0, 1, 2, \ldots) \qquad (32a)$$

and

$$\blacktriangleright \qquad b_n = \frac{1}{\pi a^n} \int_0^{2\pi} f(\theta) \sin n\theta \, d\theta \qquad (n = 1, 2, 3, \ldots). \qquad (32b)$$

For instance, if $F(\theta) = +T_0$ for $0 < \theta < \pi$ and $F(\theta) = -T_0$ for $\pi < \theta < 2\pi$, so that

$$F(\theta) = \frac{4T_0}{\pi} \sum_{n \text{ odd}} \frac{1}{n} \sin n\theta,$$

then $a_n = 0$ for all $n \geq 0$, $b_n = 0$ for n even, and $b_n = 4T_0/(\pi n a^n)$ for n odd. So Eqs. (31) and (32) yield

$$u(r, \theta) = \frac{4T_0}{\pi} \sum_{n \text{ odd}} \frac{r^n}{n a^n} \sin n\theta.$$

Note: In the Dirichlet problems of this section, we have concentrated on temperature functions with preassigned boundary values. In the case of a plate with an *insulated* edge—across which no heat can flow—the boundary condition is that the derivative of $u(x, y)$ in the direction normal to this edge vanishes. For instance, consider the rectangular plate in Fig. 9.7.2. If the edge $x = 0$ is insulated, then $u_x(0, y) \equiv 0$, whereas if the edge $y = b$ is insulated, then $u_y(x, b) \equiv 0$.

9.7 Problems

In Problems 1 through 3, solve the Dirichlet problem for the rectangle $0 < x < a$, $0 < y < b$ consisting of Laplace's equation $u_{xx} + u_{yy} = 0$ and the given boundary value conditions.

1. $u(x, 0) = u(x, b) = u(0, y) = 0$, $u(a, y) = g(y)$
2. $u(x, 0) = u(x, b) = u(a, y) = 0$, $u(0, y) = g(y)$
3. $u(x, 0) = u(0, y) = u(a, y) = 0$, $u(x, b) = f(x)$
4. Consider the boundary value problem

$$u_{xx} + u_{yy} = 0;$$

$$u_x(0, y) = u_x(a, y) = u(x, 0) = 0,$$

$$u(x, b) = f(x)$$

corresponding to a rectangular plate $0 < x < a$, $0 < y < b$ with

the edges $x = 0$ and $x = a$ insulated. Derive the solution

$$u(x, y) = \frac{a_0 y}{2b} + \sum_{n=1}^{\infty} a_n \left(\cos \frac{n\pi x}{a} \right) \left(\frac{\sinh (n\pi y/a)}{\sinh (n\pi b/a)} \right),$$

where

$$a_n = \frac{2}{a} \int_0^a f(x) \cos \frac{n\pi x}{a} \, dx \qquad (n = 0, 1, 2, \ldots).$$

(*Suggestion:* Show first that $\lambda_0 = 0$ is an eigenvalue with $X_0(x) = 1$ and $Y_0(y) = y$.)

In Problems 5 and 6, find a solution of Laplace's equation $u_{xx} + u_{yy} = 0$ in the rectangle $0 < x < a$, $0 < y < b$ that satisfies the given boundary conditions (see Problem 4).

5. $u_y(x, 0) = u_y(x, b) = u(a, y) = 0, \quad u(0, y) = g(y)$

6. $u_x(0, y) = u_x(a, y) = u_y(x, 0) = 0, \quad u(x, b) = f(y)$

In Problems 7 and 8, find a solution of Laplace's equation in the semi-infinite strip $0 < x < a, \ y > 0$ that satisfies the given boundary conditions and the additional condition that $u(x, y)$ is bounded as $y \to +\infty$.

7. $u(0, y) = u(a, y) = 0, \quad u(x, 0) = f(x)$

8. $u_x(0, y) = u_x(a, y) = 0, \quad u(x, 0) = f(x)$

9. Suppose that $a = 10$ and $f(x) = 10x$ in Problem 8. Show that

$$u(x, y) = 50 - \frac{400}{\pi^2} \sum_{n \text{ odd}} \frac{1}{n^2} e^{-n\pi y/10} \cos \frac{n\pi x}{10}.$$

Then compute (with two-decimal-place accuracy) the values $u(0, 5)$, $u(5, 5)$, and $u(10, 5)$.

10. The edge $x = a$ of the rectangular plate $0 < x < a$, $0 < y < b$ is insulated, the edges $x = 0$ and $y = 0$ are held at temperature zero, and $u(x, b) = f(x)$. Use the odd half-multiple sine series of Problem 21 of Section 9.3 to derive a solution of the form

$$u(x, y) = \sum_{n \text{ odd}} c_n \sin \frac{n\pi x}{2a} \sinh \frac{n\pi y}{2a}.$$

Give a formula for c_n.

11. The edge $y = 0$ of the rectangular plate $0 < x < a$, $0 < y < b$ is insulated, the edges $x = a$ and $x = b$ are held at temperature zero, and $u(0, y) = g(y)$. Use the odd half-multiple cosine series of Problem 22 of Section 9.3 to find $u(x, y)$.

12. A vertical cross section of a long high wall 30 cm thick has the shape of the semi-infinite strip $0 < x < 30, \ y > 0$. The face $x = 0$ is held at temperature zero, but the face $x = 30$ is insulated. Given $u(x, 0) = 25$, derive the formula

$$u(x, y) = \frac{100}{\pi} \sum_{n \text{ odd}} \frac{1}{n} e^{-n\pi y/60} \sin \frac{n\pi x}{60}$$

for steady-state temperature within the wall.

Problems 13 through 15 deal with the semicircular plate of radius a shown in Fig. 9.7.8. The circular edge has a given temperature $u(a, \theta) = f(\theta)$. In each problem, derive the given series for the steady-state temperature $u(r, \theta)$ satisfying the given boundary conditions along $\theta = 0$ and $\theta = \pi$, and give the formula for the coefficients c_n.

13. $u(r, 0) = u(r, \pi) = 0$;

$$u(r, \theta) = \sum_{n=1}^{\infty} c_n r^n \sin n\theta$$

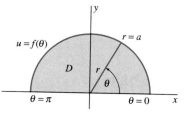

FIGURE 9.7.8. The semicircular plate of Problems 13–15

14. $u_\theta(r, 0) = u_\theta(r, \pi) = 0$;

$$u(r, \theta) = \frac{c_0}{2} + \sum_{n=1}^{\infty} c_n r^n \cos n\theta$$

15. $u(r, 0) = u_\theta(r, \pi) = 0$;

$$u(r, \theta) = \sum_{n \text{ odd}} c_n r^{n/2} \sin \frac{n\theta}{2}$$

16. Consider Dirichlet's problem for the region *exterior* to the circle $r = a$. You want to find a solution of

$$r^2 u_{rr} + r u_r + u_{\theta\theta} = 0$$

such that $u(a, \theta) = f(\theta)$ and $u(r, \theta)$ is bounded as $r \to +\infty$. Derive the series

$$u(r, \theta) = \frac{a_0}{2} + \sum_{n=1}^{\infty} \frac{1}{r^n} (a_n \cos n\theta + b_n \sin n\theta),$$

and give formulas for the coefficients $\{a_n\}$ and $\{b_n\}$.

17. The velocity potential function $u(r, \theta)$ for steady flow of an ideal fluid around a cylinder of radius $r = a$ satisfies the boundary value problem

$$r^2 u_{rr} + r u_r + u_{\theta\theta} = 0 \qquad (r > a);$$

$$u_r(a, \theta) = 0, \qquad u(r, \theta) = u(r, -\theta),$$

$$\lim_{r \to \infty} [u(r, \theta) - U_0 r \cos \theta] = 0$$

(a) By separation of variables, derive the solution

$$u(r, \theta) = \frac{U_0}{r} (r^2 + a^2) \cos \theta.$$

(b) Hence show that the velocity components of the flow are

$$u_x = \frac{\partial u}{\partial x} = \frac{U_0}{r^2} (r^2 - a^2 \cos 2\theta)$$

and

$$u_y = \frac{\partial u}{\partial y} = -\frac{U_0}{r^2} a^2 \sin 2\theta.$$

The streamlines for this fluid flow around the cylinder are shown in Fig. 9.7.9.

FIGURE 9.7.9. Streamlines for ideal fluid flow around a cylinder

Comment: The streamlines in Fig. 9.7.9 are the level curves of the function $\psi(x, y)$ given in Problem 18(b). It is troublesome to write a computer program to plot such level curves. It is far easier to plot some solutions of the differential equation $dy/dx = u_y/u_x$. We did so with initial conditions $x_0 = -5$, $y_0 = -2.7, -2.5, -2.3, \ldots, 2.5, 2.7$. The solutions were obtained numerically using the improved Euler method (Section 2.5) with step size 0.02.

18. (a) Show that the velocity potential in Problem 17(a) can be written in rectangular coordinates as

$$u(x, y) = U_0 x \left(1 + \frac{a^2}{x^2 + y^2} \right).$$

(b) The stream function for the flow is

$$\psi(x, y) = U_0 y \left(\frac{a^2}{x^2 + y^2} - 1 \right).$$

Show that $\nabla u \cdot \nabla \psi \equiv 0$. Because $\mathbf{v} = \nabla u$ is the velocity vector, this shows that the streamlines of the flow are the level curves of $\psi(x, y)$.

Problems 19 through 21 deal with a solid spherical ball of radius $r = a$ with initial temperature T_0 throughout. At time $t = 0$ it is packed in ice, so its temperature at the surface $r = a$ is zero thereafter. Its temperature then depends only upon time t and the distance r from the center of the ball, so we write $u = u(r, t)$.

19. (a) The heat content of the spherical shell with inner and outer radii r and $r + \Delta r$ is

$$Q(t) = \int_r^{r + \Delta r} c \delta u(x, t) \cdot 4 \pi s^2 \, ds.$$

Show that $Q'(t) = 4 \pi c \delta r^2 u_t(\bar{r}, t)$ for some \bar{r} in the interval $(r, r + \Delta r)$. (b) The radial heat flux is $\phi = -K u_r$ across the bounding spherical surfaces of the shell in part (a). Conclude that

$$Q'(t) = 4 \pi K [(r + \Delta r)^2 u_r(r + \Delta r, t) - r^2 u_r(r, t)].$$

(c) Equate the values of $Q'(t)$ in parts (a) and (b); then take the limit as $\Delta r \to 0$ to get the equation

$$\frac{\partial u}{\partial t} = \frac{k}{r^2} \frac{\partial}{\partial r} \left(r^2 \frac{\partial u}{\partial r} \right).$$

(d) Finally, show that this last equation is equivalent to

$$\frac{\partial}{\partial t} (ru) = k \frac{\partial^2}{\partial r^2} (ru).$$

20. It follows from Problem 19(d) that $u(r, t)$ satisfies the boundary value problem

$$\frac{\partial}{\partial t} (ru) = k \frac{\partial^2}{\partial r^2} (ru) \qquad (r < a);$$

$$u(a, t) = 0, \qquad u(r, 0) = T_0.$$

Show that the new function $v(r, t) = ru(r, t)$ satisfies a familiar boundary value problem (in Section 9.5), and thus derive the solution

$$u(r, t) = \frac{2aT_0}{\pi} \sum_{n=1}^{\infty} \frac{(-1)^{n+1}}{nr} e^{-n^2 \pi^2 kt/a^2} \sin \frac{n \pi r}{a}.$$

21. (a) Deduce from the solution to Problem 20 that the temperature at the center of the ball at time t is

$$u(0, t) = 2T_0 \sum_{n=1}^{\infty} (-1)^{n+1} e^{-n^2 \pi^2 kt/a^2}.$$

(b) Let $a = 30$ cm and $T_0 = 100°$C. Compute $u(0, t)$ after 15 min if the ball is made of iron with $k = 0.15$ cgs. (The answer is approximately $45°$C). (c) If you have access to a programmable calculator, repeat part (b) for a ball made of concrete with $k = 0.005$ in cgs units. About 15 terms are required to show that $u = 100.00°$C accurate to two decimal places.

22. In the discussion of the Dirichlet problem for a circular disk in this section, we obtained the ordinary differential equation $\Theta'' + \lambda \Theta = 0$ with the periodicity condition $\Theta(\theta) = \Theta(\theta + 2\pi)$. (a) Suppose that $\lambda = \alpha^2 > 0$. Show that the general solution

$$\Theta(\theta) = A \cos \alpha\theta + B \sin \alpha\theta$$

has period 2π only if $\lambda = n^2$ with n an integer. (b) In the case $\lambda = 0$, show that the general solution

$$\Theta(\theta) = A\theta + B$$

is periodic only if $A = 0$.

23. If $\lambda = -\alpha^2 < 0$ in Problem 22, then the general solution of the differential equation is

$$\Theta(\theta) = A e^{\alpha\theta} + B e^{-\alpha\theta}.$$

Show that this function is not periodic unless $A = B = 0$.

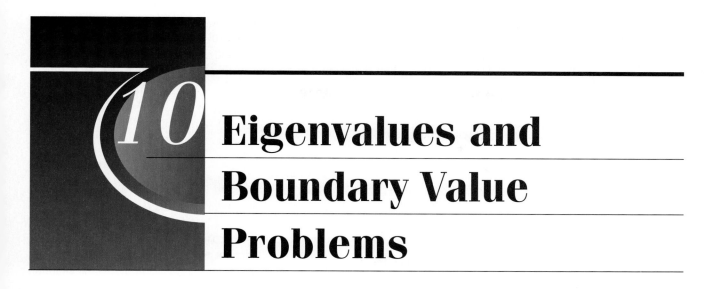

10 Eigenvalues and Boundary Value Problems

10.1 Sturm-Liouville Problems and Eigenfunction Expansions

In the last three sections of Chapter 9, we saw that numerous different boundary value problems all lead—by separation of variables—to the same ordinary differential equation

▶ $$X''(x) + \lambda X(x) = 0 \qquad (0 < x < L), \qquad (1)$$

containing an eigenvalue λ, but with different endpoint conditions, such as

$$X(0) = X(L) = 0 \qquad (2)$$

or

$$X'(0) = X'(L) = 0 \qquad (3)$$

or

$$X(0) = X'(L) = 0, \qquad (4)$$

depending upon the original boundary conditions.

For example, recall the problem (in Section 9.5) of finding the temperature $u(x, t)$ in a rod $0 \leqq x \leqq L$ with given initial temperature $u(x, 0) = f(x)$. As a boundary value

problem, the problem of the rod is the same as the problem of finding the temperature within a large slab that occupies the region $0 \leq x \leq L$ in xyz-space. If its initial temperature depends only upon x and is independent of y and z—that is, if $u(x, 0) = f(x)$—then the same will be true of its temperature $u = u(x, t)$ at time t. When we substitute

$$u(x, t) = X(x)T(t)$$

in the heat equation

▶
$$\frac{\partial u}{\partial t} = k \frac{\partial^2 u}{\partial x^2},$$

we find that $X(x)$ satisfies the endpoint conditions in (2) if the faces $x = 0$ and $x = L$ of the slab are held at temperature zero, those in (3) if both faces are insulated, and those in (4) if one face is insulated and the other is held at temperature zero. But if each face loses heat to a surrounding medium (at temperature zero) in accord with Newton's law of cooling, then (according to Problem 23 of Section 9.5) the endpoint conditions take the form

$$hX(0) - X'(0) = 0 = hX(L) + X'(L), \tag{5}$$

where h is a nonnegative heat transfer coefficient.

The point is that when we impose different endpoint conditions on the solution of Eq. (1), we get different eigenvalue problems, and hence different eigenvalues $\{\lambda_n\}$ and different eigenfunctions $\{X_n(x)\}$ to use in constructing a formal power series solution

$$u(x, t) = \sum c_n X_n(x)T_n(t) \tag{6}$$

of the boundary value problem. The final step in this construction is to choose the coefficients $\{c_n\}$ in Eq. (6) so that

$$u(x, 0) = \sum c_n T_n(0)X_n(x) = f(x). \tag{7}$$

Thus we need finally an *eigenfunction expansion* of the given function $f(x)$ in terms of the eigenfunctions of the pertinent endpoint value problem.

Sturm-Liouville Problems

In order to unify and generalize the method of separation of variables, it is useful to formulate a general type of eigenvalue problem that includes as special cases each of those mentioned above. Equation (1), with y instead of X as the dependent variable, can be written in the form

▶
$$\frac{d}{dx}\left[p(x)\frac{dy}{dx}\right] - q(x)y + \lambda r(x)y = 0, \tag{8}$$

where $p(x) = r(x) \equiv 1$ and $q(x) \equiv 0$. Indeed, we indicate in Problem 16 that essentially any linear second-order differential equation of the form

$$A(x)y'' + B(x)y' + C(x)y + \lambda D(x)y = 0$$

takes the form in (8) after multiplication by a suitable factor. For instance, if we multiply the parametric Bessel equation

$$x^2 y'' + xy' + (\lambda x^2 - n^2)y = 0 \qquad (x > 0)$$

of order n by $1/x$, the result may be written as

$$\frac{d}{dx}\left[x\frac{dy}{dx} \right] - \frac{n^2}{x}y + \lambda xy = 0,$$

which is of the form in (8) with $p(x) = r(x) = x$ and $q(x) = n^2/x$.

Now, on solutions of Eq. (8) in a bounded open interval (a, b), let us impose homogeneous [linear] endpoint conditions of the form

$$\alpha_1 y(a) - \alpha_2 y'(a) = 0, \qquad \beta_1 y(b) + \beta_2 y'(b) = 0, \tag{9}$$

where the coefficients α_1, α_2, β_1, and β_2 are constants. In addition to being homogeneous, these two conditions are *separated,* in that one of them involves the values of $y(x)$ and $y'(x)$ at one endpoint $x = a$, whereas the other involves values at the other endpoint $x = b$. For instance, note that the conditions $y(a) = y'(b) = 0$ are of the form in (9) with $\alpha_1 = \beta_2 = 1$ and $\alpha_2 = \beta_1 = 0$.

An eigenvalue problem of the form

▶
$$\frac{d}{dx}\left[p(x)\frac{dy}{dx} \right] - q(x)y + \lambda r(x)y = 0 \qquad (a < x < b); \tag{8}$$

$$\alpha_1 y(a) - \alpha_2 y'(a) = 0, \qquad \beta_1 y(b) + \beta_2 y'(b) = 0, \tag{9}$$

(with neither α_1 and α_2 nor β_1 and β_2 both zero) is called a **Sturm-Liouville problem,** named for the French mathematicians Charles Sturm (1803–1855) and Joseph Liouville (1809–1882), who investigated this type of problem in the 1830s. Note that the problem in (8)–(9) always has the trivial solution $y(x) \equiv 0$. We seek the values of λ—the **eigenvalues**—for which this problem has a *nontrivial* real-valued solution (an **eigenfunction**), and for each eigenvalue its associated eigenfunction (or eigenfunctions). Note that any constant [nonzero] multiple of an eigenfunction will also be an eigenfunction. The following theorem provides sufficient conditions under which the problem in (8)–(9) has an infinite sequence $\{\lambda_n\}_1^\infty$ of nonnegative eigenvalues, with each eigenvalue λ_n having (to within a constant multiple) exactly one associated eigenfunction $y_n(x)$. A proof of this theorem is outlined in Chapter 9 of G. P. Tolstov, *Fourier Series* (New York: Dover, 1976).

THEOREM 1: Sturm-Liouville Eigenvalues

Suppose that the functions $p(x)$, $p'(x)$, $q(x)$, and $r(x)$ in Eq. (8) are continuous in the interval $[a, b]$ and that $p(x) > 0$ and $r(x) > 0$ at each point of $[a, b]$. Then the eigenvalues of the Sturm-Liouville problem in (8)–(9) constitute an increasing sequence

$$\lambda_1 < \lambda_2 < \lambda_3 < \cdots < \lambda_{n-1} < \lambda_n < \cdots \tag{10}$$

of real numbers with

$$\lim_{n \to \infty} \lambda_n = +\infty. \tag{11}$$

To within a constant factor, only a single eigenfunction $y_n(x)$ is associated with each eigenvalue λ_n. Moreover, if $q(x) \geqq 0$ on $[a, b]$ and the coefficients α_1, α_2, β_1, and β_2 in (9) are all nonnegative, then the eigenvalues are all nonnegative. ∎

Note: It is important to observe the signs in (8) and (9) when verifying the hypotheses of Theorem 1. Sometimes the Sturm-Liouville problem in (8)–(9) is called **regular** if it satisfies the hypotheses of Theorem 1; otherwise it is **singular.** In this section we will confine our attention to regular Sturm-Liouville problems. Singular Sturm-Liouville problems associated with Bessel's equation will appear in Section 10.4.

EXAMPLE 1 In Example 3 of Section 3.8, we saw that the Sturm-Liouville problem

$$y'' + \lambda y = 0 \qquad (0 < x < L);$$
$$y(0) = 0, \qquad y(L) = 0 \tag{12}$$

has eigenvalues $\lambda_n = n^2\pi^2/L^2$ and associated eigenfunctions $y_n(x) = \sin(n\pi x/L)$ ($n = 1, 2, 3, \ldots$). There we had to consider the cases $\lambda = -\alpha^2 < 0$, $\lambda = 0$, and $\lambda = \alpha^2 > 0$ separately. Here $p(x) = r(x) \equiv 1$, $q(x) \equiv 0$, $\alpha_1 = \beta_1 = 1$, and $\alpha_2 = \beta_2 = 0$, so we know from Theorem 1 that the problem in (12) has only nonnegative eigenvalues. Hence only the two cases $\lambda = 0$ and $\lambda = \alpha^2 > 0$ would need to be considered if we were starting afresh. ∎

We are also familiar (from the problems in Section 9.5) with the Sturm-Liouville problem

$$y'' + \lambda y = 0 \qquad (0 < x < L);$$
$$y'(0) = 0, \qquad y'(L) = 0, \tag{13}$$

which has eigenvalues $\lambda_0 = 0$, $\lambda_n = n^2\pi^2/L^2$ ($n = 1, 2, 3, \ldots$) and associated eigenfunctions $y_0(x) \equiv 1$, $y_n(x) = \cos(n\pi x/L)$. We will customarily write $\lambda_0 = 0$ if 0 is an eigenvalue and otherwise write λ_1 for the smallest eigenvalue; thus λ_1 always denotes the smallest positive eigenvalue.

EXAMPLE 2 Find the eigenvalues and associated eigenfunctions of the Sturm-Liouville problem

$$y'' + \lambda y = 0 \qquad (0 < x < L);$$
$$y'(0) = 0, \qquad y(L) = 0. \tag{14}$$

Solution This is a Sturm-Liouville problem satisfying the hypotheses of Theorem 1 with $\alpha_1 = \beta_2 = 0$ and $\alpha_2 = \beta_1 = 1$, so there are no negative eigenvalues. If $\lambda = 0$, then $y(x) = Ax + B$, and thus $y'(0) = A = 0$ and $y(L) = B = 0$. Therefore 0 is not an eigenvalue. If $\lambda = \alpha^2$, then

$$y(x) = A \cos \alpha x + B \sin \alpha x \qquad \text{and} \qquad y'(x) = -A\alpha \sin \alpha x + B\alpha \cos \alpha x.$$

Hence $y'(0) = 0$ implies that $B = 0$, and then $y(L) = A \cos \alpha L = 0$, so it follows that αL is an *odd* integral multiple of $\pi/2$: $\alpha L = (2n - 1)\pi/2$. Thus we have eigenvalues and associated eigenfunctions

$$\lambda_n = \alpha_n^2 = \frac{(2n - 1)^2\pi^2}{4L^2} \qquad \text{and} \qquad y_n(x) = \cos \frac{(2n - 1)\pi x}{2L}$$

for $n = 1, 2, 3, \ldots .$

EXAMPLE 3 Find the eigenvalues and associated eigenfunctions of the Sturm-Liouville problem

$$y'' + \lambda y = 0 \qquad (0 < x < L);$$

$$y(0) = 0, \qquad hy(L) + y'(L) = 0 \qquad (h > 0). \tag{15}$$

Solution This problem satisfies the hypotheses of Theorem 1 with $\alpha_1 = \beta_2 = 1$, $\alpha_2 = 0$, and $\beta_1 = h > 0$, so there are no negative eigenvalues. If $\lambda = 0$, then $y(x) = Ax + B$, thus $y(0) = B = 0$. Then

$$hy(L) + y'(L) = h \cdot AL + A = A \cdot (hL + 1) = 0,$$

and it follows that $A = 0$ as well. Thus 0 is not an eigenvalue.

If $\lambda = \alpha^2$, then

$$y(x) = A \cos \alpha x + B \sin \alpha x.$$

Hence $y(0) = A = 0$, so

$$y(x) = B \sin \alpha x \qquad \text{and} \qquad y'(x) = B\alpha \cos \alpha x.$$

Therefore

$$hy(L) + y'(L) = hB \sin \alpha L + B\alpha \cos \alpha L = 0.$$

If $B \neq 0$, it follows that

$$\tan \alpha L = -\frac{\alpha}{h} = -\frac{\alpha L}{hL}. \tag{16}$$

Thus $\beta = \alpha L$ is a [positive] solution of the equation

$$\tan x = -\frac{x}{hL}. \tag{17}$$

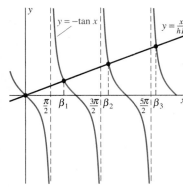

$y = -\tan x$ $y = \frac{x}{hL}$

$\frac{\pi}{2}$ β_1 $\frac{3\pi}{2}$ β_2 $\frac{5\pi}{2}$ β_3 x

FIGURE 10.1.1. The solution of Eq. (17) by geometric methods

The solutions of Eq. (17) are the points of intersection of the graphs of $y(x) = -\tan x$ and $y(x) = x/hL$, as indicated in Fig. 10.1.1. It is apparent from the figure that there is an infinite sequence of positive roots $\beta_1, \beta_2, \beta_3, \ldots$, and that when n is large, β_n is only slightly larger than $(2n - 1)\pi/2$. See the table in Fig. 10.1.2, in which the first eight solutions of Eq. (17) are listed for the case $hL = 1$. At any rate, the eigenvalues and associated eigenfunctions of the problem in (15) are given by

$$\lambda_n = \alpha_n^2 = \frac{\beta_n^2}{L^2}, \qquad y_n(x) = \sin \alpha_n x = \sin \frac{\beta_n x}{L} \tag{18}$$

n	x_n	$(2n - 1)\pi/2$
1	2.0288	1.5708
2	4.9132	4.7124
3	7.9787	7.8540
4	11.0855	10.9956
5	14.2074	14.1372
6	17.3364	17.2788
7	20.4692	20.4204
8	23.6043	23.5619

FIGURE 10.1.2. Approximate values of the first eight positive solutions of $\tan x = -x$

for $n = 1, 2, 3, \ldots$. Equation (17) appears frequently in certain applications (mechanical vibrations and heat conduction are only two of many examples), and its solutions for various values of hL are tabulated in Table 4.19 of Abramowitz and Stegun, *Handbook of Mathematical Functions* (New York: Dover, 1965).

Orthogonal Eigenfunctions

Recall from Section 9.1 that the familiar formulas for the coefficients in a Fourier series follow from the orthogonality of the sine and cosine functions. Similarly, the expansion of a given function in terms of the eigenfunctions of a Sturm-Liouville problem depends upon a crucial orthogonality property of these eigenfunctions. The

functions $\phi(x)$ and $\psi(x)$ are said to be **orthogonal** on the interval $[a, b]$ with respect to the **weight function** $r(x)$ provided that

$$\int_a^b \phi(x)\psi(x)r(x)\, dx = 0. \tag{19}$$

The following theorem implies that any two eigenfunctions of a regular Sturm-Liouville problem that are associated with distinct eigenvalues are orthogonal with respect to the weight function $r(x)$ in Eq. (8).

THEOREM 2: Orthogonality of Eigenfunctions

Suppose that the functions p, q, and r in the Sturm-Liouville problem in (8)–(9) satisfy the hypotheses of Theorem 1, and let $y_i(x)$ and $y_j(x)$ be eigenfunctions associated with the distinct eigenvalues λ_i and λ_j. Then

$$\int_a^b y_i(x)y_j(x)r(x)\, dx = 0. \tag{20}$$

Proof: We begin with the equations

$$\frac{d}{dx}\left[p(x)\frac{dy_i}{dx}\right] - q(x)y_i + \lambda_i r(x)y_i = 0,$$

$$\frac{d}{dx}\left[p(x)\frac{dy_j}{dx}\right] - q(x)y_j + \lambda_j r(x)y_j = 0. \tag{21}$$

These equations imply that λ_i, y_i, and λ_j, y_j are eigenvalue-eigenfunction pairs. If we multiply the first equation by y_j and the second by y_i, then subtract the results, we get

$$y_j\frac{d}{dx}\left[p(x)\frac{dy_i}{dx}\right] - y_i\frac{d}{dx}\left[p(x)\frac{dy_j}{dx}\right] + (\lambda_i - \lambda_j)r(x)y_i y_j = 0.$$

Hence

$$(\lambda_i - \lambda_j)y_i y_j\, r(x) = y_i\frac{d}{dx}\left[p(x)\frac{dy_j}{dx}\right] - y_j\frac{d}{dx}\left[p(x)\frac{dy_i}{dx}\right]$$

$$= \frac{d}{dx}\left[p(x)\left(y_i\frac{dy_j}{dx} - y_j\frac{dy_i}{dx}\right)\right],$$

the latter of the two equalities being verifiable by direct differentiation. Therefore integration from $x = a$ to $x = b$ yields

$$(\lambda_i - \lambda_j)\int_a^b y_i(x)y_j(x)r(x)\, dx = \left[p(x)\left(y_i(x)y_j'(x) - y_j(x)y_i'(x)\right)\right]_a^b. \tag{22}$$

From the endpoint condition in (9), we have

$$\alpha_1 y_i(a) - \alpha_2 y_i'(a) = 0 \quad \text{and} \quad \alpha_1 y_j(a) - \alpha_2 y_j'(a) = 0.$$

Because α_1 and α_2 are not both zero, it follows that the determinant of coefficients must be zero:

$$y_i(a)y_j'(a) - y_j(a)y_i'(a) = 0.$$

Similarly, the second endpoint condition in (9) implies that

$$y_i(b)y_j'(b) - y_j(b)y_i'(b) = 0.$$

Thus the right-hand side in Eq. (22) vanishes. Inasmuch as $\lambda_i \neq \lambda_j$, the result in (20) follows, and the proof is complete. ∎

Eigenfunction Expansions

Now suppose that the function $f(x)$ can be represented in the interval $[a, b]$ by an **eigenfunction series**

$$\blacktriangleright \qquad\qquad f(x) = \sum_{m=1}^{\infty} c_m y_m(x), \qquad\qquad (23)$$

where the functions y_1, y_2, y_3, \ldots are the eigenfunctions of the regular Sturm-Liouville problem in Eqs. (8)–(9). To determine the coefficients c_1, c_2, c_3, \ldots, we generalize the technique by which we determined the ordinary Fourier coefficients in Section 9.1. First we multiply each side of Eq. (23) by $y_n(x)r(x)$, then integrate from $x = a$ to $x = b$. Under the assumption that termwise integration is valid, we obtain

$$\int_a^b f(x)y_n(x)\, r(x)\, dx = \sum_{m=1}^{\infty} c_m \int_a^b y_m(x)y_n(x)\, r(x)\, dx. \qquad (24)$$

But because of the orthogonality in (20), the only nonzero term on the right-hand side in Eq. (24) is the one for which $m = n$. Thus Eq. (24) takes the form

$$\int_a^b f(x)y_n(x)\, r(x)\, dx = c_n \int_a^b [y_n(x)]^2\, r(x)\, dx,$$

and therefore

$$\blacktriangleright \qquad\qquad c_n = \frac{\displaystyle\int_a^b f(x)y_n(x)\, r(x)\, dx}{\displaystyle\int_a^b [y_n(x)]^2\, r(x)\, dx}. \qquad\qquad (25)$$

We therefore *define* the eigenfunction series in (23)—representing $f(x)$ in terms of the eigenfunctions of the given Sturm-Liouville problem—by means of the choice of the coefficients specified by Eq. (25).

For instance, suppose that the Sturm-Liouville problem is the familiar

$$y'' + \lambda y = 0 \qquad (0 < x < \pi); \qquad\qquad (26)$$
$$y(0) = y(\pi) = 0,$$

for which $r(x) \equiv 1$ and the eigenfunctions are $y_n(x) = \sin nx$ for $n = 1, 2, 3, \ldots$. Then Eq. (25) yields

$$c_n = \frac{\displaystyle\int_0^\pi f(x)\sin nx\, dx}{\displaystyle\int_0^\pi \sin^2 nx\, dx} = \frac{2}{\pi}\int_0^\pi f(x)\sin nx\, dx,$$

because $\int_0^\pi \sin^2 nx \, dx = \frac{1}{2}\pi$. This is the familiar formula for the Fourier sine coefficients, and so the eigenfunction series in (23) is simply the familiar Fourier sine series

$$f(x) = \sum c_n \sin nx$$

of $f(x)$ on $[0, \pi]$.

The following theorem, stated without proof, generalizes the Fourier convergence theorem of Section 9.2.

THEOREM 3: Convergence of Eigenfunction Series

Let y_1, y_2, y_3, . . . be the eigenfunctions of a regular Sturm-Liouville problem on $[a, b]$. If the function $f(x)$ is piecewise smooth on $[a, b]$, then the eigenfunction series in Eq. (23) converges for $a < x < b$ to the value $f(x)$ wherever f is continuous, and to the average $\frac{1}{2}[f(x+) + f(x-)]$ of right-hand and left-hand limits at each point of discontinuity. ∎

EXAMPLE 4 For the Sturm-Liouville problem $y'' + \lambda y = 0$ $(0 < x < L)$, $y'(0) = y(L) = 0$ of Example 2, we found the eigenfunctions $y_n(x) = \cos(2n-1)\pi x/(2L)$, $n = 1, 2, 3, \ldots$. The corresponding eigenfunction series for a function $f(x)$ is

$$f(x) = \sum_{n=1}^{\infty} c_n \cos \frac{(2n-1)\pi x}{2L} \tag{27}$$

with

$$c_n = \frac{\int_0^L f(x) \cos([2n-1]\pi x/2L)\, dx}{\int_0^L \cos^2([2n-1]\pi x/2L)\, dx}$$

$$= \frac{2}{L} \int_0^L f(x) \cos \frac{(2n-1)\pi x}{2L}\, dx, \tag{28}$$

because $\int_0^L [\cos^2(2n-1)\pi x/2L]\, dx = L/2$. Thus (27) is the odd half-multiple cosine series of Problem 22 of Section 9.3. Similarly, the Sturm-Liouville problem $y'' + \lambda y = 0$, $y(0) = y'(L) = 0$ leads to the odd half-multiple sine series

$$f(x) = \sum_{n=1}^{\infty} c_n \sin \frac{(2n-1)\pi x}{2L}, \qquad c_n = \frac{2}{L} \int_0^L f(x) \sin \frac{(2n-1)\pi x}{2L}\, dx \tag{29}$$

of Problem 21 of Section 9.3.

EXAMPLE 5 Represent the function $f(x) = A$ (a constant) for $0 < x < 1$ as a series of eigenfunctions of the Sturm-Liouville problem

$$y'' + \lambda y = 0 \qquad (0 < x < 1);$$
$$y(0) = 0, \qquad y(1) + 2y'(1) = 0. \tag{30}$$

Solution Comparing (30) with (15), we see that this is the Sturm-Liouville problem of Example 3 with $L = 1$ and $h = \frac{1}{2}$. From (17) and (18) we see that the eigenfunctions of this problem are therefore $y_n(x) = \sin \beta_n x$, where $\beta_1, \beta_2, \beta_3, \ldots$ are the positive roots of the equation $\tan x = -2x$. Hence the coefficients in the desired series are given by

$$c_n = \frac{\int_0^1 A \sin \beta_n x \, dx}{\int_0^1 \sin^2 \beta_n x \, dx}. \tag{31}$$

Now $\int_0^1 A \sin \beta_n x \, dx = A(1 - \cos \beta_n)/\beta_n$ and

$$\int_0^1 \sin^2 \beta_n x \, dx = \int_0^1 \frac{1}{2} (1 - \cos 2\beta_n x) \, dx = \frac{1}{2} \left[x - \frac{1}{2\beta_n} \sin 2\beta_n x \right]_0^1$$

$$= \frac{1}{2} \left(1 - \frac{\sin \beta_n \cos \beta_n}{\beta_n} \right).$$

Consequently,

$$\int_0^1 \sin^2 \beta_n x \, dx = \frac{1}{2} (1 + 2 \cos^2 \beta_n).$$

In the last step we used the fact from Eq. (17) that $(\sin \beta_n)/\beta_n = -2 \cos \beta_n$. Substituting these values for the integrals in (31), we get the eigenfunction series

$$f(x) = \sum_{n=1}^{\infty} \frac{2A(1 - \cos \beta_n)}{\beta_n(1 + 2 \cos^2 \beta_n)} \sin \beta_n x. \tag{32}$$

Summary

According to the theorems in this section, every regular Sturm-Liouville problem has the following three properties:

- It has an infinite sequence of eigenvalues diverging to infinity (Theorem 1).
- The eigenfunctions are orthogonal with appropriate weight function (Theorem 2).
- Any piecewise smooth function can be represented by an eigenfunction series (Theorem 3).

There are other types of eigenvalue problems in applied mathematics that also enjoy these three important properties. Some isolated examples will appear in subsequent sections, though we will confine our attention largely to applications of Sturm-Liouville problems.

10.1 Problems

The problems for Section 3.10 deal with eigenvalues and eigenfunctions and may be used here as well. In Problems 1 through 5, verify that the eigenvalues and eigenfunctions for the indicated Sturm-Liouville problem are those listed.

1. $y'' + \lambda y = 0$, $y'(0) = y'(L) = 0$; $\lambda_0 = 0$, $y_0(x) \equiv 1$ and $\lambda_n = n^2\pi^2/L^2$, $y_n(x) = \cos n\pi x/L$

2. $y'' + \lambda y = 0$, $y(0) = y'(L) = 0$; $\lambda_n = (2n-1)^2\pi^2/4L^2$, $y_n(x) = \sin(2n-1)\pi x/2L$, $n \geq 1$

3. $y'' + \lambda y = 0$, $y'(0) = hy(L) + y'(L) = 0$ $(h > 0)$; $\lambda_n = \beta_n^2/L^2$, $y_n(x) = \cos \beta_n x/L$ $(n \geq 1)$, where β_n is the nth positive root of $\tan x = hL/x$. Sketch $y = \tan x$ and $y = hL/x$ to estimate the value of β_n for n large.

4. $y'' + \lambda y = 0$, $hy(0) - y'(0) = y(L) = 0$ $(h > 0)$; $\lambda_n = \beta_n^2/L^2$, $y_n(x) = \beta_n \cos \beta_n x/L + hL \sin \beta_n x/L$ $(n \geq 1)$, where β_n is the nth positive root of $\tan x = -x/hL$.

5. $y'' + \lambda y = 0$, $hy(0) - y'(0) = hy(L) + y'(L) = 0$ $(h > 0)$; $\lambda_n = \beta_n^2/L^2$, $y_n(x) = \beta_n \cos \beta_n x/L + hL \sin \beta_n x/L$ $(n \geq 1)$, where β_n is the nth positive root of $\tan x = 2hLx/(x^2 - h^2L^2)$. Estimate β_n for n large by sketching the graphs of $y = 2hL \cot x$ and the hyperbola $y = (x^2 - h^2L^2)/x$.

6. Show that the Sturm-Liouville problem $y'' + \lambda y = 0$, $y(0) = y'(L) = 0$ leads to the odd half-multiple sine series in Eq. (29) (see Problem 2).

In Problems 7 through 10, represent the given function $f(x)$ as a series of eigenfunctions of the indicated Sturm-Liouville problem.

7. $f(x) \equiv 1$, the Sturm-Liouville problem of Example 3

8. $f(x) \equiv 1$, the Sturm-Liouville problem of Problem 3

9. $f(x) = x$; the Sturm-Liouville problem of Example 3 with $L = 1$

10. $f(x) = x$; the Sturm-Liouville problem of Problem 3 with $L = 1$

Problems 11 through 14 deal with the regular Sturm-Liouville problem

$$y'' + \lambda y = 0 \qquad (0 < x < L);$$
$$y(0) = 0, \qquad hy(L) - y'(L) = 0, \tag{33}$$

where $h > 0$. Note that Theorem 1 does not exclude the possibility of negative eigenvalues.

11. Show that $\lambda_0 = 0$ is an eigenvalue if and only if $hL = 1$, in which case the associated eigenfunction is $y_0(x) = x$.

12. Show that the problem in (33) has a single negative eigenvalue λ_0 if and only if $hL > 1$, in which case $\lambda_0 = -\beta_0^2/L^2$ and

$y_0(x) = \sinh \beta_0 x/L$, where β_0 is the positive root of the equation $\tanh x = x/hL$. (*Suggestion*: Sketch the graphs of $y = \tanh x$ and $y = x/hL$.)

13. Show that the positive eigenvalues and associated eigenfunctions of the problem in (33) are $\lambda_n = \beta_n^2/L^2$ and $y_n(x) = \sin \beta_n x/L$ $(n \geq 1)$, where β_n is the nth positive root of $\tan x = x/hL$.

14. Suppose that $hL = 1$ in (33) and that $f(x)$ is piecewise smooth. Then show that

$$f(x) = c_0 x + \sum_{n=1}^{\infty} c_n \sin \frac{\beta_n x}{L},$$

where $\{\beta_n\}_1^{\infty}$ are the positive roots of $\tan x = x$, and

$$c_0 = \frac{3}{L^3} \int_0^L x f(x)\, dx,$$

$$c_n = \frac{2}{L \sin^2 \beta_n} \int_0^L f(x) \sin \frac{\beta_n x}{L}\, dx.$$

15. Show that the eigenvalues and eigenfunctions of the Sturm-Liouville problem

$$y'' + \lambda y = 0 \qquad (0 < x < 1);$$

$$y(0) + y'(0) = 0, \qquad y(1) = 0$$

are given by $\lambda_0 = 0$, $y_0(x) = x - 1$ and

$$\lambda_n = \beta_n^2, \quad y_n(x) = \beta_n \cos \beta_n x - \sin \beta_n x$$

for $n \geq 1$, where $\{\beta_n\}_1^{\infty}$ are the positive roots of $\tan x = x$.

16. Beginning with the equation

$$A(x)y'' + B(x)y' + C(x)y + \lambda D(x)y = 0,$$

first divide by $A(x)$ and then multiply by

$$p(x) = \exp\left(\int \frac{B(x)}{A(x)}\, dx \right).$$

Show that the resulting equation can be written in the Sturm-Liouville form

$$\frac{d}{dx}\left[p(x) \frac{dy}{dx} \right] - q(x)y + \lambda r(x)y = 0$$

with $q(x) = -p(x)C(x)/A(x)$ and $r(x) = p(x)D(x)/A(x)$.

Loaded Uniform Beam

Consider a uniform beam with [downward] load $w(x)$, whose deflection function $y(x)$ satisfies the fourth-order equation

$$EIy^{(4)} = w(x)$$

for $0 < x < L$ and the endpoint conditions

- $y = y'' = 0$ at a hinged (or simply supported) end;
- $y = y' = 0$ at a fixed (built-in) end;
- $y'' = y''' = 0$ at a free end.

In the case in which each end is hinged, $y(x)$ can be found by the Fourier series method discussed in Section 9.4—that is, by substituting the Fourier series

$$y(x) = \sum b_n \sin \frac{n\pi x}{L}$$

in the differential equation

$$EIy^{(4)} = w(x) = \sum_{n=1}^{\infty} c_n \sin \frac{n\pi x}{L} \qquad (34)$$

(where c_n is the nth Fourier sine coefficient of $w(x)$) to determine the coefficients $\{b_n\}$.

17. Suppose that w is constant in Eq. (34). Apply the method described above to obtain the deflection function

$$y(x) = \frac{4wL^4}{EI\pi^5} \sum_{n\ \text{odd}} \frac{1}{n^5} \sin \frac{n\pi x}{L}.$$

18. Suppose that $w = bx$ in (34). Derive the deflection function

$$y(x) = \frac{2bL^5}{EI\pi^5} \sum_{n=1}^{\infty} \frac{(-1)^{n+1}}{n^5} \sin \frac{n\pi x}{L}.$$

The method used in Problems 17 and 18 succeeds because the functions $\sin n\pi x/L$ satisfy the hinged/hinged conditions $y(0) = y''(0) = y(L) = y''(L) = 0$, so that $y(x)$ does also.

If, instead, both ends of the beam are fixed, in place of the sine functions we can use the eigenfunctions of the problem

$$y^{(4)} - \lambda y = 0 \qquad (0 < x < L);$$
$$y(0) = y'(0) = 0, \qquad y(L) = y'(L) = 0, \qquad (35)$$

because these eigenfunctions satisfy the fixed/fixed endpoint conditions. The eigenvalues of this problem are all positive, and by Problem 22 below the associated eigenfunctions are orthogonal with weight function $r(x) \equiv 1$. Hence we can write

$$w(x) = \sum_{n=1}^{\infty} c_n y_n(x), \qquad c_n = \frac{\displaystyle\int_0^L w(x)y_n(x)\,dx}{\displaystyle\int_0^L [y_n(x)]^2\,dx}, \qquad (36)$$

according to the analogue of Theorem 3 that holds for the problem in (35). If we write $\lambda = \alpha^4$, then $y_n(x)$ is of the form

$$y(x) = A \cosh \alpha x + B \sinh \alpha x + C \cos \alpha x + D \sin \alpha x, \quad (37)$$

with $\alpha = \alpha_n$, so it follows that $y_n^{(4)}(x) = \alpha_n^4 y_n(x)$. When we substitute the series $y(x) = \sum b_n y_n(x)$—which evidently satisfies the fixed/fixed endpoint conditions—in (35), we obtain

$$EI \sum_{n=1}^{\infty} b_n \alpha_n^4 y_n(x) = \sum_{n=1}^{\infty} c_n y_n(x).$$

Hence $EIb_n \alpha_n^4 = c_n$, so the deflection function of the beam is

$$y(x) = \sum_{n=1}^{\infty} \frac{c_n}{EI\alpha_n^4} y_n(x). \qquad (38)$$

The following problems deal with the eigenvalues and eigenfunctions of the problem in (35) and similar problems.

19. Begin with the general solution in (37) of $y^{(4)} - \alpha^4 y = 0$. First note that $y(0) = y'(0) = 0$ implies that $C = -A$ and $D = -B$. Then impose the conditions $y(L) = y'(L) = 0$ to get two homogeneous linear equations in A and B. Hence the determinant of coefficients of A and B must vanish; deduce from this that $\cosh \alpha L \cos \alpha L = 1$. Conclude that the nth eigenvalue is $\lambda_n = \beta_n^4/L^4$ where $\{\beta_n\}_1^{\infty}$ are the positive roots of the equation $\cosh x \cos x = 1$ (see Fig. 10.1.3). Finally, show that an associated eigenfunction is

$$y_n(x) = (\sinh \beta_n - \sin \beta_n)\left(\cosh \frac{\beta_n x}{L} - \cos \frac{\beta_n x}{L}\right)$$

$$- (\cosh \beta_n - \cos \beta_n)\left(\sinh \frac{\beta_n x}{L} - \sin \frac{\beta_n x}{L}\right).$$

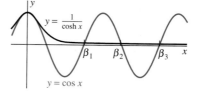

FIGURE 10.1.3. The solutions of $\cosh x \cos x = 1$ (the graph is not drawn to scale)

20. For the case of a cantilever (fixed/free) beam, we need to solve the eigenvalue problem

$$y^{(4)} - \lambda y = 0 \qquad (0 < x < L);$$
$$y(0) = y'(0) = 0, \qquad y''(L) = y'''(L) = 0.$$

Proceeding as in Problem 19, show that the nth eigenvalue is $\lambda_n = \beta_n^4/L^4$, where $\{\beta_n\}_1^{\infty}$ are the positive roots of the equation $\cosh x \cos x = -1$. Then find the associated eigenfunction.

21. For the eigenvalue problem

$$y^{(4)} - \lambda y = 0, \qquad y(0) = y'(0) = 0 = y(L) = y''(L)$$

corresponding to a fixed/hinged beam, show that the nth eigenvalue is $\lambda_n = \beta_n^4 / L^4$, where $\{\beta_n\}_1^\infty$ are the positive roots of the equation $\tanh x = \tan x$.

22. Suppose that $y_m^{(4)} = \lambda_m y_m$ and $y_n^{(4)} = \lambda_n y_n$. Apply the method of proof of Theorem 2 and integrate by parts twice to show that

$$(\lambda_m - \lambda_n) \int_0^L y_m(x) y_n(x)\, dx = \left[y_n(x) \frac{d^3 y_m}{dx^3} - y_m(x) \frac{d^3 y_n}{dx^3} - \frac{dy_n}{dx} \frac{d^2 y_m}{dx^2} + \frac{dy_m}{dx} \frac{d^2 y_n}{dx^2} \right]_0^L.$$

Conclude that if each endpoint condition is either $y = y' = 0$, $y = y'' = 0$, or $y'' = y''' = 0$, then y_m and y_n are orthogonal if $\lambda_m \neq \lambda_n$.

10.2 Applications of Eigenfunction Series

This section is devoted to three examples that illustrate the application of the eigenfunction series of Section 10.1 to boundary value problems. In each, the method of separation of variables leads to a Sturm-Liouville problem in which the eigenfunctions are used as building blocks to construct a solution satisfying the nonhomogeneous boundary condition in the original problem.

EXAMPLE 1 A uniform slab of material with thermal diffusivity k occupies the region $0 \leq x \leq L$ and initially has temperature U_0 throughout. Beginning at time $t = 0$, the face $x = 0$ is held at temperature zero; at the face $x = L$, heat exchange takes place with a surrounding medium at temperature zero, so $hu + u_x = 0$ there (by Problem 23 of Section 9.5; the constant h is an appropriate heat transfer coefficient). We want to find the temperature $u(x, t)$ of the slab at position x at time t; $u(x, t)$ satisfies the boundary value problem.

$$u_t = ku_{xx} \qquad (0 < x < L, \quad t > 0); \tag{1}$$

$$u(0, t) = 0, \tag{2}$$

▶

$$hu(L, t) + u_x(L, t) = 0, \tag{3}$$

$$u(x, 0) = U_0. \tag{4}$$

Solution As in Section 9.5, we begin by substituting $u(x, t) = X(x)T(t)$ in Eq. (1) and thereby obtain

$$\frac{X''}{X} = \frac{T'}{kT} = -\lambda$$

as usual, so

$$X'' + \lambda X = T' + \lambda kT = 0. \tag{5}$$

Now Eq. (2) gives $X(0) = 0$, and Eq. (3) yields $hX(L)T(t) + X'(L)T(t) = 0$. We naturally assume that $T(t)$ is not identically zero (because we are not looking for a trivial solution); it follows that $X(x)$ and λ satisfy the Sturm-Liouville problem

$$X'' + \lambda X = 0 \qquad (0 < x < L);$$

$$X(0) = 0, \qquad hX(L) + X'(L) = 0. \tag{6}$$

In Example 3 of Section 10.1, we found that the eigenvalues and associated eigenfunctions of this problem are

$$\lambda_n = \frac{\beta_n^2}{L^2}, \qquad X_n(x) = \sin \frac{\beta_n x}{L} \tag{7}$$

for $n = 1, 2, 3, \ldots$, where β_n denotes the nth positive root of the equation

$$\tan x = -\frac{x}{hL}. \tag{8}$$

When we substitute $\lambda = \beta_n^2/L^2$ in the right-hand equation in (5), we get the first-order equation

$$T_n' = -\frac{\beta_n^2 k}{L^2} T_n$$

with solution (to within a multiplicative constant)

$$T_n(t) = e^{-\beta_n^2 kt/L^2}. \tag{9}$$

Consequently, each of the functions

$$u_n(x, t) = X_n(x)T_n(t) = e^{-\beta_n^2 kt/L^2} \sin \frac{\beta_n x}{L}$$

satisfies the homogeneous conditions in (1)–(3) of the boundary value problem. It remains only for us to choose the coefficients so that the formal series

$$\blacktriangleright \qquad u(x, t) = \sum_{n=1}^{\infty} c_n e^{-\beta_n^2 kt/L^2} \sin \frac{\beta_n x}{L} \tag{10}$$

also satisfies the nonhomogeneous condition

$$u(x, 0) = \sum_{n=1}^{\infty} c_n \sin \frac{\beta_n x}{L} = U_0. \tag{11}$$

Now $r(x) \equiv 1$ in the Sturm-Liouville problem in (6), so by Theorem 3 and Eq. (25) of Section 10.1, we can satisfy (11) by choosing

$$\blacktriangleright \qquad c_n = \frac{\displaystyle\int_0^L U_0 \sin (\beta_n x/L)\, dx}{\displaystyle\int_0^L \sin^2(\beta_n x/L)\, dx}.$$

But

$$\int_0^L U_0 \sin \frac{\beta_n x}{L}\, dx = \frac{U_0 L}{\beta_n} (1 - \cos \beta_n),$$

and by essentially the same computation as in Example 5 of Section 10.1 we find that

$$\int_0^L \sin^2 \frac{\beta_n x}{L}\, dx = \frac{1}{2h} (hL + \cos^2 \beta_n).$$

Hence

$$c_n = \frac{2U_0 hL(1 - \cos \beta_n)}{\beta_n(hL + \cos^2 \beta_n)},$$

and substitution of this value in (10) yields the formal series solution

$$u(x, t) = 2U_0 hL \sum_{n=1}^{\infty} \frac{1 - \cos \beta_n}{\beta_n(hL + \cos^2 \beta_n)} e^{-\beta_n^2 kt/L^2} \sin \frac{\beta_n x}{L}. \tag{12}$$

∎

Longitudinal Vibrations of Bars

Suppose that a uniform elastic bar has length L, cross-sectional area A, and density δ (mass per unit volume) and occupies the interval $0 \le x \le L$ when it is unstretched. We consider longitudinal vibrations in which each cross section (normal to the x-axis) moves only in the x-direction. We can then describe the motion of the bar in terms of the displacement $u(x, t)$ at time t of the cross section whose unstretched position is x. It follows (see Problem 13) from Hooke's law and the definition of the Young's modulus E of the material of the bar that the force $F(x, t)$ exerted on the cross section x by the part of the bar to the *left* of this section is

$$F(x, t) = -AEu_x(x, t), \tag{13}$$

the minus sign signifying that F acts to the left when $u_x > 0$ (so the bar is then stretched near x rather than compressed) (Fig. 10.2.1).

We take Eq. (13) as the starting point for our derivation of the partial differential equation that the displacement function $u(x, t)$ satisfies when the displacements are sufficiently small that Hooke's law may be applied. If we apply Newton's second law of motion to the segment of the bar between cross section x and cross section $x + \Delta x$, we get

$$(\delta A \, \Delta x) u_{tt}(\bar{x}, t) \approx -F(x + \Delta x, t) + F(x, t)$$
$$= AE[u_x(x + \Delta x, t) - u_x(x, t)], \tag{14}$$

FIGURE 10.2.1. A small segment of the bar

where \bar{x} denotes the midpoint of $[x, x + \Delta x]$, because this segment has mass $\delta A \, \Delta x$ and approximate acceleration $u_{tt}(\bar{x}, t)$. When we divide the expression in (14) by $\delta A \, \Delta x$ and then take the limit as $\Delta x \to 0$, the result is the one-dimensional wave equation

$$\frac{\partial^2 u}{\partial t^2} = a^2 \frac{\partial^2 u}{\partial x^2}, \tag{15}$$

where

$$a^2 = \frac{E}{\delta}. \tag{16}$$

Because Eq. (15) is identical to the equation of the vibrating string, it follows from our discussion of the d'Alembert solution in Section 9.6 that the [free] longitudinal vibrations of a bar with fixed ends are represented by waves of the form $u(x, t) = F(x \pm at)$. The velocity $a = \sqrt{E/\delta}$ with which these waves travel is the velocity of sound in the material of the bar. Indeed, the wave equation in (15) also describes ordinary one-dimensional sound waves in a gas in a pipe. In this case, E in Eq. (16) denotes the bulk modulus (fractional increase in density per unit increase in pressure) of the gas and δ is its equilibrium density.

EXAMPLE 2 A bar has length L, density δ, cross-sectional area A, Young's modulus E, and total mass $M = \delta AL$. Its end $x = 0$ is fixed and a mass m is attached to its free end (Fig. 10.2.2). The bar initially is stretched linearly by moving m a distance $d = bL$ to the right; at time $t = 0$ the system is released from rest. To determine the subsequent vibrations of the bar, we must solve the boundary value problem

FIGURE 10.2.2. The bar-and-mass system of Example 2

$$u_{tt} = a^2 u_{xx} \qquad (0 < x < L, \quad t > 0); \tag{17a}$$

$$u(0, t) = 0, \tag{17b}$$

$$mu_{tt}(L, t) = -AEu_x(L, t), \tag{17c}$$

$$u(x, 0) = bx, \qquad u_t(x, 0) + 0. \tag{17d}$$

Solution The endpoint condition at $x = L$ in (17c) comes from equating $ma = mu_{tt}$ for the mass with the force $F = -AEu_x$ given in (13)—the mass being acted on only by the bar. Substitution of $u(x, t) = X(x)T(t)$ in $u_{tt} = a^2 u_{xx}$ leads, as usual, to the equations

$$X'' + \lambda X = 0, \qquad T'' + \lambda a^2 T = 0. \tag{18}$$

The boundary condition in (17b) yields $u(0, t) = X(0)T(t) = 0$, so one endpoint condition is $X(0) = 0$. Because $u_{tt} = XT''$ and $u_x = X'T$, Eq. (17c) yields

$$mX(L)T''(t) = -AEX'(L)T(t)$$

as the other endpoint condition. Substitution of

$$T''(t) = -\lambda a^2 T(t) = -\frac{\lambda E}{\delta} T(t),$$

followed by division by $-ET(t)/\delta$, gives $m\lambda X(L) = A\delta X'(L)$. Thus the eigenvalue problem for $X(x)$ is

$$X'' + \lambda X = 0; \tag{19}$$
$$X(0) = 0, \qquad m\lambda X(L) = A\delta X'(L).$$

It is important to note that—because of the presence of λ in the right-endpoint condition—this is *not* a Sturm-Liouville problem, so Theorems 1 through 3 of Section 10.1 do not apply. Nevertheless, all eigenvalues of (19) are positive (Problem 9). We therefore write $\lambda = \alpha^2$, and note that $X(x) = \sin \alpha x$ satisfies $X(0) = 0$. The right-endpoint condition in (19) then yields

$$m\alpha^2 \sin \alpha L = A\delta\alpha \cos \alpha L,$$

and thus

$$\tan \alpha L = \frac{A\delta}{m\alpha} = \frac{M/m}{\alpha L}, \tag{20}$$

where $M = A\delta L$. We put $\beta = \alpha L$; it follows that the eigenvalues of (19) and associated eigenfunctions are

$$\lambda_n = \frac{\beta_n^2}{L^2}, \qquad X_n(x) = \sin \frac{\beta_n x}{L} \tag{21}$$

for $n = 1, 2, 3, \ldots$, where $\{\beta_n\}_1^\infty$ are the positive roots of the equation

$$\tan x = \frac{M/m}{x}, \tag{22}$$

indicated in Fig. 10.2.3.

Next, we deduce in the usual way from

$$T_n'' + \frac{\beta_n^2 a^2}{L^2} T_n = 0, \qquad T_n'(0) = 0$$

that $T_n(t) = \cos \beta_n at/L$ to within a multiplicative constant. Thus it remains only to find coefficients $\{c_n\}_1^\infty$ so that the series

$$\blacktriangleright \qquad u(x, t) = \sum_{n=1}^{\infty} c_n \cos \frac{\beta_n at}{L} \sin \frac{\beta_n x}{L} \tag{23}$$

satisfies the nonhomogeneous condition

$$u(x, 0) = \sum_{n=1}^{\infty} c_n \sin \frac{\beta_n x}{L} = f(x) = bx. \tag{24}$$

Caution is required because (19) is not a Sturm-Liouville problem. Indeed, we ask you to show in Problems 14 and 15 that the eigenfunctions $\{\sin \beta_n x/L\}_1^\infty$ are *not* orthogonal on $[0, L]$, so the coefficient formula in Eq. (25), Section 10.1, is not applicable here.

But the following sly trick succeeds. Differentiation of the expressions in Eq. (24) yields

$$\sum_{n=1}^{\infty} \frac{c_n \beta_n}{L} \cos \frac{\beta_n x}{L} = f'(x) = b. \tag{25}$$

The extreme members in Eq. (24) are zero when $x = 0$, so it suffices (assuming the validity of termwise integration of Eq. (25)) to find $\{c_n\}_1^\infty$ so that Eq. (25) holds. It happens that the terms $\{\cos \beta_n x/L\}_1^\infty$ *are* orthogonal on $[0, L]$. In fact, we ask you in Problem 8 to show that they are precisely the eigenfunctions of the regular Sturm-Liouville problem

$$y''(x) + \lambda y(x) = 0 \qquad (0 < x < L);$$
$$y'(0) = 0, \qquad My(L) + mLy'(L) = 0. \tag{26}$$

Consequently we *can* use Eq. (25) of Section 10.1 to find the coefficients in Eq. (25):

$$\blacktriangleright \qquad \frac{c_n \beta_n}{L} = \frac{\int_0^L b \cos(\beta_n x/L)\, dx}{\int_0^L \cos^2(\beta_n x/L)\, dx}.$$

Routine computations give

$$\int_0^L b \cos \frac{\beta_n x}{L}\, dx = \frac{bL}{\beta_n} \sin \beta_n = \frac{bLM}{m\beta_n^2} \cos \beta_n$$

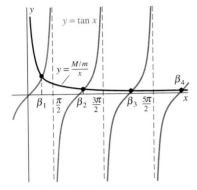

FIGURE 10.2.3.

and

$$\int_0^L \cos^2 \frac{\beta_n x}{L} \, dx = \frac{L}{4\beta_n} (2\beta_n + \sin 2\beta_n),$$

so

$$c_n = \frac{4bLM}{m} \cdot \frac{\cos \beta_n}{\beta_n^2(2\beta_n + \sin 2\beta_n)}.$$

On substituting these values in Eq. (23), we finally get the formal series solution

$$u(x, t) = \frac{4bLM}{m} \sum_{n=1}^{\infty} \frac{\cos \beta_n \sin (\beta_n x/L) \cos (\beta_n at/L)}{\beta_n^2(2\beta_n + \sin 2\beta_n)}. \tag{27}$$

It is of interest to note that this series converges rapidly because $\beta_n \approx (n-1)\pi$ for n large, and that the nth term circular frequency is

$$\omega_n = \frac{\beta_n a}{L} = \frac{\beta_n}{L} \sqrt{\frac{E}{\delta}}. \tag{28}$$

∎

Transverse Vibrations of Bars

We now discuss vibrations of a uniform elastic bar in which the motion of each point is not longitudinal, but instead is perpendicular to the x-axis (the axis of the bar in its equilibrium position). Let $y(x, t)$ denote the transverse displacement of the cross section at x at time t, as indicated in Fig. 10.2.4. We merely want to outline a derivation of the partial differential equation that the deflection function $f(x, t)$ satisfies. Recall first that in Section 3.8 we introduced the equation $EIy^{(4)} = F$ for the static deflection of a bar or beam under the influence of a transverse external force F (per unit length). According to a general dynamical principle, we can transform the static equation $EIy^{(4)} = F$ into a dynamical equation (with no external force) by replacing F with the reversed inertial force $F = -\rho y_{tt}$, where ρ is the linear density (mass/length) of the bar, and also by replacing $y^{(4)}$ with y_{xxxx}. This gives

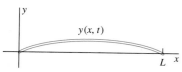

FIGURE 10.2.4. A bar undergoing transverse vibrations

$$\blacktriangleright \qquad EI \frac{\partial^4 y}{\partial x^4} = -\rho \frac{\partial^2 y}{\partial t^2},$$

which may be written in the form

$$\frac{\partial^2 y}{\partial t^2} + a^4 \frac{\partial^4 y}{\partial x^4} = 0, \tag{29}$$

where

$$a^4 = \frac{EI}{\rho}. \tag{30}$$

The following example illustrates the solution of this fourth-order partial differential equation by the method of separation of variables.

EXAMPLE 3 A uniform bar with linear density ρ, Young's modulus E, and cross-sectional moment of inertia I is simply supported (or hinged) at its two ends $x = 0$ and $x = L$. If the bar

is set in motion from rest with given initial position $f(x)$, then its displacement function $y(x, t)$ satisfies the boundary value problem

$$y_{tt} + a^4 y_{xxxx} = 0 \qquad (0 < x < L, \quad t > 0); \tag{31a}$$

▶
$$y(0, t) = y_{xx}(0, t) = y(L, t) = y_{xx}(L, t) = 0, \tag{31b}$$

$$y(x, 0) = f(x), \qquad y_t(x, 0) = 0. \tag{31c}$$

Find $y(x, t)$. The boundary conditions in (31b) are the hinged end conditions that we accept without proof, and those in (31c) are the initial conditions.

Solution Substitution of $y(x, t) = X(x)T(t)$ in the differential equation yields $XT'' + a^4 X^{(4)} T = 0$, so

$$\frac{X^{(4)}}{X} = -\frac{T''}{a^4 T} = \lambda. \tag{32}$$

To determine the sign of λ, we reason that the equation

$$T'' + \lambda a^4 T = 0 \tag{33}$$

must have trigonometric rather than exponential solutions. The reason is that on the basis of practical experience—with tuning forks or xylophone bars, for instance—one expects periodic vibrations to take place. This could not occur if λ were negative and Eq. (33) had exponential solutions. Hence λ must be positive, and it is convenient to write $\lambda = \alpha^4 > 0$. Then $X(x)$ must satisfy the equation

$$X^{(4)}(x) - \alpha^4 X(x) = 0, \tag{34}$$

which has the general solution

$$X(x) = A \cos \alpha x + B \sin \alpha x + C \cosh \alpha x + D \sinh \alpha x,$$

with

$$X''(x) = \alpha^2(-A \cos \alpha x - B \sin \alpha x + C \cosh \alpha x + D \sinh \alpha x).$$

The endpoint conditions in (31) yield

$$X(0) = X''(0) = X(L) = X''(L) = 0. \tag{35}$$

Hence

$$X(0) = A + C = 0 \qquad \text{and} \qquad X''(0) = -A + C = 0,$$

and these two equations imply that $A = C = 0$. Therefore,

$$X(L) = B \sin \alpha L + D \sinh \alpha L = 0$$

and

$$X''(L) = \alpha^2(-B \sin \alpha L + D \sinh \alpha L) = 0.$$

It follows that

$$B \sin \alpha L = 0 \qquad \text{and} \qquad D \sinh \alpha L = 0.$$

But $\sinh \alpha L \neq 0$ because $\alpha \neq 0$; consequently $D = 0$. Hence $B \neq 0$ if we are to have a nontrivial solution, so $\sin \alpha L = 0$. Thus α must be an integral multiple of π/L.

Therefore, the eigenvalues and associated eigenfunctions of the problem determined by Eqs. (34) and (35) are

$$\lambda_n = \alpha_n^4 = \frac{n^4 \pi^4}{L^4}, \quad X_n(x) = \sin \frac{n \pi x}{L} \tag{36}$$

for $n = 1, 2, 3, \ldots$.

With $\lambda = n^4 \pi^4 / L^4$ in (33) we get the equation

$$T_n'' + \frac{n^4 \pi^4 a^4}{L^4} T_n = 0. \tag{37}$$

Because the initial condition $y_t(x, 0) = 0$ yields $T_n'(0) = 0$, we take

$$T_n(t) = \cos \frac{n^2 \pi^2 a^2 t}{L^2}. \tag{38}$$

Combining the results in (36) and (38), we construct the series

$$\blacktriangleright \qquad y(x, t) = \sum_{n=1}^{\infty} c_n \cos \frac{n^2 \pi^2 a^2 t}{L^2} \sin \frac{n \pi x}{L} \tag{39}$$

that formally satisfies the partial differential equation in (31) and the homogeneous boundary conditions. The nonhomogeneous condition is

$$y(x, 0) = \sum_{n=1}^{\infty} c_n \sin \frac{n \pi x}{L} = f(x),$$

so we choose the Fourier sine coefficients, given by

$$\blacktriangleright \qquad c_n = \frac{2}{L} \int_0^L f(x) \sin \frac{n \pi x}{L} \, dx, \tag{40}$$

in order for Eq. (39) to provide a formal series solution. ∎

Note that the circular frequency of the nth term in (39) is

$$\omega_n = \frac{n^2 \pi^2 a^2}{L^2} = n^2 \omega_1, \tag{41}$$

where the fundamental frequency of the bar is

$$\omega_1 = \frac{\pi^2 a^2}{L^2} = \frac{\pi^2}{L^2} \sqrt{\frac{EI}{\rho}}. \tag{42}$$

Because the frequency of each of the higher harmonics is an integral multiple of ω_1, the sound of a vibrating bar with simply supported ends is musical. Because the higher frequencies $\{n^2 \omega_1\}_2^{\infty}$ are sparser than the higher frequencies $\{n \omega_1\}_2^{\infty}$ of a vibrating string, the tone of a vibrating bar is purer than that of a vibrating string. This partly accounts for the silkiness of the sound of the vibraphone as played by Milt Jackson, former member of the Modern Jazz Quartet.

10.2 Problems

Find formal series solutions of the boundary value problems in Problems 1 through 6. Express each answer in the form given in Problem 1.

1. $u_t = ku_{xx}$ $(0 < x < L, \ t > 0)$;
$u_x(0, t) = hu(L, t) + u_x(L, t) = 0, u(x, 0) = f(x)$
(*Answer:*

$$u(x, t) = \sum_{n=1}^{\infty} c_n e^{-\beta_n^2 \, kt/L^2} \cos \frac{\beta_n x}{L},$$

where $\{\beta_n\}_1^\infty$ are the positive roots of the equation $\tan x = hL/x$ and

$$c_n = \frac{2h}{hL + \sin^2 \beta_n} \int_0^L f(x) \cos \frac{\beta_n x}{L} \, dx.)$$

2. $u_{xx} + u_{yy} = 0$ $(0 < x < L, \ 0 < y < L)$;
$u(0, y) = hu(L, y) + u_x(L, y) = 0, u(x, L) = 0,$
$u(x, 0) = f(x)$

3. $u_{xx} + u_{yy} = 0$ $(0 < x < L, \ 0 < y < L)$;
$u_y(x, 0) = hu(x, L) + u_y(x, L) = 0, u(L, y) = 0,$
$u(0, y) = g(y)$

4. $u_{xx} + u_{yy} = 0$ $(0 < x < L, \ y > 0)$; $u(0, y) =$
$hu(L, y) + u_x(L, y) = 0, u(x, y)$ bounded as $y \to +\infty$,
$u(x, 0) = f(x)$

5. $u_t = ku_{xx}$ $(0 < x < L, \ t > 0)$;
$hu(0, t) - u_x(0, t) = u(L, t) = 0, u(x, 0) = f(x)$

6. $u_t = ku_{xx}$ $(0 < x < L, \ t > 0)$;
$hu(0, t) - u_x(0, t) = hu(L, t) + u_x(L, t) = 0,$
$u(x, 0) = f(x)$

7. Let $u(x, y)$ denote the bounded steady-state temperature in an infinitely high wall with base $y = 0$ and faces $x = 0$ and $x = 1$. The face $x = 0$ is insulated, the base $y = 0$ is kept at temperature $100°C$, and heat transfer with $h = 1$ takes place at the face $x = 1$. Derive the solution

$$u(x, y) = 200 \sum_{n=1}^{\infty} \frac{e^{-\alpha_n y} \sin \alpha_n \cos \alpha_n x}{\alpha_n + \sin \alpha_n \cos \alpha_n},$$

where $\{\alpha_n\}_1^\infty$ are the positive roots of the equation $\cot x = x$. Given $\alpha_1 = 0.860$, $\alpha_2 = 3.426$, $\alpha_3 = 6.437$, and $\alpha_4 = 9.529$, calculate the temperature $u(1, 1)$ accurate to $0.1°C$.

8. Verify that the eigenvalues and eigenfunctions of the regular Sturm-Liouville problem in (26) are

$$\lambda_n = \frac{\beta_n^2}{L^2} \quad \text{and} \quad y_n(x) = \cos \frac{\beta_n x}{L}$$

for $n = 1, 2, 3, \ldots$, where $\{\beta_n\}_1^\infty$ are the positive roots of the equation $\tan x = M/mx$.

9. (a) Show that $\lambda = 0$ is not an eigenvalue of the problem in (19). (b) Show that this problem has no negative eigenvalues. (*Suggestion:* Sketch the graphs $y = \tanh x$ and $y = -k/x$ with $k > 0$.)

10. Calculate the speed (in miles per hour) of longitudinal sound waves in each case. (a) Steel, with $\delta = 7.75$ g/cm³ and $E = 2 \times 10^{12}$ in cgs units. (b) Water, with $\delta = 1$ g/cm³ and bulk modulus $K = 2.25 \times 10^{10}$ in cgs units.

11. Consider a mass $m = nm_0$ of an ideal gas of molecular weight m_0 whose pressure P and volume V satisfy the law $PV = nRT_K$, where n is the number of moles of the gas, $R = 8314$ in mks units, and $T_K = T_C + 273$, where T_C is the Celsius temperature. The bulk modulus of the gas is $K = \gamma P$, where the value of the dimensionless constant γ is 1.4 for air having molecular weight $m_0 = 29$. (a) Show that the velocity of sound in this gas is

$$a = \sqrt{\frac{K}{\delta}} = \sqrt{\frac{\gamma RT_K}{m_0}}$$

(b) Use this formula to show that the speed of sound in air at Celsius temperature T_C is approximately $740 + (1.36)T_C$ miles per hour.

12. Suppose that the free end of the bar of Example 2 is attached to a spring (rather than to a mass), as shown in Fig. 10.2.5. The endpoint condition then becomes $ku(L, t) + AEu_x(L, t) = 0$. (Why?) Assume that $u(x, 0) = f(x)$ and that $u_t(x, 0) = 0$. Derive a solution of the form

$$u(x, t) = \sum_{n=1}^{\infty} c_n \cos \frac{\beta_n at}{L} \sin \frac{\beta_n x}{L},$$

where $\{\beta_n\}_1^\infty$ are the positive roots of the equation $\tan x = -AEx/kL$.

FIGURE 10.2.5.

13. If a bar has natural length L, cross-sectional area A, and Young's modulus E, then (as a consequence of Hooke's law) the axial force at each end required to stretch it the small amount ΔL is $F = (AE \, \Delta L)/L$. Apply this result to a segment of the bar of natural length $L = \Delta x$ between the cross sections at x and $x + \Delta x$ that is stretched by the amount $\Delta L = u(x + \Delta x, t) - u(x, t)$. Then let $\Delta x \to 0$ to derive Eq. (13).

14. Show that the eigenfunctions $\{X_n(x)\}_1^\infty$ of the problem in (19) are not orthogonal. (*Suggestion:* Apply Eq. (22) of Section 10.1 to show that if $m \neq n$, then

$$\int_0^L X_m(x)X_n(x)\,dx = -\frac{m}{A\delta}X_m(L)X_n(L).)$$

15. Show that the eigenfunctions $\{\sin \beta_n x/L\}_1^\infty$ of the problem in (19) are not orthogonal; do so by obtaining the explicit value of the integral

$$\int_0^L \sin\frac{\beta_m x}{L}\sin\frac{\beta_n x}{L}\,dx.$$

(*Suggestion:* Use the fact that $\{\beta_n\}_1^\infty$ are the roots of the equation $x \tan x = M/m$.)

16. According to Problem 19 of Section 9.7, the temperature $u(r, t)$ in a uniform solid spherical ball of radius a satisfies the partial differential equation $(ru)_t = k(ru)_{rr}$. Suppose that the ball has initial temperature $u(r, 0) = f(r)$ and that its surface $r = a$ is insulated, so that $u_r(a, t) = 0$. Substitute $v(r, t) = ru(r, t)$ to derive the solution

$$u(r, t) = c_0 + \sum_{n=1}^\infty \frac{c_n}{r} e^{-\beta_n^2 kt/a^2} \sin\frac{\beta_n r}{a},$$

where $\{\beta_n\}_1^\infty$ are the positive roots of the equation $\tan x = x$ and

$$c_0 = \frac{3}{a^3}\int_0^a r^2 f(r)\,dr,$$

$$c_n = \frac{2}{a \sin^2 \beta_n}\int_0^a rf(r)\sin\frac{\beta_n r}{a}\,dr$$

(see Problem 14 of Section 10.1).

17. A problem concerning the diffusion of gas through a membrane leads to the boundary value problem

$$u_t = ku_{xx} \qquad (0 < x < L, \quad t > 0);$$

$$u(0, t) = u_x(L, t) + hku_x(L, t) = 0,$$

$$u(x, 0) = 1.$$

Derive the solution

$$u(x, t) = 4\sum_{n=1}^\infty \frac{1 - \cos\beta_n}{2\beta_n - \sin 2\beta_n} e^{-\beta_n^2 kt/L^2}\sin\frac{\beta_n x}{L},$$

where $\{\beta_n\}_1^\infty$ are the positive roots of the equation $x \tan x = hL$.

18. Suppose that the simply supported uniform bar of Example 3 has, instead, initial position $y(x, 0) = 0$ and initial velocity $y_t(x, 0) = g(x)$. Then derive the solution

$$y(x, t) = \sum_{n=1}^\infty c_n \sin\frac{n^2\pi^2 a^2 t}{L^2}\sin\frac{n\pi x}{L},$$

where

$$c_n = \frac{2L}{n^2\pi^2 a^2}\int_0^L g(x)\sin\frac{n\pi x}{L}\,dx.$$

19. To approximate the effect of an initial momentum impulse P applied at the midpoint $x = L/2$ of a simply supported bar, substitute

$$G(x) = \begin{cases} \dfrac{P}{2\rho\epsilon} & \text{if } \dfrac{L}{2} - \epsilon < x < \dfrac{L}{2} + \epsilon, \\ 0 & \text{otherwise} \end{cases}$$

in the result of Problem 18. Then let $\epsilon \to 0$ to obtain the solution

$$y(x, t) = C\sum_{n=1}^\infty \frac{1}{n^2}\sin\frac{n\pi}{2}\sin\frac{n^2\pi^2 a^2 t}{L^2}\sin\frac{n\pi x}{L},$$

where

$$C = \frac{2PL}{\pi^2\sqrt{EI\rho}}.$$

20. (a) If $g(x) = v_0$ (a constant) in Problem 18, show that

$$y(x, t) = \frac{4v_0 L^2}{\pi^3 a^2}\sum_{n \text{ odd}} \frac{1}{n^3}\sin\frac{n^2\pi^2 a^2 t}{L^2}\sin\frac{n\pi x}{L}.$$

This describes the vibrations of a hinged bar lying crosswise in the back of a pickup truck that hits a brick wall with speed v_0 at time $t = 0$. (b) Now suppose that the bar is made of steel ($E = 2 \times 10^{12}$ dyn/cm², $\delta = 7.75$ g/cm³), has a square cross section with edge $a = 1$ in. (so that $I = \frac{1}{12}a^4$), and length $L = 19$ in. What is its fundamental frequency (in hertz)?

10.2 Computing Project

First let's investigate numerically the temperature function

$$u(x, t) = 2U_0 hL\sum_{n=1}^\infty \frac{1 - \cos\beta_n}{\beta_n(hL + \cos^2\beta_n)}\exp\left(-\frac{\beta_n^2 kt}{L^2}\right)\sin\frac{\beta_n x}{L} \qquad (1)$$

of the heated slab of Example 1, given its thickness $L = 50$ cm, constant initial temperature $U_0 = 100$, thermal diffusivity $k = 0.15$ (for iron), and heat transfer coefficient $h = 0.1$ at the right-hand boundary $x = L$. According to Eq. (8), the eigenvalues $\{\beta_n\}$ are the positive solutions of the equation $\tan x = -x/(hL)$. As in Fig. 10.1.1, we see that β_n is slightly larger than $(2n - 1)\pi/2$ for each integer $n = 1, 2, 3, \ldots$. Using *Mathematica* we can therefore solve for the first 20 of these eigenvalues as follows:

```
L = 50;  h = 0.1;

solutions =
       Table[ FindRoot[ Tan[x] == -x/(h*L),
               {x, (2*n - 1)*Pi/2 + 0.1}], {n, 1, 20} ];
beta = x /. solutions
```

```
{2.65366, 5.45435, 8.39135, 11.4086, 14.4699,
  17.5562, 20.6578, 23.7693, 26.8874, 30.0102,
  33.1365, 36.2653, 39.3961, 42.5285, 45.6622,
  48.7968, 51.9323, 55.0684, 58.2052, 61.3424}
```

The following *Mathematica* function then sums the first 20 nonzero terms of the series in Eq. (1).

```
b = beta;   U0 = 100;   k = 0.15;

u[x_,t_] := 2*U0*h*L*Apply[ Plus,
                ((1 - Cos[b])/(b*(h*L + (Cos[b])^2)))*
                Exp[-b*b*k*t/L^2]*Sin[b*x/L]] // N
```

As a practical matter, this suffices to give the value $u(x, t)$ after 10 seconds (or more) with two-place accuracy throughout the interval $0 \leqq x \leqq 50$. (How might you verify this assertion?)

The graph of $u(x, 900)$ in Fig. 10.2.6 shows that after 15 minutes the right boundary $x = 50$ of the slab has cooled below $40°$, whereas interior temperatures near $x = 30$ remain above $80°$. The graph of $u(50, t)$ shown in Fig. 10.2.7 indicates that the right boundary temperature of the slab falls to $25°$ in a bit less than 2000 seconds. The computation

```
t1 = t /. FindRoot[ u[50,t] == 25, {t, 2000}]
```

```
1951.24
```

shows that this actually takes about $t_1 = 1951$ seconds. Figure 10.2.8 indicates that interior temperatures of the slab at time t_1 still remain above $50°$ at some points. We can find the maximum value of the temperature $u(x, t_1)$ by finding the minimum value of its negative $-u(x, t_1)$:

```
FindMinimum[ -u[x,t1], {x,30}]
```

```
{-53.804, {x -> 29.3586}}
```

FIGURE 10.2.6. Temperatures in the slab after 15 minutes

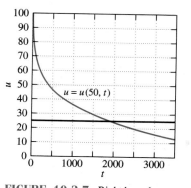

FIGURE 10.2.7. Right boundary temperatures of the slab

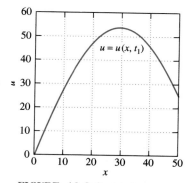

FIGURE 10.2.8. Interior temperatures when the right boundary temperature is 25 degrees

Thus the maximum temperature within the slab when $u(50, t) = 25$ is about $53.8°$.

For your very own slab with constant initial temperature $f(x) = U_0 = 100$ to investigate in this manner, let $h = 0.1$,

$$L = 5 \cdot (10 + p), \quad \text{and} \quad k = (0.1) \cdot q,$$

where p is the largest and q is the smallest nonzero digit of your student I.D. number. Then carry out the investigation outlined above to find:

- When the right boundary temperature of the slab is $25°$.
- The maximum temperature within the slab at this instant.

If your computational system does not include functions like **FindRoot** and **FindMinimum**, you can approximate these values graphically.

*10.3 Steady Periodic Solutions and Natural Frequencies

In Section 9.6 we derived the solution

$$y(x, t) = \sum_{n=1}^{\infty} \left(A_n \cos \frac{n\pi at}{L} + B_n \sin \frac{n\pi at}{L} \right) \sin \frac{n\pi x}{L}$$

$$= \sum_{n=1}^{\infty} C_n \cos \left(\frac{n\pi at}{L} - \gamma_n \right) \sin \frac{n\pi x}{L} \tag{1}$$

of the vibrating string problem

$$\frac{\partial^2 y}{\partial t^2} = a^2 \frac{\partial^2 y}{\partial x^2} \quad \left(a = \sqrt{\frac{T}{\rho}} \right); \tag{2}$$

$$y(0, t) = y(L, t) = 0, \tag{3}$$

$$y(x, 0) = f(x), \quad y_t(x, 0) = g(x). \tag{4}$$

The solution in Eq. (1) describes the *free* vibrations of a string with length L and linear

density ρ under tension T; the constant coefficients in Eq. (1) are determined by the initial conditions in (4).

In particular, we see from the terms in Eq. (1) that the natural [circular] frequencies of vibration (in radians per second) of the string are given by

$$\omega_n = \frac{n\pi a}{L}, \qquad n = 1, 2, 3, \ldots . \tag{5}$$

These are the only values of ω for which Eq. (2) has a steady periodic solution of the form

$$y(x, t) = X(x) \cos(\omega t - \gamma) \tag{6}$$

that satisfies the endpoint conditions in (3). For if we substitute Eq. (6) in (2) and cancel the factor $\cos(\omega t - \gamma)$, we find that $X(x)$ must satisfy the equation

$$a^2 X''(x) + \omega^2 X(x) = 0,$$

whose general solution

$$X(x) = A \cos \frac{\omega x}{a} + B \sin \frac{\omega x}{a}$$

satisfies the conditions in (3) only if $A = 0$ and $\omega = n\pi a/L$ for some positive integer n.

Forced Vibrations and Resonance

Now suppose that the string is influenced by a periodic external force $F(t) = F_0 \cos \omega t$ (force per unit mass) that acts uniformly on the string along its length. Then, according to Eq. (1) of Section 9.6, the displacement $y(x, t)$ of the string will satisfy the nonhomogeneous partial differential equation

$$\frac{\partial^2 y}{\partial t^2} = a^2 \frac{\partial^2 y}{\partial x^2} + F_0 \cos \omega t \tag{7}$$

together with boundary conditions such as those in (3) and (4). For instance, if the string is initially at rest in equilibrium when the external force begins to act, we want to find a solution of Eq. (7) that satisfies the conditions

$$y(0, t) = y(L, t) = y(x, 0) = y_t(x, 0) = 0. \tag{8}$$

To do this, it suffices first to find a particular solution $y_p(x, t)$ of Eq. (7) that satisfies the fixed endpoint conditions in (3), and second to find a solution $y_c(x, t)$ like Eq. (1) of the familiar problem in (2)–(4) with

$$f(x) = -y_p(x, 0) \qquad \text{and} \qquad g(x) = -D_t y_p(x, 0).$$

Evidently

$$y(x, t) = y_c(x, t) + y_p(x, t)$$

will then satisfy Eqs. (7) and (8).

So our new task is to find $y_p(x, t)$. Examination of the individual terms in Eq. (7) suggests that we try

$$y_p(x, t) = X(x) \cos \omega t. \tag{9}$$

Substitution of this in Eq. (7) and cancellation of the common factor $\cos \omega t$ yields the ordinary differential equation

$$a^2 X'' + \omega^2 X = -F_0$$

with general solution

$$X(x) = A \cos \frac{\omega x}{a} + B \sin \frac{\omega x}{a} - \frac{F_0}{\omega^2}. \tag{10}$$

The condition $X(0) = 0$ requires that $A = F_0/\omega^2$, and then $X(L) = 0$ requires that

$$X(L) = \frac{F_0}{\omega^2}\left(\cos \frac{\omega L}{a} - 1\right) + B \sin \frac{\omega L}{a} = 0. \tag{11}$$

Now suppose that the frequency ω of the periodic external force is *not* equal to any one of the natural frequencies $\omega_n = n\pi a/L$ of the string. Then $\sin \omega L/a \neq 0$, so we can solve Eq. (11) for B and then substitute the result in Eq. (10) to obtain

$$X(x) = \frac{F_0}{\omega^2}\left(\cos \frac{\omega x}{a} - 1\right) - \frac{F_0[\cos(\omega L/a) - 1]}{\omega^2 \sin(\omega L/a)} \sin \frac{\omega x}{a}. \tag{12}$$

Then Eq. (9), with this choice of $X(x)$, gives the desired particular solution $y_p(x, t)$.

Note, however, that as the value of ω approaches $\omega_n = n\pi a/L$ with n odd, the co-efficient of $\sin \omega x/a$ in Eq. (12) approaches $\pm\infty$; thus *resonance* occurs. This explains the fact that when [only] one of two nearby identical strings is plucked, the other will begin to vibrate as well, due to its being acted on (through the medium of the air) by an external periodic force at its fundamental frequency. Observe also that if $\omega = \omega_n = n\pi a/L$ with n even, then we can choose $B = 0$ in Eq. (11), so resonance does not occur in this case. Problem 20 explains why some of the resonance possibilities are absent.

The vibrating string is typical of continuous systems that have an infinite sequence of natural frequencies of vibration. When a periodic external force acts on such a system, potentially destructive resonance vibrations may occur if the imposed frequency is close to one of the natural frequencies of the system. Hence an important aspect of proper structural design is the avoidance of such resonance vibrations.

Natural Frequencies of Beams

$y(x, t)$

$x = 0$ $x = L$

FIGURE 10.3.1. A bar clamped at each end

Figure 10.3.1 shows a uniform beam of length L, linear density ρ, and Young's modulus E, clamped at each end. For $0 < x < L$ and $t > 0$, its deflection function $y(x, t)$ satisfies the fourth-order equation

$$\frac{\partial^2 y}{\partial t^2} + a^4 \frac{\partial^4 y}{\partial x^4} = 0 \qquad \left(a^4 = \frac{EI}{\rho}\right) \tag{13}$$

that we discussed in Section 10.2; I denotes the moment of inertia of the cross section of the beam about its horizontal axis of symmetry. Because both the displacement and the slope are zero at each fixed end, the endpoint conditions are

$$y(0, t) = y_x(0, t) = 0 \tag{14}$$

and

$$y(L, t) = y_x(L, t) = 0 \tag{15}$$

Here we want only to find the natural frequencies of vibration of the beam, so we will not be concerned with initial conditions. The natural frequencies are the values of ω for which Eq. (13) has a nontrivial solution of the form

$$y(x, t) = X(x) \cos(\omega t - \gamma) \tag{16}$$

that satisfies the conditions in Eqs. (14) and (15). When we substitute $y(x, t)$ from (16) into (13) and then cancel the common factor $\cos(\omega t - \gamma)$, we obtain the fourth-order ordinary differential equation $-\omega^2 X + a^4 X^{(4)} = 0$; that is,

$$X^{(4)} - \frac{\omega^2}{a^4} X = 0. \tag{17}$$

If we write $\alpha^4 = \omega^2/a^4$, we can express the general solution of Eq. (17) as

$$X(x) = A \cosh \alpha x + B \sinh \alpha x + C \cos \alpha x + D \sin \alpha x,$$

with

$$X'(x) = \alpha(A \sinh \alpha x + B \cosh \alpha x - C \sin \alpha x + D \cos \alpha x).$$

The conditions in (14) give

$$X(0) = A + C = 0 \quad \text{and} \quad X'(0) = \alpha(B + D) = 0,$$

so $C = -A$ and $D = -B$. Hence the conditions in (15) give

$$X(L) = A(\cosh \alpha L - \cos \alpha L) + B(\sinh \alpha L - \sin \alpha L) = 0$$

and

$$\frac{1}{\alpha} X'(L) = A(\sinh \alpha L + \sin \alpha L) + B(\cosh \alpha L - \cos \alpha L) = 0.$$

In order for these two linear homogeneous equations in A and B to have a nontrivial solution, the determinant of coefficients must be zero:

$$(\cosh \alpha L - \cos \alpha L)^2 - (\sinh^2 \alpha L - \sin^2 \alpha L) = 0;$$

$$(\cosh^2 \alpha L - \sinh^2 \alpha L) + (\cos^2 \alpha L + \sin^2 \alpha L) - 2 \cosh \alpha L \cos \alpha L = 0;$$

$$2 - 2 \cosh \alpha L \cos \alpha L = 0.$$

Thus $\beta = \alpha L$ must be a nonzero root of the equation

$$\cosh x \cos x = 1. \tag{18}$$

From Fig. 10.3.2 we see that this equation has an increasing sequence of positive roots $\{\beta_n\}_1^\infty$. Now $\omega = \alpha^2 a^2 = \beta^2 a^2/L^2$ and $a^2 = \sqrt{EI/\rho}$, so it follows that the natural [circular] frequencies of vibration of the beam with clamped ends are given by

$$\omega_n = \frac{\beta_n^2}{L^2} \sqrt{\frac{EI}{\rho}} \quad \text{(rad/s)} \tag{19}$$

for $n = 1, 2, 3, \ldots$. The roots of Eq. (18) are $\beta_1 \approx 4.73004$, $\beta_2 \approx 7.85320$, $\beta_3 \approx 10.99561$, and $\beta_n \approx (2n + 1)\pi/2$ for $n \geq 4$ (as indicated in Fig. 10.3.2).

For example, suppose the basic structural element of a bridge is a 120-ft-long steel I beam with the cross section indicated in Fig. 10.3.3, having moment of inertia

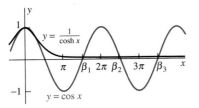

FIGURE 10.3.2. Solutions of $\cosh x \cos x = 1$

FIGURE 10.3.3. An idealized I beam

$I = 9000 \text{ cm}^4$. If we substitute the values

$$L = (120 \text{ ft})\left(30.48 \frac{\text{cm}}{\text{ft}}\right), \quad r = \left(7.75 \frac{\text{g}}{\text{cm}^3}\right)(40 \text{ cm}^2), \quad E = 2 \times 10^{12} \frac{\text{dyn}}{\text{cm}^2},$$

and the values of β_1 and β_2 in Eq. (19), we find that the lowest two natural frequencies of the beam are

$$\omega_1 \approx 12.74 \frac{\text{rad}}{\text{s}} \quad \left(122 \frac{\text{cycles}}{\text{min}}\right) \quad \text{and} \quad \omega_2 \approx 35.13 \frac{\text{rad}}{\text{s}} \quad \left(335 \frac{\text{cycles}}{\text{min}}\right).$$

If a company of soldiers marching at about 120 steps per minute approaches this bridge, they therefore would be well-advised to break cadence before crossing. From time to time bridges collapse because of resonance vibrations. Recall the Kansas City hotel disaster of July 17, 1981, in which a skywalk filled with dancers collapsed. Newspapers quoted investigators who speculated that the rhythmic movement of the dancers had set up destructive resonance vibrations in the steel I beams that supported the skywalk.

Underground Temperature Oscillations

Let us assume that the underground temperature at a particular location is a function $u(x, t)$ of time t and the depth x beneath the surface. Then u satisfies the heat equation $u_t = ku_{xx}$, with k being the thermal diffusivity of the soil. We may regard the temperature $u(0, t)$ at the surface $x = 0$ as being known from weather records. In fact, the periodic seasonal variation of monthly average surface temperatures, with a maximum in midsummer (July in the Northern hemisphere) and a minimum in midwinter (January), is very close to a sine or cosine oscillation. We shall therefore assume that

$$u(0, t) = T_0 + A_0 \cos \omega t, \tag{20}$$

where we take $t = 0$ at midsummer. Here T_0 is the average annual temperature, A_0 the amplitude of seasonal temperature variation, and ω is chosen to make the period of $u(0, t)$ exactly one year. (In cgs units, for instance, ω would be 2π divided by the number of seconds in a year.)

It is reasonable to assume that the temperature at a fixed depth also varies periodically with t. If we introduce $U(x, t) = u(x, t) - T_0$ for convenience, then we are interested in periodic solutions of the heat equation of the form

$$U(x, t) = A(x) \cos(\omega t - \gamma) = V(x) \cos \omega t + W(x) \sin \omega t \tag{21}$$

of the problem

$$\frac{\partial U}{\partial t} = k \frac{\partial^2 U}{\partial x^2} \quad (x > 0, \quad t > 0), \tag{22}$$

$$U(0, t) = A_0 \cos \omega t. \tag{23}$$

To solve this problem, let us regard $U(x, t)$ in Eq. (21) as the real part of the complex-valued function

$$\tilde{U}(x, t) = X(x)e^{i\omega t}. \tag{24}$$

Then we want $\tilde{U}(x, t)$ to satisfy the conditions

$$\tilde{U}_t = k\tilde{U}_{xx}, \tag{22'}$$

$$\tilde{U}(0, t) = A_0 e^{i\omega t}. \tag{23'}$$

If we substitute Eq. (24) in Eq. (22′), we get $i\omega X = kX''$; that is,

$$X'' - \alpha^2 X = 0, \tag{25}$$

where

$$\alpha = \pm\sqrt{\frac{i\omega}{k}} = \pm(1 + i)\sqrt{\frac{\omega}{2k}} \tag{26}$$

because $\sqrt{i} = \pm(1 + i)/\sqrt{2}$. Hence the general solution of Eq. (25) is

$$X(x) = Ae^{-(1+i)x\sqrt{\omega/2k}} + Be^{+(1+i)x\sqrt{\omega/2k}}. \tag{27}$$

In order that $\tilde{U}(x, t)$, and hence $X(x)$, be bounded as $x \to \infty$, it is necessary that $B = 0$. Also we see from Eqs. (23′) and (24) that $A = X(0) = A_0$. So

$$X(x) = A_0 e^{-(1+i)x\sqrt{\omega/2k}}. \tag{28}$$

Finally, the solution of our original problem in (22)–(23) is

$$U(x, t) = \operatorname{Re}\tilde{U}(x, t) = \operatorname{Re}X(x)e^{i\omega t} = \operatorname{Re}\left(A_0 e^{i\omega t}e^{-(1+i)x\sqrt{\omega/2k}}\right)$$

$$= \operatorname{Re}\left(A_0 e^{-x\sqrt{\omega/2k}}e^{i(\omega t - x\sqrt{\omega/2k})}\right);$$

hence

$$U(x, t) = A_0 e^{-x\sqrt{\omega/2k}} \cos\left(\omega t - x\sqrt{\frac{\omega}{2k}}\right). \tag{29}$$

Thus the amplitude $A(x)$ of the annual temperature is exponentially damped as a function of the depth x:

$$A(x) = A_0 e^{-x\sqrt{\omega/2k}}. \tag{30}$$

In addition, there is a phase delay $\gamma(x) = x\sqrt{\omega/2k}$ at the depth x. With $k = 0.005$ (a typical value for soil in cgs units) and the value of ω previously mentioned, we find that $\sqrt{\omega/2k} \approx 0.00446$ cm^{-1}. For instance, we then see from Eq. (30) that the amplitude is one-half the surface amplitude, $A(x) = \frac{1}{2}A_0$, when $(0.00446)x = \ln 2$; that is, when $x \approx 155.30$ cm ≈ 5.10 ft. If $A_0 = 16°$, it follows that at a depth of about 20 ft, the amplitude of annual temperature variation is only 1°. Another interesting consequence of Eq. (29) is the "reversal of seasons" that occurs when $\gamma(x) = (0.00446)x = \pi$; that is, at a depth of $x \approx 704.39$ cm ≈ 23.11 ft.

10.3 Problems

A uniform bar of length L is made of material with density δ and Young's modulus E. In Problems 1 through 6, substitute $u(x, t) = X(x) \cos \omega t$ in $\delta u_{tt} = Eu_{xx}$ to find the natural frequencies of longitudinal vibration of the bar with the two given conditions at its ends $x = 0$ and $x = L$.

1. Both ends are fixed.

2. Both ends are free.

3. The end at $x = 0$ is fixed; the end at $x = L$ is free.

4. The end at $x = 0$ is fixed; the free end at $x = L$ is attached to a mass m as in Example 2 of Section 10.2.

5. Each end is free, but the end at $x = L$ is attached to a spring with Hooke's constant k as in Problem 12 of Section 10.2.

6. The free ends are attached to masses m_0 and m_1.

7. Suppose that the mass on the free end at $x = L$ in Problem 4 is attached also to the spring of Problem 5. Show that the natural frequencies are given by $\omega_n = (\beta_n/L)\sqrt{E/\delta}$, where $\{\beta_n\}_1^\infty$ are the positive roots of the equation

$$(mEx^2 - k\delta L^2)\sin x = MEx \cos x.$$

(*Note:* The condition at $x = L$ is $mu_{tt} = -AEu_x - ku$.)

Problems 8 through 14 deal with transverse vibrations of the uniform beam of this section, but with various end conditions. In each case show that the natural frequencies are given by the formula in Eq. (19), with $\{\beta_n\}_1^\infty$ being the positive roots of the given frequency equation. Recall that $y = y' = 0$ at a fixed end, $y = y'' = 0$ at a hinged end, and $y'' = y''' = 0$ at a free end (primes denote differentiation with respect to x).

8. The ends at $x = 0$ and $x = L$ are both hinged; the frequency equation is $\sin x = 0$, so that $\beta_n = n\pi$.

9. The end at $x = 0$ is fixed and the end at $x = L$ is hinged; the frequency equation is $\tanh x = \tan x$.

10. The beam is a cantilever with the end at $x = 0$ fixed and the end at $x = L$ free; the frequency equation is $\cosh x \cos x = -1$.

11. The end at $x = 0$ is fixed and the end at $x = L$ is attached to a vertically sliding clamp, so $y' = y''' = 0$ there; the frequency equation is $\tanh x + \tan x = 0$.

12. The cantilever of Problem 10 has total mass $M = \rho L$ and has a mass m attached to its free end; the frequency equation is

$$M(1 + \cosh x \cos x) = mx(\cosh x \sin x - \sinh x \cos x).$$

The conditions at $x = L$ are $y_{xx} = 0$ and $my_{tt} = EIy_{xxx}$.

13. The free end at $x = L$ of the cantilever in Problem 10 is attached (as in Fig. 10.3.4) to a spring with Hooke's constant k; the frequency equation is

$$EIx^3(1 + \cosh x \cos x) = kL^3(\sinh x \cos x - \cosh x \sin x).$$

The conditions at $x = L$ are $y_{xx} = 0$ and $ky = EIy_{xxx}$.

FIGURE 10.3.4. The cantilever of Problem 13

14. Suppose that the mass m on the free end of the cantilever of Problem 12 is attached to the spring of Problem 13. The conditions at $x = L$ are $y_{xx} = 0$ and $my_{tt} = EIy_{xxx} - ky$. Derive the frequency equation

$$MEIx^3(1 + \cosh x \cos x)$$
$$= (kML^3 - mEIx^4)(\sinh x \cos x - \cosh x \sin x).$$

Note that the frequency equations in Problems 12 and 13 are the special cases $k = 0$ and $m = 0$, respectively.

15. Suppose that the cantilever of Problem 10 is a diving board made of steel with density $\delta = 7.75$ g/cm³. The diving board is 4 m long and its cross section is a rectangle of width $a = 30$ cm and thickness $b = 2$ cm. The moment of inertia of this rectangle about its horizontal axis of symmetry is $I = \frac{1}{12}ab^3$. Given that the least positive root of the equation $\cosh x \cos x = -1$ is $\beta_1 \approx 1.8751$, determine the frequency (in hertz) with which a person should bounce up and down at the tip of the diving board for maximal (resonant) effect.

16. If a uniform bar hinged at each end is subjected to an axial force of compression P, then its transverse vibrations satisfy the equation

$$\rho\frac{\partial^2 y}{\partial t^2} + P\frac{\partial^2 y}{\partial x^2} + EI\frac{\partial^4 y}{\partial x^4} = 0.$$

Show that its natural frequencies are given by

$$\omega_n = \frac{n^2\pi^2}{L^2}\left(1 + \frac{PL^2}{n^2\pi^2 EI}\right)^{1/2}\sqrt{\frac{EI}{\rho}}$$

for $n = 1, 2, 3, \ldots$. Note that with $P = 0$, this reduces to the result in Example 3 of Section 10.2 and that the effect of $P > 0$ is to increase the value of each of the ω_n.

17. A beam hinged at each end is sufficiently thick that its kinetic energy of rotation must be taken into account. Then the differential equation for its transverse vibrations is

$$\rho\frac{\partial^2 y}{\partial t^2} - \frac{I}{A}\frac{\partial^4 y}{\partial x^2 \partial t^2} + EI\frac{\partial^4 y}{\partial x^4} = 0.$$

Show that its natural frequencies are given by

$$\omega_n = \frac{n^2\pi^2}{L^2}\left(1 + \frac{n^2\pi^2 I}{AL^2}\right)^{-1/2}\sqrt{\frac{EI}{\rho}}$$

for $n = 1, 2, 3, \ldots$.

18. Suppose that the end $x = 0$ of a uniform bar with cross-sectional area A and Young's modulus E is fixed, while the longitudinal force $F(t) = F_0 \sin \omega t$ acts on its end $x = L$, so $AEu_x(L, t) = F_0 \sin \omega t$. Derive the steady periodic solution

$$u(x, t) = \frac{F_0 a \sin(\omega x/a)\sin \omega t}{AE\omega \cos(\omega L/a)}.$$

19. Repeat Problem 18, except here a transverse force $F(t) = F_0 \sin \omega t$ acts at the free end $x = L$, so that

$$y_{xx}(L, t) = EIy_{xxx}(L, t) + F_0 \sin \omega t = 0.$$

Determine the steady periodic transverse oscillations of the cantilever in the form $y(x, t) = X(x) \sin \omega t$.

20. A string with fixed ends is acted on by a periodic force

$F(x, t) = F(x) \sin \omega t$ per unit mass, so

$$y_{tt} = a^2 y_{xx} + F(x) \sin \omega t.$$

Substitute

$$y(x, t) = \sum_{n=1}^{\infty} c_n \sin \frac{n\pi x}{L} \sin \omega t$$

and

$$F(x) = \sum_{n=1}^{\infty} F_n \sin \frac{n\pi x}{L}$$

to derive the steady periodic solution

$$y(x, t) = \sum_{n=1}^{\infty} \frac{F_n \sin(n\pi x/a) \sin \omega t}{\omega_n^2 - \omega^2},$$

where $\omega_n = n\pi a/L$. Hence resonance does not result if $\omega = \omega_n$ but $F_n = 0$.

21. Suppose that the string of Problem 20 is also subject to air resistance proportional to its velocity, so that

$$y_{tt} = a^2 y_{xx} - c y_t + F(x) \sin \omega t.$$

Generalize the method of Problem 20 to derive the steady periodic solution

$$y(x, t) = \sum_{n=1}^{\infty} \rho_n F_n \sin \frac{n\pi x}{L} \sin(\omega t - \alpha_n),$$

where

$$\rho_n = [(\omega_n^2 - \omega^2)^2 + \omega^2 c^2]^{-1/2} \text{ and } \alpha_n = \tan^{-1} \frac{\omega c}{\omega_n^2 - \omega^2}.$$

Note the similarity to damped forced motion of a mass on a spring.

22. The **telephone equation** for the voltage $e(x, t)$ in a long transmission line at the point $x \geq 0$ at time t is

$$\frac{\partial^2 e}{\partial x^2} = LC \frac{\partial^2 e}{\partial t^2} + (RC + LG) \frac{\partial e}{\partial t} + RGe,$$

where R, L, G, and C denote resistance, inductance, conductance, and capacitance (all per unit length of line), respectively. The condition $e(0, t) = E_0 \cos \omega t$ represents a periodic signal voltage at the origin of transmission at $x = 0$. Assume that $e(x, t)$ is bounded as $x \to +\infty$. Substitute $\tilde{e}(x, t) = E(x)e^{i\omega t}$ to derive the steady periodic solution

$$e(x, t) = E_0 e^{-\alpha x} \cos(\omega t - \beta x),$$

where α and β are the real and imaginary parts, respectively, of the complex number

$$[(RG - LC\omega^2) + i\omega(RC + LG)]^{1/2}.$$

23. The temperature $u(x, t)$ at the point $x \geq 0$ at time t of water moving with velocity $\gamma \geq 0$ in a long pipe satisfies the equation

$$\frac{\partial u}{\partial t} = k \frac{\partial^2 u}{\partial x^2} - \gamma \frac{\partial u}{\partial x}.$$

Suppose that $u(0, t) = A_0 \cos \omega t$ and that $u(x, t)$ is bounded as $x \to +\infty$. Substitute $\tilde{u}(x, t) = X(x)e^{i\omega t}$ to derive the steady periodic solution

$$u(x, t) = A_0 e^{-\alpha x} \cos(\omega t - \beta x),$$

where

$$\alpha = \frac{1}{2k}(\gamma^4 + 16k^2\omega^2)^{1/4} \cos \frac{\phi}{2} - \frac{\gamma}{2k},$$

$$\beta = \frac{1}{2k}(\gamma^4 + 16k^2\omega^2)^{1/4} \sin \frac{\phi}{2},$$

$$\phi = \tan^{-1} \frac{4k}{\gamma^2}.$$

Show also that when $\gamma = 0$, this solution reduces to that in Eq. (29).

10.3 Computing Project

In this project you are to investigate further the vibrations of an elastic bar or beam of length L whose position function $y(x, t)$ satisfies the partial differential equation

$$\rho \frac{\partial^2 y}{\partial t^2} + EI \frac{\partial^4 y}{\partial x^4} = 0 \qquad (0 < x < L)$$

and the initial conditions $y(x, 0) = f(x)$, $y_t(x, 0) = 0$.

First separate the variables (as in Example 3 of Section 10.3) to derive the formal series solution

$$y(x, t) = \sum_{n=1}^{\infty} c_n \left(\cos \frac{\beta_n^2 a^2 t}{L^2} \right) X_n(x),$$

where $a^4 = EI/\rho$, the $\{c_n\}$ are the appropriate eigenfunction expansion coefficients of the initial position function $f(x)$, and $\{\beta_n\}_1^\infty$ and $X_n(x)$ are determined by the end conditions imposed on the bar. In a particular case, one wants to find both the **frequency equation** whose positive roots are the $\{\beta_n\}_1^\infty$ and the eigenfunctions $\{X_n(x)\}$. In this section we saw that the frequency equation for the fixed-fixed case (with $y(0) = y'(0) = y(L) = y'(L) = 0$) is $\cosh x \cos x = 1$.

Case 1. Hinged at each end
 The boundary conditions are

$$y(0) = y''(0) = y(L) = y''(L) = 0.$$

According to Problem 8, the frequency equation is $\sin x = 0$, so $\beta_n = n\pi$ and $X_n(x) = \sin n\pi x$. Suppose that the bar is made of steel (with density $\delta = 7.75$ g/cm^3 and Young's modulus $E = 2 \times 10^{12}$ dyn/cm^2), 19 in. long with square cross section of edge $w = 1$ in. (so its moment of inertia is $I = \frac{1}{12}w^4$). Determine its first few natural frequencies of vibration (in Hz). How does this bar sound when it vibrates?

Case 2. Free at each end
 The boundary conditions are

$$y''(0) = y'''(0) = y''(L) = y'''(L) = 0.$$

This case models, for example, a weightless bar suspended in space in an orbiting spacecraft. Now show that the frequency equation is $\cosh x \cos x = 1$ (although the eigenfunctions differ from those in the fixed-fixed case). Solve this equation (either graphically or numerically, as in the Section 10.2 project) to approximate the first several natural frequencies of vibration of the same bar considered in case 1. How does it sound now?

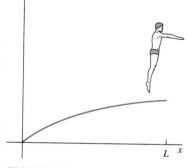

Case 3. Fixed at $x = 0$, free at $x = L$
 Now the boundary conditions are

$$y(0) = y'(0) = y''(L) = y'''(L) = 0.$$

This is a **cantilever** like the diving board illustrated in Fig. 10.3.5. According to Problem 15, the frequency equation is $\cosh x \cos x = -1$. Approximate the first several positive solutions of this equation and show graphically that $\beta_n \approx (2n - 1)\pi/2$ for n large. Thence determine the first several natural frequencies (in Hz) of vibration of the particular diving board described in Problem 15. These are the frequencies at which a diver on this board should bounce up and down at the free end for maximal resonant effect.

FIGURE 10.3.5. The most spectacular dives are determined by the frequency equation of case 3.

10.4 Applications of Bessel Functions

When the Laplacian $\nabla^2 u = u_{xx} + u_{yy} + u_{zz}$ of a function $u = u(x, y, z)$ is transformed by means of the substitution $x = r \cos \theta$, $y = r \sin \theta$, the result is the **Laplacian in cylindrical coordinates,**

$$\nabla^2 u = \frac{\partial^2 u}{\partial r^2} + \frac{1}{r}\frac{\partial u}{\partial r} + \frac{1}{r^2}\frac{\partial^2 u}{\partial \theta^2} + \frac{\partial^2 u}{\partial z^2}. \qquad (1)$$

For a typical application, consider a very long uniform solid cylinder of radius c that lies along the z-axis. Suppose that it is heated to an initial temperature depending only upon the distance r from the z-axis, and that at time $t = 0$ the condition

$$\beta_1 u + \beta_2 u_r \Big|_{r=c} = 0 \tag{2}$$

is imposed on its surface $r = c$. Note the following special cases for Eq. (2):

- It reduces to the condition $u = 0$ if $\beta_1 = 1$ and $\beta_2 = 0$.
- It reduces to the insulation condition $u_r = 0$ if $\beta_1 = 0$ and $\beta_2 = 1$.
- It reduces to the heat transfer condition $hu + u_r = 0$ if $\beta_1 = h$ and $\beta_2 = 1$.

It is reasonable to expect the temperature u within the cylinder at time t to depend only upon r, so we write $u = u(r, t)$. Then $u_{\theta\theta} = u_{zz} = 0$, so substitution of (1) in the heat equation $u_t = k\nabla^2 u$ yields the boundary value problem

$$\frac{\partial u}{\partial t} = k\left(\frac{\partial^2 u}{\partial r^2} + \frac{1}{r}\frac{\partial u}{\partial r}\right) \qquad (r < c, \quad t > 0); \tag{3}$$

$$\beta_1 u(c, t) + \beta_2 u_r(c, t) = 0, \tag{4}$$

$$u(r, 0) = f(r) \qquad \text{(initial temperature)}. \tag{5}$$

To solve this problem by separation of variables, we substitute

$$u(r, t) = R(r)T(t)$$

in Eq. (3); thus we obtain

$$RT' = k\left(R''T + \frac{1}{r}R'T\right). \tag{6}$$

Division by kRT yields

$$\frac{R'' + R'/r}{R} = \frac{T'}{kT} = -\lambda. \tag{7}$$

Hence $R(r)$ must satisfy the equation

$$R'' + \frac{1}{r}R' + \lambda R = 0, \tag{8}$$

as well as the equation $\beta_1 R(c) + \beta_2 R'(c) = 0$ that follows from Eq. (4). Moreover, the equation

$$T' = -\lambda kT$$

implies that $T(t) = e^{-\lambda kt}$ to within a constant multiple. Because the diffusivity k is positive, it follows that λ must be nonnegative if $T(t)$ is to remain bounded as $t \to +\infty$, as is required by the physical problem that Eqs. (3)–(5) model. We therefore write $\lambda = \alpha^2$, so Eq. (8) takes the form

$$r^2 R'' + rR' + \alpha^2 r^2 R = 0. \tag{8'}$$

A Singular Sturm-Liouville Problem

Equation (8') is—with $x = r$ and $y(x) = R(r)$—the parametric Bessel equation

$$x^2 y'' + xy' + \alpha^2 x^2 y = 0 \qquad (9)$$

of order zero that we discussed in Section 8.5. More generally, recall that the parametric Bessel equation

▶
$$x^2 y'' + xy' + (\alpha^2 x^2 - n^2)y = 0 \qquad (10)$$

has general solution

▶
$$y(x) = AJ_n(\alpha x) + BY_n(\alpha x) \qquad (11)$$

if $\alpha > 0$. Upon division by x, the Bessel equation in (10) takes the Sturm-Liouville form

▶
$$\frac{d}{dx}\left[x \frac{dy}{dx} \right] - \frac{n^2}{x} y + \lambda xy = 0 \qquad (12)$$

with $p(x) = x$, $q(x) = n^2/x$, $r(x) = x$, and $\lambda = \alpha^2$. We want to determine the nonnegative values of λ for which three is a solution of (12) in $(0, c)$ that is *continuous* (along with its derivative dy/dx) on the closed interval $[0, c]$ and satisfies the endpoint condition

$$\beta_1 y(c) + \beta_2 y'(c) = 0, \qquad (13)$$

where β_1 and β_2 are not both zero.

The Sturm-Liouville problem associated with Eqs. (12) and (13) is *singular* because $p(0) = r(0) = 0$ and $q(x) \to +\infty$ as $x \to 0^+$, whereas we assumed in Theorem 1 of Section 10.1 that $p(x)$ and $r(x)$ were positive and that $q(x)$ was continuous on the whole interval. This problem also fails to fit the pattern of Section 10.1 in that no condition like (13) is imposed at the left endpoint $x = 0$. Nevertheless, the requirement that $y(x)$ be continuous on $[0, c]$ plays the role of such a condition. Because $Y_n(x) \to -\infty$ as $x \to 0$, the solution in Eq. (11) for $\alpha > 0$ can be continuous at $x = 0$ only if $B = 0$, so

$$y(x) = J_n(\alpha x)$$

to within a constant multiple. It remains only to impose the condition in Eq. (13) at $x = c$.

It is convenient to distinguish the cases $\beta_2 = 0$ and $\beta_2 \neq 0$. If $\beta_2 = 0$, then Eq. (13) takes the simple form

▶
$$y(c) = 0. \qquad (13a)$$

If $\beta_2 \neq 0$, we multiply each term in Eq. (13) by c/β_2 and then write $h = c\beta_1/\beta_2$ to obtain the equivalent condition

▶
$$hy(c) + cy'(c) = 0. \qquad (13b)$$

We assume hereafter that $h \geqq 0$.

The case $\lambda = 0$

First we consider the possibility of a zero eigenvalue $\lambda = 0$. If both $\lambda = 0$ and $n = 0$, then Eq. (12) reduces to the equation $[xy']' = 0$ with general solution

$$y(x) = A \ln x + B,$$

and continuity on $[0, c]$ requires that $A = 0$. But then Eq. (13a) implies that $B = 0$ as well, as does Eq. (13b) unless $h = 0$, in which case $\lambda = 0$ is an eigenvalue with associated eigenfunction $y(x) \equiv 1$.

If $\lambda = 0$ but $n > 0$, then Eq. (12) is simply the equation

$$x^2 y'' + xy' - n^2 y = 0$$

with general solution (substituting the trial solution $y = x^k$ as in Section 9.7)

$$y(x) = Ax^n + Bx^{-n},$$

and continuity on $[0, c]$ requires that $B = 0$. But it is easy to check that $y(x) = Ax^n$ satisfies neither Eq. (13a) nor Eq. (13b) unless $A = 0$. Thus $\lambda = 0$ is not an eigenvalue if $n > 0$. We have therefore shown that $\lambda = 0$ *is an eigenvalue of the problem* (12)–(13) *if and only if* $n = h = 0$ *and the endpoint condition at* $x = c$ *is* $y'(c) = 0$, *in which case an associated eigenfunction is* $y(x) \equiv 1$. In this case we write

$$\lambda_0 = 0 \quad \text{and} \quad y_0(x) = 1.$$

The case $\lambda > 0$

Now suppose that $\lambda = \alpha^2 > 0$, in which case the only solution of Eq. (12) that is continuous on $[0, c]$ is, to within a constant multiple,

$$y(x) = J_n(\alpha x).$$

Then Eq. (13a) implies that $J_n(\alpha c) = 0$; in other words, αc must be a positive root of the equation

$$J_n(x) = 0. \tag{14a}$$

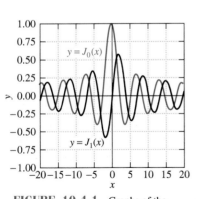

Recall from Section 8.5 that the graphs of $J_0(x)$ and $J_1(x)$ look as indicated in Fig. 10.4.1. The graph of $J_n(x)$ for $n > 1$ resembles that of $J_1(x)$, even in the detail that $J_n(0) = 0$. In particular, for each $n = 1, 2, 3, \dots$, Eq. (14a) has an increasing infinite sequence $\{\gamma_{nk}\}_{k=1}^{\infty}$ of positive roots with $\lim_{k \to \infty} \gamma_{nk} = \infty$. These roots for $n \leq 8$ and $k \leq 20$ are given in Table 9.5 of Abramowitz and Stegun's *Handbook of Mathematical Functions.*

If $y(x) = J_n(\alpha x)$, so that $dy/dx = \alpha J_n'(\alpha x)$, then Eq. (13b) implies that

$$h J_n(\alpha c) + \alpha c J_n'(\alpha c) = 0$$

—that is, that αc be a positive root of the equation

$$h J_n(x) + x J_n'(x) = 0. \tag{14b}$$

FIGURE 10.4.1. Graphs of the Bessel functions $J_0(x)$ and $J_1(x)$

It is known that this equation also has an increasing infinite sequence $\{\gamma_{nk}\}_{k=1}^{\infty}$ of positive roots diverging to $+\infty$. If $h = 0$, then Eq. (14b) reduces to the equation $J_n'(x) = 0$; the roots of this equation appear in Table 9.5 of Abramowitz and Stegun. In the important case $n = 0$, the first five roots of (14b) for various values of h can be found in Table 9.7 of the same reference.

If either of the boundary conditions in Eqs. (13a) and (13b) holds, then the kth positive eigenvalue is

$$\lambda_k = \frac{\gamma_k^2}{c^2},$$

	Endpoint Condition	**Eigenvalues**	**Associated Eigenfunctions**
Case 1:	$y(c) = 0$	$\lambda_k = \gamma_k^2/c^2$; $\{\gamma_k\}_1^\infty$ the positive roots of $J_n(x) = 0$	$y_k(x) = J_n\left(\dfrac{\gamma_k x}{c}\right)$
Case 2:	$hy(c) + cy'(c) = 0$; h and n not both zero	$\lambda_k = \gamma_k^2/c^2$; $\{\gamma_k\}_1^\infty$ the positive roots of $hJ_n(x) + xJ_n'(x) = 0$	$y_k(x) = J_n\left(\dfrac{\gamma_k x}{c}\right)$
Case 3:	$y'(c) = 0$, $n = 0$	$\lambda_0 = 0,\ \lambda_k = \gamma_k^2/c^2$; $\{\gamma_k\}_1^\infty$ the positive roots of $J_0'(x) = 0$	$y_0(x) = 1$, $y_k(x) = J_0\left(\dfrac{\gamma_k x}{c}\right)$

FIGURE 10.4.2. Eigenvalues and eigenfunctions of the singular Sturm-Liouville problem

$$\frac{d}{dx}\left[x\,\frac{dy}{dx}\right] - \frac{n^2}{x}y + \lambda xy = 0, \qquad \beta_1 y(c) + \beta_2 y'(c) = 0 \quad \text{on } [0, c]$$

where we write γ_k for the kth positive root of the appropriate one of Eqs. (14a) and (14b); the associated eigenfunction is

▶
$$y_k(x) = J_n\left(\frac{\gamma_k x}{c}\right).$$

The table in Fig. 10.4.2 summarizes this situation for ready reference. The exceptional case $n = h = 0$ corresponding to the endpoint condition $y'(c) = 0$ is listed separately. We have discussed only nonnegative eigenvalues, but it can be proved that the problem in (12)–(13) has no negative eigenvalues. (See Section 78 of R. V. Churchill and J. W. Brown, *Fourier Series and Boundary Value Problems,* 3rd ed. (New York: McGraw-Hill, 1978).)

Fourier-Bessel Series

Now that we know that the singular Sturm-Liouville problem in (12)–(13) has an infinite sequence of eigenvalues and associated eigenfunctions similar to those of a regular Sturm-Liouville problem, we can discuss eigenfunction expansions. In either case 1 or case 2 of Fig. 10.4.2, we expect a piecewise smooth function $f(x)$ on $[0, c]$ to have an eigenfunction series of the form

▶
$$f(x) = \sum_{k=1}^{\infty} c_k y_k(x) = \sum_{k=1}^{\infty} c_k J_n\left(\frac{\gamma_k x}{c}\right), \tag{15}$$

while in the exceptional case 3, the series will also contain a constant term c_0 corresponding to $\lambda_0 = 0$, $y_0(x) \equiv 1$. If the conclusion of Theorem 2 of Section 10.1 is to hold (despite the fact that its hypotheses are not satisfied), then the eigenfunctions

$$J_n\left(\frac{\gamma_k x}{c}\right), \qquad k = 1, 2, 3, \dots$$

must be orthogonal on $[0, c]$ with weight function $r(x) = x$. Indeed, if we substitute

$p(x) = r(x) = x$ and

$$y_k(x) = J_n\left(\frac{\gamma_k x}{c}\right), \qquad y_k'(x) = \frac{\gamma_k}{c} J_n'\left(\frac{\gamma_k x}{c}\right)$$

in Eq. (22) of Section 10.1, the result is

$$(\lambda_i - \lambda_j) \int_0^x x J_n\left(\frac{\gamma_i x}{c}\right) J_n\left(\frac{\gamma_j x}{c}\right) dx$$

$$= \left[x\left\{ \frac{\gamma_j}{c} J_n\left(\frac{\gamma_i x}{c}\right) J_n'\left(\frac{\gamma_j x}{c}\right) - \frac{\gamma_i}{c} J_n\left(\frac{\gamma_j x}{c}\right) J_n'\left(\frac{\gamma_i x}{c}\right) \right\} \right]_0^c$$

$$= \gamma_j J_n(\gamma_i) J_n'(\gamma_j) - \gamma_i J_n(\gamma_j) J_n'(\gamma_i). \tag{16}$$

It is clear that the quantity in Eq. (16) is zero if γ_i and γ_j are both roots of Eq. (14a), $J_n(x) = 0$, whereas if both are roots of Eq. (14b) it reduces to

$$J_n(\gamma_i)[-h J_n(\gamma_j)] - J_n(\gamma_j)[-h J_n(\gamma_i)] = 0.$$

In either event we thus see that if $i \neq j$, then

$$\int_0^c x J_n\left(\frac{\gamma_i x}{c}\right) J_n\left(\frac{\gamma_j x}{c}\right) dx = 0. \tag{17}$$

This orthogonality with weight function $r(x) = x$ is what we need to determine the coefficients in the eigenfunction series in Eq. (15). If we multiply each term in Eq. (15) by $x J_n(\gamma_k x/c)$ and then integrate termwise, we get

$$\int_0^c x f(x) J_n\left(\frac{\gamma_k x}{c}\right) dx = \sum_{j=1}^{\infty} c_j \int_0^c x J_n\left(\frac{\gamma_j x}{c}\right) J_n\left(\frac{\gamma_k x}{c}\right) dx$$

$$= c_k \int_0^c x \left[J_n\left(\frac{\gamma_k x}{c}\right) \right]^2 dx$$

by Eq. (17). Hence

$$\blacktriangleright \qquad\qquad c_k = \frac{\int_0^c x f(x) J_n(\gamma_k x/c)\, dx}{\int_0^c x [J_n(\gamma_k x/c)]^2\, dx}. \tag{18}$$

With these coefficients, series of the form in Eq. (15) are often called **Fourier-Bessel series**. It is known that a Fourier-Bessel series for a piecewise smooth function $f(x)$ satisfies the convergence conclusion of Theorem 3 of Section 10.1. That is, it converges to the average value $\frac{1}{2}[f(x+) + f(x-)]$ at each point of $(0, c)$, and hence to the value $f(x)$ at each interior point of continuity.

The Fourier-Bessel Coefficients

In spite of their appearance, the denominator integrals in Eq. (18) are not difficult to evaluate. Suppose that $y(x) = J_n(\alpha x)$, so that $y(x)$ satisfies the parametric Bessel equation of order n,

$$\frac{d}{dx}\left[x \frac{dy}{dx} \right] + \left(\alpha^2 x - \frac{n^2}{x} \right) y = 0. \tag{19}$$

By multiplying this equation by $2xy'(x)$ and integrating by parts (Problem 10), one can readily derive the formula

$$2\alpha^2 \int_0^c x[J_n(\alpha x)]^2\, dx = \alpha^2 c^2 [J_n'(\alpha c)]^2 + (\alpha^2 c^2 - n^2)[J_n(\alpha c)]^2. \qquad (20)$$

Now suppose that $\alpha = \gamma_k/c$, where γ_k is a root of the equation $J_n(x) = 0$. We apply Eq. (20) as well as the recurrence formula

$$xJ_n'(x) = nJ_n(x) - xJ_{n+1}(x)$$

of Section 8.5, which implies that $J_n'(\gamma_k) = -J_{n+1}(\gamma_k)$. The result is

$$\int_0^c x\left[J_n\left(\frac{\gamma_k x}{c}\right)\right]^2\, dx = \frac{c^2}{2}[J_n'(\gamma_k)]^2 = \frac{c^2}{2}[J_{n+1}(\gamma_k)]^2. \qquad (21)$$

The other entries in the table in Fig. 10.4.3 follow similarly from Eq. (20). Fourier-Bessel series with $n = 0$ are the most common (Problem 9). The forms they take in our three cases are listed below.

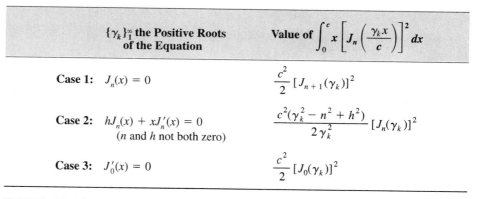

	$\{\gamma_k\}_1^\infty$ the Positive Roots of the Equation	Value of $\displaystyle\int_0^c x\left[J_n\left(\frac{\gamma_k x}{c}\right)\right]^2 dx$
Case 1:	$J_n(x) = 0$	$\dfrac{c^2}{2}[J_{n+1}(\gamma_k)]^2$
Case 2:	$hJ_n(x) + xJ_n'(x) = 0$ (n and h not both zero)	$\dfrac{c^2(\gamma_k^2 - n^2 + h^2)}{2\gamma_k^2}[J_n(\gamma_k)]^2$
Case 3:	$J_0'(x) = 0$	$\dfrac{c^2}{2}[J_0(\gamma_k)]^2$

FIGURE 10.4.3.

Case 1 with $n = 0$

If $\{\gamma_k\}_{k=1}^\infty$ are the positive roots of the equation $J_0(x) = 0$, then

$$f(x) = \sum_{k=1}^\infty c_k J_0\left(\frac{\gamma_k x}{c}\right);$$

$$c_k = \frac{2}{c^2[J_1(\gamma_k)]^2}\int_0^c xf(x) J_0\left(\frac{\gamma_k x}{c}\right) dx. \qquad (22)$$

Case 2 with $n = 0$

If $\{\gamma_k\}_{k=1}^\infty$ are the positive roots of the equation $hJ_0(x) + xJ_0'(x) = 0$ with $h > 0$, then

$$f(x) = \sum_{k=1}^\infty c_k J_0\left(\frac{\gamma_k x}{c}\right);$$

$$c_k = \frac{2\gamma_k^2}{c^2(\gamma_k^2 + h^2)[J_0(\gamma_k)]^2}\int_0^c xf(x) J_0\left(\frac{\gamma_k x}{c}\right) dx. \qquad (23)$$

Case 3

If $\{\gamma_k\}_{k=1}^{\infty}$ are the positive roots of the equation $J_0'(x) = 0$, then (Problem 10)

$$f(x) = c_0 + \sum_{k=1}^{\infty} c_k J_0\left(\frac{\gamma_k x}{c}\right);$$ (24a)

$$c_0 = \frac{2}{c^2} \int_0^c xf(x)\, dx,$$ (24b)

$$c_k = \frac{2}{c^2 [J_0(\gamma_k)]^2} \int_0^c xf(x) J_0\left(\frac{\gamma_k x}{c}\right) dx.$$ (24c)

Applications

EXAMPLE 1 Suppose that a long circular cylinder of radius c has initial temperature $u(r, 0) = u_0$, a constant. Find $u(r, t)$ in each of the three cases

(a) $u(c, t) = 0$ (zero boundary temperature);

(b) The boundary of the cylinder is insulated, so that $u_r(c, t) = 0$;

(c) Heat transfer takes place across the boundary of the cylinder, so that
$Hu(c, t) + Ku_r(c, t) = 0$ with H and K positive.

Solution With $u(r, t) = R(r)T(t)$, we saw previously that $\lambda = \alpha^2 > 0$ in Eq. (7), so

$$r^2 R'' + rR' + \alpha^2 r^2 R = 0$$ (25)

and

$$T' = -\alpha^2 kT.$$ (26)

Equation (25) is Bessel's parametric equation of order zero, and its only continuous nontrivial solutions on $[0, c]$ are of the form

$$R(r) = AJ_0(\alpha r).$$ (27)

But the possible values of α depend upon the boundary conditions that are imposed.

(a) Zero boundary temperature

The condition $u(c, t) = 0$ yields $R(c) = AJ_0(\alpha c) = 0$, so αc must be one of the roots $\{\gamma_n\}_1^{\infty}$ of the equation $J_0(x) = 0$. Thus the eigenvalues and eigenfunctions are

$$\lambda_n = \frac{\gamma_n^2}{c^2}, \qquad R_n(r) = J_0\left(\frac{\gamma_n r}{c}\right)$$ (28)

for $n = 1, 2, 3, \ldots$. Then the equation

$$T_n' = -\left(\frac{\gamma_n^2}{c^2}\right) kT_n$$

yields

$$T_n(t) = \exp\left(\frac{-\gamma_n^2 kt}{c^2}\right)$$

to within a constant coefficient. Hence the series

$$u(r, t) = \sum_{n=1}^{\infty} c_n \exp\left(\frac{-\gamma_n^2 kt}{c^2}\right) J_0\left(\frac{\gamma_n r}{c}\right) \tag{29}$$

satisfies formally the heat equation and the boundary condition $u(c, t) = 0$. It remains to choose the coefficients so that

$$u(r, 0) = \sum_{n=1}^{\infty} c_n J_0\left(\frac{\gamma_n r}{c}\right) = u_0.$$

Because $J_0(\gamma_n) = 0$, Eq. (22) yields

$$c_n = \frac{2u_0}{c^2[J_1(\gamma_n)]^2} \int_0^c r J_0\left(\frac{\gamma_n r}{c}\right) dr$$

$$= \frac{2u_0}{\gamma_n^2[J_1(\gamma_n)]^2} \int_0^{\gamma_n} x J_0(x) \, dx = \frac{2u_0}{\gamma_n^2[J_1(\gamma_n)]^2}\left[x J_1(x)\right]_0^{\gamma_n} = \frac{2u_0}{\gamma_n J_1(\gamma_n)}.$$

Here we have used the integral

$$\int x J_0(x) \, dx = x J_1(x) + C.$$

On substitution of the coefficients above in Eq. (29), we finally obtain

$$u(r, t) = 2u_0 \sum_{n=1}^{\infty} \frac{1}{\gamma_n J_1(\gamma_n)} \exp\left(\frac{-\gamma_n^2 kt}{c^2}\right) J_0\left(\frac{\gamma_n r}{c}\right). \tag{30}$$

Because of the presence of exponential factors, only a few terms are ordinarily needed for numerical computations. The data required for the first five terms are listed in Fig. 10.4.4. For instance, suppose that the cylinder has radius $c = 10$ cm, is made of iron with thermal diffusivity $k = 0.15$, and has initial temperature $u_0 = 100°C$ throughout. Then, because $J_0(0) = 1$, we find from Eq. (30) that the temperature at its axis $(r = 0)$ after two minutes $(t = 120)$ will be

$$u(0, 120) = 200 \sum_{n=1}^{\infty} \frac{1}{\gamma_n J_1(\gamma_n)} \exp(-[0.18]\gamma_n^2)$$

$$\approx 200 \cdot (0.28283 - 0.00221 + 0.00000 - \cdots);$$

thus $u(0, 120)$ will be approximately $56.12°C$.

n	γ_n	$J_1(\gamma_n)$
1	2.40483	+0.51915
2	5.52008	−0.34026
3	8.65373	+0.27145
4	11.79153	−0.23246
5	14.93092	+0.20655

FIGURE 10.4.4. Roots of $J_0(\gamma) = 0$

(b) Insulated boundary

In this case no heat ever escapes from the heated cylinder, so we certainly should find that its temperature remains constant: $u(r, t) = u_0$. Inasmuch as $u_r(c, t) = 0$ implies that $R'(c) = 0$, we have $n = h = 0$ in Eq. (14b), and hence case 3 in Table 10.4.2. Therefore $\lambda_0 = 0$ is an eigenvalue with associated eigenfunction $R_0(r) \equiv 1$. A corresponding solution of Eq. (26) is $T_0(t) = 1$. The positive eigenvalues are again given by (28), except that now the numbers $\{\gamma_n\}_1^\infty$ are the positive roots of $J_0'(x) = 0$. The solution is therefore of the form

$$u(r, t) = c_0 + \sum_{n=1}^{\infty} c_n \exp\left(\frac{-\gamma_n^2 kt}{c^2}\right) J_0\left(\frac{\gamma_n r}{c}\right),$$

and we want

$$u(r, 0) = c_0 + \sum_{n=1}^{\infty} c_n J_0\left(\frac{\gamma_n r}{c}\right) = u_0.$$

But now the case 3 coefficient formulas in (24) yield

$$c_0 = \frac{2}{c^2} \int_0^c r u_0 \, dr = \frac{u_0}{c^2}\left[\frac{1}{2}r^2\right]_0^c = u_0;$$

$$c_n = \frac{2u_0}{c^2[J_0(\gamma_n)]^2} \int_0^c r J_0\left(\frac{\gamma_n r}{c}\right) dr = \frac{2u_0}{\gamma_n^2[J_0(\gamma_n)]^2} \int_0^{\gamma_n} x J_0(x) \, dx$$

$$= \frac{2u_0}{\gamma_n^2[J_0(\gamma_n)]^2}\left[x J_1(x)\right]_0^{\gamma_n} = \frac{2u_0 J_1(\gamma_n)}{\gamma_n[J_0(\gamma_n)]^2} = 0$$

because $J_1(\gamma_n) = -J_0'(\gamma_n) = 0$. Thus we find that $u(r, t) \equiv u_0$, as expected.

(c) Heat transfer at the boundary

Substitution of $R(r) = J_0(\alpha r)$ in the boundary condition $HR(c) + KR'(c) = 0$ gives the equation

$$HJ_0(\alpha c) + K\alpha J_0'(\alpha c) = 0$$

that takes the form

$$hJ_0(\alpha c) + \alpha c J_0'(\alpha c) = 0 \tag{31}$$

with $h = cH/K > 0$. Comparing Eq. (31) with Eq. (14b), we see that we have case 2 in Table 10.4.2 with $n = 0$. Hence our eigenvalues and associated eigenfunctions are given by

$$\lambda_n = \frac{\gamma_n^2}{c^2}, \qquad R_n(r) = J_0\left(\frac{\gamma_n r}{c}\right), \tag{32}$$

where $\{\gamma_n\}_1^{\infty}$ are the positive roots of the equation $hJ_0(x) + xJ_0'(x) = 0$. Now $T' = -\lambda kt$ as before; consequently, the solution is of the form

$$u(r, t) = \sum_{n=1}^{\infty} c_n \exp\left(\frac{-\gamma_n^2 kt}{c^2}\right) J_0\left(\frac{\gamma_n r}{c}\right), \tag{33}$$

and Eq. (23) yields

$$c_n = \frac{2u_0\gamma_n^2}{c^2(\gamma_n^2 + h^2)[J_0(\gamma_n)]^2} \int_0^c r J_0\left(\frac{\gamma_n r}{c}\right) dr$$

$$= \frac{2u_0}{(\gamma_n^2 + h^2)[J_0(\gamma_n)]^2} \int_0^{\gamma_n} x J_0(x) \, dx = \frac{2u_0\gamma_n J_1(\gamma_n)}{(\gamma_n^2 + h^2)[J_0(\gamma_n)]^2}.$$

Hence

$$u(x, t) = 2u_0 \sum_{n=1}^{\infty} \frac{\gamma_n J_1(\gamma_n)}{(\gamma_n^2 + h^2)[J_0(\gamma_n)]^2} \exp\left(\frac{-\gamma_n^2 kt}{c^2}\right) J_0\left(\frac{\gamma_n r}{c}\right). \tag{34}$$

EXAMPLE 2 Suppose that a flexible circular membrane of radius c vibrates under tension T in such a way that its [normal] displacement u depends only upon time t and the distance r

from its center. (This is the case of *radial vibrations.*) Then $u = u(r, t)$ satisfies the partial differential equation

$$\frac{\partial^2 u}{\partial t^2} = a^2 \nabla^2 u = a^2 \left(\frac{\partial^2 u}{\partial r^2} + \frac{1}{r} \frac{\partial u}{\partial r} \right) \tag{35}$$

where $a^2 = T/\rho$, and $u(c, t) = 0$ if the boundary of the membrane is fixed. Find the natural frequencies and normal modes of radial vibration of the membrane.

Solution We apply the method of Section 10.3: Substitution of the function $u(r, t) = R(r) \sin \omega t$ in Eq. (35) yields

$$-\omega^2 R \sin \omega t = a^2 \left(R'' \sin \omega t + \frac{1}{r} R' \sin \omega t \right).$$

Thus ω and $R(r)$ must satisfy the equation

$$r^2 R'' + r R' + \frac{\omega^2}{a^2} r^2 R = 0, \tag{36}$$

as well as the condition $R(c) = 0$ that follows from $u(c, t) = 0$. Equation (36) is the Bessel equation of order zero with parameter $\alpha = \omega/a$, and its only nontrivial solution is (to within a constant multiple)

$$R(r) = J_0 \left(\frac{\omega r}{a} \right); \qquad \text{hence} \quad R(c) = J_0 \left(\frac{\omega c}{a} \right) = 0,$$

so $\omega c/a$ must be one of the positive roots $\{\gamma_n\}_1^\infty$ of the equation $J_0(x) = 0$. Thus the nth natural [circular] frequency and a corresponding natural mode of vibration are

$$\omega_n = \frac{\gamma_n a}{c}, \qquad u_n(r, t) = J_0 \left(\frac{\gamma_n r}{c} \right) \sin \frac{\gamma_n a t}{c}. \tag{37}$$

On inspection of the table of values of $\{\gamma_n\}$ in Fig. 10.4.4, we see that the higher natural frequencies ω_n are *not* integral multiples of $\omega_1 = \gamma_1 a/c$; this is why the sound of a vibrating circular drumhead is not perceived as being harmonious. The vibration of the membrane in the nth normal mode in (37) is illustrated in Fig. 10.4.5, which shows a vertical cross section through the center of the drumhead. In addition to the boundary $r = c$, there are $n - 1$ fixed circles, called *nodal circles*, with radii $r_i = \gamma_i c/\gamma_n$, $i = 1$, $2, \ldots, n - 1$. The annular regions of the membrane between consecutive pairs of

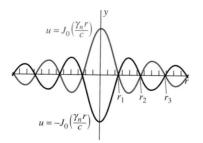

FIGURE 10.4.5. Cross section of the vibrating circular membrane

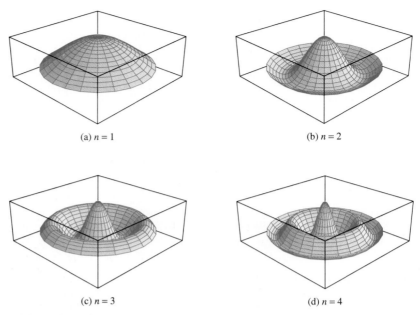

(a) $n = 1$ (b) $n = 2$

(c) $n = 3$ (d) $n = 4$

FIGURE 10.4.6. The surface $u = J_0(\gamma_n r/c)$:
(a) $n = 1$; (b) $n = 2$; (c) $n = 3$; (d) $n = 4$

nodal circles move alternately up and down between the surfaces $u = \pm J_0(\gamma_n r/c)$. Figure 10.4.6 shows how the surface $u = J_0(\gamma_n r/c)$ looks for $n = 1, 2, 3$, and 4.

10.4 Problems

1. Suppose that the circular membrane of Example 2 has initial position $u(r, 0) = f(r)$ and initial velocity $u_t(r, 0) = 0$. Derive by separation of variables the solution

$$u(r, t) = \sum_{n=1}^{\infty} c_n J_0\left(\frac{\gamma_n r}{c}\right) \cos \frac{\gamma_n a t}{c},$$

where $\{\gamma_n\}_1^{\infty}$ are the positive roots of $J_0(x) = 0$ and

$$c_n = \frac{2}{c^2 [J_1(\gamma_n)]^2} \int_0^c r f(r) J_0\left(\frac{\gamma_n r}{c}\right) dr.$$

2. Assume that the circular membrane of Example 2 has initial position $u(r, 0) = 0$ and initial velocity $u_t(r, 0) = v_0$ (constant). Derive the solution

$$u(r, t) = \frac{2cv_0}{a} \sum_{n=1}^{\infty} \frac{J_0(\gamma_n r/c) \sin (\gamma_n a t/c)}{\gamma_n^2 J_1(\gamma_n)},$$

where $\{\gamma_n\}_1^{\infty}$ are the positive roots of $J_0(x) = 0$.

3. (a) Find $u(r, t)$ in the case the circular membrane of Example 2 has initial position $u(r, 0)$ and initial velocity

$$u_t(r, 0) = \begin{cases} \dfrac{P_0}{\rho \pi \epsilon^2} & \text{if } 0 \leqq r < \epsilon, \\ 0 & \text{if } \epsilon < r \leqq c. \end{cases}$$

(b) Use the fact that $[J_1(x)]/x \to \frac{1}{2}$ as $x \to 0$ to find the limiting value of the result in part (a) as $\epsilon \to 0$. You should obtain

$$u(r, t) = \frac{a P_0}{\pi c T} \sum_{n=1}^{\infty} \frac{J_0(\gamma_n r/c) \sin (\gamma_n a t/c)}{\gamma_n [J_1(\gamma_n)]^2},$$

where $\{\gamma_n\}_1^{\infty}$ are the positive roots of $J_0(x) = 0$. This function describes the motion of a drumhead resulting from an initial momentum impulse P_0 at its center.

4. (a) A circular plate of radius c has insulated faces and heat capacity s calories per degree per square centimeter. Find $u(r, t)$ given $u(c, t) = 0$ and

$$u(r, 0) = \begin{cases} \dfrac{q_0}{s \pi \epsilon^2} & \text{if } 0 \leqq r < \epsilon, \\ 0 & \text{if } \epsilon < r \leqq c. \end{cases}$$

(b) Take the limit as $\epsilon \to 0$ of the result in part (a) to obtain

$$u(r, t) = \frac{q_0}{s\pi c^2} \sum_{n=1}^{\infty} \frac{1}{[J_1(\gamma_n)]^2} \exp\left(-\frac{\gamma_n^2 kt}{c^2}\right) J_0\left(\frac{\gamma_n r}{c}\right),$$

(where $\{\gamma_n\}_1^{\infty}$ are the positive roots of $J_0(x) = 0$) for the temperature resulting from an initial injection of q_0 calories of heat at the center of the plate.

Problems 5 through 7 deal with the steady-state temperature $u = u(r, z)$ in a solid cylinder of radius $r = c$ with bottom $z = 0$ and top $z = L$, given that u satisfies Laplace's equation

$$\frac{\partial^2 u}{\partial r^2} + \frac{1}{r}\frac{\partial u}{\partial r} + \frac{\partial^2 u}{\partial z^2} = 0.$$

5. If $u(r, L) = u_0$ and the rest of the surface of the cylinder is held at temperature zero, use separation of variables to derive the solution

$$u(r, z) = 2u_0 \sum_{n=1}^{\infty} \left(\frac{J_0(\gamma_n r/c)}{\gamma_n J_1(\gamma_n)}\right)\left(\frac{\sinh \gamma_n z/c}{\sinh \gamma_n L/c}\right),$$

where $\{\gamma_n\}_1^{\infty}$ are the positive roots of $J_0(x) = 0$.

6. (a) If $u(r, L) = f(r)$, $u(r, 0) = 0$, and the cylindrical surface $r = c$ is insulated, derive a solution of the form

$$u(r, z) = c_0 z + \sum_{n=1}^{\infty} c_n J_0\left(\frac{\gamma_n r}{c}\right) \sinh \frac{\gamma_n z}{c},$$

where $\{\gamma_n\}_1^{\infty}$ are the positive roots of $J_0'(x) = 0$. (b) Suppose that $f(r) = u_0$ (constant). Deduce from the result in part (a) that $u(r, z) = u_0 z/L$.

7. Let $c = 1$ and $L = +\infty$, so that the cylinder is semi-infinite. If $u(r, 0) = u_0$, $hu(1, z) + u_r(1, z) = 0$ (heat transfer on the cylindrical surface), and $u(r, z)$ is bounded as $z \to +\infty$, derive the solution

$$u(r, z) = 2hu_0 \sum_{n=1}^{\infty} \frac{\exp(-\gamma_n z) J_0(\gamma_n r)}{(\gamma_n^2 + h^2) J_0(\gamma_n)},$$

where $\{\gamma_n\}_1^{\infty}$ are the positive roots of the equation $hJ_0(x) = xJ_1(x)$.

8. Begin with the parametric Bessel equation of order n,

$$\frac{d}{dx}\left[x\frac{dy}{dx}\right] + \left(\alpha^2 x - \frac{n^2}{x}\right) y = 0. \quad (38)$$

Multiply each term by $2x\, dy/dx$, then write the result as

$$\frac{d}{dx}\left[\left(x\frac{dy}{dx}\right)^2\right] + (\alpha^2 x^2 - n^2)\frac{d}{dx}(y^2) = 0.$$

Integrate each term, using integration by parts for the second term, to obtain

$$\left[\left(x\frac{dy}{dx}\right)^2 + (\alpha^2 x^2 - n^2) y^2\right]_0^c - 2\alpha^2 \int_0^c xy^2\, dx = 0.$$

Finally, substitute $y(x) = J_n(\alpha x)$, a solution of Eq. (38), to get the formula in Eq. (20) in the text.

9. This problem provides the coefficient integrals for Fourier-Bessel series with $n = 0$. (a) Substitute $n = 0$ in the result of Problem 8 to obtain the integral formula

$$\int_0^c x[J_0(\alpha x)]^2\, dx = \frac{c^2}{2}\{[J_0(\alpha c)]^2 + [J_1(\alpha c)]^2\}. \quad (39)$$

(b) Suppose that $\alpha = \gamma_k/c$ where γ_k is a root of the equation $J_0(x) = 0$. Deduce that

$$\int_0^c x\left[J_0\left(\frac{\gamma_k x}{c}\right)\right]^2\, dx = \frac{c^2}{2}[J_1(\gamma_k)]^2.$$

(c) Suppose that $\alpha = \gamma_k/c$ where γ_k is a root of the equation $J_0'(x) = 0$. Deduce that

$$\int_0^c x\left[J_0\left(\frac{\gamma_k x}{c}\right)\right]^2\, dx = \frac{c^2}{2}[J_0(\gamma_k)]^2.$$

(d) Suppose that $\alpha = \gamma_k/c$ where γ_k is a root of the equation $hJ_0(x) + xJ_0'(x) = 0$. Deduce that

$$\int_0^c x\left[J_0\left(\frac{\gamma_k x}{c}\right)\right]^2\, dx = \frac{c^2(\gamma_k^2 + h^2)}{2\gamma_k^2}[J_0(\gamma_k)]^2.$$

10. Suppose that $\{\gamma_m\}_1^{\infty}$ are the positive roots of the equation $J_0'(x) = 0$ and that

$$f(x) = c_0 + \sum_{m=1}^{\infty} c_m J_0\left(\frac{\gamma_m x}{c}\right). \quad (40)$$

(a) Multiply each side of Eq. (40) by x and then integrate termwise from $x = 0$ to $x = c$ to show that

$$c_0 = \frac{2}{c^2} \int_0^c xf(x)\, dx.$$

(b) Multiply each side of Eq. (40) by $xJ_0(\gamma_n x/c)$ and then integrate termwise to show that

$$c_m = \frac{2}{c^2[J_0(\gamma_m)]^2} \int_0^c xf(x)\, J_0\left(\frac{\gamma_m x}{c}\right)\, dx.$$

11. If a circular membrane with fixed boundary is subjected to a periodic force $F_0 \sin \omega t$ per unit mass uniformly distributed over the membrane, then its displacement function $u(r, t)$ satisfies the equation

$$\frac{\partial^2 u}{\partial t^2} = a^2\left(\frac{\partial^2 u}{\partial r^2} + \frac{1}{r}\frac{\partial u}{\partial r}\right) + F_0 \sin \omega t.$$

Substitute $u(r, t) = R(r) \sin \omega t$ to find a steady periodic solution.

12. Consider a vertically hanging cable of length L and weight w per unit length, with fixed upper end at $x = L$ and free lower end at $x = 0$, as shown in Fig. 10.4.7. When the cable vibrates

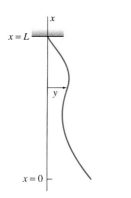

FIGURE 10.4.7. The vertical hanging cable of Problem 12

transversely, its displacement function $y(x, t)$ satisfies the equation

$$\frac{w}{g}\frac{\partial^2 y}{\partial t^2} = \frac{\partial}{\partial x}\left(wx\frac{\partial y}{\partial x}\right)$$

because the tension is $T(x) = wx$. Substitute the function $y(x, t) = X(x)\sin\omega t$, then apply the theorem of Section 8.6 to solve the ordinary differential equation that results. Deduce from the solution that the natural frequencies of vibration of the hanging cable are given by

$$\omega_n = \frac{\gamma_n}{2}\sqrt{\frac{g}{L}}\quad\left(\frac{\text{rad}}{\text{s}}\right),$$

where $\{\gamma_n\}_1^\infty$ are the roots of $J_0(x) = 0$. Historically, this problem was the first in which Bessel functions appeared.

Problems 13 through 15 deal with a canal of length L off the ocean (see Fig. 10.4.8 for a top view). Its vertical cross section at x is rectangular with width $w(x)$ and depth $h(x)$; the latter is the equilibrium depth of the water at x. Consider a periodic

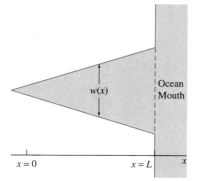

FIGURE 10.4.8. The canal of Problems 13–15

canal tide such that the vertical displacement of the water surface is $y(x, t) = X(x)\cos\omega t$ at time t. Then $y(x, t)$ satisfies the equation

$$\frac{w(x)}{g}\frac{\partial^2 y}{\partial t^2} = \frac{\partial}{\partial x}\left[w(x)\,h(x)\frac{\partial y}{\partial x}\right].$$

Let $y_0 = X(L)$ be the amplitude of the tide at the mouth of the canal.

13. Suppose that $w(x) = wx$ and $h(x) = h$ (a constant). Show that

$$y(x, t) = y_0\frac{J_0(wx/\sqrt{gh})}{J_0(wL/\sqrt{gh})}\cos\omega t.$$

Apply the theorem of Section 8.6.

14. Suppose that $w(x) = w$ (a constant) and that $h(x) = hx$. Show that

$$y(x, t) = y_0\frac{J_0(2w\sqrt{x/gh})}{J_0(2w\sqrt{L/gh})}\cos\omega t.$$

15. Suppose that $w(x) = wx$ and $h(x) = hx$ with w and h both constant. Show that

$$y(x, t) = y_0\sqrt{\frac{L}{x}}\frac{J_1(2w\sqrt{x/gh})}{J_1(2w\sqrt{L/gh})}\cos\omega t.$$

16. If $0 < a < b$, then the eigenvalue problem

$$\frac{d}{dx}\left[x\frac{dy}{dx}\right] + \lambda xy = 0,\qquad y(a) = y(b) = 0$$

for the parametric Bessel equation of order zero is a regular Sturm-Liouville problem. By Problem 1 of Section 10.1, it therefore has an infinite sequence of nonnegative eigenvalues. (a) Prove that zero is not an eigenvalue. (b) Show that the nth eigenvalue is $\lambda_n = \gamma_n^2$, where $\{\gamma_n\}_1^\infty$ are the positive roots of the equation

$$J_0(ax)\,Y_0(bx) - J_0(bx)\,Y_0(ax) = 0. \tag{41}$$

The first five roots of Eq. (41) for various values of a/b are listed in Table 9.7 of Abramowitz and Stegun, *Handbook of Mathematical Functions*. (c) Show that an associated eigenfunction is

$$R_n(x) = Y_0(\gamma_n a)\,J_0(\gamma_n x) - J_0(\gamma_n a)\,Y_0(\gamma_n x). \tag{42}$$

17. Suppose that an annular membrane with constant density ρ (per unit area) is stretched under constant tension T between the circles $r = a$ and $r = b\ (a < b)$. Show that its nth natural [circular] frequency is $\omega_n = \gamma_n\sqrt{T/\rho}$, where $\{\gamma_n\}_1^\infty$ are the positive roots of Eq. (41).

18. Suppose that the infinite cylindrical shell $a \leqq r \leqq b$ has

initial temperature $u(r, 0) = f(r)$, and thereafter $u(a, t) = u(b, t) = 0$. By separation of variables, derive the solution

$$u(r, t) = \sum_{n=1}^{\infty} c_n \exp(-\gamma_n^2 kt) R_n(r),$$

where $R_n(r)$ is the function in Eq. (42) and

$$c_n \int_a^b r[R_n(r)]^2 \, dr = \int_a^b rf(r) R_n(r) \, dr.$$

19. Consider the semi-infinite cylindrical shell

$$0 < a \leq r \leq b, \qquad z \geq 0.$$

If $u(a, z) = u(b, z) = 0$ and $u(r, 0) = f(r)$, derive by separation of variables the steady-state temperature

$$u(r, z) = \sum_{n=1}^{\infty} c_n e^{-\gamma_n z} R_n(r),$$

where $\{c_n\}$ and $\{R_n\}$ are as given in Problems 18 and 16.

10.4 Computing Project

First let's investigate numerically the temperature function

$$u(r, t) = \sum_{n=1}^{\infty} a_n \exp\left(-\frac{\gamma_n^2 \, kt}{c^2}\right) J_0\left(\frac{\gamma_n r}{c}\right) \tag{1}$$

of the heated cylindrical rod of Example 1, with radius $c = 10$ cm, having constant initial temperature $u_0 = 100$ and thermal diffusivity $k = 0.15$ (for iron). The coefficients $\{a_n\}_1^{\infty}$ depend on the boundary condition imposed at $r = c$.

In the case of the zero boundary condition $u(c, t) = 0$, Eq. (30) in this section implies that

$$a_n = \frac{2u_0}{\gamma_n J_1(\gamma_n)},$$

where the $\{\gamma_n\}_1^{\infty}$ are the positive solutions of the equation $J_0(x) = 0$. Knowing that $\gamma_1 \approx 2.4$ and that successive roots differ approximately by an integral multiple of π, we can approximate the first m values of γ_n by using the *Mathematica* command

```
m = 20;

solutions =

Table[ FindRoot[ BesselJ[0,x] == 0,

                    {x, 2.4 + (n - 1)*Pi} ], {n, 1, m} ];

gamma = x /. solutions

{2.40483, 5.52008, 8.65373, 11.7915, 14.9309,

  18.0711, 21.2116, 24.3525, 27.4935, 30.6346,

  33.7758, 36.9171, 40.0584, 43.1998, 46.3412,

  49.4846, 52.6241, 55.7655, 58.9070, 62.0485}
```

Then the first m coefficients in (1) are given by

```
g = gamma;

c = 10; u0 = 100; k = 0.15;

a = 2*u0/(g*BesselJ[1,g]);
```

and the following *Mathematica* function sums the corresponding terms of the series.

```
u[r_,t_] := Apply[ Plus,

        a*Exp[-g*g*k*t/c^2]*BesselJ[0,g*r/c] ] // N
```

The graph of $u(r, 120)$ in Fig. 10.4.9 shows how the temperature within the rod after 2 minutes varies with the distance r from its center, and we see that the centerline temperature has already fallen below 60°. The graph of $u(0, t)$ for a 5-minute period shown in Fig. 10.4.10 indicates that the centerline temperature takes a bit more than 200 seconds to fall to 25°. Indeed, the computation

```
FindRoot[ u[0,t] == 25, {t, 200} ]

{t -> 214.013}
```

shows that this occurs after about 214 seconds.

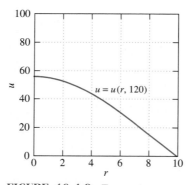

FIGURE 10.4.9. Temperature as a function of distance r from the rod's centerline

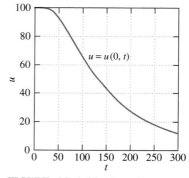

FIGURE 10.4.10. Centerline temperature as a function of time t

For your very own cylindrical rod with constant initial temperature $u_0 \equiv 100°$ to investigate in this manner, let $c = 2p$ and $k = (0.1)q$, where p is the largest and q the smallest nonzero digit of your student I.D. number.

1. If the cylindrical boundary of the rod is held at zero temperature $u(c, t) = 0$, plot graphs as above, then determine how long it will take for the rod's centerline temperature to fall to 25°.

2. Now suppose that heat transfer occurs at the rod's cylindrical boundary, so that the coefficients in the series in (1) are those appearing in Eq. (34) of the text. Assume that $h = 1$ and that the $\{\gamma_n\}_1^\infty$ are now the positive roots of the equation

$$J_0(x) + xJ_0'(x) = J_0(x) - xJ_1(x) = 0 \qquad (2)$$

(because $J_0'(x) = -J_1(x)$). Figure 10.4.11 shows the graph of the left-hand side in (2) and indicates that $\gamma_1 \approx 1.25$, with successive roots differing (as usual) by approximately π. Determine in this case *both* how long it takes the centerline temperature to fall to 25° *and* how long it takes the boundary temperature at $r = c$ to fall to 25°.

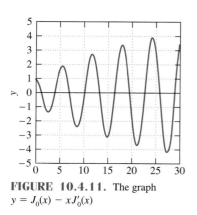

FIGURE 10.4.11. The graph $y = J_0(x) - xJ_0'(x)$

10.5 Higher-Dimensional Phenomena

In this section we discuss the application of the method of separation of variables to heat flow and vibration problems in which two or more space variables are involved. The section consists largely of illustrative examples, problems, and projects grouped according to whether rectangular, cylindrical, or spherical coordinates are most appropriate for their solutions.

Rectangular Coordinate Applications and Two-Dimensional Fourier Series

As indicated in Section 9.7, the Laplacian in two dimensions takes the form

$$\nabla^2 u = \frac{\partial^2 u}{\partial x^2} + \frac{\partial^2 u}{\partial y^2}.$$

For instance, consider a thin plate lying in the xy-plane with its two parallel faces insulated, so that heat flows within the plate only in the x- and y-directions. If $u(x, y, t)$ denotes the temperature at time t at the point (x, y) within the plate, then under standard assumptions it follows that u satisfies the **two-dimensional heat equation**

$$\frac{\partial u}{\partial t} = k\nabla^2 u = k\left(\frac{\partial^2 u}{\partial x^2} + \frac{\partial^2 u}{\partial y^2}\right). \tag{1}$$

Here k denotes the thermal diffusivity of the material comprising the plate. If the plate is rectangular and homogeneous boundary conditions are imposed along its four edges, then the method of separation of variables can be applied in a straightforward manner.

EXAMPLE 1 Suppose that a thin rectangular plate occupies the plane region $0 \leqq x \leqq a, 0 \leqq y \leqq b$, that its top and bottom faces are insulated, and that its four edges are held at temperature zero. If the plate has the initial temperature function $u(x, y, 0) = f(x, y)$, then its temperature function $u(x, y, t)$ satisfies the boundary value problem consisting of the heat equation in (1) and the boundary conditions

$$u(0, y, t) = u(a, y, t) = u(x, 0, t) = u(x, b, t) = 0, \tag{2}$$

$$u(x, y, 0) = f(x, y). \tag{3}$$

Find $u(x, y, t)$.

Solution We substitute $u(x, y, t) = X(x)Y(y)T(t)$ in Eq. (1). After division by $kXYT$, we obtain

$$\frac{T'}{kT} = \frac{X''}{X} + \frac{Y''}{Y}.$$

This relation can hold for all x, y, t only if each term is a constant, so we write

$$\frac{X''}{X} = -\lambda, \qquad \frac{Y''}{Y} = -\mu, \qquad \frac{T'}{kT} = -(\lambda + \mu). \tag{4}$$

Taking into account the boundary conditions in (2), we see that $X(x)$ and $Y(y)$ satisfy

the separate Sturm-Liouville problems

$$X'' + \lambda X = 0, \qquad X(0) = X(a) = 0 \tag{5}$$

and

$$Y'' + \mu Y = 0, \qquad Y(0) = Y(b) = 0. \tag{6}$$

The eigenvalues and eigenfunctions of the familiar problem in (5) are

$$\lambda_m = \frac{m^2 \pi^2}{a^2}, \qquad X_m(x) = \sin \frac{m\pi x}{a} \tag{7}$$

for $m = 1, 2, 3, \ldots$. Similarly, the eigenvalues and eigenfunctions of the problem in (6) are

$$\mu_n = \frac{n^2 \pi^2}{b^2}, \qquad Y_n(y) = \sin \frac{n\pi y}{b} \tag{8}$$

for $n = 1, 2, 3, \ldots$. We use distinct indices m and n in (7) and (8) because the two problems in (5) and (6) are independent of each other.

For each pair m, n of positive integers, we must solve the third equation in (4),

$$T'_{mn} = -(\lambda_n + \mu_n)kT_{mn} = -\left(\frac{m^2}{a^2} + \frac{n^2}{b^2} \right) \pi^2 k T_{mn}. \tag{9}$$

To within a multiplicative constant, the solution of Eq. (9) is

$$T_{mn}(t) = \exp(-\gamma_{mn}^2 kt), \tag{10}$$

where

$$\gamma_{mn} = \pi \sqrt{ \frac{m^2}{a^2} + \frac{n^2}{b^2} }. \tag{11}$$

Thus we have found a "doubly infinite" collection of building blocks, and it follows that the "doubly infinite" series

$$u(x, y, t) = \sum_{m=1}^{\infty} \sum_{n=1}^{\infty} c_{mn} \exp(-\gamma_{mn}^2 kt) \sin \frac{m\pi x}{a} \sin \frac{n\pi y}{b} \tag{12}$$

formally satisfies the heat equation in (1) and the homogeneous boundary conditions in (2).

It remains only to determine the coefficients $\{c_{mn}\}$ so that the series satisfies also the nonhomogeneous condition

$$u(x, y, 0) = \sum_{m=1}^{\infty} \sum_{n=1}^{\infty} c_{mn} \sin \frac{m\pi x}{a} \sin \frac{n\pi y}{b} = f(x, y). \tag{13}$$

To do so, we first group the terms in this *two-dimensional Fourier series* to display the total coefficient of $\sin(n\pi y/b)$ and write

$$f(x, y) = \sum_{n=1}^{\infty} \left(\sum_{m=1}^{\infty} c_{mn} \sin \frac{m\pi x}{a} \right) \sin \frac{n\pi y}{b}. \tag{14}$$

For each fixed x, we want (14) to be the Fourier sine series of $f(x, y)$ on $0 \leq y \leq b$. This will be so provided that

$$\sum_{m=1}^{\infty} c_{mn} \sin \frac{m\pi x}{a} = \frac{2}{b} \int_0^b f(x, y) \sin \frac{n\pi y}{b} \, dy. \tag{15}$$

The right-hand side in (15) is, for each fixed n, a function $F_n(x)$; viz.,

$$F_n(x) = \sum_{m=1}^{\infty} c_{mn} \sin \frac{m\pi x}{a}. \tag{16}$$

This requires that c_{mn} be the mth Fourier sine coefficient of $F_n(x)$ on $0 \leq x \leq a$; that is, that

$$c_{mn} = \frac{2}{a} \int_0^a F_n(x) \sin \frac{m\pi x}{a} \, dx. \tag{17}$$

Substituting the right-hand side in Eq. (15) for $F_n(x)$ in Eq. (17), we finally get

$$c_{mn} = \frac{4}{ab} \int_0^a \int_0^b f(x, y) \sin \frac{m\pi x}{a} \sin \frac{n\pi y}{b} \, dy \, dx \tag{18}$$

for $m, n = 1, 2, 3, \ldots$. With these coefficients, the series in (13) is the double Fourier sine series of $f(x, y)$ on the rectangle $0 \leq x \leq a$, $0 \leq y \leq b$, and the series in (12) formally satisfies the boundary value problem in (1)–(3). ∎

Problem 1
Suppose that $f(x, y) = u_0$, a constant. Compute the coefficients in (18) to obtain the solution

$$u(x, y, t) = \frac{16 u_0}{\pi^2} \sum_{m \text{ odd}} \sum_{n \text{ odd}} \frac{\exp(-\gamma_{mn}^2 kt)}{mn} \sin \frac{m\pi x}{a} \sin \frac{n\pi y}{b}.$$

Problem 2
Replace the boundary conditions (2) in Example 1 with

$$u(0, y, t) = u(x, 0, t) = 0,$$

$$hu(a, y, t) + u_x(a, y, t) = hu(x, b, t) + u_y(x, b, t) = 0.$$

Thus the edges $x = 0$ and $y = 0$ are still held at temperature zero, but now heat transfer takes place along the edges $x = a$ and $y = b$. Then derive the solution

$$u(x, y, t) = \sum_{m=1}^{\infty} \sum_{n=1}^{\infty} c_{mn} \exp(-\gamma_{mn}^2 kt) \sin \frac{\alpha_m x}{a} \sin \frac{\beta_n y}{b}$$

where $\gamma_{mn}^2 = (\alpha_m/a)^2 + (\beta_n/b)^2$, $\{\alpha_m\}$ are the positive roots of $ha \tan x = -x$, $\{\beta_n\}$ are the positive roots of $hb \tan x = -x$, and

$$c_{mn} = \frac{4}{A_m B_n} \int_0^a \int_0^b f(x, y) \sin \frac{\alpha_m x}{a} \sin \frac{\beta_n y}{b} \, dy \, dx,$$

where $A_m = (ha + \cos^2 \alpha_m)/h$ and $B_n = (hb + \cos^2 \beta_n)/h$.

Now let's consider a two-dimensional flexible membrane whose equilibrium position occupies a region in the horizontal xy-plane. Suppose that this membrane vibrates up and down, with $u(x, y, t)$ denoting the vertical displacement of the point (x, y) of the membrane at time t. If T and ρ denote the membrane's tension and density (per unit area), respectively, then under standard assumptions it follows that its displacement

function $u(x, y, t)$ satisfies the **two-dimensional wave equation**

$$\frac{\partial^2 u}{\partial t^2} = c^2 \nabla^2 u = c^2 \left(\frac{\partial^2 u}{\partial x^2} + \frac{\partial^2 u}{\partial y^2} \right), \tag{19}$$

where $c^2 = T/\rho$.

Problem 3

Suppose that the rectangular membrane $0 \leq x \leq a$, $0 \leq y \leq b$ is released from rest with given initial displacement $u(x, y, 0) = f(x, y)$. If the four edges of the membrane are held fixed thereafter with zero displacement, then the displacement function $u(x, y, t)$ satisfies the boundary value problem consisting of the wave equation in (19) and the boundary conditions

$$u(0, y, t) = u(a, y, t) = u(x, 0, t) = u(x, b, t) = 0,$$

$$u(x, y, 0) = f(x, y) \quad \text{(initial position)}, \tag{20}$$

$$u_t(x, y, 0) = 0 \qquad \text{(initial velocity)}.$$

Derive the solution

$$u(x, y, t) = \sum_{m=1}^{\infty} \sum_{n=1}^{\infty} c_{mn} \cos \gamma_{mn} ct \sin \frac{m\pi x}{a} \sin \frac{n\pi y}{b}, \tag{21}$$

where the numbers $\{\gamma_{mn}\}$ and the coefficients $\{c_{mn}\}$ are given by the formulas in (11) and (18), respectively.

The mnth term in Eq. (21) defines the rectangular membrane's mnth *natural mode of oscillation,* with displacement function

$$u_{mn}(x, y, t) = \sin \frac{m\pi x}{a} \sin \frac{n\pi y}{b} \cos \gamma_{mn} ct. \tag{22}$$

In this mode the membrane travels up and down between the (imaginary) surfaces

$$u = \pm \sin \frac{m\pi x}{a} \sin \frac{n\pi y}{b}$$

with circular frequency $\omega_{mn} = \gamma_{mn} c$ of oscillation. Figure 10.5.1 illustrates how these surfaces look for typical small values of m and n. If $c = 1$ and $a = b = \pi$ (for instance), then the successive frequencies

$$\omega_{12} = \omega_{21} = \sqrt{5} \approx 2.24, \qquad \omega_{22} = \sqrt{8} \approx 2.83,$$

$$\omega_{13} = \omega_{31} = \sqrt{10} \approx 3.16, \qquad \omega_{23} = \omega_{32} = \sqrt{13} \approx 3.61,$$

$$\omega_{33} = \sqrt{18} \approx 4.24, \ldots,$$

are *not* integral multiples of the fundamental frequency $\omega_{11} = \sqrt{2} \approx 1.41$. This correctly suggests that the sound of a vibrating rectangular membrane is not harmonious, and therefore is usually perceived as noise rather than music.

Problem 4

Suppose that the membrane is Problem 3 is a square tambourine lying upright and crosswise in a pickup truck that hits a brick wall at time $t = 0$. Then the membrane is set in motion with zero initial displacement and constant initial velocity, so the initial

(a) $m = 2, n = 1$ (b) $m = 2, n = 2$

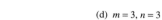

(c) $m = 3, n = 2$ (d) $m = 3, n = 3$

FIGURE 10.5.1. Surfaces of the form $u = \sin \dfrac{m\pi x}{a} \sin \dfrac{n\pi y}{b}$

conditions are

$$u(x, y, 0) = 0, \qquad u_t(x, y, 0) = v_0 \qquad \text{(a constant)}.$$

Then derive the solution

$$u(x, y, t) = \frac{16 v_0}{\pi^2 c} \sum_{m \text{ odd}} \sum_{n \text{ odd}} \frac{\sin \gamma_{mn} ct}{mn \gamma_{mn}} \sin \frac{m\pi x}{a} \sin \frac{n\pi y}{b}.$$

Project A

Suppose that the three edges $x = 0$, $y = 0$, and $y = b$ of the plate of Example 1 are held at temperature zero, but the fourth edge $x = a$ is insulated, with corresponding boundary conditions

$$u(0, y, t) = u(x, 0, t) = u(x, b, t) = u_x(a, y, t) = 0.$$

If the plate's initial temperature is $u(x, y, 0) = f(x, y)$, show that its temperature function is given by

$$u(x, y, t) = \sum_{m=1}^{\infty} \sum_{n=1}^{\infty} c_{mn} \exp\left(- \gamma_{mn}^2 \, kt\right) \sin \frac{(2m-1)\pi x}{2a} \sin \frac{n\pi y}{b}, \qquad (23)$$

where

$$\left(\frac{\gamma_{mn}}{\pi}\right)^2 = \left(\frac{2m-1}{a}\right)^2 + \left(\frac{n}{b}\right)^2$$

and

$$c_{mn} = \frac{4}{ab} \int_0^a \int_0^b f(x, y) \sin \frac{(2m-1)\pi x}{2a} \sin \frac{n\pi y}{b} \, dy \, dx.$$

The result of Problem 21 in Section 9.3 may be useful. If $f(x, y) \equiv u_0$ (a constant), show that Eq. (2) yields

$$u(x, y, t) = \frac{16u_0}{\pi^2} \sum_{m=1}^{\infty} \sum_{n \text{ odd}} \frac{\exp(-\gamma_{mn}^2 kt)}{(2m-1)n} \sin \frac{(2m-1)\pi x}{2a} \sin \frac{n\pi y}{b}. \quad (24)$$

For your personal plate to investigate numerically, take $u_0 = 100$, $a = 10p$, $b = 10q$, and $k = r/10$, where p and q are the two largest digits and r is the smallest nonzero digit in your student I.D. number. Plot $z = u(x, y, t)$ for typical values of t to verify that each such graph is symmetric with respect to the midline $y = b/2$, so it follows (why?) that the maximum temperature in the plate occurs at a point of this midline. Then determine (perhaps using the method of the Section 10.2 project):

- How long it takes for the maximum temperature on the edge $x = a$ to fall to 25°;
- What is then the maximum interior temperature in the plate.

Project B

Suppose that the square membrane $0 \le x \le \pi$, $0 \le y \le \pi$ is plucked at its center point and set in motion from rest with the initial position function

$$u(x, y, 0) = f(x, y) = \min\{x, y, \pi - x, \pi - y\}, \quad (25)$$

whose graph over the square $0 \le x \le \pi$, $0 \le y \le \pi$ resembles a square-based tent or pyramid with height $\pi/2$ at its center. Thus the "tent function" $f(x, y)$ is the two-dimensional analogue of the familiar one-dimensional triangle function. It can be defined piecewise as indicated in Fig. 10.5.2.

Use a computer algebra system as *Maple* or *Mathematica* to show that the double integral formula in (18) yields $c_{mn} = 0$ if $m \ne n$ and

$$c_{nn} = \frac{2[1 - (-1)^n]}{\pi n^2} = \begin{cases} \dfrac{4}{\pi n^2} & \text{for } n \text{ odd,} \\[2mm] 0 & \text{for } n \text{ even.} \end{cases}$$

It therefore follows from (21) that the membrane's resulting displacement function is given by

$$u(x, y, t) = \frac{4}{\pi} \sum_{n \text{ odd}} \frac{\sin nx \sin ny \cos nt \sqrt{2}}{n^2}. \quad (26)$$

Is it clear that—because the summand in (26) contains no terms with $m \ne n$—the function $u(x, y, t)$ is periodic (in t) with period $\pi\sqrt{2}$? The fact that the tent function in (25) thus yields a "musical" vibration of a square membrane was first pointed out to us by John Polking. Figure 10.5.3 shows some typical snapshots of this vibration.

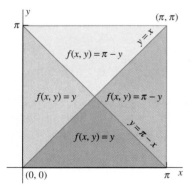

FIGURE 10.5.2. Piecewise definition of the tent function

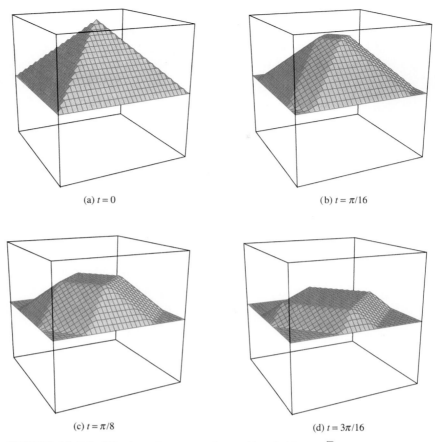

(a) $t = 0$

(b) $t = \pi/16$

(c) $t = \pi/8$

(d) $t = 3\pi/16$

FIGURE 10.5.3. Vibrations of square membrane with period $P = \pi\sqrt{2}$

Polar Coordinate Applications

In problems involving regions that enjoy circular symmetry around the origin in the plane (or the vertical z-axis in space), the use of polar (or cylindrical) coordinates is advantageous. In Section 9.7 we discussed the expression of the two-dimensional Laplacian in terms of the familiar plane polar coordinates (r, θ), for which $x = r\cos\theta$ and $y = r\sin\theta$. The three-dimensional Laplacian for a function $u(r, \theta, z)$ expressed in cylindrical coordinates is given by

$$\nabla^2 u = \frac{\partial^2 u}{\partial r^2} + \frac{1}{r}\frac{\partial u}{\partial r} + \frac{1}{r^2}\frac{\partial^2 u}{\partial\theta^2} + \frac{\partial^2 u}{\partial z^2}. \tag{27}$$

If u is independent of either θ or z then the corresponding second derivative is absent from the right-hand side in Eq. (27).

EXAMPLE 2 Suppose that the solid cylinder $0 \leqq r \leqq c$, $0 \leqq z \leqq h$ of Fig. 10.5.4 is made of a uniform material with thermal diffusivity k and has an axially symmetric initial temperature $u(r, z, 0) = f(r, z)$ that is independent of θ. If the cylinder's boundary—consisting of the vertical cylindrical surface $r = c$ and its circular top and bottom—are thereafter held at temperature zero (perhaps because the cylinder is embedded in ice at

FIGURE 10.5.4. The solid
cylinder of Example 2

time $t = 0$), then the resulting axially symmetric temperature function $u(r, z, t)$ satisfies the boundary value problem

$$\frac{\partial u}{\partial t} = k\nabla^2 u = k\left(\frac{\partial^2 u}{\partial r^2} + \frac{1}{r}\frac{\partial u}{\partial r} + \frac{\partial^2 u}{\partial z^2}\right), \tag{28}$$

$$u(c, z, t) = u(r, 0, t) = u(r, h, t) = 0$$
(boundary temperature zero), $\tag{29}$

$$u(r, z, 0) = f(r, z)$$
(given initial temperature). $\tag{30}$

The following two problems outline a solution of this heat problem for the case of constant initial temperature. ∎

Problem 5
Show that the substitution
$$u(r, z, t) = R(r)\, Z(z)\, T(t)$$
in Eq. (28) yields the separation of variables

$$r^2 R'' + rR' + \alpha^2 r^2 R = 0, \qquad R(c) = 0; \tag{31}$$

$$Z'' + \beta^2 Z = 0, \qquad\qquad Z(0) = Z(h) = 0; \tag{32}$$

$$T' = -(\alpha^2 + \beta^2)kT. \tag{33}$$

Note that the differential equation in (31) is the parametric Bessel equation of order zero for $R(r)$, and so (31) has the eigenvalues and eigenfunctions given in case 1 of the table in Fig. 10.4.2. Of course, the differential equations in (32) and (33) have familiar trigonometric and exponential solutions. Hence derive the formal series solution

$$u(r, z, t) = \sum_{m=1}^{\infty}\sum_{n=1}^{\infty} c_{mn}\exp(-\lambda_{mn}kt)\, J_0\left(\frac{\gamma_m r}{c}\right)\sin\frac{n\pi z}{h}, \tag{34}$$

where the $\{\gamma_m\}_1^{\infty}$ are the positive solutions of the equation $J_0(x) = 0$ (as listed in the Section 10.4 project),

$$\lambda_{mn} = \frac{\gamma_m^2}{c^2} + \frac{n^2\pi^2}{h^2}, \tag{35}$$

and the coefficients in Eq. (34) are given by the formula

$$c_{mn} = \frac{4}{hc^2[J_1(\gamma_m)]^2}\int_0^c\int_0^h rf(r, z)\, J_0\left(\frac{\gamma_m r}{c}\right)\sin\frac{n\pi z}{h}\, dz\, dr. \tag{36}$$

The derivation of Eq. (36) is similar to that of the double Fourier series coefficient formula in (18).

Problem 6
If the initial temperature function is constant, $f(r, z) \equiv u_0$, deduce from Eqs. (34) and (36) that

$$u(r, z, t) = \frac{8u_0}{\pi}\sum_{m=1}^{\infty}\sum_{n=1\ n\ \text{odd}}^{\infty} \frac{\exp(-\lambda_{mn}kt)\, J_0\left(\dfrac{\gamma_m r}{c}\right)\sin\dfrac{n\pi z}{h}}{n\gamma_m J_1(\gamma_m)}, \tag{37}$$

where λ_{mn} is defined by (35).

Project C

For your personal heated cylinder to investigate numerically, take $u_0 = 100$, $h = 10p$, $c = 5q$, and $k = r/10$ where p and q are the two largest digits and r is the smallest nonzero digit in your student I.D. number. Assume zero boundary temperatures as in Problems 5 and 6. Plot the surface $z = u(r, z, t)$ for typical values of t to substantiate the physically plausible conjecture that, at any time t, the maximum temperature within the cylinder occurs at its center point where $r = 0$ and $z = h/2$. It may help to plot also graphs of:

1. u as a function of r with $z = h/2$ and t constant; and
2. u as a function of z with $r = 0$ and t constant.

Then determine how long it takes for the maximum temperature within the cylinder to fall to $25°$.

Repeat this investigation with the temperature held at zero on the cylinder's bottom and curved surface, but with its top now insulated, so that the boundary conditions in (29) are replaced with

$$u(c, z, t) = u(r, 0, t) = u_z(r, h, t) = 0.$$

Using (as in Project A) the result of Problem 21 in Section 9.3, you should find that (37) is replaced with

$$u(r, z, t) = \frac{8u_0}{\pi} \sum_{m=1}^{\infty} \sum_{n=1}^{\infty} \frac{\exp(-\lambda_{mn}kt)J_0\left(\frac{\gamma_m r}{c}\right)\sin\frac{(2n-1)\pi z}{2h}}{(2n-1)\,\gamma_m J_1(\gamma_m)}, \qquad (38)$$

where

$$\lambda_{mn} = \frac{\gamma_m^2}{c^2} + \frac{(2n-1)^2\pi^2}{4h^2}.$$

Is it plausible that the cylinder's maximum temperature now always occurs at the center of its top? Substantiate this conjecture with appropriate graphical investigations. Again, determine how long it takes for this maximum temperature to fall to $25°$.

Project D

This project deals with a vibrating uniform circular membrane of radius a. If the membrane's initial displacement and velocity functions depend on both polar coordinates r and θ, then the wave equation in (19) takes the polar coordinate form

$$\frac{\partial^2 u}{\partial t^2} = c^2 \nabla^2 u = c^2 \left(\frac{\partial^2 u}{\partial r^2} + \frac{1}{r}\frac{\partial u}{\partial r} + \frac{1}{r^2}\frac{\partial^2 u}{\partial \theta^2} \right). \qquad (39)$$

If the membrane is released from rest at time $t = 0$ and thereafter its boundary is held fixed (so on the circle $r = a$ we have the displacement u always zero), then the membrane's displacement function $u(r, \theta, t)$ satisfies both Eq (39) and the boundary conditions

$$u(a, \theta, t) = 0 \qquad \text{(fixed boundary)}, \qquad (40)$$

$$u(r, \theta, 0) = f(r, \theta) \quad \text{(given initial displacement)}, \qquad (41)$$

$$u_t(r, \theta, 0) = 0 \qquad \text{(zero initial velocity)}. \qquad (42)$$

Fill in the details in the following outline of a solution. Show first that the substitution

$$u(r, \theta, t) = R(r)\Theta(\theta)T(t)$$

in Eq. (39) yields the separation of variables

$$\frac{T''}{c^2 T} = \frac{R'' + \frac{1}{r}R'}{R} + \frac{\Theta''}{r^2\Theta} = -\alpha^2 \quad \text{(constant)}. \tag{43}$$

Then

$$T'' + \alpha^2 c^2 T = 0, \qquad T'(0) = 0 \tag{44}$$

implies that, to within a constant multiple,

$$T(t) = \cos \alpha c t. \tag{45}$$

Next, the right-hand equality in (43) yields the equation

$$\frac{r^2 R'' + rR'}{R} + \alpha^2 r^2 + \frac{\Theta''}{\Theta} = 0, \tag{46}$$

from which it follows that

$$\frac{\Theta''}{\Theta} = -\beta^2 \quad \text{(constant)}. \tag{47}$$

In order that a solution $\Theta(\theta)$ of $\Theta'' + \beta^2\Theta = 0$ have the necessary periodicity of period 2π, the parameter β must be an integer, so we have the θ-solutions

$$\Theta_n(\theta) = \begin{cases} \cos n\theta \\ \sin n\theta \end{cases} \tag{48}$$

for $n = 0, 1, 2, 3, \ldots$.

Substitution of $\Theta''/\Theta = -n^2$ in (46) now yields the parametric Bessel equation

$$r^2 R'' + rR' + (\alpha^2 r^2 - n^2)R = 0 \tag{49}$$

of order n, with bounded solution $J_n(\alpha r)$. Because the zero boundary condition in (40) yields $J_n(\alpha a) = 0$, case 1 in the table of Fig. 10.4.2 yields the r-eigenfunctions

$$R_{mn}(r) = J_n\left(\frac{\gamma_{mn}r}{a}\right) \quad (m = 1, 2, 3, \cdots; n = 0, 1, 2, \cdots), \tag{50}$$

where γ_{mn} denotes the mth positive solution of the equation $J_n(x) = 0$. The numerical value of γ_{mn} can be approximated by first estimating the value $r_1 \approx \gamma_{1n}$ of the first root by inspecting a graph of $J_n(x)$ as in Fig. 10.5.5, and then using a command such as *Mathematica's*

```
FindRoot[ BesselJ[n,x] == 0, {r, r1 + (m - 1)*Pi} ]
```

Finally, substitution of $\alpha_{mn} = (\gamma_{mn})/a$ in (45) yields the t-function

$$T_{mn}(t) = \cos\frac{\gamma_{mn}ct}{a}. \tag{51}$$

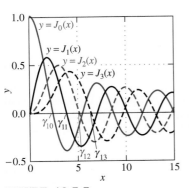

FIGURE 10.5.5. Graphs and initial zeros of the first several Bessel functions

Combining (48), (50), and (51), we see that our boundary value problem for the circular membrane released from rest has the formal series solution

$$u(r, \theta, t) = \sum_{m=1}^{\infty} \sum_{n=0}^{\infty} J_n\left(\frac{\gamma_{mn}r}{a}\right)(a_{mn}\cos n\theta + b_{mn}\sin n\theta)\cos\frac{\gamma_{mn}ct}{a}. \qquad (52)$$

Thus the vibrating circular membrane's typical natural mode of oscillation with zero initial velocity is of the form

$$u_{mn}(r, \theta, t) = J_n\left(\frac{\gamma_{mn}r}{a}\right)\cos n\theta\cos\frac{\gamma_{mn}ct}{a} \qquad (53)$$

or the analogous form with $\sin n\theta$ in place of $\cos n\theta$. In this mode the membrane vibrates with $m - 1$ fixed *nodal circles* (in addition to its boundary $r = a$) with radii

$$r_{jn} = \frac{\gamma_{jn}a}{\gamma_{mn}} \quad \text{for } j = 1, 2, \ldots, m - 1.$$

It also has $2n$ fixed *nodal radii* spaced at angles of π/n starting with $\theta = \pi/(2n)$. Figure 10.5.6 shows some typical configurations of these nodal circles and radii, which divide the circle into annular sectors that move alternately up and down as the membrane vibrates.

Formulas for the coefficients in (52) often are not required for practical applications involving vibrating circular membranes. We suggest that you explore vibrating membrane possibilities by graphing convenient linear combinations of eigenfunctions defined as in (53). For instance, Fig. 10.5.7 shows snapshots of the oscillation de-

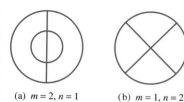

(a) $m = 2, n = 1$ (b) $m = 1, n = 2$

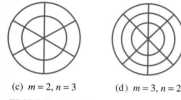

(c) $m = 2, n = 3$ (d) $m = 3, n = 2$

FIGURE 10.5.6. Typical nodal circles and radii for a vibrating circular membrane

FIGURE 10.5.7. Snapshots of the circular membrane vibration defined by Eq. (54)

fined by

$$u(r, \theta, t) = J_1(\gamma_{21}r) \cos \theta \cos \gamma_{21}t + J_2(\gamma_{32}r) \cos 2\theta \cos \gamma_{32}t \qquad (54)$$

for a circular membrane with $c = 1$ and radius $a = 1$. If multimedia hardware and software are available you might enjoy constructing a movie showing such an oscillation.

Spherical Coordinate Applications

In problems involving regions that enjoy spherical symmetry around the origin in space, it is appropriate to use the spherical coordinates indicated in Fig. 10.5.8. The three-dimensional Laplacian for a function $u(\rho, \phi, \theta)$ expressed in spherical coordinates is given by

$$\nabla^2 u = \frac{1}{\rho^2} \left[\frac{\partial}{\partial \rho} \left(\rho^2 \frac{\partial u}{\partial \rho} \right) + \frac{1}{\sin \phi} \frac{\partial}{\partial \phi} \left(\frac{\partial u}{\partial \phi} \sin \phi \right) + \frac{1}{\sin^2 \phi} \frac{\partial^2 u}{\partial \phi^2} \right]. \qquad (55)$$

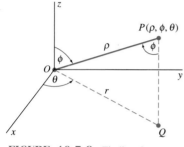

FIGURE 10.5.8. Finding the spherical coordinates of the point P

Note that $\rho = \sqrt{x^2 + y^2 + z^2}$ denotes the distance of the point P from the origin O, ϕ is the angle down from the positive z-axis to OP, and θ is the ordinary polar coordinate angle in the xy-plane (although some texts reverse the roles of ϕ and θ). Observe also that if u is independent of either ρ, ϕ, or θ, then the corresponding second derivative term is missing on the right-hand side in Eq. (55).

EXAMPLE 3 Suppose that a given axially symmetric temperature function $g(\phi)$ is imposed on the boundary sphere $\rho = a$ of the solid ball $\rho \leqq a$, and we seek the resulting axially symmetric steady-state temperature function $u(\rho, \phi)$ within the sphere. Because u is independent of θ, Laplace's equation $\nabla^2 u = 0$ takes (after multiplication by ρ^2 in Eq. (55)) the form

$$\frac{\partial}{\partial \rho} \left(\rho^2 \frac{\partial u}{\partial \rho} \right) + \frac{1}{\sin \phi} \frac{\partial}{\partial \phi} \left(\frac{\partial u}{\partial \phi} \sin \phi \right) = 0, \qquad (56)$$

and we have the single boundary condition

$$u(a, \phi) = g(\phi) \quad \text{(given boundary temperature)}. \qquad (57)$$

The following problems outline a solution of this boundary value problem to find the temperature function $u(\rho, \phi)$. ∎

Problem 7

Show that the substitution $u(\rho, \phi) = R(\rho) \, \Phi(\phi)$ in Eq. (56) yields the separation of variables

$$\rho^2 R'' + 2\rho R' - \lambda R = 0, \qquad (58)$$

$$[(\sin \phi) \, \Phi']' + \lambda(\sin \phi) \, \Phi = 0, \qquad (59)$$

where λ is the usual separation constant. We have no homogeneous boundary conditions to impose, but we do seek *continuous* functions $R(\rho)$ for $0 \leqq \rho \leqq a$ and $\Phi(\phi)$ for $0 \leqq \phi \leqq \pi$. Equation (58) is one for which the trial solution $R(\rho) = \rho^k$ suggests itself, but Eq. (59) appears to be completely unfamiliar.

Problem 8

Show that the substitution

$$x = \cos\phi, \qquad y(x) = \Phi(\cos^{-1}x) = \Phi(\phi) \qquad (-1 \leq x \leq 1)$$

in Eq. (59) yields the *Legendre equation*

$$(1 - x^2)y'' - 2xy' + \lambda y = 0$$

that we discussed in Section 8.2. This equation has a solution $y(x)$ that is continuous for $-1 \leq x \leq 1$ only if $\lambda = n(n + 1)$, where n is a nonnegative integer. In this case $y(x)$ is a constant multiple of the nth *Legendre polynomial* $P_n(x)$. Thus we have eigenvalues and eigenfunctions of Eq. (59) given by

$$\lambda_n = n(n + 1), \qquad \Phi_n(\phi) = P_n(\cos\phi) \tag{60}$$

for $n = 0, 1, 2, 3, \ldots$. Recall from Section 8.2 that the first several Legendre polynomials are

$$P_0(x) \equiv 1, \qquad\qquad P_1(x) = x,$$

$$P_2(x) = \frac{1}{2}(3x^2 - 1), \qquad P_3(x) = \frac{1}{2}(5x^3 - 3x),$$

$$P_4(x) = \frac{1}{8}(35x^4 - 30x^2 + 3), \quad \ldots .$$

Problem 9

With $\lambda = n(n + 1)$, Eq. (58) takes the form

$$\rho^2 R'' + 2\rho R' - n(n + 1)R = 0.$$

Show that the trial solution $R(\rho) = \rho^k$ yields the general solution

$$R(\rho) = A\rho^n + \frac{B}{\rho^{n+1}}.$$

But continuity at $\rho = 0$ implies that $B = 0$ here, so it follows that the eigenfunction of Eq. (58) corresponding to $\lambda_n = n(n + 1)$ is (a constant multiple of) $R_n(\rho) = \rho^n$. Thus we have found the building-block solutions

$$u_n(\rho, \phi) = \rho^n P_n(\cos\phi) \qquad (n = 0, 1, 2, \ldots)$$

of Laplace's equation in (56). In the usual fashion our next step is to write the formal series solution

$$u(\rho, \phi) = \sum_{n=0}^{\infty} b_n \rho^n P_n(\cos\phi). \tag{61}$$

Problem 10

It remains only to discuss the choice of coefficients in (61) to satisfy the nonhomogeneous condition

$$u(a, \phi) = g(\phi) = \sum_{n=0}^{\infty} b_n a^n P_n(\cos\phi).$$

With $x = \cos\phi$, $f(x) = g(\phi) = g(\cos^{-1} x)$, and $c_n = b_n a^n$, this equation takes the form of the *Fourier-Legendre series*

$$f(x) = \sum_{n=0}^{\infty} c_n P_n(x), \tag{62}$$

expressing the function $f(x)$ on $[-1, 1]$ in terms of Legendre polynomials. Given that the Legendre polynomials $\{P_n(x)\}_0^{\infty}$ are mutually orthogonal on $[-1, 1]$ with weight function $r(x) \equiv 1$, apply the formal eigenfunction series method of Section 10.1—multiplying each side in Eq. (62) by $P_k(x)$ and integrating termwise—to derive the *Fourier-Legendre coefficient formula*

$$c_n = \frac{\displaystyle\int_{-1}^{1} f(x) P_n(x)\, dx}{\displaystyle\int_{-1}^{1} [P_n(x)]^2\, dx}.$$

But then the known integral

$$\int_{-1}^{1} [P_n(x)]^2\, dx = \frac{2}{2n + 1}$$

gives

$$c_n = \frac{2n + 1}{2} \int_{-1}^{1} f(x) P_n(x)\, dx. \tag{63}$$

Show, finally, that this choice of coefficients yields the formal series solution

$$u(\rho, \phi) = \sum_{n=0}^{\infty} c_n \left(\frac{\rho}{a}\right)^n P_n(\cos\phi) \tag{64}$$

of the boundary value problem in Eqs. (56) and (57).

Problem 11

Recall the notation

$$k!! = k(k - 2)(k - 4)\,\cdots\,4\cdot 2$$

for k even and

$$k!! = k(k - 2)(k - 4)\,\cdots\,3\cdot 1$$

for k odd. Use the integral

$$\int_0^1 P_n(x)\, dx = \begin{cases} 1 & \text{if } n = 0, \\[2mm] \frac{1}{2} & \text{if } n = 1, \\[2mm] 0 & \text{if } n = 2, 4, 6, \cdots, \\[2mm] (-1)^{(n-1)/2} \dfrac{(n - 2)!!}{(n + 1)!!} & \text{if } n = 3, 5, 7, \cdots \end{cases} \tag{65}$$

to derive the Fourier-Legendre series

$$s(x) = \frac{3}{2} P_1(x) - \frac{7}{8} P_3(x) + \frac{11}{16} P_5(x) - \frac{75}{128} P_7(x) + \cdots$$

$$= \frac{3}{2} P_1(x) + \sum_{n=3,5,\cdots} (-1)^{(n-1)/2} (2n+1) \frac{(n-2)!!}{(n+1)!!} P_n(x) \quad (66)$$

of the square wave function

$$s(x) = \begin{cases} -1 & \text{if } -1 < x < 0, \\ +1 & \text{if } 0 < x < 1. \end{cases}$$

FIGURE 10.5.9. Graph of 25-term partial sum of the rectangular wave series in (66)

Figure 10.5.9 shows the graph of the partial sum with 25 terms of the series in Eq. (66), exhibiting a characteristic Gibbs phenomenon near $x = 0$.

Project E

Figure 10.5.10 shows a solid spherical buoy of radius $a = 1$ meter floating in water. If the buoy has uniform specific gravity $\delta = 0.5$ (density half that of water), then it sinks to a depth $h = 1$ meter as shown. Suppose that the temperature of the water is $10°$ and that of the air is $20°$. Then we want to find the temperature function $u(\rho, \phi)$ within the buoy subject to the boundary condition

FIGURE 10.5.10. A floating spherical buoy with specific gravity $\delta = 0.5$

$$u(1, \phi) = g(\phi) = \begin{cases} 20 & \text{if } 0 < \phi < \pi/2, \\ 10 & \text{if } \pi/2 < \phi < \pi. \end{cases}$$

Then

$$f(x) = g(\cos^{-1} x) = \begin{cases} 10 & \text{if } -1 < x < 0 \\ 20 & \text{if } 0 < x < 1 \end{cases} = 15 + 5s(x)$$

in terms of the step function $s(x)$ of Problem 11. Hence use Eqs. (64) and (66) to show that

$$u(\rho, \phi) = 15 + \frac{15}{2} \rho P_1(\cos \phi)$$

$$+ \sum_{n=3,5,\cdots} 5 \cdot (-1)^{(n-1)/2} (2n+1) \frac{(n-2)!!}{(n+1)!!} \rho^n P_n(\cos \phi). \quad (67)$$

Because the odd-degree Legendre polynomials have only terms of odd degree, it follows from Eq. (67) that the buoy has a constant average temperature of $15°$ on its water-level cross section (where $\phi = \pi/2$). As a first step in using the series in (67) to investigate the temperature distribution within the buoy, sum enough terms to plot u as a function $u(z)$ of height z ($-1 \leq z \leq 1$) on the vertical axis of symmetry of the buoy. Knowing that $u(0) = 15$, find the numerical values of z for which $u = 12.5°$ and $u = 17.5°$.

FIGURE 10.5.11. The floating buoy with $\delta < 0.5$

The buoy problem is more interesting if the specific gravity of the buoy is less than half that of water, $0 < \delta < 0.5$, so the buoy lies higher in the water as in Fig. 10.5.11. Archimedes' law of buoyancy implies that the buoy floats with the fraction δ of its total volume $4\pi/3$ submerged. Hence the part of the buoy lying beneath the wa-

terline has volume $V = 4\pi\delta/3$. But this volume also is given by the sphere-segment volume formula

$$V = \frac{\pi h}{6}(3r^2 + h^2).$$

Equate the two expressions for V to show that the depth h to which the buoy sinks in the water is a solution of the cubic equation

$$h^3 - 3h^2 + 4\delta = 0. \tag{68}$$

With your own choice of δ—perhaps one-tenth the smallest nonzero digit in your student I.D. number—graph this equation to see that it has a single root in the interval $0 < h < 1$. Approximate this root h accurate to at least two decimal places. Then our boundary condition (water temperature 10°, air temperature 20°) corresponds to

$$f(x) = \begin{cases} 10 & \text{if } -1 < x < h-1, \\ 20 & \text{if } h-1 < x < +1, \end{cases}$$

so (63) gives the formula

$$c_n = \int_{-1}^{h-1} 10 P_n(x)\, dx + \int_{h-1}^{1} 20 P_n(x)\, dx \tag{69}$$

for the coefficients $\{c_n\}_0^\infty$ in the series

$$u(\rho, \phi) = \sum_{n=0}^{\infty} c_n \rho^n P_n(\cos\phi). \tag{70}$$

Now the questions—as to the temperature at the waterline level within the buoy, and as to where within the buoy the temperature is exactly 12.5°, 15°, and 17.5°—are more interesting. If $h \neq 0$ then numerical integration is necessary to evaluate the integrals in (69). For instance, the *Mathematica* command

```
c[n] = ((2*n + 1)/2)*

        (10*NIntegrate[LegendreP[n,x], {x, -1, h-1}] +

        20*NIntegrate[LegendreP[n,x], {x, h-1,  1}])
```

can be used. Explain why Eq. (70) implies that the temperature $u(z)$ at the point $(0, 0, z)$ (on the buoy's vertical axis of symmetry with $-1 \leq z \leq 1$) is then given by

$$u(z) = \sum_{n=0}^{\infty} c_n z^n. \tag{71}$$

With δ chosen so that $h = 0.5$, the partial sum consisting of 50 terms in (71) was used to plot the graph of $u(z)$ shown in Fig. 10.5.12, where we see the temperature increasing nonlinearly from $u(-1) = 10$ to $u(1) = 20$. Using the *Mathematica* **FindRoot** function we found that $u(-0.6335) \approx 12.5$, $u(-0.3473) \approx 15$, and $u(0) = 17.5$.

Now the temperature at the center point of the buoy's cross section at the water-level is $u(-0.5) \approx 13.6603$ (rather than the average temperature of 15° that one might naively expect). In Fig. 10.5.13 we see that

$$\rho = \sqrt{x^2 + 0.25} \qquad \text{and} \qquad \phi = \pi - \arctan|2x|$$

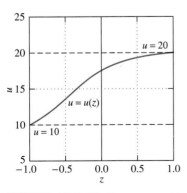

FIGURE 10.5.12. Temperature $u(z)$ at point z on the vertical axis of the buoy with $h = 0.5$

FIGURE 10.5.13. The waterline cross section with

$$z = -0.5, \quad -\frac{\sqrt{3}}{2} \leqq x \leqq \frac{\sqrt{3}}{2}$$

FIGURE 10.5.14. Temperature $u(x)$ in the waterline cross-section of the buoy with $h = 0.5$

at a point of the waterlevel cross section at distance x from the buoy's vertical axis. The graph of u (now as a function of x) shown in Fig. 10.5.14 was plotted by substituting these expressions for ρ and ϕ in a 50-term partial sum of the series in (67). Can you see intuitively why, as x increases starting at zero, the temperature $u(x)$ first decreases and then rises rapidly to $u = 15°$ at the boundary circle of the waterlevel cross section?

References for Further Study

The literature of the theory and applications of differential equations is vast. The following list includes a selection of books that might be useful to readers who wish to pursue further the topics introduced in this book.

1. M. ABRAMOWITZ and I. A. STEGUN, *Handbook of Mathematical Functions.* New York: Dover, 1965. The comprehensive collection of tables to which frequent reference is made in the text.

2. G. BIRKHOFF and G.-C. ROTA, *Ordinary Differential Equations* (2nd ed.). New York: John Wiley, 1969. An intermediate-level text that includes more complete treatment of existence and uniqueness theorems, Sturm-Liouville problems, and eigenfunction expansions.

3. F. BRAUER and J. NOHEL, *Qualitative Theory of Ordinary Differential Equations.* New York: W. A. Benjamin, 1969. A more complete treatment of linear systems and of qualitative properties of solutions.

4. M. BRAUN, *Differential Equations and Their Applications* (3rd ed.). New York: Springer-Verlag, 1983. An introductory text at a slightly higher level than this book; it includes several interesting "case study" applications.

5. R. V. CHURCHILL, *Operational Mathematics* (3rd ed.). New York: McGraw-Hill,

1972. The standard reference for theory and applications of Laplace transforms, starting at about the same level as Chapter 7 of this book.

6. R. V. CHURCHILL and J. W. BROWN, *Fourier Series and Boundary Value Problems* (3rd ed.). New York: McGraw-Hill, 1978. At about the same level as Chapters 9 and 10 of this book.

7. E. A. CODDINGTON, *An Introduction to Ordinary Differential Equations.* Englewood Cliffs, N.J.: Prentice Hall, 1961. An intermediate-level introduction; Chapters 3 and 4 include proofs of the theorems on power series and Frobenius series solutions stated in Chapter 8 of this book.

8. E. A. CODDINGTON and N. LEVINSON, *Theory of Ordinary Differential Equations.* New York: McGraw-Hill, 1955. An advanced theoretical text; Chapter 5 discusses solutions near an irregular singular point.

9. S. D. CONTE and C. DEBOOR, *Elementary Numerical Analysis* (3rd ed.). New York: McGraw-Hill, 1980. An introductory text; Chapter 8 treats numerical solution of differential equations, and includes FORTRAN programs.

10. P. HENRICI, *Discrete Variable Methods in Ordinary Differential Equations.* New York: John Wiley, 1962. A more complete and somewhat advanced treatment of numerical methods of solution.

11. M. W. HIRSCH and S. SMALE, *Differential Equations, Dynamical Systems, and Linear Algebra.* New York: Academic Press, 1974. Intermediate-level treatment of linear systems and of qualitative properties of solutions.

12. E. L. INCE, *Ordinary Differential Equations.* New York: Dover, 1956. First published in 1926, this is the classic older reference work on the subject.

13. N. N. LEBEDEV, *Special Functions and Their Applications.* New York: Dover, 1972. A comprehensive account of Bessel functions and the other special functions of mathematical physics.

14. N. N. LEBEDEV, I. P. SKALSKAYA, and Y. S. UFLYAND, *Worked Problems in Applied Mathematics.* New York: Dover, 1979. A large collection of applied examples and problems similar to those discussed in Chapter 10 of this book.

15. N. W. MCLACHLAN, *Bessel Functions for Engineers* (2nd ed.). London: Oxford University Press, 1955. Includes numerous physical applications of Bessel functions.

16. N. W. MCLACHLAN, *Ordinary Non-Linear Differential Equations in Engineering and Physical Sciences.* London: Oxford University Press, 1956. A concrete introduction to the effects of nonlinearity in physical systems.

17. B. NOBLE, *Applied Linear Algebra* (2nd ed.). Englewood Cliffs, N.J.: Prentice Hall, 1977. An introduction to linear algebra and its applications.

18. W. H. PRESS, B. P. FLANNERY, S. A. TEUKOLSKY, and W. T. VETTERLING, *Numerical Recipes: The Art of Scientific Computing.* Cambridge: Cambridge University Press, 1986. Chapter 15 discusses modern techniques for the numerical solution of differential equations. This edition includes FORTRAN programs; Pascal and C editions have also been published.

19. E. RAINVILLE, *Intermediate Differential Equations* (2nd ed.). New York: Macmillan, 1964, Chapters 3 and 4 include proofs of the theorems on power series and Frobenius series solutions stated in Chapter 8 of this book.

20. H. SAGAN, *Boundary and Eigenvalue Problems in Mathematical Physics*. New York: John Wiley, 1961. Discusses the classical boundary value problems and the variational approach to Sturm-Liouville problems, eigenvalues, and eigenfunctions.

21. G. F. SIMMONS, *Differential Equations*. New York: McGraw-Hill, 1972. An introductory text with interesting historical notes and fascinating applications and with the most eloquent preface in any mathematics book currently in print.

22. W. G. STRANG, *Linear Algebra and Its Applications* (2nd ed.). New York: Academic Press, 1980. An introductory treatment of linear algebra with motivating applications.

23. G. P. TOLSTOV, *Fourier Series*. New York: Dover, 1976. An introductory text including detailed discussion of both convergence and applications of Fourier series.

24. H. F. WEINBERGER, *A First Course in Partial Differential Equations*. New York: Blaisdell, 1965. Includes separation of variables, Sturm-Liouville methods, and applications of Laplace transform methods to partial differential equations.

25. R. WEINSTOCK, *Calculus of Variations*. New York: Dover, 1974. Includes variational derivations of the partial differential equations of vibrating strings, membranes, rods, and bars.

Appendix: Existence and Uniqueness of Solutions

In Chapter 1 we saw that an initial value problem of the form

$$\frac{dy}{dx} = f(x, y), \qquad y(a) = b \tag{1}$$

can fail (on a given interval containing the point $x = a$) to have a unique solution. For instance, in Example 4 of Section 1.3, we saw that the initial value problem

$$x^2 \frac{dy}{dx} + y^2 = 0, \qquad y(0) = b \tag{2}$$

has no solutions at all unless $b = 0$, in which case there are infinitely many different solutions. According to Problem 31 of Section 1.3, the initial value problem

$$\frac{dy}{dx} = -\sqrt{1 - y^2}, \qquad y(0) = 1 \tag{3}$$

has the two distinct solutions $y_1(x) \equiv 1$ and $y_2(x) = \cos x$ on the interval $0 \leqq x \leqq \pi$. In this Appendix we investigate conditions on the function $f(x, y)$ that suffice to guarantee that the initial value problem in (1) has one and only one solution, and then proceed to establish appropriate versions of the existence-uniqueness theorems that were stated without proof in Sections 1.3, 3.1, 3.2, and 4.1.

Existence of Solutions

The approach we employ is the **method of successive approximations,** which was developed by the French mathematician Emile Picard (1856–1941). This method is based on the fact that the function $y(x)$ satisfies the initial value problem in (1) on the open interval I containing $x = a$ if and only if it satisfies the integral equation

$$y(x) = b + \int_a^x f(t, y(t))\, dt \tag{4}$$

for all x in I. In particular, if $y(x)$ satisfies Eq. (4), then clearly $y(a) = b$, and differentiation of both sides in (4)—using the fundamental theorem of calculus—yields the differential equation $y'(x) = f(x, y(x))$.

To attempt to solve Eq. (4), we begin with the initial function

$$y_0(x) \equiv b, \tag{5}$$

and then define iteratively a sequence y_1, y_2, y_3, \ldots of functions that we hope will converge to the solution. Specifically, we let

$$y_1(x) = b + \int_a^x f(t, y_0(t))\, dt \quad \text{and} \quad y_2(x) = b + \int_a^x f(t, y_1(t))\, dt. \tag{6}$$

In general, y_{n+1} is obtained by substitution of y_n for y in the right-hand side in Eq. (4):

$$y_{n+1}(x) = b + \int_a^x f(t, y_n(t))\, dt. \tag{7}$$

Suppose we know that each of these functions $\{y_n(x)\}_0^\infty$ is defined on some open interval (the same for each n) containing $x = a$, and that the limit

$$y(x) = \lim_{n \to \infty} y_n(x) \tag{8}$$

exists at each point of this interval. Then it will follow that

$$y(x) = \lim_{n \to \infty} y_{n+1}(x) = \lim_{n \to \infty} \left[b + \int_a^x f(t, y_n(t))\, dt \right]$$

$$= b + \lim_{n \to \infty} \int_a^x f(t, y_n(t))\, dt \tag{9}$$

$$= b + \int_a^x f\left(t, \lim_{n \to \infty} y_n(t)\right) dt \tag{10}$$

and hence that

$$y(x) = b + \int_a^x f(t, y(t))\, dt,$$

provided that we can validate the interchange of limit operations involved in passing from (9) to (10). It is therefore reasonable to expect that, under favorable conditions, the sequence $\{y_n(x)\}$ defined iteratively in Eqs. (5) and (7) will converge to a solution $y(x)$ of the integral equation in (4), and hence to a solution of the original initial value problem in (1).

EXAMPLE 1 To apply the method of successive approximations to the initial value problem

$$\frac{dy}{dx} = y, \qquad y(0) = 1, \tag{11}$$

we write Eqs. (5) and (7), thereby obtaining

$$y_0(x) \equiv 1, \qquad y_{n+1}(x) = 1 + \int_0^x y_n(t) \, dt. \tag{12}$$

The iteration formula in (12) yields

$$y_1(x) = 1 + \int_0^x 1 \, dt = 1 + x,$$

$$y_2(x) = 1 + \int_0^x (1 + t) \, dt = 1 + x + \frac{1}{2}x^2,$$

$$y_3(x) = 1 + \int_0^x \left(1 + t + \frac{1}{2}t^2\right) dt = 1 + x + \frac{1}{2}x^2 + \frac{1}{6}x^3,$$

and

$$y_4(x) = 1 + \int_0^x \left(1 + t + \frac{1}{2}t^2 + \frac{1}{6}t^3\right) dt$$

$$= 1 + x + \frac{1}{2}x^2 + \frac{1}{6}x^3 + \frac{1}{24}x^4.$$

It is clear that we are generating the sequence of partial sums of a power series solution; indeed, we immediately recognize the series as that of $y(x) = e^x$. There is no difficulty in demonstrating that the exponential function is indeed the solution of the initial value problem in (11); moreover, a diligent student can verify (using a proof by induction on n) that $y_n(x)$, obtained in the manner above, is indeed the nth partial sum for the Taylor series with center zero for $y(x) = e^x$.

EXAMPLE 2 To apply the method of successive approximations to the initial value problem

$$\frac{dy}{dx} = 4xy, \qquad y(0) = 3, \tag{13}$$

we write Eqs. (5) and (7) as in Example 1. Now we obtain

$$y_0(x) \equiv 3, \qquad y_{n+1}(x) = 3 + \int_0^x 4t y_n(t) \, dt. \tag{14}$$

The iteration formula in (14) yields

$$y_1(x) = 3 + \int_0^x (4t)(3) \, dt = 3 + 6x^2,$$

$$y_2(x) = 3 + \int_0^x (4t)(3 + 6t^2) \, dt = 3 + 6x^2 + 6x^4,$$

$$y_3(x) = 3 + \int_0^x (4t)(3 + 6t^2 + 6t^4) \, dt = 3 + 6x^2 + 6x^4 + 4x^6,$$

and

$$y_4(x) = 3 + \int_0^x (4t)(3 + 6t^2 + 6t^4 + 4t^6)\, dt$$

$$= 3 + 6x^2 + 6x^4 + 4x^6 + 2x^8.$$

It is again clear that we are generating partial sums of a power series solution. It is not quite so obvious what function has such a power series representation, but the initial value problem in (13) is readily solved by separation of variables:

$$y(x) = 3e^{2x^2} = 3 \sum_{n=0}^{\infty} \frac{(2x^2)^n}{n!}$$

$$= 3 + 6x^2 + 6x^4 + 4x^6 + 2x^8 + \frac{4}{5}x^{10} + \cdots. \qquad \blacksquare$$

In some cases it may be necessary to compute a much larger number of terms, either in order to identify the solution or to use a partial sum of its series with large subscript to approximate the solution accurately for x near its initial value. Fortunately, computer algebra systems such as *Maple* and *Mathematica* can perform the symbolic integrations (as opposed to numerical integrations) of the sort in the examples above. If necessary, you could generate the first hundred terms in Example 2 in a matter of minutes.

In general, of course, we apply Picard's method because we cannot find a solution by elementary methods. Suppose that we have produced a large number of terms of what we believe to be the correct power series expansion of the solution. We *must* have conditions under which the sequence $\{y_n(x)\}$ provided by the method of successive approximations is guaranteed in advance to converge to a solution. It is just as convenient to discuss the initial value problem

$$\frac{d\mathbf{x}}{dt} = \mathbf{f}(\mathbf{x}, t), \qquad \mathbf{x}(a) = \mathbf{b} \tag{15}$$

for a system of m first-order equations, where

$$\mathbf{x} = \begin{bmatrix} x_1 \\ x_2 \\ x_3 \\ \vdots \\ x_m \end{bmatrix}, \qquad \mathbf{f} = \begin{bmatrix} f_1 \\ f_2 \\ f_3 \\ \vdots \\ f_m \end{bmatrix}, \qquad \text{and} \qquad \mathbf{b} = \begin{bmatrix} b_1 \\ b_2 \\ b_3 \\ \vdots \\ b_m \end{bmatrix}.$$

It turns out that with the aid of this vector notation (which we introduced in Section 5.1), most results concerning a single [scalar] equation $x' = f(x, t)$ can be generalized readily to analogous results for a system of m first-order equations, as abbreviated in (15). Consequently, the effort of using vector notation is amply justified by the generality it provides.

The method of successive approximations for the system in (15) calls for us to

compute the sequence $\{\mathbf{x}_n(t)\}_0^\infty$ of vector-valued functions of t,

$$\mathbf{x}_n(t) = \begin{bmatrix} x_{1n}(t) \\ x_{2n}(t) \\ x_{3n}(t) \\ \vdots \\ x_{mn}(t) \end{bmatrix},$$

defined iteratively by

$$\mathbf{x}_0(a) \equiv \mathbf{b}, \qquad \mathbf{x}_{n+1}(t) = b + \int_a^t \mathbf{f}(\mathbf{x}_n(s), s) \, ds. \tag{16}$$

Recall that vector-valued functions are integrated componentwise.

EXAMPLE 3 Consider the m-dimensional initial value problem

$$\frac{d\mathbf{x}}{dt} = \mathbf{A}\mathbf{x}, \qquad \mathbf{x}(0) = \mathbf{b} \tag{17}$$

for a homogeneous linear system with $m \times m$ constant coefficient matrix \mathbf{A}. The equations in (16) take the form

$$\mathbf{x}_0(t) = \mathbf{b}, \qquad \mathbf{x}_{n+1}(t) = \mathbf{b} + \int_0^t \mathbf{A}\mathbf{x}_n(s) \, ds. \tag{18}$$

Thus

$$\mathbf{x}_1(t) = \mathbf{b} + \int_0^t \mathbf{A}\mathbf{b} \, ds = \mathbf{b} + \mathbf{A}\mathbf{b}t = (\mathbf{I} + \mathbf{A}t)\mathbf{b};$$

$$\mathbf{x}_2(t) = \mathbf{b} + \int_0^t \mathbf{A}(\mathbf{b} + \mathbf{A}\mathbf{b}s) \, ds = \mathbf{b} + \mathbf{A}\mathbf{b}t + \frac{1}{2}\mathbf{A}^2\mathbf{b}t^2 = \left(\mathbf{I} + \mathbf{A}t + \frac{1}{2}\mathbf{A}^2t^2\right)\mathbf{b}$$

and

$$\mathbf{x}_3(t) = \mathbf{b} + \int_0^t \mathbf{A}\left(\mathbf{b} + \mathbf{A}\mathbf{b}s + \frac{1}{2}\mathbf{A}^2\mathbf{b}s^2\right) ds = \left(\mathbf{I} + \mathbf{A}t + \frac{1}{2}\mathbf{A}^2t^2 + \frac{1}{6}\mathbf{A}^3t^3\right)\mathbf{b}.$$

We have therefore obtained the first several partial sums of the exponential series solution

$$\mathbf{x}(t) = e^{\mathbf{A}t}\mathbf{b} = \left(\sum_{n=0}^\infty \frac{(\mathbf{A}t)^n}{n!}\right)\mathbf{b} \tag{19}$$

of (17), which was derived earlier in Section 5.5. ■

The key to establishing convergence in the method of successive approximations is an appropriate condition on the rate at which $\mathbf{f}(\mathbf{x}, t)$ changes when \mathbf{x} varies but t is held fixed. If R is a region in $(m+1)$-dimensional (\mathbf{x}, t)-space, then the function $\mathbf{f}(\mathbf{x}, t)$ is said to be **Lipschitz continuous** on R if there exists a constant $k > 0$ such

that

$$|\mathbf{f}(\mathbf{x}_1, t) - \mathbf{f}(\mathbf{x}_2, t)| \leqq k |\mathbf{x}_1 - \mathbf{x}_2| \tag{20}$$

if (\mathbf{x}_1, t) and (\mathbf{x}_2, t) are points of R. Recall that the **norm** of an m-dimensional point or vector \mathbf{x} is defined to be

$$|\mathbf{x}| = \sqrt{x_1^2 + x_2^2 + x_3^2 + \cdots + x_m^2}. \tag{21}$$

Then $|\mathbf{x}_1 - \mathbf{x}_2|$ is simply the Euclidean distance between the points \mathbf{x}_1 and \mathbf{x}_2.

EXAMPLE 4 Let $f(x, t) = x^2 e^{-t^2} \sin t$ and let R be the strip $0 \leqq x \leqq 2$ in the xt-plane. If (x_1, t) and (x_2, t) are both points of R, then

$$|f(x_1, t) - f(x_2, t)| = |e^{-t^2} \sin t| \cdot |x_1 + x_2| \cdot |x_1 - x_2| \leqq 4 |x_1 - x_2|,$$

because $|e^{-t^2} \sin t| \leqq 1$ for all t and $|x_1 + x_2| \leqq 4$ if x_1 and x_2 are both in the interval $[0, 2]$. Thus f satisfies the Lipschitz condition in (20) with $k = 4$ and is therefore Lipschitz continuous in the strip R.

EXAMPLE 5 Let $f(x, t) = t\sqrt{x}$ on the rectangle R consisting of the points (x, t) in the plane for which $0 \leqq x \leqq 1$ and $0 \leqq t \leqq 1$. Then, taking $x_1 = x$, $x_2 = 0$, and $t = 1$, we find that

$$|f(x, 1) - f(0, 1)| = \sqrt{x} = \frac{1}{\sqrt{x}} |x - 0|.$$

Because $x^{-1/2} \to +\infty$ as $x \to 0^+$, we see that the Lipschitz condition in (20) cannot be satisfied by any (finite) constant $k > 0$. Thus the function f, though obviously continuous on R, is *not* Lipschitz continuous on R. ∎

Suppose, however, that the function $f(x, t)$ has a continuous partial derivative $f_x(x, t)$ on the closed rectangle R in the xt-plane, and denote by k the maximum value of $|f_x(x, t)|$ on R. Then the mean value theorem of differential calculus yields

$$|f(x_1, t) - f(x_2, t)| = |f_x(\overline{x}, t) \cdot (x_1 - x_2)|$$

for some \overline{x} in (x_1, x_2), so it follows that

$$|f(x_1, t) - f(x_2, t)| \leqq k |x_1 - x_2|$$

because $|f_x(\overline{x}, t)| \leqq k$. Thus a continuously differentiable function $f(x, t)$ defined on a closed rectangle *is* Lipschitz continuous there. More generally, the multivariable mean value theorem of advanced calculus can be used similarly to prove that a *vector-valued function* $\mathbf{f}(\mathbf{x}, t)$ *with continuously differentiable component functions on a closed rectangular region R in (\mathbf{x}, t)-space is Lipschitz continuous on R.*

EXAMPLE 6 The function $f(x, t) = x^2$ is Lipschitz continuous on any closed [bounded] region in the xt-plane. But consider this function on the infinite strip R consisting of the points (x, t) for which $0 \leqq t \leqq 1$ and x is arbitrary. Then

$$|f(x_1, t) - f(x_2, t)| = |x_1^2 - x_2^2| = |x_1 + x_2| \cdot |x_1 - x_2|.$$

Because $|x_1 + x_2|$ can be made arbitrarily large, it follows that f is *not* Lipschitz continuous on the infinite strip R. ∎

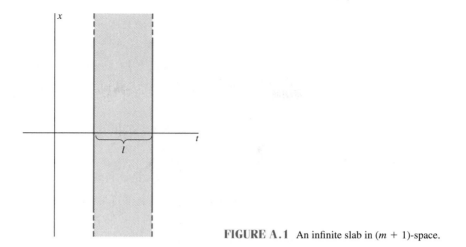

FIGURE A.1 An infinite slab in $(m + 1)$-space.

If I is an interval on the t-axis, then the set of all points (\mathbf{x}, t) with t in I is an infinite strip or slab in $(m + 1)$-space (as indicated in Fig. A.1). Example 6 shows that Lipschitz continuity of $\mathbf{f}(\mathbf{x}, t)$ on such an infinite slab is a very strong condition. Nevertheless, the existence of a solution of the initial value problem

$$\frac{d\mathbf{x}}{dt} = \mathbf{f}(\mathbf{x}, t), \qquad \mathbf{x}(a) = \mathbf{b} \tag{15}$$

under the hypothesis of Lipschitz continuity of \mathbf{f} in such a slab is of considerable importance.

THEOREM 1: Global Existence of Solutions

Let \mathbf{f} be a vector-valued function (with m components) of $m + 1$ real variables, and let I be a [bounded or unbounded] open interval containing $t = a$. If $\mathbf{f}(\mathbf{x}, t)$ is continuous and satisfies the Lipschitz condition in (20) for all t in I and for all \mathbf{x}_1 and \mathbf{x}_2, then the initial value problem in (15) has a solution on the [entire] interval I.

Proof: We want to show that the sequence $\{\mathbf{x}_n(t)\}_0^\infty$ of successive approximations determined iteratively by

$$\mathbf{x}_0(a) = \mathbf{b}, \qquad \mathbf{x}_{n+1}(t) = \mathbf{b} + \int_0^t \mathbf{f}(\mathbf{x}_n(s), s)\, ds \tag{16}$$

converges to a solution $\mathbf{x}(t)$ of (15). We see that each of these functions in turn is continuous on I, as each is an [indefinite] integral of a continuous function.

We may assume that $a = 0$, because the transformation $t \to t + a$ converts (15) into an equivalent problem with initial point $t = 0$. Also, we will consider only the portion $t \geqq 0$ of the interval I; the details for the case $t \leqq 0$ are very similar.

The main part of the proof consists in showing that if $[0, T]$ is a closed (and bounded) interval contained in I, then the sequence $\{\mathbf{x}_n(t)\}$ converges *uniformly* on I to a limit function $\mathbf{x}(t)$. This means that, given $\epsilon > 0$, there exists an integer N such

that

$$|\mathbf{x}_n(t) - \mathbf{x}(t)| < \epsilon \tag{22}$$

for all $n \geq N$ and all t in $[0, T]$. For ordinary (perhaps nonuniform) convergence the integer N, for which (22) holds for all $n \geq N$, may depend upon t, with no single value of N working for all t in I. Once this uniform convergence of the sequence $\{\mathbf{x}_n(t)\}$ has been established, the following conclusions will follow from standard theorems of advanced calculus (see pages 620–622 of A. E. Taylor and W. R. Mann, *Advanced Calculus*, 3rd ed. (New York: John Wiley, 1983)):

1. The limit function $\mathbf{x}(t)$ is continuous on $[0, T]$.

2. If N is so chosen that the inequality in (22) holds for $n \geq N$, then the Lipschitz continuity of f implies that

$$|\mathbf{f}(\mathbf{x}_n(t), t) - \mathbf{f}(\mathbf{x}(t), t)| \leq k|\mathbf{x}_n(t) - \mathbf{x}(t)| < k\epsilon$$

for all t in $[0, T]$ and $n \geq N$, so it follows that the sequence $\{\mathbf{f}(\mathbf{x}_n(t), t)\}_0^\infty$ converges uniformly to $\mathbf{f}(\mathbf{x}(t), t)$ on $[0, T]$.

3. But a uniformly convergent sequence or series can be integrated termwise, so it follows that, upon taking limits in the iterative formula in (16),

$$\mathbf{x}(t) = \lim_{n \to \infty} \mathbf{x}_{n+1}(t) = \mathbf{b} + \lim_{n \to \infty} \int_0^t \mathbf{f}(\mathbf{x}_n(s), s)\, ds$$

$$= \mathbf{b} + \int_0^t \lim_{n \to \infty} \mathbf{f}(\mathbf{x}_n(s), s)\, ds;$$

thus

$$\mathbf{x}(t) = \mathbf{b} + \int_0^t \mathbf{f}(\mathbf{x}(s), s)\, ds. \tag{23}$$

4. Because the function $\mathbf{x}(t)$ is continuous on $[0, T]$, the integral equation in (23) (analogous to the one-dimensional case in (4)) implies that $\mathbf{x}'(t) = \mathbf{f}(\mathbf{x}(t), t)$ on $[0, T]$. But if this is true on every closed subinterval of the open interval I, then it is true on the entire interval I.

It therefore remains only to prove that the sequence $\{\mathbf{x}_n(t)\}_0^\infty$ converges uniformly on the closed interval $[0, T]$. Let M be the maximum value of $|\mathbf{f}(\mathbf{b}, t)|$ for t in $[0, T]$. Then

$$|\mathbf{x}_1(t) - \mathbf{x}_0(t)| = \left| \int_0^t \mathbf{f}(\mathbf{x}_0(s), s)\, ds \right| \leq \int_0^t |\mathbf{f}(\mathbf{b}, s)|\, ds \leq Mt. \tag{24}$$

Next,

$$|\mathbf{x}_2(t) - \mathbf{x}_1(t)| = \left| \int_0^t [\mathbf{f}(\mathbf{x}_1(s), s) - \mathbf{f}(\mathbf{x}_0(s), s)]\, ds \right| \leq k \int_0^t |\mathbf{x}_1(s) - \mathbf{x}_0(s)|\, ds,$$

and hence

$$|\mathbf{x}_2(t) - \mathbf{x}_1(t)| \leq k \int_0^t Ms\, ds = \frac{1}{2} kMt^2. \tag{25}$$

We now proceed by induction. Assume that

$$\left| \mathbf{x}_n(t) - \mathbf{x}_{n-1}(t) \right| \leqq \frac{M}{k} \cdot \frac{(kt)^n}{n!}. \tag{26}$$

It then follows that

$$\left| \mathbf{x}_{n+1}(t) - \mathbf{x}_n(t) \right| = \left| \int_0^t [\mathbf{f}(\mathbf{x}_n(s), s) - \mathbf{f}(\mathbf{x}_{n-1}(s), s)] \, ds \right|$$

$$\leqq k \int_0^t \left| \mathbf{x}_n(s) - \mathbf{x}_{n-1}(s) \right| ds;$$

consequently,

$$\left| \mathbf{x}_{n+1}(t) - \mathbf{x}_n(t) \right| \leqq k \int_0^t \frac{M}{k} \cdot \frac{(ks)^n}{n!} \, ds.$$

It follows upon evaluating this integral that

$$\left| \mathbf{x}_{n+1}(t) - \mathbf{x}_n(t) \right| \leqq \frac{M}{k} \cdot \frac{(kt)^{n+1}}{(n+1)!}.$$

Thus (26) holds on $[0, T]$ for all $n \geqq 1$.

Hence the terms of the infinite series

$$\mathbf{x}_0(t) + \sum_{n=1}^{\infty} [\mathbf{x}_n(t) - \mathbf{x}_{n-1}(t)] \tag{27}$$

are dominated (in magnitude on the interval $[0, T]$) by the terms of the convergent series

$$\sum_{n=1}^{\infty} \frac{M}{k} \cdot \frac{(kT)^{n+1}}{(n+1)!} = \frac{M}{k} (e^{kT} - 1), \tag{28}$$

which is a series of positive constants. It therefore follows (from the Weierstrass *M*-test on pages 618–619 of Taylor and Mann) that the series in (27) converges uniformly on $[0, T]$. But the sequence of partial sums of this series is simply our original sequence $\{(\mathbf{x}_n(t)\}_0^{\infty}$ of successive approximations, so the proof of Theorem 1 is finally complete. ∎

Linear Systems

An important application of the global existence theorem just given is to the initial value problem

$$\frac{d\mathbf{x}}{dt} = \mathbf{A}(t)\mathbf{x} + \mathbf{g}(t), \qquad \mathbf{x}(a) = \mathbf{b} \tag{29}$$

for a linear system, where the $m \times m$ matrix-valued function $\mathbf{A}(t)$ and the vector-valued function $\mathbf{g}(t)$ are continuous on a [bounded or unbounded] open interval I containing the point $t = a$. In order to apply Theorem 1 to the linear system in (29), we note first that the proof of Theorem 1 requires only that, for each closed and bounded subinterval J of I, there exists a Lipschitz constant k such that

$$\left| \mathbf{f}(\mathbf{x}_1, t) - \mathbf{f}(\mathbf{x}_2, t) \right| \leqq k \left| \mathbf{x}_1 - \mathbf{x}_2 \right| \tag{20}$$

for all t in J (and all \mathbf{x}_1 and \mathbf{x}_2). Thus we do not need a single Lipschitz constant for the entire open interval I.

In (29) we have $\mathbf{f}(\mathbf{x}, t) = \mathbf{A}\mathbf{x} + \mathbf{g}$, so

$$\mathbf{f}(\mathbf{x}_1, t) - \mathbf{f}(\mathbf{x}_2, t) = \mathbf{A}(t)\,(\mathbf{x}_1 - \mathbf{x}_2). \tag{30}$$

It therefore suffices to show that, if $\mathbf{A}(t)$ is continuous on the closed and bounded interval J, then there is a constant k such that

$$|\mathbf{A}(t)\mathbf{x}| \leqq k|\mathbf{x}| \tag{31}$$

for all t in J. But this follows from the fact (Problem 17) that

$$|\mathbf{A}\mathbf{x}| \leqq \|\mathbf{A}\| \cdot |\mathbf{x}|, \tag{32}$$

where the **norm** $\|\mathbf{A}\|$ of the matrix \mathbf{A} is defined to be

$$\|\mathbf{A}\| = \left(\sum_{i,j=1}^{m} (a_{ij})^2 \right)^{1/2}. \tag{33}$$

Because $\mathbf{A}(t)$ is continuous on the closed and bounded interval J, the norm $\|\mathbf{A}\|$ is bounded on J, so Eq. (31) follows, as desired. Thus we have the following global existence theorem for the linear initial value problem in (29).

THEOREM 2: Existence for Linear Systems

Let the $m \times m$ matrix-valued function $\mathbf{A}(t)$ and the vector-valued function $\mathbf{g}(t)$ be continuous on the [bounded or unbounded] open interval I containing the point $t = a$. Then the initial value problem

$$\frac{d\mathbf{x}}{dt} = \mathbf{A}(t)\mathbf{x} + \mathbf{g}(t), \qquad \mathbf{x}(a) = \mathbf{b} \tag{29}$$

has a solution on the [entire] interval I. ∎

As we saw in Section 4.1, the mth-order initial value problem

$$x^{(m)} + a_1(t)x^{(m-1)} + \cdots + a_{m-1}(t)x' + a_m(t)x = p(t) \tag{34}$$

$$x(a) = b_0, \qquad x'(a) = b_1, \qquad \ldots, \qquad x^{(m-1)}(a) = b_{m-1}$$

is readily transformed into an equivalent $m \times m$ system of the form in (29). It therefore follows from Theorem 2 that if the functions $a_1(t), a_2(t), \ldots, a_m(t)$ and $p(t)$ in (34) are all continuous on the [bounded or unbounded] open interval I containing $t = a$, then the initial value problem in (34) has a solution on the [entire] interval I.

Local Existence

In the case of a *nonlinear* initial value problem

$$\frac{d\mathbf{x}}{dt} = \mathbf{f}(\mathbf{x}, t), \qquad \mathbf{x}(a) = \mathbf{b}, \tag{35}$$

the hypothesis in Theorem 1 that \mathbf{f} satisfies a Lipschitz condition on a slab (\mathbf{x}, t) (t in I, all \mathbf{x}) is unrealistic and rarely satisfied. This is illustrated by the following simple example.

EXAMPLE 7 Consider the initial value problem

$$\frac{dx}{dt} = x^2, \qquad x(0) = b > 0. \tag{36}$$

As we saw in Example 6, the equation $x' = x^2$ does not satisfy a "strip Lipschitz condition." When we solve (36) by separation of variables, we get

$$x(t) = \frac{b}{1 - bt}. \tag{37}$$

Because the denominator vanishes for $t = 1/b$, Eq. (37) provides a solution of the initial value problem in (36) only for $t < 1/b$, despite the fact that the differential equation $x' = x^2$ "looks nice" on the whole real line—certainly the function appearing on the right-hand side of the equation is continuous everywhere. In particular, if b is large, then we have a solution only on a very small interval to the right of $t = 0$. ∎

Although Theorem 2 assures us that *linear* equations have global solutions, Example 7 shows that, in general, even a "nice" nonlinear differential equation can be expected to have a solution only on a small interval about the initial point $t = a$, and that the length of this interval of existence can depend upon the initial value $\mathbf{x}(a) = \mathbf{b}$, as well as upon the differential equation itself. The reason is this: If $\mathbf{f}(\mathbf{x}, t)$ is continuously differentiable in a neighborhood of the point (\mathbf{b}, a) in $(m + 1)$-dimensional space, then—as indicated in the discussion preceding Example 6—we can conclude that $\mathbf{f}(\mathbf{x}, t)$ satisfies a Lipschitz condition on some rectangular region R centered at (\mathbf{b}, a), of the form

$$|t - a| < A, \qquad |x_i - b_i| < B_i \tag{38}$$

$(i = 1, 2, \ldots, m)$. In the proof of Theorem 1, we need to apply the Lipschitz condition on the function \mathbf{f} in analyzing the iterative formula

$$\mathbf{x}_{n+1}(t) = \mathbf{b} + \int_a^t \mathbf{f}(\mathbf{x}_n(s), s)\, ds. \tag{39}$$

The potential difficulty is that unless the values of t are suitably restricted, the points $(\mathbf{x}_n(t), t)$ appearing in the integrand in (39) may not lie in the region R where \mathbf{f} is known to satisfy a Lipschitz condition. On the other hand, it can be shown that—on a sufficiently small open interval J containing the point $t = a$—the graphs of the functions $\{\mathbf{x}_n(t)\}$ given iteratively by the formula in (39) remain within the region R, so the proof of convergence can then be carried out as in the proof of Theorem 1. A proof of the following *local* existence theorem can be found in Chapter 6 of G. Birkhoff and G.-C. Rota, *Ordinary Differential Equations,* 2nd ed. (New York: John Wiley, 1969).

THEOREM 3: **Local Existence of Solutions**

Let \mathbf{f} be a vector-valued function (with m components) of the $m + 1$ real variables x_1, x_2, \ldots, x_m, and t. If the first-order partial derivatives of \mathbf{f} all exist and are continuous in some neighborhood of the point $\mathbf{x} = \mathbf{b}$, $t = a$, then the initial value problem

$$\frac{d\mathbf{x}}{dt} = \mathbf{f}(\mathbf{x}, t), \qquad \mathbf{x}(a) = \mathbf{b}, \tag{35}$$

has a solution on some open interval containing the point $t = a$. ∎

Uniqueness of Solutions

It is possible to establish the existence of solutions of the initial value problem in (35) under the much weaker hypothesis that $\mathbf{f}(\mathbf{x}, t)$ is merely continuous; techniques other than those used in this section are required. By contrast, the Lipschitz condition that we used in proving Theorem 1 is the key to *uniqueness* of solutions. In particular, the solution provided by Theorem 3 is unique near the point $t = a$.

■ THEOREM 4: Uniqueness of Solutions

Suppose that on some region R in $(m + 1)$-space, the function \mathbf{f} in (35) is continuous and satisfies the Lipschitz condition

$$\left|\mathbf{f}(\mathbf{x}_1, t) - \mathbf{f}(\mathbf{x}_2, t)\right| \leq k\cdot\left|\mathbf{x}_1 - \mathbf{x}_2\right|. \tag{20}$$

If $\mathbf{x}_1(t)$ and $\mathbf{x}_2(t)$ are two solutions of the initial value problem in (35) on some open interval I containing $t = a$, such that the solution curves $(\mathbf{x}_1(t), t)$ and $(\mathbf{x}_2(t), t)$ both lie in R for all t in I, then $\mathbf{x}_1(t) = \mathbf{x}_2(t)$ for all t in I. ■

We will outline the proof of Theorem 4 for the one-dimensional case in which x is a real variable. A generalization of this proof to the multivariable case can be found in Chapter 6 of Birkhoff and Rota.

Let us consider the function

$$\phi(t) = [x_1(t) - x_2(t)]^2 \tag{40}$$

for which $\phi(a) = 0$, because $x_1(a) = x_2(a) = b$. We want to show that $\phi(t) \equiv 0$, so that $x_1(t) \equiv x_2(t)$. We will consider only the case $t \geq a$; the details are similar for the case $t \leq a$.

If we differentiate each side in (40), we find that

$$\begin{aligned}
\left|\phi'(t)\right| &= \left|2[x_1(t) - x_2(t)]\,[x_1'(t) - x_2'(t)]\right| \\
&= \left|2[x_1(t) - x_2(t)]\,[f(x_1(t), t) - f(x_2(t), t)]\right| \\
&\leq 2k\left|x_1(t) - x_2(t)\right|^2 = 2k\phi(t),
\end{aligned}$$

using the Lipschitz condition on f. Hence

$$\phi'(t) \leq 2k\phi(t). \tag{41}$$

Now let us temporarily ignore the fact that $\phi(a) = 0$ and compare $\phi(t)$ with the solution of the differential equation

$$\Phi'(t) = 2k\,\Phi(t) \tag{42}$$

such that $\Phi(a) = \phi(a)$; clearly

$$\Phi(t) = \Phi(a)e^{2k(t-a)}. \tag{43}$$

In comparing (41) with (42), it seems inevitable that

$$\phi(t) \leq \Phi(t) \quad \text{for } t \geq a, \tag{44}$$

and this is easily proved (Problem 18). Hence

$$0 \leq [x_1(t) - x_2(t)]^2 \leq [x_1(a) - x_2(a)]^2 e^{2k(t-a)}.$$

On taking square roots, we get

$$0 \leq |x_1(t) - x_2(t)| \leq |x_1(a) - x_2(a)| e^{k(t-a)}. \tag{45}$$

But $x_1(a) - x_2(a) = 0$, so (45) implies that $x_1(t) \equiv x_2(t)$.

EXAMPLE 8 The initial value problem

$$\frac{dx}{dt} = 3x^{2/3}, \qquad x(0) = 0 \tag{46}$$

has both the obvious solution $x_1(t) \equiv 0$ and the solution $x_2(t) = t^3$ that is readily found by separation of variables. Hence the function $f(x, t)$ must *fail* to satisfy a Lipschitz condition near $(0, 0)$. Indeed, the mean value theorem yields

$$|f(x, 0) - f(0, 0)| = |f_x(\bar{x}, 0)| \cdot |x - 0|$$

for some \bar{x} between 0 and x. But $f_x(x, 0) = 2x^{-1/3}$ is unbounded as $x \to 0$, so no Lipschitz condition can be satisfied. ∎

Well Posed Problems and Mathematical Models

In addition to uniqueness, another consequence of the inequality in (45) is the fact that solutions of the differential equation

$$\frac{dx}{dt} = f(x, t) \tag{47}$$

depend *continuously* on the initial value $x(a)$; that is, if $x_1(t)$ and $x_2(t)$ are two solutions of (47) on the interval $a \leq t \leq T$ such that the initial values $x_1(a)$ and $x_2(a)$ are sufficiently close to one another, then the values of $x_1(t)$ and $x_2(t)$ remain close to one another. In particular, if $|x_1(a) - x_2(a)| \leq \delta$, then (45) implies that

$$|x_1(t) - x_2(t)| \leq \delta e^{k(T-a)} = \epsilon \tag{48}$$

for all t with $a \leq t \leq T$. Obviously, we can make ϵ as small as we wish by choosing δ sufficiently close to zero.

This continuity of solutions of (47) with respect to initial values is important in practical applications where we are unlikely to know the initial value $x_0 = x(a)$ with absolute precision. For example, suppose that the initial value problem

$$\frac{dx}{dt} = f(x, t), \qquad x(a) = x_0 \tag{49}$$

models a population for which we know only that the initial population is within $\delta > 0$ of the assumed value x_0. Then even if the function $f(x, t)$ is accurate, the solution $x(t)$ of (49) will only be an approximation to the actual population. But (45) implies that the actual population at time t will be within $\delta e^{k(t-a)}$ of the approximate population $x(t)$. Thus, on a given closed interval $[a, T]$, $x(t)$ will be a close approximation to the actual population, provided that $\delta > 0$ is sufficiently small.

An initial value problem is usually considered *well posed* as a mathematical model for a real-world situation only if the differential equation has unique solutions that are continuous with respect to initial values. Otherwise it is unlikely that the initial value problem adequately mirrors the real-world situation.

An even stronger "continuous dependence" of solutions is often desirable. In addition to possible inaccuracy in the initial value, the function $f(x, t)$ may not model precisely the physical situation. For instance, it may involve physical parameters (such as resistance coefficients) whose values cannot be measured with absolute precision. Birkhoff and Rota generalize the proof of Theorem 4 to establish the following result.

THEOREM 5: Continuous Dependence of Solutions

Let $\mathbf{x}(t)$ and $\mathbf{y}(t)$ be solutions of the equations

$$\frac{d\mathbf{x}}{dt} = \mathbf{f}(\mathbf{x}, t) \quad \text{and} \quad \frac{d\mathbf{y}}{dt} = \mathbf{g}(\mathbf{y}, t) \tag{50}$$

on the closed interval $[a, T]$. Let \mathbf{f} and \mathbf{g} be continuous for $a \leqq t \leqq T$ and for \mathbf{x} and \mathbf{y} in a common region D of n-space and assume that \mathbf{f} satisfies the Lipschitz condition in (20) in the region D. If

$$\left| \mathbf{f}(\mathbf{z}, t) - \mathbf{g}(\mathbf{z}, t) \right| \leqq \mu \tag{51}$$

for all t in the interval $[a, T]$ and all \mathbf{z} in D, it then follows that

$$\left| \mathbf{x}(t) - \mathbf{y}(t) \right| \leqq \left| \mathbf{x}(a) - \mathbf{y}(a) \right| \cdot e^{k(t-a)} + \frac{\mu}{k} \left[e^{k(t-a)} - 1 \right] \tag{52}$$

on the interval $[a, T]$. ∎

If $\mu > 0$ is small, then (51) implies that the functions \mathbf{f} and \mathbf{g} appearing in the two differential equations, though different, are "close" to each other. If $\epsilon > 0$ is given, then it is apparent from (52) that

$$\left| \mathbf{x}(t) - \mathbf{y}(t) \right| \leqq \epsilon \tag{53}$$

for all t in $[a, T]$ if both $\left| \mathbf{x}(a) - \mathbf{y}(a) \right|$ and μ are sufficiently small. Thus Theorem 5 says (roughly) that if both the two initial values and the two differential equations in (50) are close to each other, then the two solutions remain close to each other for $a \leqq t \leqq T$.

For example, suppose that a falling body is subject both to constant gravitational acceleration g and to resistance proportional to some power of its velocity, so (with the positive axis directed downward) its velocity v satisfies the differential equation

$$\frac{dv}{dt} = g - cv^p. \tag{54}$$

Assume, however, that only an approximation \bar{c} to the actual resistance coefficient c and an approximation \bar{p} to the actual exponent p are known. Then our mathematical model is based on the differential equation

$$\frac{du}{dt} = g - \bar{c}u^{\bar{p}} \tag{55}$$

instead of the actual equation in (54). Thus if we solve Eq. (55), we obtain only an approximation $u(t)$ to the actual velocity $v(t)$. But if the parameters \bar{c} and \bar{p} are suffi-

ciently close to the actual values c and ρ, then the right-hand sides in (54) and (55) will be close to each other. If so, then Theorem 5 implies that the actual and approximate velocity functions $v(t)$ and $u(t)$ are close to each other. In this case the approximation in (55) will be a good model of the actual physical situation.

Problems

In Problems 1 through 8, apply the successive approximations formula to compute $y_n(x)$ for $n \leq 4$. Then write the exponential series for which these approximations are partial sums (perhaps minus the first term or two; for example,

$$e^x - 1 = x + \frac{1}{2}x^2 + \cdots).$$

1. $\dfrac{dy}{dx} = y, \quad y(0) = 3$

2. $\dfrac{dy}{dx} = -2y, \quad y(0) = 4$

3. $\dfrac{dy}{dx} = -2xy, \quad y(0) = 1$

4. $\dfrac{dy}{dx} = 3x^2y, \quad y(0) = 2$

5. $\dfrac{dy}{dx} = 2y + 2, \quad y(0) = 0$

6. $\dfrac{dy}{dx} = x + y, \quad y(0) = 0$

7. $\dfrac{dy}{dx} = 2x(1 + y), \quad y(0) = 0$

8. $\dfrac{dy}{dx} = 4x(y + 2x^2), \quad y(0) = 0$

In Problems 9 through 12, compute the successive approximations $y_n(x)$ for $n \leq 3$; then compare them with the appropriate partial sums of the Taylor series of the exact solution.

9. $\dfrac{dy}{dx} = x + y, \quad y(0) = 1$

10. $\dfrac{dy}{dx} = y + e^x, \quad y(0) = 0$

11. $\dfrac{dy}{dx} = y^2, \quad y(0) = 1$

12. $\dfrac{dy}{dx} = \dfrac{1}{2}y^3, \quad y(0) = 1$

13. Apply the iterative formula in (16) to compute the first three successive approximations to the solution of the initial value problem

$$\frac{dx}{dt} = 2x - y, \qquad x(0) = 1;$$

$$\frac{dy}{dt} = 3x - 2y, \qquad y(0) = -1.$$

14. Apply the matrix exponential series in (19) to solve (in closed form) the initial value problem

$$\mathbf{x}'(t) = \begin{bmatrix} 1 & 1 \\ 0 & 1 \end{bmatrix}\mathbf{x}, \qquad \mathbf{x}(0) = \begin{bmatrix} 1 \\ 1 \end{bmatrix}.$$

(*Suggestion:* Show first that

$$\begin{bmatrix} 1 & 1 \\ 0 & 1 \end{bmatrix}^n = \begin{bmatrix} 1 & n \\ 0 & 1 \end{bmatrix}$$

for each positive integer n.)

15. For the initial value problem $dy/dx = 1 + y^3$, $y(1) = 1$, show that the second Picard approximation is

$$y_2(x) = 1 + 2(x - 1) + 3(x - 1)^2 + 4(x - 1)^3 + 2(x - 1)^4.$$

Then compute $y_2(1.1)$ and $y_2(1.2)$. The fourth-order Runge–Kutta method with step size $h = 0.005$ yields $y(1.1) \approx 1.2391$ and $y(1.2) \approx 1.6269$.

16. For the initial value problem $dy/dx = x^2 + y^2$, $y(0) = 0$, show that the third Picard approximation is

$$y_3(x) = \frac{1}{3}x^3 + \frac{1}{63}x^7 + \frac{2}{2079}x^{11} + \frac{1}{59535}x^{15}.$$

Compute $y_3(1)$. The fourth-order Runge–Kutta method yields $y(1) \approx 0.350232$, both with step size $h = 0.05$ and with step size $h = 0.025$.

17. Prove as follows the inequality $|\mathbf{Ax}| \leq \|\mathbf{A}\| \cdot |\mathbf{x}|$, where \mathbf{A} is an $m \times m$ matrix with row vectors $\mathbf{a}_1, \mathbf{a}_2, \ldots, \mathbf{a}_m$, and \mathbf{x} is an m-dimensional vector. First note that the components of the vector \mathbf{Ax} are $\mathbf{a}_1 \cdot \mathbf{x}, \mathbf{a}_2 \cdot \mathbf{x}, \ldots, \mathbf{a}_m \cdot \mathbf{x}$, so

$$|\mathbf{Ax}| = \left[\sum_{n=1}^m (\mathbf{a}_i \cdot \mathbf{x})^2 \right]^{1/2}.$$

Then use the Cauchy–Schwarz inequality $(\mathbf{a} \cdot \mathbf{x})^2 \leq |\mathbf{a}|^2|\mathbf{x}|^2$ for the dot product.

18. Suppose that $\phi(t)$ is a differentiable function with

$$\phi'(t) \leq k\phi(t) \qquad (k > 0)$$

for $t \geq a$. Multiply both sides by e^{-kt}; then transpose to show

that

$$\frac{d}{dt}\left[\phi(t)e^{-kt}\right] \leq 0$$

for $t \geq a$. Then apply the mean value theorem to conclude that

$$\phi(t) \leq \phi(a)e^{k(t-a)}$$

for $t \geq a$.

Answers to Selected Problems

CHAPTER 1

Section 1.1

11. If $y = y_1 = x^{-2}$, then $y'(x) = -2x^{-3}$ and $y''(x) = 6x^{-4}$, so $x^2 y'' + 5xy' + 4y = x^2(6x^{-4}) + 5x(-2x^{-3}) + 4(x^{-2})$ $= 6x^{-2} + 10x^{-2} + 4x^{-2} = 0$. If $y = y_2 = x^{-2} \ln x$, then $y'(x) = x^{-3} - 2x^{-3} \ln x$ and $y''(x) = -5x^{-4} + 6x^{-4} \ln x$, so $x^2 y'' + 5xy' + 4y = x^2(-5x^{-4} + 6x^{-4} \ln x) +$ $5x(x^{-3} - 2x^{-3} \ln x) + 4(x^{-2} \ln x) = (-5x^{-2} + 5x^{-2}) +$ $6x^{-2} - 10x^{-2} + 4x^{-2}) \ln x = 0$.

13. $r = \frac{2}{3}$ **14.** $r = \pm \frac{1}{2}$ **15.** $r = -2, 1$

17. $C = 2$ **18.** $C = 3$ **19.** $C = 6$

20. $C = 11$ **21.** $C = 7$ **22.** $C = 1$

23. $C = -56$ **24.** $C = 17$ **25.** $C = \pi/4$

26. $C = -\pi$ **27.** $y' = x + y$ **28.** $y' = 2y/x$

29. $y' = x/(1 - y)$ **31.** $y' = (y - x)/(y + x)$

32. $dP/dt = k\sqrt{P}$ **33.** $dv/dt = kv^2$

35. $dN/dt = k(P - N)$ **37.** $y \equiv 1$ or $y = x$

39. $y = x^2$ **41.** $y = \frac{1}{2}e^x$

42. $y = \cos x$ or $y = \sin x$

43. (a) $C = 10.1$; (b) No such C, but the constant function $y(x) \equiv 0$ satisfies the conditions $y' = y^2$ and $y(0) = 0$.

Section 1.2

1. $y(x) = x^2 + x + 3$ **3.** $y(x) = \frac{1}{3}(2x^{3/2} - 16)$

5. $y(x) = 2\sqrt{x + 2} - 5$ **7.** $y(x) = 10 \tan^{-1} x$

9. $y(x) = \sin^{-1} x$

11. $x(t) = 25t^2 + 10t + 20$

13. $x(t) = \frac{1}{2}t^3 + 5t$

15. $x(t) = \frac{1}{3}(t + 3)^4 - 37t - 26$

17. $x(t) = \frac{1}{2}[(t + 1)^{-1} + t - 1]$

19. The car stops when $t \approx 2.78$ (s), so the distance traveled before stopping is approximately $x(2.78) \approx 38.58$ (m).

21. $y_0 \approx 178.57$ (m)

23. $v_0 = 544/3$ (ft/s)

25. $v_0 = 150$ (ft/s), about 102 mi/h

27. $20\sqrt{10} \approx 63.25$ (ft/s)

31. 25 (mi)

Section 1.3

1.

2.

3.

4.

5.

6.

7.

8.

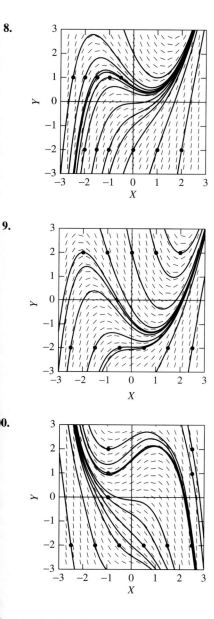

9.

0.

. Each isocline is a vertical straight line.

. Each isocline is a horizontal straight line.

. Each isocline is a straight line through the origin.

. Each isocline $xy = C$ is a rectangular hyperbola that opens along the line $y = x$ if $C > 0$, along the line $y = -x$ if $C < 0$.

. Each isocline is a parabola symmetric around the y-axis.

. A unique solution exists in some neighborhood of $x = 1$.

. A unique solution exists in some neighborhood of $x = 0$.

25. Neither existence nor uniqueness is guaranteed in any neighborhood of $x = 2$.

27. A unique solution exists in some neighborhood of $x = 0$.

29. A unique solution exists in some neighborhood of $x = 0$.

31. $\partial y/\partial x$ is not continuous when $y = 1$, so the theorem does not guarantee uniqueness.

Section 1.4

1. $y(x) = C\exp(-x^2)$ **3.** $y(x) = C\exp(-\cos x)$

5. $y(x) = \sin(C + \sqrt{x})$ **7.** $y(x) = (2x^{4/3} + C)^{3/2}$

9. $y(x) = C(1 + x)/(1 - x)$ **11.** $y(x) = (C - x^2)^{-1/2}$

13. $\ln(y^4 + 1) = C + 4\sin x$

15. $1/(3y^3) - 2/y = 1/x + \ln|x| + C$

17. $\ln|1 + y| = x + \frac{1}{2}x^2 + C$

19. $y(x) = 2\exp(e^x)$ **21.** $y^2 = 1 + \sqrt{x^2 - 16}$

23. $\ln(2y - 1) = 2(x - 1)$ **25.** $\ln y = x^2 - 1 + \ln x$

27. About 51,840 persons **29.** About 14,735 years

31. $21,103.48 **33.** 2585 mg

35. About 4.86 billion years ago

37. After a total of about 63 min have elapsed

39. (a) 0.495 m; (b) $(8.32 \times 10^{-7})I_0$; (c) 3.29 m

41. (a) $dA/dt = rA + Q$; (b) $Q = 0.70482$, so you make deposits at the rate of $704.82 per year.

43. After about 66 min 40 s

45. After about 46 days

47. 972 s

48. At time $t = 2048/1562 \approx 1.31$ (in hours)

50. 1:20 P.M.

51. $y(t) = (8 - 7t)^{2/3}$; (b) at 1:08:34 P.M.;

 (c) $r = \frac{1}{60}\sqrt{\frac{7}{12}} \approx 0.15$ (in.)

53. Approximately 14 min 29 s

54. $r = \frac{1}{720}\sqrt{3}$ ft, about $\frac{1}{35}$ in.

55. At approximately 10:29 A.M.

Section 1.5

1. $y(x) = 2(1 - e^{-x})$ **2.** $\rho(x) = e^{-2x}$

3. $y(x) = e^{-3x}(x^2 + C)$ **4.** $\rho(x) = \exp(-x^2)$

5. $y(x) = x + 4x^{-2}$ **6.** $\rho(x) = x^5$

7. $y(x) = 5x^{1/2} + Cx^{-1/2}$ **8.** $\rho(x) = x^{1/3}$

9. $y(x) = x(7 + \ln x)$ **10.** $\rho(x) = x^{-3/2}$

11. $y(x) \equiv 0$ **12.** $\rho(x) = x^3$

13. $y(x) = (e^x + e^{-x})/2$ **14.** $\rho(x) = x^{-3}$

15. $y(x) = [1 - 5\exp(-x^2)]/2$

16. $\rho(x) = e^{\sin x}$

17. $y(x) = (1 + \sin x)/(1 + x)$

18. $\rho(x) = x^{-2}$

19. $y(x) = \frac{1}{2}\sin x + C\csc x$

20. $\rho(x) = \exp(-x - \frac{1}{2}x^2)$

21. $y(x) = x^3\sin x$

22. $\rho(x) = \exp(-x^2)$

23. $y(x) = x^3(2 + Ce^{-2x})$

24. $\rho(x) = (x^2 + 4)^{3/2}$

25. $y(x) = [\exp(-3x^2/2)][3(x^2 + 1)^{3/2} - 2]$

26. $\rho(y) = y^4$

27. $x(y) = e^y(C + \frac{1}{2}y^2)$

28. $\rho(y) = (1 + y^2)^{-1}$

29. $y(x) = [\exp(x^2)][C + \frac{1}{2}\sqrt{\pi}\,\mathrm{erf}(x)]$

33. After about 7 min 41 s

34. About 22.2 days

35. After about 10.85 years

37. 393.75 lb

39. (b) $y_{\max} = 100e^{-1} \approx 36.79$ (gal)

41. (b) Approximately $1,308,283

Section 1.6

1. $x^2 - 2xy - y^2 = C$

3. $y(x) = x(C + \ln|x|)^2$

5. $\ln|xy| = C + xy^{-1}$

7. $y^3 = 3x^3(C + \ln|x|)$

9. $y(x) = x/(C - \ln|x|)$

11. $y = C(x^2 + y^2)$

13. $y + \sqrt{x^2 + y^2} = Cx^2$

15. $x^2(2xy + y^2) = C$

17. $y(x) = -4x + 2\tan(2x + C)$

19. $y^2 = x/(2 + Cx^5)$

20. Substitute $v = y^3$

21. $y^2 = 1/(Ce^{-2x} - 1)$

22. Substitute $v = y^{-3}$

23. $y(x) = (x + Cx^2)^{-3}$

24. Substitute $v = y^{-2}$

25. $2x^3y^3 = 3\sqrt{1 + x^4} + C$

26. Substitute $v = y^3$

27. $y(x) = (x^4 + Cx)^{1/3}$

28. Substitute $v = e^y$

29. $\sin^2 y = 4x^2 + Cx$

31. $x^2 + 3xy + y^2 = C$

33. $x^3 + 2xy^2 + 2y^3 = C$

35. $3x^4 + 4y^3 + 12y\ln x = C$

37. $\sin x + x\ln y + e^y = C$

39. $5x^3y^3 + 5xy^4 + y^5 = C$

41. $x^2y^{-1} + y^2x^{-3} + 2y^{1/2} = C$

46. Substitute $v = \ln y$

47. $x^2 - 2xy - y^2 - 2x - 6y = C$

49. $x = \tan(x - y) + \sec(x - y) + C$

53. $y(x) = x + (C - x)^{-1}$

57. Approximately 3.68 mi

<div align="center">

CHAPTER 1 REVIEW PROBLEMS

</div>

1. Linear: $y(x) = x^3(C + \ln x)$

2. Separable: $y(x) = x/(3 - Cx - x\ln x)$

3. Homogeneous: $y(x) = x/(C - \ln x)$

4. Exact: $x^2y^3 + e^x - \cos y = C$

5. Separable: $y(x) = C\exp(x^{-3} - x^{-2})$

6. Separable: $y(x) = x/(1 + Cx + 2x\ln x)$

7. Linear: $y(x) = x^{-2}(C + \ln x)$

8. Homogeneous: $y(x) = 3Cx/(C - x^3) = 3x/(1 + Kx^3)$

9. Bernoulli: $y(x) = (x^2 + Cx^{-1})^2$

10. Separable: $y(x) = \tan(C + x + \frac{1}{3}x^3)$

11. Homogeneous: $y(x) = x/(C - 3\ln x)$

12. Exact: $3x^2y^3 + 2xy^4 = C$

13. Separable: $y(x) = 1/(C + 2x^2 - x^5)$

14. Homogeneous: $y^2 = x^2/(C + 2\ln x)$

15. Linear: $y(x) = (x^3 + C)e^{-3x}$

16. Substitution: $v = y - x$; solution:
$(1 + Ce^{2x})y = 1 + x + C(1 - x)e^{2x}$

17. Exact: $e^x + e^y + e^{xy} = C$

18. Homogeneous: $y^2 = Cx^2(x^2 - y^2)$

19. Separable: $y(x) = x^2/(x^5 + Cx^2 + 1)$

20. Linear: $y(x) = 2x^{-3/2} + Cx^{-3}$

21. Linear: $y(x) = [C + \ln(x - 1)]/(x + 1)$

22. Bernoulli: $y(x) = (2x^4 + Cx^2)^3$

23. Exact: $xe^y + y\sin x = C$

24. Separable: $y(x) = x^{1/2}/(6x^2 + Cx^{1/2} + 2)$

25. Linear: $y(x) = (x + 1)^{-2}(x^3 + 3x^2 + 3x + C) = x + 1 + K(x + 1)^{-2}$

26. Exact: $3x^{3/2}y^{4/3} - 5x^{6/5}y^{3/2} = C$

27. Bernoulli: $y(x) = x^{-1}(C + \ln x)^{-1/3}$

28. Linear: $y(x) = x^{-1}(C + e^{2x})$

29. Linear: $y(x) = (x^2 + x + C)(2x + 1)^{-1/2}$

30. Substitution: $v = x + y$; solution:
$x = 2(x + y)^{1/2} - 2\ln[1 + (x + y)^{1/2}] + C$

<div align="center">

CHAPTER 2

</div>

Section 2.1

1. 20 weeks

2. (b) 256

3. (b) At 6 months

4. It approaches zero.

6. Approximately 4.87 million

7. (a) Approximately 271.15 million; (b) approximately 282.22 million

9. If $P_0 < 0$, then $\lim\limits_{t \to \infty} P(t) = -\infty$.

11. (a) 200 g; (b) $\frac{5}{4}\ln 3$ (s)

12. $\frac{20}{3}\ln 4$ (days)

. (a) $M = 100$ and $k = 0.0002$;　(b) in the year 2035

. $50 \ln \frac{9}{8}$ months

. (a) $100 \ln \frac{9}{5}$ months;　(b) $100 \ln 2$ months

. $\alpha \approx 0.3915$; 2.15×10^6 cells

ction 2.2

. $x(t) = x_0 e^{-t}$;　$x = 0$ is a stable critical point.

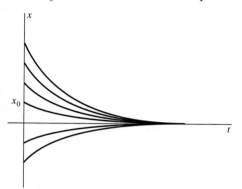

$x(t) = 2 + (x_0 - 2)e^t$;　$x = 2$ is an unstable critical point.

$x(t) = \dfrac{x_0}{x_0 + (1 - x_0)e^{-t}}$;　$x = 1$ is a stable critical point, whereas $x = 0$ is an unstable critical point.

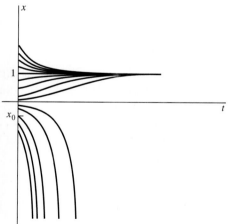

$x(t) = \dfrac{2x_0}{x_0 + (2 - x_0)e^{2t}}$;　$x = 0$ is a stable critical point, whereas $x = 2$ is an unstable critical point.

$x(t) = \dfrac{x_0}{(x_0 + 1)e^{-t} - x_0}$;　$x = 0$ is an unstable critical point, whereas $x = -1$ is a stable critical point.

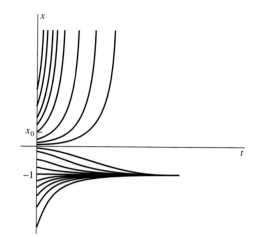

6. $x(t) = \dfrac{x_0 - t(x_0 - 1)}{1 - t(x_0 - 1)}$;　$x = 1$ is an unstable critical point.

7. $x(t) = \dfrac{1 + x_0 + (x_0 - 1)e^{-2t}}{1 + x_0 - (x_0 - 1)e^{-2t}}$;　$x = 1$ is a stable critical point, whereas $x = -1$ is an unstable critical point.

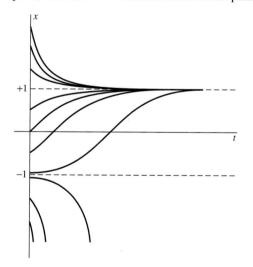

8. $x(t) = 2\,\dfrac{x_0 + 2 + (x_0 - 2)e^{4t}}{x_0 + 2 - (x_0 - 2)e^{4t}}$;　$x = -2$ is a stable critical point, whereas $x = 2$ is an unstable critical point.

9. $x(t) = \dfrac{x_0 + 2 + 2(x_0 - 1)e^{-3t}}{x_0 + 2 - (x_0 - 1)e^{-3t}}$;　$x = 1$ is a stable critical point, whereas $x = -2$ is an unstable critical point.

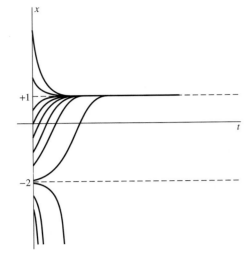

10. $[x(t)]^2 = \dfrac{(x_0)^2}{(x_0)^2 + [1 - (x_0)^2]e^{-2t}}$; $x = 0$ is an unstable

critical point, whereas $x = -1$ and $x = 1$ are stable critical points.

11. $x(t) = \dfrac{2(x_0 - 3) - 3(x_0 - 2)e^{-t}}{x_0 - 3 - (x_0 - 2)e^{-t}}$; $x = 2$ is a stable

critical point, whereas $x = 3$ is an unstable critical point.

12. $x(t) = 2 + \dfrac{x_0 - 2}{\sqrt{1 + 2t(2 - x_0)^2}}$; $x = 2$ is a stable

critical point.

14. $x(t) = \dfrac{ax_0}{bx_0 + (a - bx_0)e^{-at}}$

15. $x(t) = \dfrac{ax_0 e^{-at}}{a - bx_0 + bx_0 e^{-at}}$

16. (a) $M = (a - k)/b$

Section 2.3

1. Approximately 31.5 s

3. $400/(\ln 2)$ ft

5. $400 \ln 7$ ft

8. (b) About 71 mi/h; about 102 mi/h

9. 50 ft/s

10. 5 min 47 s

11. Time of fall: about 12.5 s

12. Approximately 649 ft

15. Approximately 30.46 ft/s; exactly 40 ft/s

18. Approximately 1044.14 ft in approximately 7.8003 s

19. Approximately 8.362 s; about 233.72 ft/s

20. Approximately 20.66 ft/s; about 484.57 s

22. (a) About 0.88 cm; (b) about 2.91 km

24. (b) About 11 min 33 s; about 11,230 mi/h

26. Height: about 56,711 ft; velocity: about 7858 ft/s

27. If its exhaust velocity is greater than 800 ft/s, it lifts off immediately. If $160 < c \leq 800$, then the rocket lifts off sometime during the 20 s its fuel is burning. If $c < 160$, then the rocket never leaves the ground.

32. Velocity: about 5337 ft/s; height: about 136,925 ft

Section 2.4

Note: Most of the problems in this section call for a table of values. Space limitations prohibit reproduction of the complete table in this book; we have chosen in most cases to give only data from the last line of the table. Your answers may differ slightly because of variations in hardware and software.

1. $y_{n+1} = y_n + h(-y_n)$; $y(x) = 2e^{-x}$. Results:

	$h = 0.1$	$h = 0.05$	**Actual**
x	y	y	y
0.0	2.0000	2.0000	2.0000
0.1	1.8000	1.8050	1.8097
0.2	1.6200	1.6290	1.6375
0.3	1.4580	1.4702	1.4816
0.4	1.3122	1.3268	1.3406
0.5	1.1810	1.1975	1.2131

2. $y_{n+1} = y_n + h(2y_n)$; $y(x) = \frac{1}{2}e^{2x}$. At $x = 0.5$ we should see $y = 1.2442$ ($h = 0.1$), 1.2969 ($h = 0.05$), and 1.3591 (true value).

Note: In the answers to Problems 3 through 24, we give first the x-value, then the y-values obtained with decreasing values of h, and finally the true value of y.

3. 0.5, 2.2210, 2.2578, 2.2974

4. 0.5, 0.6810, 0.6975, 0.7131

5. 0.5, 0.8895, 0.8711, 0.8513

6. 0.5, 1.6272, 1.5912, 1.5576

7. 0.5, 2.7373, 2.6930, 2.6475

8. 0.5, 0.4198, 0.4124, 0.4055

9. 0.5, 1.2785, 1.2828, 1.2874

10. 0.5, 1.2313, 1.2776, 1.3333

11. 1.0, -0.7048, -0.7115, -0.7183

12. 1.0, 2.9864, 2.9931, 3.0000

2.0,	4.8890,	4.8940,	4.8990	
2.0,	3.2031,	3.2304,	3.2589	
3.0,	3.4422,	3.4433,	3.4444	
3.0,	8.8440,	8.8445,	8.8451	
1.0,	0.2925,	0.3379,	0.3477,	0.3497
2.0,	1.6680,	1.6771,	1.6790,	1.6794
2.0,	6.1831,	6.3653,	6.4022,	6.4097
2.0,	−1.3792,	−1.2843,	−1.2649,	−1.2609
2.0,	2.8508,	2.8681,	2.8716,	2.8723
2.0,	6.9879,	7.2601,	7.3154,	7.3265
1.0,	1.2262,	1.2300,	1.2306,	1.2307
1.0,	0.9585,	0.9918,	0.9984,	0.9997

x	$h = 0.15$ y	$h = 0.03$ y	$h = 0.006$ y
−1.0	1.0000	1.0000	1.0000
−0.7	1.0472	1.0512	1.0521
−0.4	1.1213	1.1358	1.1390
−0.1	1.2826	1.3612	1.3835
0.2	0.8900	1.4711	0.8210
0.5	0.7460	1.2808	0.7192

x	$h = 0.1$ y	$h = 0.01$ y
1.8	2.8200	4.3308
1.9	3.9393	7.9425
2.0	5.8521	28.3926

x	$h = 0.1$ y	$h = 0.01$ y
0.7	4.3460	6.4643
0.8	5.8670	11.8425
0.9	8.3349	39.5010

ction 2.5

x	Improved Euler y	Three-term Taylor y	Actual y
0.1	1.8100	1.8100	1.8097
0.2	1.6381	1.6381	1.6375
0.3	1.4824	1.4824	1.4816
0.4	1.3416	1.3416	1.3406
0.5	1.2142	1.2142	1.2131

Note: In Problems 2 through 10, we give the value of x, the corresponding improved Euler value of y, the three-term Taylor value of y, and the true value of y.

2. 0.5, 1.3514, 1.3514, 1.3591

3. 0.5, 2.2949, 2.2949, 2.2974

4. 0.5, 0.7142, 0.7142, 0.7131

5. 0.5, 0.8526, 0.8526, 0.8513

6. 0.5, 1.5575, 1.5542, 1.5576

7. 0.5, 2.6405, 2.6580, 2.6475

8. 0.5, 0.4053, 0.4046, 0.4055

9. 0.5, 1.2873, 1.2871, 1.2874

10. 0.5, 1.3309, 1.3233, 1.3333

In Problems 11 through 16 we give the final value of x, the corresponding values of y with $h = 0.01$ and with $h = 0.005$, and the true value of y.

11. 1.0, −0.71824, −0.71827, −0.71828

12. 1.0, 2.99995, 2.99999, 3.00000

13. 2.0, 4.89901, 4.89899, 4.89898

14. 2.0, 3.25847, 3.25878, 3.25889

15. 3.0, 3.44445, 3.44445, 3.44444

16. 3.0, 8.84511, 8.84509, 8.84509

In Problems 17 through 24 we give the final value of x and the corresponding values of y for $h = 0.1, 0.02, 0.004$, and 0.0008.

17. 1.0, 0.35183, 0.35030, 0.35023, 0.35023

18. 2.0, 1.68043, 1.67949, 1.67946, 1.67946

19. 2.0, 6.40834, 6.41134, 6.41147, 6.41147

20. 2.0, −1.26092, −1.26003, −1.25999, −1.25999

21. 2.0, 2.87204, 2.87245, 2.87248, 2.87247

22. 2.0, 7.31578, 7.32841, 7.32916, 7.32920

23. 1.0, 1.22967, 1.23069, 1.23073, 1.23073

24. 1.0, 1.00006, 1.00000, 1.00000, 1.00000

25. $y_{n+1} = y_n +$
$[1 + (y_n)^2]\{h + h^2 y_n + \frac{1}{3} h^3 [1 + 3(y_n)^2]\}$

27. $y_{n+1} = y_n +$
$h(x_n + y_n)^2 + h^2 [(x_n + y_n) + (x_n + y_n)^3] +$
$\frac{1}{3} h^3 [1 + 4(x_n + y_n)^2 + 3(x_n + y_n)^4]$

Section 2.6

1. $y(0.25) \approx 1.55762$; $y(0.25) = 1.55760$.
$y(0.5) \approx 1.21309$; $y(0.5) = 1.21306$.
Solution: $y = 2e^{-x}$.

In Problems 2 through 10 we give the approximation to $y(0.5)$, its true value, and the solution.

2. 1.35867, 1.35914; $y = \frac{1}{2}e^{2x}$

3. 2.29740, 2.29744; $y = 2e^x - 1$

4. 0.71309, 0.71306; $y = 2e^{-x} + x - 1$

5. 0.85130, 0.85128; $y = -e^x + x + 2$

6. 1.55759, 1.55760; $y = 2\exp(-x^2)$

7. 2.64745, 2.64749; $y = 3\exp(-x^3)$

8. 0.40547, 0.40547; $y = \ln(x + 1)$

9. 1.28743, 1.28743; $y = \tan\frac{1}{4}(x + \pi)$

10. 1.33337, 1.33333; $y = (1 - x^2)^{-1}$

11. *Solution:* $y(x) = 2 - e^x$.

x	$h = 0.2$ y	$h = 0.1$ y	**Exact** y
0.0	1.00000	1.00000	1.00000
0.2	0.77860	0.77860	0.77860
0.4	0.50818	0.50818	0.50818
0.6	0.17789	0.17788	0.17788
0.8	-0.22552	-0.22554	-0.22554
1.0	-0.71825	-0.71828	-0.71828

In Problems 12 through 16 we give the final value of x, the corresponding Runge–Kutta approximations with $h = 0.2$ and with $h = 0.1$, the exact value of y, and the solution.

12. 1.0, 2.99996, 3.00000, 3.00000,
 $y = 1 + 2/(2 - x)$

13. 2.0, 4.89900, 4.89898, 4.89898,
 $y = \sqrt{8 + x^4}$

14. 2.0, 3.25795, 3.25882, 3.25889,
 $y = 1/(1 - \ln x)$

15. 3.0, 3.44445, 3.44444, 3.44444,
 $y = x + 4x^{-2}$

16. 3.0, 8.84515, 8.84509, 8.84509,
 $y = (x^6 - 37)^{1/3}$

In Problems 17 through 24 we give the final value of x and the corresponding values of y with $h = 0.2, 0.1, 0.05$, and 0.025.

17. 1.0, 0.350258, 0.350234, 0.350232, 0.350232

18. 2.0, 1.679513, 1.679461, 1.679459, 1.679459

19. 2.0, 6.411464, 6.411474, 6.411474, 6.411474

20. 2.0, -1.259990, -1.259992, -1.259993, -1.259993

21. 2.0, 2.872467, 2.872468, 2.872468, 2.872468

22. 2.0, 7.326761, 7.328452, 7.328971, 7.32913

23. 1.0, 1.230735, 1.230731, 1.230731, 1.23073

24. 1.0, 1.000000, 1.000000, 1.000000, 1.00000

25. $v(10) \approx 104.98$, $s(10) \approx 839.56$, $v(20) \approx 105.05$, $s(20)$ ≈ 1889.95; $s(t) = 0$ when $t \approx 97.2$

26. (b) $s(20) \approx 1461.43$; true value: about 1461.37; (c) termi nal velocity 80 ft/s; $s(t) = 0$ when $t \approx 127$

27. (a) 100 ft/s; (b) about 368 ft, about 63.21 ft/s; (c) approximately 21 s

28. (a) 100 ft/s; (b) about 434 ft, about 76.16 ft/s; (c) approximately 14 s

29. (a) About 302.5 ft, about 4.05 s; (b) about 4.7 s, about 120 ft/s

30. (a) About 294 ft, about 4.08 s; (b) about 4.5 s, about 119 ft/s

CHAPTER 3

Section 3.1

1. $y(x) = \frac{5}{2}e^x - \frac{5}{2}e^{-x}$

3. $y(x) = 3\cos 2x + 4\sin 2x$

5. $y(x) = 2e^x - e^{2x}$ **7.** $y(x) = 6 - 8e^{-x}$

9. $y(x) = 2e^{-x} + xe^{-x}$ **11.** $y(x) = 5e^x \sin x$

13. $y(x) = 5x - 2x^2$ **15.** $y(x) = 7x - 5x \ln x$

21. Linearly independent **23.** Linearly independent

25. Linearly independent

29. There is no contradiction because if the given differential equation is divided by x^2 to get the form in Eq. (8), then the resu ing coefficient functions $p(x) = -4/x$ and $q(x) = 6/x^2$ are not continuous at $x = 0$.

33. $y(x) = c_1 e^x + c_2 e^{2x}$

35. $y(x) = c_1 + c_2 e^{-5x}$

37. $y(x) = c_1 e^{-x/2} + c_2 e^x$

39. $y(x) = (c_1 + c_2 x)e^{-x/2}$

41. $y(x) = c_1 e^{-4x/3} + c_2 e^{5x/2}$

Section 3.2

1. $15 \cdot (2x) - 16 \cdot (3x^2) - 6 \cdot (5x - 8x^2) \equiv 0$

3. $1 \cdot (0) + 0 \cdot \sin x + 0 \cdot e^x \equiv 0$

5. $1 \cdot 17 - 34 \cdot \cos^2 x + 17 \cdot \cos 2x \equiv 0$

13. $y(x) = \frac{4}{3}e^x - \frac{1}{3}e^{-2x}$

15. $y(x) = (2 - 2x + x^2)e^x$

17. $y(x) = \frac{1}{9}(29 - 2\cos 3x - 3\sin 3x)$

19. $y(x) = x + 2x^2 + 3x^3$

1. $y(x) = 2 \cos x - 5 \sin x + 3x$

3. $y(x) = e^{-x} + 4e^{3x} - 2$

ection 3.3

1. $y(x) = c_1 e^{2x} + c_2 e^{-2x}$

3. $y(x) = c_1 e^{2x} + c_2 e^{-5x}$

5. $y(x) = c_1 e^{-3x} + c_2 x e^{-3x}$

7. $y(x) = c_1 e^{3x/2} + c_2 x e^{3x/2}$

9. $y(x) = e^{-4x}(c_1 \cos 3x + c_2 \sin 3x)$

1. $y(x) = c_1 + c_2 x + c_3 e^{4x} + c_4 x e^{4x}$

3. $y(x) = c_1 + c_2 e^{-2x/3} + c_3 x e^{-2x/3}$

5. $y(x) = c_1 e^{2x} + c_2 x e^{2x} + c_3 e^{-2x} + c_4 x e^{-2x}$

7. $y(x) = c_1 \cos(x/\sqrt{2}) + c_2 \sin(x/\sqrt{2}) + c_3 \cos(2x/\sqrt{3}) + c_4 \sin(2x/\sqrt{3})$

9. $y(x) = c_1 e^x + c_2 e^{-x} + c_3 x e^{-x}$

. $y(x) = 5e^x + 2e^{3x}$

3. $y(x) = e^{3x}(3 \cos 4x - 2 \sin 4x)$

5. $y(x) = \frac{1}{4}(-13 + 6x + 9e^{-2x/3})$

7. $y(x) = c_1 e^x + c_2 e^{-2x} + c_3 x e^{-2x}$

9. $y(x) = c_1 e^{-3x} + e^{3x/2}(c_1 \cos \frac{3}{2} x\sqrt{3} + c_2 \sin \frac{3}{2} x\sqrt{3})$

. $y(x) = c_1 e^x + e^{-2x}(c_2 \cos 2x + c_3 \sin 2x)$

3. $y(x) = c_1 e^{3x} + e^{-3x}(c_2 \cos 3x + c_3 \sin 3x)$

5. $y(x) = c_1 e^{-x/2} + c_2 e^{-x/3} + c_3 \cos 2x + c_4 \sin 2x$

9. $y(x) = c_1 e^{-ix} + c_2 e^{3ix}$

. $y(x) = c_1 \exp([1 + i\sqrt{3}]x) + c_2 \exp(-[1 + i\sqrt{3}]x)$

3. $y(x) = 2e^{2x} - 5e^{-x} + 3 \cos x - 9 \sin x$

ction 3.4

1. Frequency: 2 rad/s $(1/\pi$ Hz); period: π s

3. Amplitude: 2 m; frequency: 5 rad/s; period: $2\pi/5$ s

7. About 10,450 ft

. About 3.8 in.

5. $x(t) = 4e^{-2t} - 2e^{-4t}$; overdamped

6. $x(t) = 5e^{-4t} + 10te^{-4t}$; critically damped

7. $x(t) = \frac{1}{3}\sqrt{313}\, e^{-5t/2} \cos(6t - 0.8254)$; underdamped

9. $x(t) = e^{-5t}(6 \cos 10t + 8 \sin 10t)$
$\approx 10e^{-5t} \cos(10t - 0.9273)$; underdamped

9. (b) The time-varying amplitude is $\frac{2}{3}\sqrt{3}$, the frequency is $4\sqrt{3}$ rad/s, and the phase angle is $\pi/6$.

. (a) $k \approx 7018$ lb/ft; (b) after about 2.47 s

. Damping constant: $c \approx 11.5$ lb/ft; spring constant: $k \approx 189.68$ lb/ft

Section 3.5

1. $y_p(x) = \frac{1}{25} e^{3x}$

3. $y_p(x) = \frac{1}{39}(\cos 3x - 5 \sin 3x)$

5. $y_p(x) = \frac{1}{26}(13 + 3 \cos 2x - 2 \sin 2x)$

7. $y_p(x) = -\frac{1}{6}(e^x - e^{-x}) = -\frac{1}{3} \sinh x$

9. $y_p(x) = -\frac{1}{3} + \frac{1}{16}(2x^2 - x) e^x$

11. $y_p(x) = \frac{1}{8}(3x^2 - 2x)$

13. $y_p(x) = \frac{1}{65} e^x(7 \sin x - 4 \cos x)$

15. $y_p(x) \equiv -17$

17. $y_p(x) = \frac{1}{4}(x^2 \sin x - x \cos x)$

19. $y_p(x) = \frac{1}{8}(10x^2 - 4x^3 + x^4)$

21. $y_p(x) = xe^x(A \cos x + B \sin x)$

23. $y_p(x) = Ax \cos 2x + Bx \sin 2x + Cx^2 \cos 2x + Dx^2 \sin 2x$

25. $y_p(x) = Axe^{-x} + Bx^2 e^{-x} + Cxe^{-2x} + Dx^2 e^{-2x}$

27. $y_p(x) = Ax \cos x + Bx \sin x + Cx \cos 2x + Dx \sin 2x$

29. $y_p(x) = Ax^3 e^x + Bx^4 e^x + Cxe^{2x} + Dxe^{-2x}$

31. $y_p(x) = \cos 2x + \frac{3}{4} \sin 2x + \frac{1}{2} x$

33. $y(x) = \cos 3x - \frac{2}{15} \sin 3x + \frac{1}{5} \sin 2x$

35. $y(x) = e^x(2 \cos x - \frac{5}{2} \sin x) + \frac{1}{2} x + 1$

37. $y(x) = 4 - 4e^x + 3xe^x + x - \frac{1}{2} x^2 e^x + \frac{1}{6} x^3 e^x$

39. $y(x) = -3 + 3x - \frac{1}{2} x^2 + \frac{1}{6} x^3 + 4e^{-x} + xe^{-x}$

41. $y_p(x) = 255 - 450x + 30x^2 + 20x^3 + 10x^4 - 4x^5$

43. (b) $y(x) = c_1 \cos 2x + c_2 \sin 2x + \frac{1}{4} \cos x - \frac{1}{20} \cos 3x$

45. $y(x) = c_1 \cos 3x + c_2 \sin 3x + \frac{1}{24} - \frac{1}{10} \cos 2x - \frac{1}{56} \cos 4x$

47. $y_p(x) = \frac{2}{3} e^x$ **49.** $y_p(x) = x^2 e^{2x}$

51. $y_p(x) = -\frac{1}{4}(\cos 2x \cos x - \sin 2x \sin x) + \frac{1}{20}(\cos 5x \cos 2x + \sin 5x \sin 2x) = -\frac{1}{5} \cos 3x$ (!)

53. $y_p(x) = \frac{2}{3} x \sin 3x + \frac{2}{9}(\cos 3x) \ln|\cos 3x|$

55. $y_p(x) = \frac{1}{8}(1 - x \sin 2x)$ **59.** $y_p(x) = \frac{1}{4} x^4$

61. $y_p(x) = \ln x$

Section 3.6

1. $x(t) = 2 \cos 2t - 2 \cos 3t$

3. $x(t) = \frac{1}{15}\sqrt{138,388} \cos(10t - \alpha) + \frac{1}{3} \cos(5t - \beta)$, where $\alpha = 2\pi - \tan^{-1}\left(\frac{1}{186}\right) \approx 6.2778$ and $\beta = \tan^{-1}\left(\frac{4}{3}\right) \approx 0.9273$

5. $x(t) = (x_0 - C) \cos \omega_0 t + C \cos \omega t$, where $C = F_0/(k - m\omega^2)$

7. $x_{sp}(t) = \frac{10}{13} \cos(3t - \alpha)$, where $\alpha = \pi - \tan^{-1}\left(\frac{12}{5}\right) \approx 1.9656$

9. $x_{sp}(t) = \left(3/\sqrt{40,001}\right) \cos(10t - \alpha)$, where $\alpha = \pi + \tan^{-1}(199/20) \approx 4.6122$

11. $x_{sp}(t) = \frac{1}{4}\sqrt{10}\cos(3t - \alpha)$, where $\alpha = \pi - \tan^{-1}(3) \approx$ 1.8925; $x_{tr}(t) = \frac{5}{4}\sqrt{2}\,e^{-2t}\cos(t - \beta)$, where $\beta = 2\pi - \tan^{-1}(7) \approx 4.8543$

13. $x_{sp}(t) = \left(3/\sqrt{9236}\right)\cos(10t - \alpha)$, where $\alpha = \pi - \tan^{-1}\left(\frac{10}{47}\right) \approx 2.9288$; $x_{tr}(t) = (10.9761)\,e^{-t}\cos(t\sqrt{5} - \beta)$, where $\beta \approx 0.4181$

15. $\omega = \sqrt{384}$ rad/s (approximately 3.12 Hz)

17. $\omega_0 = \sqrt{(g/L) + (k/m)}$

19. (a) Natural frequency: $\sqrt{10}$ rad/s (approximately 0.50 Hz);
 (b) amplitude: approximately 10.625 in.

Section 3.7

1. $I(t) = 4e^{-5t}$

3. $I(t) = \frac{4}{145}(\cos 60t + 12\sin 60t - e^{-5t})$

5. $I(t) = \frac{5}{6}e^{-10t}\sin 60t$

7. (a) $Q(t) = E_0 C(1 - e^{-t/RC})$; $I(t) = (E_0/R)\,e^{-t/RC}$

9. (a) $Q(t) = \frac{1}{1480}(\cos 120t + 6\sin 120t - e^{-20t})$;
 $I(t) = \frac{1}{74}(36\cos 120t - 6\sin 120t + e^{-20t})$;
 (b) steady-state amplitude: $3/\sqrt{37}$

11. $I_{sp}(t) = \left(10/\sqrt{37}\right)\sin(2t - \delta)$, where $\delta = 2\pi - \tan^{-1}\left(\frac{1}{6}\right) \approx 6.1180$

13. $I_{sp}(t) = \left(20/\sqrt{13}\right)\sin(5t - \delta)$ where $\delta = 2\pi - \tan^{-1}\left(\frac{2}{3}\right) \approx 5.6952$

15. $I_0 = 33\pi[(1000 - 36\pi^2)^2 + (30\pi)^2]^{-1/2} \approx 0.1591$;
 $\delta = 2\pi - \tan^{-1}[(1000 - 36\pi^2)/(30\pi)] \approx 4.8576$

17. $I(t) = -25e^{-4t}\sin 3t$

19. $I(t) = 10e^{-20t} - 10e^{-10t} - 50te^{-10t}$

21. $I(t) = \frac{20}{13}(2\cos 5t + 3\sin 5t)$
 $- \frac{10}{39}e^{-t}(12\cos 3t + 47\sin 3t)$

23. Critical frequency: $\omega_0 = 1/\sqrt{LC}$

Section 3.8

1. Eigenvalues: $\{(2n + 1)^2\pi^2/4\}$;
 associated eigenfunctions: $\{\cos([2n + 1]\pi x/2)\}$ $(n \geq 0)$

3. Eigenvalues: $\{n^2/4\}$ for $n > 0$;
 associated eigenfunctions: $y_n(x) = \cos(nx/2)$ for n odd and $y_n(x) = \sin(nx/2)$ for n even

5. Eigenvalues: $\{(2n + 1)^2\pi^2/64\}$ for $n \geq 0$;
 associated eigenfunctions: $y_n(x) = \cos([2n + 1]\pi x/8) + (-1)^n\sin([2n + 1]\pi x/8)$

CHAPTER 4

Section 4.1

1. $x_1' = x_2$, $x_2' = -7x_1 - 3x_2 + t^2$

2. $x_1' = x_2$, $x_2' = x_3$, $x_3' = x_4$,
 $x_4' = -x_1 + 3x_2 - 6x_3 + \cos 3t$

3. $x_1' = x_2$, $t^2 x_2' = (1 - t^2)x_1 - tx_2$

5. $x_1' = x_2$, $x_2' = x_3$, $x_3' = x_2^2 + \cos x_1$

7. $x_1' = x_2$, $y_1' = y_2$, $x_2' = -kx_1 \cdot (x_1^2 + y_1^2)^{-3/2}$,
 $y_2' = -ky_1 \cdot (x_1^2 + y_1^2)^{-3/2}$

9. $x_1' = x_2$, $y_1' = y_2$, $z_1' = z_2$, $x_2' = 3x_1 - y_1 + 2z_1$,
 $y_2' = x_1 + y_1 - 4z_1$, $z_2' = 5x_1 - y_1 - z_1$

11. $x(t) = A\cos t + B\sin t$,
 $y(t) = B\cos t - A\sin t$

12. $x(t) = Ae^t + Be^{-t}$, $y(t) = Ae^t - Be^{-t}$

13. $x(t) = A\cos 2t + B\sin 2t$,
 $y(t) = -B\cos 2t + A\sin 2t$; $x(t) = \cos 2t$,
 $y(t) = \sin 2t$

14. $x(t) = A\cos 10t + B\sin 10t$,
 $y(t) = B\cos 10t - A\sin 10t$;
 $x(t) = 3\cos 10t + 4\sin 10t$,
 $y(t) = 4\cos 10t - 3\sin 10t$

15. $x(t) = A\cos 2t + B\sin 2t$,
 $y(t) = 4B\cos 2t - 4A\sin 2t$

16. $x(t) = A\cos 4t + B\sin 4t$,
 $y(t) = \frac{1}{2}B\cos 4t - \frac{1}{2}A\sin 4t$

17. $x(t) = Ae^{-3t} + Be^{2t}$, $y(t) = -3Ae^{-3t} + 2Be^{2t}$;
 $x(t) = e^{2t}$, $y(t) = 2e^{2t}$

18. $x(t) = Ae^{-2t} + Be^{-5t}$, $y(t) = 2Ae^{-2t} + 5Be^{-5t}$;
 $A = \frac{17}{3}$ and $B = -\frac{11}{3}$ in the particular solution.

19. $x(t) = -e^{-2t}\sin 3t$,
 $y(t) = e^{-2t}(3\cos 3t + 2\sin 3t)$

20. $x(t) = (A + Bt)\,e^{3t}$, $y(t) = (3A + B + 3Bt)\,e^{3t}$

27. $2(I_1' - I_2') + 50I_1 = 100\sin 60t$,
 $2(I_2' - I_1') + 25I_2 = 0$

28. $I_1' = -20(I_1 - I_2)$, $I_2' = 40(I_1 - I_2)$

Section 4.2

1. $x(t) = a_1 e^{-t} + a_2 e^{2t}$, $y(t) = a_2 e^{2t}$

2. $x(t) = (c_1 + c_2 t)e^{-t}$, $y(t) = (c_1 - \frac{1}{2}c_2 + c_2 t)e^{-t}$

3. $x(t) = \frac{4}{5}(e^{3t} - e^{-2t})$, $y(t) = \frac{2}{5}(6e^{3t} - e^{-2t})$

4. $x(t) = \frac{1}{2}(3e^{2t} - e^{-2t})$, $y(t) = \frac{1}{2}(3e^{2t} - 5e^{-2t})$

5. $x(t) = e^{-t}(a_1\cos 2t + a_2\sin 2t)$,
 $y(t) = -\frac{1}{2}e^{-t}[(a_1 + a_2)\cos 2t + (a_2 - a_1)\sin 2t]$

6. $x(t) = e^{-2t}(3 \cos 3t + 9 \sin 3t),$
$y(t) = e^{-2t}(2 \cos 3t - 4 \sin 3t)$

7. $x(t) = a_1 e^{2t} + a_2 e^{3t} - \frac{1}{3} t + \frac{1}{18},$
$y(t) = -2a_1 e^{2t} - a_2 e^{3t} - \frac{2}{3} t - \frac{5}{9},$

8. $x(t) = c_1 e^t + c_2 e^{3t} + e^{2t},$ $y(t) = -c_1 e^t + c_2 e^{3t}$

9. $x(t) = 3a_1 e^t + a_2 e^{-t} - \frac{1}{5}(7 \cos 2t + 4 \sin 2t),$
$y(t) = a_1 e^t + a_2 e^{-t} - \frac{1}{5}(2 \cos 2t + 4 \sin 2t)$

10. $x(t) = e^t,$ $y(t) = -e^t$

11. $x(t) = a_1 \cos 3t + a_2 \sin 3t - \frac{11}{20} e^t - \frac{1}{4} e^{2t},$
$y(t) = \frac{1}{3}[(a_1 - a_2) \cos 3t + (a_1 + a_2) \sin 3t] + \frac{1}{10} e^t$

12. $x(t) = c_1 e^{2t} + c_2 e^{-2t} + c_3 e^{3t} + c_4 e^{-3t},$
$y(t) = -c_1 e^{2t} - c_2 e^{-2t} + \frac{3}{2} c_3 e^{3t} + \frac{3}{2} c_4 e^{-3t}$

13. $x(t) = a_1 \cos 2t + a_2 \sin 2t + b_1 \cos 3t + b_2 \sin 3t,$
$y(t) = \frac{1}{2}(a_1 \cos 2t + a_2 \sin 2t) - 2(b_1 \cos 3t + b_2 \sin 3t)$

14. $x(t) = c_1 \cos 2t + c_2 \sin 2t + \frac{1}{3} \sin t,$
$y(t) = c_1 \cos 2t + c_2 \sin 2t + c_3 \cos 2t\sqrt{2} +$
$c_4 \sin 2t\sqrt{2} + \frac{4}{21} \sin t$

15. $x(t) = a_1 \cos t + a_2 \sin t + b_1 \cos 2t + b_2 \sin 2t,$
$y(t) = a_2 \cos t - a_1 \sin t + b_2 \cos 2t - b_1 \sin 2t$

16. $x(t) = a_1 \cos t + a_2 \sin t + b_1 e^{2t} + b_2 e^{-2t},$
$y(t) = 3a_2 \cos t - 3a_1 \sin t + b_1 e^{2t} - b_2 e^{-2t}$

17. $x(t) = \frac{1}{6}(4c_1 e^{3t} - 3c_2 e^{-4t}),$ $y(t) = c_1 e^{3t} + c_2 e^{-4t},$
$z(t) = \frac{1}{6}(-4c_1 e^{3t} + 3c_2 e^{-4t})$

18. $x(t) = a_1 + a_2 e^{4t} + a_3 e^{8t},$ $y(t) = 2a_1 - 2a_3 e^{8t},$
$z(t) = 2a_1 - 2a_2 e^{4t} + 2a_3 e^{8t}$

19. $x(t) = a_1 e^{2t} + a_2 e^{-t} + \frac{2}{3} t e^{-t},$
$y(t) = a_1 e^{2t} + b_2 e^{-t} - \frac{1}{3} t e^{-t},$
$z(t) = a_1 e^{2t} - \left(a_2 + b_2 + \frac{1}{3}\right) e^{-t} - \frac{1}{3} t e^{-t}$

20. Infinitely many solutions

21. No solution

22. Infinitely many solutions

23. Two arbitrary constants

24. No arbitrary constants

25. No solution

26. Four arbitrary constants

27. $I_1(t) = 2 + e^{-5t}[-2 \cos(10t/r) + 4r \sin(10t/r)],$
$I_2(t) = (20/r)e^{-5t} \sin(10t/r)$ where $r = \sqrt{6}$

28. $I_1(t) = \frac{1}{1321}(120e^{-25t/3} - 120 \cos 60t + 1778 \sin 60t),$
$I_2(t) = \frac{1}{1321}(-240e^{-25t/3} + 240 \cos 60t + 1728 \sin 60t)$

29. $I_1(t) = \frac{2}{3}(2 + e^{-60t}),$ $I_2(t) = \frac{4}{3}(1 - e^{-60t})$

30. (a) $x(t) = a_1 \cos 5t + a_2 \sin 5t + b_1 \cos 5t\sqrt{3} +$
$b_2 \sin 5t\sqrt{3},$ $y(t) = 2a_1 \cos 5t + 2a_2 \sin 5t -$
$2b_1 \cos 5t\sqrt{3} - 2b_2 \sin 5t\sqrt{3};$ (b) In the natural mode with
frequency $\omega_1 = 5$, the masses move in the same direction,

whereas in the natural mode with frequency $\omega_1 = 5\sqrt{3}$ they
move in opposite directions. In each case the amplitude of the
motion of m_2 is twice that of m_1.

39. $x(t) = a_1 \cos t + a_2 \sin t + b_1 \cos 3t + b_2 \sin 3t,$
$y(t) = a_1 \cos t + a_2 \sin t - b_1 \cos 3t - b_2 \sin 3t$

40. In the natural mode with frequency $\omega_1 = 1$, the two masses
move in the same direction with equal amplitudes of oscilla-
tion. In the natural mode with frequency $\omega_2 = 2$ the two
masses move in opposite directions with the amplitude of
motion of m_1 twice that of m_2.

41. $x(t) = a_1 \cos t + a_2 \sin t + b_1 \cos t\sqrt{5} + b_2 \sin t\sqrt{5},$
$y(t) = a_1 \cos t + a_2 \sin t - b_1 \cos t\sqrt{5} - b_2 \sin t\sqrt{5}$

42. In the natural mode with frequency $\omega_1 = \sqrt{2}$, the two masses
move in the same direction; in the natural mode with fre-
quency $\omega_2 = 2$, they move in opposite directions. In each nat-
ural mode their amplitudes of oscillation are equal.

43. $x(t) = a_1 \cos t\sqrt{2} + a_2 \sin t\sqrt{2} +$
$b_1 \cos 2t\sqrt{2} + b_2 \sin 2t\sqrt{2},$
$y(t) = a_1 \cos t\sqrt{2} + a_2 \sin t\sqrt{2} -$
$\frac{1}{2} b_1 \cos 2t\sqrt{2} - \frac{1}{2} b_2 \sin 2t\sqrt{2}$

Section 4.3

The format for the first eight answers is this: $(x(t), y(t))$ at
$t = 0.2$ by the Euler method, by the improved Euler method, by
the Runge-Kutta method, and finally the actual values.

1. $(0.8800, 2.5000),$ $(0.9600, 2.6000),$ $(1.0027, 2.6401),$
$(1.0034, 2.6408)$

2. $(0.8100, -0.8100),$ $(0.8200, -0.8200),$
$(0.8187, -0.8187),$ $(0.8187, -0.8187)$

3. $(2.8100, 2.3100),$ $(3.2200, 2.6200),$
$(3.6481, 2.9407),$ $(3.6775, 2.9628)$

4. $(3.3100, -1.6200),$ $(3.8200, -2.0400),$
$(4.2274, -2.4060),$ $(4.2427, -2.4205)$

5. $(-0.5200, 2.9200),$ $(-0.8400, 2.4400),$
$(-0.5712, 2.4485),$ $(-0.5793, 2.4488)$

6. $(-1.7600, 4.6800),$ $(-1.9200, 4.5600),$
$(-1.9029, 4.4995),$ $(-1.9025, 4.4999)$

7. $(3.1200, 1.6800),$ $(3.2400, 1.7600),$
$(3.2816, 1.7899),$ $(3.2820, 1.7902)$

8. $(2.1600, -0.6300),$ $(2.5200, -0.4600),$
$(2.5320), -0.3867),$ $(2.5270, -0.3889)$

9. At $t = 1$ we obtain $(x, y) = (3.99261, 6.21770)$
$(h = 0.1)$ and $(3.99234, 6.21768)$ $(h = 0.05);$
the actual value is $(3.99232, 6.21768).$

10. At $t = 1$ we obtain $(x, y) = (1.31498, 1.02537)$
$(h = 0.1)$ and $(1.31501, 1.02538)$ $(h = 0.05);$
the actual value is $(1.31501, 1.02538).$

11. At $t = 1$ we obtain $(x, y) = (-0.05832, 0.56664)$ $(h = 0.1)$ and $(-0.05832, 0.56665)$ $(h = 0.05)$; the actual value is $(-0.05832, 0.56665)$.

12. We solved $x' = y$, $y' = -x + \sin t$, $x(0) = y(0) = 0$. With $h = 0.1$ and also with $h = 0.05$ we obtain the actual value $x(1.0) \approx 0.15058$.

13. Runge-Kutta, $h = 0.1$: about 1050 ft in about 7.7 s

14. Runge-Kutta, $h = 0.1$: about 1044 ft in about 7.8 s

15. Runge-Kutta, $h = 1.0$: about 83.83 mi in about 168 s

16. At $40°$: 5.0 s, 352.9 ft; at $45°$: 5.4 s, 347.2 ft; at $50°$: 5.8 s, 334.2 ft (all values approximate)

17. At $39.0°$ the range is about 352.7 ft. At $39.5°$ it is 352.8; at $40°$, 352.9; at $40.5°$, 352.6; at $41.0°$, 352.1.

18. Just under $57.5°$

19. Approximately 253 ft/s

20. Maximum height: about 1005 ft, attained in about 5.6 s; range: about 1880 ft; time aloft: about 11.6s

21. Runge-Kutta with $h = 0.1$ yields these results:
(a) 21,400 ft, 46 s, 518 ft/s; (b) 8970 ft, 17.5 s;
(c) 368 ft/s (at $t \approx 23$).

CHAPTER 5

Section 5.1

1. (a) $\begin{bmatrix} 13 & -18 \\ 23 & 17 \end{bmatrix}$; (b) $\begin{bmatrix} 0 & -1 \\ 2 & 19 \end{bmatrix}$; (c) $\begin{bmatrix} -9 & -i1 \\ 47 & -9 \end{bmatrix}$;

(d) $\begin{bmatrix} -10 & -37 \\ 14 & -8 \end{bmatrix}$

2. $(\mathbf{AB})\mathbf{C} = \mathbf{A}(\mathbf{BC}) = \begin{bmatrix} -33 & -7 \\ -27 & 103 \end{bmatrix}$;

$\mathbf{A}(\mathbf{B} + \mathbf{C}) = \mathbf{AB} + \mathbf{AC} = \begin{bmatrix} -18 & -4 \\ 68 & -8 \end{bmatrix}$

3. $\mathbf{AB} = \begin{bmatrix} -1 & 8 \\ 46 & -1 \end{bmatrix}$; $\mathbf{BA} = \begin{bmatrix} 11 & -12 & 14 \\ -14 & 0 & 7 \\ 0 & 8 & -13 \end{bmatrix}$

4. $\mathbf{Ay} = \begin{bmatrix} 2t^2 - \cos t \\ 3t^2 - 4\sin t + 5\cos t \end{bmatrix}$, $\mathbf{Bx} = \begin{bmatrix} 2t + 3e^{-t} \\ -14t \\ 6t - 2e^{-t} \end{bmatrix}$

5. (a) $\begin{bmatrix} 21 & 2 & 1 \\ 4 & 44 & 9 \\ -27 & 34 & 45 \end{bmatrix}$; (b) $\begin{bmatrix} 9 & 21 & -13 \\ -5 & -8 & 24 \\ -25 & -19 & 26 \end{bmatrix}$;

(c) $\begin{bmatrix} 0 & -6 & 1 \\ 10 & 31 & -15 \\ 16 & 58 & -23 \end{bmatrix}$; (d) $\begin{bmatrix} -10 & -8 & 5 \\ 18 & 12 & -10 \\ 11 & 22 & 6 \end{bmatrix}$;

(e) $\begin{bmatrix} 3-t & 2 & -1 \\ 0 & 4-t & 3 \\ -5 & 2 & 7-t \end{bmatrix}$

7. $\det(\mathbf{A}) = \det(\mathbf{B}) = 0$

8. $\det(\mathbf{AB}) = \det(\mathbf{BA}) = 144$

9. $(\mathbf{AB})' = \begin{bmatrix} 1 - 8t + 18t^2 & 1 + 2t - 12t^2 + 32t^3 \\ 3 + 3t^2 - 4t^3 & 8t + 3t^2 + 4t^3 \end{bmatrix}$

11. $\mathbf{x} = \begin{bmatrix} x \\ y \end{bmatrix}$, $\mathbf{P}(t) = \begin{bmatrix} 0 & -3 \\ 3 & 0 \end{bmatrix}$, $\mathbf{f}(t) = \begin{bmatrix} 0 \\ 0 \end{bmatrix}$

13. $\mathbf{x} = \begin{bmatrix} x \\ y \end{bmatrix}$, $\mathbf{P}(t) = \begin{bmatrix} 2 & 4 \\ 5 & -1 \end{bmatrix}$, $\mathbf{f}(t) = \begin{bmatrix} 3e^t \\ -t^2 \end{bmatrix}$

15. $\mathbf{x} = \begin{bmatrix} x \\ y \\ z \end{bmatrix}$, $\mathbf{P}(t) = \begin{bmatrix} 0 & 1 & 1 \\ 1 & 0 & 1 \\ 1 & 1 & 0 \end{bmatrix}$, $\mathbf{f}(t) = \begin{bmatrix} 0 \\ 0 \\ 0 \end{bmatrix}$

17. $\mathbf{x} = \begin{bmatrix} x \\ y \\ z \end{bmatrix}$, $\mathbf{P}(t) = \begin{bmatrix} 3 & -4 & 1 \\ 1 & 0 & -3 \\ 0 & 6 & -7 \end{bmatrix}$, $\mathbf{f}(t) = \begin{bmatrix} t \\ t^2 \\ t^3 \end{bmatrix}$

19. $\mathbf{x} = \begin{bmatrix} x_1 \\ x_2 \\ x_3 \\ x_4 \end{bmatrix}$, $\mathbf{P}(t) = \begin{bmatrix} 0 & 1 & 0 & 0 \\ 0 & 0 & 2 & 0 \\ 0 & 0 & 0 & 3 \\ 4 & 0 & 0 & 0 \end{bmatrix}$, $\mathbf{f}(t) = \begin{bmatrix} 0 \\ 0 \\ 0 \\ 0 \end{bmatrix}$

21. $W(t) = e^{3t}$; $\mathbf{x}(t) = \begin{bmatrix} 2c_1e^t + c_2e^{2t} \\ -3c_1e^t - c_2e^{2t} \end{bmatrix}$

23. $W(t) \equiv 4$, $\mathbf{x}(t) = \begin{bmatrix} c_1e^{2t} + c_2e^{-2t} \\ c_1e^{2t} - 5c_2e^{-2t} \end{bmatrix}$

25. $W(t) = 7e^{-3t}$, $\mathbf{x}(t) = \begin{bmatrix} 3c_1e^{2t} + c_2e^{-5t} \\ 2c_1e^{2t} + 3c_2e^{-5t} \end{bmatrix}$

27. $W(t) \equiv 3$, $\mathbf{x}(t) = \begin{bmatrix} c_1e^{2t} + c_2e^{-t} \\ c_1e^{2t} + c_3e^{-t} \\ c_1e^{2t} - (c_2 + c_3)e^{-t} \end{bmatrix}$

9. $W(t) = e^{2t}, \quad \mathbf{x}(t) = \begin{bmatrix} 3c_1e^{-2t} + c_2e^t + c_3e^{3t} \\ -2c_1e^{-2t} - c_2e^t - c_3e^{3t} \\ 2c_1e^{-2t} + c_2e^t \end{bmatrix}$

1. $\mathbf{x} = 2\mathbf{x}_1 - \mathbf{x}_2$

33. $\mathbf{x} = 3\mathbf{x}_1 + 4\mathbf{x}_2$

5. $\mathbf{x} = \mathbf{x}_1 + 2\mathbf{x}_2 + \mathbf{x}_3$

37. $\mathbf{x} = 3\mathbf{x}_1 - 3\mathbf{x}_2 - 5\mathbf{x}_3$

9. $\mathbf{x} = 3\mathbf{x}_1 + 7\mathbf{x}_2 + \mathbf{x}_3 - 2\mathbf{x}_4$

0. $\mathbf{x} = 13\mathbf{x}_1 + 41\mathbf{x}_2 + 3\mathbf{x}_3 - 12\mathbf{x}_4$

1. (a) $\mathbf{x}_2 = t\mathbf{x}_1$, so neither is a constant multiple of the other.
(b) $W(\mathbf{x}_1, \mathbf{x}_2) \equiv 0$, whereas Theorem 2 implies that $W \neq 0$ if \mathbf{x}_1 and \mathbf{x}_2 were independent solutions of a system of the indicated form.

ection 5.2

1. Eigenvalues: $\lambda_1 = -1$, $\lambda_2 = 3$, eigenvectors:
$\mathbf{v}_1 = [1 \ -1]^T$, $\mathbf{v}_2 = [1 \ 1]^T$; solution:
$x_1 = c_1e^{-t} + c_2e^{3t}$, $x_2 = -c_1e^{-t} + c_2e^{3t}$

2. Eigenvalues: -1 and 4; solution:
$x_1 = c_1e^{-t} + 3c_2e^{4t}$, $x_2 = -c_1e^{-t} + 2c_2e^{4t}$

3. $x_1 = \frac{1}{7}(-e^{-t} + 8e^{6t})$, $x_2 = \frac{1}{7}(e^{-t} + 6e^{6t})$

4. $x_1 = c_1e^{-2t} + c_2e^{5t}$, $x_2 = -6c_1e^{-2t} + c_2e^{5t}$

5. $x_1 = c_1e^{-t} + 7c_2e^{5t}$, $x_2 = c_1e^{-t} + c_2e^{5t}$

6. Eigenvalues: 3 and 4

7. $x_1 = c_1e^t + 2c_2e^{-9t}$, $x_2 = c_1e^t - 3c_2e^{-9t}$

9. Eigenvalue: $4i$; solution:
$x_1 = 2\cos 4t - \frac{11}{4}\sin 4t$, $x_2 = 3\cos 4t + \frac{1}{2}\sin 4t$

1. $x_1 = -4e^t\sin 2t$, $x_2 = 4e^t\cos 2t$

3. $x_1 = 3e^{2t}(c_1\cos 3t - c_2\sin 3t)$,
$x_2 = e^{2t}[(c_1 + c_2)\cos 3t + (c_1 - c_2)\sin 3t]$

4. Eigenvalue: $3 + 4i$

5. $x_1 = 5e^{5t}(c_1\cos 4t - c_2\sin 4t)$,
$x_2 = e^{5t}[(2c_1 + 4c_2)\cos 4t + (4c_1 - 2c_2)\sin 4t]$

7. $x_1 = c_1e^{9t} + c_2e^{6t} + c_3$, $x_2 = c_1e^{9t} - 2c_2e^{6t}$,
$x_3 = c_1e^{9t} + c_2e^{6t} - c_3$

9. $x_1 = c_1e^{6t} + c_2e^{3t} + c_3e^{3t}$, $x_2 = c_1e^{6t} - 2c_2e^{3t}$,
$x_3 = c_1e^{6t} + c_2e^{3t} - c_3e^{3t}$

1. $x_1 = 6c_1 + 3c_2e^t + 2c_3e^{-t}$, $x_2 = 2c_1 + c_2e^t + c_3e^{-t}$,
$x_3 = 5c_1 + 2c_2e^t + 2c_3e^{-t}$

3. $x_1 = c_1e^{2t} + c_3e^{3t}$, $x_2 = -c_1e^{2t} + c_2e^{-2t} - c_3e^{3t}$,
$x_3 = -c_2e^{-2t} + c_3e^{3t}$

5. Eigenvalues: $0, 2 \pm 3i$; solution:
$x_1 = c_1 + e^{2t}[(-c_2 + c_3)\cos 3t + (c_2 + c_3)\sin 3t]$
$x_2 = -c_1 + 2e^{2t}(c_2\cos 3t - c_3\sin 3t)$,
$x_3 = 2e^{2t}(-c_2\cos 3t + c_3\sin 3t)$

7. $x_1(t) = 15e^{-(0.2)t}$, $x_2(t) = 15(e^{-(0.2)t} - e^{-(0.4)t})$;
the maximum of x_2 is 3.75 (lb)

29. $x_1(t) = 10 + 5e^{-(0.6)t}$, $x_2(t) = 5 - 5e^{-(0.6)t}$

31. $x_1(t) = 3c_1e^{-(0.5)t}$,
$x_2(t) = -5c_1e^{-(0.5)t} + c_2e^{-(0.2)t}$,
$x_3(t) = 4c_1e^{-(0.5)t} + 4c_2e^{-(0.2)t} + c_3e^{-(0.25)t}$

33. $x_1(t) = 2c_0 + e^{-(0.6)t}[5c_1\cos (0.3)t - 5c_2\sin (0.3)t]$,
$x_2(t) = 5c_0 + e^{-(0.6)t}[(-c_1 - 3c_2)\cos (0.3)t +$
$(-3c_1 + c_2)\sin (0.3)t]$,
$x_3(t) = 2c_0 + e^{-(0.6)t}[(-4c_1 + 3c_2)\cos (0.3)t +$
$(3c_1 + 4c_2)\sin (0.3)t]$

35. $x_1(t) = 3c_1e^t + c_4e^{-2t}$,
$x_2(t) = -2c_1e^t + c_3e^{2t} - c_4e^{-2t}$, $x_3(t) = 4c_1e^t + c_2e^{-t}$,
$x_4(t) = c_1e^t$

37. $x_1(t) = x_4(t) = 2e^{10t} + e^{15t}$
$x_2(t) = x_3(t) = -e^{10t} + 2e^{15t}$

Section 5.3

1. Natural frequencies: $\omega_1 = 0$, $\omega_2 = 2$ (rad/s). In the first degenerate natural mode, the two masses move by translation without oscillation. In the second natural mode, they oscillate in opposite directions with equal amplitudes.

2. Natural frequencies: $\omega_1 = 1$, $\omega_2 = 3$. In the first natural mode, the two masses move in the same direction with equal amplitudes of oscillation. In the second natural mode, they move in opposite directions with equal amplitudes.

3. Natural frequencies: $\omega_1 = 1$, $\omega_2 = 2$. In the natural mode with frequency $\omega_1 = 1$, the two masses move in the same direction with equal amplitudes of motion. In the natural mode with frequency $\omega_2 = 2$, the two masses move in opposite directions, with the amplitude of motion of m_1 twice that of m_2.

5. Natural freqencies: $\omega_1 = \sqrt{2}$, $\omega_2 = 2$. In each natural mode the two masses have equal amplitudes of oscillation. They move in the same direction at frequency ω_1, in opposite directions at frequency ω_2.

7. $\omega_1 = \sqrt{2 - \sqrt{2}}$ with amplitude ratios $1 : \sqrt{2} : 1$; $\omega_2 = \sqrt{2}$ with amplitude ratios $1 : 0 : -1$; $\omega_3 = \sqrt{2 + \sqrt{2}}$ with amplitude ratios $1 : -\sqrt{2} : 1$

9. $x_1(t) = a_1\cos t + a_2\sin t + b_1\sin 2t - \frac{7}{40}\cos 3t$,
$x_2(t) = a_1\cos t + a_2\sin t - \frac{1}{2}(b_1\cos 2t + b_2\sin 2t)$
$+ \frac{1}{40}\cos 3t$

10. $x_1(t) = c_1\cos t + c_2\sin t + c_3\cos t\sqrt{5} + c_4\sin t\sqrt{5} +$
$\frac{2}{3}\sin 2t$,
$x_2(t) = c_1\cos t + c_2\sin t - c_3\cos t\sqrt{5} -$
$c_4\sin t\sqrt{5} - \frac{4}{3}\sin 2t$

11. $x(t) = a_1\cos t\sqrt{2} + a_2\sin t\sqrt{2} + b_1\cos 2t +$
$b_2\sin 2t + \frac{4}{3}\cos t$,
$y(t) = a_1\cos t\sqrt{2} + a_2\sin t\sqrt{2} -$
$b_1\cos 2t - b_2\sin 2t + \frac{5}{3}\cos t$

13. $x_1(t) = \frac{2}{3} \cos 5t - 2 \cos 5t \sqrt{3} + \frac{4}{3} \cos 10t,$
$x_2(t) = \frac{4}{3} \cos 5t + 4 \cos 5t \sqrt{3} + \frac{16}{3} \cos 10t$

19. (a) $\omega_1 \approx 1.0293$ Hz; $\omega_2 \approx 1.7971$ Hz.
(b) $v_1 \approx 28$ mi/h; $v_2 \approx 49$ mi/h

21. $\omega_1 = 2\sqrt{10}, \quad v_1 \approx 40.26$ ft/s (about 27 mi/h),
$\omega_2 = 5\sqrt{5}, \quad v_2 \approx 71.18$ ft/s (about 49 mi/h)

23. $\omega_1 \approx 5.0424, \quad v_1 \approx 32.10$ ft/s (about 22 mi/h),
$\omega_2 \approx 9.9158, \quad v_2 \approx 63.13$ ft/s (about 43 mi/h)

Section 5.4

1. Repeated eigenvalue $\lambda = -3$, eigenvector
$\mathbf{v} = [1 \ -1]^T; \quad x_1(t) = (c_1 + c_2 + c_2 t)e^{-3t},$
$x_2(t) = (-c_1 - c_2 t)e^{-3t}$

2. Repeated eigenvalue $\lambda = 2$

3. Repeated eigenvalue $\lambda = 3$, eigenvector
$\mathbf{v} = [-2 \ 2]^T; \quad x_1(t) = (-2c_1 + c_2 - 2c_2 t)e^{3t},$
$x_2(t) = (2c_1 + 2c_2 t)e^{3t}$

4. Repeated eigenvalue $\lambda = 4$

5. Repeated eigenvalue $\lambda = 5$, eigenvector
$\mathbf{v} = [2 \ -4]^T; \quad x_1(t) = (2c_1 + c_2 + 2c_2 t)e^{5t},$
$x_2(t) = (-4c_1 - 4c_2 t)e^{5t}$

6. Repeated eigenvalue $\lambda = 5$

7. Eigenvalues $\lambda = 2, 2, 9; \quad x_1(t) = c_1 e^{2t} + c_2 e^{2t},$
$x_2(t) = c_1 e^{2t} + c_3 e^{9t}, \quad x_3(t) = c_2 e^{2t}$

8. Eigenvalues $\lambda = 7, 13, 13$

9. Eigenvalues $\lambda = 5, 5, 9;$
$x_1(t) = c_1 e^{5t} + 7c_2 e^{5t} + 3c_3 e^{9t}, \quad x_2(t) = 2c_1 e^{5t},$
$x_3(t) = 2c_2 e^{5t} + c_3 e^{9t}$

10. Eigenvalues $\lambda = 3, 3, 7$

11. Triple eigenvalue $\lambda = -1$ of defect 2;
$x_1(t) = (-2c_2 + c_3 - 2c_3 t)e^{-t},$
$x_2(t) = (c_1 - c_2 + c_2 t - c_3 t + \frac{1}{2}c_3 t^2)e^{-t},$
$x_3(t) = (c_2 + c_3 t)e^{-t}$

13. Triple eigenvalue $\lambda = -1$ of defect 2;
$x_1(t) = (c_1 + c_2 t + \frac{1}{2}c_3 t^2)e^{-t},$
$x_2(t) = (2c_2 + c_3 + 2c_3 t)e^{-t}, \quad x_3(t) = (c_2 + c_3 t)e^{-t}$

15. Triple eigenvalue $\lambda = 1$ of defect 1;
$x_1(t) = (3c_1 - 3c_2 + c_3 - 3c_3 t)e^{t},$
$x_2(t) = (-c_1 + c_2 + c_3 t)e^{t}, \quad x_3(t) = (c_2 + c_3 t)e^{t}$

17. Triple eigenvalue $\lambda = 1$ of defect 1; $x_1(t) = 2c_1 e^{t},$
$x_2(t) = (6c_2 + c_3 + 6c_3 t)e^{t}, \quad x_3(t) = -(9c_1 + 9c_2 + 9c_3 t)e^{t}$

19. Double eigenvalues $\lambda = -1$ and $\lambda = 1$, each with
defect 1;
$x_1(t) = c_1 e^{-t} + c_4 e^{t}, \quad x_2(t) = c_3 e^{t}, \quad x_3(t) = c_2 e^{-t} + 3c_4 e^{t}, \quad x_4(t) = c_1 e^{-t} - 2c_3 e^{t}$

20. Eigenvalue $\lambda = 2$ with multiplicity 4 and defect 3;
$x_1(t) = (c_1 + c_3 + c_2 t + c_4 t + \frac{1}{2}c_3 t^2 + \frac{1}{6}c_4 t^3)e^{2t},$
$x_2(t) = (c_2 + c_3 t + \frac{1}{2}c_4 t^2)e^{2t}, \quad x_3(t) = (c_3 + c_4 t)e^{2t},$
$x_4(t) = c_4 e^{2t}$

21. Eigenvalue $\lambda = 1$ with multiplicity 4 and defect 2;
$x_1(t) = (-2c_2 + c_3 - 2c_3 t)e^{t}, \quad x_2(t) = (c_2 + c_3 t)e^{t},$
$x_3(t) = (c_2 + c_4 + c_3 t)e^{t}, \quad x_4(t) = (c_1 + c_2 t + \frac{1}{2}c_3 t^2)e^{t}$

22. Eigenvalue $\lambda = 1$ with multiplicity 4 and defect 2;
$x_1(t) = (c_1 + 3c_2 + c_4 + c_2 t + 3c_3 t + \frac{1}{2}c_3 t^2)e^{t},$
$x_2(t) = -(2c_2 - c_3 + 2c_3 t)e^{t}, \quad x_3(t) = (c_2 + c_3 t)e^{t},$
$x_4(t) = -(2c_1 + 6c_2 + 2c_2 t + 6c_3 t + c_3 t^2)e^{t}$

23. $\mathbf{x}(t) = c_1 \mathbf{v}_1 e^{-t} + (c_2 \mathbf{v}_2 + c_3 \mathbf{v}_3)e^{3t}$ with $\mathbf{v}_1 = [1 \ -1 \ 2]^T,$
$\mathbf{v}_2 = [4 \ 0 \ 9]^T, \quad \mathbf{v}_3 = [0 \ 2 \ 1]^T$

24. $\mathbf{x}(t) = c_1 \mathbf{v}_1 e^{-2t} + (c_2 \mathbf{v}_2 + c_3 \mathbf{v}_3)e^{3t}$ with $\mathbf{v}_1 = [5 \ 3 \ -3]^T,$
$\mathbf{v}_2 = [4 \ 0 \ -1]^T, \quad \mathbf{v}_3 = [2 \ -1 \ 0]^T$

25. $\mathbf{x}(t) = [c_1 \mathbf{v}_1 + c_2(\mathbf{v}_1 t + \mathbf{v}_2) + c_3(\frac{1}{2}\mathbf{v}_1 t^2 + \mathbf{v}_2 t + \mathbf{v}_3)]e^{2t}$
with $\mathbf{v}_1 = [-1 \ 0 \ -1]^T, \quad \mathbf{v}_2 = [-4 \ -1 \ 0]^T, \quad \mathbf{v}_3 = [1 \ 0 \ 0]$

26. $\mathbf{x}(t) = [c_1 \mathbf{v}_1 + c_2(\mathbf{v}_1 t + \mathbf{v}_2) + c_3(\frac{1}{2}\mathbf{v}_1 t^2 + \mathbf{v}_2 t + \mathbf{v}_3)]e^{3t}$
with $\mathbf{v}_1 = [0 \ 2 \ 2]^T, \quad \mathbf{v}_2 = [2 \ 1 \ -3]^T,$
$\mathbf{v}_3 = [1 \ 0 \ 0]^T$

27. $\mathbf{x}(t) = [c_1 \mathbf{v}_1 + c_2(\mathbf{v}_1 t + \mathbf{v}_2) + c_3 \mathbf{v}_3]e^{2t}$ with
$\mathbf{v}_1 = [-5 \ 3 \ 8]^T, \quad \mathbf{v}_2 = [1 \ 0 \ 0]^T, \quad \mathbf{v}_3 = [1 \ 1 \ 0]^T$

28. $\mathbf{x}(t) = [c_1 \mathbf{v}_1 + c_2(\mathbf{v}_1 t + \mathbf{v}_2) + c_3(\frac{1}{2}\mathbf{v}_1 t^2 + \mathbf{v}_2 t + \mathbf{v}_3)]e^{2t}$
with $\mathbf{v}_1 = [119 \ -289 \ 0]^T, \quad \mathbf{v}_2 = [-17 \ 34 \ 17]^T,$
$\mathbf{v}_3 = [1 \ 0 \ 0]^T$

29. $\mathbf{x}(t) = [c_1 \mathbf{v}_1 + c_2(\mathbf{v}_1 t + \mathbf{v}_2)]e^{-t} + [c_3 \mathbf{v}_3 + c_4(\mathbf{v}_3 t + \mathbf{v}_4)]e^{2t}$
with $\mathbf{v}_1 = [1 \ -3 \ -1 \ -2]^T, \quad \mathbf{v}_2 = [0 \ 1 \ 0 \ 0]^T,$
$\mathbf{v}_3 = [0 \ -1 \ 1 \ 0]^T, \quad \mathbf{v}_4 = [0 \ 0 \ 2 \ 1]^T$

30. $\mathbf{x}(t) = [c_1 \mathbf{v}_1 + c_2(\mathbf{v}_1 t + \mathbf{v}_2)]e^{-t} + [c_3 \mathbf{v}_3 + c_4(\mathbf{v}_3 t + \mathbf{v}_4)]e^{2t}$
with $\mathbf{v}_1 = [0 \ 1 \ -1 \ -3]^T, \quad \mathbf{v}_2 = [0 \ 0 \ 1 \ 2]^T,$
$\mathbf{v}_3 = [-1 \ 0 \ 0 \ 0]^T, \quad \mathbf{v}_4 = [0 \ 0 \ 3 \ 5]^T$

31. $\mathbf{x}(t) = [c_1 \mathbf{v}_1 + c_2(\mathbf{v}_1 t + \mathbf{v}_2) + c_3(\frac{1}{2}\mathbf{v}_1 t^2 + \mathbf{v}_2 t + \mathbf{v}_3) + c_4 \mathbf{v}_4]e$
with $\mathbf{v}_1 = [42 \ 7 \ -21 \ -42]^T, \quad \mathbf{v}_2 = [34 \ 22 \ -10 \ -27]^T,$
$\mathbf{v}_3 = [1 \ 0 \ 0 \ 0]^T, \quad \mathbf{v}_4 = [0 \ 1 \ 3 \ 0]^T$

32. $\mathbf{x}(t) = [c_1 \mathbf{v}_1 + c_2 \mathbf{v}_2]e^{2t} + (c_3 \mathbf{v}_3 + c_4 \mathbf{v}_4 + c_5 \mathbf{v}_5)]e^{3t}$ with
$\mathbf{v}_1 = [8 \ 0 \ -3 \ 1 \ 0]^T, \quad \mathbf{v}_2 = [1 \ 0 \ 0 \ 0 \ 3]^T,$
$\mathbf{v}_3 = [3 \ -2 \ -1 \ 0 \ 0]^T, \quad \mathbf{v}_4 = [2 \ -2 \ 0 \ -3 \ 0]^T,$
$\mathbf{v}_5 = [1 \ -1 \ 0 \ 0 \ 3]^T$

33. $\mathbf{x}_1(t) = [\cos 4t \ \sin 4t \ 0 \ 0]^T e^{3t},$
$\mathbf{x}_2(t) = [-\sin 4t \ \cos 4t \ 0 \ 0]^T e^{3t},$
$\mathbf{x}_3(t) = [t \cos 4t \ t \sin 4t \ \cos 4t \ \sin 4t]^T e^{3t},$
$\mathbf{x}_4(t) = [-t \sin 4t \ t \cos 4t \ -\sin 4t \ \cos 4t]^T e^{3t}$

34. $\mathbf{x}_1(t) = \begin{bmatrix} \sin 3t \\ 3\cos 3t - 3\sin 3t \\ 0 \\ \sin 3t \end{bmatrix} e^{2t},$

$$\mathbf{x}_2(t) = \begin{bmatrix} -\cos 3t \\ 3\sin 3t + 3\cos 3t \\ 0 \\ -\cos 3t \end{bmatrix} e^{2t},$$

$$\mathbf{x}_3(t) = \begin{bmatrix} 3\cos 3t + t\sin 3t \\ (3t - 10)\cos 3t - (3t + 9)\sin 3t \\ \sin 3t \\ t\sin 3t \end{bmatrix} e^{2t},$$

$$\mathbf{x}_4(t) = \begin{bmatrix} -t\cos 3t + 3\sin 3t \\ (3t + 9)\cos 3t + (3t - 10)\sin 3t \\ -\cos 3t \\ -t\cos 3t \end{bmatrix} e^{2t}$$

$x_1(t) = x_2(t) = v_0(1 - e^{-t});$
$\lim\limits_{t \to \infty} x_1(t) = \lim\limits_{t \to \infty} x_2(t) = v_0$

$x_1(t) = v_0(2 - 2e^{-t} - te^{-t}),$
$x_2(t) = v_0(2 - 2e^{-t} - te^{-t} - \frac{1}{2}t^2 e^{-t});$
$\lim\limits_{t \to \infty} x_1(t) = \lim\limits_{t \to \infty} x_2(t) = 2v_0$

ction 5.5

$\boldsymbol{\Phi}(t) = \begin{bmatrix} e^t & e^{3t} \\ -e^t & e^{3t} \end{bmatrix},$ $\mathbf{x}(t) = \dfrac{1}{2}\begin{bmatrix} 5e^t + e^{3t} \\ -5e^t + e^{3t} \end{bmatrix}$

$\boldsymbol{\Phi}(t) = \begin{bmatrix} 5\cos 4t & -5\sin 4t \\ 2\cos 4t + 4\sin 4t & 4\cos 4t - 2\sin 4t \end{bmatrix},$

$\mathbf{x}(t) = \dfrac{1}{4}\begin{bmatrix} -5\sin 4t \\ 4\cos 4t - 2\sin 4t \end{bmatrix}$

$\boldsymbol{\Phi}(t) = \begin{bmatrix} 2\cos 3t & -2\sin 3t \\ -3\cos 3t + 3\sin 3t & 3\cos 3t + 3\sin 3t \end{bmatrix},$

$\mathbf{x}(t) = \dfrac{1}{3}\begin{bmatrix} 3\cos 3t - \sin 3t \\ -3\cos 3t + 6\sin 3t \end{bmatrix}$

$\boldsymbol{\Phi}(t) = \begin{bmatrix} 6 & 3e^t & 2e^{-t} \\ 2 & e^t & e^{-t} \\ 5 & 2e^t & 2e^{-t} \end{bmatrix},$ $\mathbf{x}(t) = \begin{bmatrix} -12 + 12e^t + 2e^{-t} \\ -4 + 4e^t + e^{-t} \\ -10 + 8e^t + 2e^{-t} \end{bmatrix}$

In the next six answers we give the eigenvector matrix **P**, the ̱gonal eigenvalue matrix **D**, and the fundamental matrix **Φ**.

$\mathbf{P} = \begin{bmatrix} 2 & 1 \\ 1 & 1 \end{bmatrix},$ $\mathbf{D} = \begin{bmatrix} 3 & 0 \\ 0 & 1 \end{bmatrix},$

$$\boldsymbol{\Phi}(t) = \begin{bmatrix} 2e^{3t} - e^t & -2e^{3t} + 2e^t \\ e^{3t} - e^t & -e^{3t} + 2e^t \end{bmatrix}$$

11. P $= \begin{bmatrix} 3 & 1 \\ 2 & 1 \end{bmatrix},$ **D** $= \begin{bmatrix} 3 & 0 \\ 0 & 2 \end{bmatrix},$

$$\boldsymbol{\Phi}(t) = \begin{bmatrix} 3e^{3t} - 2e^{2t} & -3e^{3t} + 3e^{2t} \\ 2e^{3t} - 2e^{2t} & -2e^{3t} + 3e^{2t} \end{bmatrix}$$

13. P $= \begin{bmatrix} 4 & 1 \\ 3 & 1 \end{bmatrix},$ **D** $= \begin{bmatrix} 3 & 0 \\ 0 & 1 \end{bmatrix},$

$$\boldsymbol{\Phi}(t) = \begin{bmatrix} 4e^{3t} - 3e^t & -4e^{3t} + 4e^t \\ 3e^{3t} - 3e^t & -3e^{3t} + 4e^t \end{bmatrix}$$

15. P $= \begin{bmatrix} 5 & 2 \\ 2 & 1 \end{bmatrix},$ **D** $= \begin{bmatrix} 2 & 0 \\ 0 & 1 \end{bmatrix},$

$$\boldsymbol{\Phi}(t) = \begin{bmatrix} 5e^{2t} - 4e^t & -10e^{2t} + 10e^t \\ 2e^{2t} - 2e^t & -4e^{2t} + 5e^t \end{bmatrix}$$

17. P $= \begin{bmatrix} 1 & 1 \\ 1 & -1 \end{bmatrix},$ **D** $= \begin{bmatrix} 4 & 0 \\ 0 & 2 \end{bmatrix},$

$$\boldsymbol{\Phi}(t) = \dfrac{1}{2}\begin{bmatrix} e^{4t} + e^{2t} & e^{4t} - e^{2t} \\ e^{4t} - e^{2t} & e^{4t} + e^{2t} \end{bmatrix}$$

19. P $= \begin{bmatrix} 2 & -1 \\ 1 & 2 \end{bmatrix},$ **D** $= \begin{bmatrix} 10 & 0 \\ 0 & 5 \end{bmatrix},$

$$\boldsymbol{\Phi}(t) = \dfrac{1}{5}\begin{bmatrix} 4e^{10t} + e^{5t} & 2e^{10t} - 2e^{5t} \\ 2e^{10t} - 2e^{5t} & e^{10t} + 4e^{5t} \end{bmatrix}$$

21. $e^t \begin{bmatrix} 1 & 2t \\ 0 & 1 \end{bmatrix}$ **22.** $e^{3t}\begin{bmatrix} 1 & 5t \\ 0 & 1 \end{bmatrix}$ **23.** $e^t \begin{bmatrix} 1 & t & \frac{1}{2}t^2 \\ 0 & 1 & t \\ 0 & 0 & 1 \end{bmatrix}$

27. x$(t) = \begin{bmatrix} c_1\cosh t + c_2\sinh t \\ c_1\sinh t + c_2\cosh t \end{bmatrix}$

29. x$(t) = e^t \begin{bmatrix} c_1 + 2c_2 t + 2c_3 t^2 \\ c_2 + 2c_3 t \\ c_3 \end{bmatrix}$

CHAPTER 6

Section 6.1

1. 6.1.11 **2.** 6.1.13 **3.** 6.1.16 **4.** 6.1.10
5. 6.1.9 **6.** 6.1.15 **7.** 6.1.12 **8.** 6.1.14

9. $x(t) = 0, 2, -2$ **10.** $x(t) = 0$

11. $x(t) = n\pi$ where n is an integer.

12. $x(t) = 0$

13. The origin $(0, 0)$ is a stable proper node, similar to the one shown in Fig. 6.1.3.

14. The origin is an unstable saddle point; reverse all arrows in Fig. 6.1.5 to see the trajectories.

15. The origin is a stable improper node, similar to the one shown in Fig. 6.1.4, except that the trajectories consist of the x-axis and parabolas of the form $x = ky^2$.

16. The origin is an unstable improper node.

17. The origin is a stable center.

18. The origin is a stable center.

19. The origin is a stable center.

20. The origin is an asymptotically stable spiral point.

23. The origin and the circles $x^2 + y^2 = C > 0$.

24. The origin and the hyperbolas $y^2 - x^2 = C$.

25. The origin and the ellipses $x^2 + 4y^2 = C > 0$.

26. The origin and the ovals of the form $x^4 + y^4 = C > 0$.

Section 6.2

1. Asymptotically stable node

2. Unstable improper node

3. Unstable saddle point

4. Unstable saddle point

5. Asymptotically stable node

6. Unstable node

7. Unstable spiral point

8. Asymptotically stable spiral point

9. Stable, but not asymptotically stable, center

10. Stable, but not asymptotically stable, center

11. Asymptotically stable node: $(2, 1)$

12. Unstable improper node: $(2, -3)$

13. Unstable saddle point: $(2, 2)$

14. Unstable saddle point: $(3, 4)$

15. Asymptotically stable spiral point: $(1, 1)$

16. Unstable spiral point: $(3, 2)$

17. Stable center: $(5/2, -1/2)$

18. Stable (but not asymptotically stable) center: $(-2, -1)$

19. Asymptotically stable node

20. Unstable improper node

21. Unstable saddle point

22. Here, $(0, 0)$ is either a center or a spiral point, but its stability is not determined by Theorem 2.

23. Asymptotically stable spiral point

24. Unstable spiral point

25. Asymptotically stable node or spiral point

26. Either an unstable node or an unstable spiral point

27. The origin is either a center or a spiral point, but its stability is not determined by Theorem 2.

28. The origin is either a center or a spiral point, but its stability is not determined by Theorem 2.

29. The origin is an unstable saddle point. The point $(1, 1)$ is either a center or a spiral point, but its stability is indeterminate.

30. There is an unstable saddle point at $(1, 1)$ and an asymptotically stable spiral point at $(-1, 1)$.

31. There is an unstable saddle point at $(1, 1)$ and an asymptotically stable spiral point at $(-1, -1)$.

32. There is an unstable saddle point at $(2, 1)$ and an asymptotically stable spiral point at $(-2, -1)$.

37. Note that the differential equation is homogeneous.

Section 6.3

3. At $(0, 0)$ the linearized system is $x' = 60x, \quad y' = 42y$, with general solution $x(t) = Ae^{60t}, \quad y(t) = Be^{42t}$.

4. At $(0, 14)$ the linearized system has eigenvalues $\lambda_1 = 4$ and $\lambda_2 = -42$.

5. At $(20, 0)$ the linearized system has eigenvalues $\lambda_1 = 2$ and $\lambda_2 = -60$.

6. At $(12, 6)$ the linearized system has the two negative eigenvalues $-27 + 3\sqrt{73}$ and $-27 - 3\sqrt{73}$.

8. At $(0, 0)$ the linearized system is $x' = 5x, \quad y' = -2y$, with general solution $x(t) = Ae^{5t}, \quad y(t) = Be^{-2t}$.

9. Substitute $u = x - 5, \quad v = y$; then show that the linearized uv-system has eigenvalues -5 and 3.

10. Substitute $u = x - 2, \quad v = y - 3$; then show that the linearized uv-system has eigenvalues $-1 + i\sqrt{5}$ and $-1 - i\sqrt{5}$.

13. At $(0, 0)$ the linearized system has general solution $x(t) = Ae^{-2t}, \quad y(t) = Be^{-4t} = kx^2$.

15. Substitute $u = x - 2, \quad v = y$.

16. Substitute $u = x - 3, \quad v = y - 1$.

20. Approximately 200.43 days

Section 6.4

1. Eigenvalues: $-2, -3$; stable node

2. Eigenvalues: $1, 3$; unstable node

3. Eigenvalues: $-3, 5$; unstable saddle point

4. Eigenvalues: $-1 \pm 2i$; stable spiral point

5. Critical points: $(0, n\pi)$, n an integer; an unstable saddle point if n is even, a stable spiral point if n is odd

6. Critical points: $(n, 0)$, n an integer; an unstable saddle point if n is even, a stable spiral point if n is odd

7. Critical point: $(n\pi, n\pi)$, n an integer; an unstable saddle point if n is even, a stable spiral point if n is odd

8. Critical points: $(n\pi, 0)$, n an integer; an unstable node if n is even, an unstable saddle point if n is odd

10. Unstable saddle points at $(2, 0)$ and $(-2, 0)$, a stable center at $(0, 0)$

11. Unstable saddle points at $(2, 0)$ and $(-2, 0)$, a stable spiral point at $(0, 0)$

12. Stable centers at $(2, 0)$ and $(-2, 0)$, an unstable saddle point at $(0, 0)$

13. A stable center at $(0, 0)$ and an unstable saddle point at $(-4, 0)$

14. Stable centers at $(2, 0)$, $(0, 0)$, and $(-2, 0)$, unstable saddle points at $(1, 0)$ and $(-1, 0)$

CHAPTER 7

Section 7.1

1. $1/s^2$, $s > 0$

2. $2/s^3$, $s > 0$

3. $e/(s - 3)$, $s > 3$

4. $s/(s^2 + 1)$, $s > 0$

5. $1/(s^2 - 1)$, $s > 1$

7. $(1 - e^{-s})/s$, $s > 0$

8. $(e^{-s} - e^{-2s})/s$, $s > 0$

9. $(1 - e^{-s} - se^{-s})/s^2$, $s > 0$

1. $\frac{1}{2}\sqrt{\pi}\, s^{-3/2} + 3s^{-2}$, $s > 0$

3. $s^{-2} - 2/(s - 3)$, $s > 3$

5. $s^{-1} + s/(s^2 - 25)$, $s > 5$

6. $(s + 2)/(s^2 + 4)$, $s > 0$

7. $\cos^2 2t = \frac{1}{2}(1 + \cos 4t)$; $\frac{1}{2}[s^{-1} + s/(s^2 + 16)]$, $s > 0$

8. $3/(s^2 + 36)$, $s > 0$

9. $s^{-1} + 3s^{-2} + 6s^{-3} + 6s^{-4}$, $s > 0$

0. $1/(s - 1)^2$, $s > 1$

1. $(s^2 - 4)/(s^2 + 4)^2$, $s > 0$

2. $\frac{1}{2}[s/(s^2 - 36) - s^{-1}]$

3. $\frac{1}{2}t^3$

24. $2\sqrt{t/\pi}$

5. $1 - \frac{8}{3}t^{3/2}\,\pi^{-1/2}$

26. e^{-5t}

7. $3e^{4t}$

28. $3\cos 2t + \frac{1}{2}\sin 2t$

9. $\frac{5}{3}\sin 3t - 3\cos 3t$

30. $-\cosh 2t - \frac{9}{2}\sinh 2t$

31. $\frac{3}{5}\sinh 5t - 10\cosh 5t$

32. $2u(t - 3)$

37. $f(t) = 1 - u_a(t) = 1 - u(t - a)$

Section 7.2

1. $x(t) = 5\cos 2t$

2. $x(t) = 3\cos 3t + \frac{4}{3}\sin 3t$

3. $x(t) = \frac{2}{3}(e^{2t} - e^{-t})$

4. $x(t) = \frac{1}{2}(7e^{-3t} - 3e^{-5t})$

5. $x(t) = \frac{1}{3}(2\sin t - \sin 2t)$

6. $x(t) = \frac{1}{3}(\cos t - \cos 2t)$

7. $x(t) = \frac{1}{8}(9\cos t - \cos 3t)$

8. $x(t) = \frac{1}{9}(1 - \cos 3t)$

9. $x(t) = \frac{1}{6}(2 - 3e^{-t} + e^{-3t})$

10. $x(t) = \frac{1}{4}(2t - 3 + 12e^{-t} - 9e^{-2t})$

11. $x(t) = 1$, $y(t) = -2$

13. $x(t) = -(2/r)\sinh(t/r)$, $y(t) = \cosh(t/r) + (1/r)\sinh(t/r)$, where $r = \sqrt{3}$

15. $x(t) = \frac{1}{3}\{2 + e^{-3t/2}[\cos(rt/2) + r\sin(rt/2)]\}$, $y(t) = \frac{1}{21}\{28 - 9e^t + 2e^{-3t/2}[\cos(rt/2) + 4r\sin(rt/2)]\}$ where $r = \sqrt{3}$

16. $x(t) = \cos t + \sin t$, $y(t) = e^t - \cos t$, $z(t) = -2\sin t$

17. $f(t) = \frac{1}{3}(e^{3t} - 1)$

18. $f(t) = \frac{3}{5}(1 - e^{-5t})$

19. $f(t) = \frac{1}{4}(1 - \cos 2t) = \frac{1}{2}\sin^2 t$

20. $f(t) = \frac{1}{9}(6\sin 3t - \cos 3t + 1)$

21. $f(t) = t - \sin t$

22. $f(t) = \frac{1}{9}(-1 + \cosh 3t)$

23. $f(t) = -t + \sinh t$

24. $f(t) = \frac{1}{2}(e^{-2t} - 2e^{-t} + 1)$

Section 7.3

1. $24/(s - \pi)^5$

2. $\frac{3}{4}\sqrt{\pi}(s + 4)^{-5/2}$

3. $3\pi/[(s + 2)^2 + 9\pi^2]$

4. $\sqrt{2}(2s + 5)/(4s^2 + 4s + 17)$

5. $\frac{3}{2}e^{2t}$

6. $(t - t^2)e^{-t}$

7. te^{-2t}

8. $e^{-2t}\cos t$

9. $e^{3t}(3\cos 4t + \frac{7}{2}\sin 4t)$

10. $\frac{1}{36}e^{2t/3}(8\cos\frac{4}{3}t - 5\sin\frac{4}{3}t)$

11. $\frac{1}{2}\sinh 2t$

12. $2 + 3e^{3t}$

13. $3e^{-2t} - 5e^{-5t}$

14. $2 + e^{2t} - 3e^{-t}$

15. $\frac{1}{25}(e^{5t} - 1 - 5t)$

16. $\frac{1}{125}[e^{2t}(-2 + 5t) + e^{-3t}(2 + 5t)]$

17. $\frac{1}{16}(\sinh 2t - \sin 2t)$

18. $e^{4t}(1 + 12t + 24t^2 + \frac{32}{3} t^3)$

19. $\frac{1}{3}(2 \cos 2t + 2 \sin 2t - 2 \cos t - \sin t)$

20. $\frac{1}{32}[e^{2t}(2t - 1) + e^{-2t}(2t + 1)]$

21. $\frac{1}{2} e^{-t}(5 \sin t - 3t \cos t - 2t \sin t)$

22. $\frac{1}{64} e^{t/2}[(4t + 8) \cos t + (4 - 3t) \sin t]$

27. $\frac{1}{4} e^{-3t}(8 \cos 4t + 9 \sin 4t)$

28. $\frac{1}{4}(1 - 2e^{2t} + e^{4t})$ **29.** $\frac{1}{8}(-6t + 3 \sinh 2t)$

30. $\frac{1}{10}[2e^{-t} - e^{-2t}(2 \cos 2t + \sin 2t)]$

31. $\frac{1}{15}(6e^{2t} - 5 - e^{-3t})$ **32.** $\frac{1}{2}(\cosh t + \cos t)$

33. $x(t) = r(\cosh rt \sin rt - \sinh rt \cos rt)$ where $r = 1/\sqrt{2}$

34. $\frac{1}{2} \sin 2t + \frac{1}{3} \sin 3t$ **35.** $\frac{1}{16}(\sin 2t - 2t \cos 2t)$

36. $\frac{1}{50}[2e^{2t} + (10t - 2) \cos t - (5t + 14) \sin t]$

37. $\frac{1}{50}[(5t - 1) e^{-t} + e^{-2t}(\cos 3t + 32 \sin 3t)]$

38. $\frac{1}{510} e^{-3t}(489 \cos 3t + 307 \sin 3t) +$
 $\frac{1}{170} (7\cos 2t + 6 \sin 2t)$

Section 7.4

1. $\frac{1}{2} t^2$ **2.** $(e^{at} - at - 1)/a^2$

3. $\frac{1}{2} (\sin t - t \cos t)$ **4.** $2(t - \sin t)$

5. te^{at} **6.** $(e^{at} - e^{bt})/(a - b)$

7. $\frac{1}{3} (e^{3t} - 1)$ **8.** $\frac{1}{4} (1 - \cos 2t)$

9. $\frac{1}{54} (\sin 3t - 3t \cos 3t)$ **10.** $(kt - \sin kt)/k^3$

11. $\frac{1}{4} (\sin 2t + 2t \cos 2t)$

12. $\frac{1}{5} [1 - e^{-2t} (\cos t + 2 \sin t)]$

13. $\frac{1}{10} (3e^{3t} - 3 \cos t + \sin t)$

14. $\frac{1}{3} (\cos t - \cos 2t)$ **15.** $6s/(s^2 + 9)^2, \quad s > 0$

16. $(2s^3 - 24s)/(s^2 + 4)^3, \quad s > 0$

17. $(s^2 - 4s - 5)/(s^2 - 4s + 13)^2, \quad s > 0$

18. $2(3s^2 + 6s + 7)/[(s + 1)^2(s^2 + 2s + 5)^2], \quad s > 0$

19. $\frac{1}{2} \pi - \arctan s = \arctan (1/s), \quad s > 0$

20. $\frac{1}{2} \ln (s^2 + 4) - \ln s, \quad s > 0$

21. $\ln s - \ln(s - 3), \quad s > 3$

22. $\ln(s + 1) - \ln(s - 1), \quad s > 1$

23. $-(2 \sinh 2t)/t$ **24.** $2(\cos 2t - \cos t)/t$

25. $(e^{-2t} + e^{3t} - 2 \cos t)/t$

26. $(e^{-2t} \sin 3t)/t$ **27.** $2(1 - 2 \cos t)/t$

28. $\frac{1}{8} (t \sin t - t^2 \cos t)$

29. $(s + 1)X'(s) + 4X(s) = 0; \quad x(t) = Ct^3 e^{-t}, \quad C \neq 0$

30. $X(s) = A/(s + 3)^3; \quad x(t) = Ct^2 e^{-3t}, \quad C \neq 0$

31. $(s - 2)X'(s) + 3X(s) = 0; \quad x(t) = Ct^2 e^{2t}, \quad C \neq 0$

32. $(s^2 + 2s)X'(s) + (4s + 4)X(s) = 0;$
 $x(t) = C(1 - t - e^{-2t} - te^{-2t}), \quad C \neq 0$

33. $(s^2 + 1)X'(s) + 4sX(s) = 0;$
 $x(t) = C(\sin t - t \cos t), \quad C \neq 0$

34. $x(t) = Ce^{-2t}(\sin 3t - 3t \cos 3t), \quad C \neq 0$

Section 7.5

1. $f(t) = (t - 3)u_3(t)$

3. $f(t) = e^{-2(t - 1)}u_1(t)$

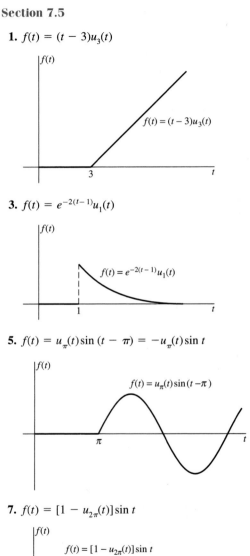

5. $f(t) = u_\pi(t) \sin (t - \pi) = -u_\pi(t) \sin t$

7. $f(t) = [1 - u_{2\pi}(t)] \sin t$

9. $f(t) = [1 - u_3(t)] \cos \pi t$

11. $f(t) = 2[1 - u_3(t)]; \quad F(s) = 2(1 - e^{-3s})/s$

2. $F(s) = 3(e^{-s} - e^{-4s})/s$

3. $F(s) = (1 - e^{-2\pi s})/(s^2 + 1)$

4. $F(s) = s(1 - e^{-2s})/(s^2 + \pi^2)$

5. $F(s) = (1 + e^{-3\pi s})/(s^2 + 1)$

6. $F(s) = 2(e^{-\pi s} - e^{-2\pi s})/(s^2 + 4)$

7. $F(s) = \pi(e^{-2s} + e^{-3s})/(s^2 + \pi^2)$

8. $F(s) = 2\pi(e^{-3s} + e^{-5s})/(4s^2 + \pi^2)$

9. $F(s) = e^{-s}(s^{-1} + s^{-2})$

10. $F(s) = (1 - e^{-s})/s^2$

11. $F(s) = (1 - 2e^{-s} + e^{-2s})/s^2$

13. $F(s) = (1 - e^{-as} - ase^{-as})/[s^2(1 - e^{-2as})]$

14. $x(t) = \frac{1}{2}[1 - u_\pi(t)] \sin^2 t$

2. $x(t) = g(t)$ if $t < 2$; $x(t) = g(t) - g(t - 2)$ if $t \geq 2$

3. $x(t) = \frac{1}{8}[1 - u_{2\pi}(t)](\sin t - \frac{1}{3} \sin 3t)$

4. $x(t) = t - \sin t$ if $t < 1$,
$x(t) = -\sin t + \sin(t - 1) + \cos(t - 1)$ if $t > 1$

5. $x(t) = \frac{1}{4}\{t - 1 + (t + 1)e^{-2t} + u_2(t)[1 - t + (3t - 5)e^{-2(t-2)}]\}$

6. $i(t) = e^{-10t} - u_1(t)e^{-10(t-1)}$

7. $i(t) = [1 - u_{2\pi}(t)] \sin 100t$

8. $i(t) = g(t)$ if $t < \pi$, $i(t) = 0$ if $t > \pi$

9. $i(t) = \frac{1}{50}(1 - e^{-50t})^2 - \frac{1}{50}u_1(t)[1 + 98e^{-50(t-1)} - 99e^{-100(t-1)}]$

10. $i(t) = g(t) - u_1(t)g(t - 1) - u_1(t)h(t - 1)$

11. The complete solution $x(t) = 2|\sin t| \sin t$ is periodic, so the transient solution is zero.

12. $x(t) = g(t) + 2\sum(-1)^n u_{n\pi}(t)g(t - n\pi)$

ection 7.6

1. $x(t) = \frac{1}{2} \sin 2t$

2. $x(t) = \frac{1}{2} \sin 2t$ if $t < \pi$, $x(t) = \sin 2t$ if $t > \pi$

3. $x(t) = \frac{1}{4}(1 - e^{-2t}) - \frac{1}{2}te^{-2t} + u_2(t)(t - 2)e^{-2(t-2)}$

4. $x(t) = t - 2 + 2e^{-t} + 3te^{-t}$

5. $x(t) = 0$ if $0 \leq t < \pi$, $x(t) = -2e^{-(t-\pi)} \sin t$ if $t \geq \pi$

6. $x(t) = -\frac{1}{3}u_{3\pi}(t) \sin 3t + \frac{1}{6}t \sin t$

7. $x(t) = [2 - e^{2\pi}u_\pi(t) + e^{4\pi}u_{2\pi}(t)]e^{-2t} \sin t$

8. $x(t) = (5t + 2)e^{-t} - u_2(t)(t - 2)e^{-(t-2)}$

9. $x(t) = \int_0^t \frac{1}{2}(\sin 2\tau)f(t - \tau) \, d\tau$

10. $x(t) = \int_0^t \tau e^{-3\tau}f(t - \tau) \, d\tau$

11. $x(t) = \int_0^t (e^{-3t} \sinh t)f(t - \tau) \, d\tau$

12. $x(t) = \frac{1}{2}\int_0^t (e^{-2\tau} \sin 2\tau)f(t - \tau) \, d\tau$

13. (a) $mx_\epsilon(t) = p[t^2 - u_\epsilon(t)(t - \epsilon)^2]/(2\epsilon)$;
(b) If $t > \epsilon$, then $mx_\epsilon(t) = p(2\epsilon t - \epsilon^2)/(2\epsilon)$,
and hence $mx_\epsilon(t) \to pt$ as $\epsilon \to 0$;
(c) $mv = (mx)' = (pt)' = p$.

15. The transform of each of the two given initial value problems is $(ms^2 + k)X(s) = mv_0 = p_0$.

17. (b) $i(t) = e^{-100(t-1)}u_1(t) - e^{-100(t-2)}u(t)$.
If $t > 2$, then $i(t) = -(e^{100} - 1)e^{100(1-t)} < 0$.

CHAPTER 8

Section 8.1

1. $y = c_0(1 + x + x^2/2! + x^3/3! + \cdots) = c_0e^x$; $\rho = +\infty$

2. $c_{n+1} = 4c_n/(n + 1)$

3. $y = c_0(1 - 3x/2 + 3^2x^2/(2!2^2) - 3^3x^3/(3!2^3) + 3^4x^4/(4!2^4) - \cdots) = c_0e^{-3x/2}$; $\rho = +\infty$

4. $c_1 = 0$; $c_{n+2} = -2c_n/(n + 2)$

5. $y = c_0(1 + x^3/3 + x^6/(2!3^2) + x^9/(3!3^3) + \cdots) = c_0 \exp(x^3/3)$; $\rho = +\infty$

6. $c_{n+1} = c_n/2$

7. $y = c_0(1 + 2x + 4x^2 + 8x^3 + \cdots) = c_0/(1 - 2x)$; $\rho = \frac{1}{2}$

8. $y = c_0(1 + x)^{1/2}$

9. $y = c_0(1 + 2x + 3x^2 + 4x^3 + \cdots) = c_0/(1 - x)^2$; $\rho = 1$

10. $y = c_0(1 - x)^{3/2}$

11. $y = c_0(1 + x^2/2! + x^4/4! + x^6/6! + \cdots) + c_1(x + x^3/3! + x^5/5! + x^7/7! + \cdots) = c_0 \cosh x + c_1 \sinh x$; $\rho = +\infty$

12. $c_{n+2} = 4c_n/((n + 1)(n + 2))$

13. $y = c_0(1 - 3^2x^2/2! + 3^4x^4/4! - 3^6x^6/6! + \cdots) + (c_1/3)(3x - 3^3x^3/3! + 3^5x^5/5! - 3^7x^7/7! + \cdots) = c_0 \cos 3x + (c_1/3)\sin 3x$; $\rho = +\infty$

14. $y = x + c_0 \cos x + (c_1 - 1)\sin x$

15. $(n + 1)c_n = 0$ for all $n \geq 0$, so $c_n = 0$ for all $n \geq 0$

16. $2nc_n = c_n$ for all $n \geq 0$, so $c_n = 0$ for all $n \geq 0$

17. $c_0 = c_1 = 0$ and $c_{n+1} = -nc_n$ for $n \geq 1$, thus $c_n = 0$ for all $n \geq 0$

18. $c_n = 0$ for all $n \geq 0$

19. $c_n = -4c_{n-2}/(n(n - 1))$ for $n \geq 2$; $c_0 = 0$ and $c_1 = 3$; $y = (3/2)\sin 2x$

20. $y = 2 \cosh 2x$

21. $c_{n+1} = (2nc_n - c_{n-1})/(n(n + 1))$ for $n \geq 1$; $c_0 = 0$, $c_1 = 1$, and $y = xe^x$

22. $y = e^{-2x}$

23. As $c_0 = c_1 = 0$ and $(n^2 - n + 1)c_n + (n - 1)c_{n-1} = 0$
for $n \geqq 2$, $c_n = 0$ for all $n \geqq 0$

Section 8.2

1. $c_{n+2} = c_n;\ y = c_0 \sum\limits_{n=0}^{\infty} x^{2n} + c_1 \sum\limits_{n=0}^{\infty} x^{2n+1} =$

$(c_0 + c_1 x)/(1 - x^2);\quad \rho = 1$

2. $c_{n+2} = -\frac{1}{2}c_n;$

$y = c_0 \sum\limits_{n=0}^{\infty} (-1)^n x^{2n}/2^n + c_1 \sum\limits_{n=0}^{\infty} (-1)^n x^{2n+1}/2^n;\quad \rho = 2$

3. $c_{n+2} = -c_n/(n + 2);\quad y = c_0 \sum\limits_{n=0}^{\infty} (-1)^n x^{2n}/(n!\,2^n) +$

$c_1 \sum\limits_{n=0}^{\infty} (-1)^n x^{2n+1}/(2n + 1)!!;\quad \rho = \infty$

4. $c_{n+2} = -[(n + 4)/(n + 2)]c_n;$

$y = c_0 \sum\limits_{n=0}^{\infty} (-1)^n (n + 1) x^{2n} +$

$\frac{1}{3}c_1 \sum\limits_{n=0}^{\infty} (-1)^n (2n + 3)x^{2n+1};\quad \rho = 1$

5. $c_{n+2} = nc_n/[3(n + 2)];\quad y = c_0 +$

$c_1 \sum\limits_{n=0}^{\infty} x^{2n+1}/[(2n + 1)3^n];\quad \rho = 3$

6. $c_{n+2} = [(n - 3)(n - 4)/(n + 1)(n + 2)]c_n;$
$y = c_0(1 + 6x^2 + x^4) + c_1(x + x^3);\quad \rho = \infty$

7. $c_{n+2} = -[(n - 4)^2/3(n + 1)(n + 3)]c_n;$
$y = c_0(1 - \frac{8}{3}x^2 + \frac{8}{27}x^4) + c_1(x - \frac{1}{2}x^3 + \frac{1}{120}x^5 +$

$9 \cdot \sum\limits_{n=3}^{\infty} \{[(2n - 5)!!]^2(-1)^n/(2n + 1)!3^n\}x^{2n+1})$

8. $c_{n+2} = [(n - 4)(n + 4)/2(n + 1)(n + 2)]c_n;$
$y = c_0(1 - 4x^2 + 2x^4) + c_1(x - \frac{5}{4}x^3 + \frac{7}{32}x^5 +$

$\sum\limits_{n=3}^{\infty} [(2n - 5)!!(2n + 3)!!/(2n + 1)!2^n]x^{2n+1})$

9. $c_{n+2} = [(n + 3)(n + 4)/(n + 1)(n + 2)]c_n;$

$y = c_0 \sum\limits_{n=0}^{\infty} (n + 1)(2n + 1) x^{2n} +$

$\frac{1}{3}c_1 \sum\limits_{n=0}^{\infty} (n + 1)(2n + 3) x^{2n+1};\quad \rho = 1$

10. $c_{n+2} = -[(n - 4)/3(n + 1)(n + 2)]c_n;$
$y = c_0(1 + \frac{2}{3}x^2 + \frac{1}{27}x^4) + c_1(x + \frac{1}{6}x^3 + \frac{1}{360}x^5 +$

$3 \cdot \sum\limits_{n=3}^{\infty} [(-1)^n(2n - 5)!!/(2n + 1)!3^n]x^{2n+1})$

11. $c_{n+2} = [2(n - 5)/5(n + 1)(n + 2)]c_n;$
$y = c_1(x - \frac{4}{15}x^3 + \frac{4}{375}x^5) + c_0(1 - x^2 + \frac{1}{10}x^4 + \frac{1}{750}x^6 +$

$15 \cdot \sum\limits_{n=4}^{\infty} [(2n - 7)!!2^n/(2n)!5^n]x^{2n})$

12. $c_2 = 0;\quad c_{n+3} = c_n/(n + 2);$

$y = c_0\left(1 + \sum\limits_{n=1}^{\infty} x^{3n}/[2 \cdot 5 \cdots (3n - 1)]\right) + c_1 \sum\limits_{n=0}^{\infty} x^{3n+1}/(n!$

13. $c_2 = 0;\quad c_{n+3} = -c_n/(n + 3);$

$y = c_0 \sum\limits_{n=0}^{\infty} (-1)^n x^{3n}/(n!3^n) +$

$c_1 \sum\limits_{n=0}^{\infty} (-1)^n x^{3n+1}/[1 \cdot 4 \cdots (3n + 1)]$

14. $c_2 = 0;\quad c_{n+3} = -c_n/[(n + 2)(n + 3)];$

$y = c_0\left(1 + \sum\limits_{n=1}^{\infty} (-1)^n x^{3n}/[3^n \cdot n! \cdot 2 \cdot 5 \cdots (3n - 1)]\right) +$

$c_1 \sum\limits_{n=0}^{\infty} (-1)^n x^{3n+1}/[3^n \cdot n! \cdot 1 \cdot 4 \cdots (3n + 1)]$

15. $c_2 = c_3 = 0,\quad c_{n+4} = -c_n/[(n + 3)(n + 4)];$

$y = c_0\left(1 + \sum\limits_{n=1}^{\infty} (-1)^n x^{4n}/[4^n \cdot n! \cdot 3 \cdot 7 \cdots (4n - 1)]\right) +$

$c_1 \sum\limits_{n=0}^{\infty} (-1)^n x^{4n+1}/[4^n \cdot n! \cdot 5 \cdot 9 \cdots (4n + 1)]$

16. $y(x) = x$

17. $y(x) = 1 + x^2$ **18.** $c_{n+2} = -c_n/(n + 2)$

19. $y = \dfrac{1}{3} \sum\limits_{n=0}^{\infty} (2n + 3)(x - 1)^{2n+1};$ converges if $0 < x < 2$

20. $y = 2 - 6(x - 3)^2;$ converges for all x

21. $y = 1 + 4(x + 2)^2;$ converges for all x

23. $2c_2 + c_0 = 0;\quad (n + 1)(n + 2)c_{n+2} + c_n + c_{n-1} = 0$ for
$n \geqq 1;\ y_1 = 1 - \frac{1}{2}x^2 - \frac{1}{6}x^3 + \cdots;$
$y_2 = x - \frac{1}{6}x^3 - \frac{1}{12}x^4 + \cdots$

25. $c_2 = c_3 = 0,\quad (n + 3)(n + 4)c_{n+4} + (n + 1)c_{n+1} +$
$c_n = 0$ for $n \geqq 0;\ y_1 = 1 - \frac{1}{12}x^4 + \frac{1}{126}x^7 + \cdots;$
$y_2 = x - \frac{1}{12}x^4 - \frac{1}{20}x^5 + \cdots$

26. $y = c_0(1 - x^6/30 + x^9/72 + \cdots) +$
$c_1(x - x^7/42 + x^{10}/90 + \cdots)$

27. $y = 1 - x - \frac{1}{2}x^2 + \frac{1}{3}x^3 - \frac{1}{24}x^4 + \frac{1}{30}x^5 + \frac{29}{720}x^6 -$
$\frac{13}{630}x^7 - \frac{143}{40,320}x^8 + \cdots;\ y(0.5) \approx 0.4156$

28. $y = c_0(1 - x^2/2 + x^3/6 + \cdots) +$
$c_1(x - x^3/6 + x^4/12 + \cdots)$

$y_1 = 1 - \frac{1}{2}x^2 + \frac{1}{720}x^6 + \cdots; \quad y_2 = x - \frac{1}{6}x^3 - \frac{1}{60}x^5 + \cdots$

$y = c_0(1 - x^2 + 13x^4/72 + \cdots) +$
$\quad c_1(x - x^3/3 + x^5/24 + \cdots)$

ection 8.3

1. Ordinary point **2.** Ordinary point

3. Irregular singular point **4.** Irregular singular point

5. Regular singular point; $r_1 = 0, \quad r_2 = -1$

6. Regular singular point; $r_1 = 1, \quad r_2 = -2$

7. Regular singular point; $r = -2, -3$

8. Regular singular point; $r = 1/2, -3$

9. Regular singular point $x = 1$

10. Regular singular point $x = 1$

11. Regular singular points $x = 1, -1$

12. Irregular singular point $x = 2$

13. Regular singular points $x = 2, -2$

14. Irregular singular points $x = 3, -3$

15. Regular singular point $x = 2$

16. Irregular singular point $x = 0$, regular singular
point $x = 1$

17. $y_1 = \cos \sqrt{x}, \quad y_2 = \sin \sqrt{x}$

18. $y_1 = \sum_{n=0}^{\infty} x^n/[n!(2n+1)!!], \quad y_2 = x^{-1/2} \sum_{n=0}^{\infty} x^n/[n!(2n-1)!!]$

19. $y_1 = x^{3/2}\left(1 + 3\sum_{n=1}^{\infty} x^n/[n!(2n+3)!!]\right),$

$y_2 = 1 - x - \sum_{n=2}^{\infty} x^n/[n!(2n-3)!!]$

20. $y_1 = x^{1/3} \sum_{n=0}^{\infty} (-1)^n 2^n x^n/[n! \cdot 4 \cdot 7 \cdots (3n+1)],$

$y_2 = \sum_{n=0}^{\infty} (-1)^n 2^n x^n/[n! \cdot 2 \cdot 5 \cdots (3n-1)]$

21. $y_1 = x\left(1 + \sum_{n=1}^{\infty} x^{2n}/[n! \cdot 7 \cdot 11 \cdots (4n+3)]\right),$

$y_2 = x^{-1/2} \sum_{n=0}^{\infty} x^{2n}/[n! \cdot 1 \cdot 5 \cdots (4n+1)]$

22. $y_1 = x^{3/2}\left(1 + \sum_{n=1}^{\infty} (-1)^n x^{2n}/[n! \cdot 9 \cdot 13 \cdots (4n+5)]\right),$

$y_2 = x^{-1}\left(1 + \sum_{n=1}^{\infty} (-1)^{n-1} x^{2n}/[n! \cdot 3 \cdot 7 \cdots (4n-1)]\right)$

23. $y_1 = x^{1/2}\left(1 + \sum_{n=1}^{\infty} x^{2n}/[2^n \cdot n! \cdot 19 \cdot 31 \cdots (12n+7)]\right),$

$y_2 = x^{-2/3}\left(1 + \sum_{n=1}^{\infty} x^{2n}/[2^n \cdot n! \cdot 5 \cdot 17 \cdots (12n-7)]\right)$

24. $y_1 = x^{1/3}\left(1 + \sum_{n=1}^{\infty} (-1)^n x^{2n}/[2^n \cdot n! \cdot 7 \cdot 13 \cdots (6n+1)]\right),$

$y_2 = 1 + \sum_{n=1}^{\infty} (-1)^n x^{2n}/[2^n \cdot n! \cdot 5 \cdot 11 \cdots (6n-1)]$

25. $y_1 = x^{1/2} \sum_{n=0}^{\infty} (-1)^n x^n/(n! \, 2^n) = x^{1/2} e^{-x/2},$

$y_2 = 1 + \sum_{n=1}^{\infty} (-1)^n x^n/(2n-1)!!$

26. $y_1 = x^{1/2} \sum_{n=0}^{\infty} x^{2n}/(n! \, 2^n) = x^{1/2} \exp(x^2/2),$

$y_2 = 1 + \sum_{n=1}^{\infty} 2^n x^{2n}/[3 \cdot 7 \cdots (4n-1)]$

27. $y_1 = (\cos 3x)/x, \quad y_2 = (\sin 3x)/x$

28. $y_1 = (\cosh 2x)/x, \quad y_2 = (\sinh 2x)/x$

29. $y_1 = (1/x)\cos x/2, \quad y_2 = (1/x)\sin x/2$

30. $y_1 = \cos x^2, \quad y_2 = \sin x^2$

31. $y_1 = x^{1/2}\cosh x, \quad y_2 = x^{1/2}\sinh x$

32. $y_1 = x + 3x^2/5 + 3x^3/35 + x^4/315$ (terminates),
$y_2 = x^{-1/2}(1 - 3x/2 - 3x^2/8 + x^3/48 + \cdots)$

33. $y_1 = x^{-1}(1 + 10x + 5x^2 + 10x^3/9 + \cdots),$
$y_2 = x^{1/2}(1 + 11x/20 - 11x^2/224 + 671x^3/24{,}192 + \cdots)$

34. $y_1 = x(1 - x^2/42 + x^4/1320 + \cdots),$
$y_2 = x^{-1/2}(1 - 7x^2/24 + 19x^4/3200 + \cdots)$

Section 8.4

1. $y_1 = x^{-2}(1 + x), \quad y_2 = 1 + 2\sum_{n=1}^{\infty} x^n/(n+2)!$

2. $y_1 = x^{-4}(1 + x + \frac{1}{2}x^2 + \frac{1}{6}x^3),$

$y_2 = 1 + 24\sum_{n=1}^{\infty} x^n/(n+4)!$

3. $y_1 = x^{-4}(1 - 3x + \frac{9}{2}x^2 - \frac{9}{2}x^3),$

$y_2 = 1 + 24\sum_{n=1}^{\infty} (-1)^n 3^n x^n/(n+4)!$

4. $y_1 = x^{-5}(1 - \frac{3}{5}x + \frac{9}{50}x^2 - \frac{9}{250}x^3 + \frac{27}{1000}x^4),$

$y_2 = 1 + 120\sum_{n=1}^{\infty} (-1)^n 3^n x^n/[(n+5)! \, 5^n]$

5. $y_1 = 1 + \frac{3}{4}x + \frac{1}{4}x^2 + \frac{1}{24}x^3,$

$y_2 = x^5\left(1 + 120\sum_{n=1}^{\infty} (n+1)x^n/(n+5)!\right)$

6. $y_1 = x^4\left(1 + \dfrac{8}{5}\displaystyle\sum_{n=1}^{\infty}\dfrac{(2n+5)!!x^n}{n!(n+4)!2^n}\right)$

7. $y_1 = x^{-2}(2 - 6x + 9x^2),\quad y_2 = \displaystyle\sum_{n=1}^{\infty}(-1)^{n-1}3^n x^n/(n+2)!$

8. $y_1 = 3 + 2x + x^2,\quad y_2 = x^4/(1-x)^2$

9. $y_1 = 1 + x^2/2^2 + x^4/(2^2\cdot 4^2) + x^6/(2^2\cdot 4^2\cdot 6^2) + \cdots,$
$y_2 = y_1\cdot(\ln x - x^2/4 + 5x^4/128 - 23x^6/3456 + \cdots)$

10. $y_1 = x(1 - x^2/2^2 + x^4/(2^2\cdot 4^2) - x^6/(2^2\cdot 4^2\cdot 6^2) + \cdots),$
$y_2 = y_1\cdot(\ln x + x^2/4 + 5x^4/128 + 23x^6/3456 + \cdots)$

11. $y_1 = x^2(1 - 2x + \tfrac{3}{2}x^2 - \tfrac{2}{3}x^3 + \cdots),$
$y_2 = y_1\cdot(\ln x + 3x + \tfrac{11}{4}x^2 + \tfrac{49}{18}x^3 + \cdots)$

12. $y_1 = x^2(1 - x/2 + 3x^2/20 - x^3/30 + x^4/168 - \cdots),$
$y_2 = y_1\cdot(-\tfrac{1}{3}x^{-3} + \tfrac{1}{20}x^{-1} + \tfrac{3}{100}x + \cdots)$

13. $y_1 = x^3(1 - 2x + 2x^2 - \tfrac{4}{3}x^3 + \cdots),$

$y_2 = y_1\cdot(2\ln x - \tfrac{1}{2}x^{-2} - 2x^{-1} + \tfrac{4}{3}x + \cdots)$

14. $y_1 = x^2(1 - 2x/5 + x^2/10 - 2x^3/105 + x^4/336 - \cdots),$
$y_2 = y_1\cdot(-\tfrac{1}{4}x^{-4} + \tfrac{1}{15}x^{-3} + \tfrac{1}{100}x^{-2} - \tfrac{13}{1750}x^{-1} + \cdots);$
y_2 contains no logarithmic term.

16. $y_1 = x^{3/2}\left(1 + \displaystyle\sum_{n=1}^{\infty}(-1)^n x^{2n}/[2^n\cdot n!\cdot 5\cdot 7\cdots(2n+3)]\right),$

$y_2 = x^{-3/2}\left(1 + \displaystyle\sum_{n=1}^{\infty}(-1)^n x^{2n}/[2^n\cdot n!\cdot(-1)\cdot 1\cdot 3\cdots(2n-3)]\right)$

Section 8.5

5. $J_4(x) = (1/x^2)(x^2 - 24)J_0(x) + (8/x^3)(6 - x^2)J_1(x)$

12. 3

13. $x^2 J_1(x) + xJ_0(x) - \displaystyle\int J_0(x)\,dx + C$

14. $(x^3 - 4x)J_1(x) + 2x^2 J_0(x) + C$

15. $(x^4 - 9x^2)J_1(x) + (3x^3 - 9x)J_0(x) + 9\displaystyle\int J_0(x)\,dx + C$

16. $-xJ_0(x) + \displaystyle\int J_0(x)\,dx + C$

17. $2xJ_1(x) - x^2 J_0(x) + C$

18. $3x^2 J_1(x) + (3x - x^3)J_0(x) - 3\displaystyle\int J_0(x)\,dx + C$

19. $(4x^3 - 16x)J_1(x) + (8x^2 - x^4)J_0(x) + C$

20. $-2J_1(x) + \displaystyle\int J_0(x)\,dx + C$

21. $J_0(x) - (4/x)J_1(x) + C$

Section 8.6

1. $y = x[c_1 J_0(x) + c_2 Y_0(x)]$
2. $y = x^{-1}[c_1 J_1(x) + c_2 Y_1(x)]$
3. $y = x[c_1 J_{1/2}(3x^2) + c_2 J_{-1/2}(3x^2)]$
4. $y = x^3[c_1 J_2(2x^{1/2}) + c_2 Y_2(2x^{1/2})]$

5. $y = x^{-1/3}[c_1 J_{1/3}(\tfrac{1}{3}x^{3/2}) + c_2 J_{-1/3}(\tfrac{1}{3}x^{3/2})]$
6. $y = x^{-1/4}[c_1 J_0(2x^{3/2}) + c_2 Y_0(2x^{3/2})]$
7. $y = x^{-1}[c_1 J_0(x) + c_2 Y_0(x)]$
8. $y = x^2[c_1 J_1(4x^{1/2}) + c_2 Y_1(4x^{1/2})]$
9. $y = x^{1/2}[c_1 J_{1/2}(2x^{3/2}) + c_2 J_{-1/2}(2x^{3/2})]$
10. $y = x^{-1/4}[c_1 J_{3/2}(\tfrac{2}{5}x^{5/2}) + c_2 J_{-3/2}(\tfrac{2}{5}x^{5/2})]$
11. $y = x^{1/2}[c_1 J_{1/6}(\tfrac{1}{3}x^3) + c_2 J_{-1/6}(\tfrac{1}{3}x^3)]$
12. $y = x^{1/2}[c_1 J_{1/5}(\tfrac{4}{5}x^{5/2}) + c_2 J_{-1/5}(\tfrac{4}{5}x^{5/2})]$

CHAPTER 9

Section 9.1

1. $2\pi/3$ **2.** 1 **3.** $4\pi/3$

4. 6 **5.** π **6.** $\tfrac{1}{2}$

7. Not periodic **8.** Not periodic **9.** π

10. $\pi/3$

11. $a_0 = 2;\ a_n = b_n = 0$ for $n \geq 1$

12. $-12\pi^{-1}(\sin t + \tfrac{1}{3}\sin 3t + \tfrac{1}{5}\sin 5t + \cdots)$

13. $\tfrac{1}{2} + 2\pi^{-1}(\sin t + \tfrac{1}{3}\sin 3t + \tfrac{1}{5}\sin 5t + \cdots)$

14. $\tfrac{1}{2} - 10\pi^{-1}(\sin t + \tfrac{1}{3}\sin 3t + \tfrac{1}{5}\sin 5t + \cdots)$

15. $2(\sin t - \tfrac{1}{2}\sin 2t + \tfrac{1}{3}\sin 3t - \cdots)$

16. $\pi - 2(\sin t + \tfrac{1}{2}\sin 2t + \tfrac{1}{3}\sin 3t + \cdots)$

17. $\tfrac{1}{2}\pi - 4\pi^{-1}(\cos t + \tfrac{1}{9}\cos 3t + \tfrac{1}{25}\cos 5t + \cdots)$

18. $\tfrac{1}{2}\pi + 4\pi^{-1}(\cos t + \tfrac{1}{9}\cos 3t + \tfrac{1}{25}\cos 5t + \cdots)$

19. $a_0 = \pi/2;\ a_n = [1 - (-1)^n]/(\pi n^2)$ for $n \geq 1;$
$b_n = -1/n$ for $n \geq 1$

20. $\tfrac{1}{2} + 2\pi^{-1}(\cos t - \tfrac{1}{3}\cos 3t + \tfrac{1}{5}\cos 5t - \cdots)$

21. $\tfrac{1}{3}\pi^2 - 4(\cos t - \tfrac{1}{4}\cos 2t + \tfrac{1}{9}\cos 3t - \cdots)$

22. $a_0 = \tfrac{8}{3}\pi^2;\ a_n = 4/n$ for $n \geq 1;\ b_n = -4\pi/n$
for $n \geq 1$

23. $a_0 = \tfrac{1}{3}\pi^2;\ a_n = 2\cdot(-1)^n/n^2)$ for $n \geq 1;$
$b_n = 2\cdot[(-1)^n - 1]/(\pi n^3) - \pi\cdot(-1)^n/n$ for $n \geq 1$

24. $b_n = 0$ for $n \geq 1;\ a_n = 0$ if n is odd;
$a_n = -4/[\pi(n^2 - 1)]$ for $n = 0, 2, 4, \ldots$

25. $a_0 = 1, a_4 = \tfrac{1}{2}$, and all other coefficients are zero.

26. $\dfrac{1}{2}\sin t + \dfrac{1}{\pi}$

$\quad - \dfrac{2}{\pi}\left(\dfrac{1}{1\cdot 3}\cos 2t + \dfrac{1}{3\cdot 5}\cos 4t + \dfrac{1}{5\cdot 7}\cos 6t + \cdots\right)$

Section 9.2

1. $8\pi^{-1}(\sin\tfrac{1}{3}\pi t + \tfrac{1}{3}\sin\tfrac{3}{3}\pi t + \tfrac{1}{5}\sin\tfrac{5}{3}\pi t + \cdots)$

2. $\tfrac{1}{2} + 2\pi^{-1}(\sin\tfrac{1}{5}\pi t + \tfrac{1}{3}\sin\tfrac{3}{5}\pi t + \tfrac{1}{5}\sin\tfrac{5}{5}\pi t + \cdots)$

3. $\frac{1}{2} - 6\pi^{-1}(\sin\frac{1}{2}t + \frac{1}{3}\sin\frac{3}{2}t + \frac{1}{5}\sin\frac{5}{2}t + \cdots)$

4. $4\pi^{-1}(\sin\frac{1}{2}\pi t - \frac{1}{2}\sin\frac{2}{2}\pi t + \frac{1}{3}\sin\frac{3}{2}\pi t - \cdots)$

5. $4(\sin\frac{1}{2}t - \frac{1}{2}\sin\frac{2}{2}t + \frac{1}{3}\sin\frac{3}{2}t - \cdots)$

6. $\frac{2}{3} - 3\pi^{-1}(\sin\frac{2}{3}\pi t + \frac{1}{2}\sin\frac{4}{3}\pi t + \frac{1}{3}\sin\frac{6}{3}\pi t + \cdots)$

7. $\frac{1}{2} - 4\pi^{-2}(\cos\pi t + \frac{1}{9}\cos 3\pi t + \frac{1}{25}\cos 5\pi t + \cdots)$

8. $\frac{1}{3} - \sqrt{3}\,\pi^{-1}(\cos\frac{2}{3}\pi t - \frac{1}{2}\cos\frac{4}{3}\pi t + \frac{1}{4}\cos\frac{8}{3}\pi t -$
$\frac{1}{5}\cos\frac{10}{3}\pi t + \cdots)$

9. $\frac{1}{3} - 4\pi^{-2}(\cos\pi t - \frac{1}{4}\cos 2\pi t + \frac{1}{9}\cos 3\pi t - \cdots)$

10. $\frac{2}{3} - 8\pi^{-2}(\cos\frac{1}{2}\pi t - \frac{1}{4}\cos\frac{2}{2}\pi t + \frac{1}{9}\cos\frac{3}{2}\pi t - \cdots) +$
$4\pi^{-1}(\sin\frac{1}{2}\pi t - \frac{1}{2}\sin\frac{2}{2}\pi t + \frac{1}{3}\sin\frac{3}{2}\pi t - \cdots) -$
$16\pi^{-3}(\sin\frac{1}{2}\pi t + \frac{1}{27}\sin\frac{3}{2}\pi t + \frac{1}{125}\sin\frac{5}{2}\pi t + \cdots)$

11. $a_0 = 4/\pi$; $a_n = (4/\pi)[(-1)^{n+1}/(4n^2 - 1)]$;
$b_n = 0$ for all $n \geq 1$

12. $L = \frac{1}{2}$, $a_0 = 4/\pi$; $a_n = -4/[\pi(4n^2 - 1)]$ for
$n \geq 1$; $b_n = 0$ for all $n \geq 1$

13. $a_0 = 2/\pi$; $a_1 = 0$; $a_n = -[1 + (-1)^n]/[\pi(n^2 - 1)]$
for $n \geq 2$; $b_1 = \frac{1}{2}$; $b_n = 0$ if $n \geq 2$

14. $\frac{1}{2}\sin t + 4\pi^{-1}(\frac{1}{3}\cos\frac{1}{2}t - \frac{1}{5}\cos\frac{3}{2}t - \frac{1}{21}\cos\frac{5}{2}t - \cdots)$

Section 9.3

1. Cosine series: $a_0 = 2$; the coefficient of $\cos(n\pi t/L)$ is $a_n = 0$ for $n \geq 1$. Sine series: the coefficient of $\sin(n\pi t/L)$ is $b_n = 4/(n\pi)$ for n odd, $b_n = 0$ for n even.

2. Cosine series: $a_0 = 1$; the coefficient of $\cos n\pi t$ is $a_n = 4/(n\pi)^2$ for n odd, $a_n = 0$ for n even. Sine series: the coefficient of $\sin n\pi t$ is $b_n = 2/(n\pi)$ for $n \geq 1$.

3. Cosine series: $a_0 = 0$; the coefficient of $\cos(n\pi t/2)$ is $a_n = 4 \cdot [1 - (-1)^n]/(n\pi)$ for $n \geq 1$, so $a_n = 0$ for n even, $a_n = 8/(n\pi)^2$ for n odd. Sine series: the coefficient of $\sin(n\pi t/2)$ is $b_n = 2 \cdot [1 + (-1)^n]/(n\pi)$ for $n \geq 1$, so $b_n = 4/(n\pi)$ for n even, $b_n = 0$ for n odd.

4. Cosine series: $a_0 = 1$; the coefficient of $\cos(n\pi t/2)$ is $a_n = 0$ for n odd and for n an integral multiple of 4. Otherwise (for $n = 2, 6, 10, \ldots$), $a_n = -16/(n\pi)^2$. Sine series: the coefficient of $\sin(n\pi t/2)$ is $b_n = 0$ for n even. If n is odd and of the form $4k + 1$ then $b_n = 8/(n\pi)^2$, whereas if n is odd and of the form $4k + 3$ then $b_n = -8/(n\pi)^2$.

5. Cosine series: $a_0 = \frac{2}{3}$; the coefficient of $\cos(n\pi t/3)$ is $a_n = -(2\sqrt{3})/(n\pi)$ if n is of the form $6k + 2$, $a_n = (2\sqrt{3})/(n\pi)$ if n is of the form $6k + 4$, and $a_n = 0$ otherwise. Sine series: the coefficient of $\sin(n\pi t/3)$ is $b_n = 0$ if n is even, $b_n = -4/(n\pi)$ if n is of the form $6k + 3$, and $b_n = 2/(n\pi)$ otherwise.

7. Cosine series: $a_0 = \frac{1}{3}\pi^2$; the coefficient of $\cos nt$ is

$a_n = -2 \cdot [1 + (-1)^n]/n^2$ for $n \geq 1$. Sine series: the coefficient of $\sin nt$ is $b_n = 4 \cdot [1 - (-1)^n]/(\pi n^3)$ for $n \geq 1$.

9. Cosine series: $a_0 = 4/\pi$ and $a_1 = 0$; if $n \geq 2$ then $a_n = -2 \cdot [1 + (-1)^n]/[\pi(n^2 - 1)]$ is the coefficient of $\cos nt$. Sine series: $b_1 = 1$ and $b_n = 0$ for $n \geq 2$.

11. $x(t) = -\dfrac{4}{\pi} \displaystyle\sum_{n\text{ odd}} \dfrac{1}{n(n^2 - 2)} \sin nt$

13. $x(t) = \displaystyle\sum_{n=1}^{\infty} \dfrac{2 \cdot (-1)^n}{n\pi(n^2\pi^2 - 1)} \sin n\pi t$

15. $x(t) = \dfrac{\pi}{2} + \dfrac{2}{\pi} \displaystyle\sum_{n=1}^{\infty} \dfrac{1 - (-1)^n}{n^2(n^2 - 2)} \cos nt$

17. *Suggestion:* Substitute $u = -t$ in the left-hand integral.

Section 9.4

1. $x_{sp}(t) = \dfrac{12}{\pi} \displaystyle\sum_{n\text{ odd}} \dfrac{1}{n(5 - n^2)} \sin nt$

3. $x_{sp}(t) = 4 \displaystyle\sum_{n=1}^{\infty} \dfrac{(-1)^n}{n(n^2 - 3)} \sin nt$

5. $x_{sp}(t) = \dfrac{8}{\pi^3} \displaystyle\sum_{n\text{ odd}} \dfrac{1}{n^3(10 - n^2\pi^2)} \sin n\pi t$

7. Resonance will occur.

8. Pure resonance will not occur.

9. Resonance will not occur.

10. Pure resonance will occur.

11. Resonance will not occur.

12. Pure resonance will occur.

13. $x_{sp}(t) \approx (1.2725)\sin(t - 0.0333) +$
$(0.2542)\sin(3t - 3.0817) + (0.0364)\sin(5t - 3.1178) + \cdots$

14. $x_{sp}(t) \approx (0.2500)\sin(t - 0.0063) -$
$(0.2000)\sin(2t - 0.0200) + (4.444)\sin(3t - 1.5708) -$
$(0.0714)\sin(4t - 3.1130) + \cdots$

15. $x_{sp}(t) \approx (0.08150)\sin(\pi t - 1.44692) +$
$(0.00004)\sin(3\pi t - 3.10176) + \cdots$

17. (a) $x_{sp}(t) \approx (0.5687)\sin(\pi t - 0.0562) +$
$(0.4721)\sin(3\pi t - 0.3891) + (0.1396)\sin(5\pi t - 2.7899) +$
$(0.0318)\sin(7\pi t - 2.9874) + \cdots$

Section 9.5

1. $u(x, t) = 4e^{-12t}\sin 2x$

2. $u(x, t) \equiv 7$

3. $u(x, t) = 5\exp(-2\pi^2 t)\sin\pi x - \frac{1}{5}\exp(-18\pi^2 t)\sin 3\pi x$

4. $u(x, t) = 2e^{-4t}\sin 2x + 2e^{-36t}\sin 6x$

5. $u(x, t) = 4\exp(-8\pi^2 t/9)\cos(2\pi x/3) -$
$2\exp(-32\pi^2 t/9)\cos(4\pi x/3)$

6. $u(x, t) = \exp(-2\pi^2 t)\sin 2\pi x + \frac{1}{2}\exp(-8\pi^2 t)\sin 4\pi x$

7. $u(x, t) = \frac{1}{2} + \frac{1}{2} \exp(-16\pi^2 t/3) \cos 4\pi x$

8. $u(x, t) = 5 \exp(-4\pi^2 t) \cos 2\pi x +$
$\quad 5 \exp(-16\pi^2 t) \cos 4\pi x$

9. $u(x, t) = \dfrac{100}{\pi} \displaystyle\sum_{n \text{ odd}} \dfrac{1}{n} \exp(-n^2\pi^2 t/250) \sin \dfrac{n\pi x}{5}$

11. $u(x, t) = 20 - \dfrac{160}{\pi^2} \displaystyle\sum_{n \text{ odd}} \dfrac{1}{n^2} \exp(-n^2\pi^2 t/500) \cos \dfrac{n\pi x}{10}$

13. (a) $u(x, t) = \dfrac{400}{\pi} \displaystyle\sum_{n \text{ odd}} \dfrac{1}{n} \exp(-n^2\pi^2 kt/1600) \sin \dfrac{n\pi x}{40}$;

 (b) with $k = 1.15$, $u(20, 300) \approx 15.16°C$;
 (c) about 19 h 16 min

14. (b) $u(10, 60) \approx 25.15°C$; (c) 6 min 54.3 s

16. (b) 15 h

Section 9.6

1. $y(x, t) = \frac{1}{10} \cos 4t \sin 2x$

2. $y(x, t) = \frac{1}{10} \cos \pi t \sin \pi x - \frac{1}{20} \cos 3\pi t \sin 3\pi x$

3. $y(x, t) = \frac{1}{10} (\cos \frac{1}{2} t + 2 \sin \frac{1}{2} t) \sin x$

4. $y(x, t) = \frac{1}{10} \cos \pi t \sin 2\pi x$

5. $y(x, t) = \frac{1}{4} \cos 5\pi t \sin \pi x + \pi^{-1} \sin 10\pi t \sin 2\pi x$

6. $y(x, t) = \displaystyle\sum_{n \text{ odd}} \dfrac{8}{\pi n^3} \cos 10nt \sin nx$

7. $y(x, t) = \displaystyle\sum_{n=1}^{\infty} \dfrac{(-1)^{n+1}}{5\pi^2 n^2} \sin 10n\pi t \sin n\pi x$

9. $y(x, t) = y_B(x, t) = \displaystyle\sum_{n \text{ odd}} \dfrac{4}{n^4 \pi^4} \sin 2n\pi t \sin n\pi x$

11. Fundamental frequency 256 Hz; velocity: 1024 ft/s

Section 9.7

1. $u(x, y) = \displaystyle\sum_{n=1}^{\infty} c_n \sinh \dfrac{n\pi x}{b} \sin \dfrac{n\pi y}{b}$ where

$c_n = \dfrac{2}{b \sinh (n\pi a/b)} \displaystyle\int_0^b g(y) \sin \dfrac{n\pi y}{b} \, dy$

3. $u(x, y) = \displaystyle\sum_{n=1}^{\infty} c_n \sin \dfrac{n\pi x}{a} \sinh \dfrac{n\pi y}{a}$ where

$c_n = \dfrac{2}{a \sinh (n\pi b/a)} \displaystyle\int_0^a f(x) \sin \dfrac{n\pi x}{a} \, dx$

5. $u(x, y) = \dfrac{a_0}{2a} (a - x) +$

$\displaystyle\sum_{n=1}^{\infty} a_n \dfrac{\sinh (n\pi[a - x]/b)}{\sinh (n\pi a/b)} \cos \dfrac{n\pi y}{b}$,

where $a_n = \dfrac{2}{b} \displaystyle\int_0^b g(y) \cos \dfrac{n\pi y}{b} \, dy$

7. $u(x, y) = \displaystyle\sum_{n=1}^{\infty} b_n e^{-n\pi y/a} \sin \dfrac{n\pi x}{a}$ where

$b_n = \dfrac{2}{a} \displaystyle\int_0^a f(x) \sin \dfrac{n\pi x}{a} \, dx$

9. $u(0, 5) \approx 41.53$; $u(5, 5) = 50$; $u(10, 5) \approx 58.47$

11. $u(x, y) = \displaystyle\sum_{n \text{ odd}} c_n \sinh \dfrac{n\pi(a - x)}{2b} \cos \dfrac{n\pi y}{2b}$ where

$c_n = \dfrac{2}{b \sinh (n\pi a/2b)} \displaystyle\int_0^b g(y) \cos \dfrac{n\pi y}{2b} \, dy$

13. $c_n = \dfrac{2}{\pi a^n} \displaystyle\int_0^\pi f(\theta) \sin n\theta \, d\theta$

15. $c_n = \dfrac{2}{\pi a^{n/2}} \displaystyle\int_0^\pi f(\theta) \sin \dfrac{n\theta}{2} \, d\theta$

CHAPTER 10

Section 10.1

7. $1 = 2hL \displaystyle\sum_{n=1}^{\infty} \dfrac{1 - \cos \beta_n}{\beta_n(hL + \cos^2 \beta_n)} \sin \dfrac{\beta_n x}{L}$, $\quad 0 < x < L$

9. $x = 2h(1 + h) \displaystyle\sum_{n=1}^{\infty} \dfrac{\sin \beta_n \sin \beta_n x}{\beta_n^2(h + \cos^2 \beta_n)}$, $\quad 0 < x < 1$

Section 10.2

3. $u(x, y) = \displaystyle\sum_{n=1}^{\infty} A_n \sinh \dfrac{\beta_n(L - x)}{L} \cos \dfrac{\beta_n y}{L}$,

where $\{\beta_n\}_1^\infty$ are the positive roots of the equation
$\beta \tan \beta = hL$ and $A_n \sinh \beta_n =$

$\dfrac{2h}{hL + \sin^2 \beta_n} \displaystyle\int_0^L g(y) \cos \dfrac{\beta_n y}{L} \, dy$

5. $u(x, t) = \displaystyle\sum_{n=1}^{\infty} c_n \exp(-\beta_n kt/L^2) X_n(x)$, where $\{\beta_n\}_1^\infty$
are the positive roots of the equation $hL \tan \beta =$
$-\beta$, $X_n(x) = \beta_n \cos(\beta_n x/L) + hL \sin(\beta_n x/L)$, and

$c_n \displaystyle\int_0^L [X_n(x)]^2 \, dx = \displaystyle\int_0^L f(x) X_n(x) \, dx$

7. $u(1, 1) \approx 31.4°$

Section 10.3

In these answers, ω_n denotes the nth natural circular
frequency (in rad/s).

1. $\omega_n = \dfrac{n\pi}{L} \sqrt{\dfrac{E}{\delta}}$ **3.** $\omega_n = \dfrac{(2n - 1)\pi}{2L} \sqrt{\dfrac{E}{\delta}}$

5. $\omega_n = \dfrac{\beta_n}{L}\sqrt{\dfrac{E}{\delta}}$, where β_n is th nth positive

root of the equation $AE\beta \tan \beta = kL$.

15. 1.03 Hz

Section 10.4

11. $u(r, t) = \dfrac{F_0}{\omega^2 J_0(\omega b / a)}\, [J_0(\omega r / a) - J_0(\omega b / a)] \sin \omega t,$

where b is the radius of the circular membrane

APPENDIX

1. $y_0 = 3, y_1 = 3 + 3x, \quad y_2 = 3 + 3x + \frac{3}{2}x^2,$
$y_3 = 3 + 3x + \frac{3}{2}x^2 + \frac{1}{2}x^3,$
$y_4 = 3 + 3x + \frac{3}{2}x^2 + \frac{1}{2}x^3 + \frac{1}{8}x^4; \quad y(x) = 3e^x$

3. $y_0 = 1, y_1 = 1 - x^2, \quad y_2 = 1 - x^2 + \frac{1}{2}x^4,$
$y_3 = 1 - x^2 + \frac{1}{2}x^4 - \frac{1}{6}x^6, \quad y_4 = 1 - x^2 + \frac{1}{2}x^4 - \frac{1}{6}x^6 + \frac{1}{24}x^8;$
$y(x) = \exp(-x^2)$

5. $y_0 = 0, \ y_1 = 2x, \ y_2 = 2x + 2x^2, \ y_3 = 2x + 2x^2 + \frac{4}{3}x^3,$
$y_4 = 2x + 2x^2 + \frac{4}{3}x^3 + \frac{2}{3}x^4; \ y(x) = e^{2x} - 1$

7. $y_0 = 0, \ y_1 = x^2, \ y_2 = x^2 + \frac{1}{2}x^4,$
$y_3 = x^2 + \frac{1}{2}x^4 + \frac{1}{6}x^6, \ y_4 = x^2 + \frac{1}{2}x^4 + \frac{1}{6}x^6 + \frac{1}{24}x^8;$
$y(x) = \exp(x^2) - 1$

9. $y_0 = 1, \ y_1 = (1 + x) + \frac{1}{2}x^2, \ y_2 = (1 + x + x^2) + \frac{1}{6}x^3, y_3 = (1 + x + x^2 + \frac{1}{3}x^3) + \frac{1}{24}x^4;$
$y(x) = 2e^x - 1 - x = 1 + x + x^2 + \frac{1}{3}x^3 + \cdots$

11. $y_0 = 1, \ y_1 = 1 + x, \ y_2 = (1 + x + x^2) + \frac{1}{3}x^3,$
$y_3 = (1 + x + x^2 + x^3) + \frac{2}{3}x^4 + \frac{1}{3}x^5 + \frac{1}{9}x^6 + \frac{1}{63}x^7;$
$y(x) = 1/(1 - x) = 1 + x + x^2 + x^3 + x^4 + \cdots$

12. $y_0 = 1, \ y_1 = 1 + \frac{1}{2}x, \ y_2 = 1 + \frac{1}{2}x + \frac{3}{8}x^2 + \frac{1}{8}x^3 + \frac{1}{64}x^4,$
$y_3 = 1 + \frac{1}{2}x + \frac{3}{8}x^2 + \frac{5}{16}x^3 + \frac{13}{64}x^4 + \cdots ;$
$y(x) = (1 - x)^{-1/2}$

13. $\begin{bmatrix} x_0 \\ y_0 \end{bmatrix} = \begin{bmatrix} 1 \\ -1 \end{bmatrix}, \quad \begin{bmatrix} x_1 \\ y_1 \end{bmatrix} = \begin{bmatrix} 1 + 3t \\ -1 + 5t \end{bmatrix}, \quad \begin{bmatrix} x_2 \\ y_2 \end{bmatrix} =$

$\begin{bmatrix} 1 + 3t + \frac{1}{2}t^2 \\ -1 + 5t - \frac{1}{2}t^2 \end{bmatrix}, \quad \begin{bmatrix} x_3 \\ y_3 \end{bmatrix} = \begin{bmatrix} 1 + 3t + \frac{1}{2}t^2 + \frac{1}{3}t^3 \\ -1 + 5t - \frac{1}{2}t^2 + \frac{5}{6}t^3 \end{bmatrix}$

14. $\mathbf{x}(t) = \begin{bmatrix} e^t + te^t \\ e^t \end{bmatrix}$ **16.** $y_3(1) \approx 0.350185$

Index

Boldface page numbers indicate where terms are defined.